THE HANDBOOK OF REAL ESTATE PORTFOLIO MANAGEMENT

Edited by
Joseph L. Pagliari, Jr., CFA

IRWIN
Professional Publishing
Chicago • Bogotá • Boston • Buenos Aires • Caracas
London • Madrid • Mexico City • Sydney • Toronto

© RICHARD D. IRWIN, INC., 1995

This publication is designed to provide accurate and authoritative information in regard to
the subject matter covered. It is sold with the understanding that neither the author nor the
publisher is engaged in rendering legal, accounting, or other professional service. If legal
advice or other expert assistance is required, the services of a competent professional person
should be sought.

*From a Declaration of Principles jointly adopted by a Committee of the American Bar
Association and a Committee of Publishers.*

Project editor: Rebecca Dodson
Production supervisor: Dina L. Treadaway
Designer: Heidi J. Baughman
Graphics supervisor: Charlene Breeden
Compositor: TCSystems, Inc.
Typeface: 11/13 Century Schoolbook
Printer: Quebecor Printing

Library of Congress Cataloging-in-Publication Data

Handbook of real estate portfolio management / [edited by] Joseph L.
    Pagliari, Jr.
        p.   cm.
    Includes index.
    ISBN 1-55623-539-9
    1. Real estate investment.   2. Portfolio management.
I. Pagaliari, Joseph L.
HD1382.5.H37 1995
332.63'24—dc20   94–38584

Printed in the United States of America
1 2 3 4 5 6 7 8 9 0 QF 2 1 0 9 8 7 6 5

To my wife Karen and our children, Joe, Mike, and Laura:
When it comes to the richness of life,
I count myself among the most wealthy.
Thank you!

To my parents, Fran and Joe:
When it comes to the indebtitudes of life,
I count myself among the most owing.
Thank you!

CONTRIBUTING AUTHORS

Helen R. Arnold is a Senior Director at Jones Lang Wootton USA. Ms. Arnold received her bachelor's degree from Vassar College (Phi Beta Kappa) and her master's degree and M. Phil. from Yale University. She has managed the Investment Research Division at Jones Lang Wootton since 1983, concentrating on real asset allocation for investors combined with regional and local market research in North America. For the last 5 years, her specialization has been worldwide investment strategies for institutional investors.

Daniel J. Coughlin currently heads Copley's Investment Management and Services area. He came to Copley as a founder of the company. He holds a bachelor's degree from Stonehill College and a master's degree from Boston University and has held the Certified Property Manager designation. Mr. Coughlin is a member of the reporting and valuation committees of several trade organizations and is a past board member and a former President of the National Council of Real Estate Investment Fiduciaries. He is a licensed real estate broker in Massachusetts.

Werner F. M. De Bondt is a Frank Graner Professor of Investment Management in the School of Business at the University of Wisconsin–Madison, where he teaches security analysis and portfolio management. He earned his doctorate degree in business administration from Cornell University in 1985. He has published articles in a number of professional journals and is the author of *Earnings Forecasts and Share Price Reversals,* published in 1992 by the Research Foundation of The Institute of Chartered Financial Analysts. He has served as a visiting professor at Cornell University, the Catholic University of Louvain in Belgium, and Erasmus University in the Netherlands.

Joseph J. Del Casino is Chief Real Estate Investment Officer and Assistant Director of the $3 billion real estate portfolio of the New York State Common Retirement Fund, a $65 billion pension plan for the state and local employees. His responsibilities include creating and monitoring the Fund's real estate portfolio strategy, originating new acquisitions and mortgage investments, and overseeing the Fund's relationships with a dozen real estate investment advisory firms. Mr. Del Casino holds a bachelor's degree from

Brown University and a master's degree from the University of Pennsylvania. He is a frequent contributor to a variety of real estate and business journals.

Geoffrey Dohrmann is the Chairman and CEO of Institutional Real Estate, Inc., and is the publisher and editor-in-chief of *The Institutional Real Estate Letter, Real Estate Capital Markets Report,* and the *European Real Estate Quarterly.* He is also a member of the editorial advisory board of the *REIT Report,* the *National Real Estate Index,* and the *Handbook of Real Estate Portfolio Management,* and is a member of the board of directors of the National Investment Conference for Senior Housing and Long Term Care, and the Institute of Chartered Real Estate Analysts. A graduate of the University of California–Berkeley, Mr. Dohrmann is a member of the American Real Estate Society, the American Association of Real Estate and Urban Economics, the Urban Land Institute, and the National Association of Real Estate Editors.

Robert J. Domrese is a real estate investment consultant and an attorney in private practice. He was a founding principal and Chief Operating Officer of Grubb & Ellis Realty Advisers, an institutional investment management firm specializing in warehouse/distribution properties. He is co-author of *Strategic Investment Opportunities in the Industrial/Warehouse Sector,* prepared with the research department of Grubb & Ellis. Mr. Domrese holds degrees from Harvard College, the Woodrow Wilson School at Princeton University, and Harvard Law School, where he was an editor of the *Harvard Law Review.*

David H. Downs is a Ph.D. candidate at the Kenan-Flagler Business School of the University of North Carolina at Chapel Hill. While in the Ph.D. program, Mr. Downs received a research award from the Eastern Finance Association, a funded grant from the Real Estate Research Institute, and an award for outstanding teaching at the University of North Carolina. He worked as a management consultant with Booz-Allen & Hamilton, Inc., and earned his master's degree in business administration from George Washington University. He is co-author of an updated examination of the size of the U.S. real estate market.

Jeffrey A. Duni is Vice President of Hotel Development for Sage Hospitality Resources, LP, a national hotel management, investment, and consulting company. He was formerly Director of Hotel Investments, Western Region, for the Prudential Realty Group, a subsidiary of The Prudential Insurance Company of America. Prior to that Mr. Duni spent 8 years in several management positions in the hospitality industry. Mr. Duni is an adjunct professor at the University of Denver's School of Hotel, Restaurant, and Tourism Management.

Richard T. Garrigan, Professor of Finance at the Kellstadt Graduate School of Business at DePaul University, received his bachelor's degree from Ohio State University and his master's and doctorate degrees from the University of Wisconsin–Madison. A member of the American Society of Real Estate Counselors, he is a director of Chicago's Bell Federal Savings and Loan Association and Bell Bancorp, Inc., and a member of the Midwestern Regional Advisory Board of the Federal National Mortgage Association. Dr. Garrigan co-edited *The Handbook of Mortgage Banking*.

Adam K. Gehr, Jr. is a Professor of Finance at DePaul University in Chicago. He received his bachelor's and master's degrees in economics from Miami University and his doctorate degree from Ohio State University. He has taught at the University of Missouri and Pennsylvania State University. He currently does research and consults in the areas of design and derivative instruments and markets for derivative instruments, valuation, and financial market structure. Mr. Gehr has published articles in many professional journals on topics related to financial management and analysis.

Jacques N. Gordon joined LaSalle Partners in June 1994, where he is responsible for portfolio strategies and capital markets research. He served as Chairman of the Research Committee of the National Council of Real Estate Investment Fiduciaries from 1991 to 1993 and continues as chair of the Index Subcommittee. Mr. Gordon is an Adjunct Professor at New York University's Real Estate Institute where he teaches a course on Portfolio Management and serves on the curriculum committee. He earned his bachelor's degree from the University of Pennsylvania, his master's from the London School of Economics, and his doctorate degree from the Massachusetts Institute of Technology.

Roy L. Gordon, Jr., MAI, CRE, is Managing Director of Cushman & Wakefield's Appraisal Services and Consulting Group and the National Director of Appraisal Standards. Mr. Gordon holds a MAI designation of the Appraisal Institute and the CRE designation of the American Society of Real Estate Counselors. He is a former Chairman of the National Professional Practice Committee of the Society of Real Estate Appraisers and presently serves on the Appraisal Standards Council of the Appraisal Institute. He is the immediate past Chairman of the Appraisal Institute's seven-state Region IV and is currently a member of the Board of Directors.

W. Cabell Grayson, Jr. is Managing Director of CB Commercial Realty Advisors. He is a member of the Realty Advisors Management Committee as well as the CB Commercial Real Estate Investment Committee, which holds the responsibility for final approval of all real estate investments made by CB Commercial. Realty Advisors manages a portfolio of over 80 commercial real estate properties valued at approximately $1 billion, in 30 metropolitan areas across the country. He is also a member of the National Association of Real Estate Investment Managers and the Pension Real Estate Association. Mr. Grayson earned his bachelor's degree in history at Yale University.

D. Wylie Greig is a Partner and Director of Research for The RREEF Funds, a San Francisco-based real estate investment manager for U.S. institutional pension funds. Mr. Greig directs a research program that supports strategic decision making in all major areas of operation, including acquisitions, dispositions, asset management, portfolio management, and client reporting. Mr. Greig is the current President of the National Council of Real Estate Investment Fiduciaries (NCREIF) and a member of the Board of Real Estate Research Institute (RERI).

Charles Grossman is a Managing Director of Jones Lang Wootton Realty Advisors, which manages $3 billion in real estate assets on behalf of U.S. pension fund clients. He is a graduate of Harvard College, Columbia University School of Law, and Columbia University School of Business Administration. From 1971 to 1987, he was chief executive of Schroder Real Estate Associates, a real estate investment management firm. Mr. Grossman is a member of the Pension Real Estate Association, where he is the Chairman of the PREA Institute Committee. He is also a member of the International Council of Shopping Centers, the Urban Land Institute, and the Real Estate Board of New York.

David J. Hartzell is Associate Professor of Finance and Director of the Real Estate Program at the Kenan-Flagler School of Business at the University of North Carolina at Chapel Hill. He earned his bachelor's and master's degrees from the University of Delaware and his doctorate degree from the University of North Carolina at Chapel Hill. Formerly, he was a vice president at Salomon Brothers Inc. in New York, where his primary focus was on institutional real estate finance and investments. He has published numerous academic and professional articles on issues related to the construction of institutional real estate portfolios, real estate finance, and mortgage-backed securities.

Michael Herzberg, Co-Chairman and Chief Executive Officer of FPL Associates, has extensive experience in providing consulting services to many sectors of the real estate industry. FPL Associates is involved in the fields of management, strategic, organizational, and compensation consulting. In addition to Mr. Herzberg's consulting role, he also serves as Chairman and CEO of EMH Financial, a financial advisory firm which is a sister company to FPL Associates. Prior to his current associations, Mr. Herzberg was an Executive Vice President with JMB Realty Corporation. He attended Northwestern University and the University of Chicago Graduate School of Business and School of Law.

Aileen M. Hooks received her B.S.F.S. from Georgetown University magna cum laude in 1979 and her J.D. with high honors from the University of Texas in 1982. As a member of the Government Regulation Group of Jones, Day, Reavis & Pogue, Ms. Hooks practices in the areas of environmental law and commercial real estate. She has substantial experience in multi-asset acquisitions, dispositions, and financings and in counseling clients concerning the application of environmental regulatory requirements, the performance of environmental audits, and the assessment and resolution of liability concerns in real estate, corporate, and lending transactions.

David T. Johnstone is a Principal and Executive Vice President, Investment Advisory Services Division of Sage Hospitality Resources, Inc. He directs the division, which provides asset management and advisory services to hotel owners. Mr. Johnstone has a bachelor's degree in hotel, restaurant, and institutional management from Michigan State University and a master's degree in real estate and construction management from the University of Denver. He is the founding President of the Hospitality Asset Managers Association.

Gary T. Kachadurian is Partner in Charge of the Apartment Group for The RREEF Funds. He received his bachelor's degree in accounting from the University of Illinois and has 15 years of real estate experience, specializing in land acquisition, development, and financing and management of rental apartments. At RREEF, Mr. Kachadurian has full responsibility for acquisitions and management of apartments nationwide and is a member of the RREEF Investment Committee. He serves on the Multi-Family Advisory Council of the Urban Land Institute (ULI) and is currently Secretary of the National Multi-Housing Council.

Richard Kateley is Executive Vice President and a member of the Executive Committee at Heitman Financial Ltd. He also serves on the Investment Committee of Heitman/JMB Advisory Corporation, one of the nation's largest real estate money managers and pension fund advisors. Prior to joining Heitman, he was President and CEO of Real Estate Research Corporation (RERC), a national consulting and appraisal firm, where he worked on projects in the Middle East, China, and Europe, as well as in major U.S. markets. Mr. Kateley earned his bachelor's degree from the University of Texas, his master's degree from the University of Chicago, and was a Fulbright Fellow. He has authored numerous articles in professional and trade publications and the well known industry forecast, *Emerging Trends in Real Estate*.

Mary Ellen Kris is a partner in the New York office of Jones, Day, Reavis & Pogue, in charge of that office's Environmental, Health, & Safety practice. She is a civil and criminal litigator and environmental lawyer with substantial experience in environmental, criminal, civil, and administrative investigations, litigations, and negotiations. She received her B.A. and J.D. with honors from Fordham University. For 10 years she served in the U.S. Attorney's Office for the Southern District of New York, in both the Civil and Criminal Division and as Chief of the Environmental Protection Unit. Formerly an Adjunct Professor at Fordham University School of Law, she is a frequent lecturer on environmental prosecutions and other environmental topics.

Frank P. Liantonio, MAI, CRE, is Executive Managing Director of Cushman & Wakefield's National Appraisal Services and its Real Estate Asset Recovery Services Groups. He is a member of the company's National Management Committee, Board of Directors, and Executive Committee of the Board. Mr. Liantonio is a full member of the Urban Land Institute and the International Council of Shopping Centers. He holds professional designations in the Appraisal Institute and the American Society of Real Estate Counselors. He is a graduate of Marist College with a bachelor's degree in economics. He is also a member of the Board of Directors of the American Cancer Society.

Frederich Lieblich is Director of Real Estate Research for MetLife Realty Group where he assists in the integration of property, market, and portfolio research and analysis in the real estate investment management process. Mr. Lieblich received his bachelor's degree from the University of Illinois–Urbana and his master's degree from the University of Chicago. He has had extensive experience in many facets of real estate investment/management, including production, asset management, and portfolio management. He is currently Co-Chair of the Micro/Macro Research Subcommittee for the National Council of Real Estate Investment Fiduciaries (NCREIF) and a CFA candidate.

Marc A. Louargand is Managing Director of Cornerstone Real Estate Advisers, Inc., and the founding director of the Pension Real Estate Association Institute. Prior to joining Cornerstone, he was a consultant to institutional investment portfolios, industrial and financial corporations, and domestic and foreign governments. Mr. Louargand earned his bachelor's degree from the University of California at Santa Barbara and his master's and doctorate degrees from UCLA. He is an associate editor of the *Journal of*

Real Estate Literature, a member of the editorial board of the *Journal of Real Estate Portfolio Management,* and a frequent speaker at professional and academic gatherings.

Glenn R. Mueller is Director of Strategic Research at LaSalle Advisors Ltd. and a Professor of Real Estate at Johns Hopkins University's Allen L. Berman Real Estate Institute. He is responsible for portfolio, market, and strategic research. A graduate of the University of Denver, Mr. Mueller received his master's degree from Babson College and his doctorate degree in real estate from Georgia State University. He has been a lender, developer, builder, and professor in the real estate field. He has published numerous articles in academic and professional journals on real estate related topics.

Scott R. Muldavin is Managing Director of The Roulac Group, a strategy and financial economics consulting firm that advises senior management and investors in complex high stakes real estate decisions. Mr. Muldavin received his M.C.R.P. from Harvard University and his bachelor's degree in environmental science from the University of California at Berkeley. He has published over 100 papers, columns, and articles, and his quarterly Real Estate Capital Flows Database in the *Real Estate Capital Markets Report* is the premier source of real estate capital markets data published.

Joseph L. Pagliari, Jr. is President of Citadel Realty, Inc. and Special Consultant, Quantitative Analysis for the Research Department at MetLife Realty Group. He is active and experienced in virtually all areas of real estate investment and management. He has written numerous articles for professional and academic journals, has lectured at the graduate schools of business at DePaul University and the University of Chicago, has taught the portfolio management and real estate sections of the review class for the Chartered Financial Analysts examination in conjunction with DePaul University and the Investment Analysts Society of Chicago, and has given speeches to a number of professional and academic organizations. Mr. Pagliari is a Chartered Financial Analyst and a Certified Public Accountant. He received his bachelor's degree from the University of Illinois–Urbana and his master's degree in business administration from DePaul University.

John F. C. Parsons is the founder and Managing Director of MacGregor Associates, where he provides institutional investor relations services to real estate organizations. Prior to founding MacGregor Associates, Mr. Parsons was a Managing Director with Ferguson Partners, a Chicago-based real estate consulting firm. He is the author of numerous articles discussing management issues for real estate organizations and is also a frequent public speaker at various real estate symposiums. Mr. Parsons was educated at McMaster University in Hamilton, Ontario, Canada, where he received his bachelor's and master's degrees.

James R. Proud is currently a Managing Director of Heitman/JMB Advisory Corporation and is a Senior Client Portfolio Manager with responsibility for implementing investment strategies and achieving client objectives. Mr. Proud graduated from Princeton University and received his master's degree from the Amos Tuck School at Dartmouth College. He has more than 20 years of real estate development and investment management experience and is a member of the Pension Real Estate Association, the National Council of Real Estate Investment Fiduciaries, the State Association of County Retirement Systems, the Urban Land Institute, the National Association of Industrial and Office Parks, and the California Business Properties Association.

Stephen E. Roulac heads The Roulac Group, a strategy and financial economics consulting firm that advises on significant decisions of businesses, individuals, and government agencies with real estate involvements. He earned his bachelor's degree from Pomona College and graduate degrees from Harvard University, the University of California–Berkeley, and Stanford University. Mr. Roulac taught at the Stanford Graduate School of Business for 10 years and held a joint appointment at the College of Environmental Design and the School of Business Administration of the University of California–Berkeley. He has also taught at Hastings College of Law, UCLA School of Management, and Texas A&M. Mr. Roulac is a Certified Public Accountant and an expert on real estate securitization, pension and institutional investment, financing, property analysis and valuation, and strategic management. Mr. Roulac has written over 200 articles in professional journals and authored/edited a dozen books. He is President-Elect of the American Real Estate Society and Chair of the Society's Strategic Planning Task Force, and is involved in numerous other professional associations.

Paul Sack received his bachelor's degree magna cum laude in economics from Harvard College, his master's degree from Harvard Business School, and his doctorate degree in political economy from the University of California–Berkeley. Mr. Sack was one of the founders of RREEF and actively participated in the growth of RREEF portfolios from 1975 until his retirement in 1992. For 17 years prior to the formation of RREEF, Mr. Sack's principal business activity had been in real estate, always as a principal. He has formed 14 partnerships known as The Paul Sack Properties for the acquisition, development, ownership, and management of specific projects, chiefly multifamily residential.

Anthony B. Sanders is a Professor of Finance at Ohio State University. He holds the title of Research Associate at the University of Chicago. His research interests include real estate valuation, interest rate behavior, and risk-return analysis of alternative real estate investment vehicles. Mr. Sanders has published extensively on the subjects of real estate investment and finance. He currently teaches an innovative stock market course at Ohio State University (with Prof. Stephen Buser), where students manage approximately $10 million of stocks for the University's endowment fund.

Allan J. Sweet is President of Amli Institutional Advisors, Inc., and of Amli Residential Properties Trust, a real estate investment trust traded on the New York Stock Exchange. Mr. Sweet received his bachelor's degree from the University of Michigan in 1968 and his law degree from the University of Michigan Law School in 1973. Prior to joining Amli in 1985, Mr. Sweet was a partner in the Chicago law firm of Schiff, Mardin & White. He is a member of the National Association of Real Estate Investment Trusts, the Pension Real Estate Association, and the National Multi-Housing Council.

Raymond G. Torto is a principal in CB Commercial/Torto Wheaton Research and is a Professor of Economics at the University of Massachusetts–Boston and Interim Director of the John W. McCormack Institute of Public Affairs at the University. Torto Wheaton Research is a market research firm for major institutional investors in commercial real estate. Mr. Torto is a member of the Boston Real Estate Board, the American Society of Real Estate Counselors, a director of the Boston Municipal Research Bureau, a director of Associated Industries of Massachusetts, and Chairman of their Counsel of Economic Advisors. He has written numerous scholarly articles and four books and holds a Ph.D in economics from Boston College.

Scott E. Tracy is Managing Director of CB Commercial Realty Advisors, where he is in charge of the daily operating responsibilities of Realty Advisors, the real estate investment and portfolio manager for the CB Commercial Real Estate Group. He earned his bachelor's degree in economics from the University of California–Santa Barbara (magna cum laude) and received his master's degree in business administration from UCLA. Mr. Tracy is a member of the National Association of Real Estate Investment Managers, the Pension Real Estate Association, the National Council of Real Estate Investment Fiduciaries, and the American Institute of Certified Public Accountants.

Christopher H. Volk is Senior Vice President and Secretary of Franchise Finance Corporation of America, a publicly traded real estate investment trust, where he is responsible for the company's research and investment underwriting. Previously, Mr. Volk served in various capacities in the property management and underwriting areas and was a Director of the company. He received his bachelor's degree from Washington and Lee University in 1979 and his master of business administration degree in finance from Georgia State University in 1987. Mr. Volk is a member of the Association for

Investment Management and Research and the Phoenix Society of Financial Analysts.

James R. Webb is a Professor of Finance and Director of the Center for the Study of Real Estate Brokerage and Markets at the James J. Nance College of Business of Cleveland State University. He is the Executive Director and also a past president of the American Real Estate Society, Chairman of the Board of the National Bureau of Real Estate Research, and a founding member of the Institute of Chartered Real Estate Analysts. In 1990 he was the first recipient of the James A. Graaskamp award. He has served as a consultant to numerous organizations, including the Department of Energy and NLO on the Fernald Nuclear facility, Ohio State University Research Foundation, and the Ohio Real Estate Commission. Mr. Webb has also written two books—*The Theory and Practice of Real Estate Finance* (co-author) and *Micro-Real Estate: The Quintessential Dictums*.

William C. Wheaton has worked at the vanguard studying urban economics for more than 10 years. His theoretical work contributed to the founding and development of the field as an academic discipline, and his original research has been applied by major private and public sector institutions. Repeatedly, Mr. Wheaton's innovative perspective and integrated economic modeling have provided a practicable framework for decision making. Mr. Wheaton has a doctorate degree in economics and holds a Professorship of Economics and Urban Planning at the Massachusetts Institute of Technology and is the Director of the MIT Center of Real Estate. He is a principal in CB Commercial/Torto Wheaton Research.

Michael S. Young is Vice-President and Director of Quantitative Research of The RREEF Funds, San Francisco, California. He has been involved in a broad array of real estate activities for over 20 years, including development, consulting, land use economics, valuation, investment management, and computer systems design and implementation. Mr. Young is the author of over 30 works on the theory and application of individual property and portfolio investment analysis, valuation, and computer applications in real estate. He received his bachelor's degree from Cornell University and his master's degree from the University of Chicago.

CONSULTING EDITORS

Robert M. Angland
Cabot Partners, Ltd.

Mary M. Briggs
MacFarlane Partners, LP

Joshua M. Brown
Security Capital Group

John M. Burlingame
*Hyatt Development
  Corporation*

Michael M. Caron
Block & Caron

Karl E. Case, Jr.
Wellesley College

Daniel M. Cashdan, Jr.
Aldrich, Eastman, & Waltch

Peter F. Colwell
University of Illinois–Urbana

Cornelius Daly
*Pennsylvania Public School
  Employees' Retirement
  System*

Joseph B. Diehl

Jeffrey J. Diermeier
Brinson Partners

Richard M. Ennis
Ennis, Knupp & Associates

Roger C. Franz
CalPERS

Jack Friedman
The Roulac Group

Joseph Garrett
Garrett Realty Advisors

Bruce Garrison
*Kidder, Peabody & Company,
  Inc.*

Robert H. Gidel
Brazos Asset Management

S. Michael Giliberto
Lehman Brothers

Jacques N. Gordon
LaSalle Partners

Richard A. Graff
Electrum Partners

Joseph E. Gyourko
*The Wharton School of
  Business*

John Hart
Hart Advisors

Thomas A. Hassard
Virginia Retirement System

Peter Jeans
Alaska Permanent Fund

Howard Kaplan
Farmvest, Inc.

Jonathon Kerester
Realty Investment Advisors

Donald A. King, Jr.
The RREEF Funds

Paula K. Konikoff
Valuation Advisory Services

PREFACE

The well-documented collapse of commercial real estate values in the late 1980s and early 1990s caused many of us involved in the serious issues of real estate investment to carefully re-examine our investment paradigms and methodologies. This re-examination has resulted in an interesting dichotomy: the simple virtues of cash flow versus the mind-numbing advances of the capital markets. On the one hand, we have again focused our sights on cash flow ("cash is king"). The collapse of "paper" profits, the hype of "trophy" properties, and so on has led more than one real estate investor back to the virtues of buying properties based on their "fundamentals." It strikes me as no coincidence that investors in common stocks fled to the common-sense practicalities advocated by Benjamin Graham and David Dodd (in their classic book *Security Analysis*) as a result of the stock market crash of the 1930s. In fact, the jargon of the stock market describes as fundamentalists those investors who attempt to analyze a corporation's long-term growth prospects (in light of a host of considerations: balance sheet strength, liquidity, industry position, etc.) and its current earnings, while those who trade based on recent price behavior and trends are called technicians (or, worse yet, chartists). The fundamental analyst/investor is considered to be more likely to uncover discrepancies between price and value[1] and to invest on a long-term basis to profitably capture the divergence and convergence between the two. The real estate market crash in the 1980s and 1990s has caused (rightfully, in my opinion) a similar conversion of the previously "unwashed" to a more fundamental approach.

On the other hand, we attempt to apply the ever-increasing technological advances of the capital markets to real estate investment. Concepts like modern portfolio theory (MPT), duration, securitization, option-based-pricing, and so on were mere blips on the radar screens

---

[1] Yes, many investors and most regulators seem to confuse these two, often to the misfortune of the appraisal community.

of most practitioners 10 or so years ago. Today these concepts (and others) explode on our radar screens like giant supernovas. The difficulties for even the most savvy practitioners are manifold: How does the practicality of such concepts interplay with the mathematical rigor that most of these concepts engender? What does all the math really mean? Since most of these concepts have stock and/or bond origins, how should they be tempered given the difference between these markets and the real estate market? Despite these uncertainties, many of us cannot help but feel that somewhere in the midst of this confusion lies a better approach to real estate investment and portfolio management. Thus, the quest continues unabated, with the "quants" (i.e., those analysts/investors with a severe quantitative bent) leading the way.

This book addresses two issues: the quantitative influences of an evolving capital market tempered by a "fundamental" perspective. Yet this is not enough. To offer practical relevance, this book must offer at least two additional perspectives. First, while much of it also applies to individual investors, this book is oriented primarily toward institutional investors. This orientation reflects the increasing prominence of such investors as leaders in the area of real estate investment and portfolio management. Second, the book's emphasis is on real estate equities as opposed to real estate debt (or mortgages). This emphasis reflects the role real estate equities play (or at least are hoped to play) in the context of mixed-asset portfolios; namely, real estate equities, in the long run, are expected to offer attractive risk-adjusted returns that are negatively to moderately correlated with stock and bond returns. Thus, the inclusion of real estate equities is expected to enhance the risk-return characteristics of the mixed-asset portfolio. Simply stated, real estate debt (mortgages) is a bond for which the underlying collateral happens to be real estate. While mortgage investments may be attractive to investors because of their spread in interest rates (i.e., mortgage interest rates vis-à-vis other sectors of the bond market), mortgages remain essentially a "credit play" within the bond manager's investment universe. However, when one considers the option-based aspects of mortgage lending (i.e., the borrower owns a put option that enables him or her to "put" the property back to the lender if the real estate performance is unsatisfactory) and the recent real estate crash (which has made many mortgages into equities "in waiting"), much of what this book has to say can also be applied to mortgage investing. The other practical reason for essentially excluding mortgages is that the appropriate coverage of the mortgage markets would have made the length of the book unwieldy. Thus, this book uses the terms *real estate* and *real estate equities* interchangeably, both referring to unleveraged real equity investments (unless otherwise noted).

Finally, to meet the daunting challenges of addressing the issues outlined above, this book is divided into six parts:

1. *Players and Paradigms*
   Part 1 overviews the force that institutional players have become in the real estate investment arena and many of the conceptual frameworks these sophisticated investors use to assemble and manage real estate portfolios.

2. *Sticks and Bricks*
   Part 2 overviews the major property types in terms of their historical performance and the key factors affecting their past and future performance. An understanding of the nuances of each property type is an essential ingredient in (1) forming efficient real estate portfolios and (2) considering the impacts of the electronic revolution (telecommuting, virtual offices, etc.) and its attendant changes in the demand for real estate by tenants.

3. *Capital Structure*
   Institutional real estate investment has traditionally been characterized by unleveraged, unsecuritized transactions (or portfolios). Part 3 explores the impacts of both leverage and securitization.

4. *Elements of Real Estate Investment*
   Unlike the highly evolved securities markets for stocks and bonds and due to the legal complications present in real estate, certain aspects of real estate investment require special appreciation: appraisal practices and issues, environmental issues, and real estate due diligence. Part 4 addresses these issues.

5. *How Do We Get There from Here?*
   Having laid much of the foundation for effective real estate portfolio management, it is important to also understand the organizational requirements. How can consultants best be used? How should a real estate department or firm be structured? What role should real estate research play? Part 5 attempts to answer these questions.

6. *Portfolio Management Revisited*

Part 6 revisits real estate portfolio management. These chapters present state-of-the-art thinking on crucial issues: diversification considerations, portfolio strategies, the portfolio management process, real estate's role in a mixed-asset portfolio, the application of options and futures to real estate, and the influences of investor behavior and psychology.

The authors of these chapters are some of the most respected practitioners and academicians in and outside the world of real estate investment management. It has been my great pleasure to work with them, and I hope you will benefit from their invaluable counsel.

ACKNOWLEDGMENTS

It is appropriate that my first acknowledgment extends to Richard Garrigan (DePaul University) for persuading me to tackle this project and for his encouragement and insight along the way. Next, I would like to thank the members of the Editorial Advisory Board; their guidance and input helped mold the better parts of this book. In particular, I would like to thank Marc Louargand (Cornerstone Realty Advisers, née MIT) and Jim Webb (Cleveland State University) for countless hours of advice and guidance. My first contact with Jim was at the University of Illinois–Urbana, where I was a beer-swilling, know-it-all undergraduate and he was an intolerant, in-a-hurry doctoral candidate. It is comforting to note that the passage of time has only slightly smoothed our rough edges.

Obviously, any project such as this one owes its lifeblood to the contributing authors. The experience, expertise, enthusiasm, and persistence that they brought to bear on each chapter must be marveled at. I extend my sincere thanks to each of them. Similarly, the consulting editors (two per chapter) helped fine-tune chapters or argued for wholesale revisions, where they thought appropriate. The book surely benefited from their input.

I also thank the people at Irwin Professional Publishing, Ralph Rieves and Rebecca Dodson in particular, for their professionalism and understanding.

Last but not least, I would like to thank and acknowledge my colleagues at Citadel Realty, Inc. Their indulgence of my editorial odyssey often meant that a heavier load fell on their shoulders. Most of all, I would like to thank Carol Miklica; her perseverance, personality, and proficiency were invaluable and indispensable. This book would have never emerged without her.

Thanks to one and all!

Joseph L. Pagliari, Jr., CFA

CONTENTS

PART 6
PORTFOLIO MANAGEMENT REVISITED

PART 1

PLAYERS AND PARADIGMS

CHAPTER 1

THE EVOLUTION OF INSTITUTIONAL INVESTMENT IN REAL ESTATE

Geoffrey Dohrmann
Institutional Real Estate, Inc.

Institution: an established organization; especially, one dedicated to public service
Institutionalize: to make or treat as an institution

The American Heritage Dictionary of the English Language

INTRODUCTION

Since the late 1960s, the ownership and management of commercial real estate have been shifting from the hands of gut-driven, deal-oriented entrepreneurs to those of more information-driven and more strategic institutional investors. This is a secular, not a cyclical, change, and it is revolutionizing the real estate investment industry.

The term *institutional investor* here refers to life insurance companies, commercial banks, thrifts, credit companies, pension funds, publicly held real estate investment trusts (REITs) and real estate operating companies, private real estate investment trusts, mortgage conduits and mortgage-backed securities (MBSs), and both public and private real estate syndications. All of these are established organizations dedicated to managing investments for the benefit of

The author would like to thank Ellen Beckett Brown for her assistance on the initial chapter draft. Much of this chapter is based upon her thesis topic prepared as a graduate student at the Massachusetts Institute of Technology. Some of the passages were used nearly verbatim from her dissertation.

third parties or the public. For an overview of relative market strength, see Exhibit 1–1.

Compared to their involvement in other asset classes, institutional investors' interest in real estate is a relatively new phenomenon. Even as recently as 1952, life insurance companies and pension funds held the majority of their assets in long-term bonds. Over the next 20 years, stock investments gradually grew until by 1972, they

EXHIBIT 1–1

The Institutional Real Estate Investment Market (Real Estate Assets Held by Institutional Investors as of January 31, 1993)

	Equity		Debt**		Combined Total	
	Amount*	%	Amount*	%	Amount*	%
Life insurance companies	$51	16.6%	$246	22.7%	$297	21.3%
Thrifts and savings banks	20	6.5	165	15.2	185	13.3
Credit companies	N/A	0.0	15	1.4	15	1.1
Commercial banks	28	9.1	427	39.3	455	32.6
RTC, FDIC, SIDs	28	9.1	53	4.9	81	5.8
Pension funds	68	22.1	90	8.3	158	11.3
Endowments	3	1.0	3	0.3	6	0.4
Foundations	2	0.6	1	0.1	3	0.2
Equity REITs	28	9.1	N/A	0.0	28	2.0
Mortgage and hybrid REITs	3	1.0	23	2.1	23	1.7
Syndications	77	25.0	20	1.8	97	7.0
Commercial MBSs	N/A	0.0	42	3.9	42	3.0
Total	$308	100.0%	$1,085	100.0%	$1,393	100.0%
	22.1%		77.9%		100.0%	

* In billions of dollars.
** Nonsecuritized mortgage loans and mortgage-backed securities.

Sources: Institutional Real Estate, Inc.; *Real Estate Capital Markets Report.*

comprised nearly 40 percent of total pension fund assets. Today they range between 40 and 60 percent of most institutional portfolios; as a result, institutional investors now control roughly 25 percent of all financial assets. The institutionalization of real estate, which is now well under way, is simply an extension of this long-term trend.

The first wave of real estate institutionalization occurred in the late 1940s, when enabling legislation was passed in New York and other states increasing allowable investment limits for owned real estate. This legislation was intended to ease the flow of capital into postwar civilian construction of housing and office facilities and came at a time when the insurance industry's portfolios were heavy with government bonds at low interest rates. The effect was a dramatic increase in life company real estate lending and investment, driving real estate and mortgage investments as a percentage of total portfolios from 18.5 percent to nearly 40 percent in just 10 years—an average annual asset growth rate of 30 percent per year. See Exhibit 1–2. Much of this early activity focused on financing or investing in properties triple net leased to large, creditworthy corporate tenants.[1]

EXHIBIT 1–2

U.S. Life Insurance Companies' Real Estate Holdings as Percentage of Total Assets ($ Millions/Book Values, End of Year)

	Mortgages		Real Estate		Total	
	Amount	%	Amount	%	Amount	%
1947	$8,675	16.8%	$887	1.7%	$9,562	18.5%
1957	35,236	34.8	3,119	3.1	35,236	37.9
1965*	60,013	37.8	4,681	3.0	64,694	40.8
1987	213,450	20.4	34,172	3.3	247,622	23.7
1992	246,702	14.8	50,595	3.1	297,297	17.9

* 1967 data not available.

Source: *Life Insurance Fact Book.*

---

[1] Bruce Ricks, *Recent Trends in Institutional Real Estate Investments,* The Center for Real Estate and Urban Economics, Institute of Urban and Regional Development, University of California, Berkeley, 1964.

The first pension fund investments in real estate were conducted by bank trust departments on behalf of their large pension fund clients like General Electric and GM. Most of these investments focused on sale leaseback transactions.[2] Real estate owned or managed by bank trust departments grew from $512 million or 3.3 percent of total assets in 1947 to $1.7 billion or 3.8 percent of total assets in 1961.

Compared to the activities of university endowments and life companies, pension fund investment in real estate is a relatively new phenomenon. Pension funds began investing in real estate initially as lenders and later as investors in net leased property. According to data compiled from various sources, corporate pension fund investments in real estate grew from roughly $313 million or 1.6 percent of total assets in 1957 to $907 million or 2.8 percent of total assets by 1961.

Growth in pension fund investment was hampered until the late 1960s and early 1970s by, among other things, a lack of appropriate vehicles. While larger funds were able to achieve sufficient diversification by investing directly, smaller funds needed to pool their assets to achieve the same level of diversification.[3]

The first real estate commingled fund was offered in 1968, but it was not until the latter half of the 1970s that pension funds began to seriously consider realty allocations as an integral part of their broad portfolio strategy. Several motivating factors converged at that time, prompting the shift into real estate. First, the passage of ERISA in 1974 mandated diversification across asset classes. Second, the geometric growth in pension fund contributions necessitated investments capable of absorbing large amounts of long-term capital, while double-digit inflation and the demand for space in an expanding economy drove realty returns higher and higher. Perhaps most important, in the rising-interest-rate, inflation-driven economy of the 1970s, total returns on pension fund stock and bond portfolio holdings were falling dramatically.

The increasing demand for institutional investment grade properties stimulated the growth of the commingled funds and the life company, bank, and independent real estate investment advisory

---

[2] Ibid.

[3] Stephen Roulac, *Institutional Investment in Real Estate,* 1973.

firms that sponsored them. These firms provided professional real estate products and services to clients who had no prior experience in real estate investment. They worked with clients to define their individual investment objectives; helped clients form specific investment strategies based on those objectives; researched the markets in light of those strategies; originated specific investment opportunities within selected markets; underwrote (established value and performed due diligence on) potential acquisitions; negotiated and closed specific transactions; developed projections, budgets, and operating plans for specific assets; developed and guided the implementation of asset and property management strategies; managed properties on-site with their own in-house staff or contracted with third-party property management companies; compiled portfolio and property level information for reports to clients and their consultants; prepared client and consultant reports; responded to client and consultant inquiries; monitored portfolio performance against original client objectives; and timed and negotiated the sale of specific clients' assets. The tasks were far more complex than those executed by traditional equity and fixed-income managers, and the fees reflected that complexity, being from 50 to 150 basis points higher as a percentage of assets under management.

While no more than 15 such advisory firms operated in the mid-1970s, by 1983 nearly 70 such firms were actively managing pension fund real estate assets. By 1993 there were well over 100, not including the 50 or so firms vying to enter the business.

To assist pension funds in developing and executing their investment strategies, investment consultants and, later, specialized real estate investment consultants also began to emerge. These firms assisted pension funds in developing strategic asset allocation plans, executing asset and liability matching strategies, formulating formal investment strategies and policies, and later preparing specific real estate investment strategies and policies. In addition, consultants helped guide pension fund investment decision-making patterns by maintaining databases on the universe of investment manager options available to them; conducting investment manager searches; monitoring investment manager and portfolio performance; and providing independent fiduciary services, including independent reviews of the fairness and reasonableness of specific transactions and of the merits of specific investment opportunities.

In 1987, there was really only one specialized institutional real

estate investment consulting shop: the real estate consulting group
of Frank Russell Company. Today there are at least four independent
consulting firms (Institutional Property Consultants, the Townsend
Group; Pension Real Estate Services, and Saylor Property Capital)
and at least four major shops within the four largest general consulting firms (Callan & Associates, SEI Realty, Pension Consulting
Alliance, Wilshire Associates, and, of course, Frank Russell Company). In addition, a variety of smaller firms offer real estate consulting as part of their total service package; these include Asset
Consulting Group, DeMarche & Associates, the Marco Group, Ronald
A. Karp and Associates, Rogers Casey and Associates, and Evaluation
Associates, among others.

Pension fund investment followed a predictable pattern. To obtain adequate diversification, investors began by investing in commingled funds. As core portfolio positions were established and investors became more comfortable and sophisticated, they began to gravi-
tate toward more direct forms of investment.

Initially, open-end commingled funds, patterned after the open-
end stock and bond mutual funds that enabled investors to buy in
and out of the funds at net asset values, were the favored means
of investment. Almost always sponsored by either a large bank or
insurance company, these funds usually were structured as insurance
company separate accounts or bank trust accounts and focused primarily on so-called core-diversified investment strategies. Most of
these funds eventually assembled large, nationally diversified portfolios of large, trophy-type CBD office towers, regional shopping centers,
and class A industrial office parks.

In the late 1970s and early 1980s, dissatisfaction with the structure and performance of such funds eventually led sponsors to embrace closed-end commingled funds. These funds, structured as group
trusts or limited partnerships, were patterned after closed-end stock
and bond mutual funds, focusing on myriad specialized investment
strategies ranging from core diversified to regional and property
specific. (Closed-end funds typically ranged between $50 million and
$500 million in size versus $500 million or more for the average
open-end fund.) However, closed-end funds failed to be the panacea
for which most investors had hoped. Relatively high fees and conflicts
of interest compounded investor dissatisfaction when these funds'
performance began to falter in the late 1980s and early 1990s.

As of 1992, the smaller pension, foundation, and endowment fund
investor had all but withdrawn from the market. Larger funds, for

the most part, had abandoned commingled fund investment in favor of more direct forms of investment administered by either in-house real estate personnel or separate accounts managed by an advisory firm.

As larger funds became more heavily involved in the direction of their real estate investments, the relationship between investors and their advisors also evolved from being fully discretionary (where the advisory firm made all the critical decisions) to being completely nondiscretionary (where the advisor recommends, but the investor makes all the critical decisions).

When transaction volume dwindled and property values nose-dived in the late 1980s and early 1990s, research, portfolio management, asset management, and fiduciary reporting capabilities replaced acquisition expertise and deal flow as the primary criteria for selecting an advisory firm. As performance dropped, investors placed greater and greater demands on investment managers for information about their portfolios, while dramatically cutting the fees paid to managers.

The role of the advisory firm today is to originate and underwrite potential acquisitions or loans and to act as an operating company on behalf of its investors. The primary focus of most managers today is to oversee the management and eventual disposition of properties on behalf of their investors.

In the early 1990s, the advisory industry began to contract in response to the slowdown in the national economy, the low level of activity in the real estate market, and the demand by pension funds for increased service and lower fees. To survive this period of restructuring, advisory firms had to have a substantial base of assets under management—a minimum of $500 million to $1 billion—to stay in business. Research also began to play an increasingly important role in the decisions of advisory firms. Institutional investors are information-driven rather than gut-driven investors. They demand and require quantifiable, economically justified, well-documented investment decisions. Research helps fulfill this need.

TAX-SHELTER SYNDICATION

According to data supplied by the Stanger *Register* and *Questor,* tax-driven syndication activity peaked between 1981 and 1986. The upswing was stimulated by the passage of the Economic Recovery Tax

Act of 1981 (ERTA). The downswing resulted from the passage of the Tax Reform Act of 1986 (TRA). For example, from 1974 to 1981, public syndications raised over $2 billion in real estate capital, while during the three-year period between 1980 and 1983 alone, syndicators raised well over $10 billion, or five times the amount raised in the previous six years. This volume peaked in 1984 at nearly $10 billion, dropped precipitously to $8 billion in 1985, climbed a little in 1986, and then continued to drop in 1987 and 1988. See Exhibit 1–3. By 1988, however, the industry had raised a total of $49 billion and, despite the change in the tax laws, raised substantially more money between 1985 and 1989 than it did between 1980 and 1984. Since most of these partnerships were highly leveraged, this meant the industry had been able to acquire real estate portfolio holdings between $120 billion and $160 billion.

Throughout the early 1980s, these tax-driven institutional investors had been encouraged by the Tax Code to pay increasingly higher prices for properties to generate greater tax benefits for their limited partners. The willingness of tax-driven investors to pay up

EXHIBIT 1–3
Registrations of Public Limited Partnership Offerings, 1974–88 ($ Millions)

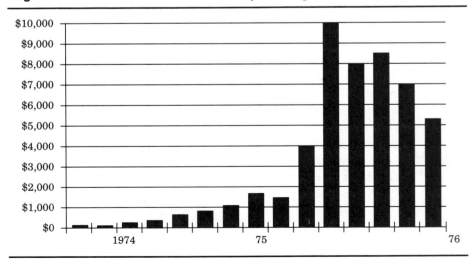

Source: *Questor Real Estate Syndication Yearbook 1984*, Robert A. Stanger & Company.

for property was the first major capital stimulus driving up property appreciation. The emergence of these investors as a dominant force during the 1980s marked the turning point for the real estate markets. Once driven primarily by fundamental supply and demand and controlled by inherent market disciplines, they now shifted to being driven primarily by the availability of capital. In turn, market disciplines crumbled.

The TRA had been passed too late, and an irresistible momentum in the market already had been well established. Foreign investment institutions, U.S. pension funds, and developers, levered to a greater or lesser degree by bank, savings and loan, and life company borrowings, continued to feed the fires. Consequently, property values continued to rise or hold firm throughout much of the remainder of the decade.

FOREIGN INVESTORS

Throughout the 1980s, foreign investors with a long history of global real estate investment generally viewed the U.S. market as a safe haven for long-term investment of their considerable assets. Between 1985 and 1987, the 40 percent drop in the dollar relative to the yen, deutsche mark, and pound also made U.S. realty seem inexpensive by comparison. Japanese institutions and individuals were particularly keen on U.S. markets. Due to the high rate of savings in Japan, institutional investors had more capital than they could invest domestically, while the favorable balance of payments situation produced the liquidity needed to fund U.S. acquisitions. Even more of an impetus were the 6 to 8 percent yields for U.S. trophy properties, a bonanza compared to Japanese domestic returns of between 2 and 4 percent.[4]

Between 1980 and 1989 (the peak year for foreign investment in U.S. real estate), 45 foreign investment institutions invested nearly $39 billion of new capital in U.S. property. See Exhibit 1–4. Assuming these investments were leveraged between 40 and 60 percent, foreign investors now controlled between $66 billion and $97 billion of U.S. property.

---

[4] Larry Bacow, *Understanding Foreign Investment in Real Estate*, MIT, Center for Real Estate Development, 1987.

EXHIBIT 1–4
Total Foreign Capital Invested in U.S.
Real Estate, 1980–92 ($ Billions)

1980	$7.3
1981	10.7
1982	13.5
1983	17.2
1984	20.7
1985	22.8
1986	26.2
1987	31.8
1988	40.0
1989	45.9
1990	34.9
1991	34.4
1992	35.3

Sources: The Real Estate Consulting Group of Deloitte & Touche; U.S. Department of Commerce.

The devaluation of U.S. property, coupled with wide swings in currency exchange rates and a worldwide economic recession, hammered foreign investors, particularly the Japanese, who since 1990 have gradually been paring down their U.S. real estate property holdings. The outlook for renewed foreign real estate investment for the remainder of the decade was relatively positive, however. In a 1993 survey of its membership, the Association for Foreign Investment in U.S. Real Estate (AFIRE) found that a clear majority of respondents viewed the prospects for U.S. realty markets to be better in 1994 than in 1993 and better than those for the European property markets. An even larger majority indicated they planned to either retain or expand their investment posture in the U.S. rather than reduce their exposures.[5]

REAL ESTATE INVESTMENT TRUSTS

According to the National Association of Real Estate Investment Trusts (NAREIT), the history of REITs dates back to the 19th century, when the very first real estate investment trusts were organized as

---

[5] Association of Foreign Investors in U.S. Real Estate, *Annual Survey of Membership*, 1993.

Massachusetts business trusts. However, the viability of these early REITs was undermined by a 1935 federal tax court ruling that required all business trusts to be taxed as corporations.[6]

In 1960, Congress passed the Real Estate Investment Trust Act of 1960, creating a new form of institutional investor: the real estate investment trust, or REIT. By electing REIT status under the 1960 REIT act, a real estate investment management corporation or trust now could become exempt from corporate taxation. Most states recognize this federal exemption and do not require REITs to pay state income tax. REITs therefore are able to distribute income directly to shareholders, thus avoiding double taxation of dividends and distributions.[7]

A REIT essentially is a corporation or trust that enables individual and/or institutional investors to combine their capital to acquire or provide financing for all forms of real estate, provided it qualifies for REIT election and makes a successful election. To qualify for REIT status, a REIT must:

- Be a corporation, business trust, or similar association.
- Be managed by a board of directors or trustees.
- Have shares that are fully transferable.
- Have a minimum of 100 shareholders.
- Have no more than 50 percent of its shares held by five or fewer individuals during the last half of each taxable year (since 1993, pension funds are treated as a collection of the beneficiaries of the pension trust).
- Invest at least 75 percent of total assets in real estate.
- Derive at least 75 percent of gross income from rents from real property or interest on mortgages on real property.
- Derive no more than 30 percent of gross income from the sale of real property held for less than four years, securities held for less than six months, or certain prohibited transactions.
- Pay dividends of at least 95 percent of REIT taxable income.

---

[6] National Association of Real Estate Investment Trusts, *REIT Fact Book*, 1993.

[7] National Association of Real Estate Investment Trusts, *REIT: All About It*, 1993.

Analysts typically classify REITs as using one of three investment approaches: equity REITs, which invest directly in real property; mortgage REITs, which lend money on real property; and hybrid
REITs, which do both. REITs are further categorized by investment
strategy. The most common groupings include retail, office, multifamily residential, industrial, health care, and other (which includes
hotels, manufactured housing, mobile home parks, and even golf
course investments).

A REIT's investments are determined by the REIT's board of
directors or trustees. Directors are elected by and responsible solely
to the shareholders. Directors then appoint management, either by
hiring or retaining managers as employees of the REIT or by contracting with independent REIT advisors.

The first real estate investment trusts organized in the wake of
the 1960 REIT act were equity trusts. Between 1961 and 1973, REITs
raised nearly $6.6 billion in new capital in a total of 371 offerings
(approximately $4.3 billion in 189 initial public offerings, or IPOs,
and approximately $2.3 billion in 182 secondary offerings.)[8]

Industry growth between 1960 and 1968, however, was slow by
all standards, including assets, market capitalization, earnings per
share, and share price appreciation. But in 1969, the market began to
take off. Market capitalization doubled each year for four consecutive
years between 1969 and 1972. The bull market for REIT stocks of
1969 to 1972 occurred during a climate of tight monetary policy, high
interest rates, and limited availability of funds for new construction
and development. Sensing the opportunity to grow dividends by capitalizing on the high yields offered by the market, REITs stepped in
to fill the development and construction financing gap. By 1972, over
50 percent of REIT industry investments were in the form of development or construction loans. REIT initial public and secondary offerings accounted for more than 11 percent of the total equity IPO and
secondaries sold in the United States during this period.

While rates in general were high, REITs were able to borrow
from the public and private markets at much lower rates than they
could lend to the development community. To lever their yields and
increase their lending power, REITs therefore went to the public and

---

[8] National Association of Real Estate Investment Trusts, *REIT Handbook,* 1994.

private debt markets through the issuance of commercial paper and bank borrowings. Aggregate REIT industry borrowings outstanding, totaling roughly $90 million in 1968, tripled for each of the next four years to over $6 billion in 1972 and over $10 billion in 1973 and 1974. The industry's average debt-to-equity ratio had risen from 1 to 1 in 1968 to 3.4 to 1 in 1974.[9]

Many of the REITs formed in the early 1970s were designed primarily as financing vehicles; many of these were set up by commercial banks to make riskier commercial construction loans that the banks didn't want to (or weren't allowed) to keep in their own portfolios. As noted above, most of these mortgage REITs were highly leveraged, some with debt-to-equity ratios as high as 8 to 1.[10] By late 1972 and early 1973, many of the developers to whom the REITs had lent their money found themselves in the uncomfortable position of being unable to lease up or sell their projects as a result of a national recession and an overbuilt real estate market. Plagued by rising interests rates, many were unable to meet the debt service on their loans. Borrowers defaulted, and the highly leveraged REITs in turn saw their earnings drop considerably. As a result, many REITs were no longer able to meet the debt service on their own borrowings.

To resolve their problems, many REITs started surrendering deeds in lieu of foreclosure in exchange for cancellation of some of this debt, which further reduced profit margins. As a result, a number of REITs were forced to omit dividends, and share prices plummeted. The NAREIT share price index fell by 3.3 percent in 1972 and by a whopping 50 percent in 1973.

Because of the hammering investors had taken, money for new REIT IPOs literally dried up; very little new money was raised between 1973 and 1974, and no new money was raised between 1975 and 1977.[11] Developing lending by REITs, in turn, all but evaporated, falling from $10 billion in 1974 to less than $4 billion in 1975 and roughly $2 billion in 1976.

While common, however, not all REITs shared this fate. Sixty-three trusts were able to maintain regular dividend payments

---

[9] National Association of Real Estate Investment Trusts, *REIT Fact Book*, 1986.

[10] Tim Legesse, "Securitization," *The Institutional Real Estate Letter* 5, no. 12, December 1993.

[11] National Association of Real Estate Investment Trusts, *REIT Handbook*, 1994.

throughout the 1972–78 real estate recession. Equity REITs in particular fared better; many of these were able to continue to grow, albeit at a much slower but nevertheless steady pace. Equity investments grew, for example, from $4 billion in 1974 to $5 billion in 1976.

By 1976, most of the REITs that had survived the recession began to resume normal operations. Mortgage REITs gradually began to expand their loan portfolios once again. Mortgage REITs particularly hard hit by the downturn, however, were forced to continue to focus internally on restructuring their existing loan portfolios.

During the reconstruction period of 1976 to 1983, total industry assets remained virtually unchanged, ranging between $7 billion and $8 billion, but balance sheet health improved considerably, returning to a debt-to-equity ratio of 1 to 1 by 1983. Share prices doubled during this time, while dividend yields remained high, between 8 and 10 percent.

This recovery was clearly reflected in a resurgence of new IPO activity beginning in 1976.[12] In 1975, the first limited or finite-life REITs (FREITs) were introduced. Prior to that time, REITs universally had been organized as traditional corporate entities, that is, organized to have perpetual or infinite life. Sixteen of these new entities were formed in 1985, five in 1985, and five more in 1987. Most of these finite-life REITs were organized as advised rather than self-administered REITs. (Over the long term, the FREIT concept has largely been rejected by the public markets, partly because of the perception of conflicts of interest between FREIT advisors and shareholders. In general, FREIT share prices have traded down relative to other REITs.) When the markets cooled in the recession of 1981 and 1982, IPO activity took a slight dip, but continued to grow from 1983 through 1987, initially fueled by the real estate–favorable provisions of the Economic Recovery Tax Act of 1981.[13]

The REIT industry experienced its first year of truly strong growth in 1984, when 10 IPOs were registered, raising $449 million, and existing REITs raised $2.7 billion in secondary equity ($700 million) and debt ($2 billion) offerings. Levered by the acquisition

---

[12] Ibid.
[13] Ibid.

opportunities and strong operating results delivered by a recovering real estate market, this new capital helped boost industry assets from $7.5 billion to $12 billion, with the NAREIT share price index hitting four new highs. Generating an average yield of 9 percent and earning an average 4 percent appreciation in share price, REIT stocks outperformed the market considerably.[14]

Legislative activity and several Treasury Department proposals enacted in 1984, along with the passage of the Tax Reform Act of 1986 (TRA), severely undermined the viability of tax-driven limited partnership syndication offerings, but actually enhanced the appeal of REITs as an alternative real estate investment option. Despite concerns over the pending tax legislation, for example, an additional 33 companies registered to qualify as REITs and completed public stock offerings in 1985. In total, 59 initial public and secondary offerings were completed that year, raising $3.2 billion in equity and $1.1 billion in debt. This $4.3 billion raised in one year set another new record for the industry, only to be surpassed in 1986, when 63 offerings were completed. These raised an additional $4.7 billion, most of it ($2.84 billion) in debt. IPO activity fell substantially, with most of the equity ($623 million) raised in secondary offerings. The market correction of 1987 (roughly 28.5 percent) resulted in an 18 percent correction in REIT prices; as a result, IPO activity slackened considerably, but rebounded in 1988 and 1989.[15]

The 1980s also witnessed the emergence of more specialized REITs, including a sector focused on the purchase of mortgage-backed securities, single-family loans, or single-family residential lending and subsequent packaging and selling of these packages into the capital markets in the form of collateralized mortgage obligations (CMOs) and other mortgage-backed securities.

With bad news abounding and property values free falling, REIT prices and IPO activity also adjusted downward in 1990 through 1991. The successful initial public offering of KIMCO in November 1992, however, opened the door to the most successful bull market in the history of publicly traded real estate securities. In 1992, a total of $6.6 billion was raised in 8 IPOs and 24 secondaries, and in the

---

[14] Ibid.
[15] Ibid.

landmark 1993 bull market, a record $11.4 billion was raised: $8.15 billion in 41 IPOs and $3.2 billion in 38 secondaries. See Exhibit 1–5.

Unlike the first great wave of securitization in the 1970s, the new REITs launched in 1992 and 1993 for the most part were operating companies rather than financing vehicles. Some were designed to enable entrepreneurial operators to cash out, but most were designed to allow operators to restructure their balance sheets by paying down debt and to better access the global capital markets. By ensuring that they would be able to finance the ongoing growth of their businesses, these operators created for themselves a significant competitive advantage over the operators of privately held portfolios.

As a result of all this new activity, the market capitalization of the REIT industry grew in 1993 by a record 67 percent in one year alone. Perhaps more important, the average market capitalization of the new crop of REITs had grown to new record highs in 1992 and 1993, from $110 in 1987 and $115 in 1992 to an average of $199 in 1993. By the end of 1993, 16 REITs had obtained a market capitalization in excess of $500 million and four REITs had market caps over the $1 billion mark.[16]

The larger capitalization of the market in general, the much larger number of REITs, and the larger average market capitalization of individual issues made it much easier for other financial institutions like mutual funds, pension funds, life companies, and professional money managers to participate in the real estate securities market by buying REIT shares and debt securities. Participate they did, driving REIT yields down to historically low levels and driving pricing up to record high multiples.[17]

Pension funds, however, have been slower to participate in this market directly, primarily because smaller pension funds that typically invest in pooled investment vehicles like REITs had not been as active in the real estate markets of the early 1990s. As their consultants gear up to help them access the public markets, and as they once again begin to become more active in building their real estate portfolios, pension fund interest in REIT stocks is expected to increase significantly.[18]

---

[16] Ibid.

[17] Legesse, "Securitization."

[18] Ibid.

EXHIBIT 1–5
Offerings of Equity Securities by REITs, 1961–93 ($ Millions)

	Total Offerings		IPOs		Secondaries	
	Number	*Total*	*Number*	*Total*	*Number*	*Total*
1961	14	$71.9	14	$71.9	0	$0.0
1962	16	105.9	12	81.8	4	24.1
1963	9	25.8	6	4.0	3	21.8
1964	19	36.2	11	1.4	8	34.8
1965	14	32.6	5	3.0	9	29.6
1966	3	5.8	1	0.0	2	5.8
1967	7	41.5	1	0.0	6	41.5
1968	14	122.4	4	67.6	10	54.8
1969	58	1,256.7	33	976.7	25	280.0
1970	72	1,687.4	41	1,358.4	31	329.0
1971	78	1,987.3	32	1,183.4	46	803.9
1972	67	1,223.3	29	563.2	38	660.1
1973	68	852.1	18	156.8	50	695.3
1974	17	23.7	5	1.5	12	22.2
1975	5	0.4	1	0.0	4	0.4
1976	8	19.7	0	0.0	8	19.7
1977	8	91.9	0	0.0	8	91.9
1978	12	91.5	3	8.4	9	83.1
1979	18	110.5	4	0.0	14	110.5
1980	20	264.0	4	30.0	16	234.0
1981	22	244.7	5	100.0	17	144.7
1982	9	435.1	3	315.0	5	115.1
1983	23	747.0	4	159.0	15	438.0
1984	18	1,438.4	6	140.0	8	173.0
1985	59	4,270.6	29	2,791.9	17	412.7
1986	63	4,668.9	20	1,204.4	17	623.7
1987	50	2,929.2	12	634.4	15	733.0
1988	37	3,068.7	13	1,374.2	13	785.0
1989	34	2,440.8	11	1,074.5	15	722.1
1990	24	1,765.2	10	882.0	8	389.2
1991	35	2,288.6	8	808.4	20	786.2
1992	58	6,615.1	8	919.2	24	1,054.5
1993	79	11,398.4	41	8,158.7	38	3,239.7
Total	1,038	$50,361.30	394	$23,069.80	515	$13,159.40

Source: National Association of Real Estate Investment Trusts, *Realty Stock Review*.

Perhaps one of the most important developments in the REIT industry was the emergence in the mid-1980s and early 1990s of a cadre of REIT analysts at Wall Street firms like Salomon Brothers, Dean Witter, and Kidder Peabody; research firms like Greenstreet Advisors, Penobscot, and the Townsend Group; and money management firms like Alex. Brown & Sons (and its affiliate, Alex. Brown Kleinwort Benson), Cohen & Steers, PRA Securities, RREEF Real Estate Securities, The Invesco Realty Advisors, European Investors, Columbia Asset Managers, and The Franklin Funds and Fidelity.[19] These analysts and portfolio managers rapidly began shaping market perceptions.[20] Partly as a result of their efforts, the markets today tend to favor REITs that:

- Are structured as self-administered rather than externally advised REITs.
- Have experienced, seasoned management teams with strong track records of operating the established portfolios or property types to be taken public.
- Have a significant proportion of shares owned by managment, creating alignment of interests between management and shareholders.
- Have a majority of outside versus inside directors who are both well qualified and clearly independent of mind.
- Are oriented toward a particular geographic region and property type, providing a clear management focus.
- Are designed with a simple corporate structure, such as real estate operating companies, rather than with complex structures like the so-called UpREIT and DownREIT structures introduced in the 1992 and 1993 markets.
- Have market capitalizations of at least $250 million or more to facilitate greater liquidity.

In the meantime, as conduits, REITs are in a particularly good position to raise capital in the private and public debt and equity markets. Private market lenders like commercial banks, life companies, and credit companies are assured of multiple takeouts of their debt positions in either the private or public equity or debt markets. This ability to raise capital in four dimensions (private equity, private debt, public equity, public debt) provides REITs with a significant competitive advantage, particularly given the long-term outlook for the capital markets. See Exhibit 1–6. Competition for capital should

---

[19] Ibid.
[20] Ibid.

EXHIBIT 1–6
Total Market Capitalization of the REIT Industry, 1972–92 ($ Millions)

	All	Equity	Mortgage	Hybrid
1972	$1,880.9	$377.3	$774.7	$728.9
1973	1,393.5	336.0	517.3	540.2
1974	712.4	241.9	238.8	231.7
1975	885.9	275.7	298.2	312.0
1976	1,308.0	409.6	415.6	482.8
1977	1,528.1	538.1	398.3	591.6
1978	1,412.4	575.7	340.3	496.4
1979	1,754.0	743.6	377.1	633.3
1980	2,298.6	942.2	509.5	846.8
1981	2,438.9	977.5	541.3	920.1
1982	3,298.6	1,071.4	1,133.4	1,093.8
1983	4,329.1	1,782.8	1,434.9	1,111.4
1984	5,152.3	2,285.6	1,801.3	1,065.4
1985	7,711.8	3,314.4	3,128.5	1,231.8
1986	10,079.4	4,390.1	3,651.5	2,037.8
1987	9,702.4	4,758.5	3,161.4	1,782.4
1988	11,435.2	6,141.7	3,620.8	1,672.6
1989	11,662.2	6,769.6	3,536.3	1,356.3
1990	8,737.1	5,551.6	2,549.2	636.3
1991	12,968.2	8,785.5	2,586.3	1,596.4
1992	15,689.2	11,008.9	1,948.8	2,722.5

Source: National Association of Real Estate Investment Trusts.

only intensify throughout the remainder of the decade and beyond, driven by the insatiable demand for financing the exploding economies of the rapidly developing nations of the Pacific Rim and, to a lesser extent, South America and the African continent. Massive amounts of capital also will be needed to rebuild war-torn economies throughout the world and to finance the privatization of the nations of the former Soviet Union and, to a lesser extent, China.[21]

Clearly, the prospects for continued expansion of the REIT market are very good, particularly given that most of the REITs being formed today are low leveraged and purchasing new properties at the bottom (rather than the top) of a real estate market cycle. Many

---

[21] Mayree Clarke, Morgan Stanley Real Estate, from a speech delivered to the Pension Real Estate Association, 1991.

existing REITs also have used the markets to raise new equity and fixed-rate debt to pay down variable-rate debt and thereby improve their balance sheets and posture in the markets. As history demonstrates, however, the IPO and secondary markets for new issues of REIT securities will continue to ebb and flow in volume each year, along with the tide of the overall equity and fixed-income markets in which they operate.

THE COMMERCIAL MORTGAGE-BACKED SECURITIES MARKET[22]

Rating agency and regulatory pressure on life companies and commercial banks slowed commercial mortgage flows to the real estate markets considerably during the early and mid-1990s. In 1991, 1992, and 1993, for example, net flows actually were negative as major financial institutions sought to pare down their real estate lending portfolios. See Exhibit 1–7.

In addition to bulk portfolio sales, mortgage-backed securities have provided these financial institutions with one of the primary vehicles for spinning these assets off their balance sheets (or changing the balance sheet classification of these assets) and will continue to do so throughout the remainder of the 1990s.

Commercial mortgage-backed securities (CMBSs), like mortgage REITs, are conduits structured as pass-through securitized interests in whole loans or loan interests. The sponsors of CMBSs therefore can be classified, by definition, as institutional investors. A *conduit* is defined as any intermediary between a lender and an investor, but typically a conduit is a private investment company that purchases or originates loans and issues mortgage-backed securities (MBSs) under their own name and without a federal guarantee. Active conduits, according to Tax Management, Inc. (TMI), include investment bankers, home builders, life insurance companies, commercial banks, savings and loans, real estate investment trusts (REITs), and mutual funds.

---

[22] The discussion of commercial mortgage-backed securities is based on an analysis prepared by Tax Management, Inc., and by information provided by David L. Smith and David McWhorter of JMB Institutional Realty Corp., Anne Russell of Baring Advisors, and Debra Kops and Steve Leiter of Arthur Andersen Real Estate Service Group.

'HIBIT 1–7

New Mortgage Capital Flows to the Real Estate Markets, 1985–92

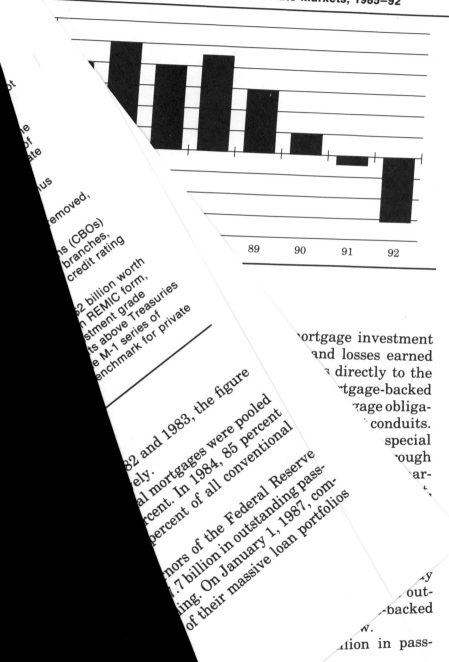

89   90   91   92

ot

he
of
ate

us

moved,

s (CBOs)
branches,
credit rating

2 billion worth
REMIC form,
stment grade
ts above Treasuries
e M-1 series of
enchmark for private

ortgage investment
and losses earned
directly to the
rtgage-backed
gage obliga-
conduits.
special
ough
ar-

82 and 1983, the figure
ely.
al mortgages were pooled
cent. In 1984, 85 percent
percent of all conventional

nors of the Federal Reserve
7 billion in outstanding passing. On January 1, 1987, com-
of their massive loan portfolios

y
out-
backed
w.

lion in pass-

EXHIBIT 1–8

Milestones in the Development of the Markets for Mortgage-Backed Securities

1984	Standard & Poor's Corp. issues guidelines for procedures it would use to attach a credit rating to mortgages.
1985	Lincoln Mutual Life Insurance Co. issues the first pass-through MBS backed by commercial mortgages.
	Standard & Poor's rates its first multifamily MBS.
	Salomon Brothers issues the first REMIC securities in the form of deb[t] instruments backed by Fannie Mae pass-through securities.
1986	Thrift institutions create a new type of MBS that divides a pool of mortgages into two subpools or "pieces," where income from th[e] pieces passes to the investors separately. The Tax Reform Act [of] 1986 (1986 TRA) is enacted, creating a new entity: the real est[ate] mortgage investment conduit (REMIC).
1987	Fannie Mae is authorized by HUD to issue REMIC securities, th[us] expanding the potential market for REMICs.
1988	All restrictions on Fannie Mae's ability to issue REMICs are [ ] further expanding the potential market for REMICs.
1989	First Boston issues so-called collateralized bond obligatio[ns] backed by junk bonds. These CBOs are issued in three [ ] two of which are overcollateralized and thus receive a[ ] of AA.
1992	The RTC issues C-1 and C-2, consisting of more than [ ] of performing and nonperforming loans packaged i[n] the A tranche of which was rated with an A or inve[stment] rating and priced between 200 and 300 basis poin[ts] of comparable maturities. These, coupled with th[e] transactions launched in 1991, have created a b[ ] issuance of similarly structured securities.

through MBSs were created each year. In 19[ ]
rose to $54 billion and $85 billion, respectiv[ely]

In 1980, 40 percent of all new residenti[al]
into MBSs. In 1982, the figure was 43 pe[rcent]
of all FHA and VA loans and 15 to 20 [ ]
loans were securitized.

In April 1984, the Board of Gover[nors]
System determined that there was $29[ ]
through MBS pools or trusts outstand[ing]
mercial banks held only $37 billion[ ]

in MBS form. By September 1989, however, MBSs had grown to over $120 billion.

The growth in MBSs has been driven in part because securitization through the creation of MBS eliminates most of the disadvantages traditionally connected with more direct forms of mortgage investment, including:

- *Servicing problems,* which securitization overcomes by separating the origination and servicing functions from the mortgage investment function.
- *Lack of marketability,* which securitization overcomes by establishing uniform underwriting standards that create homogeneous mortgage pools.
- *Default risk,* which securitization significantly reduces through the diversification resulting from pooling individual mortgages or from purchasing the certificates of multiple MBSs, strict underwriting standards, guarantees of payments or the creation of preferences, and insurance or credit enhancement on the underlying mortgages.
- *Cash flow uncertainty,* which securitization helps alleviate in part by structuring the cash flow similarly to bond payments.

In the future, continued growth of the pass-through MBS market will be stimulated in part by the tremendous demand by institutional investors. Traditionally, institutional investors have been attracted by yield spreads as high as 150 to 300 basis points above Treasury bonds with nearly comparable safety and liquidity.

Financial institutions traditionally have purchased MBSs to:

- Satisfy regulatory standards for mortgage holdings.
- Increase balance sheet liquidity.
- Serve as collateral for borrowing in the money markets.[23]
- Defer losses through the employment of swap strategies.
- Park money otherwise reserved for mortgage loan originations when the supply of quality loan opportunities has temporarily waned in local markets.

---

[23] MBSs are frequently used as collateral for repurchase agreements and tax and loan accounts.

In deciding what do with a mortgage loan, a lender has four alternatives:

1. Retain the mortgage loan in its portfolio.
2. Sell the mortgage as a whole loan.
3. Carve up and sell direct participations in the underlying loan.
4. Carve up any securitized interests in the underlying loan through a mortgage-backed security or real estate mortgage investment conduit instrument.

With an MBS or a REMIC, the lender typically trades or "swaps" its mortgage loans for pass-through MBS or REMIC certificates issued by an MBS or REMIC trust formed by the lender or by Fannie Mae, Freddie Mac, or another entity operating on MBS program. The pass-through MBS or REMIC can then be retained, sold, or used in various other financial transactions such as collateral for a collateralized mortgage obligation (CMO), builder bond, or other debt obligations.

Perhaps the most significant innovation in the evolution of the mortgage-backed security occurred in 1986 when thrift institutions created the new type of MBS that divided a pool of mortgages into two subpools or *pieces*. The senior piece typically contained about 90 percent of the pool's loans. (It is called *senior* because any foreclosure loss from the pooled loans was to be subtracted from the income paid to the holders of the smaller "subordinated" subpool, sometimes called the *junior* or *subpiece*. Because of the allocation of foreclosure losses to the subordinated piece, the senior security was able to obtain a triple-A rating without pool insurance (which costs 15 to 25 basis points per year).

The ability to earn a triple-A rating without pool insurance was a particularly important feature, because it set the stage for the future securitization of commercial mortgages. Pool insurance is sometimes difficult, if not impossible, to obtain for commercial mortgages, and if an issuer personally guarantees the securities, the securities must be carried on the issuer's books as a contingent liability.

The savings derived from not having to purchase pool insurance were offset in part by special costs associated with the security. These costs included:

- Potential foreclosure losses from the entire pool that now must be borne solely by the holders of the junior subordinated certificates.

- The substantially lower sales price per dollar of mortgage principal earned from selling the junior piece versus selling the senior piece.
- The opportunity cost of retaining the junior piece if not sold.

The holder or purchaser of the junior piece, however, enjoyed the benefits of a significantly enhanced yield, derived from the difference between the yield of the underlying mortgage and the yield at which the senior piece was priced.

The REMIC

In 1986, Congress modified the Tax Code, thereby creating a new mortgage securities vehicle called a real estate mortgage investment conduit, or REMIC. The volume of such issues has grown remarkably since 1986 (see Exhibit 1–9). Issuers are able to issue securities backed by mortgages without the regulatory and economic obstacles impeding the issuance of other forms of MBSs. While the concept is fairly simple, the legal and accounting issues surrounding the application of the concept can be quite complex.

Under the Code, a REMIC is any entity (e.g., partnership, corpo-

EXHIBIT 1–9
History of Commercial Mortgage-Backed Securities Issuance, 1987–93

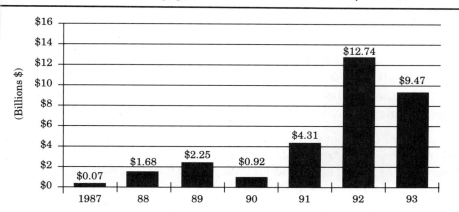

Sources: Arthur Andersen; Lehman Brothers.

ration, trust) allowed under state law that has assets consisting of a pool of mortgages and elects REMIC status on a partnership federal tax return in its first taxable year. A REMIC may also be formed as a segregated pool of assets rather than as a separate entity. To constitute a REMIC, the assets identified as part of the segregated pool must all be treated for federal income tax purposes as assets of the REMIC, and interests in the REMIC must be based solely on the assets of the REMIC. To elect REMIC status, the entity must satisfy requirements concerning the composition of its assets and the nature of the investors' interests.

To qualify as a REMIC, as of the close of the fourth month ending after the entity's start-up day and each quarter thereafter, substantially all of the entity's assets must consist of *qualified mortgages* and *permitted investments*. *Qualified mortgages* generally include any obligation that is secured principally by an interest in real property that is either (1) transferred to the REMIC on the start-up day in exchange for regular or residual interests in the REMIC or (2) purchased by the REMIC within three months after the start-up day under a fixed-price contract that was in effect on the start-up day.

Qualified mortgages may include:

- Interests in pass-through MBSs in grantor trusts that contain assets that qualify.
- Mortgage participations.
- Stripped mortgage bonds and coupons that contain assets that qualify.
- First and/or second mortgages on residential or commercial real estate.
- Mortgages on mobile homes that satisfy the definition of a single-family residence.
- Loans secured by stock in a cooperative housing corporation.
- Money purchase loans under installment land contracts.

Any of the above may be replaced with a replacement mortgage. A *replacement mortgage* is an obligation that would be a qualified mortgage if it had been transferred on the start-up day. Replacement mortgages may be exchanged for any interest in the REMIC, provided it is exchanged for another obligation within the three-month period beginning on the start-up day. Replacement mortgages may also be exchanged for a defective obligation if exchanged within the two-year period beginning on the start-up day. A *defective obligation* is a qualified mortgage in which there is a default or a threatened default by the borrower or obligator and as that term is commonly understood in the case of a single-class grantor trust.

If a REMIC loan becomes delinquent more than two years after the REMIC's start-up day, the REMIC may sell or otherwise liquidate the loan, but after the initial two-year period, it may not replace the delinquent loan with another mortgage loan.

Permitted investments generally include temporary investments that earn passive income such as interest. Under the Code, this means any *cash flow investment, qualified reserve asset,* or *foreclosure property.*

A *cash flow investment* is any investment of amounts received under qualified mortgages for a temporary period before distribution to holders of interests in the REMIC. Cash flow investments may not be sold from the REMIC, unless the REMIC is currently engaged in a qualified liquidation (i.e., a final liquidation of 100 percent of the REMIC's assets). Any gain from the disposition of a cash flow investment other than that pursuant to a qualified liquidation is subject to a 100 percent prohibited transactions penalty tax.

A *qualified reserve asset* is an intangible asset that is held for investment as part of a qualified reserve fund. A *qualified reserve fund* is a reasonably required (e.g., required by a credit rating agency) reserve to provide for full payment of expense of the REMIC or amounts due on regular interests in the event of defaults on qualified mortgages or lower than expected returns on cash flow investments. The REMICs issued during the first quarter of 1992 by the RTC, for example, had established a substantial qualified reserve fund, which helped the REMICs qualify for their relatively high investment grade rating.

Foreclosure property is property that would be foreclosure property if acquired by a REIT and that is acquired in connection with the default or imminent default of a qualified mortgage held by the REMIC.

To qualify as a REMIC, the REMIC must also make reasonable arrangements to ensure that residual interests are not held by disqualified organizations and that information necessary for the application of the tax on transfers of residual interests to disqualified organizations is available. (Residual interests are discussed below.)

To qualify as a REMIC, all of the interests in the REMIC must consist of one or more classes of *regular interests* and a single class of *residual interests*. Generally, a *regular interest* is an interest in the underlying mortgages of a REMIC, which is analogous to the pass-through certificate issued by a grantor trust. A regular interest may be in the form of debt, stock, partnership interests, interests in a trust, or any other form permitted by state law. It must be issued on the start-up day of the REMIC, be designated as a regular interest, and have fixed terms. The holder of a regular interest must have an unconditional right to receive a specified principal amount (or other similar amount), and the interest payments (or similar amounts), if any, at or before maturity must be payable based on a fixed rate (or, to the extent provided in the regulations, at a variable rate).

A *residual interest* in a REMIC generally is an equity interest in the REMIC's assets that do not belong to the regular interest holders. It is issued on the start-up day, is not a regular interest, and is designated as a residual interest. A REMIC may have only one class of residual interest.

A residual interest typically arises from so-called *excess interest*, wherein, for example, the certificate holders purchase certificates with a coupon rate of 10 percent, the underlying mortgage pool contains loans bearing an interest rate of 11 percent, and the mortgage servicer receives $1/8$ of 1 percent as a servicing fee. Here the residual interest is equal to $7/8$ of 1 percent, that is, to the interest rate differential between the 11 percent interest rate earned by the underlying mortgage and the REMIC coupon rate of 10 percent plus the servicing fee. Usually the value of the residual interest is quite small; they may even carry a zero value.

With a few exceptions, a REMIC is not subject to tax, although it is required to file an annual federal income tax return. A REMIC's income is taxed to the regular interest holders and residual interest holders. A REMIC would be subject to tax, however, if:

- The prohibited transactions tax applies.
- The tax on contributions to the REMIC after the start-up day applies.
- The withholding taxes imposed on REMICs applies.

Benefits Offered by the REMIC Structure

An investor in a REMIC does not recognize any gain or loss on the transfer of property to the REMIC in exchange for regular or residual interests in the REMIC. A taxable gain or loss is incurred, however, when the REMIC securities are sold.

As with grantor trust pass-through securities, regular and residual interests in a REMIC qualify as qualifying real property loans for financial institutions and REITs. CMOs and other mortgage cash flow bonds do not. The REMIC eliminates the cumbersome requirements associated with the structuring of a CMO issue. With a REMIC, the regular interests automatically are treated as debt securities to the investors. REMICs do not require any minimum equity. The REMIC can pay its regular interest holders monthly as it receives its funds.

Another advantage of REMICs is that they eliminate owners' trust disadvantages for selling residual interests. CMO residuals typically are sold through owners' trusts, which impose, for tax reasons, restrictions on transfers of equity interests and personal liability on equity investors. These restrictions and limitations do not apply when selling REMIC residual interests. Perhaps equally important, a senior-subordinated grantor trust does not allow the transfer of a subordinated interest, *unless* the REMIC vehicle is used. Transferability of subordinated interests is therefore one of the most significant benefits offered by the REMIC structure.

REMICs also provide flexibility in issuing securities. With a REMIC, the sponsor can select any vehicle to issue the securities (trust, partnership, corporation, etc.) and any type of securities (debt, pass-throughs, striped bonds, etc.) to obtain business, regulatory, and state tax objectives, but generally, whatever form is selected is treated as a partnership for tax treatment. Unlike CMOs (which do allow for different maturities), REMICs allow issuers to structure securities with different priorities for servicing as well as different maturities.

REMICs can also facilitate more advantageous trading conditions. The sale of CMO residuals requires that complex adjustments be made to their tax basis at transfer; this is not the case with REMIC residuals.

Not all pass-through securities held by REMICs are taxed to foreign investors, which makes the REMIC particularly attractive to foreign investors who otherwise might have to pay the 30 percent withholding tax required on interest income paid to nonresident foreign investors. However, by international treaty, most European nations already are exempted from this provision.

In a REMIC, both residual and regular interests are tax exempt to pension plan investors, while in a CMO, only regular interests are tax exempt. For this reason, REMIC residual interests may be attractive to pension funds, despite the fact that CMO residuals traditionally have not been. (Residual interests in a REMIC are only partially tax exempt to pension investors, however.)

One of the most significant benefits of the REMIC structure, and the primary reason for its creation, is that REMICs are easy to use relative to other MBS structures. REMIC status can be elected simply by filing a partnership tax return and provides for flexible tax treatment selection.

Perhaps most important, REMICs are able to issue multiclass securities. To issuers of pass-through MBSs, this is the most important feature of the REMIC. A trust cannot qualify for grantor status if it issues multiple classes of interests that divide ownership of investment assets, such as mortgages, or the cash flow from such assets into non–pro rata portions. Because of the inability to issue multiclass pass-through securities in a grantor trust, fund raisers that wanted to issue multiclass securities had to use CMO-type instruments and were forced to abandon the pass-through MBS vehicle. With a REMIC, multiclass securities in a grantor trust are allowed. This reduces the complexity and associated costs of administering pass-through MBS vehicles through CMOs. The ability to issue multiclass securities also enables MBS issuers to reduce their credit enhancement needs. This is because the senior MBS class (or tranche) of securities would have less risk of default and thus would require less credit enhancement to obtain an adequate credit rating. For seasoned properties, the senior security might even receive a rating with no surety or other credit enhancement. In either case, the junior or subordinated security would carry most of the risk and would not receive a credit rating. The security would have no credit enhancement but would carry a higher yield.

REMICs also afford issuers of pass-through MBSs much more flexibility in managing the underlying mortgages than the grantor trust tax rules allow. Unlike CMO issuers, however, REMIC issuers cannot make minimum or maximum prepayment guarantees.

Complexity

As with all forms of MBSs, as the vehicle has evolved, REMIC structures gradually have become more sophisticated and complex. REMICs now typically contain, for example, numerous classes of securities with different payment schedules. In 1990, for example, Fannie Mae issued two REMIC offerings, one with 13 classes and one with 11 classes. The 11-class issuance contained the added feature of stripped securities (wherein the principal and interest portions of a security are separated, or stripped, and sold separately).

Complexity is not a requirement of the REMIC structure, however. By utilizing the REMIC vehicle in its simplest form, investors still can benefit fully from all of the positive attributes and characteristics outlined above.

TAX-EXEMPT REAL ESTATE INVESTORS

A Historical Overview

Pension, endowment, and foundation fund assets constitute the largest and fastest-growing single pool of capital in the United States.[24] From 1983 to 1993, for example, total tax-exempt assets roughly doubled in size from approximately $1.6 trillion to nearly $3.2 trillion—an average annual growth rate of around 7.2 percent.[25]

While current real estate allocations continue to hover between 3 and 5 percent of total pension assets, most pension fund investment consultants continue to recommend an allocation to real estate ranging between 5 and 15 percent. Institutional Real Estate, Inc., estimates total tax-exempt fund real estate investments (including equity, mortgages, and mortgage-backed securities) at roughly $167 billion as of January 1, 1993, of which $73 billion, or about 44 percent, is equity and $94 billion, or 56 percent, is debt. Equity real estate allocations therefore are currently approximately 2.3 percent of total assets, or at a historical low. Therefore, if 10 percent of the current pool of assets were allocated to real estate, a total of $247 billion in additional new capital would be available for real estate investment today.

For a variety of reasons, pension funds are unlikely to achieve their targeted allocations. If pension funds are able to maintain investment allocations between 2 and 5 percent, however, then, assuming a continued growth rate of total assets of approximately 7.2 percent between 1994 and 2004, pension real estate investments should

---

[24] Flow of Funds Account, Board of Governors of the Federal Reserve System.

[25] Institutional Real Estate, Inc., *Money Market Directory of Pension Funds and Their Managers,* 1993.

double from over \$167 billion in 1994 to over \$334 billion by 2004. In other words, in the 10-year period between 1994 and 2004, pension, foundation, and endowment funds can be expected to invest as much or more new money in real estate as they have invested over the previous 22 years.

Prior to 1968, pension funds had relatively little capital invested in real estate. Lack of available vehicles, lack of in-house expertise, lack of experience, and concerns over real estate's relative illiquidity all served to inhibit more widespread investment.[26] If pension funds were going to be involved in the real estate markets, they clearly needed a better way to access those markets.

In 1968, the first real estate commingled fund was offered to U.S. institutional investors by the First Wachovia Bank in North Carolina.[27] Then, in 1970, Prudential introduced the Prudential Real Estate Income Separate Account (PRISA), which revolutionized pension investment patterns. Spurred by the pioneering efforts of large financial institutions like Prudential, First Wachovia, First Chicago, Metropolitan Life, Connecticut General (now CG), John Hancock, Aetna, and Equitable and by innovative independent investment advisors like RREEF and CB Commercial, real estate was slowly accepted as a legitimate institutional investment over the next 20 years. Not until the late 1980s, however, did real estate earn core portfolio asset status alongside stocks and bonds.

Like life insurance companies and other institutional investors, throughout this 20-year time span pension funds' attitudes toward real estate investment have changed considerably, reflecting investor response to shifts in the U.S. economic cycles and reactions to imposed regulatory measures.

The Nature of the Pension Fund Investment Community

Pension funds by definition are a collection of liabilities—promises to pay pension benefits to the workers or "participants" covered by the plan. Pension plans are governed by independent boards of trustees who are personally responsible for arranging the financial affairs

---

[26] Roulac, *Institutional Investment in Real Estate.*

[27] Meyer Melnikoff, "A Note on the Dawn of Property Investment by American Pension Funds," *AREUEA Journal* 12, no. 3 (1984).

of the plan for the sole benefit of the beneficiaries or participants. The agency—government, corporation, or, in the case of labor unions, multiple employers—that creates and finances those pension plan liabilities is called a *plan sponsor*. The board or the plan sponsor may appoint fully or partially dedicated staff to implement the policy decisions established by the board.

Three sources can be used to finance pension liabilities: contributions of new money (which, by definition, decrease corporate earnings or increase funding burdens on taxing agencies), investment returns, or reductions in benefits.

Underwriting a pension plan's liabilities is an actuarial exercise, similar to underwriting a life insurance pool of liabilities. Actuaries must take into account the collective anticipated employment and mortality experience of the pool of employees covered by the plan and must factor in an actuarial investment return assumption and an inflation assumption. In general, the lower the investment assumption, the higher the funding requirement, which is why plan sponsors resist lowering the actuarial investment assumptions underlying their plans.

If a pension fund actuarially lacks sufficient assets (in light of current assets, current contribution levels, and actuarial investment return assumptions), it is considered to be *underfunded*. If a pension fund has more than sufficient assets to finance its anticipated liabilities, it is considered either *fully funded* or *overfunded*.

Managers of underfunded pension plans usually are willing to assume more risk than managers of fully or overfunded plans in order to reduce contribution requirements. Underfunded plans by definition also require that plan sponsors contribute new dollars to the fund and therefore typically generate positive cash flow (i.e., more money paid in as contribution than is paid out in benefits). Since pension real estate investments typically are funded out of positive cash flow, underfunded pension plans tend to be more active real estate investors than fully funded or overfunded pension plans.

If a plan becomes overfunded, the only way a plan sponsor can recapture the surplus or *overcontribution* is to terminate the plan and distribute the assets to the beneficiaries. Typically this is accomplished by purchasing an immunized bond portfolio or annuity contract. But terminating a pension plan requires the approval of the Department of Labor and the Internal Revenue Service, and such approval is very difficult to obtain.

Because volatility of investment returns can lead plan sponsors to overcontribute to their plans, and because it is difficult to recapture those overcontributions, plan sponsors tend to be extremely conservative in the management of their portfolios, seeking to stabilize rather than optimize portfolio returns. Stress is placed on diversifying assets across assets (i.e., stocks, bonds, cash, real estate) and within assets (high-cap versus low-cap stocks and, within real estate, by property type, geographic and economic region, property size, tenant mix, lease maturity, and so forth).

In constructing portfolios, plan sponsors tend to build the core of the portfolio out of assets they consider to be stable and therefore relatively low yielding (cash, investment grade bonds of blue chip companies, high-cap stocks of blue chip companies, trophy real estate assets). Total portfolio yield is then enhanced by adding higher-yielding, more volatile specialty assets (low-cap stocks, venture capital, specialty real estate). Exhibit 1–10 summarizes the asset mix of the 1,000 largest pension plans.

As of 1990, total pension fund assets were split approximately 50-50 between public and private funds. For example, according to the 1990 Greenwich Associates annual survey of the 2,000 largest pension funds, corporate sponsors represented 49 percent of total pension assets. Public pension funds, sponsored by state and local governments, represented 45 percent, while labor union pension plans, endowments, and foundations accounted for roughly 6 percent.[28]

As noted above, pension funds are governed by boards of trustees and investment committees. The people who serve on these boards and committees typically are unpaid volunteers (public, foundation, and endowment funds) or employees or directors of the firms that sponsor them (corporate and Taft-Hartley funds). They are also fiduciaries, meaning they are personally liable for the prudent management of fund assets. This also partly explains the conservative posture of most pension funds.

Pension fund administrators are charged with administering pension contributions, investments, and disbursements. Their primary objective is to ensure that sufficient funds will be available for disbursement when vested employees reach retirement age. Pen-

---

[28] Greenwich Associates, *Report to Participants,* 1991.

Pensions and Investments' 1993 survey of the top 1,000 pension funds revealed that defined benefit plans had $20.8 billion invested in real estate compared to $4.6 billion for defined contribution plans. While 123 defined benefit sponsors used real estate in 1990, only 11 defined contribution sponsors did so. The aging of the U.S. work force, coupled with the move from defined benefit to defined contribution plans, is affecting the way pension funds will invest in real estate in the future.

Equity real estate allocations traditionally have been funded from positive cash flow (total contributions minus total distributions). Unfortunately, most pension funds are not cash flowing positively today, and negative cash flows are growing. Net pension industry cash flows were a negative $7 million in 1990, for example, compared to a negative $1 billion in 1989.

As a result, in the future pension plans will have to look to investment gains rather than contributions to maintain asset growth sufficient to match their funds' growing liabilities. While real estate can play a role, the illiquidity of more direct forms of investment is not well matched to a negative cash flow enviroment. This fact most likely will promote greater securitization. As the total capitalization of both the equity and debt real estate securities markets grows, pension funds most likely will invest in real estate more indirectly through their existing equity and fixed-income investment managers and through specialized real estate securities portfolio managers.

Negative cash flows are distributed unequally between market segments. In the corporate sector, for example, cash flow is strongly negative. In 1990, distributions of roughly $51 billion far exceeded the total contributions of $38 billion, a difference of $13 billion. The public sector, however, showed a positive cash flow of $6 billion ($45 billion in contributions, $38 billion in distributions). But positive cash flow in the public sector is also shrinking, falling from $16 billion in 1988 to $12 billion in 1989, to $6 billion in 1991. (Interestingly, although exacerbated by the decline in performance precipitated by the 1987 downturn in the stock markets, the decline in direct pension fund investment activity in real estate almost parallels this decline in positive cash flow.)

In late 1993, the Securities and Exchange Commission (SEC) issued an advisory letter to the Financial Accounting Standards

Board (FASB) urging the FASB to promulgate rule changes requiring pension funds to lower their actuarial investment assumptions from a maximum of 8 percent to a maximum of 6 percent. The SEC's reasoning is that the higher investment assumptions created in the sizzling 1980s are no longer appropriate in the lower interest rate environment of the mid-1990s. Should the FASB adopt the SEC's recommendations, the impact would be to turn many funds that now are fully funded into underfunded plans. This, in turn, would stimulate a rash of termination requests and further growth in defined contribution plans at the expense of defined benefit plans. Most important, it would force pension plans to take on more risk to finance future pension liabilities and would create positive cash flow, both of which would promote renewed interest in real estate as an asset class.

Market Segmentation

The tax-exempt institutional investor market can be segmented by type of plan sponsor (corporate, public, multi-employer, foundation, endowment) and size of plan. See Exhibits 1–13 through 1–15.

EXHIBIT 1–13
Total Number of Pension Plans by Plan Sponsor Type (as of September 1992)

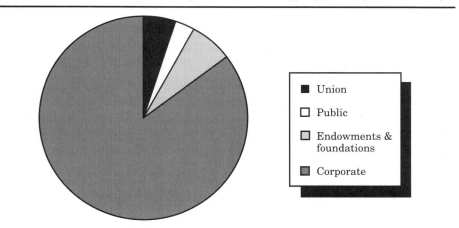

Union
Public
Endowments & foundations
Corporate

Sources: *Pensions and Investments;* Institutional Real Estate, Inc.

EXHIBIT 1–14
Market Size of Pension Plans by Plan Sponsor Type (as of September 1992)

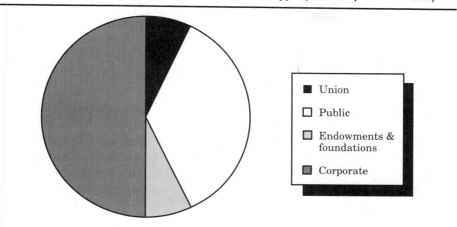

- ■ Union
- □ Public
- ▨ Endowments & foundations
- ▩ Corporate

Sources: *Pensions and Investments;* Institutional Real Estate, Inc.

Public Plans

The 1993 *Money Market Directory of Pension Funds and Their Managers* lists 1,175 public pension funds, with total assets of $1.055 billion. Public plans are not subject to ERISA but are constrained in their investment practices by the municipal or state statutes that govern them. (Many public funds have voluntarily adapted ERISA standards of investment practice. They technically are not bound by ERISA, however.)

Public plans are governed by boards of trustees, which typically are composed of *ex officio* members (state or municipal treasurers), representatives appointed by officials or legislative bodies (governors, mayors, state legislatures, county boards of supervisors, city councils), and elected representatives of both active members (those participants currently employed by the public agency) and retired members (those currently drawing pension benefits from the plan). Because of the makeup of these boards, boards typically meet on schedule rather than on demand—as little as once a month or as frequently as three to four times a month.

Historically, public fund investment strategies tended to be more conservative than corporate strategies, with their portfolios more

EXHIBIT 1–15
Tax-Exempt Real Estate Investment by Sector ($ Billions)

	Corporate	Public	Taft-Hartley	Total Pension	Endow-ments	Founda-tions	Total Tax Exempt
Real estate:							
Equity	$28,263	$34,652	$5,184	$68,099	$2,489	$2,360	$72,948
Mortgages	1,849	20,842	1,944	24,635	483	261	25,379
Mortgage-backed securities	6,293	54,234	4,968	65,495	2,728	1,118	69,341
Total real estate	$36,405	$109,728	$12,096	$158,229	$5,700	$3,739	$167,668
Summary:							
Equity	$28,263	$34,652	$5,184	$68,099	$2,489	$2,360	$72,948
Debt	8,142	75,076	6,912	90,130	3,211	1,379	94,720
Total assets	$1,529,000	$1,055,000	$216,000	$2,800,000	$109,000	$118,000	$3,027,000
% of total:							
Equity	1.8%	3.3%	2.4%	2.4%	2.3%	2.0%	2.4%
Mortgages	0.1	2.0	0.9	0.9	0.4	0.2	0.8
Mortgage-backed securities	0.4	5.1	2.3	2.3	2.5	0.9	2.3
Total real estate	2.4%	10.4%	5.6%	5.7%	5.2%	3.2%	5.5%
Summary:							
Equity	1.8%	3.3%	2.4%	2.4%	2.3%	2.0%	2.4%
Debt	0.5	7.1	3.2	3.2	2.9	1.2	3.1

heavily weighted toward bonds and other fixed-income securities. Many public funds were forbidden by statute to invest in real estate. If they invested in real estate at all, residential mortgages and government agency–guaranteed residential mortgage-backed securities were the preferred alternative, being less risky than equity ventures and without the management hassle.

By the mid-1980s many funds' legislative constraints had been loosened, allowing public plans to invest a portion of their considerable assets in real estate. Public plans now represent 45 percent of total pension fund assets and have become the most active in allocating new monies for real estate investment.

Corporate Funds

The 1993 *Money Market Directory of Pension Funds and Their Managers* lists 33,799 corporate pension funds, with total assets of $1.529 billion. Corporate funds are governed by ERISA.

Typically, a corporate fund has a master trustee rather than a board of trustees. Investment decisions usually are directed by an investment committee composed of corporate executives, employee representatives, and members of the company's board of directors. Corporate boards often meet on demand rather than on schedule.

Multi-Employer Benefits Funds

The 1993 *Money Market Directory of Pension Funds and Their Managers* lists 1,581 multi-employer benefits funds, with total assets of $216 billion. Multi-employer plans (also known as Taft-Hartley or labor union plans) are also governed by ERISA. Plans are chartered under the statutes of the Taft-Hartley Act of 1939, which created the legal basis for collective bargaining in the United States.

In a Taft-Hartley plan, multiple employers contribute to each plan, and each employer typically contributes to a variety of plans. The Retail Food Workers plan, for example, receives contributions from Alpha Beta, Safeway, Von's, and a host of other grocery store chain operators. A grocery chain store operator like Safeway, in turn, contributes to a variety of union pension plans, including the Teamsters (for drivers), the retail clerks' union, and the meatcutters' union, among others. (Many of these employers also contribute to a single-employer plan on behalf of their salaried versus hourly employees.)

Multi-employer plans are governed by boards of trustees, half of which typically represent the interests of management and the other half the interests of labor. Management trustees usually are appointed by the various management councils formed to conduct collective bargaining with the different unions. Examples include the Western Steel Council and the Food Employers Council. Labor trustees typically are elected by the participants covered by the plan and usually include key union officials and representatives of both the active and retired participants.

Most union plans are administered by third-party administration companies. These third-party administrators may also have representation on the investment board. The union's (or management's) counsel may be appointed as well.

Endowment Funds

The 1993 *Money Market Directory of Pension Funds and Their Managers* lists 1,439 endowment funds, with total assets of $118 billion. Endowments are created to fund specific programs or to fund the general activities of a college, university, or other eleemosynary institution. While tax exempt, these funds are not retirement funds and therefore are not subject to ERISA. Endowment funds typically are governed by a board of trustees, which is composed of representatives from the constituency served by the endowment.

By definition, endowments are designed to fund programs from earnings, not principal. Therefore, the primary objective of foundation trustees is, first, to preserve principal and, second, to maximize earnings.

Foundation Funds

The 1993 *Money Market Directory of Pension Funds and Their Managers* lists 1,439 foundation funds, with total assets of $118 billion. Foundations, like endowments, are established to finance particular objectives, with a bias toward preservation of capital. Like endowments, foundations are governed by independent boards of trustees, whose composition typically reflects the constituency the foundation is designed to serve.

Size of Plan

According to the *Money Market Directory of Pension Funds and Their Managers,* the largest U.S. tax-exempt plans (i.e., those with $500 million or more in assets) control more than 25 percent of all pension, foundation, and endowment fund assets. Larger funds, however, clearly dominate pension fund real estate investment activity. The largest corporate sponsors, for example, control $25.5 billion of the $28 billion currently invested by corporate pension funds in real estate, or roughly 90.3 percent of all such investments. The largest public and Taft-Hartley plan sponsors control $33.9 billion of the total of $34.7 billion invested by such funds in real estate, or roughly 98 percent of all such investments. Larger funds typically invest directly, either individually or by coinvesting with one or two other financial institutions, rather than in commingled or pooled investment vehicles. Most larger funds have full-time professional investment staffs, and many have full-time real estate investment staffs.

Most smaller funds (those under $500 million) lack sufficient capital to invest directly in real estate and therefore limit their real estate investment activities to pooled investment funds. Smaller funds also tend to have smaller staffs. Funds with $100 million or less in total assets may have no full-time dedicated pension adminis-trative or investment staff at all; they fill these roles out of the treasury or financial departments of the plan sponsor.

Early Tax-Exempt Fund Investment in Real Estate

As noted earlier, real estate equity funds were first provided by bank trust departments and insurance companies, which had been the leading historical providers of investment opportunities for pension funds. The first investment vehicles to be offered were open-end, commingled real estate equity funds. The first such fund was estab-lished by the First Wachovia Bank in 1968. The Prudential Property Separate Account (PRISA), the precursor of the large open-end com-mingled equity funds, was first activated in July 1970. These vehicles were conceived for and marketed exclusively to pension funds.[29]

The open-end vehicle appealed to this new group of real estate investors because it offered a partially specified pool of diversified real estate assets in which they could immediately invest, without having to learn the nuances of real estate investment. The promise of liquidity also was a key feature, allowing investors a potential way to both enter and eventually exit the asset class. The open-end fund structure also simply "felt" familiar, and therefore "comfortable," to most institutional investors, because its structure mirrored the structure of mutual funds, the predominant investment vehicle for institutional investment in the corporate securities markets at that time.

Despite the emergence of these early real estate equity invest-ment vehicles, pension funds did not begin to consider real estate seriously as an asset class until the mid-1970s. Their emergence,

---

[29] Melnikoff, "A Note on the Dawn of Property Investment."

however, did signal the beginning of the gradual institutionalization of the commercial real estate markets—a process that continues today. This process of institutionalization was the logical evolution of a much broader trend: the institutionalization and globalization of the capital markets worldwide.

Pension Funds and the Stock Market

Until 1952, U.S. pension funds held little stock, preferring the safety of high-grade corporate bonds.[30] Worried about the effect of inflation on pension liabilities, administrators slowly began shifting assets into the stock market. Twenty years later, in 1972, stocks represented nearly three-quarters of total pension fund assets, and institutional investment management had become a growth industry.

The increasing presence of pension assets changed the underlying structure of the stock market. Due to the sheer size of their collective pools, pension funds brought about "block" trading: trades of 10,000 shares or more. Coupled with the introduction of powerful new mini- and microcomputer programs, this promoted the emergence of program trading, which also transformed the behavior of the markets.

In 1965, 3 percent of all trades on the New York Stock Exchange were block trades. By 1984, increasing pension fund participation had brought the block trading percentage up to 50 percent. It is estimated that as of the first quarter of 1991, U.S. institutional investors owned 39 percent of the total market value of the stock market.[31]

Institutionalization of the equity and fixed-income markets fostered the emergence of the investment management business: professional securities investment managers who operated as co-fiduciaries rather than as principals. As institutionalization progressed, the investment decision-making process also shifted from a purely gut-driven approach to a much more information-driven process. (This shift affected other sectors of the American economy as well. The fastest-growing subsector of the American economy in the 1970s, for example, was the information business. The fastest-growing subsector of the information business was the financial services business. Driv-

---

[30] Natalie McKelvy, *Pension Fund Investments in Real Estate*, p. 14.

[31] Tobin, *New York Stock Exchange.*

ing this rapid growth was the institutionalization of the capital markets.)

Within 10 short years, pension funds had become the dominant players in the U.S. capital markets. By 1972, 74 percent of U.S. pension fund assets were in common stocks.

By the mid-1980s, pension funds had clout and were beginning to exercise it. Led by the multibillion-dollar California Public Employees' Retirement System (CalPERS), the largest funds banded together to form the Council of Institutional Investors, with the primary objective of advocating shareholder rights and influencing the management of the companies they now literally controlled. (It is ironic that at the same time communism is dying as an economic system throughout much of the world, most of the productive capacity of America is now in the hands of the American workers, albeit indirectly, through their pension funds.)

Pension fund clout also transformed the organization, pricing, and delivery of financial services. Most large brokerage houses eventually formed separate institutional trading and client-servicing groups to meet the unique needs of pension fund investors; research became an absolute requirement to support and substantiate the prudence of recommended investment strategies; and both transactions fees and investment management fees were forced way, way down. Those pressures—increased demand for service, coupled with continual pressure on fees—continue to shrink investment manager margins, transforming the investment management business itself from a once entrepreneurial, gut-driven industry to one that is much more managerial and institutional in character. In effect, the industry has become a reflection of the market it serves.

REAL ESTATE INVESTMENT IN THE EARLY 1970s

Real estate had been riding the crest of demand generated during the 1960s. It too boomed until it peaked in 1973, laid low by inflation and recession. With interest rates and construction costs at historic highs, demand for new space evaporated. With it went the availability of capital. Millions of square feet of vacant office space lay fallow on the market; new construction came to a halt. The 1974 collapse of the real estate investment trusts brought even more properties onto the market. From 1974 to 1976, the market was awash with properties that developers and investors were desperate to unload at bargain prices.[32] Commingled real estate funds could purchase these properties for less than replacement cost. When the real estate market began to tighten in 1977 and the economy floated toward double-digit inflation, these commingled funds were able to post returns that outperformed the equity and bond markets.[33] As a result of this performance, pension funds for the first time began to consider real estate seriously as a key component of their asset allocation strategies.

Performance was not the only impetus for pension investment in real estate, however. Two other conditions compelled pension funds to consider real estate investment: the passage of the Employee Retirement Income Security Act (ERISA) and the geometric increase of investable contributions to pension fund coffers.

The Impact of ERISA

Prior to 1974, only a relatively few regulations governed corporate pension funds. With the passage of ERISA in 1974, private pension fund fiduciaries (administrators, trustees, investment managers, and others with direct or indirect control over pension assets) were legally bound by law to arrange the financial affairs of the funds entrusted to their care in a manner consistent with the way a prudent person of like means would arrange his or her own financial affairs. This in effect mandated broader diversification of pension plan assets. As stated earlier, if a corporation's pension plan fails to meet its fiduciary responsibility to vested beneficiaries, a federal tax lien could be placed on up to 30 percent of the corporation's net worth.[34]

The application of the "prudent person" rule, later interpreted as the "prudent expert" rule, in pension fund investment is found in Section 404 of ERISA. Under this section, a fiduciary is defined as anyone with discretionary authority in the administration of a plan or anyone who provides advice to a plan for compensation or has authority or responsibility to do so.[35] Section 404 prescribes that the fiduciary shall

---

[32] McKelvy, *Pension Fund Investments,* p. 213.

[33] Ibid.

[34] ERISA, Article 3, paragraph 1002.

[35] Hillary Gray, *New Directions in the Investment and Control of Pension Funds,* Investor Responsibility Research Center, Washington, DC, 1983.

discharge his or her duties solely in the interest of plan participants or beneficiaries, and A) for the sole purpose of providing plan benefits to them; B) with care, skill, prudence and diligence under the circumstances then prevailing that a prudent man acting in a like capacity and familiar with such matters would use; C) by diversifying the investments of the plan so as to minimize the risk of large losses, unless under the circumstances it would be prudent not to do so, and D) in accordance with plan documents and instruments. (ERISA, Section 404[a])

The prudence regulations and the clause governing investment policies, 404(c), did not specifically tell a manager how to invest. Unsure of how the new law would subsequently be interpreted in court, pension funds invested in conservative, "prudent" investments. The Department of Labor (DOL) later clarified that the prudence rule did not rule out risky investments or investments in nontraditional assets.[36] In addition, the DOL specifically stated that a nontraditional investment could "improve diversification if it includes new investment opportunities in such areas such as small business and real estate."[37] Nor did ERISA define any specific percentage of assets to be allocated to nontraditional investments, such as 10 percent to real estate. (This convention has been attributed to a misinterpretation of section 404[a], which limits the inclusion of a sponsor's own assets within the fund to "10% of the sponsor's securities or real property.")[38]

Under ERISA, plan sponsors also were bound to abide by certain rules of fiduciary conduct, and were prohibited from engaging in any transactions that might be considered self-dealing.

The passage of ERISA effectively promoted a "herd instinct" among pension fund investors. Absent a clearer definition of what constitutes "prudent" behavior, what the majority elected to do became the standard. The fact that the majority of funds were invested in equities, for example, actually defined stock investment as a prudent thing to do. Conversely, if fewer than 51 percent of the funds were invested in a relatively new area like real estate, the burden of proof that investing in that area indeed was a prudent thing to do rested on the pension fund's shoulders. The same would be true when considering moving into more specialized types of real property investments

---

[36] ERISA Committee Reports, paragraph 5035.

[37] Gray, *New Directions,* p. 55.

[38] Ned Merkle, "The Do's and Don'ts of Pension Management" (New York: AMACON, 1981).

or when contemplating hiring new or emerging real estate investment managers. This herd instinct would become a critical factor in the decision-making processes pension funds would exercise over the formation and execution of their real estate investment strategies. Ironically, the herd instinct actually worked against the best interests of the funds by promoting concentration rather than diversification.

A 1993 study of the data presented each year in *Pension and Investments'* annual survey of the top 100 real estate investment managers shows that concentration of assets among the top 25 investment managers gradually increased over the 10-year period from 1983 to 1993.[39] In other words, fewer and fewer managers are controlling more and more of the pension funds' real estate portfolios, concentrating control of those assets in the hands of a relatively few investment managers.

Exhibit 1–16 graphically portrays the geometric increase of pension assets from 1950 to 1990, increasing rapidly from the mid-1970s and helping to fuel the building boom of the 1980s. (This growth rate, averaging between 7 and 15 percent per year, has persisted throughout the 1990s.)

Two distinct sources fueled the real estate boom of the early 1980s. One, of course, was the growth in the actual demand for space due to demographics and structural changes in the nation's economy. The second source was a change in the capital markets and the demand for real estate as an investment asset.[40] Three sources have been identified as contributing to the demand for space. First, the baby boomers came of age, entered the work force, and formed their own households. Second, women entered the labor force in unprecedented numbers, increasing their participation rate from 50 to 70 percent. Third, there was a structural shift in the economy as the United States moved from being a manufacturing-based economy to a service-based economy.[41] These events gave economic credence to the boom in office construction. It was investment demand, however—the need of institutions to place large sums of capital in invest-

---

[39] Joseph Pagliari, unpublished white paper, 1993.

[40] Larry Bacow, "A Look at the Real Estate Cycle," MIT, Center for Real Estate Development *Newsletter,* Spring 1991.

[41] Lynn Sagalyn and Marc Louargand, "Real Estate in the Next Recession," MIT, Center for Real Estate Development *Newsletter,* 1989.

EXHIBIT 1–16
Total Pension Fund Financial Assets and Rate of Growth, 1950–90 ($ Billions)

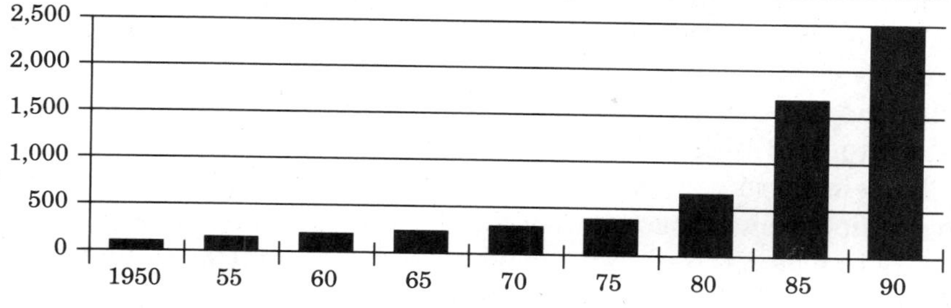

Source: Employee Benefit Research Institute.

ments—that caused the market to overshoot the traditional points of equilibrium.

THE GREAT FLOOD OF REAL ESTATE CAPITAL

Meyer Melnikoff, the pioneer of institutional real estate investment, described 1980 as the "threshold year" for real estate.[42] *Pensions and Investments'* 1980 survey of the pension fund community found that 22 percent of the sponsors were invested in real estate compared to 15 percent the previous year.[43] Most notably, over half of the large funds were invested in real estate. Large corporate plans, with their more aggressive investment policies, had pioneered pension real estate investment. Lagging the corporations, large public pension plans began their initial forays into real estate investment in 1984. Continued high inflation, combined with the incipient recession and poor stock market performance, fueled the trend toward "alternative" non–stock and bond investments.

Pension funds were not the only players fueling the real estate investment feeding frenzy. They were joined by syndicators and private investors, foreign institutions, and commercial banks.

---

[42] Melnikoff, "A Note on the Dawn of Property Investment."
[43] *Pensions and Investments,* December 20, 1980.

The Economic Recovery Tax Act of 1981 (ERTA) provided additional incentive for real estate investment. Though it had no direct effect on tax-exempt investors, by effectively creating a federal subsidy to the real estate market, ERTA did fuel a flurry of new real estate investment activity by taxable investors. As a result, combined public and private syndication investments jumped from $1.9 billion in 1980 to $8.3 billion in 1983.[44]

Developers and syndicators alike took advantage of the shortened 15-year depreciation schedules and interest write-offs, selling those benefits to wealthy individuals who needed to shelter their high personal incomes. The underlying economics of a project, including concerns such as marketability and cash flow generation, were given only secondary consideration by most syndicators (and developers as well).

Adding to the competition were foreign individuals and institutions looking to invest in U.S. real estate. Lacking large-scale investment opportunities in their own countries, offshore investors viewed the United States as a safe harbor for their long-term investments. Unlike their U.S. counterparts, foreign funds always considered property to be a core asset class. As discussed below, these funds would be active players in the late 1980s market. With tremendous amounts of capital from a variety of sources chasing too few properties, capitalization rates were driven lower and projected yields began to diminish.

By late 1980 and early 1981, U.S. pension funds began to reconsider the wisdom of investing in real estate. Still initiates to the real estate game, they were not convinced that real estate could deliver on its promise. In April 1982, for example, *Pensions and Investments* reported that the "bloom is off the real estate rose."[45] As inflation drifted downward and interest rates upward, pension funds shuffled their assets into the bond market. With the stock market also rebounding, financial assets offered better value than real estate.

Reallocation strategies such as this are a typical reflex for institutional investors, who have been trained to believe that changing market conditions demand a realignment of asset allocation to take advantage of inefficiencies in the market. Real estate, the new asset

---

[44] Robert A. Stanger & Company.
[45] "Realty Interest Slows for Sponsors," *Pensions and Investments,* April 1982.

class, was treated no differently than its stock and bond brethren. Real estate had been sold as an inflationary hedge, and expectations about inflation were changing. If the economy was entering a period of disinflation, why hold real estate assets?

This reasoning prompted investors in PRISA (Prudential's multi-billion-dollar open-end commingled real estate fund) to liquidate their holdings. Responding to the change in direction of the herd, pension funds lined up at Prudential's doors to redeem their shares. (According to John Streiker of Security Capital, which also manages a large open-end commingled fund, investors seek to exit open-end funds only when they perceive the valuation of fund units is too high. When the units are marked to market, Streiker asserts, investors lose interest in exiting, and the queue disappears.)

In Prudential's case, that didn't happen. Plan sponsors who thought they had invested in a more liquid real estate investment vehicle found themselves waiting in line to recover their investments. In the meantime, ostensibly to protect the integrity of the fund, Prudential refused to sell assets at below appraised value to meet redemption requirements.[46] This well-publicized event sent a shock wave throughout the pension fund community, raising issues about valuation and liquidity. The ultimate result was that many plan sponsors who already were well invested in real estate began to reconsider their proportional allocation, while those not already invested began to rethink their commitment.

By September 1984, articles heralding Armageddon due to over-building began to appear in the pension fund and real estate press.[47] With no signs of a slowing in new construction activity, vacancy rates rose steadily in most major markets, and returns on real estate investments correspondingly began to suffer.

The fact that the construction boom continued unabated despite these early warning signs merely reflects the institutionalization of the real estate markets that had begun in the early 1970s.[48] No longer

---

[46] "PRISA Sticks to Its Guns in Dealing with Withdrawals," *Pensions and Investments,* March 7, 1983.

[47] Steve Hemmerick, "Glut of Office Buildings Flattens Rental Income," *Pensions and Investments,* September 3, 1984.

[48] Mark Westerbeck, "Pension Funds Cautious about Realty," *Pensions and Investments,* October 31, 1981.

was development activity held in check by local lender knowledge. Prior to institutionalization, most construction was financed by local banks that knew their markets and would have refused to lend construction funds unless a take-out commitment was in place. Locally based developers understood the vagaries of their particular markets and ran their businesses profitably within the disciplines imposed on them by local lenders.

With the nationalization and institutionalization of the development and lending industries, traditional disciplines eroded. A development company from Boston could build in Houston with financing from a New York bank. The banks' traditional customers, corporations, were flush with cash and had no incentive to borrow. Third-world lending had proven to be far too risky and unprofitable. Banks therefore were eager to finance construction projects.[49] But surprisingly, the culprit that probably did more to unleash the flow of funds in the market was not a key participant in the real estate markets at all.

In 1978, Merrill Lynch introduced its Lynch cash management account, a money market mutual fund that enabled Merrill Lynch to offer investors a much higher current yield than banks and life companies were able to offer their depositors. Investors could even borrow against the account and write checks on it. Other brokers, unfettered by the restrictive lending practices under which the banks and savings institutions were forced to operate, quickly followed suit. When interest rates skyrocketed in 1980, 1981, and 1982, the process of disintermediation began in earnest. Savers cashed in their 5.25 percent passbook savings accounts and transferred their capital to the higher yields and relative safety of the brokerage-sponsored money market accounts. By the end of 1980, the banking industry in general and the thrift industry in particular were on the verge of a catastrophic collapse. In 1981, Congress responded in kind with the passage of new legislation deregulating the financial institutions. With the objective of creating "a more level playing field," under the new regulations banks and thrift institutions could now pay depositors more competitive rates on government-insured deposits. Most important, they were now free to expand their loan portfolios in general and their real estate portfolios in particular.

---

[49] Sharon Reirer, "The Office Market Time Bomb," *Institutional Investor,* June 1985.

The net result was an unprecedented run-up in mortgage lending. With billions of new financing dollars available for the asking, competition intensified and lending disciplines collapsed. Loan-to-value ratios rose from traditional 50 to 75 percent limits to 80, 90, 100 percent, and higher. Debt coverage ratios shrank from 1.5 or better to 1.1 or lower. Loan covenants all but disappeared.

The first sector to collapse was the savings and loan industry, which had attracted neither the talent nor the experience to compete effectively in such a highly inflammatory environment. Savings and loan institutions historically had served the residential market, limiting their real estate lending practices to providing fixed-rate, long-term mortgages to home buyers. By the time deregulation brought S&Ls into the commercial market, they were already in a weakened financial condition. The practice of borrowing short and lending long had decimated earnings during high inflation, and savers' preference for the new money market funds was further eroding their earnings. In the rush to generate fees and interest payments to bolster their bottom lines, these inexperienced commercial lenders failed to carefully analyze the underlying economics of their real estate ventures. Deals were struck to generate fees and interest payments. Many of these projects were considered second tier, below the acquisition standards of more experienced financial institutions. To cope with the catastrophe that ensued, Congress created the Federal Asset Disposition Agency (FADA) and later the Resolution Trust Corporation (RTC).

While the collapse of the thrift industry clearly was a precursor to the decline of the real estate markets in the late 1980s, the thrifts alone were not to blame. Life companies and, to a much greater extent, commercial banks were the real culprits in undermining market discipline. Life company commercial and multifamily real estate loan portfolios grew at an average annual rate of 13 percent per year from 1980 through the peak year 1991, for example, while savings and loan commercial real estate loan portfolios grew from 1980 to peak at an annual rate of 14.8 percent. But commerical banks went wild, increasing their commercial real estate and multifamily loan portfolios at an annual rate of 33.7 percent per year from 1980 through the peak year 1989, tripling total bank-held commercial and multifamily real estate loans outstanding. See Exhibit 1–17. Commercial banks' market share of total annual commercial real estate loan volume also increased 2.5-fold from 15.1 percent in 1980 to 45.8 per-

EXHIBIT 1-17
Real Estate Loans Held by Commercial Banks, 1982-92

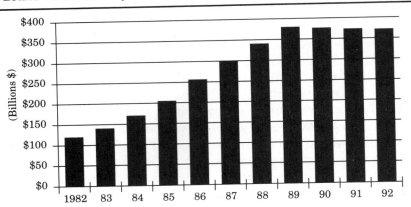

Source: *Real Estate Market Review*, Goldman Sachs, April 1993.

cent in 1989.[50] From 1980 to 1990, real estate loans accounted for roughly 64 percent of the annual increase in total commercial bank loan volume.[51]

Before the regulators loosened the reigns, commercial banks had served as short-term construction lenders only, making construction loans on projects provided that long-term financing commitments from insurance companies were already in place. As life companies retreated from the take-out market, commercial banks filled the void with mini-perm loans that financed construction and operations for a year or two beyond the lease-up stage. Typically, mini perms, or *bullet loans,* provided for a specified maximum construction loan amount and interest-only debt service. The full loan balance was due from five to seven years after the initial loan closing.

Insurance companies joined the fray, scrambling to grow assets under management in the form of guaranteed investment contracts (GICs). In a GIC, the life company promises to make a stated fixed-interest payment to a pension fund over a stipulated 5-, 7-, or 10-

---

[50] William Brueggeman, *Real Estate Market Review,* Goldman Sachs, April 1993.

[51] Ken Rosen, speech to Berkeley Real Estate Associates, University of California, Center for Real Estate and Urban Economics, December 1991.

year term backed by the performance of a pool of 5-, 7-, or 10-year mortgages. Pension funds were offered the additional advantage of book value accounting, meaning their GIC investments could be held on their books at acquisition cost without having to be marked to market whenever interest rates swung. Even more important, the GICs were backed by the full faith and credit of the respective insurers' own names, providing pension funds with relative safety.

To cover the issuers' expenses and still make a profit, the yield promised by borrowers was marked down 150 to 200 basis points (the spread). This marked-down figure became the expressed yield that was guaranteed to the pension fund. The problem was that as more and more life companies got into the GIC business, the business became more and more competitive, not only in terms of the yields being promised but also in the narrowness of the spreads.

The maturities of the 10-year bullet loans underlying these contracts posed a real threat to the integrity of the financial community, because in most cases, values were not sufficient to fully fund principal repayment, and few borrowers had the means to finance the gap. Between 1990 and 1994, these maturities totaled nearly $61 billion. See Exhibit 1–18. The need to refinance these obligations, coupled with increasing rating agency and regulatory pressures, severely curtailed the inventory of capital available to make new loan originations or to help refinance surplus savings and loan and bank debt.

Life company general accounts also suffered. Equitable Real Estate Investment Management in particular, under increasing pres-

EXHIBIT 1–18
Maturities of 10-Year Bullet Loans Underlying Life Company Portfolios and Guaranteed Investment Contracts, 1990–94

	($ Billions)
1990	$ 6.8
1991	8.0
1992	12.0
1993	17.0
1994	17.0

Source: Morgan Stanley Real Estate.

sure from rating agencies to reduce Equitable Life's real estate holdings and from Equitable's board to raise cash, was forced to sell off
some of the best assets held in Equitable's general account, significantly weakening the company's own portfolio. (This sell-off had no
impact on Equitable's pension and other institutional investors' portfolios, however.) Other insurers, including Travellers, Aetna, and
Prudential, announced plans in 1993 to sell off billions of dollars of
loans from their general accounts, either privately or in the public
markets.

Rating agency and regulatory pressures on the banking and life
company industries to reduce their real estate portfolio holdings and
restructure their balance sheets continued through the mid-1990s.
The Financial Institutions Reform, Recovery and Enforcement Act of
1988 (FIRREA) led the charge by creating tougher risk-based capital
rules for banks and savings institutions, discouraging riskier lending
practices, particularly construction lending and the financing of commercial real estate properties. Insurers followed by promulgating
their own, tougher set of lending requirements.[52] FIRREA also promoted more uniform (and more conservative) appraisal practices by,
among other measures, requiring a nationwide uniform state licensing procedure for appraisers.

Finally, in 1993, the National Association of Insurance Commissioners (NAIC) proposed much tougher guidelines—see Exhibit
1–19—for loan underwriting, including a proposal that a maximum
loan-to-value ratio of 70 percent be established for loans that are
fully amortizing and a maximum loan-to-value ratio of 60 percent be
established for loans that are not.[53]

Developing the Case for Real Estate in an Institutional Portfolio

The passage of ERISA and increasing interest in the comparative
performance of real estate to other asset classes have prompted a
wave of real estate research activity and heightened the importance
of research's contribution to the institutional real estate investment
process.

---

[52] Dennis Yeskey, "NAIC Criteria for Reserves Set Aside for Investments by Insurance
Companies," National Association of Real Estate Investment Trusts, *The REIT Report*, XIV,
no. 1 (Winter 1994).

[53] Salomon Brothers, *Update on NAIC Guideline Proposals*, November 1993.

EXHIBIT 1–19

Statutory Risk-Based Capital Requirements for Insurers (Selected Assets)

Asset Category	Statutory Risk-Based Capital (% of Assets)
Mortgages:	
1- to 4-family residential	0.6%–1.0%
Commercial and multifamily—current	1.0%–3.0%
Commercial and multifamily—delinquent	3.0%–6.0%
Mortgages in foreclosure	20.0%
Real estate:	
Company occupied	10.0%
Investment property	10.0%
Foreclosed property (REO)	15.0%
Stocks:	
Common	0.0%–30.0%
Preferred	2.3%–30.0%
Bonds:	
Class 1 (A or higher)	0.3%
Classes 2 to 3 (BBB to BB)	1.0%–4.0%
Classes 4 to 6 (B, CCC, D)	9.0%–30.0%

Source: National Association of Insurance Commissioners.

Early academic research efforts focusing on real estate performance were hampered during the 1970s by the lack of reliable data.
Compared to the established securities markets, real estate had long
been criticized for its peculiarities that stymied efforts to standardize
it as an asset class: It was not traded on an open market; no two
transactions were alike; transactions were private, not open to public
inspection; and it was an illiquid asset, usually held for long durations.

In 1977, under the leadership of Blake Eagle and Frank Russell
Co., the National Council of Real Estate Investment Fiduciaries
(NCREIF) was organized to help resolve the data problem. In 1978,
the Russell/NCREIF Property Index was founded, which created a
benchmark against which institutional investors could measure their
portfolios' (and investment managers') performance.

Today the Russell/NCREIF Property Index is derived from the
aggregate property returns of 1,861 nondevelopmental, income-
producing properties held by tax-exempt funds. As of fourth quarter
1992, those properties were valued at $23.97 billion, representing
roughly 33 percent of all tax-exempt investor equity real estate hold-

ings. Property returns in the Russell/NCREIF Property Index are reported on an unlevered, all-cash basis, before investment management fees, and are broken into income, appreciation, and total return components. Appreciation components are based primarily on appraised values; all data are contributed by NCREIF members on a voluntary, self-reported basis.

By the mid-1980s, several of the commingled real estate funds had been in existence for a decade or more. These funds supplied the necessary data for a number of studies, several of which were published in the fall of 1984, the *American Real Estate and Urban Economics Association (AREUEA) Journal,* and the spring 1982 edition of the *Journal of Portfolio Management.*[54,55,56]

In their *AREUEA* article, Ibbotson and Siegel stated that real estate could improve the risk-adjusted portfolio in one of two ways. First, market inefficiencies could be taken advantage of to produce a "good buy." Second, the addition of real estate may reduce overall portfolio risk, even if it is not a "good buy." Brueggeman, Chen, and Thibodeau published in the same *AREUEA* edition the results of a study that pointed to the diversification benefits to be derived from real estate, showing that it was negatively correlated to stocks and bonds. Furthermore, since real estate returns were positively correlated to the consumer price index, using real estate assets, inflation protection could also be engineered into a portfolio, while portfolios containing only stock and bond investments were shown to exhibit no such inflation protection. From their examination of the databases, they also concluded that real estate generally outperformed stocks and bonds. Concurrently, Zerbst and Cambon's study published in the *Journal of Portfolio Management* concluded that real estate returns generally equaled or exceeded stock returns and that real estate consistently outperformed bonds, Treasury bills, and the rate of inflation. As their colleagues discovered, real estate was shown to be negatively correlated to stocks and bonds, offering a viable diversification strategy. Later these early studies would be criticized for their use of unreliable and unrepresentative data. On the other hand, they were unquestionably based on the best data available at the time

---

[54] Ibbotson and Siegel (1984).

[55] Brueggeman, Chen, and Thibodeau (1984).

[56] R. H. Zerbst and B. R. Cambon, "Everything You Wanted to Know about Real Estate Returns, but Were Afraid to Ask," *Journal of Portfolio Management,* Spring 1982.

and helped change real estate's image as an exotic, or alternative, investment class, pushing it toward acceptance as a legitimate, core asset class. As unreliable as the data may have been, however, these studies did form a rational basis for wholesale pension fund entry into the feeding frenzy of the 1980s. Their timing couldn't have been worse.

The Tax Reform Act of 1986

The explosive growth of the stock market in the mid-1980s resulted in the real estate component of overall portfolios dropping as much as 5 percentage points. Corporate plans, pessimistic about the health of the overbuilt real estate market and disenchanted with falling returns, were not so willing to increase their real estate allocation. Fears about the real estate market were somewhat alleviated by the passage of the Tax Reform Act of 1986 (TRA). This act placed stringent statutory limitations on the utilization of tax shelters, completely shutting off the flow of funds from tax-driven syndicators.[57]

Under TRA, depreciation schedules were lengthened from 15 years to 27.5 years for residential rental and 31 years for nonresidential. Both classes had to be depreciated by straight-line methods. Distinctions were made between active and passive income and their respective tax deductions. No longer could passive losses from real estate investments be offset against active income received from wages.

When TRA was enacted, popular opinion held that the exclusion of tax-driven deals would exert a downward pressure on prices. Not so. Prices remained high despite the surplus of space, due to steadily growing investment demand from public pension funds and a sharp increase in foreign investment.[58] Many of the public plans, recently freed from legislative investment constraints, were anxious to invest in real estate. (CalPERS did not receive legislative authority to invest in real estate until 1983; many public pension plans, including Texas Teachers Retirement System and the Wyoming Public Employees Retirement System, are still prohibited from investing directly in real estate.) Likewise, small and mid-size corporate pension plans were looking to emulate their bigger corporate brothers and sisters.

---

[57] Sheldon Schwartz, "Real Estate and the Tax Reform Act of 1986," *Real Estate Review*, Winter 1987.

[58] Joel Chernoff, "Real Estate Prices Stay High," *Pensions and Investments*, October 27, 1986.

According to *Pensions and Investments'* annual survey of the top 200 pension funds, public funds increased their commitment from $8.6 billion in 1985 to $12.9 billion in 1987, a 50 percent increase (see Exhibit 1–20).[59] Foreign investor presence also grew steadily throughout the 1980s, increasing by more than $40 billion between 1980 and 1980.

Reaction to the Market

From 1980 to 1987, the pension fund press reported the industry's wavering commitment to real estate. Though pension fund investments had increased from $19 billion in 1980 to $87.8 billion in 1987, real estate was still considered by most pension funds and their consultants as an alternative asset class, not on a par with stocks and bonds as a core asset class.[60]

In the meantime, turmoil and unrest characterized the real estate markets of the mid-1980s. The recovery anticipated in 1986 was delayed by concerns over unusually low oil prices, the economic fallout from tax reform, an overbuilt real estate market, and a generally sluggish economy.

Returns for commingled funds continued to slide as portfolios

EXHIBIT 1–20
Real Estate Holdings of the Top 200
Public Pension Plans, 1985–92 (Market Value in $ Billions)

1985	$ 8.6
1986	10.0
1987	12.9
1988	12.8
1989	24.2
1990	30.3
1991	31.4
1992	30.8

Source: "Top 200 Funds Invested in Real Estate," *Pensions and Investments.*

[59] Equitable Real Estate Management and the Roulac Group, *Real Estate Capital Flows,* 1989.

[60] Ibid.

began to be marked down. PRISA lost $1 billion in assets in 1986 as a result of client withdrawals.[61] The recession in oil-producing regions forced the write-down of properties in those markets. Pension fund administrators began to get edgy, questioning the fiduciary wisdom of investing in such an apparently risky asset class.

Then, on October 19, 1987, the stock market plummeted in value by nearly 29 percent. Pension portfolios, heavily weighted toward equities, lost as much as 12 percent of their value. In the same year, unleveraged pension fund real estate investments on the Russell/NCREIF index posted a record low total return of 5.4 percent, with office properties returning a miserable 0.6 percent. Some within the industry wondered if the same fate awaited real estate: that a drastic correction was needed to deal with overvaluation in the market.[62]

After the Crash

The October crash induced a temporary state of paralysis. In the aftermath, investors took another look at the diversification benefits attributed to real estate. Many of those already invested saw that their real estate holdings, as a percentage of assets, had increased due to the relative devaluation of equities. This being the case, many of these investors delayed any new allocations to real estate. Other investors, those who had shirked real estate investment during the bull market, became born-again real estate investors.

The crash had a sobering effect on everyone, but within a year's time, the pension fund press was reporting that sponsors were "ready for a real estate buying spree."[63]

One thing had changed since the early 1980s, however. Pension fund staffs and investment boards had evolved and progressed up the learning curve into a more sophisticated group of investors than ever before. The stock market crash brought home the fact that real estate would have to become a core portfolio asset to more completely diversify the overall portfolio and lower its volatility. At the same time, pension fund administrators faced a fundamentally unstable real

---

[61] Steve Hemmerick, "Plagued by Withdrawals," *Pensions and Investments,* July 21, 1986.

[62] Andy Reinbach, "Values to Drop as Realty Prices Rise," *Pensions and Investments,* November 14, 1988.

[63] Steve Hemmerick, "Funds Ready for a Buying Spree," *Pensions and Investments,* September 1988.

estate market characterized by oversupply, increasing vacancies, and declining returns. This being the case, fund administrators began to reassess their real estate investment strategies and redefine their relationship with real estate investment advisory firms.

In the meantime, investors of all kinds got caught up in the dynamics of Newton's law of inertia (a body in motion tends to remain in motion, and a body at rest tends to remain at rest). Everyone was seduced by the forward psychology of the markets.

The problem was that the psychology of the markets was seductive indeed. First, syndicators drove prices up in search of write-offs. Foreign investors, particularly the Japanese, arrived on the scene in force just as the syndicators were getting ready to vacate the market. They looked around and saw prices approaching those they had grown accustomed to at home. In fact, properties priced at what U.S. investors knew were historically low capitalization rates for U.S. markets actually looked cheap to the Japanese. U.S. market participants literally were drunk with excitement as prices continued to be bid up to unprecedented highs.

Wall Street formed real estate capital markets groups to participate in the feeding frenzy. The Wall Streeters pointed out that capitalization rates in the United States traditionally had been significantly higher than capitalization rates in Europe and the Far East. The drop in capitalization rates, they argued, was merely a reflection of the repricing of U.S. real estate assets in the global capital markets—a secular, not a cyclical, shift in pricing.

Wall Street's point of view eventually would be proven wrong, but for the time being, pension fund investment managers, after being on the outside for the third, fourth, or fifth deal in a row, began to believe. This psychology continued to fuel the feeding frenzy long after the leading indicators supported continued capitalization of the real estate investment markets.

THE EMERGENCE AND GROWTH OF THE REAL ESTATE INVESTMENT MANAGEMENT BUSINESS

The passage of ERISA and the growth of pension portfolio managers in search of real estate investment opportunities combined to spawn the emergence of the real estate investment advisory industry.

Prior to 1980, few independent advisory firms existed. In the mid-1970s, no more than 15 such firms were in existence. By 1981 that number had risen to 40,[64] and two years later 65 independent firms were polled for *Pensions and Investments'* annual survey. By 1991, the survey listed well over 100 firms.

The genealogy of real estate investment vehicles begins with the large, open-end funds offered by bank trust departments and insurance companies. Placing funds through an established, reputable, experienced commercial bank or life company real estate investment management group appeared to the pension funds to be the "prudent" way to access the real estate markets.

Before the diversification clause of ERISA was clarified by the Department of Labor (DOL), however, there was some doubt as to how the DOL might subsequently rule on the inclusion of real estate assets. The liquidity of the open-end commingled funds appealed to investors. Should the DOL rule that real estate was not a responsible investment for an investment fiduciary to make, investors could liquidate their holdings—or so they thought.

Another feature that favored the large, open-end funds was their experienced real estate staff. Pension fund administrators were well versed in the securities markets. Real estate, however, was unfamiliar to most pension funds, requiring specialized skills and knowledge for prudent investment decision making. Commercial banks and insurance companies, with their history of long-term mortgage financing and their experience as equity investors for their own general accounts and trust account customers, were deemed to possess the requisite skills for institutional real estate investment.

Closed-End Commingled Funds

Emerging first in 1976 with the introduction of Coldwell Banker's (now CB Commercial) first commingled fund, closed-end funds represented the next generation of real estate investment vehicles. Unlike an open-end fund, which by definition is always open to subscription, a closed-end fund is closed to additional investment capital once it has reached its target subscription level. Typically no money changes hands until properties are actually ready to be acquired. Once the fund is fully subscribed, dollars sufficient to acquire each property

---

[64] McKelvy, *Pension Fund Investments*, p. 214.

are called from each investor in precise proportion to the amount of money each investor has committed. Properties then are held for a predetermined period, typically 10 years. When the due date arrives, the fund is supposed to be liquidated and proceeds distributed to the investors. Exhibit 1–21 shows the dates and values of maturing closed-end funds.

Closed-end commingled real estate funds tended to be much smaller in total assets than the large, open-end, commingled real estate funds.[65] Portfolios tended to have fewer properties. To support the diversification requirements mandated by ERISA, properties acquired by such funds also tended to be smaller in scale. An open-end fund such as PRISA, for example, could easily acquire properties valued at $100 million or above without risking underdiversification, while closed-end funds typically were constrained to properties in the $5 million to $20 million range.

Other than the difference in typical property size, the early investment strategies of both closed-end and open-end funds essentially were identical: Target the most prestigious, best-located properties and purchase 100 percent equity interests on an all-cash basis.[66]

EXHIBIT 1–21
Closed-End Fund Maturities ($ Billions)

	Number of Funds	Value	Cumulative
1990–1993	25	$2,006	$3,796
1994	7	1,144	3,150
1995	8	1,440	4,590
1996	5	1,224	5,813
1997	13	2,024	7,837
1998	5	1,079	8,916
1999	8	1,605	10,522
2000–2005	15	2,817	13,339
Total	86	$13,339	$13,339

Source: *The Institutional Real Estate Letter* 5, no. 12 (December 1993) (from data provided by Frank Russell Co.).

---

[65] J. Rohrer, "How Pension Funds Are Making Their Great Leap into Real Estate," *Institutional Investor*, June 1981.

[66] McKelvy, *Pension Fund Investments*, p. 218.

rates on loans. This worked to the benefit of owners, of course. Mortgaged property owners not only paid a negative real rate of interest; they could write off that interest and enjoy increasing property appreciation from demand pressures. Lenders, however, learned their lessons from that experience. During the 1980s, shorter-term, high-rate (and in many cases variable-rate) mortgages were underwritten to protect lenders from unexpected inflation, undermining real estate's ability to hedge returns against inflation.

The inability of real estate returns in general and office property returns in particular to capture the majority of inflation effects consistently across market cycles has been well documented in a series of research papers completed in 1994 by Pagliari and Webb.[111] Since real estate values in the form of housing prices constitute such a large percentage of the CPI, however, real estate still should be considered to provide a reasonable inflation hedge throughout most of the cycle.[112]

Changing Pension Fund/Advisory Firm Relationships

Because smaller funds became inactive in the late 1980s and early 1990s, the larger funds became the dominant force in the markets. The prevailing trend toward separate accounts among these larger funds gave them the upper hand. Between 1990 and 1993, these larger pension funds began demanding more from their real estate advisors: nondiscretionary relationships (where the fund pulled the trigger on major decisions), more stringent reporting requirements, higher performance standards, and lower fees.

Under discretionary relationships, the pension fund delegates full or partial responsibility for acquiring, underwriting, managing, and disposing of real estate assets on behalf of the penison fund. Most commingled funds structured during the 1980s were fully discretionary accounts, providing investment managers with a great deal of latitude in managing their clients' portfolios.

Under nondiscretionary relationships, the pension funds retain the right to approve any and all deals submitted for acquisition.

---

[111] The series of papers began with: Joseph L. Pagliari and James R. Webb, "Fundamental Returns of the Office Sector," *The Institutional Real Estate Letter,* January 1994.

[112] William Brueggeman, from a speech delivered to the semiannual real estate conference of the Institute for Fiduciary Education, Dallas, TX, 1992.

Increasingly, funds also retain the right to approve major leases; control the initial valuation and ongoing appraisal process; and dictate uniform acquisition submittal, underwriting, management, and reporting processes and procedures.

In the late 1980s and early 1990s, mid-size pension funds (and even some larger funds) that remained active but still needed to pool their capital with like-minded investors began participating in coinvestment programs sponsored by specialty investment management firms like L&B Real Estate Counsel, Kennedy Associates, and Metric Institutional Realty Advisors. Co-investment enabled these mid-size investors to acquire positions in larger properties than otherwise would have been possible, while retaining some measure of control over their investments. Coinvestment also enabled investors to tailor investment management relationships with their managers rather than being subjected to the kind of uniform investment management contract required with a traditional commingled fund.

Smaller pension funds began returning to the market in late 1993. By necessity, these smaller funds were forced to invest in pooled investment programs, lacking sufficient capital to invest directly or in coinvestment programs. By 1993, however, the pooled form of investment had changed dramatically. The group trust and limited partnership form of investment had been replaced by the private real estate investment trust (REIT) as the favored investment structure.

The primary appeal of these private REITs was better corporate governance. Shareholders could vote their shares to elect independent trustees without having to assume fiduciary liability for other investors. Trustees, in turn, had the power to remove and replace the advisor, approve or disapprove deals submitted by the advisor, approve or disapprove major leases, contract with independent appraisers to value the portfolio, and negotiate with the advisor on its compensation, among other powers. In addition, REIT advisors could be paid in the form of incentive compensation; many of the new REITS proposed to pay advisors a portion of their compensation in REIT shares, which purportedly aligned their interests more closely with those of the shareholders in the REIT. Private REITs also offered investors the option to eventually go public, which, in the hot REIT market of 1993 and early 1994, appealed to many investors as a potential exit strategy. Most of these private REITs also were organized as open-end, infinite-life vehicles, eliminating the conflicts arising between investors wishing to liquidate property holdings at fund maturity and managers' desire to extend the life of the fund and keep assets under management. Unlike with open-end commingled funds, which promised to redeem shares at net asset value, liquidity of shares would depend on market pricing mechanisms. If buyers and sellers of units could come to some form of agreement over price, shares would trade, and investors could achieve liquidity without the manager needing to take action.

Many smaller investors began investing in publicly traded REIT shares in 1993 as well. As the market capitalization of public real estate stocks continues to expand, pension fund involvement in these markets can only be expected to continue to grow.

In addition to a shift in the vehicles preferred by pension funds, the players also changed in the 1990s. In the early 1980s, for example, the dominant players in the pension market were the corporate funds. Most of these funds selected investment managers through an informal search process, with or without the help of a real estate consultant. Because of the character of their boards, they were able to make such selections relatively quickly.

By the late 1980s, most of the corporate funds were overfunded, meaning little new cash flow was available to fund new real estate investments. The real estate allocations of many of these large corporate funds also were now fully invested. As a result, corporate funds became less active in selecting new investment managers.

During the late 1980s and mid-1990s, many of these funds began to retrench, focusing on their existing portfolios, removing and replacing some managers, and restructuring fees and the nature of their relationships with others.

By the mid-1980s to early 1990s, public funds became the dominant force in the market. Public funds typically utilized lower investment assumptions in underwriting their plans and, consequently, tended to be more underfunded than corporate pension plans. Most also were neophytes to real estate investing and therefore became the most active in conducting searches for new investment managers.

Because most public pension plans are subject to the same contracting guidelines as the entities or agencies that sponsor them, the manager selection process tended to be much more process oriented and almost always involves a real estate consultant. First, the funds issue a request for proposal (RFP). The RFP states the products and services to be provided, the requirements for contractor qualifications, and any other parameters that define the contract. Responses to the

RFPs are then screened by a series of objective criteria, and the candidate list is narrowed to a list of finalists, who are then invited to make formal presentations to the board of trustees and investment staff. Prior to the presentations, staff typically will conduct due diligence on each finalist. Presentations usually last between 20 minutes to an hour per finalist; selections typically follow immediately upon completion of the formal presentations. Then contracts are negotiated over the following three to eight months. Once an advisor is under contract, the process of acquiring assets begins.

With separate accounts, this process typically is nondiscretionary, meaning deals must be submitted to staff for screening and final approval. (With larger funds, staff typically will be empowered to make or break the deal up to a certain limit, ranging between $10 million and $80 million per transaction. Acquisitions larger than this limit will require the approval of the investment committee or the entire board.)

The collapse of the property markets in oil-producing states spurred renewed interest in real estate research during the 1980s, creating even greater demands for quantitative sophistication in all levels of the business. Despite this emphasis on the quantitative side of the business, however, the most significant investment manager selection criterion in the 1990s continued to be trust and comfort: trust in the capabilities of an advisory firm to perform its duties in the best interest of the pension fund, trust in the accuracy and reliability of the manager's valuations and reports, and comfort in dealing with managers interpersonally.

Investor underwriting criteria also had changed. In the 1980s, investors viewed real estate primarily as a long-term asset, emphasizing appreciation potential over current cash flow when underwriting specific transactions. In the 1990s, cash-on-cash returns replaced projected appreciation as the primary underwriting criterion; perceived risk in the current marketplace as well as pessimism about future performance prompted investors to demand cash-on-cash returns that exceeded the risk-free rate of 5- or 10-year Treasury bills. Income streams typically were expected to remain flat over the next two to three years, with a slight improvement after that. Expenses, on the other hand, typically were expected to increase between 4 and 5 percent annually. Capitalization rates had increased nationwide on most property types, reflecting investor pessimism. See Exhibit 1–27.

EXHIBIT 1–27
Real Estate Investment Criteria by Property Type, Third Quarter 1993

	Office	Retail	Industrial	Apartment
Expected cap rate*	9.7%	8.8%	9.6%	9.1%
Actual cap rate†	9.2%	9.6%	9.6%	9.6%
Expected IRR*	12.45%	11.91%	11.88%	11.43%
Actual rent/sq. ft.†	$20.14	$13.84	$4.28	$9.65

* Peter F. Korpacz, Korpacz Investor Survey, third quarter 1993.
† National Real Estate Index, the Liquidity Fund, third quarter 1993.

Properties in need of renovation or purchased from distressed sellers were registering capitalization rates in the 10 to 12 percent range.[113]

By 1993, investors increasingly expressed confidence in real estate as an asset class but doubts about the reliability or trustworthiness of their investment managers. By way of amplifying the earlier-mentioned study for the National Association of Real Estate Investment Managers:[114]

- 64 percent of plan sponsors surveyed reported they planned to continue to invest in real estate to meet their target allocations.
- 81 percent of respondents said they planned to increase their overall allocations to real estate.
- An additional 14 percent said that after a hiatus, they will begin to allocate additional assets to real estate again.
- Only 4 percent said they planned to abandon the asset class altogether.

However, the survey also showed that the real estate investment management industry must "reinvent itself" to better meet plan sponsors' needs and correct the perceived excesses of poor performance, extravagant fees, unresolved conflicts of interest, and bad advice of the past.

---

[113] "Investors' Higher Yield Expectations Aren't Being Met," *Pensions and Investments*, May 1991.

[114] Opinion survey of 60 large plan sponsors, conducted by Real Estate Consulting Associates for the National Association of Real Estate Investment Managers, 1993.

According to the survey, reform was required in four specific areas:

- Investment practices and reporting need to be standardized on an industrywide basis.
- Investment managers need to increase their understanding of client needs and must express a sincere desire to meet those needs (particularly in the areas of investment management fees and honest, forthright communications).
- Investment managers need to develop a better understanding of pension fund culture and obligations and work diligently to remove any conflicts that might inhibit their operating in the best interests of their plan sponsor clients.
- Investment managers must become more forward thinking about the industry in general and the portfolios entrusted to their stewardship in particular.

To regain the trust of the plan sponsor community, the study therefore recommended the following action plans:

- Investment managers must take the appropriate steps to align their interests more closely with those of their clients.
- Investment managers must develop a better understanding of the responsibilities associated with being a plan fiduciary and must eliminate the structural and financial conflicts of interest that inhibit their ability to fulfill their fiduciary obligations.
- Investment managers must provide plan sponsors with a clearer vision for the future of the real estate investment industry.

The State of the Institutional Real Estate Investment Industry in the 1990s

In the mid-1990s, securities managers—those who manage pension funds' stock and bond portfolios—were experiencing similar changes in their relationship with pension fund clients. Track record and long-term performance had become the prime determinants for choosing a management firm.

As the money management business became more competitive, consolidation was inevitable. Money managers complained that consultants were forcing them to specialize. To placate the consultants, a management firm had to have a definable investment focus, for example, specializing in growth-oriented stocks or mutual funds. If an advisor did not a have a clearly defined specialty, it became more and more unlikely that it would appear on a consultant's list.

Between 1980 and 1990, the number of pension funds relying exclusively on internal management shrank. *Pensions and Investments'* 1990 survey of the top 200 funds disclosed that the number of funds managed entirely in-house had fallen from 30 in 1980 to 10.[115] Passive investment strategies, such as indexed portfolios, are managed in-house, but when diversifying into asset classes that require special skills, outside managers almost always are contracted.

The downward pressure on fees that real estate managers experienced in the late 1980s and early 1990s reflects three factors. First, the process of institutionalization has a tendency to lower fees in general. As the investment management business has become increasingly institutionalized, for example, fees for common stock portfolio management services have come down from as high as 100 to 150 basis points on assets under management to between 20 and 80 basis points on such assets.[116] Second, as investors have become more sophisticated, investment management services have begun to be perceived as being more commoditylike and therefore are being priced as commodities. Third, poor investment performance has meant that fees had been taking a proportionately bigger and bigger bite out of investor returns.[117]

However, as real estate investment management performance improves and as investment managers become better able to demonstrate how they add value to the investment management process, fees can be expected to increase somewhat. In the equity investment management business, for example, the average annual fee paid by pension funds to their outside managers in 1991 was 38.8 basis points, an 8 percent increase over the 35.7 basis points paid to outside managers in 1988.[118]

---

[115] Terry Williams, "The Dawn of a New Age for Internal Portfolios," *Pensions and Investments,* June 10, 1991.

[116] Ibid.

[117] From an unpublished study by Institutional Real Estate, Inc., January 1993.

[118] Williams, "The Dawn of a New Age."

In general, corporations and foundations tend to pay more than public pension funds for the same services. In 1991, for example, corporate funds paid their stock managers an average of 44 basis points on assets under management, while public funds paid an average of 32.2 basis points on such assets. Corporate and foundation funds also appeared willing to pay more to their real estate investment managers in the 1990s than were public funds.[119]

Among both corporate and public funds, there was a trend toward performance-based fees. Fifteen percent of both corporate and public pension funds now use performance-based fees; 8 percent expect to implement them in the future, bringing the expected total to 23 percent.[120]

In keeping with the growth of government and, concurrently, the downsizing of the private sector, public pension plans were more disposed to develop in-house expertise than were corporate pension plans. In addition, public plan trustees tend to be more actively involved in administering their funds and therefore more willing to build in-house management operations. In contrast, private sector senior managers typically do not want to add fiduciary risk to their business risk. For corporate pension plans, the art of pension administration presents an entirely different culture than business management and is far removed from the plan sponsor's core business.[121]

To carve out a place for themselves in today's more competitive market, advisory firms have had to reassess their business strategies. "Asset management" has become the catchword of the 1990s as investors seek to improve the quality and competitiveness of the assets already in their portfolios.

Since the early 1980s, real estate investment managers could always be divided into one of three camps: those who advocate in-house property management, those who favor using third-party property managers, and those who employ both approaches. Advocates of the in-house property management approach stress the added control in-house property management provides and the benefits of standardization it facilitates. Advocates of the third-party approach stress the flexibility that this approach provides, enabling them to acquire the best talent available in local markets. Pension funds, however, appear

---

[119] Ibid.

[120] Ibid.

[121] Ibid.

indifferent to the issue; what matters to most pension funds is that the property leasing, maintenance, and operations be well controlled, not the manner in which they are controlled.[122]

In the 1980s, most clients were content with simply receiving aggregate portfolio information. In the 1990s, they increasingly requested property-level information that would enable them to monitor the performance of the portfolio on a property-by-property basis and thereby avoid surprises. Each client defined those needs differently, however. Managers therefore had to invest in the development of integrated, flexible, sophisticated property management and portfolio management systems that would enable them to deliver custom-tailored reports to meet the unique information requests of their many different clients. Systems had to be designed to meet these specific reporting requirements cost effectively, while presenting that information in the precise format requested on a nearly real-time basis.[123]

To help them organize, slice, and dice the volumes of information now being reported to them by multiple managers on their real estate holdings, large pension funds like Ameritech, CalPERS, State of Connecticut Trust Funds, and the Colorado Public Employee Retirement Association began developing their own in-house, computerized portfolio management systems. These systems, in turn, helped create reporting standards that filtered back to their managers' other accounts.[124]

In response to investor needs, during the mid- to late 1980s, a number of investment management firms began establishing themselves as specialists in specific property types or geographic locations, primarily to help pension fund investors overweighted in specific markets (like the oil patch or California) or specific property types (like office or retail) to balance out their real estate investment portfolios.[125]

In addition to these specialty shops, large, established, full-service firms like Aldrich, Eastman and Waltch, Alex. Brown Kleinwort Benson, Equitable Real Estate Investment Management, Mellon/McMahan Real Estate Advisors, and Prudential Real Estate

---

[122] "MegaShifts," *The Institutional Real Estate Letter,* December 1989, 1990, 1991, 1992, 1993.

[123] Ibid.

[124] Ibid.

[125] Ibid.

began positioning themselves in the 1990s as portfolio specialists, with the ability to help investors balance their portfolios via a one-stop shopping approach. This particularly appealed to large pension funds like Ameritech and California Public Employees Retirement System, which were seeking to limit the number of investment managers with whom they worked.[126]

In general, the trend in pension real estate investment strategy during the early to mid-1990s was away from core portfolio acquisitions toward more specialized property types that offered unique diversification benefits and higher potential returns. Alternative products attracting investor attention in the 1990s included multifamily residential, industrial property, community and neighborhood shopping centers, single-family home-building finance, single-tenant net leased offices, industrial and retail property, franchise finance investments, health care facilities, senior living facilities, and land, land-income, timberland, and farmland investment offerings. Retail and industrial properties in need of revitalization also were popular, though acquisition prices were determined primarily by current cash flow rather than upside appreciation potential. A number of more adventuresome funds, like the Illinois State Teachers and Ohio Public Employees, also became involved in underwriting purchases of distressed loans or bulk portfolio loan packages, and some, like the State of Connecticut Trust Funds, IBM Pension Funds, and Ohio State Teachers, were involved in securitized transactions or in capitalizing on the tidal wave of equity real estate securitization of 1991 to 1993.[127]

While pension funds were becoming more adventuresome during the mid-1990s, life companies and commercial banks were becoming more conservative, focusing almost exclusively on financing or refinancing fully stabilized retail and apartment properties that they perceived as offering more reliable, more predictable revenue streams to cover debt service.[128] Credit companies like GE Capital and GMAC, on the other hand, began focusing their investment resources on niche markets like home-building finance and senior living, as well as the more traditional areas of multifamily and retail finance.[129]

---

[126] Ibid.

[127] Ibid.

[128] John Levy, "Debt Real Estate," *Real Estate Capital Markets Report,* Winter 1992, Spring 1992, Fall 1992, Winter 1993, Spring 1993, Fall 1993.

[129] Institutional Real Estate, Inc., unpublished research, December 1993.

The decision-making process utilized by most successful real estate investors relied on insights into the underlying forces that affect market demand. The ability to make these subjective judgments was based on a real estate professional's experience, network of contacts, and "gut instincts." In the 1990s, growing institutionalization has increasingly demanded that even the most subjective decisions be backed up by quantitative support.[130]

Institutions and their advisors now have to access and analyze data from a variety of sources. Demographic changes and employment growth must be monitored to determine the supply and demand dynamics of individual markets. Changes in business and industry must be tracked to determine their effect on demand.[131] Revolutions in communication, transportation, and information technologies, for example, are redefining space usage patterns, undermining the utility and therefore the value of certain types of properties and certain geographic locations.

The advent of the European Union has focused considerable interest on Europe, while the passage of the North American Free Trade Agreement has focused renewed investment interest in Mexico and Canada.[132,133] Conversion of that interest to investment activity was inhibited in the early 1990s, however, by a number of factors:[134,135]

1. The collapse of JMB's Randsworth Trust (primarily London office properties) investment program in the early 1990s.
2. Investor dissatisfaction with the continued (although anticipated) capital calls by JMB to help finance the ongoing operations of its Cadillac Fairview portfolio of Canadian real estate holdings.
3. Declining performance in European property markets during the early 1990s that mirrored difficulties in U.S. markets.

---

[130] "MegaShifts," *The Institutional Real Estate Letter,* December 1989, 1990, 1991, 1992, 1993.

[131] Leanne Lachman, "Changing Demographics," *The Institutional Real Estate Letter* 12, no. 5 (May 1993).

[132] "Investors Explore International Markets," *The Institutional Real Estate Letter* 5, no. 5 (May 1993).

[133] Equitable Real Estate Investment Management and Real Estate Research Corp., *Emerging Trends in Real Estate,* 1991, 1992, 1993.

[134] Steve Hemmerick, "U.S. Funds Wary of Overseas Realty Pitch," *Pensions and Investments,* April 1993.

[135] Institutional Real Estate, Inc.

4. Lack of familiarity with the intricacies of foreign property markets, including ignorance of local market customs, regulations, and tax provisions.

5. Lack of available, comparable data about foreign property investment markets.

6. Concerns over the political stability and currency risks associated with offshore investing.

Long term, however, there are a number of reasons U.S. pension funds can be expected to adopt a more globalized approach to developing their real estate investment portfolios:[136,137,138]

1. The U.S. market accounts for only 6 percent of the world's physical real estate inventory, 5 percent of the world's total population, and only 5 percent of all cities with a population of 1 million or more. Given the amount of investable funds now controlled by U.S. pension funds relative to the ability of U.S. markets to absorb those funds, new investment fund managers have no choice but to seek opportunities in foreign investment (and property) markets.

2. The continued trend toward globalization of the world's economy necessitates the inclusion of foreign holdings to diversify the portfolio. Many pension funds already have incorporated international investment strategies into their stock and bond portfolios.

3. The globalization of information resources, coupled with the institutionalization of real estate worldwide, will make information about global property investment markets and transactions more readily available and eventually will lead to standardization of the collection and reporting of property- and market-related information throughout the world. The emergence of the Institutional Property Database in Great Britain during the 1980s, for example, reflects this trend.

---

[136] Hemmerick, "U.S. Funds Wary."

[137] *Capital Flows 1990: Real Estate Alternatives for Institutional Investors;* Equitable Real Estate Investment Management; and the Roulac Group.

[138] Institutional Real Estate, Inc.

4. A number of experienced global real estate investment management firms with competitive track records have been emerging in the 1990s to help investors and their consultants bridge the gap in international real estate knowledge and expertise. Prudential's PRICOA Property Services, Ltd., and the merger of Baring, Houston and Saunders with Baring Institutional Realty Advisors in 1992 are just two examples.

Some public pension funds, however, will not be able play in the international real estate game until they are freed from legislative constraints. It is likely, however, that these constraints eventually will be lifted, just as they have been for other sectors of the portfolio.[139]

Though other areas of the world may contain larger populations and greater aggregate real estate values, those real estate values consist mainly of agricultural, residential, and small retail uses. For this reason, institutional investors most likely will initially concentrate their international investments in the top three areas: the European Union, Japan, and the United States—see Exhibit 1–28.[140]

Though foreign investment no doubt will gain acceptance as an integral part of a cohesive institutional investment strategy in the 1990s, it is doubtful that U.S. advisory firms will play a significant role. Few pension funds queried in a 1991 minisurvey,[141] for example, said they would use one of their existing investment advisors for international investment. When asked if they would consider a U.S. advisory firm that was linked with a foreign firm, most responded negatively, asserting there was no reason to pay an additional layer of fees. Most said they would consider investing only with foreign investment management firms, provided, however, that they are experienced in their targeted local markets and already are well respected by institutional investors in the countries in which they are domiciled.

---

[139] Ibid.

[140] *Capital Flows 1990: Real Estate Alternatives for Institutional Investors;* Equitable Real Estate Investment Management; and the Roulac Group.

[141] Ellen Beckett Brown, *The Evolution of Pension Fund Investment in Real Estate,* MIT, Center for Real Estate Development, September 1991.

EXHIBIT 1–28
Global Real Estate (1989 Value Estimates)

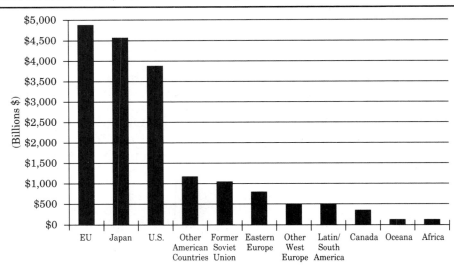

Sources: The Roulac Group; *The Economist.*

CONCLUSION

The real estate markets in the 1990s are undergoing a series of major evolutionary changes in the underlying structure of the real estate investment industry.[142] Portfolio managers must be prepared to cope with these changes, which include:

- The growing institutionalization and globalization of investment in general and real estate ownership and management in particular, which is shifting decision making from an entrepreneurial, gut-driven, transaction-based, short-term orientation to a more managerial, more asset-based, more information-driven, more long-term orientation.
- The transformation of the U.S. economy from a manufacturing base to a service base.
- Lowered expectations about the prospects for sustained, long-term U.S. economic growth.

---

[142] "MegaShifts," *The Institutional Real Estate Letter,* December 1989, 1990, 1991, 1992, 1993.

- Rising expectations about the prospects for growth in the rapidly industrializing nations of the Third World, particularly in the Pacific Rim.
- The demise of communism as a competitive economic model and the spread of more capitalistic models throughout the world. (In the long run, the spread of capitalism throughout the world should increase competition for scarce capital resources.)
- An unprecedented oversupply of nearly every property type in the United States, prolonging the recovery stage of the normal real estate cycle.
- Changing U.S. population demographics, which in turn are decreasing the growth in demand for most property types while recasting the ethnic character of that demand.
- Growing international economic competition, which is forcing U.S. companies to automate and downsize to remain competitive.
- Technological innovations in transportation, inventory management, communications, and financial management, which are changing the volume and nature of space user requirements and thereby undermining values of some property types and markets while increasing values in others.
- The recent restructuring of the U.S. real estate capital markets, shrinking the availability of capital from traditional debt sources while stimulating newer, more dynamic sources of both equity and debt capital.
- The growing securitization in the United States of all asset classes, placing greater emphasis on current cash yields and income growth expectations rather than longer-term capital values.

With these changes as a backdrop, the outlook for institutional real estate investment for the remainder of the 1990s includes the following:[143]

- Securitization of commercial mortgage debt will increase, with insurance companies (and, to a lesser extent, commercial banks) leading the way. Current and proposed NAIC guidelines will combine to encourage life company portfolio managers to

---

[143] Ibid.

spin more and more of their existing real estate portfolio holdings into the public markets. A growing number of conduits will emerge to help facilitate this trend.

- Commercial banks will continue to spin off assets in bulk portfolio sales to raise cash and pare down their real estate portfolios.
- The RTC will become less and less important in the secondary commercial mortgage and equities markets as it winds down its activities toward the middle of the decade. The absence of RTC inventory will further stimulate Wall Street securitization of private debt and equity portfolios.
- Conservative underwriting policies and relatively low new loan origination volume (when compared with traditional levels) will persist among both commercial banking institutions and life companies.
- Savings and thrift institutions will continue to limit real estate lending to traditional residential mortgage lending activities and will not be players in the commercial mortgage or equity real estate markets.
- As rating agency pressures relax, credit companies eventually will return to the real estate debt markets.
- The process of equity securitization of private real estate operating companies will continue, although initial public offering volume will continue to wax and wane with the fortunes of the public markets (i.e., with the opening and closing of the public market window for initial public offerings). Securitization of institutional equity holdings will increase.
- Pension fund assets will continue to grow at their historical growth rates, ranging between 7 and 15 percent.
- Allocations for those pension funds electing to participate in real estate (including mortgage debt) will continue to range between 10 and 15 percent of total assets, a small but growing percentage of which will be diverted to fund international real estate investment strategies.
- Pension fund investment in both the debt and equity real estate markets therefore will continue to grow on an absolute basis, and pension funds consequently will become the dominant providers of private and public equity capital to the markets.
- Pension funds will increase their allocations to equity real

estate securities as well, through existing stock managers, specialty realty stock managers, and mutual funds and by direct investing.

- Pension fund equity investors and lenders of all kinds will continue to underwrite property values based primarily on current cash returns until yields on stocks and bonds return to traditional levels and general investor expectations about the economy in general and the real estate markets in particular improve.
- Modern portfolio theory will continue to be applied at the pension fund/consultant level in an effort to achieve optimal portfolio diversification benefits. Consultants will increasingly be called upon to assist in developing overall real estate investment strategies, particularly in the international real estate arena. If they fail to gear up to meet this challenge, investment advisors will step in to fill the gap.
- The pace of closing transactions will continue to slow due to the increasing due diligence demands of institutional investors.
- Demand for information of all kinds about potential acquisitions and portfolio holdings will continue to increase.
- Information at all levels will become more standardized, reducing market inefficiencies and facilitating even greater securitization and institutionalization.

The effects on advisory firms and others seeking to serve an increasingly institutionalized market include the following:

- The trend toward separate accounts will continue as larger pension funds seek more control over their realty assets. Advisors to such funds will operate in a nondiscretionary capacity, with fund administrators exercising more and more control over all important decisions.
- The move toward separate accounts will allow clients to change advisors more readily than they have in the past. Within the industry, 30-day cancellation notices have become standard and in the future will be executed more frequently.
- The facilities offered investors by the new private REIT structures will enable investors to more readily remove and replace investment managers, and, in the long run, more managers

will in fact be removed and replaced for nonperformance and poor communications.

- Pension funds will continue to balance their portfolios with specialty properties that can provide additional diversification and enhance portfolio yields.
- Acquisitions will be more research and information driven. Sponsors will demand quantifiable expectations of the future performance of an asset. Advisors will have to verify that the underlying economics of supply and demand justify acquisition. Portfolio holdings will increasingly be monitored, and advisor performance will be measured against original expectations.
- Asset management will play an increasingly important role. Until transaction volume picks up dramatically, management capabilities will be more important to clients than acquisition skills. Advisory firms will act more as operating companies than as deal-driven brokers and will find themselves increasingly competing with publicly traded operating companies for capital.
- Consolidation within the advisory industry will continue. New firms will find it virtually impossible to survive unless they can quickly acquire a critical mass of assets to manage. Three types of firms will exist: very large firms offering multifaceted service capabilities, boutique firms specializing in certain types of properties or services, and operating companies willing to share in the risks of specific transactions by coinvesting their own funds alongside those of their investor/clients.
- Greater securitization will facilitate more active trading of portfolio holdings as investors continue to reposition their portfolios in an increasingly volatile world environment. This ability to move into and out of markets will facilitate even greater securitization and institutionalization.

REFERENCES

Books

Brueggeman, W. B.; Jeffrey Fisher; and Leo Stone. *Real Estate Finance.* Boston: Irwin, 1989.

McKelvy, Natalie. *Pension Fund Investments in Real Estate.* Westport, CT: Quorum Books, 1983.

Reilley, Frank. *Investments*. Hinsdale, IL: Dryden Press, 1986.

Roulac, Stephen E. *Modern Real Estate Investment—An Institutional Approach*. San Francisco: Property Press, 1978.

Periodicals

Bacow, Larry. *Understanding Foreign Investment in Real Estate*. MIT, Center for Real Estate Development, 1987.

Bacow, Larry. "A Look at the Real Estate Cycle." *C.R.E.D. Newsletter,* MIT, Spring 1991.

Bergsman, S. "Extravagant 80s Produce Grim 90s." *National Real Estate Investor* 33, no. 2 (1991).

Brueggeman, W. B.; T. Sheldon Chang; and Matthew James. *The Real Estate Report*. Goldman Sachs Real Estate Research, October 1993.

Brueggeman, W. B.; A. H. Chen; and T. G. Thibodeau. "Real Estate Investment Funds: Performance and Portfolio Considerations." *AREUEA Journal* 12, no. 3 (1984), pp. 333–54.

Carey, S. A. "Shared Appreciation Loans by Tax-Exempt Pension Funds." *Real Estate Finance Journal* 6, no. 4 (1991), pp. 19–23.

Chadwick, W. J. "The Need for Asset Location." *Pension World,* June 1990.

Cheng, A. "Marketing Real Estate to Pension Funds." *Real Estate Review* (1982), pp. 61–64.

Chernoff, J. "Outlook for Office Buildings Still Gloomy." *Pensions & Investments,* October 13, 1986.

Chernoff, J. "Real Estate Prices Stay High." *Pensions & Investments,* October 27, 1986.

Christman, E. "Allocations for Real Estate Drop." *Pensions & Investments,* August 4, 1986.

Christman, E. "Syndicators' Pain to be Plans' Gain." *Pensions & Investments,* July 7, 1986.

Clark, S. "Taking a Big Bite." *Institutional Investor,* September 1990, pp. 67–70.

Cole, R.; D. Guilkey; and M. Miles. "Pension Fund Investment Managers' Unit Values Deserve Confidence." *Real Estate Review,* Spring 1987, pp. 84–89.

Cole, R.; D. Guilkey; M. Miles; and B. Webb. "More Scientific Diversification Strategies for Commercial Real Estate." *Real Estate Review,* Spring 1989, pp. 59–66.

Covaleski, J. "Pullout Goes On; PRISA Loses CIBA-Geigy." *Pensions & Investments,* January 12, 1987.

Covaleski, J. "Hancock Fund Faces Pressure." *Pensions & Investments,* October 5, 1987.

Covaleski, J. "Appraisal Guidelines Eyed." *Pensions & Investments,* March 9, 1987.

Covaleski, J. "Commitments Up 52.6%." *Pensions & Investments,* February 8, 1988.

Crawford, T. K., and C. H. Volk. "Real Estate Portfolio Enhancement." *Pension World,* April 1991, pp. 51–52.

Dellagrotta, S. Q. "Trustee Considerations for Safeguarding Real Estate Investments." *Pension World* 27 (1991), pp. 26–27.

Dohrmann, Geoffrey. "MegaShifts 1989." *The Institutional Real Estate Letter* 1, no. 12 (December 1989).

Dohrmann, Geoffrey. "MegaShifts 1990." *The Institutional Real Estate Letter* 2, no. 12 (December 1990).

Dohrmann, Geoffrey. "MegaShifts 1991." *The Institutional Real Estate Letter* 3, no. 12 (December 1991).

Dohrmann, Geoffrey. "MegaShifts 1992." *The Institutional Real Estate Letter* 4, no. 12 (December 1992).

Dohrmann, Geoffrey. "MegaShifts 1993." *The Institutional Real Estate Letter* 5, no. 12 (December 1993).

Doran, Pietro. *Real Estate Investment for Defined Contribution Pension Plans: An Analysis.* Master's thesis, MIT, Center for Real Estate Development, 1991.

Downs, Anthony, and S. Michael Gilberto. "How Inflation Erodes the Income of Fixed-Rate Lenders." *Real Estate Review,* Spring 1981.

"Dramatic Increases During 1980: Over Half of Large Funds in Real Estate." *Pensions and Investments,* December 22, 1980.

"Editorial: Open-End Funds Are Fighting Back." *Pensions & Investments,* August 1983.

"Editorial: Real Estate Looks Good Long Term." *Pensions & Investments,* December 22, 1986.

"Editorial: Threshold of a New Era." *Pensions & Investments,* February 4, 1991.

Edwards, R. G. J. "Pension Funds and Real Estate: Assessing Opportunities and Risks." *Real Estate Finance* 4 (Fall 1987), pp. 53–61.

Elebash, C. C., and W. A. Christiansen. "State Pension Funds: What Is Their Future in Real Estate?" *Journal of Real Estate Research* 4 (Summer 1989), pp. 71–79.

Elgin, P. R. "Real Estate Slump Burns Pension Trends, Offers Opportunities." *Corporate Cash Flow,* April 1991, pp. 7–8.

Evans, M. "Real Estate 1991—The Party's Over." *Journal of Property Management,* January 1991.

Faggen, I. "Supply to Hamper Pensions' Real Estate Goals." *National Real Estate Investor,* June 1990.

Firstenberg, P. B., and Wurtzbach, C. H. "Managing Portfolio Risk and Reward." *Real Estate Review,* 1990, pp. 61–65.

Fulton, W. "Trends Show Soft Market Will Stay Awhile." *Pensions & Investments,* March 7, 1988.

Garner, R. L. "Consider Economic Cycles in Real Estate Investing." *Pension World,* September 1987, pp. 35–37.

Giliberto, S. M., and Hopkins, R. E. "Metropolitain Employment Trends: Analysis and Portfolio Considerations." *Salomon Brothers Bond Market Research: Real Estate Report,* 1990.

Gordon, J. "Real Estate Research for Institutional Investors." *Real Estate Finance Journal,* Winter 1990, pp. 37–42.

Gorman, B. "Is Real Estate Still an Inflationary Hedge?" Interviews with Blake and Michael Miles. *Journal of Property Management* 56 (January–February 1991), pp. 46–50.

Gray, Hillary. *New Directions in the Investment and Control of Pension Funds.* Investor Responsibility Research Center, Washington, DC, 1983.

Graydon, Linda. *Survey of 60 Large Plan Sponsors.* Study conducted by Real Estate Consulting Associates for the National Association of Real Estate Investment Managers, 1993.

Greenwich Associates. "Report to Participants." Annual study of the investment management practices of U.S. tax-exempt funds, Greenwich, CT, 1991.

Greer, R. "The Role of the Financial Advisor." *Real Estate Finance Journal,* Fall 1990, pp. 53–60.

Gropper, D. "Real Estate: Going Direct." *Institutional Investor,* June 1984.

Hartzell, D.; David Shulman; Terrance Langetieg; and Martin Leibowitz. "A Look at Real Estate Duration." *CFA Readings in Real Estate,* The Institute of Chartered Financial Analysts, Susan Hudson-Wilson and Katrina F. Sherrerd, 1990.

Hartzell, D.; D. Shulman; and C. Wurtzebach. "Refining the Analysis of Regional Diversification for Income-Producing Real Estate." *Journal of Real Estate Research* 2, no. 2 (1987), pp. 85–95.

Hemmerick, S. "Recession Triggers Building Surplus." *Pensions & Investments,* April 12, 1982.

Hemmerick, S. "Glut of Office Buildings Flattens Rental Income." *Pensions & Investments,* September 3, 1984.

Hemmerick, S. "Standardization of Appraisals Eyed." *Pensions & Investments,* July 8, 1985.

Hemmerick, S. "No Rush Seen to Get Out of Real Estate." *Pensions & Investments,* June 24, 1985.

Hemmerick S. "Switch to Paper Securities: Large Withdrawals Continue." *Pensions & Investments,* August 19, 1985.

Hemmerick, S. "Real Estate Outlook Dim." *Pensions & Investments,* December 8, 1986.

Hemmerick, S. "Plagued by Withdrawals." *Pensions & Investments,* July 21, 1986.

Hemmerick, S. "Report Cites Appraisal Flaws." *Pensions & Investments,* December 12, 1986.

Hemmerick, S. "Investors Place $5.6 Billion of New Business in Direct Accounts." *Pensions & Investments,* September 15, 1986.

Hemmerick, S. "Separate Accounts Draw More Assets." *Pensions & Investments,* February 3, 1986.

Hemmerick, S. "Funds Are Poised to Re-enter Market." *Pensions & Investments,* October 13, 1986.

Hemmerick, S. "Contributions Fall Short." *Pensions & Investments,* August 4, 1987.

Hemmerick, S. "Plan Executives Pledge to Stay with PRISA." *Pensions & Investments,* March 23, 1987.

Hemmerick, S. "Two Public Funds Take Charge." *Pensions & Investments,* May 2, 1988.

Hemmerick, S. "Funds Ready for Buying Spree." *Pensions & Investments,* September 1988.

Hemmerick, S. "Assets Swell by 20%." *Pensions & Investments,* October 2, 1989.

Hemmerick, S. "Gap Found in Realty Returns." *Pensions & Investments,* 1990.

Hemmerick, S. "Outlook Is Bleak for Pooled Real Estate Fund Returns," *Pensions & Investments,* 1990.

Hemmerick, S. "1989's Realty Deals Try to Reduce Risk." *Pensions & Investments,* January 8, 1990.

Hemmerick, S. "JMB Set to Close 5th Fund, Properties to Come from Cash-Strapped Developers." *Pensions & Investments,* July 9, 1990.

Hemmerick, S. "Separate Accounts Top Commingled Funds." *Pensions & Investments,* September 3, 1990.

Hemmerick, S. "Loyalty Fading in Bumpy Realty Market." *Pensions & Investments,* February 19, 1990.

Hemmerick, S. "Fund Caps Realty Advisers' Fee." *Pensions & Investments,* October 15, 1990.

Hemmerick S. "Preparing for Shock: Big Writedowns Coming for Northeast." *Pensions & Investments,* December 10, 1990.

Hemmerick, S. "Gap Found in Realty Turns." *Pensions & Investments,* October 29, 1990.

Hemmerick, S. "Outlook Is Bleak for Pooled Real Estate Fund Returns." *Pensions & Investments,* November 26, 1990.

Hemmerick, S. "Real Estate Managers Admit Their Mistakes." *Pensions & Investments,* July 23, 1990.

Hemmerick, S. "Four Hunt for Real Estate Niches." *Pensions & Investments,* January 22, 1990.

Hemmerick, S. "Apartment Hunt: Investors Seek Once-Shunned Property Type." *Pensions & Investments,* April 30, 1990.

Hemmerick, S. "Liquidity Crunch Hits Realty Funds." *Pensions & Investments,* August 6, 1990.

Hemmerick, S. "RREEF Funds Maturing." *Pensions & Investments,* 1991.

Hemmerick, S. "Real Estate Values Fall by $5.4 Billion." *Pensions & Investments,* May 13, 1991.

Hemmerick, S. "Dismal Performance Imperils Realty Firms." *Pensions & Investments,* March 18, 1991.

Hemmerick, S. "Specialty Real Estate Funds Dominate Period." *Pensions & Investments,* February 18, 1991.

Hemmerick, S. "RREEF Kills Planned Fund." *Pensions & Investments,* April 29, 1991.

Hemmerick, S. "RREEF Funds Maturing." *Pensions & Investments,* February 4, 1991.

Hemmerick, S. "Pension Funds Cut Allocations to Realty." *Pensions & Investments,* March 4, 1991.

Hemmerick, S. "IBM Sticks with Realty but Freezes New Buys." *Pensions & Investments,* June 10, 1991.

Hemmerick, S. "U.S. Funds Wary of Overseas Realty Pitch." *Pensions & Investments,* April 29, 1991, pp. 21–24.

Hemmerick, S., and E. Christman. "Advisers Close Open-End Funds." *Pensions & Investments,* July 7, 1986.

Hemmerick, S., and J. Covaleski. "RREEF Writedown Spurs Fee Debate." *Pensions & Investments,* August 10, 1987.

Hollie, L. J. "More Pension Plans Eye Real Estate." *Pensions & Investments,* September 4, 1989.

Hudson-Wilson, S. "Doubt Surrounds Realty Return Data." *Pensions & Investments,* 1990.

Ibottson, R., and J. Siegel. "Real Estate Investment Funds: Performance and Portfolio Considerations." *AREUEA Journal* 12, no. 3 (1984).

"Is the Syndications Boom a Blessing in Disguise for Pension Funds?" *Institutional Investor,* November 1983, pp. 237–43.

Jaffe, A. J., and C. F. Sirmans. "The Theory and Evidence on Real Estate Financial Decisions: A Review of Issues." *AREUEA Journal* 12, no. 3 (1984), pp. 378–95.

Jansson, S. "The Hot New Opportunities in Real Estate." *Institutional Investor,* June 1980, pp. 79–90.

Jansson, S. "The Retreat from Real Estate." *Institutional Investor,* June 1982, pp. 91–107.

Kalson, G. "Make Room for New Managers." *Pensions & Investments,* February 4, 1991.

Kinney, R. "Fertile Domestic Real Estate Market Ahead." *Pensions & Investments,* January 21, 1980.

Kolman, J. "The Boom in Real Estate Development Funds." *Institutional Investor,* November 1984, pp. 165–72.

Levy, John. "Debt Real Estate." *Real Estate Capital Markets Report,* Spring 1992.

Levy, John. "Debt Real Estate." *Real Estate Capital Markets Report,* Summer 1992.

Levy, John. "Debt Real Estate." *Real Estate Capital Markets Report,* Fall 1992.

Levy, John. "Debt Real Estate." *Real Estate Capital Markets Report,* Winter 1992.

Levy, John. "Debt Real Estate." *Real Estate Capital Markets Report,* Spring 1993.

Levy, John. "Debt Real Estate." *Real Estate Capital Markets Report,* Summer 1993.

"Measuring the Real Estate Move." *Institutional Investor,* June 1981, pp. 131–38.

"Measuring the Unmeasurable." *Institutional Investor,* November 1984, pp. 149–60.

"New Copley Tactic." *Pensions & Investments,* February 7, 1983.

Nitzberg, K. "Realty Management Fees: Sponsor Scrutiny Needed." *Pensions & Investments,* June 7, 1982.

Pagliari, J., and J. Weiss, "Fundamental Returns to the Office Sector." *The Institutional Real Estate Letter,* January 1994.

Paustian, C. "Supply vs. Demand: Existing Closed-end Fund Shares at a Premium." *Pensions & Investments,* February 22, 1988.

Paustian, C. "Next Year's Strategies Are This Year's Trends." *Pensions & Investments,* September 1988.

Paustian, C. "Closer Look Given to Realty Projections." *Pensions & Investments,* May 1990.

"Pension Forum: Putting Real Estate on Hold." *Institutional Investor,* November 1990, p. 159.

"Pension Forum: Real Estate Moves Ahead." *Institutional Investor,* May 1988, pp. 115–16.

"Pension Management: The 1989 Pension Olympics." *Institutional Investor,* February 1989, pp. 85–89.

Pershing, A. "Silver Linings?" *Institutional Investor,* June 1990, pp. 142–47.

Pershing, A. "The Post-Vulture Culture." *Institutional Investor,* June 1990.

"Piedmont, RREEF Merge." *Pensions & Investments,* January 7, 1991.

Pygman, J. "How to Plan a Direct Investment Program in Real Estate." *Pension World,* September 1986, pp. 32, 34–35.

Ramseyer, W. L. "Public Pension Funds: A New, But Cautious Participant in Real Estate Finance." *Real Estate Finance,* Summer 1984, pp. 56–61.

Real Estate Research Corp. *Emerging Trends in Real Estate: 1991.* Report prepared for Equitable Real Estate Investment Management, Inc.

"Real Estate Slump Burns Pension Funds, Offers Opportunities." *Corporate Cash Flow,* April 1991.

Reier, S. "The Office Market Time Bomb." *Institutional Investor,* June 1985, pp. 172–86.

Reinbach, A. "Values to Drop as Realty Prices Rise." *Pensions & Investments,* November 14, 1988.

Reinbach, A. "33% of Assets Left in Cash." *Pensions & Investments,* January 9, 1989.

Retkwa, R. "Well Funded Institutional Investors Are Demanding More from Their Real Estate." *National Real Estate Investor* 32, no. 10 (1990), pp. 74–80.

Retkwa, R. "Pension Funds: Financiers of the 90's?" *National Real Estate Investor,* June 1990.

Rohrer, J. "How Pension Funds Are Making Their Great Leap into Real Estate." *Institutional Investor,* June 1981, pp. 85–126.

Rohrer, J. "Real Estate Managers Tough It Out." *Institutional Investor,* June 1983, pp. 101–16.

Rohrer, J. "Why RREEF Keeps RRolling Along." *Institutional Investor,* June 1983, pp. 119–120.

Roulac Group of Deloitte and Touche. *Capital Flow 1990: Real Estate Alternatives for Institutional Investors.* Report prepared for Equitable Real Estate Management, Inc.

Roulac Group of Deloitte and Touche. *Real Estate Capital Flows 1989.* Report prepared for Equitable Real Estate Investment Management, Inc.

Roulac, S. E., and N. F. Dimick. "Real Estate Capital Markets Undergo Fundamental Changes." *Real Estate Finance Journal,* Winter 1991, pp. 7–17.

Roulac, S. E., and L. Lynford. "Real Estate Decision Making in an Information Era." *Real Estate Finance Journal,* Summer 1990.

Sagalyn, Lynne, and Marc Louargand. *Real Estate in the Next Recession.* MIT, Center for Real Estate Development, 1989.

Sandler, L. "Wall Street Enters the Pension Fray." *Institutional Investor,* November 1982, pp. 267–82.

Sass, M. D. "Distressed Opportunities Plentiful in the 90's." *Pensions & Investments,* March 5, 1990.

Schwartz, Sheldon. "Real Estate and the Tax Reform Act of 1986." *Real Estate Review,* Winter 1987.

Selby, B. "Downtown Strategies." *Institutional Investor,* June 1986, pp. 214–22.

Smedley, R. "Pension Funds Plunge into Property Development." *Pension World,* June 1984, pp. 37–39, 54.

Sojacy, L. "Melnikoff Puts PRISA into Perspective." *Pensions & Investments,* September 14, 1981.

Sojacy, L., and N. Webman. "Realty Interest Slows for Sponsors." *Pensions & Investments,* April 12, 1982.

Stoesser, J. W. "Real Estate Investing in a Weakened Market." *Pension World,* June 1987, pp. 16–20, 32.

Upsata, M. "Pension Funds Face Opportunity." *National Real Estate Investor* 33, no. 2 (1991), pp. 58–62.

Vosti, C. "Consulting Slump Shows Industry Shift." *Pensions & Investments,* March 18, 1991.

Vosti, C. "Panacea or Problem Child? Questions Surround Popular Defined Contribution Plans." *Pensions & Investments,* April 1, 1991.

Webman, N. "Sponsor's Real Estate Interest Rebuilding." *Pensions & Investments,* April 4, 1983.

Welles, C. "Modern Portfolio Theory: Reprogramming the Money Manager; How the New Investment Technology Evolved; How the New Technology Will Change the Business." *Institutional Investor,* April 1977, pp. 35–52.

Westerbeck, M. "Hot 1981 Alternative Cools Off." *Pensions & Investments,* December 20, 1982.

Westerbeck, M. "No Quick Sales to Meet Requests: PRISA Sticks to Its Guns in Dealing with Withdrawals." *Pensions & Investments,* March 7, 1983.

Westerbeck, M. "Open-End Fund Drops May Flag Arbitraging." *Pensions & Investments,* March 7, 1983.

Westerbeck, M. "Fund Fighting Closed-End Tide." *Pensions & Investments,* August 8, 1983.

Westerbeck, M. "Pension Funds Cautious about Realty." *Pensions & Investments,* October 31, 1983.

Westerbeck, M. "Syndicators Push for Pension Business." *Pensions & Investments,* April 4, 1983.

Westerbeck, M. "Real Estate Investment Game Attracts Rookies as Well as Pros." *Pensions & Investments,* July 25, 1983.

Westerbeck, M. "Syndicators Load Real Estate Bases." *Pensions & Investments,* December 12, 1983.

Westerbeck, M. "Pooled Vehicles Insulate the Risk: Pension Funds, Developers Break New Ground." *Pensions & Investments,* April 2, 1984.

Westerbeck, M. "Plans Cooling in Expanding Positions." *Pensions & Investments,* October 1, 1984.

Westerbeck, M. "Salomon, Balcor/American Express: Firms Fade From Field." *Pensions & Investments,* September 17, 1984.

Westerbeck, M. "Corporate Interests in Real Estate Seen Eroding." *Pensions & Investments,* January 12, 1985.

Westerbeck, M. "Withdrawals from PRISA High, Calmer." *Pensions & Investments,* April 29, 1985.

Westerbeck, M. "How Small Funds Get into Real Estate Action." *Pensions & Investments,* June 10, 1985.

White, Norku N. "Return of the Leaseback." *Pensions & Investments,* March 7, 1988.

Wiley, C. "Assets' Rise Hailed." *Pensions & Investments,* January 23, 1989.

Williams, T. "Cash Flow, Growth Lag." *Pensions & Investments,* January 23, 1989.

Williams, T. "Funds to Maintain Financing Pace." *Pensions & Investments,* October 30, 1989.

Williams, T. "Funds to Stay Tight with Real Estate." *Pensions & Investments,* October 29, 1990.

Williams, T. "Realty Fund Shifts Gears amid Withdrawals." *Pensions & Investments,* April 2, 1990.

Williams, T. "Property Fills Cash Needs." *Pensions & Investments,* September 17, 1990.

Williams, T. "Funds to Stay Tight with Real Estate." *Pensions & Investments,* October 29, 1990.

Williams, T. "The Dawn of a New Age for Internal Portfolios." *Pensions & Investments,* March 18, 1991.

Williams, T. "AEW Sells Stake in Firm." *Pensions & Investments,* April 1, 1991.

Zerbst, R. H., and Cambon, B. R. "Real Estate: Historical Returns and Risks." *Journal of Portfolio Management,* Spring 1984, pp. 5–20.

Zilberstein, S. "How Has ERISA Impacted Real Estate Co-investing?" *Pension World,* September 1985, pp. 32–38.

Telephone Interviews

Anonymous private pension fund.

Mary Ann Briggs, Mellon/McMahan, San Francisco.

Kevin Comer, Ohio Public Employees Retirement System.

Michael Ervolini, Aldrich, Eastman and Waltch.

Joan Fallon, TIAA.

Roger Franz, California Public Employees Retirement System.

Wiley Greig, RREEF, San Francisco.

Mary Ann Hoffman, Trammell Crow Real Estate Advisors.

Steven Hoover, General Electric.

Pete Jeans, Alaska Permanent Fund.

Laurie Ann Kloppenbug, Loomis-Sayles, Boston.

Karen Seplak, Illinois Municipal Retirement Fund.

Scott Westphal, IBM.

CHAPTER 2

PORTFOLIO MANAGEMENT CONCEPTS AND THEIR APPLICATION TO REAL ESTATE

Anthony B. Sanders
Faculty of Finance
The Ohio State University

Joseph L. Pagliari, Jr.
Citadel Realty, Inc.

James R. Webb
Real Estate Research Center
James J. Nance College of Business
Cleveland State University

INTRODUCTION

This chapter highlights various techniques central to the issue of portfolio management and applies these techniques to real estate investment management. To apply these techniques, it will be necessary to review the following theoretical constructs:

- Returns.
- Variance of returns.
- Covariance of returns.
- "Random walk."
- Systematic versus unsystematic risk.

After reviewing these topics, the chapter discusses various portfolio management techniques. These portfolio management techniques include:

- Mean/variance efficiency.
- Capital asset pricing model.
- Arbitrage pricing theory.

- Duration matching.
- Option pricing theory.
- Chaos theory.

The chapter examines the principles underlying each of these techniques and their application to real estate investing. Collectively, these techniques comprise what is often referred to as Modern Portfolio Theory (MPT). However, the acceptance of each technique varies among leading practitioners and theorists. Moreover, some of these techniques represent competing schools of thought. They are perhaps best viewed as complementary or supplementary, helping to create a rich mosaic of portfolio management considerations.

THEORETICAL CONSTRUCTS

The application of the following theoretical constructs to historical real estate returns must be viewed with some suspicion. Unlike studies on the stock and bond markets, where market-based daily and monthly returns are readily available, real estate studies must often rely on either appraisal-based returns or real estate investment trust (REIT) returns. Appraisal-based returns are often criticized for their failure to represent market sentiment in the sense that appraisals reflect opinions of value on which there is no transaction. An advantage of equity REITs is that they represent market-based transactions of participants purchasing and selling the assets in question. On the other hand, one potential problem with using REITs as a proxy for real estate is that REIT returns may be more representative of common stock behavior than of the actual assets in the REIT's portfolio. Existing research on appraisal-based return indices has thus far found that real estate earned risk-adjusted returns substantially higher than those for bonds and common stocks (e.g., see Hartzell, Hekman, and Miles [1987]). Using equity REITs as a proxy for real estate returns, however, Chan, Hendershott, and Sanders (1990) find no evidence that real estate has earned superior risk-adjusted returns.

The following sections introduce the fundamentals of risk and return. A variety of models are examined, along with empirical evidence from the real estate market. For a general review of real estate returns, see Chapter 3, which, along with Chapter 16, also discusses the problem of appraisal lags and biases. In addition, Chapter 14 contains an in-depth discussion of REITs.

Return

The historical return (i.e., the *ex post,* or realized, return) on any investment is defined as the appreciation (or depreciation) in the asset's price plus any cash flow (e.g., dividends) received[1] as compared to the asset's beginning price:

$$R_t = \frac{P_t - P_{t-1} + CF_t}{P_{t-1}} \tag{1}$$

where R_t = Return on investment over time period t.
  P_t = Asset price at end of period t.
  CF_t = Cash flow received during period t.

For example, assume an investment was purchased for $100 and at the end of one year, it had appreciated to $106 and generated a $4 dividend. This investment would have then generated a 10 percent return for the year.

The expected return (i.e., the *ex ante,* or prospective, return) for a single-asset investment is represented by the return realized under each possible scenario weighted by the probability of each scenario's occurrence. Following from equation (1), the expected return can be formulated:

$$E(R_t) = \sum_{n=1}^{N} R_{t,n} P(R_{t,n}) \tag{2}$$

where $E(R_t)$ = Expected return on investment over future time period t.
  $R_{t,n}$ = Expected return on investment over time period t under outcome n.
  $P(R_{t,n})$ = Probability of outcome n occurring.

Moreover, it is axiomatic that the probability of all outcomes must sum to 1:

$$\sum_{n=1}^{N} P(R_{t,n}) = 1.0 \tag{3}$$

For example, an asset with a 25 percent probability of generating

---

[1] To simplify the calculation, it was assumed that cash flow is received at the end of the period.

a -3 percent return and a 75 percent probability of generating a 9 percent return has an expected return of 6.0 percent:

$$E(R_t) = -.03 \times .25 + .09 \times .75$$
$$= .06$$

Alternatively stated, the expected return of 6 percent represents a weighted average of the various outcomes.

Volatility of Returns

One of the statistics portfolio managers use to measure risk is the variance of returns. Essentially this statistic measures the dispersion of returns around an average value. To examine the dispersion of historical returns, the variance[2] of these returns can be written as:

$$\sigma^2 = \frac{\sum_{t=1}^{T}(R_t - \overline{R})^2}{T} \qquad (4)$$

where σ^2 = Variance of returns.
       T = Total number of time periods under analysis.
       $\overline{R}$ = Average return over T time periods.

Alternatively, the expected variance of returns can be examined by slightly modifying equation (4) to incorporate the expected return generated in each future scenario and then weight each scenario by the probability of its occurrence:

$$E(\sigma^2) = \sum_{t=1}^{N} P(R_{t,n}) \times [R_{t,n} - E(R_t)]^2 \qquad (5)$$

where $E(\sigma^2)$ = Expected variance of returns.

Using the earlier example, an asset generating an expected return of 6.0 percent, with a 25 percent probability of returning -3 percent and a 75 percent probability of returning 9 percent, would lead to an expected variance of 0.27 percent:

---

[2] Note that statistical purists divide variance by $T - 1$ to account for the loss of 1 degree of freedom; see, among others, Chao (1980).

$$E(\sigma^2) = .25(-.03 - .06)^2 + .75(.09 - .06)^2$$
$$= .0027$$

The "squaring" of the deviations from the expected return is used to treat equally both positive and negative variances from the average return. The standard deviation removes the distorting impact associated with the squaring process found in the variance calculation. This distortion is removed by taking the square root of the variance figure:

$$\sigma = \sqrt{\sigma^2} \tag{6}$$

where σ = Standard deviation of returns.

Continuing the example, the standard deviation of the hypothetical asset equals approximately 5.2 percent:

$$\sigma = \sqrt{.0027} \approx .052$$

When the dispersion of returns is a normal bell-shaped curve, the standard deviation also lends itself to some important benchmarks: Approximately 68 percent of the returns lie within plus and minus 1 standard deviation from the expected return (or average, mean return if using historical data), 95 percent of the returns lie within plus and minus 2 standard deviations, and 99 percent of the returns lie within 3 standard deviations, as shown in Exhibit 2–1.

EXHIBIT 2–1
Probabilities under the Normal Curve

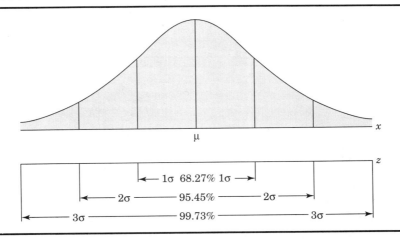

Source: Adapted from Lincoln L. Chao, *Statistics for Management* (Monterey, CA: Brooks/Cole Publishing, 1980), p. 195.

Normal Returns and Passage of Time

Long-term, historical return series are often used to frame an analysis of anticipating ex ante returns—$E(R_t)$. While this is a sound starting point, it should be remembered that the reliability of using historical returns to forecast future returns depends on the commonalities between the two time periods. It should also be noted that much of portfolio management is based on the assumption that the distribution of future returns is represented by the normal bell-shaped curve, as shown in Exhibit 2–1. However, not all distributions are normal. Exhibit 2–2 shows two examples of non-normal (or skewed) distributions.

A recent study by Myer and Webb (1994) suggests that quarterly nominal real estate returns (as measured by the Russell/NCREIF Property Index) are non-normal. However, this non-normality is greatly reduced when semiannual or annual nominal returns are used. Also, the non-normality is also lower for quarterly real (inflation-adjusted) returns than it is for quarterly nominal returns.

Fortunately, even if the underlying distribution is non-normal, as the number of repetitions increases, the realized return will converge to the mean (or expected) return. Continuing with the example used up to this point, even though the distribution of possible returns is non-normal—a 75 percent probability of a 9 percent return and a 25 percent probability of a −3 percent return, as shown in Exhibit

EXHIBIT 2–2
Three Probability Distributions with Different Types of Skewness

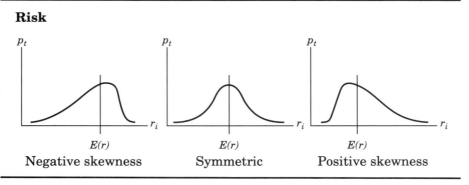

| Negative skewness | Symmetric | Positive skewness |

Source: Adapted from Jack Clark Francis, *Investments: Analysis and Management*, 3rd ed. (New York: McGraw-Hill, 1980), p. 347.

2–3—as the number of times this investment is repeated, its average return will converge to 6.0 percent.

Exhibit 2–4 illustrates a random series of "draws" from the probability distribution shown in Exhibit 2–3. When examining these series, it is apparent that, on average, one -3 percent return is realized and three 9 percent returns are realized in each four-period time frame. This is consistent with their 25/75 percent probabilities. However, the pattern can vary dramatically from series to series. Nevertheless, by the 30th repetition in each series, the cumulative average return begins to converge at the expected return of 6 percent. As the number of repetitions[3] per series is extended, this convergence becomes even more pronounced.

The number of repetitions required to have the average return of the randomly generated returns approach the expected return will

EXHIBIT 2–3
Non-Normal Distribution of Assumed Asset Returns

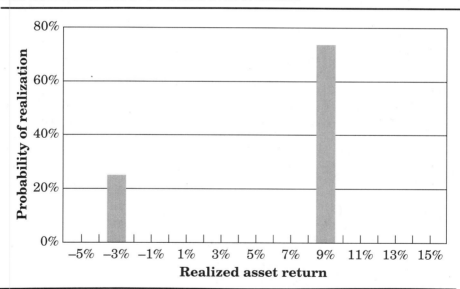

---

[3] Exhibit 2–4 was prepared using 100 trials per series. However, 30 repetitions are often cited as the minimum number of observations needed to employ the central limit theorem, which suggests that the mean and standard deviation of a sample population will be approximately normal regardless of the shape of the population's underlying asset distribution as long as the sample size is sufficiently large. See, among others, Chao (1980).

EXHIBIT 2–4
Random Patterns of Asset Returns Based on Assumed Underlying Asset Distribution

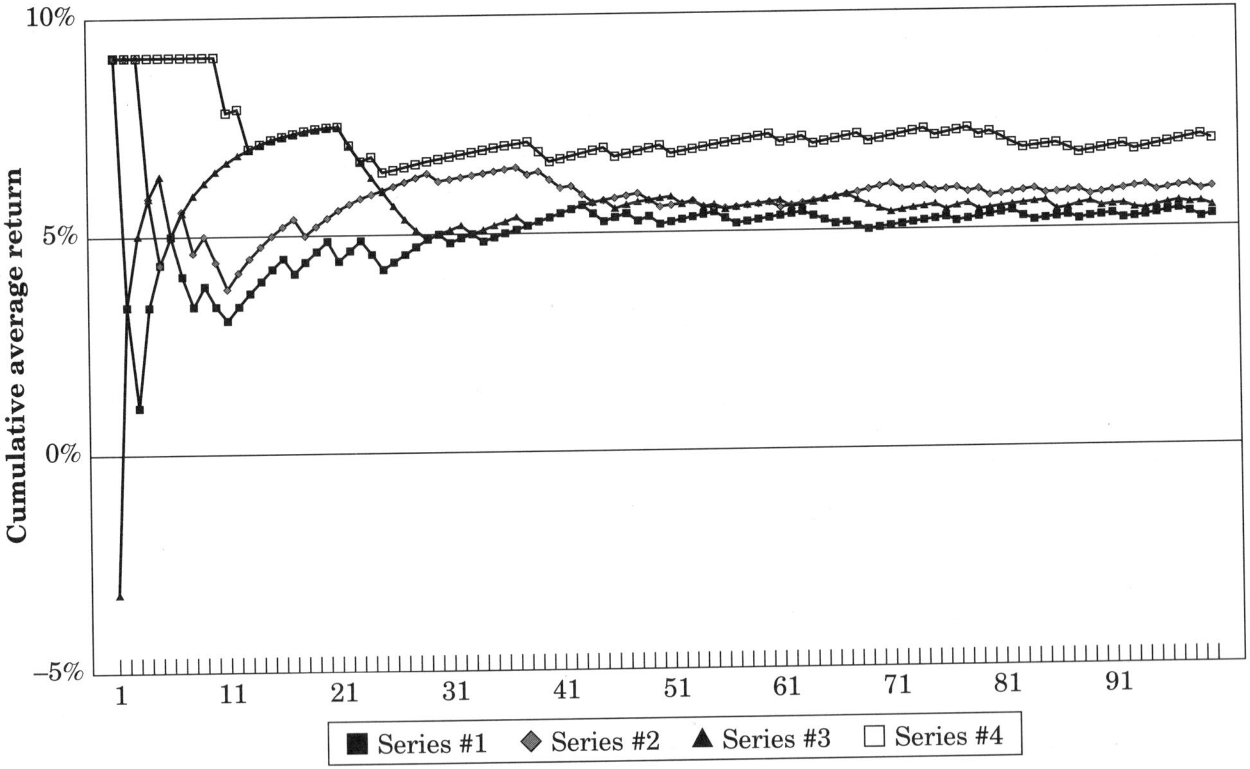

decrease (increase) when the probability of either return is narrowed (widened). For example, if the chance of -3 percent and 9 percent returns were instead 50/50 percent, the series would be more likely to converge around the expected return (3 percent) more quickly and smoothly than that depicted in Exhibit 2–4.

Exhibit 2–4 nicely captures the notion that risk, or the dispersion of returns, declines with the passage of time. This characteristic is captured by restating variance (or standard deviation) as a function of time:

$$\sigma_T^2 = \frac{\sigma^2}{\sqrt{T}} \tag{7}$$

where σ_T^2 = Annualized variance over T time periods.

Equation (7) is predicated on the assumption that an asset's returns over time behave randomly. If so, the asset's annualized volatility is constant across all time horizons (see Holton [1992]), even though the asset's overall volatility (i.e., over the entire holding period) increases with the square root of time.

Conversely, an asset's multiperiod return reflects the compounding of the single-period return over the longer, multiple periods:

$$R_t = (1 + R_t)^T - 1 \tag{8}$$

Continuing with our earlier example, over a five-year investment horizon the investment's total return is expected to be 33.82 percent (i.e., $[1 + .06]^5 - 1$) with a standard deviation of 11.62 percent (i.e., $.052 + \sqrt{5}$), assuming returns are normally and randomly distributed.

Thus, when using such statistics, it is critical to understand the time frames involved in the investor's time horizon. The time horizon and the investor's risk tolerance are critical components to understanding, on an ex ante basis, likely risk-return experiences and the investor's satisfaction.

Real Estate's Risk and Return

Myer and Webb (1992) compared the mean returns and standard deviations of various real estate investments. They examined quarterly returns on an equity REIT portfolio as well as several Russell/

NCREIF indices from 1978 through 1990. The results are quite interesting:

	Mean Return	Standard Deviation
Equity REITs	4.19%	7.06%
Russell/NCREIF index	2.63	1.56
S&P 500	1.59	4.62

A comparison of these historical means and standard deviations reveals that equity REITs had a greater return than the S&P 500 index (4.19 percent versus 1.59 percent), but greater risk as well (7.06 percent versus 4.62 percent). It would seem that the real estate returns, as measured by the Russell/NCREIF index, are superior to the S&P 500 index. However, the equity REIT return index is not necessarily superior to the S&P 500 return index, because it is much riskier.

There are several problems with the aforementioned information. First, the data are historical and may not be representative of the future. Second, the Russell/NCREIF index may be biased, since a number of the values on which returns are being calculated have been generated by appraisals rather than market transactions. Third, equity REITs may be more representative of stocks than of real estate. Fourth, the investment management fees tend to be much higher for the Russell/NCREIF properties than the stocks represented by equity REITs and the S&P 500. Fifth, the Russell/NCREIF returns are unleveraged, while the underlying assets of the other two indices are leveraged. The use of leverage can lead to higher but more volatile returns. Sixth, an investment decision made on the basis of an individual asset's expected return (mean) and variance ignores the benefits of diversification that are potentially gained by combining two or more assets together in a portfolio (discussed in the mean/variance efficiency section).

Covariance

Another measure of risk is covariance, which measures the way the total variance of two assets is altered when the assets' returns are held in the same portfolio. Covariance, in turn, is dependent on the correlation between the returns of the two assets, as measured by the correlation coefficient. This coefficient can range from $+1$ to -1. The formulae for computing the covariance and correlation coefficient are given, respectively, in equations (9) and (10):

$$\sigma_{1,2}^2 = \sigma_1 \times \sigma_2 \times \rho_{1,2} \tag{9}$$

where $\sigma_{1,2}^2$ = Covariance between the returns for asset 1 and asset 2.

σ_1 = Standard deviation of asset 1's return distribution.

σ_2 = Standard deviation of asset 2's return distribution.

$\rho_{1,2}$ = Correlation coefficient between the returns of asset 1 and asset 2.

$$\rho_{1,2} = \frac{\sum\limits_{t=1}^{T} (R_{1,t} - \overline{R}_1) \times (R_{2,t} - \overline{R}_2)}{\sqrt{\sum\limits_{t=1}^{T} (R_{1,t} - \overline{R}_1)^2 \times \sum\limits_{t=1}^{T} (R_{2,t} - \overline{R}_2)^2}} \tag{10}$$

The notion of identifying the degree to which asset returns move together (i.e., their correlation) is central to what Markowitz (1952) described as mean/variance efficiency and later became the foundation for Modern Portfolio Theory. This notion is central to efficient diversification, which fundamentally rests on identifying assets with different return patterns (that is, having low to negative correlation coefficients with one another) while enjoying high absolute returns.

Real Estate's Correlation with Other Assets

The correlation coefficient between real estate and other assets in the economy is of particular interest to portfolio managers. Gyourko and Keim (1992) examined the period from 1978:1 through 1990:4. They found equity REITs have a correlation coefficient of .65 with the S&P 500 index. However, the Russell/NCREIF index has a correlation coefficient of only $-.04$ with the S&P 500 index. Clearly, the Russell/NCREIF index can reduce total variance of the portfolio more dramatically than equity REITs. On the other hand, the well-documented appraisal smoothing problem with the Russell/NCREIF index may tend to generate such a low correlation. The low correlation may have nothing to do with the intrinsic value of real estate per se. It could be due to the smoothness of the data, to the method of valuation, and/or lags in reporting values.

Another interesting finding of Gyourko and Keim (1992) is that the equity REITs have a correlation coefficient of .82 with small stocks. This should not really be a surprise, since the vast majority of REITs are very small in terms of market capitalization. The pertinent question is whether REITs behave like small firms. While this has not been fully resolved, it appears that REITs may behave like other small firms (see Pozsonyi and Sanders [1994]).

"Random Walk" and Efficient Markets

One of the most important cornerstones of modern finance is the efficiency of the capital markets. This efficiency is, in large part, based on the belief that an asset's price fully reflects all currently available information and that the arrival of new, unanticipated information, which may be good or bad but occurs randomly, will be quickly reflected in the price. Given that unanticipated information arrives randomly, price changes are unpredictable (or random). Accordingly, asset prices follow a "random walk" through time; that is, future prices cannot be predicated on the basis of past price movements. To state the theory another way, if past price movements could foretell future price investments, people with access to the necessary information would bid current asset prices up (or down) in accordance with that foretold by past price movements. Thus, current prices should, in efficient markets, reflect the value implied by past price movements (see Malkiel [1990]).

Financial theorists have described financial markets as having differing degrees of efficiency. The so-called efficient market hypothesis (EMH) has three forms. A description of each, from Bodie et al. (1992) follows:

- *Weak form:* The assertion that asset prices reflect all information contained in the history of past trading (price, volume, etc.).
- *Semi-strong form:* The assertion that asset prices reflect all publicly available information (in addition to all information contained in the history of past trading).

- *Strong form:* The assertion that asset prices reflect all relevant information, including inside information (in addition to all information contained in the history of past trading and all publicly available information).

However, the testing of the market's efficiency is inherently ambiguous. Any such testing of whether information is properly reflected in an asset's price necessarily involves using some asset-pricing model to determine the proper price. In turn, this leads to what is referred to as the joint-hypothesis problem, namely, that any test of market efficiency also necessarily involves a test of the asset-pricing model (see Fama [1991]).

Real Estate and Market Efficiency

The following factors, as they distinctly apply to real estate, might suggest that the real estate market is less efficient than the stock and bond markets:

- High transaction costs.
- Lack of publicly available, audited information.
- Large transaction size.
- Uniqueness of each real estate investment.
- Complexity of possible transaction structures.
- Varying state laws for acquisition, finance, and operations.
- Complexity of state and federal income tax codes.

Accordingly, it should come as little surprise that real estate is generally considered to be weak-form efficient. That is, past real estate prices, on average, provide little (if any) guidance to future (inflation-adjusted) real estate prices. However, access to nonpublic information may provide significant guidance to future real estate prices.

Systematic versus Unsystematic Risk

Closely aligned with the concept of risk diversification (and the covariance of asset returns) is the concept that an asset's total risk can be identified as having two components: systematic and unsystematic risk. The first component, known as market risk, cannot be diversified away, as it is common to (or systematically found in) all assets. The second component, known as asset-specific risk, is unique to that particular asset. It can be diversified away by increasing the number of assets randomly assembled in the portfolio. On average, this results in portfolios in which the underlying assets have less than perfect correlation with one another. Fisher and Lorie (1970) illustrated this concept with Exhibit 2–5. As you can see, a portfolio's total risk (as measured by its standard deviation) is reduced as the number of securities is increased. Approximately 95 percent of the reduction in the portfolio's standard deviation occurred after the inclusion of 20 stocks.

Since unsystematic risk can be diversified away, investors should be compensated for bearing only systematic risk. In other words,

EXHIBIT 2–5
Systematic Risk and the Number of Securities in the Portfolio

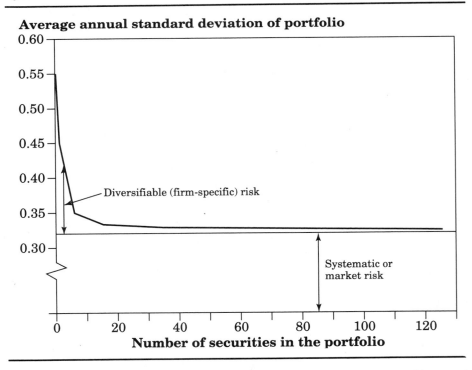

Source: Adapted from Zvi Bodie, Alex Kane, and Alan J. Marcus, *Essentials of Investment* (Homewood, IL: Richard D. Irwin, 1992), p. 212, as excerpted from Lawrence Fisher and James H. Lorie, "Some Studies of the Variability of Returns on Investments in Common Stocks," *Journal of Business*, April 1970.

investors should not be rewarded for a type of risk (i.e., unsystematic risk) that can be costlessly reduced to zero.

Real Estate's Systematic and Unsystematic Risks

Due to the inherently more localized nature of real estate investments, it has been suggested that real estate possesses greater unsystematic risk than either stock or bond investments. While a computer manufacturer/distributor can sell its product across the country and across the globe, the owner of real estate must sell (or, more accurately, rent) its space to those buyers (or renters) that are located in (or are willing to consider relocating to) the same geographic market as the subject building.

   If it is true that real estate contains higher unsystematic risk, holding a poorly diversified real estate portfolio is more costly than holding a poorly diversified stock and/or bond portfolio. This would be true, in theory at least, because the market compensates real estate investors only for the systematic risk of their portfolios. Investors are not compensated for the diversifiable (unsystematic) risk contained in their portfolios. Accordingly, a naively diversified portfolio potentially incurs more risk, but yields the same reward as a well-diversified portfolio. For real estate (because of its greater unsystematic risk), this predicament is thought to be more damaging than for stock and/or bonds. Alternatively stated, real estate portfolios may have more to gain (than either stock or bond portfolios) from efficient diversification, since it would remove a greater percentage of unsystematic risk.

PORTFOLIO MANAGEMENT TECHNIQUES

Having viewed some of the important portfolio management constructs, it is now possible to explore various portfolio management techniques.

Mean/Variance Efficiency

Markowitz (1952) demonstrated that the focus on maximizing the expected return is not a sufficient portfolio consideration; rather, the returns and variances of assets must be considered in combination.

Furthermore, the law of large numbers is an insufficient criterion from which to achieve an efficiently diversified portfolio, which is taken to be the portfolio with the least variance (i.e., risk) for a given level of return or the portfolio with the highest return for a given level of variance.

To find the optimal combination of portfolios offering the least variance for given levels of return, it is necessary to expand the theoretical constructs described earlier to include portfolio return and variance. The portfolio's expected return[4] is a simple, weighted return of each asset's expected return multiplied by its weighting in the portfolio:

$$E(R_p) = \sum_{i=1}^{I} x_i \times E(R_i) \tag{11}$$

where $E(R_p)$ = Expected return on the multiple-asset portfolio.
    x_i = Percentage of the portfolio invested in the ith asset.
    $E(R_i)$ = Expected return on the ith asset.

However, the portfolio variance is less straightforward. It is a combination of the different assets' variances, their weighting in the portfolio, and the correlation of one asset's variance with that of another. In its general form, it appears as follows:

$$E(\sigma_p^2) = \sum_{i=1}^{I} x_i^2 E(\sigma_i^2) + \sum_{i=1}^{I}\sum_{j=1}^{J} x_i x_j E(\sigma_{i,j}) \tag{12}$$

where $E(\sigma_p^2)$ = Expected variance of the multiple-asset portfolio.
    $E(\sigma_i^2)$ = Expected variance of the ith asset.
    $E(\sigma_{i,j})$ = Expected covariance between the ith and jth assets = $\rho_{o,j}\sigma_i\sigma_j$.

For all correlation coefficients less than 1.0, the portfolio's variance will be a nonlinear combination of asset variances, their weightings, and their correlation.

---

[4] At this point, the chapter will concentrate on expected returns and variances of the portfolio. However, the conversion between ex ante and ex post calculations is straightforward and can be derived by comparing earlier equations, such as equations (1) versus (2) and (4) versus (5).

Two-Asset Portfolio

Much of the foregoing discussion is intimidating to all but the most facile users of comparative statistics. To illustrate the powerful insights offered by Markowitz, consider the case of a two-asset portfolio. For purposes of illustration, let's assume a portfolio consists of only two assets with the following risk-return characteristics:

Asset	Return	Standard Deviation
A	12%	15%
B	8	10

As noted above, the portfolio return can be written as the linear combination of the assets' returns and their weights; see equation (11). Thus, a portfolio with a 50/50 allocation, for example, would have a 10 percent return:

$$E(R_\rho) = x_A E(R_A) + x_B E(R_B)$$
$$= .5(.12) + .5(.08) \qquad (13)$$
$$= .10$$

In the case of the two-asset portfolio, the portfolio's variance can be written as

$$E(\sigma_\rho^2) = x_A^2 E(\sigma_A^2) + x_B^2 E(\sigma_B^2) + \rho_{A,B} x_A x_B \sigma_A \sigma_B \qquad (14)$$

Only in the case where the returns are perfectly correlated (i.e., $\rho_{A,B} = 1.0$) will the portfolio's variance also be a linear combination of the assets' variances, weighted by their respective portfolio allocations as the portfolio combinations range from and between a 100 percent allocation to asset A to a 100 percent allocation to asset B.

In all other cases, the portfolio's variance will be less than the weighted sum of the individual assets' variances. Exhibit 2–6 illustrates the relationship of portfolio variance to the correlation of asset returns. There are four cases, with correlation coefficients ranging from 1.0 to -0.5. Case 1 represents the special instance of perfect correlation, while the remaining three cases are based on successively lower correlation between the two assets.

As the correlation between the asset returns decreases from 1.0, the combinations of assets A and B result in a portfolio of declining

EXHIBIT 2-6 Impact on Efficient Frontier Based on Changes in Correlation Coefficients

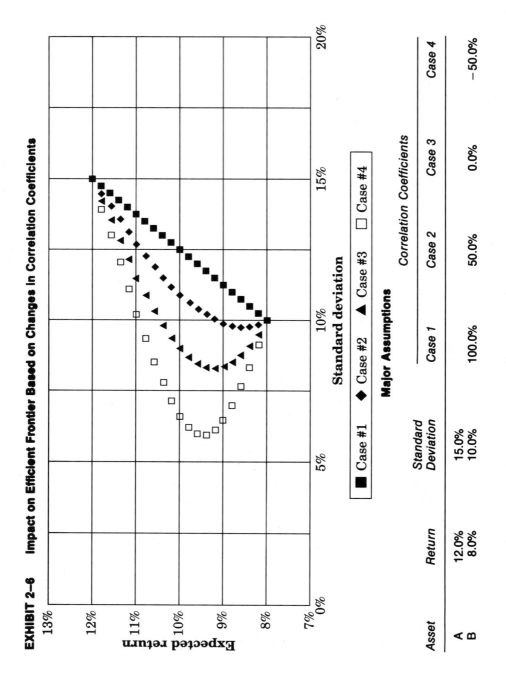

Major Assumptions

Asset	Return	Standard Deviation	Correlation Coefficients			
			Case 1	Case 2	Case 3	Case 4
A	12.0%	15.0%	100.0%	50.0%	0.0%	−50.0%
B	8.0%	10.0%				

variance for each level of return. This relationship is highlighted in Exhibit 2–6. For example, it shows that at an expected portfolio return of 10 percent, a decrease in the correlation from 1.0 to 0.5 results in more than a 150-basis-point decline in the portfolio's variance, while a decrease in the correlation from 0.5 to 0.0 results in a little less than an additional 200-basis-point decline in the portfolio's variance and a decrease from 0.0 to −0.5 in the correlation coefficient results in a little more than an additional 200-basis-point decline in portfolio variance. This reduction in portfolio variance, through the combination of assets with little positive correlation and without greatly forsaking expected return, is the essence of mean/variance efficiency. Exhibit 2–7 presents the underlying portfolio combinations for the graph displayed in Exhibit 2–6.

Exhibits 2–6 and 2–7 also help illustrate another important aspect of diversification, namely, that the portfolio combinations that lie beneath the curve's inflection point[5] are inefficient. That is, portfolios that lie above the inflection point—also known as minimum variance portfolios—offer less return but the same volatility as those portfolios that lie below the inflection point. For example, using Case 4 ($\rho = -0.5$), a portfolio allocation of 15/85 (assets A and B, respectively) offers a 8.60 percent return with a standard deviation of 7.63 percent, while a portfolio allocation of 55/45 offers a 10.20 percent return with a 7.15 percent standard deviation. Clearly, the 15/85 portfolio allocation is superior to the 55/45 allocation.[6]

The case of a three-asset portfolio is illustrated in Appendix 2A.

The Efficient Frontier

Following the procedure outlined by Markowitz (1952), the optimal combination of portfolio weights can be determined based on the return, variance, and correlation coefficients for each asset in the portfolio. Assuming short sales are prohibited, equations (11) and (12) can be used to determine the optimal combinations of asset weights

---

[5] Technically, the inflection point is found at the point formed by a perfectly vertical line (i.e., parallel to the y axis) that is tangent to the combination of efficient portfolios plotted in risk/return space. At this point, the tangent line is of an infinite slope.

[6] The portfolio combination that offers an identical standard deviation to the 15/85 portfolio is approximately 58.7/41.3, and its expected return is approximately 12.93 percent.

EXHIBIT 2–7
Inputs and Outputs to Two-Asset Portfolio Optimization Process

Asset	Expected Return	Standard Deviation	Correlation Coefficient ($P_{A,B}$)			
			Case 1	Case 2	Case 3	Case 4
A	12.0%	15.0%				
B	8.0%	10.0%	100.0%	50.0%	0.0%	−50.0%

Portfolio Weighting				Standard Deviation Based on Correlation Coefficients of:			
A	B	Total	Expected Return	100.0%	50.0%	0.0%	−50.0%
0.0%	100.0%	100.0%	8.00%	10.00%	10.00%	10.00%	10.00%
5.0	95.0	100.0	8.20	10.25	9.90	9.53	9.15
10.0	90.0	100.0	8.40	10.50	9.84	9.12	8.35
15.0	85.0	100.0	8.60	10.75	9.82	8.79	7.63
20.0	80.0	100.0	8.80	11.00	9.85	8.54	7.00
25.0	75.0	100.0	9.00	11.25	9.92	8.39	6.50
30.0	70.0	100.0	9.20	11.50	10.04	8.32	6.14
35.0	65.0	100.0	9.40	11.75	10.19	8.36	5.97
40.0	60.0	100.0	9.60	12.00	10.39	8.49	6.00
45.0	55.0	100.0	9.80	12.25	10.63	8.71	6.22
50.0	50.0	100.0	10.00	12.50	10.90	9.01	6.61
55.0	45.0	100.0	10.20	12.75	11.20	9.40	7.15
60.0	40.0	100.0	10.40	13.00	11.53	9.85	7.81
65.0	35.0	100.0	10.60	13.25	11.89	10.36	8.55
70.0	30.0	100.0	10.80	13.50	12.28	10.92	9.37
75.0	25.0	100.0	11.00	13.75	12.69	11.52	10.23
80.0	20.0	100.0	11.20	14.00	13.11	12.17	11.14
85.0	15.0	100.0	11.40	14.25	13.56	12.84	12.07
90.0	10.0	100.0	11.60	14.50	14.03	13.54	13.03
95.0	5.0	100.0	11.80	14.75	14.51	14.26	14.01
100.0	−0.0	100.0	12.00	15.00	15.00	15.00	15.00

necessary to construct a series of portfolios offering the least risk for a given level of return (or the highest return for a given level of risk). These optimal portfolios are said to comprise what is known as the efficient frontier, as shown in Exhibit 2–8.

The portfolio possibility set is defined as every stock, bond, real estate, venture capital, commodity fund, currency fund, mutual fund, and index fund, with the expected return plotted on the vertical axis and the standard deviation of returns plotted on the horizontal axis. Since investors are risk averse, they will prefer the security that has the least risk for a given level of expected return. The collection of

EXHIBIT 2-8
The Opportunity Set without Borrowing and Lending Opportunities

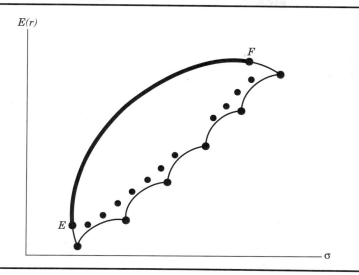

Source: Adapted from Jack Clark Francis, *Investments: Analysis and Management,* 3rd ed. (New York: McGraw-Hill, 1980), p. 529.

securities that have the least risk for a given level of return is called the efficient frontier of risky assets. Although it seems possible that individual securities can exist on the efficient frontier, this is not in fact true. There will always exist some combination of two or more securities that will dominate the individual security. Thus, the only inhabitants of the efficient frontier will be portfolios of more than one security.

Real Estate: Mean/Variance Efficiency and the Efficient Frontier

Several studies have documented that real estate's inclusion in a mixed-asset portfolio will serve to favorably shift the efficient frontier. As one early example, consider Webb, Curcio, and Rubens (1988). Given real estate's strong performance vis-à-vis stocks and bonds over the 1947–83 period and its low correlation with these financial assets, they showed that mean/variance portfolio efficiency was greatly enhanced by the inclusion of real estate in the mixed-asset portfolio.

Firstenberg, Ross, and Zisler (1988) were also among the first to apply MPT to real estate investment management. They analyzed real estate's role in a mixed-asset portfolio as well as the intra-allocation questions of property type and geographic diversification within the real estate sector. Since then, much work has been done on geographic diversification in particular. See Chapters 23 and 24 for additional information.

The Risk-Free Asset and Capital Market Equilibrium

Thus far, we have considered only risky assets. In addition to risky assets, investors can choose short-term assets that have no default or interest rate risk. These assets are called risk-free assets. They have expected returns with zero variance. Suppose we wish to invest part (x) of our wealth in the risk-free asset (R_f) and the remainder $(1 - x)$ in risky asset i. The expected return and variance, respectively, for such a portfolio are defined as

$$E(R_\rho) = xR_f + (1 - x)E(R_i) \qquad (15)$$

$$\sigma_\rho^2 = (1 - x)^2\sigma_i^2 \qquad (16)$$

The variance of a portfolio with a riskless asset and a risky asset reduces to equation (16) because the variance of the riskless asset is zero and the covariance between the riskless and risky asset is zero.

Investors face many possible combinations of the riskless and risky assets. Risk-averse investors will select the combination that maximizes the slope of the line connecting the riskless asset and a risky asset in the portfolio possibility set. As it turns out, there is one combination that maximizes this slope: the tangency point of the line that connects the risk-free asset with the efficient frontier. This relationship is shown in Exhibit 2–9. This tangency point (M) represents the market portfolio, and it dominates all other risky assets. Therefore, investors can combine the market portfolio with the risk-free asset and dominate any other combination for any given level of risk. Furthermore, assuming investors can borrow at the risk-free rate and invest in additional shares of the market portfolio, it still dominates any other combination.

EXHIBIT 2–9
The Optimal Risky Portfolio

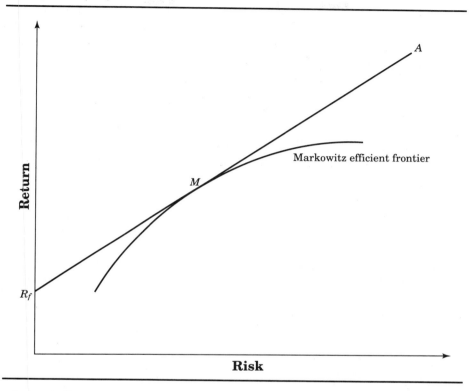

Source: Adapted from Jerome B. Cohen, Edward D. Zingburg, and Arthur Zeikel, *Investment Analysis and Portfolio Management,* 5th ed. (Homewood, IL: Richard D. Irwin, 1987), p. 138.

Capital Asset Pricing Model (CAPM)

Sharpe (1963), among others, recognized the computational problems associated with Markowitz (1952) diversification. For example, to create an optimized portfolio of the 500 common stocks utilized in the S&P 500 would require the calculation (or estimation) of 124,750 paired correlation coefficients.[7] Thus, the required calculations can

---

[7] The required number of paired correlation coefficients equals $\dfrac{N^2 - N}{2}$, *where* $N =$ the number of securities (or assets). Thus, for the Wilshire 5000, the required number of paired correlation coefficients equals approximately 12.5 million!

become quite burdensome if the ex ante correlation coefficients are to be estimated using any kind of probabilistic approach.

Moreover, Sharpe (1964) also suggested that the return on any risky security would equal a linear combination of the risk-free rate of interest plus the sensitivity of the security's systematic risk to the market portfolio's risk. The latter element is commonly referred to as *beta*. These results follow from the assumption that if risk-averse investors find it disadvantageous to bear unsystematic risk, only the systematic risk of an individual asset matters. That is, it is not the total risk of the asset's return that matters. How the asset's returns are correlated with the returns on the market portfolio is what matters.

Sharpe suggests that the expected return on any investment can be viewed as

$$E(R_i) = R_f + [E(R_m) - R_f] \times \beta_i \qquad (17)$$

where $E(R_m)$ = Expected return on the market portfolio
$\beta_i = \sigma_{i,m}/\sigma_m^2$

This equation highlights the fact that the investment's pricing is a function of the investment's relative volatility, as measured by its beta (β), and the market's risk premium, $[E(R_m) - R_f]$. The underpinnings of the CAPM are discussed in Appendix 2B.

EXHIBIT 2–10
The Security Market Line (SML)

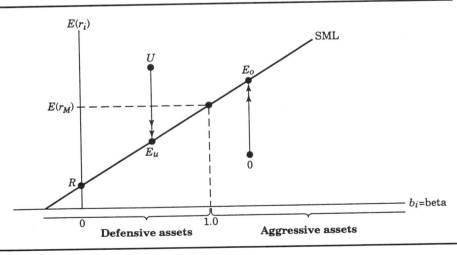

Source: Adapted from Jack Clark Francis, *Investments: Analysis and Management*, 3rd ed. (New York: McGraw-Hill, 1980), p. 371.

Equation (17) also represents the basis for what is known as the security market line (SML). See Exhibit 2–10. This graphical depiction of the SML highlights the notion that a security's expected return increases as the security's beta increases. The market portfolio, quite obviously, has a beta of 1.0. Securities with a beta greater than 1.0 are considered aggressive assets (i.e., they increase in value faster than the market). They should be held in the investor's portfolio depending on the investor's risk tolerance and expectation of future market movements.[8] Securities with a beta less than 1.0 are considered defensive assets (i.e., they decrease in value more slowly than the market). Likewise, they should be held in the portfolio depending on the investor's risk tolerance and market expectations.

Real Estate's Role in the Market Portfolio

An important point to re-emphasize is that given the CAPM's assumptions, any portfolio other than the market portfolio represents an inefficient combination with the risk-free asset. Only the market portfolio maximizes the investor's return. Improperly specifying the market portfolio can lead to serious biases in the calculated efficient frontier (see Roll [1977] and Webb [1990]). By a variety of estimates (see Hartzell [1992], Karnosky [1988], Miles [1990], and Webb and Rubens [1987]), real estate occupies a significant percentage of the market portfolio. As an example, Karnosky estimated investment real estate (excluding single-family homes) to comprise 16.5 percent of the U.S. investable capital market at year-end 1988. Thus, any portfolio that excludes real estate is, theoretically at least, inefficient.

CAPM and Investment Performance

Since not all assets will lie directly on the security market line as the capital asset pricing model suggests, several measures have been offered to gauge investment performance. Those reviewed here include (1) alpha, (2) the Treynor ratio, and (3) the Sharpe ratio.

Jensen (1969) employed the CAPM to test whether an asset earns positive risk-adjusted returns using the following regression model:

$$R_{i,t} - R_{f,t} = \alpha_i + \beta_i[R_{m,t} - R_{f,t}] + \varepsilon_{i,t} \qquad (18)$$

---

[8] That is, if the market is expected to rise in price (and therefore return), the investor is better served by greater exposure to the aggressive assets ($\beta > 1.0$).

where $R_{i,t}$ = Return on the ith security during time period t.

α_i = The regression equation's intercept (at $\beta = 0$).

β_i = The regression equation's slope coefficient.

$R_{m,t}$ = Return on the market portfolio during time period t.

$R_{f,t}$ = Return on the risk-free security during time period t.

$\varepsilon_{i,t}$ = Residual risk premium for the ith security during time period t that is unexplained by the regression equation.

This approach is based on the theory that if the ith security was correctly priced, there would be no excess return and the alpha value (α_i) would equal zero. If alpha is significantly greater than zero, it can be concluded that the investment has earned excess risk-adjusted returns. Unfortunately, the empirical evidence indicates that few investments can consistently earn positive excess risk-adjusted returns after the costs associated with trading and portfolio management are considered.

Treynor (1965) also employed the CAPM to determine whether a security or a portfolio offers a competitive risk-adjusted return. His performance-ranking measurement takes the following form:

$$T_{i,t} = \frac{R_{i,t} - R_{f,t}}{\beta_{i,t}} \tag{19}$$

where $T_{i,t}$ = Treynor risk-adjusted measure of performance of the ith security (or portfolio) during time period t.

$\beta_{i,t}$ = CAPM β of the ith security (or portfolio) during time period t.

Sharpe (1966) employed a slight variation for his measure of performance, as follows:

$$S_{i,t} = \frac{R_{i,t} - R_{f,t}}{\sigma_{i,t}} \tag{20}$$

where $S_{i,t}$ = Sharpe risk-adjusted performance measure for the ith security (or portfolio) during time period t.

$\sigma_{i,t}$ = Standard deviation of the returns of the ith security (or portfolio) during time period t.

Both the Treynor and Sharpe measures utilize the risk premium (i.e., the security's return less the risk-free rate) as the numerator in their respective calculations. However, they slightly diverge in the denominator. Treynor's measure focuses on the security's (or portfolio's) systematic risk (as measured by beta). Sharpe's measure focuses on the security's (or portfolio's) total risk (as measured by its standard deviation). Thus, Treynor's measure may be more appropriate to a security (rather than a portfolio) when one is trying to measure the contribution of a security to a portfolio's overall risk-return parameters.[9] On the other hand, Sharpe's measure may be more appropriate to a portfolio (rather than an underlying security) when one is trying to measure the adequacy of a portfolio's return relative to its risk characteristics. The difference between the investment performance (or ranking) of these two measures will, in large part, be determined by the unsystematic risk found in the security (or portfolio).

Real Estate: CAPM and Investment Performance

Chan, Hendershott, and Sanders (1990) estimated equation (18) for a portfolio of equity REIT returns from the period 1973 through 1988. The results indicate that the portfolio of equity REITs has a beta of .635 and an alpha of .0056 when the value-weighted NYSE index was employed as the market portfolio for the entire sample period. When the equally weighted NYSE index was employed, the equity REITs had a beta of .659 and an alpha of .0031 for the same sample period. The alpha was (statistically) significant only when the value-weighted NYSE was employed.

The authors examined subperiods as well. For the 1973–79 subperiod, the betas for equity REITs were .734 (equally weighted NYSE index) and .750 (value-weighted index). The alphas were statistically insignificant. For the 1980–87 subperiod, the betas were .556 (equally weighted) and .541 (value-weighted). The alphas were positive and statistically significant.

The Jensen performance test indicates that equity REITs are approximately 60 percent as risky as the market (as proxied by the NYSE indices) and that excess risk-adjusted returns were found for the 1980s but not the 1970s.

---

[9] Along the same lines, it could be used to measure the contribution of a smaller portfolio to that of a larger portfolio.

Challenges to the CAPM

Several challenges have been made to the CAPM's assumption that risk can be captured in a one-factor model (the covariance between the ith security and the market portfolio, as measured solely by beta). Generally, studies from the 1970s empirically support the relationship between beta and security returns (see Fama and MacBeth [1973] and Black, Jensen, and Scholes [1972]), while studies from the 1980s detect an insignificant relationship between beta and returns (see Reinganum [1982], Lakonishok and Shapiro [1986], and Ritter and Chopra [1989]). Recently Fama and French [1992] found two factors (book-to-market value and firm size) to be more explanative than the single-factor CAPM.

The evidence in support of beta is mixed. With 51 years of data through 1982, the statistical support for beta is quite strong; however, the 1983–91 period showed little support. On balance (i.e., over the 60-year period ended in 1991), beta was not significant at the 5 percent confidence level. Were the last nine years an aberration that damaged the overall results? Is the increased popularity of index funds contributing to beta's demise? Are other institutional/behavioral matters at work? If so, are they cyclical or secular? While these questions go unanswered, it is also clear that "the very noisy and constantly changing environment [for] generating stock returns . . ." makes it difficult to assert that beta should be discarded—particularly "[g]iven that no other widely accepted risk measure exists . . ." (Chan and Lakonishok [1993]).

The Arbitrage Pricing Model

A long-standing alternative to the capital asset pricing model for measuring the risk-adjusted investment performance is the arbitrage pricing theory (APT) model. According to Ross (1976), returns are assumed to be generated by a number of factors, as follows:

$$r_i = E(R_i) + B_{i,k}F_K + \varepsilon_I \qquad (21)$$

where
$r_i = N \times 1$ vector of returns.
$E(R_i) = N \times 1$ vector of expected returns.
$B_{i,k} = N \times K$ matrix of factor sensitivities.
$F_k = K \times 1$ vector of random factors with means equal to zero.
$\varepsilon_i = N \times 1$ vector of residuals.

While the number of factors is unspecified (i.e., $N \geq 1$), the model generally attempts to capture informational factors (such as unanticipated inflation, unanticipated changes in domestic GNP, changes in the term structure of interest rates, etc.) that are intended to measure new information concerning the macroeconomy (relating to systematic risk). This new information has an equal chance of positively or negatively affecting security prices. The error term (ε_i), representing the firm's unsystematic risk, is expected to cancel out in the context of a well-diversified portfolio.

Generally speaking, the assumptions underlying APT are less restrictive than those of the CAPM. Specifically, where CAPM relies on, among other matters, investors with homogeneous expectations about the risk-reward characteristics of all securities, APT does not. Rather, APT suggests that in the context of a well-diversified portfolio, investors can locate securities (or groups of securities) that offer risk-adjusted arbitrage opportunities. However, locating these securities is predicated on the underlying systematic factors themselves (e.g., industrial production, inflation rates, term structure of interest rates, etc.) rather than using the market portfolio as a proxy for these factors. The existence of such opportunities will tend to move security prices into alignment with those predicated by the multifactor APT. In other words, the use of APT will generate its own security market line where excess return is a function of the underlying, systematic components hypothesized in the N-factor model.

Real Estate and APT

Chan, Hendershott, and Sanders (1990) employed the arbitrage pricing model approach to studying real estate return behavior. They regressed excess real estate returns on the excess returns of portfolios whose returns mimicked prespecified factors (see Chen, Roll, and Ross [1986]). The prespecified factors were changes in expected inflation and industrial production, the risk and term structure of interest rates, and unexpected inflation. They derived an APT-based model that estimates real estate risk exposure. Furthermore, the constant term in the model is analogous to Jensen's alpha, which permits testing for risk-adjusted excess returns. That is, rather than controlling for one type of risk (systematic) as in the CAPM, they sought to control for a variety of risks to which real estate investors are exposed. After controlling for these macroeconomic factors (risks), they found that real estate in the form of equity REITs did not earn risk-adjusted excess returns. This conclusion contradicts previous studies that found real estate did earn risk-adjusted excess returns. The interested reader is encouraged to read Titman and Warga (1986) as well.

Duration Matching

Long ago, Macaulay (1938) introduced the concept of duration, which attempts to measure the sensitivity of a bond's price to relatively small movements in interest rates. His approach was to weight the bond's maturity by the product of the relative portion of present value received and the year in which it is received. This weighted maturity became known as duration. A related concept, modified duration, was later introduced to more easily identify a bond's sensitivity to interest rate fluctuations. Both of these measures (adapted from Fabozzi, Pitts, and Dattatrega [1991]) are, respectively, as follows:

$$D = \sum_{t=1}^{T} \frac{t \times \text{PVCF}_t}{k \times \text{PVTCF}} \qquad (22)$$

$$\text{Modified } D = \frac{D}{\left[\dfrac{1 + \text{YTM}}{k} \right]} \qquad (23)$$

where D = Duration.

t = Period when cash flow is to be received.

T = Number of years to maturity.

k = Number of periods per year.

PVCF_t = Present value of cash flow received in period t, discounted at the yield to maturity.

PVTCF = Present value of all cash flows discounted at the yield to maturity (this equals the initial price).

YTM = Yield-to-maturity discount rate.

For example, consider two bonds. Bond A has level (semiannual) payments at 8 percent and matures in 10 years, while bond B is a zero-coupon bond accreting at 8 percent and also maturing in 10 years. The respective duration calculations for each bond are shown in Exhibit 2–11.

The pricing impact of a change in the level of interest rates on each bond can be estimated through the use of the respective duration measures. For example, if interest rates increased from 8.00 to 8.50 percent, the price of the level-coupon bond (bond A) would drop by 3.40 percent while the zero-coupon bond (bond B) would drop by 4.81 percent. This and other duration-estimated examples are presented in Exhibit 2–12.

The concept of duration matching, also known as either immunized or dedicated portfolios, grew from estimating the duration of a firm's liabilities. For example, a pension fund sponsor can, with some precision, estimate its future liabilities (i.e., retirement benefits paid to plan beneficiaries). Accordingly, the duration of the outflow stream can be calculated as shown in equations (22) and (23). Moreover, this pension fund sponsor can, theoretically at least, match the market (or present) value and duration of its liability stream with an asset (or a portfolio of assets) that has an equivalent duration and an equal or greater market (or present) value (see, among others, Christensen, Fabozzi, and LoFaso [1991]).

In theory, at least, this strategy would result in equal changes in the value of the assets and liabilities for a given and relatively small change in interest rates. Thus, the pension fund's net worth or surplus (i.e., assets minus liabilities) would be "immunized" (i.e., the fund's surplus would remain unchanged even though interest rates changed) if a portfolio of assets were dedicated to this duration-matching approach.

However, several pragmatic problems with a duration-matching strategy should also be noted.

Convexity

While duration (and its first cousin, modified duration) implies a linear relationship between changes in interest rates and, say, bond prices, the relationship is in fact curvilinear, as shown in Exhibit 2–13. The exhibit shows that increases in interest rates have a smaller impact on bond prices than do decreases in interest rates. In other words, bond prices decrease at a decreasing rate as the interest rate increases. This relationship is known as convexity.

Convexity implies that price changes caused by interest rate changes will be approximated by the duration measurement for small

EXHIBIT 2–11

Duration Comparison of Constant-Coupon versus Zero-Coupon Bonds with Equivalent Yields to Maturity

Period	Bond A				Bond B			
	Cash Flow	Present Value Factor	Present Value of Cash Flow	Time-Weighted Present Value	Cash Flow	Present Value Factor	Present Value of Cash Flow	Time-Weighted Present Value
1	$ 40	0.9615	$ 38.46	$ 38.46	$ 0	0.9615	$ 0.00	$ 0.00
2	40	0.9246	36.98	73.96	0	0.9246	0.00	0.00
3	40	0.8890	35.56	106.68	0	0.8890	0.00	0.00
4	40	0.8548	34.19	136.77	0	0.8548	0.00	0.00
5	40	0.8219	32.88	164.39	0	0.8219	0.00	0.00
6	40	0.7903	31.61	189.68	0	0.7903	0.00	0.00
7	40	0.7599	30.40	212.78	0	0.7599	0.00	0.00
8	40	0.7307	29.23	233.82	0	0.7307	0.00	0.00
9	40	0.7026	28.10	252.93	0	0.7026	0.00	0.00
10	40	0.6756	27.02	270.23	0	0.6756	0.00	0.00
11	40	0.6496	25.98	285.82	0	0.6496	0.00	0.00

Coupon bond

Period	Cash flow	Discount factor	Present value	Time-weighted present value
12	40	0.6246	24.98	299.81
13	40	0.6006	24.02	312.30
14	40	0.5775	23.10	323.39
15	40	0.5553	22.21	333.16
16	40	0.5339	21.36	341.70
17	40	0.5134	20.53	349.09
18	40	0.4936	19.75	355.41
19	40	0.4746	18.99	360.73
20	1,040	0.4564	474.64	9,492.85
	$1,800		$1,000.00	$14,133.94

Time-weighted present value	$14,133.94
Present value of cash flow	1,000.00
	14.13
Number of coupon payments per year	2
Duration (in years)	7.07
Duration (in years)	7.07
1 + Periodic yield to maturity	1.04
Modified duration (in years)	6.80

Zero-coupon bond

Period	Cash flow	Discount factor	Present value	Time-weighted present value
12	0	0.6246	0.00	0.00
13	0	0.6006	0.00	0.00
14	0	0.5775	0.00	0.00
15	0	0.5553	0.00	0.00
16	0	0.5339	0.00	0.00
17	0	0.5134	0.00	0.00
18	0	0.4936	0.00	0.00
19	0	0.4746	0.00	0.00
20	2,191	0.4564	1,000.00	20,000.00
	2,191		$1,000.00	$20,000.00

Time-weighted present value	$20,000.00
Present value of cash flow	1,000.00
	20.00
Number of coupon payments per year	2
Duration (in years)	10.00
Duration (in years)	10.00
1 + Periodic yield to maturity	1.04
Modified duration (in years)	9.62

EXHIBIT 2–12
Duration-Estimated Pricing Impact Due to Interest Rate Changes

Revised Interest (or Discount) Rate	Change From Initial Rate	Percentage Price Change in	
		Bond A	Bond B
7.0%	−1.0%	6.80%	9.62%
7.1	−0.9	6.12	8.65
7.2	−0.8	5.44	7.69
7.3	−0.7	4.76	6.73
7.4	−0.6	4.08	5.77
7.5	−0.5	3.40	4.81
7.6	−0.4	2.72	3.85
7.7	−0.3	2.04	2.88
7.8	−0.2	1.36	1.92
7.9	−0.1	0.68	0.96
8.0	0.0	−0.00	−0.00
8.1	0.1	−0.68	−0.96
8.2	0.2	−1.36	−1.92
8.3	0.3	−2.04	−2.88
8.4	0.4	−2.72	−3.85
8.5	0.5	−3.40	−4.81
8.6	0.6	−4.08	−5.77
8.7	0.7	−4.76	−6.73
8.8	0.8	−5.44	−7.69
8.9	0.9	−6.12	−8.65
9.0	1.0	−6.80	−9.62

Note: Duration-estimated price change = −Modified duration × Discount rate change.

changes in the interest rate. However, as the interest rate changes increase in magnitude, the estimate of the changes in bond prices will become increasingly understated.

Parallel Yield Curve Shifts

The calculations underlying duration's accuracy rely on the assumption that interest rate changes via parallel shifts in the yield curve (i.e., short- and long-term rates move by an equal amount). This assumption is not very pragmatic, as short-term rates tend to be more volatile than long-term rates, even though an equivalent change in short- and long-term interest rates will more dramatically affect the pricing of the long-term bonds.

EXHIBIT 2–13
Price Approximation Using Duration

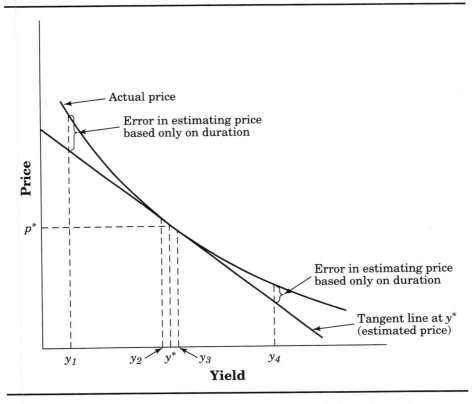

Source: Adapted from Frank J. Fabozzi, Mark Pitts, and Ravi Dattatrega, "Price Volatility Characteristics of Fixed-Income Securities," in F. J. Fabozzi, ed., *The Handbook of Fixed Income Securities,* 3rd ed. (Homewood, IL: Business One Irwin, 1991), p. 130.

Rebalancing

The duration of a portfolio (of assets and/or liabilities) is continuously changing. The passage of time alone will alter the calculated duration measures. In addition, a change in the level of interest rates will quite obviously cause assets and liabilities to be revalued. Accordingly, the immunized portfolio must be periodically rebalanced. Depending on the magnitude of the changes in the duration of the asset and liability portfolios, the transaction costs associated with the portfolio rebalancing may be substantial.

Default Risk

Duration-based calculations do not explicitly account for the default risk contained in the asset portfolio. While such risk is indirectly incorporated into the yield-to-maturity pricing, there is no explicit differentiation of the duration associated with Treasury bonds as compared to junk bonds. Thus, the impact of forgone principal and/or interest is not directly incorporated into an asset-liability immunization program. In practice, the solution has often been to use investment grade bonds exclusively. However, this approach implies a substantial cost for the investor (e.g., pension fund) that forsakes the potentially higher returns associated with common stocks, real estate, venture capital, junk bonds, and so on—all of which is compounded by the lack of diversification and the preclusion of reducing the standard deviation of returns on risky assets with the passage of time.

There are also a host of technical problems in utilizing the immunization (or duration) strategy. While many of the problems have solutions, they come with a cost and/or compromise the theoretically elegant (and appealing) aspects of duration matching. Again, see Christensen, Fabozzi, and LoFaso (1991), among others.

Real Estate and Duration

The application of duration has been extended to equities in general and real estate in particular; see Giliberto (1989) and Hartzell et al. (1988). Essentially, this research suggests that real estate's duration increases as the underlying property is encumbered with leases of lengthening expiration dates. Properties with short-term leases (e.g., apartments and hotels) have duration measures approaching zero (i.e., their prices are insensitive to changes in interest rates) where the change in the interest rate is related to a change in the expected inflation rate (as opposed to the risk premium). Conversely, properties with long-term leases (e.g., net-leased industrial facilities) can offer durations of three to six years (approximately those found with intermediate-term bonds). When the change in the interest rate is related to a change in the risk premium (and not the expected inflation rate), the prices of all properties (regardless of lease term) show greater sensitivity.

Investors may have some control over the duration of their real estate investments by selection of the lease term. However, lease terms are generally set by the marketplace (e.g., a retail tenant is often unwilling to sign a short-term lease). Accordingly, real estate's duration can effectively be altered based on selecting those property types that tend to operate with the longer or shorter lease term and/or to utilize mortgage leverage to shorten the duration of properties encumbered with long-term leases. The utilization of mortgage debt (with a maturity equal to the lease expiration) can effectively reduce the combination of the tenant's lease payments and the debt service expenditure to zero, which in turn transforms the real estate into an investment that generates its return solely from the property's reversionary value (upon lease expiration). If market rental rates keep pace with inflation, this reversionary value should have a duration approaching zero. Thus, investors can alter the duration of their real estate investments by changing the degree of leverage used to finance their property investments.

Duration Applied to Real Estate

The following illustration uses duration to measure the pricing sensitivity of two hypothetical properties to changes in the discount rate. For ease of exposition, let us compare two single-tenant buildings that are identical in every respect except the specified rents. While both properties have signed tenants to 10-year leases, building A's lease calls for level rental payments of $1,000 per year, and building B's lease calls for "stepped" rental payments as indicated below. At lease expiration, the leases "roll" to the market rate, which is assumed to be growing at 3.5 percent per annum. Upon lease expiration, the building's reversionary value is determined by capitalizing—using the prevailing discount rate (which, by the assumptions utilized here, is equivalent for both properties)—the market rental rate. Assume the initial discount rate is 10 percent per annum and all cash flows are received at year's end.

At this assumed discount rate, the properties have an identical (or nearly so) value of $11,581. Moreover, the component values of the two properties are also nearly identical; approximately 53 percent of the value is attributable to the lease income, and the remaining

47 percent is derived from the reversionary value. See Exhibit 2–14 for the specifics of these calculations.

From Exhibit 2–14, we observe that the duration of building A's lease is 4.73 years (i.e., 29,036/6,145) while building B's lease is 6.59 years (i.e., 40,523/6,145). These duration measures indicate that the value of the lease on building A is less sensitive to changes in the discount rate than is that for building B. Specifically, the modified duration would provide an estimate of the change in lease value for a given change in the discount rate:

	Lease Value- Only	
	Building A	Building B
Duration	4.73	6.59
1 + Discount rate	1.10	1.10
Modified duration	4.30	5.99

These figures indicate that for every 100-basis-point increase (or decrease) in the discount rate, the value of the lease decreases (or increases) by approximately 4.30 percent for building A and by 5.99 percent for building B. Intuitively, this appears reasonable, as the back-end skewing of building B's lease payments would make it more sensitive to changes in the discount rate.

The value of the entire building will change based on the duration (or modified duration) of the lease component and the residual component. It is the weighted average of these components that determines the building's overall duration (D), as follows:

$$D = \frac{\text{Lease value}}{\text{Total value}} \times \frac{\text{Lease}}{\text{duration}} + \frac{\text{Reversion value}}{\text{Total value}} \times \frac{\text{Reversion}}{\text{duration}} \quad (24)$$

$$\text{Duration}_A = (.5306)(4.73) + (.4694)(10.00)$$
$$= 7.20 \quad (24a)$$
$$\text{Duration}_B = (.5306)(6.59) + (.4694)(10.00) \quad (24b)$$
$$= 8.19$$

The impact of a change in the discount rate on total building value can be estimated using duration (or modified duration). The percentage change in building value for a relatively small range of

EXHIBIT 2–14 Duration Comparison of Two Identical Buildings, Each with 10-Year Leases

Lease/Income Value

Building A: Level Rents

Year	Annual Net Rent	Present Value Factor	Present Value of Rent	Time-Weighted Present Value
1	$1,000.00	0.9091	$ 909.09	909
2	1,000.00	0.8264	826.45	1,653
3	1,000.00	0.7513	751.31	2,254
4	1,000.00	0.6830	683.01	2,732
5	1,000.00	0.6209	620.92	3,105
6	1,000.00	0.5645	564.47	3,387
7	1,000.00	0.5132	513.16	3,592
8	1,000.00	0.4665	466.51	3,732
9	1,000.00	0.4241	424.10	3,817
10	1,000.00	0.3855	385.54	3,855
Total			$6,144.57	29,036

Building B: Stepped Rents

Year	Annual Net Rent	Present Value Factor	Present Value of Rent	Time-Weighted Present Value
1	$ 0.00	0.9091	$ 0.00	0
2	0.00	0.8264	0.00	0
3	1,000.00	0.7513	751.31	2,254
4	1,000.00	0.6830	683.01	2,732
5	1,000.00	0.6209	807.20	4,036
6	1,300.00	0.5645	733.82	4,403
7	1,300.00	0.5132	769.74	5,388
8	1,500.00	0.4665	699.76	5,598
9	1,500.00	0.4241	890.60	8,015
10	2,100.00	0.3855	809.64	8,096
10	2,100.00			
Total			$6,145.09	40,523

Reversionary Value

Building A: Level Rents

Year	Then-Current Capitalized Value	Present Value Factor	Present Value of Capitalized Value	Duration of Each	Time-Weighted Present Value
10	$14,100.00	0.3855	$5,436.16	10.00	54,362

Building B: Stepped Rents

Year	Then-Current Capitalized Value	Present Value Factor	Present Value of Capitalized Value	Duration of Each	Time-Weighted Present Value
10	$14,100.00	0.3855	$5,436.16	10.00	54,362

Total Value

Building A: Level Rents

	Present Value of Cash Flow	Percentage of Value	Duration of Each	Weighted-Average Duration
Lease	$ 6,144.57	53.06%	4.73	2.51
Reversion	5,436.16	46.94	10.00	4.69
Total	$11,580.73	100.00%		7.20

Building B: Stepped Rents

	Present Value of Cash Flow	Percentage of Value	Duration of Each	Weighted-Average Duration
Lease	$ 6,145.09	53.06%	6.59	3.50
Reversion	5,436.16	46.94	10.00	4.69
Total	$11,581.25	100.00%		8.19

Notes and assumptions
1. For simplicity, assume rents are received at year-end.
2. Rents increase at growth rate and are capitalized at discount rate. Discount rate: 10.0% per annum; growth rate: 3.5% per annum.

EXHIBIT 2–15
Analysis of Pricing Impact Due to Change in Discount Rate

Revised Discount Rate	Change in Discount Rate	Percentage Price Change	
		Building A	Building B
9.0%	−1.0%	6.55%	7.45%
9.1	−0.9	5.89	6.70
9.2	−0.8	5.24	5.96
9.3	−0.7	4.58	5.21
9.4	−0.6	3.93	4.47
9.5	−0.5	3.27	3.72
9.6	−0.4	2.62	2.98
9.7	−0.3	1.96	2.23
9.8	−0.2	1.31	1.49
9.9	−0.1	0.65	0.74
10.0	0.0	−0.00	−0.00
10.1	0.1	−0.65	−0.74
10.2	0.2	−1.31	−1.49
10.3	0.3	−1.96	−2.23
10.4	0.4	−2.62	−2.98
10.5	0.5	−3.27	−3.72
10.6	0.6	−3.93	−4.47
10.7	0.7	−4.58	−5.21
10.8	0.8	−5.24	−5.96
10.9	0.9	−5.89	−6.70
11.0	1.0	−6.55	−7.45

Duration − Estimated percentage price change = − Modified duration ×
Discount rate change.

possible changes is shown in Exhibit 2–15. For purposes of this analysis, changes in the discount rate are assumed to be independent of changes in the growth rate of market rents. To the extent that rates are positively correlated, the estimates of duration would be reduced.

Option Pricing Theory

As more fully described in Chapter 27, option pricing theory is essentially predicated on the notion that an asset can be synthetically mimicked by the combination of the option (or futures) contract and (borrowing or lending) the risk-free security. The pricing of the synthetic security will be derived from the asset and (plus or minus) the risk-free security.

The following example, adopted from Bodie et al. (1992) and Kritzman (1990), assumes there exists some risky asset, currently priced at $100, that with equal probability will be worth either $130 or $80 at the end of one year. Further assume a call option exists with an exercise (or strike) price of $105. (The purchaser of this option has the right, but not the obligation, to purchase the risky asset from the seller of the option at the exercise price.) At the end of one year, the value of the call option will either be $25 or $0. These relationships are shown in Exhibit 2–16.

Alternatively, investors can synthetically create a payoff pattern of the same magnitude (i.e., in one year's time, receive a multiple of either $25 or $0 with equal probability) by borrowing the present value of the lower ending stock price. To see that this is true, examine the payoff patterns illustrated below:

				Year 1 Stock Price	
	Year 0			Rise	Fall
Buy security	$100.00	Sell security		$130.00	$80.00
Borrow funds	76.19	Repay loan		80.00	80.00
Net investment	$ 23.81	Net proceeds		$ 50.00	$ 0

Note that at the end of year 1, the stock may either rise in value to $130 or fall to $80. If the former occurs, the investor will receive

EXHIBIT 2–16
Stock and Option Call Values Using Binomial Model

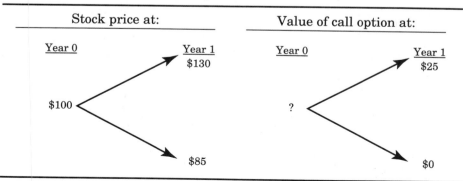

$50 after having repaid an $80 loan (of which $76.19 is principal and $3.81 is accrued interest at 5 percent per annum) from the proceeds of the stock sale. If the latter occurs, the investor's sale proceeds will be exactly equal to the loan payoff amount. Because the investor borrowed funds (equal to the present value of the lower stock price), the net investment at acquisition was only $23.81. For this amount, the investor receives a payoff pattern that is equal to exactly twice that expected by the option purchaser. This is illustrated (using the same method as before) in Exhibit 2–17.

From Exhibit 2–17, it is apparent that an investor with a riskless opportunity to make either $50 or $0 at the end of one year would indeed pay $23.81 for the opportunity. Similarly, an investor offered two call options (such that the payoff in one year would total either $50 or $0) would also be willing to pay $23.81 for the opportunity. Accordingly, if two call options are worth $23.81, one call option must be worth $11.90. At any other price, option purchasers (or sellers) could synthetically create their own option (by combining the risky and risk-free assets) and arbitrage the mispriced option against the synthetic option. To understand this, note that an investor who owns the stock could sell two such call options, thereby creating a perfectly hedged portfolio which earns the risk-free rate of return. Examine the payoff patterns under either stock price movement:

	Year 0		Year 1	
			Rise	Fall
Buy security	$100.00	Stock value	$130.00	$80.00
Sell two call options	23.81	Option obligation	50.00	0.00
Net investment	$ 76.19	Net payoff	$ 80.00	$80.00

Notice that, no matter the stock price movement, the investor will receive $80.00 for which the initial investment was $76.19. The rate of return on this investment is equal to the risk-free rate, assumed to be 5 percent.

Obviously, this example (often referred to as the binomial option model) oversimplifies the possible payoff patterns associated with most risky assets. Fortunately, the binomial model can be revised to accommodate a variety of considerations, such as multiple time periods, multiple payoff possibilities, differing payoff probabilities, and

EXHIBIT 2–17
A Synthetic Option's Payoff Patterns

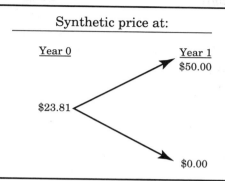

so on. Perhaps even more fortunately, we will spare the reader (and ourselves) an introduction to these more complex models here; interested readers are referred to Cox and Rubenstein (1985). The Black-Scholes (1973) option pricing model does away with the constraints of a binomial (or modified binomial) model and utilizes a continuous-time approach.[10]

The application of option pricing to portfolio management is primarily in the context of portfolio insurance. While there are different approaches to portfolio insurance, the effect of portfolio insurance is illustrated in Exhibit 2–18. In essence, portfolio insurance is equivalent to an investment in a risky asset combined with a put option (which is the converse of a call option; i.e., it is the right, but not the

---

[10] The Black-Scholes (1973) option pricing model is written as

$$C_0 = S_0 N(d_1) - X_e^{-rT} N(d_2)$$ (25)

where $d_1 = \dfrac{\ln(S_0/X) + (r + \sigma^2/2)T}{\sigma\sqrt{T}}$.

$d_2 = d_1 - \sigma\sqrt{T}$.

C_0 = Current value of call option.

S_0 = Current stock price.

$N(d_n)$ = Cumulative normal density function of d_n.

X = Exercise price.

e = 2.71828 (the base of the natural log function).

r = Risk-free interest rate.

T = Time to option's maturity.

ln = Natural logarithm function.

σ = Standard deviation of stock's return.

EXHIBIT 2–18
Portfolio Insurance Payoff Diagram

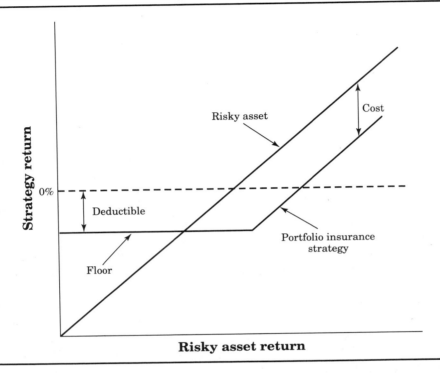

Source: Adapted from Mark P. Kritzman, *Asset Allocation for Institutional Portfolios* (Homewood, IL: Richard D. Irwin, 1990), p. 35.

obligation, to sell the risky asset to the seller of the option at the exercise price) or an investment in the risk-free asset combined with a call option. The intention is to ensure that a portion of the portfolio's value (and/or rate of return) does not fall below a prescribed "floor." Such investors are willing to forsake some "upside" return in exchange for a fixed "downside" exposure.

Real Estate and Options

Readers interested in the application of synthetic (or derivative) securities are referred to Chapter 27 for a host of insightful applications. However, it should be noted that much of option (and futures) pricing is based on the ability to (1) synthetically mimic the risky portfolio and (2) arbitrage away any riskless opportunities with the simultaneous sale and purchase of like assets. The real estate securities market, in its present form, offers little opportunity for such trading. However, there are indications that the institutional market is taking steps in this direction. Consider several recent market-based transactions: (1) a swap of returns from a corporate pension fund's equity real estate with a swap for floating-rate notes provided by an investment bank (see Williams [March 8, 1993]); (2) a corporate pension fund's exchange of seven shopping centers for cash and stock from a real estate investment trust (see Williams [February 8, 1993]); and (3) a public pension plan reduces its exposure to net-lease transactions by selling the leases on 59 properties to a real estate investment trust for cash and a convertible note (see Williams [August 23, 1993]).

Chaos Theory

Chaos theory, contrary to what its name might otherwise suggest, is not about purely random events. Rather, it attempts to describe nonlinear systems. Such systems exhibit a long-term dependency, but in the shorter term may often appear to be random in nature. Moreover, such systems often exhibit an increasing level of complexity as they are examined at increasing levels of detail, sometimes referred to as fractals (see Mandelbrot [1982]).

An example may best illustrate the nature of this theory. The following example is adapted from Feigenbaum as described by Paulos (1991). Consider an animal species that has population growth based on

$$x_{t+1} = rx_t(1 - x_t) \tag{26}$$

where x_t = Population scaled from 0 to 1 in year t.
   r = Constant parameter ranging from 0 to 4.

If we assume the current population (x_0) is .3 (e.g., .3 × 1,000,000) and the constant parameter current (r) is 2, the next year's population is .41 and the following year it is .48; thereafter, the population stabilizes at .5. If instead a parameter (r) of 1 or less is chosen, the population quickly stabilizes at 0 (i.e., moves to extinction). Conversely, if the parameter (r) is 3.2, the population eventually settles into alternating between .5 and .8. If the parameter (r) is raised to 3.5, the population eventually settles down to four alternating values—.38, .83, .50, and .88—in successive years. If r is increased slightly, the population settles down to regularly alternat-

EXHIBIT 2–19   Illustration of Nonlinear System Using Hypothetical Species Population

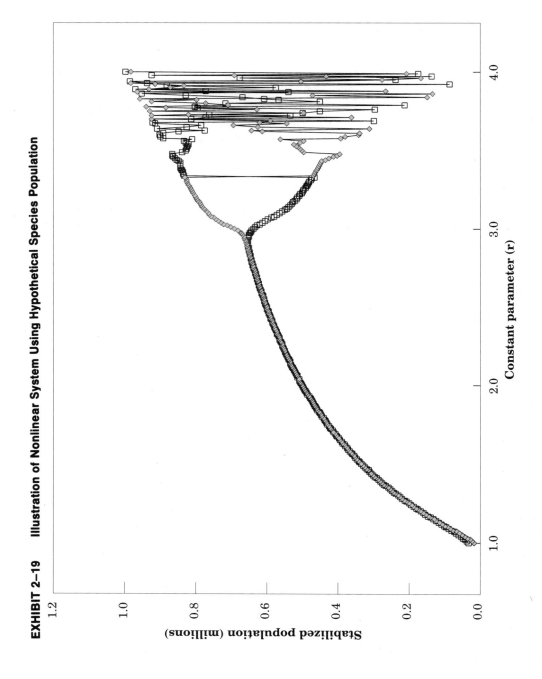

ing among eight variables. Yet successively smaller increases in r will result in more doubling of the number of eventual values. This pattern increases until r reaches 3.57, at which the species' population grows randomly from year to year. This pattern is reflected in Exhibit 2–19.

From Exhibit 2–19, it is apparent that the constant parameter (r) proxies the system's volatility. However, it is also apparent that small changes in the value of r can have a substantial impact on the predicted variable—species population in this case.

This type of nonlinear system has been applied to hydrodynamics, physics, and biology, among other fields of the natural sciences. It has also been applied to the social science of finance. Peters (1989) used this type of nonlinear approach to analyze the "random walk" of security prices. He used rescaled range (R/S) analysis in an attempt to estimate a volatility parameter—similar to the r described earlier—as a way of estimating the persistence of investor sentiment in securities price. Specifically, Peters found that from 1950 through 1988, 16.8 percent of stock returns, 21.5 percent of bond returns, and 24.5 percent of relative stock/bond returns were influenced by past returns. For this period, it seems market trends continued in one direction (i.e., a biased random walk) until some exogenous event occurred to change the bias.

Chaos Theory and Real Estate

Chaos/fractal theory has not yet been applied to real estate investments. Nevertheless, the application of nonlinear systems in viewing real estate returns has some intuitive appeal. Real estate has long been characterized as experiencing pronounced cyclical patterns.

However, liberally applying the techniques of data analysis from the natural sciences to the investment setting may not be appropriate. While natural scientists benefit from studying "closed" systems (i.e., natural phenomena are repeatable and largely unaffected by outside factors), social scientists—among others, those in the field of finance—are burdened by studying "open" systems where the results of previous experiences are fed back into the system. That is, any financial "rosetta stone" would soon lose its predictive power once a large group of investors incorporated it into their investment decision-making calculus. Accordingly, any predictive model that exhibits a goodness of fit using historical data may quickly become obsolete as investors successfully use it to predict future prices and thereby arbitrage away its predictive accuracy.

CONCLUSION

This chapter provided a broad overview of portfolio management concepts used by leading theorists and practitioners. In turn, these concepts have been applied to real estate portfolio management.

Most of these concepts were initially developed to be applied to assets with known cash flow streams and/or assets that trade in large, securitized markets with liquid, continuous trading over long periods of time. Real estate meets neither of these criteria, though the burgeoning REIT market may at some future date deliver the latter. Consequently, the applications of the portfolio management techniques must be viewed cautiously. At present, however, the fact that the real estate market is still largely characterized as an illiquid, private market makes the application of much of the portfolio management artillery problematic.

Moreover, the existence of competing portfolio management techniques (e.g., CAPM versus APT) indicates that there is no one optimal way to manage an investment real estate (or other) portfolio. This is compounded by our ex ante ability to optimize a portfolio which is based on the assumption that (1) the past will be repeated in the future, (2) the portfolio manager has some risk-adjusted ability to profitably engage in either security selection and/or market timing, or (3) the manager has no such (selection and/or timing) abilities and therefore opts to passively manage the portfolio. In the final analysis, a mix of financial theory and human judgment is needed to efficiently manage real estate portfolios.

APPENDIX 2A THE THREE-ASSET PORTFOLIO

Expanding the analysis in the chapter to a three-asset portfolio is a little more complex than the two-asset case. Assume the three assets represent the following choices (a slight modification of the two-asset example):

Asset	Return	Standard Deviation
A	12%	15%
B	10	10
C	4	5

As before, a variety of correlation coefficients will be illustrated. However, because each pair of assets must be separately examined, it is necessary to construct a matrix of correlation coefficients[11] for each case. These assumed matrices are presented in Exhibit 2A–1.

Again, the portfolio's return is a linear combination of each asset's weighting. For our initial purpose, the portfolio's return with equal weighting to each of the three assets would result in an 8.33 percent portfolio return:

$$
\begin{aligned}
E(R_p) &= x_A \times E(R_A) + x_B \times E(R_B) + x_C \times E(R_C) \\
&= 1/3(.12) + 1/3(.08) + 1/3(.05) \\
&= .0833
\end{aligned}
\tag{28}
$$

With each increase in the number of assets in the portfolio, the calculation of the portfolio's variance becomes a little more unyielding, as the number of terms increases geometrically. The variance of the three-asset portfolio is calculated as

$$
\begin{aligned}
E(\sigma_p^2) &= x_A^2 E(\sigma_A^2) + x_B^2 E(\sigma_B^2) + x_C E(\sigma_C^2) \\
&+ 2\rho_{A,B} x_A x_B \sigma_A \sigma_B + 2\rho_{A,C} x_A x_C \sigma_A \sigma_C \\
&+ 2\rho_{B,C} x_B x_C \sigma_B \sigma_C
\end{aligned}
\tag{29}
$$

---

[11] The bounds for any three interlinked correlation coefficients (say, ρ_{12}, ρ_{13}, and ρ_{23}) can be described as

$$
\rho_{12} \times \rho_{13} + \sqrt{(1 - \rho_{12}^2)(1 - \rho_{13}^2)} \geq \rho_{23} \geq \rho_{12} \times \rho_{13} - \sqrt{(1 - \rho_{12}^2)(1 - \rho_{13}^2)}
\tag{27}
$$

Thus, in Exhibit 2A–1, the bounds for Case 4, which has correlation coefficients of $\rho_{AB} = -.25$ and $\rho_{AC} = .25$, relative to ρ_{BC} are given by

$$
1.0 \geq \rho_{BC} \geq -.875
$$

Accordingly, the assumed value ($\rho_{BC} = -.25$) for the third correlation coefficient falls within these limits.

EXHIBIT 2A–1
Inputs to Three-Asset Portfolio Optimization

Asset	Expected Return	Standard Deviation
A	12.0%	15.0%
B	10.0	10.0
C	4.0	5.0

Case 1: Correlation Matrix

Asset	A	B	C
A	1.00		
B	0.75	1.00	
C	0.75	0.75	1.00

Case 2: Correlation Matrix

Asset	A	B	C
A	1.00		
B	0.50	1.00	
C	0.50	0.50	1.00

Case 3: Correlation Matrix

Asset	A	B	C
A	1.00		
B	0.00	1.00	
C	0.00	0.00	1.00

Case 4: Correlation Matrix

Asset	A	B	C
A	1.00		
B	−0.25	1.00	
C	−0.25	−0.25	1.00

Exhibit 2A–2 combines the expected returns of each of three assets (as shown above) and computes an optimal combination of portfolio weights for each of the four correlation matrices shown in Exhibit 2A–1. Like Exhibit 2–6, Exhibit 2A–2 indicates the powerful reduction in portfolio volatility that accompanies the combination of asset returns with low to negative correlations. For example, consider

EXHIBIT 2A-2
Three-Asset Portfolio under Different Correlation Matrices

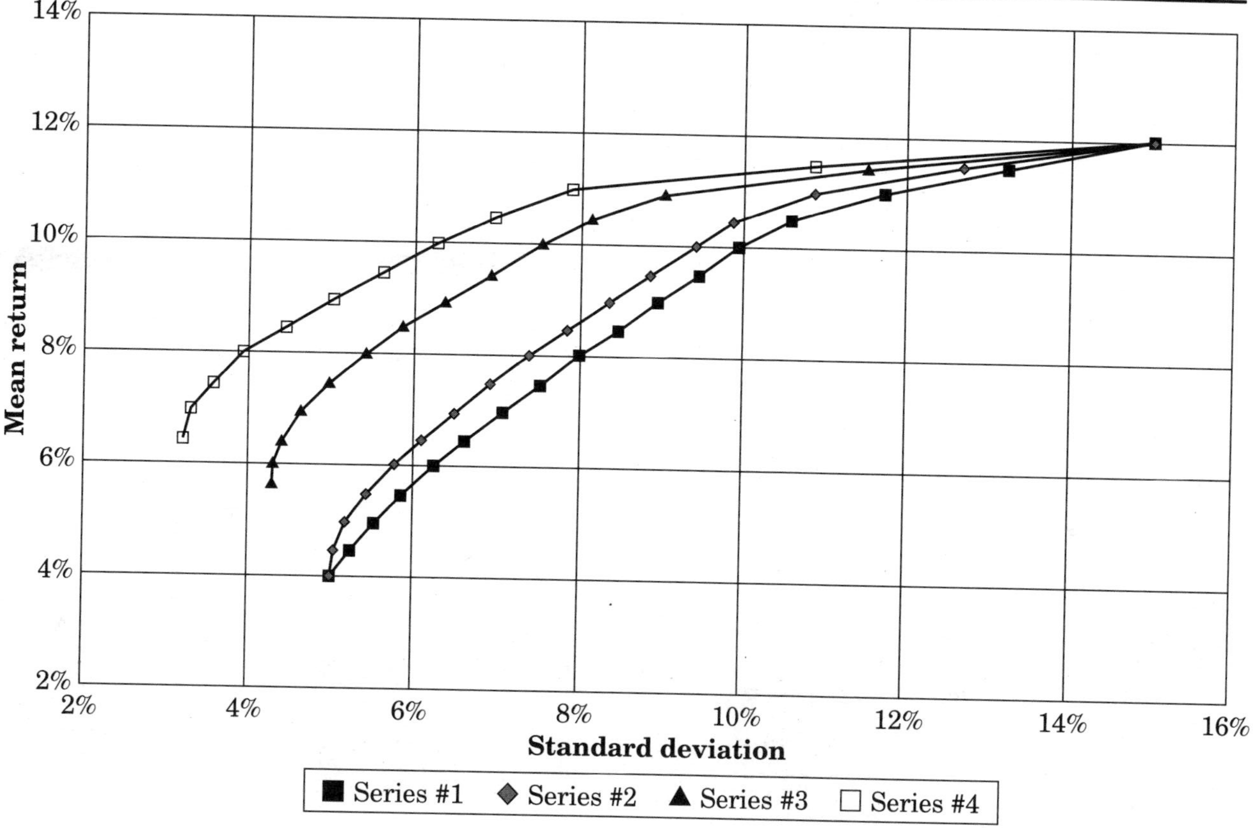

Mean return (y-axis): 2%, 4%, 6%, 8%, 10%, 12%, 14%

Standard deviation (x-axis): 2%, 4%, 6%, 8%, 10%, 12%, 14%, 16%

Legend: Series #1, Series #2, Series #3, Series #4

the four portfolios at the 8 percent return level. Under Case 1, the portfolio's standard deviation is also approximately 8 percent, while under Case 4, the portfolio's standard deviation is reduced by approximately half.

APPENDIX 2B THE UNDERPINNINGS OF THE CAPM

Investors can purchase various combinations of the risk-free asset and the market portfolio. The combinations are a linear function of the risk-free rate (R_f), the expected return on the market portfolio $[E(R_m)]$, and the degree of portfolio risk that the investor wishes to bear (σ_p). The expected return on such a portfolio is defined as

$$E(R_p) = R_f + \frac{E(R_m) - R_f}{\sigma_m} \times \sigma_p \qquad (30)$$

where σ_m = Standard deviation of market portfolio.

Fundamentally, equation (30) suggests that investors should hold only the market portfolio and the risk-free asset in proportions that depend on their degree of preferred risk exposure. That is, one investor may want to hold only the market portfolio, another investor may want to hold only the risk-free asset, and a third investor may choose to hold equal shares of both. In any case, investors will want to hold some combination of the risk-free rate and the market portfolio.

Equation (30) can be rewritten to reflect the importance of the asset's correlation with the market portfolio:

$$E(R_i) = R_f + \left[\frac{E(R_m) - R_f}{\sigma_m}\right]\rho_{i,m}\sigma_i \qquad (31)$$

where $\rho_{i,m}$ = Correlation coefficient between the return on the ith asset and the market portfolio.

A little algebra allows us to rewrite equation (31) as

$$E(R_i) = R_f + \left[\frac{E(R_m) - R_f}{\sigma_m}\right]\frac{\rho_{i,m}\sigma_i\sigma_m}{\sigma_m} \qquad (32)$$

Since the covariance of the individual asset and the market portfolio $(\sigma_{i,m})$ is defined as $\rho_{i,m}\sigma_i\sigma_m$, we can rewrite equation (32) in the following form:

$$E(R_i) = R_f + \left[\frac{E(R_m) - R_f}{\sigma_m}\right]\frac{\sigma_{i,m}}{\sigma_m} \qquad (33)$$

A final bit of algebra allows us to present the capital asset pricing model (CAPM) in its best-known form:

$$E(R_i) = R_f + [E(R_m) - R_f]\beta_i \qquad (34)$$

The variance of returns on asset i is shown as

$$\sigma_i^2 = \beta_i^2\sigma_m^2 + \sigma_\varepsilon^2 \qquad (35)$$

where $\sigma_\varepsilon^2 =$ Variance of the residual terms.

REFERENCES

Black, Fischer; Michael C. Jensen; and Myron Scholes. "The Capital Asset Pricing Model: Some Empirical Tests." In M. Jensen, ed., *Studies on the Theory of Capital Markets.* New York: Praeger, 1972.

Black, Fischer, and Myron Scholes. "The Pricing of Options and Corporate Liabilities." *Journal of Political Economy,* May–June 1973, pp. 637–59.

Bodie, Zvi; Alex Kane; and Alan J. Marcus. *Essentials of Investment.* Homewood, IL: Richard D. Irwin, 1992.

Chan, K. C.; Patric Hendershott; and Anthony Sanders. "Risk and Return and Real Estate: Evidence from Equity REITs." *AREUEA Journal,* Winter 1990.

Chan, K. C., and Josef Lakonishok. "Are Reports of Beta's Death Premature?" *Journal of Portfolio Management,* Summer 1993, pp. 51–62.

Chao, Lincoln L. *Statistics for Management.* Monterey, CA: Brooks/Cole, 1980, pp. 225–27.

Chen, Nai-fu; Richard Roll; and Stephen Ross. "Economic Forces and the Stock Market: Testing the APT and Alternative Asset Pricing Theories." *Journal of Business* 59 (July 1986), pp. 383–403.

Christensen, Peter E; Frank J. Fabozzi; and Anthony LoFaso. "Bond Immunization: An Asset Liability Optimization Strategy" and "Dedicated Bond Portfolios." In F. J. Fabozzi, ed., *The Handbook of Fixed Income Securities.* 3rd ed. Homewood, IL: Business One Irwin, 1991, pp. 912–58.

Cox, John C., and Mark Rubenstein. *Option Markets.* Englewood Cliffs, NJ: Prentice Hall, 1985.

Fabozzi, Frank J.; Mark Pitts; and Ravi Dattatrega. "Price Volatility Characteristics of Fixed Income Securities." In F. J. Fabozzi, ed., *The Handbook
of Fixed Income Securities*. 3rd ed. Homewood, IL: Business One Irwin,
1991, pp. 124–26.

Fama, Eugene F. "Efficient Capital Markets: II." *Journal of Finance,* December 1991, pp. 1575–1617.

Fama, Eugene F., and Kenneth R. French. "The Cross-Section of Expected
Stock Returns." *Journal of Finance Studies* 47 (1992), pp. 427–65.

Fama, Eugene F., and James MacBeth. "Risk, Return, and Equilibrium:
Empirical Tests." *Journal of Political Economy* 81 (1973), pp. 607–36.

Firstenberg, Paul M.; Stephan A. Ross; and Randall C. Zisler. "Real Estate:
The Whole Story." *Journal of Portfolio Management,* Spring 1988, pp.
22–34.

Fisher, Lawrence, and James H. Lorie. "Some Studies of the Variability of
Returns on Investments in Common Stocks." *Journal of Business,* April
1970, pp. 99–134.

Giliberto, S. Michael. "Managing Real Estate Duration: A New Perspective
on the Use of Leverage." New York: Salomon Brothers, Inc., October 1989.

Gyourko, Joseph, and Donald Keim. "What Does the Stock Market Tell Us
about Real Estate Returns?" *AREUEA Journal,* Fall 1992, pp. 457–85.

Hartzell, David. "An Updated Look at the Size of the Institutional Grade
Property Market." *Journal of Real Estate Research,* Spring 1994, pp.
197–212.

Hartzell, David; J. Hekman; and M. Miles. "Real Estate Returns and Inflation." *AREUEA Journal* 15 (1987).

Hartzell, David J.; David G. Shulman; Terrence C. Langetieg; and Martin
L. Leibowitz. "A Look at Real Estate Duration." *Journal of Portfolio Management,* Fall 1988, pp. 16–24.

Holton, Glyn A. "Time: The Second Dimension of Risk." *Financial Analysts
Journal,* November–December 1992, pp. 38–45.

Jensen, Michael C. "Risk, the Pricing of Capital Assets, and the Evolution
of Investment Portfolios." *Journal of Business,* April 1969, pp. 167–247.

Karnosky, Denis S. "Management of the Asset Allocation Decision: Part
I." In Susan Hudson-Wilson, ed., *Real Estate: Valuation Techniques and
Portfolio Management* seminar proceedings, October 1988.

Kritzman, Mark P. "Asset Allocation for Institutional Portfolios." Homewood, IL: Richard D. Irwin, 1990.

Lakonishok, Josef, and Alan C. Shapiro. "Systematic Risk, Total Risk and
Size as Determinants of Stock Market Returns." *Journal of Banking and
Finance* 10 (1986), pp. 115–32.

Macaulay, Frederick. "Some Theoretical Problems Suggested by the Movements of Interest Rates, Bond Yields, and Stock Prices in the United States Since 1856." New York: National Bureau of Economic Research, 1938.

Malkiel, Burton G. *A Random Walk Down Wall Street*. New York: W. W. Norton, 1990, pp. 24, 181–85.

Mandelbrot, Benoit B. *The Fractal Geometry of Nature*. New York: W. M. Freeman, 1982.

Markowitz, Harry. "Portfolio Selection." *Journal of Finance,* March 1952, pp. 77–91.

Miles, Mike. "What Is the Value of All U.S. Real Estate?" *Real Estate Review,* Summer 1990, pp. 69–75.

Myer, Neil, and James R. Webb. "Return Properties of Equity REITs, Common Stocks, and Commercial Real Estate: A Comparison." Unpublished mimeo, Cleveland State University, 1992.

Myer, F. C. Neil, and James R. Webb. "Statistical Properties of Returns: Financial Assets versus Commercial Real Estate." Forthcoming in *Journal of Real Estate Finance and Economics*.

Paulos, John Allen. *Beyond Numeracy: Ruminations of a Numbers Man*. New York: Alfred A. Knopf, 1991, p. 35.

Peters, Edgar E. "Fractal Structure in the Capital Markets." *Financial Analysts Journal*, July–August 1989, pp. 32–37.

Pozsonyi, Deborah, and Anthony B. Sanders. "REITs and the Small-Firm Effect." Unpublished mimeo, University of Chicago, 1994.

Reinganum, Marc R. "A Direct Test of Roll's Conjecture on the Firm Size Effect." *Journal of Finance* 37 (1982), pp. 27–35.

Ritter, Jay R., and Navin Chopra. "Portfolio Rebalancing and the Turn-of-the-Year Effect." *Journal of Finance* 44 (1989), pp. 149–66.

Roll, Richard. "A Critique of the Asset Pricing Theory's Tests; Part I: On Past and Potential Testability of the Theory." *Journal of Financial Economics,* March 1977, pp. 129–76.

Ross, Stephen A. "Arbitrage Theory of Capital Asset Pricing." *Journal of Economic Theory,* December 1976, pp. 341–60.

Sharpe, William F. "Capital Asset Prices: A Theory of Market Equilibrium under Conditions of Risk." *Journal of Finance,* September 1964, pp. 425–42.

Sharpe, William F. "Mutual Fund Performance." *Journal of Business,* supplement on security prices, January 1966, pp. 119–38.

Sharpe, William F. "A Simplified Model for Portfolio Analysis." *Management Science,* January 1963, pp. 277–93.

Titman, Sheridan, and Arthur Warga. "Risk and Performance of Real Estate Investment Trusts: A Multiple Index Approach." *AREUEA Journal,* Fall 1986, pp. 414–31.

Treynor, Jack. "How to Rate Management of Investment Funds." *Harvard Business Review,* January–February 1965, pp. 63–75.

Webb, James R. "On the Exclusion of Real Estate from the Market Portfolio." *Journal of Portfolio Management,* Fall 1990, pp. 78–84.

Webb, James R.; Richard J. Curcio; and Jack H. Rubens. "Diversification Gains from Including Real Estate in Mixed-Asset Portfolios." *Decision Sciences,* Spring 1988, pp. 434–52.

Webb, James R., and Jack H. Rubens. "How Much in Real Estate? A Surprising Answer." *Journal of Portfolio Management,* Spring 1987, pp. 10–14.

Williams, Terry. "AEW Uses Swaps in Realty Deal." *Pensions & Investments,* March 8, 1993, pp. 2, 31.

Williams, Terry. "IBM Swaps Property for REIT Shares." *Pensions & Investments,* February 8, 1993, pp. 1, 39.

Williams, Terry. "Ohio Sells Properties to REIT." *Pensions & Investments,* August 23, 1993, pp. 1, 33.

CHAPTER 3

THE CHARACTERISTICS OF REAL ESTATE RETURNS AND THEIR ESTIMATION

James R. Webb
Real Estate Research Center
James J. Nance College of Business
Cleveland State University

Joseph L. Pagliari, Jr.
Citadel Realty, Inc.

INTRODUCTION

The heterogeneity of real estate investments is a theme echoed throughout this book. At a minimum, real estate can be classified along the dimensions of property type, geographic location, and its stage in the property life cycle, among others. Moreover, there exists a rich stratification reflecting the subtleties and nuances found within each of these coarse dimensions. Layered on these three dimensions are various investment and capital structures.[1]

Notwithstanding the virtually limitless combinations of property characteristics and investment and capital structures, the investor's goal is always to maximize the risk-adjusted return. This objective is best achieved when the primary focus is on the real estate itself, as the asset value is largely independent of the degree and type of leverage used (see Modigliani and Miller [1958]).

Accordingly, this chapter provides a framework for analyzing real estate returns and the nature of their risks. As an extension of

---

[1] Examples of various investment structures include partnerships, commingled open- and closed-end funds, real estate investment trusts, and so on. Examples of various capital structures include a range of leverage ratios and use a variety of debt structures, including conventional, participating, and convertible debt.

examining risk and return, real estate returns are broken down into their component parts. This attribution of returns should enable investors to better understand historical and prospective returns. Next, the chapter examines the question of real estate's volatility. Essentially, the question of measured (or reported) volatility largely depends on the reliability of appraised values. Conventional wisdom suggests that appraisal values understate real estate's reported volatility. Finally, the chapter analyzes real estate's correlation within the asset class itself. This analysis begins to address the systematic versus unsystematic risk components of real estate's investment performance.

The three focal points of this chapter—return, volatility, and covariance—are the key inputs to optimizing a multi-asset portfolio (see Markowitz [1952]). Since investors setting future portfolio allocations must estimate these measures of investment performance, a thorough understanding of these components is paramount to successful real estate and/or mixed-asset portfolio allocations. This chapter offers some insights into this daunting challenge. Much of the discussion and analysis is directed toward estimating the return-generating process, and successively less time is devoted to variances and covariances. In part, this is due to the assertion (see Chopra and Ziemba [1993]) that in the context of optimizing a multi-asset portfolio according to its mean/variance efficiency, errors in predicting mean returns are significantly more damaging than errors in variances, which in turn are more damaging than errors in covariances.

GENERAL FINANCIAL FRAMEWORK

A widely accepted premise of finance is that the current value of an asset equals the discounted value of its future cash flow stream.[2] Algebraically, this relationship is shown in equation (1):

---

[2] This proposition can be found in any number of finance textbooks. For example, see Francis (1980).

$$P_0 = \sum_{n=1}^{N} \frac{CF_n}{(1 + k)^n} \tag{1}$$

where P_0 = Today's price.

CF_n = Cash flow in the nth period.

n = Discrete time periods of equal length.

N = Terminal time period.

k = Discount rate.

With various degrees of precision, this general financial framework is applied to stocks, bonds, real estate, and other assets.

The solutions derived from this valuation approach can sometimes also be given by the dividend discount model (DDM). This model serves as a platform for a more specific analysis of real estate returns known as IRR attribution. Each is discussed next.

The Dividend Discount Model

The so-called Gordon-Shapiro (1956) dividend discount model simplifies equation (1) to the following:

$$P_0 = \frac{CF_0(1 + g)}{k - g} = \frac{CF_1}{k - g} \tag{2}$$

where g = Constant growth rate of cash flow.

The result, in terms of P_0, from equation (2) will exactly equal the result as computed by equation (1) when the following conditions are met:

- The growth rate (g) of cash flow is constant (i.e., $CF_n = CF_0(1 + g)^n$ and $g_1 = g_2 = \ldots g_n$).
- The discount rate (k) is constant (i.e., $k_1 = k_2 = \ldots k_n$).
- The holding period (N) is infinite (i.e., $N = \infty$) or, at the end of some finite holding period, the asset is sold at the same capitalization rate at which it was purchased (i.e., $CF_0/P_0 = CF_N/P_N$).
- Transaction costs are ignored.

In the area of common stock valuation, this model and its many variations are widely used by so-called fundamental (versus technical) analysts. However, in applying the DDM (and its simplifying assumptions) to common stocks, the stock analyst often encounters the following obstacles:

- The need to convert projected earnings per share (often based on inconsistently applied accounting principles) into dividends per share.
- The complexity of estimating earnings per share in companies with several operating divisions and very different product lines.
- The rapid obsolescence of many companies' products (compared to real estate's long useful life).
- The threat of domestic and foreign competition for many publicly held companies.
- The potential for foreign exchange losses in companies with overseas operations.

In addition, stock analysts are typically required to estimate the portion of the firm's earnings that will be retained to help fuel future income growth.

The DDM Applied to Real Estate

The dividend discount model can also be applied to real estate; see Pagliari (1991), from which much of the following discussion is adapted.

Because of the nature of the stabilized cash flow patterns generally associated with seasoned, unleveraged real estate equity investments, the DDM may be more suitable to the valuation of real estate than to that of common stocks. Consider: The typical real estate pro forma assumes stabilized revenues and expenses that often grow at some constant rate over the projected holding period. At the conclusion of the expected holding period, the pro forma assumes the property will be sold for a price based on a capitalization rate approximately equal to the rate used to acquire the property. These assumptions are generally in keeping with the requirements of the DDM noted above.

The application of the DDM to real estate equity investments involves adhering to the simplifying assumptions noted above (and these assumptions can sometimes be unrealistic). However, their simplistic purity reveals three meaningful insights:

1. The IRR (k) equals the capitalization rate plus growth.
2. The real (versus nominal) yield is largely a function of the capitalization rate.
3. The DDM approach can be used to decompose the nominal yield (or IRR) into its meaningful attributes.

IRR Equals Capitalization Rate Plus Growth Rate

The first insight is that, given the simplifying assumptions noted previously are met, the yield (IRR) of a stabilized, unleveraged real property portfolio is equal to the capitalization rate plus the growth rate. Exhibit 3–1 provides an example of this additive relationship. If, for example, a property is bought and sold at a capitalization rate of 7 percent and the growth rate is 4 percent, these two factors provide

EXHIBIT 3–1

Relationship among Capitalization Rate, Growth Rate, and Expected Return for Hypothetical Unleveraged Property: Example 1

Major assumptions:	
Purchase price	$10,000,000
Expected NOI (upcoming 12 months)	$700,000
Growth rate	4.0%
Holding period	5 years
Capitalization rate at disposition	7.0%
Transaction costs	0.0%
Income taxes	0.0%
Leverage	0.0%

Present Value of Property Operations

	Year 1	Year 2	Year 3	Year 4	Year 5
Expected NOI	$700,000	$728,000	$757,120	$787,405	$818,901
Discount factor @ 11%	0.9009	0.8116	0.7312	0.6587	0.5935
Present value	$630,631	$590,861	$553,600	$518,688	$485,978

Present Value of Disposition (Year 5)

Expected NOI (year 6)	$ 851,657
Capitalization rate	7.0%
Expected selling price	$12,166,529
Discount factor @ 11%	0.5935
Present value	$ 7,220,243

Summary of Present Value Contributors

From operations:	
Year 1	$ 630,631
Year 2	590,861
Year 3	553,600
Year 4	518,688
Year 5	485,978
From disposition	7,220,243
Total	$10,000,000

the unleveraged equity investor with a yield of 11 percent per annum. Provided the constraints of the DDM are met, this relationship between the yield and the capitalization and growth rates holds true across all combinations of capitalization and growth rates.

As another example, assume a property is bought and sold at a capitalization rate of 9 percent with a 3 percent growth rate (see Exhibit 3–2). As before, the yield (k) equals the sum of the capitalization and growth rates.

The terms of equation (2) can be rearranged as follows:

$$k = \frac{CF_1}{P_0} + g \qquad (3)$$

Thus, equation (3) reiterates that the yield (k) equals the sum of the capitalization rate (CF_1/P_0) and the constant rate of growth (g).

EXHIBIT 3–2

Relationship among Capitalization Rate, Growth Rate, and Expected Return for Hypothetical Unleveraged Property: Example 2

Major assumptions:

Purchase price	$10,000,000
Expected NOI (upcoming 12 months)	$900,000
Growth rate	3.0%
Holding period	5 years
Capitalization rate at disposition	9.0%
Transaction costs	0.0%
Income taxes	0.0%
Leverage	0.0%

Present Value of Property Operations

	Year 1	Year 2	Year 3	Year 4	Year 5
Expected NOI	$900,000	$927,000	$954,810	$983,454	$1,012,958
Discount factor @ 12%	0.8929	0.7972	0.7118	0.6355	0.5674
Present value	$803,571	$738,999	$679,615	$625,003	$ 574,780

Present Value of Disposition (Year 5)

Expected NOI (year 6)	$ 1,043,347
Capitalization rate	9.0%
Expected selling price	$11,592,741
Discount factor @ 12%	0.5674
Present value	$ 6,578,032

Summary of Present Value Contributions

From operations:	
Year 1	$ 803,571
Year 2	738,999
Year 3	679,615
Year 4	625,003
Year 5	574,780
From disposition	6,578,032
Total	$10,000,000

Alternatively, this may be stated as follows: The capitalization rate equals the total yield less the expected growth rate. This perspective offers certain insights that may be overlooked if the investor focuses merely on the IRR (or k). It reveals the importance of the capitalization rate (or initial yield) and the meaninglessness of the IRR in the absence of knowledge about the growth (or inflation) rate.

Growth Rates and Inflation

In many instances, the property's cash flow growth rate can be conceptually linked to the economywide inflation rate. The growth rate can be thought of as the product of the economy's inflation rate (ρ) and the asset's ability (λ) to pass through this inflationary increase in prices to increased cash flow. That is,

$$g = \lambda\rho \tag{4}$$

where λ = Inflation pass-through rate.
ρ = Inflation rate.

This relationship can also be used to amend equation (2) as follows:

$$P_0 = \frac{CF_0(1 + \lambda\rho)}{k - \lambda\rho} \tag{5}$$

In the special case of a 100 percent inflation pass-through (i.e., $\lambda = 1.0$), the growth rate (g) equals the inflation rate. This can be thought of as the equilibrium case, where the property markets' supply and demand factors operate in harmony.

In all other instances (i.e., $\lambda \neq 1.0$), the market can be said to be operating in disequilibrium. In these instances, supply and demand are out of balance, creating either a renters' or a landlords' market depending in which direction the relative advantage has swung.

Cap Rates, Inflation, and Real Returns

The conversion from the nominal return (k) to a real (i.e., inflation-adjusted) return (r) is accomplished via

$$r = \frac{1 + k}{1 + \rho} - 1 \tag{6}$$

In the special case of 100 percent inflation pass-through, the capitalization rate is a rough first approximation of the investment's real (as opposed to nominal) yield. However, the capitalization rate (in this special case) overstates the real yield by the inflationary increase embedded in the first year's (or first period's) net operating income. The real yield (r) equals the first year's capitalization rate divided by 1 plus the inflation rate. Algebraically, this relationship and its variations can be summarized as follows:

$$r = \frac{\frac{CF_1}{P_0}}{1 + g} = \frac{CF_0}{P_0} = \frac{k - g}{1 + g} = \frac{1 + k}{1 + g} - 1 \tag{7}$$

if and only if $g = \rho$

Thus, under these simple assumptions, real estate is an inflation-indexed asset and the capitalization rate (based on CF_0) indicates the investment's real return. Applying the terms of equation (7) to Exhibit 3–1 indicates that although this investment provides a nominal yield of 11 percent, its real yield is 6.73 percent. This can be computed as follows:

$$r = \frac{\frac{CF_1}{P_0}}{1 + g} = \frac{CF_0}{P_0} = \frac{k - g}{1 + g} = \frac{1 + k}{1 + g} - 1 \tag{7}$$

$$r = \frac{.07}{1 + .04} = \frac{700,000/1.04}{10,000,000} = \frac{.11 - .04}{1 + .04} = \frac{1 + .11}{1 + 0.4} - 1$$
$$= 6.73\% \tag{7a}$$

This approach can also be applied to Exhibit 3–2. However, in this case the inflation pass-through rate is 75 percent (i.e., $g = 3\%$ and $\rho = 4\%$; therefore, $\lambda = 75\%$). Thus, equation (6) must be used:

$$r = \frac{1 + k}{1 + \rho} - 1 \tag{6}$$

$$r = \frac{1 + .12}{1 + .04} - 1 = 7.69\% \tag{6a}$$

This presentation can also be interpreted to suggest, as have Hartzell et al. (1988), that the pricing of real estate will be unaffected by changes in the inflation rate that are fully reflected in the growth rate (i.e., $\lambda = 1.0$) and the discount rate (k).[3] In all other cases (i.e., $\lambda \neq 1.0$), the pricing will be affected by a change in the inflation rate. To see why this is the case, let's expand the basic DDM (equation [2]) by incorporating the more general form of the growth rate (noted in equation [5]) and a restatement of the discount rate (k) from equation (6). Then equation (2) can be expanded to

$$P_0 = \frac{CF_0(1 + \lambda\rho)}{(1 + r)(1 + \rho) - 1 - \lambda\rho} \tag{9}$$

In the special case of $\lambda = 1.0$, equation (9) reduces to

$$P_0 = \frac{CF_0}{r} \tag{10}$$

Equation (10) suggests that today's price (as measured by its investment value) for an asset with cash flows fully indexed to inflation is simply the asset's initial cash flow (CF_0) capitalized at the investor's required real return. Alternatively stated, the real yield in this special case is found in the capitalization rate (CF_0/P_0), which is also equation (7).

A simple view of the relationships between the inflation pass-through (λ) and the real return (r) as they affect price (P_0) is illustrated in Exhibit 3–3. As shown, when the inflation pass-through rate (λ) equals 100 percent, the price of the property does not change for a given real return. For example, at a 5 percent real return, the value of a property (P_0) generating initial cash flow (CF_0) of $1,000 is $20,000, regardless of whether the inflation rate is 3.0 percent or 5.0 percent.

However, as the inflation pass-through rate drops below 100 percent, the value of the property decreases, at a decreasing rate. Using the sample of a 3 percent inflation rate and a 5 percent required real return, the property's value drops from $20,000 to $17,331 (or by 13.3 percent) as the inflation pass-through rate drops from 100 to 75 percent; when the inflation pass-through rate drops from 25 to 0

---

[3] For these purposes, it is assumed that k is determined by

$$k = (1 + \rho)(1 + \bar{r}) - 1 \tag{8}$$

where $\bar{r}$ = Expected real, risk premium.

EXHIBIT 3–3

Relationship between Inflation Pass-Through Rate and Required Real Return Measured by Required Price (P_0)

Assumptions:
Lease length   1 year
Initial cash flow, CF_0 $1,000

		Inflation Pass-Through Rate					
		0%	25%	50%	75%	100%	125%
	3.0%	$16,420	$18,867	$22,113	$26,628	$33,333	$44,338
Required	4.0	14,045	15,816	18,060	20,996	25,000	30,786
real	5.0	12,270	13,615	15,263	17,331	20,000	23,580
return	6.0	10,893	11,951	13,216	14,755	16,667	19,107
	7.0	9,794	10,650	11,653	12,845	14,286	16,060
	8.0	8,897	9,604	10,421	11,374	12,500	13,852

Inflation rate = 3.0%

		Inflation Pass-Through Rate					
		0%	25%	50%	75%	100%	125%
	3.0%	$12,270	$14,674	$18,142	$23,580	$33,333	$55,921
Required	4.0	10,870	12,736	15,299	19,037	25,000	36,017
real	5.0	9,756	11,250	13,226	15,962	20,000	26,563
return	6.0	8,850	10,075	11,648	13,742	16,667	21,040
	7.0	8,097	9,122	10,406	12,064	14,286	17,418
	8.0	7,463	8,333	9,404	10,751	12,500	14,860

Inflation rate = 5.0%

Note: Assumes either an infinite holding period or property is sold at the same capitalization rate at which it was purchased.

percent, the property's value drops from $13,615 to $12,270 (or by 9.9 percent). The opposite is true when the inflation pass-through rate increases above 100 percent. Then the property's value rises at an increasing rate.

A decline in the desired real return (r) translates into an increasing property value, at an increasing rate. Using the example of a 3 percent inflation rate and a 100 percent inflation pass-through rate, the property's value increases from $20,000 to $25,000 (or by 25 percent) as the required real return decreases from 5 to 4 percent; when the required real return drops yet further from 4 to 3 percent, the property's value increases to $33,333 from $20,000 (or by 66.7 percent). The opposite is also true when the desired real return decreases. Then the property's value decreases at a declining rate.

Obviously, the sensitivity of property values to changes in the desired real return and the inflation pass-through rate is important and complex.[4] Moreover, there is reason to believe that these two variables are inversely correlated on an ex ante basis. That is, when investors are unsure of the disequilibrium in the market (which manifests itself in an inflation pass-through rate of less than 100 percent), they may increase their required real (ex ante) return requirements to compensate themselves for the lack of inflation indexation and an uncertain ex ante inflation rate. Using a 50 percent inflation pass-through rate combined with a 5 percent required real return suggests, at a 3 percent inflation rate, a property value of $15,263, while an increase to a 5 percent inflation rate causes a decline in the price to $13,226. Clearly, investors should want some form of compensation (i.e., additional return) for bearing the uncertainty of future inflation rates.[5]

As shown in Exhibit 3–3, when the inflation pass-through rate (λ) equals 100 percent, the price of the property does not change for a given required real return. For example, at a 5 percent required real return, the value of a property (P_0) generating initial cash flow (CF_0) of $1,000 is $20,000, regardless of whether the inflation rate is 3.0 percent or 5.0 percent.

As the real estate community grows more sophisticated, it increasingly views its assets in terms of their ability to generate real

---

[4] More formally, the sensitivity of the property's value (P_0) can be given by taking the first derivative of the pricing function given by equation (9):

$$P_0 = \frac{CF_0(1 + \lambda\rho)}{(1 + r)(1 + \rho) - (1 + \lambda\rho)} \tag{9}$$

With respect to the inflation pass-through rate (λ) and the required real return (r), the partial derivative of the pricing function yields

$$\frac{\partial P_0}{\partial \lambda} = \frac{CF_0 \times \rho \times (1 + r)(1 + \rho)}{[(1 + r)(1 + \rho) - (1 + \lambda\rho)]^2} \tag{11}$$

$$\frac{\partial P_0}{\partial r} = \frac{-CF_0(1 + \lambda\rho)(1 + r)}{[(1 + r)(1 + \rho) - (+\lambda\rho)]^2} \tag{12}$$

The sensitivity of price can be estimated via equations (11) and (12). A similar approach can be found in Grieg and Young (1991).

[5] This analysis has assumed one-year leases. If leases are fixed and long term, a property's effective inflation pass-through rate declines, even if the property operates in a market characterized by equilibrium (see Hartzell et al. [1988]).

returns. Furthermore, performance-based compensation of advisors and syndicators is often tied to real returns. Thus, a clear understanding of the determinants of real return is crucial.

IRR Attribution

Any violation of the assumptions needed to satisfy the requirements of the DDM assumptions will potentially convey additional useful information. All operating, financial, and/or valuation "frictions" that violate the DDM assumptions must be separately identified. These violations, along with the fundamental factors (of CF_0/P_0 and g), result in the ability to specifically attribute a project's return (or yield) to its individual components. This technique can be used to analyze and attribute prospective (ex ante) or historical (ex post) returns.

Real-world complexities are perhaps best described by example. Exhibit 3–4 describes two hypothetical investments with equivalent

EXHIBIT 3–4
IRR Attribution for Two Hypothetical Investments

	To-Be-Developed Office Building	Existing Apartment Complex
Stabilized yield*	10.0%	7.0%
Inflationary expectation	4.0	4.0
Base yield	14.0%	11.0%
Construction period	−0.3	0.0
Lease-up period	−0.4	0.0
Rent concessions	−0.6	0.0
Fixed leases	−0.5	0.0
Market disequilibrium	−1.0	0.2
Operating frictions	−1.0	0.0
Change in capitalization rates	1.6	−0.8
Disposition costs	−0.2	−0.2
Real estate yield	11.6%	10.2%
Benefits/(costs) of leverage	0.0	0.0
Benefits/(costs) of income taxes	0.0	0.0
Costs of partners/advisors	−1.5	−1.0
Investor's nominal yield	10.1%	9.2%
Investor's real yield	5.9%	5.0%

* Capitalization rate based on CF_1, which for commercial properties is before tenant improvements and leasing commissions.

long-term holding periods. Both the to-be-developed office building and the stabilized apartment complex are (or will be) well built, located, and operated.

Those complications that violate the assumptions of the DDM can be explicitly attributed to various components of a project's total return (IRR attribution). As indicated in Exhibit 3–4, the "base yield" is an approximation of the high end of the project's overall nominal yield. However, the base yield is eroded by real-world complications that should be incorporated into the analysis. Because the buildings illustrated in Exhibit 3–4 differ in terms of property type and stage of the life cycle, the complications or "frictions" also differ.

Construction Period.   Obviously, with new construction some time delay occurs before the development begins to produce income. This delayed receipt of cash flow needs to be identified in the analysis.

Lease-up Period.   Similarly, until the newly developed property is fully leased, the expected stabilized yield will not be realized. This delay also needs to be identified.

Rental Concessions.   Many commercial tenants in "soft markets" have been able to negotiate substantial rent abatements. This has had the effect of "kinking" the growth in the income stream, and therefore rental income does not exhibit the continuous growth required under the DDM. Rent abatements are not features of most residential markets because lease terms are typically a year or less, and consequently concessions do not substantially affect the residential analysis.

Fixed Leases.   Many commercial leases fix all or a portion of the lease payments for a number of years. Thus, commercial rents may violate the DDM assumptions of constant growth; if so, these violations must be factored into the office building's disaggregated IRR. Most residential leases are written for one-year terms and are renewed annually at the then-prevailing market rental rate. If residential rental rates grow at a constant rate, they more closely conform to the growth requirement of the DDM.

Market Disequilibrium.   To the extent that markets operate in disequilibrium (i.e., $\lambda \neq 1.0$), the growth in rental rates is either faster or slower than the inflation rate. In the short run, no amount of inflation can fill the vacant space in a soft market. Conversely, in a "tight" market, landlords may be able to increase rental rates at a pace that exceeds the inflation rate. Of course, in the long run, all markets tend to move toward equilibrium. Exhibit 3–4 reduces the office building's base yield by 2 percent (i.e., assumed $\lambda = .50$) because it assumes the commercial landlord is unable to increase rental rates to match the rate of inflation. Exhibit 3–4 adds 0.2 percent (i.e., assumed $\lambda = 1.05$) to the apartment investment's yield to reflect the ability of that landlord to increase rental rates slightly faster than the rate of inflation.

Operating Frictions. The leasing of commercial properties involves substantial, periodic costs (primarily tenant improvements and leasing commissions). As with fixed leases and rental concessions, leasing costs change the income stream from a smooth curve that increases gradually to one with discrete periodic changes. Thus, for example, the operating income of a single-tenant commercial project is essentially understated in the years in which leasing commissions and tenant improvements are incurred and overstated in nonleasing years. In residential properties, rental costs typically recur annually, and they are usually incorporated into annual net operating income.

All of the preceding situations violate the continuous growth requirement of the DDM. The following violate other constraints.

Change in Capitalization Rates. Investments in newly developed properties should benefit from the "positive arbitrage" of capitalization rates. That is, the initial yield (defined as net income divided by the all-in development costs) should be, for example, 200 to 400 basis points higher than the capitalization rate used in the property's ultimate disposition.[6] Stabilized properties, on the other hand, tend to experience a slight increase in capitalization rates. In other words, the capitalization rate at which the property was acquired tends to

---

[6] New construction should provide an initial yield that is higher than existing facilities. Otherwise, there is no motivation to undertake the development risk. Nevertheless, in practice this may not be the case.

be lower than that used in pricing its sale. Regardless of property type, the increase in the capitalization rate over time for an individual property tends to occur because a building's finite life (or declining useful life) suggests that the present value of the remaining cash flow is less than that when the property was purchased or developed. This decline is reflected in an increasing capitalization (or discount) rate as the property ages. This notion of declining utility can also be used to explain why, in addition to market disequilibrium, the growth in cash flow (CF_n) fails to keep pace with inflation.

The significance of capitalization rate arbitrage declines with the projected holding period. In addition, changes in capitalization rates may also be a function of shifting investor perceptions (e.g., regarding risk and the relative attractiveness of real estate compared to stocks, bonds, etc.) and changes in interest rates.

Disposition Costs.   The disposition costs of real estate are very high compared to the disposition costs of financial assets. Thus, real estate also violates the DDM assumptions concerning transaction costs.

In Exhibit 3–4, each of the previously discussed elements was assumed to increase or decrease the base yield to produce a total yield. Once the total yield has been calculated, the deal's capital structure and the investor's income tax situation combine to reduce or enhance the yield of the particular real estate investment. These factors, along with the costs of any joint venture, partnership, or advisory relationship, then determine the investor's nominal yield, which in turn is adjusted for inflation, as described in equation (6), to determine the investor's real yield.

The amount attributed to each of the "frictions" (i.e., violations of the DDM) is computed by sequentially layering the frictions onto the cash flow pattern used to generate the base yield. A new internal rate of return (IRR) is then computed at each iteration. This difference in the IRR provides the amount attributed to that element. Additionally, the interaction between each of the frictions can result in some joint impacts. For purposes of this analysis, these joint impacts have been ratably allocated to each friction. In the future, perhaps some standardized convention will be adopted to ensure comparability among analyses.

Exhibit 3–4 has identified, through IRR attribution, the significant attributes of the total yield generated from two real estate equity investments. This attribution allows the sophisticated real estate investor to prospectively focus on the pro forma's key assumptions and make judgments about their reasonableness. Or, retrospectively, the investor can assess the violations of the DDM's simplifying assumptions that altered the historical yield. IRR attribution distills the attributes of an investment into its essential ingredients. Moreover, IRR attribution provides a framework for understanding the dynamics of the marketplace. These changing elements currently include the following: increasing capitalization (discount) rates, net operating income that fails to keep pace with inflation, operating frictions (e.g., fixed rent, free rent, tenant improvements) that further erode net operating income, and construction and lease-up periods that exert a downward drag on yield. While IRR attribution estimates the effect (or the expected effect) of a changing marketplace on the investor's yield, it does not determine the causes. The investor is simply directed toward those items affecting the yield.

IRR ATTRIBUTION APPLIED TO PROPERTY RETURNS

This section applies IRR attribution to the Russell/NCREIF Property Index.[7] This index comprises a large sample—approximately $22.0 billion as of December 31, 1993—of unleveraged institutional real estate investments for the period 1978 through 1993.

   While the preceding analysis attributed IRR components to a multitude of factors, the following analysis attributes the IRR to three fundamental sources: initial current yield, growth in net operating income (NOI), and pricing movements (i.e., capitalization rate changes). Given the growth in NOI (g) and inflation (ρ), the inflation pass-through rate (λ) can be calculated. See Pagliari and Webb (1992), and Webb and Pagliari (1994), from which much of the following discussion is adapted. As reported therein, several biases in the data and methodology should be noted.

   In addition to the total index, the Russell/NCREIF real estate returns can be disaggregated by property type and geographic location:

---

[7] As reported in the Russell/NCREIF Property Index, *Index Detail*, December 1993.

Property Type	Geographic Location
Office	East
Retail	Midwest
R&D/office	South
Warehouse	West
Apartment	

Based on the quarterly income and appreciation returns reported by Russell/NCREIF, it is possible to estimate the underlying NOI and property values used to create the index. From this reconstructed data series, the following elements of IRR attribution were identified.

Total Property Index

For the period January 1978 through December 1993, Exhibit 3–5 divides the Russell/NCREIF Total Property Index into the three fundamental components discussed above. The return components are grouped into four-year increments. The data are then summarized for the entire 16-year period. Several interesting observations about the return components can be made from Exhibit 3–5.

First, the initial current yield and the going-in capitalization rate followed a fairly steady downward path from the beginning of 1978 until an upturn appeared in early 1990. Thereafter, capitalization rates rose steadily through 1993. The period ended with an average capitalization rate of 9.15 percent, the highest reported over the 16-year history of the Russell/NCREIF index.

Second, for about the first subperiod, real estate returns benefited greatly from the downward pressure on capitalization rates. Especially in the first four-year period, a substantial positive return was generated from "cap rate arbitrage" (increasing property values due to declining capitalization rates). The middle subperiods experienced a general slowdown in the decline in capitalization rates, which contributed more modestly to each subperiod's return. The final subperiod witnessed a tremendous increase in capitalization rates, which in turn led to a dramatic decrease in the subperiod's total return.

More specifically with regard to capitalization rates, two observations are noteworthy:

- Even while the inflation rate grew substantially (at 10.5 percent per annum on average) in the 1978–81 period, capitaliza-

EXHIBIT 3–5

Total Index: Annualized Yield Attributes from 1978:1 through 1993:4

	1978–81 (4 Years)	1982–85 (4 Years)	1986–89 (4 Years)	1990–93 (4 Years)	1978–93 (16 Years)
Initial yield	8.66%	7.43%	7.16%	6.37%	8.66%
Growth in earnings*	4.62	2.33	-3.16	-0.49	0.79
Change in cap rate†	3.70	1.04	1.83	-7.44	-0.19
Estimated return	16.98%	10.80%	5.82%	-1.56%	9.25%
Timing/methodology differences	0.83%	0.66%	0.52%	-0.57%	-1.13%
Russell/NCREIF time-weighted returns:					
Nominal	17.81%	11.46%	6.34%	-2.14%	8.12%
Real	6.22%	7.33%	2.61%	-5.60%	2.51%
* Inflation:					
Annual rate	10.91%	3.85%	3.64%	3.67%	5.47%
Pass-through rate	42.30%	60.41%	-86.93%	-13.33%	14.39%
† Capitalization rates:					
Going-in rate	8.56%	7.35%	7.04%	6.51%	8.56%
Going-out rate	7.35%	7.04%	6.51%	9.15%	9.15%

tion rates fell (from 8.6 to 7.4 percent) during this period. This suggests that the capital markets did not necessarily require real estate equity investments to increase their current yield to keep pace with inflation. Thus, these periods of high inflation exhibited a negative spread between commercial real estate's current yield (or capitalization rate) and coupon rates on long-term bonds (which were increasing in response to higher inflation rates).

• The impact of pricing movements (i.e., capitalization rate changes) diminishes as the investment horizon lengthens. For example, the 1986–89 period saw an approximate 53-basis-point decline in capitalization rates, which translated into a 1.83 percent increase in total (annualized) return. However, the 1978–93 period saw a 60-basis-point increase in capitalization rates, but with a corresponding 0.19 percent decline in total (annualized) return. Clearly, the length of the holding period has a significant impact on the influence of pricing movements on total return.

At least as measured by the Russell/NCREIF Total Property Index, one of the more disappointing aspects of real estate's investment performance has been the inability of NOI growth to keep pace with inflation. Over the 16-year period of the Russell/NCREIF experience, the implied NOI grew at a rate of 0.78 percent per annum while inflation increased at 5.36 percent per annum. Alternatively stated, real estate investments saw NOI grow at approximately 15 percent of the inflation rate. If real estate investments are to act as an inflation hedge, NOI growth must be much closer to the rate of inflation. However, this inability may be partly a function of the composition of property types in the aggregate Russell/NCREIF Property Index. For example, NOI (as measured per square foot) for the apartment sector, which does not have the same available history as the other property types, has been shown to substantively keep pace with inflation (see Garrigan and Pagliari [1992]).

As time progresses, all three components generally weakened. Of these three components, the growth in net operating income and the pricing movements show the most serious declines.

The impact of data and methodology limitations is capsulized in the line item "timing/methodology differences" in Exhibit 3–5, which represents the difference between the estimated return (k) and the time-weighted, total Russell/NCREIF return. Generally, the differences are quite small.

Property Types

Of course, an analysis of aggregate data masks the performance of underlying property types and geographic regions. The following sections review the five major property types. An examination of regional variations in property returns follows.

The Office Sector

As shown in Exhibit 3–6, the return components for the office sector have been similar to the total index. Understandably, this similarity is attributable in part to the large weighting the office sector has in the total index. During certain periods, the office sector represented more than 50 percent of the total. However, the office sector's total returns have been more volatile than those of other property types (and therefore those of the total index as well). In the first subperiod, the office sector substantially outperformed the total index. In the two final subperiods, the performance of the office sector substantially lagged the overall index.

The capitalization rates found in the office sector also tend to be more volatile and generally lower than those in the total index. However, capitalization rates can be particularly deceiving, as this property class, particularly since the early 1980s, has been noted for the high cost of tenant improvements and leasing commissions, which tend to reduce cash flow.

The growth in net operating income is particularly disappointing. The average annual nominal growth rate of net operating income is slightly negative (-0.49 percent). On a nominal basis, net operating income (or cash flow) ended up below where it started. On a real (i.e., inflation-adjusted) basis, cash flow deteriorated at a fairly constant pace throughout the period. Some of this decline can be attributed to the inclusion of newly developed properties into the index, especially since the mid-1980s, which depressed actual NOI as these properties went through the lease-up phase. However, this does not explain the entire decline. Most of the explanation may reside in the substantial supply-demand imbalances that have occurred since the mid-1980s, which depressed rental and occupancy rates.

EXHIBIT 3–6

Office Index: Annualized Yield Attributes, 1978:1–1993:4

	1978–81 (4 Years)	1982–85 (4 Years)	1986–89 (4 Years)	1990–93 (4 Years)	1978–93 (16 Years)
Initial yield	8.97%	7.00%	6.84%	5.89%	8.97%
Growth in earnings*	6.97	3.24%	−6.79%	−3.38%	−0.49%
Change in cap rate†	5.31	0.79%	3.14%	−9.35%	−0.17%
Estimated return	21.25%	11.03%	3.19%	−6.84%	8.31%
Timing/methodology differences	0.49%	−0.25%	−0.23%	−0.68%	−1.86%
Russell/NCREIF time-weighted returns:					
Nominal	21.74%	10.78%	2.97%	−7.52%	6.45%
Real	9.76%	6.67%	−0.65%	−10.79%	0.93%
* Inflation:					
Annual rate	10.91%	3.85%	3.64%	3.67%	5.47%
Pass-through rate	63.90%	84.17%	−186.41%	−92.22%	−8.91%
† Capitalization rates:					
Going-in rate	8.82%	7.14%	6.91%	6.05%	8.82%
Going-out rate	7.14%	6.91%	6.05%	9.45%	9.45%

In addition to the issues raised for the aggregate index, certain particular caveats should be noted with regard to the office sector:

- There is a substantial "overhang" of existing supply.
- Demand/absorption rates appear to be slowing down.
- The future costs of tenant improvements, leasing commissions, "free rent," and so on as existing leases expire are expected to be high.
- No attempt is made to differentiate these forces and their impact on CBD versus suburban office properties.

Given historical precedent and adjustment to future trends (based on currently foreseeable market forces), it seems that the office sector's total real return over the upcoming 10 years may lag returns available from other property types.

The Retail Sector

Unlike in the office sector, the pattern of returns from the retail sector is significantly less volatile than the total index; see Exhibit 3–7. Again, several observations can be gleaned from examining the component returns of the retail sector:

- Throughout the mid-1980s, the retail sector enjoyed high capitalization rates, which helped to buoy returns in these periods. Since then, implied capitalization rates tended to decline through 1990. Beginning in 1991, capitalization rates began to increase.
- The retail sector's growth in net operating income has exceeded the total index. Nonetheless, net operating income growth has averaged less than 1.4 percent per annum, which was substantially below the rate of inflation, which averaged 5.36 percent per annum. The result has been slight increases in nominal NOI, with steadily deteriorating real NOI.
- The 1982–85 and 1986–89 subperiods represent an interesting example of how the marketplace can send mixed signals. While nominal NOI was increased at only 0.27 percent (on average) per annum,[8] capitalization rates dropped by approximately 172

---

[8] Of course, real (i.e., inflation-adjusted) net operating income actually declined at the rate of approximately 3.2 percent per annum.

EXHIBIT 3–7

Retail Index: Annualized Yield Attributes, 1978:1–1993:4

	1978–81 (4 Years)	1982–85 (4 Years)	1986–89 (4 Years)	1990–93 (4 Years)	1978–93 (16 Years)
Initial yield	8.14%	7.95%	7.24%	6.33%	8.14%
Growth in earnings*	2.12	0.38	0.16	0.54	1.39
Change in cap rate†	0.86	2.80	3.12	–6.01	0.07
Estimated return	11.12%	11.13%	10.52%	0.85%	9.61%
Timing/methodology differences	0.37%	1.38%	1.23%	0.74%	–0.37%
Russell/NCREIF time-weighted returns:					
Nominal	11.49%	12.50%	11.75%	1.60%	9.24%
Real	0.52%	8.33%	7.82%	–2.00%	3.57%
* Inflation:					
Annual rate	10.91%	3.85%	3.64%	3.67%	5.47%
Pass-through rate	19.44%	9.91%	4.52%	14.60%	25.39%
† Capitalization rates:					
Going-in rate	8.10%	7.81%	6.93%	6.09%	8.10%
Going-out rate	7.81%	6.93%	6.09%	7.93%	7.93%

basis points. Thus, investors were buying marginally increasing income streams at substantially more expensive multiples. Clearly, such a long-run practice is not in the investor's best interests.

- Of course, the perverse economics of the 1982–89 period could not last indefinitely (i.e., there is some limit to an environment in which both NOI and cap rates are declining). Beginning in the early 1990s, capitalization rates appear to have "bottomed out."

In the retail sector, several questions that could affect future returns need to be addressed:

- The economy and consumer spending.
- The financial problems with national and regional retailers.
- The changing purchasing patterns of consumers.
- The fact that the current yield is the lowest of any property type surveyed here.
- The lack of an attempt to differentiate between regional shopping centers (which generally trade at substantially lower capitalization rates) and community shopping centers.

The R&D/Office Sector

The R&D/office sector also displayed strong fundamentals through the mid-1980s. Thereafter, these fundamentals began to weaken substantially; see Exhibit 3–8.

Two additional observations should be made:

- Generally speaking, capitalization rates have been higher for this sector. However, like the other property types, there are indications that capitalization rates have also "bottomed out" here.
- This sector's growth in nominal earnings was also anemic. Its inflation pass-through rate was only slightly better than 10 percent. Consequently, NOI growth still significantly lagged the pace of inflation.

The underlying fundamentals of this property sector resemble a combination of the office sector and the warehouse sector. Accordingly, please review the office and warehouse sections.

EXHIBIT 3–8
R&D/Office Index: Annualized Yield Attributes, 1978:1–1993:4

	1978–81 (4 Years)	1982–85 (4 Years)	1986–89 (4 Years)	1990–93 (4 Years)	1978–93 (16 Years)
Initial yield	9.33%	7.36%	7.91%	7.43%	9.33%
Growth in earnings*	2.37	6.44	-3.67	-4.62	0.59
Change in cap rate†	4.89	0.69	0.65	-6.39	-0.11
Estimated return	16.59%	14.49%	4.89%	-3.58%	9.81%
Timing/methodology differences	0.78%	0.09%	1.66%	0.89%	-1.14%
Russell/NCREIF time-weighted returns:					
Nominal	17.37%	14.58%	6.55%	-2.69%	8.67%
Real	5.82%	10.34%	2.80%	-6.13%	3.03%
* Inflation:					
Annual rate	10.91%	3.85%	3.64%	3.67%	5.47%
Pass-through rate	21.76%	167.39%	-100.84%	-125.96%	10.72%
† Capitalization rates:					
Going-in rate	9.27%	7.55%	7.34%	7.14%	9.27%
Going-out rate	7.55%	7.34%	7.14%	9.66%	9.66%

The Warehouse Sector

The warehouse sector has been the strongest and most consistent performer of the major property types examined; see Exhibit 3–9. A review of its fundamental factors includes the following observations:

- In almost all periods, it has maintained fairly high (in a relative sense) and consistent capitalization rates. However, in 1993 capitalization rates increased dramatically.
- This sector had the highest rate of nominal NOI growth: 1.83 percent per annum. However, it was still unable to pass through increases in net operating income that were more than 35 percent of the inflation rate over the 16-year period. Somewhat surprising is the relatively high net operating income growth rate by a property type that is typically thought of as having long-term, fixed-rate leases.
- Like many other property sectors, this sector showed negative net operating income growth during the last two periods (1987–89 and 1990–91).

Compared to the office and retail markets, the warehouse sector has some very different fundamental factors:

- Much of the tenant demand is owner occupied (or single-user) and is customized.
- Relatively speaking, little of the market is built on "spec."
- Leases tend to be longer in length.
- Conversion of land to a higher use at some later date is sometimes possible.
- Concerns about the future course of the economy are combined with the financial leverage taken on by some industrial users during the 1980s LBO frenzy.

Again, these factors provide a partial context for estimating future industrial returns.

The Apartment Sector

Unfortunately, the data for the apartment sector begin 10 years later than those for the other property sectors. Nevertheless, some guarded observations (see Exhibit 3–10) can still be made:

- Capitalization rates have trended upward over the abbreviated time horizon. Moreover, the quarterly capitalization rates

EXHIBIT 3–9
Warehouse Index: Annualized Yield Attributes, 1978:1–1993:4

	1978–81 (4 Years)	1982–85 (4 Years)	1986–89 (4 Years)	1990–93 (4 Years)	1978–93 (16 Years)
Initial yield	8.26%	7.59%	7.36%	6.92%	8.26%
Growth in earnings*	4.90	3.08	0.16	−1.01	1.83
Change in cap rate†	2.43	−0.50	2.52	−7.29	−0.44
Estimated return	15.59%	10.17%	10.04%	−1.38%	9.66%
Timing/methodology differences	0.88%	1.00%	−0.05%	0.29%	−0.71%
Russell/NCREIF time-weighted returns:					
Nominal	16.47%	11.17%	10.00%	−1.09%	8.94%
Real	5.01%	7.05%	6.13%	−4.59%	3.29%
* Inflation:					
Annual rate	10.91%	3.85%	3.64%	3.67%	5.47%
Pass-through rate	44.92%	80.07%	4.49%	−27.58%	33.43%
† Capitalization rates:					
Going-in rate	8.16%	7.38%	7.54%	6.78%	8.16%
Going-out rate	7.38%	7.54%	6.78%	9.46%	9.46%

EXHIBIT 3–10
Apartment Index: Annualized Yield Attributes, 1988:1–1993:4

	1988–89 (2 Years)	1990–93 (4 Years)	1988–93 (6 Years)
Initial yield	6.64%	6.88%	6.64%
Growth in earnings*	3.12	5.59	4.14
Change in cap rate†	−2.97	−7.45	−5.50
Estimated return	6.79%	5.02%	5.29%
Timing/methodology differences	−0.17%	−0.66%	−0.18%
Russell/NCREIF time-weighted returns:			
Nominal	6.63%	4.36%	5.11%
Real	2.00%	0.67%	1.11%
* Inflation:			
Annual rate	4.53%	3.67%	3.96%
Pass-through rate	68.76%	152.27%	104.76%
† Capitalization rates:			
Going-in rate	6.64%	7.05%	6.64%
Going-out rate	7.05%	9.73%	9.73%

showed less volatility over this six-year period. This reduced volatility, in part, may be attributed to lower capital improvement and leasing commission costs, as well as their accounting treatment, since apartments typically expense (rather than capitalize) these normally recurring items.

- For the 1990–93 period (which is comparable to the other sectors), this sector had the largest net operating income increase of any property type. (In fact, the retail sector was the only other property type to show positive growth in NOI for this subperiod.)

- As a result of the interplay between capitalization rates and net operating income growth, reported property values had been fairly consistent through much of 1990. However, the dramatic increase in capitalization rates beginning in 1991 have more than offset increases in NOI such that nominal property values fell substantially in the 1990–93 subperiod.

Of course, certain supply/demand factors specific to apartments should be reviewed. These issues include

- The aging of the population.
- The affordability of owner-occupied housing.
- Rent control/governmental intervention.
- Relatively "tight" markets.
- Quality of construction vis-à-vis other property sectors.

The issues raised above provide an overview of the factors affecting such future returns.

Regional Patterns

Each of the four major regional classifications reported in the Russell/ NCREIF index are examined next.

The East Index

Of the regional indices, the East index showed the highest total return, averaging 10.77 percent per annum (or 5.02 percent as adjusted for inflation). The disaggregated yield for the East index is shown in Exhibit 3–11.

Certain elements of Exhibit 3–11 highlight the East's historical strength:

- The East index began with the highest initial yield (10.82 percent) of any regional sector. As noted previously, the initial yield is often the single most important determinant of total returns.
- There was substantial volatility in the estimated inflation pass-through rates. In the 1982–85 subperiod, the East had an inflation pass-through rate in excess of 280 percent. Nevertheless, the region had the second highest inflation pass-through rate (32.80 percent) over the 16-year period of any of the four regions.
- In part because of its high initial yield, the East also benefited from the period of falling capitalization rates. Over the 16-year period, the East region realized the highest yield increase due to pricing movements—0.34 percent per annum—of the four regions.

The East region merits several observations. First, the value of properties within the region is about equally divided between the Northeast (New York, Pennsylvania, New Jersey, and New England) and the Mideast (Virginia, the Carolinas, Maryland, Kentucky, and

EXHIBIT 3–11

East Index: Annualized Yield Attributes, 1978:1–1993:4

	1978–81 (4 Years)	1982–85 (4 Years)	1986–89 (4 Years)	1990–93 (4 Years)	1978–93 (16 Years)
Initial yield	10.82%	6.37%	7.39%	6.33%	10.82%
Growth in earnings*	2.73	10.79	−0.15	0.57	1.79
Change in cap rate†	8.48	0.84	2.06	−7.43	0.34
Estimated return	22.03%	17.99%	9.30%	−0.53%	12.96%
Timing/methodology differences	0.50%	−3.82%	0.49%	−1.44%	−2.19%
Russell/NCREIF time-weighted returns:					
Nominal	22.52%	14.18%	xf −9.79%	−1.98%	10.77%
Real	10.47%	9.94%	5.93%	−5.44%	5.02%
* Inflation:					
Annual rate	10.91%	3.85%	3.64%	3.67%	−5.47%
Pass-through rate	24.98%	280.31%	−4.24%	15.53%	32.80%
† Capitalization rates:					
Going-in rate	10.75%	7.56%	7.31%	6.72%	10.75%
Going-out rate	7.56%	7.31%	6.72%	9.44%	9.44%

Delaware). Second, this region is obviously diverse. Using the classification system initiated by Garreau (1981) and later adapted by
Hartzell, Shulman, and Wurtzebach (1987), this region is composed
of New England, the Mid-Atlantic, Old South, and the Industrial
Midwest (in whole or in part). Third, recent research (see Mueller
and Ziering [1992]) has suggested that cities can be grouped as being
economically similar even though they are not geographically linked.
For example, the cities of Fort Lauderdale, Phoenix, San Francisco,
Boston, and Pittsburgh can all be characterized as having a similar
proportion of economic activity devoted to the financial services area.
Fourth, as also suggested by Garreau (1988), autonomous "edge cities"
may operate within the boundaries of a metropolitan area. For example, the quintessential (for Garreau, at least) edge city is the Tyson's
Corner area of Virginia, located four miles from the old downtown
of the District of Columbia. Taken as a whole (including other edge
cities along and near the Beltway), the Washington, DC, area may
be the most significant market in the region designated by Russell/
NCREIF as the Mideast. The economics of these edge cities can be
very different from those of the older downtown areas from which
they evolved. Fifth, the mix of property types within a region (or a
submarket) can vary dramatically from one region (or submarket) to
the next. In addition, the typical locations of the various property
types may also differ (e.g., retail in suburban settings versus large
office buildings located in the urban core). Thus, the changing dynamics of market socioeconomic factors can vary dramatically.

In conclusion, the coarse four-region definition (or even the eight-
subregion definition) of the Russell/NCREIF index can blur the subtle
(and not so subtle) distinctions between local economies and how the
property (i.e., space-time) markets operate within those economies
and how the capital markets price this divergent set of economic and
property interactions.

The Midwest Region
Of the regional indices, the Midwest region began the period with
the lowest initial yield: 6.05 percent. Ultimately, this greatly contributed to the region having the second lowest total return—6.79 percent
(or 1.25 percent as adjusted for inflation)—over the 16-year period.
The disaggregated yield for the Midwest index is shown in Exhibit
3–12.

As just noted above, the region's low initial yield at the outset
of the analysis period led to several predictable implications:

EXHIBIT 3–12
Midwest Index: Annualized Yield Attributes, 1978:1–1993:4

	1978–81 (4 Years)	1982–85 (4 Years)	1986–89 (4 Years)	1990–93 (4 Years)	1978–93 (16 Years)
Initial yield	6.05%	8.07%	7.43%	6.37%	6.05%
Growth in earnings*	7.22	2.55	-1.99	1.30	1.98
Change in cap rate†	-3.98	-3.56	4.00	-7.46	-1.60
Estimated return	9.29%	7.05%	9.45%	0.21%	6.43%
Timing/methodology differences	1.92%	3.33%	-1.87%	-1.74%	0.36%
Russell/NCREIF time-weighted returns:					
Nominal	11.22%	10.39%	7.58%	-1.53%	6.79%
Real	0.28%	6.30%	3.80%	-5.01%	1.25%
* Inflation:					
Annual rate	10.91%	3.85%	3.64%	3.67%	5.47%
Pass-through rate	66.17%	66.15%	-54.64%	35.45%	36.19%
† Capitalization rates:					
Going-in rate	5.94%	7.01%	8.12%	6.84%	5.94%
Going-out rate	7.01%	8.12%	6.84%	9.62%	9.62%

- By the end of the first four-year period, the low initial yield increased to a more typical yield of 7.01 percent. This was just slightly below the average (7.35 percent) for the total index and predictably led to a dramatic decrease in return——3.98 percent—attributable to negative capitalization rate arbitrage. In other words, the region's reversion to a more typical capitalization rate led to a substantial (and negative) repricing consequence (i.e., a decline in property values).
- However, the negative impacts of this first-period repricing adjustment were superseded by the region's phenomenal growth in net income. Over the first four-year period, NOI grew at an average rate of 7.22 percent per annum. This was the highest observed growth rate in any period. Also, this period had the second highest inflation pass-through rate (66.17 percent) of the four regional indices.
- The growth rate of NOI, however, is very uncertain for the Midwest region. The volatility is even more evident when the inflation pass-through rates are examined by period. Nevertheless, this region ended the analysis period with the highest inflation pass-through rate (36.19 percent) of any region.

The Midwest region is composed of two subregions: the East North Central (Ohio, Michigan, Indiana, Illinois, and Wisconsin) and the West North Central (Missouri, Iowa, Minnesota, the Dakotas, Kansas, and Nebraska). As of December 1993, the East North Central subregion was approximately the same size as the Northeast and Mideast subregions of the East index, which are approximately of average size for the total index. Conversely, the West North Central subregion is clearly the smallest of any of the subregions and is approximately one-fourth the size of the East North Central subregion. Accordingly, the results of the Midwest region as a whole are dominated by the market activities of an area largely consisting of "The Foundry," as described by Garreau (1988), or the "Industrial Midwest," as described by Hartzell et al. (1987).

The South Region
The South region had the lowest total return of any of the regional indices over the 16-year period. The disaggregated yield components for this region are shown in Exhibit 3–13.

Exhibit 3–13 reveals several interesting patterns:

EXHIBIT 3–13
South Index: Annualized Yield Attributes, 1978:1–1993:4

	1978–81 (4 Years)	1982–85 (4 Years)	1986–89 (4 Years)	1990–93 (4 Years)	1978–93 (16 Years)
Initial yield	8.66%	8.42%	6.37%	6.45%	8.66%
Growth in earnings*	6.14	-3.86	-7.64	1.07	-1.04
Change in cap rate†	0.67	5.01	1.95	-8.88	-0.19
Estimated return	15.46%	9.57%	0.68%	-1.37%	7.43%
Timing/methodology differences	0.15%	0.26%	-0.81%	1.33%	-1.32%
Russell/NCREIF time-weighted returns:					
Nominal	15.61%	9.83%	-0.13%	-0.04%	6.11%
Real	4.24%	5.76%	-3.64%	-3.58%	0.60%
* Inflation:					
Annual rate	10.91%	3.85%	3.64%	3.67%	5.47%
Pass-through rate	56.28%	-100.34%	-209.91%	29.18%	-19.00%
† Capitalization rates:					
Going-in rate	8.53%	8.30%	6.68%	6.13%	8.53%
Going-out rate	8.30%	6.68%	6.13%	9.10%	9.10%

- The most striking component of the South's disaggregated return is the persistent decline in NOI throughout most of the 1980s. Even including the positive growth experience in the initial and final four-year periods, the region experienced an average growth in earnings of − 1.04 percent per annum over the 16-year period.
- As a corollary to the decline in NOI, the South region also experienced a negative inflation pass-through rate, − 19.0 percent. Clearly, this type of growth will severely curtail real returns.
- As noted with some of the property types, this region exhibited declining capitalization rates while NOI was declining. However, this investment aberration cannot last indefinitely. Beginning in 1990, capitalization rates substantially increased (implying relative price declines).

The South region is composed of two subregions: the Southeast (Florida, Georgia, Alabama, Mississippi, and Tennessee) and the Southwest (Louisiana, Texas, Arkansas, and Oklahoma). Both are approximately the same size, as measured by market value of properties reported to the Russell/NCREIF index, and both are slightly smaller than the median subregion. While Hartzell et al. (1987) ascribed two socioeconomic regions (the "Old South" and the "Mineral Extraction" regions) to the area covered by this index, Garreau (1988) had initially ascribed four: Dixie, the Breadbasket, the Islands, and MexAmerica. Garreau's characterization may more fully capture the diversity of this region.

The West Region
Of the regional indices, the West index had the second highest total return, 8.47 percent (or 2.84 percent as adjusted for inflation), over the 16-year period. The disaggregated yield components for the West index are shown in Exhibit 3–14.

Perhaps not coincidentally, the West region had the second highest initial yield (9.05 percent) at the beginning of the 16-year period. (The East region had the highest initial yield and the highest total return.) Other aspects of the West's return pattern are also revealed in Exhibit 3–14:

- As measured by both its overall growth rate (of NOI) and its inflation pass-through rate, the West region had the third low-

EXHIBIT 3–14

West Index: Annualized Yield Attributes, 1978:1–1993:4

	1978–81 (4 Years)	1982–85 (4 Years)	1986–89 (4 Years)	1990–93 (4 Years)	1978–93 (16 Years)
Initial yield	9.05%	7.12%	7.28%	6.37%	9.05%
Growth in earnings*	4.02	1.41	-2.88	-2.74	0.70
Change in cap rate†	6.16	1.55	0.48	-6.83	0.05
Estimated return	19.23%	10.08%	4.87%	-3.21%	9.80%
Timing/methodology differences	0.61%	1.28%	2.58%	-0.26%	-1.33%
Russell/NCREIF time-weighted returns:					
Nominal	19.84%	11.36%	7.45%	-3.47%	8.47%
Real	8.05%	7.24%	3.68%	-6.88%	2.84%
* Inflation:					
Annual rate	10.91%	3.85%	3.64%	3.67%	5.47%
Pass-through rate	36.81%	36.69%	-79.21%	-74.73%	12.82%
† Capitalization rates:					
Going-in rate	8.96%	6.97%	6.53%	6.40%	8.96%
Going-out rate	6.97%	6.53%	6.40%	8.80%	8.80%

est increase (0.70 percent) in earnings. It surpassed only the South, which had negative growth, on average, over the 16-year period.

- The level of capitalization rates for properties in the West tended to be lower than those in the East and Midwest. While its level of capitalization rates was often similar to those in the South, this may more likely represent the slow downward repricing of assets in the South (and not the movement of capitalization rates for newly acquired properties in the South).

The West region is composed of two subregions: Mountain (Arizona, New Mexico, Utah, Colorado, Wyoming, Montana, and Idaho) and Pacific (California, Oregon, and Washington). The Pacific subregion, by far the largest subregion, comprises nearly a third of the Russell/NCREIF index. Conversely, the Mountain subregion is the second smallest. Hartzell et al. (1987) characterized the West region as being part of three regional economies: Southern California, Northern California, and Mineral Extraction. Similarly, Garreau (1988) described this region, with greater embellishment, as belonging to MexAmerica, Ecotopia, the Breadbasket, and the Empty Quarter. Obviously, such a varied region shows disparate tendencies and trends.

PROJECTED REAL RETURNS

One of the primary reasons for reviewing the past is to assist in making estimates about future returns. However, while the past is a prologue to the future, it will not be perfectly replicated. Thus, the review of past returns acts as a backdrop for framing estimates of future returns.

From the proposition that a property's (or portfolio's) total return consists of the three fundamental components identified here, an estimate of possible future outcomes can be developed. Given that today's going-in capitalization rate (in this case, as of January 1, 1994) is known (or at least closely estimated), only estimates of the rate of NOI growth and pricing movements are needed. Since most investors are concerned with real returns, the growth rate can be replaced with the percentage of the inflation rate that the investment is expected to pass through.

In addition, the use of ranges for the inflation pass-through and the pricing movements (or capitalization rate shifts) generates a two-dimensional matrix of real returns. Adapting Hartzell et al. (1988), the nominal return (from which the real return is derived) is computed as follows:

$$P_o = \sum_{n=1}^{N} \frac{NOI_0 (1 + \lambda\rho)^n}{(1 + k)^n} + \frac{NOI_0(1 + \lambda\rho)^N \cdot \nabla\left[\frac{NOI_0}{P_0}\right]}{(1 + k)^N} \tag{13}$$

where P_0 = Initial price.
    NOI_0 = Initial net operating income.
    ρ = Inflation rate.
    λ = Inflation pass-through rate.
    ∇ = Capitalization rate shift upon sale.
    k = Nominal yield (or IRR).

More exactly, the capitalization rate shift (∇) is defined as:

$$\nabla = \frac{\dfrac{NOI_N}{P_N}}{\dfrac{NOI_0}{P_0}} \tag{14}$$

So, for example, if the initial capitalization rate was 10 percent and the ending rate (NOI_N/P_N) was 12 percent, this would then equal to a shift of 120 percent.

Equation (13) was used to produce Exhibit 3–15 (similar matrices can be generated for the individual property types and regional locations discussed previously). This approach implicitly assumes the property has predominantly short-term leases and/or has a nearly constant proportion of leases "rolling over." For those properties that have a significant portion of long-term, fixed-rate leases that roll over near or beyond the 10-year time horizon, investors will need to effectuate the growth rate by discounting the market rents expected at the rollover date. For such properties, the return and growth can be estimated using the differential income valuation model discussed in Chapter 4 and in Grieg and Young (1991).

Assuming reasonable ranges for the expected pass-through of inflation and the shift of capitalization rates (from the time of purchase to the time of sale), a going-in capitalization rate of 9.15

EXHIBIT 3–15
Russell/NCREIF Total Property Index: Estimated Real Yields (10-Year Holding Period) Based on Various Inflation Pass-Through Rates and Cap Rate Shifts

		Pass-through of inflation rate				
		25%	50%	75%	100%	125%
	120%	5.24%	6.34%	7.44%	8.54%	9.64%
Capitalization rate	110%	5.74%	6.85%	7.95%	9.06%	10.17%
shift at	100%	6.32%	7.43%	8.54%	9.66%	10.77%
sale	90%	6.97%	8.10%	9.22%	10.34%	11.47%
	80%	7.74%	8.87%	10.01%	11.14%	12.28%

Major assumptions
9.15% = Going-in capitalization rate
4.00% = Inflation rate

percent, and a 4 percent annual inflation rate, this matrix generates annual real returns (before transaction fees and advisory costs) ranging from 5.24 to 12.28 percent over an assumed 10-year holding period.[9] Due to the high going-in capitalization rate (the highest in the 16 years of the Russell/NCREIF index), this range exceeds the index's historical annual real return of 2.39 percent. Moreover, the shaded area would seem to represent the most likely range (6.34 to 9.66 percent) of possible future returns, given the following assumptions:

1. Given the supply-demand imbalances plaguing many markets, it seems unlikely that rental rates will keep pace with inflation. If this is true, real estate's ability to act as an inflation hedge will be diminished. In turn, this suggests that the inflation pass-through rate (λ) will be less than 100 percent. Other analysts have taken the approach of demonstrating

---

[9] It should be noted that a shorter (or longer) holding period would attribute more (or less) impact to the assumed shift in capitalization rates.

real estate's ability to hedge inflation by examining income, appreciation, and total return movements relative to anticipated and unanticipated inflation; see Rubens, Bond, and Webb (1989).

2. Capitalization rates should naturally increase gradually as a property ages. As noted previously, as any property ages, its useful life and ability to generate real income decline.[10] This then translates into a higher capitalization rate for a subsequent buyer if that investor is to receive the same total risk-adjusted return as the current owner. If investors seek higher returns to compensate themselves for acquiring older properties, this increase in capitalization rates will be more pronounced.

3. The Russell/NCREIF returns are reported before advisory fees. Both the amount and the structure of such fees can have a significant negative impact on these projected returns (see Saint-Pierre [1990]).

As an aside, other published sources (e.g., *Crittenden's Pension Funds and Real Estate* and the *National Real Estate Index*) seem to indicate that higher capitalization rates[11] than discussed here are obtainable. At least three possible explanations come to mind. First, the methodology used herein relies on a trailing-earnings (NOI_n/P_n) basis as opposed to the more commonly used forecasted-net operating income (NOI_{n+1}/P_n) basis. Second, it is unclear how these other sources treat large, periodic costs (such as capital improvements, leasing commissions, "free rent," etc.) in determining the capitalization rate. Third, the property values reported in the NCREIF data may be overstated and have yet to be fully written down. Of these elements, the third may have been the most important. At the beginning of the 1990s there was a large spread between buyers' bidding prices and sellers' asking prices. This spread, which Giliberto (1992) suggests may have been as large as 330 basis points in 1991, would have caused the carrying values of these properties to be overstated. However, the

---

[10] Again, for purposes of calculating these returns, capital improvements have been assumed to be zero. This is not the case in practice, as the frequency and intensity of capital improvements can shorten or lengthen a property's useful life.

[11] This analysis assumes the capitalization rate is determined by NOI_n/P_n as opposed to NOI_{n+1}/P_n. It is largely unimportant which approach is taken, so long as the user correctly identifies the computation and correctly incorporates the figure into the total yield calculation.

increases in capitalization rates for 1992–93 and the corresponding decline in property values would suggest a narrowing of the bid-ask spread. Accordingly, the figures used in these analyses are assumed to be representative of properties already in the institutional investor's portfolio. To the extent that acquisitions can be made at higher going-in capitalization rates, portfolio performance will improve (as a function of the mix of the values of newly acquired properties versus property values already in the portfolio).

Projected Real Returns: A Question of Growth

In the long run, shifts in the capitalization rate have relatively little impact on total returns. For example, and as noted previously, compare the impact of a 53-basis-point decline in capitalization rates for the total index in the 1986–89 period, which resulted in a yield increase of 1.83 percent per annum to a 60-basis-point decline over the entire 16-year period, which led to a yield increase of −0.19 percent per annum (see Exhibit 3–5).

If, as the holding period lengthens, capitalization rate shifts have a relatively benign impact on total return, projecting real ex ante returns essentially rests on the initial yield and the growth of those earnings over time relative to inflation. The relative growth in earnings is essentially reflected in three attributes:

1. *Lease length.* As the lengths of tenants' leases increase, the duration (or inflation rate sensitivity) also increases (see Hartzell et al. 1988), assuming the lease contracts are written without CPI (or similar) escalation clauses. That is, an increase in inflation effectively translates into a lower inflation pass-through rate as the length of the lease increases.
2. *Market disequilibrium.* Notwithstanding the length of the lease contract, the supply and demand balance (or imbalance) of the local property market will also affect the property's ability to grow its NOI in relation to inflationary increases; see Garrigan and Pagliari (1992) and Wurtzebach, Mueller, and Macchi (1991), among others.
3. *Obsolescence/decay.* Like any other physical asset, the improvements situated on a fixed piece of land have a finite useful life. Over time, the improvements decline in utility because of physical and/or functional obsolescence as well as potential site externalities adverse to the existing use. These

forces imply that a property's ability to realize growth in NOI commensurate with the rate of inflation declines as it ages, all other things being equal (see Pagliari and Webb [1994]).

More often than not, investors can exercise some choice over lease length via property-type selection rather than attempting to "buck" the market by shortening or lengthening contracted lease terms vis-à-vis market lease terms.[12] However, the second two attributes, market disequilibrium and obsolescence/decay, are risks all investors must bear.

From the perspective of forecasting real returns, the key question becomes: Is growth random? If so, the investor's job is easy: Pick the properties with the highest initial yields. If future growth is just as likely for the high-capitalization-rate properties as it is for the low-capitalization-rate properties (and the impact of capitalization rate shifts declines with time), high-yield properties will generate the highest returns. However, if growth tends to be higher for properties offering low initial yields and lower for properties offering high initial yields, total returns may be approximately equal for low- and high-initial-yield properties. This, of course, is another way of examining market efficiency.

While real estate research in this area is scant, considerable research has been performed on common stocks in an attempt to address the question of whether or not changes in corporate earnings are randomly distributed over time. This general body of research has often been termed "higgledy-piggledy growth." Recent papers by Fuller, Huberts, and Levinson (1992, 1993) suggest that earnings growth (actually excess earnings) is related to initial earnings-to-price ratios (or capitalization rates, in the parlance of the real estate industry). Thus, firms with high E/P ratios "tend to have considerably lower earnings changes" and firms with low E/P ratios "tend to have considerably higher earnings changes." Moreover, "high E/P stocks generated above-normal returns, and low E/P stocks generated below-normal returns." Of course, the existence of these relationships in the stock market does not necessarily imply similar relationships for the real estate market.

---

[12] Investors can also reduce the duration of their property investments, even though it is encumbered by long-term leases, by utilizing leverage. See Giliberto (1989).

VOLATILITY

Exhibit 3–16 shows the quarterly mean returns and their standard deviations for real estate, common stocks, and short- and long-term bonds. As shown, real estate has exhibited considerably less volatility (as measured by the standard deviation of its return) than its counterparts in the stock and/or long-term bond markets. Unlike stocks and bonds, which are frequently traded in an auction market, real estate is infrequently traded in a negotiated market. Since property trades are infrequent, the real estate community relies on appraised values to estimate the market value at the end of each (quarterly) period. Most real estate practitioners and academics believe these appraisals tend to lag movements in the underlying property values and, consequently, appraised values understate the true volatility of real estate.

Appraisal Lags

Firstenberg, Ross, and Zisler (1988) were among the early observers of appraisal lags. They developed a statistical estimation procedure by which this lag could be inferred through a linear regression model that attempts to estimate the excessive autocorrelation of the Russell/NCREIF returns. The essence of this approach is to view the true

EXHIBIT 3–16

Comparison of Annualized (Quarterly) Returns for Real Estate, Stocks, Bonds, and Bills for the Period Ended 1978–93

	Mean Return		Standard Deviation	Coefficient of Variation
	Arithmetic	*Geometric*		
Real estate (Russell/ NCREIF)	8.21%	8.12%	4.10%	50.01%
Common stocks (S&P 500)	16.31	15.04	15.04	92.21
Corporate/government bonds (Shearson Lehman)	10.86	10.49	8.47	78.01
Treasury bills	8.11	8.10	1.47	18.15

Sources: Russell/NCREIF Property Index, December 31, 1993; authors' calculations.

appraised value as a function of previous appraised values. Moreover, this sluggishness of appraised values manifests itself in understating the volatility of returns.

From their statistical approach,[13] Firstenberg et al. attempted to reflect greater volatility in the real return series than was otherwise reported. This approach may be particularly appropriate for those properties that are externally appraised once every four quarters (the other three quarters have internally prepared appraisals), as is the case for many of the contributors to the Russell/NCREIF index. The general notion is that the lag in appraised values is a result of apprais- ers anchoring, to some extent, their estimates of previous values. This is both (1) typical human behavior (see Russo and Schoemaker [1989]) and (2) a function of the large search costs and inefficiencies associated with the real estate market (see Quan and Quigley [1991]). A series of articles by Geltner (September 1991; Spring 1991; 1989) discusses why "smoothing" of appraisal-based returns must be explic- itly considered when comparing real estate's estimated volatility (and all risk-return statistics) to that of stocks and bonds. Geltner further asserts that since appraisal-based returns understate the true volatil- ity of real estate returns, they should be used only after correcting for appraisal smoothing.

Real Estate versus REITs

Part of the contention that real estate's volatility is understated is derived from the comparison between the volatility of real estate compared to equity real estate investment trust (REITs). As shown

---

[13] A summary of their statistical approach to estimating appraisal lags is shown below:

$$R_t = a + b_1 R_{t-1} + b_2 R_{t-2} + b_3 R_{t-3} + b_4 R_{t-4} + z_t \tag{15}$$

where R_t = Observed return in period t.
  a = A constant.
  b_n = A coefficient modifying the observed return.
  z_t = Residual error term.

These parameters from the regression equation are then used to estimate the true mean re- turn (M):

$$M = \frac{a}{[1 - (b_1 + b_2 + b_3 + b_4)]} \tag{16}$$

in Exhibit 3–17, equity REITs (as measured by the leveraged, institutional holdings represented in the NAREIT index) have exhibited substantially greater volatility than real estate (as measured by the unleveraged, institutional holdings represented in the Russell/NCREIF index). Over the time period 1978–91, equity REITs averaged a quarterly return of 3.82 percent with a standard deviation of 6.89 percent, while the Russell/NCREIF index averaged 2.35 percent with a standard deviation of 1.88 percent. (The former is leveraged real estate reported after advisory fees, while the latter is unleveraged real estate reported before advisory fees.) Moreover, a recent survey by Giliberto (1992) indicated that many real estate practitioners and academics believe real estate's "true" volatility ranges from 15 to 200 percent (with 63 percent as the mean response) of the volatility exhibited by common stocks.

Dissenting Opinion

As noted above, opinion about the true volatility of real estate is varied. While most believe it to be higher than reported in the Russell/NCREIF index, many are unwilling to believe it approaches the volatility exhibited by REITs and/or common stocks. The reasons fall into four broad categories: (1) REITs are not directly comparable to real estate; (2) the volatility of the stock market (and, accordingly, REITs) is overstated; (3) as the history of the Russell/NCREIF return series lengthens, more volatility can be observed; and (4) the reliability of commercial real estate appraisals. Each of these arguments is explored in greater detail next.

Real Estate versus REITs
There are a number of reasons equity REITs should not be directly compared to real estate.

Leverage. Many equity REITs employ a substantial degree of leverage, while the properties in the Russell/NCREIF index are

---

and the true standard deviation of return (σ):

$$\sigma = \frac{\sigma_z}{[1 - (b_1 + b_2 + b_3 + b_4)]} \qquad (17)$$

EXHIBIT 3–17

Comparison of Total Quarterly Returns, NAREIT Equity Index versus Russell/NCREIF Index, 1978–93

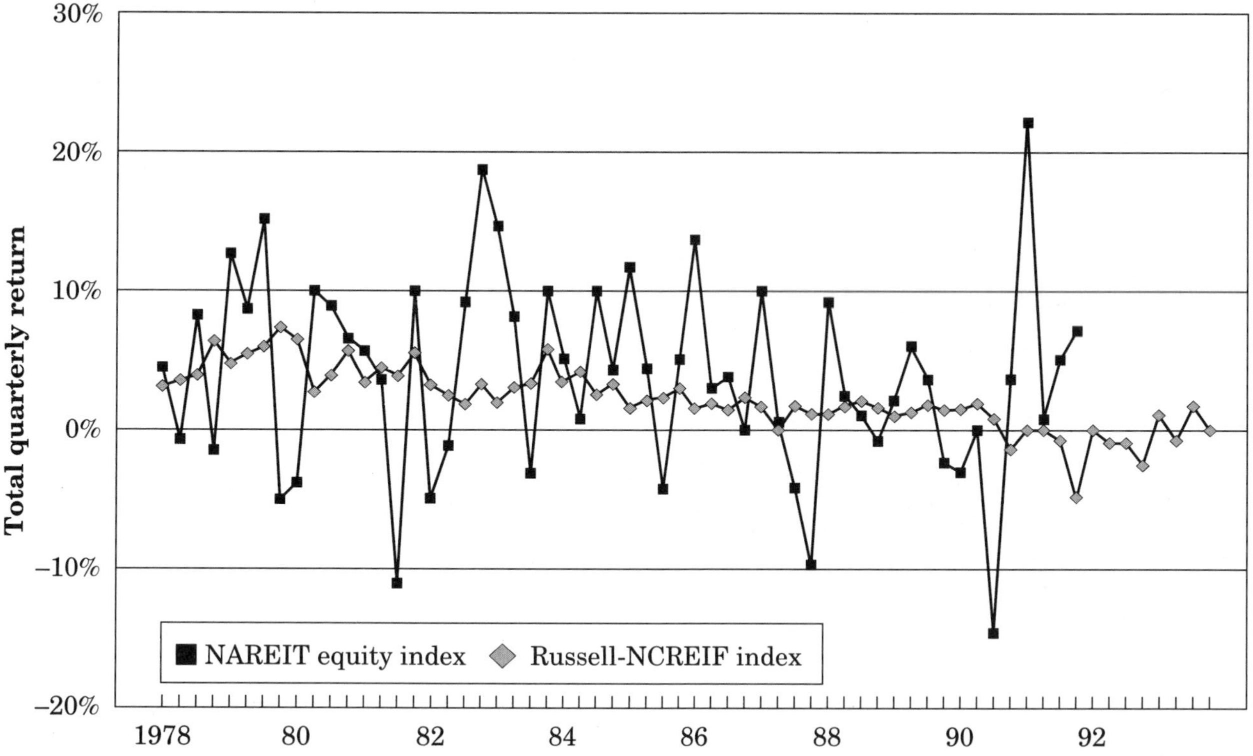

unleveraged. The existence of mortgage debt will necessarily increase volatility. As Ross and Zisler (1991) pointed out, "[w]ere we to unleverage the S&P 500, we might find that its volatility would more nearly resemble that of real estate." Shulman (1986) reached a similar conclusion.

Fractional versus Majority Interest. As described more fully below, REITs or common stocks represent a fractional interest in the underlying asset. Real estate interests, as reported in the Russell/NCREIF index, represent the entire interest in the asset. To see why this is an important distinction, consider, say, IBM (or any large corporation) and the 1 to 2 percent of its common stock that typically trades on the NYSE every day. The interests that trade are generally thought to represent less than what the entire company (or a controlling interest) would sell for. This is due to a number of factors, including the "control" premium paid for a controlling interest. That the "controlling" price is not represented by the "trading" price can be observed from a number of vantage points. First, the prices paid to shareholders in leveraged buyouts were considerably higher than the share price recognized by the Exchange before the company was "put in play." Second, the impact of trading large block shares is often suggested as having a significant impact on trading prices. Third, the fact that 1 to 2 percent of the shares exchanged hands at the trading price also indicates that 98 to 99 percent of the shareholders were unwilling to sell their shares at the trading price.

Differing Mix of Assets. The mix of property types in the Russell/NCREIF index is composed largely of office, retail, and industrial properties (with office buildings occupying the dominant position). Equity REITs, on the other hand, comprise a different mix of property types with an emphasis on retail, apartment, and "other" property types (where "other" include raw land, nursing home/health care facilities, and race tracks). Clearly, there appear to be differences in the risk-return parameters of these property types. If so, the reported risk-return parameters of these indexes would also differ.[14]

---

[14] So, for example, even if the retail component of the Russell/NCREIF index reported the same returns as the retail component of the equity REIT index (after having adjusted for leverage and fractional interests), the returns of the aggregate indexes would differ if they

(*cont.*)

Property Quality. It is largely assumed that the asset quality comprising the Russell/NCREIF index is "better" (as measured by the assets' age, construction quality, tenant roster, etc.) than that generally found among the equity REITs (this is perhaps more true of the REIT portfolios, excluding those brought to market in the 1992–94 surge and on which these historical statistics are computed). If this is true, it is reasonable to assume the lesser-quality properties (or portfolios of properties) are accompanied by higher risk (i.e., greater volatility) and higher expected returns.

Therefore, if equity REIT returns are controlled for these differences, the volatility of the equity REITs may come more closely into line with the reported real estate volatility. In particular, controlling the first two factors, leverage and fractional interests, may remove much of the volatility associated with REITs.

Excess Stock Market Volatility

Shulman (1986) suggested that if common stocks are valued through the use of the dividend discount model, their riskiness declines dramatically.[15] Significantly, Shulman adopted this approach to "[a]ssume that the market for corporations was a private one with only an occasional transaction for an entire corporation," as in the real estate investment arena. The implication is that the short-term trading orientation of the stock market overshadows a more fundamental, long-term approach, such as the DDM.

Other authors have also suggested that there may be excess volatility in the stock market. One of the early voices was Shiller (1981), who suggested that stock prices move too much to be justified by the present value of the subsequent dividend payments. Along similar lines, DeBondt and Thaler (1985) suggested that the stock market systematically overvalues stocks that have recently outperformed the market and undervalues those stocks that recently under-

---

had different weightings attributable to the retail sectors and assuming the other property types had different return series than the retail series. The volatility of these aggregate returns would be dampened by the lack of perfect correlation among the various return series of the underlying property-type components.

[15] This chapter, of course, utilized the DDM earlier to analyze historical real estate returns and project future returns.

performed the market. Moreover, a simple strategy of selling the "winners" and buying the "losers" would have resulted in a portfolio that substantially outperformed a simple buy-and-hold strategy. Another interesting study, by Cutler, Poterba, and Summers (1989), suggested that the movements in stock prices "reflect something other than news about fundamental values." They examined stock market returns factored by various financial proxies (e.g., dividend yields, industrial production, the money supply) and found that only about one-third of the variance in stock market returns was explained. They then expanded their analysis to include major noneconomic events (wars, presidential elections, major tax law changes, etc.). Here they found that the combination of economic and noneconomic events explained less than half of the variance in stock market returns.

Thus, it would appear that the stock market (and therefore REITs) may exhibit too much volatility. Perhaps Fisher Black, as reported in Gross (1989), described it best: "[T]he short-term volatility of price will be greater than the short-term volatility of value." Accordingly, real estate's volatility may more accurately represent the pattern of returns associated with unleveraged, controlling interests.

Time Period Dependency

In part, the need to attribute more volatility in real estate returns may have resulted from the early studies of real estate's role in a mixed-asset portfolio. These studies (see, for example, Brueggeman, Chen, and Thibodeau [1984]; Folger [1984]; Webb [1990]; and Webb and Rubens [1987]) generally suggested that real estate be allocated 20 to 40 percent of the total portfolio. However, these optimal portfolios were generally constructed using historical returns concluding in the mid-1980s. Many investors and their advisors felt uncomfortable with such a high allocation to real estate. One way to decrease the allocation to real estate is to increase its standard deviation, thereby causing the portfolio optimization process to allocate a lesser percentage to real estate.[16]

---

[16] There may be other reasons real estate occupies a lesser allocation. Ennis and Burik (1991) describe other characteristics of real estate that are beyond the scope of standard portfolio (or mean/variance) optimization. These characteristics include "absence of freely available information, relatively high transaction costs, limited trading liquidity, largely indivisible ownership of interests, and tax advantages embedded in some property investments."

Importantly, this was before the large decreases in reported values. Consequently, real estate returns through the early 1990s show lower mean returns and higher standard deviations. See, for example, Exhibit 3–18, which tracks how the cumulative average real estate returns peaked out in the early to mid-1980s and average returns thereafter declined while volatility increased.

If the optimal portfolios were reconstructed with more recent data, real estate's optimal allocation would decrease substantially as a result of real estate's deteriorating performance and the increasing relative performance of the stock and bond markets since the mid-1980s. In turn, this may somewhat lessen the "need" to increase real estate's volatility. Alternatively stated, the period-specific results throughout the mid-1980s may have understated real estate's volatility more because this period had yet to witness the significant trough of the late 1980s and early 1990s than because of appraisal lags. With a more complete real estate cycle recorded, real estate's risk and return parameters translate into a portfolio allocation that is more in keeping with investor intuition.

Reliability of Appraisals
A series of papers (see Cole, Guilkey, and Miles [1986]; Guilkey, Miles, and Cole [1989]; and Miles, Guilkey, Webb, and Hunter [1991]) have indicated that appraised values are reasonably close to actual transaction prices (as adjusted for inflation, transaction costs, and capital improvements). Cole, Guilkey, and Miles (1986) found, for example, that the mean absolute difference between actual net sales price (which on average included approximately 2 percent selling and transaction costs) and appraised value was roughly 10 percent. Had the researchers used simply mean differences (so that negative and positive differences would tend to cancel out each other), this reported difference may have been reduced dramatically. These "signed" differences are more appropriate when examining the confidence level that might be placed on an individual property than a portfolio of real estate.

In addition, if the difference between appraised values and actual selling prices were constant over time, the volatility of real estate returns would generally be accurately reported. Of course, it is possible that these differences are not constant.[17] The appraisal function

---

[17] In addition, there appears to be some bias in the properties sold. See Guilkey, Miles, and Cole (1989).

EXHIBIT 3–18
Risk-Return Features of Cumulative FRC Data for the Period 1978:1–1993:4

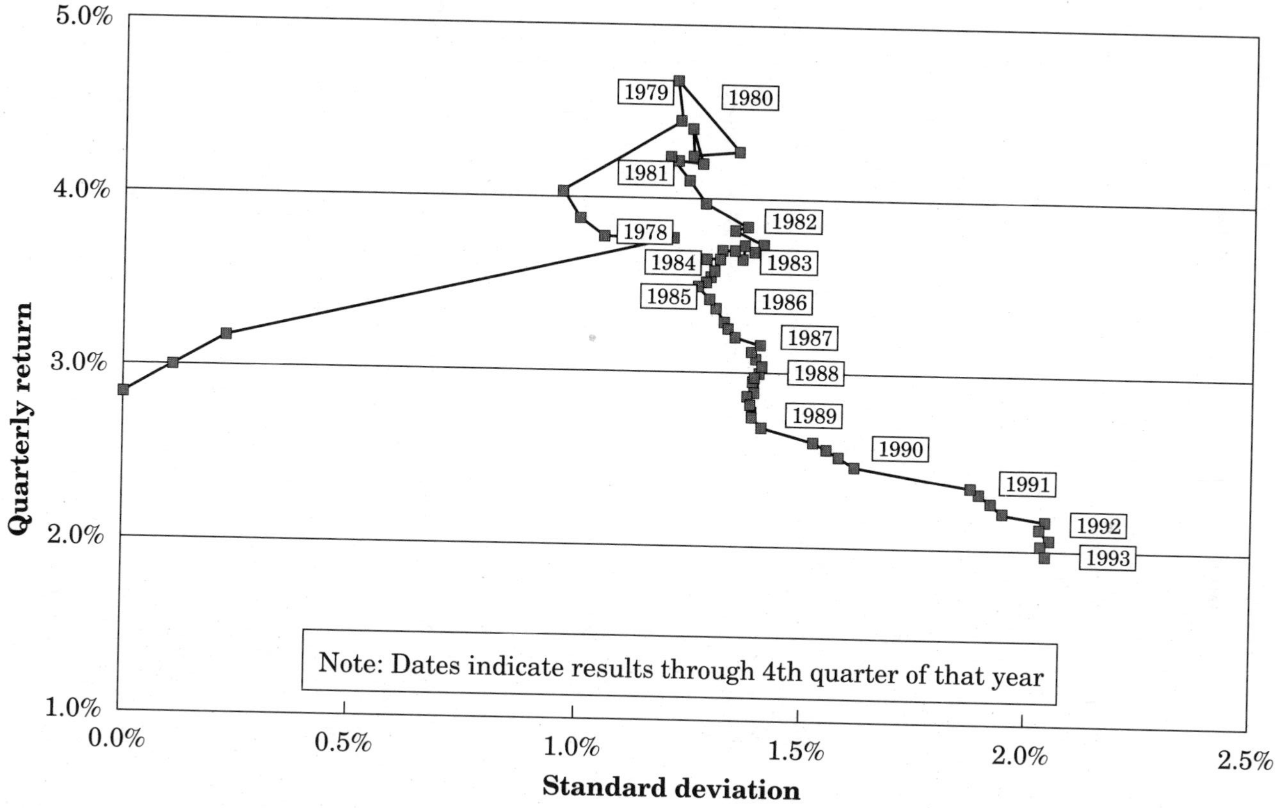

Note: Dates indicate results through 4th quarter of that year

is inherently retrospective in that it examines historical sales to estimate current values. In a rising real estate market, appraised values tend to be understated; in a falling market, these values tend to be overstated.

In summary, appraised values may represent a reasonable approximation of the property's true market value. While the inherent sluggishness of the appraisal process will dampen the volatility of market values, and therefore estimated returns, other factors—most notably leverage and fractional versus controlling interests—may contribute to the greater volatility of REITs and common stocks. That the volatility of historical real estate returns appeared to be understated relative to stocks and bonds is, in part, time period dependent. As the real estate cycle peaked in the mid-1980s, the subsequent decline generated increased volatility in the return series as well as decreasing its average return. With data containing a more complete real estate cycle, real estate's risk-return parameters now suggest a portfolio allocation more in keeping with investors' actual allocations.

COVARIANCE/SYSTEMATIC VERSUS UNSYSTEMATIC RISK

The pattern in which real estate returns move (i.e., their covariance) is important in two respects. First, as an asset class, real estate's covariance with stock and bond returns has historically been low to negative. This characteristic, combined with its historically high returns and low standard deviation of returns, has led many researchers to conclude that real estate should have historically occupied a large allocation of the mixed-asset portfolio (see Brueggeman, Chen, and Thibodeau [1984]; Folger [1984]; Webb [1990]; and Webb and Rubens [1987]). Second, within the asset class, the covariance of individual properties with a market basket of real estate properties is important in analyzing the amount of systematic and unsystematic risk contained in an individual property. The diversification gained from owning a number of individual properties will tend to reduce unsystematic risk, as discussed more fully in Chapter 2, so that what remains is the undiversifiable, systematic risk. This section explores this second aspect of covariance, namely, that real estate's covariance within the asset class has a direct bearing on the systematic and unsystematic components of real estate risk.

Before statistically examining real estate's historical covariance patterns, it may be helpful to review some of the factors relating to real estate's unsystematic risk. Perhaps it is best to think of real estate's unsystematic risk relative to that of common stocks. Whereas the real estate investment often constitutes a controlling interest in a single building, common stock typically represents a fractional interest in leveraged corporate assets. These corporate assets may represent multiple product lines, each of which operates nationally (or internationally). Therefore, in a sense the corporation already represents a portfolio of assets with some amount of diversification. Thus, if one product line experiences a decrease, the decrease may be offset by an increase in another product line. Even within a single product line, there is often the possibility that when sales in one area of the country slow due to regional recessionary forces (e.g., Houston in the mid-1980s), this effect is offset by regional growth in other areas of the country (e.g., Boston in the mid-1980s).

Take Hewlett-Packard as an example. It has multiple product lines (pocket calculators, laser printers, engineering equipment, etc.) and sells these products internationally. It has already diversified much of its unsystematic risk. However, it still faces the unsystematic risk of the engineering/computer industry. A stock market investor can diversify away this risk by investing in other, dissimilar industries.

Relatively speaking, a property investment (e.g., an office building in Boston) would entail substantially more unsystematic (or idiosyncratic) risk than a common stock investment. Consider the following elements of such risk: (1) the particular building (with regard to its construction, tenancy, market penetration, etc.), (2) the dynamics of the office market (increased supply, slowing absorption, changing preferences for CBD versus suburban office space, etc.), (3) the regional economy of the Boston area, (4) the property's submarket, and (5) the quality of the operator (i.e., the asset/property manager).

The notion of systematic risk seems rather abstract. What factors systematically affect real estate returns? Two such factors might include tax law changes and interest rate movements. However, even these risks can have different impacts. For example, different tax treatments often apply to hotel, apartment, and commercial properties. Similarly, a change in interest rates will have a declining impact as lease length shortens (see Hartzell et al. [1988]). Generally speaking, lease terms lengthen as one moves from hotel to apartment to commercial properties. Thus, even such "macro" factors cannot be said to affect all real properties equally.

Assuming real estate's unsystematic risk is higher than that of, say, common stocks, the appropriate portfolio strategy is one of efficient diversification. That is, investors should diversify across property types and locations to eliminate the unsystematic risk of the real estate portfolio, leaving it with only the undiversifiable, systematic risk. More will be said specifically about such strategies in Chapter 24. The following section provides some historical perspectives on past correlations of returns by property type and region.

Historical Covariance Characteristics

As before, the reconstructed Russell/NCREIF data series is used to examine the relationships among net operating income, capitalization rates, and total return for the period 1978 through 1993. As Exhibit 3–19 shows, the four main property type categories possess generally similar cumulative returns.[18] However, when the components of total return—principally net operating income and capitalization rates—are viewed separately, the correlation among the property type components seems less uniform; see Exhibits 3–20 and 3–21. As can be seen from Exhibit 3–20, the erratic path of implied NOI is quite pronounced. However, it appears less so for capitalization rates, as Exhibit 3–21 indicates.

The interplay of NOI, capitalization rates and total returns can be observed via the following simplified formulation[19] of total returns:

---

[18] Cumulative total returns assume the 100 percent reinvestment of "dividends" (i.e., net operating income) into the property type basket of properties.

[19] The Russell/NCREIF return calculation is more complicated than the simplified version presented here. Its calculation is

$$R_t = \frac{NOI_t + (P_t - P_{t-1}) + PS_t - CI_t}{P_{t-1} + .5(CI_t - PS_t) - .33\,NOI_t} \tag{18}$$

where NOI_t = Income in quarter t.
  CI_t = Capital improvements in quarter t.
  PS_t = Partial sales in quarter t.
  P_t = Market value at end of quarter t.

EXHIBIT 3-19

Cumulative Total Returns by Property Type, 1978:1–1993:4

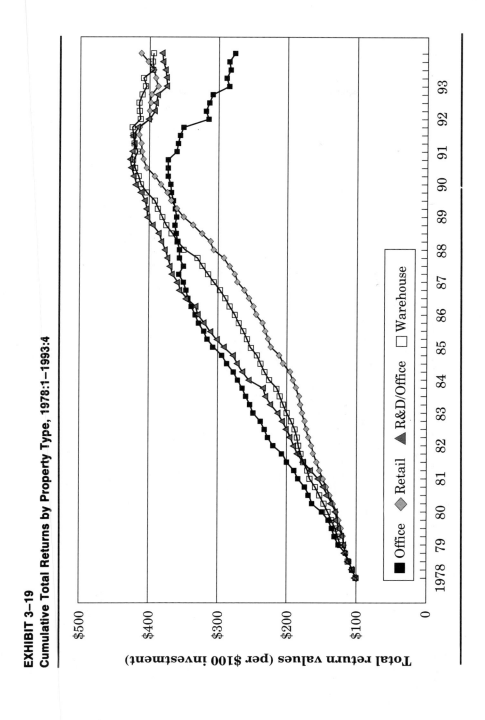

EXHIBIT 3–20
Nominal NOI by Property Type, 1978:1–1993:4

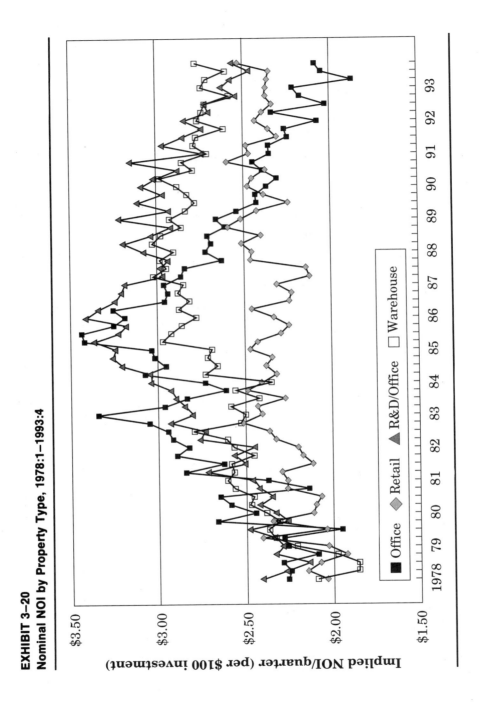

EXHIBIT 3–21
Capitalization Rates by Property Type, 1978:1–1993:4

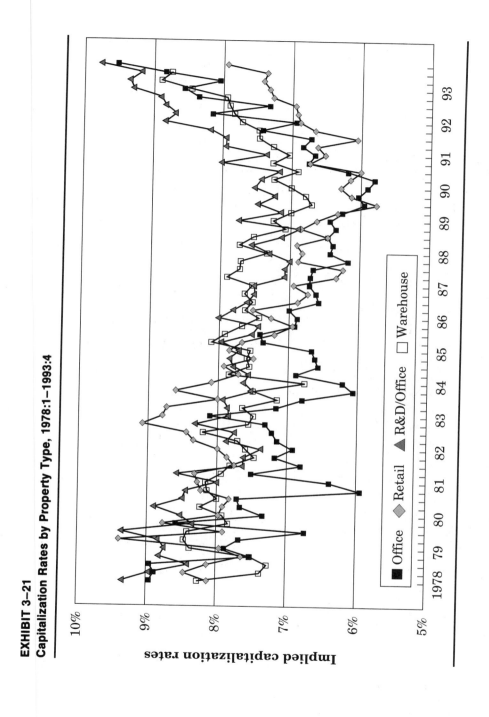

$$P_t = \frac{NOI_t}{\text{Cap rate}_t} \qquad (19)$$

$$R_t = \frac{NOI_t + P_t - P_{t-1}}{P_{t-1}} \qquad (20)$$

$$R_t = \frac{NOI_t + \dfrac{NOI_t}{\text{Cap rate}_t} - \dfrac{NOI_{t-1}}{\text{Cap rate}_{t-1}}}{\dfrac{NOI_{t-1}}{\text{Cap rate}_{t-1}}} \qquad (21)$$

$$R_t = \frac{NOI_t}{NOI_{t-1}} \times \left[\text{Cap rate}_{t-1} + \frac{\text{Cap rate}_{t-1}}{\text{Cap rate}_t} \right] - 1 \qquad (22)$$

where P_t = Property's price at end of time t.
NOI_t = Net operating income generated by property in time t.
Cap rate$_t$ = Property's capitalization rate at end of time t.

This simplified approach can be used to examine the covariance of total returns and its components.[20]

From the reconstructed quarterly nominal NOI, capitalization rates and total returns, a matrix of correlation coefficients was generated for the 1978–91 period (see Exhibit 3–22). From Exhibit 3–22, we can see that there is relatively little correlation of nominal NOI among the four major property types. The largest correlation coefficient is between office and retail (22.8 percent), and the smallest is between office and R&D/office (–9.2 percent). In the long run, it is the initial level and growth of NOI that determines a property's (or portfolio's) total return. However, the observed correlation of total returns among property types was quite high. For example, the correlation coefficient between the office sector's total return and that of

---

[20] In general, given the correlation coefficients for any two groups of assets ($\rho_{1,2}$ and $\rho_{2,3}$), the correlation coefficient for the linked asset group ($\rho_{1,3}$) is bounded by

$$\rho_{1,3} \geq \rho_{1,2} \times \rho_{2,3} - \sqrt{(1 - \rho_{1,2}^2)(1 - \rho_{2,3}^2)} \text{ and} \qquad (23)$$

$$\rho_{1,3} \leq \rho_{1,2} \times \rho_{2,3} + \sqrt{(1 - \rho_{1,2}^2)(1 - \rho_{2,3}^2)}$$

For example, if the correlation coefficients between stocks and bonds ($\rho_{\text{Stocks, Bonds}}$) and bonds and real estate ($\rho_{\text{Bonds, Property}}$) were known, a bounded range of the correlation between the returns of stocks and real estate ($\rho_{\text{Stocks, Property}}$) could be identified.

EXHIBIT 3–22
Russell/NCREIF Correlation Characteristics by Property Type (Excluding Apartments), 1978–93

	Implied Nominal Income				Implied Capitalization Rates				Total Returns			
	Office	Retail	R&D/Office	Warehouse	Office	Retail	R&D/Office	Warehouse	Office	Retail	R&D/Office	Warehouse
Implied nominal income:												
Office	1.000											
Retail	0.228	1.000										
R&D/office	−0.092	0.079	1.000									
Warehouse	−0.008	0.053	0.197	1.000								
Implied capitalization rates:												
Office	0.924	0.224	−0.173	−0.076	1.000							
Retail	0.213	0.964	0.078	0.023	0.273	1.000						
R&D/office	−0.116	0.045	0.880	0.112	−0.048	0.133	1.000					
Warehouse	−0.045	0.032	0.155	0.925	0.019	0.079	0.215	1.000				
Total returns:												
Office	0.091	−0.016	0.229	0.191	−0.292	−0.169	−0.145	−0.139	1.000			
Retail	0.057	0.105	0.026	0.117	−0.196	−0.162	−0.314	−0.176	0.609	1.000		
R&D/office	0.051	0.084	0.244	0.187	−0.248	−0.091	−0.244	−0.102	0.758	0.676	1.000	
Warehouse	0.113	0.069	0.097	0.122	−0.225	−0.130	−0.277	−0.262	0.850	0.761	0.749	1.000

the warehouse sector was 85.0 percent. What explains this abnormality? Two factors. First, the comparison made in Exhibit 3–22 is of quarterly returns. The fundamental approach (which states that the important determinants of return are the initial level and growth of NOI) is based on longer holding periods. To the extent that these holding periods vary, it is not surprising that there are different observed correlation coefficients. Second, the deviation from the long-run expected relationship (between nominal NOI growth and total return) is also attributable to the perverse movement of capitalization rates over the observed period. Specifically, there was a very high degree of correlation between property type NOI and its capitalization rates (ranging from 88.0 to 96.4 percent). This relationship is the opposite of what should occur. That is, in the long run, capitalization rates should move inversely with NOI growth. Investors should be willing to accept lower capitalization rates for growing NOI.[21] In the 1980s, investors broke from this relationship by purchasing properties with declining NOI at lower and lower capitalization rates (see Pagliari and Webb [1992]). Not coincidentally, this perverse economic behavior coincided with the well-chronicled capital frenzy of the 1980s.

Notwithstanding the perverse pricing (as measured by capitalization rates) of the 1980s, the low correlation of NOI from the various property types suggests that a portfolio diversified by property type will substantially reduce the long-run risk (for a given level of return) by virtue of these low correlation coefficients (i.e., portfolio risk is reduced by combining properties with less than perfect correlations). Reducing risk also entails eliminating much of the unsystematic risk associated with individual properties as well as property types.

Because the apartment index was first reported in 1988, a decade after the total index's commencement, the correlation matrix of property type returns was re-estimated to cover the period 1988:1 to 1993:4 (see Exhibit 3–23). When reviewing the correlation of nominal NOI, two observations merit comment. First, the apartment sector generally has strong positive correlations with other property types. This suggests that the inclusion of the apartment sector would have

---

[21] More accurately, real NOI growth should be inversely linked to capitalization rate movements. See Hartzell et al. (1988).

EXHIBIT 3–23

Russell/NCREIF Correlation Characteristics by Property Type, 1988–93

	Implied Nominal Income					Implied Capitalization Rates					Total Returns				
	Office	Retail	R&D/Office	Warehouse	Apartments	Office	Retail	R&D/Office	Warehouse	Apartments	Office	Retail	R&D/Office	Warehouse	Apartments
Implied nominal income:															
Office	1.000														
Retail	0.112	1.000													
R&D/office	-0.068	0.312	1.000												
Warehouse	-0.029	0.331	0.614	1.000											
Apartments	0.480	0.475	0.259	0.449	1.000										
Implied capitalization rates:															
Office	0.915	0.219	-0.089	-0.088	0.498	1.000									
Retail	0.145	0.930	0.262	0.227	0.440	0.359	1.000								
R&D/office	-0.022	0.345	0.940	0.556	0.262	0.063	0.408	1.000							
Warehouse	-0.027	0.424	0.552	0.891	0.498	0.079	0.453	0.623	1.000						
Apartments	0.487	0.453	0.198	0.342	0.974	0.559	0.480	0.256	0.440	1.000					
Total returns:															
Office	-0.119	-0.295	0.073	0.168	-0.203	-0.509	-0.570	-0.201	-0.237	-0.340	1.000				
Retail	-0.103	0.003	0.078	0.226	0.009	-0.407	-0.365	-0.233	-0.145	-0.155	0.785	1.000			
R&D/office	-0.134	-0.053	0.236	0.228	0.039	-0.430	-0.377	-0.108	-0.124	-0.128	0.771	0.885	1.000		
Warehouse	0.001	-0.244	0.049	0.107	-0.157	-0.355	-0.532	-0.233	-0.354	-0.263	0.876	0.813	0.771	1.000	
Apartments	-0.036	0.093	0.239	0.445	0.083	-0.240	-0.148	0.025	0.272	-0.144	0.532	0.649	0.669	0.372	1.000

moderately reduced the risk of a real estate portfolio over the longer term. Second, the correlations of the other property types are generally stronger with one another than was observed for the longer time horizon (compare to Exhibit 3–22). For example, the warehouse and R&D/office sectors had a 19.7 percent correlation of nominal NOI over the 1978:1–1993:4 time period, while in the shorter time period (1988:1–1993:4) their correlation was 61.4 percent. This illustrates the notion that real estate return data can be very period specific, and its application to future periods must be judged very carefully.

In addition to stronger correlations of nominal NOI among the property types, capitalization rates generally exhibited greater levels of correlation over the shorter time period. Similarly, the hypothesized inverse relationship between a property type's capitalization rate and its total return strengthened considerably over the shortened time period. For example, the retail sector's capitalization rate had a -16.2 percent correlation with its total return over the longer (1978:1–1993:4) time period, while over the shorter time period, the relationship was -36.5 percent. Finally, comparing the correlation of total returns indicates a much higher degree of correlation among the property types over the shorter time period (a range of 77.1 to 87.6 percent compared to the longer time period (60.9 to 85.0 percent, excluding the apartment sector). It is also interesting to note in the shorter time period (see Exhibit 3–23) the apartment sector's correlation with the other property types (37.2 to 66.9 percent) compared to the narrower ranges for the other property type total returns.

A similar analysis was prepared for the four major geographic regions of the Russell/NCREIF index. See Exhibit 3–24, which covers the 1978:1–1993:4 period. Again, by examining the correlation of nominal NOI among the regions, it is obvious that portfolios diversified by region are also likely to reduce portfolio risk to a more systematic level. For the regions, there were strong negative correlations between a region's capitalization rate and its total return (e.g., the West's capitalization rates had a correlation of -34.8 percent with its total return, and the South had a correlation of -22.4 percent). However, the correlations among regional total returns were in a very narrow band, ranging from 54.1 to 69.5 percent, but at a level generally lower than that for property types.

EXHIBIT 3–24

Russell/NCREIF Correlation Characteristics by Region, 1978–93

	Implied Nominal Income				Implied Capitalization Rates				Total Returns			
	East	Midwest	South	West	East	Midwest	South	West	East	Midwest	South	West
Implied nominal income:												
East	1.000											
Midwest	0.332	1.000										
South	0.056	-0.136	1.000									
West	-0.159	-0.108	0.385	1.000								
Implied capitalization rates:												
East	0.976	0.317	0.047	-0.167	1.000							
Midwest	0.324	0.976	-0.126	-0.119	0.346	1.000						
South	0.041	-0.122	0.964	0.328	0.069	-0.080	1.000					
West	-0.200	-0.100	0.360	0.893	-0.135	-0.040	0.384	1.000				
Total returns:												
East	-0.036	0.029	0.101	0.076	-0.244	-0.117	-0.064	-0.240	1.000			
Midwest	0.009	0.005	-0.006	0.085	-0.160	-0.211	-0.160	-0.245	0.690	1.000		
South	0.089	-0.009	0.040	0.154	-0.043	-0.120	-0.224	-0.131	0.599	0.541	1.000	
West	0.134	0.018	0.003	0.110	-0.026	-0.131	-0.171	-0.348	0.691	0.695	0.632	1.000

Caveat: Return Distributions

The notion of systematic risk as it relates to real estate is an evolving area of research. Webb, Miles, and Guilkey (1992) used a hedonic, transaction-driven model in an attempt to circumvent the potential problems of appraisal-based returns. While they found greater volatility with the hedonic (versus appraisal-based) model, they also found that "[t]he variance of returns on well diversified portfolios of real estate may not be understated, however, as the risk in transaction-driven real estate returns is predominately diversifiable." Young and Graff (1993) examined the continuously compounded annual total returns for specific office, retail, research and development, and industrial properties in the Russell/NCREIF index for the period 1980–92. They concluded that property return distributions are not normal and do not have finite variance. Myer and Webb (1994) reached a similar conclusion using quarterly returns generated from the Russell/NCREIF Property Index. In addition, Liu, Hartzell, and Grissom (1992) note the negative skewedness (i.e., more than 50 percent of the distribution of property returns lie to the left of the mean of the distribution) of real estate returns. These studies cast doubt on the assumption of a normal distribution of property returns necessary to optimize a portfolio using the tenets of modern portfolio theory. Accordingly, care should be exercised when attempting to incorporate the preceding statistics into a portfolio optimization strategy.

CONCLUSION

This chapter overviewed real estate's historical investment characteristics in terms of the three components—average return, volatility, and covariance—needed to optimize any portfolio. (Notwithstanding the above caveat regarding the assumed distribution of returns, modern portfolio theory is still used by many academics and practitioners to set portfolio allocation standards.) As befits its importance, this chapter focused primarily on the return component. More specifically, it advocated examining the long-term fundamental components of return, namely, initial yield and growth in earnings. The concept of an inflation pass-through rate has been utilized to measure earnings growth relative to inflation. As the holding period lengthens, the impact of changing capitalization rates on the investment's total return diminishes.

Real estate's volatility has increased substantially over the last several years. Not surprisingly, this development resulted from the crash of property values beginning in the late 1980s. However, where real estate's volatility stands in relation to common stocks is still a matter of some debate.

Real estate's historical covariance shows an interesting pattern. While total quarterly returns have been highly correlated (more so by property type than by geographic region), the changes in nominal NOI and capitalization rates show significantly less correlation. Consequently, investors may find the correlation of total returns decreasing as their holding period lengthens, provided the low correlation found historically continues in the future. In turn, this long-term approach would be in keeping with the fundamental approach used to analyze returns.

REFERENCES

Breuggeman, William B.; A. H. Chen; and T. G. Thibodeau. "Real Estate Investment Funds: Performance and Portfolio Considerations." *AREUEA Journal*, Fall 1984, pp. 333–54.

Chopra, Vijay K., and William T. Ziemba. "The Effect of Errors in Means, Variances and Covariances on Optimal Portfolio Choice." *Journal of Portfolio Management*, Winter 1993, pp. 6–11.

Cole, Rebel; David Guilkey; and Mike Miles. "Toward an Assessment of the Reliability of Commercial Appraisals." *Appraisal Journal*, July 1986.

Cutler, David M.; James M. Poterba; and Lawrence H. Summers. "What Moves Stock Prices?" *Journal of Portfolio Management*, Spring 1989, pp. 4–12.

DeBondt, Werner F. M., and Richard H. Thaler. "Does the Stock Market Overreact?" *Journal of Finance*, July 1985, pp. 798–805.

Ennis, Richard M., and Paul Burik. "Pension Fund Real Estate Investment under a Simple Equilibrium Pricing Model." *Financial Analysts Journal*, May–June 1991, pp. 20–30.

Firstenberg, Paul M.; Stephen A. Ross; and Randall C. Zisler. "Real Estate: The Whole Story." *Journal of Portfolio Management*, Spring 1988, pp. 22–34.

Fogler, H. Russell. "20% in Real Estate: Can Theory Justify It?" *Journal of Portfolio Management,* Winter 1984, pp. 6–13.

Francis, Jack Clark. *Investments Analyses and Management.* New York: McGraw-Hill, 1980.

Fuller, Russell J.; Lex C. Huberts; and Michael Levinson. "Its Not Higgledy-Piggledy Growth." *Journal of Portfolio Management,* Winter 1992, pp. 38–45.

Fuller, Russell J.; Lex C. Huberts; and Michael J. Levinson. "Returns to E/P Strategies, Higgledy-Piggledy Growth, Analysts' Forecasts Errors, and Omitted Risk Factors." *Journal of Portfolio Management,* Winter 1993, pp. 13–24.

Garreau, Joel. *The Nine Nations of North America.* Boston: Houghton Mifflin, 1981.

Garreau, Joel. *Edge City: Life on the New Frontier.* New York: Doubleday, 1988.

Garrigan, Richard T., and Joseph L. Pagliari, Jr. "The Impact of Supply Changes on Real Net Operating Income: The Multi-family Perspective." *Real Estate Issues,* Spring–Summer 1992, pp. 24–32.

Geltner, David Michael. "Bias in Appraisal-Based Returns." *AREUEA Journal,* Fall 1989, pp. 338–52.

Geltner, David Michael. "A Further Examination of Appraisal Data and the Potential Bias in Real Estate Indexes: A Comment and Clarification." *AREUEA Journal,* Spring 1991, pp. 102–12.

Geltner, David Michael. "Smoothing in Appraisal-Based Returns." *Journal of Real Estate Finance and Economics,* September 1991, pp. 327–45.

Giliberto, S. Michael. *Managing Real Estate Duration: A New Perspective on the Use of Leverage.* New York: Salomon Brothers, October 1989.

Giliberto, S. Michael. *Real Estate Risk and Return: 1991 Survey Results.* New York: Salomon Brothers, March 31, 1992.

Gordon, Myron J., and Eli Shapiro. "Capital Equipment Analysis: The Required Rate of Profit." *Management Science,* October 1956, pp. 102–10.

Grieg, D. Wylie, and Michael S. Young. "New Measures of Future Property Performance and Risk." *Real Estate Review,* Spring 1991, pp. 17–25.

Gross, William H. "Selling the Noise." *Journal of Portfolio Management,* Spring 1989, pp. 61–63.

Guilkey, David; Mike Miles; and Rebel Cole. "The Motivation for Institutional Real Estate Sales and Implications for Asset Class Returns." *AREUEA Journal,* Spring 1989, pp. 70–86.

Hartzell, David J.; David G. Shulman; Terrence C. Langetieg; and Martin L. Leibowitz. "A Look at Real Estate Duration." *Journal of Portfolio Management,* Fall 1988, pp. 16–24.

Hartzell, David J.; David G. Shulman; and Charles H. Wurtzebach. "Refining the Analysis of Regional Diversification for Income-Producing Real Estate." *Journal of Real Estate Research,* Winter 1987, pp. 85–95.

Liu, Crocker H.; David J. Hartzell; and Terry V. Grissom. "The Role of Co-Skewness in the Pricing of Real Estate." *Journal of Real Estate Finance and Economics,* September 1992, pp. 299–319.

Markowitz, Harry. "Portfolio Selection." *Journal of Finance,* March 1952, pp. 77–91.

Miles, Mike; David Guilkey; Brian Webb; and Kevin Hunter. "An Empirical Evaluation of the Reliability of Commercial Appraisals, 1978–1990." Working paper, August 20, 1991.

Modigliani, Franco, and Merton M. Miller. "The Cost of Capital, Corporation Finance and the Theory of Investment." *American Economic Review,* June 1958, pp. 261–97.

Mueller, Glenn R., and Barry A. Ziering. "Real Estate Portfolio Diversification Using Economic Diversification." *Journal of Real Estate Research,* Fall 1992, pp. 375–86.

Myer, F. C. Neil, and James R. Webb. "Statistical Properties of Returns: Financial Assets versus Commercial Real Estate." *Journal of Real Estate Finance and Economics,* May 1994, pp. 267–82.

Pagliari, Joseph L., Jr. "Inside the Real Estate Yield." *Real Estate Review,* Fall 1991, pp. 48–53.

Pagliari, Joseph L., Jr., and James R. Webb. "Past and Future Sources of Commercial Real Estate Returns." *Journal of Real Estate Research,* Fall 1992, pp. 387–421.

Pagliari, Joseph L., Jr., and James R. Webb. "Real Estate Decay: A Paradigm." Working paper, November 1992.

Quan, Daniel C., and John M. Quigley. "Price Formation and the Appraisal Function in Real Estate Markets." *Journal of Real Estate Finance and Economics,* June 1991, pp. 127–46.

Ross, Stephen A., and Randall C. Zisler. "Risk and Return in Real Estate." *Journal of Real Estate Finance and Economics,* June 1991, pp. 175–90.

Rubens, Jack M.; Michael T. Bond; and James R. Webb. "The Inflation-Hedging Effectiveness of Real Estate." *Journal of Real Estate Research,* Summer 1989, pp. 45–55.

Russo, J. Joseph, and Paul J. M. Schoemaker. *Decision Traps: The Ten Barriers to Brilliant Decision-Making and How to Overcome Them.* New York: Simon & Schuster, 1989.

Saint-Pierre, Paul S. "Performance Fees: An Evaulation with Historical Industry Performance." *Strategies* (by Pension Realty Advisors, Inc.), Spring 1990, pp. 1–5.

Shiller, Robert. "Do Stock Prices Move Too Much to be Justified by Subsequent Changes in Dividends?" *American Economic Review,* June 1981, p. 421–36.

Shulman, David. *The Relative Risk of Equity Real Estate and Common Stocks: A New View.* New York: Salomon Brothers, Inc., June 30, 1986.

Webb, Brian; Mike Miles; and David Guilkey. "On the Nature of Systematic Risk in Commercial Real Estate." Working paper presented at the Real Estate Research Institute Conference, 1992.

Webb, James R. "On the Exclusion of Real Estate from the Market Portfolio." *Journal of Portfolio Management,* Fall 1990, pp. 78–84.

James R. Webb, and Pagliari, Joseph L., Jr. "Past and Future Sources of Commercial Real Estate Returns: A Regional Approach." Working paper, August 1994.

Webb, James R., and Jack H. Rubens. "How Much in Real Estate? A Surprising Answer." *Journal of Portfolio Management,* Spring 1987, pp. 10–14.

Wurtzebach, Charles H.; Glenn R. Mueller; and Donna Macchi. "The Impact of Inflation and Vacancy on Real Estate Returns." *Journal of Real Estate Research,* Summer 1991, pp. 153–68.

Young, Michael S., and Richard A. Graff. "Real Estate Is Not Normal: A Fresh Look at Real Estate Return Distributions." Paper presented at the American Real Estate Society Annual Meeting, April 1993.

CHAPTER 4

LEASES AS A KEY TO PERFORMANCE AND VALUE: UNDERSTANDING WHAT YOU HAVE VERSUS WHAT YOU HOPE FOR

Michael S. Young
The RREEF Funds

D. Wylie Greig
The RREEF Funds

INTRODUCTION

Commercial real estate can be viewed in financial terms as a hybrid of debt—the existing lease obligations—and equity—the right to release the property after the existing leases expire.[1] Its investment performance is either more bondlike or more equitylike (sensitive to inflation and market fluctuations), depending on the nature of the leases in place, the market demand for space, and the current and

Special appreciation is owed to William Knudson, portfolio analyst at RREEF, for his assistance in developing and analyzing the lease-level data used in the examples provided.

[1] David G. Booth, Daniel M. Cashdan, Jr., and Richard A. Graff, "Real Estate: A Hybrid of Debt and Equity," *Real Estate Review* 19 (Spring 1989), pp. 54–58; Richard A. Graff and Daniel M. Cashdan, Jr., "Some New Ideas in Real Estate Finance," *Journal of Applied Corporate Finance* 3 (Spring 1990), pp. 77–89; Richard A. Graff, "The Impact of Tax Issues on Real Estate Debt and Equity Separation," *Real Estate Review* 20 (Fall 1990), pp. 50–58; D. Wylie Greig and Michael S. Young, "New Measures of Future Property Performance and Risk," *Real Estate Review* 21 (Spring 1991), pp. 17–25; Daniel M. Cashdan, Jr., "Single-Tenant Properties Add Stability to Real Estate Portfolios," *Real Estate Review* 22 (Spring 1992), pp. 45–52; Richard A. Graff, "Perspectives on Debt-and-Equity Decomposition for Investors and Issuers of Real Estate Securities," *Journal of Real Estate Research* 7 (Fall 1992), pp. 449–67.

expected interest rate environment. Explicit recognition of these differences at the property level provides a powerful tool for understanding property values, predicting future performance, and measuring risk.

Understanding income properties as a hybrid of bondlike and equitylike components represents a paradigm shift in thinking about commercial real estate. It helps explain performance characteristics and allows comparison of individual investments to the generalized performance expectations often used to set portfolio strategy. Currently pension funds and other managers of mixed-asset portfolios must use generalized performance information for real estate when they make their asset allocation decisions. However, it is difficult, given the current investment performance technology, to determine whether the specific property investments will conform to general expectations.

This chapter describes the hybrid nature of commercial real estate. It also outlines a methodology for explicitly measuring performance expectations for multitenant commercial properties based on the character of existing leases and the credit quality of the lessee. The methodology is demonstrated on both a property and a portfolio level using an institutional-quality portfolio of retail and industrial properties. The chapter concludes by outlining ways the methodology can be employed by both real estate and mixed-asset fund managers to evaluate acquisitions and dispositions, monitor property and portfolio management decisions, and determine more precise performance expectations.

EQUITYLIKE AND DEBTLIKE ELEMENTS OF INCOME PROPERTY

The most basic distinction investors make among different asset classes is that between debt and equity. Debt involves a contractual obligation to make predetermined payments over a specified period of time. Equity represents ownership of an investment whose returns will be determined by its success or failure at its business activity over any given time period. The risk characteristics and expected returns from each type of asset are distinctly different. Ownership of commercial real estate is usually viewed as equity. The true nature of income property, however, lies somewhere between debt and equity.

Its performance embodies some of the characteristics of both bonds (debt) and stocks (equity). As a result, it tends to produce total returns that fall between those for bonds and those for common stocks over time.

Bonds, by virtue of the more predictable, contractual nature of their income, are seen as safer than stocks. Bonds have tended to produce lower returns than equity real estate. On the other hand, common stocks have generally outperformed equity real estate. A portfolio of the two assets, stocks and bonds, can be expected to achieve a total return equal to the weighted average of total returns for each component. Equity real estate appears to produce a similar result.

THE REAL ESTATE "FACTORY"

One useful way to think about real estate is as a factory. This real estate factory produces space to house business ventures, households, or other entities. The space is purchased by people or corporations that need it for a specific purpose. James Graaskamp described real estate as "artificially delineated space (cubage) with a fourth dimension of time."[2] Further, he asserted that "the real estate enterprise is concerned with the conversion of space-time to money-time." In his view, developers and owners create space and sell discrete cubage for a specified period of time. When the space is vacated by the tenant, the developer/owner is free to resell the same space to another user. Thus, real estate can be viewed as a long-lived asset that is sold to different users over an extended period of time.

The hybrid nature of real estate stems from the manner in which its space is "sold." Contractual obligations in the form of leases encumber the property and determine its income for as long as the leases are in effect. Leases are, in essence, obligations of tenants, whether individuals, partnerships, or corporations, to make periodic payments for predetermined lengths of time. In virtually all economically significant respects, a lease on commercial real estate is analogous to a

---

[2] Stephen P. Jarchow, ed., *Graaskamp on Real Estate* (Washington, DC: Urban Land Institute, 1991).

corporate bond. Leases resemble fixed-income securities and as such take on many of the same economic characteristics. The performance of fully leased income properties is decidedly "bondlike" during the time the leases are in force. The amount and quality of the income stream are determined by specified rent payments, lease maturities (termination dates), and the creditworthiness of the tenants. While some inflation protection may be provided in the leases through participation in sales made by the tenant, CPI clauses, expense pass-throughs, or other conditional rent provisions, these clauses do not change the essentially bondlike nature of the contractual obligation.

Once the existing leases expire, the property owner is exposed to changes in market conditions and may take advantage of his or her marketing skill to "resell" the property to the same or a different tenant. Investment performance becomes equitylike, akin to the opportunities and risks associated with ownership of any business venture, at the moment leases expire. Equity opportunities carry the risks that the space may remain vacant, may require extensive capital outlays to release, and may not be rented on as favorable terms as before. Equity risks are generally higher than risks on fixed-income investments. On the bright side, equity risks generally produce a commensurately higher return than bond risks.

The most significant differences between the debtlike and equity-like components of real estate are summarized in Exhibit 4–1.

The nature of the leases used to "sell" space to tenants determines whether a property's performance will be more bondlike or more equitylike. Long-term net-leased properties and sale/leasebacks are primarily bondlike. The investment performance of bondlike properties is determined primarily by the terms of the lease and the credit quality of the lessee. Conversely, multitenant properties with short-term leases are more equitylike; that is, the bulk of the property value is imbedded in leases yet to be written, the property's residual value. The investment performance of equitylike properties is more dependent on the physical, functional, and locational quality of the asset, ongoing market conditions, and the skill of the operator.

Investors typically require a higher return for a greater level of risk. Thus, all other things being equal, a property having more of its total value in the residual can be expected to produce a higher return owing to the uncertainty of future rental conditions. Future leases would have to be discounted at higher rates than current, more certain leases.

EXHIBIT 4–1
The Debt and Equity Components of Real Estate Ownership

Existing Leases: *The Debt Component*	*Future Leases:* *The Equity Component*
The portion of the property "sold" to tenants for a specified period of time.	The "unsold" portion of real estate.
Owner's occupancy rights are precluded by the "sale" for the term of the lease.	Occupancy rights retained by the property owner for subsequent sale or use.
Bondlike features. Obligations to pay a specified rent for a fixed term. The return is "capped" by conditions of the lease.	Equitylike features. Speculative.
Credit quality of the tenant's obligation to pay can be rated, at least informally. A form of asset-backed bond.	No specified "cap" on returns, except what the market will allow.
Nominal assets—fixed payments with minimal inflation protection features.	Real assets—unoccupied space is repriced over time at future rent levels. Rents are adjusted for inflation when markets are balanced.
Individual leases differ by credit and default characteristics.	Unleased space can be regarded as zero-coupon equity. The space has future value but no income stream until available for releasing.
Building space is priced according to "spot" prices—rents currently available in the market for similar credit and maturity.	Priced according to "future" prices—the prices that reflect futures for similar credit and maturity.
Low income volatility.	Higher income volatility driven by market conditions and the manager's expertise and relative negotiating strength.
Volatility in valuations driven by changes in interest rates and spreads for credit.	Volatility in valuations driven by operating risks as well as changes in interest rates and spreads for credit.

CATEGORIZING INVESTMENTS BY PERFORMANCE CHARACTERISTICS

There is growing evidence that particular property types do not exhibit a characteristic type of performance as measured by total return (income plus appreciation) over time.[3] An industrial property, for example, may exhibit the same sequence of total returns over time as an apartment project or office building despite the yearly differences. The performance of a multitenant industrial property on a relatively short-term lease is more likely to look like that of an apartment or multitenant office building on a short-term lease than that of another industrial building subject to a long-term lease.

Investments in the securities markets are routinely categorized as much by their expected return characteristics as by the physical nature (if any) of their underlying assets. Common stocks, for example, are described as *small-capitalization, large-capitalization, growth,* or *income* as much as they are by their industry groups or underlying companies. Real estate investments can also be categorized in more meaningful ways than property type or geographic location, the traditional way of viewing differences among real estate assets. Understanding the essential equitylike and debtlike attributes of individual property investments would facilitate this new view of real estate as a productive asset having a multifaceted nature. Real estate analogues to securities investments, such as those suggested in Exhibit 4–2, might improve investor understanding of expected real estate performance and encourage new investment from those seeking particular investment characteristics to complement or augment existing multi-asset-class portfolios.

USES FOR THE NEW PARADIGM

The state of the art of performance measurement for income-producing real estate has been relatively static for nearly 20 years. Real estate owners—including the most rapidly growing class of own-

---

[3] Michael S. Young and D. Wylie Greig, "Drums along the Efficient Frontier," *Real Estate Review* 22 (Winter 1939), pp. 18–29.

EXHIBIT 4–2
Real Estate Analogues to Stock and Bond Investments

Stock & Bond Category	Real Estate Analogue
Growth stock	Below-market rents, short-term leases, supply-constrained markets
Income stock	High current capitalization rate, long-term leases
Small capitalization	Lower-priced, smaller properties
Large capitalization	Larger, higher-valued properties
Leveraged equity	Leveraged equity
Blue chip	Dominant or trophy properties
High-grade bond	Low loan-to-value mortgages on high-quality properties
High-yield bond	Second mortgage investments or bridge financing

ers, the pension funds—receive relatively little information about assets in their portfolios that provides substantive insight into the character of expected returns and risks.

Typically, a real estate investment manager reports once a quarter on performance at the portfolio level in terms of a rate of return earned (or accrued) on income, capital appreciation, and a total of the two. Investment managers also often supply some descriptive information about the portfolio, such as its composition by value, property type, geographic area, size of individual properties, life cycle, or the like. Few managers routinely provide tenant-level statistics for property investments. All too often, property- or tenant-level data are viewed as proprietary for fear that the data will be used improperly or misconstrued or will give ammunition to critics or competitors.

Nonetheless, a 1990 survey of pension funds by Standard & Poor's found a substantial desire for improved performance reporting.[4] Pension funds and their consultants complain that the information managers provide is inadequate to enable forecasting of future returns, either in absolute terms or relative to other asset classes. This is important in a period when the contribution of real estate to a mixed-asset portfolio is being questioned and real estate is increasingly

---

[4] Presentation by Charles Dorris of Standard & Poor's to the winter meeting of the Pension Real Estate Association, Santa Monica, California, February 1990.

being justified as a portfolio diversifier rather than as a generator of stellar returns.

One explanation for the dearth of data reported by managers may be the lack of an analytical framework able to capture salient features of properties or tenants in a way that is meaningful to asset managers, portfolio managers, and owners alike. On the following pages, we present a workable framework based on existing finance principles and techniques. We show how to use readily obtainable information on properties, tenants, and leases in place to:

- Measure tenant quality related to default risk, contribution to income, and the value of current leasehold interests.
- Determine the proportion to total property (or portfolio) value associated with existing leases versus anticipated future income streams.
- Understand the essential nature of real estate on the continuum from equitylike to bondlike investment.

The uses of these and derivative measures are legion in predicting future investment performance and evaluating tenant and market risk. The prediction of future investment performance, however, is beyond the scope of this discussion.

On the following pages, we introduce a basic analytical model that underlies the framework. An example of a portfolio of multitenant retail and industrial properties will highlight interpretations of model results. Finally, we present a range of possible uses of the model related to portfolio construction and management, acquisitions, and property management.

TRADITIONAL VIEWS OF VALUE

The notion that a substantial portion of the value of commercial real estate is imbedded in the value of its underlying leases is widely understood. With few exceptions, real estate investment managers, acquisition specialists, and appraisers make explicit income forecasts based on existing and anticipated future lease conditions. Analysis of current and future leases follows discounted cash flow techniques developed over the past 20 years.

In short, real estate analysts routinely perform tenant-by-tenant cash flow forecasts to produce a stream of anticipated annual net receipts, usually for 10 or 11 years. To boil these numbers into a current-value estimate, the 10th or 11th year's net operating income is "capitalized" into a reversionary amount, and the resulting annual net cash flows and reversionary amount are discounted to a present value figure at some rate presumed to represent the *cost of capital* or *hurdle rate* of the most probable investor.

Without getting into the details of how capitalization and discount rates are determined, suffice it to say that rigor seldom characterizes the process of selecting these important assumptions. We suggest there are better ways utilizing finance principles and current knowledge of conditions in the broader capital markets.

THE DEBT-EQUITY MODEL

If commercial real estate is viewed as a combination of debt, that is, leases from corporations as an obligation analogous in financial terms to corporate debt, and of equity, or ownership in a productive "factory" for creating future leases, the techniques of debt and equity analysis may also be applied to the two components.[5]

Extracting Returns from the Capital Markets

Algebraically, the value of a property is the sum of the present values of existing leases and future leases (residuals), all net of operating expenses and capital costs:

> Property value = Present value of existing leases + Present value of future leases (or residuals)

Exhibit 4–3 further illustrates the debt-equity model by showing

---

[5] The dynamic capitalization model proposed by Gordon Blackadar of Metropolitan Life Insurance Co. utilizes actuarial techniques and terminology in its view that property values are composed of the sum of the individual lease values. Unlike the traditional discounted cash flow technique used by appraisers and other analysts in which 10 or more years of cash flow are projected and the resulting stream is discounted at a single rate, the dynamic capitalization technique discounts each lease separately and then sums the present values to arrive at the current valuation. The debt-equity model presented here is more in the spirit of Blackadar's dynamic capitalization. See C. Gordon Blackadar, *Dynamic Capitalization: Appraising with Real Rates of Interest,* 3 supplements (New York: Metropolitan Life Insurance Co., 1981–82).

EXHIBIT 4–3
The Debt-Equity Model

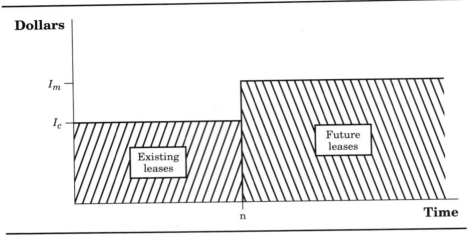

that a property's total value, the total shaded area, is composed of the present value of existing leases at current rents of I_c with a term remaining of n years plus the present value of future leases (residuals) at some market rent I_m deferred n years but extending into perpetuity by presuming releasing. In the remainder of this section, we adapt the inflation, stock, real estate, and bond data from Graff and Cashdan.[6]

By adapting the above equation, we can extract estimates of lease returns and residual returns from publicly available data series. The value equations can be expressed as return equations as follows:

Property return = (Value of existing leases/
Property value) × Return on existing leases + (Value of the
residual/ Property value) × Return on residual

From this equation we can derive the return of residuals once we have estimates of the other variables. We can approximate the return for existing leases by recognizing that leases should behave somewhat like corporate bonds. The estimates of bond, and therefore lease, returns shown in Exhibits 4–4 and 4–5 are the Shearson Leh-

---

[6] Graff and Cashdan, "Some New Ideas in Real Estate Finance."

EXHIBIT 4–4
Nominal Rates of Return for Various Assets and Computed Residual Returns, 1975–89

Year	Inflation	S&P 500	Real Estate	Bonds/Leases	Residuals at Various Fractions of Total Value		
					@80%	@70%	@60%
1975	7.01	37.20	9.90	9.49	10.00	10.08	10.17
1976	4.81	23.84	11.20	12.32	10.92	10.72	10.45
1977	6.77	-7.18	12.00	3.32	14.17	15.72	17.79
1978	9.03	6.56	16.00	2.13	19.47	21.94	25.25
1979	13.31	18.44	20.78	5.99	24.48	27.12	30.64
1980	12.40	32.42	18.06	6.42	20.97	23.05	25.82
1981	8.94	-4.91	16.57	10.51	18.09	19.17	20.61
1982	3.87	21.41	9.39	26.11	5.21	2.22	-1.76
1983	3.80	22.51	13.23	8.60	14.39	15.21	16.32
1984	3.95	6.27	13.07	14.37	12.75	12.51	12.20
1985	3.77	32.16	9.85	18.06	7.80	6.33	4.38
1986	1.13	18.47	6.34	13.14	4.64	3.43	1.81
1987	4.41	5.12	5.39	3.66	5.82	6.13	6.54
1988	4.42	16.81	7.15	6.68	7.27	7.35	7.46
1989	4.64	31.49	6.03	12.74	4.35	3.15	1.56
Mean	6.15	17.37	11.66	10.24	12.02	12.28	12.62
Standard deviation	3.31	13.20	4.49	6.08	6.23	7.59	9.49

EXHIBIT 4–5
Real Rates of Return for Various Assets and Computed Residual Returns, 1975–89

Year	S&P 500	Real Estate	Bonds/Leases	Residuals at Various Fractions of Total Value		
				@80%	@70%	@60%
1975	28.21	2.70	2.32	2.80	2.86	2.96
1976	18.16	6.10	7.17	5.83	5.64	5.38
1977	-13.07	4.90	-3.23	6.93	8.38	10.32
1978	-2.27	6.39	-6.33	9.57	11.84	14.87
1979	4.53	6.59	-6.46	9.86	12.19	15.29
1980	17.81	5.04	-5.32	7.62	9.47	11.94
1981	-12.71	7.00	1.44	8.39	9.39	10.71
1982	16.89	5.31	21.41	1.29	-1.58	-5.42
1983	18.03	9.08	4.62	10.20	11.00	12.06
1984	2.23	8.77	10.02	8.46	8.24	7.94
1985	27.36	5.86	13.77	3.88	2.47	0.58
1986	17.15	5.15	11.88	3.47	2.27	0.67
1987	0.68	0.94	-0.72	1.35	1.65	2.04
1988	11.87	2.61	2.16	2.73	2.81	2.91
1989	25.66	1.33	7.74	-0.27	-1.42	-2.95
Mean	10.70	5.19	4.03	5.47	5.68	5.95
Standard deviation	13.01	2.34	7.80	3.38	4.53	6.24

man Brothers Intermediate Government/Corporate Bond Index (later we will propose a method for estimating returns on leases based on a risk premium over equivalent-duration Treasury instruments).[7] The real estate returns for the years 1978 to 1989 are the returns on the Russell/NCREIF Property Index, and the real estate returns for earlier years are those published by Real Estate Research Corp.[8] Returns for stocks are from the Standard & Poor's 500 Stock Index, and inflation is measured by the consumer price index.[9]

As we will find later, when we apply the debt-equity model to actual properties, the value of current leases generally constitutes less than half of the total value of a property unless the leases are exceptionally long term. Thus, we depart from the Graff and Cashdan approach of starting with a 50–50 split between current leases and residuals and letting the split for future years be the result of prior years' estimates. Instead, we hold the proportions of current lease value and residual value constant for each year of calculation at three different amounts: 20–80, 30–70, and 40–60, respectively. There are merits and demerits to either approach, but we note that holding the proportions constant avoids the possible situation where either the current lease value or the residual value exceeds 100 percent, a distinct possibility in the Graff and Cashdan approach.

By way of example, we will use the information for 1975 from Exhibit 4–4 and apply the formula shown above to compute the residual return. When the value of the residual represents 80 percent of the total value, the value of the existing leases represents the remaining 20 percent of value. In 1975, the returns for real estate and bonds/leases were 9.90 and 9.49 percent, respectively. Therefore, the formula can be written as follows:

$$9.90\% = 0.20 \ (9.49\%) + 0.80(\text{Return on residual})$$

or

$$\text{Return on residual} = [9.90\% - 0.20(9.49)]/0.80 = 10.00\%$$

Exhibit 4–4 shows the computed residual returns for the period

---

[7] Shearson Lehman Hutton Inc., *The Shearson Lehman Hutton Bond Market Report* (New York, 1990).

[8] National Council of Real Estate Investment Fiduciaries and Frank Russell Co., *Russell/ NCREIF Property Index* (Tacoma, WA); Equitable Real Estate Investment Management Inc. and Real Estate Research Corp., *Emerging Trends* (Chicago).

[9] Ibbotson Associates, Inc., *Stocks, Bonds, Bills, and Inflation Yearbook* (Chicago, 1990).

1975 to 1989 in nominal terms, and Exhibit 4–5 shows the computed residual returns in real terms. The mean annual returns for the 15 years are not notably different in either nominal or real terms as we move from a 20–80 split between current leases and residuals to a 40–60 split. Indeed, the results are similar to those of Graff and Cashdan. As expected, the residual returns fall between the returns of bonds and stocks in both nominal and real terms.

Most researchers have observed that the published returns of aggregate real estate performance such as the Russell/NCREIF Property Index show real estate to be a high-return/low-risk asset class where risk is measured as the standard deviation of returns. This seems odd, since other assets having high returns also exhibit relatively high risk. Notice that the S&P 500 returns have a high-return/high-risk pattern. The answer to this riddle can be found in the hybrid nature of real estate as part bondlike and part equitylike, with each component having a higher risk than the aggregate. But aggregating two less than perfectly correlated assets produces a lower standard deviation than either of the assets separately, exactly what our exercise has shown.

VALUING LEASES AND RESIDUALS: AN EXAMPLE

Leases may be valued by bond valuation techniques that have been in use for decades. Only three variables are needed to value leases treated as bonds: the pattern of net rents, the credit quality of the tenant, and the risk premium corresponding to the credit quality. The present value of a lease is simply the present value of the stream of net rents at the appropriate discount rate. This is represented as a premium over the risk-free rate (Treasury rate) at a point in time equal to the "duration" of the lease.

Duration is a term of art in bond analysis defined as the time-weighted present value of the lease net cash flows.[10] While duration varies with the discount rate and the pattern of cash flows, a very good approximation to the duration in years at current interest rates results from dividing the term of the lease in months by 25.

---

[10] See Chapter 2, "Portfolio Management Concepts and Their Application to Real Estate," for an introduction to this concept.

EXHIBIT 4–6
Tenant Credit Quality versus Risk Premium and Default Risk

Credit Rating	Description	Risk Premium over Treasuries	Default Risk
A	Highest possible rating Better than commercial credit Little default risk	0.75%	1%
B	Best commercial credit Very low probability of default	0.95	4
C	Good commercial credit Small probability of default	1.40	8
D	Average commercial credit Real potential for default	1.90	14
E	No credit or little business experience New "mom and pop" or undercapitalized start-up	2.30	22

Thus, the duration of a 60-month lease would be approximately 2.4 years.

Credit quality of the tenant may be difficult to determine if the tenant does not have publicly traded debt. This is, unfortunately, the most common case in commercial properties.[11] One possible approach, and the one taken here, is to have the asset manager most familiar with the tenants rate them on a relative basis using a numerical or letter scale. Naturally, without an objective source of credit information and credit-processing technology, differences in judgment will occur from manager to manager. This inconsistency is unavoidable, but with experience and across many managers, the differences should diminish over time.

For purposes of exposition, we used a five-point letter scale of A through E, where A represents the highest-quality tenant. Credit quality is interpreted as a tenant's likelihood of meeting its lease obligations. Taken another way, credit quality is a measure of the risk of loss or default on lease obligations that can be expressed in percentage terms. We used the scales described in Exhibit 4–6 to

---

[11] KMV Corp. (Kealhofer, McQuown, Vasicek) of San Francisco produces a monthly assessment of the credit quality of more than 6,900 domestic firms with publicly traded debt and equity. The ratings are described along three measures: the Standard & Poor's rating, the implicit debenture rating (IDR), and the expected default frequency (EDF).

express two distinct ideas: the risk premium over Treasuries implied by the credit rating and the default risk expressed as a percentage of expected rent subject to loss. The risk premium will be used later to determine the appropriate discount rate for a tenant's lease, and the default risk will be used as a separate measure of the possibility of rental loss. The estimates presented in Exhibit 4–6 were subjectively chosen and bear no particular relation to empirical research in this new field. Indeed, the real estate industry would be well served by fundamental research into the relations among tenant credit, risk premia, and probability of default.

Most tenants fall in the C or D credit categories rather than at the top of the scale. A-rated tenants are relatively rare and are often shunned by landlords, as they demand heavily discounted rental rates or preferential lease terms.

The risk premia associated with the different credit ratings are added to prevailing Treasury yields that represent the risk-free rate at the time of the valuation. The Treasury yield curve summarized in Exhibit 4–7 was used for this analysis.

EXHIBIT 4–7
Risk-Free (Treasury) Yield Curve

Years to Maturity	Annualized Yield
0.00	7.00%
0.25	7.10
0.50	7.50
0.75	7.90
1.00	8.10
3.00	8.30
5.00	8.50
7.00	8.80
10.00	9.10
15.00	9.00
20.00	8.95
25.00	8.95
30.00	8.92

CALCULATING THE PRESENT VALUE OF EACH LEASE

There are several ways to estimate the discount rate with which to calculate the present value of a lease in a manner analogous to bond valuation, including yield to maturity, yield equivalent to zero-coupon Treasury "strips," or yield at equivalent Treasury duration. Because we are concerned principally with institutional grade, income-producing property owned by pension plans and insurance companies that routinely match the duration of liabilities to some multiple of the duration of assets, we chose the later approach, but others are equally valid if consistently applied.

To compute the present value of each lease with the Treasury duration-matching technique, we follow these five steps:

1. Determine the net rent month by month for each lease, taking care to include all scheduled rental increases, anticipated percentage or other contingent rent for the current year, current operating expense reimbursements, and a proportionate share of total operating expenses not recovered from tenants.

2. Approximate the duration of the lease by dividing the remaining term of the lease in months by 25.[12]

3. Interpolate along the Treasury yield curve to find the risk-free discount rate appropriate to the duration found in step 2. For example, a lease with 60 months remaining would have a duration of 2.40 years. Using the Treasury yield curve from Exhibit 4–8, the estimated risk-free rate would be 8.24 percent.

4. Add the risk premium appropriate to the credit of the tenant to arrive at the risk-adjusted discount rate. For example, from Exhibit 4–4, a lease with a C credit having a risk premium of 1.40 percent would produce a 9.64 percent risk-adjusted discount at a duration of 2.40 years.

---

[12] Alternatively, the duration of each lease can be computed directly, thereby bypassing reliance on this appropriation. Additionally, we have chosen to use the intercept of duration and the credit risk–adjusted yield curve as the point at which to select the appropriate discount rate for each lease. We could just as well have chosen to use the "average life" of the lease analogous to the average life or weighted-average maturity of a bond. The choice is immaterial as long as the method is consistently and logically applied. Duration uses the time until payments as the weights, while average life uses the payments as weights.

EXHIBIT 4–8
Yield Curves for Tenants with Various Credit Ratings

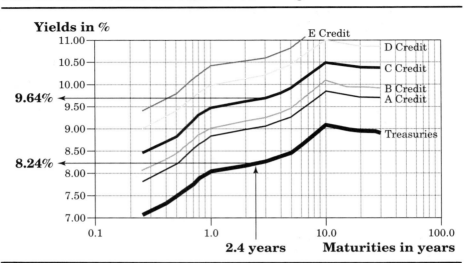

5. Discount the net monthly rents resulting from step 1 at the risk-adjusted discount rate from step 4 to determine the current present value of the lease.

This process is repeated for each lease. The sum represents the value of all current leasehold interests, adjusted by tenant quality. The present value of future leasehold interests (the pure equity value of the property) is the total market value of the property computed by traditional means less the present value of current leases.[13]

APPLICATION TO AN INSTITUTIONAL PORTFOLIO

The application of the model was tested using detailed property and tenant-specific data from a portfolio of eight properties managed by a major institutional real estate advisor on behalf of a group of domestic pension investors. The properties consist of four community shopping

---

[13] The traditional approaches to income property valuation can be found in textbooks such as *The Appraisal of Real Estate*, 8th ed. (Chicago: The Appraisal Institute, 1992).

centers having a total of 95 tenants and an aggregate market value of about $51 million and four industrial properties with 105 tenants and an aggregate market value of about $54 million. All the properties had been acquired and managed by the same investment manager for over nine years. Extensive historical and current information was available.

Tenant Credit Quality and Default Risk

There are several ways to measure the credit quality of leases in a particular property. Each has its particular usefulness and can be used either as absolute measures or for comparative purposes. They include:

- *An implicit credit rating,* expressed as a letter score, which represents the weighted average of the credit ratings for each tenant in the property.

- *An estimated default risk,* expressed as a percentage estimate of the likelihood of a default. This is the average of the default risk associated with each existing tenant, weighted by the present value of each lease.

- *The actual lease yield* is the risk-adjusted discount rate for the existing leases computed as the weighted average by value of the risk-adjusted discount rates applied to each lease. For a particular lease duration, we would expect that a higher lease yield would indicate a lower-quality, higher-risk collection of leases. (The estimated default risk and actual lease yields in Exhibit 4–9 for the retail and industrial groups seem to contradict this statement. As we will see in Exhibit 4–11, however, the apparent anomaly can be explained by the difference in the respective lease durations.)

- *The market lease yield* is what the risk-adjusted discount rate for the property would be if all tenants had leases with a term of years typical of the market. This is considered a better estimate of property yield over the longer term than the actual lease yield, which is calculated from actual unexpired terms of the existing leases, which are likely to be shorter than market rent terms. (In Exhibit 4–9, it is merely a coincidence that the market lease yields of the retail and industrial groups are nearly identical. The market lease yield is a function of future

EXHIBIT 4–9
Measures of Tenant Credit Quality and Default Risk

Property	Implicit Credit Rating	Estimated Default Risk	Actual Lease Yield	Market Lease Yield
Retail:				
Property A	C+	6.43%	9.59%	9.49%
Property B	C	7.96	9.70	9.72
Property C	C	9.00	9.57	9.88
Property D	C−	9.44	9.72	10.03
Average	C	8.26%	9.67%	9.79%
Industrial:				
Property W	C−	10.47%	9.68%	9.80%
Property X	D	14.41	9.80	10.05
Property Y	D+	11.18	9.47	9.88
Property Z	C	8.45	9.47	9.63
Average	D+	10.45%	9.61%	9.80%
Portfolio average	C−	9.45%	9.64%	9.80%

lease terms, credit, and relative space values within the property.)

Each of these measures is shown in Exhibit 4–9 for the eight properties evaluated.

Implicit credit rating is perhaps the most easily communicated measure of the relative quality of a property's tenancy. The letter rankings of implicit credit ratings are more easily assimilated than the numerical rankings of the other three measures and are similar to the letter rankings of the major bond rating agencies: Standard & Poor's, Moody's, and Duff and Phelps.

Proportion of Total Property Value Associated with Existing Leases

The debt-equity model was used to calculate the proportion of each property's value associated with the existing lease portfolio. These figures are given in Exhibit 4–10.

The retail properties are more bondlike (as measured by the ratio of lease value to total value) than the industrial properties, but this may be just a reflection of the particular properties in our sample. We would expect less dramatic differences from a wider variety of

EXHIBIT 4–10
Value of Existing Lease Portfolios

Property	Lease Portfolio Value	Residual Equity Value	Total Property Value
Retail:			
Property A	33.6%	66.4%	100.0%
Property B	29.4	70.6	100.0
Property C	26.4	73.6	100.0
Property D	21.9	78.1	100.0
Average	27.7%	72.3%	100.0%
Industrial:			
Property W	17.1%	82.9%	100.0%
Property X	9.9	90.1	100.0
Property Y	10.9	89.1	100.0
Property Z	17.6	82.4	100.0
Average	15.3%	84.7%	100.0%
Portfolio average	21.3%	78.7%	100.0%

properties. Indeed, property type may be a distinction with less economic meaning than generally ascribed.

In all properties examined, the value of the current leases represent significantly less than half of total property value. For the industrial properties, current leases represent less than 20 percent of total value. This result reflects management's short-term leasing strategy and, for the industrial properties, a coincident short average period to rollover for the existing leases. In general, properties must have average lease terms of greater than 10 years for the lease portfolio value to exceed 50 percent of total property value at current interest rates. Because such long-term leases are relatively uncommon, a property's total value is most often composed of more residual value than current lease value, which may account for the widely presumed riskiness of real estate relative to other asset classes.

The ratio of lease portfolio value to total property value is a powerful indicator of how property performance is likely to respond to different market conditions. The higher the ratio of current lease value to residual value, the less sensitive the property value change will be to changes in market rent, for example.

Clearly, some properties are more bondlike than others. Existing leases are obligations of tenants to pay fixed rents in a manner similar to the obligations of a corporation issuing a bond. Future leases, leases yet to be written, are equity interests retained by the property owner and driven up or down in value by changes in market rent, that is, changes in the value that will be available once the existing lease expires. In the extreme, a property with a perpetual lease could be considered 100 percent bondlike, while an empty building could be considered 100 percent equity. Naturally, most properties fall somewhere in between, as shown in these examples.

The fact that properties—indeed, entire portfolios—can be described by the fraction of the total value imbedded in existing leases suggests an important distinguishing characteristic of properties and portfolios. Investors that desire properties or portfolios with strong inflation-hedging characteristics, for example, would prefer that this statistic be relatively low. On the other hand, if an asset manager expects market rents to remain low or to decline for several years in a particular market, he or she might prefer properties that exhibit a relatively high value for this statistic.

In short, this seemingly simple statistic has applications for investors and asset managers alike. The value of the statistic is enhanced by the notion that leases are nominally denominated instruments that correlate poorly with inflation, while the property's residual value—the value of future leases—captures the significant inflation-hedging quality that investors expect from real estate as a distinct asset class.

Lease Durations versus Time until Rollover as a Measure of Future Market Exposure

Exhibit 4–11 shows statistics for lease duration, years to rollover, the ratio of duration to years to rollover, and the weighted-average property duration. The *weighted-average property duration* is defined as the product of lease duration and the fraction of total value attributable to the existing leases, plus the product of the average years to rollover and the fraction attributable to the residual.

All other things being equal, properties with shorter lease durations will be less subject to changes in valuation due to changes in interest rates. This finding comes directly from the mathematics of the duration measure and is one of the most common interpretations of duration.

As a measure of a property's exposure to rollover risk, lease duration is superior to the more conventional measure of average number of years until rollover in that duration incorporates the time value of the lease payments into its calculation. For example, two

EXHIBIT 4–11
Lease Duration and Years to Rollover

Property	Lease Duration	Average Years to Rollover	Duration/ Rollover	Weighted-Average Property Duration
Retail:				
Property A	3.77 years	7.25 years	0.52	6.08 years
Property B	3.60	8.60	0.42	7.13
Property C	2.66	4.68	0.57	4.15
Property D	2.33	5.85	0.40	5.08
Average	3.18 years	7.18 years	0.45	6.05 years
Industrial:				
Property W	1.33 years	2.21 years	0.60	2.06 years
Property X	1.22	1.56	0.78	1.53
Property Y	1.07	1.46	0.73	1.42
Property Z	1.56	2.41	0.65	2.26
Average	1.33 years	2.05 years	0.66	1.94 years
Portfolio average	2.23 years	4.54 years	0.56	3.94 years

properties having a similar average number of years to rollover but differing markedly in terms of lease duration would have different exposures to changes in interest rates, with the property having the shortest duration being the least exposed and the least risky.

Leases that have uniform payments over the entire term of the lease would exhibit a ratio of lease duration to lease term of about 0.50. This ratio would vary with the discount rate such that flat leases at higher discount rates would have higher ratios than leases at lower discount rates. Nonetheless, if a lease (or property) had a ratio greater than 0.50, the lease (or property) would have a disproportionately high share of its rent in the later years or large increases in rents over the lease term. All other things being equal, risk-averse owners would prefer properties with lower ratios of duration to rollover (i.e., given interest rate and credit rate risk, it is better to have your money sooner rather than later). By this argument, the retail properties in our example would appear less risky than the industrial properties.

PROPERTY DURATION DEFINED

Weighted-average property duration combines the durations of the existing leases with the durations of the spaces encumbered by those leases, that is, the individual space residuals. Residuals can be thought of as zero-coupon equity interests and as such have a duration exactly equal to their terms, which we have called average years to rollover.[14]

We noted earlier that lease duration is a measure of a lease's sensitivity to value change due to changes in interest rates. By analogy, we suggest that the weighted-average property duration is a measure of a property's sensitivity to capital value change due to changes in interest rates.

LEASE EXPIRATIONS REVISITED

In an attempt to describe the exposure of a property or portfolio of properties to market releasing risk, investment managers publish lease expiration schedules. Typically, the schedule consists of the yearly and cumulative yearly number of square feet on which existing leases will expire. There are other useful ways to describe exposure to releasing risk. Since pictures can be more expressive than numbers, we have created graphs of the cumulative distribution of lease expirations for each of the four retail properties and for the aggregate of those properties, that is, the retail property portfolio.

Each graph presents the cumulative distribution of lease expirations computed three different ways: the conventional way by area leased, the debt-equity measure by current lease value, and the measure of total value attributable to each leasable space. Among individual properties, different measurement approaches can produce considerably different results and interpretations. Exhibit 4–12 shows the individual retail property results, and Exhibit 4–13 shows the retail property aggregation from our sample.

In Exhibit 4–12, property A illustrates a property with near perfect correspondence between leasable space and its current lease

[14] While duration is widely used in the management of fixed-income portfolios, the efforts to extend duration into equity arenas are more recent and still in the formative stages. For example, see David J. Hartzell, David G. Shulman, Terence C. Langetieg, and Martin L. Leibowitz, "A Look at Real Estate Duration," *Journal of Portfolio Management,* Fall 1988, pp. 16–24; Martin L. Leibowitz, Erich H. Sorensen, Robert D. Arnott, and H. Nicholas Hanson, "A Total Differential Approach to Equity Duration," *Financial Analysts Journal,* September–October 1989, pp. 30–37.

EXHIBIT 4–12
Cumulative Distribution of Lease Expirations for Four Retail Properties

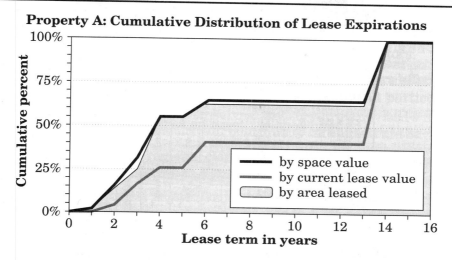

Property A: Cumulative Distribution of Lease Expirations

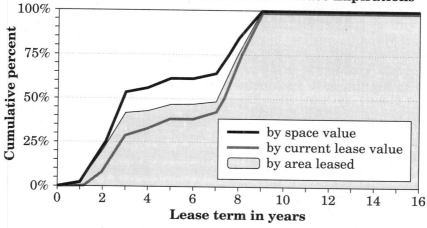

Property B: Cumulative Distribution of Lease Expirations

value. Conversely, the gap between current lease value and space value suggests an opportunity to enhance returns by releasing space over the next six years.

Property B illustrates a relatively large discrepancy between expirations by area leased and expirations by space value. For example, 50 percent of the area leased will expire within the next seven

EXHIBIT 4–12 *(concluded)*

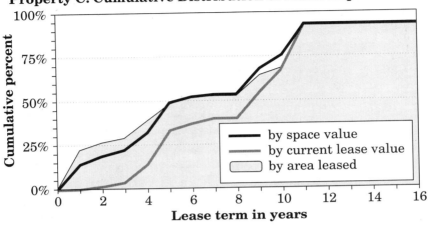

Property C: Cumulative Distribution of Lease Expirations

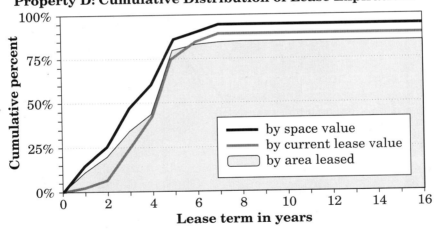

Property D: Cumulative Distribution of Lease Expirations

years. However, 50 percent of the leasable space in terms of total value will expire within the next three years. In other words, the value of the space subject to releasing is large relative to its physical size.

While the cumulative distribution of lease expirations among properties differs substantially, the aggregation of retail property lease expirations shown in Exhibit 4–13 dramatizes the effect of

EXHIBIT 4–13
Retail Properties

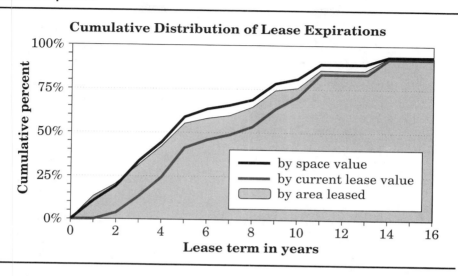

Cumulative Distribution of Lease Expirations

pooling properties into portfolios. Notice that the rate of lease expirations is more uniform at the portfolio level than at any individual property level. Similarly, the value of spaces relative to their areas is close so that, for example, there is no year in which an exceptionally valuable amount of space is subject to releasing risk.

The spread between current lease value and space value indicates the spread between existing rents and future market rents. Property A exhibits the largest difference, while property D has the smallest. Thus, we would expect the future value of property A to be much more closely tied to the prospect of achieving anticipated market rents than property D. In a sense, property A may be regarded as a somewhat riskier investment than property D, but in improving markets property A would also have more opportunity to experience increases in value relative to property D. In other words, responsiveness to changing market rent can be seen as either a problem or an opportunity, depending on the manager's perception of future trends. Some properties are simply more or less responsive to market rent changes, which implies that all properties within a given market, for example, are unlikely to respond identically to changing macroeconomic forces.

IMPLICATIONS FOR REAL ESTATE INVESTORS

The approach to individual lease and property valuation outlined in this chapter allows the analyst to measure significant differences in the risk and performance characteristics of individual properties or portfolios that are largely invisible or only hinted at by conventional analytic techniques. This creates the opportunity for strategic investment planning and management based on individual property or portfolio characteristics rather than on generic property types or geographic performances. The analytical tools that can be developed are both powerful and extensive.

These techniques can be used by real estate owners and managers in a variety of ways. For *strategic investment planning,* they can be used for:

- Development of explicit investment strategies that capitalize on the more bondlike or equitylike characteristics of individual properties, allowing investors to develop "long" or "short" strategies in response to expected market conditions.
- Measurement of the property or portfolio value's sensitivity to interest rate changes via duration measures and to market conditions, particularly rent levels and capitalization rates.

For *acquisitions and dispositions,* these techniques can be used for:

- Determination of whether proposed acquisitions or dispositions fit with explicit investment strategy.
- Identification of potential market pricing imperfections that can be exploited.
- Identification of disposition candidates based on the impact of changing market conditions on property value.

For *portfolio or property management,* they can be used for:

- Understanding default risks for individual tenants and properties.
- Guidance to tactics for asset and risk management.
- Measurement of trade-offs between risks and returns for specific properties and determination of proper return premia for different levels of risk.
- Guidance for altering the property, tenant, or lease term mix to maintain or adjust portfolio strategy.

For *measuring investment manager performance,* they can provide:

- A methodology for monitoring investment managers' adherence to explicit portfolio strategies.
- An assessment of managers' property valuations by comparison to capital market conditions.
- An objective measurement of investment managers' ability to alter portfolio performance in light of changing market conditions.

IS THE DEBT-EQUITY MODEL PRACTICAL?

To date, no one has actually separated the existing lease income stream from the equity residual to produce two financial instruments. Fortunately, the debt-equity model offers insights into property performance as an abstract or theoretical construct. Nonetheless, it may be useful to consider some of the reasons the separation has not taken place. The problems that need to be resolved cover a wide range of disciplines, including economics, law, accounting, operations, and marketing. We can only touch on some of the problems here. (See the references in footnote 1 for more complete discussions of the topics covered briefly here.)

First, does the separation of leases from residuals make economic sense? Arbitrage arguments would suggest they do not. Separating leases from residuals sounds like separating skimmed milk from cream: The value should be the same whether separated or combined into whole milk. This argument does not account for the "clientele effect," where there are different buyers for the components than there are for the totality. This effect is most apparent in the fixed-income arena, where Treasuries or other fixed-income instruments are split into several instruments having different terms and income streams and often one instrument having a zero coupon similar to the concept of equity real estate residuals.

Equity real estate residuals may be particularly attractive to high-income individuals as an alternative to zero-coupon bonds. Zero-coupon bonds carry an imputed interest income component that is taxable, while equity real estate residuals have none. Also, equity real estate residuals would seem to embody some of the most important characteristics that pension plans in particular say they desire or expect from the real estate assets class: protection from unanticipated inflation and low correlation with stocks and bonds. Clearly, virtually all of the upside potential of income-producing real estate is contained in the residuals, not the leases. While some leases offer some inflation protection in the form of operating expense pass-throughs or percentage rent clauses, the protection is not absolute.

Existing leases packaged like bonds may be attractive to any investor who would ordinarily purchase fixed-income instruments. As noted earlier, leases look like fully amortized bonds and have a duration roughly half that of bonds with an equivalent term. All other things being equal, fixed-income investors tend to prefer shorter-duration investments to longer-duration ones because shorter-duration investments are less sensitive or risky with respect to unanticipated interest rate changes.

From a practical standpoint, leases would have to be more standardized to be widely marketable. Unfortunately, leases often contain myriad, difficult to price terms, conditions, and imbedded options. To be viable as a financial instrument, leases would have to be relatively simple with few, if any, options; in essence, lease documents should look like bond documents.

Surprisingly few corporations have publicly traded debt, so few corporations have ratings published by the major rating companies. In addition, many firms are partnerships or individual proprietorships, making credit rating difficult, if not impossible. Nonetheless, just as lively markets developed in below–investment grade bonds—junk bonds—so too could we expect markets to develop in unrated leases sold individually or in packages.

Finally, a property owner could mimic the effect of lease separation by means of a carefully constructed mortgage in which 100 percent of the net income goes to the lender and 100 percent of the residual is retained by the borrower. If the property being financed had several leases with varying terms and credits, the job of financing would be difficult, but not impossible. Actually, such a mortgage exists, but it invariably stems from default by the borrower and, not surprisingly, has a poor reputation: the cash flow mortgage. To get the same financial effect as debt-equity separation, there has to be a "good" cash flow mortgage. Since lenders already are comfortable with mortgage instruments and the conditions necessary to protect the rights of both parties to the transaction, this would appear to be the best approach, albeit a transitional one, to separating leases from residuals.

PART 2

STICKS AND BRICKS

CHAPTER 5

LAND INVESTMENT

*Allan J. Sweet**
Amli Institutional Advisors, Inc.

INTRODUCTION

This chapter discusses land investment and management. It is predicated on the notion that the land in question will ultimately be developed, though not necessarily by the owner. We present the subject in six distinct parts:[1]

- Historical Perspective.
- Definition of *Land*.
- Evolution of Land Investment.
- The Land Investment Process.
- Investment Risks.
- Conclusion.

Despite the large number of variables connected with land investment, we hope this chapter will give a foundation from which the reader can focus on the critical issues and pose the most effective questions.

---

* The author wishes to acknowledge the considerable assistance of John F. Woldenberg in the preparation of this chapter.

[1] Land for which the highest and best use is timber or agricultural is covered in Chapter 13, "Nontraditional Real Estate."

HISTORICAL PERSPECTIVE

Land is a blank canvas on which people can paint the American Dream.

Land investment is an inexact science. Both success and failure have come to all types of people and institutions, from individuals and small partnerships to national corporations. Sometimes land investment results from someone's hunch, without any research. At other times, land investment takes place only after extensive due diligence. Some transactions have been executed on the back of a napkin, and others have been documented in lengthy and cryptic contracts. There is no correct method, and there is certainly no shortage of formulas.

Land has come to symbolize growth and prosperity. Control of land seems to translate into power. The discovery of America was based, in part, on the desire for wealth that would accrue to the conquerors of the New World and, with small poetic license, can be thought of as one large land speculation. It should come as no surprise that acquiring, selling, and developing land has produced a large share of the country's greatest and oldest fortunes, its most colorful entrepreneurs, its most vicious battles, and its greatest failures and scandals.

One of the first recognized American real estate moguls was Robert Morris,[2] a banker in the 18th century. Morris's rise and fall was a precursor to a dangerous business cycle common to many land speculators. A patriotic banker, Morris grew wealthy financing the American Revolution with capital from foreign banks. As a businessperson, he could not resist the opportunities for land dealing in the new United States. Morris used little to none of his own money to buy land, financing transactions through the same European lenders that helped fund the war. All land acquisitions were located in what he believed to be the path of future population growth. He bought land at deeply discounted prices from Indians and Revolutionary War veterans who were anxious to convert their government-granted warrants for land into cash. Morris then actively marketed the virtues of the property to foreigners who were in no position to discern truth from embellishment. Over a period of years, Morris assembled in excess of 7 million acres. He was recognized, on paper at least, as one of the wealthiest Americans of his time.

---

[2] *Lords of the Lands,* "Magnificent Bankrupts," pp. 11–31.

Morris relinquished his empire under circumstances not dissimilar to many real estate failures. He attempted to capitalize on the announcement to locate the national capital in an area surrounding the intersection of the Potomac and Anacostia rivers in what is now Washington, DC. Morris led a group of investors who acquired 7,000 lots in the proposed new city, declaring that "Washington building lots will continue to rise for 100 years to come." Morris's projections were conservative; in fact, he would probably be amazed at today's real estate values in Washington. Unfortunately, however, Morris was one of the first U.S. land speculators to fall victim to timing. Three Napoleonic wars shut down credit from European banks and stopped the flow of immigrants on whom Morris had hoped to unload his properties. While he was one of the richest men in America on paper, Morris's real estate portfolio generated little or no cash with which to pay lenders. Morris's overleveraged real estate empire toppled in spectacular fashion, and he died penniless in debtor's prison five years later.

The high risk and opportunity for reward in land investment have produced many more colorful stories—the much-publicized $24 purchase of Manhattan from the Algonquin Indian tribe, for example—but Robert Morris typified the dynamic breed of American businesspeople who sought land and capitalized on land investment opportunities in colonial times. These people influenced the development of the country's largest urban centers and shaped the character of the nation from wilderness.

If history is any indication, one can see a clear pattern showing real estate as one of the more volatile American industries, characterized by boom and bust cycles. Land often is either severely undervalued or ridiculously inflated. Typically, land is a slow-moving, illiquid asset that requires great patience and precise timing for successful investment.

The economics of land investment can be thought of as (1) the interaction of basic supply and demand forces and/or (2) an option-based approach to development.[3] In reality, each approach influences the other. The basic economic model of supply and demand generates

---

[3] This does not suggest that the land is purchased using an option contract (which is a common practice); rather, it implies that the valuation of land for purchase can be viewed using options/futures pricing. If the buyer were to purchase the land option, this would further lever the return pattern inherent in any option/futures contract.

an ever-changing equilibrium point (or "market-clearing price") as the factors affecting both supply and demand change. Within reasonable bounds (given slowly changing zoning laws and high opportunity cost related to razing the existing stock of buildings), supply changes slowly. Demand, on the other hand, results from a large, and often volatile, set of socioeconomic factors for developed property. In this factor of demand, land values are sometimes viewed as a residual or "plug" value. That is, land value represents the difference between the capitalized value of the income stream generated by the improvements and the costs (including the developer's overhead and profit) of putting the improvements in place, as adjusted by the project's perceived riskiness. With fairly stable development costs and volatile capitalized income values, it is apparent that the value of this residual or plug value can also be quite volatile.

The option-based approach recognizes that the land owner has, in effect, an option to develop the property (or sell the property to someone else who wants to develop it) at any future point in time. This approach tends to view the payoff in a more asymmetrical fashion, meaning the capital appreciation from a successful land investment may be substantial while the loss is limited to the investment. This is analogous to a stock options contract, where the option purchaser enjoys the advances of stock prices but his or her loss if the stock declines in value is limited to the price paid for the contract.[4]

Regardless of the valuation model used, it is apparent that the land investment process is complex and uncertain. The balance of this chapter discusses some of these complexities and removes some of these uncertainties to improve the investor's risk-adjusted return. Hopefully, this will help the reader to capitalize on one of the world's greatest finite resources: land.

DEFINITION OF *LAND*

A discussion of land must begin with the fundamental elements that help to define it. While a precise definition is impossible, a good description can be derived from (1) a clear identification of the types

---

[4] For more information about options and futures, see Chapter 27, "Application of Derivative Instruments."

of the land, (2) the important attributes of land, and (3) the status of a land parcel in the development cycle. This information is essential in the process of building a case for land investment. To begin with, unless otherwise stated, all references to land in this chapter are to vacant or unimproved land.

Locational Categories

To adequately understand land, one must become familiar with the investment categories into which it is broken down and their respective attributes. Although there are no hard and fast rules about describing and labeling undeveloped land, land is usually categorized by either its location or its use, because these descriptions are broad enough to encompass most land and clear enough to differentiate among parcels. Some commonly cited categories of undeveloped land are:

- *Land at the edge of development,* situated at the fringes of a developed area or just beyond active development, usually in suburban or rural locations.
- *Infill sites,* surrounded by developed real estate or development in process. Infill sites, which were passed over during the first phase of development of an area, are typically smaller and have a shorter development horizon.
- *Urban renewal sites,* developed land that becomes ripe for redevelopment in the foreseeable future.
- *Parking lots,* which may represent land being "parked," literally and figuratively, in anticipation of development demand.
- *Farm land* and *commodity land,* rural settings with an abundance of open space.

Stages of Development

The existing development status of every site is a gauge of the site's potential profitability. As will be discussed later in this chapter, land investment may be active, where value is added through active involvement with the site, or passive, where value is added simply by the passage of time, inflation, and the course of surrounding development.

Before acquiring a piece of land, most investors determine the stage in the development cycle of the site and consider the resulting risks and potential returns of the acquisition before committing to proceed, whether on the basis of active or passive investment.

As indicated in Exhibit 5–1, there are five stages in the land cycle: (1) raw/unimproved, (2) pre-development, (3) development, (4) improved, and (5) redevelopment.

Raw/Unimproved Land

Raw land is real property without any physical improvements (including sewers, roads, utilities, etc.) and without the required zoning approvals and/or entitlements for the intended use. It is land that is not actively or passively being developed. It is an investment in the future.

Essentially open space, the property is situated in any demographic or geographic location and can range in size from less than one acre to thousands of acres. Management is limited to the ongoing maintenance of the property, if any. Interim use, a variation of raw land (agriculture, timber, parking, etc. while the property is being held for the highest and best use), would require consideration of additional management responsibilities such as daily monitoring, collecting income, and managing personnel.

Investors in raw land are generally more risk oriented, especially given the uncertain nature of the exit strategy. Some investors prefer to take the property through the process of pre-development (and possibly development) given the high return that can be achieved through value enhancement. Others are content to allow the passage of time to create value.

Pre-Development Land[5]

Predevelopment land is ready for physical land development, namely, the construction of all infrastructure, but such activities have not yet begun. Pre-development activities include:

- Zoning.
- Subdivision.
- Utilities.
- Easement agreements.

---

[5] Both the pre-development and development processes are examined in greater detail in Chapter 6, "Real Estate Development."

EXHIBIT 5–1
The Land Acquisition Cycle

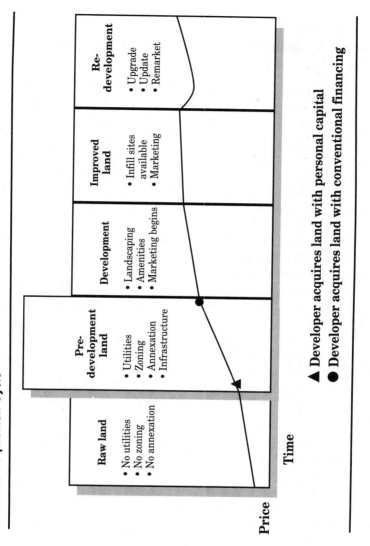

Raw land	Pre-development land	Development	Improved land	Re-development
• No utilities • No zoning • No annexation	• Utilities • Zoning • Annexation • Infrastructure	• Landscaping • Amenities • Marketing begins	• Infill sites available • Marketing	• Upgrade • Update • Remarket

Price

Time

▲ Developer acquires land with personal capital
● Developer acquires land with conventional financing

- Off-site/proffer agreements.
- Land planning, grading, and engineering plans.

Location, size, and seller disposition are some of the characteristics that determine the chances for a successful return when investing in pre-development land. Location in a growth corridor not only takes away some of the absorption risk; it also provides greater certainty with regard to forecasting and market conditions. Purchasing a large parcel can generate a discount price that greatly enhances return, as can a motivated seller.

Pre-development land may have an interim use, similar to that of raw land, provided the cost of implementation does not exceed the income over the anticipated holding period. In this case, the manager would need to control the interim activities described above, as well as determining the fulfillment of the property's highest and best use.

The manager accomplishes this goal through the assembly and management of a team that includes such professionals as attorneys, architects, land planners, engineers, traffic consultants, brokers, marketing analysts, and so on. A team approach is implemented to evaluate, understand, plan, and effectuate all necessary permits and approvals. The team serves as a liaison between the project and the government authorities, zoning boards, city councils, planning departments, the EPA, the Corps of Engineers, neighbors, highway/tollway authorities, and utility companies. The ultimate goal of the manager is to achieve a fully entitled parcel that can be either immediately developed or sold as immediately developable.

The timing for achieving full entitlements varies by jurisdiction. It can be affected dramatically by neighborhood opposition, government moratoriums, and market conditions. The manager can make the decision to proceed with pre-development activities only after being reasonably assured that the market will accept the development of the parcel upon its completion or if the property will receive considerable value enhancement after completion for subsequent sale to a buyer. A key element in most jurisdictions is the length of a permit's life (for example, if a permit is good for only five years, one will not proceed with entitling the property if the market will not be ready to absorb it for longer than five years).

When reviewing land as an investment, the pre-development stage is certainly one in which timing is extremely critical. This is because site preparation is costly, especially if it is incurred prematurely. For suburban properties, the costs of site preparation and infrastructure construction can range from 30 percent to over 100 percent of actual land cost. Although such costs can be closely forecasted through hard- and soft-cost budgets prepared under the direction of the manager, their value is determined by the speed at which the land use is absorbed. Thus, the manager in this position is required to be highly familiar with market conditions, including planned and existing competition and their absorption rates.

The value of pre-developed land is appreciated most by passive land investors, for risk-oriented investors will prefer to take the property through the process of pre-development themselves given the high return they can realize through the value enhancement. In addition, tenant/users, land developers, and construction companies prefer the benefits of pre-development land. The largest variables challenging the manager are the timing of (1) the period over which to accomplish full entitlement, which could be one month to five years (or greater), and (2) the demand for the pre-developed parcel upon its completion.

Development Land

Development land is land that is fully entitled, with full infrastructure in place on- and off-site and all utilities present and serviceable. It is property ready for immediate construction of a building(s), and typically the investor's goal at this stage is to market the property to users of the site. Rarely would a passive investor acquire or hold such property absent some special circumstance on the buy side. At this point, the land cost (though not necessarily the value) is substantial, for it includes not only the land component but also the pre-development costs.

In the development stage, the manager continues to interact with the pre-development team to preserve and enhance existing entitlements. In addition, the manager is responsible for overseeing the development/construction team (which includes the pre-development team), bidding to all contractors, awarding and executing all service agreements pertaining thereto, and completion documents and draw orders. Timing for completion of full development varies greatly, depending on the size of the parcel, the amount of infrastructure necessary, and the physical constraints of the property.

Although land development is an intensive "hands-on" investment requiring decidedly more technical expertise on an ongoing basis than pre-development land, it is closer to the end-user, and thus to the return stage, than either the raw land or pre-development stage.

Improved Land

Improved land is a parcel with a structure(s) already in place. The total area of the land is typically allocated to a building structure (except, for instance, open space or common areas that are attributed to a residential community or business park as a whole on a pro rata basis). Thus, the use of the property is primarily that which is rentable or usable. The land maintenance is insignificant relative to the structure, and the value of the land is inconsequential as it is incorporated into the project cost, until the structure reaches obsolescence.

The manager's responsibilities at this point vary greatly, depending on the use of the improved land. Management of improved land is discussed in Chapters 7 through 13.

The investment value of an improved parcel is a function of the net income flow generated by the occupants of the leased facility against the cost of the land, the cost (or imputed cost) of carrying the land, and the construction costs and their respective carry. In the case of for-sale (as opposed to rental) residential property, the investment value is determined by a function of the land cost (plus carry) and the construction cost versus the sales revenue generated from the net sales of homes.

Redevelopment Land

As the physical improvements (on the improved land) age, the development is subject to economic and functional obsolescence. This, in turn, suggests a shortening of the remaining useful life for the physical improvements. As the aging process continues, it becomes more economical to consider one of the following three options.

Raze.   Demolish the existing facility and hold as undeveloped land until such time as new construction would be economically justified. This was the case in the mid-1980s, when the Houston multifamily sector took a precipitous fall. The lower carrying cost of carrying land as opposed to apartments made some investors find it prudent to raze the properties and then hold the land.

Renovate.   A substantial renovation can dramatically lengthen the useful life of a property. For some investors, this represents a better economic alternative than either holding or razing the current structure. Renovation does not necessarily imply a continuation of the existing use; consider, for example, industrial loft buildings that have been converted to commercial/residential space.

Redevelop.   The existing facility is demolished, and new improvements are immediately constructed. Redevelopment is often associated with greater density; an example is the demolition of one or more CBD office buildings to enable the development of a new, denser office building. However, as with renovation, this approach does not necessarily imply a continuation of the existing use.

The foregoing examples illustrate the renewable investment cycle that land and buildings can provide.

Existing versus Future Use

Since demand is a function of the potential use for the site, the end-user ultimately determines the value of a piece of land. Existing versus future use is a critical consideration in land investment. Historically, investors have made fortunes by upgrading the use of their land. One example is Carl G. Fisher[6], a wealthy northern investor, who is credited with buying up swampland and reptile-infested jungle and transforming it into a vacation paradise called Miami Beach. Fisher's success netted him millions in profit.

To seek the "highest and best use" means to seek the use that renders the greatest value from the land. Seven commonly accepted uses for land are *office, retail, industrial, residential, mixed-use, agricultural,* and *special,* each with a variety of subuses. For example, retail use can be broken down into regional malls, community centers, power centers, strip centers, and stand-alone stores. Residential use includes single-family homes, condominiums, apartments, and mobile homes. The land investment process involves some speculation as to what use is appropriate for a particular parcel.

Consider the Van Sweringen brothers from Cleveland[7]. They

---

[6] Dan Cortz, "Land Lords," *FW Magazine,* November 12, 1991, pp. 49–54.
[7] Ibid.

successfully identified the highest and best use for a 1,400-acre tract northeast of downtown Cleveland. In 1905, the Van Sweringens purchased the site for a deeply discounted price and proceeded to plan a community named Shaker Heights, considered one of the first planned suburban residential developments in the country. Part of the Van Sweringens' master plan included providing reliable transportation linking this "bedroom community" with jobs in downtown Cleveland. The rapid transit system established by the Van Sweringens remains intact today. The Van Sweringens' stewardship of this project was rewarded with tremendous personal wealth, and the brothers went on to become the primary developers of downtown Cleveland. At the height of their success, the Van Sweringens assembled a business empire worth approximately $4 billion.

Active versus Passive Investment

Ultimately, land acquisition reflects an investor's understanding of existing market conditions and his or her perceptions of future market conditions. If investors simply acquire a property to hold it, they are *passive*. If investors acquire land not only for such appreciation due to the passage of time but also to enhance its value, through active management, to move the property into the next stage of the cycle, they are *active*.

Passive Investors
A passive investor's post-acquisition costs are kept to a minimum due to the owner's passive role in the land development process. Investment value is based primarily on the ability to intelligently acquire assets in anticipation of future economic and demographic trends. The passive investor may even have a short-term mentality, with a focus on quick sales with potentially smaller margins and greater volume. Short-term investment relies, in part, on quick and sometimes violent swings in the market caused by announcements of other projects, road improvements, or special developments such as airports or convention centers. The passive investor may, however, also have a long-term mentality, viewing land as an asset that can build equity and protect capital over time.

Active Investors
In contrast, the active investor has considerable overhead, often with a large staff sufficient to successfully execute the investment strategy.

An active investor relies, as does the passive one, on the ability to buy wisely, but will actively continue to influence post-acquisition value through horizontal and vertical development activities. Horizontal development includes all activities affecting land prior to the construction of a building; vertical development is the actual construction of buildings. An active investor's goal is to successfully orchestrate these activities to maximize the value of the land investment. Active investors with a short-term mentality may become merchant builders who buy land, build and quickly sell it, or "flip" it. Development strategy with a long-term outlook will improve land as the market dictates, without forcing any transactions. Both are accepted development strategies that take on different risk-reward profiles.

General Considerations

Land is one of the more complex subclasses within the full spectrum of real estate investments. It is definitely one of the least understood. A number of general considerations provide some insight into land investment. However, every site still necessitates independent and comprehensive study.

The following factors have both confounded and encouraged those interested in land investment.

Uniqueness.   Land is frequently cited as a heterogeneous product. No two locations or uses are exactly the same.

Market Knowledge.   Land investment is a localized business. Market-specific politics, demographic trends, and economic trends are all factors that determine the success of any parcel. For example, rent control ordinances are frequently cited as a limiting factor in residential land investment in New York City, while favorable demographic trends are credited with fueling a heated land market in Dallas. It is difficult to compete in the land business without superior knowledge of the local market enabling one to react to rapidly changing market conditions.

Limited Supply.   A finite number of prime sites exist at any one time. The definition of *prime* may change from person to person, as well as over time as cities evolve, but the supply of quality sites will always be limited.

Holding Costs and Illiquidity. Land normally does not generate an income stream. This is one reason land is so difficult to value. In addition, land is an illiquid asset that does not have an efficient market.

Risks and Reward. Land is an investment that possesses substantial natural leverage. That is, the value of the land is a small component of the finished use, and the ultimate use determines the overall value. Thus, swings in the ultimate value of the finished product cause exaggerated swings in the value of the land.

EVOLUTION OF LAND INVESTMENT

In recorded history, land has always played an important role for every living thing. Possession and control over land is a fundamental and natural imperative. Even fish, birds, and rats fight over territory. In fact, most of nature reflects this continuous struggle to defend and expand territory. Over time, control over land has taken on added meaning for humankind. Prehistoric humans fought over it to protect means of survival such as food and water supplies. Medieval lords and the church owned or controlled land for power and profit and to preserve the social order. The British claimed land to establish global political power. Land represents a major portion of the wealth of many of the world monarchies, and for centuries in America, land ownership has allowed many people and organizations to accumulate considerable wealth.

Over the 20th century, however, land has become vastly more complex to own and manage as environmental, political, and lifestyle issues gain increasing importance. A real estate specialist can provide the services necessary to maximize the value of a land investment. Taking a parcel from raw land through the pre-development stage to the fully developed stage requires skill, experience, and knowledge in many areas. Successful completion of this process allows the landowner to realize the full value of his or her investment.

Some historical trends in land investment warrant consideration. The 18th and 19th centuries saw wealthy families, the government, and the church as the dominant ownership groups. Land was owned as a long-term asset that preserved wealth. However, middle-class farmers and homeowners were increasing in number. The 20th century witnessed dramatic growth in population with increasing immigration, increased longevity, the baby boom, and the "echo" baby boom. Migratory patterns in America redistributed the population with shifts from north to south and east to west, rural to urban, then city to suburb. In the last 20 years, the proliferation of the two-income household increased the labor pool, which accommodated unprecedented business activity. Growth is translating into demand for space to live in, work in, sell from, and distribute from.

In the 1970s and 1980s, tax incentives providing paper losses and sheltered income persuaded people to invest in uneconomic real estate. The syndication industry prospered and in doing so financed large quantities of poor-quality real estate. Lenders and investors could not place money fast enough. By the mid-1980s, the industry had gone wild with the concept of tax-incentive-driven real estate. Much of America's real estate was leveraged or releveraged during this period. Thus, land investment became capital driven to satisfy investor and lender. In 1986, changes in the Tax Code removed the tax benefits that had fueled the syndication business. Investors were stunned by this change, yet continued to invest in real estate, adding to the existing oversupply. The damage resulting from these turbulent years is still being felt in the 1990s, but land is slowly regaining its status as a prudent long-term investment.

This shift in the land investment arena was caused in part by America's worsening economy, which was rocked by recession as well as the long-term displacement due to structural changes in U.S. and world economics. The financial industry collapsed around real estate. Credit, which fueled one of America's most prolific periods of growth, was cut off, bringing real estate investment to its knees. Contraction, not expansion, was generally considered to be the trend for most American businesses in the early 1990s. Speculative development has saturated every asset class in real estate, leaving most major metropolitan markets with high vacancy rates.

Many experts predict that going into the 21st century, real estate development will remain depressed, with little to no office and retail construction throughout the 1990s. However, the industry is cyclical, and many experts believe the supply and demand will again reach equilibrium sometime around the turn of the century. Looking into the future, some demographic and socioeconomic trends may have a significant impact on land. For example, how will the aging population affect business and housing in the late 1990s? Will cities continue to lose people to the suburbs? How will the growing electronic "cottage industries" affect real estate trends? Will cold climates continue to lose to warm climates? Will water supply dictate development patterns? Will lifestyles focus more heavily on environment and leisure? Will American business redirect dollars and efforts to production, research, and development? Will convenience be of prime importance to everyone from leisure to business activities? Will major urban centers expand or contract? Will large domestic institutional investors control the supply of real estate products to corporate America and homes to American families? These are just a few of the forward-looking questions one must consider when making a land investment.

THE LAND INVESTMENT PROCESS

Land has few quantifiable characteristics that allow for an objective analysis of value—no cash flow, no physical structure, no lease, just plain dirt. These characteristics have kept the perception of land investment as somewhat mysterious, often political, and frequently speculative. But ultimately, land has value based on when and for what purpose it is used, and an assessment and determination of those issues is the ultimate goal of the investment process, which attempts to remove uncertainty and lower the risk. Being able to draw talent from a variety of important fields (law, development, finance, construction, landscaping, accounting, environmental) is helpful for successful land analysis, but it is not the complete answer. Beyond the boilerplate due diligence and "post-buy" financial projections that participants in any successful land program execute vigorously is an intangible component that must harness the collective knowledge and experience of many people into a methodical and prudent decision-making process. The land investment process should be anything but speculative.

Research

Land investment relies heavily on the ability to collect and organize vast amounts of information necessary to understand and analyze potential profitability in geographic areas and submarkets targeted for land acquisition. It is critical that an investor know such things as the local political environment, educational system, financial community, social infrastructure, transportation system (planned or improved), and demographic trends. The competitive edge goes to the investor who has the largest pool of accurate information from which to make decisions and knows how to apply it.

Knowledge is the key. Investors should monitor every detail of each growing community or metropolitan area where they own land or actively seek to acquire it. Creating a comprehensive land research library of aerial photographs, maps, and files fuels the acquisition process. Land investment should tap the power of state-of-the-art computer software specifically designed to track information based on geographic location. Such software can organize text information by map location, making land searches and information gathering faster and much more efficient. Of course, the most costly and difficult part of establishing a land library is orchestrating the initial collection and inputting data, as well as continuously updating the database. To get started, one must seek local sources of information, including appraisers, developers, brokers, local businesses, financial institutions, city planners, and economists.

Land Analysis

A prudent land acquisition program requires careful review of targeted geographic areas to determine whether the region meets prespecified criteria for land acquisition and has prospects for future growth. The logical next step is to examine site-specific issues pertaining to each potential acquisition. Exhibit 5–2 depicts in flowchart form the many issues that must be examined prior to land purchase. The exhibit borrows the macro/micro terminology from the study of economics to distinguish the broad area from the site-specific issues that must be analyzed.

Macro Stage
Optimally, a land team should bring diverse backgrounds in real estate investment and consulting experience to the collection and interpretation of information specific to targeted markets. Research and land libraries should be repositories of data on demographics, road systems, railroads, airports, school districts, and landfill sites,

EXHIBIT 5–2   The Land Acquisition Process

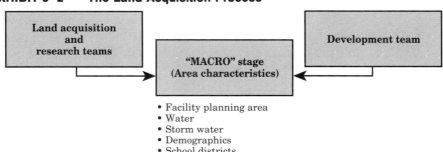

Land acquisition
and
research teams

"MACRO" stage
(Area characteristics)

Development team

- Facility planning area
- Water
- Storm water
- Demographics
- School districts
- Landfills
- Location of superfund sites
- Road systems
- Commuter and freight systems
- Airports
- Wetlands
- Area business trends
- Area political analysis
- Property and income taxes

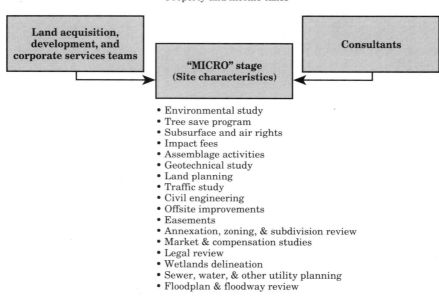

Land acquisition,
development, and
corporate services teams

"MICRO" stage
(Site characteristics)

Consultants

- Environmental study
- Tree save program
- Subsurface and air rights
- Impact fees
- Assemblage activities
- Geotechnical study
- Land planning
- Traffic study
- Civil engineering
- Offsite improvements
- Easements
- Annexation, zoning, & subdivision review
- Market & compensation studies
- Legal review
- Wetlands delineation
- Sewer, water, & other utility planning
- Floodplan & floodway review

Apartment acquisition
team, finance, and
legal departments

Negotiations

Legal counsel,
banks, and
mortgage lenders

- Negotiation
- Letter of intent
- Seller representations & warranties
- Purchase contract
- Closing (6-18 mos)

to name a few factors. In addition to drawing on federal and state sources, original research relating to special issues such as school districts and landfill sites aids in determining interest in a given area. Prior to actually seeing a piece of land, this research often enables the purchaser to gain a competitive advantage by knowing more about the forces of growth in the vicinity of a given land parcel than other real estate firms.

The outcome of this macro stage is to isolate particular sites that are located in areas that meet criteria for growth, quality of life, economic stability, and demographic profile.

Micro Stage

At the micro stage, or site level of analysis, land teams focus on specific parcels targeted for acquisition. Exhibit 5–3 depicts a land analysis checklist that chronicles the minimum information needed to begin a proper analysis of a particular site.[8]

As a known land investor, the purchaser will receive frequent submissions from sellers or brokers. However, a purchaser can also independently uncover an attractive land parcel. On-site property reviews, as well as discussions with owners, local and regional officials, and lawyers, will help to identify potential acquisitions and determine interest in issuing a letter of intent on a parcel.

In this stage of the acquisition process, several physical aspects of the land are also examined. Land teams review land use restrictions, availability of utilities, and the existing and proposed transportation network for the site. Outside consultants complement internal efforts regarding geo-technical issues (such as soil analysis), civil engineering studies, and hazardous waste studies and environmental reviews.

Landscaping and natural terrain are important elements of any land parcel. In the course of developing a land use plan, the overall topography, existing vegetation, and other natural conditions are analyzed. Though not inexpensive, the survival of irreplaceable trees and shrubs enhances the attractiveness of a site for end-users and the community at large.

---

[8] A more comprehensive land acquisition study is available on written request to the author. A review of this survey suggests the depth of knowledge necessary to adequately assess the merits of a potential land acquisition.

EXHIBIT 5–3   Preliminary Land Analysis

Completed by: _____   Date: _____

Property/Ownership

Property ID number—PIN				
Project manager				
Date of purchase				
Original acquisition price				

Location

Access		
Visibility		
Other		

Property Description

Zoning		
Annexation		
Approvals		
Subdivision (# lots)		

Infrastructure	
Sewer	
Water	
Roads	
Landscaping	
Other/soft	
Cost to complete	

Geo-Environmental

	Date	Consultant	Summary	Estimated Cost
Hazardous waste				
Soils report				
Wetlands delineation				
Floodplain delineation				
Other				

(continued)

EXHIBIT 5-3 (continued)

Appraisal

	Date	Consultant	Value
Competitive market survey			
Market feasibility survey			

Economics

Original purchase price	
Assessed value	
Real estate taxes	
Required impact fee study/issues	
Impact fees	
Farming or other income	
Estimated annual maintenance	

Consultants/Advisors/Project Team

Engineer	
Architect	
Attorneys	
General Contractor	
Other	

Agreements

	Date	Amount	Consultant
Management company			
Broker/leasing agent			
Construction agreements			
Other			

(continued)

EXHIBIT 5–3 *(continued)*

Debt and Encumbrances	Rate	Amount	Maturity	Lender	Grantee
Financing (Muni, MUD, TIF, SSD)					
Purchase money mortgages					
Easements					
Bonds					
Guarantee agreement, litigation, claims					
L/C					
Liens and mortgages					
Other					

Sales		
Owner		
Acres		
Closed/pending		
Price/price per square foot		
Date		

Leases

Term	
Square feet	
Net/gross/% increase	
Rate	
Buildout	

Operating Expenses

	Sq. Ft.	Tenant	Owner
Real estate taxes			
Operating expenses			
Management			
Current elec., water, sewer, gas			
Other			

(continued)

EXHIBIT 5–3 (continued)

Analyst Observations	
Development	
Marketing	
Other	

Original gross acres: _____ Offer/total offer: _____

Current gross acres: _____ Bid/total offer: _____

Estimated loss: _____ Bid/offer ratio: _____

Current net acres: _____

	Total Offer	Net Acre	Net Sq. Ft.
Offer price	_____	_____	_____
Estimated value/bid	_____	_____	_____

At any point in the analysis, an issue may arise that can delay or halt the acquisition process. The ability to weigh the costs versus the benefits of pursuing or terminating the acquisition proves vital to successful land investment. Purchase agreements should be structured to recognize the needs and objectives of sellers while protecting the interests of investors.

INVESTMENT RISKS

Once one has analyzed a given land site and knows the macro and micro characteristics of that site as thoroughly as possible, one must assess the investment risks that apply. These risks also have a macro and a micro component. Some relate to land investment generally, as compared to alternative investments that may be available at that time, while others have a site-specific orientation.

Macro Investment Risks

Liquidity

One obvious, but not fully appreciated, characteristic of land investment is its high degree of illiquidity. It is widely acknowledged that real estate is extremely illiquid relative to most other investments. The relatively large size of an investment, the lack of homogeneity among properties, the large number of forces that affect the income stream (if one exists), the variety of ownership alternatives and tax issues related to ownership, and high transaction costs all act to keep liquidity at low levels.

Real estate illiquidity also seems to increase precisely when an investor does not want it to, that is, when times are bad. The real estate recession of the early 1990s magnified this problem. The stock market can fall 500 points in one day and still have willing buyers and sellers immediately thereafter. When real estate falls in value, sellers withdraw from the market, and the spread between the bid and ask for real estate property grows. This phenomenon led some real estate professionals to ask whether real estate is a viable asset class without some method of improving its liquidity; the issue of real estate investment trusts, commonly known as REITs, is addressed in Chapter 14, "Real Estate Investment Trusts."

Not surprisingly, within the continuum of real estate investment, undeveloped land is probably the most illiquid of assets. There are several reasons for this. First, the long list of macro and micro concerns makes land a more complex investment to understand than other property types. Second, land's principal intrinsic value is as a component in a finished income-producing property. To the extent that development of the land is in the future rather than current, its value becomes increasingly uncertain and its liquidity reduced. Thus, land's illiquidity increases when economic activity slows down. Third, the fact that land typically does not generate an income stream further hampers the ease with which its value can be assessed. It also reduces the universe of buyers willing to make it a long-term investment. When land is "hot," meaning development ready, its value becomes more readily ascertainable and its liquidity improves rapidly. Unfortunately, since liquidity is defined as the ability to find a willing buyer at all times during an investment cycle, land simply does not trade easily when development is not readily foreseeable.

Timing
Most investments, even appreciating ones, do not appreciate on a straight-line basis. Nevertheless, the larger a predictable income component is to the total return from the investment, the closer the return is to straight-line growth. Likewise, the greater the certainty of future value, the more straight-line the appreciation at any given point in time. Land investment possesses neither of these risk-reducing elements. However, the universe of land buyers increases dramatically as land becomes appropriate for development. Developers and land users are added to land investors in the class of eligible buyers. This exponential increase in buyers dramatically affects pricing, sometimes stimulating an auctionlike bidding war. These reasons help explain why timing is very important in a land acquisition. For the most part, increases in land value are small to nonexistent for a long period of time and then spike up sharply. Consequently, an extended holding period is one of the greatest enemies to successful land investment, reducing the total return with each passing day. Given the uncertainty that now exists, and probably always will, in measuring when a given site will become development ready (especially as that date moves out beyond a year or two), it is clear that a heavy discount factor must be used in evaluating a land site's future development value. Enormous profit potential exists to the extent that the holding period is less than projected if appreciation is constant.

Leverage

The use of leverage is generally treated in Chapter 15, "Leveraged Investments for Tax-Exempt Investors," but the use of debt for land acquisition has two special considerations to be added to this basic theme. First, as mentioned, most land buyers use a relatively high discount factor in determining the present value of a land site whose development use is at least several years away (the process is almost meaningless if development is more than five years away). For this reason, given the high risk and high potential return, leverage will often be positive if expectations prove close to reality. Thus, land purchases whose development is anticipated to be within two or three years commonly use leverage.

On the other hand, since land does not generate a current cash flow, there is no reliable cash stream from the land investment to service the debt. Thus, little margin for error exists if the property cannot be converted into cash within the projected time frame. Interest reserves, often built into the land loan itself, solve the cash flow problem during the anticipated length of the loan. However, when these reserves run out, land borrowing can become an unpleasant experience.

Another subtle disadvantage of land leveraging is the pressure it places on land use decisions. Typically, land can be sold for some "lower" uses at earlier points in time as opposed to the hoped-for higher use that may require time for the site to mature. So, for example, a land site may be perceived as a high-rise or mid-rise suburban office site in the future. Currently there is demand only for single-story office use or perhaps outparcel uses such as gas stations or fast-food restaurants. Another example might be a business park site with future desirability as a pure office location. Currently warehouse or office/warehouse uses are more appropriate. In each of these cases, plus many others, leverage may force the owner to sell the land for a use lower than optimal because of current cash obligations. This can occur even though the owner knows that allowing the site to mature would enhance total return.

The credit crunch in the early 1990s introduced another variable into leveraged land acquisitions. In the past, land loans were possible as long as the lending source viewed the collateral as having a much greater value than the loan amount, a percentage known as the loan-to-value (LTV). This would be a so-called balance sheet approach to lending. However, lenders now require for most real estate loans both the balance sheet approach *and* an income statement approach. That is, in addition to the loan being some percentage of the property's value, the debt service coverage should be some percentage of the property's annual cash flow (or, the borrower must demonstrate sufficient liquidity from other sources to reasonably service the debt). When land loans need to satisfy both of these tests, they are obviously much more difficult to come by. Thus, an additional risk to land purchasers who want to use debt is periods in the business cycle when the land loan cannot be extended or replaced even though the collateral has real value in excess of the debt. It will be precisely during periods like the early 1990s, when economic growth has slowed down and extension of existing loans is needed, that such loans will not be available.

In the author's view, land investment already contains a high level of risk. Because leverage may force poor land use decisions, we do not recommend the use of leverage in most land purchases, especially purchases of pre-development land.

Inefficient Market
To the astute investor, inefficient markets mean opportunity. The abilities to learn more, decipher better, analyze more thoroughly, and negotiate with greater skill should create value that can be realized through land transactions. Unfortunately, inefficient markets introduce an additional level of luck into the process. Undiscovered factors can be critical to value, although difficult to uncover. In some cases, the process of discovering all the relevant facts may simply be too expensive to undertake, even if possible to accomplish. Thus, it may be desirable or necessary to assume some level of calculated risk.

Esoteric and Complex Attributes
Closely related to the risk of inefficient markets, and one reason the land market remains small, is the high number of esoteric and complex attributes that apply to land valuation. These attributes, which were discussed previously in the market analysis section, require a land investor to constantly assess their interrelated characteristics and take calculated risks as to the future value of a given site. Clearly, the ability to assess these risks and receive appropriate compensation for taking them is a key component of successful investing. Unfortunately, there is no "black box" for this process, and the investment risk remains high.

Tax Risks

Most income-producing real estate purchased by individuals or other taxable entities is subject to an intricate set of taxable gain and loss provisions. The passive loss limitation, at-risk rules, and the effect of nonrecourse debt on the investor's tax all serve to add a level of tax complexity to real estate investing. For taxable entities, land investing is delightfully simple. Usually, the only taxable event of consequence occurs at sale of the property, when gain or loss is realized and recognized. The absence of both nonrecourse financing and depreciable real property reduces the tax complexities.

Unfortunately, for tax-exempt investors, the situation is reversed. Income generated from an operating real estate asset is not subject to the rules on unrelated business taxable income (UBTI) unless the property is purchased with acquisition indebtedness. Even when debt is used to purchase a property, it is relatively easy to structure an acquisition to avoid UBTI for the purchaser. A land investment will not generate UBTI if the property is bought, held, and sold without any form of "value-added" activity. However, almost any action by a land site owner to enhance the value of the site will create UBTI income for the tax-exempt owner. Thus, zoning changes, subdivision activity, site grading, utility enhancement, or other active value-enhancing pursuits will likely turn a passive non-UBTI land investment gain into active UBTI development-oriented income.

Micro Investment Risks

Political Environment: Municipal

The political environment that surrounds a given land site introduces a high level of investment risk and economic uncertainty. The political process begins at the municipal level with zoning, annexation, utilities, and entitlement issues. Many land investors will not buy a land site that does not have the appropriate zoning and entitlements already in place because of the vagaries of the political process at the municipal level. For those who choose to invest in a site before it is zoned, annexed, and entitled, it is necessary to judge the likelihood of success and price the risk accordingly. Zoning and annexation issues are greater the further the site is from its development-ready state. When land investments are in the "path of progress" but not yet touching fully developed land and certainly not "infill" land, where development on all sides has pretty much set the use for the site, the cooperativeness of the local municipality in assisting in the development process can be a key factor. After zoning, annexation, and entitlements issues are resolved, there are other political issues to consider. The costs of services such as road systems, water, sewers, and schools are often tied to the land. Analysis of the anticipated costs of these services should be done during the market analysis phase. This process involves a careful and detailed picture of the political environment.

Regulations and Enforcement
In addition to the above municipal issues, wetlands, hazardous waste, and floodplain are three examples of site characteristics that may involve municipal, county, state, or national regulations. The practices of the bodies having jurisdiction for the enforcement of these regulations are often as important to know as the rules themselves.

Economic and Demographic Facts
It is hard to think of an investment class that is not affected by economic and demographic factors. The practical correlation between these factors and land values seems especially high. As previously mentioned, land has value principally as a component in an income-producing property use. Its value will be quickly and adversely affected by weak national and local economic conditions or adverse demographic shifts. Conversely, economic growth, population growth, and job growth are the three driving forces of improving land value.

The Value-Added Component

A term that has become a cliché with respect to real estate investment is value-added. Most investment advisors who offer their services to the investment community ascribe great weight to how they add value to the real estate assets they manage. This position improves as more work is required in connection with managing the real estate asset. For the most part, the effort needed to enhance and improve a property is tied to an understanding of the construction and lease-up needs of the assets. Something that is already built and fully occupied on a long-term lease has reduced opportunities for value-added services, triple-net-leased warehouses, or office buildings on long-term leases, for example. Most of the value differential ascribed to these assets relates to assessing residual value at some future time and determining the creditworthiness of the tenant. This latter fact is critical in maintaining the income stream and is rarely subject to manipulation—only evaluation. Not surprisingly, this category of real estate is actually more like a bond, and notions of value added are rarely emphasized. Fully constructed and well-leased office buildings or shopping centers might be next on the continuum. Some efforts are needed to maintain asset quality and occupancy. Proper maintenance programs reduce unnecessary costs and hamper the effects of depreciation and obsolescence. Leases are usually long term, but some turnover must be addressed over the life of the investment. Nevertheless, there is not a lot of opportunity to add value, and after the "buy" decision has been made and until the sell decision, there is little differentiation among advisors with respect to their value-added capabilities.

In contrast, apartments and hotels have more frequent turnover of tenants and thus a greater need for value-added efforts. Likewise, rehabilitation efforts or new construction dramatically increase the value-added component with respect to construction needs. Curiously, land can be an asset category with a high or a very low level of value added, and legitimate investment strategies can be developed either way.

Low-Level Value-Added Investment Strategy

As previously discussed under investment risks, many complex, esoteric, interdependent, and uncontrollable factors affect the value of land over time until it is ready to be a part of an income-producing property. Because of the high level of uncertainty that surrounds its future value and the minimal (e.g., farm income or parking revenues) to nonexistent cash flow during the holding period, most investors place a high discount value on a site's future value to determine its present value. This discount factor obviously fluctuates (as do all other investment discount factors), but seems to range between 15 and 30 percent. For instance, if everyone expected that a land parcel would be development ready for a high-rise office building to be built in five years and, based on expected development costs and leasing revenues, the land at that time would have a value of $10 million, its present value might range from $2 million to $5 million. The more uncertainty surrounding the holding period or the ultimate value of the land, the greater the discount factor. This means the patient investor, especially one who can forgo current cash flow, has the opportunity to earn relatively high rates of return even without anticipating a large value-added activity by the investment advisor. Undeniably, great skill is required on the "buy side" and "sell side" of the transaction. But once the land is purchased and until its sale, there is little need for active management and a small value-added component.

This "buy-hold-sell" strategy for land, where the value-added component is minimized, is usually applied on the commercial side to smaller infill locations where economic cycles or some specific identifiable external factor has prevented development. Single-family land sites can be larger and closer to the outskirts of civilization and still be appropriate for passive investment without the need for value enhancement. In general, however, the larger the land site and the less certain its future use, the more likely it is that the investor will have an active rather than passive investment approach.

High-Level Value-Added Investment Strategy

Different from a buy-hold-sell strategy is active land investment, which might also be characterized as horizontal land development. Land development must be distinguished from typical real estate development activities, which might be characterized as vertical development. Horizontal development encompasses all activities necessary to prepare a land site ready for vertical development and includes most, if not all, of the activities listed previously in the discussion of pre-development land (zoning, utilities, roads, etc.)

To the extent that the process of construction, or horizontal development, adds value to the site (in excess of the cost associated with the development work), the opportunity for land profit has increased. The complexity of the horizontal development process and the plethora of alternatives that exist throughout the process place a premium on the skills of the active manager. Using this strategy, time alone is not the principal factor creating profit.

Contrary to the buy-hold-sell strategy, which favors smaller infill sites or sites with an obvious use, the active management strategy works best on larger sites on the edge of development where ultimate use is less certain and more activities are required. An unzoned site without defined entitlements is a rarity for any commercial land parcel being analyzed for a buy-hold-sell strategy. It is far more typical for a site to be unzoned when part of the value-added process includes that activity.

One note: There is clearly a blurring between horizontal development (land development) and vertical development (building) with respect to large-acreage land projects such as business parks, industrial parks, and mixed-use parks. Many developers of this product that intend to construct office buildings, research and development buildings, distribution centers, or warehouses often engage in most, if not all, of the previously described horizontal land development activities. It is possible, however, to separate the vertical and horizontal activities. When this is done, the land developer can sell "development-ready" sites to users or other developers. In some cases, it may be desirable for the land developer to assist the development process with build-to-suit for sale transactions. This latter activity clearly involves vertical development and goes beyond typical land development. Nevertheless, it still falls below the higher-risk development areas of build-to-suit for lease or speculative development.

Risk-Reward Profile

As should be clear from the preceding discussions of investment risk, the risk level for land investment as it relates to expected return is high. There are simply too many interconnected, uncontrollable, unknowable variables to create any sense of value certainty. Illiquidity of the asset class also increases the risk and requires an additional reward premium. On the other hand, land is somewhat favored in that it seldom depreciates or becomes obsolete, and its long-term value seems inextricably tied to the number of people who would exploit its location. Thus, to the extent that land is in the path of progress or already positioned at a location that will become more in demand over time as the population and economy expand, it is commonly believed that the capital risk for land investment is low.

In most cases, an investor should be able to sell a land parcel for cost or greater over time, although the return on that capital may be minimal to nonexistent. This is likely if a development use does not become obvious and imminent. On the other hand, there is a reduced risk that high operating costs will eliminate any chance of future profit or the land's use will equate with buggy whips.

CONCLUSION

Vacant land has the potential to create great wealth or great disaster. Values can change overnight. The desire to take on the risk associated with land in the hope of superior returns has always attracted investment dollars. The process of land investment, however, even with all of its complexities, can be accomplished in a prudent, risk-averse manner. Of course, this investment is not without a cost. Land demands detailed study. It requires a broad knowledge of markets and a comprehensive understanding of the host of factors influencing the development of land. Since the world is in a constant state of change, a land investor's job is never done. All information must be maintained as fresh, because the buy is only one component of the overall investment, which relies on timing and ultimately on the sale. The key is always to know more than anyone else so that quick decisions may be made from a position of strength. If an investor understands the mechanics of a land investment and accepts the responsibilities and the risks of the process, there is money to be made.

CHAPTER 6

REAL ESTATE DEVELOPMENT

Daniel J. Coughlin*
Copley Real Estate Advisors

INTRODUCTION

As with any financial asset, an investment in existing (i.e., constructed and leased) real estate is subject to significant fluctuations in value. Investment in real estate development (i.e., unconstructed and unleased) is even more volatile, as the process entails even greater uncertainty than that presented by investments in existing real estate. Because many markets are characterized by historically high vacancy rates and socioeconomic factors that suggest a slower absorption rate over this decade than the last, real estate development in the 1990s has changed dramatically from earlier times. To be successful in the 1990s, real estate development must be carried out with prudent management of the cyclical and secular risks presented in most real estate markets. If these risks can be prudently managed, real estate development in certain instances may prove to generate satisfactory risk-adjusted returns.

To understand real estate development, one must understand real estate as an asset class. Dr. James Grasskamp indicated that "real estate can be defined generally as space delineated by man relative to a fixed geography intended to contain an activity for a specific period of time."[1] Consequently, real estate is sometimes described as operating in space-time markets.

Dr. Grasskamp also said, "the real estate development process involves three major groups: a consumer group, a production group and a public infrastructure group." The confluence of these major groups in the context of fixed geography presents a series of inherent

---

* The author would like to thank Joseph Pagliari for his help in creating the risk/return analysis shown later in this chapter.

risks. These risks are examined at the various stages of the development process (land assembly, product design, product leasing and management, and the space-time market). This chapter describes the risks found in each of these stages and identifies important property/market characteristics that must be reviewed in the process of undertaking real estate development.

Development is sometimes thought of as a vision that ends in bricks and mortar. It brings together management, land, capital, and labor to create a product that in itself becomes associated with providing a service. Real estate development (i.e., the bricks and mortar) becomes a factor of production that others use in providing their manufacturing or service-oriented products.

DEVELOPMENT'S EVOLVING NATURE

In the past, real estate development often relied on a single individual's vision. In the late 1940s, Trammell Crow merged industrial development with speculation by building the first industrial building for "to-be-identified," or speculative, tenants (previously, industrial buildings were constructed for identified tenants). This change was the result of one person's vision to provide a supply of product before the specific demand user had been identified.

In today's complicated economic environment, development is a collective process that relies on the wisdom and consensus of many individuals. These individuals are frequently both public and private institutions and include the developer, the architect, the city planner, the marketing agent, the lender, the equity investor, the landscape architect, the general contractor, and myriad others. Each works in concert and provides a product that meets the needs of the (sometimes unidentified) consumer.

Today, more than ever, there is pressure to reflect the urban environment, support public policy, and respond to social needs. Of course, the product must also reflect local ordinances and controls, be underwritten to conform to state and local tax structures, and always be constructed in light of current and future market economics. Each of these pressure points must be addressed by the developer, who today is no longer simply a visionary but also a conductor, orchestrating a multitude of divergent talents toward the production of a building.

Time Frames

Among the various development risks, one of the most important is time. In the earliest development stage, individuals have a vision that they intend to bring to the market. As the complicated issues described above play themselves out against that vision, changes and concessions are made and the vision is modified. The construction of an industrial building can take as little as three months, while an office building can take as long as five or six years. Issues such as land assemblage, control, zoning, public policies, and design/engineering matters can significantly lengthen the period of time necessary to bring a product from the vision stage to the physical stage. As time and market dynamics evolve, the demand for the real estate product and the competing supply for that product can change dramatically. These issues place significant financial pressure on the project and generate uncertainty for the investors and financiers.

Volatile Space Markets

In a number of cases, the 1990s have shown that the dramatic and volatile changes in market dynamics can leave even well-conceived projects in financial ruin. When demand does not grow as anticipated or supply characteristics change, the market results can be drastic. At the same time, changes in public and social policy issues sometimes occur in a five-to-six year development period, while the asset becomes part of the physical landscape for perhaps 50 to 75 years.

Environmental Pressures

At the same time, increased environmental pressures have placed many projects in jeopardy. At a minimum, environmental issues frequently complicate the development process. The uncertainty of site excavation results from the possibility of historical and archeological finds, topographical and geological transfigurations of the environment, disruption to wildlife and other environmental species, and the discovery of environmentally sensitive materials on or beneath the land surface.

Changing Capital and Space Markets

The issue of time also relates to the financial success of the project. As market dynamics change, capital market pressures can also change. Many projects that are identified in strong markets reach the point of fruition in weak financial and economic times. This was clearly the case in the early 1990s, when many projects that were started as early as 1988 reached a marketplace that no longer needed the product.

Submarket configurations can also change during the development period. The site and its impact on the local market and the confluence of this development with others can have important impacts on the project's success in the marketplace. In addition, the uncertainty of construction costs that are not always controlled is clearly a risk for a time-delayed or time-intensive real estate development.

DEVELOPMENT VERSUS ACQUISITION

Real estate development should be compared to the more prevalent practice of acquiring fully developed real estate. The risks associated with real estate development are more extensive than those related to the acquisition of a building. The pertinent question is whether or not the investor in real estate development is adequately compensated for the incremental development risks.

Each approach has a number of common risks. These common elements are the economic environment, market conditions, and environmental and public policy issues, though in the case of the latter two elements, an existing building may be "grandfathered" from having to adopt such policies. The expanded risks relate to longer time frames for real estate development and more frequent public input and planning. The public domain has increasingly taken a jaundiced view of real estate development as altering the social and economic structure of the community. As a result, public-interest groups have taken a greater interest in real estate and its impact. Increasingly, public authorities are providing a forum for these special-interest groups to articulate their concerns and are encouraging, and in some cases mandating, that developers be responsive to those concerns.

LEVERAGE

In addition to introducing the concept of speculative real estate development, Trammell Crow was one of the first developers to use the financial tool of leverage. As any student of finance knows, this tool has the effect of amplifying the rewards as well as the risks of an investment. This is no less true in a real estate investment.

In the 1980s, the use of leverage grew dramatically, when savings and loans, commercial banks, and insurance companies were increasingly motivated to lend on real property. In part, their motivation stemmed from the high total returns generated by real estate through the mid-1980s (e.g., the Russell/NCREIF Total Property Index showed an annual average return of 13.03 percent from 1978 through 1986). These high returns and the perceived security obtained from growing rental streams made real estate an attractive investment for these institutions. The use of debt magnified these high total returns. (The Russell/NCREIF returns are reported on an unleveraged basis.) However, since much of the total return was generated by appreciation (rather than income growth), these higher leveraged and total returns proved to be illusory "paper" returns and were subsequently lost when market values declined in the second half of the 1980s and the early 1990s.

The use of leverage in the development of a project magnifies the risk. The use of debt capital to acquire and develop land creates a mismatch of income and expenses.

Obviously, unimproved land provides no income stream while the lender requires current debt service payment. Accordingly, the equity investor must "come out of pocket" to fund the current land costs. In this instance, the investor essentially makes a bet on the future land appreciation and development profits. In the 1980s this bet proved to be a virtual sure thing in the eyes of many developers and land speculators. In the 1990s, the use of leverage on land has proven to be fatal for a number of developers and land speculators.

While land development in any of its stages presents significant risks, the effective management of a development process can mitigate these risks and at the same time identify substantial rewards as compensation to the investor for having taken this land and development risk. The following sections review the potential risks of various stages of the development cycle.

The use of leverage during the 1980s included a number of structural concepts. Some lending institutions were providing floating-rate, short-term debt in the form of construction loans that were intended to have a relatively short life. These loans were secured prior to development and were funded by the lenders on an incremental basis to cover the costs associated with the development and construction. These construction loans were generally intended to be "taken out" (i.e., refinanced) with a fixed-rate, long-term, permanent loan once the property was constructed and leased.

In the 1980s, the overbuilding crisis and the deterioration in real estate markets made it virtually impossible to refinance construction loans. As a result, many short-term construction lenders became long-term, permanent lenders by default. This situation changed the nature of the relationship between lender and borrower and created an adversarial circumstance. The less restrictive capital market of the 1980s provided for construction loans without a traditional take-out requirement which led in part to the development boom in that decade. As a result of these rather lenient funding requirements, commercial banks and other mortgage lenders ended the 1980s with a significant, uncovered position of floating-rate constructions loans for which permanent loans could not be secured.

THE FIRST STAGE OF DEVELOPMENT: LAND CONTROL

It is important to note that land represents a unique raw material in the development of a real estate investment. Each land parcel is unique. Consequently, the positioning, topography, and configuration of the land parcel are the first elements to be assessed in the development process. The right parcel in the right location with the right configuration can spell the difference between success and failure.

Real estate development has many stages. The first, or primary, stage includes the control of the land that will ultimately be used for real estate development. In this process, the ownership and control of the land occur in a number of ways, including options, partnership, direct acquisitions, and leases.

Option Agreements

The developer can seek an option agreement that will allow the land to be acquired (at a specified strike, or option, price) in its vacant condition once certain events have taken place. Thus, the developer can control the land while minimizing up-front acquisition costs and at the same time try to initiate a program that will result in the construction of a facility in concert with market demand. The use of fixed-price options essentially provides a "free look" (i.e., the option price is usually quite small in relation to the strike price) to the developer. It mitigates the risk associated with owning the land during the period of time when the developer is assessing market conditions. It also precludes the opportunity for competing developers to take control of that parcel.

Partnerships/Joint Ventures

Frequently public entities and private investors team together with the intention of developing a particular site. This occurs mostly in urban settings where a city has identified its desire for urban renewal in the form of building new residential, retail, office, and/or industrial projects in a certain part of the city. The use of enterprise zones is a typical vehicle that combines support from the public sector and the use of private capital toward the achievement of social and economic objectives. In these public and private partnerships, the public sector answers the needs of the social and political environment, while the economic needs of the investor are similarly serviced. It is important that the public and private sectors have common goals and complementary skills. The early identification of these goals is critical to the success of this public/private partnership.

Direct Acquisition

The strongest form of land control is the direct acquisition of the land. This can be done with a combination of equity and debt capital. Land acquisition is generally done after the risks associated with zoning, entitlement, and planning have been identified. These risks, which are described in greater detail later in this chapter, are important economic components of land acquisition. It is important to identify the presence of these risks and assess the cost of managing them when acquiring a piece of land.

Ground (or Land) Lease

Another form of land control is the use of a ground (or land) lease. The characteristics of a ground lease are distinct from those of an operating lease (used to lease space in the ultimately developed building). In the case of a ground lease, terms are usually written for a period of 50 to 100 years, a period well in excess of the financing period to be used in borrowing money to develop the building and generally longer than the useful physical life of the developed building. In addition, the ground lease itself provides a number of unique financial and tax characteristics. It frequently represents a form of risk sharing among the developer, the equity investor, and the ground lessor.

The structure of ground leases varies in relationship to the overall financing of a development. The major forms of ground leases are subordinated and unsubordinated.

The subordinated ground lease is subordinated to other forms of financing and receives a distribution of cash flow after debt service has been paid on the primary mortgage indebtedness and prior to the distribution to the equity owner or developer. In the unsubordinated or senior ground lease, this debt instrument is senior to other obligations of the project, including the mortgage loan. The returns required under these two forms of ground lease vary directly with the nature of the risk the ground lessor assumes. In this case, the subordinated lease usually carries a premium or higher interest rate and may share in the operational cash flow of the property. The typical senior ground lease does not share in a cash flow and carries a lower coupon rate reflecting its inherently lower risk.

THE SECOND STAGE OF DEVELOPMENT: PRE-DEVELOPMENT

Once the land is controlled through any of the above-mentioned processes, the developer enters the pre-development stage. Pre-development land investing differs sharply from investing in developed properties. Investment in a fully operational facility usually involves a fairly predictable return on the capital invested. An investor can accept a lower return in a class A property because of the relative certainty of the rental structure. In contrast, an investment in raw land provides only a speculative return. This is because the development of the land and its ultimate resale are both subject to substantial uncertainties. The uncertainties of the market timing, market demand, rental rates, and/or sale price all affect the ultimate return resulting from a raw land investment.

Estimating Likely Returns and Risks

Since the land's ultimate development influences the fundamental supply and demand relationship in the real estate market, it is critical that the developer assess in the pre-development stage the ultimate use and anticipated returns for the new development. It is also important to assess the relative probability of achieving those returns and the ability of the investor to service their financing and other obligations with uncertain returns.

Mitigating Holding Period Risks

A key strategic element in managing the risks of the pre-development stage is the investment strategy. The appropriate strategy can vary by the type of marketplace. In the case of office development, downtown and suburban markets frequently pose relatively different land and pre-development issues. In many urban centers, underdeveloped or undeveloped lots located near thriving metropolitan centers have already been zoned for commercial development. The ability to maximize the value of the land and generate a profit from the ownership and/or development of that land can be measured in the context of the supply of competing real estate products and the time and cost associated with developing a new building.

   In today's marketplace, a frequently utilized strategy is the acquisition of land in a low-intensity use, such as a parking lot. The owner/ investor holds the land while generating income from the operation of the parking facility. This income frequently covers the facility's operating costs and provides cash flow to fund debt service and ownership costs (such as taxes and insurance). As the office market conditions improve, the property is then positioned for future development. This pre-development strategy can mitigate the ownership costs and

risks and at the same time position an asset for the market's anticipated improvement. Another important risk this strategy avoids is
the zoning risk. The fact that the property has already been zoned
for its ultimate use means the developer's risk is essentially that of
waiting for the market demand to return to the point where it makes
economic sense to begin construction.

The pre-development strategy associated with suburban parcels
differs substantially. In the case of suburban parcels, zoning risks,
neighborhood risks, and competition risks frequently exist. The urban
location generally presents a unique location that cannot be readily
duplicated. Frequently, a suburban location has a large supply of
land that is not yet zoned and could invite competition at any point
in time. In a suburban setting, the developer/investor must be able
to conceptualize in great detail the actual product to be developed. The
conceptualization should be based on the fundamentals of anticipated
real estate supply and demand, with the knowledge of the economic,
demographic, political, and legal issues that can affect the property at
each stage. In suburban locations, multiple buildings are frequently
developed over a longer period of time. The economic, demographic,
political, and legal issues can change dramatically from one phase to
the other as changes occur in the economic environment, the political
infrastructure, and/or the social fabric of the community.

These risks require intensive personal management and involvement in the community environment. The ability to anticipate and
meet the community's needs is critical for the development of a successful product.

Land Risks

Zoning ordinances present one of the more significant risks associated
with the ownership of land. These ordinances are an important part
of the land control process in the United States. Ninety-eight percent
of all cities with over 10,000 people have some form of zoning or
entitlement process. The zoning ordinances typically have three elements. The first element is the zoning map, which reflects the city
and town planner's desired plan for land use. The second element is
the regulation text, which describes the infrastructure and the specific
controls on the parcel itself (set-back requirements, building height,
parking availability, etc.). The third element is the zoning adminis-

tration's level of control and regulatory authority utilized to ensure that the development meets the municipal requirements.

Zoning places restrictions on land use, which are often the most significant impact on the value of land. The uses are intended to promote public safety and welfare. However, public desire and purpose and economic need are not always aligned. The rezoning process therefore can create substantial value where the public purpose is consistent with the land's highest and best use in an economic sense. Conversely, the use of land for social and public purposes can strain value creation (or realization) in an economic sense. It is also important to note that the "value" of a project cannot always be measured in economic terms. For example, the value to a community of a new recreational center can be more appropriately measured in social and cultural terms.

Zoning affects the transfer of real estate wealth. For example, it allows for large land tracts to be subdivided and prepares parcels for development as a residential subdivision. In this way, the parcel becomes affordable to the residential consumer. Typically, the residential consumer would be financially precluded from owning a large parcel of land. At the same time, zoning regulations related to office development can affect the nature of the ownership rights by requiring larger parcels, more highly improved parcels, restricted building ordinances, and so on. The result is a varied, economic characteristic for the area in a city or, in some cases, for the entire city. Zoning is a very powerful and influential municipal control. It can dramatically alter the physical, cultural, and economic landscape.

Environmental Issues

Environmental management is an increasingly critical element in the ownership of real estate. Developers face the responsibility of ensuring that the property is environmentally safe. A developer that ignores the magnitude of the environmental issue can find that the economic characteristics of the investment are drastically changed. Consequently, the developer must carefully assess and plan for the building's environmental impact. Much potential liability can be mitigated if the developer carefully assesses the site prior to acquiring the land and certainly before beginning construction.

A prudent developer will carefully review a site with the help of a qualified environmental risk management firm to identify potential hazards and assess the cost of remediating those hazards. (See Chapter 17, "Environmental Issues," for a detailed discussion of these issues.) Failure to undertake this review can have catastrophic investment consequences.

THE THIRD STAGE OF DEVELOPMENT: PRODUCT DESIGN

The third stage in real estate development is product design. This includes architectural, engineering, landscaping and planning, and regulatory approvals. At this point, the developer must have clearly identified the type of project, its location, its general configuration, and the general tenant and market segment(s) to be attracted to the site. It is also important to have assembled the architectural, landscaping, engineering, and environmental teams, which will be critical to the development of the property. At this time, the developer must have also evaluated the financial feasibility of and the public need for the project.

The developer's reputation is critical to the success of a new product in a variety of ways. The developer's reputation will affect the leasing of the facility (and its perceived attractiveness to new tenants). It will also be critical to the identification of financial capital sources for project construction. In addition, it will be important to the local community. A community's concern is not solely financial. The community is more likely to consider the project in the context of its cultural, social, and municipal influence than in terms of its financial impact. The impact on a city or town is subjectively measured based on the net cost or benefit to it in terms of traffic, aesthetics, long-term use, and character of the project. These noneconomic costs are critical to the municipal perception of a new real estate development.

Product Definition

The first element in the product design is product definition. At this stage, the developer must identify (1) the market need, (2) how that the need will be met, and (3) how the building's marketing and management staff will access those who need the real estate product itself. This is generally done through the use of a series of feasibility studies.

Initially, the developer undertakes a simple economic review of the potential project. At this point, not every alternative justifies a great deal of research and analysis. To prepare a quick financial review and pro forma, developers frequently use their general understanding of potential tenants' needs and willingness to pay for a certain type of real estate product and contrast this with their own expectations and analyses of the cost of operating and constructing the facility. The result of this income and cost analysis is the identification of a potential return from the development concept. After analyzing a number of these potential alternatives and estimates of market acceptance, the developer narrows the potential uses for the real estate development.

The next stage is to identify a more definitive strategic plan for development. At this stage, the developer conducts a more thoughtful level of market research and feasibility analysis. The developer must recognize the importance of planning and control in a highly competitive market. Market research will be directed toward the individual market segments the developer has identified. The research will attempt to assess the relative growth in the demand for that market need and will also measure the relative supply of space that meets such demand. If the developer identifies a growing demand that is not being met by existing or planned supply, the marketplace offers a real estate investment opportunity.

The full feasibility study, the formal study of a project's viability, is an important step in the identification of the ultimate real estate product. A full feasibility study includes the following steps:

1. Macro- and microeconomic comparisons of project alternatives and the full scope and cost of each project.
2. Market demand analysis reflecting the potential use for the product in the marketplace.
3. Preliminary review and drawings for the property.
4. Cost estimates, alternative value estimates, profit estimates, and rental structure associated with the investment.
5. Analysis of projected debt and equity costs and returns.

6. Governance and municipal impacts.
    a. Restrictions/limitations.
    b. Requirements.
    c. Zoning.
    d. Local ordinances and building codes.
7. A risk profile of the project, including the above-mentioned items and land development risks.
8. Identification of the development team, including contractor, developer, marketer, political consultant, architects, engineers, equity investors, financiers, and so on.

The feasibility study generally includes components relating to the market, preliminary physical drawings, estimated construction costs, information about potential investors and lenders, and an evaluation of general government considerations and the resultant economic value of the project.

The nature and extent of the feasibility study can vary widely, depending on the use of the property. Planned economic communities, sometimes encompassing thousands of acres of land, will require frequent and extensive multiyear feasibility studies that are updated constantly during the development process. This contrasts with the feasibility study associated with the development of a single industrial facility, which may be completed in relatively short order and rely on readily ascertainable data about the marketplace.

The Enterprise Concept

Increasingly, real estate development includes the operating business and the value of that business as an enterprise. This value can affect the financial feasibility of a project. In planning the feasibility study, care should be taken to recognize the unique and separate rights of the facility and the operating group. Valuation of these unique entities is conducted separately and generally reported to the owners. An example of this activity is the land owner/developer that is also the builder of residential homes. In this case, the profit associated with the land development is derived by the developer in two ways. The first is the profit associated with owning and developing the land; the second is the profit associated with building the residential product.

In this case, the developer's contributions to the project are not only the land and infrastructure development but also the residential development skills. Accordingly, the developer in this instance is paid for both contributions to the real estate development enterprise. This is an important assessment in identifying the potential profitability of a project and is critical in reviewing its feasibility.

The enterprise concept can also be applied to the developer's motivation for owning and operating the property. In many situations, the developer funds none of the project costs and anticipates that the benefit of ownership will be in the form of distant residual value and/or, more immediately, the fee income generated from ongoing services such as property management, leasing, and coordination of tenant improvements. This fee income, generated while operating the project, will provide longer-term incentives for the developer—besides the fees, if any, associated with the construction and development of the project. This form of operational compensation may create conflicts between the developer and the lender/investor. To resolve this issue, incentive management contracts are often used.

Impact Fees

Impact (or mitigation) fees are an increasingly important item regarding the cost of land development. These fees, which are generally assessed by the local municipal jurisdiction, are a form of taxation that allows the municipality to cover the incremental costs associated with the development and its "impact" on the community. Proceeds from these impact fees can be used for a number of community-related projects, many of which often benefit the new development. In the case of residential development, impact fees frequently help finance the construction of fire stations, elementary schools, and other municipal costs that grow dramatically as land is developed and new residents move into the area. Note that while these fees increase the cost of development, they frequently provide the ancillary benefit of an improved community, which in turn may ultimately create and/or enhance values.

A particular issue affecting many municipalities is the lack of standard development impact fees. Planning and zoning acts generally have been relatively standardized over the years. Impact fees are a relatively new phenomenon as many municipalities have experienced a diminution of their tax base and tax revenues. As this has occurred, a number of communities have sought to shift the burden for this incremental growth by exacting these fees.

These charges are frequently challenged by real estate owners, and suits are sometimes brought in state court. There does not appear to be unanimity among the state courts with respect to the charge for impact fees.

A prime example of the use of impact fees is in California. Municipal revenue pressures increased dramatically in California with the passage of Proposition 13 in 1978. This legislation decreased property tax assessments, limited property tax rates, and prevented the use of "special" taxes such as income, liquor, sales, use, vehicle, and property transfer taxes from being levied without a majority vote. As a result of Proposition 13, a number of California municipalities sought alternative ways to raise revenues. Among the options was an expanded use of impact fees to pay for new facilities and services. This alternative has become particularly important in growth communities experiencing new demands for services but a restriction on municipal revenues. These communities tend to use impact fees to bridge the gulf between their limited revenues and their increased service demand.

An important distinction exists between impact fees and local property taxes. Local property taxes are raised by municipalities and other taxing bodies (school districts, county hospitals, etc.) in the form of an annual levy on real estate. The community can then aggregate those funds in its general account and expend them in whatever fashion it deems appropriate. In the case of impact fees, the fees raised are generally earmarked for a specific use. That use usually relates to the impact the new development has on the community. It is generally believed that impact fees may be assessed on a development when it appears that the project will have an adverse impact on the overall municipality. As a result, the project is assumed to mitigate the increased costs to the community. However, it is difficult to precisely determine whether or not the actual dollars paid by the development equal the (subjectively measured) costs incurred by the community.

In other areas, different fees have been exacted for similar purposes. In Oregon, for example, communities have developed a system of development charges. These arose as a result of Oregon's statewide land use planning program, which requires all communities to prepare comprehensive land use plans consistent with the state-mandated goals. Among these goals is a requirement that the communities provide public facilities and services in line with their needs and implement processes to pay for those facilities and services. System development charges are an example of a revenue-raising process.

As a result of a dramatic growth in population and real estate development, development and impact fees have been widely used in Florida. Between 1970 and 1980, Florida grew by nearly 50 percent. In the first half of the 1980s, it grew by more than 15 percent. The strain of growing infrastructure costs and a limited tax revenue base has affected several communities in that state. A number of taxation programs have been used to try to allocate costs of new projects to the developers rather than the existing residents in the community.

In each of these cases, one concern is that impact fees are an unauthorized form of taxation. Many developers contend that the specific benefit associated with impact fees lacks a specific relationship to their ultimate use. Others argue that increased community infrastructure benefits all community residents and all other real estate development in that community; therefore, it is inappropriate to make one-for-one comparisons between individual projects and the specific municipal improvements. Infrastructure projects should be reviewed in the larger, communitywide context.

As they are levied by varied municipalities, impact fees reflect the needs of that political jurisdiction. Accordingly, the specific needs of a municipality and of a given real estate project lead to significant negotiation of the size, nature, and economic consequence of the impact fees. This is particularly true in the pre-annexation stage. Many governing bodies have been creative and flexible when contemplating the inclusion of a large tract of land that has been previously unincorporated into their jurisdictions.

Market Analysis

An important component of real estate feasibility analysis relates to the assessment of the individual market to be served by the new project. It is important to identify potentially competing products in the form of undeveloped land, projects in the planning stages, buildings suitable for renovation, and so on. In the feasibility study, the market analysis will focus on these possibilities and also on barriers to entry into that marketplace. These barriers include land that is zoned for nonconforming or noncompetitive uses, as well as configurations of competing parcels, age and obsolescence of competing buildings, attitudes of city officials toward growth and development, and other factors. It is important to assess the current market size and analyze its potential to change dramatically through new development.

Assessment of competing real estate products is an element of concern to all new developments. Market studies vary significantly in their complexity and sophistication. In individual markets, inventory analysis and vacancy/occupancy reports can provide an important indication of competitive position. These analyses frequently do not consider product size, obsolescence, and location. In declining real estate markets, ownership and sponsorship of projects have been critical, as they indicate the financial strength of the landlord and the ability to maintain the project in a competitive, cost-effective manner. In analyzing a new development versus an existing competitive product, it is important to conduct an analysis of the strengths and weaknesses in terms of location, product size, age, configuration, sponsorship, and so on so that an estimate of potential rents and absorption rates can be made.

Since the potential increase in the number and quality of competitive buildings will affect the project's ability to retain tenants, expand its lease roll, and, hopefully, achieve rent increases, many developers frequently focus on markets that limit future supply increases. These limitations include zoning, current ownership, physical configuration, and barriers such as rivers, railroad, highways, and so on. An important assessment in this analysis is whether these limitations are permanent or temporary in nature.

Market constraints also exist in a legal and physical sense. There are legal limitations on the type of use that relate to zoning and entitlement processes. In addition, legal limitations exist on the use of sites for food and liquor, music, gambling casinos, and so on. Physical limitations concern height, density, set-back requirements, and other zoning factors.

In assessing the market size, it is important to also consider the inventory of product owned by users. This product, while not currently considered to be competition for new development, may be relet or become an excess facility for the user. When this property is "dumped on the market," it becomes part of the market inventory and influences market supply characteristics.

Similarly, market dumping can be the result of the "foreclosure cycle." That is, after the substantial decline in rents and values following an overheated market, many of those projects heavily laden with debt fall into disrepair as borrowers trim back discretionary expenditures. In time, these poorly maintained projects are often deeded to the lender via foreclosure actions. Many of these lenders, including thrifts, commercial banks, and life insurance companies, are motivated (in large part because of their regulatory environment) to sell these assets quickly. Such sales are often transacted at bargain prices (as measured by percentage of replacement costs, previous market highs, or some other benchmark). The dumping of these properties on the market can have a substantial adverse impact on market rents and values, as owners with a substantially lower cost basis can afford to undercut market rents.

In reviewing the demand side of the market analysis, it is important to focus on five major areas: demographics, growth constraints, market diversification, sector growth, and noneconomic factors.

In the area of demographics, an analysis of the future market demand for the product focuses on economic forces (e.g., population size, employment patterns, age distribution, wealth indices) that affect employment opportunities, including those in smaller, growth-oriented companies. It also focuses on the economic vitality of an area. Another element is the desirability of living in the area. This can be influenced by cultural, educational, and recreational amenities, as well as by municipal services and the political environment.

Growth constraints are very similar to the market constraints described above. They can be due to the municipality, political pressures, and the public's perception of a given location or marketplace.

The degree of the market's diversification is also an important consideration. Market diversification includes the community's economic base, that is, the various employers' products, services, and manufacturing elements. It is important to identify these diversification issues in light of the proposed real estate development.

Still another consideration is sector growth. Will the new development benefit from a single sector or multiple sectors of the economy? How diversified is the economy? Which sectors of this economy are growing? What growth factors will affect this area in terms of population, business expansion, municipal requirements, taxation, regulation, and so on?

Another demand-side characteristic of the market relates to non-economic factors. The desirability of the project and its use can significantly determine its success. The growing NIMBY ("not in my back yard") phenomenon has resulted in some projects having very low market acceptance and poor economic success. The location of the project, its placement in the community, its proximity to schools, recreational facilities, residential areas and other factors can be critical elements in the determination of the project's ultimate economic success.

The market feasibility study must clearly assess each of these supply and demand issues. It is important to assess them within a common time frame and context and to overlay given market conditions concerning growth, space absorption, and demographics. Once these items have been determined, the developer will frequently assess the market's growth potential in light of the anticipated supply of space. The result is the market share that the project must capture to achieve its investment objectives. This market share analysis is critical to the success of the project. It is an area where developers frequently wear "rose-colored glasses," assuming they can capture an inordinately large share of the market. In cases where developers have entered a new market, this is a particularly dangerous assumption.

DEVELOPMENT: RISK-RETURN

As discussed earlier, real estate development presents inherent risks. In taking these risks, investors anticipate higher returns as compensation. The following example offers a simplified illustration of this risk-return trade-off.

Major Assumptions

Assume that a project can be develped for $10 million. The construction period is to last one year, over which time the average outstanding cost balance will be $5 million. Moreover, it is expected to take an additional year to lease up and stabilize property operations. It is assumed that the most likely stabilized net operating income is $1.1

million. However, given market uncertainties about future rents and operating expenses, it is also estimated that the standard deviation[2] of the estimated net operating cost is $220,000. When the project is stabilized, it is expected to be sold at a capitalization rate of 8.5 percent. These assuumptions are summarized in Exhibit 6–1. Furthermore, the terms of a proposed joint venture investment are such that in return for funding all of the expected costs ($10 million), the investor receives a preferred return of 12 percent per annum and 60 percent of the residual profits.

Expected Distribution of NOI

At the time the joint venture partner makes the investment decision (i.e., before construction begins), the property's stabilized NOI is inherently uncertain. Stabilized NOI can only be estimated.

EXHIBIT 6–1
Assumed Real Estate and Investment Parameters Using a Joint Venture Approach

Development cost	$10,000,000
Construction parameters:	
Construction period	1 year
Average balance outstanding	50.00%
Stabilization parameters:	
Stabilization period	1 year
Average balance outstanding	100.0%
First-year (stabilized) NOI:	
Mean (average)	$1,100,000
Standard deviation	$220,000
First-year (stabilized) capitalization rate	8.50%
Investor parameters:	
Preferred return	12.00%
Residual participation	60.00%

---

[2] One standard deviation from the expected NOI (of $1.1 million) in either direction accounts for approximately 68 percent of the variation in projected NOI, two standard deviations account for approximately 95 percent, and three standard deviations account for approximately 99 percent. See Chapter 2 for more details.

Exhibit 6–2 illustrates the probable distribution of stabilized NOI based on the assumptions discussed earlier: The distribution has a mean of $1.1 million with a standard deviation of $220,000. This implies that, on average, the actual stabilized NOI will fall between $880,000 and $1,320,000 (i.e., $1,100,000 ± $220,000) 68 percent of the time. Obviously, as values move farther from the mean ($1.1 million), their likelihood diminishes.

Expected Property Values

Each possible stabilized NOI figure, capitalized at 8.5 percent, corresponds to a possible property value (at the time the property is to be sold); see Exhibit 6–3. The expected distribution of property values has a mean of approximately $12.94 million (i.e., $1.1 million capitalized at 8.5 percent) with a standard deviation of approximately $2.59 million (i.e., $220,000 capitalized at 8.5 percent). Similar to the treatment of forecasted NOI, this distribution implies that, on average, the actual property value (once the property is constructed, leased, and sold) will fall between approximately $10.35 million and $15.53 million 68 percent of the time. Again, as values move farther from the mean ($12.94 million), their likelihood diminishes.

Expected Return

The joint venturer's expected return can be determined based on the distribution of forecasted sales prices (see Exhibit 6–3), the assumed construction cost ($10 million) and construction/stabilization period (2 years), and the terms of the joint venture. This requires examining the returns for each forecasted sales price and weighting each by its estimated probability. The result is shown in Exhibit 6–4. The distribution of investor returns shown in Exhibit 6–4 has a mean of approximately 14.8 percent and a standard deviation of approximately 12.0 percent.

To examine these returns more thoroughly, let's look at the return associated with the most likely sales price, approximately $12.94 million:

EXHIBIT 6-2
Estimated Distribution of First Year (Stabilized) NOI Alternative

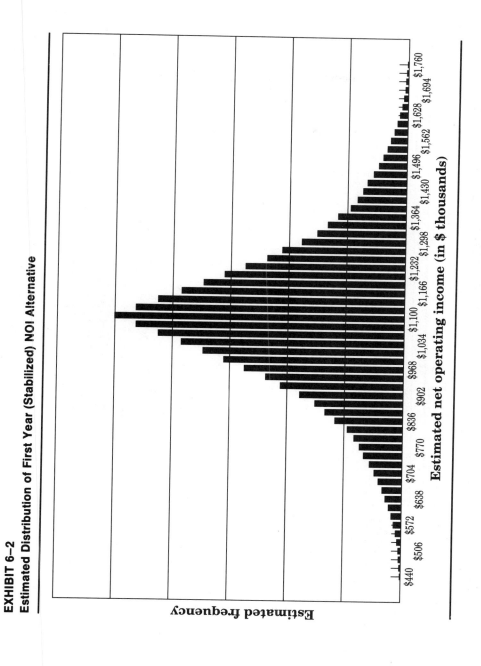

EXHIBIT 6–3
Estimated Distribution of Property Values

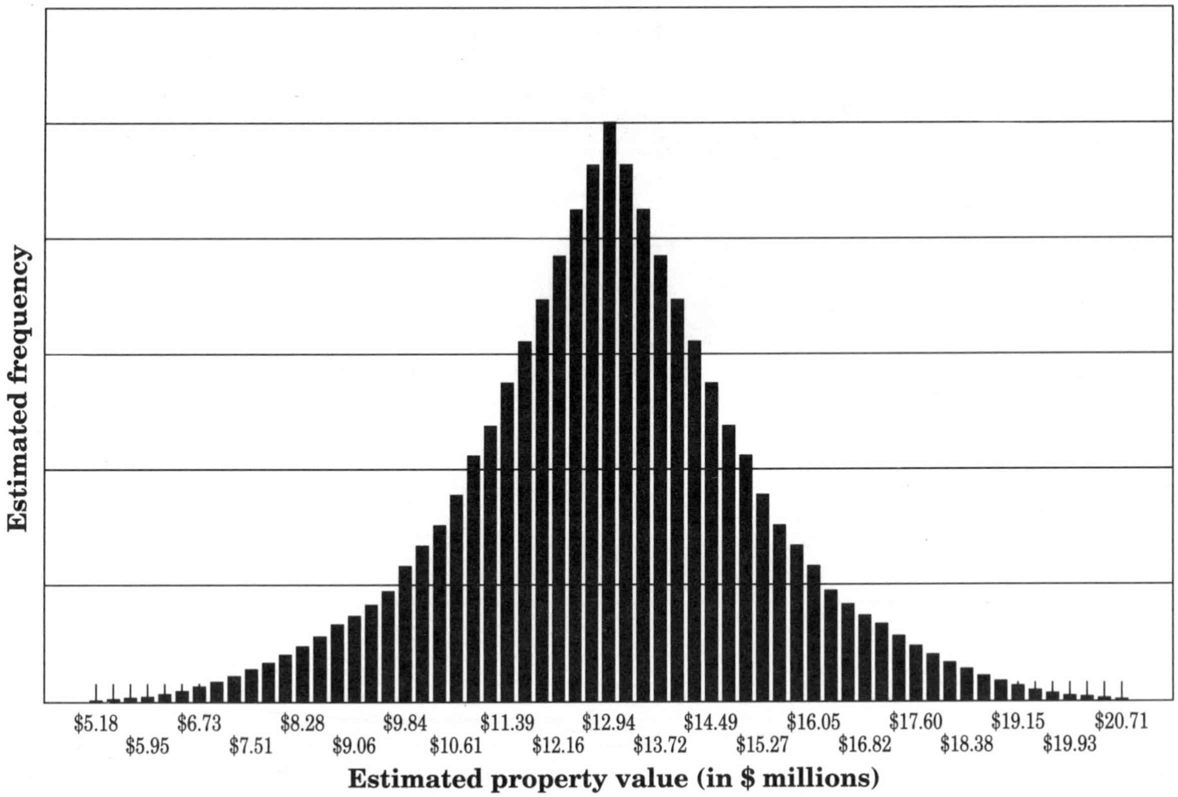

Estimated frequency

Estimated property value (in $ millions)

$5.18 $5.95 $6.73 $7.51 $8.28 $9.06 $9.84 $10.61 $11.39 $12.16 $12.94 $13.72 $14.49 $15.27 $16.05 $16.82 $17.60 $18.38 $19.15 $19.93 $20.71

EXHIBIT 6-4
Estimated Distribution of Joint Venturer's Return

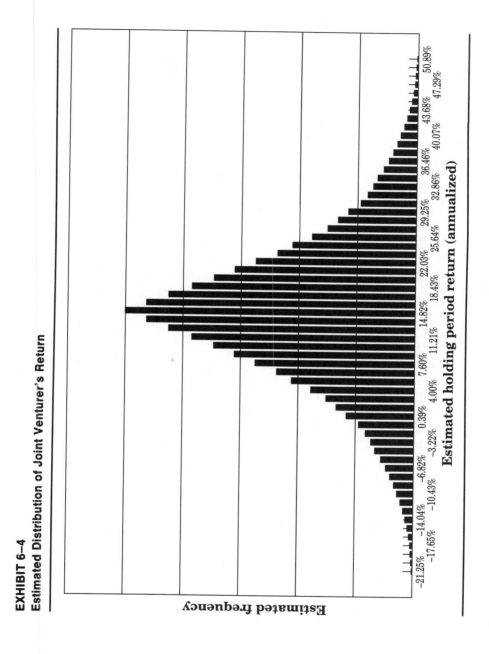

New sales proceeds	$12,941,176
Return of capital	− 10,000,000
Preferred return	− 1,800,000*
Residual profits	$ 1,141,176
Joint venturer's share (%)	60%
Joint venturer's share ($)	$ 684,706
Annualized return on equity	15.9%†

* Preferred return of 12 percent per annum computed over (effective) 1.5-year holding period.

† Based on annual compounding with assumed (effective) 1.5-year holding period.

Note that the 15.9 percent return represents an estimated return that is higher than the mean of the distribution shown in Exhibit 6–4. Why? Because the underlying distribution of the returns to the joint venturer is asymmetrical: On the upside (a sales price of more than $11.8 million), the investor participates in only 60 percent of the residual profits, while on the downside (a sales price of less than $10.0 million), the investor incurs 100 percent of the loss. (At a sales price between $10.0 million and $11.8 million, the investor keeps, in the form of the preferred return, 100 percent of the profits.) The nature of the investment made by the joint venturer suggests that he or she incurs the risk of losing his or her capital in return for a partial participation in the potential profits of the development.

Developer's Expected Cash Flow

The nature of the developer's expected cash flow is the corollary to that of the investor: The developer incurs none of the downside risk and gains a partial participation in the potential profits of the development. Exhibit 6–5 graphically illustrates the developer's limited downside and virtually unlimited upside.

Other Considerations

For ease of presentation, only the uncertainty of the forecasted stabilized NOI has been illustrated. However, savvy investors will note that similar uncertainty exists for all critical assumptions of the joint venturer's abbreviated pro forma. Each critical element (construction

EXHIBIT 6–5
Distribution of Developer's Estimated Profits

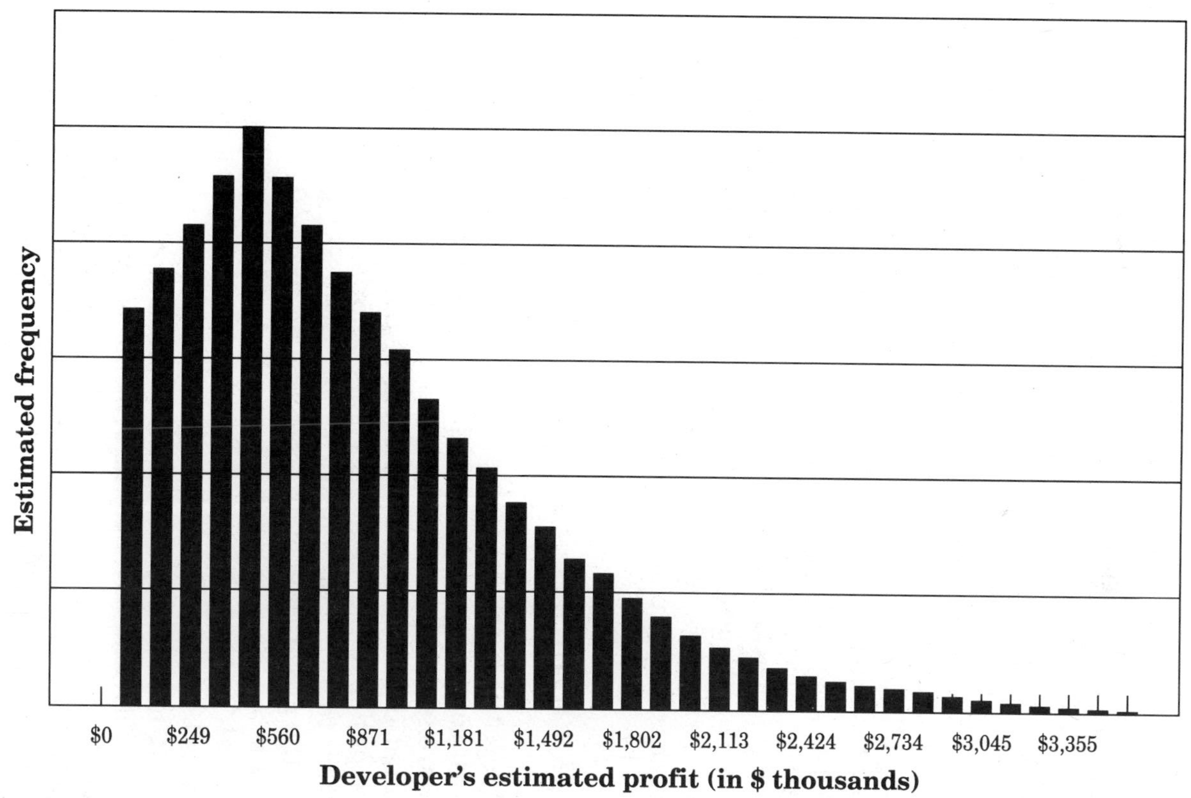

costs, construction period, stabilization period, and reversionary capitalization rate) could be similarly described, with an estimated mean and standard deviation. If so, the range of possible outcomes for the joint venture investor would widen, and his or her expected return might decline further (depending on the assumptions chosen).

The foregoing discussion is not intended to dissuade investors from using real estate development to earn superior risk-adjusted returns. Rather, it is intended to simplistically demonstrate the substantial risks found in real estate development so that investors can be adequately compensated for bearing such risks. In fairness, it should also be noted that the investor in existing real estate faces similar uncertainties (e.g., reversionary capitalization rates, growth rates); however, the uncertainty about stabilized NOI should be much diminished once the property is leased. In this regard, the investor in existing properties bears less risk and accordingly should earn a lower return premium.

THE FUTURE OF DEVELOPMENT

The real estate "landscape" has changed dramatically in the last 5 to 10 years. The wide swings in real estate returns have heightened awareness of the risks inherent in owning real estate. This has resulted in a significant repricing of the asset class and will change the profile of real estate investment for many investors as they construct their investment portfolios. The aforementioned forces affecting the private and public sectors have and will continue to influence real estate development. The impact of these changing product and capital market forces on development organizations will remain critical.

It has become increasingly important that developers manage their activities as a long-term business enterprise. The inherent mismatch of future profitability from a new development and current operating expenses has traditionally made it difficult for developers to survive. This difficulty has been exacerbated of late by declining real estate profitability and increased front-end development costs. It is therefore critical that developers recognize the current certain nature of their expense load and the speculative long-term nature of their payback when they participate in the "future profitability" of a new investment. In the future, developers may rely more on current pay for services rendered and less on future profitability of transactions, provided that leaders and investors agree to such an arrangement.

This change will also spur a significant realignment of the interests of developers and their investor partner/capital providers. These investor entities will require greater control of product development, design, ownership, and management. It is important to the strategy of the investor/owner to have ultimate control of the destiny of the project, including the right to replace the developer at any stage from conception through management of the enterprise.

In addition, developers are required to provide increasing amounts of information, research, and management services. In addition, their industry is changing from a product-driven to a service-oriented one. This trend reflects the overall national change toward a knowledge- and information-based economy.

The world of the developer enterprise is changing dramatically. It has been very volatile over the last several years, and the profile for the future is a very different business enterprise than what it has been in the last 20 years. This is a maturing industry that has changed significantly from the speculative development activity introduced by Trammell Crow nearly 50 years ago.

CONCLUSION

Industry Consolidation

The real estate development industry has gone through a tremendous consolidation. One of the bigger casualties may have been the mid-size developer. Large, national developers can maintain their (limited) access to the capital markets and concentrate their (diminished) resources on fewer projects. Small, local developers can use their flexibility, responsiveness, and entrepreneurial talents to seize small market niches. The result is the "hourglass" effect: the mid-size developers squeezed out of both ends by the large and small developers.

Merchant Building

As the speculative excesses (and then some) are wrung from the marketplace, developers focus more on merchant building. This requires their involvement in the development, but not ownership, of the asset.

Service Income

The well-worn developer's business strategy of shifting more of the company's revenue stream to recurring service income (property management, leasing, consulting, asset management, investment advisory work, etc.) is an attempt to smooth out the peaks and troughs of the developer's operating income. The market's reaction, however, has been decidedly mixed (with many skeptical that the "deal junkie" mentality of some developers can remain subservient to a more operational/institutional approach).

Changing Product Type

The last 10 to 15 years would surely reinforce the traditional notion that the development of commercial properties is countercyclical to that of developing residential properties. Some developers may have hung on to the office market too long when a burgeoning uptick in single-family housing was getting under way. The real question is: Are real estate developers able to "retool" to a new product type, or are the barriers to entry too strong to allow transition?

This chapter has illustrated that real estate development is a risk-prone adventure. In markets such as those experienced in the late 1980s and early 1990s, development has become a life-and-death struggle for many developers and real estate investors alike. The large market imbalance has yielded a number of significant changes in the real estate industry.

This chapter dealt with issues of environmental and legal pressures and briefly touched on financial market conditions. As the market moves forward in the 1990s, the advent of securitized offerings on both the debt and equity sides will further change the real estate and development ownership businesses. The use of private market sources is likely to diminish, and the use of public market capital is likely to increase. The nature and structure of these capital programs are quite varied, and developers need to keep pace with these changing capital sources. Investment capital is the lifeblood of the real estate development business.

In terms of market product, the changing demographics, both nationally and internationally, as well as emerging technologies have influenced the design and delivery of real estate products. These changes have affected existing real estate investments, rendering some obsolete and others much more attractive. They will also significantly influence the design of new products as market conditions return to balance and new development is ultimately required. These changing trends, particularly as they relate to a more service-oriented U.S. real estate economy, will require dramatic redesign of existing real estate stock and potentially an entirely new type of office research and development and industrial real estate base. These will present selective opportunities for developers, particularly with emerging high-tech tenant prospects. These emerging market forces present yet another risk for the balance of this decade and beyond.

CHAPTER 7

THE OFFICE SECTOR

W. Cabell Grayson, Jr.
CB Commercial Realty Advisors

Raymond G. Torto
CB Commercial/Torto Wheaton Research

Scott E. Tracy
CB Commercial Realty Advisors

William C. Wheaton
Massachusetts Institute of Technology
MIT Center of Real Estate

Almost one out of every three jobs in the United States is office related today. These jobs, of course, are generally white-collar, professional positions, and many are located in suburban office parks or towering city high-rises. During the 1980s, much was written about the dynamic growth of these types of jobs and the corresponding growth in the supply of office space. We will turn to this latter issue shortly. We wish to emphasize at the outset of this chapter that the purpose of office real estate is to provide the space for office-related jobs. In other words, the demand for office space is a derived demand where the ultimate "driver" of office space demand is the growth in such professions as law, brokerage, consulting, accounting, and the like.

Theoretically, it is possible that many of the professional jobs could be performed in another setting, such as the home. The current location and structure of the office sector today is a product of land use policies resulting from location and urban transportation policies of earlier periods in our economic history. Downtown cores that are densely populated with office jobs that are "stacked" in high-rise towers are examples of the results of these policies. However, the technology and transportation system of this earlier time period is changing as we move into the 21st century.

This chapter:

- Describes the dimensions of the office sector as measured by size, age, and location.
- Reviews market conditions and market history.
- Outlines the key dimensions from the demand side (office-related employment growth is important, but so are issues of home offices, "just-in-time" offices, and technological impacts on office layouts).
- Carefully analyzes the major two measures of office market conditions: rents and vacancy.
- Describes intermetropolitan and intrametropolitan variations in the office sector, with a particular emphasis on the suburban versus downtown competition of office jobs.
- Examines the office sector as an investment class.

DIMENSIONS OF THE OFFICE SECTOR

Supply

Estimates of the size of the U.S. office sector vary considerably, and various analysts define the sector differently. Some include all office buildings, whether owner occupied or single tenant. Others count only those that are multitenanted. Other issues to consider are size, quality, and, correlated with quality, age. For instance, some analysts track only buildings of 10,000 square feet or larger; others use a 20,000-square-foot criterion. The choice usually depends on the analyst's purposes.

Also, real estate brokers often look only at "competitive" buildings. These are usually class A (another term that has subjective dimensions) buildings, which are newer, well located, and technologically efficient.

For the purpose of this chapter, we define the office sector as those multitenanted buildings of 20,000 or more square feet that are competitive in today's marketplace. We also focus on aggregated statistics for the 50 larger metropolitan areas for which we have a consistent, accurate, and up-to-date database.

Before turning to these statistics one caveat is in order. This chapter focuses on the *space* market. This is the market for the demand for and supply of space where on the demand side we find the tenants and on the supply side we find the developer/investor. We wish to distinguish the space market from the capital market for office buildings. In the latter market, investors buy and sell office buildings based on calculated rates of return, and the availability of capital is a very important factor.

The U.S. office market as of the end of 1992 contained approximately 26,000 buildings with 2.6 billion square feet, of which 18.9 percent was vacant. The amount of space in the country grew exponentially during the 1980s, leading to severe overbuilding and serious damage to the health of many financial institutions. Prior to 1980, there were about 1.1 billion square feet of office space. From 1980 to 1987, about 41 percent of the current stock of space was built! Office development slowed in 1988, but between that year and 1992, another 373 million square feet were added to the market. In sum, the 1980s saw about 50 percent of the market developed and built. Exhibit 7–1 shows the supply of office space by the period built.

Naturally, aggregate statistics mask differences in underlying markets. Generally speaking, more mature urban areas grew at slower rates, though not necessarily in absolute amounts of new construction. For example, Austin more than doubled its office stock, while New York City's office stock grew by only 16 percent. Yet the office vacancy rate in Austin dropped from 40 to 11 percent during 1993 (and some speculative building is occurring again), while New

EXHIBIT 7–1
Office Completions by Year Built

	Square Feet (x 1,000)	Percent of Stock	Percent Vacant
Pre-1960	405,769	15.5%	20.7%
1960–69	233,801	8.9	18.2
1970–79	526,638	20.1	18.3
1980–89	1,291,155	49.3	17.1
1990–92	163,802	6.2	31.6
Total	2,621,165	100.0%	18.9%

Source: CB Commercial/Torto Wheaton Research.

York City's vacancy rate hovers around 14 percent. Clearly, there is a spectrum of office markets.

In the aggregate, about 60 percent of the office market is in the suburbs, where the vacancy rate averages 19.8 percent versus 17.7 percent in the downtowns. Since about the mid-1980s the vacancy trend in the downtown markets has been slowly rising while the vacancy trend in the suburban markets has been declining. The rising downtown rate has been induced primarily by an overbuilding that has continued in the downtowns while it has been curtailed in the suburbs for several years. Exhibit 7–2 shows the annual completion statistics for the downtowns and suburbs for the 1986–92 period. Fortunately for the immediate future, the pipeline is dry in both the downtowns and the suburbs!

Exhibit 7–3 shows office completions over a longer time period, 1970 to 1992. The completion rate is the ratio of new space brought to the market over the stock of then-existing space. The exhibit shows that two significant periods of development occurred in the United States. The first was in the early 1970s, when completions reached 9 percent, and the second was in the early 1980s, when completions

EXHIBIT 7–2
Office Completions, 1986–92 (Suburban versus Downtown)

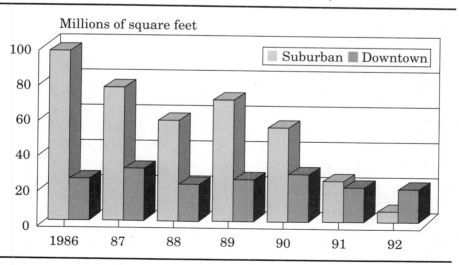

Source: CB Commercial/Torto Wheaton Research.

EXHIBIT 7–3
Office Completions Rate, 1970–92 (Nationwide)

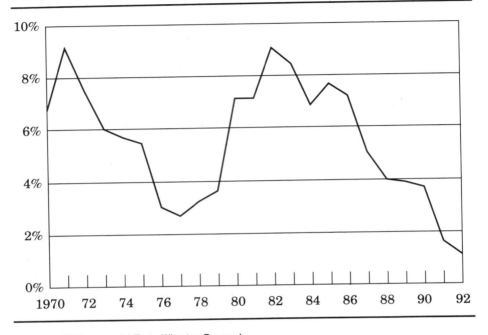

Source: CB Commercial/Torto Wheaton Research.

also reached 9 percent. The completion rate steadily declined from both peaks for several years. The current situation as of this writing (1993), will show a completions rate of almost 0 percent for 1993 and 1994!

With a seriously overbuilt market and the availability of much newer space, uninhibited by asbestos or technologically outmoded heating, cooling, fire protection, and electrical systems, some analysts believe the office market will see the "obsolete" buildings boarded up or torn down as tenants move into the "better" space in a flight to quality. Underlying this presumption are the vacancy figures presented in Exhibit 7–1. Vacancy rates are above 20 percent for buildings built in the 1950s. For the newer buildings, vacancy rates have declined until reaching the most recently completed buildings, many of which are undergoing a lease-up phase. This is what we would expect: Older buildings and those most recently brought to the market have more availability. The question is whether the older buildings will fade out of the market as tenants move into the newer space.

Demand

The demand for office space is driven primarily by employment within certain sectors of the economy. Annual and five-year surveys of establishments, or sites, conducted by the Bureau of Labor Statistics can be used to distinguish those employees located in separate office facilities from office-type workers located at the site of production, distribution, or retailing. In processing these data, a remarkably uniform pattern emerges across metropolitan areas in the distribution of office building employment. The figures given in Exhibit 7–4 for Dallas and Chicago are very representative of most of the nation's major metropolitan areas.

Two important conclusions emerge from examining these data. First, the fraction of manufacturing workers located in separate office

EXHIBIT 7–4
"Office" Employment[a] (Thousands of Employees)

SIC[c]	Dallas[b] Employment		Chicago[b] Employment	
	Total	"Office"	Total	"Office"
Manufacturing	184.7	16.2	499.1	49.4
Mining	17.4	10.3	1.3	0.6
Construction	47.5	.6	93.8	0.4
TCU[d]	92.4	7.1	148.5	6.2
Trade	287.9	28.1	613.6	51.1
FIRE[e]	122.9	122.9	246.0	246.0
Services	314.8	105.8[f]	730.2	227.0[f]
Total private	1,067.6	291.0	2,332.5	580.7
Office/total		27.3%		24.9%
(FIRE + service)/office		78.6%		81.5%

[a] Those employees occupying "separate" office space from on-site manufacturing, retailing, or distribution activity.
[b] Dallas County; Cook County.
[c] Standard Industrial Classification codes.
[d] Transportation, communication, and utilities.
[e] Finance, insurance, and real estate.
[f] Includes advertising, computer and data processing, credit reporting, mailing and reproduction, legal and social services, membership organizations, and engineering and management services.

Sources: CB Commercial/Torto Wheaton Research; Bureau of Labor Statistics.

facilities (roughly 10 percent) is far smaller than the current fraction of the manufacturing work force whose activity is white-collar in character (management, clerical, research and development). The latter occupations now account for roughly 35 percent of manufacturing employment. Any large shift toward moving these workers off-site (i.e., into office buildings) in the future might create considerable office demand. Current trends in management theory, however, suggest this would not necessarily be in the interest of productivity.

The second and perhaps more important conclusion is that almost 80 percent of office employment comes from the finance, real estate, and service sectors. The service sector in particular has grown enormously over the last two decades and covers accountants, lawyers, consultants, lobbyists, architects, and a range of other producer-related service professions.

Exhibit 7–5 shows the number of office and manufacturing em-

EXHIBIT 7–5
National Employment Levels, 1970–92

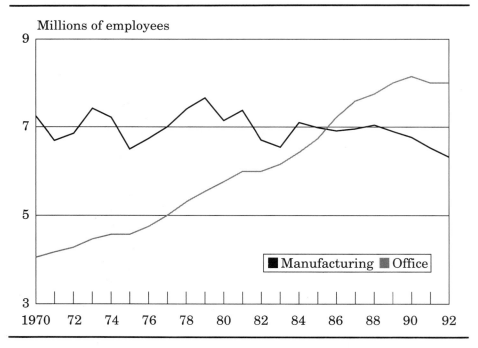

Source: CB Commercial/Torto Wheaton Research.

ployees nationwide for the period 1970 through 1992. Over this period, office employment doubled while manufacturing employment fell slightly. Meanwhile, total employment rose by 64 percent.

As shown in Exhibit 7–6, the growth rates of office and manufacturing employment are quite disparate. The growth of office employment has been steadier over the years, while manufacturing has been more volatile. The growth of manufacturing employment turns negative during recessions and rebounds during early recoveries. This is most evident in the 1970, 1975, 1982, and 1990–91 recessions; it is of note that the 1990–91 recession was relatively milder for manufacturing employment losses than the earlier recessions. Office employment growth turns lower during recessions, such as those in 1975 and 1982, but only during the 1990–91 recession did office employment actually lose jobs. This reflects the major restructuring occurring in the real estate and finance sectors.

EXHIBIT 7–6
Employment Growth, 1970–92 (Office versus Manufacturing)

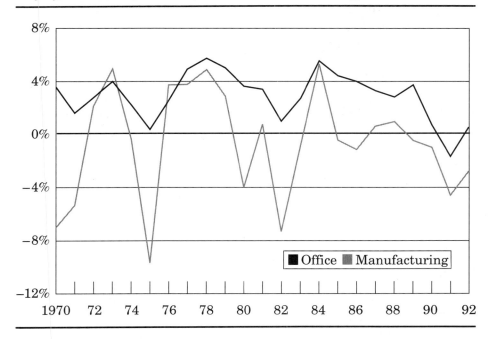

Source: CB Commercial/Torto Wheaton Research.

The most significant factor in determining the demand for office space is the growth in office employment. As companies need more space to house their employees, net absorption (the change in occupied space) increases. However, the relationship between office employment growth and net absorption is not proportional or constant over time. Put another way, the demand for office space also depends on the level of rent, expectations about future economic and market considerations, technological factors, and tenant tastes.

For example, evidence has clearly shown that tenants are sensitive to rent levels and changing expectations about those levels. High rents reduce the amount of space demanded, while lower rents increase demand. In fact, we have seen in recent years that falling rents are stimulating net absorption, even while office employment growth is negligible. Price-conscious tenants are "bargain shopping" for space in anticipation of future growth. This helps to fill buildings during a recession, but it has ominous implications. During the following expansion, as office employment growth picks up, there will not be concomitant net absorption. Rather, these bargain-shopping tenants will have already leased the space for their new employees.

In the third quarter of 1992, a very strong rebound in absorption occurred when 12.4 million square feet were absorbed. This was well above the average for the first two quarters of the year and for 1991. Also, it was a respectable comparison to the 24 million square foot average of 1987, which was a peak year for net absorption. See Exhibit 7–7.

Was this strong showing of absorption a sign of renewed demand

EXHIBIT 7–7
National Absorption: Quarterly Averages
(Millions of Square Feet)

	1992:3	1992	1991	1987
Downtown	6.3	3.2	1.2	8
Suburban	6.1	4.3	7.8	16
Total	12.4	7.5	9.0	16

in the office market? Given the uncertain state of the economy and the very modest growth, if any, of office-related employment, the strong absorption figures are the result of "bargain basement" rents and the leasing of office space *today* by tenants who expect to grow in the future. Tenants are occupying office space today with the expectation that they will use it more intensively in the future. This interpretation of the figures implies that when these tenants have new office-related employment in the future, they will already have "bought" the space today at the low price now available. Hence, future economic growth will not lead to historical absorption levels.

The above example is one of cyclical variation in the ratio of square feet to office employees. This ratio will vary from time period to time period because of short-term market factors. It will also vary across markets, depending on the structure of tenant industries. There are also long-term considerations. For instance, the technological advances in communications have helped disperse economic activity. As an example, major New York City banks locate back offices in other parts of the region, other parts of the country, and in some cases other countries for check clearing or credit card processing. When one calls an 800 telephone number, the respondent can be anywhere in the United States.

Exhibit 7–8 plots the long-run trend in the ratio of square feet per employee in the country. As can be seen, this ratio rises significantly. Some analysts are concerned that the trend will reverse itself in the 1990s, and by implication this would reduce the demand for office space. Some might even argue that the office sector is a mature industry. They cite such phenomena as the growth in the number of people who are working out of their homes or the "just-in-time" office. The latter concept is employed by large accounting firms. Many of their employees are out of the office performing their job functions on the client's premises. To save overhead expenses, more than one employee (even senior partners) share offices. When the employee is in the firm's office, his or her papers and other necessary accoutrements are wheeled in. When he or she is out, out go the papers and in roll somebody else's—a just-in-time office! Naturally, real estate professionals are concerned about the long-run trend of office space per employee. Many analysts believe this historical trend will not continue and will reverse itself in the future. Accordingly, the implication is that the demand for space will be less.

EXHIBIT 7–8
Office Square Feet per Worker (Nation)

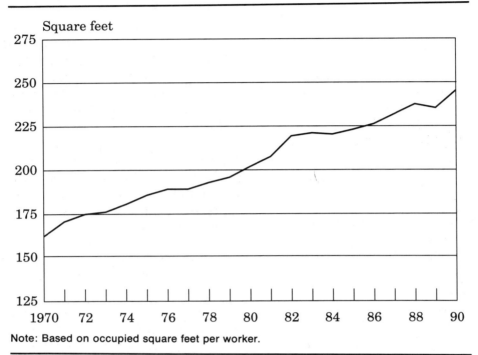

Note: Based on occupied square feet per worker.

Source: CB Commercial/Torto Wheaton Research.

MARKET INDICATORS

The previous two sections discussed office space supply and demand. This section focuses on market indicators: rents and vacancy.

Vacancy survey results reported by the national brokerage companies for both office and industrial property vary widely. In 1988, the variation in reported vacancy rates in some markets was as wide as 7 percentage points. The variations are not "errors" but are due to different definitions of geography, building size, and building quality that are surveyed. Because of differing methodologies, we would strongly urge analysts to know their vacancy surveys and not use different surveys in different markets for comparison! They might be comparing apples to oranges!

Also, and probably more compelling, we have found that a correct net absorption calculation requires a complete understanding of how the vacancy survey is conducted. The implications for net absorption calculations are the most important reasons for understanding vacancy survey construction.

For example, the CB Commercial survey[1] covers competitively leased space of a minimum size, usually 20,000 square feet; other brokerage surveys often have a different minimum size. After setting a minimum size, the next step is to define the types of buildings to be surveyed. In the CB Commercial survey, certain buildings are excluded, such as owner-user or corporate headquarter buildings, government-owned buildings, and medical buildings. Only multitenant buildings are included, while single-tenant buildings are excluded. However, if a single owner-user decides to rent out some of its own space, the building is reclassified and picked up in the competitive space survey. The amount of office space occupied by single tenants in most markets is small—usually less than 15 percent of all space. In areas such as Hartford, Indianapolis, St. Louis, and Washington, DC, however, such space can account for up to 35 percent of the market.

Other factors that affect vacancy survey results are the handling of rehabilitational space and the handling of new buildings. New buildings in the CB Commercial survey are added to the existing stock when the occupancy permit is issued.

It is very important to understand what it means to say that the data come from a "survey." Not all of the office space within a given market is included, but only that portion of it that is defined by the survey standards. One implication of different standards is that two surveys done by different firms are not comparable either at a moment in time or over time. But a more fundamental implication is that even the same survey might not be comparable over time, because the buildings included in it are not necessarily the same from period to period. For example, a building that has several tenants may be sold to a large corporation that wishes to use the entire building as its home office; then, in the next period, this building will no longer

---

[1] Though other surveys could be discussed here, the CB Commercial survey is emphasized because (1) the authors are obviously familiar with it and (2) it is the data source from which many of the calculations presented in this chapter are derived.

be considered "competitively leased" space and will therefore not be included in the survey. Or a building that was built as a warehouse may be rehabilitated into an office building and added to the survey.

It should also be noted that the CB Commercial survey of office space is a vacancy survey; that is, space that is vacant is counted. It is not an availability survey. In the latter, space that is occupied but soon to be available is counted. Other brokerage and research firms may handle this issue differently, which obviously can lead to reported vacancy rate disparity.

NET ABSORPTION

The most important reason to understand the vacancy survey methodology is to be able to calculate the net absorption rate (NAR) correctly. Net absorption is the change in occupied space (as defined by the survey's methodology) from period to period. Occupied space is calculated as 1 minus the vacancy rate multiplied by the stock of space.

Market analysts need to be sure that in calculating this figure, they are using a vacancy rate and stock number that is a correct measure of what happened in the market. Sometimes vacancy rates and stock figures can simply reflect survey changes. The following example will illustrate.

From our description of survey methodology, it should be obvious that the net rentable square feet in a survey can vary from quarter to quarter due simply to definitional changes and/or survey coverage. For example, if a building of 1 million square feet was multitenant in the last quarter but has since been bought and occupied fully by a single tenant, the surveyed net rentable square footage in the market would fall (the building is no longer multitenant and competitive). If the market had a stock of 40 million square feet and a 10 percent vacancy last quarter, with no new completions this quarter, this definitional change (i.e., a nonmarket change) alone would cause the existing stock of space surveyed to decline to 39 million square feet and the vacancy rate to increase to 10.3 percent. (Note that 4 million square feet are still vacant and the change occurred due to market forces.)

However, the rise in the vacancy rate is not an indication of a slackening market! Rather, it is simply a reflection of the survey coverage. CB Commercial has a fairly complicated method for deciding what vacancy rate to actually print in this instance. It begins by calculating four different vacancy rates: (1) the published rate for the previous quarter, (2) the rate for the previous quarter when previous-quarter stock and vacancy figures have been adjusted by the nonmarket changes, (3) the rate for the current quarter when nonmarket changes are removed from the stock and vacancy, and (4) the rate for the current quarter when stock and vacancy figures include the nonmarket changes. See Exhibit 7–9 for a summary.

Then the rates, as well as the changes in rates, are compared: the two rates calculated without adjustments (rates 1 and 3), the two rates that include adjustments (rates 2 and 4), and finally the published rate from the last quarter with the proposed rate for this quarter (rates 1 and 4). In our example, the first two sets of rates show no change in vacancy, while the last set shows an increase in vacancy over the quarter. At this point, a decision is made in the local office as to whether the market changes make a sufficient difference to warrant a revision of the previous quarter's rate. The current rate will always reflect the changes of the current quarter. Thus, the 10.3 percent rate would be published for the current quarter, while the previous quarter's rate of 10.0 percent may be revised to 10.3 percent. It is of interest to us that CB Commercial, as a brokerage company, would make an adjustment in the history (10.0 to 10.3 percent). We would surmise that an analyst would do the reverse, that is, revise the figure to show 10.0 percent in the current period, consistent with last period's reported figure. It should be noted that such revisions are seldom made.

Continuing the example, we have assumed that in period 2 the survey coverage dropped by 1 million square feet, as explained above. Period 3 shows the building returning to the survey; hence, the NAR is again 40 million square feet.

Period 4 shows an increase in the NAR of 1 million square feet due to new completions of that amount, while period 5 has new comple-

EXHIBIT 7–9
Vacancy Rate Calculations

Rate 1 (published previous quarter)	= 10.0%
Rate 2 (adjusted previous quarter)	= 10.3%
Rate 3 (base current quarter)	= 10.0%
Rate 4 (adjusted current quarter)	= 10.3%

tions of 500,000 square feet *and* additional coverage, bringing the total square feet surveyed to 42 million.

We think the biggest effect of changes in survey coverage is found in calculating net absorption. It has been our experience that many analysts, brokers, and others make egregious errors in this calculation. Exhibit 7–10 presents the data for our illustration. Our question is: What is the net absorption in each period?

Before tackling the arithmetic, let us present what we consider the best formula for measuring net absorption. In these equations, S is stock and V is the vacancy rate.

$$\text{Abs} = S_t(1 - V_t) - S_{t-1}(1 - V_{t-1}) \quad \text{(absorption equals the change in occupied stock)} \quad (1)$$

$$= S_t - V_t S_t - S_{t-1} + V_{t-1}S_{t-1} \quad \text{(multiplying through . . .)} \quad (2)$$

$$= (S_t - S_{t-1}) - (V_t S_t - V_{t-1}S_{t-1}) \quad \text{(and rearranging)} \quad (3)$$

$$= \text{Completions} - \Delta\text{Vacant space} \quad \text{(our formula for absorption)} \quad (4)$$

Note that net absorption can be measured as new space constructed and entering the market (what we call completions) minus the change in vacant space.

Real estate researchers usually collect historic supply-side information consisting of vacancy rates and stock. They calculate absorption by multiplying $(1 - \text{Vacancy rate})$ by stock to obtain occupied square footage and then take the change in occupied square feet over time as the measure of absorption (method 1, the same as in equation [1] above). In Exhibit 7–10, this calculation would generate a net absorption figure of -1 million square feet in period 1, $+1$ million square feet in period 2, $+1$ million in period 4, and -1 million in period 5—all of which would be incorrect, except for period 4. The correct figures can be put together by equation (4) (method 2), which requires the use of columns 3 (vacant square feet) and 5 (new completions).

Most analysts have available to them the net rentable area and the vacancy rate over time from which to calculate absorption. However, as we showed above, using these figures alone will lead to errors. We would suggest that analysts also collect completion figures and calculate absorption via equation (4) above.

EXHIBIT 7–10
Hypothetical NRA Problem*

Period	Net Rentable Area	Vacancy		New Completions	Occupied	Absorption Methodology	
		Amount	Percentage			1	2
1	40m	4m	10.0%	0m	36m	0m	0m
2	39	4	10.3	0	35	−1	0
3	40	4	10.0	0	36	1	0
4	41	4	9.7	1.0	37	1	1

* In millions of square feet, with the exception of vacancy percentage.

Clearly, the survey methodology affects the reported vacancy rate and the underlying, supporting statistics. Proper adjustment must be made for both market and nonmarket factors in the survey. Unfortunately, one can accomplish this only if one knows these changes for each quarter.

MEASURING RENTS

Collecting data on effective or contract rents in a consistent, systematic way has been fairly impossible. Most deals between landlord and tenant are private. Observers of the marketplace may know what the asking rent was, but the final negotiation and the final lease terms are a private transaction.

Nevertheless, everybody in the real estate business looks to measure "market" rents to gauge market direction, plan leasing strategy, and estimate building income in the future. To overcome this paucity of data, we have developed a rent measure that has the advantage of consistency with regard to source. We will discuss it next.

When leasing agreements for office space are made available, they normally display a series of features that warrant careful discussion. Seemingly slight differences in these features can often involve significant differences in the "value" of a lease. The major provisions of office leases are as follows:

- *Rental payments over time.* Leases may specify a fixed rental payment, a payment that rises over time contingent on some index (CPI escalation), or a payment that involves a number of specified changes ("jumps" or "bumps"). The undiscounted sum of rental payments over the term of the lease is usually called the lease's total consideration. Longer-term leases rarely specify a fixed rent level.

- *Net versus gross rents.* Lease rents may or may not include the payment of property taxes, utilities, and certain maintenance costs by the tenant. A lease rent that requires the tenant to pay current taxes, utilities, and maintenance is termed triple net, while one that requires the tenant to pay none of these is termed gross. Net and double net refer to cases in between. Gross leases place the risk of increases in operating costs with the owner, while net leases shift these various risks to the tenant.

- *Free rent periods*. During the last decade, office leases have frequently involved periods of rent abatement (or, "free" rent) for up to as much as the first year of the lease term. This seems to be a fairly common practice, particularly in soft markets.
- *Tenant improvements*. Particularly when a tenant is new, the office space to be leased must be refitted or remodeled to suit the new lessee. Such tenant improvements are paid for by the landlord, who usually amortizes the cost over the lease term. The exact definition of the work to be done is normally specified in the lease.

In the real estate industry, two measures of office "rent" tend to be frequently quoted. These are gross asking rent and net effective rent. Gross asking rent is the gross rent to be paid during the first year of the lease, as advertised by the landlord to brokers seeking space for their clients. Surveys of quoted asking rents are frequently produced by brokerage firms and are viewed as the starting point in tenant-landlord negotiations.

Net effective rent is the present or discounted value of all lease payments minus reimbursable operating expenses actually to be received by the landlord during the term of the lease. In the language of the above lease features, net effective rent would be the present value of net rents, including any period of free rent minus the value of tenant improvements. It is important to note that the practice of discounting all the terms of a lease at face value assumes both parties are risk neutral, with no capital market constraints. It could be argued, for example, that the value of future rent increases must incorporate the risk of tenant default and that in some situations, the value of space improvements will accrue to the landlord for use by future tenants. In such cases, leases with identical terms could command different rents, depending on tenant or landlord characteristics.

Given all of the previous provisions in most commercial leases, the notion of a single market "rent" is often difficult to define. Two common terms are used in practice: total consideration and net effective rent. The first refers to the sum of all gross payments made over the lease term. Frequently this figure is divided by the square footage of space and the lease term. This yields an "average" payment per square foot over the length of the lease, undiscounted by when those payments are made.

Net effective rent takes the discounted present value of this total consideration less estimated total operating expenses during the lease term, as well as the initial cost of tenant improvements. This figure too is often divided by lease term and square footage.

It is clear that any meaningful measure of market "rent" must be based on a careful analysis of individual leases. Given the proprietary nature of rental contracts, it is perhaps not surprising that there have been no standard surveys or indices, especially over time, documenting movements in either office or industrial space "rents." An innovation in this regard is an office rental index recently prepared by CB Commercial/Torto Wheaton Research, which is based on the brokerage fees received by its leasing agents. Leasing commissions are typically a variable percentage of each year's rent during the lease term.

In calculating the commission, the brokerage company normally determines the total consideration of the lease. The payroll records of CB Commercial go back to the late 1970s in a number of metropolitan areas and were used to retrospectively create a measure of "consideration rent" for each market.

Designing a rental index based on the sample of leases from only one brokerage company raises the issue of whether that company's business is always representative of the overall market. In particular, if the company's properties or the structure of its leases were to change from year to year, movements in the average rent of the company's transactions might not represent true changes in market conditions. To allow for this possibility, the CB Commercial index statistically "adjusts" the data on consideration rent. This can be done in one of two ways: Either leases for the same space can be repeatedly surveyed, or a statistical (or, hedonic) model can be estimated to predict how consideration rent varies by such factors as type and location of building, lease term, and square footage, as well as the year the lease was signed. The CB Commercial index uses the latter method.

In Exhibit 7–11, the dark line represents the average consideration rent each year in San Francisco, based on 1,932 leases brokered by CB Commercial since 1979. The gray line is the predicted rent (i.e., the Torto Wheaton rent index), based on the statistical corrections discussed above. Both rental measures have been adjusted for inflation and are in (constant) 1990 dollars. While the long-term trend in the two measures is the same, the year-to-year movements sometimes differ. Between 1987 and 1988, for example, the simple average consideration rose by $1.70 (adjusted for inflation), while the hedonic index rose by $.30.

EXHIBIT 7–11
Average Rent versus TW Rent Index, 1979–92 (San Francisco)

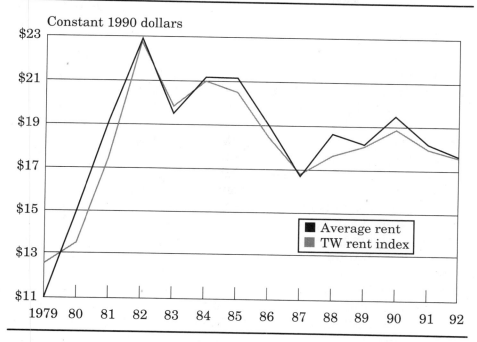

Constant 1990 dollars

Legend: ■ Average rent   ▪ TW rent index

Source: CB Commercial/Torto Wheaton Research.

This says that the sample of buildings and leases in 1988 was different than in 1987, and in fact was worth roughly 10 percent more. Correcting these differences, the same buildings and leases would have commanded a 1.5 percent increase in consideration rent that year.

The bottom line is that this approach provides a data set on rents that is consistent over time and across markets. It allows the analyst to provide an "apples-to-apples" comparison based on leases of similar size and length.

VACANCY AND THE MOVEMENT IN OFFICE RENTS

Just as households may change their desired home during their life cycle, firms experience change and periodically seek to relocate. If the average lease length were, say, five years, 20 percent of all leases would expire each year, creating quite a large pool of tenants who were in a position to move if they so desired. The ratio of the amount of vacant space to the space needed by the pool of moving tenants represents a measure of the *time* it will likely take a landlord to rent his or her space. The inverse of this ratio is the probability that space is rented at any interval of time.

The search by tenants for appropriate space can be an extensive process. Not only does space vary by location and building, but parcels of space come in widely different sizes and configurations, especially in existing buildings. When a tenant has found appropriate space, the stage is set for a round of bargaining between tenant and landlord over both the rent and the other terms of the lease. It is in this bargaining process that the market for commercial rental space differs from the market for owner-occupied housing.

In a rental market, the risk of vacancy lies mainly with the landlord. When an appropriate potential tenant arrives, the landlord has to consider the "cost" of not accepting the tenant's offer—the prospect of the property remaining vacant. A landlord establishes a reservation or minimum rent that would make him or her indifferent between renting the space and keeping it vacant. The longer the expected lease-up time for vacant space, the lower will be the landlord's reservation rent: "A bird in the hand is worth two in the bush." Greater vacancy and fewer relocating tenants raise the expected leasing time and hence lower the minimum rent that landlords are willing to accept.

On the tenant's side of the negotiation, when there are few other searching tenants and much vacant space, it becomes easier to find appropriate new space. This reduces the "cost" to the tenant of not closing any particular deal, since the search for some other suitable parcel will be less difficult. Thus, the maximum rent the tenant is willing to offer likewise will be less when vacant space is plentiful and there are few competing tenants. The eventual contract rent that emerges in the bargaining process must lie between the tenant's maximum offer and the landlord's minimum reservation. Both of these move figures inversely with vacancy and positively with the number of tenants in the market.

The impact of residential vacancy rates on house rents and prices has been clearly demonstrated. Many researchers have found that similar relationships exist in commercial markets as well. For example, Exhibit 7–12 illustrates these relationships for the San Francisco office sector for the period 1980 through 1992. Exhibit 7–12 compares

EXHIBIT 7–12
Real Rent Change versus Vacancy Rate, 1980–92 (San Francisco)

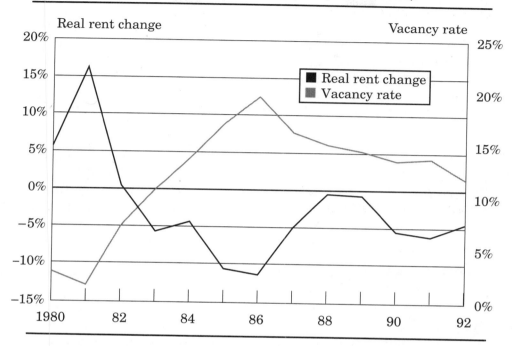

Source: CB Commercial/Torto Wheaton Research.

the annual change (in real or constant dollars) to the office vacancy rate series for the same market. Clearly, there appears to be some form of negative relationship between the level of vacancy and the change in rents.

While simple relationships between vacancy and rents are intuitively appealing, if the theory of tenant search and bargaining is correct, the relationship is more complicated. First, some measure of tenant activity or market growth should also influence rental movements, in addition to the level of vacancy. This is because it is the combination of the two that determines the expected leasing time for vacant space. While direct estimates of tenant leasing activity or mobility are largely unknown, net space absorption should be a close proxy. Thus, a function predicting real rental changes might include the level of current office space absorption (AB_{t-1}) as well as current vacancy (V_{t-1}).

The theory of tenant search and landlord bargaining also suggests that for a given level of vacancy and absorption, there eventually emerges a stable level of market rent. Rents do not fall (rise) continuously in response to overly high (low) vacancy. This is also suggested by Exhibit 7–12. In the early 1980s, rents eventually stabilized (in constant dollars), even though vacancy remained low. Conversely, they stabilized in the late 1980s after falling for several years in response to continuously high vacancy. A rental adjustment model that incorporates these features is shown below:

$$R^* = \mu_0 + \mu_1 V_{t-1} + \mu_2 AB_{t-1}$$
$$R_t - R_{t-1} = \mu_3(R^* - R_{t-1})$$
$$= \mu_3(\mu_0 + \mu_1 V_{t-1} + \mu_2 AB_{t-1}) - \mu_3 R_t - 1 \tag{5}$$

In equation (5), R^* represents the equilibrium rent that eventually emerges in the market as a linear function of absorption and vacancy rates.

THE FUTURE OF OFFICE LOCATIONS

Recently a concern has developed in both the academic and professional communities over the future of America's inner cities. How will they compete in the late 1990s with the seemingly ever-growing ranks of suburban edge cities? Institutions that have invested heavily in "premier" downtown high-rise office space now wonder if these investments are as secure as they once thought. What kinds of firms will occupy this space? What kinds of workers will be employed in those firms? Will inner cities and downtowns come back and be able to compete with newer suburban centers as the sites that firms desire for the location of new jobs?

To begin, we will put the competition between city and suburb into context. The historical numbers tell an interesting and important story. The spatial structure of metropolitan areas is changing in America. After decades of population decentralization, jobs are decentralizing every bit as rapidly. It is interesting that there is also some fairly strong evidence that similar changes are occurring in many foreign cities as well. At a 1987 conference in Europe, researchers described the widespread decentralization of employment in many of that continent's cities.

Europeans have a strong belief in urban centrality, and many have expressed concern about these changes. There have also been several academic conferences on this topic that predated Joel Garreau's book *Edge Cities*. The consensus from these gatherings is that the extensive movement of jobs away from urban centers challenges the traditional model of a city—where people commute to a center and where the ratio of jobs to people is high at the center and very low at the periphery. The argument is that cities are now moving from what is called a monocentric form to one of polycentricity.

It is useful to illustrate these trends with an example. We have chosen the Boston metropolitan area and selected some employment statistics covering the last 20 years. Boston is one of the cities showing only a very small trend toward suburbanization. Boston has a strong central city that has withstood the challenge from the suburbs relatively better than the downtowns of many other metropolitan areas. We should also note that it is easy to trace these changes in the case of Boston, because the city lines up perfectly with a county. Where this is not the case, tracking center city employment often can be quite difficult. After Boston, we will examine some examples of weaker cities.

Let's begin with the changes in employment that occurred in the Boston metropolitan area between 1970 and 1990 (Exhibit 7–13). Looking at the industrial categories first, we focus on three SIC groups: manufacturing, transportation/communication/utilities (TCU), and wholesaling. You can see that Boston city's industrial base has been declining rapidly and steadily over the last 20 years. It is half now what it was in 1970. Earlier data suggest that this absolute decline started to occur as early as the late 1950s. In the suburbs, on the other hand, manufacturing employment increased until 1980 (the "Massachusetts miracle") and declined slightly since. Manufacturing in the suburbs reflects the area's general economic cycle. Suburban wholesale employment has grown a whopping 150 percent, and the suburban TCU sectors have increased a healthy 60 percent. Thus, in Boston's case, not only is incremental industrial growth occurring only in the suburbs, but the area's industrial sectors have been rapidly abandoning the city in absolute terms.

The explanation for industrial decentralization is now a couple of decades old. Since the 1920s, America's industries have moved toward a technology that uses horizontal assembly and storage. This obviously requires lots of land, and so industrial uses are called land extensive. As such, industrial development can't possibly compete

EXHIBIT 7–13
Employment Trends in the Boston Metropolitan Area, 1976–90

Employment Category	Boston, City		
	1970	1980	1990
Mining	165	213	15
Construction	20,427	19,405	13,148
Manufacturing	84,172	57,467	39,508
TCU[a]	47,693	37,853	37,921
Wholesale	40,419	24,473	18,896
Retail	70,812	64,712	92,297
FIRE[b]	70,573	64,712	92,297
Service	131,019	176,866	248,793
Total nonagricultural employment	466,200	440,234	520,187

Employment Category	Boston, Suburban		
	1970	1980	1990
Mining	775	780	1,251
Construction	37,557	42,781	73,014
Manufacturing	342,065	365,516	334,523
TCU	37,522	48,836	57,949
Wholesale	49,589	74,630	117,849
Retail	184,838	235,455	301,406
FIRE	32,015	52,679	85,006
Service	172,488	303,653	509,991
Total nonagricultural employment	859,654	1,130,601	1,492,323

[a] *Transportation, communications, and utilities.*
[b] Finance, insurance, and real estate.

Source: CB Commercial/Torto Wheaton Research.

with more land-intensive uses, such as offices or retail, in inner-city, high-rent areas. In a 1970s survey of firms moving to beltways such as Route 128, firms universally reported that expansion capability, access to labor, and cheap land were the most important factors causing them to develop in the suburbs. The point here is that this trend still seems to be continuing. Even in the last decade, the decline of wholesale and manufacturing employment in the city has still been very pronounced.

The second category of employment to focus on is retail trade. Retail employment declined in Boston quite significantly from 1970 to 1980 and then managed a small rebound. The city of Boston is a relatively strong retail center, and many such strong cities saw a slight recovery in retail employment from 1980 to 1990. Much of this reflects the redevelopment of inner-city shopping districts and ancillary new construction. If we trace the retail employment numbers back to the 1950s, to the opening of the early suburban shopping centers, the decline of inner-city retail employment is even more pronounced. So retail employment in a strong city such as Boston declined in the 1970s (and 1960s), but managed some slight growth in the 1980s.

Over this time, however, retail employment almost doubled in the suburbs. Furthermore, this enormous and expansive growth shows little sign of abating. The explanation for the movement of retail employment is quite simple: People want to shop closer to where they live. Obviously, it makes strong economic sense for stores to go to where people wish to shop. As long as residences are dispersing, stores will follow.

The last category of employment is one that many said would never leave the city: office employment. The traditional view is that offices must be concentrated, or clustered in central business districts, because the firms occupying office space rely heavily on face-to-face communication. In this view, the future of the central business district is ensured as a center where service-type firms communicate with clients, creating knowledge and learning in the process. To some extent, there is a little truth in this prognosis. If we look at a strong city like Boston, FIRE and service employment is the one sector that has actually experienced job growth. You can see that downtown FIRE employment grew about 30 percent, while service employment grew almost 90 percent. Growth of this magnitude also occurred in other strong central cities, such as New York, Chicago, and San

Francisco. In fact, in almost any city, one finds significant growth in FIRE and service employment over the last 20 years. For urban enthusiasts this is good news, because it is that growth alone that has saved the inner cities from economic collapse. Were it not for the growth of FIRE and services in the central business district (CBD), total employment in many cities would have dropped 25 or 30 percent over the last two decades. This would have resulted in large tracks of vacant city land and falling property values. The office sectors in Boston clearly have saved the city.

When we look further at the Boston area, we find that while FIRE employment grew 30 percent in the city, it grew 200 percent in the suburbs. The good news about 90 percent service growth in the city again is overshadowed by more than 200 percent growth in the suburbs. In 1970, the city of Boston had 70 percent of the region's FIRE employment and 45 percent of its service jobs. By 1990, these percentages had dropped to 50 and 32 percent, respectively.

There is another way to look at these changes. Think of the following question: What share of the incremental growth in jobs went to the city or the suburbs? Every new job that was created had a choice of locating in some existing downtown or going out to the suburbs. In Boston's case, if we do this for FIRE and service sectors combined, we find that 78 percent of the new jobs created went to the suburbs. Put differently, when a new job was created, the probability that it wanted to locate in the suburbs was .78 as opposed to only .22 for locating in the city.

The city still has some power to attract new FIRE and service jobs, but on the margin, suburban development is preferred by about a three-to-one ratio. Of course, in the trade and industrial sectors, where the city lost absolute employment, this probability notion is misleading. Not only did all incremental growth go to the suburbs, but some existing firms picked up and moved there as well.

A case can be made that these trends for the office sector are not just a Boston phenomenon. To compare other cities, however, we switch to analyzing the growth of occupied office space rather than looking at employment growth in the office using FIRE and service sectors (Exhibit 7–14). The second and third columns in Exhibit 7–14 list the percentage changes in downtown (CBD) and suburban occupied office space from 1980 to 1990.

In Atlanta, for example, space demand grew 74 percent downtown and 196 percent in the suburbs. We have labeled groups of cities "strong" and "weak," but this categorization is not based on relative

EXHIBIT 7–14
Office Market Indicators by Downtown and Suburban Locations, 1980–90

	Percentage Change in Occupied Space		Percentage of Growth to Suburbs	Downtown versus Suburbs	
	Down-town	Suburban		Vacancy Rates	TW Rent Index
Weak markets:					
Atlanta	74%	196%	86%	29.5%/18.6%	$15.17/$13.30
Dallas	99	244	81	28.1%/25.0%	$12.85/$11.20
Denver	94	177	71	20.3%/19.4%	$10.66/$10.40
Los Angeles	114	118	79	19.9%/19.3%	$20.09/$18.80
Phoenix	69	132	81	18.5%/22.4%	$12.77/$10.30
Strong markets:					
Boston	49	251	71	15.5%/16.2%	$16.02/$13.00
Chicago	48	153	56	17.4%/19.4%	$17.91/$14.60
Minneapolis	72	137	55	17.9%/18.6%	$13.50/$12.30
Seattle	113	169	54	13.6%/14.1%	$15.90/$14.10
Washington, DC	91	225	68	10.6%/15.9%	$20.48/$14.50
National	43	173	73	17.6%/19.4%	$16.09/$13.60

Source: CB Commercial/Torto Wheaton Research.

city-suburban growth rates. In the stronger cities, the growth rates of the downtown markets often were lower because those cities had bigger downtowns to begin with. With smaller suburban markets in 1980, the suburban growth rates were therefore often higher.

A better measure of city/suburban strength is the probability notion used for Boston: What percentage of the overall area's growth occurred downtown as opposed to in the suburbs? This is shown in the fourth column of Exhibit 7–14. There the weak and strong categorization becomes clear: In the weak markets, between 80 and 85 percent of the new office development that emerged in the boom of the last decade occurred in the suburbs. In contrast, in the strong cities, only about 60 percent of the incremental growth occurred in the suburbs and about 40 percent of the growth still occurred in downtowns.

Moving to the next column, we have the 1990 vacancy rates in the downtowns versus the suburbs of each of these metropolitan areas. The reader can see that in the weak markets, vacancy rates downtown are generally higher than in the suburbs, whereas in the stronger markets, the vacancy rates are all lower downtown than in the suburbs. If one looks at average contract rental payments for comparable space (a rent index from CB Commercial), one can see that in the weak markets, the rent premium for downtown space is less than $2 per square foot. Sometimes there is no rent premium (see Denver) in the downtown market. In the strong markets, on the other hand, the rent premium is still in the $2 to $5 range. The numbers at the bottom of the exhibit represent national average values for a composite of 50 metropolitan areas.

Looking across metropolitan areas, it is not difficult to identify those areas with strong central cities and downtown markets. They are those that had a higher share of their area's incremental growth, with lower vacancy rates and higher rents relative to their suburbs. Weaker downtowns are those with the opposite pattern.

Turning to Exhibit 7–15, we can more closely examine the phe-

EXHIBIT 7–15
Office Space by Downtown and Suburban Location, 1968–92 (50 Largest Metropolitan Markets)

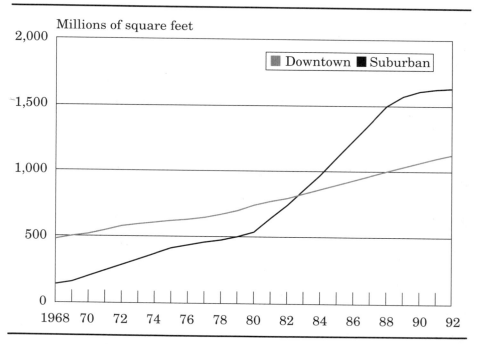

Source: CB Commercial/Torto Wheaton Research.

nomenon of suburban office development over time. This exhibit tracks the stock of office space for the largest 50 metropolitan areas in downtown and suburban markets. Clearly, the downtown stock of office space grew pretty smoothly over those 25 years. The stock of suburban office space, on the other hand, started out in 1968 at only 25 percent of the downtown stock, but in 1992 wound up being one-and-a-half times as great. Until the late 1970s, downtown and suburban stocks were moving roughly in parallel. Over the following decade, a major change occurred: The growth rate of office space tripled in the suburbs, and the stock increased 300 percent over only 10 years. This was not just a supply phenomenon, because current downtown and suburban vacancy rates were quite close. It reflected a major shift of the location of office space demand as well.

Now that we have put the economic development of cities and suburbs into a historical context, we are in a position to examine why these changes occurred. We have already argued that industrial space left the central city because it is land extensive and retail development moved out to be closer to its market. But what of the office sectors that are the major remaining employer in the city? Will they eventually follow the path of retail and industrial space? In thinking about the future, it is important to evaluate the arguments that have been advanced for the historical changes just described. Let's take them one by one.

A common question economists often ask when analyzing growth is: Did the suburbs grow much faster than the cities because the suburbs had the "right" mix of firms and industries? In the late 1970s, did the suburbs simply have a concentration of the types of industries that were destined to grow fast in the 1980s? To answer this question, we turn to Exhibit 7–16, where the bar graphs show the tenant characteristics of downtown and suburban office space. This is a new data set produced from a joint effort by CB Commercial and Dun & Bradstreet. You can see that corporate headquarters constitute more than 30 percent of the occupied space in the suburbs but only about 17 percent in the downtown. Lawyers, on the other hand, have the opposite location pattern: They occupy 15 percent of the space downtown but only 3 percent of the office space in the suburbs. Banking, finance, and insurance are pretty evenly distributed, while brokerage has a much higher share downtown. Business services (such as advertising and copying) are more prevalent in the suburbs, while con-

EXHIBIT 7–16

Office SIC Employment Shares by Downtown and Suburban Location, 1970–90

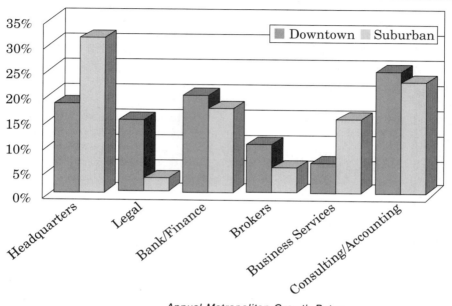

Annual Metropolitan Growth Rates

	Headquarters	Legal	Bank/ Finance	Brokers	Business Services	Consulting/ Accounting
1970–80	3.1%	7.8%	3.7%	3.4%	5.6%	1.8%
1980–90	1.4	6.7	2.4	6.4	4.3	4.7

Sources: CB Commercial/Torto Wheaton Research; Dun & Bradstreet.

sulting, accounting, and professional services (architects and engineers) are quite evenly distributed.

At the bottom of Exhibit 7–16 are the long-term growth rates of
these employment categories over the last two decades for the 50
largest metropolitan areas as a whole. The exercise to be undertaken
is to apply these growth rates to the employment mixes in the downtown and the suburbs and see which markets should have grown
faster based on industry mix. The answer is that the downtowns
should have grown faster. The downtowns actually had the better
industrial or tenant mix. More of their tenants were in faster-growing
industries (SICs). Despite this advantage, downtowns actually grew

far more slowly than the suburbs. It is clear, then, that the mix of tenants had nothing to do with the success or failure of downtowns versus suburbs. There must have been some large shift in the locational preferences of firms, one large enough to overwhelm any industrial mix effect.

The prime candidate for explaining this shift in locational demand is the theory of urban labor markets. One theoretical argument, known as the urban gradient theory, goes as follows. First, cities tend to develop horizontally before they develop vertically. Once housing is constructed, it presents an opportunity cost that delays any eventual replacement for decades and even centuries. Thus, residential development always moves outward (horizontally) first, with vertical redevelopment occurring only after considerable time. With horizontal development, residents' commute into the center for work becomes increasingly burdensome, much more so than if development occurred vertically. As worker commuting increases, firms begin to consider the prospect of a suburban location. At a suburban location, firms in principle can attract workers for a lower wage, because such workers will have little or no commute. This simple theory predicts that urban employment patterns will follow what is called an urban wage gradient. The wages paid for comparable workers in the CBD should be higher than wages in the closer suburbs, which in turn are higher than wages paid by firms even farther out.

Over the years, economic researchers have collected data that do tend to support the wage gradient theory. For example, secretarial salaries in Suffolk County, Long Island, are 25 percent lower than those in Manhattan, while those in Nassau County (closer to Manhattan) are only 15 percent lower. Secretaries who commute an hour and a half on the train to Manhattan get paid for it. Urban employment agencies will reinforce the fact that not only are suburban wages lower, but suburban workers tend to be more stable, productive, and loyal to their employers. The anecdotal evidence is widespread that the suburbs offer some real labor market advantages.

With all these savings, why don't all firms move to the suburbs? The answer is that several factors put the brakes on this process. First, employers using a diverse labor force can't always find a broad range of workers in one suburb. Workers with different skills often are scattered across various suburbs because of the historical pattern by which housing developed. Current community zoning standards only reinforce these patterns. If executives reside on the North Shore while technicians live on the South Shore, the location of easiest access may still be the central business district. The explosive growth of corporate headquarters in southern Connecticut was well suited to the living patterns of executives, but what about the clerical work force that is so important to office headquarters? Firms locating in exclusive Fairfield County now must pay to import their clerical workers.

A second factor is the transportation system. In some metropolitan areas, the transportation system makes it difficult to collect workers between suburbs, because it has been designed for radial use rather than circumferential travel. King of Prussia, Pennsylvania, for example, has become an ideal satellite city now that the Blue Route makes a circumferential link around Philadelphia. For years, development in this area was delayed by the absence of a complete circular route. Rail transit systems, on the other hand, can provide strong radial links that help the central business district and slow the development of the suburbs. Thus, the idiosyncrasies of each city's transportation system strongly influence the ability of firms to decentralize.

A third factor is the hypothesized importance of face-to-face communication. Large, central concentrations of office space may create an information productivity advantage, or "agglomeration," that is not easily duplicated in the suburbs. In the mid-1980s, a Hartford survey of several hundred office firms queried why they had chosen downtown over suburban locations. Companies that located in the suburbs said they wanted to gain access to workers and reduce commuting. Downtown firms said they needed to communicate with clients, suppliers, and other firms.

Now we come to the last question: Why did decentralization occur in the 1980s? What was it about the last decade, as opposed to the 1960s or the 1970s, that led these events to occur when they did? Here again, there are several arguments.

First, as cities grow, there simply may exist threshold effects. Firms won't move to the suburbs until the city gets to such a size that commuting creates a significant burden. However, the facts suggest that decentralization occurred across the board in large, medium-size, and smaller metropolitan areas. If a threshold effect was responsible, decentralization would have occurred only in selected cities.

Second, cities have increasingly harbored an underclass, which cannot provide the appropriate labor force for the financial and service office firms that make up the major inner-city job base. The problem with this argument is that it is not clear that inner-city poverty was more of a problem in the 1980s than it was in the 1960s and 1970s.

The two arguments that seem to stand up best involve transportation and telecommunications. By the end of the 1970s, many metropolitan areas had completed their systems of circumferential highways that had been planned and begun in the late 1960s. Thus, the timing of the decentralization phenomenon is quite consistent with some major changes in the pattern of road networks. In Paris, for example, the suburbanization of employment seems to have moved closely with the suburbanization of the Metro. As Paris's transit system developed circumferential linkages, the large-scale decentralization of employment seems to have followed rapidly.

The telecommunications and information revolution is another event whose timing closely matches that of office decentralization. Computers, mobile phones, faxes, hard-wired networks, and so on have all meant that face-to-face communication is much less important in the operations of many firms. It is far easier today to locate various branches of a company at widely different sites. Sales, marketing, and other forms of business communication likewise have become less dependent on direct interpersonal contact. As business contact costs are reduced, firms will be able to take advantage of the lower wages suburban sites offer.

What about the future? Will growth continue to go to the suburbs? Will center cities continue to decline? The answer depends on four factors, some of which are quite likely to vary significantly from city to city.

First, continued telecommunications improvements represent one factor that is both universal and ongoing. Widespread teleconferencing is around the corner, and seemingly every day some new video phone or other new communications device is announced. All such changes will continue to assist the suburbanization process.

Second, future infrastructure improvements can work in either direction. Proposed rail rapid transit systems will tend to assist center cities. The continued development of suburban circumferential highways, on the other hand, would only hasten the exodus of firms out to the suburbs. Federal transportation policy over the next decade bears close watching.

The final two considerations involve changes in inner-city housing and social policy. Can neighborhoods be revitalized to attract middle-class workers back into the city, where they can provide an office work force within a reasonable commute? Without this work force, central city employers will continue to be forced to draw workers from 10, 20, or 30 miles away. Paying for this commute will continue to place them at a disadvantage relative to firms that have chosen to locate in the suburbs. The absence of an appropriate inner-city work force might partly be addressed through a range of urban social policies. Can inner-city youth develop the white-collar skills needed for employment in the service firms that now locate downtown? The answer will depend on some kind of new educational initiative from federal and state governments.

The specific way these issues play out in the future undoubtedly will differ city by city. Keeping the factors we have mentioned in mind, we might consider Minneapolis, which often shows up as a strong city in our analysis. That is because there are many middle-class residential areas within a city that has been able to retain many upper-middle-income households. It provides just the right infrastructure policy and a progressive educational system. The labor force within the city is well matched to the financial and service sector industries that reside downtown. Downtown Minneapolis will face competition from its edge cities, but wise public policies should enable it to withstand the challenge.

THE OFFICE SECTOR AS AN INVESTMENT

Prior to the mid-1980s, office building investments provided stable cash flow and the potential for significant long-term appreciation. The relatively stable cash flow was created by a growing office employment base (service and FIRE sectors) and significant barriers to the supply of new space (time to construct, the governmental approval process, capital constraints, etc.).

Beginning in the early to mid-1980s, the supply side of this equation was put under severe strain due to a dramatic increase in the flow of capital directed toward office building investment. This flow of capital provided funds for construction and the purchase of property, creating substantial profit for lenders and developers.

From 1982 through 1990, the supply of office space increased approximately 100 million square feet per year nationally, a 120 percent increase from the 46 million square feet completed per year during the prior comparable period. From 1982 to 1990, absorption of office space averaged 64 million square feet per year, an increase of only 33 percent from the prior comparable period. The result was that supply exceeded demand by approximately 320 million square feet during the nine-year period ended 1990. National office vacancy increased from 5.1 to 18.5 percent. This excess supply has been compounded by the national recession, driving down demand for office space to approximately 25 percent of that which occurred during the 1980s.

Office Building Investment Returns

As a result of this disequilibrium condition and restrictions on financing, capital essentially "dried up" from the real estate marketplace beginning in 1990. The lack of capital and the decline in rental rates and income have resulted in a dramatic revaluation of office buildings. Office buildings have lost approximately 25 percent of their value over the past three years, according to the Russell/NCREIF Property Index. The Russell/NCREIF Property Index provides quarterly reports for property-level returns from data collected by members of the National Council of Real Estate Investment Fiduciaries (NCREIF) and reports returns on office and other real estate investments by geographic region. The index reports income, appreciation (both realized and unrealized gains/losses on investments), and total returns, before fees, by quarter. The income return represents net operating income as a percentage of current value, *not cash flow distributed to the investor*. The appreciation return includes gains or losses on investment as a result of appraisals and, in some cases, actual sales. Exhibit 7–17 presents a 10-year summary of office returns from the Russell/NCREIF Property Index.

The office returns in the East, Midwest, South, and West categories of the United States are shown in Exhibit 7–18. The returns by region are published for the most recent 10 years.

Since 1983, "income" returns have averaged 6.83 percent while total returns have averaged 2.20 percent on an arithmetic basis and 1.90 percent on a geometric basis. Income returns increased in 1992, reflecting the significant devaluation of office buildings. This is not an indication of better performance. Operating cash flow (net operating income reduced by tenant improvement costs, leasing commissions, and other capitalized costs) would be significantly less than the in-

EXHIBIT 7–17
Total Index: Office, Annual Performance, Years Ending December 31

Period	Total	Income	Appreciation
1983	12.28%	7.30%	4.72%
1984	12.08	6.87	4.96
1985	8.94	7.34	1.52
1986	4.35	6.91	−2.44
1987	0.93	6.63	−5.43
1988	3.05	6.54	−3.33
1989	3.57	6.29	−2.59
1990	−2.73	6.16	−8.50
1991	−11.68	6.67	−17.47
1992	−8.81	7.59	−15.51
Ten-year mean return:			
Geometric	1.90%	6.83%	−4.69%
Arithmetic	2.20%	6.83%	−4.41%
Standard deviation	7.69%	0.44%	7.25%

Source: Russell/NCREIF Property Index.

come return of 7 percent, reflecting the high cost of attracting and retaining tenants. This is significant because existing cash flow is today's single greatest determinant of value.

The "Repricing" of Office Buildings

Real estate investment, particularly in the office building area, is becoming "institutionalized." Institutional ownership (broadly defined as financial institutions, insurance companies, tax-exempt funds and their advisors, major corporations, etc.) and control of commercial real estate has dramatically increased and will dominate the market throughout the 1990s. The institutional orientation/mindset will clearly dominate real estate decision-making processes and therefore how real estate is "priced."

The institutionalization of the real estate investment marketplace has changed the way investors underwrite real estate investments. Investors are no longer looking at real estate mainly for diversification or as an inflation hedge. As an investment class, real estate must compete on a risk-adjusted return basis with alternative investments.

Before the mid-1980s, returns on real estate were at the higher end of the investment grade yield spectrum, approximately 300 to 400 basis points over longer-term Treasury rates. In the mid-1980s, returns were driven down below yields on longer-term Treasury rates due to the huge infusions of debt and equity capital and unrealistic expectations for appreciation.

Currently, exaggerated yield premiums exist due to the lack of capital directed toward investment real estate and the market risk associated with the disequilibrium condition (i.e., too much supply, too little demand) described above. These exaggerated yield premiums (in some cases 600 to 700 basis points over longer-term Treasury rates) should remain in place over the near term.

Investments are currently priced based on the variability of returns given changes in key operating assumptions (e.g., the predictability of cash flow). Risk premiums (which ultimately determine required returns and therefore pricing) are assessed in this manner. Key operating assumptions include market rent growth, the level of occupancy a building will maintain, and the ultimate reversionary value.

The exaggerated yield premiums described above exist for multitenant properties where the buyer is exposed to "leasing risk." Properties with long-term investment grade tenants in place for, say, 15 years or longer trade at returns significantly below those with leasing risk.

Underwriting in the current environment also considers the potential for tenants to exercise termination options and/or renegotiate existing lease rates to capture fallen market rents. In many cases, properties are priced based on the assumption that termination options will be exercised and above-market rents will not be realized as had been the case in years past. These so-called worst-case scenarios typically determine "purchase" value for most properties today.

Yield premiums should decline in the future as office space supply and demand move toward equilibrium. This decline should occur because of a decrease in the risk premium and the interrelated return of capital to the real estate investment marketplace. Ultimately, real estate returns should stabilize at the high end of the investment grade yield spectrum, approximately 400 to 500 basis points over longer-term Treasury rates. A significant component of this risk premium and the primary reasons premiums should remain high from a historical perspective are (1) the volatility of returns and (2) the lack of liquidity inherent in real estate investment. This lack of liquidity has been clearly demonstrated in the 1990s.

EXHIBIT 7–18

Russell/NCREIF Property Index: Office, Annual Performance, Years Ending December 31

	East				Midwest		
Period	Total	Income	Appreciation	Period	Total	Income	Appreciation
1983	19.65%	7.29%	11.71%	1983	12.14%	7.14%	4.75%
1984	21.73	6.58	11.46	1984	11.50	7.44	3.84
1985	12.59	7.22	5.10	1985	11.84	8.50	3.14
1986	11.37	7.61	3.56	1986	7.67	7.17	0.47
1987	10.74	7.03	3.53	1987	7.39	7.47	-0.07
1988	6.97	7.58	-0.57	1988	2.54	5.85	-3.16
1989	5.14	6.87	-1.65	1989	3.36	6.35	-2.85
1990	-3.56	6.73	-9.80	1990	-5.29	6.20	-11.01
1991	-10.95	7.24	-17.26	1991	-16.12	7.27	-22.16
1992	-7.84	8.10	-15.01	1992	-4.91	8.40	-12.53
Ten-year mean return:				Ten-year mean return:			
Geometric	6.05%	7.22%	-1.12%	Geometric	2.61%	7.17%	-4.33%
Arithmetic	6.58%	7.23%	-0.89%	Arithmetic	3.01%	7.18%	-3.96%
Standard deviation	10.47%	0.43%	9.66%	Standard deviation	8.79%	0.83%	8.23%

South

Period	Total	Income	Appreciation
1983	7.72%	6.82%	0.85%
1984	5.93	6.44	−0.49
1985	4.17	6.66	−2.37
1986	−3.29	5.72	−8.64
1987	−16.17	5.45	−20.76
1988	−3.02	5.63	−8.30
1989	−2.85	5.57	−8.09
1990	−4.40	6.26	−10.18
1991	−14.18	7.17	−20.24
1992	−9.30	8.84	−16.99
Ten-year mean return:			
Geometric	−3.85%	6.45%	−9.82%
Arithmetic	−3.54%	6.46%	−9.52%
Standard deviation	7.64%	0.97%	7.36%

West

Period	Total	Income	Appreciation
1983	9.78%	7.86%	1.82%
1984	9.21	7.20	1.91
1985	7.55	7.31	0.23
1986	2.06	6.92	−4.62
1987	1.16	6.64	−5.22
1988	2.87	6.40	−3.36
1989	4.91	6.10	−1.13
1990	−0.47	5.69	−5.91
1991	−9.43	5.96	−14.72
1992	−10.88	6.51	−16.58
Ten-year mean return:			
Geometric	1.44%	6.66%	−4.96%
Arithmetic	1.68%	6.66%	−4.76%
Standard deviation	6.74%	0.64%	6.07%

Source: Russell/NCREIF Property Index.

Office Building Economics

The evaluation of an office building investment relies on reasonable assumptions relating to the factors that dictate returns. This section deals with several of these factors, which are vital to accurate evaluation:

- Physical characteristics: building age, location, functionality, and efficiency.
- Projecting revenues.
- Projecting operating and nonoperating expenses and capital costs.

Physical Characteristics

Investment evaluation starts with a broad view and works down to the detail. One flaw in the past was that evaluation of office building investments was limited to simple, static cash flow models with little or no consideration given to the physical improvements and how the building would perform physically and functionally in the long run. Many investors have learned that solid leases do not guarantee long-term success in office building investments; this may occur only after significant capital has been invested to improve or recondition the physical asset. An assessment of what an office building can achieve in the future given its physical constraints, location, age, and efficiency is critical.

The concept of competitive position is a good starting point for the physical evaluation of an office building investment. The question to be asked is: What type of tenant is this office building capable of attracting given its location, functionality, and so on? A well-located but old and inefficient office building will most likely not compete for the same tenants in current or future real estate markets. As newer, more efficient buildings are built, the existing buildings inevitably slide downward on the scale. Any long-term evaluation that does not reflect this reality, especially in a market where significant new efficient space has been or will be added in the future, will cause the investment to underperform its expectations.

Today's tenants are more sensitive and better educated. Tenant representation in the brokerage community has given rise to detailed, side-by-side evaluation of tenant alternatives, including physical issues in office buildings. And in many cases, no amount of financial incentive can overcome these physical issues. One fallacy is that a "facelift" can be used to bring a building back to a competitive position. This type of quick fix may work in the short run to attract tenants, but functional and mechanical obsolescence usually cannot be overcome with cosmetic upgrades.

In general, older office buildings, even if well located and in good condition, suffer greatly in soft markets where new projects are able to attract tenants who can "buy up" to a high quality level. For older buildings to keep occupancy high, a greater occupancy cost differential must be demonstrated to tenants so that they will not be lured to the newer, more efficient projects.

Specific factors to review in evaluation of the physical attributes of an office building are:

- Location.
- Building size, floor sizes, space efficiency.
- HVAC capacity and efficiency.
- Elevator capacity, speed, and efficiency.
- Building structural components, age, life span.
- Hazardous materials issues (asbestos, PCBs, etc.).
- ADA requirements.

Although this list is not meant to be exhaustive, it hopefully suggests a framework for viewing these issues as they related to office building analysis.

Projecting Revenues

All analysis methods, whether static or dynamic (e.g., discounted cash flow, or DCF), rely on accurate and realistic assessments of future revenues. The *static* or *stabilized* approach relies on capitalizing a projected net operating income. This approach tends to deal with these issues with a broad brush and, by its nature, does not take into account all of the subtle yet critical factors necessary in effective office building evaluation. The *dynamic* (DCF) analysis provides the ability to specifically model each tenant or space using a variety of assumptive factors to not only predict short- and long-term revenues but also strategically position a property for disposition. Some of the revenue/tenant assumptions that will be discussed are as follows:

- Demand for office space.
- Occupancy trends.
- Current and future market rental rates.
- Existing tenant renewal probabilities.
- Tenant expense reimbursement considerations and gross-ups.
- Additional tenant rights and options/encumbrances.

As described in prior sections, two important factors in determining demand for office space are the trends in office building employment and the change in tenant mentality concerning use of office space. With tenants attempting to become more efficient with their office space, it is especially necessary to make certain that an accurate net absorption figure is utilized in calculating space estimates for office tenants.

Although the office building may be able to capture a significant portion of the market's net absorption, the remaining vacant space created by tenants moving from one building to another and the resulting desperation on the part of those landlords to lease that space may drive future expectations for rents downward. Office sector supply was discussed earlier in this chapter.

Another factor influencing office building evaluation is office occupancy trends. Generally, office demand has been growing in suburban areas in relation to urban areas. In the past, most retail activities, banking, and legal services were located in the urban cores of the major cities throughout the United States. In the last 20 to 30 years, with major retailing centers being constructed in the suburban bedroom communities and the financial service providers locating branch offices in the suburbs, it has become increasingly difficult to attract high-quality workers to the urban core to fill the office requirements. Therefore, in the last 20 years a dynamic shift in the direction tenants are going has occurred, from urban to suburban. Office space users took a careful look at the true need to be in the urban core, the costs of doing business in that area, and the availability of workers. A substantial number decided that the quality of their business and workers' environments was best served in suburban locations. Therefore, it is critical in the evaluation of an office building to consider its location not only within its submarket but also in terms of urban versus suburban. This is not to say that urban-located office buildings do not still have a consistent draw of tenants; rather, it suggests that future demand for office space will most likely be more highly skewed to the suburbs.

For buildings of like size and quality (whether urban or suburban), it is typically not difficult to evaluate the rent level currently achievable. The big question arises as to the future trend in market rental rates used in long-term evaluation of the office building as an investment. An assumption of continually rising rental rates, given the recent historically significant declines in rental rates, would most likely be an erroneous one. Combinations of factors were discussed earlier in this chapter, including supply of product, demand from tenants, and age, location, and size of buildings. All play a part in creating assumptions for future rental rate growth. Some large, national markets may contain as much as a 10-year supply of office space at predicted tenant demand levels. Therefore, conservative, well-researched, and well-documented database analysis must be conducted to justify the rental rate growth assumptions used in an office building evaluation.

Whether conducting a static or a dynamic analysis, existing tenant renewal probabilities play a major part. In a static approach, capitalization rates adjusting current market rents for certain tenants, deductions for tenant improvements, downtime, free rent, and so on are the tools used to adjust the value. The dynamic approach uses the tenant renewal probability concept to adjust future cash flows for the probability of tenant renewal and the expenses associated with that renewal or replacement of that tenant. Every asset manager must try to ascertain a tenant's intentions if the lease expires within the next few years. At a minimum, the asset manager must attempt to determine if the tenant's business is in a growth cycle or in a decline/consolidation mode (as well as the past expansion, contraction, and renewal tendencies of this tenant). In general, as tenants are renewing in a market where their rental rates will be significantly higher than before, there will be substantial competition from other buildings in the marketplace. Therefore, tenant renewal probability may be very low. However, in a situation where a tenant's lease is expiring with a rental rate below current market conditions, it follows that the current landlord has the upper hand in negotiating a renewal with this tenant. The current landlord can avoid downtime and provide the tenant with economic advantages over the market (because of the lack of downtime and risk and potentially because of the savings in tenant improvement dollars).

Tenant expense reimbursements are an additional factor in evaluating revenues. In the past, many owners used expense stops or base year calculations to extract additional revenues because of tenants' lack of understanding regarding expense reimbursements. However, tenants are now more knowledgeable about this concept. Generally, office buildings still rely on a gross lease and usually some base or stop over which the tenant pays the increases. Typically this allows a landlord to be repaid for increased expenses. However, in buildings that suffer from low occupancy and/or slow lease-up, the landlord bears all of the expenses for the vacant space until the property reaches a higher occupancy level.

Recently net leases have regained favor in the office building community. This concept tends to restore some sanity to the rent-versus-expense relationship. The net lease is also favorable to the landlord, as it does not penalize the landlord for dramatic shifts in occupancy. Whether gross or net leases are used, tenants will typically require some combination of caps, stops, limits, or projections within the operating expense pool. The real estate tax protection concept started in California, and it is typically a substantial risk for the owner, especially a prospective seller who has owned a building for a significant period of time. The new buyer will most likely discount the purchase price due to limits imposed by tenants on tax reimbursements because of reassessment of the building's value at sale. Careful attention must be paid to any of these concessions, as they may not greatly affect the current ownership revenue but could severely affect the ultimate purchase price.

Finally, larger tenants in softer markets are consistently asking for additional rights and options, including early releases, extensions, expansions, and contractions. These factors, if not negotiated strongly by the landlord in light of the overall leasing strategy of the building, can create a situation where vacant space becomes available but cannot be leased for unreasonable periods of time (e.g., 5 or 10 years) because it is encumbered by expansion options from major tenants. This situation can create instances where large blocks of space in an office building are basically "off the market" for significant periods of time until the tenant with the right to expand either exercises that right or declines it. If the tenant exercises that right, at least some revenue will be attributed to this space at a fixed point in time. However, if, after waiting several years for a tenant's decision, the tenant declines to expand into that space, many years and dollars will have been lost, and market conditions may have changed significantly during that period.

Projecting Expenses

Operating expenses for an office building can have a dramatic effect on the building's return characteristics. Any increases in building operating expenses without a corresponding increase in rents results in a net loss of revenue. For example, if two office buildings are competing for tenants in a market where the rental rate is well established, the building with the higher expenses will neither achieve as great a return nor be as competitive in the tenant market. As discussed previously, operating expenses in office buildings are frequently attributable to the age, construction, and efficiencies of a building and its mechanical systems, but they can also be a reflection of management and ownership inefficiencies or prolonged deferred maintenance.

In understanding and evaluating an office building as an investment it is critical to understand the characteristics not only in total but within the subcategories as well. Following are some of the subcategories of expenses that are critical to office building valuations:

- HVAC.
- Property taxes.
- Insurance.

For example, the HVAC systems in an office building are typically the second largest consumer of utility expenses (lighting typically being the largest), and by their very design and nature can create significant inefficiencies in delivery of the conditioned air to the property. Older, outdated equipment (or equipment that has been maintained less than adequately) will not be able to supply tenants with the comfort they require. Many of the systems in older buildings were not designed to accommodate the heavy use of personal computers, data processing equipment, and copier equipment in today's offices. Not only are these systems inefficient in their use of electricity, but the general control systems for delivery of the conditioned air may leave wide variances in temperatures in different parts of the building, depending on exterior temperature and sun exposure.

Another issue that must be taken into account and that will substantially affect office building values is the eventual compliance with the Clean Air Act as enacted by the United States Environmental Protection Agency (EPA). This requires the discontinuance of production of CFC refrigerants used in air conditioning and refrigeration equipment because of their contribution to important environmental issues, notably the depletion of the ozone layer. The EPA expects many owners of air conditioning equipment to face higher prices and even refrigerant shortages before the production phaseout is completed on January 1, 1996, unless they prepare now. Building owners and managers that fail to take action in advance of the phaseout may have difficulty maintaining an adequate supply of recyclable CFCs to service old units and are likely to bear significantly higher prices or substantial delays in retrofitting or purchasing new equipment that uses CFC alternatives. It will be critical for future office building evaluation to not only map out a strategy for compliance with the EPA regulations but also to determine whether compliance costs associated with these regulations can be passed back to tenants through the operating expense pool or must be borne by the owner as a capital expenditure.

Another significant operating expense for an office building is real estate taxes. Taxes can be assessed by all levels of state, county, and city governments on the assessed value of the real estate (in addition to any personal property in the building in some jurisdictions). Most agencies rely on an assessed valuation of the building that equates in some fashion to a determination of market value as determined by their assessment staff. Many jurisdictions use the sales price of an investment as the market value for assessment purposes for the new ownership entity. This system puts properties that have recently been sold at a disadvantage, because their tax burden will probably be significantly higher than that of a competing property that has not changed hands in the recent past (assuming assessed values for properties not recently sold lag their fair market values). Most jurisdictions, however, also utilize an overriding concept of equalized values, which, if argued appropriately by a tax consulting firm, can typically lower the assessed values to a more equitable level in the marketplace. It is absolutely critical that effective real estate tax consultation services be retained at all times to ensure that the real estate tax assessments and corresponding tax burdens are equitable among competing projects in the marketplace.

Owners of CBD office buildings should also consider the potential tax impact of the increasing flight of jobs, retail sales, and homeowners to suburban locales. The urban taxpayers are left with the debt and infrastructure costs that remain; the tax burden remains long after the jobs and people are gone. This is especially true for commercial properties, which typically carry a disproportionate share of the real estate tax burden.

Management/Accounting and Reporting Issues

Effective management of an office investment rests on a foundation of reliable financial analysis and reporting. The asset manager's accounting and reporting function provides the linkage among the property, the portfolio, and the investor. The asset manager must provide accurate and timely results to investors, act as a critical resource to the portfolio management function by providing meaningful financial review and analysis, and safeguard the assets under management.

Accurate and timely reporting is critical to successful portfolio management. Given the constant changing of the real estate investment industry and its focuses, significant flexibility must be built into the system to meet investors' changing and varied needs. As the goals of the investment account change, so do the types of analysis and reporting.

Management reports used in the analysis of portfolio strategy start with the property manager. An on- or off-site property management team captures the day-to-day workings of each property. The property manager typically transfers available cash flow to the portfolio manager or investor representative on a daily basis and provides monthly reporting on tenant billings, receipts, delinquencies, disbursements, and property operational status. An operational status update addresses property issues such as collectibility of outstanding billings, tenant financial strength, rent roll, property maintenance, progress on tenant and building improvements, and analyses of variances from the financial plan.

It is the responsibility of the portfolio management group to ensure the accuracy of the property managers' reports. The detailed property information must be subjected monthly to stringent auditing procedures. These procedures generally include detailed reviews of property operating statements, tenant billings, leasing status, compliance of expenditures with the guidelines published in a predetermined financial and operational plan, a review of bank reconciliations, and annual review of tenant expense escalations. A detailed analytical review of the property operating statements is performed monthly to detect timing differences and bring potential operating problems to light.

Cash management policies must be tailored to meet the needs and requirements of the investor. The following objectives, however, can be generally applied to all investor funds: to maintain an efficient and controlled flow of receipts and disbursements to and from property bank accounts; to maintain adequate minimum property cash operating reserves; and, when requested by the investor, to prudently invest cash operating reserves to maximize return.

The portfolio manager must assimilate property-level information into portfolio-level reports. The information must be presented in such a format as to facilitate the understanding of property and portfolio performance not only currently but also historically and prospectively. Only then can effective portfolio strategies be formulated, implemented, and evaluated.

Following is a brief summary of a few of the more typical investor reports:

- Financial statements, prepared at both the property and the portfolio level.
- Performance returns, prepared at both a property and a portfolio level (returns are shown before and after fees and are compared to various benchmarks such as the Russell/NCREIF Property Index).
- Summary of historical and projected net income, appreciation, and capital costs.
- Projected cash performance and distributions.
- Summary of actual cash activity.
- Rent roll.
- Strategic reports, including operational, leasing, and disposition strategies.
- Summary of appraisal results.

There are three divergent methods of accounting for real estate investments: traditional historical-cost accounting, current-value accounting, and cash-basis accounting.

The accounting for an office investment on a traditional historical-cost basis is well documented in authoritative literature. Historical-cost accounting guidance is provided through officially established accounting principles, Financial Accounting Standards Board (FASB) statements, FASB interpretations, American Institute of Certified Public Accountants (AICPA) Accounting Principles Board opinions, and AICPA Accounting Research Bulletins, among others. Certain gray areas exist with respect to accounting for complex real estate investment structures, such as accounting for guarantees and joint ventures (with preferred returns), but for the most part, guidance on accounting treatment is available. Comparing performance on real estate investments using historical-cost accounting is not particularly meaningful, however, since the current values of real estate investments dramatically affect their overall yield.

The second method of accounting, current-value accounting, presents more challenges. Many institutional owners are required to account for their investments on a current-value basis as opposed to a historical-cost basis. Current-value reporting is considered GAAP (generally accepted accounting principles) for entities that are required to carry their investments at value. Given the relatively recent status of substantial institutional ownership of office buildings (commencing generally in the 1970s, with the heaviest acquisition activity in the latter half of the 1980s), current-value accounting is a relatively new concept for real estate and lacks the authoritative accounting literature on other, more established investments. There exists, however, some general industry consensus on many major reporting issues.

Several industry groups, such as NCREIF, survey their members frequently on important accounting policies and attempt to show dominant industry positions. Areas that such industry groups have addressed include accounting for leasing costs, lease termination fees, loan fees, free rent, joint ventures, guaranteed and/or preferred returns, the discounting of loans to prevailing rates, and the calculation of performance returns.

Current-value financial statements necessitate the performance of periodic property appraisals. Investments in real estate are typically valued annually. The investments are carried at market value.

Appraisal methodologies or policies of portfolio managers also affect performance returns through the appreciation component of return. Real estate appraisals are inherently subjective and thus affect comparability of investments. An investor needs to understand the appraisal assignment and method of valuation (see Chapter 16) to evaluate the appraisal results.

While the primary method of accounting remains accrual-basis accounting, the third method, cash-basis accounting, has become paramount. Cash flow from an office investment may vary widely from period to period, depending on the rental market, the vacancy rate, lease rollovers, and other factors. Relative to other real estate investments, the office sector requires heavy leasing costs—free rent, leasing commissions, and tenant improvements. Currently, no indices of cash-basis real estate performance have been published, making cash-basis comparisons among investments difficult, if not impossible. The current investor focus on cash yields as opposed to the standard accrual-based returns may reorient the efforts of real estate consulting firms to publishing such information. Given the office sector's heavy leasing costs, it is not surprising that attention has turned to cash-on-cash returns.

Different methods of accounting or calculating peformance returns can dramatically affect the reported results. An investor needs to understand the more important accounting policies to effectively evaluate performance results. As the current-value reporting industry matures, effective comparability among investments will increase.

CHAPTER 8

THE RETAIL SECTOR

Richard Kateley
Heitman Financial Ltd.

Retail real estate is a population-driven land use. That is, it responds primarily to demographic patterns—numbers of people, their ages, family compositions, ethnic identities, and income levels. Retail properties also closely reflect changing lifestyles and broad consumer behavior trends that evolve out of demographic shifts.[1] As a result, retail properties are among the most dynamic and diverse property types.

The first section of this chapter presents a typology of retail investment products, ranging from the typical neighborhood center to the largest regional malls, and describes their function and position in the retail spectrum. The second section presents an analysis of the key determinants of retail investment performance: trade area, competitive alignment, tenant/merchandise mix, and leasing and management. The third section identifies emerging issues in retail investment. The last section describes the major data sources used in the analysis and evaluation of retail properties.

RETAIL INVESTMENT PRODUCTS

A shopping center, as defined by the Urban Land Institute (ULI), is "a group of commercial establishments planned, developed, owned and managed as a unit related in location, size and type of shops to the trade area the unit serves; it provides on-site parking in definite relationship to the types and sizes of stores."[2] There were 39,000

---

[1] The unit of consumption for retail properties (as with residential) is the individual or the household. The unit of demand for office and industrial real estate is a business, a firm, or a corporation.

[2] ULI, *Shopping Center Development Handbook* (1992), p. iv.

EXHIBIT 8–1
Shopping Center Floor Space, 1992

Center Size (Thousands of Square Feet)	Number of Centers	Total GLA (Thousands of Square Feet)	Percentage of Total GLA
Under 100	24,578	1,190,196	25%
100–200	9,467	1,288,856	28
200–400	3,086	806,881	17
400–800	1,170	652,702	14
800–1,000	294	264,448	6
Over 1,000	371	475,446	10
Total	38,966	4,678,529	10

Sources: *Shopping Center World*, March 1993; Merrill Lynch.

shopping centers in operation in the United States in 1992. The vast majority (see Exhibit 8–1) are small, less than 100,000 square feet of GLA.[3] In total, retail centers account for almost 70 percent of the nation's nonautomotive retail sales and employ one out of every nine nonfarm workers. In a typical month, 95 percent of the population age 18 and over shops at shopping centers.[4]

Not only are shopping centers ubiquitous; they have been expanding at a rapid rate, both in absolute numbers and in relation to the population they serve (see Exhibit 8–2). Shopping center floor space per capita increased 26 percent in the 1970s and another 34 percent in the 1980s. The largest increases were in smaller centers (under 400,000 square feet), which are easier to finance and build than the larger projects.

The phenomenal growth in shopping centers reflects more than a parallel growth in the number of consumers. It was driven as well by the expansion in retail stores as chains have sought to retain and expand their market share by creating new concepts.

Types of Centers

The proliferation of shopping centers has changed the face of retailing. Up until the mid-1950s shopping venues consisted of downtown and the neighborhood convenience retail strip. The first enclosed mall

---

[3] GLA is gross leasable area, the space measure most often used in retail analysis.

[4] ICSC, *The Scope of the Shopping Center Industry in the United States* (1977), p. 13.

EXHIBIT 8–2
Growth in Shopping Center Floor Space, 1970–90

Center Size (Thousands of Square Feet)	GLA per Capita (Square Feet)			Percentage Change	
	1990	1980	1970	1980–90	1970–80
Under 100	4.52	2.75	1.46	64	89
100–200	4.81	3.47	2.85	39	22
200–400	2.95	2.15	1.80	37	20
400–800	2.49	2.11	1.81	18	17
800–1,000	1.04	0.99	0.98	5	1
Over 1,000	1.84	1.67	1.55	10	8
Total	17.65	13.14	10.45	34%	26%

Sources: *NRB Shopping Center Census*, 1991; U.S. Bureau of the Census; F. W. Dodge; Merrill Lynch.

(Southdale in Minneapolis) opened in 1956. As recently as 1963, there were only 7,500 shopping centers, representing 20 percent of the current total.

As of the mid-1990s, shopping centers can be divided into five investment categories according to their size, their tenants, and the predominant type of merchandise they provide.[5] Exhibits 8–3 and 8–4 indicate the major distinguishing features of the different types of centers.

Neighborhood strip centers comprise the majority of shopping centers. The neighborhood center provides for the sale of daily living needs or convenience goods, such as food, drugs, hardware, and personal services. The anchors are supermarkets and drugstores or combination grocery and drug formats. The locational orientation of neighborhood centers is to major local arterials. These centers range in size from 50,000 to 100,000 square feet. Typically, the trade area of a neighborhood facility is limited to two to three miles, no more than 10 minutes' drive time. The major risk in neighborhood centers is the leasing of the nonanchor shop space to local noncredit tenants that may not be able to pay required rents and may turn over frequently.

---

[5] This typology of shopping centers is based on the categories used by the Urban Land Institute (ULI) and the International Council of Shopping Centers (ICSC), the two dominant professional organizations conducting research on retail real estate.

EXHIBIT 8–3
Typology of Retail Centers

Center Type	Dominant Tenancy/ Merchandising	Typical Stores
Neighborhood	Grocery and drugstore; convenience stores (dry cleaning, card shop, shoe repair) Not enclosed	Safeway, Jewel-Osco, Alpha Beta
Community	Junior department, discount, off-price stores, restaurants, banks, apparel, and personal service stores Not enclosed	Wal-Mart, Marshalls, Price/Costco
Power center	Category killer retailers (drugs, sporting goods, consumer electronics, toys, home improvement)	Toys "R" Us, Circuit City, Sports Authority
Outlet center	Unanchored group of stores offering deeply discounted goods sold directly by manufacturer; sometimes includes off-price or close-out stores	Polo, Liz Claiborne, Dansk
Regional/super-regional	Anchored by department stores; 40–50% of space is fashion-oriented mall shops, mostly national chains Enclosed	Macy's, Nordstrom, Dayton-Hudson

Community centers, which range in size from 100,000 to 400,000 square feet, in addition to convenience goods, feature stores carrying apparel and accessories, furniture and home furnishings, and miscellaneous shoppers' goods. Shoppers' goods include toys, hobbies, sporting goods, garden and lawn supplies, books, candy, and the like. Newer community centers are anchored by large discount stores, off-price stores, warehouse clubs, and "super" grocery or drug facilities. The locational orientation of community centers is to major arterials serving the market, and many are located in proximity to a regional mall. The risk of community centers lies in the strength of the anchors (they must be dominant in their merchandise line throughout the trade area in order to draw sufficient traffic) and in the space allotted

EXHIBIT 8–4
Characteristics of Retail Centers

Center Type	Center Size (Square Feet)	Site Size (Acres)	Trade Area Minimum (Population)	Maximum Drive Time (Minutes)
Neighborhood	Over 100,000	3–10	10,000	10
Community	100,000–400,000	10–30	50,000–150,000	20
Power	250,000–500,000	50 +	200,000	40
Outlet	100,000–250,000	40 +	200,000	90
Regional/super-regional	400,000–1,000,000 +	50 +	200,000	60

Source: Heitman Investment Research.

to small tenants and the mix of those tenants. Community centers require "cross-shopping"—that is, the shopper who visits more than one store on a trip to the center—so the quality and mix of stores are critical.

Power centers are a new retail distribution channel. These centers first appeared in the mid-1980s and now number about 2,000. They range in size between 200,000 and 500,000 square feet; 80 percent or more of the space is taken by large "category killer" stores. These "big box" retailers sell a wide array of merchandise within a single product line, such as toys, home electronics, sporting goods, and home improvement items. These stores sell merchandise at a discount and are heavily promoted. They are destination stores that draw shoppers from a wide trade area, usually the same dimensions as that of a regional mall. Small shops in power centers do not perform well, largely because there is little cross-shopping. The risk in power centers is the staying power of the category killer stores. While many qualify as credit tenants, others do not, and the competition among these stores is intense.

Outlet centers are located 20 to 50 miles away from major metropolitan areas or near tourist destinations. They bring together shops operated directly by manufacturers that sell their merchandise at deep discounts, usually 25 to 70 percent off full retail. These centers number only about 300 (as of mid-1992) and range in size between 100,000 and 250,000 square feet. Outlet malls draw from large trade areas and offer a recreational experience as well as discounts on major name brand goods. Unlike power centers, which sell commodity products, outlet centers focus on fashion-oriented goods. The outlet shopper profile is similar in demographic and income characteristics to the regional mall shopper. The primary risk in outlet centers is the continued willingness of consumers to drive long distances for discounts that may be matched by more convenient retail formats.

Regional and super-regional malls are enclosed (all of the other types of centers are open) and are the venue of fashion-oriented department stores. The department store anchors occupy 50 to 60 percent of mall GLA. The remaining mall shop space is composed of apparel, accessory, jewelry, shoe, and other specialty stores. Typically, strong national concept stores (The Limited, The Gap, Edison Brothers, etc.) occupy 80 percent or more of the small-shop space and function as a draw to the center. Regional malls range in size from 400,000 to over 2 million square feet and serve a minimum trade area of 200,000 people. They offer food, movies, and entertainment as well as fashion shopping. There are about 1,800 malls, for the most part located in middle- and upper-middle-income suburban locations. Dominant regional malls, if anchored by locally strong department stores, offer a complement of retail stores not duplicated in other retail formats.

In addition to size, tenancy, and trade area, retail properties are also distinguished by their position on the spectrum of shopper requirements. Exhibit 8–5 arrays the shopping centers along the five most important dimensions of shopping: price, convenience, selection, service, and recreation/entertainment. Each center has a position on these dimensions that sets it apart from the others. Community centers offer convenience and selection, for example, while power centers

EXHIBIT 8–5
Retail Center Attraction

Primary Shopper Attraction	Center Type				
	Neighborhood	Community	Power	Regional	Outlet
Price		✓	✓		✓
Convenience	✓		✓		
Selection			✓	✓	
Service				✓	
Recreation/ entertainment				✓	✓

stress price. However, as will be seen shortly, as the number of shopping centers has increased, there is more and more overlap among categories and therefore increasing competition among centers.

Performance Characteristics

Each type of retail center serves a different retail niche and a different segment of the consumer market. As national retail chains—department stores, discount stores, warehouse clubs, and specialty or concept stores—strive to successfully identify and interpret demographic trends and consumer behavior, the performance of the traditional retail venues has been affected.

Retail performance data are collected and disseminated by a variety of organizations (see Appendix 8A for a guide to data sources). Sales (total and same-store) and other information for individual chains (i.e., Macy's, Wal-Mart, The Limited) are reported for publicly held companies. Statistics are available from government sources on retail sales for merchandise categories (i.e., apparel, furniture, food, and drugs) or store types (i.e. auto dealers, eating and drinking establishments, mass merchandisers). However, few consistent and reliable sources of performance-related data exist at the "real estate" level, that is, at the level of the different types of shopping centers identified earlier. Therefore, investors in retail properties must be especially careful in judging center performance.

Traditional measures of performance in the retail sector include total sales, sales per square foot, achieved rental levels, net operating income, and vacancy. Investment returns, current income, and capital appreciation for the different categories for retail centers remain sketchy but will improve as more experience is gained. The growth of the REIT market, which is heavily invested in retail properties, will contribute to the development of retail investment benchmarks.

Sales productivity data are shown in Exhibits 8–6 and 8–7. The data in Exhibit 8–6 show the relationship between total sales per square foot in all centers and GLA per capita. On an inflation-adjusted basis, productivity has actually declined for retail properties in general. Exhibit 8–7 lists the levels of productivity achieved by centers of varying size in 1992. The pattern in these data is revealing: Neighborhood centers (less than 100,000 square feet) and regional malls (400,000 square feet and over) outperformed the intermediate-size centers.

EXHIBIT 8–6
Shopping Center Productivity, 1987–92

	1987	1988	1989	1990	1991	1992	Compound Annual Growth Rate, 1987–92
GLA square feet per capita	15.3	16.1	17.0	17.6	18.1	18.8	4.2%
Inflation-adjusted sales per square foot	$162	$159	$156	$151	$144	$142	−2.6%

Sources: International Council of Shopping Centers; Management Horizons, Division of Price Waterhouse.

EXHIBIT 8–7
Center Sales Productivity, 1992

Center Size (Thousands of Square Feet)	Average Sales per Square Foot
Under 100	$182
100–200	147
200–400	141
400–800	148
800–1,000	180
Over 1,000	171
Total	$160

Sources: *Shopping Center World*, March 1993; Merrill Lynch.

Net operating income (NOI) figures for four categories of shopping centers that are tracked by ULI are consistent with the sales productivity numbers: The largest and the smallest centers are better performers than the community and/or power centers. However, care needs to be taken in interpreting these data, as centers are categorized by size rather than by function. Outlet centers, for example, are probably included in the community center category by virtue of their size even though their retail function is entirely different, as is their financial profile.

Vacancy data are an important indicator of overall market conditions and individual center performance. Unfortunately, vacancy data are rarely available for the retail sector. Unlike for the office, industrial, apartment, and hotel markets, no firms or other organizations consistently report on retail occupancy levels and trends. Surveys by ICSC, based on self-reports from member retail center owners, are available but are too narrow in focus to serve as benchmarks for investors. Anecdotal evidence suggests that outlet centers and neighborhood centers, along with regional malls, have the lowest levels of vacancy. But in the absence of good information, investors must be wary of generalizations about this important dimension of retail center performance.

Measures of the investment performance of retail properties have heretofore been available from the Russell/NCREIF data set only in highly aggregated form.[6] Preliminary investigation of the components of the retail segment of the Russell/NCREIF database breaks the retail category into four subsets as shown in Exhibit 8–8.[7] Returns are shown for holding periods ranging from 1 year to 11 years. The return profile matches the sales productivity and NOI data: The regional malls and the neighborhood centers posted the best returns over the longer time horizons.

The same database, composed of tax-exempt pension fund investments, affords a look at the movement of the annual returns of the four major retail categories: neighborhood, community, regional, and super-regional. The correlations (Exhibit 8–9) are uniformly high (ranging between .814 to .928), indicating that at the portfolio level, there is little difference among the retail subcategories in terms of diversification benefit. Studies of the volatility of the subcomponents of the retail sector may yield additional insight into the portfolio implications of diversification across different retail shopping centers.

Distinctions among retail shopping centers are blurring. This is especially true for the intermediate-size centers, those larger than the traditional neighborhood strips and smaller than the regional mall with its department store anchors. The addition of power centers, outlet centers, and a number of other specialized properties (festival malls, unanchored specialty centers, "value" malls, etc.) may meet emerging consumer needs, but the sheer growth in the amount of space relative to slow population growth raises serious questions. The next section outlines the key investment parameters of retail shopping centers.

RETAIL INVESTMENT PARAMETERS

As seen in the previous section, shopping centers have a variety of sizes, shapes, and, most important, functions in their markets. The performance of a center, from an equity investment perspective, depends largely on its dominance in the marketplace vis-à-vis existing

---

[6] The Russell/NCREIF Property Index (RNPI) is the standard benchmark for real estate performance. The RNPI reports on "retail" as one category including all types of centers.

[7] Young and Kateley (1993) use an expanded database that includes the standard RNPI properties and leveraged real estate not included in the formal index.

EXHIBIT 8–8
Returns by Retail Subcategory*

	Neighbor-hood	Community	Regional	Super-Regional	Other†
11 years	8.55%	7.36%	8.34%	N/A	8.52%
10	8.35	7.47	8.72	11.81	8.50
9	7.89	7.01	8.08	11.54	8.16
8	7.39	6.30	6.96	10.65	7.51
7	6.68	5.21	6.43	9.43	7.05
6	5.79	4.27	5.66	8.58	5.86
5	4.86	3.77	4.56	7.23	4.29
4	3.52	2.32	2.18	4.69	2.14
3	2.10	1.34	−0.84	1.44	−1.27
2	0.80	−0.50	−3.76	−1.35	−3.47
1	2.26	0.92	−3.08	−3.19	−1.34

* Total return = income and capital appreciation for year-end fourth quarter, 1992 Russell/NCREIF.
† Other = power, outlet, festival malls.

and proposed competition and the expenditure potential of the trade area residents for the specific types of goods and services the center offers. Therefore, in the context of its functional trade area, shopping centers should be viewed as a merchandising venture as well as a real estate investment. Sales performance, lease rates and terms, and net operating income all depend on the center's merchandising dominance in its marketplace.

Each center type has slightly different sales, lease, and operating characteristics that make it more or less attractive to an investor. Neighborhood centers, for example, with locally strong drug and supermarket anchors on long leases, represent a stable return, but with little upside. Similarly, power centers offer long (usually 20-year)

EXHIBIT 8–9
Correlation among Returns, 1982:4–1992:4

	Neighborhood	Community	Regional	Super-Regional
Neighborhood	1.000			
Community	0.931	1.000		
Regional	0.873	0.867	1.000	
Super-regional	0.912	0.866	0.906	1.000

Source: Young and Kateley (1993), p. 12.

leases with credit tenants, but with little or no promise of residual value at the time of anchor lease expirations. Both these types of centers may be better suited to mortgage investment (low risk, bond-like yield) than equity investment, where rental income growth and capital appreciation are part of the investment calculus. Regional mall investors, on the other hand, participate in the sales growth of the mall shops and the anchor department stores and, in the long term, real estate value that is created by the dominance a strong mall has in a marketplace.

The following sections describe the four key merchandising dimensions against which shopping center investments can be arrayed and assessed. These are (1) the extent of the trade area and the expenditure potential of its residents; (2) the competitive alignment of other centers offering similar merchandise; (3) the tenancy and merchandise mix, as well as the locational orientation to potential shoppers, of the center; and (4) the management and operation of the center as a merchandising venture. Restated, these four dimensions relate to demand, supply, product differentiation, and management. The critical difference between a retail investment and office, industrial, or residential assets is that the retail investor has two target markets to attract and retain: retailers *and* shoppers.

Demand: The Trade Area

The trade area for shopping center represents the total potential sales available to the center. In practice, it is the geographic area from which a major portion of the retail center's sales is drawn. The actual extent of the trade area depends on the function of the center (i.e., the type of merchandise), accessibility and driving time, and intercepting competition (both existing and planned). In most instances, a primary trade area represents 60 to 70 percent of the area's sales potential. The secondary trade area usually comprises the areas from which an additional 20 to 35 percent of the sales are derived. The remaining proportion of sales is derived from outside the trade area. These percentages vary considerably. Some regional malls serving a large hinterland may have as much as 20 percent of sales from outside the primary and secondary trade areas. Outlet centers, which may be near tourist attractions or in a drive-by location between metropolitan areas, may have huge trade areas without identifiable geographic boundaries.

Trade areas do not consist of perfect circles of three- or five-mile radii, although such naive and simplistic approaches to defining trade areas are sometimes observed. Rather, trade areas (see Exhibit 8–10) are irregular in shape, reflecting physical (and psychological) barriers, roadway vectors, drive times, preferred shopping patterns, and competition.

The trade area defines the center's expenditure potential, from which a share, or capture rate, is derived. The number of individuals and households in the trade area, their income levels, and their patterns of spending for different categories of retail goods comprise the three indicators of trade area potential. Many complicated statistical refinements, and much experienced judgment, are required to assess expenditure potential. In general, however, empirical studies support the notion that certain merchandise types—shoppers' goods, for example—consume a fairly constant percentage of household income regardless of income level, slightly higher at low income levels and slightly lower at high income levels. Food, on the other hand, is just the opposite; food accounts for a much higher percentage of income at lower income levels than at higher income levels.

Exhibit 8–11 shows how a trade area profile is typically defined. Starting with the number of households and their mean incomes, a series of ratios are applied to derive the total expected retail expenditure levels. These expenditures can then be projected out over three- and five-year horizons using population, income, and inflation assumptions. A final refinement, shown in Exhibit 8–12, indicates how the total retail expenditure potential (the bottom line of Exhibit 8–11) can be allocated into the types of goods found in each of the typical types of retail centers.[8]

Clearly, the critical demand-side analysis of trade area potential is based on many assumptions and judgments by retailers and shopping center investors. Industry rules of thumb that have been used to generate such crucial variables as percentage shares of spending on each retail category or the proportion of household retail dollars spent outside the trade area (*leakage* in retail jargon) may no longer be reliable. In fact, there is considerable evidence, in the form of

---

[8] Real Estate Research Corp., *Handbook for Analysis of the Impact of New Development on Older Commercial Areas* (1982) has an excellent "how to" review of trade area analysis methods and data sources.

EXHIBIT 8–10

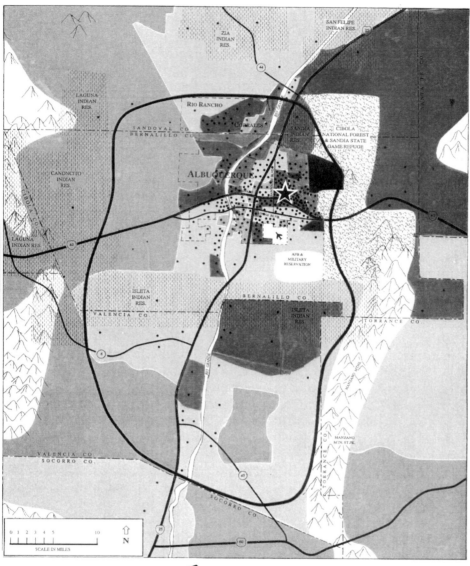

THE CENTER OF THE GREAT SOUTHWEST®

★ Coronado Center

—— Effective Trade Area

Parks

Indian reservations

• **1993 Population Distribution**
(one dot equals 2,000 persons)

1993 Average Household Income

Under $25,000
$25,000 - $34,999
$35,000 - $49,999
$50,000 - $74,999
$75,000 & Over

EXHIBIT 8–11
Retail Expenditures by Trade Area Residents

	Actual		Projected	
	1987	*1990*	*1995*	*2000*
Households	120,563	124,528	130,198	135,849
Average household income	$38,135	$42,000	$48,000	$55,000
Total household income*	$4,597.7	$5,230	$6,249	$7,472
Percentage disposable income	85.1%	85.0%	85.0%	85.0%
Total disposable income*	$3,914.4	$4,446	$5,312	$6,351
Percentage consumption expenditures	90.4%	90.0%	90.0%	90.0%
Total consumption expenditures*	$3,537.9	$4,001	$4,781	$5,716
Percentage retail expenditures	30.5%	30.0%	30.0%	30.0%
Total retail expenditures*	$1,078.3	$1,200	$1,434	$1,715

* In millions.

Source: John McMahon, *Real Estate Development,* (New York: McGraw Hill), 1989, p. 132.

EXHIBIT 8–12
1992 Retail Sales by Category

	Amount ($ Billions)	Percentage
Shoppers' goods:		
Apparel	$ 90.9	10.1%
General merchandise	185.3	20.5
Household furnishings	89.3	9.9
Specialty stores	20.7	2.3
Subtotal	386.2	42.8
Convenience goods	463.9	51.4
Personal services	20.3	2.3
Specialized services	31.7	3.5
Total	$902.1	100.0%

Source: Bureau of the Census.

center failures and retailer bankruptcy, to suggest that these rules and standards do not work.

Changing demographics and shifts in lifestyles, attitudes, and behaviors are the causal factors behind the fact that old rules of thumb and industry standards no longer work well. The major population changes include (1) the middle-aging of the population as the nearly 80 million baby boomers enter their high earning years; (2) the rise of nontraditional households, especially singles living alone, single parents with children, and empty-nesters; and (3) the emergence of multi-ethnic and multiracial majorities in many cities as Asian, Hispanic, and African-American households increase. In terms of lifestyle, many families have two wage earners but less time to shop. These and other changes have complicated trade area analysis. The trickiest part of the equation, translating disposable income into expenditure estimates for each category of retail spending, is rendered more difficult than in the past when mass market assumptions could be used. Looking forward, retail markets will be much more highly segmented, and retail investment will have to adjust for the additional risks that will be encountered.

Supply: The Competitive Alignment
The trade area retail potential is shared by competitive shopping centers. The capture rate of a particular center depends on its location and its drawing power in the context of competition for market share. Various models—gravitational, vacuum, shift share, and cumulative attraction—have been advanced to account for the capture rate for shopping centers.[9]

Industry rules of thumb suggest that a regional shopping center in a metropolitan area with multiple centers typically will not capture more than 25 percent—and at most 35 percent—of the potential

---

[9] Locational studies can be roughly divided into two classes: academic and pragmatic. The two best examples of the pragmatic class are Richard Nelson, *The Selection of Retail Location* (1958), and John Thompson, *Retail Site Selection* (1978). A good review of the theoretical literature as applied to real estate issues is Michael Webber, *Impact of Uncertainty on Location* (1972). Anthony Catanese's *Scientific Methods of Urban Analysis* (1972) provides an overview of optimization models and simulation techniques. The classic text on location theory is Walter Isard, *Location and Space-Economy* (1956). One of the earliest and still cited theories of retail location is William Reilly's "Law of Retail Orientation," elaborated in *Methods for the Study of Retail Relationships* (1929). His concept is that people will stop at the largest retail center that is closest to them. Although this single model does not hold in the economic and demographic environment of the 1990s, it still has an intuitive appeal.

expenditures of its primary and secondary trade areas. In the case of smaller community and neighborhood centers, with more compact trade areas, the standard capture rate is no more than 50 to 60 percent of potential expenditures. For the newer retail formats—power centers, outlet centers, festival malls, and so on—no reliable ratios of center sales to trade area capacity have yet evolved. One noted retail analyst states that capture estimates "should be a judgment evaluation based upon location and character of competition, driving time distance studies, and home interviews. I do not believe it is possible to reduce these to a formula; I would rather see the analyst make an arbitrary judgment for each trade area based upon his analysis of all the data for that area and the indicated consumer preferences."[10]

The judgmental factors that in practice are used to define the competitive environment of a center and estimate its share of the potential include:

- Relative travel times and ease of travel for each center.
- Relative size of competing centers in square feet of comparable goods.
- Mix of stores in the center (to promote optimal cross-shopping and lengthen each shopping trip).
- Proximity to major employment concentrations (to maximize lunch times and after-work shopping by workers).
- General attractiveness of the center vis-à-vis the competition, including such variables as age, operating hours, vacancy, parking and ingress/egress, security, and advertising/promotion.

As shown in Exhibit 8–1, the square footage of retail space has grown dramatically, at a rate far outpacing population and real income growth. Accordingly, the competition for retail spending has heightened. The relative attractiveness of centers offering the same lines of merchandise at similar price points is now very difficult to gauge. Therefore, as in trade area definition, the identification of competitive centers and the assignment of a reasonable market share capture rate is inherently judgmental.

Exhibit 8–13 illustrates the conceptual complexity of changing economic and demographic factors. In this exhibit, sales performance is a function of economic conditions, demographic factors, shopper

---

[10] Applebaum et al. (1968), p. 102.

EXHIBIT 8–13
Major Influences on Store Sales

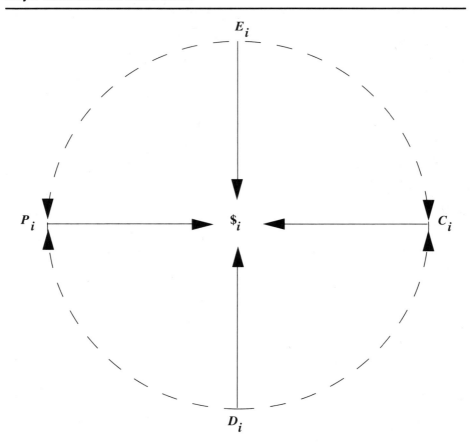

$$\$_i \quad = \text{Sales performance}$$
$$E_i \quad = \text{Economics}$$
$$D_i \quad = \text{Demographics}$$
$$P_i \quad = \text{Psychographics}$$
$$C_i \quad = \text{Competition}$$

Source: Charles A. Ingene, "Using Economic Data in Retail Industry Analysis," in *The Retail Industry* (Chicago: AIMR, 1992), pp. 18–24.

preferences (psychographic tendencies), and the competition. But the competition also evolves in response to the same variables, leading to the dynamic quality of retail real estate. In fact, the successful shopping center is one that is continuously changing in anticipation of trade area and competitive pressures, not just in response to them. The role of the tenant and merchandise mix and the ability of center owners to change that mix to meet macro changes and competitive forces are discussed in the next section.

Tenancy and Merchandise Mix

According to Real Estate Research Corp.,[11] an investment grade shopping center is one that has "an appropriate mix of locally dominant anchors and a complement of smaller retail stores and service establishments targeted to the specific market area and its competitive requirements."

The question of what constitutes "an appropriate mix" is elusive. Exhibit 8–14 shows the percentage of GLA typically devoted to anchor stores in each of the different types of centers. At one extreme, power centers have few, if any, mall shops, while regional malls have traditionally had 40 to 50 percent of space devoted to smaller stores. Meanwhile, some newer types of centers, such as outlet malls, have no anchors at all.

Anchor tenants are large tenants that sign long (10-to-25-year) leases. They are "credit tenants" in the sense that their financial track records, earnings, and balance sheets reduce turnover risk. In many cases, anchor tenants own their stores and may own the land as well. Most important, however, anchor tenants serve as the primary draw for the retail center. This is true whether the anchor is a supermarket, a discounter, a category killer, or a department store.

Traditionally, center owners have sought anchors that dominate their trade areas, that is, command a meaningful share of local expenditures within the consumer lines that they merchandise.[12] In recogni-

---

[11] Real Estate Research Corp., *Handbook for Analysis*, p. 45.

[12] The distinction of anchors as dominant does not hold true for all types of centers. In most markets other than the largest metropolitan areas, an identifiable number of chains capture most of the consumer expenditures and achieve dominance. In most markets, for example, no more than three department stores and grocery store chains command the lion's share of food and shoppers' goods expenditures. However, the anchors for newer retail formats—discount stores, off-price stores, category killers, warehouse clubs, and so on—are more numerous and therefore less likely to have significant market share. The lack of clear anchor dominance in these retail formats may add to the risk of investment.

EXHIBIT 8–14
The Importance of Anchor Stores

Center Type	Typical Anchor Store	Percentage of Space Occupied by Anchor
Neighborhood	Drug, grocery	80–90%
Community	Discount, junior department store, off-price, "super drug"	60–80
Power	Category killer, discount, warehouse clubs	80–100
Regional	Department store	50–60
Outlet	None	0
Specialty*	None	0

* Specialty centers include festival malls, fashion centers, and off-price/value centers.

Source: ICSC, *The Source* (ICSC: New York, 1992).

tion of their drawing power, anchor stores are courted by center owners, and they contribute much less in rent than do the small shops. In fact, in the prevailing economics of most retail centers, mall shop rents are the major source of revenue. Accordingly, the risk—and the upside—in retail center investment lies largely with the mall shop space. As seen in Exhibit 8–14, small-shop space is less significant for neighborhood centers and power centers than for community centers and regional malls. However, in all cases the effective leasing and management of the small shops is important. In large centers, base rents from mall shops are on the order of five times higher, on a square foot basis, than the anchor stores. The successful concept merchants that account for a substantial portion of nonanchor regional mall space allocate 1 to 12 percent of their sales for occupancy costs, including rent and their share of expenses.

The mix of mall shops is especially critical for regional malls and community centers. Small shops are kept to short leases (three to five years) so that they can be moved out if they don't perform and expanded if they do. The mix of tenants among apparel, gifts and accessories, stores, home furnishings, books, and so on and the location of "hot" retailers within a center are constantly modified. Retail center management and leasing in large measure succeeds or fails on the basis of juggling the appropriate mix of small-shop space.

Leasing and Management

As stated earlier, retail investment is an investment in a merchandising venture as well as in real estate. The "art" of that investment is in reading the local market correctly, anticipating changes, and providing the most advantageous mix of tenants, merchandise, and price points for the trade area. The "science" of the investment is using management and leasing tools to ensure that store sales translate into investor returns. Standard lease terms and conditions, the importance of credit tenants, expense control pass-throughs, and capital expenditures for remodeling, retenanting, and merchandising centers are discussed in this section.

The retail lease is the most advantageous of all real estate leases to investors and owners. It allows owners to participate in the success of the center's merchants by sharing in the sales achieved in each store, over and above a negotiated minimum or base rent. Retail leases also feature pass-through of most expenses to the tenant. Office and industrial leases also provide for full or partial pass-throughs of expenses, but do not provide for percentage rent or overages. Typically, base rents—secured by long leases signed by credit tenants—comprise up to two-thirds of a retail center's revenue. Overages, or percentage rents, account for the remaining one-third.

The standard conditions in retail leases are summarized in Exhibit 8–15. This listing provides a good overview of the types of issues addressed in retail negotiations. In particular, it illustrates the importance of owners' ability to creatively manage the tenancy of the center as balanced against the need for long-term, stable leases from anchor tenants. This balance is the key to financial success: Too much reliance on low-rent anchors or on higher-rent-paying but less stable mall shops is to be avoided. For department stores, which are the critical tenants in regional malls, there are also operating covenants that protect owners and investors. The covenants, which extend for a fixed period, require the department store to remain operational as a "name" department store over the course of the period. This assures investors that a major draw for the mall will be in place. Mall shop tenants also count on the presence of the anchors, and their leases may be contingent on the continued operation of the majors.

Some institutional investors will not consider an equity position in a mall unless operating covenants are in place for their projected holding period. Others, on a case-by-case basis, will invest in regional

EXHIBIT 8–15
Retail Lease Terms

- *Base rent:* fixed and guaranteed minimum rental payments, usually quoted on an annual basis but payable monthly. Based on the total volume of gross leasable space being leased by the tenant (e.g., $X per square foot per year).
- *Percentage rent:* variable rental payments, usually set as a proportion of a tenant's sales volume above a minimum threshold or *break-even point.* This provision gives property owners a vested interest in their tenants' success.
- *Lease period:* the term of the lease, in years. The term typically ranges between 10 and 35 years for large tenants occupying blocks of space of 10,000 square feet or more. In contrast, the term ranges from three to five years for smaller tenants.
- *CAMs:* common area maintenance charges, covering the costs of operating and maintaining the common areas within a shopping center.
- *Expense recoveries:* payments by the tenants to reimburse shopping center owners for CAMs, property taxes, insurance payments, and specified capital expenses.
- *Use clauses:* restrictions on the types of goods and services that a tenant is permitted to sell from the premises. Property owners select tenants to achieve an overall tenant mix suitable to the property's customer base. Use clauses enable property owners to ensure that the desired tenant mix is realized.
- *Exclusive or "noncompete" clauses:* restrictions granting tenants the exclusive rights to sell certain kinds of merchandise within specified boundaries, that is, either a wing or the whole shopping center. Tenants want to limit the number of rival retailers against which they must compete—preferably to zero.
- *Kick-out clauses:* the right (or obligation) of a tenant to either close its store or move to another location within the shopping center if its retail sales volume falls short of some threshold level as of a specified point in time—for example, two to three years after a lease has taken effect.
- *Go-dark clause:* the rights of tenants that apply if a major anchor in a shopping center shuts down and is not replaced within a reasonable time period. In this event, tenants often are able to cancel their leases, go on percentage rent, or get an outright rent reduction.

Source: Sahling (1993), p. 22.

centers where department store covenants have expired if the stores are productive and their ownership is strong.

Credit tenants are the backbone of retail centers. In the neighborhood center, they are the drug and grocery stores chains; in regional malls, they are the department stores and the national concept and specialty stores. In all cases, owners and investors strive for a high percentage of credit tenant occupancy. However, in no case does today's credit guarantee tomorrow's occupancy. The faltering and failure of some department stores in the 1980s, the regular demise of overextended discount operators, and the traditional ebb and flow of specialty stores indicate that credit risk is extremely important for retail investors. This is particularly important in power centers, where virtually all of the revenues are derived from a small number of big box retailers.

Expenses are another key retail center management issue. Most retail leases are net leases in which the tenant pays a fixed amount or a pro rata share of the significant expense items. Exhibit 8–16 identifies typical expense items for a regional mall. Expense lines for small centers are similar, with the exception of the interior common area maintenance, which is unique to the enclosed regional mall. The CAM expenses are large and are the focus of intense negotiation between tenants and owners as retailers strive to improve margins by reducing their total occupancy costs. The nonrecoverable expenses indicated in Exhibit 8–16 include the owner's share of the merchants' association marketing expense and legal, accounting, and other costs. Department stores and other anchors that own their own stores pay their own taxes, insurance, and other expenses and contribute a negotiated amount to interior and exterior CAM costs.

Lease negotiations—for base rents, percentage rent breaking points, terms and conditions, and expense pass-through—are critical to retail investment performance. In these negotiations, the strong retailers, especially the anchors but also including popular specialty

EXHIBIT 8–16
Typical Expense Summary for an Enclosed Mall

Expense	Percentage
Exterior CAM	17.4%
Enclosed CAM	39.1
Insurance	2.3
Real estate taxes	7.3
Management fee	17.9
HVAC expense	6.2
Food court	3.9
Nonrecoverables	5.9
Total operating expenses	100%

Source: Heitman Financial Ltd.

stores, are in a strong position. They typically negotiate many leases each year, and they understand their importance to the center. This situation is entirely different from the usual office or industrial investment, where the tenants are local. Accordingly, investors need to be assured that leases do not overly favor the anchors and other strong credit tenants.

The final important management issue relevant to investors is capital budgeting. To consistently meet changing market conditions and competitive pressures, all but the most "vanilla" neighborhood centers need to be upgraded, retenanted/remerchandised, and even expanded over the course of an investment holding period. The costs of replacing tenants and upgrading the physical plant can be significant. The investor's return on this relatively frequent reinvestment must be known at the outset. The costs of keeping a center viable are higher than keeping an office building or industrial facility competitive. Not all retail centers warrant the ongoing capital demands they may face. As the large number of retail projects that were built in the 1970s and 1980s age, capital calls will increase in frequency. Investors are well advised to investigate the life cycle costs of retail center investment and understand the pros and cons of attempting to keep the center competitive in its trade area.

As indicated in this section, shopping centers are operating businesses. Management and leasing, capital budgeting, and accommodating economic, demographic, and lifestyle changes all require strong, active management.

EMERGING ISSUES IN RETAIL INVESTMENT

Driven by demographic and economic shifts and guided by changing consumer attitudes toward shopping, retail real estate is dynamic and diverse. There are three fundamental, structural issues facing prospective retail property investors.

The first issue, as shown in Exhibit 8–17, is the evolution of retail distribution channels. The left-hand panel illustrates the continuing segmentation of retail stores, which now include formats with more and more focused markets. Outlet, off-price and close-out stores, for example, all compete within a very narrow range of overall consumer spending. Stores have also steadily increased in size. A typical supermarket was 25,000 square feet in the 1970s, 40,000 in the 80s, and

EXHIBIT 8–17
Retail Distribution Channels

Store Type	Retail Format	Nonstore
Convenience (food/drug)	Neighborhood center	
Off-price	Community center	Catalog
Discount		
Category killer	Power center	
Clearance	Freestanding store	Interactive television
Warehouse club		
Specialty	Specialty (festival, fashion)	On-line computer
Outlet	Outlet center	
Department	Regional/super-regional mall	

in the 90s the new generation of superstores are in the 60,000 to 80,000 square foot range.[13] The proliferation of category killer stores also warrants attention. Shoppers are demanding more and more selection (merchandise depth) within product lines that can only be economically accommodated in very large store formats. However, at some point saturation will be achieved and not all of the big box stores proliferating in the 1990s will stand the test of time.

Retail center formats are also more numerous and competitive with one another. The center column of Exhibit 8–17 identifies the major competitive venues for the shopper's retail expenditure. While some of these centers command a very small market share (outlet centers accounted for 1 percent of 1992 total retail sales, for example), cumulatively they have added to the inventory of GLA. Nonstore formats—catalog shopping, on-line computer shopping, and interactive television—are also increasingly vying for the consumer dollar at the expense of the traditional shopping center.

Product segmentation, in which small and more specialized niche markets are targeted, means investors need to carefully assess the possibilities of market saturation and trade area cannibalization. Most markets can support only so much retail space.

The second issue is the change in trade area demand characteris-

[13] *National Mall Monitor* and *Chain Store Executive* regularly collect data on store sizes.

tics. The demographics of demand suggest that retail sales will be dominated by discretionary purchasers—middle-aged and older Americans who can afford to be selective and can elect not to spend at all. This factor, plus the increasing importance of ethnic populations, means that old rules of thumb about demand will have to be constantly re-evaluated. As existing populations mature and trade areas change household composition, not all retail centers will successfully make the transition. Demographic and economic patterns also suggest an increasing bifurcation of retail markets into a value- and price-conscious low end and a service-oriented, fashion-conscious high end. The middle market will grow more slowly and will comprise a smaller proportion of total retail spending.

Finally, the structure of retail center ownership is changing. Institutional owners (pension funds in particular) and public ownership (e.g., REITs) are beginning to influence the ownership of shopping centers. With a universe of 39,000 retail centers, these changes will play out slowly. However, as institutional owners become more important in the limited universe of large centers, they will affect the balance of power between retailers and investors/owners. As institutions and REITs gain market share, they will be in a stronger position to negotiate directly with the key anchor store chains. Heretofore, that power rested with the entrepreneurial development organizations (largely family owned) that created the retail center inventory in the 1970s and 1980s.

In conclusion, retail real estate presents a host of challenges to investors. As operating businesses, shopping centers demand significant levels of management skill. As real estate investments, they command the attention of investors willing to carefully assess the risks that will accompany the evolution of retail shopping patterns.

APPENDIX 8A
RETAIL DATA AND SOURCES

Specialized data on retail markets, retail centers, and stores are available from a wide variety of sources. These sources are quite distinct from those used for office, industrial, residential, and other real estate investment analysis. This appendix lists the most useful and reliable sources.

Government

U.S. Census of Population	Trade area demographics
Census of Retail Trade	Sales by major retail category
Survey of Current Business	Income per capita
Census Expenditure Survey	Spending by category of merchandise

Industry Associations

International Council of Shopping Centers (ICSC)	Several specialty publications on shopping center expenses, operating ratios, productivity, and so on. Based on surveys.
Urban Land Institute (ULI)	*Dollars and Cents of Shopping Centers* provides sales and operating data. Based on surveys.

Private Sources

Wall Street investment banks	Analysis of publicly traded retailers and assessments of general retail trends.
Specialty trade magazines	*Shopping Center World, National Mall Monitor, Chain Store Age Executive, Sales and Marketing Management, American Demographics, Value Retail News.*
Russell/NCREIF	Performance data on pension fund retail investments. Standard industry benchmark.
Property data vendors	CACI, 1915 North Fort Myer Drive, Arlington, VA 22209; National Decision Systems, 861 Sixth Avenue, San Diego, CA 92101; National Planning Data Corporation, P.O. Box 610, Ithaca, NY 14850; Urban Decision Systems, Inc., P.O. Box 25953, Los Angeles, CA 90025.

Geographic Information Systems (GISs)

GIS refers to the matching of databases (population, sales, retail centers, etc.) with digitized mapping so that data can be displayed in areal formats. GIS provides a means for plotting any type of information that can be geocoded, that is, that has identifiable longitude and latitude (SW corner of Main Street, ZIP Code 10001, 217 Broadway, etc.). A wide variety of proprietary GIS firms sell software, hardware (plotters, etc.), and databases. A good source of listings of GIS firms is *American Demographics*.

REFERENCES

Applebaum, William, et al. *Guide to Store Location Research*. Reading, MA, Addison-Wesley, 1968.

Association for Investment Management and Research. *The Retail Industry—General Merchandisers and Discounters, Specialty Merchandisers, Apparel Specialty and Food/Drug Retailers*. Chicago: AIMR, 1992.

Catanese, Anthony J. *Scientific Methods of Urban Analysis*. Urbana, IL: University of Illinois, 1972.

Equitable Real Estate Investment Management. *The Evolution of Regional Shopping Centers*. Atlanta, GA: Equitable Real Estate, 1990.

Homart Development. *The Future of Regional Malls*. Chicago: Homart Development, 1993.

International Council of Shopping Centers. *The Scope of the Shopping Center Industry in the United States*. New York: ICSC, 1992.

ICSC Research Bulletin; monthly report.

ICSC SCORES; Shopping Center Operations, Revenues, and Expenses; annual.

Isard, Walter. *Location and Space-Economy*. Cambridge, MA: MIT Press, 1956.

Kratovitz, Robert, and Raymon Weiner. *Real Estate Law*. 9th ed. Englewood Cliffs, NJ: Prentice Hall, 1988.

Kateley, Richard. *Investment in Regional Malls*. Chicago: Heitman Financial Ltd., 1992.

McMahon, John. *Property Development*. New York: McGraw-Hill, 1989.

McKeever, J. Ross, et al. *Shopping Center Development Handbook*. Washington, DC: Urban Land Institute, 1977.

Nelson, Richard. *The Selection of Retail Locations*. New York: McGraw-Hill, 1958.

Peiser, Richard B. *Professional Real Estate Development*. Chicago: Dearborn Financial Publishing, 1992.

Real Estate Research Corp. *Handbook for Analysis of the Impact of New Development on Older Commercial Areas*. Chicago: Estate Research Corporation, 1982.

Reilly, William. *Methods for the Study of Retail Relationships*. Austin, TX: University of Texas, 1958 (originally published in 1929).

Sahling, Leonard. *The New Wave Shopping Center Industry of the 1990s*. New York: Merrill Lynch, 1993.

Thompson, John. *Retail Site Selection*. New York: F. W. Dodge, 1978.

Urban Land Institute. *Dollars and Cents of Shopping Centers*. Washington, DC: ULI, 1992.

Webber, Michael J. *Impact of Uncertainty on Location*. Cambridge, MA: MIT Press, 1972.

Young, Michael, and Richard Kateley. "Retail Revisited and Dissected." *Russell-NCREIF Report*. Tacoma, WA: 1993.

CHAPTER 9

THE INDUSTRIAL SECTOR

Robert J. Domrese
Domrese & Associates

James R. Proud
Heitman/JMB Advisory Corporation

INTRODUCTION

This chapter provides a conceptual and practical overview of the industrial warehouse sector. The conceptual considerations include a description of the subsectors and property types that make up the "industrial" warehouse and distribution sector, an examination of the nature of the tenancy base and the supply-demand considerations that define the markets for warehouse space, a review of the sources of capital and how these sources affect the pace of new construction, and a historical review of the investment performance of the industrial sector.

These analyses are closely related. The hallmarks of the warehouse sector's investment performance—above-average total returns, a high current yield, and low volatility—can be traced to the relatively efficient balancing of supply and demand in the markets for leased space and the relatively moderate flows of capital to fund new construction. Because the availability of capital for warehouse development has not been distorted by tax incentives, foreign capital flows, excessive lending, or widespread speculative development, the warehouse sector has not experienced the degree of overbuilding that has characterized other property sectors.

The chapter also addresses several practical considerations. Which market segments are most likely to generate the most stable returns? The least likely? The highest? Which geographic markets are the most favored, and how should these markets be tracked and selected? What are the likely effects of technological change, such as the increasing use of robotics, computer technologies, and just-in-time inventory control systems? Do these changes favor larger or smaller properties? Outlying or close-in locations? What will be the impact of other emerging trends in the nation's wholesale distribution system, such as the increased importance of trucking and air transport and the growth of overnight delivery system providers like UPS and Federal Express? What is the near-term outlook for warehouse investments?

Finally, the chapter examines several portfolio management issues. In particular, it questions the basis for determining an "optimal" allocation to warehouse properties. Can there really be an allocation that will approach an "efficient frontier" in which returns are enhanced and portfolio risks are most effectively minimized? Several risk-spreading and risk-mitigating strategies are examined and applied to warehouse portfolios.

Throughout these discussions, several suggestive themes emerge. The economies of wholesale distribution should tend, over the long term, to encourage more intensive use of existing space. It should favor space located close to major distribution centers and lead users to select smaller tenancies and property sizes. The warehouse sector is the most "commoditylike" of all real estate sectors. Tenancies are broad based and highly substitutable. Perhaps more than office, retail, or apartment portfolios, warehouse portfolios, if carefully assembled, should therefore lend themselves to portfolio-wide risk-spreading and risk management techniques.

WAREHOUSE SUBSECTORS AND MARKET SEGMENTATION

Warehouses come in a wide variety of types and sizes. Each represents a distinct property segment and presents a different set of risks and returns on investment. Not all are equally suitable for institutional investment.

Minor Warehouse Market Subsectors

Examples of the minor warehouse subsectors include incubator, single-user, and R&D/office buildings.

Incubator Buildings
Incubator warehouses are very small, "tilt-up" warehouses, typically less than 25,000 square feet and accommodating very small tenants in 2,000- to-10,000-square-foot bays. They are called *incubator* warehouses because they may be used by small, start-up businesses. These properties can be management intensive and typically will not attract credit tenants. They are generally much too small to attract institutional investment.

Single-User Buildings
At the other end of the spectrum are specialized, typically very large, single-user industrial buildings that are constructed to meet the needs of a single tenant. These include large manufacturing, operating, or storage facilities located near a large manufacturing plant. The dedication of these properties to a specific use makes them less suitable for general warehouse/distribution functions if their underlying special purpose should disappear. Frequently they are a part of large-scale, vertically integrated operations and are either owned by the users, are sale/leasebacks, or are subject to long-term leases. These building values derive from a specific use and application and from the creditworthiness of the user. The investment should normally be fully amortized over the initial lease term. The residual value of the property at the end of the holding period will depend on the property's continuing suitability for its dedicated use or, depending on location and zoning restrictions, the value of the underlying land for alternative uses.

R&D/Office Buildings
Another subsector is research and development properties, or R&D/office properties, which make up a significant high-tech property subsector of their own. These are a hybrid property type, typically consisting of 50 percent office space to accommodate emerging high-tech companies' front office operations and 50 percent warehouse space for assembly and/or storage uses. The prospective tenant base for R&D buildings is much smaller than that for warehouse buildings, since the large office component does not make the building appropriate for pure distribution functions, and the warehouse component makes the building inappropriate for pure office use. Investment performance is usually dependent on the health of the local high-tech industry. R&D properties have attracted institutional investment

and are sometimes included in the "industrial" allocation of many pension portfolios, but they really represent a specialized and unique market subsector.

Major Warehouse Market Subsectors

In addition to these special segments are the "generic" or "pure" warehouse/distribution properties that play the central role in the wholesale and retail trade and distribution network in the United States. These warehouses are generally considered to present the most attractive opportunities for institutional investment. These properties have recurring, common requirements. Ceiling heights range from 18 feet in smaller buildings to 24 feet or more in larger, newer buildings. Loading docks should be well located and easily accessible, taking into consideration truck turning radius and parking requirements. Building configuration should be simple and adaptable and should be divisible into multiple bays for several users or adaptable for use by a single user. Office buildout should usually be less than 25 percent and often is less than 10 percent. Location should be appropriate to the user's storage and distribution requirements.

These pure warehouse/distribution properties may be broken down into three broad categories:

1. "High-cube" regional distribution centers.
2. Planned industrial parks.
3. Small and intermediate-size freestanding warehouses.

Each type draws on a different part of the tenant market and therefore has different requirements for size, location, and buildout. Each type has somewhat different investment characteristics, which are summarized in Exhibit 9–1.

High-Cube Regional Distribution Centers

A major segment of the market involves the very large regional distribution center. Building sizes ranging from 350,000 to 1,000,000 square feet or more are common. The facilities are used for the storage and distribution of bulk goods. Ceiling heights are typically 24 to 30 feet or more to facilitate the storage of cubical-shaped, pallet-size bundles; hence the name *high cube*. The facility is typically used by a single tenant. Rail service as well as freeway access is important,

EXHIBIT 9–1
Major Warehouse Market Subsectors

Category	Size	Location	Tenant	Strategic Importance
High-cube bulk distribution	350,000 sq. ft. and above	Outlying areas	Owner/single tenant	Cost and efficiency
Park-based	50,000– 350,000 sq. ft.	Planned business park	Owner/single tenant	Cost and location
Freestanding	50,000– 100,000 sq. ft.	Close in	Single/ multitenant	Location and amenities

Source: Grubb & Ellis Realty Advisers, Inc.

and the properties are nearly always located on the outskirts of a major population center, where low-cost land is abundant.

For properties located in outlying, peripheral areas, location is not the critical factor. Cost is much more important. Since these facilities are typically used for the distribution of bulk, low-margin goods, tenants tend to be very cost sensitive and will be willing to relocate some distance to competing low-cost distribution facilities. Competition for inexpensive space will therefore tend to keep rents low, even where there are few existing competing facilities. Because replacement costs for new warehouses are relatively low and land in outlying areas may be abundant and cheap, competing facilities can be built as rents begin to rise. Accordingly, the relatively few barriers to the new supply (whether build-to-suit or spec, though the latter is less likely with facilities of this size) of warehouse space will then bring rents down.

The return on investment in a large, regional distribution center acts more like a bond than an equity investment, since most of the return is dependent on the income stream generated by the operations of the user, and the prospects for significant appreciation in the residual value of the land is low. When a large amount of land is available, there is usually only a minimal prospect for real (i.e., inflation-adjusted) rent growth.

Planned Industrial Parks/Suburban Parks

Warehouse properties located in planned industrial parks represent a second major market segment. Individual warehouse buildings in these parks tend to be mid-range in size, usually from 50,000 to 350,000 square feet, depending on the region of the country. The size of the parks, however, can run into millions of square feet. Users of park-based space are usually less cost sensitive than users of large high-cube bulk distribution space. Park-based warehouse space caters to a broader range of tenants.

Over the last decade, industrial parks have increased the percentage of property devoted to office buildout, as the location has become attractive to low-end office users and corporate users looking for a single location. Except for those parks still specializing in distribution-oriented space, many parks are now characterized by higher-end, mixed uses. Tenants locating in parks are usually more location sensitive than bulk distribution warehouse users.

The planned industrial park represents a purer "real estate play" than the regional distribution center. Once built in emerging markets along interstate highways, they are becoming engulfed by suburban growth. Increasingly, less land is available for new parks, so the prospects for competition from new construction are reduced. In addition, many industrial/suburban parks are subject to deed restrictions, which tend to preserve quality standards and protect investment values. Parks may also evolve to higher mixed uses as they serve both traditional warehousing/distribution and office or retail functions. Because of the synergies of property management and tenant diversification and because well-located parks will become increasingly difficult to replicate, industrial parks can offer attractive returns, combining both current income and the prospect of appreciation.

Small and Intermediate-Size Freestanding Warehouses

This last category is also the most diverse. It includes small and intermediate-size freestanding warehouse properties. Properties are usually less than 300,000 square feet and are typically 50,000 to 150,000 square feet. Small and intermediate-size warehouses suitable for institutional investments are usually located more centrally along the close-in distribution corridors of major metropolitan areas and near major airports, rail connections, or port facilities. These properties cater to tenants whose primary criterion is location rather than cost. Tenants require less space and therefore can afford the higher rents per square foot associated with more centrally located land. They may be single-tenant buildings but are frequently multitenant buildings owing to the relatively smaller size of the average tenant. Many of these properties may be converted to higher uses as the location becomes more valuable for office or retail purposes.

The small and intermediate-size warehouse subsector offers a broad range of opportunities for redevelopment, evolution to higher use, and capital appreciation. It therefore still represents a pure "real estate play" and relatively good inflation-hedging potential. Because these properties are located close to major metropolitan areas where there is little available land, competition from newly constructed facilities is limited. Tenants requiring access to close-in distribution points are less price sensitive than users of the large bulk distribution warehouses. Many of these smaller properties are not professionally managed and therefore offer the possibility for adding value through more intensive management. Frequently opportunities for upgrading or expansion exist.

Because of their proximity to major metropolitan areas, some of these properties are evolving to higher uses, such as discount retail or retail "clubs," or to high-intensity distribution uses, records storage, and services applications. Single-tenant buildings, if properly configured, may be converted to multitenant facilities and marketed to smaller users willing to pay higher rents per square foot. Computerized just-in-time inventory management control systems, to the extent that they become cost effective for small users, should enable these growing tenants to remain in their current space for a longer period of time. These small and intermediate-size warehouses thus offer a range of opportunities for increasing yields and appreciation.

One conclusion that emerges from an analysis of these three warehouse segments is that one sector with a good prospect for superior investment returns is the small and intermediate-size freestanding warehouses located in the older, central distribution corridors of major trading centers. This is the segment of the industrial market that is most frequently overlooked by institutional investors, primarily because of the high transaction costs of making small individual investments. Both the large, regional distribution centers and the suburban industrial and office parks have attracted institutional capital and present differing investment returns. If institutional investors could tap into the small warehouse subsector, the result should be to enhance both industrial and total real estate portfolio performance. However, there are three important risks to this strategy: (1) close-in facilities usually are acquired at a substantial premium to other facilities, (2) the cost of upgrades may be substantial in light of the new market rents, and (3) close-in locations are more subject to congestion and neighborhood deterioration.

WAREHOUSE FUNDAMENTALS

Warehouse/distribution properties have had a strong and stable performance record and, even in the current recessionary environment, make up one of the healthier property sectors. While demand slightly weakened in the early 1990s, it generally has been steady and broad based. The construction boom of the mid-1980s created a glut of many types of commercial real estate, but the supply of warehouse and distribution properties has generally responded to demand and has not been characterized by excessive overbuilding. Warehouse construction tends to be held back by capital constraints, leaving the forces of tenant demand to dictate the pace of new supply. Accordingly, supply and demand have tended to balance better. Construction of new warehouse space tends to go up when rents increase and vacancies decline. When rents fall and vacancies rise, new construction comes to a halt.

Broad-Based, Diversified Demand

Warehouse properties represent the least specialized land use category within commercial real estate. Tenant demand is generated by the activities associated with the storage and distribution of both consumer and manufacturing goods. This diversification and nonspecialization of demand means there is a great deal of substitutability among tenants in warehouses. Warehouses are the most "commodity-like" of all major real estate categories. While this can expose properties to greater lease turnover due to tenants' ability to more readily substitute space, these same substitutional characteristics offer a broader, more stable supply of tenants for vacant space, leading to generally better performance from well-managed properties.

On the other hand, because demand is broad based, a slow national economy can affect warehouse rents and investment returns. A large cross-section of the economy contributes to the demand for warehouse space. These sectors include domestic consumption, wholesale trade, and import and export trade. Thus, the cyclical aspects of demand are related to trends in the broader economy rather than to any single economic sector.

By far, most of the demand for warehouse space is generated by domestic consumption. Consequently, trends in retail sales will affect the strength of tenant demand. This exposure to the retail sector and to consumer demand explains why warehouse returns are more closely correlated to shopping center returns than to any other property sector.

The wholesale trade sector, particularly merchant wholesalers, is also very important to the demand for investment grade warehouse space. We estimate that merchant wholesalers make up from 40 to 60 percent of the overall distribution market, depending on the metropolitan area, with the balance accounted for by captive distribution networks in built-to-suit, owner-user operations that are often vertically integrated.

Trends in import and export trade also influence the demand for warehouse space. In the last half-decade, U.S. trade competitiveness has increased, primarily because of the decline of the dollar. Since exports make up 15 percent of U.S. gross domestic product, export growth can have an important impact on the demand for warehouse space. U.S. export trade, however, does not actually have to increase to boost demand for warehouse space. Foreign suppliers exporting to the United States also require local distribution space. Foreign tenants now make up a larger percentage of users of warehouse/distribution space than a decade ago. Many of these users are expected to expand in the future and may establish local production facilities or operations to access U.S. markets more easily. Foreign exporters began to establish U.S. operations in the early 1980s and still focus most of their activities in major trade centers. Eventually secondary centers may see more activity as foreign exporters seek greater market penetration.

Supply-Demand Balance: Less Overbuilding

Construction of warehouse space has historically followed trends in demand. Exhibit 9–2 displays the very close relationship between construction and demand as revealed by growth in employment. Data collected from 1970 through 1990 shows that these trends have tracked very closely.

The close relationship between supply and demand is one of the hallmarks of warehouse investments. The warehouse sector has been relatively insulated from the extraneous forces that have distorted the supply-demand balance and led to excessive speculative development and overbuilding in other property sectors. There are several reasons for this.

First, compared to other property types, relatively low rents and relatively high land costs tend to discourage speculative warehouse development. Developers seek the highest use possible for a given land parcel to maximize the spread between land basis and the discounted income stream generated by the leases in the fully developed space. As one of the least improved land use categories, warehouse lease rates are lower than lease rates for other commercial property types. In contrast, land costs as a percentage of total project costs are among the highest of any category of commercial real estate. This results from low construction cost per square foot, minimal landscaping requirements, and low coverage ratios for warehouses. As a consequence, warehouse properties generally have the lowest lease rate to land cost ratios of any commercial use. Development is usually feasible only where land costs are very low or projected rents are unusually high.

Much of the construction of new warehouse space has been accounted for by bulk distribution facilities, or so-called high-cube warehouses. These facilities have been constructed in outlying areas where land is readily available and therefore less expensive. Typically, this development has been build-to-suit projects (i.e., constructed after the tenant has committed to the space). In these instances, the lease-up risk can be eliminated and the rental income stream can be fixed in advance. Some construction has also occurred in larger warehouse parks. Close-in traditional distribution locations have seen much less new construction because of limited land availability. With close-in, high-demand areas zoned for industrial use, construction has favored

EXHIBIT 9–2
Warehouse Construction Tied to Demand

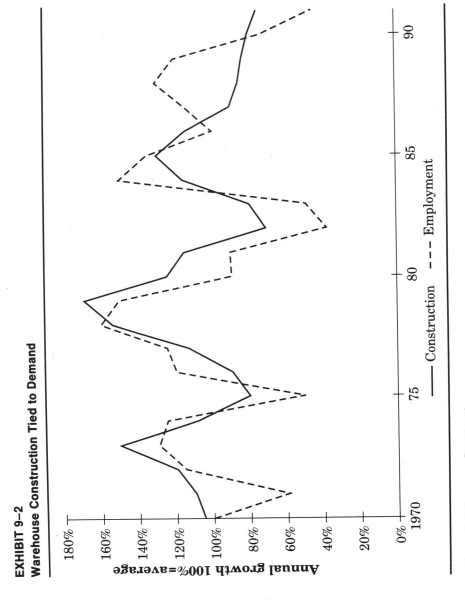

Source: U.S. Commerce Department.

430

higher uses, such as R&D/office properties. Land prices have been bid up in anticipation that higher-end buildings that could push rents up will be developed. This has kept the rent-land cost spread for warehouse space high and has made speculative development relatively less attractive than other categories of more highly improved real estate.

Second, warehouse properties have been less susceptible to the aggressive real estate lending that led to the banking and savings and loan crises and fueled much of the overbuilding in other property sectors. One striking illustration of this fact is that almost no industrial properties ended up being included on Resolution Trust Corp.'s (RTC) list of properties recovered from failed savings and loans. This fact suggests two extremely important implications for investment in industrial properties:

1. The supply of available warehouse space has been less distorted by the lending practices that fueled speculative development in other property sectors.
2. The values of institutional grade warehouse properties were not depressed by a constant stream of RTC-owned properties placed on the market for sale. Without this overhang of excess inventory typical of some other property types, the forces of supply and demand continued to be the main factors determining the values and returns on industrial properties.

A third factor that has limited excessive warehouse development is that warehouse properties have traditionally received relatively little institutional money to support new construction. This is particularly true of small and medium-size warehouse properties. Industrial properties targeted by institutional investors for development have usually been large-scale industrial parks or very large build-to-suit bulk distribution centers, because they offer a more convenient way to place large fund commitments. The investment market for large industrial parks is limited, since warehouse space in master planned parks represent only an estimated 25 to 30 percent of the total investment grade warehouse base, and not all large-scale parks offer sufficient returns to justify institutional investment. Such parks require a substantial amount of industrially zoned contiguous land, which is often available only in outlying areas, where demand for warehouse space is relatively low. Large-scale, build-to-suit projects must be supported by long-term leases and may require a 15-to-20-year time horizon to recover the investment. All of these factors have contributed to limited capital flows from institutional sources in the past and will continue to influence institutional development activity in the future.

A fourth factor limiting overbuilding is that warehouse properties have generally been passed over by tax-motivated investors. As noted previously, land cost as a percentage of total project cost for industrial properties is among the highest of any category of commercial real estate. Conversely, the cost of building improvements—that is, the total depreciable basis in the project for tax purposes—is a much lower percentage of total project cost than in other property categories. This results from the low cost of construction for warehouses, which are fairly uncomplicated building structures, and low land coverage ratios. Depreciation tax benefits as a proportion of total investment have always been much lower than those for office, apartment, and retail real estate. However, since the Tax Reform Act of 1986, the benefits have not been a significant factor in the investor's decision-making calculus.

A fifth factor is the historically limited extent to which warehouse space has attracted foreign investment. Plain-vanilla warehouse properties have not been susceptible to the "herd instinct" that has sometimes characterized the movement of international real estate capital flows that have traditionally been drawn to high-profile "trophy" properties.

Finally, new warehouse construction has been constrained by the fact that the available land for optimally located warehouse space is limited. Much of the properties zoned for industrial use, especially in major metropolitan areas, has been devoted to existing industrial uses for some time, and these areas have experienced pressures to move to higher uses. In areas where land is available, construction has favored R&D/office properties.

In summary, supply and demand tend to balance in the warehouse sector largely because of the absence of the distorting influences in the capital markets that have led to overbuilding in the other property sectors. Real estate market forces, rather than distortion in the capital markets, have historically tended to govern the investment performance of warehouse/distribution properties.

Will this continue to be the case? The answer is probably yes. Warehouse properties will continue to offer only limited opportunities for attractive returns on speculative new construction. Banks are not likely to step up to finance much new construction in the near future, and foreign investors are not likely to pour money into the industrial sector for some time to come. Institutional investors, attracted to warehouse/distribution investment by the properties' steady return history, may increase the rate of their investment, and this increased availability of capital for warehouses could keep warehouse yields down. But the fundamental supply-demand balance in the leasing markets should continue to generate steady current yields and attractive total returns in the warehouse sector relative to other property sectors throughout the 1990s.

PERFORMANCE CHARACTERISTICS

The relative responsiveness of supply and demand for warehouse space at the property level leads directly to the steady, stable performance of warehouse properties' investment returns. Intuitively, one would expect this result. If supply responds to increasing tenant demand, as manifested in rising rents and falling vacancies, or in decreasing tenant demand, as reflected in declining rents and increased vacancies, investment returns should not be distorted by excessive overbuilding. In fact, warehouse returns have historically performed pretty much as expected.

Historical Risk-Return Characteristics

According to data collected nationwide from institutional real estate investors by Frank Russell Co. and the National Council of Real Estate Investment Fiduciaries (NCREIF), warehouse/distribution properties have recorded an above-average performance record among all types of real estate over the 15-year period from 1978 through 1992. As shown in Exhibit 9–3, total returns have been above average for all real estate, current yields have been relatively high, and returns and have been steady. Above-average total returns, above-average current yields, and low volatility are now considered hallmarks of warehouse investments. One other characteristic of warehouse properties, particularly small and intermediate-size properties, became apparent during the real estate recession of the early 1990s: Warehouse property investments are also relatively liquid. In part

EXHIBIT 9–3
Historical Property Performance, 1978–92

	Total Returns					
Property Type	15-Year Return	10-Year Return	5-Year Return	3-Year Return	5-Year Current Income	10-Year Standard Deviation
Warehouse	9.6%	7.0%	3.0%	−1.3%	7.4%	6.2%
Total index	8.6%	5.0%	0.6%	−3.3%	7.0%	6.6%
R&D/office	9.1	5.6	−0.4	−4.6	7.8	8.8
Office	7.4	1.9	−3.5	−7.8	6.7	8.1
Retail	9.6	9.0	4.9	0.4	6.7	6.7
Apartment	N/A	N/A	3.7	1.8	7.4	N/A

Sources: Russell/NCREIF Property Index; Grubb & Ellis Realty Advisers, Inc.

because the average size of a warehouse investment is small, the investment market has greater depth than other property types. A wide range of prospective investors can afford to participate.

The Russell/NCREIF Property Index (RNPI), which tracks (as of December 31, 1992) the real estate returns for 1,738 properties held by the nation's largest institutional investors, valued at $22.9 billion, shows warehouse performance to be above average for all real estate and over all time periods. As of December 31, 1992, the 10-year return for warehouses was 200 basis points above the average return for all properties. The seven-year, six-year, five-year, four-year, three-year, and two-year returns average approximately 250 basis points above the average. Part of this difference can be attributed to the very poor performance of the office sector, which has recently tended to pull the entire index down. But the warehouse sector shows consistently above-average returns for all time periods since the inception of the Russell/NCREIF series. Over the 15-year period, warehouses have outperformed all other property types.

Current yields are also considerably above the average for all real estate. Over all time periods, from 15-year to 5-year returns, the current income return is typically 30 to 50 basis points above the index for all real estate. Because the development of warehouses is closely tied to demand, there is generally less fluctuation in vacancy levels than for other property types. This is because there is less threat to the income flow from warehouse properties due to excess supply. As a result, the current yield on investment in warehouse properties has exceeded the average for all real estate and has been highly consistent.

Low volatility—the investment characteristic that can bring consistency, stability, and balance to real estate portfolio performance—is also evident in the Russell/NCREIF data. By one measure of the steadiness of returns, the comparison of the standard deviations for several historical series of returns, warehouse returns are less volatile than the returns for all other real estate categories combined. Only retail properties have historically offered similar benefits. Even in the current real estate downturn, which has been characterized by substantial write-downs in value and declining income returns for all properties, warehouses have performed relatively well compared to other property types. This means warehouse properties should generate relatively attractive returns year after year throughout an investment cycle. More stable returns are, by definition, less cyclical. Less cyclical investment performance gives investors the luxury of not having to worry about timing their decisions to enter the market.

Exhibit 9–3 shows the trends in annualized weighted rates of return for five types of investment properties and for the entire RNPI for the 15-year period 1978 through 1992. Three-year overall returns and five-year current income returns are also shown.

A further advantage of the stability of warehouse returns is that warehouses should offer a more predictable inflation hedge than other property types within the real estate category. Although real estate's inflation-hedging potential has perhaps been oversold and is of marginal concern in today's economic environment, the available data do suggest that warehouses should offer long-term inflation-hedging capabilities. Exhibits 9–4 and 9–5 detail the ability of warehouse lease rates to track inflation during periods of high and low inflation. The correlation suggests that warehouse returns should continue to offer effective hedging abilities. Other property types are more subject to cycles (e.g., apartment, office, R&D) so an investor may find that such properties will not be well positioned to pass on inflation because of high vacancies or slack demand depressing rental increases. In such property sectors, rent growth and inflation can become "decoupled," and the ability of real estate to act as an inflation hedge can be lost. While warehouse properties are not immune to economic

EXHIBIT 9–4

Rent Increases during High Inflation (Average for Industrial Properties, 1970–80)

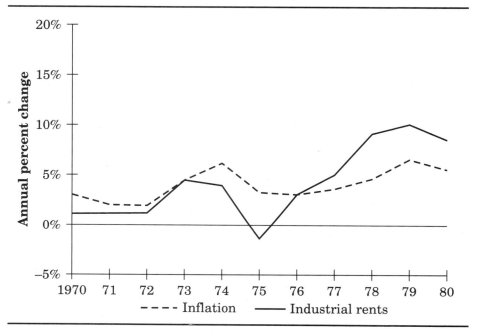

Sources: U.S. Department of Labor: Grubb & Ellis Realty Advisers, Inc.

slowdowns, they are much less attractive as speculative developments and thus are less susceptible to the boom and bust cycles of other categories of real estate, which degrade their capability to hedge inflation.

Correlations among returns from different property types also show warehouse returns to be the least correlated to any of the other real estate categories tracked in the index. That is, fluctuations between industrial property returns and the returns of other property sectors do not move entirely in step. Warehouses represent a broader exposure to the general economy than any other type of real estate. Warehouses tap into nearly all sectors of the economy, including retail, manufacturing, and services, while other property types are more concentrated in their exposure. Thus, the pattern of returns for

EXHIBIT 9–5
Rent Increases during Low Inflation (Average for Industrial Properties, 1980–90)

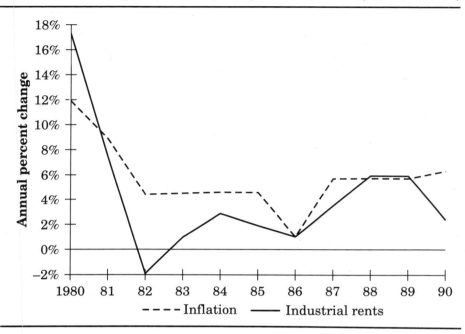

Sources: U.S. Department of Labor: Grubb & Ellis Realty Advisers, Inc.

warehouses are dependent on a more diversified base of demand. Correlations among property returns show warehouses to be a very good diversifier in the context of a portfolio of properties. Exhibit 9–6 indicates the pattern of correlations based on returns of the 1982–92 period. The strongest correlation is with shopping centers and R&D properties, two related categories in terms of user demand. Yet warehouses show very limited correlation with other categories of real estate and have the lowest overall correlation to other real estate categories of any other property type. Overall, warehouses act as a balance to other types of real estate in a portfolio. For this reason, warehouses can be considered a core holding in any real estate portfolio. Industrial properties can not only add stability and consistency to portfolio performance but also dampen the cyclical movements of the core real estate portfolio.

EXHIBIT 9–6
Historical Correlations among Property Returns, 1982–92

	Warehouse	Office	Retail	R&D	Apartment
Warehouse	1.00	—	—	—	—
Office	.15	1.00	—	—	—
Retail	.40	.25	1.00	—	—
R&D	.30	.60	.15	1.00	—
Apartment*	.10	.30	.50	.20	1.00

* Apartment correlations are for the period 1989–92.

Sources: Russell/NCREIF Property Index; Grubb & Ellis Realty Advisers, Inc.

Prospective Risk-Return Estimates

Demand for warehouse space declined in 1991 and 1992, and warehouse vacancies rose. As expected, new speculative construction virtually stopped to allow the oversupply to be absorbed. The markets are not nearly as overbuilt as other property sectors, however, and supply will continue to be significantly constrained over the next five years, even if economic growth returns to normal, due to capital constraints. As demand grows, vacancy rates should decline within the existing base of distribution space. Exhibit 9–7 details trends in available distribution space from 1970 forecast to 1995. Vacancy rates have declined since the recession-related highs of the early 1980s as demand picked up with general economic growth. The 1991–92 recession resulted in an increase in vacancies due to reduced demand. Most of the vacancies occurred in noncentral locations as areas with marginal demand experienced greater contraction in their local economy. As the economy recovers, vacancies should decline through 1995.

Under any set of inflationary conditions, declining vacancies should translate into stable to improving rents as tenants compete for a shrinking range of available options. Exhibit 9–8 shows the change in U.S. average lease rates for distribution space from 1975 forecast through 1995. Reflecting trends in the balance between supply and demand, lease rates experienced weaknesses during both the 1981–82 and 1991–92 recessions. As the economy improved following

EXHIBIT 9–7
National Vacancy Rate in Warehouses, 1970 Forecast to 1995

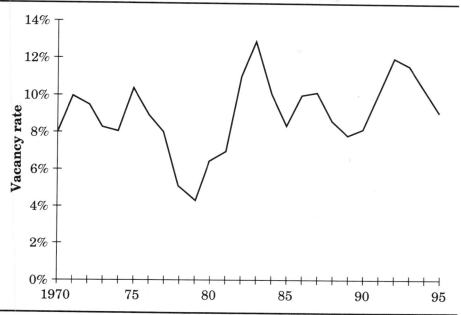

Sources: Grubb & Ellis Co.; Grubb & Ellis Realty Advisers, Inc.

1982, rental increases accelerated as demand picked up and vacancies were worked down. Looking forward, we expect a similar pattern of events to unfold in the next two to four years. As the economy returns to stable growth, rents should increase.

Because warehouse rents are historically low relative to other land use categories, we do not expect rising rents to stimulate significant new construction. Land prices have not declined sufficiently to generate an attractive return on cost and make the development of distribution space feasible at current lease rates. When land prices decline enough to justify development, markets will be well supplied and competition among competing properties for tenants will depress rent increases and increase leasing risk. These conditions exist today in many outlying areas (with a surplus of available land) that have low potential for rental growth. Conversely, there should be ample

EXHIBIT 9–8
Inflation and Industrial Rents (National Average)

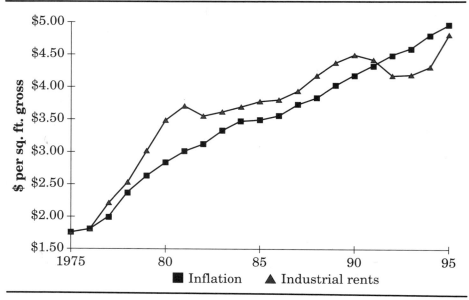

Sources: Grubb & Ellis Co.; Grubb & Ellis Realty Advisers, Inc.

opportunity for rental appreciation in those warehouse markets with good transportation linkages near major metropolitan areas with developed local economies. In many of these markets, lease rates can rise substantially before current land prices provide attractive rent-cost spreads.

Summary

Warehouse properties are currently well positioned for new investment, although the availability of institutional capital for this asset class may tend to keep capitalization rates and total yields low. Among all real estate sectors, warehouse properties have shown the best balance between construction and demand, with the consequence being relatively stable growth in rents. Essentially, the only disruptions to stable rent growth have come from the changes in the growth rate of the domestic economy. In this respect, warehouse properties are not unlike most other investment assets in drawing their fortune from the general economy. Particularly important, however, is the fact that warehouse properties have proven to be less susceptible to the excesses that have been characteristic of certain other real estate sectors.

DEREGULATION AND TECHNOLOGICAL CHANGE

Warehouse properties serve several basic economic functions involving the storage and distribution of goods. The central factors influencing demand for space are the amount of inventory needed at a given place at any given time and the most efficient mode of transportation among given locations. Over the last 15 years, several forces have altered the way inventories are managed and moved.

One major influence on this process has been the deregulation of many of the transportation services industries. As a result of deregulation, a shift has occurred in the relative fortunes of rail, water, air, and truck transportation, with truck and air transport emerging as increasingly important modes of transportation and the nature and range of transportation services undergoing fundamental changes.

Another factor is the impact of technological change, particularly the effects of computerized inventory control systems, bar code and laser-based management systems, and robotics, on the way inventories are managed and moved.

Deregulation: The Decline of Rail and Water and the Growth of Trucking and Air Transport

As Exhibit 9–9 suggests, the 1980s witnessed the decline of rail and water as preferred modes of transportation. Rail has suffered the most dramatic depression in both employment and cargo demand. Inland domestic river and lake shipping has been stagnant or declining, although international shipping (excluding oil) offers one bright spot. Some ports, such as Los Angeles–Long Beach, have seen increasing activity, much of it due to increased Pacific Rim trade. But overall, employment in the water transport and rail transportation sectors has continued to shrink at a rate of almost 2 and 4 percent per year, respectively, over the last decade.

In contrast, growth in the trucking, freight forwarding, and air cargo industries has been phenomenal. Since the beginning of the

EXHIBIT 9–9
Changing Modes of Transportation: Annual Employment Growth of Transportation

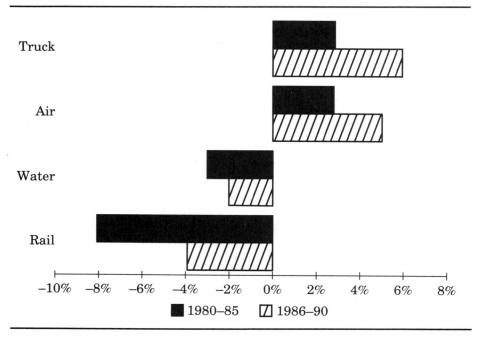

Sources: U.S. Department of Labor; Grubb & Ellis Realty Advisers, Inc.

1980s, employment in trucking and air has grown at an annual average of almost 5 percent, outpacing employment growth in the more highly touted high-tech and service-related industries. Moreover, as Exhibit 9–9 shows, the rate of growth increased at the end of the decade. Air cargo and express package shipments are the strongest-growing areas of the business. International air cargo is also an important growing segment. Trucking shipments increased more than 6 percent per year over the five years ending in 1990.

Trucking and air transportation, where the most dramatic growth in employment has occurred, cater to high-margin goods. High-margin goods are favored by merchant wholesalers, which account for the greatest proportion of speculative warehouse demand.

Bulk goods and heavier equipment are more typically handled by ship or rail. Captive operations are generally vertically integrated to achieve cost savings. These operations are more often found in the bulk goods, heavy materials, and equipment sectors.

The juxtaposition of these two trends—the incredible growth in trucking and air transportation, supported by the high-margin wholesale goods trade, and the stagnation and shrinkage of water and rail transport that is oriented toward the high-bulk, low-margin goods and equipment distribution sector—has important implications for investors in warehouse properties. The best opportunities for investment in the warehouse sector are in warehouse/distribution properties catering to the merchant wholesale trade and served by air and truck transportation.

A second implication is that these opportunities will be focused on key distribution corridors used by the trucking and air transport industry. From the standpoint of demand for warehouse space, trucking and air transportation place greater emphasis on certain types of locations and properties. Business parks with easy truck access to freeways are the most obvious attractive location, but also important may be internodal locations. "Piggyback" truck-rail shipping is a growing segment, with warehouse locations well placed for rail-freeway connections. Air-truck transfer locations are also driving demand for warehouse space in and around many airports. Not all airports will benefit. Those airports not in a major regional hub or serving as an international transfer point are less likely to see growth in air cargo traffic.

A third implication of deregulation and the emergence of trucking and air transport is a tendency toward more frequent ordering. Deregulation of shipping rates and more flexibility in licensing carriers has led to greater competition among providers and a willingness to customize services to each shipper's needs. On the side of the customer, several forces have changed the way goods are stored and shipped. A significant factor has been the expense of inventory carrying costs. These costs have motivated manufacturers, retailers, and wholesalers to minimize carried inventory and order more often and in smaller quantities. Deregulation and rate competition among transportation service companies have allowed the cost equation to favor more frequent ordering. A corollary to more frequent ordering is a decline in the need for large storage spaces.

Just-in-Time Systems: Technology and Inventory Obsolescence

At the same time deregulation opened up distribution markets to wider competition and the introduction of new services, the computer revolution has allowed greater integration and coordination of the relationship among sales, manufacturing, and shipment. Computerized inventory management systems provide greater control over existing inventory and greater precision in the quantities ordered from suppliers in relation to requirements. Wholesalers can operate from multiple locations and a common inventory management system to locate bulk versus small-package inventories efficiently with respect to transportation modes and storage costs. Automated entry systems link customers and suppliers electronically for fast-response order filling. Satellite technology has aided in the tracking and routing of transportation services.

These changes are creating a different distribution system than that which existed in the past. No longer is a strict hierarchical system required in which regional bulk centers feed subregional centers, which in turn feed end-point customers. Computers and customized shipping allow a variety of inventories to be assembled for final distribution to customer outlets directly from local staging areas. Large-scale, bulk, high-cube warehouse buildings are becoming less important. Smaller buildings located close in to major distribution centers, air transport hubs, and international transfer points are becoming more important.

The changes in transport and computerized inventory management systems that began in the 1980s will continue throughout the 1990s. These changes may favor small and medium-size warehouse properties strategically placed near air and trucking distribution points and catering to the high-margin wholesale trade.

TARGETING INVESTMENT MARKETS

The recession of the early 1990s was far more regionalized than previously experienced; the economy was (and still is) marked by major extremes in regional economic activity. Similarly, even before the current recession began, when the general economy was growing, many areas were experiencing decline. As the national economy recovers, many areas may remain depressed for some time. Real estate construction cycles have varied considerably across markets as well as for different types of property within markets, and the differences are likely to persist. Therefore, a disciplined, continually updated approach to targeting and selecting markets for investment is required.

Close-in staging areas within warehouse markets seem to be favored by the shifting distribution economics in the 1990s. But because of widely different real estate returns among urban areas across the country, investors will still need to know which markets will be most favorably positioned to benefit from these trends. By the proper selection of geographic markets, risks, and return potential can be balanced and spread across an industrial portfolio.

What is needed is a systematic approach to tracking and targeting the nation's top warehouse markets.

A Systematic Approach

Periodically—say, every six months—investors and/or their advisors should analyze and rank the industrial markets with particular reference to wholesale trade, trucking services, air and cargo activity, warehouse construction, vacancy, absorption, leasing activity, and rental trends. The analysis is best prepared using transaction-based data (the data for the analysis described here were collected by over 100 researchers in more than 50 of Grubb & Ellis' commercial real estate offices nationwide and from other sources). Such an approach seeks to identify markets with the greatest potential for rental appreciation and total return given average capitalization rates and vacancy patterns. It also attempts to identify low-risk markets and to incorporate factors related to economic diversification and the balance or imbalance between supply and demand.

An example of a systematic approach is the following analysis, which is based on a model of market risks and potential returns for each of more than 50 major metropolitan markets. Estimates of total returns are adjusted to reflect these risks so that a final risk-adjusted total return is calculated. This risk-adjusted return is then used to rank and select targeted markets.

The top metropolitan areas are then selected for further analysis of submarkets. Within each area are a number of different microeconomies with different rates of growth and varying importance to the overall strength of the metropolitan economy. These microeconomies are defined by transportation networks, local employers, housing patterns, population growth, access to other markets, and relationships to the centers of finance and administration.

The complexity of the analysis can vary. What is important is that the analysis be systematic, consistent, and periodically updated. The factors that we believe should be considered in selecting targeted markets are outlined next.

The Importance of Infrastructure

Critical to real estate is the quality of infrastructure resources. The age and condition of roads, power grids, water, and sewage capacity all contribute to the health of a local economy and therefore the health of a real estate market. Such infrastructure investments vary widely among communities owing to the history of development in different areas, the wealth of the tax base, and the shifting fortunes of local land use planning initiatives. As a result, certain areas are blessed with an abundance of resources, while other areas have met severe capacity constraints. Such differences are often idiosyncratic and cannot be explained by simple urban-suburban distinctions.

The condition and quality of the country's infrastructure resources in many communities is in serious decline. Over the last decade, government spending for infrastructure has been less than half the rate of depreciation of public infrastructure. This has occurred even in communities where the local economy is undergoing historically accelerated growth. The backlog in unfunded improvements will be carried over to a time when governments at all levels will face rising deficits and declining tax revenues from slower economic growth.

Some governments will find themselves with fewer resources to replace decaying infrastructure at the very time new infrastructure investment will be critical. They will be embroiled in a catch-22 situation: Slow economic growth will impede government's ability to modernize infrastructure, and decaying infrastructure will impede further economic growth.

Two consequences can be foreseen. First, infrastructure expenditures will be increasingly privatized, often in the form of developer fees, making new development more expensive and more the province of well-capitalized developers. Fewer projects will be built as the burden of developer fees drives the cost of developing new properties up and the returns on investment down. Second, infrastructure will become an increasingly scarce commodity. Those communities or metropolitan areas well endowed with infrastructure from past investments or current wealth in tax revenues and bonding capacity will be more favored as sites of future economic growth. Such communities may also be in a position to use political or land use planning constraints to limit growth or place increasingly heavy burdens on the developers or owner of real estate.

The cumulative effect of higher development costs, fewer locations with good infrastructure, and more burdensome planning requirements will be to further limit supply of new warehouse space. The resulting constraints on supply will support rents and returns on existing real estate investments.

The implications for warehouse investment are clear. Market areas with deteriorating infrastructure and local governments with weak financial capacity should be avoided. Markets with new infrastructure or the capacity to rebuild aging infrastructure should be favored.

A Framework for Assessing Market Risks and Returns

We have already discussed the framework for evaluating and selecting targeted geographic markets. The process of targeting investment markets should be based on an analysis of the factors that contribute to the market risks and potential returns of each local economy. Again, it is important that this process be systematic.

Selecting Markets Based on Local Economies' Strengths and Diversification

Not every major city will offer the same economic base to support warehouse investment returns and reduce risk. Markets could be selected, for example, by (1) ranking markets for specific supply-demand criteria, such as leasing activity, absorption, new construction, vacancy, estimated years of supply, and so on; (2) selecting markets that are well diversified; (3) identifying pricing opportunities; and (4) ranking each market by prevailing rent growth rates, capitalization rates, and changes in the consumer price index. In the warehouse sector, an analysis like this can help identify and rank the top 10 to 15 warehouse markets that present the best risk-adjusted warehouse investment opportunities.

The analysis is based on an estimation of market risks and potential returns for each of the major metropolitan markets. The approach seeks to identify those markets with the greatest potential for rental appreciation and total return given average capitalization rates and vacancy patterns. At the same time, an attempt is made to identify low-risk markets and incorporate factors related to economic diversification and macro balances or imbalances between supply and demand. Factors considered in estimating market risks and potential returns are listed in Exhibit 9–10. Estimates of total returns are adjusted to reflect these risks so that a final risk-adjusted total return can be calculated. This risk-adjusted return can be used to rank and then select targeted markets.

Where will this process lead? In the warehouse sector, a geographically diversified portfolio will include investments in the nation's three major warehouse distribution markets: on the East Coast in northern and central New Jersey, in the central Midwest region in the Chicago market, and on the West Coast in the metro areas surrounding Los Angeles. Up to 50 percent of the portfolio might be represented in these markets, with the balance parceled out to other distribution centers such as Baltimore, Washington, DC, and Philadelphia in the East; Atlanta in the South; selected Ohio cities in the Midwest; Dallas and Houston in the Southwest; and Seattle, San Francisco, Sacramento, and San Diego in the West.

Factors Contributing to Market Risk

Understanding market risk requires careful evaluation of each of the factors identified in Exhibit 9–10.

Growth in Demand. Long-term growth in demand is studied by looking at past trends in employment and population growth, together with projections based on expectations for trade and regional importance in serving wholesale trade in surrounding areas. An estimate of relative growth over the next three years is formed for each market based on a common assumption of national growth.

Availability of Supply. The supply of warehouse properties is assessed by measuring current trends in construction relative to

EXHIBIT 9–10
Market Risks and Return

Market Risk	Potential Returns
Assess long-term growth in demand: Growth in employment and population Growth in trade Regional importance	**Supply constraints:** Regulatory environment Barriers to new construction Land use profile
Assess availability of supply: Growth in construction Current speculative vacancies Planned construction	**Projected lease rates:** Lease rates catch up Land price increases Market balance
Determine market balance: Equilibrium vacancy rate Years of supply Relative balance	**Property pricing:** Current capitalization rate Availability Price per square foot
Economic diversification and resiliency: Industry composition Economic volatility Firm concentration Incidence of business formation	**Potential return:** Current income and appreciation Risk-adjusted return

Source: Grubb & Ellis Realty Advisers, Inc.

absorption. Current vacancies, together with planned construction, are monitored to assess the potential growth rate in new construction.

Market Balance. Current conditions of available supply are compared with expected growth to determine market balance. The equilibrium vacancy rate is assessed by historical analysis of how vacancy rates have affected rent increases. The equilibrium rate is that rate that allows rents to keep pace with inflation. The length of time needed to reach equilibrium given current supply is calculated.

Diversification and Resiliency. Vulnerability to economic shocks can be minimized by identifying local economies that are well diversified and dependent on industries that have the best chances of weathering and adjusting to downturns. Each market is examined to assess the size and composition of the potential tenant base for warehouse properties.

Screening Markets for Low Risk.   These factors are combined into a summary measure of relative market risk. Markets with greater economic diversification and resiliency to economic shocks, together with limited prospects for increased competition from current or new supply, are identified as having lower risk.

Factors Contributing to Potential Returns

As with market risk, understanding an individual market's return potential requires close examination of the relevant factors.

Supply Constraints.   The presence or absence of regulatory controls on new construction, along with the degree to which the availability of land for new development limits expansion, is assessed. To the extent that barriers to new supply exist, markets are rated as having a higher potential for inflation in lease rates.

Projected Lease Rates.   Growth in rents is forecast by using long-term inflation in rents and estimating the stage of the rent cycle within each market. Supply constraints, low current vacancies, and trends in prices for industrially zoned land are examined to forecast relative rent growth.

Pricing Trends.   The average going-in cash-on-cash return is surveyed from relevant market transactions to develop an estimate of capitalization rate yields. This information is reconciled with price data on a square foot basis.

Potential Returns.   Using capitalization rates and estimated rental growth, pro forma total returns are calculated on an unleveraged, before-tax basis. Average rent growths are plotted against going-in yields, or capitalization rates, for all markets, and the resulting trade-offs are analyzed to identify markets with the most favorable growth-adjusted capitalization rates. For each level of expected rent growth, certain markets offer higher going-in yields. When adjusted for market risk, this analysis can indicate where favorable pricing opportunities may exist.

Risk-Adjusted Returns.   Finally, total return estimates are adjusted up or down to reflect relative risk of the market. The result is an estimate of risk-adjusted total return that measures the relative attractiveness of markets on a common footing.

Identifying Local Industrial Submarkets

Within each selected metropolitan area are microeconomies with different rates of growth, each having varying importance to the overall strength of the metropolitan economy. These microeconomies are defined by transportation networks, local employers, housing patterns and population growth, access to other markets, and relationship to the center of finance and administration. Each of these areas is analyzed to identify those that have characteristics of the warehouse opportunities listed in Exhibit 9–10.

Targeting Property Types

Because of the submarkets chosen, certain property types may be ruled out as possible investments. For example, bulk warehouses suitable for high-volume, single-tenant users are not likely to be found in these submarkets, primarily because these properties are cost sensitive and therefore seek the lower land costs of outlying areas. Larger suburban warehouse parks are also less evident. Because of the nature of tenant demand, properties will most often be multitenant, smaller facilities, usually less than 300,000 square feet.

These submarkets tend to have a large proportion of the properties previously identified as representing the small, freestanding warehouse subsector:

- Multitenanted, seasoned properties.
- Well located, with freeway access.
- 50,000 to 300,000 square feet in size.
- Less than 25 percent office buildout.
- Not more than 20 years from year of construction or rehabilitation.

All of the submarkets represent at least a third of the overall market within each of the top 10 metropolitan areas. In many markets, these submarkets comprise as much as 65 to 70 percent of the total market. Due to their sheer size and diversity of ownership, these submarkets offer an ample supply of investment grade opportunities.

APPLYING PORTFOLIO MANAGEMENT TOOLS TO A WAREHOUSE PORTFOLIO

Institutions have long accepted the role portfolio management techniques can play in diversifying the risks associated with traditional stock and bond asset classes. As more fund sponsors have invested in real estate, they have also begun to ask how to apply portfolio management techniques to insulate their real estate investments from market risks. Past experiences with real estate holdings in boom and bust markets, concerns about overbuilding, and the declining value of many real estate assets during the current recession have highlighted the importance of controlling and diversifying market risks in real estate.

Risk control techniques applied to real estate have traditionally involved simply ensuring that not all investments were exposed to the same geographic market. But scattering investments geographically will not always minimize risks. Geographic diversification can, in some circumstances, increase risks and reduce returns because of inefficient combinations of markets and the increased management costs associated with excessive geographical dispersion. A preferable portfolio risk management approach would balance the need to achieve stated performance objectives with the need to minimize, manage, and spread real estate risks across each portfolio and over time. This balancing exercise must take place within the practical constraints imposed by asset size and management costs.

Risk control is often seen as an "up front" decision-making process. Markets are chosen according to a plan for diversification when properties are acquired. Investors frequently forget that portfolio risk management techniques can also be built into the asset management process. Decisions as to tenant mix, tenant credit, and lease structures can mitigate market risks. Even if all properties within a portfolio are in diversified geographic markets but all tenants are in the same or similar industries, the portfolio will still be subject to considerable risk. Diversification and active management go hand in hand not only up front in the acquisition phase but also during the asset management phase and at the time of property disposition.

A transaction-driven portfolio—that is, a portfolio of properties assembled over time because each individual investment seemed to represent a "good deal" at the time—is not likely to lend itself to effective portfolio management techniques. Properties may not represent similar real estate risks, tenancies may not be comparable, properties may vary widely in size or other building characteristics, and properties may be located in diverse markets where management skills are thinly spread. Individual investments or tenancies may be too big to allow risk spreading among markets or sectors or to permit much flexibility in allocating management resources to markets or properties.

However, carefully assembled portfolios may lend themselves to rudimentary portfolio management techniques. For example, including a portfolio of small, close-in warehouse properties in a larger, balanced portfolio provides an opportunity to apply risk management techniques to spread and minimize real estate risks on a portfolio-wide basis. The relatively small size of individual buildings permits risks to be easily spread among geographic markets and industry sectors. While smaller properties have certain diseconomies of scale, these can be minimized by concentrating these investments and management resources in favored markets. Since the small-warehouse subsector consists of essentially similar properties, comparisons among tenancies on a portfoliowide basis can be meaningful. Risks can be minimized and long-term risk-adjusted yields enhanced in both the acquisition and asset management phases of the portfolio's holding period.

Risks can be mitigated by:

1. Selecting markets that are geographically diversified.
2. Selecting markets whose local economies are themselves strong and diversified. Not all local economies are as strong or as balanced as others.
3. Selecting markets that are resistant to economic shocks or are highly cyclical or volatile. This process can help minimize the adverse effects on the local economy of, for example, changes in oil prices, interest rates, or defense spending.
4. Managing tenant selection, on a portfoliowide basis, to spread the portfolio's tenant base across a broad range of industries.

5. Managing tenant selection, on a portfoliowide basis, to avoid concentrations in cyclical or volatile industries, such as defense or real estate.

6. Managing tenancy expirations, on a portfoliowide basis, to spread leasing risks and projected vacancies over time so that tenancy turnover will not substantially and adversely affect returns in any one year.

7. Timing any redevelopment or expansion programs to spread development and lease-up risks across the portfolio and over time.

Many of these techniques are often applied to real estate portfolios in an incomplete and unplanned way.

Markets and Sectors Resistant to Economic Shocks and Cycles

Markets can also be characterized by their vulnerability to economic shocks and cycles. Industries can be grouped and ranked according to their relative sensitivity to national cycles and fundamental economic shocks such as:

- Changes in the value of the dollar.
- Energy-related prices.
- Commodity-related prices (excluding energy).
- Defense expenditures.
- Interest rates.
- Changes in GDP.
- International conditions.

Industry categories can be separated into two groups according to whether they exhibit high or low sensitivity to these economic factors. Highly vulnerable industries might include heavy manufacturing, construction and real estate, mining and petroleum, chemicals, and defense technology. On the other hand, industries showing greater resilience to economic shocks could include utilities, transportation, finance, communications, insurance, health and education, and the federal, state, and local governments. This categorization can be a useful guide in both selecting geographic markets and evaluating optimal tenant mixes across a portfolio.

Geographic markets whose industry mix might emphasize one or more of the highly vulnerable industries might be given lower weight in the portfolio unless there are mitigating circumstances. Markets with concentrations in industries with greater resiliency can be given higher allocations of portfolio value.

Exhibit 9–11 can be a useful guide in both selecting geographic markets and evaluating optimal tenant mixes across a portfolio. For example, major metropolitan markets that might currently be considered more or less vulnerable or resistant to these economic shocks are shown in Exhibit 9–12.

Markets whose industry mix may be skewed toward one or more of the highly vulnerable industries might be given lower weight in the portfolio unless there are mitigating circumstances from an asset management perspective. Markets with concentrations in industries with greater resiliency can be given high allocations of portfolio value. Larger markets having such mixes might be permitted to have a higher weight owing to the greater diversification they provide. To the extent that a core set of diversified markets comprises a greater amount of portfolio value, special exposures may be taken on in markets considered more vulnerable, which may enhance returns. Tilting allocations to markets to minimize cyclical correlations can add further value to portfolio returns.

EXHIBIT 9–11
Industry Sensitivity to Economic Shocks

Highly Vulnerable	*More Resilient*
Heavy manufacturing	Utilities
Construction, real estate	Transportation
Mining, petroleum	Finance
Consumer goods	High technology
Chemicals	Communications
Defense technology	Insurance
Tourism	Health and education
Wholesale/retail trade	Federal government
	State and local governments

Source: Grubb & Ellis Realty Advisers, Inc.

EXHIBIT 9-12
Economic Exposures

	Geographic Market
Vulnerable industries:	
Aerospace	Atlanta, Los Angeles, Orange County, Orlando, San Diego, San Jose, Seattle
Durable manufacturing	Cleveland, Chicago, Baltimore, Philadelphia
Construction	Orlando, Washington, DC, Sacramento, San Diego, Orange County
Motor vehicles	Atlanta, Chicago, Columbus, Philadelphia
Defense	Boston, Los Angeles, Orange County, Orlando, San Jose, San Diego, Seattle, Washington, DC
Tourism	Orlando, Orange County, San Francisco
Resilient industries:	
Transportation/utilities	Atlanta, northern New Jersey, San Francisco, Seattle
Finance/insurance	San Francisco, Cleveland, Columbus, Boston, Chicago
Trade	Northern New Jersey, Atlanta, Orlando, Chicago, Sacramento
Government	Washington, DC, Baltimore, Columbus, Sacramento, San Francisco
Health/education	Baltimore, Boston, Cleveland, Columbus, San Francisco
Civilian technology	Boston, Los Angeles, northern New Jersey, Seattle, San Jose, San Diego

Source: Grubb & Ellis Realty Advisers, Inc.

Industry concentrations within the portfolio's tenant base can also be examined to control the sensitivity of the portfolio to external shocks, depending on the size of the portfolio and the tenants' exposure to resilient or vulnerable industries.

Portfoliowide Tenant Selection

In the asset management phase, the screening and selection of tenants can help minimize and spread economic exposure to weak industries and favor tenants in sectors in strong or emerging industries on a portfoliowide basis. The tenants in all properties in a portfolio can be classified by the Standard Industrial Classification (SIC) code to uncover portfoliowide exposures to key industries. High percentage concentrations of a portfolio's tenant base in any one economic sector can be tracked and adjusted as required when leases expire. Industry concentrations within the portfolio's tenant base can also be examined to control the sensitivity of the portfolio to external shocks, depending on the size of the portfolio and the tenants' exposure to the resilient or vulnerable industries described above.

Portfoliowide Tenant Expirations

It is common in—and essential to—effective property management to track lease maturities for each property. It is less common, but equally important, to track lease maturities across an entire portfolio. Spreading the leasing risk in a portfolio over longer time periods so that tenancy expirations are less than 20 percent in any one year (with the actual incidence of nonrenewing tenants being much lower) can considerably reduce rollover risk on a portfoliowide basis.

Spreading Development Risks

Portfolio managers can be guided by these techniques in the timing and implementation of value-enhancing strategies. Renovations, re-structuring, and expansions should be done to the extent that this will lead, on a cost-justified basis, to a better market position. Initial lease-up can be timed during periods of low projected lease rollover. Understanding the trade-offs among properties within the portfolio can do much to enhance the stability of income and the probability of increasing cash flows.

Systematic risk control policies can be effective in adding value. A laundry list approach to risk spreading can create the appearance of a well-diversified portfolio, but in reality may involve underlying market uncertainties and reduce management efficiency. Targeting property types and markets with known risk-return characteristics, diversifying unwanted economic exposures, planning to minimize cy-clicity, and adding value through active management are the corner-stones of effective portfolio risk control.

CONCLUSION

A historical review of investment performance shows that warehouse properties have outperformed the average real estate investment over the last decade. Given the factors that influence the market, the prospect is for above-average performance to continue into the 1990s.

Market health is in part due to the fact that institutional capital flows and unconstrained lending practices have not led to as much overbuilding as they have for other real estate categories such as shopping centers and office buildings. Limited construction has tended to keep supply and demand in better balance.

Although warehouse properties offer attractive returns and significant diversification benefits, they remain underweighted in most institutional portfolios. We believe warehouse properties should play a valuable role in enhancing performance of real estate portfolios and deserve a core allocation on a par with other principal categories of real estate properties. Accomplishing this objective is made more difficult by the typical small size of warehouse investments, but investors who follow a focused investment process, which incorporates disciplines similar to those we have outlined, should achieve their targeted allocation and expected performance.

CHAPTER 10

THE APARTMENT SECTOR

Paul Sack
The Paul Sack Properties

Gary T. Kachadurian
The RREEF Funds

WHY APARTMENTS?

Managers of institutional portfolios are giving apartments a prominent place in their real estate allocations for the 1990s for three
reasons: superior returns, diversification benefits, and inflation protection.

Superior Returns, Past and Future

As shown in Exhibit 10–1, cumulative returns from investments in
apartments have exceeded those from industrial, office, and retail
investment since 1981, although not for every period, according to the
Russell/NCREIF Property Index. A greater proportion of the returns
from apartments is also in current cash, as apartments do not face the
same onerous costs for tenant improvements and leasing commissions
that commercial properties do. For instance, 90 percent of net operating income (before depreciation) is typically distributable for
apartments versus 60 percent or less for office buildings. Moreover,
because of the forecasts for supply and demand described in the next
section, returns on apartments are expected to exceed those from
other property types by an even wider margin in the 1990s.

Important Diversification within the Real Estate Portfolio

Apartments offer several attractive forms of diversification within
the real estate portfolio compared to commercial property. First, *demand* for commercial properties is highly correlated with the business

EXHIBIT 10–1

Russell/NCREIF Index: Property-type Subindices, Cumulative Value Index, 1977–93

Year*	Total Index	Apartments	R&D/Office	Warehouse	Office	Retail
1977	100.0	100.0	100.0	00.0	100.0	100.0
1979	140.2	154.1	128.4	137.5	145.0	124.6
1981	193.1	208.0	189.8	184.0	219.6	156.0
1983	239.4	286.1	257.7	222.2	270.9	192.2
1985	298.0	357.1	327.2	281.0	330.7	249.9
1987	335.2	396.5	373.8	340.2	348.3	308.0
1989	381.1	450.5	421.9	411.3	371.8	386.0
1991	363.2	467.2	399.1	413.5	319.4	400.0
1993	349.4	537.3	371.9	396.0	271.2	412.3

* As of December 31.

Sources: National Council of Real Estate Investment Fiduciaries; calculations prepared by The RREEF Funds.

cycle. Recessions reduce demand for office space as companies cut work forces, for industrial space as real inventories decline, and for retail space as consumers spend less time in shopping centers during recessions. However, demand for apartments is based more on household growth than on economic expansion or contraction. While household growth is not immune to the effects of recession (as potential renters double up or move back with their parents), these effects are much less obvious than the reduction in demand for office and industrial space or for consumer goods. Indeed, the high interest rates that often lead to recession can actually help apartments. High interest rates reduce the ability of apartment developers to construct new competing apartment projects and make it difficult or impossible for households to leave the rental market by becoming homeowners. Apartments are not wholly immune to the business cycle but are *much* less subject to it than commercial properties.

Second, *greater tenant diversification* within each building makes apartment vacancies less "lumpy" and income streams smoother than in the case of commercial properties. For instance, a typical industrial building contains only three or four tenants, and a single tenant often occupies 25 percent or more of an office building. When these large tenants move out, a sudden high vacancy occurs in the building, even in the best of times. In contrast, an apartment building typically has 100 or more tenants, and the loss of any one tenant makes very little difference to the cash flow. None of them are large enough to command special concessions.

Third, *apartments are underweighted in present portfolios*. During the 1980s, tax-exempt investors believed they could not compete with taxable investors for apartments. They reasoned that prices included a premium for tax benefits, which had no value for tax-exempt institutions. For this reason, apartments are vastly underweighted in almost all institutional portfolios. Salomon Brothers estimates that apartments comprise approximately 35 percent of the nation's investment real estate[1] and, given the prognosis for favorable returns in the 1990s, there is no reason allocations to apartments within the real estate portfolio should not approach that figure.

Inflation Protection

Inflation protection in the portfolio is enhanced by apartments, as rents can be renegotiated annually or even more often. In times of inflation, the fact that the owner does not have to wait 3 to 10 years for rent increases, as with commercial buildings, makes it possible to achieve the same compound rate of return or IRR with an initial return (capitalization rate) that is 100 to 150 basis points lower on apartments than those on commercial properties, all other growth factors being equal.

Exhibit 10–2 shows that net operating income per square foot from apartments has generally kept up with inflation since 1975, even though inflation from 1975 to 1983 was dominated by increases in the price of oil and despite the fact that these are national figures that include the NOI disasters in Texas, Arizona, Colorado, and Florida.

SUPPLY AND DEMAND IN THE 1980s VERSUS THE 1990s

Supply

During the last half of the 1980s, oversupply dominated the apartment markets as a result of severe overbuilding from 1984 through 1987, resulting in declining rents and net operating income. (See

---

[1] Robert E. Hopkins and David Shulman, "Toward an Indexed Portfolio of Real Estate, Part II: Recent Construction" (New York: Salomon Brothers, January 1989).

EXHIBIT 10–2
Net Operating Income per Square Foot, Inflation as Measured by the Consumer Price index, and "Real" Net Operating Income per Square Foot, 1975–90

Year	NOI Amount	NOI Change	Inflation Index	Inflation Change	"Real" NOI Amount	"Real" NOI Change
1975	$1.21		53.8		$1.21	
1976	1.27	4.96%	56.9	5.76%	1.20	−0.76%
1977	1.41	11.02	60.6	6.50	1.25	4.24
1978	1.52	7.80	65.2	7.59	1.25	0.20
1979	1.66	9.21	72.6	11.35	1.23	1.92
1980	1.81	9.04	82.4	13.50	1.18	−3.93
1981	2.00	10.50	90.9	10.32	1.18	0.16
1982	2.24	12.00	96.5	6.16	1.25	5.50
1983	2.33	4.02	99.6	3.21	1.26	0.78
1984	2.44	4.72	103.9	4.32	1.26	0.39
1985	2.44	0.00	107.6	3.56	1.22	−3.44
1986	2.48	1.64	109.6	1.86	1.22	−0.22
1987	2.47	−0.40	113.6	3.65	1.17	−3.91
1988	2.62	6.07	118.3	4.14	1.19	1.86
1989	2.73	4.20	124.0	4.82	1.18	−0.59
1990	3.02	10.62	130.7	5.40	1.24	4.95
Average		6.36%		6.14%		0.22%
Standard deviation		3.91%		3.17%		2.87%
Annual growth	6.29%		6.10%		0.18%	

Sources: Richard T. Garrigan and Joseph L. Pagliari, Jr., "The Impact of Supply Changes on Real Net Operating Income: The Multi-Family Perspective," *Real Estate Issues*, 1992; *Income/Expense Analysis Conventional Apartments, 1991* (Chicago: Institute of Real Estate Management), Table 20, "Garden Buildings," p. 18; *Statistical Abstract of the United States, 1990* (Washington, DC: Bureau of the Census, 1990), Table 762, "Consumer Price Indexes," p. 471; U.S. Bureau of Labor Statistics.

"Real" NOI for 1985–89 in Exhibit 10–2.) The overbuilding was driven almost equally by tax considerations and the easy availability of generous mortgage financing. The 1990s promise to be very different. The Tax Reform Act of 1986 removed or greatly diluted the tax benefits that had overstimulated apartment syndication, and structural changes among financial institutions are very likely to make the decade one of capital shortage for all types of real estate.

During the four years from 1983 through 1986, the nation averaged 403,000 multifamily housing starts per year, or 40 percent more than the average from 1978 through 1991 of 288,000. The cumulative *excess* above the 14-year average was 460,000 units for these four years alone, or 1.6 years' total construction (see Exhibit 10–3). The predictable results were double-digit vacancies almost everywhere, declining rents, and financial distress for both lenders and borrowers.

However, the removal of tax benefits in 1986, combined with a credit crunch on construction loans, caused construction starts (for properties with five or more units) to plummet to 108,000 units by 1991. The Tax Reform Act of 1986 reduced the top marginal tax rate from 50 percent to 28 percent, proportionately reducing the value of tax write-offs; eliminated the capital gains exclusion, so that the tax at the time of sale would be at the same rate as that applied to the original deductions; lengthened depreciable lives, reducing the magnitude of any tax benefits; and, most important, made it virtually impossible for investors to offset reportable losses from investment in apartments against income from other sources. The great syndicators who had been earning enormous fees on billions of dollars' worth of new deals every year became simple property management organizations or went out of business.

EXHIBIT 10–3
New Privately Owned Multifamily Rental
Units, 1978–91 (Five Units or More)

1978	373,000
1979	303,000
1980	213,000
1981	167,000
1982	206,000
1983	350,000
1984	381,000
1985	451,000
1986	431,000
1987	305,000
1988	272,000
1989	253,000
1990	216,000
1991	108,000
1992	109,000
1993	99,000
1994 (2nd quarter)	76,000

Source: Bureau of the Census, *Construction Reports,* Series C-20, *Housing Starts.*

Economists at the University of California at Berkeley estimate that as a result of the loss of tax benefits, the construction of new apartments will not be financially feasible in most markets until rents have risen by approximately 23 percent from their 1991 levels.[2] Meanwhile, other economists have estimated that real rents may rise, on average, by 0.5 percent per annum from their pre-TRA 1986 levels through the end of this century.[3]

To produce all of those tax benefits, it had been necessary to maintain a high ratio of depreciable assets to equity investment, a feat accomplished by the use of leverage; 70 percent or more of the money was borrowed—approximately 40 percent from savings and loans, 10 percent from banks, and 12 percent from insurance companies. Clearly, the 1990s will see little money for new apartments from the savings and loan industry, which is beset with loan losses and increased capital requirements. It is also unlikely that banks or insurance companies will even match, much less increase, their lending to apartment developers in the 1990s, given the lessons of the past decade and the banks' capital requirements. Thus, the supply of new apartments is likely to be less than demand at least through 1995 and then to increase no more rapidly than demand, largely avoiding the conditions of excess supply that dominated the last half of the 1980s.

Demand

Although much has been made of the fact that demographic trends are less favorable for apartments in the 1990s than they were in the 1980s, absolute demand for rental units will increase significantly during the 1990s, albeit at a lower rate. Specifically, the Population Division of the U.S. Bureau of the Census has estimated that the population aged 15 to 24 decreased by 4.2 million persons (10.5 percent) between 1985 and 1990, reflecting the drop in births that occurred after 1962. This age group is a heavy user of rental housing. On the other hand, the Population Division has projected an increase of 1.7 million (4.2 percent) in the population aged 25 to 34 and an

[2] S. J. Maisel and J. M. Quigley, "Tax Reform and Real Estate," Working paper series, Center for Real Estate and Urban Economics, University of California at Berkeley, July 1985, p. 3.

[3] Denise DiPasquale and William C. Wheaton, "The Cost of Capital, Tax Reform and the Future of the Rental Housing Market," Working paper W89-5, Harvard University, Joint Center for Housing Studies, October 1990.

increase of 3.1 million (11.0 percent) in the population over age 64 during the same time period.[4] Both these latter populations are increasingly becoming users of rental housing, especially as the proportion of unmarried persons and nonfamily units in our society increases as reflected in the trend toward smaller households. Singles now represent one-fourth of all households, are the only growing segment, and are expected to increase by 8 million households during the 1990s, rapidly enough to represent one-third of all households by the end of the decade. Both men and women are marrying later and many not at all, significantly expanding demand for rental housing.

Moreover, the widely publicized problem of affordability makes it increasingly difficult for renters to become owners. And, as indicated earlier, the revised tax law (with some slight modifications since the passage of TRA '86) will only increase that problem. As everyone well knows, the median income household cannot qualify for a 90 percent loan to purchase a median-priced home in much of the United States.

As a result of all these factors, economists at the University of California at Berkeley estimate that annual demand for additional rental units in the United States will decline from 243,000 in the 1980s to 167,000 in the 1990s.

Conclusion

The combination of increasing demand and restricted supply should result in strong upward pressure on apartment rents as soon as the excess supply with which the industry entered the 1990s is absorbed. Absorption and rent increases will, of course, arrive at different times in different markets.

SELECTION OF TARGET MARKETS: METRO AREAS AND SUBMARKETS

For Steady Growth, Longer Holding Periods

To protect against possible localized unfavorable demographic trends and take advantage of favorable ones, investors must concentrate purchases of apartments in markets and submarkets where popula-

---

[4] Kenneth T. Rosen, *Affordable Housing: New Policies for the Housing and Mortgage Markets* (Cambridge, MA: Ballinger Publishing) p. 15; U.S. Bureau of the Census, Population Division.

tion growth is expected. There *are* entire metropolitan areas where population will decline during the 1990s, and even expanding metro areas almost always have submarkets where population is shrinking. Expanding demand is a necessary prerequisite for increasing rents.

On the supply side, it is at least equally important to seek out markets where there are political or physical constraints on supply and avoid markets—except for short-term opportunistic investments—that have been frequently overbuilt in the absence of those constraints, for instance, Houston, Dallas, Denver, Orlando, Fort Lauderdale, and Miami.

The ideal submarket is in an area where population and demand are growing but it is hard to build new units because of the lack of suitably zoned land and a political climate that is hostile to growth. It is also important that there be a significant gap between monthly rents and the monthly cost of ownership of starter housing, including condominiums. Otherwise, in times of low interest rates, demand for rental housing will decline as renters opt for home ownership.

While the reduced rate of inflation has removed the threat of rent control from most markets, investors must remain concerned about the re-emergence of pressure for rent control if the economy returns to higher rates of inflation or the shortage of apartments produces double-digit rent increases. Many investors avoid jurisdictions where more than 50 percent of the electorate are renters and/or students. It is also a good idea to secure, wherever possible, the authorizations necessary for conversion to condominiums to provide an escape route if onerous forms of rent control are enacted. Nevertheless, the very conditions that might cause rent controls to be enacted (rapid increases in apartment rents) would mean these investments had been unusually successful.

For Market Turnarounds, Shorter Holding Periods

Market conditions in the 1990s offer a possibility of unusual profits from short-term investments (two to four years) in turnaround situations. For the most part, these are the very metropolitan areas and submarkets that one would eschew for longer-term investments because of the ability and propensity of developers to overbuild. These areas were the greatest disasters of the late 1980s, with falling rents, foreclosures, and deferred maintenance piling up. Shrewd investors have monitored such markets and been alert to the economic turnarounds that have increased jobs, brought in population, and led to absorption of vacant units. Until credit becomes available for new construction (perhaps in the mid-1990s), these markets offer the prospect of increasingly high occupancy rates and increased rents and values.

However, these markets have few constraints, political or otherwise, on new construction and will become overbuilt as soon as credit is available. Investment in these markets can be highly rewarding, but requires almost continuous and careful monitoring of supply and demand so that properties can be sold before buyers recognize incipient market weakness.

Mismanaged properties also offer an attractive turnaround opportunity and can be found in both growth and turnaround markets. These properties are typically more than 10 years old and in need of refurbishing and modernization. In many cases, the needs are clear, but the work has not been done because the owner lacks the necessary capital. The combination of good management and available funds for capital improvement projects can create a very sound property in a supply-constrained market or a near-term profit in a turnaround market.

HIGH-RISE VERSUS GARDEN APARTMENTS: A MATTER OF SUPPLY AND DEMAND

Demand

In some markets, there is good acceptance of and demand for apartments in high-rise buildings. These are generally in the core cities or in dense suburban nodes of large metropolitan areas. New York, Chicago, and San Francisco are good examples. High-density, high-rise living goes hand in hand with high land costs, close proximity to jobs, transportation, and cultural amenities. Even outside of these markets, there are always some people who prefer high-rise living. The sense of security is increased, because access to the entire complex, which serves dozens or even hundreds of families, can be controlled at a single entrance and residents can go directly to their apartments from a locked garage. Also, views can be spectacular.

However, the investor needs to evaluate carefully whether a specific market has demonstrated a widespread acceptance of high-rise apartments. One or two successful high-rises amid a sea of suburban garden apartments and single-family homes are not enough.

Supply

Even if a significant number of renters seem to have accepted or even prefer high-rise living, the investor needs to consider carefully the potential for construction of additional competition. Does the area have a lot of land that is empty or is presently developed to relatively low uses and whose locations are comparable to the high-rise being considered for purchase with respect to views and access to jobs and transportation? If comparable, undeveloped land is available, there is a high probability that developers will continue to build until they have oversupplied the market; and to pay for the expensive land, developers will have to build high-density, high-rise buildings. The results will be a high level of vacancies and an inability to raise rents in proportion to the rate of inflation.

The ability of developers to oversupply the market for so-called luxury high-rises is a particular concern. Unless the appropriate land has been almost entirely built out, the high rents such buildings command will easily support the costs of new construction. Moreover, residents in such buildings can easily afford and be tempted to cease being renters and become owners of single-family homes.

CHARACTERISTICS OF A GOOD GARDEN APARTMENT PROPERTY

Location

Residential areas are best, and it is always preferable to be among lower densities. An apartment house in an area of single-family homes or duplexes is better, for instance, than one surrounded by other apartment buildings. Most apartments, however, will be near other apartments. The investor in apartments should beware of apartment "ghettos" dominated by lower-grade properties; such buildings compete on the basis of price alone and often do not achieve the rent increases of higher-quality locations.

Visibility, identification, and ease of access are important. A location on a small, hard-to-find street is a detriment. A location on a noisy, busy street or in a retail/commercial area is also undesirable.

In summary, the best locations are in close proximity to major arteries but in residential areas.

Ambiance and Amenities

The physical attractiveness and "feel" of the property as one walks through it are important. Nice landscaping, attractive architecture, and quality materials all make a property more desirable. Lakes, ponds, and waterfalls are pluses.

A building's amenity package should be competitive in its marketplace. Most garden apartment communities in many areas have a swimming pool, a hot-water whirlpool, and/or a recreation building. For more than 200 units, one might expect two pools and possibly two recreation buildings. The recreation building should include a comfortable lounge with color television, possibly one or two pool tables, a properly equipped exercise room, and saunas. A large property may include tennis courts.

What a particular property needs depends on the competition in the market and in the immediate area. Higher-density areas obviously offer little opportunity to do extensive landscaping or waterscapes. But high-density properties can nevertheless be very successful.

Unit Mix

With the trend toward single-person households and the affordability problem, demand generally seems to be strongest for one-bedroom units. On the other hand, developers like to put in as many larger units as possible, because such units are more profitable. Rents per square foot are only slightly lower (perhaps 10 percent) for two-bedroom than for one-bedroom units, but construction costs per square foot are much lower. Each unit has only one kitchen, no matter how many bedrooms, and kitchens and bathrooms are the most expensive square feet to build. Having 40 to 60 percent of the units one-bedroom or studio is, in most markets, the desirable norm, with studios being no more than half the number of one-bedroom units. If three-bedroom units are more than 10 to 15 percent of the mix, a hard look at the rental history of these units is in order.

Questions concerning the appropriateness of the unit mix can best be answered by looking at the rental history, surveying current vacancies in the market, and interviewing resident managers at the property and at competing buildings.

Layout of the Site

In high-density neighborhoods, the layout of buildings on the site is not a problem. The building will fill the site and will probably have interior hallways with apartments opening off both sides (known as *double-loaded corridors.*)

In garden apartments of lesser density, it is best that the automobile parking be separated from the landscaping and out of view from the apartments. For instance, one would want as few living rooms and decks as possible looking out over the parking lot; units are more desirable if they look out on the landscaping.

A common problem is a layout where the access to upstairs apartments is via an outside hall with windows fronting on that hall. This means people are walking past bedroom or living room windows, creating noise and requiring the residents to keep their draperies permanently drawn.

Usually tenants are willing to walk up one or two flights of stairs to their units, but anything more requires an elevator or a rent concession unless offset by an unusually attractive view.

Living room windows that look in on each other from relatively short distances are undesirable; tenants will feel they need to keep their draperies permanently drawn. Bedroom windows that face each other are less of a problem, as people spend less time in their bedrooms and will probably draw the draperies most of that time anyway.

It is important to study both the target property and its competition to determine how the layout and ambiance of the property stack up.

Parking

Ample, properly dispersed parking is very important to residents and should be carefully reviewed by the investor. Adequacy of overall parking spaces is not enough. Spaces for residents and guests must be dispersed so that a sufficient number of spaces are within a very short walk of the apartment building they serve. Residents will move out, especially in northern climates, if they cannot park within a reasonable distance of their apartments.

Covered parking, either underground or in attached and detached garages, is very desirable in both northern and southern climates. Carports (covered spaces without walls) are also a good addition but are best in warmer areas. Covered parking not only provides an additional source of income but also improves the image of the community to the renter prospect. However, attention must be given to the management of garage spaces. Renters often choose to use garages as inexpensive storage sheds and then park in surface spaces. This can cause severe parking shortages in the surface spaces, so strict rules prohibiting garage use for storage must be implemented.

Unit Sizes

The required unit sizes obviously depend on the rental range and the market. The following comments apply to apartments below the luxury level.

Studio units of less than about 425 square feet are very small, and studio units of over 550 square feet are unusually generous. A unit of more than 550 square feet can usually accommodate a one-bedroom configuration.

One-bedroom units of under 600 square feet are so small that they can appeal to tenants only on a price basis. In most markets, 650 to 750 square feet are the norm for one-bedroom units. Anything over 800 square feet is generally considered "large" except in the genuine luxury category.

Two-bedroom units of under 800 square feet are like one-bedroom units of under 600 square feet. In most markets, 850 to 950 square feet are probably the norm, and anything over 1,000 square feet is generous, again except in the genuine luxury markets.

Three-bedroom units appeal largely to families with children, and many institutional investors will attempt to avoid buildings catering largely to families with children. Children are hard on a building and hard on tenants who do not have children, as children and adults keep very different hours. Two or three children can also take over a swimming pool and make it intolerable for adults. Nevertheless, most apartment buildings include a few three-bedroom units for people who can afford them. It is hard to fit three bedrooms and two or more baths into less than 1,100 square feet.

Unit Floor Plans

The best way to evaluate floor plans is to walk into the living/dining area, see how it "feels," and visualize furniture layouts. (One way to visualize this is to see how the furnished model unit, if there is one, or a tenant-occupied unit lays out.) There needs to be a wall for a couch, a wall for a TV and stereo, and so forth. There should be enough space in the living room area for seating as many people as will occupy the unit, plus two to four guests. It is important to have enough windows in the living room area that it seems light and airy. Dark units are harder to rent and often command lower rents.

A dining area that has some physical separation from the living room area (e.g., as an "el" or alcove) giving definition to the dining space, is a great advantage. Except in studios, the dining area should be large enough to accommodate a table with at least four, and preferably six, people.

The kitchen should not appear too small. It is an advantage to have a window in the kitchen, but that is not always possible. In any event, illumination should be substantial. Appliances should include a two-door, self-defrosting refrigerator; a range and oven, preferably self-cleaning; a disposal; and a dishwasher. The drawer and cabinet space should be adequate for the needs of a two- or three-person household, which is probably the maximum that will occupy most one- and two-bedroom units.

Closets should have at least six lineal feet of hanging space for each occupant, counting two occupants for one-bedroom units, three occupants for two-bedroom units, and four occupants for three-bedroom units. Well-designed walk-in closets are a plus. There should also be a linen closet of some sort.

Every unit should have at least one bedroom that measures a minimum of 13 by 10 feet. Otherwise, it becomes difficult to accommodate a double dresser plus twin beds with nightstands on either side. There should be an identifiable wall against which the bed or beds will be placed and another wall for a double dresser, including space for a person to stand in front of the dresser and open a drawer. Mirrored sliding doors on the closet are a plus.

Two-bedroom units ideally should have two baths. Two-bedroom, one-bath apartments often rent only at a substantial discount from those with two baths. The most popular two-bedroom floor plans are what is known as "splits" or "roommate" plans. In these two-bedroom, two-bath units, each bedroom has easy access to an adjacent (or very nearby) full bathroom, and the bedrooms are located on opposite sides of the living/dining/kitchen area. Such an arrangement gives each of the two occupants of the unit considerable privacy and facilitates entertaining guests. It should always be possible for guests to get to a bathroom from the living room without having to go through a bedroom.

The first door one opens on entering a unit should not be the bathroom; preferably, it should be a coat closet. Since doors are often left open, the toilet should not be opposite the entrance to the apartment and therefore visible from the entry when the bathroom door is open.

In the bathrooms, a vanity with some drawer space is preferable to a wall-hung basin. At a minimum, there must be a medicine cabinet and some storage space in the bathrooms. Every unit should have one bathtub. The second bath can have a shower. A showerhead over the tub is common. A glass or other enclosure is vastly preferable to a shower curtain.

Balconies less than 5 feet deep are not very useful; 6 feet is a better minimum. Balconies should be able to accommodate some furniture.

The rules for hallways are the same as those for office buildings, the halls should be attractive and not look like long, boring chutes. Obviously, hallways can be redecorated.

If the building has a lobby, it should be clean and attractively decorated. One gets more for one's money by spending a few thousand dollars on the lobby than spending $25 on each unit.

Fireplaces, wood paneling, wallpaper, and higher ceilings (usually on the top floor) are all pluses. A fireplace is probably worth at least $20 per month in additional rent. Views can also be important. In a garden complex, a nice view might add 5 percent to the rent; a magnificent bay view in San Francisco could add 25 percent. A market survey should enable one to quantify the values.

REVIEWING THE INCOME STATEMENT

The investor must review the property's actual expenses and critically evaluate each line item. Often income and expenses are higher or lower for one management company than for another due to management style, operational philosophy, strategy, and/or length of the intended holding period. Operating costs also vary on the basis of local conditions and a building's age and design, so the experience of seemingly comparable buildings may be only indicative.

Income Accounts

Gross Potential Rental Income.   This is the current rent roll of the occupied units plus vacant units at market rent, including any furnished models and employee-occupied units.

Miscellaneous Income.   Subcategories include security deposits or portions of security deposits that are retained as residents vacate, receipts from common-area laundry facilities, fees received from applicants in applying for credit approval, late fees received as charges for late payment of rent, gross amount of interest revenue on security deposits and any other investments from the operating proceeds, transfer fees or "early termination fees" received for special relocation clauses, rental income received for storage spaces, and income received from any covered parking spaces or garages, as well as any other miscellaneous source of income.

Gross Potential Income.   This is the sum of gross potential rental income and miscellaneous income.

Vacancy Expense.   Vacancy expense represents the amount of money that is lost when vacant units are costed at their market rents. Traditional thinking suggests a normal vacancy rate of 5 percent, which should be adequate for most analyses. However, the national vacancy rate is often higher and varies from market to market.

Credit Expense.   Credit expense represents the bad debt expense. Depending on the nature of the property, the location, and the resident profile, the credit expense might range from 0.05 to 1.25 percent as a percentage of gross potential income.

Concession Allowance.   This represents deductions from gross potential rental income that are necessary to rent the units.

Effective Gross Income.   Effective gross income is gross potential income minus vacancy expense, credit expense, and concession allowance.

Expense Accounts

Real Estate Taxes.   Real estate taxes are generally based on the property's market value, though this definition varies widely from one taxing jurisdiction to the next. Investors should consult the local assessor's office to determine what the future tax liability will be. There may also be local special assessments that might create additional liabilities in the future, possibly because of certain agreements made during development of the property. The preliminary title report should give notice of any special assessment districts or development agreements that are attached to the property.

Utilities.   Utility costs will vary depending on tenant- versus landlord-paid utilities, type of heat source (gas, electricity, forced air, hot water), management style, and so forth. The future cost of utilities should be estimated by combining historical usage figures (which will vary with occupancy and weather fluctuations) and future utility rates (per unit of measurement—kilowatts, therms, gallons, etc.). Variances should then occur only if the investor is anticipating higher vacancies or occupancies based on the rental strategy to be implemented or if the buyer has plans to implement practices that will increase or reduce utility costs. Vendors should be contacted regarding anticipated trends in utility rates. After acquisition, many utility conservation methods, such as relamping with more efficient fixtures, installing water saver faucets and shower heads, and so forth, can be instituted to lower these expenses.

Insurance.   The investor should receive quotations on insurance for the property based on his or her required coverages. These coverages typically include fire and extended loss on the building and contents, rental income loss, and liability.

Payroll.   Payroll includes the following:

1. Administrative payroll for the property manager, leasing agents, and part-time leasing employees.
2. Commissions and bonuses payable to these same employees.
3. Maintenance payroll, including any part-time employees and gardeners. Maintenance payroll is directly related to the

amount of work the current owner does in-house versus hiring outside vendors. While it is generally preferable to do as many tasks in-house as possible, market conditions sometimes make the use of outside vendors advantageous.

4. The value of any free apartments or percentage discount on apartment rents given to employees as part of their compensation. It is good practice, and often legally required, to have at least one manager or the maintenance person live on-site.

It is important that the investor understand the payroll, not in terms of how the seller operates the property but in terms of how the investor will operate the property.

Payroll Taxes and Benefits. Subcategories include the cost to the owner of payroll taxes, worker's compensation, health insurance, and any other benefits offered to employees. Worker's compensation and other categories vary from state to state, and benefits vary for full-time and part-time employees. Health insurance should be evaluated based on the investor's policies.

Maintenance Supplies. These include all the supplies required for use by the maintenance staff in normal operation of the apartment community, including paint, cleaning supplies, filters, light bulbs, plumbing items, all items not qualifying as capital expenditures, and any materials the on-site staff will require for repairs. The category does not include replacements of capital items such as carpets, boilers, or appliances, but does include parts for their repair.

Contract Services. These include all services routinely provided on a contract basis by outside vendors. Subcategories include elevator service, security services, maintenance of fire extinguishers, painting (when not performed by in-house staff), carpet cleaning (when not performed by in-house staff), trash removal, landscape services, and pool cleaning and maintenance. Again, close attention should be paid to the cost of contracting these services relative to the cost of doing them in-house.

Repairs and Maintenance by Outside Contractors. These include expenditures for repairs that the maintenance staff cannot handle. A rule of thumb provides for $30 to $75 per unit per year to be allocated to this category, depending on the staffing at the property and the age and condition of the improvements.

Management Fee.   The management fee is the percentage, typically of gross collected income, paid monthly for supervision and services that are not provided on-site. The percentage should be based on local and market conditions. The services typically include hiring, training, and support of on-site staff; bill paying and bookkeeping; market surveys and rent setting; selection of vendors and contractors; placing insurance; recommendations on and implementation of major capital programs (though a separate fee may be charged for this service); and supervision of the on-site operations through regular site visits. For buildings of over 100 units, typical management fees would be 4 to 5 percent.

Marketing Expenses.   These expenses include

1. *Advertising*. Generally advertisements are placed in local newspapers, magazines, and apartment guides. The cost of preparation of the collateral material would be included.
2. *Promotions and tenant functions*. These include open houses, parties, and other functions that are used to generate community involvement and help tenant retention.
3. *Resident referrals*. At many communities, the current residents are paid a fee or commission for referring someone who subsequently signs a lease. This fee typically ranges from $100 to $300 on a one-time basis.
4. *Model apartments*. In this category are the gross rental value of any model apartment(s) and any related expense such as plant or furniture rental. Many owners simply deduct the rental value of model apartments from gross potential income or as part of the vacancies. The authors strongly recommend that the cost of model apartments be included both as income and as an expense so that the managers of the community will realize that keeping model apartments has a cost and will evaluate whether it is necessary.
5. *Locator/broker fees*. Depending on market conditions, fees may be paid to local real estate residential brokerage companies for referral of residents (typically half a month's rent on a one-time basis). Also, most major markets have one or more

apartment locator companies whose sole business is to assist prospects in identifying an apartment community in the area. The fee is typically the same as the brokerage fee described above.

Other Expenses.   These include:

1. *Administrative expenses and supplies* associated with operating the administrative and leasing office. Some examples would be telephone, brochures, and office supplies. The category includes many small items that should make up no more than 1 percent of effective gross income.
2. *Professional fees* paid to attorneys, collection agencies, engineers, and so forth.
3. *Other expenses* is a catch-all that should be a minimal amount for anything not covered elsewhere.

Net Operating Income

Effective gross income less total operating expenses equals net operating income. It is especially important to understand real estate taxes, payroll, and maintenance, since these three categories typically total approximately 70 percent of operating expenses. It is also important to review a full year's operating history, preferably from monthly operating statements, to pick up seasonal variations in income and expenses.

Since gross potential rental income is based on the current rents of the occupied units and some of those units may have been rented at less than market rent, there may be an opportunity to improve the financial performance of the property. Adding these potential rent increases to gross potential rental income results, after carrying out the above analysis, in an increased net operating income known as *stabilized net operating income*.

These projected increases from current rents to market rents may be easy or difficult to achieve. For instance, the property may already have a program to increase rents to market rents as current leases expire so that only the passage of time will be necessary. Usually some cause other than simply misreading the market rents created the disparity between actual and market rents. Accordingly, some imaginative or costly alterations to the property or services to tenants may be necessary to achieve the increased rents: improving the landscaping or amenities, redecorating the kitchens, recarpeting, repainting, or replacing the facades.

Capital Items and Replacements

Carpets and dishwashers are good for 5 to 10 years, roofs for probably 10 to 15 years, and exterior paint jobs for 5 to 10 years. If the carpets appear to be approaching the end of their useful lives, it would be well to reserve funds now to replace them during the next three years of ownership. Otherwise, an annual reserve equal to one-tenth of the cost of new carpeting, new dishwashers, and a new roof would probably be sufficiently conservative. If the roof has just been replaced, it is probably not necessary to budget for its replacement during the holding period.

The annual budget for replacement reserves is clearly related to the age and condition of the asset. After all, as with people, more things go wrong as years go by! For an apartment community that was built with high-quality materials and workmanship, the following replacement reserves might be appropriate:

Years 1–3	$150/unit/year
Years 4–5	$200/unit/year
Years 6–9	$250/unit/year
Years 10+	$325/unit/year

However, for older properties, these figures could be higher and are highly dependent on the level of maintenance performed over the previous years and the quality of the original construction.

Cash Flow

Net operating income less capital items and replacements equals cash flow.

Valuing the Property: Capitalization Rate versus Internal Rate of Return

As indicated earlier, rents in almost all non-rent-controlled apartments can be increased annually by as much as the market will allow, a characteristic of rental apartments that greatly enhances their value as an inflation hedge. This potential for annual rent increases makes it much less important, in pricing apartment properties, to rely on internal or discounted rates of return than is the case with commercial properties. Thus, the capitalization rate, defined as net annual operating income divided by price, is a much more reliable indication of value and/or return for apartments than for commercial properties.

The big difference is that in the case of commercial properties, leases are generally for much longer periods of time—3, 5, or 10 years—so that contract rents can lag significantly behind market rents; also, there can be long lags before the inflation-hedging opportunities can be exercised. Turnover costs at the time of lease renewal or renting to a new tenant are also considerably higher for commercial properties and typically include leasing commissions, allowances for tenant improvements, and, in soft markets, an extended period of free rent. Indeed, in high-rise office buildings in the softest downtown markets, the turnover costs in the early 1990s almost equaled the total cost of constructing the building.

THE IMPORTANCE OF PROPERTY MANAGEMENT

What Is "Management Intensive"?

The management of apartments might be compared to that of commercial properties on two dimensions: (1) the *frequency* and (2) the *magnitude* of the problems. The greater intensity of apartment management lies in the greater frequency of demands for action or decisions. Fortunately, the magnitude of the problems is lower in apartments than in commercial properties, so decision making and action can frequently be delegated to a resident manager and on-site staff. While a $15 million industrial property or shopping center would have no on-site employees, an apartment project of that size would have five or six full-time staff members to service the tenants and the property. The major tasks of the off-site property manager operating out of the local management office are to select, support, and monitor the on-site staff.

Apartment tenants have myriad needs for service. A kitchen appliance needs repair. A towel bar comes off the wall. A faucet is leaking. The tenant upstairs has left the sink running, and water is dripping through the ceiling. With 100 tenants, these problems are at least 100 times as frequent as in a single-family home, but all are items that should be handled by the on-site maintenance personnel. In many buildings, the resident and on-site staff also clean and paint the apartments.

A good on-site maintenance staff can handle almost all the repairs, even complicated ones, at tremendous savings from the costs that would be incurred by using outside contractors. Similarly, properly selected and/or trained on-site staff is less expensive than outside gardening or pool services. The authors prefer to use more on-site employees and fewer contractors than some other managers. While some tasks are too large or technical, we have frequently had on-site personnel who could jackhammer through concrete to repair a water main and then repour the slab, completely take apart and repair an electric stove, install dishwashers to upgrade the building's amenities, and do extensive patching of the parking lot and the roof. Such tasks arise with sufficient frequency that maintaining and repairing apartment projects through on-site staff instead of outside contractors can add 50 to 100 basis points to the return.

Renting apartments is much more marketing/sales oriented than renting commercial property (which tends to be more financially oriented). It requires that a competent rental agent be on-site, ready to show the units and screen potential tenants seven days a week, including the early evening hours. All such rental agents must be able to show the property to its advantage, handle questions and objections, recognize and reject undesirable tenants (usually for credit unworthiness), and close the sale. On the other hand, there are no complicated lease provisions to negotiate. While the consummation of a commercial lease may require the services of an attorney, the best apartment rental agents may not even have a high school diploma.

The off-site property manager must select and hire the manager, approve the manager's selection of subordinate staff, train the manager in company procedures and policies (all of which should be available in a printed manual), help the resident manager with problems that are beyond his or her capacity, ensure through physical inspections that any unit for which rent is not being received is in fact vacant, keep a tight rein on expenses, physically inspect the property at least monthly to ensure the quality of maintenance, and, when necessary, make the decision to change resident managers. In addition, the off-site manager can help design advertising and promotional campaigns, negotiate regional and national vendor contracts (paint, carpet, appliances, etc.), and generally seek opportunities to improve the competitive position of the property at minimum cost in ways that are appropriate to the nature of the property—for instance, new recreational amenities, special events for tenants, additional or upgraded appliances, or improved landscaping or storage facilities.

In summary, intensive management means giving attention to a host of problems, all of which occur frequently but almost none of which is overly complicated or highly technical.

Whether the off-site property management will be performed by the owner or the portfolio manager or subcontracted to a third party is a portfolio management decision. Other major duties of the portfolio manager include approving the annual operating and capital budgets, monitoring performance against those budgets and the prior year's results, and evaluating the competitiveness of the property in its market and the potential for growth of that market. An early recognition of competitive failures or of future market weakness could prompt the portfolio manager or owner to undertake a program of capital improvements or place the property on the market for sale.

In the authors' opinion, the intensity of management of apartments makes it difficult for the owner or the owner's portfolio manager to subcontract the off-site property management to a third party. The owner and the portfolio manager are interested in the performance and net income from the property, but a third-party manager is interested in his or her own profits from the management of the property. Even though the quality of personnel may be identical, the third-party manager tends to assign more properties per person and even the added responsibility of bringing in new business. As a result, third-party managers tend to be less responsive to the owner's and tenants' needs, less likely to engage in time-consuming analyses of ways to improve appearance and performance, and more reluctant to take on the difficult and time-consuming tasks of firing resident staff and hiring and training their replacements. As a result of our combined 40 years of experience in the apartment field, the authors believe strongly in in-house property management.

Setting Rents and Maximizing Effective Gross Income

There are three important determinants of leasing success:

- A strong marketing program with qualified leasing personnel.
- Maintaining and showing the property and units well.

- Proper setting of rental rates and discriminating use of concessions.

Rental rates should reflect an assessment of the property in relation to its key competitors, taking into account factors such as age, size of units, scope of the amenity package, location, and quality of improvements. To determine the rents the market will support, it is important to survey at least three (and preferably five) competing buildings regularly—preferably monthly—keeping in mind that a project with exceptionally high rents but low occupancy is usually making a mistake and that the same is true for a project that is 100 percent occupied and is not raising rates. Traditionally, a property in the 95 to 97 percent occupancy range is considered stabilized and a good indicator of rates accepted by the market.

The same considerations apply to rent concessions, typically a move-in bonus or a free rental period. In the late 1980s, concessions became ingrained into numerous markets throughout the country. Even when markets improve, renters often remain so deal conscious that asking rates are often artificially inflated so that concessions continue to give the illusion of a deal. Ideally, as the market firms, concessions should dissipate before real movement in rental rates occurs.

Signals to raise or lower rents and/or concessions come from three sources: the information secured by frequent shopping of competitive buildings, the number of vacancies in each floor plan or location in one's own building, and the number of units whose tenants have given notice of intent to vacate at a specified future date, usually the end of the month.

In general, it makes sense to discriminate by unit type when raising rents. A property may have a waiting list for one-bedroom units but be unable to lease its two-bedroom units. Normally, an occupancy of 97 percent or better in any given unit type, coupled with a relatively stable anticipated turnover, indicates an opportunity to increase rents. Conversely, if vacancy and move-out notices exceed the market rate for one or more unit types or for the entire building, increased concessions and/or reduced rents may be in order.

As soon as sufficient units have been rented at the newly increased rental rate to prove its acceptance by the market, rents can be increased to tenants-in-place as their leases expire and are renewed.

Marketing the Units

Maintaining Curb Appeal

Successful marketing of apartments begins with careful attention to *curb appeal* (an industry term for the general impression the property gives when entered or driven through). Design and maintenance of the landscaping are important to creating a favorable impression. Weather permitting, an owner can enhance the property by planting flowers, usually annuals, strategically throughout the property. Signs should be attractive, parking lots clearly striped and free of debris, recreation areas, rooms, and lawns well groomed, and the model apartments (if any) attractively accessorized and sparkling clean.

The Presentation

An effective sales presentation has two components: the telephone presentation and the personal tour. The telephone sales presentation has the sole purpose of convincing a prospective renter to visit the property. The leasing agent's goal is to communicate an emotionally appealing portrait of the property and secure a commitment to visit. To do this, he or she should attempt to get some idea of the needs and motivation of the prospect. The answer to "Why are you moving?" is often the catalyst to a well-crafted phone presentation.

The personal tour also requires focusing on the needs and motivations of the prospect. This requires information gathering through 5 to 10 minutes spent with the prospect before setting out to show the property. By knowing what is important to the prospect, the leasing agent can shape the tour to highlight the factors that count. The presentation should include a tour of the amenities of the property, a model apartment if one is being used, and a visit to the specific unit(s) being proposed for occupancy.

Monitoring the Sales Force

To ensure that a leasing presentation is personable and effective, leasing agents should be "shopped" at least once a quarter. Shopping entails sending an individual to the property posing as a potential renter in order to critique the leasing agent(s). The shopper should make initial contact by phone and should evaluate both the phone presentation and the in-person tour.

Advertising

Good advertising brings qualified prospects to the property. The tone and focus of the ad should aim at the type of resident the owner wants to attract. Sheer volume of traffic does not make an ad successful. If 50 people respond to a particular ad but not one can afford the rent, the ad is a failure. For that reason, many ads include a price point to indicate the starting rates to potential renters.

As the size of local apartment magazines and the advertising sections of Sunday newspapers continues to grow, the distinctiveness of an ad becomes more and more important. Keeping an ad different yet tasteful is a challenge, but a rewarding one. One of the most common shortcomings of an advertising policy, however, is the failure to quantify the results from the various media and different ads.

Promotional Events and Aids, Including Model Apartments

Collateral sales materials are an important supplement to the sales presentation. Attractive brochures embellish the property's image, provide site and floor plans for reference, and leave the prospect with a tangible tie to the community for future decision making.

The use of model apartments is controversial. What exactly do model apartments provide to the marketing effort? By furnishing and accessorizing a particular unit, the leasing agent can convey to prospects that it indeed offers ample room for furnishings and an attractive lifestyle.

However, models are expensive, in terms of both the cost of furnishings and the opportunity cost of rent lost. When a property is new and filling up for the first time, there are large numbers of vacant units of every floor plan, so the opportunity cost is virtually nil. However, when occupancy has stabilized at close to 95 percent, keeping units vacant as furnished models has a real cost. Moreover, since there are normally at least four or five different floor plans and generally no more than two or three models, the units available to rent often do not have the same floor plans as the model. Even more important, they almost never have the same views, location, light, and airiness as the models. It is therefore important to show the prospect the exact unit(s) available for occupancy unless extensive renovations or clean-up are intended. For instance, if the to-be-vacated unit has a magnificent view or a cathedral ceiling that sells the unit, it is a waste to show the prospect only the model and attempt to describe those important amenities in words rather than by demonstration. Too often, leases do not contain a clause giving the owner permission to show the unit after the tenant has given notice of intent to vacate, or managers refuse to take advantage of that opportunity.

Promotional events at a property are generally more valuable for resident retention than for recruiting new residents. However, it is generally a good idea to use a resident party or function as a vehicle to involve prospective new residents. Offering a prospect who has just toured a property an invitation to an upcoming resident function is a good way to personalize the tour and can help close a new rental.

Minimizing Time between Tenants

With the exception of badly damaged units or a particularly high inventory of vacant units, an apartment generally should be made ready for showing and occupancy within three business days of the time it becomes vacant, especially if a new tenant is waiting to move in. Managers who regularly schedule 15 to 30 days between tenants are far from profit maximizers.

Maintenance of the Property

Proper maintenance of the property is essential to retaining existing residents and attracting new ones. A community should have a regular program of maintaining good curb appeal, keeping all amenities and common areas in excellent condition, and responding efficiently and effectively to resident work orders.

It is becoming increasingly common for management companies to complete the majority of resident requests within 24 hours; in fact, some now guarantee it.

Expense Control

Following is a summary of specific strategies for maintaining good expense control:

• Look for efficiencies in staffing where possible. Hire in-house maintenance employees capable of doing the bulk of apartment turnover work, such as painting, shampooing the carpets, and appliance repair. Evaluate traffic and workload for administrative staff, and consolidate where possible. Reduce paperwork and nonessential corporate reporting. Adjust staffing seasonally and throughout the week to match demands for services. Gear leasing and manager bonuses to performance, with leasing agents rewarded for the value and term of leases and managers for net operating income.

• Appeal property taxes when appropriate. Many local and national professional firms and attorneys provide services to monitor property taxes and assessment levels. Depending largely on local custom and historical effectiveness, these firms can be hired either on a flat fee, on an hourly fee with a maximum, or on a sliding scale based on savings.

• Implement utility conservation measures such as the use of fluorescent light fixtures and putting common area amenities on timers.

• Install water conservation devices in showers, faucets, and toilets, and educate residents to report any problems with them. Monitor timing and efficiency of irrigation systems.

• Audit utility bills to ensure that accounts are set up correctly with regard to type of account, peak measuring periods, and other pertinent billing conditions. As with tax appeal firms, energy auditors will work for a percentage of savings.

• Scrutinize advertising expenses to minimize cost-benefit ratios.

• Rebid necessary outside vendor contracts regularly to keep prices down.

• Keep administrative supplies and expenses on a short leash, with office products and phone bills regularly scrutinized. Open accounts with major discounters for maintenance and cleaning supplies, and then control and audit usage. Reduce stocks of supplies to easily accountable levels.

In summary, resident managers should be encouraged and given incentives to run the operation as though it were their own business.

THE IMPACT OF GOVERNMENT REGULATIONS

This section briefly addresses risks and constraints that are generally beyond the control of the investor. As political committees are formed and legislation is proposed, the investor must engage legal and other professional assistance (engineers, architects, etc.) in sorting through the requirements for compliance.

Americans with Disabilities Act

This Americans with Disabilities Act (ADA), which took effect in January 1992, generally affects the development of new apartments rather than existing properties. However, the ADA does address the need to reasonably provide access to areas that are for public use (versus one's own apartment) relative to existing properties. Information can be obtained through both legal counsel and national organizations such as the National Multi-Housing Council in Washington, DC.

Fair Housing Laws

Though it is axiomatic that no one should discriminate among tenants or potential tenants, the investor should understand all of the issues involved in compliance (leasing, management, use of common areas and amenities on-site, etc.) and the risks associated with their violation.

Environmental Issues

It is assumed that the investor, in the course of normal due diligence prior to acquisition, will perform adequate environmental assessments of the property. At a minimum, these include testing for hazardous waste either on the property or nearby, investigating for the existence of any significant levels of lead in the paint or water, checking records for the existence or prior removal of underground storage tanks, and the possible presence of asbestos in any of the physical improvements.

The investor should also be aware that investigations have begun, though conclusive evidence not yet been found, on other issues that may have a dramatic effect on the value of the investment. Some of the more recent and important issues include radon gas, lead-based paint (found in most older buildings), and electromagnetic fields (adjacent power lines). Though it is impossible to accurately predict the final resolution of such issues, the investor must be aware of them and again consult with professionals who continually monitor the legal and legislative processes.

CONCLUSION

The successful acquisition and operation of apartment communities require different skills and analytical tools than those necessary for office, industrial, and retail properties. This chapter described the various facets of apartment acquisitions and operations. Experience, however, is no doubt the best teacher.

There are excellent reasons to believe that apartments in correctly chosen markets will provide the best returns of any type of U.S. real estate during the 1990s. All three types of commercial properties are in significant oversupply in almost every U.S. market. With economists widely projecting very slow economic growth in the United States for most of the decade, until worker productivity and international competitiveness improve, absorption of vacant commercial space is likely to be extremely slow. The best apartment markets, on the other hand, are already achieving occupancies of 95 percent or better; and population growth guarantees increased demand, while there are significant constraints on the supply of new competition. At the very least, apartments add welcome diversification to the real estate portfolio as it works through the economic cycles. At best, and as the authors anticipate, apartments will provide the highest returns of any type of real estate for at least the next five years.

CHAPTER 11

THE HOTEL SECTOR

David T. Johnstone
Sage Hospitality Resources, Inc.

Jeffrey A. Duni
Sage Hospitality Resources, Inc.

INTRODUCTION

This chapter explores the unique characteristics of the hospitality industry through a historical industry overview and detailed discussions of the competitive environment, investment performance, and portfolio issues.

At the most basic level, hotel real estate differs from other property types in the following ways:

1. Hotels are operating businesses. Aside from the component of leasing real estate, hotels conduct many other businesses such as restaurants, equipment rentals, business services, and so on.

2. Hotel leases are only 24 hours in duration. As such, hotel room nights are perishable, and countless transactions are involved in leasing hotel rooms during the course of a year.

3. To accomplish the goals of executing 24-hour leases and operating other related businesses, hotels are very labor intensive.

4. Hotels are also capital intensive. The excessive wear and tear on hotel real estate due to the public nature of the facilities requires annual expenditures for property renovation and improvements that other real estate types do not require.

5. Hotels are typically "branded" with a chain affiliation. In essence, the chain affiliation partially replaces the real estate broker as a leasing agent.

INDUSTRY OVERVIEW

History of Lodging

Over the centuries, the hotel industry has evolved into its current profile of highly specialized properties that serve specific users' needs. The evolution of the industry has been directly tied to people's ability, desire, and need to travel.

The inception of the hospitality industry began in England around the mid-1700s, when the English inn came into prominence during the Industrial Revolution.[1] From there, inns spread rapidly throughout Europe and then into the Americas. The first hotel constructed in the United States was the City Hotel in New York City, which was built in 1794.[2] The primary method of travel during this time was by horseback or coach.

During the 1800s, the development of rooming and boarding houses, inns, and hotels in the United States tended to parallel railroad growth westward. Demand for overnight accommodations grew as numerous small towns sprang up across the country. In the second half of the 1800s, more luxurious properties were constructed in major cities along the railroad lines. As railroad transportation became more affordable and more people began to travel, the first modern, commercial hotels were built. The affluence spawned from the industrialization of the U.S. economy in the late 1800s. The invention of the automobile in the early 1900s further precipitated hotel growth. The origins of national chains, such as Hilton and Sheraton, began during the stock market crash and the depression of the 1930s as hotel entrepreneurs expanded their holdings by buying financially distressed properties.

The first post–World War II boom in hospitality development occurred in the late 1950s and early 1960s, when roadside motels were heavily developed. This property type provided lodging and parking in a facility whose rooms were usually accessible from an outdoor parking area. Motels were primarily located adjacent to the increasing number of interstate and state highways to allow the traveler easy access to the facility.

---

[1] Stephen Rushmore, "The Origins of the Lodging Industry," *Hotels, Motels, and Restaurants,* 1983, p. 1.

[2] Ibid.

The 1950s boom was further fueled by tax law changes and the emergence of franchising. Franchising provided the vehicle for hotel companies to expand their concept without being owners or operators. Holiday Inn is perhaps the best example of franchise growth during this period. The development boom continued throughout the 1950s and early 1960s, resulting in a trend of steadily decreasing hotel occupancies and a curtailment of new hotel construction.

From the late 1960s to the mid-1970s, lodging's franchise industry began to mature as companies began focusing on standardizing quality and achieving increased brand recognition. In exchange for an established identity, franchisees were required to perform ongoing regular maintenance of hotel facilities and periodically renovate major portions of the hotel as mandated by the franchisor's product improvement plan. Providing a consistent-quality room, coupled with the franchise's toll-free reservation system, allowed franchise hotels to significantly outperform independent hotels in highly competitive markets. Hotel owners realized that identification with a nationally recognized hotel name was crucial to their efforts to maximize revenues and profits.

Major convention hotels emerged as the number of special-interest groups and associations increased in the 1970s and 1980s. To accommodate these lucrative meetings, hoteliers, in concert with local civic organization and politicians, pushed for the construction of convention centers.

The second great postwar boom of hospitality industry development occurred in the 1970s, when real estate investment trusts (REITs) provided enormous amounts of financing for real estate development. REITs offered attractive financing packages for new construction and allowed small investors to participate in real estate mortgages and equities. This phase of new development ended in the mid-1970s, however, when inflation and interest rates skyrocketed and the energy crisis interrupted travel. The resulting recession caused absolute demand for rooms to decrease 7 percent in 1975 (it did not exceed the 1974 level until 1978). In turn, nationwide occupancy declined from 65.9 percent in 1974 to 62.2 percent in 1975.

As demand for lodging rebounded in the late 1970s, hotel chains more clearly recognized that consumers travel for a variety of reasons and under varying circumstances. In essence, the market could be stratified into various economic segments that would appeal to specific consumers' income levels and buying habits. To meet the varying needs of the consumer traveling for either business or pleasure, the hotel industry evolved specialized property types. Product and demand segmentation would accelerate in the decade to come.

The third, and possibly the most dramatic, post–World War II hotel-building boom was unleashed during the capital-rich 1980s. Hotel chains, management companies, lenders, consultants, and developers all made decisions to build in the belief that their respective hotels could capture a disproportionate share of a market's lodging demand. The frenzy of hotel development was augmented by several sources of capital- and tax-based incentives. Thus, lodging developers were flooded with capital in the 1980s, often resulting in mistimed, misplaced, and unprofitable hotel developments.

Market Supply Segmentation

Paradoxically, hotel companies segmented the industry into increasingly narrower strata, providing developers with the opportunity to build a variety of property types to offer the consumer at all levels of economic orientation. For example, the low-cost hotel segment was further subdivided into "budget" and "economy." Roadside motels were either limited-service or full-service, depending on whether or not the property had an on-site restaurant. A limited-service hotel could call itself a convention property if it converted a guestroom to a meeting room. Extended-stay hotels were initially considered to be "first class" due to the spacious suites these properties offered. By the end of the 1980s, a budget, extended-stay suite hotel at a roadside limited-service location had emerged. Was the consumer confused? Yes. Even those in the industry couldn't adequately explain their own segmentation.

Let's try to decipher the multitiered brand segmentations that have developed in recent years by creating two classification parameters: economic orientation and property type. Economic orientation generally refers to the hotel's room rate. The economic categories can be defined as follows:

- Budget: room rates under $30.
- Economy: room rates between $30 and $50.
- Mid-market: room rates between $50 and $90.
- First-class: room rates between $90 and $140.
- Luxury: room rates in excess of $140.

The preceding dollar amounts are room rates, as of 1994, in an average U.S. metropolitan area representing a cost-of-living index of 1.00.

Property type refers to the nature of the facilities the hotel offers and the specific needs these properties fulfill for the different types of hotel guests. Property types are categorized as follows:

- Resort: A hotel, usually located in a suburban or isolated rural location, with special recreational facilities to attract pleasure-seeking guests.[3]
- Convention: A hotel that provides facilities and services geared to meet the needs of large-group and association meetings and trade shows. Typically, these hotels have in excess of 400 guest rooms and contain substantial function and banquet space flexibly designed for use by large meeting groups. They often work in concert with other convention hotels and convention centers to provide facilities for citywide conventions and trade shows.[4]
- Full-service: A hotel that provides a wide variety of facilities and amenities, including food and beverage outlets, meeting rooms, and recreational activities.[5]
- Extended-stay: A transient lodging facility that derives more than 50 percent of its occupied room nights from travelers who stay at the property for five or more consecutive room nights.[6] These hotels typically contain a separate living area and some type of kitchen facilities.
- Limited-service: A hotel that provides only some of the facilities and amenities of a full-service property. This category includes properties commonly referred to as *motels* or *motor hotels*.[7] In the strictest sense, this type of hotel is a rooms-only operation, with food and beverage service provided by an independent, freestanding restaurant adjacent to the hotel site.

Exhibit 11–1 places the two classification parameters in a matrix and offers examples of each property type at varying economic orientations. These examples are neither empirical nor exhaustive.

---

[3] Pannell Kerr Forster, *Trends in the Hotel Industry,* USA edition, 1991.

[4] Ibid.

[5] Ibid.

[6] Michael Cahill and Stephen Rushmore, *The Hotel Valuation Journal,* Fall 1990.

[7] Ibid.

EXHIBIT 11–1
Segmentation Matrix

	Resort	Convention	Full-Service	Extended-Stay	Limited-Service
Luxury	The Phoenician	Waldorf-Astoria	Four Seasons	Sara Hotel (New York, NY)	Kimco Hotels (San Francisco, CA)
First-class	Ritz-Carlton, Aspen	Loews Anatole	Ritz-Carlton		
	Sheraton Waikiki Club Med	Chicago Hilton New York Hilton	Westin St. Francis Marriott	Embassy Suites	De La Poste (New Orleans, LA)
Mid-market	Holiday Inn Cancun	Red Lion Hotels	Holiday Inns Hilton Inns	Residence Inns	Holiday Express Marriott Courtyard
Economy	Comfort Inn (Vail, CO)	Days Inn Hotel (Orlando, FL)		Hawthorn Suites	Hampton Inns
Budget	Super 8 (Jackson, WY)			Comfort Suites	Super 8 Motel 6

495

With hotel companies racing to establish a presence on almost every street corner of well-trafficked interchanges and with seemingly unlimited sources of capital, the industry has experienced unprecedented growth. According to Salomon Brothers, Inc., at least 750,000 new rooms entered the national hotel supply during the 1980s.[8]

Capital Market Conditions

In the midst of this development frenzy, the Tax Reform Act of 1986 (TRA 1986) greatly curtailed the tax advantages associated with real estate investment. As a result, hotels, along with other real estate investments, lost their tax-based justification and were forced to stand on the basis of economic merit alone. Nevertheless, new hotel construction did not substantially decline until 1989, as projects that were under development prior to TRA 1986 were finally completed. As growth in demand tapered, overbuilt market became the buzzword of every industry expert.

By the end of the 1980s, the extent of the dramatic increases in supply, in conjunction with decreasing growth in demand, became apparent as competitive pressures forced many hotels to deeply discount room rates to attract demand. In essence, hotels were buying market share, seeking occupancy at the expense of room rate, to cover as much of their fixed operating costs as possible. Cutthroat discounting became a standard "marketing" practice. Not surprisingly, the ultimate effect was substantially decreased revenues and income available for debt service.

In 1986, Japanese investors began to make significant investments in American real estate. The devaluation of the U.S. dollar relative to the yen, the Japanese government's promotion of foreign investment, and the low interest rates of Japanese banks with low reserve requirements combined to create a temporarily inflated environment of "market values." Soon thereafter, transactions on institutional grade and trophy properties were occurring at prices that were not economically justifiable to domestic investors. Nevertheless, market-based capitalization rates decreased, and comparable sales were numerous. As a result, property values appreciated as appraisers applied the then-current market data, failing to realize that many

---

[8] Salomon Brothers Stock Research, The Lodging Industry, January 1989.

transactions during that period failed to meet the definition of market value (i.e., a fully informed buyer). Perhaps the best-known example was the 1990 purchase of the Pebble Beach Golf Resort for $841 million and subsequent resale, less than 16 months later, for $500 million. Unfortunately, many refinancings occurred based on the "market values" that appeared supportable at the time.

By early 1991, the onset of the Persian Gulf war clearly marked the end of the Japanese "bubble economy." Comparable sales transactions would soon be virtually nonexistent, and capitalization rates for valuation purposes would skyrocket. In the face of the competitive environment of the early 1990s, debt coverage ratios dipped below 1:1, and many owners found themselves in negative equity positions as loan balances exceeded market values.

In markets across the country, the turmoil created by the excesses of the 1980s meant hotel properties would be the cause of headaches for hotel and real estate executives for years to come.

CURRENT TRENDS

Since 1986, the hospitality industry has embarked on a difficult journey of transition and restructuring. The journey is expected to continue well into the 1990s. Every facet of the industry will continue to be affected, including developers, lenders, hotel chains, franchise companies, operators, and educators.

Development and Redevelopment

The 1980s real estate boom led to the building of over 750,000 hotel rooms. This caused a nationwide imbalance between supply and demand. Exacerbating the situation was the fact that fewer than 1 percent of all hotel rooms leave the inventory each year, according to Coopers & Lybrand. In response, development of new hotel rooms has fallen to the lowest point since 1975.

New hotel construction of full-service, first-class luxury products will likely be very slow nationwide until the late 1990s, when lodging demand is expected to catch up to the large oversupply. For certain brands, the construction of limited service hotels has begun again. In addition, although 1991 saw the first decline in hotel development costs since 1976, the large number of financially distressed properties of quality condition that are available to investors at substantially below replacement cost suggest that new construction will continue to be minimal over the next several years.

For those companies that can still access the capital markets, there has been a shift from development of hotels to renovation and repositioning of outdated hotel properties which allows them to maintain their competitiveness in the marketplace. Repositioning can involve either upgrading the property to match improvements in the competitive supply, scaling back a facility and its services to accommodate shifts in market demand or external economic conditions, reaffiliating the hotel with a new franchise, or simply directing management to refocus marketing strategies. A successful repositioning typically involves a comprehensive approach concerning every aspect of a hotel property in terms of its operating strategy and the physical improvements to the real estate.

To illustrate, consider a 225-room Travelodge located in a suburban section of a major metropolitan area. The hotel is situated at a dominant intersection of two interstate highways. The facility was improved such that it exceeded the standards and, more important, the perceived public image of a typical Travelodge. The subject property achieved an occupancy of 52 percent at an average daily rate (ADR) of $49, which is significantly below the market yet above the typical Travelodge occupancy and rate performance. The hotel captured only 13 percent of its total reservations from the Travelodge central reservation system compared to an average of approximately 25 percent for all other Travelodges. Evaluation of alternative franchises revealed that Holiday Inn's reservation system was denying, on an annual basis, approximately 17 percent of its reservation requests for the area. The average daily rate for the Holiday Inns in the surrounding market was estimated to be in the low $60s. By reaffiliating with a Holiday Inn franchise and making approximately $200,000 worth of physical improvements to the subject property to meet the new franchisor's standards, the subject property's market identity was more accurately matched to the facility type. As a result, occupancy rose to 59 percent at an ADR of $65 within the first year of the repositioning, representing a 50 percent increase in gross rooms revenue.

With hotel development relatively dormant in the United States, developers and chains are finding opportunities in Eastern Europe, Latin America, and Asia. Currently hotel developments are proposed in Moscow; Mexico is supporting an initiative to promote hospitality development on the Yucatán Peninsula; and the tourism industry in several Pacific Rim nations, among them Thailand, Malaysia, and Indonesia, is in its infancy.

Developers and owners of hotels are also looking for opportunities to convert hotels to other uses. As a result of the oversupply of hotels in the United States, many older facilities have become functionally obsolete. In some cases, these obsolete hotels can be converted to other uses such as student housing, apartments, and senior housing. However, difficulties sometimes arise due to location, the presence of hazardous materials, outdated floor plans and/or life safety systems, and structural items required by current building code.

Lending

In today's market, finding mortgage lenders willing to invest in hotel financing is very difficult, and for luxury hotels almost impossible. Underwriting on lodging properties has become increasingly stringent, perhaps excessively so. However, the lender's wariness is easily understood, since many institutions are still struggling to work out a significant number of problem loans. Exhibit 11–2 presents historical foreclosures on hotel mortgage loans as reported by the American Council of Life Insurance. Indicating the higher level of risk in hotel loans is the fact that in 1992, foreclosures represented 3.2 percent of loans outstanding in this category, while the foreclosure rate for all commercial property was 2.3 percent. Overall, 13 percent of the hotel loans outstanding since 1988 have been foreclosed.

EXHIBIT 11–2
Hotel Loan Foreclosure Experience of Life Insurance Companies, 1988–93

Year	Loans Outstanding	Foreclosures	Percent of Total
1988	1,471	47	3.2%
1989	1,345	19	1.4
1990	1,263	31	2.5
1991	1,260	35	2.8
1992	1,104	35	3.2
1993	917	22	2.4

Source: American Council of Life Insurance.

Compounding the situation is the fact that many of the loans made to hotels during the 1980s were miniperms of five to seven years or construction loans that were refinanced by the same lender because takeout financing was never found. A large number of these mid-term loans came due during the early 1990s. Since there are few viable outlets for refinancing, the current lenders will be forced to either foreclose, refinance, or restructure their loans.

Hotel Chains, Franchise Companies, and Operators

The 1980s witnessed tremendous growth by the chains and operating companies in response to the increased supply of hotel rooms and the subsequent need for brand identity, national marketing prowess, and professional management. To date, the 1990s have witnessed two distinct trends for hotel chains and franchise companies: (1) increasing market share in an effort to achieve growth in management and franchise fees and (2) consolidating to realize economies of scale. With regard to the latter, the major hotel chains such as Hyatt, Marriott, and Sheraton "reorganized" and laid off hundreds of corporate personnel to reduce expenses and improve profitability.

Concurrent with the development boom of the 1980s was a large increase in the number of hotel management companies. Worldwide membership of hotel properties in the American Hotel and Motel Association rose from 7,357 in 1980 to 8,800 in 1990, an increase of 19.6 percent. Exhibit 11–3 illustrates the growth in independent management companies over the last eight years.

EXHIBIT 11–3
Independent Management Companies, 1986–94

Year	Number of Companies
1986	587
1987	641
1988	714
1989	790
1990	838
1991	853
1992	868
1993	906
1994	912

Source: American Hotel and Motel Association.

The proliferation of new management companies, many with less than adequate expertise and personnel resources, may have contributed to the poor performance realized by many hotel owners. Consequently, the early 1990s witnessed a shakeout as less able operators found themselves without contracts and quality operators were acquired by or merged with larger management companies. Perhaps the most widely recognized merger of solidly performing management companies was the consolidation of Motor Hotel Management, Regal-Aircoa, and Hospitality Management Systems to form Richfield Hotel Management.

The Educational Sector

In the 1980s, the industry could not produce qualified general managers fast enough to keep pace with the number of properties being constructed. This need for experienced and skilled managers frequently resulted in mid-management-level personnel being promoted faster than was advisable. Ultimately, property performance suffered as management failed to achieve ownership's financial goals.

The response by academic institutions around the country was to develop new and expand existing hospitality programs. From 1980 to 1990, the number of two- and four-year programs in hospitality and tourism education increased by 300 percent from 40 in 1980 to 160 in 1990. Approximately 700 associate degree programs now exist, offering a more vocational orientation to hospitality education.

Unfortunately, the dramatic decline in construction activity has left the industry with an oversupply of trained students with bleak job opportunities. According to the placement departments of major hospitality programs such as those at Cornell University, Michigan State, and the University of Denver, interviewing by the major hotel companies for new hires has dropped significantly.

Outlook

Despite the turmoil in the hospitality industry, demand for lodging will continue to grow, resulting in a better balance between supply and demand. According to the American Hotel and Motel Association, tourism is the number two employer in the United States (behind health care) and is number three in sales (behind autos and food). By the year 2000, tourism is projected to be the number one industry in both employment and sales. Much of this strength is expected to be based on increasing international travel to the United States.

Worldwide, tourism is expected to grow to a $5.5 trillion industry by 2005, according to the WEFA Group in Philadelphia. Employment estimates reveal that approximately 2.5 million jobs per year will be created in the travel and tourism industry, bringing total tourism employment to 157 million jobs by 2005.

THE COMPETITIVE ENVIRONMENT

Historical Supply and Demand

Exhibit 11–4 depicts the historical growth in hotel room supply and demand on a national level. Of particular interest is the 14-year period beginning in 1977, during which room supply grew at a compound annual growth rate of 2.3 percent. This represents net additions to national room supply of approximately 827,000 units. During the same period, lodging demand increased at 1.6 percent compound annual growth. The effect on occupancy is demonstrated by the 69.2 percent level achieved in 1978 compared to 60.7 percent in 1991.

The performance of average daily rate for the 10-year period beginning in 1973 demonstrates why hotel investments were historically thought of as excellent hedges against inflation, given a hotel's ability to adjust its lease rates every 24 hours. With the ability to adjust room rates on a daily basis, average room rate grew at 11.6 percent compound annual growth from 1973 to 1982. The consumer price index increased at 9.0 percent for the same period, according to the U.S. Bureau of Labor Statistics. From 1985 to 1991, the peak years of the last development boom, when net additions to room supply averaged 88,000 rooms per year, average room rate displayed compound annual growth of 2.9 percent, while the consumer price index grew at 4.0 percent per year. The effect of the supply-demand imbalance was clearly evident as operators reacted to competitive markets by lowering rates.

Factors Affecting Supply and Demand

Many factors influence the supply-demand relationship for lodging rooms that are either external or internal to the hotel industry. On the supply side, external influences can be government related, such

EXHIBIT 11–4

Hotel Supply and Demand Statistics, 1973–92

Year	Supply (1)	Demand (1)	Room Rate	Occupancy	CPI Levels	Inflation Rate	Inflation-Adjusted Room Rate (2)	Inflation-Adjusted REVPAR (3)
1973	2,331	1,486	$15.64	63.7%	44.4		$49.42	$31.51
1974	2,327	1,533	17.19	65.9	49.3	11.04%	48.92	32.23
1975	2,293	1,426	19.22	62.2	53.8	9.13	50.12	31.17
1976	2,264	1,459	21.07	64.4	56.9	5.76	51.95	33.48
1977	2,240	1,496	23.45	66.8	60.6	6.50	54.29	36.26
1978	2,271	1,572	26.72	69.2	65.2	7.59	57.50	39.80
1979	2,303	1,656	31.27	71.9	72.6	11.35	60.43	43.45
1980	2,321	1,639	36.03	70.6	82.4	13.50	61.35	43.32
1981	2,356	1,600	39.64	67.9	90.9	10.32	61.18	41.55
1982	2,372	1,581	42.02	66.7	96.5	6.16	61.09	40.72
1983	2,400	1,545	44.21	64.4	99.6	3.21	62.28	40.09
1984	2,436	1,559	47.27	64.0	103.9	4.32	63.83	40.85
1985	2,504	1,582	49.45	63.2	107.6	3.56	64.48	40.74
1986	2,587	1,616	51.04	62.5	109.6	1.86	65.34	40.81
1987	2,685	1,661	52.68	61.9	113.6	3.65	65.06	40.25
1988	2,796	1,738	54.58	62.2	118.3	4.14	64.73	40.24
1989	2,895	1,824	56.50	63.0	124.0	4.82	63.93	40.28
1990	2,992	1,859	58.40	62.1	130.7	5.40	62.69	38.95
1991	3,067	1,861	58.82	60.7	136.2	4.21	60.59	36.77
1992	3,106	1,929	59.61	62.1	140.3	3.01	59.61	37.02
Average compound growth	1.45%	1.31%	6.92%	0.65%	5.92%			
Average (mean) value							$59.44	$38.47
Standard deviation				0.03%			$5.36	$3.67

(1) Supply and demand data represent the average number of daily available rooms (supply) and occupied rooms (demand).
(2) In 1992 dollars.
(3) REVPAR = revenue per available room.

Sources: Smith Travel Research; Laventhol & Howath; U.S. Bureau of the Census.

as tax law changes, banking deregulation, construction of interstate highway systems, and legal and regulatory actions that affect the availability of capital. Factors internal to the hospitality industry affecting the supply of hotel rooms center mainly on the proliferation of multitiered brands developed by chains and franchise companies to appeal to perceived consumer demand segmentation.

On the demand side, external influences are global, national, and regional economic conditions such as foreign trade, employment, government spending, corporate restructurings, and personal disposable income; demographic factors such as growth in population and age distribution; social factors such as attitudes toward family and time away from work; political events such as war and the creation of new sovereign states; and environmental factors such as weather and natural disasters.

Internal factors influencing demand concern what is termed *induced demand,* that is, demand that is created due simply to the development of new or expansion of existing lodging facilities. For example, a small resort area may be achieving only a 60 percent market occupancy. The development of a 300-room hotel and conference center boosts market occupancy to 65 percent as a result of the new facility's ability to attract demand by groups that previously would have been unable to visit the area.

The interaction of these diverse external and internal supply and demand factors determine the strength or weakness of a particular market. Since these factors are dynamic, most markets experience substantial volatility in their occupancy and (inflation-adjusted) average room rate levels. Thus, from an investor standpoint, gauging where a particular property in a specific market is or, more important, will be along the equilibrium continuum is crucial to making a prudent investment in a lodging property.

Previously we examined how the explosive growth in hotel segmentation contributed to increased supply. This section will focus on the external factors that affect lodging demand.

Nationally, the oil embargo of the 1970s brought domestic leisure travel to a virtual standstill as both air and automobile travel became prohibitively expensive for many Americans. The effect on hotel demand during this period was profound; nationwide occupancies dipped 3.7 percentage points to 62.2 percent in 1975. The oil crisis of the 1970s resulted in a substantial structural change to the U.S. oil industry, the effects of which were felt for a decade later in the oil belt states of Texas, Oklahoma, and Colorado. Consequently, there was a lasting regional impact on the lodging industry in markets in the southwest United States.

Still, most lodging markets are most directly affected by the specific economic and demographic activity occurring in the immediate surrounding area, especially within a five-mile radius of the hotel. For example, the 1995 opening of Denver International Airport, the newest major international airport since the expanded Atlanta's Hartsfield International Airport opened in the 1970s, will generate lodging demand requiring the construction of numerous hotel properties over the next decade.

Conversely, as new hotel construction is completed and supply reaches critical mass, hotels located at the existing Denver Stapleton International Airport may be closed. Owners of many of these hotel properties will consequently face the challenge of adapting their facilities to alternative uses such as senior housing or apartments.

There is no question that increasing globalization is helping to shape the future course of the hospitality industry. During the meteoric rise in Japanese financial markets in the late 1980s, there was a dramatic increase in Japanese visitors to the United States, particularly to the Hawaiian Islands. In 1989, estimates were that fully one-third of total demand for lodging in the state of Hawaii originated in Japan. The onset of the Persian Gulf war in January 1991 precipitated a slowdown in overseas travel by the Japanese and other foreign travelers to the United States, thus demonstrating the impact of political events on hotel demand.

Demand Segmentation

Sources of hotel demand are categorized according to the nature of and reason for the travel involved. Thus, demand is segmented into business (individual or group); association, which includes social, educational, religious and fraternal organizations; and leisure, typically the individual, or transient, traveler.

The individual business traveler has been greatly affected by the corporate cost-cutting measures prevalent in the early 1990s. Electronic media have replaced many in-person meetings, which are being consolidated or held only when absolutely necessary. Many corporations have mandated that company travelers downscale their accommodations from first class to mid-market or even economy.

Perhaps even more drastic have been the cutbacks in corporate group travel. Attendance at industry meetings is being approved only when absolutely necessary, and where previously several members of a department would attend, the current trend is for a senior staff member to travel and report back to the group. According to *Meetings & Conventions,* the number of corporate meetings fell from 886,800 in 1989 to 806,200 in 1991. Expenditures associated with these meetings decreased from $9.7 billion to $8.7 billion during the same period, a drop of over 10 percent in two years.

Other types of group demand (e.g., association, fraternal, educational), have shown similar decreases in terms not only of group members' attendance but also of attendance by spouses and family. The impact of this trend is significant, for the associated spouse/family events typically contribute greatly to the meeting location's general economy. Furthermore, the tendency for meeting attendees to add on a day of leisure travel following the meeting has diminished. Convention attendance nationwide is estimated to have declined from 13.6 million in 1989 to 8.6 million in 1991, a decrease of almost 37 percent.

The leisure segment meanwhile remains relatively strong, bolstered by increased political freedom abroad that is encouraging foreign travel to the United States and Americans' interest in exploring their own "backyard." The trend toward more frequent but shorter vacations has been well publicized, and this fact by its very nature is maintaining domestic demand in this segment.

It is also helpful to consider the existence of other types of real estate, infrastructure, or natural attraction in determining the nature of demand for lodging. Exhibit 11–5 overviews the type of demand generated for lodging by the respective improvement or amenity.

Additionally, in the 1980s, the much improved sophistication and education of lodging consumers resulted in unforeseen shifts in demand and buying practices. Corporations that generated significant amounts of demand developed guidelines to control travel and entertainment expenditures, hired meeting and travel planners to negotiate volume discounts with national hotel companies, and developed information and control systems to monitor compliance and measure savings. The dramatic growth in size and buying power of travel industry consortia, as well as the sophistication and prevalence of airline automated reservation systems, significantly strengthened corporate and group travelers' buying power.

Even the individual traveler, both business and leisure, was educated by the media as to how to negotiate corporate rates, book last

EXHIBIT 11–5
Relationship of Real Estate Improvements to Hotel Demand

Type of Real Estate	Type of Demand Generated
Commercial office space	Individual business travelers, corporate groups, training
Interstate and state highways	Individual business travelers, leisure travelers, trucking
Convention center	National, regional, and state conventions and conferences, and trade shows
Manufacturing plants	Individual business travelers, training, groups
Major amenity (theme park, beach, shopping center, sports team)	Primarily leisure travelers, groups

minute walk-in reservations, and exploit the competitive nature of oversupplied hotel markets. The perishability of a hotel's inventory—one sleeping room for one night—became widely known by individual travelers who were aware that if rooms were available at 11 o'clock P.M., a hotel operator would rather sell a room at a 50 percent discount than lose the revenue-producing potential of a room night forever.

In summary, the challenge of capturing demand for lodging is one of the most dynamic of all consumer marketing disciplines. Peter Yesawich, a nationally recognized researcher of the hospitality industry, offers the following observation:

> As we settle into the 1990s and survey the horizon, it becomes increasingly clear that one of the greatest challenges will be sizing up the market preferences and behavior of future guests . . . The demography of the U.S. is changing dramatically as the baby boom generation matures and the number of people over 65 years old grow to an unprecedented level.

He continues,

- The distribution of wealth in our society will skew even further in favor of our older population . . .
- The percentage of dual income households (now estimated at 60 percent) will continue to rise . . .
- The incidence of business travel by women will continue to outpace the corresponding figure for men (women currently account for 40 percent of commercial room night demand) . . .

- The percentage of nontraditional households will grow, led primarily by increases in single-person and single-parent units.
- The general educational levels of the population will rise . . .
- [T]he influence of status as a purchase motive is declining and consumers now make more prudent selections for everything from automobiles to vacations.
- People have embraced a genuine commitment to personal health and fitness . . .
- Consumers are genuinely concerned [about the environment and] are now displaying their convictions through their purchase behavior.

These changes, according to Yesawich, suggest that "the guest of the 90s will be unlike any other served by the lodging industry before: older, more affluent, better educated, more discerning, and more demanding."[9] The implication is that to gain a competitive advantage in the future, hotel operators will need to spend greater resources in studying their market segments. Furthermore, the implementation of marketing strategies designed to capture targeted demand segments will require close cooperation with hotel owners such that capital expenditure programs for facility renovations reflect the needs of the changing demographics. It is incumbent upon hotel owners to employ the proper resources to understand the operators' marketing goals and develop a strategic long-term asset plan that functions in concert with the marketing plan, thereby maximizing investment returns.

Human Resources

Labor issues greatly affect the operating competitiveness and profitability of hotels. The service nature of the hospitality industry means that hotels, particularly resort properties, are extremely labor intensive. Direct labor costs, payroll taxes, and benefits are usually the single greatest expense associated with operating a hotel, often representing up to 40 percent of all costs. This is due, in large part, to the high degree of fixed labor required to adequately staff a hotel. The continuing increases in health insurance and medical costs have had

---

[9] Peter C. Yesawich, "Who Are the Guests of the 90's?" *Lodging Hospitality,* October 1991, p. 50.

a profound negative impact on the financial performance of many hotel properties.

Employee turnover is extremely high at the entry level, as in most service industries. Thus, training and orientation are an ongoing activity and carry significant cost. Cost of turnover estimates range from $4,000 to $6,000 per occurrence.

The Americans with Disabilities Act of 1991 mandates that employee areas be accessible to all qualified individuals, regardless of disability. Consequently, capital expenditures are required to modify existing workstations to provide access and comply with the law. In addition, new hiring guidelines were implemented by employers to avoid discriminatory employment practices. In summary, ongoing human resource administration will be more challenging and potentially more costly as a result of the legislation. However, providing accessible work areas is expected to bring a new source of labor to the hospitality industry.

Computer-Based Technology

Given its challenges, the hospitality industry has been quick to embrance computer technology to maximize revenue, minimize expense, and accurately account for both.

Hospitality technology is categorized according to the following functions:

1. Property management systems (PMSs), which handle front office management, rooms inventory, accounting, and yield management. Hotel operators and owners should perform a needs analysis as the first stage in a PMS purchase. For smaller hotels without abundant meeting facilities and with fairly stable levels of demand, a basic accounting and front office system should suffice. If the hotel handles a great deal of banquet and meeting business, an automated function book will assist greatly the sales team's efforts in planning events. If demand for the hotel larger than 200 rooms is extremely seasonal and exhibits high variability, then a yield management module would be helpful.

2. Reservation systems, which are networked to a central facility operated by a hotel chain or franchise organization. This component is typically the single greatest benefit to franchisees in terms of increasing revenues. Users at the property level have the capability of structuring room rates and availability by season, room type, and day of the week. This system is often interfaced with a yield management (i.e., occupancy and room rate—or revenue—maximization) module.

3. Telecommunications systems, including sophisticated call accounting systems and user-features such as guest voicemail and conferencing.

4. Energy management systems, which control heating, air-conditioning, ventilation, and lighting for entire buildings such that a certain meeting or guest room can be controlled from a single, remote computer terminal. Owners of larger facilities have found these systems can increase energy utilization efficiency thereby providing significant savings.

5. Risk management systems, which continually monitor, at a central location, guest security areas, sprinkler systems, and smoke and fire detection systems.

6. Audio visual systems, for meeting and function rooms; also video checkout systems which preclude the need for guests to visit the front desk upon departure.

With any technology purchase, it is critical to perform a needs analysis. Determining what functions, type of required reports, the physical attributes of the subject hotel, and the hotel's target market will reduce the ultimate cost of the system. Consideration should also be given to the user-friendliness of the system, ease of training new users, system support, and annual maintenance costs. As a service industry, the bottom line is: Will the high-tech equipment allow hotel employees to provide more friendly and gracious service in a more efficient and quick manner?

INVESTMENT PERFORMANCE

Critical Success Factors

Location/Market
As with any real estate development, location is paramount to the hotel's ability to successfully attract lodging demand. The site should be close to demand generators, possess good visibility, be easily accessible, and be surrounded by compatible land uses. The improvements should be situated to take advantage of the natural topography. From an engineering standpoint, the land itself should be free of hazardous materials and possess adequate load-bearing capacity. Zoning and

entitlement issues must be considered with respect to building height restrictions, density, signage controls, parking requirements, and so on.

An assessment of growth patterns will provide assurance that what appears to be a strong location today will continue to be so 10 years hence. Therefore, it is crucial to develop an in-depth understanding of market demand generators, potential users of the hotel, and the profiles of competitive hotels.

Brand Affiliation

Franchise affiliation is critical to the hotel investment process and, some would argue, is the single most important factor to the success of the hotel. The selection of hotel brand or flag brings together the elements of location, site characteristics, property type, and economic orientation into a coherent theme and market image. Three major elements to consider when selecting the franchise are the central reservation system (CRS), the frequent-guest program, and national marketing support. Essentially, a cost-benefit analysis should be performed on each element of the proposed affiliation. From the owner and operator standpoint, franchise costs are often highly uncontrollable, in that the franchisor dictates the property contribution to a national marketing fund and directs the spending with little direction from the franchisee. Reservation charges can be unilaterally changed, and frequent-user program redemption costs may dilute a hotel's average daily rate as well as incur direct cost to the property.

Yet, the ability of some franchises and hotel chains, in particular, Holiday Inn and Marriott, to generate a significant percentage (as much as 30 percent) of a hotel's total room nights can outweigh the costs, and allow a property to establish a dominant position in its competitive market. The most successful franchise systems can generate high reservation volume by offering consistent room quality, a well-defined identity, and lucrative frequent-guest programs.

Management Company Selection

It is germane to the understanding of hotel franchises to distinguish between an independent management company, a hotel chain management company, a franchise system, and a reservation referral network. An independent management company operates any number of different types of hotels under different franchise affiliations. In this case, the owner would pay both a management fee to the independent operator, and a franchise fee as described previously. A hotel chain management company operates under only its name—Ritz-Carlton, for example. The owner involved in this arrangement would pay a fee only to the operating company.

The franchise organization typically offers only the right to use its name, reservation system, and other sales and marketing resources, in exchange for a fee, but does not provide management services. A reservation referral network simply permits the hotel to be part of the national reservation system while retaining its own name. Best Western is the foremost referral network in the industry. Boutique or luxury hotels can join the Leading Hotels of the World, Hotels of Distinction, or Preferred Hotels network, which caters to a more upscale clientele.

Hybrids do exist. For example, Hilton operates its own hotels and franchises the Hilton Inn name for use by independent management companies. In general, the hotel company name displayed on the marquee typically has little or no ownership interest in the property.

The selection of a hotel management company can be a complex process. It is best to organize the selection criteria into a formal request for proposal (RFP), then categorize the responses into a matrix and rank each company within the category. A relative weighting for each category prioritizes the importance of the category to develop an overall rating. Following are several key areas to consider when selecting a hotel operator:

- Accounting system (centralized/decentralized).
- Corporate office support.
- Marketing.
- Technical services.
- Human resources.
- Management fee structure.
- Number of hotels managed.
- Management contracts lost.
- Franchise affiliations managed.
- Similarity of managed hotels to subject.
- Proven turnaround capability.
- References.

While quantifying the responses to the RFP is a useful exercise, it does not replace the intuitive sense that a management company has the right personality or corporate culture for a particular property. The ability of a hotel operator to understand a specific marketplace, especially resorts, can mean the difference between a management company that attracts and retains the most qualified employees in key positions and one that suffers from constant turnover. The downside scenario brings about fragmented marketing efforts; poor staff morale, resulting in substandard guest service; and a tarnished property image that ultimately leads to lower repeat guest patronage.

The major expense involved in hiring a management company is the management fee. Such fees should be evaluated by calculating each company's proposed base plus incentive fee structure against a static set of projections to draw a meaningful comparison among proposed operators.

The management contract itself forms the basis for the relationship, legal and otherwise, between owner and operator. One of the most essential elements of the contract is the relationship of the parties. An agency relationship should be avoided; the operator should be an independent contractor. This prevents actions of the operator from being construed as those of the owner. In addition, performance standards should be clearly defined, and failure to meet them should be cause for termination.

Capital Improvements Program

A final factor critical to the long-term success of hotel properties is the need for renovation capital, which is best fulfilled by funding a reserve for replacement from cash flow on an ongoing basis. This does not mean, however, that such a reserve need be spent in its entirety each year. To the extent that funds remain after typical operating equipment is replaced, such funds should be invested in low-risk, insured accounts to provide for the major renovation that inevitably occurs in hotels every five to seven years. The financial pain will thus be lessened at renovation time, and the long-term value of the property will be maintained by the ability to proceed with the renovation as soon as needed. In contrast, delaying the renovation, for whatever reason, defeats the purpose of the affiliation and management company selection, for the *property itself* is no longer appropriate to the target market.

Operating Performance: Understanding Hotel Profitability

Exhibit 11–6 summarizes the performance of three types of hotel properties: full-service, limited-service, and all-suites. It represents the results of a national survey of hotel operating performance in 1991. The data are presented as a ratio to total sales (except for departmental expenses, which are presented as a percentage of departmental revenue) and on a dollars per available room (PAR) basis. The exhibit will serve as a framework within which to discuss basic revenue and expense relationships.

Financial Overview

Examining first the revenue mix of the three property types, it is readily apparent how the facility type affects the ratio of food and beverage (F&B) sales to total revenues. With the full-service hotel offering at times multiple restaurant outlets along with extensive banquet facilities, these properties tend to generate one-third of their total revenues in food and beverage. Extended-stay hotels (all-suites) typically include only a complimentary breakfast and evening cocktails, on a self-service basis, as part of the room rate charge. Whatever food and beverage sales are generated result from the occasional meeting or small reception that may be held in the guest suite itself or in the small meeting room typically located adjacent to the residential-style lobby of suite hotels. Limited-service hotels by definition do not offer food service; hence, almost all of such hotels' revenues are derived from room sales.

The impact of food and beverage sales on the overall profitability of hotels is significant. Note that as the ratio of F&B sales to total revenues declines, the departmental operating profit margin increases. This is due to the higher expense ratio in F&B compared to rooms, which in turn dilutes departmental operating profit. Furthermore, F&B contributes to a substantial increase in overhead expense in the form of credit card commissions, accounting support, energy usage, and maintenance of restaurant equipment. Consequently, net operating income (NOI) margins for full-service properties are diluted, with all-suites and limited-service NOI hotels generating profit margins substantially more than those of full-service hotels. Note that the benefit of food and beverage operations to larger full-service hotels is as an amenity to generate room sales, particularly in the group meeting demand segment.

The single largest difference in line item expense that further contributes to the higher NOI margin in limited-service hotels is sales and marketing, which is typically three to four times higher (as measured by PAR) in full-service hotels. Reviewing a sample of sales and marketing departments expense budgets reveals that staffing constitutes approximately 25 percent of the increase. With a variety of demand segments to market to, full-service hotels must employ a sales manager for each major segment (transient corporate, commercial group, and association), with some segments further divided by region of the country. In contrast, a limited-service hotel typically has less rooms than a full-service property and one major demand segment—transient tourists or commercial travelers—which does not require a strong direct sales effort. The limited-service hotel instead relies primarily on the reservation system, travel directories, and other print advertising. Typically only one individual comprises the sales staff at this type of hotel.

Yield Management

The maximization of rate and occupancy, known as yield management, further affects hotel profitability. The basic yield measurement, which quantifies top-line performance (i.e., occupancy and ADR), is revenue per available room (REVPAR). The REVPAR measurement incorporates the offsetting effects of occupancy and ADR by dividing total room revenue for a period by the number of available room nights in that period. Typically ADR and occupancy move inversely to each other such that higher occupancies can be achieved by offering lower rates, while ADR can be increased, resulting in lower occupancy. The REVPAR calculation can assist in determining whether a property should pursue maximizing room revenue yield by seeking an increase in ADR or in occupancy. Exhibit 11–7 illustrates two alternatives.

Thus, it is hypothesized that the 5-percentage-point increase in occupancy combined with a $5 decrease in ADR would increase the revenue performance of the hotel more favorably than a $10 increase in ADR combined with a 5-percentage-point decrease in occupancy, all other things being equal. Yet REVPAR does not provide all of the necessary insight into maximizing rooms profitability; the expense component must be considered as well.

With rooms revenue and profit constituting the bulk of hotel income, precise management of both revenue and expenses of this

EXHIBIT 11–6

Representative Hotel Financial Statements

	Full-Service		All-Suites		Limited-Service	
	%	PAR	%	PAR	%	PAR
Revenues:						
Rooms	62.2%	$17,062	84.4%	$17,684	94.0%	$10,544
Food	24.3	6,677	7.4	1,579	N/A	N/A
Beverage	6.9	1,909	2.0	432	N/A	N/A
Telephone	2.4	663	3.5	746	2.2	251
Other operated departments	2.3	643	1.6	349	1.4	156
Rentals and other income	1.9	528	1.5	223	2.4	267
Total revenues	100.0%	$27,482	100.0%	$21,193	100.0%	$11,218
Departmental expenses:						
Rooms	27.2	4,730	23.8	$ 4,263	26.4	$ 2,787
Food and beverage	84.6	7,247	83.0	1,658	N/A	N/A
Telephone	67.1	445	87.7	379	82.5	207
Other operated departments	75.9	488	92.2	322	35.3	55
Total departmental expenses	47.0%	$12,910	31.2%	$ 6,622	27.1%	$ 3,049
Gross operating income	53.0%	$14,572	68.8%	$14,571	72.9%	$ 8,169

Undistributed operating expenses:

	%	Amount	%	Amount	%	Amount
Administrative and general	10.4	2,871	10.5	2,227	10.0	1,120
Franchise fees	0.9	243	1.4	305	1.7	192
Marketing and guest entertainment	6.8	1,879	7.2	1,525	4.9	555
Property operation and maintenance	5.6	1,550	5.2	1,103	6.5	733
Energy costs	5.1	1,394	5.7	1,213	5.2	582
Other unallocated operated departments	0.2	52	0.9	199	0.2	21
Total undistributed expenses	29.0%	$ 7,989	30.9%	$ 6,572	28.5%	$ 3,203
Gross operating profit	14.0%	$ 6,583	37.9%	$ 7,999	44.4%	$ 4,966
Fixed charges:						
Management fees	2.8	766	3.5	733	4.4	499
Property taxes and other municipal charges	3.3	907	4.7	1,005	4.3	480
Insurance on buildings and contents	0.7	182	0.6	127	1.0	111
Total fixed charges	6.8%	$ 1,855	8.8%	$ 1,865	9.7%	$ 1,090
Net operating income	17.2%	$ 4,728	29.1%	$ 6,134	34.7%	$ 3,876

PAR = per available room.

SOURCE: PKF Consulting, *Trends in the Hotel Industry*, USA edition (1992).

EXHIBIT 11–7
Yield Management Example

	Occupancy	ADR	REVPAR
Current	75%	$125.00	$93.75
Proposal 1	80	120.00	96.00
Proposal 2	70	135.00	94.50

department is integral to achieving financial returns. To illustrate, let's embellish upon our example in Exhibit 11–7. Assume a 100-room hotel at which the cost per occupied room (CPOR) is $30. This represents all expenses of renting, operating, and cleaning one hotel room for one night. The sales director indicates that, based on market research, the hotel should be able to increase occupancy to 80 percent by reducing the current rate structure to an average daily rate (ADR) of $120. However, the sales director believes that if an ADR strategy is pursued, the hotel can achieve a $135 ADR while reducing occupancy to 70 percent. The marketing strategy that optimizes profitability can be determined only by calculating the projected rooms department expense and profit margin. As shown in Exhibit 11–8, the analysis suggests that a rate maximization strategy should be pursued (proposal 2 in Exhibit 11–7), as it provides for a higher profit percentage of room revenue.

While oversimplified, the example points out some of the intricacies of maximizing hotel profitability, particularly given that the yield management exercise occurs on the basis of a 24-hour lease. If

Exhibit 11–8
Financial Comparison of Market Strategies

	At 80% Occupancy	At 70% Occupancy
Occupied rooms	29,200	25,550
Average daily rate	$120	$135
Rooms revenue	$3,504,000	$3,449,250
CPOR	$30	$30
Rooms expense	$876,000	$766,500
Profit margin	75%	78%

Total available rooms = 36,500 (Number of rooms × Days in a year)

the owner takes into account the additional wear and tear the guest rooms would endure as a result of the higher occupancy, thereby causing the furniture, fixtures, and equipment (FF&E) to be replaced more frequently, the equation becomes more complex. Such an exercise provides a hypothetical framework within which to make yield management decisions. In practice, pricing strategies are often based on research of competitive hotels, general manager experience and feel for the market, and yield management analysis.

Monthly Financial Statements

In evaluating operating performance, the monthly financial statement is utilized as the ongoing management and ownership information tool. Since such a report represents historical information, one can only react to results. Therefore, it is crucial that the operator's annual plan be developed by a zero-based budgeting model that sets accurate staffing levels and challenging performance standards. If the budget is properly prepared, taking into full account the relationship of fixed and variable labor components, variances to the plan are more readily explained and therefore can be acted on.

A review of the monthly operating statement should be conducted, employing variance analysis to understand the deviations in operating expenses relative to fluctuations in revenue. Profit retention, the percentage of positive variances to revenue that flow to the bottom line, is the broadest and most important measurement of an operator's ability to plan for or react to varying levels of business activity. Fully understanding the breakpoints at which additional staff must be added to handle increased occupancy will allow for thorough performance review of the hotel manager as actuals are compared to plan. Many hotel companies chart worker-hours, or full-time equivalents (FTEs), as productivity measurements. However, they are often reluctant to share such information with ownership since it might expose labor inefficiencies.

On the downside, the ability of the hotel operator to contain costs when revenues decline is judged by evaluating the corresponding reduction in controllable expenses such as supplies, minimal use of overtime, combining of job functions, replacement of salaried managers with hourly employees, and innovative means of providing the same guest experience with fewer worker-hours. The percentage, or absolute dollar amount, of decline in NOI should be less than the same measurement's decrease in revenue if the management company is truly taking the steps necessary to contain costs.

Asset Supervision

Finally, the need for specialized hotel asset managers to safeguard the investment by exercising close oversight of the hotel operator is becoming widely recognized in the institutional investment arena as a factor critical to the success of a hotel property. This is best accomplished by individuals who possess a working knowledge of hotel operations, combined with advanced training in real estate finance and appraisal. The sometimes contradictory objectives of management companies (increase revenues through greater marketing efforts and capital improvements) and owners (maximize return on investment via expense containment and sound capital expenditures) can often be reconciled by the process of goal sharing, nurtured by an owner's representative or asset manager.

How can this best be accomplished? The most potent method of developing a common agenda between operator and owner is to more closely tie the compensation of the management company to bottom-line results. Ownership should share with management its investment measurements that quantify the financial performance of the asset. This education process will aid the management company in understanding how the owner thinks and perhaps will become one of the manager's decision criteria in evaluating operational issues or capital projects. Furthermore, it is incumbent upon the hotel owner to inform the operator as to the long-term strategy for the property. The process of developing the long-term objective must, by its very nature, involve the hotel manager.

PORTFOLIO MANAGEMENT

Portfolio Strategy

Hotel portfolio diversification strategy has historically received little, if any, attention. Hotel portfolios, like many other real estate portfolios in the late 1970s, were assembled in a haphazard manner, based on whatever good deal came along next. For example, if a portfolio was assembled that was heavily weighted in the large, first-class, convention hotel segment in major metropolitan areas, it would have been extremely susceptible to the recent dramatic increase in convention center development and the resulting competition in that market segment.

In line with the maturation of the hotel real estate industry, consideration should be given to the thoughtful and well-planned development of a hotel portfolio. As a starting point, the two major components of hotel portfolio diversification should be the segmentation matrix model applied in conjunction with the distribution of properties by economic region.

In its most basic form, the combination of these two elements calls for a value-weighted distribution of portfolio dollars to various economic regions, further subdivided by the classifications set forth in the segmentation matrix. More detailed analysis will be necessary to determine growth trends within and across economic regions, which, in conjunction with current and anticipated supply, will identify a particular property type and/or economic orientation that may exhibit opportunity and the timing associated with the proposed investment. Overlaying the current position in the real estate cycle will dictate whether the portfolio will be assembled via acquisition or development.

In practice, noninstitutional, multi-unit hotel owners tend to limit their investment strategy to a specific property type and economic orientation. This approach favors concentrating the bulk of a portfolio in, for example, a Comfort Inn such that economies of scale can be achieved in terms of accounting systems employed, bulk purchasing agreements, and furniture, fixture, and equipment expenditures. Furthermore, operating expertise can be more easily transferred throughout a portfolio when properties are segmentationally homogeneous.

Current real estate markets dictate that almost every need for portfolio diversification can likely be fulfilled via acquisition, except for the rare occasion when economic analysis demonstrates an unexploited market niche.

Strategic Asset Planning

With an understanding of diversification and risk reduction at the portfolio level, attention should be focused on developing a long-term strategy for each asset in the portfolio. This comprehensive planning process incorporates every facet relating to the ownership and operation of a hotel property.

Exhibit 11–9 provides an overview of the strategic planning process. As with any such process, one must first have a firm understand-

EXHIBIT 11–9   The Strategic Asset Management Planning Process

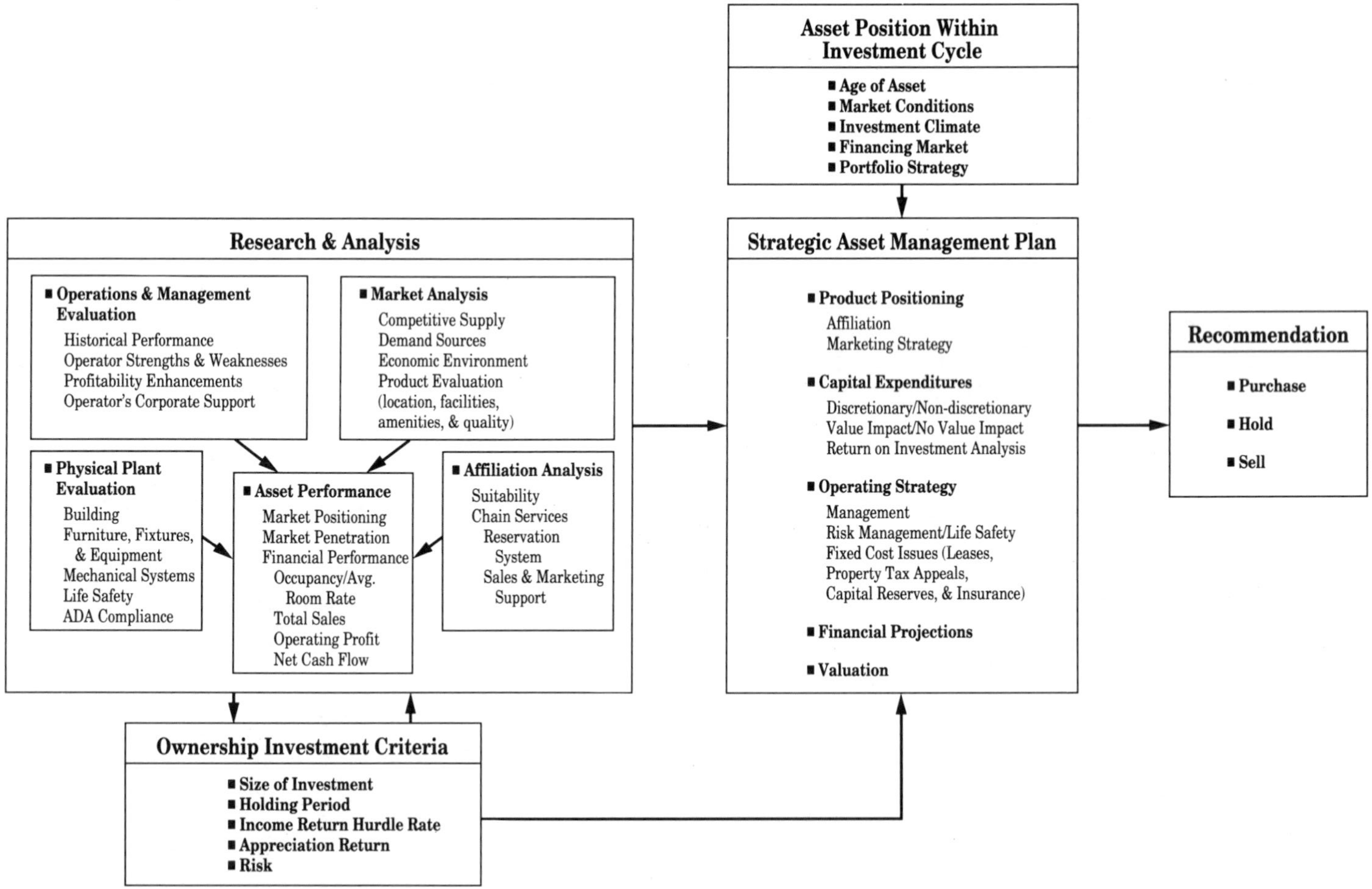

Research & Analysis

■ Operations & Management Evaluation

Historical Performance
Operator Strengths & Weaknesses
Profitability Enhancements
Operator's Corporate Support

■ Physical Plant Evaluation

Building
Furniture, Fixtures, & Equipment
Mechanical Systems
Life Safety
ADA Compliance

■ Market Analysis

Competitive Supply
Demand Sources
Economic Environment
Product Evaluation (location, facilities, amenities, & quality)

■ Asset Performance

Market Positioning
Market Penetration
Financial Performance
Occupancy/Avg. Room Rate
Total Sales
Operating Profit
Net Cash Flow

■ Affiliation Analysis

Suitability
Chain Services
Reservation System
Sales & Marketing Support

Ownership Investment Criteria

■ Size of Investment
■ Holding Period
■ Income Return Hurdle Rate
■ Appreciation Return
■ Risk

Asset Position Within Investment Cycle

■ Age of Asset
■ Market Conditions
■ Investment Climate
■ Financing Market
■ Portfolio Strategy

Strategic Asset Management Plan

■ Product Positioning

Affiliation
Marketing Strategy

■ Capital Expenditures

Discretionary/Non-discretionary
Value Impact/No Value Impact
Return on Investment Analysis

■ Operating Strategy

Management
Risk Management/Life Safety
Fixed Cost Issues (Leases, Property Tax Appeals, Capital Reserves, & Insurance)

■ Financial Projections

■ Valuation

Recommendation

■ Purchase

■ Hold

■ Sell

ing of the history of the asset. The research and analysis phase should include a review of the following five areas: (1) operations and management evaluation, (2) market analysis, (3) physical plant evaluation, (4) affiliation analysis, and (5) asset performance.

Operations and Management Evaluation

The operations and management evaluation phase should review operating procedures, including a financial operational audit to ensure accuracy of financial statements and a proper system of accounting controls. Operator compliance with the management agreement should be checked during this phase as well. The capability of the hotel operator should be reviewed in conjunction with historical financial statements to determine, among other things, how the management company anticipated operating trends or shifts in market demand. The support of the operator's corporate office should be examined in terms of its ability to provide profitability enhancements (i.e., systemwide implementation of cost-cutting measures) or the benefit to the property of national marketing programs.

The hotel's financial statements should be subjected to a thorough ratio analysis. Ratio analysis is an exploration of line item revenue and expense categories on a per-available-room, per-occupied-room, and percentage basis as they relate to sales by department, mix of demand (i.e., group versus transient), and mix of sales within the department. Year-to-year comparisons are typically made to discover trends.

Market Analysis

The hotel operator should be enlisted to assist in the market analysis phase, wherein a thorough review is performed of the competitive market supply via product evaluations, noting strengths and weaknesses of the subject property relative to its primary competitors. An overview of prevailing economic and demographic conditions and projections relating to those factors influencing lodging demand is crucial to understanding the macroenvironment in which the hotel operates. Specific assessments of changes to generators of hotel demand should be made in conjunction with the economic-demographic analysis. The sum of these data will provide a picture of the external environment in which the hotel operates and permit an understanding of what strategic direction the hotel should take in light of the market analysis.

Physical Plant Evaluation

The physical plant evaluation is performed by the hotel asset manager with the support of the subject property's chief engineer, general manager, and, if conditions warrant, specialized consultants from one or more of the engineering disciplines. A thorough inspection of all building systems, furniture, fixtures, and equipment (FF&E), guest rooms, meeting rooms, public space, and service areas should be performed by the evaluation team. Appropriate to this phase is a review of compliance to building codes, life safety requirements, and special legislation such as the Americans With Disabilities Act. The physical plant evaluation will provide the basis for the strategic plan's projection of capital expenditures during the desired holding period of the asset.

Affiliation Analysis

An affiliation analysis, where appropriate, will determine the suitability of the subject property's flag, or brand name. Does consumers' perception of the property name (Hilton Inn, for example) match the perceived quality level of the hotel in the eyes of the traveling public within its competitive marketplace? The degree of congruity between consumer perception and quality influences the performance of the affiliation's (or franchise system's) chain services, that is, its reservation system and sales and marketing support. A decision to reaffiliate is an involved process, often incurring substantial cost, due to the terms of the existing franchise or management agreement. However, the proper affiliation is paramount to the hotel's long-term financial success.

Asset Performance

The asset performance phase incorporates the above findings as a basis for understanding the historical financial performance of the property. The primary goal should be to fully understand the hotel's market positioning in a broad sense. In this context, market positioning refers to the overall combination of consumer perception of the hotel, its physical condition, its marketing strategy, its guest service level and amenities, and its performance relative to its primary competition.

Initially, a comparison of the hotel's occupancy and average daily rate (ADR) achievement relative to its primary competitive set, commonly referred to as market penetration analysis, should be performed. It is important to consider any extraordinary external market factors or property-specific events (e.g., business interruption due to renovation) that may have affected the hotel's ability to penetrate the market. Conclusions drawn during the market analysis phase will provide insight into the market penetration observations.

Many of the findings of the operations evaluation phase, particularly the ratio analyses, will relate directly to the analysis of historical financial performance conducted during the asset performance phase. Conclusions reached during other phases will provide insight into the factors that affect annual operating results (such as changes in union contracts, a shrinking available labor pool, or revisions to employee benefit and worker compensation programs).

Certainly the condition of the physical plant will have a tremendous bearing on the trends in revenue and profitability performance. The lack of a coherent and well-planned ongoing replacement program for FF&E will almost surely result in deteriorating market penetration and a decreased bottom line. Conversely, a property that has reserved and expended appropriate funds, typically 3 to 5 percent of total revenues, on an annual basis will benefit twofold: The property will have maintained its competitive position in the market, and the cost associated with a major renovation at the end of the FF&E life cycle (five to seven years) will be substantially reduced.

In conjunction with the research and analysis activity, the asset manager should determine the ownership investment criteria. This involves eliciting input from ownership with respect to its goals for the asset. Chief among these concerns is the desired holding period and the willingness to invest additional capital. The timing of a sale (i.e., knowing when and how to execute a sale) is critical to maximizing investment returns. Though this may seem obvious, hotel owners often become emotionally attached (especially when times are "good") to their hotels and, accordingly, fail to sell at the right time. Ownership's appetite for risk, capital availability, and required rate of return will dictate the long-term strategy for the property.

The resulting plan details the overall positioning of the hotel, in light of proposed capital expenditures, and the recommended operating and marketing strategy to support the positioning. As with any real estate investment, the key focus of the strategic plan is increasing the value of the asset by an amount greater than the expenditure involved in the repositioning.

The strategic planning process is an iterative one, involving continual interplay among operator, owner, and asset manager. Goal sharing is an important element in developing a long-term strategy that will be diligently supported by ownership and enthusiastically implemented by the operator.

Valuation Issues

Going-concern value, the ongoing requirement of capital expenditures, and long-term management contract encumbrances represent the key elements that distinguish valuations of hotel properties from appraisals of more traditional real estate types.

As an operating business, a hotel generates, on average, at least a third of its revenues from sources unrelated to the rental of real estate in the form of food and beverage sales, equipment rentals, sundry sales, and telephone charges. Consequently, the total appraised value of a hotel property is composed of a real estate component, representing income derived from the land and improvements, and the going-concern value, representing the management company's ability to maximize income from the operating departments. Yet the distinction of going-concern value is not simply that which is associated with the management company, for the management company is also responsible for maximizing income derived from the improvements, that is, room rentals. Moreover, the start-up costs the owner incurs to establish business operations is clearly also a part of the going-concern value. Intuitively, going-concern value should account for the expenses associated with preopening and the maintenance of items required for the daily operation of the business, such as working capital, inventories, and necessary licenses.

A more difficult question is whether the benefit of the assembled staff and organizational structure should be considered part of going-concern value. Legally, the hotel staff typically consists of employees of the management company, and the organization structure is specific to the management company as well; thus, both represent value to the operator. Yet it is obvious that without both, the hotel could not operate as a going concern. Quantifying this human resource component's contribution to business value remains clearly in the realm of an art rather than a science.

In summary, "separating the value of a hotel's business from the value of its real estate is a controversial topic. It is difficult to determine exactly where income attributed to the business stops and income from the real estate begins."[10]

Capital expenditure projections are another area that distinguishes hotel valuations from appraisals of more traditional property types. As a result of the daily rental of rooms and the high-traffic nature of their public facilities, hotel properties are extremely capital intensive, requiring ongoing maintenance on an annual basis, as well as complete replacements of furniture, fixtures, and equipment (FF&E) every five to seven years. Consequently, capital expenditures must be accounted for when calculating net operating income (NOI) for appraisal purposes.

A drawback of many hotel appraisals is that a constant 3 percent of total revenues is generally deducted as an FF&E reserve in deriving NOI, which often is insufficient to adequately fund necessary capital projects. Furthermore, many appraisals fail to account for the position of the hotel in its life cycle; that is, does the hotel require, by virtue of its age and position relative to the competitive market, a substantial capital investment in excess of the funds expended for the seven-year replacement of FF&E? If a 20-year-old hotel facility, despite being well maintained, is located in a market where significant new supply has been added within the last five years (a realistic scenario in today's market), the likelihood is great that the hotel will exhibit some degree of functional obsolescence. Consequently, a capital expenditure often approximating 10 to 30 percent of the market value of the property will be required to maintain the hotel's competitive standing in the marketplace. The importance to the hotel owner of incorporating the expenditure into the long-term projection and realizing the valuation implication cannot be understated.

Most hotel properties today operate under the auspices of a management contract or are affiliated with a nationally known brand via a franchise agreement. These agreements are in fact an encumbrance, for their terms typically run 20 years or more, with little opportunity for cancellation or termination. Effectively, such contracts limit the ability of hotel owners to sell their property by reducing the potential universe of purchasers to those willing to retain the current management company or franchise. If a disposition of the property is hindered

---

[10] Rushmore, "The Origins of the Lodging Industry," p. 104.

by the limiting conditions of the management or franchise agreement, the owner is forced to discount the sale price accordingly. Often the only method available to terminate such long-term contracts is a negotiated buyout, wherein the present value of future years' fees is tendered as compensation that the franchisor or operator would have earned had the contract not been canceled.

Thus, appraised market value can be substantially diminished, depending on investor perception of the capability of the management company or the suitability of the franchise affiliation. Given that appraisals in theory reflect the market's perception and expectation of investment yields, an understanding should be derived, and quantified, of the potential negative impact on the value of an unfavorable management contract, management company, or franchise agreement. If not the appraisal itself, certainly the astute hotel owner should consider the contract encumbrance when planning a hotel property transaction.

INDUSTRY OUTLOOK

Many hotel analysts conclude that the early 1990s will be looked back at as a turning point in the hotel industry, particularly from the investor standpoint. In 1993, the last of the pooled asset sales were sold off by Resolution Trust Corp., eliminating from the market much of the inventory of hotel properties for sale below replacement cost. Capitalization rates on hotel properties appear to have stopped increasing as investors perceived the outstanding values available in the hotel sector and began to bid up prices. In addition, in certain markets around the country, the prospect of development of new hotels became more than just wishful thinking.

Yet mortgage financing of hotel properties remains difficult to obtain. Even well-capitalized hotels in mature markets with barriers to entry, excellent debt coverage, and low loan-to-value ratios have been unable to secure new debt. According to the American Council of Life Insurance, mortgage commitments on hotel property represented only 1.5 percent of the total dollar volume of new loans in the third quarter of 1993. However, it appears that debt financing is becoming more readily available for acquisitions of nationally franchised, limited-service hotels with at least three years of profitable operating history.

According to Smith Travel Research, demand for lodging accommodations in 1993 posted the largest annual increase since 1988, rising approximately 4 percent to over 730 million occupied room nights. Nationwide occupancy in 1993 increased to almost 64 percent in the face of a less than 1 percent increase in hotel room supply. Average daily room rate rose 2.3 percent, the largest increase in three years, to $61. Thus, it is apparent that the hotel industry has begun its climb out of the doldrums in which it has been mired since the late 1980s. Barring any unforeseen national economic calamity, the hotel business is expected to continue its slow but steady recovery.

CHAPTER 12

INTERNATIONAL REAL ESTATE INVESTMENT: A REALISTIC LOOK AT THE ISSUES

Helen R. Arnold
Jones Lang Wootton USA

Charles Grossman
Jones Lang Wootton Realty Advisors

INTRODUCTION

The last decade has seen the accelerated perception and acceptance of the international economic linkages that influence and constrain the American economy. Trade deficits, European and Asian investment in both real estate and major U.S. corporations, and concerns over the competitive impact of international trading blocs have all contributed to this heightened awareness. Unlike the increasing portion of international stock and bond portfolios of U.S. investors, and unlike the very substantial real estate holdings of many giant U.S.-based corporations, investment real estate has not yet become a significant component of U.S.—or, indeed, North American—institutional investor portfolios.

The late 1980s and early 1990s marked a burgeoning interest in possible international real estate investment by U.S. institutions for a variety of reasons. The weight of the evidence presented in the U.S. technical literature of the 1980s emphasized that real estate in a portfolio could enhance overall performance by increasing returns and reducing portfolio volatility, since it tended to perform inversely with U.S. stocks and bonds.[1] Moreover, the results of past return

---

[1] Earlier chapters, particularly Chapter 2, of this book provide references to the evolving technical literature.

histories indicated that international diversification paid off in the stock and bond arena.

The technical literature on long-term return results notwithstanding, the poor performance of U.S. real estate from 1987 to 1992 (shown vividly in the Russell/NCREIF index results) detracted from the allure of U.S. real estate as an investment just as many institutional investors had begun to increase the real estate portion of their portfolios. Consequently, investors questioned their previous assumptions about U.S. real estate as a viable investment. The flood of capital into real estate construction raised concerns about the possible recurrence of such an unusually long construction cycle; the difficulty of selling underperforming real estate heightened concerns about real estate's relatively illiquid nature; and the prospect of a long period of low inflation reduced the appeal of real estate as an inflation hedge. However, all of the above were good reasons for investors to ask whether or not international real estate investment could offer the benefit of reducing the volatility of the domestic real estate portfolio.

Economic expectations for the United States relative to the rest of the world in the 1990s also played a part in this increasing interest. The United States, burdened by public and private sector debt, was expected to suffer from an undersupply of capital available for economic expansion. The early economic forecasts for Europe in the 1990s—the economic speculation over EC '92—were for much higher rates of economic growth than those predicted for the United States. The Pacific Rim locations also seemed to offer the possibility of much higher rates of economic growth. Although there has been less publicity in the United States about the positive effects of EC '92 since the change of regimes in Eastern Europe and more discussion about the impact of potential capital shortages on worldwide development, many of the measures for European business and economic unification quietly moved forward throughout 1992 and 1993.

This institutional investor curiosity about international real estate investment has perforce remained primarily in the realm of potential action rather than followed up by a flood of investment. International real estate investment does present considerable decision-making, organizational, and managerial challenges above and beyond the problems of achieving the desired cash flows at the building level. Some of these problems would be inherent in the choice of this investment medium in any case, but they are accentuated by the time-distance gap from the United States and different socioeconomic and cultural structures associated with individual national markets.

Therefore, there is a need for a concentrated scrutiny of the problems and opportunities in international real estate investment, a scrutiny of the managerial issues an organization may face in making the decision to invest abroad and implementing that decision, as well as of the evidence available to help make such a decision. This chapter is written for the U.S. investor who is particularly interested in how various other institutional investors have approached the decision process, the quantitative evidence they have used to bolster their decisions, the criteria for the decisions, and the best mode of implementation. This generic approach is drawn from our experience with offshore institutions that have initiated this process in the last decade, when more rigorous decision procedures have become the mode in most organizations. This chapter attempts to bridge some gaps between theory and practice by providing some statistics on returns and portfolio volatility in an international real estate portfolio and evaluating the limits and actual use of such information to date.

THE DECISION PROCESS AND ITS REQUIREMENTS

The approach international institutional investors take to either their initial worldwide investment strategy or their updates and re-evaluations of worldwide real estate investment strategy follows a familiar pattern. Typically, the investor creates a working group of senior real estate officers, often in combination with international in-house equities experts and outside consultants, including economists, real estate experts, and tax and legal advisors. The working group has the assignment of determining whether or not international real estate investment has the appropriate risk-reward configuration for the investor and, if so, the overall strategy and subsequent managerial tactics to pursue. Each outside advisor is usually commissioned to report on his or her area of expertise. If we consider the roster of advisors in conceptual terms, it is heavily weighted toward those who can explain and minimize the systematic risks involved.

A major time cost is involved even in the initial decision to examine the feasibility of international real estate investment, given the requirements of fiduciary responsibility. Designated senior staff must become sufficiently familiar with all of the elements involved in reaching that decision, since ultimately it is this staff who must determine the rank ordering of criteria for country and market selection and live with the selection.

The conceptual complexities become readily apparent when one considers the difficulties of selecting the countries and the real estate markets within those countries. The problem entails

- Identifying the pertinent variables by which countries and local markets can be compared.
- Determining whether the characteristics of countries as a whole, as opposed to variables pertaining to a single market, have the greatest primacy in weighting a selection.
- Applying comparison and rank ordering, thus narrowing down the universe of nations to a small and numerically manageable sample that can then be studied in more detail.

In an abbreviated format (see Exhibit 12–1), country and local market variables can be conceived of as macro and micro issues. The macro issues conceptually relate to reducing systematic risks for portfolio allocation across particular nations. By extension, international diversification should reduce a portfolio's systematic risk, especially if that portfolio was previously composed of assets principally from one nation. The micro issues are more oriented toward those items that determine unsystematic risk. Exhibit 12–1 identifies some of these elements, both those easily quantified and those not so easily quantified. These variables are discussed more extensively in the following section.

An All-Encompassing, Systematic Approach

A common approach for first-time international investors is to utilize, with the advice of experts, a limited number of macroeconomic or political variables and select somewhat arbitrary performance cutoff points as benchmarks that serve to retain or eliminate nations. These variables can be static descriptors (size of market, per capita income, type of government) and/or trend descriptors (growth rates, frequency of change in the political party in power). Then, having reduced the investment universe to anywhere from 10 to 30 nations, the urban market selection process begins, following a somewhat similar methodology but with much greater emphasis on actual return performance.

EXHIBIT 12–1
Overview of Market Variables

Macro	**Micro**
National economic cycles (prices, GDP, debt, savings, household income, currency fluctuations, alternative asset returns)	Local/regional real estate returns
	Suppy/demand/vacancy rate/ absorption trends
Political stability (changing of reigning party, frequency of elections, leadership tenure, strikes)	Local economy
	Socio/political issues operating locally
Social stability (demographics, ethnic violence, popular violence or unrest, crime, etc.)	Property market structures: local planning, local companies available for management, transaction costs
Organizational/bureaucratic structures	Leasing market: lease terms and conditions
Financial system structure	
Property market structures and stability: planning, law, mode of transactions	
National real estate returns	
Political and consumer psychology and culture	

Source: JLW USA Research.

A Past Knowledge and Intuition Approach

In the case of investors with an ongoing program, those with considerable knowledge of multiple nations, or those with strong opinions, it
is common to discover a selection process that moves immediately
to certain urban markets and property types. Some international
investors have been engaged in multination real estate investment
for so long that they consciously view the world as one large economic
system wherein major metropolitan areas constitute significant regional economies. National political changes and bureaucratic regula-

tions are then simply different rules in the local game, which can be dealt with through the appropriate tax and legal advice. The focus then becomes the urban economy and local real estate market trends.

A Problem Common to Both Approaches

Above all, in the case of international real estate investors, institutional investors wish to see the kind of risk-return analysis to which they have become accustomed in the equity and fixed-income markets, in other words, the returns, standard deviations on returns, correlation coefficients, and covariances necessary to determine the impact of a new investment on a portfolio and to create the optimal portfolio. The basic premise for international investment very much rests on assumptions about reducing the variability of real estate portfolio returns. However, demonstrating the validity of those assumptions from a comparison of past return trends is formidably difficult because of the extremely mixed quality of real estate return information from the individual nations. This is easily comprehensible when one considers that the Russell/NCREIF index in the United States, a nation generally considered to be at the forefront of statistical collection and analysis, began as recently as 1978. The United Kingdom is generally considered to have the longest-running return indices comparable to the Russell/NCREIF index, and these date only to the late 1960s. By comparison, stock price data and indices in the United States have been compiled from the mid-19th century to the present.

UNDERSTANDING COUNTRY RISKS: WEIGHTING ECONOMIC AND POLITICAL/ ORGANIZATIONAL SYSTEMS

Before turning to an analysis of the evidence available on international real estate investment returns, it is useful to discuss in more detail some aspects of the way the all-encompassing systematic approach has been applied. In general, investors and their advisors are very good at identifying ways to use economic criteria to narrow down the countries to a manageable number but less accomplished at looking at the political/organizational patterns of systematic risk that may affect foreign real estate markets. Yet United States institutional investors are extremely concerned about political/organizational risk, and this aspect of international investment deserves special attention.

Some of the most common variables in the initial winnowing process used to determine the economic desirability of a nation are gross domestic product (GDP) per capita, percentage of GDP devoted to service industries, and/or per capita income. In all instances of the above, the higher, the better.

Many pitfalls lurk for the unwary investor attempting to compare multinational economic data, including the following:

- Although a national statistic may have the same name from one nation to another, it may not always be calculated or collected in the same manner.
- Concepts and/or statistics relatively unfamiliar to an American may appear and be interpreted wrongly; conversely, information that Americans automatically expect may not be available.
- Many nations are from one to three years behind in the tabulation of their national statistics. Consequently, "current" data obtained from data sellers may actually be a forecast rather than actual current information.

These issues may seem to be the kinds of problems that would crop up when dealing primarily with the lesser developed countries. Such is not the case, as anyone familiar with comparing European economic statistics may discover. Definitions published by the European Union have to be read with considerable care. For example, one of the most interesting, and frustrating concepts in the European lexicon is the one that refers to *consumption* on a national and per capita basis. Most European nations lack retail sales data and usually lack the kind of income data that are collected in the United States. The consumption data do reflect the growth in the demand for goods and services, but they are not a direct comparable for either U.S. retail sales or income.[2]

Nations such as Greece and Italy have well-known problems in the collection and tabulation of their data. Publications comparing annual European data usually have almost a three-year lag in the current quality of the data. A five-year forecast, then, may actually

---

[2] See, for example, *Eurostate: Regions: Statistical Yearbook* (Luxembourg: Office des publications officielles des communautés européennes), which is hardly annual.

be a seven-to-eight-year forecast because of the data gap. Compiling detailed time series on localized markets can also prove to be a problem, because certain nations (Greece among them again) periodically destroy their census information or surveys for reasons of confidentiality. Statistics from Eastern Europe are notoriously unreliable or biased, and presumably it may be some time before calculation methodologies are routinized.

If nothing else, these differences emphasize that an economist experienced in comparing national economies should be included in the decision process. There still remains the issue of whittling down the nations to a manageable "short list." It is, in fact, relatively easy to reduce the investment universe through the application of gross economic criteria to a list of some 30 countries. It is much more difficult to reduce that list of 30 to a short list of 5 to 10 countries, because then the investor usually scrutinizes the interrelationships among economic variables more closely and faces some difficult economic trade-offs. Typical statistics used for comparison at this stage include the savings ratio, corporate profitability, the debt-GDP ratio, household or per capita consumption, aggregate value of real estate construction, and inflation trends.

For example, a U.S. investor would probably wish to select investment locations whose basic economic cycle (measured by annual percentage change in GDP or some variation of employment growth) has been as countercyclical as possible to that of the United States. But it is questionable whether this should outweigh, for example, the importance of variables that measure the highest economic growth rates and, by extension, the expansion in demand for real estate. Even among future growth forecasts, it may be difficult to decide the appropriate level of weighting for each variable. To illustrate the differences that have appeared in rank ordering among important economic variables, Exhibit 12–2 provides forecast rankings that were tabulated in a 20-nation comparison done in early 1991.

Consider the issue of national debt, which is commonly held to be a drag on economic growth. A number of nations have fairly solid rankings in forecasts for the economic growth components noted in Exhibit 12–2 and therefore seem to be desirable locations for investment. Yet some of these nations also have a high level of public debt in relation to their GDP. Belgium, Italy, and Austria are examples of countries ranking high in the economic forecasts but having a high level of public debt. Exhibit 12–3 compares statistics on government

EXHIBIT 12–2
Rank Ordering of Forecast Growth Rates (20-Nation Study)

Real GDP Growth, 1990–94	Export Growth Forecast	Productivity Growth
Singapore	Hong Kong	Finland
Spain	Singapore	Norway
Hong Kong	United States	Italy
Germany	Spain	Belgium
Austria	Austria	France
(U.S.: 17th)		(U.S.: 12th)

Source: JLW U.K. Consulting and Research.

EXHIBIT 12–3
Government Debt as a Proportion of GDP, 1990

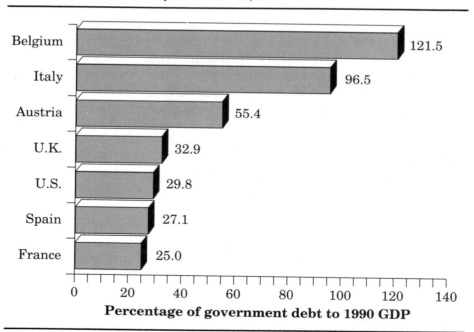

Sources: OECD, *Economic Outlook,* June 1990; JLW Consulting and Research.

debt as a proportion of GDP among various European economies and the United States.

The complicated interplay of politics and economics is reflected in any study of changing European national economic forecasts. In mid-1990, forecasts for European GDP growth rates produced by the European Community and private forecasters were extremely high; some nations were expected to see 4 to 7 percent per year growth. In the last three years, these forecasts have been drastically altered downward under the impact of recession, the slowdown in expectations for monetary union, and the economic drag expected from the diversion of resources to Eastern Europe.

A special comment should be made here about currency risk. Currency fluctuations can be treated like any other contributor to economic risk, and the volatility of nations' currencies against the dollar can be quantified and included as one of the "macro" risk elements in country comparisons. Unlike many other macro risk measures, when past real estate returns are being compared at the micro market level, the impact of currency fluctuations on real estate returns can be precisely quantified, if necessary. But in practice, international institutions seem to have been less concerned about currency risk in their decision analysis than they have been about other economic and real estate indicators. These institutions have hedging programs that apply across investments; moreover, the tax and legal structures chosen for investment often dictate the mode in which income returns can be converted or moved across national boundaries.

The Ideal Model

In an ideal research world, the results of multivariate models, with past real estate returns as the dependent variable and economic factors as the independent variables, would determine how each economic variable in the short-list comparison should be weighted. Unfortunately, the data required to construct such a model are rarely available (more on this below), and accordingly a "good fit" among the variables proves to be illusive. Moreover, even if an accurate historical model were to be created, there would be no assurance that past relationships would remain constant in the future; a forecasting model would be required. Lacking such models, the weighting attached to each economic factor is created by each investor and his or her advisors, sometimes using subjective criteria and sometimes using results drawn from other experiences.

Aspects of Political/Organizational Risk

Quantitative weights are rarely assigned to political factors in the real estate decision literature, but the literature applying quantitative techniques to a comparison of national political systems is extensive. It is possible only to highlight here certain approaches that could assist the U.S. institutional investor. These concepts assist in understanding fundamental political risks that would most heavily affect a long-term investment program. Exhibit 12–4 provides a very broad summary of the kinds of measures that quantitatively oriented social scientists use in measuring and rank ordering political volatility and organizational characteristics. The items listed under "political stability" have been the subject of extended quantitative analysis, and they are particularly useful if the investor is interested in locations other than the larger and more familiar Western European economies.

Generally, U.S. investors are most interested in the duration of governments (which generally implies stability of policy), orderly transitions between regimes, and the actual stability of economic policies pertaining to matters such as property rights and foreign

EXHIBIT 12–4
Measures of Political/Organizational Risk

Political Stability

Average durability of governments
Government effectiveness (in democracies, existence of a voting majority)
Length of tenure of major leaders
Party fractionalization
Strikes (per year, per capita)
Riots (citizens out of control destroying property)
Deaths by political violence

Bureaucratic/Managerial Behavior

Role focus (technician, advocate, broker, policymaker)
Approach to policy analysis
Attitude toward state involvement
Ideology applied to role

---

investment regulations and taxation. Contemplating political risks in international investment may involve rethinking some preconceptions about the stability of the United States itself vis à vis other nations and about what constitutes acceptable levels of political risk relative to potential return.

For example, duration of governments and maintenance of effective voting majorities are easily measured in years or months and compared. The United States is generally perceived by its citizens as an extremely stable regime, but when compared with the patterns of other industrial democracies, it has medium durability and a low voter participation in elections, which is ordinarily not considered consistent with high political stability.[3] Length of tenure of major leaders can also be examined. Leadership is more volatile in Latin America, North America, Europe, and Australia than in Africa, the Middle East, and Asia. Very high leadership turnover occurs in France, Portugal, Italy, Greece, and Japan.[4] When political volatility is actually quantified, nations somewhat more "volatile" than the United States may actually prove to have acceptable systems, especially given the expected holding period for a potential real estate investment.

Political violence, whether endemic to the system or occurring mainly at the change of a regime, has been measured worldwide through analyzing strikes, riots, and terrorist incidents. For another comparison that may affect American preconceptions, in the higher-technology industrialized nations, strikes have declined in Belgium, the United Kingdom, Denmark, the Netherlands, Norway, and Sweden but hovered at constant levels in the United States and Canada. The decline in strikes happens to be correlated with the increasing fraction of the national income passing through and allocated by the public sector.[5]

Bureaucratic behavior has not been the subject of as much extensive quantitative analysis, but bureaucrats do interpret their roles in government very differently from nation to nation. The international

---

[3] G. Bingham Powell, *Contemporary Democracies: Participation, Stability, and Violence* (Cambridge, MA: Harvard University Press, 1982).

[4] Henry Bienen and Nicolas Van De Walle, *Of Time and Power* (Stanford, CT: Stanford University Press, 1991), p. 78.

[5] Douglas A. Hibbs, *The Political Economy of Industrial Democracies* (Cambridge, MA: Harvard University Press, 1987).

real estate investment process requires extensive contact with bureaucratic elites, and, of course, governments are prime users of space for
the most common international investment of all, the office building.
In certain European nations, for instance, bureaucrats may view themselves as detached technicians and not as advocates for positions they
hold.[6] Yet, in effect, these groups can be extremely powerful and can
make important decisions about items concerning urban planning, construction, government location, and even currency without facing the
requirements for notice and consultation that exist in the United
States. Aspects of sovereign risks are often analyzed by U.S. stock and
bond managers investing internationally, albeit not necessarily with
the above degree of complexity. Nonetheless, the real estate portfolio
manager should be able to take advantage of analyses prepared by the
institutions' stock and bond managers.

A Conceptual Comparison

In addition to the above, real estate offers some special problems in
immediate country comparisons relating to the use of land in a society
and the density and spatial distribution of people and buildings within
the finite national land mass. Moreover, there are considerable differences relating to the functions, structure, and activities of the real
estate industries among various nations. There is a great difference
between nations that have extremely localized markets, dominated
by small familial real estate firms active in construction and brokerage, and nations where national or large regional banks, life insurance companies, or pension funds dominate the real estate market.
Latin America tends to be the archetypical example of the fragmented
markets, but Spain, Portugal, and Greece are not far behind. France,
Germany, and Switzerland are nations where large financial institutions predominate.

A very straightforward way to conceptualize the combination of
these criteria appears in Exhibit 12–5. The vertical axis reflects
the percentage of the economy devoted to service industries; generally, the higher that percentage, the greater the degree of higher-
technology industrialization in the society. The bars on the horizontal

---

[6] Joel D. Auerbach, ed., *Bureaucrats and Politicians in Western Democracies* (Cambridge,
MA: Harvard University Press, 1981).

EXHIBIT 12–5
Stages of Urban Development

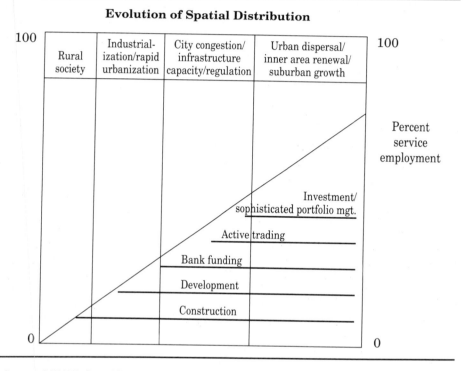

Source: JLW U.K. Consulting and Research.

axis illustrate four categories in the evolution of spatial distribution. Within the chart is a brief comment on the nature of the real estate activities characteristic of each level of development,[7] but these categories require elaboration.

Rural societies (grid 1) are nations still dominated by agriculture. They may have urban agglomerations, but the amount of modern, multiuse construction may be very slight, and the city street pattern may resemble a convoluted series of pathways rather than the linear or geometric focus of the more modern city. The construction that occurs tends to be small scale and financed by entities with a limited capital base.

---

[7] This grid was developed and quantified in detail by JLW U.K. Consulting and Research.

As industrialization proceeds (and manufacturing employment increases), rapid urbanization results (grid 2), often accompanied by extensive development projects, whether privately or publicly funded. These development projects focus on retail and business uses; the city layout changes to the linear or geometric focus. Specialized development companies emerge, but the capital base for real estate finance is still limited to an urban scope with a few rare exceptions. Smaller-scale local or neighborhood construction continues to occur.

Eventually, the city scene becomes more congested (grid 3). Stresses and strains are placed on the infrastructure, which must be upgraded and improved. As the service sector of the economy grows, banks or other financial institutions take a very significant role in the funding and structure of the real estate industry, and active trading of real estate properties owned by institutions of various types develops. The financial institutions have a sizable capital base and may be of national and large regional scope.

The final stage in the exhibit (grid 4) is typical of many larger U.S. and European metropolitan areas, where active trading of large real estate projects exists, institutional investors take a leading role in the market, and portfolio management becomes highly quantitative and organized. The real estate industry itself emerges as a complex hierarchy of companies with different functions, although large and small institutions exist side by side.

By and large, institutional investors prefer to focus on nations appearing in the last two grids. In the first two grids, the rates of economic development and real estate development are often very rapid, but the rapidity with which markets and investment uses emerge provides less protection for existing investment values. In grid 3, one would find nations such as Hungary, Bulgaria, Peru, Venezuela, Brazil, and Mexico. In grid 4, typical nations would include the United Kingdom, Singapore, Norway, Denmark, France, Germany, and Italy.

THE STATE OF THE EVIDENCE ON SAMPLE RETURNS

After the national selection process has reduced the world to a manageable list of target nations, the institutional investor usually wishes to contemplate the evidence on actual returns. Here the data allow very limited country comparisons, and the decision process must quickly begin to focus on target cities.

Return Indices

Very few markets—or institutional investors—possess the time-weighted rate of return real estate performance indices either on a national or an urban market basis. The Russell methodology has now spread to Canada, where a national index is approximately five years old. The United Kingdom happens to be far in advance of any other nation with respect to detailed return data for the nation and for its individual major markets, possessing at least six well-known indices.[8] Australia possesses a modified version of a national return index; one institutional investor commands such a large portion of the investment property market that the results of that portfolio may be considered an indicator of national performance. In addition, various discussions are under way in Australia regarding the formation of a national index.

On the Continent and around the Pacific Rim, even highly technocratic, information-oriented societies such as France and Germany lack performance indices from a database of actual returns. The reasons for this gap are complex and link technological development with real estate organizational issues. In certain relatively small nations, whether highly industrialized or not, the investment market is dominated by a few major players, and their own portfolio knowledge suffices for the creation of future investment strategy. In other nations, the organizations in the market are very small, very local entities acting in such a limited arena that familiarity with their neighborhood is sufficient. The proliferation of computers within the business and financial world also differentiates nations, and in many ways the United States is the most advanced nation in this respect. Generally, increased institutional participation in investment real estate is accompanied by an enhanced demand for market databases and performance analyses requiring extensive computer capability.

Mixed Transaction Returns

For almost all other nations around the world, estimates of real estate returns have to be derived from data drawn from leases in different properties and building prices and yields from actual sales transac-

---

[8] Jacques N. Gordon, "Property Performance Indexes in the United Kingdom and the United States," *Real Estate Review*, Summer 1991, pp. 33–40.

tions. Individual lease and property transaction information for any given year is not easily reduced to numbers that make sense for "average" rent and "average" capital value. The sample may be too small, and the properties may not be comparable. Creating a time series is equally difficult, since from one year to the next, the sample lease data and the sample transaction data may not be buildings that are strictly "comparable." Nonetheless, analysts do create the time series for rent and capital values by selecting those leases and those property transactions that seem most closely comparable. The final number for "rent" or "value" in a given year in a data set of this type will be as much an art as an arithmetic calculation. For convenience, such series will be called mixed transaction returns.

Beyond the methodological problems, even the assembling of the transaction data is not as simple as it may appear on the surface. For example, although actual rents in the United States are difficult to obtain, there are usually recording requirements relating to the ownership transfer of real estate and provisions for public access to information. In some other countries, very localized, "familial," noninstitutionalized practices with a strong incentive to avoid certain transfer taxes tend to make it highly difficult to discover the actual sales price. This comment applies to many South American markets. Other nations believe in more privacy than prevails in the United States, and there may be no provision for public access to transfer records. The United Kingdom and Germany, for instance, have much more stringent regulations on public access to records.

The interpretation of information on an international basis is also subject to a variety of challenges not seen in the U.S. For instance, Eastern European markets are having a problem with the general idea of "market rent." Fair pricing for the public benefit is still a prevalent political-psychological-social concept, and it can be difficult to select examples of leases or rents for real "market" rental growth.

Comparison of Returns: The Indices

Ideally, international return analyses should compare like-to-like data sets. As it happens, the Russell/NCREIF index for the United States and the various U.K. indices allow just such a comparison. This analysis is one of the first that American institutions usually

EXHIBIT 12–6
Comparison of JLW U.K. Property Index and Russell/NCREIF Index for the United States, 1978–91

	United Kingdom	United States	U.K. v. U.S.
Mean	13.2%	9.8%	
Standard deviation	10.5	7.2	
Correlation coefficient			+57%
Covariance			0.4%

Source: JLW Research.

perform when pondering international investment. When the U.S. quarterly real estate returns in the Russell/NCREIF index were compared with the U.K. quarterly real estate returns drawn from the JLW index[9] from 1978 to 1991, the results were as shown in Exhibit 12–6. U.K. returns have shown a higher average than U.S. returns, but the U.K. series shows a significantly higher variability (a standard deviation of 10.5 percent compared with the U.S. standard deviation of 7.2 percent). The two markets have a medium-strength positive correlation. If these results were to be maintained in the future, a U.S. investor might consider an investment in U.K. real estate. Two observations need to be made here. First, one should be cautious about attaching too much weight to relationships that span a limited number of economic and real estate cycles. Second, the addition of U.K. real estate may enhance the portfolio's (mean/variance) efficiency. If one accepts that these two real estate economies are moving less than perfectly together over time, then the inclusion of U.K. real estate extends the range of choices possible for optimal portfolio composition.

Some of the complexities of including international real estate investment in a portfolio can be portrayed by considering whether U.K. property has a low or negative correlation with U.S. stocks and bonds and/or U.K. stocks and bonds. The statistics in Exhibit 12–7 show that real estate returns in both nations do perform countercyclically with the stock and bond markets in either nation. Including

---

[9] The JLW index is a time-weighted rate of return index for properties managed and valued by JLW in the United Kingdom.

EXHIBIT 12–7
Correlation Coefficients for U.S. and U.K. Stock, Bond, and Real Estate Returns, 1978–91

	U.K. Property	U.S. Property
U.S. bonds	−.37	−.35
U.S. stocks	−.01	−.11
U.K. bonds	−.33	−.15
U.K. stocks	−.08	−.18

Sources: Analysis by JLW U.K. Research. U.K. returns from the JLW Property Index; U.S. returns from the Russell/NCREIF Property Index.

U.K. real estate in a U.S. real estate portfolio would enhance the countercyclical performance of real estate relative to an international U.S. and U.K. stock and bond portfolio.

Comparison of Returns: Mixed Transaction Returns

Investors who want a wider view of international returns than that which is confined to the United States and the United Kingdom and who also desire to focus on individual markets turn to the alternative return data sets that have been termed mixed transaction returns. To give an example of how these data can be used to understand international returns, a limited set of analyses has been performed on a selected number of international office markets: Los Angeles, New York, midtown, San Francisco, Washington, DC, Brussels, Frankfurt, London West End, Paris 8th, arrondissement, Hong Kong, Kuala Lumpur, Singapore, and Sydney (see Exhibit 12–8). Office is the only property type included here, because it is the only property type for which there is a data set on U.S. cities exactly comparable to the data on the non-U.S. cities.[10]

This particular data set applies to top-quality, downtown office properties suitable for purchase by major international institutions.

---

[10] These data sets were developed through a JLW international research program and at least offer a like-to-like comparison. There are probably other sources one could use for U.S. retail and industrial property rent/yield/capital value information (perhaps from the National Real Estate Index), but achieving the assurance of data comparability for such an analysis is an extensive undertaking beyond the scope of this chapter.

EXHIBIT 12–8
Comparison of Top-Quality, Prime Location, Downtown Office Returns, 1979–89

City	Average Return	Standard Deviation	Coefficient of Variation
Los Angeles	19.38%	17.8%	.92
San Francisco	16.69	29.5	1.77
New York, midtown	21.37	28.5	1.33
Washington, DC	17.96	12.4	.69
Brussels	19.11	5.7	.30
London West End	19.72	18.9	.96
Paris, 8th arrondissement	24.56	10.7	.43
Frankfurt	17.82	12.6	.71
Hong Kong	21.52	30.8	1.43
Kuala Lumpur	6.27	23.4	3.73
Singapore	25.02	65.0	2.60
Sydney	27.98	19.6	.70

Source: JLW International Research.

The annual capital value and yield data are derived from an analysis of comparable building sales in any given year. The rent data are net effective rents drawn from leases on comparable properties. Return figures for each year are composed of capital returns and income returns. These returns are calculated by taking each year's net income and applying the respective market capitalization rates to arrive at the estimated capital value for the hypothetical investment.

The returns therefore do not allow for any kind of obsolescence, whether physical or locational, and *this analysis is for illustrative purposes only*. This kind of analysis tacitly assumes an annual rent review, with all rents moving upward to market. The resulting returns thus show higher annual rental growth than would be seen in actual portfolio performance.

The time span shown here points out the limitations of this data set and, indeed, of valuation data in general. If the analysis were performed through 1992, the returns would naturally be lowered. However, the dearth of comparable sales in a number of cities since 1990, especially in the U.S., makes it extremely difficult to ascertain capital values and yields. Any such numbers would be quite hypothetical and subject to change after sales resume, whenever that might be in the 1990s. Exhibit 12–8 reports the office return results, the standard deviation, and the coefficient of variation for data from 1979 to 1989. The very high differences in variability should be noted, ranging from a low of 5.7 percent in Brussels to a high of 65 percent in Singapore. The coefficient of variation is obtained by dividing the standard deviation by the annual average return; an excellent coefficient of variation would be around .5, where the rate of return is twice the level of risk. In this instance, the coefficient of variation for the entire mix of cities equals .78.

Creating Sample International Office Portfolios

To better understand the inner workings among the office markets, it is also possible to calculate the correlations and covariances among these returns (see Exhibit 12–9). Correlations close to zero or negative are evidence of countercyclical behavior and suggest that the markets are influenced by outside factors in entirely different ways. Covariances (the product of the standard deviation and the correlation coefficient) approaching zero from the negative side are considered optimal.

The skillful portfolio manager, given perfect information, would be able to determine precise allocations of investments to various cities to achieve the desired combination of risk and return, most likely through the use of an optimization program. This program would produce the efficient frontier, that set of real estate investments which would produce the optimal return and risk mix of property investments.

Rather than create such an optimal model here, this return data set will be used to explore the potential benefits of international diversification through the creation of four simple hypothetical portfolios:

- The global portfolio consists of equally weighted investments in all of the office markets noted in Exhibit 12–8.
- The All America portfolio consists of equally weighted investments located only in New York, Los Angeles, San Francisco, and Washington, DC.
- The All Europe portfolio contains equally weighted investments in only the European cities.
- The All Asia/Pacific portfolio contains equally weighted investments in only the Pacific Rim office locations.

EXHIBIT 12–9

Correlation Coefficients of Returns, 1979–89

	LA	NY	SF	DC	Brussels	Frankfurt	HK	KL	London	Paris	Singapore	Sydney
Los Angeles	1.0000											
New York, midtown	0.8679	1.0000										
San Francisco	0.6256	0.6392	1.0000									
Washington, DC	0.4982	0.5032	0.9672	1.0000								
Brussels	0.1064	−0.2665	0.1221	0.1629	1.0000							
Frankfurt	−0.2013	−0.3538	−0.0691	−0.1382	0.2487	1.0000						
Hong Kong	0.6993	0.3431	0.5238	0.4691	0.6776	0.1890	1.0000					
Kuala Lampur	0.2047	0.0233	0.1684	0.1360	0.0269	0.5415	0.2610	1.0000				
London	0.5830	0.3690	0.3510	0.2472	0.6083	0.1366	0.7998	−0.1867	1.0000			
Paris, 8th arrondissement	0.0251	0.3016	0.2460	0.1926	−0.4334	0.3615	−0.2214	0.5141	−0.2647	1.0000		
Singapore	0.7172	0.7296	0.9110	0.8124	0.1888	0.0834	0.6509	0.1791	.5641	.3346	1.0000	
Sydney	0.4924	0.5140	0.9373	0.9290	0.3212	−0.0246	0.5564	0.0274	.4807	.2208	.9052	1.0000

Source: JLW USA Research.

The calculations assumed a $100 million investment in the initial year, with annual rental growth and capital appreciation having occurred in accordance with the results of the mixed transaction data. Results are given in Exhibit 12–10.

The European portfolio presented the safest strategy for prudent investors, with a return of over 20 percent and a standard deviation of 6.62 percent. An investor willing to accept higher risk might have chosen the Asia/Pacific portfolio, with its higher returns but substantially higher volatility. (Since this would have increased risk dramatically for a relatively small increase in return, such an investor might pragmatically have decided to adhere to the European portfolio or focus on selected markets in the Asia/Pacific portfolio.)

Cross-regional portfolios, consisting of equally weighted investments in each of the cities within two regions, were also created for the investor looking to perhaps increase returns while decreasing risk (see Exhibit 12–11). The addition of a 50 percent investment in European offices had significant benefits for both American and Asia/Pacific investors. An investment split between the United States and Europe provided the hypothetical American investor with a higher return and a lower standard deviation than an all-U.S. portfolio. For the Asian investor, a 50/50 split between Asian/Pacific and European locations still had high returns, but considerably reduced the coefficient of variation. The European investor, however, would be helped little by such a simplistic diversification scheme. An all-European investment scheme is hurt only by dividing the portfolios between American or Asia/Pacific properties.

EXHIBIT 12–10

Comparison of Combined Downtown Office Portfolios for Different World Regions, 1979–89

Portfolio	Average Return	Standard Deviation	Coefficient of Variation
Global	20.68%	18.77%	0.91
All U.S.	18.96	19.38	1.02
All Europe	20.56	6.62	0.32
All Asia/Pacific	22.31	31.54	1.41

Source: JLW USA Research.

EXHIBIT 12–11
Comparison of Cross-Regional Downtown Office Portfolios, 1979–89

Portfolio	Average Return	Standard Deviation	Coefficient of Variation
U.S./Europe	19.78%	11.80%	0.60
U.S./Asia Pacific	20.74	24.72	1.19
Europe/Asia Pacific	21.46	19.96	0.93

Source: JLW USA Research.

Limitations of the Evidence and Statistical Techniques

How appropriate are such statistical analyses when applied to the type of data set above compared to statistics derived from time-weighted return indices based on actual portfolio performance? Under ordinary circumstances, a 10-year return series with a single-number result derived from different building comparisons and opinions, such as the above, is not statistically significant at the 95 or 99 percent confidence level. Moreover, further statistical analyses indicate that the results cannot be counted on 30 percent of the time (30 percent being the number that many social scientists think is plausible for real-world research). Adding quarterly results to annual differences would allow the analyst to eventually achieve some level of acceptable real-world probabilities, enough perhaps to justify forecast modeling or optimal portfolio modeling, but this does not resolve the basic problems stemming from the origins of the numbers for each year or quarter.

Given the limitations of the data, it is probably fair to say that the statistical calculations provide the analyst with a greater understanding of the *possible relationships among markets. The process of attempting to apply statistical techniques to even limited data necessitates thinking about portfolio composition within a rigorous framework. It is more difficult to conclude that such data should be used in forecasting actual returns for individual portfolio composition.* This in no way denigrates the value of such market trend compilation. Rather, it emphasizes that a propensity to use the quantitative methodology available should be tempered by an understanding of the limits of information.

"FUNDAMENTALS" BEHIND LOCAL MARKET CYCLES AND QUESTIONS ABOUT WHERE THE WORLD IS GOING

The preceding section on sample returns available at the national and local market levels is one component of the decision process pursued by the potential international investor. More often than not, the exercise is pursued

1. In conjunction with expert tax and legal advice to determine whether there are significant tax and legal difficulties, and in conjunction with expert tax and legal advice obtained from appropriate sources.

2. To determine whether there is sufficient evidence on overall market return trends to warrant examining individual market investment potentials more closely and individual investments themselves. Exhibit 12–12 illustrates the decision process flow-through at this point.

Assuming the weight of the return evidence is positive, major institutions have used the individual market return data as the springboard from which to proceed to a more intensive understanding of local market fundamentals. They know the return results are due to the interplay of countercyclical conditions on both the real estate supply and the real estate demand side in the local markets in question. These conditions encompass important differences in the evolution of tenant composition, significant differences in planning and development rules and regulations, and variations in the leasing structure. Yet at the same time, forces are at work to push a number of markets into a much closer relationship with one another. It is possible to give here only a few instances of these important local trends and conditions.

Similarities in Local Market Patterns

The office market provides examples of significant similarities and differences in demand trends. Although it is very difficult to obtain consistent comparative city employment and tenant data in urban markets around the world, it certainly appears that the major office markets of the world relied heavily on the expansion of the world financial markets as a source of space demand in the last decade. For instance, in the 1980s, some 60 percent of the office market demand in London stemmed from the financial sector, Frankfurt and Paris

EXHIBIT 12–12
Stages in the Decision Process for International Real Estate Investment

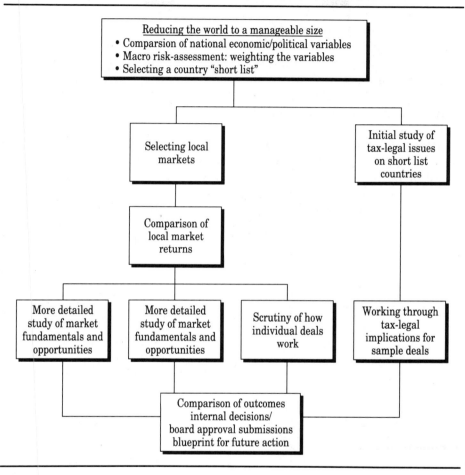

Source: JLW USA Research.

were heavily oriented toward banking and financial tenants, and New York downtown and central Chicago markets were closely tied to banking and the growth of the world securities markets. One-third of the office space in New York downtown was controlled by 50 large companies. Across the Pacific, some 40 percent of Sydney's central business district tenants were in finance and insurance industry categories.

There are markets that have served and still serve as a counterbalance to finance-based markets, markets based to a greater degree on services, government, and industrial corporations. Washington, DC, is the obvious market of this type, with its panoply of consulting firms, lawyers, accountants, and the U.S. government. New York City's midtown Manhattan has a corporation- and service-based market. Toronto also has a more diversified tenant base.

However, the recent pronounced similarity in the real estate market cycles of the United Kingdom, Canada, the United States, and Australia all point to an international investment phenomenon whose risks and outcomes would have been difficult to predict. In each of these nations, innovative financing techniques, abnormally high institutional financing available for real estate construction, and the potential for subsequent sales to Far Eastern investors (at least in the United States and Canada) largely contributed to a massive glut in real estate construction. Exhibit 12–13 illustrates the

EXHIBIT 12–13
Comparison of Selected Office Market Vacancy Rates, 1980–91

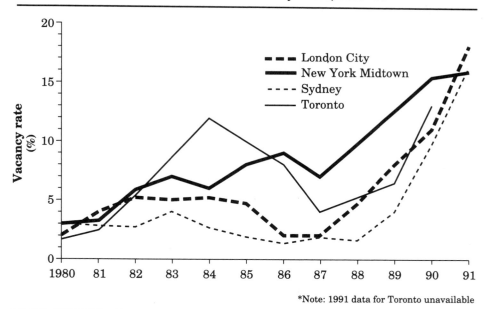

*Note: 1991 data for Toronto unavailable

Source: Jones Lang Wootton International.

confluence of their market vacancy rate trends. In many instances, the players were the same internationally. The impact of these market similarities is evident in the results of the comparison of the Russell-NCREIF index for the United States and the JLW index for the United Kingdom—a positive correlation of .57.

Despite some similarities in the tenant base, the European office markets have been following a different dynamic. The behavior of European markets has been determined by a slower pace in financial services deregulation, different industry-business mixes in the cities, and different institutional players with a much more conservative outlook on construction finance.

Various markets in Latin America and around the Pacific Rim have office markets that are tied to more trade, manufacturing, and commodities-based economies. Locations such as Jakarta, Singapore, Kuala Lumpur, and Hong Kong have the kind of volatile vacancy rates (and returns) that are characteristic of such urban areas. For example, Indonesia's main city, Jakarta, has an urban economy closely tied to oil, gas, gold-mining, and forestry corporations, and Jakarta had just begun to see the emergence of an investment market in 1987, when a few major buildings changed hands. Kuala Lumpur's tenant base is tied to exports, electronics, textiles, and rubber-based manufacturers.

Such differences in the local market office tenant base and its employment fluctuations help determine the diversification possibilities. The timing, location, and type of product demand will all vary from market to market.

Limits to New Construction

Financing practices for new construction (whether office or other property types), as well as political and bureaucratic restrictions, constitute an important factor in regulating new supply on the local scene and encouraging differences between market cycles. On the European continent, much more severe constraints are placed on construction than in the North American markets. Restrictions in North America, however, can be more severe than those in Asia. For example,

• Conservative financing practices for new construction are embodied in countries such as Germany, where insurance companies, the principal financial source, have maintained a steady, stable development program. Property funds, operated as the subsidiaries of the major banks, have had a limited role in financing development in Germany, as have pension funds.

• In countries such as France and Belgium, various limitations have been placed on new retail development (ceilings on rents and restrictions on retail leases) to protect small shopkeepers from retail mall competition. Other nations protect the supply of agricultural land, which is linked to the power of the agricultural lobby in the European Union.

• Concern for existing historical structures and restrictions on use in central cities exist across Europe and are more stringent than in North America.

• In general, land use planning in Europe is more comprehensive than in North America (although Seattle, San Francisco, and Toronto compare well with any location). Planning controls in Europe have had a longer period of evolution, and support for planning constraints is more politically acceptable. As a result, construction takes much longer.

The foregoing is not intended to suggest that Europe is a completely safe haven from cyclical construction trends. The intensive government/bureaucratic role in planning and directing urban growth in the historic cities can result in short-term overbuilding in certain areas as governments try to encourage locational shifts that will have a long-term impact. The overbuilding in the docklands area of London and the east side redevelopment of Paris are two examples. There are also signs of a market demand shift to the suburbs, which may in the future affect the focus of development financing in certain locations of Western Europe. Surveys of corporate demand in countries such as Italy, Germany, and Spain indicate that such issues as transportation access, quality of life, and technological needs are achieving primacy in corporate location thinking.

Around the Pacific Rim, regulations on new construction can be a mixture of extreme government planning combined with extreme flexibility in execution. In Kuala Lumpur, construction trends (especially in retail) indicate the relative ease of development in the country and the tendency of the sources of real estate financial supply to overanticipate the pace of demand for quality new products. Singapore land use is regulated by a master plan that is revised every five years, but the planning authorities have considerable latitude in reviewing development proposals. The burst of new construction in the late 1980s will keep vacancy rates elevated for the next four years. Appearances of some of the islands notwithstanding, Hong Kong is a highly planned agglomeration. Japan is perhaps the ultimate in restrictive land use and construction.

Lease Terms and Conditions

Lease terms and conditions are another source of important differences in local market cycles. Exhibit 12–14 illustrates differences among office, retail, and industrial properties by comparing variations in the term of the lease, lease escalation clauses, the party responsible for space improvements, special taxes on rental of space, and so on.

The international investor should be warned, though, that certain leasing practices will be under a great deal of pressure in the next decade, due to the oversupply of many types of space and the homogenization of many practices in European nations. For example, tenant concessions (or inducements) have arrived in the United Kingdom. While continuing to accept the traditional 25-year lease term, tenants are beginning to insist on having the right to cancel after a specified interval (often after 10 years) and are seeking free rent and space improvement allowances from landlords. There is some question too about whether or not the extremely protectionist laws in favor of small retail tenants (e.g., in France and Belgium) will continue to prevail under the gradual onslaught of multinational retailers and large center development.

Relative Emphasis on Different Components of Return

The analysis of local market fundamentals leads the investor to a better comprehension of the reasons for rental growth and capital appreciation (or lack thereof) in the offshore markets and the reasons for the differences in trends between U.S. real estate and markets offshore. Ultimately, the investor places the past return components in context and develops qualitative or quantitative expectations about the interrelationships among future returns. These expectations determine the relative emphasis investors have placed and still place

EXHIBIT 12–14   Commercial Leasing Practices in Western Europe

I. Office Buildings

| Market | Lease Length | Rent Review | Rent Indexation | Responsibilities | | | | Structural Repairs | Tenant Right to Cancel | Tenant Right to Renew |
				Operating Costs, Real Estate Taxes	Insurance	Ordinary Repairs				
Belgium	9 years	Every 3 years	Annual, tied to cost-of-living index	Tenant	Tenant	Tenant	Landlord	At end of each 3-year period	No	
France	9 years	No	Annual or every 3 years, tied to building cost index	Tenant	Tenant	Tenant	Landlord	At end of each 3-year period	Yes, at market rent	
Germany	5–10 years	Either review to market or index-ation linked to cost of living, every 2 to 5 years		Tenant	Tenant	Tenant	Landlord	No	No	

				Responsibilities					
	Lease Length	*Rent Review*	*Rent Indexation*	*Operating Costs, Real Estate Taxes*	*Insurance*	*Ordinary Repairs*	*Structural Repairs*	*Tenant Right to Cancel*	*Tenant Right to Renew*
Netherlands	5–10 years	No	Annual, tied to cost-of-living index	Tenant (40%) Landlord (60%)	Landlord	Tenant	Landlord	After 5 years (both landlord and tenant)	Yes, at market rent
United Kingdom	25 years	Every 5 years, upward only	No	Tenant	Tenant	Tenant	Landlord	No	Yes, at market rent

II. Retail Properties

				Responsibilities					
Market	*Lease Length*	*Rent Review*	*Rent Indexation*	*Operating Costs, Real Estate Taxes*	*Insurance*	*Ordinary Repairs*	*Structural Repairs*	*Tenant Right to Cancel*	*Tenant Right to Renew*
Belgium	9 years	Every 3 years	Annual, tied to cost-of-living index	Tenant	Tenant	Tenant	Landlord	At end of each 3-year period	Yes, for 3 terms of 9 years each; rent increased by indexation
France	9 years; increasing tendency to 12–15 years	No	Annual or every 3 years, tied to building cost index; turnover rents now appearing	Tenant	Tenant	Tenant	Landlord	At end of each 3-year period	Yes; rent increased by indexation

EXHIBIT 12–14 (continued)

II. Retail Properties

Market	Lease Length	Rent Review	Rent Indexation	Responsibilities				Tenant Right to Cancel	Tenant Right to Renew
				Operating Costs, Real Estate Taxes	Insurance	Ordinary Repairs	Structural Repairs		
Germany	5–10 years	Either review to market or index-ation linked to turnover or cost of living		Tenant	Tenant	Tenant	Landlord	No	No
Netherlands	10–15 years	Every 5 years	Annual, tied to cost-of-living index	Tenant (40%) Landlord (60%)	Landlord	Tenant	Landlord	After 5 years (both landlord and tenant)	Yes, at market rent
United Kingdom	25 years	Every 5 years, upward only	No	Tenant	Tenant	Tenant	Landlord	No	Yes, at market rent

III. Industrial Properties

Market	Lease Length	Rent Review	Rent Indexation	Operating Costs, Real Estate Taxes	Insurance	Ordinary Repairs	Structural Repairs	Tenant Right to Cancel	Tenant Right to Renew
				Responsibilities					
Belgium	9 years	Every 3 years	Annual, tied to cost-of-living index	Tenant	Tenant	Tenant	Landlord	At end of each 3-year period	No
France	9 years	No	Annual or every 3 years, tied to building cost index	Tenant	Tenant	Tenant	Landlord	At end of each 3-year period	Yes; rent increased by index-ation
Germany	5–10 years	Either review to market or indexation linked to cost of living, every 2–5 years		Tenant	Tenant	Tenant	Landlord	No	No
Netherlands	5–10 years	No	Annual, tied to cost-of-living index	Tenant (40%) Landlord (60%)	Landlord	Tenant	Landlord	After 5 years (both landlord and tenant)	Yes, at market rent
United Kingdom	25 years	Every 5 years, upward	No	Tenant	Tenant	Tenant	Landlord	No	Yes, at market rent

563

on current income yield or capital growth as the dominant component of return.

For example, during the late 1980s, investors accepted low initial capitalization rates on European office properties, since there was evidence of very strong rental growth in these markets. Recession, overbuilding in some submarkets, and political and economic uncertainties have substantially slowed rental growth in the European office sector, and near-term forecasts for rental growth dropped; consequently, capitalization rates have moved upward for European offices. The 1980s and 1990s have seen U.S. office capitalization rates that are usually higher than those in the major European office centers, reflecting the lower actual rental growth and investor perceptions of higher market risk linked to fewer supply constraints. Although many forces are at work to push international markets into a similar vacancy rate and rent cyclical pattern (which may have a two-to-three-year time lag across nations), there still seem to be sufficient economic/political differences at work such that investors constantly adapt the emphasis placed on different return components.

THE AMERICAN INSTITUTION ABROAD

International Tax Laws and Restrictions, or the Way the Game Is Played

The exploration and forecasting of local market supply-demand cycles offer the institutional investor the opportunity to attempt to determine how the promise of past returns compares to present expectations of future returns. Simultaneously (referring again to Exhibit 12–12), the potential investor usually explores the legal vehicles possible for investment and the tax laws that will affect the investment. International tax laws have a major impact on whether or not the expected returns can be realized; in certain instances, the tax laws are devised to discourage foreign ownership of real property and may coincide with overt restrictions on the percentage of foreign ownership allowed.

The institutional investor can discover the mode of investment that best facilitates the flow of returns to the home base and minimizes the tax liabilities, or is "tax neutral." No short chapter could possibly do justice to the intriguing network of corporate structures and tax treaties that govern the rules for international real estate investment. Local advice from law firms and accountants familiar with the most current market practice and legal restrictions is a necessity, as are advice and assistance from locally based real estate professionals. In the learning curve for potential international investment, one common exercise is to acquire the offering brochures for various international-class properties and work through with the advisors the manner in which the legal vehicles and tax treaties would affect the ultimate choice of product and investment mode.

The need to be familiar with local practices is one reason international real estate investors often select a form of partnership, with a local entity as the preferred vehicle, for their initial investment programs. In addition to offering some protection against the risks involved in local market real estate practice, the partnership approach minimizes the costs involved in the acquisition of knowledge and hiring of expert advice. On the negative side, partnerships generally reduce the investor's control over the property and make liquidation more difficult.

During 1991 and 1992, the international real estate investment community frequently discussed the concept of swaps between institutional investor portfolios. The best-known international swap occurred between Postel and Mitsui, in which Mitsui acquired an interest in a St. James Square location in London and Postel acquired a share of the Mitsui Building in Tokyo. Up through 1992, swaps were more often discussed than consummated, since they involved interesting issues of comparative value and avoidance or minimization of taxation for both institutions. Possible legal issues may emerge if the swap does not comply with established legal procedures for transfer of property ownership.

American Advantages

U.S. domestic players can have certain advantages in the international market, advantages that are closely tied to the fact that Americans have been forced to think about real estate investment in the context of large geographic distances and rapid technological development. Europe, for example, should experience a shift in trade route patterns in the next decade that will affect the demand for all kinds of space. Analysis of product demand requires the ability to think in terms of the transition of goods and services on a continentwide basis.

For instance, the large geographic scope of unrestricted trade, combined with greater computer use, may lead to a smaller number of really significant distribution centers needed.

In the United States, the oversupply of real estate greatly overshadows the positive lessons the industry has learned about project design and market selection. If adapted to other national tastes, these lessons could have some benefit. In the next decade, many opportunities exist in Europe for the following:

• Creation and/or upgrading of suburban retail centers. U.S. retail development had used very complex methods of identifying target markets according to socioeconomic, cultural, and psychological profiles. Coupled with retail design improvements and active property management, this expertise could be used in the creation of the next generation of European retail centers.

• Development of noncentral office parks, whether suburban or city fringe. Surveys and studies of corporate Europe indicate that central congestion and demands of technology that cannot be accommodated in centuries-old (or even 30-year-old) buildings will force a demand for out-of-center locations. Suburban business park design in Europe generally does not compare with American design in terms of convenience of layout for auto and truck access, attractiveness of the site environment, or attractiveness of the finished product. As organizations are forced out of the central cities, the supplier of the right ambiance will have a competitive advantage.

Nonetheless, the astute investor will carefully make allowances for local tastes, which can cover everything from the amount of daylight, to preferences about climate control and the ability to open windows, to carpeting.

Next Steps

The great challenge, whether for a U.S. or an offshore institution, is in the arena of comparing the results of legal, tax, and micromarket issues, moving to a blueprint for real action, and implementing that action. Truly global thinking often results in the identification of so many opportunities and varying risk patterns that actually selecting the locations and product types for what is always a limited international real estate allocation greatly taxes an organization's discipline and dedication to its original location, product type, and risk-return preferences. A hypothetical strategy on paper is one thing; the lure of the visible investment with real cash flow (and real discounted cash flow projections) is another.

To date, American institutions have for the most part studied offshore real estate through advisors and consultants, but have been reluctant to engage in offshore investment themselves. Although various organizations, such as Equitable, Baring Advisors, and Jones Lang Wootton Realty Advisors, attempted to encourage American institutional investment (especially pension fund investment) in Europe in the 1990–92 period, no major shift of funds has been forthcoming. To date, the most significant amount of U.S. institutional money invested has been through the Trans-European Property Unit Trust (MIM), in the amount of approximately $50 million.

Major shifts in the international flow of real estate investment funds by U.S. institutional investors require (among other things) the acceptance of new risks and investment vehicles designed to mitigate those risks. The great shift in world political uncertainties caused by the recession appropriately gave prudent U.S. institutions cause for further thought about international real estate in the early 1990s. It is highly probable that the rest of the decade will see a refinement and adaptation of investment vehicles suitable for the appetites of U.S. institutions as those institutions gradually determine those elements of international risk that are acceptable or unacceptable to them. Such vehicles will be offered by U.S.-based organizations, but many will be created by foreign-based financial entities seeking to attract U.S. capital that has been disillusioned with poor returns in U.S. real estate and might be persuaded to invest elsewhere with the lure of higher returns.

CHAPTER 13

NONTRADITIONAL REAL ESTATE

Christopher H. Volk
Franchise Finance Corporation of America

Broadly used performance indices often provide evidence of what is considered traditional. The most widely used index for equity real estate investments is the Russell/NCREIF index. As of December 1992, this index was composed of just over 1,600 properties, which were held by tax-exempt institutional investors. The index consists of five major real estate sectors: apartment, office, retail, R&D/office, and warehouse. In general, it can be said that these sectors comprise traditional real estate.

When addressing anything that is not traditional, it should be noted that such a label is transient. This is true when discussing nontraditional investments within any asset class and is perhaps especially so with real estate. The Russell/NCREIF index extends back only to 1978. Before 1980, equity real estate investments lacked widespread acceptance as institutional assets. In a sense, real estate as a whole was considered nontraditional. Most of the estimated $125 billion in tax-exempt institutional real estate was invested during the 1980s. During that time, industry benchmarks evolved in response to investment activity. The apartment sector was the most recent addition to the Russell/NCREIF index, with data extending back to 1988. This index was just added in 1990 and represents the changing face of mainstream institutional real estate.

Institutional investors have broadened their equity real estate investment horizons. Real estate is a capital asset. Its inclusion in a portfolio of otherwise financial assets was designed to offer greater inflation sensitivity. At the outset, real estate industry participants produced correlation matrices that illustrated a strong, positive long-term relationship to inflation. Less quantifiable, and more simplistic, was the view that capital assets tend to rise in value because their replacement costs rise. Inflation tends to drive up replacement costs, so it was believed that real estate investments would have a pronounced sensitivity to inflation. In the wake of the rapid inflation of the 1970s, the inclusion of the real estate assets class appealed to the desire of institutional investors to focus on real, not just nominal, rates of return. Thus far, history has not yet repeated itself. In the second half of the 1980s and the early 1990s, real estate investments posted weak performance results, with virtually no correlation to inflation. Consequently, the performance of institutional real estate investments is certain to precipitate further evolution.

Other chapters in this book discuss overall real estate performance issues in greater detail. The point of the above discussion is to illustrate that the definition of mainstream institutional equity real estate is dynamic. What has been traditional may be de-emphasized, and what has been nontraditional may become more mainstream. This truth has transcended all investment asset classes in response to changing business environments and a pursuit of higher risk-adjusted returns. Just as real estate investments became more mainstream in the 1980s in response to inflation concerns generated in the 1970s and 1980s, so will the real estate asset class in the 1990s change in response to its performance in the 1980s.

NONTRADITIONAL REAL ESTATE: SOME COMMON ATTRIBUTES

The prevailing view of institutional grade real estate began with larger, multitenanted properties. Large office buildings and retail and industrial properties were thought to offer superior capital preservation potential. For one thing, these properties were highly improved. In other words, the structures themselves had high values in relation to the land on which they were situated. Building such structures often involved extensive zoning changes, coupled with a long permitting process. This arduous process of creating and financing such properties posed a potential roadblock—or so the theory went—for competing locations. Each property was often viewed in light of its unique franchise. Multiple tenants and a property franchise combined to lower the perceived investment risk.

One driving force of real estate performance is tenant economics. In the end, what tenants pay for rent should be a function of what they believe is reasonably affordable given their alternatives. One problem with large, multitenanted properties is that the link between tenant economics and value is often obscured. This is because there are other variables in the rent equation, chiefly, other competing, multitenanted properties. In essence, tenant economics impose a rent barrier on the high end. On the low end, competing properties and market vacancies may force landlords to offer rents at levels well below what the tenants might otherwise be able to pay.

One thread common to nontraditional real estate is a closer link of values and rents to tenant economics. Nontraditional properties are typically less improved and often are associated with a specific industry or business purpose. With less improved real estate, property management often differs from the on-site, intensive management required for larger, highly improved, multitenanted property. More important, the less improved the real estate, the more it becomes akin to plant and equipment: a resource with definable economic tenant value. Among nontraditional real estate, some of the property types this chapter will discuss are agricultural land, franchised restaurant properties, mobile home parks, self-storage facilities, single-family housing, and timberland. Presuming investments were made in diversified pools within each of these sectors, investment risk might be expected to approximate overall industry risk. So an investment in agricultural land might entail an understanding of the prognosis for farming, timberland for wood products, and so on. The link between industry economics and real estate values is unmistakable.

The closer linkage between nontraditional real estate investments and the associated industries that use the property does not necessarily imply that such real estate investments suffer more severely from unsystematic risks than do investments in more traditional real estate. While the tenants may not be as diverse as tenants within larger, multitenanted properties, they represent industries that are generally extremely broad based. It is the large size of these nontraditional real estate sectors that attracts the attention of institutional investors.

In theory, at least, all real estate investments are effectively a form of tenant financing. Tenants have the choice of either renting or owning the space they require. With such a close linkage among real estate, tenant economic fundamentals, and industry performance, the resemblance of nontraditional real estate investments to financing is rendered more apparent. The farmer has the option to own or lease the land. The franchised restaurant operator has the option to own or lease the restaurant. The mobile home park resident has a choice of owning or leasing land. The single-family home builder may look elsewhere for project equity to finance the development. Investments in timberland effectively represent a form of long-term inventory financing for the timber industry. Whereas market rents per square foot define the income parameters for larger, multitenanted real estate, nontraditional property rents are often better compared to the financial markets. Long-term commercial mortgage interest rates are effectively the competition for many nontraditional leases. This is not to say that rents should fall below borrowing rates; there are other financial considerations. First, there is the amount of tenant capital commitment. Typically, owning real estate requires more investment than leasing real estate. Second, lease terms may be more favorable than borrowing terms. Conventional lenders are often reticent to commit to long, fixed-rate loan terms. Third, tenants may have a limited borrowing capacity. Real estate is a very costly resource that can exceed the limitations of conventional lenders.

While rents and lease terms of nontraditional real estate investments may have closer ties to the financial markets, this should not suggest that total returns are more closely correlated to financial assets than other traditional real estate sectors. The type of property and tenant does not alter the substance of the investment; real estate landlords seek not equity rates of return but returns that offer stability and the preservation of inflation-adjusted (real) capital. Should the manufactured housing or home-building industries post record performances, the real estate landlord is likely to also fare well, but not as well as the equity investor. Should the same industries post dismal performances, the landlord may also suffer, but not as much as the equity investor. In essence, a landlord is akin to a senior debt holder in the order of payment preference. Yet, unlike the senior debt holder, the real estate investor holds an asset with the capacity for income escalation and an uncertain terminal value. Absent a definitive asset class correlation model, the preceding discussion suggests that nontraditional real estate investments should intuitively offer diversification from financial assets and from traditional real estate sectors.

LOOKING AHEAD

Some of the nontraditional real estate sectors that this chapter will discuss present historic asset class correlation models that support their portfolio-enhancing attributes. However, such historic return series are not publicly available for many nontraditional real estate sectors. In part, it is this lack of information and institutional investment history that makes nontraditional real estate nontraditional. Those who invest in nontraditional real estate generally do so because it is sensible to presume that such investments will enhance overall portfolio performance in the future.

If the sources for historical real estate sector comparisons are limited, the rationale for the inclusion of nontraditional real estate will tend to focus on predicted return attributes. For this reason, each real estate sector reviewed in this chapter includes a summary analysis of predicted return attributes. In the final analysis, such a forward look is likely to be more applicable in any event. Following the commercial real estate carnage of the 1980s, historical sector performance statistics necessarily take on less importance. Few, if any, managers of nontraditional real estate will be able to say that they outperformed, or would have outperformed, the Russell/NCREIF index. Therefore, for prospective investors in nontraditional real estate, it is more important to look ahead than to take possibly deceptive comfort in looking back at comparative performance.

AGRICULTURE

Institutional investment in agricultural properties is relatively recent and is partially an outgrowth of industry restructuring following a sharp decline in farm earnings and farmland values between 1981 and 1986. The result of this downturn was a much publicized failure of many farm owners who found themselves burdened by excessive debt that they had used to acquire or borrow against land holdings. The amount of farm debt rose to all-time high levels during the early to mid-1980s in the wake of rising land values and what amounted to land speculation by the farm industry. Although farm operators continue to own most of the land they farm, land leasing has presented an avenue for expansion without the risks that leverage presented in the mid-1980s. The ability of institutional investors to fill this capital need has been facilitated through the emergence of professional financial intermediaries with expertise in the management of farmland investments. For institutional investors, farmland ownership frequently offers the ability to receive base rents, together with a crop-sharing arrangement. Whether or not a crop-sharing arrangement is used, some of the real estate income or appreciation will be effectively linked to commodity pricing.

Sector Investment Rationale

In 1992, there were more than 2 million farms in the United States, which represented more than 4 percent of total domestic wealth and accounted for more than 11 percent of U.S. exports. Together these farms comprise more than 1 billion acres with an estimated value of more than $625 billion. Farmland is estimated to account for about 11 percent of the value of all domestic real estate, but, as of 1992, comprised less than 1 percent of the over $100 billion of institutional real estate investments. The size of the agricultural real estate market suggests that its representation is appropriate within a well-diversified institutional investment portfolio.

Because the returns and values of farmland investments are largely tied to farm commodities pricing, agricultural real estate intuitively should have a low correlation to other types of real estate and other asset classes. Also, farmland investment returns can be enhanced by improving farming technologies that increase farmland efficiency. The low correlations of farmland investments to other asset classes has been borne out by the historical performance of farmland returns. According to John Hancock Economic Research, the correlation of farmland returns to commercial real estate between 1971 and 1991 was just .17, with negative correlations to financial assets during this period.

Farmland management companies believe farmland investments hold a promise for sustained long-term investment growth. Growth in prices and land values is projected because of diverging trends in global population and farmland availability. While the global population continues to rise, the availability of high-quality agricultural real estate is declining. As the world's leading competitive producers of agricultural products, farmland management companies believe the United States is positioned to realize resulting growth in farmland revenues and values. During 1992, agricultural exports exceeded 20 percent of total farm receipts. The North American Free Trade Agreement (NAFTA) and the General Agreement on Tariffs and Trade (GATT) are expected to enhance future agricultural exports.

Industry Characteristics

Farming is a foundation industry and encompasses a wide array of agricultural products with diverse return and risk profiles. Farming also encompasses a broad array of businesses, ranging from the very large to the very small. It is estimated that fewer than 20 percent of the over 2.1 million farms in the United States have sales of more than $100,000 annually, accounting for about 75 percent of total gross farm sales. In general, institutional investments are directed toward these larger farmers. Farmland leases range in term from 4 months to 10 years, but a year-to-year arrangement is most common. As noted previously, lease terms tend to have both a base payment and a crop-sharing component.

Farmland investments can essentially be broken down into two categories: row crops and permanent crops. Each category has distinct risk and return characteristics, and both are generally employed in a diversified farmland investment strategy. Row crops pertain to annual plantings, which include staples such as corn, wheat, rice, and cotton. These are typically nonperishable crops having long shelf lives. Because of their shelf lives and the fact that these crops are planted annually, there is generally less risk from weather and price conditions.

On the other hand, row crops tend to be the beneficiaries of government price support programs, which have uncertain reliability. Permanent crops pertain to trees and vines, such as citrus fruits, nuts, and grapes. Such crops have less in the way of government price supports, but have shorter shelf lives (apart from nuts) and are more susceptible to long-term weather-related damage. In general, institutional equity investments in this type of agricultural property do not entail a lease, since the investor holds title to *both* the land and the permanent crop. Therefore, investments in permanent crop property typically involve the use of contractual arrangements to manage and harvest the crop. Investor returns are accordingly tied more directly to farm performance, since property income is essentially the profit from crop sales after related management expenditures. As a result of higher risk levels, permanent crop farmland typically should be expected to generate higher targeted investment returns.

Apart from weather hazards, the most significant risk in farmland investments is regulation. Government subsidies are not the risk they once were, having fallen from $17 billion in 1987 to $9 billion in 1990. This reduction has encouraged institutional investments in the most productive farmland, which is expected to benefit over the long term from the lack of government subsidies. However, other regulations, such as the 1985 farming legislation that mandated wetlands conservation as a prerequisite to government benefits, entail constant monitoring on the part of farmland managers. In addition, certain states, such as Arizona, Iowa, Kansas, Kentucky, Minnesota, Nebraska, North Dakota, Oklahoma, South Dakota, and Wisconsin, have passive farmland ownership restrictions. The farmland in these states accounts for about 25 percent of total farmland value. Finally, government regulations can have material impacts on farm exports, which are critical to the prosperity of the farming industry. Nearly 60 percent of all farm exports go to Japan, the European Union, Canada, and Mexico, in that order.

Half of the farmland in the United States is now owned by fewer than 5 percent of the land owners. Increasingly, fewer farmland owners are farmers. According to the Census of Agriculture's Agricultural Economics and Land Ownership Survey (AELOS) conducted in 1988, farmland owners outnumber operators three to two. This survey estimated that about 41 percent of U.S. farmers now rent or own all of their farms. These farmers control, through ownership or lease, 67 percent of farmland.

Return Attributes

Historically, farmland investments have emphasized appreciation over income when viewed on a time-weighted basis. Exhibit 13–1 illustrates the historical weighting between income and appreciation. On a dollar-weighted basis, the returns should be expected to more heavily weight cash flows, which rise in tandem with agricultural prices and farm earnings. It is this alliance with commodity prices, coupled with short-term lease arrangements, that farmland managers note should make farmland investments inflation sensitive. According to John Hancock Economic Research, between 1971 and 1991, farmland investments had a higher correlation to inflation (.55) than financial assets or commercial real estate. At the same time, the natural relationship of farmland returns to agricultural commodities prices and farm earnings resulted in higher volatility than commer-

EXHIBIT 13–1
Sources of Farmland Returns, 1940–91

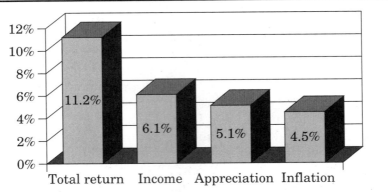

Source: John Hancock Economic Research.

cial real estate. John Hancock Economic Research estimates that from 1971 to 1991, return volatility fell below that of the S&P 500, but was almost as high as that of long-term U.S. corporate bonds. Note that volatility is less if measured over the shorter and more recent periods that followed the farmland devaluations of the early to mid-1980s.

FRANCHISED RESTAURANT PROPERTY

Franchised restaurant property investments have been offered on a fairly large scale to individual investors since the early 1980s, but are relatively new to institutional investors. These investments are typically structured using long-term sale/leaseback arrangements. Other types of investment structures, such as mortgages or participating mortgages, can also be used. In general, franchised restaurant real estate investments allow for full tenant or borrower recourse. Rents typically have escalation or percentage rent provisions as a means to some inflation indexation. Leases also often include tenant purchase options. Franchised restaurant real estate investments are typically restricted to freestanding properties. This leaves out restaurant sites located within leased shopping center space or situated on leased land. To offset the risks associated with owning single-tenant property, franchised restaurant real estate investments are generally made in a diversified portfolio of properties.

Sector Investment Rationale

Like many other nontraditional real estate investments, franchised restaurant investments effectively represent a type of long-term tenant financing, whereby investors serve as an alternative to traditional financing sources such as commercial banks, savings and loans, and insurance companies. As an alternative to tenant long-term premises financing, franchised restaurant real estate investments hold the promise for stable long-term returns that emphasize cash flow, with little dependence on real estate appreciation. Franchised restaurant real estate managers believe traditional financing sources alone cannot meet the substantial capital needs of this large and fundamental industry, and therefore, these specialized investments offer the potential for attractive risk-adjusted returns.

Industry Characteristics

As a whole, the food service industry employs more people and has more locations than any other retail industry in the United States. Total food service industry sales during 1992 were approximately $255 billion. The food service industry is composed of many segments, one of which is the limited-menu, or fast-food, segment. This segment most closely relates to franchised restaurant property investments.

There were nearly 150,000 fast-food restaurants in the United States as of December 31, 1990, the most recent year for which statistics are available. During 1992, revenues for the fast-food segment of the food service industry were estimated to be $80.3 billion. The growth rate of the fast-food restaurant segment has consistently exceeded that of other eating and drinking places for more than 20 years. As a result, its market share has steadily risen. During 1992, approximately 70 percent of the customer visits to eating and drinking places and 46 percent of the dollars spent in these establishments were garnered by fast-food restaurants.

While the growth rate of the limited-menu segment of the food service industry continues to outpace the industry as a whole, it is down from the double-digit levels of the 1970s and early 1980s.

The fall-off in the rate of sales growth has occurred as this segment of the food service industry has matured. Chiefly, fewer new restaurants have been constructed, as most markets have been substantially developed by fast-food restaurant chains. During 1991 and 1992, the largest 50 restaurant chains that chiefly use freestanding properties posted new unit development approximating 3 percent annually. This equates to roughly 2,000 new restaurants per year. As of December 31, 1992, these 50 chains had approximately 67,000 units among them.

The market for franchised restaurant property investments is large. The real estate value for the largest 50 chains is estimated to top $50 billion. Investment opportunity is derived from the refinancing of existing property, the financing of new property, and the purchase of properties that are subject to existing lease arrangements. While the market for this type of property is large, sources of franchised restaurant property investments are fragmented. Conventional financing sources account for approximately 70 percent of real estate capital, with no dominant industry participants. No source of long-term real estate financing not associated with a restaurant chain is estimated to have more than a 2 percent share of the market. The fragmented nature of the capital market suggests that few reliable sources of financing exist. As a result, many franchised restaurant industry participants employ numerous sources of real estate financing. Franchised restaurant real estate managers believe, as do home-building investment managers, that this type of capital inefficiency can translate into attractive risk-adjusted investor returns.

Return Attributes

As mentioned previously, franchised restaurant properties represent a long-term investment, with returns dominated by current cash flow. Based on dollar-weighted (internal rate of return) return estimates, appreciation is expected to account for less than 10 percent of total returns. Still, the returns are typically structured to have some indexation to inflation as a result of percentage or escalating rents and site appreciation. Here it is important to point out that the value of a restaurant site is fundamentally tied to its ability to generate operating earnings over the life of the lease. Real estate appreciation is likely to be elusive for restaurant units that post operating losses.

Another reason appreciation is apt to be comparatively less im-

portant for franchised restaurant properties is that they are not speculatively constructed. As a consequence of the commercial overdevelopment that occurred during the 1980s, many stated investment
strategies have centered around purchasing properties for fractions
of their construction or replacement cost. With real estate that was
never speculatively built, opportunities to purchase distressed properties are comparatively less. On the other hand, franchised restaurant
real estate investments should generally not exceed replacement cost,
since such costly property would be uncompetitive in the event of
tenant lease defaults and subsequent vacancy.

Investment risk can be mitigated through portfolio diversification and investment structure. Diversification can be accomplished by
tenant, geographic location, restaurant chain, and restaurant market
segment. Investments having the least risk may be structured with
full tenant recourse, with guarantor recourse, and as hybrid or participating mortgages. The use of mortgage or hybrid mortgage structures
lessens exposure to potential losses in property value. Risk can further
be mitigated through a focus on large franchisor or franchisee tenants
of the highest credit quality.

Exhibits 13–2 and 13–3 illustrate the performance of franchised

EXHIBIT 13–2
**Risk and Return: Franchised Restaurant Real Estate versus Other Real Estate
Sectors, Common Stocks, and Government/Corporate Bonds, 1983–92**

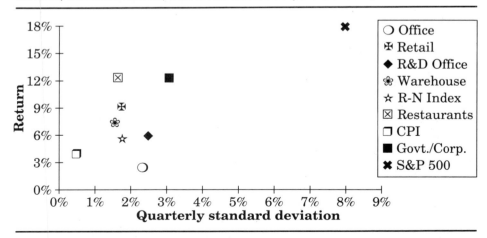

Source: Franchise Finance Corporation of America.

EXHIBIT 13–3

Comparing the Income Component: Franchised Restaurant Real Estate versus Other Real Estate Sectors, 1983–92

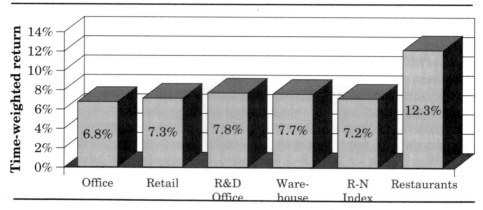

Source: Franchise Finance Corporation of America.

restaurant real estate versus the Russell/NCREIF index and its components for the 10-year period ended December 31, 1992. The total return performance of the franchised restaurant sector as shown in Exhibit 13–2 demonstrated less volatility than the index, as might be expected from the use of long-term sale/leaseback or hybrid mortgage investment structures. The majority of the total return for franchised restaurant portfolios was derived from income, which is illustrated in Exhibit 13–3.

MANUFACTURED HOUSING COMMUNITIES

Direct investments in manufactured housing communities, or mobile home parks, are relatively new to institutional investors. In effect, an investment in a manufactured housing community is an investment in improved land. The land is subdivided into small lots with utility attachments that typically range from 1,500 to 2,500 square feet. These lots are generally leased on a month-to-month basis to tenants who place their mobile homes (manufactured housing) on the sites. Many manufactured housing communities also offer amenities such as a clubhouse, a convenience store, a health care facility, and athletic facilities ranging from shuffleboard to golf courses. These communities have undergone an evolution from the days of boxy, corrugated metal trailers to today's manufactured housing, which is built to standards similar to those of residential construction. As housing has consumed an ever larger portion of the American budget, manufactured housing communities have risen in popularity to accommodate those in need of affordable housing alternatives.

Sector Investment Rationale

In a sense, manufactured housing investments can be considered an alternative to investments in multifamily housing, which recently have become widely accepted by institutional investors. As affordable housing, manufactured home communities essentially offer an alternative to renting. Because the tenants lease just the land and the manufactured homes are difficult to move, lost rent risk is perceived to be small. For the same reason, tenant turnover is likewise perceived to be small. Tenants who do move often leave their manufactured homes to be sold to replacement mobile home park tenants. In summary, the rental income streams for mobile home parks are thought to be reliable.

Apart from revenue reliability, mobile home park investments have other appeals. First, manufactured housing is the nation's fastest-growing housing type. Second, certain supply constraints exist. Mobile home park investments entail location considerations consistent with those for other single-family housing, but with added zoning requirements. Proposed manufactured housing communities are frequently opposed by neighboring residential or commercial areas. In addition, municipal zoning authorities often have less inducement to approve zoning because manufactured homes are exempt from real estate taxes. Third, manufactured housing real estate can be viewed as a defensive type of real estate investment that would be potentially less affected during an economic recession. Fourth, the short-term lease arrangements mean that rents can be continually adjusted for local market conditions. Short-term leases suggest an opportunity for enhanced inflation indexation. Fifth, ongoing maintenance and management costs are typically lower than for apartments and other, more highly improved real estate investments.

As with many other nontraditional real estate sectors, another appeal of mobile home park investments is the fragmented nature of the industry. As recently as 1987, it was reported that the 10 largest operators of manufactured housing communities held fewer than 30 properties each. The lack of market efficiencies and large participants will doubtless change, which may lead to enhanced industry property values. One sign of market activity was the formation in 1993 of Manufactured Home Communities (MHC), a New York Stock Exchange–listed REIT that, upon its initial public offering, owned 41 properties in 16 states with over 12,000 home sites that were 94 percent occupied. MHC is the first publicly traded mobile home park company. As a sign of its acceptance by investors, the price of MHC shares rose from their offering price of $25.75 on February 25, 1993, to $37.50 as of June 30, 1993.

Industry Characteristics

As noted above, manufactured housing is the nation's fastest-growing type of housing. During the 1980s, manufactured housing units grew by almost 60 percent, compared to 13 percent for other home types. This means almost one in every five homes constructed during the 1980s was a manufactured home. There are estimated to be more than 24,000 mobile home parks nationwide having a combined total in excess of 1.8 million home sites. Mobile home parks are segmented in terms of quality, with the least attractive parks having a rating of one star and those with the best appearance and amenities having five stars. It is estimated that fewer than 10 percent of the nation's mobile home parks are of the five-star variety. Home site monthly rentals typically range from $90 to $175 per month, with rents rising to as much as $300 monthly for five-star facilities. The average cost of the manufactured homes that occupy the leased land is under $30,000. Depending on the amenities offered by the mobile home park, land costs can be as little as 20 percent of the cost of development, with the remainder in utility hookups, streets, lighting, clubhouses, and other amenities.

Return Attributes

The return attributes of mobile home park investments are similar to those of multifamily housing. However, due to the nontraditional nature of this investment sector, capitalization rates have tended to be higher. Therefore, the investor should anticipate a high distributable cash component, with seasoned, highly occupied properties offering the highest immediate cash flow. Presuming the use of the property as a mobile home park remains the highest and best use, real estate appreciation should be expected to occur as rental income rises or in the event that market acceptance permits reduced investment capitalization rates.

SELF-STORAGE FACILITIES

The idea of self-storage facilities is said to have originated with free-standing industrial storage facilities in the 1960s in Texas and Oklahoma. While the industry has certainly grown since that time, no reliable statistics exist on its size. Part of the difficulty in estimating industry size is associated with definition, since many smaller self-storage properties exist that might not be considered suitable for institutional investors. Nevertheless, for an alternative real estate sector, self-storage properties have gained considerable institutional acceptance. Institutional investments in self-storage properties were estimated to exceed $1 billion as of December 31, 1992.

Perhaps more than any other alternative real estate sector, investments in self-storage real estate are tantamount to investments in the underlying industry. This is because self-storage real estate managers frequently apply their names and corporate logos to the properties they manage as a means of creating brand-name recognition among potential tenants. In this fashion, each property becomes a part of a national or regional self-storage network, a fact that is expected to enhance occupancy and rent levels and reduce operating costs associated with greater economies of scale.

Sector Investment Rationale

Self-storage facilities are an outgrowth of a highly mobile lifestyle and offer tenants a cost-effective means for storing belongings when viewed as an alternative to renting a larger apartment, purchasing a bigger house, or renting more office space. As a result, self-storage facilities have become commonplace in large urban markets. Mature self-storage properties are able to produce investor returns that emphasize distributable cash flow. Tenant lease streams tend to be reliable, because nonpayment can mean loss of access to storage contents.

Investor returns are enhanced by the comparatively low maintenance and management costs self-storage properties require. With the use of month-to-month lease arrangements, self-storage properties also hold the opportunity for enhanced inflation sensitivity when compared to real estate sectors that rely on longer-term lease arrangements.

Industry Characteristics

Self-storage properties are typically situated on land parcels ranging from 1.5 to 7.0 acres, with buildings accommodating from 300 to 700 self-contained storage spaces. Self-storage properties normally offer individual storage rooms of varying sizes ranging from 25 to 400 square feet, with an average size approximating 100 square feet. Each property typically includes office space for on-site management, and most also contain an apartment for the on-site manager. Inclusive of office space and common areas, storage buildings generally range from 40,000 to 100,000 square feet and have a cost to build ranging from $1.5 to $4.0 million.

As a rule, the self-storage industry is most conducive to large urban areas where space constraints, population lifestyles, population density, and business density combine to create sufficient demand for storage space. Managers of self-storage facilities generally look at area demographics and the per capita amount of storage space to gauge potential site success. One large manager of self-storage facilities looks for population density in a five-mile radius around a storage facility of 200,000. The population requirements to sustain self-storage properties suggest that competition from other self-storage facilities is a key risk factor to consider. The tenant market mix for self-storage facilities averages approximately 75 percent individuals and 25 percent businesses, with an average rental term of about 11 months.

Return Attributes

As with other multitenanted properties, the return characteristics and risk profile of an investment in self-storage properties varies based in large part on property maturity. New properties can require 24 to 36 months to reach a stabilized occupancy level of from 80 to 90 percent. As with any real estate investment undergoing a lease-up period, initial cash distributions can be expected to be lower during the first years of the holding period. Likewise, newly developed properties can be expected to bear a higher level of investment risk, since their acceptance by the marketplace is unknown.

SINGLE-FAMILY HOME CONSTRUCTION

Single-family home construction is relatively new to institutional real estate portfolios. During 1992, California Public Employees' Retirement System, the nation's largest state employee retirement system, made news by being one of the first public pension funds to make a commitment to this real estate sector.

Sector Investment Rationale

Like many other nontraditional real estate sectors, home-building investments essentially take the place of more traditional financing sources such as savings and loans, credit companies, banks, and insurance companies. Part of the allure of home-building investments has been the perception that the withdrawal of many traditional lenders from real estate lending has created an institutional investment opportunity. Through filling a financing and capital need, home-building investment managers perceive an opportunity for enhanced risk-adjusted performance.

Yet another allure for the home-building real estate sector has been its socially conscious investment attributes. The fact that home building generates employment and economic growth has not been lost on investors. The previously mentioned allocation by California Public Employees' Retirement System was centered around affordable housing and restricted to California housing developments.

Industry Characteristics

The home-building industry is large. Single-family homes comprise over half of total estimated real estate value in the United States. At the end of 1990, home mortgage loans outstanding amounted to roughly $2.8 trillion, with housing unit construction running at a rate of about $130 billion annually. Estimates of the size of the home-building industry range from $80 billion to $100 billion at any one time. Because home builders can turn their inventory as often as two times a year or more, new construction can result in over $130 billion in new housing units annually.

Like many other nontraditional real estate sectors, the home-building industry is highly fragmented. Thousands of home builders exist, with publicly available data on just a few; prominent participants include such companies as Centex, Pulte, Ryland, and Standard Pacific. The nation's five largest builders account for less than 8 percent of the total market. The implication of this fragmentation is that few builders have access to efficient, uninterrupted sources of capital. Hence, institutional investors who offer long-term capital commitments may be well positioned for attractive risk-adjusted earnings.

Return Attributes

Investments in home building may take on a variety of forms and therefore can have an array of return and risk profiles. Investors may or may not want a sharing in home builder profits. A recourse loan to a home builder with specified release prices per unit clearly implies less risk than a joint venture arrangement dependent on profits. Investors may also invest in various project stages ranging from undeveloped, unzoned land accumulation to land development to the actual home-building phase. The least risky phase is the actual home building, while land accumulation requires the greatest time and involves the most risk. Finally, because home building is essentially transactional (builders go from one project to the next), the investment term may be structured to suit investment term constraints.

Returns on home-building investments are essentially driven by three factors. The first is the profit margin level. The second is the speed of home inventory turnover. The third is the degree of home builder leverage used. Based on an analysis of publicly traded home builders from 1980 to 1990, unleveraged annual gross returns in home-building projects were estimated to approximate 20 percent, with a standard deviation of 7.7 percent. Using Treasury bills as a proxy for risk-free assets and standard deviation as a proxy for risk, home building was estimated to have a risk-adjusted return of 1.44 percent ([Home-building gross return − T-bill return]/Home-building standard deviation). This kind of performance outpaced the rest of the real estate industry, as measured by the Russell/NCREIF benchmark and its components over the same period, as well as the S&P 500 and the Lehman Brothers Government/Corporate Bond Index. This is shown in Exhibit 13–4.

Because home building is essentially an investment in a manufacturing enterprise, home-building real estate participants believe it has less inherent risk than many other types of institutional real estate. For one thing, the standard deviation of home-building returns, while higher than for most other real estate classes, is less subject to the appraisal-smoothing characteristic of longer-term investments. Since home builders may turn their inventory over twice or more annually, home-building returns encompass frequent asset sales, which is not the case with most traditional equity real estate investments. Therefore, the standard deviation of home-building returns can be said to be more "honest" than that of accepted institutional return benchmarks. Second, the transaction-oriented nature of home-building investments means builders are less likely to be trapped by speculative overdevelopment on the scale that commercial real estate witnessed during the late 1980s. A look at statistics on new housing starts bears this point out. New housing starts in 1990 stood at 895,000 units, down 24 percent from a high of 1.18 million

EXHIBIT 13–4
Risk and Return: Home Building versus Other Real Estate Sectors, Common Stocks, and Government/Corporate Bonds, 1980–90

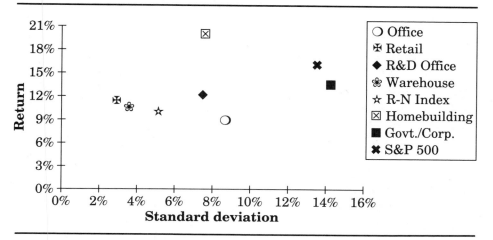

Source: Hearthstone Advisors.

housing starts in 1986. During that same period, new-home costs continued to rise, showing that the home-building industry was generally able to adjust to reduced demand levels without the adverse results that characterized more traditional institutional grade real estate.

TIMBERLAND

Timberland ownership has received increasing acceptance by institutional investors, although it is still considered an alternative real estate sector. Some institutional investors classify timberland investments as an alternative asset rather than as real estate due to its unique characteristics. Essentially, timberland ownership equates to an investment in an agricultural commodity. Agricultural properties, which were discussed earlier, are less susceptible to this claim inasmuch as they entail a base rental component from the tenant. Timberland investments, on the other hand, generally do not involve the use of a tenant. The real estate manager therefore takes on the role of business manager as well as financial intermediary.

Sector Investment Rationale

For investors seeking broad portfolio diversification, an investment in timberland represents a direct investment in the U.S. forest products industry, which is one of the nation's largest industrial sectors. The U.S. forest products industry accounts for approximately 6 percent of gross domestic product, 8 percent of the nation's work force, and about 25 percent of all domestic industrial raw materials. In addition, the U.S. forest products industry supplies about 25 percent of the world's wood products. As a real estate sector, timberland is estimated to include about 350 million acres at a value of over $150 billion.

The size of the forest products industry and of timberland in general suggests that timberland investments hold promise for prudent portfolio diversification. Exhibit 13–5 illustrates that a retrospective view of timberland versus other asset classes over a 30-year period demonstrates favorable relative performance levels. Like other alternative real estate sectors, relatively low correlations with other asset classes and other real estate suggests that overall portfolio risk-adjusted performance can be enhanced. Finally, timberland managers

EXHIBIT 13–5
Timberland Returns versus Other Asset Classes, 1960–91

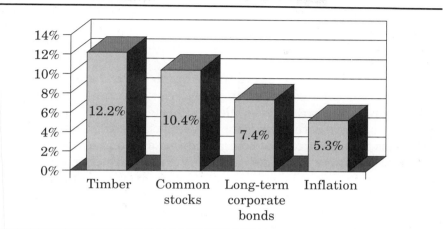

Sources: Ibbotson Associates; John Hancock Economic Research.

have pointed to predictions of increasing timber demand against a forecast backdrop of reduced timber inventory as a cause for estimates of continued favorable returns relative to other asset classes.

Industry Characteristics

As of 1992, the majority of timberland was held by individuals and forest products companies. In addition, the federal government owned approximately 58 percent of the timberland in the Pacific Northwest and 8 percent of the timberland in the Southeast. Institutional timberland investors are a relatively recent occurrence and are principally an outgrowth of the formation of timberland management companies with the expertise to serve as financial intermediaries. The formation of such companies has added to the efficiency of the timberland market by making timberland accessible for institutional investors.

Timberland investments are highly management intensive. Management of portfolio risk is targeted through diversification by age, species and geographic location, terrain, "political risk," and other considerations. The three most notable areas of diversification are age, species, and geography. Portfolios with stands of varying ages ensure an ability to employ continuous harvesting. Species diversification pertains to the different end uses that lumber types may have, ranging from pulp to sawtimber. Geographic diversification principally pertains to differences between Pacific northwestern (lumber and logs) and southeastern (furniture, pulp, and pressure treated) timber markets.

Timberland investments entail a number of risks, such as natural disasters, weather, and environmental risks, that need to be considered when compiling a diversified timberland portfolio. Timberland managers point out that many of these risks can be managed. Historically, less than 1 percent of commercial timberland owned by institutional investors is damaged annually by fire, insects, disease, and other hazards. In addition, up to 80 percent or more of timber harvested following a forest fire is merchantable. Through the use of modern forest management techniques like fire breaks and prescribed burns, timberland managers can limit the impact of fire on portfolio performance. With respect to environmental concerns, most timberland managers recommend avoiding investments in property having a concentration of old growth stands. Such property is most apt to be targeted by environmental interest groups and legislation for regulation. Timberland managers generally target for purchase newer-growth forests and properties deemed to be less susceptible to environmental challenges.

Return Characteristics

One attraction of timberland investments is that investors can somewhat tailor the return mix between cash and appreciation to meet their individual needs. Cash flow is derived from timber harvesting, which is elective and is guided by perceived market conditions and investor cash flow requirements. Timberland that remains unharvested should be expected to increase in value as trees grow. While trees remain unharvested, timberland is able to produce ancillary revenues from hunting, fishing, and camping licenses, grazing fees, and Christmas tree–cutting contracts (Christmas trees are too small to be counted as timber).

As a tangible property investment, timberland managers point out that timber should be expected to provide a measure of inflation sensitivity. One manager was targeting inflation-adjusted returns in the 6 to 10 percent range in 1992. However, it is also a commodity-driven investment and consequently has tended to have a higher standard deviation than that for real estate as a whole. According to Hancock Timber Resources Group, between 1970 and 1991, the standard deviation for timberland investments fell just slightly short of the standard deviation for the S&P 500.

OTHER OPTIONS FOR ALTERNATIVE REAL ESTATE

One by one, major equity real estate participants either curtailed or limited their real estate investment activities in the late 1980s and early 1990s. One of the first to go was the retail limited partnership investor, followed by the savings and loan, the insurance company, and, more recently, the pension fund investor. To help fill the equity investment void, real estate participants have dusted off some old vehicles and created some new ones. Public real estate investment trusts, which had been scarcely heard from in 15 years, became one such vehicle of choice, with a record amount of new issues in 1992 and again in 1993. Another prominent source of capital derived from the public markets is securitized mortgages, which can be divided into multiple tranches to suit investor risk and return profiles. The changes to the real estate capital markets have been profound and are likely to be long lasting. Therefore, many real estate industry participants have begun to look beyond the equity commingled fund and separate account vehicles that characterized institutional real estate investments in the 1980s.

The public markets seek real estate return profiles that readily accommodate the investment vehicle. The most dominant such return characteristic is recurring distributable investor cash flow. Compared to institutional private equity real estate investors, the public real estate security investor relies little on stated property appraisals. After all, the securities can be priced daily. An investor in real estate stocks (REITs) is typically most interested in the current dividend yield and the likelihood for future dividend (and therefore share price) increases. Against this backdrop are a number of nontraditional real estate sectors that can accommodate the sought-after return attributes of the public securities markets.

Nontraditional real estate sectors can accommodate the demands of the public securities markets principally because many of these sectors essentially represent a form of tenant financing. With real estate capitalization rates often tied indirectly to the financial markets, it makes sense that a variety of securitization options should be feasible. A look at the property composition among public REITs bears this point out, since nontraditional real estate sectors are well represented within the market for public real estate equities. Property types represented include small strip shopping centers, net-leased nursing home properties, public storage facilities, mobile home parks, franchised restaurant properties, and single-tenant net-leased properties, to name just a few. In effect, the return attributes of nontraditional real estate can appear quite traditional within the public securities marketplace. As real estate managers and financial intermediaries seek more efficient means to access and manage capital, the future appears to hold promise of alternatives to traditional equity real estate investments. For prospective alternative real estate investors, this promise for enhanced market efficiency has favorable implications for today's investment values and offers the ability to more readily diversify into these assets through a wider array of investment choices.

A conclusion to be drawn from the heightened activity in the public real estate securities markets is not necessarily that these markets represent the future for nontraditional real estate. Rather, a broader observation is that the real estate asset class is highly dynamic and is undergoing secular changes that are likely to result in a closer integration of private equity and public securitized investment strategies in the long term. In this regard, traditional real estate investments have historically been more highly represented in the portfolios of institutional investors than they have in the public securities markets. As noted previously, nontraditional real estate sectors are better represented in the public securities markets than in the equity real estate portfolios of institutional investors. As the universe of securitized and equity real estate converges, so too will the definitions of nontraditional and traditional real estate investments. Over the long term, the result is likely to be a revised and broader definition of optimal investment strategies.

REFERENCES

Brackey, Harriet Johnson. "Some Mobile-Home Firms on a Roll." *USA Today,* January 21, 1992.

Brooks, Nancy. "Lessons on How to Ride Out a Recession." *Los Angeles Times,* November 13, 1990.

Deloitte and Touche. *Analysis of 12 Specialized Investment Sectors,* October 16, 1990.

Deloitte and Touche. *In-Depth Analysis of Six Specialized Investment Sectors,* February 1991.

Dunn, Michael. "They Aren't Trailors Anymore." *The Tampa Tribune,* November 3, 1990.

Graydon, Linda; Marybeth Kronenwetter; and Lynn Smith. "Specialty Real Estate for the Institutional Portfolio." *Real Estate Finance Journal,* Summer 1990.

Hancock Agricultural Investment Group. *Farmland as an Institutional Asset Class,* 1992.

Hancock Agricultural Investment Group. *Farmland as an Institutional Asset Class,* Fall 1993.

Hancock Agricultural Investment Group. *Farmland Investor,* September 1993.

Hancock Timber Resource Group. *Timber Real Estate Investment,* 1992.

Hearthstone Advisors. *The Rate of Return on Investment in Single Family Homebuilding,* 1992.

Hearthstone Advisors. *The Role of Single Family Homebuilding in an Institutional Investment Portfolio,* 1991.

Holden, Meg, and Kim Redding. *The Geographic Distribution of Properties Owned by Real Estate Investment Trusts.* The RREEF Funds, September 1993.

Kane, Mary. "Mobile Homes Are Catching on with the Upwardly Mobile." *San Diego Tribune,* October 25, 1991.

Kaplan, Howard A. "Farmland Not Unreasonable as Investment." *Pensions & Investments,* April 17, 1989.

Kaplan, Howard M. "Farmland as a Portfolio Investment." *Journal of Portfolio Management,* Winter 1985.

Manufactured Housing Institute. *Quick Facts about the Manufactured Housing Industry—1990/1991.*

McGoldrick, Beth. "An Out-of-Favor Asset Class Goes Mainstream." *Corporate Finance,* January 1993.

Moss, John. "New Concerns Make Farm Management More Important Than Ever Before." *Current Thoughts.* Newsletter published by Westchester Group, Inc., August 1992.

National Restaurant Association. *1993 Foodservice Industry Forecast,* December 1992.

National Restaurant Association. *The Foodservice Industry: 1990 in Review,* 1992.

Public Storage, Inc. *Corporate Overview.*

Riazzi, Deserie; Diana Smith; and Christopher Volk. *Franchised Restaurant Industry: 1993 Review and Outlook.*

Richardson, R. G. "Manufactured Homes: Demand Outstrips Supply." *Financial Product News,* June 1987.

Rinehart, James A., and Paul S. Saint-Pierre. *Timberland: An Industry, Investment and Business Overview,* 1991.

Rogers, Denise. *Leasing Farmland in the United States.* U.S. Department of Agriculture, 1989.

Rogers, Denise, and Gene Wunderlich. *Acquiring Farmland in the United States.* U.S. Department of Agriculture, September 1993.

Stanton, Bernard F. *Market Outlook for High Quality Farmland.* Hancock Agricultural Investment Group, 1993.

Thompson, Russell, and Matthew Williams. "Calpers Gambles on California Housing." *Barron's,* July 27, 1992.

Usdansky, Margaret L. "Home 4 Sale: 3 bdr., A/C is Portable." *USA Today,* April 21, 1992.

Volk, Christopher. "What's So Special about Specialty Property?" *Commercial Real Estate Journal,* Spring 1992.

Winton, Pete. "Investors Target Mobile Home Parks." *Naples Daily News,* October 27, 1991.

Wunderlich, Gene. *Owning Farmland in the United States.* U.S. Department of Agriculture, December 1991.

Wunderlich, Gene. "Fewer Mobile Home Parks Have Higher Investment Value." *The Spectrum International,* January 1992.

Wunderlich, Gene. "Manufactured Housing an Alternative for Lenders." *National Mortgage News,* October 21, 1991.

Wunderlich, Gene. "Mobile Home Parks Provide Recession-Resistant Investments." *San Diego Daily Transcript,* March 27, 1991.

Wunderlich, Gene. "Fewer MHPs Have Higher Investment Value." *Californian,* June 1992.

Wunderlich, Gene. "Mobile Home LPs: Calm Spot in Troubled Market." *Financial Product News,* July 1990.

Wunderlich, Gene. "Affordability Crisis Fuels Mobile Home LPs." *Financial Product News,* December 1988.

PART 3

CAPITAL STRUCTURE

CHAPTER 14

REAL ESTATE
INVESTMENT TRUSTS

David H. Downs
The University of North Carolina

David J. Hartzell
The University of North Carolina

INTRODUCTION

The 1970s and 1980s brought a substantial increase in the level of pension fund investment in real estate in the United States. Indeed, virtually no pension fund real estate investment existed prior to the passage of the Employee Retirement Income Security Act of 1974 (ERISA). After passage of ERISA, however, pension funds and their advisors reasoned that the "prudent man" rule mandated diversification into assets other than the traditional bond, stock, and bill portfolios that funds had typically held until that time. In addition to its diversification benefits, real estate was thought to provide superior risk-adjusted returns to the other assets in the investment universe, as well an effective hedge against inflation. A number of investment advisors created commingled real estate funds, which were designed to attract institutional investors, particularly the pension funds. Despite recommendations from the academic and advisor communities of substantially higher real estate holdings, at the end of 1993 the proportion of overall pension portfolios held as real estate was estimated to be approximately 4 percent. This level has held fairly constant over the past decade.

While the overall pension fund exposure to real estate averages 4 percent, in general the largest pension funds have the largest proportional investment in this asset class. Studies have shown that of the more than 37,000 pension funds in the United States, only a small percentage actually hold real estate assets. One study estimates that the 500 largest pension funds hold most of the $120 billion of equity real estate accounted for in pension portfolios (Eagle, 1994).

A number of barriers exist to keep pension funds, both small and large, out of the real estate market. One barrier to investment is the requirement of unique real estate skills in both determining overall strategy for a real estate portfolio and then executing the strategy at the local market level. Because an individual pension fund might find the cost of acquiring these skills prohibitive, it might instead either hire the expertise from an investment manager or avoid the asset class altogether. Similarly, the relatively high cost of investment grade real estate may preclude smaller funds from investing in the asset and also make it difficult to acquire a diversified portfolio of real estate.

A second potential barrier to investment in real estate by pension funds involves the investment characteristics of the primary vehicle available for pension investment in real estate: the commingled real estate fund (CREF). The first CREF was created in the early 1970s to provide an opportunity for pension funds to invest in high-quality real estate. From this start, the open- and closed-end investment fund industry has grown to over $120 billion, and more than 100 investment managers now manage real estate assets for pension funds. These funds provide both core exposure and sectoral exposure to the asset class, and the performances of individual funds are published regularly by Evaluation Associates Inc. In addition, the National Council of Real Estate Investment Fiduciaries (NCREIF) publishes quarterly aggregate performance measures for the CREF community.

In effect, these commingled funds represent a fractional, undivided interest in the properties underlying the portfolios. Purchases of units of these funds are made at prices based on the net asset value of the funds. The value is determined from appraisals of the underlying properties. Similarly, any withdrawal from the fund is done through the investment advisor that operates the fund, and the withdrawal price is also determined based on appraised net asset value. Given that the commingled funds are not obligated to sell properties to meet withdrawal requests, queues form made up of pension funds looking to liquidate their real estate exposure. Therefore, it may take several quarters or even years before a fund receives a liquidation payment.

The joint problems of expertise requirements, liquidity, and pricing based on appraised values have led pension funds and investment managers to seek new ways of holding real estate. What is needed is an investment vehicle that provides all of the purported benefits of real estate, but also some degree of liquidity so that pension funds can enter into and exit out of the asset class as market conditions dictate. The recent resurgence of real estate investment trusts (REITs), from both a market size and a performance perspective, has generated arguments for extensive pension fund holdings in this sector of the stock market. Because shares of publicly held REITs are traded in organized markets at prices determined in arm's-length transactions, many argue that a significant barrier to investment is removed. The fact that these shares trade at relatively low prices (i.e., share prices typically less than $100) helps reduce the size of transaction barrier, enabling pension funds to gain exposure to real estate in increments compatible with the funds' portfolio needs. The fact that investors can diversify across many different REITs also generates opportunities for investors. However, valid questions can be raised as to whether the REIT vehicle can provide these benefits, whether sufficient liquidity for pension funds exists in the current market, and whether such liquidity will exist in the future.

This chapter addresses topics related to institutional investments in REITs. The next section identifies the traditional arguments for including real estate in institutional portfolios and examines, over several periods, whether the asset class has actually produced those benefits. To a large extent, the promised benefits of diversification, superior returns and an inflation hedge, have fallen far short of what was actually delivered. Since REITs are being touted as an alternative to the CREF vehicle, the third section of this chapter examines the potential role of REITs in institutional portfolios. That section starts with a discussion of the historical perspective on REITs. Recent changes in tax laws have reduced some significant constraints that have effectively deterred U.S. pension funds from utilizing REITs in their portfolios. In addition, current market size and current trends in the REIT market are discussed. Given the relative illiquidity of CREF units, the trading behavior of REITs is analyzed from a market liquidity perspective. In addition, the historical performance of REITs is considered and compared to the investment performances of direct forms of real estate investment. Finally, the chapter considers a number of other issues regarding pension investment in REITs as an alternative to direct CREF investment and examines the current boom in REIT underwriting.

INSTITUTIONAL REAL ESTATE
INVESTMENT: BACKGROUND

In the 1970s, several arguments, based on an intuitive understanding of real estate, were made to support the notion that pension funds should hold substantial proportions of their assets in this new class of investments. As mentioned earlier, the first CREFs were created in the early 1970s, but through 1980 there was little interest in this asset class. Among the most commonly promoted intuitive arguments for real estate investment were those of the provision of superior returns, an inflation hedge, and diversification benefits. However, without empirical verification of these investment benefits, pension funds were hesitant to invest given the uncertainties of expected performance. Further, real estate was thought to be better understood from a local market's and an individual investor's perspective, so that it would be difficult to generate investment expertise from a centralized headquarters location.

The advent of the Frank Russell Co. index in the early 1980s (later renamed the Russell/NCREIF index) allowed for empirical tests of real estate performance using holding period returns. The real estate returns were calculated based on the income and capital appreciation of the individual properties that made up the portfolios of the investment managers that contributed their data. Combined with some early work that used historical data from Prudential's PRISA commingled real estate fund, analysts could at the time investigate the performance of real estate for a period spanning 10 years. While this is a relatively short time period compared to the historical record of stock, bond, and bill performance, these new real estate data generated a great deal of new research on the relative performance of real estate.

What Was Promised

In the 1980s, proponents of real estate investment made many arguments concerning investment performance in this asset class. The first argument was that historically real estate earned significantly higher returns than stock, bond, and bill portfolios. Combined with the fact that the measured real estate returns exhibited volatility levels that were 10 percent of stock return volatility, risk-adjusted returns were found to far exceed those of other assets in the investment opportunity set. Examples of these relative returns are shown in Exhibit 14–1, using data from the third quarter of 1973 to the fourth quarter of 1983.

A second investment benefit expected from real estate investment is an inflation hedge. To provide a hedge against inflation and hence protect against losses in purchasing power, an asset class's returns should exhibit high correlations with inflation rates. Further, if the asset's returns are closely correlated with expected and unexpected inflation, investors in general and pension funds in particular will be protected in terms of meeting future liabilities that are indexed to inflation rates. Data from the underlying properties of CREF portfolios showed that real estate was indeed an effective inflation hedge, as indicated by the high correlations over the 1973–83 period between real estate returns and both the expected and unexpected components of inflation (Hartzell, Hekman, and Miles, 1986).

The final benefit expected from investment in real estate is a diversification benefit. Given the constructs of modern portfolio theory, the addition of an asset can reduce the risk of an existing portfolio if the correlation of the new asset's return with the returns of those assets already in the portfolio is significantly less than 1 and, in the best case, less than 0. By combining such assets, overall portfolio return variation can be reduced. Early real estate portfolio studies

EXHIBIT 14–1
Quarterly Asset Return Comparison, 1973:4–1983:3

Parameter	Real Estate	S&P	Bonds	T-Bills†	Inflation†	REITs
Mean	3.2%	1.4%	1.8%	2.1%	2.0%	1.0%
Median	2.7	0.2	1.2	2.0	2.0	2.9
Standard deviation	1.8	9.3	7.5	0.8	1.0	11.4
Coefficient of variation*	135.9	−1329	−2374	35.4	48.6	−997

* Except as noted below, the coefficient of variation was calculated as

$$\frac{\text{Asset's standard deviation}}{\text{Asset's excess return}} = \frac{\text{Asset's standard deviation}}{\text{Asset's return} - \text{T-bill return}}$$

† For these assets, the coefficient of variation was calculated as

$$\frac{\text{Asset's standard deviation}}{\text{Asset's return}}$$

Source: Hartzell, Hekman, and Miles (1986).

showed that correlations of real estate returns with bonds were less than 0 and with stocks close to 0, indicating significant diversification potential.

Clearly, in retrospect, these promises were extreme and seemingly too good to be true. While real estate may have outperformed other assets in this period, the results of these studies, as most authors mentioned, were period specific. From 1973 to 1983, real estate markets rose from a deep recession stemming from the REIT debacle of the 1970s to a boom during which a large number of new capital sources were providing funds to real estate, hence making debt and equity more plentiful and in turn pushing real estate values higher. Therefore, studies performed using these data captured only the trough-to-peak portion of the real estate cycle, and hence, although indicative of performance over the time period (given the usual caveat regarding appraisal-based returns), these results could not be sustained over the longer term. However, despite the caveats given in these studies regarding manager specificity, period specificity, appraisal-based returns, and so on, pension funds invested more heavily in the real estate asset class.

Exhibit 14–1 also indicates another, perhaps more compelling motivation for pension funds to strongly consider adding real estate to their stock, bond, and bill portfolios—namely, the loathsome performance of the stock and bond markets. For the five-year period ending before 1982, inflation rates averaged 10.1 percent per annum, a level previously unseen by most investors; the stock market averaged a return of 9.6 percent per annum and failed to deliver a real (i.e., inflation-adjusted) positive return; and the bond market averaged a total (nominal) return of -0.7 percent, which, of course, translates into a miserable real return (Garrigan and Pagliari, 1992). In these circumstances, it was not surprising that necessity became the "mother of (portfolio) allocation." In short, institutional investors were strongly motivated to overlook possible weaknesses in the argument for real estate's inclusion in the mixed-asset portfolio.

For individual investors, the motivation for adding real estate to the portfolio was even more compelling. In addition to the forces cited above, several tax reform measures (the Economic Recovery Tax Act of 1981, the Tax Equity and Fiscal Responsibility Act of 1982, and the Deficit Reduction Act of 1984) dramatically increased the attractiveness of real estate's after-tax return vis-à-vis such returns from stock, bond, and bill investments. These reforms created a "tails I win, heads you lose" mentality.

The confluence of these market forces caused an unprecedented rush to invest in (and, for other reasons, to lend against) real estate. In hindsight, it is no surprise that the superior returns posted by real estate in the mid-1970s and early 1980s were about to unravel.

What Was Delivered

In retrospect, the market forces that needed to be in place for a continuation of the upslope in the real estate cycle were untenable. The overbuilding of the 1980s and a general slowdown in the overall economy that restricted growth in demand for real estate space, exacerbated by the recovery in the stock and bond markets, the Tax Reform Act of 1986, and the withdrawal of many traditional real estate lenders, led to the asset class falling far short of expectations.

With regard to the provision of superior returns, panel A of Exhibit 14–2 shows that over any period since the inception of the Russell/NCREIF index, real estate has significantly underperformed stocks, bonds, and even a risk-free asset, Treasury bills. Indeed, total returns have averaged 0.0 percent over the most recent five-year period, indicating that, on average, income gains were exactly offset by loss of value for the properties that make up the Russell/NCREIF index.

Further insight into delivered performance can be ascertained from panel B of Exhibit 14–2. While the income component of return was fairly consistent over the periods listed, the appreciation component was quite volatile. The stability of the income return does not necessarily imply that NOI levels are stable. The income component is constructed as the ratio of NOI to appraised property value, and similar relative declines (or increases) in both could lead to stable income returns. Over the past 13 years, the annual decline in values for the properties within the Russell/NCREIF index has averaged 0.8 percent. While an overall downward trend is exhibited for all properties in the index, panel C shows that annualized average returns differ greatly by property type. Assuming a 7 percent average income return component, the implied average loss of value within the office sector, for example, was approximately 16 percent for each of the last three years. Declines are also indicated for all other property type sectors in the index.

The summary statistics presented in Exhibit 14–2 indicate that, as opposed to the 1973–83 period, real estate investment (as represented by the performance of the Russell/NCREIF index) has not

EXHIBIT 14–2

Historical Performance of Direct Equity Investment in Real Estate (Annualized Holding Period Returns, Year-End June 30, 1993)

A. Asset Class Comparisons

Assets	1 Year	5 Years	10 Years	13 Years
NCREIF	−3.7%	0.0%	4.6%	6.6%
CPI	2.9	4.1	3.8	4.4
Stocks	13.6	14.2	14.3	15.5
T-bills	3.1	6.2	6.8	8.0
Bonds	13.2	11.4	11.8	11.8

B. Components of Real Estate Returns

Time Periods	Total	Income	Appreciation	CPI
1993:2	−0.7%	2.1%	−2.8%	0.5%
1992:4	−3.0	1.9	−4.9	0.4
1 year	−3.7	8.2	−11.2	2.9
5 years	0.0	7.2	−6.8	4.1
7 years	1.7	7.1	−5.2	4.0
10 years	4.6	7.2	−2.5	3.8
13 years	6.6	7.4	−0.8	4.4

C. Total Returns by Property Type

Time Periods	Apartments	Office	Retail	R&D	Warehouse
1993:2	2.2%	−3.0%	1.1%	0.5%	−2.4%
1992:4	0.2	−5.6	−1.9	−3.8	−1.8
1 year	5.4	−9.9	−0.3	−3.2	−4.3
3 years	2.3	−9.1	−0.6	−4.4	−2.4
5 years	3.9	−4.4	4.1	−0.6	2.1
7 years	N/A	−2.6	6.3	1.5	4.4
10 years	N/A	1.2	8.6	5.3	6.6

Source: Russell/NCREIF index.

continued to substantially outperform other asset classes. However, Exhibit 14–3 shows that returns earned by real estate were less variable than those earned from investing in stocks and bonds. Well-known biases imparted from using appraisals to estimate the market values used to calculate holding period returns make conclusions regarding volatility suspect.

Wurtzebach, Mueller, and Machi (1990) and Hartzell and Webb (1993) have argued that for real estate investments to provide an

EXHIBIT 14–3
Asset Returns over Time 1980:1–1993:2

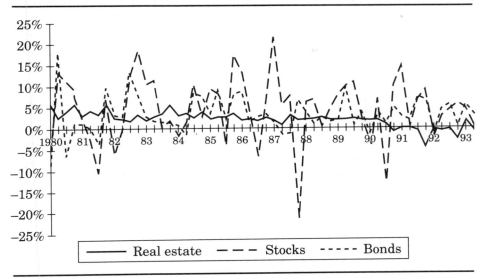

Sources: Frank Russell Co./NCREIF; the University of North Carolina Real Estate Program.

inflation hedge, supply and demand in the space markets must be in balance. When the market is in balance, as in the 1973–83 period, landlords can pass through inflationary increases to tenants in the form of higher rents. When the market is out of balance, as in the 1983–93 period, tenants are unwilling to accept inflation escalation clauses in their rental contracts. Given the alternative leasing opportunities in most real estate markets, tenants had the edge in negotiating new lease terms. Therefore, as expected, real estate has not provided a hedge against inflation in the most recent period.

Exhibit 14–4 shows these relationships graphically. In the early parts of the data period, real estate and inflation exhibited high positive correlations, indicating that real estate returns move to compensate investors for losses in purchasing power. As vacancy rates increased, correlations declined and even grew negative, indicating that real estate was for the most part unrelated to inflation, and in the worst case, returns actually declined while inflation increased. Investors in the 1980s therefore found their real estate investments providing a perverse hedge against inflation, not at all what they

EXHIBIT 14–4
Correlations between Real Estate and Inflation

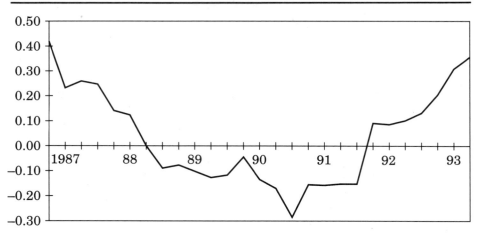

Correlations based on rolling 28-quarter periods from 1980:1 to 1993:2.

Sources: Frank Russell Co./NCREIF; the University of North Carolina Real Estate Program.

expected. This pattern has reversed itself recently, however, and a strong, positive relationship was found to exist in the most recent years of the sample period.

The final investment benefit expected from real estate is portfolio diversification. Low or negative correlations indicate that total portfolio return can be reduced by including real estate in a mixed-asset portfolio. Exhibit 14–5 shows that correlation coefficients were close to zero over the 1980–93 period, indicating there was some risk-reducing capacity. While correlations were marginally negative in the early parts of the period, they were positive in the seven-year periods ending in 1990 and 1991. In the most recent periods, correlations again became marginally negative.

From the above analyses, it appears that the touted investment benefits of real estate failed to materialize for pension investors in the 1980s and early 1990s. In addition, as pension funds recognized that the promised performance was not going to materialize, they requested withdrawals from their investment managers. The total queue waiting for liquidation from commingled real estate funds at

EXHIBIT 14–5
Correlations between Real Estate and Other Assets

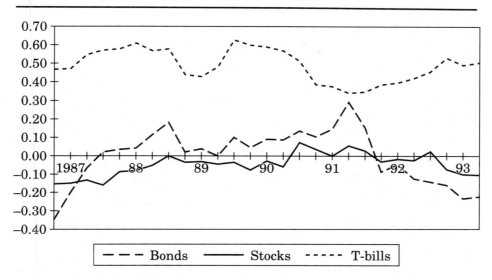

Correlations based on rolling 28-quarter periods from 1980:1 to 1993:2.

Sources: Frank Russell Co./NCREIF; the University of North Carolina Real Estate Program.

the end of 1992 was estimated at $4 billion. Some funds had been waiting over two years to liquidate their CREF real estate investments as the market turned. This lack of liquidity and inability to react to changing market conditions has led to a call for new investment vehicles that better meet the needs of investors. Although the real estate market appears poised, pension investors seem hesitant to increase their exposure to CREFs. Recent problems within the CREF industry regarding valuation of underlying properties have also led to some discussion about the viability of the CREF vehicle.

One frequently mentioned alternative is the real estate investment trust (REIT) vehicle. Since REITs may be publicly traded, investors can react more quickly to changes in market conditions if they can sell or buy shares without having a significant impact on the market. The next section provides more detail on REITs as an alternative for pension fund real estate investment.

THE REIT AS SECURITIZED REAL ESTATE

In an ideal world, securitization would solve, or at least mitigate, the myriad problems institutional investors have experienced with the real estate asset class. Unfortunately, anyone who has experienced the downside of recent real estate cycles need not be reminded that the world is far from ideal.

The REIT vehicle has the potential to become a success in the securitization of real estate. Advocates argue that the securitization of real estate will lead to an information-efficient market for all real estate transactions (Gorlow, Parr, and Taylor, 1993). We might even envision the REIT being used as a substitute for more direct forms of real estate investing and the use of REITs in hedging and market-timing techniques. However, for those who missed the bumpy ride in real estate over the past 10, 20, or 30 years, the ride in the evolution of the REIT industry has not been much smoother. Regardless, the exceptionally strong performance of REITs in the early 1990s should not be overlooked. Periods of high returns were accompanied by growth in the number and market capitalization of REITs. This combination has fueled a significant increase in interest in this part of the stock market.

How far this hot market might go is anyone's guess. The answer, though, might lie in a perspective on where the REIT industry has been and the challenges this investment vehicle faces ahead. For a discussion of the different classifications of REIT vehicles, see Appendix 14A.

Historical Perspective

Stages of Development
The REIT investment vehicle creates the opportunity for individual investors to participate in the ownership of investment grade real estate. This basic idea has always been at the heart of defining the REIT; however, the definition has transcended several generations. We consider four stages in the development of the modern REIT instrument.

The period from the late 1800s until early 1960 was, in a sense, the pre-REIT stage. The trust was first used as a means for investment in real estate in Massachusetts around the 1880s. The ancestors of the modern REIT investor pooled their resources to gain the economic advantage of real estate ownership. In 1935, Congress moved to treat trusts as taxable entities. This was an effort to curb various forms of trusts that had been created as a means of sheltering taxable income. The tax laws led to a protracted effort by real estate investors to obtain the same tax-favored treatment the growing mutual fund industry was receiving. Mutual funds at that time were recognized by federal tax codes and were designed to avoid taxation at the trust level by means of pass-through treatment. The purpose of a mutual fund, analogous to the purpose of a REIT, is the collective investment in securities. For this reason, REITs are often referred to as the "mutual funds of real estate."

Many of the rules pertaining to REITs today are a result of efforts to preclude their use as an operating tax shelter. The special tax status of REITs was authorized by Congress in 1960. The legislators intended for REITs to be a passive vehicle for real estate investment and not an operating company. However, this distinction has evolved (or blurred) to the point where REITs today are more like actively managed, strategically operated real estate companies. For a discussion of REIT qualifications, see Appendix 14B.

The passage of the 1960 law that authorized the trust form as a single-taxation ownership of real estate also marks the second stage of development in the industry. REIT industry growth began to take off in the late 1960s, when the debt REITs in particular made large loans to construction and development (C&D) projects. This practice was driven by the large spread between the REITs' borrowing and lending rates. The spreads were attributable to tight monetary policy, resulting in high interest rates and limited available funds for the C&D loans. In order to grow, the REIT continued to leverage itself with bank loans and commercial paper. Industry assets grew from $1 billion in 1968 to $20 billion in 1974, and the debt ratio went from around 50 percent to over 75 percent.

Just at this point, in 1973, the economy slowed and inflation and interest rates began to rise. The practices of the early REITs left them with many nonperforming construction loans. In turn, the trusts were forced to sell their profitable assets in an overbuilt market to buy down debt. Many REITs omitted their dividends, and the share price of the industry dropped by 50 percent. See Exhibit 14–6. Ironically, the REIT industry found itself in this position because its investment vehicle proved to be more flexible in obtaining funds than other mortgage lenders. In 1972, half of the industry's assets were C&D

EXHIBIT 14–6
NAREIT Share Price Index, 1972–93 (1972 = 100)

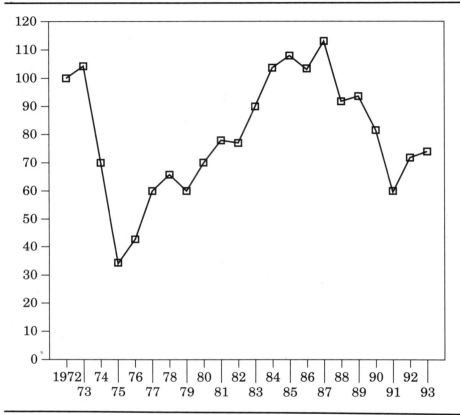

Source: *REIT Handbook*, 1993.

loans, and from 1969 to 1972, REIT offerings were 11 percent of the nation's total corporate equity securities sold. By 1974, the NAREIT index had lost more than 60 percent of its value (from its 1973 peak). Obviously, this stage involved many excesses that have helped to define prudent operating conditions for today's REIT. In addition, the REIT industry has proven to be adaptable, and many of today's managers gained their operating experience during this difficult era.

The third stage, 1976 to 1991, represents a long period of recovery and renewal for the REIT industry. By 1976 the worst was over, and the REITs that had survived the crisis of 1974 were poised to restructure their portfolios. Although the size of the industry's assets remained flat during this period, the growth in shareholder equity brought the aggregate debt ratio back to the 50 percent range. The REIT industry was beginning to prove its resilience, as evidenced by its stability in the weak real estate market of 1981 and 1982. However, competition between REIT vehicles and syndicated limited partnerships intensified in the early 1980s. Changes in tax legislation, as previously discussed, led to aggressive volumes of limited partnership offerings.

The operating experience gained in the 1970s and a stronger investment portfolio gave rise to a resurgence in REIT confidence beginning in 1984. That year saw over $500 million in new offerings, and the aggregate industry yield of 9 percent was accompanied by a 4 percent share price appreciation. Added to this, the 1984 tax laws and several Treasury Department proposals began to limit tax-motivated real estate vehicles.

The mid-1980s were also a period marked by high mortgage rates, and the REIT offered an opportunity to invest in real estate, albeit residential, when financing was expensive. REITs issued a high level of collateralized mortgage obligations (CMOs) and other debt securities backed by large pools of residential mortgages. There was a relatively strong market for mortgage REIT public offerings during 1985 and 1986.

While the introduction of the Tax Reform Act of 1986 was hard on the real estate market as a whole, the impact on REITs, whose performance did not rely as strongly on depreciation-related benefits, was far less severe. By reducing the benefits of tax shelter, the 1986 Act turned the spotlight on economically driven real estate investment. Given the full cycle of experience that management has gained and the restored strength of its balance sheets, the REIT was positioned to be the real estate vehicle of choice for investors. Despite this strong positioning, industry growth sputtered through most of the latter part of the 1980s. Oversupply in the real estate market, declining rents and occupancies, developer bankruptcies, the demise of the S&L industry, and the decline in foreign investment capital all served notice to the investor community to steer clear of real estate. This warning signal also applied to the REIT industry. However, as these pressures subsided, the fourth and most recent stage of industry development came into swing.

By the early 1990s, the REIT industry looked to be the long-term beneficiary of the downside of the real estate cycle that occurred during the mid- through late 1980s. The long-term benefit of the Tax Reform Act of 1986 was to return to the economic, as opposed to tax shelter, focus on real estate. The REIT market was situated to fill the void of financing options left by the disappearance of financial institutions and foreign investors. By this time, institutional invest-ors and developers were beginning to look for timely exit strategies for their real estate investments.

In late 1991, KIMCO Realty Corp. came to market with a success-ful offering of $128 million. This was followed by five other offerings in 1992 that each raised between $100 million and $300 million. The trend toward larger offerings of the most prominent professional real estate managers continued through 1993. By year-end 1993, the back-log of public offerings and the limited ability of investors to absorb the supply resulted in several large issues being postponed or with-drawn. The characteristically hot market for REITs at this time caused many skeptics to question the choice of properties the sponsors were placing in their offerings as well as the degree of scrutiny the underwriters were offering.

Adaptation in the Industry

The current popularity of the REIT is clear, as measured by asset growth and returns (see Exhibit 14–7). The REIT appears to have found its place among the financial options of real estate developers, owners, and investors. To a sizable degree, this popularity is the result of REIT managers who have learned to adapt and the increased flexibility of the investment vehicle.

In nature, adaptation contributes to the survival of a species. In many regards, the financial markets are also a game of survival. The 1986 Tax Reform Act represented a mortal blow to the syndicates of the early 1980s. The REIT industry has also faced its share of obsta-cles, but the lobbying success of its membership, trade affiliates, and investors has resulted in a stronger and more viable investment vehicle.

Examples of this adaptive behavior are numerous. Consider the following. As a result of the real estate downturn of the mid-1970s, debt REITs found themselves owning foreclosed property, yet federal regulations restricted the sale of these assets. Consistent with the passive intentions of the trust, REITs up to this point were not allowed

EXHIBIT 14–7
Asset and Equity Growth in the REIT Market, 1982–91

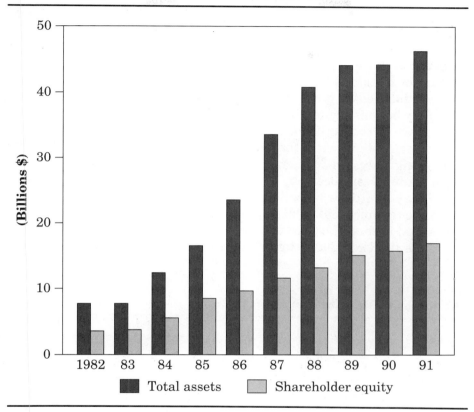

Source: *REIT Handbook*, 1993.

to hold properties for sale in the normal course of business. The law was subsequently revised to allow for special treatment in the disposition of distressed assets. Similarly, the industry pursued an opportunity to originate participating (and convertible) mortgage loans in the 1980s as a way to ensure safety and returns and to avert the problems experienced in the previous decade. In addition, rulings since the Tax Reform Act of 1986 have liberalized the opportunities for REITs to operate their own property in a sense no differently than other property owners. Prior to this, REITs could manage their properties only through independent third-party contractors.

It is difficult to separate the various reforms REITs have undergone in terms of investments, capital structure, and organizational and operational flexibility from the exodus of other sources of real estate capital. It is still harder to separate the apparent strategic motivation behind an industry trend and the economic force. A case in point is the increase in specialization among REITs. The middle ground of hybrid REITs seems to have given way to equity REITs that are focused by geographic and property type (see Exhibit 14–8). This may be consistent with an industry move toward niche posturing in the face of competition. From an economic perspective, this trend is also consistent with the notion that investors will not pay for something they can do themselves. If investors can create their own homemade diversification, across either location or property type, there may be little rationale for providing this service in a package. With the menu of real estate alternatives the REIT industry provides investors, it should be possible to structure a well-tailored portfolio.

As a final consideration of the adaptability of the REIT vehicle,

EXHIBIT 14–8
Distribution of REITs by Asset Type, 1972–92

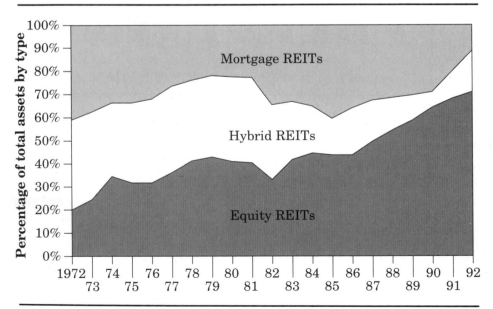

Source: *REIT Handbook*, 1993.

the five-or-fewer restriction on the concentration of ownership has been substantially revised. This rule applies principally to U.S. pension funds, since in the past foreign investors have been granted a look-through exemption, where that applied. Some of the implications of concentrated ownership by institutions are discussed later. Effectively, domestic pension funds are now also viewed on a look-through basis (i.e., each beneficiary of the pension plan is viewed as an individual investor in the REIT for purposes of the five-or-fewer test).

REIT Growth and Performance

In recent years, both total dividends paid by REITs and aggregate REIT share prices have registered impressive gains, although there was a connection in 1994. This represents a remarkable recovery from the collapse of the REIT market in the mid-1970s (see Exhibit 14–9).

The strong performance of REITs over the past several years is depicted by the historical returns for an index of all REITs and an index of equity REITs. Although often classified as income-oriented investments, REITs are best evaluated on a total return basis for their long-term benefits. The relevant cash flows, in REIT parlance, are measured as the funds-from-operations (FFO). The sustainable cash flow for paying dividends, FFO are those funds that are available for distribution to REIT shareholders out of current or projected operations. Simply stated, FFO equal net income plus depreciation less principal repayments, thus accounting for most noncash expenses and unrecognized outflows.

As noted earlier, October 1991 signaled the start of a hot market for REITs, with the $128 million initial public offering by KIMCO leading the way for several other large offerings. This was certainly not the first of the hot REIT markets. However, industry commentators are quick to point out that this may be the most sustaining leg of a migration of private real estate into a securitized form. For a perspective on the initial public offering of equity REITs, Exhibit 14–10 shows the number of offerings by year and the average size of each offering. The lower interest rates of 1984 and the possible tax reform for syndicated real estate were evident in the hot market of 1985. Interestingly, the number of secondary offerings over this same period showed a slightly different trend in which secondary offering activity picked up considerably in the early 1990s. This reflects the ability of experienced and proven REIT professionals to attract new

EXHIBIT 14–9
REIT Total Return Performance, 1972–92

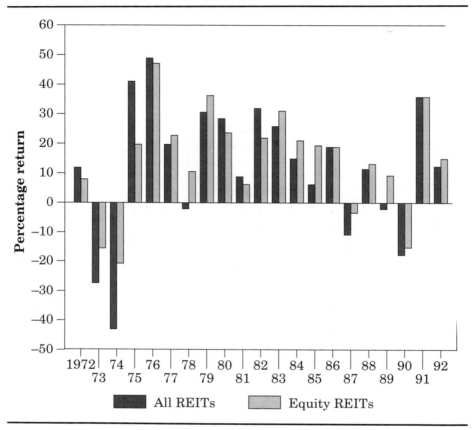

Source: *REIT Handbook*, 1993.

capital to take advantage of opportunities in a depressed real estate environment. The relative growth in equity is somewhat misleading because of the emergence of REITs issuing mortgage-backed securities in 1982. However, referring back to Exhibit 14–8, as a whole the composition of equity, mortgage, and hybrid REITs show a shift in market capitalization toward equity. The absolute level of market capitalization for mortgage REITs has diminished since their highest point in 1988.

EXHIBIT 14–10
Equity REIT Offerings: 1982–93

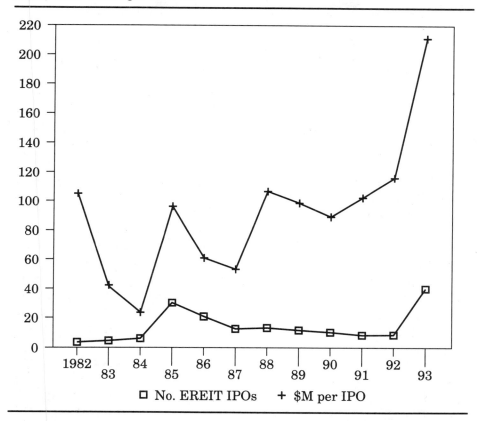

□ No. EREIT IPOs   + $M per IPO

Source: *REIT Handbook*, 1993.

Direct comparisons between the performance of the REIT index and the Russell/NCREIF index are complicated for a couple of reasons. First, since the Russell/NCREIF index is predominantly based on appraisal information, there is a well-documented smoothing bias. Although the techniques used in the de-smoothing process continue to make advances, the comparison is not an apples-to-apples match. Second, the possibility exists that the information in appraisal-based indexes actually lags that of a market-based index. The reason for the lag is most probably the result of reporting appraisals quarterly on values that essentially change daily or, in the case of the stock market, move minute by minute. Even so, there are several interesting points of comparison between REIT and Russell/NCREIF returns:

Russell/NCREIF	REIT
Appraisal based	Transaction based
Unleveraged	Leveraged
Whole interest	Fractional interest
Before fees	After fees

Separately, as an inflation hedge, REITs tend to look like common stocks. One well-touted benefit real estate has offered the investor is the hedge against inflation. As inflation rises, higher costs can often be passed along to the tenant. Income-producing real estate has traditionally been associated with assets that hedge against inflation. A recent study of the inflation characteristics of REITs finds that they perform more like equities than real estate and exhibit negative correlations with inflation and its expected and unexpected components (Park, Mullineax, and Chew, 1990). This characteristic is not consistent with the promised benefits of real estate investments.

REIT shares are often considered to be less volatile than common stock. A recent look at the change in REIT betas over time finds that this measure of systematic risk decreased significantly throughout the 1980s (Khoo, Hartzell, and Hoesli, 1993). The implication of this shift in beta is twofold. First, a low beta is consistent with the earlier arguments that real estate has a low correlation with stocks. The result is that real estate investments, and, in this case, REITs proxying for real estate, may provide diversification benefits in a portfolio of non–real estate equities. Second, the decrease in beta over time supports the argument that REITs are, in effect, behaving more like a proxy for their underlying assets. One potential reason for this effect is the increase in the number of analysts following the REIT sector. Over time, security analysts have become better equipped to reveal the value of the real estate behind the securities. This development will contribute to a more efficient REIT securities market.

Liquidity: The New Promise

From either the buy or sell side of real estate, a strong and common drawing point of the REIT vehicle is liquidity. Even for private REITs, asset managers are inclined to argue that the potential to convert to a publicly traded form represents a valuable option. Thus, a discussion of the upside of the REIT vehicle either begins with or eventually gets around to liquidity. Perhaps surprisingly, we find that the same is true when one looks at the downside. In this section, we consider several dimensions of the double-edged effects of real estate liquidity: the new promise.

Securitization and Liquidity

As a starting point, a distinction exists between the liquidity of an asset and the liquidity of a market or investment vehicle. A liquid asset is any asset that can be quickly converted to cash without significant loss of value; generally, we argue that direct holdings of real estate do not represent liquid assets. On the other hand, the U.S. stock markets are the most liquid markets in the world. This is a relative measure that implies that these markets have certain standards for information, transactions, and participation that lead to ease and low cost in the transferability of assets traded on them.

Market liquidity can be an elusive concept, in part because it can be characterized in many ways. The central point, however, is that an amount of the asset may be bought or sold quickly at a price that is close to the current market price. Real asset markets are generally not liquid. However, securities representing fractional shares of real assets can be traded in liquid markets.

Securitization has many advantages for the originator that ultimately can be expressed as a lower cost of financing. This is quite different from saying that all assets will eventually be securitized. The originator clearly chooses those assets that are perceived to lower cost by either selling the asset and taking it off the books or by issuing securities against the asset in which the proceeds may be invested. For the investor, securitization offers the opportunity to invest in assets that otherwise may be inaccessible. Securitization also permits the easy exchange of these assets. This type of liquidity offers the investor the opportunity to step in and out of the investment quickly.

Market Capitalization and Trading

Liquidity also plays an important part in the pricing of assets. For most assets, particularly stocks and bonds, the lower the liquidity of the asset, the higher the return it is required to yield. Consequently, investors with longer holding periods (e.g., institutional investors, including pension fund and endowment funds) can expect to earn higher returns from holding less liquid assets. It is clear from the discussion at the beginning of the chapter that expectations are not always realized! On the other hand, the more liquid an asset, all else being equal, the lower its expected return.

A stock's market capitalization is another aspect of liquidity that concerns institutional investors. Large institutional shareholders have a number of reasons to be averse to smaller-capitalization stocks, not the least of which are the problems associated with trades moving the price. REIT stocks have been notoriously small-capitalization issues. However, the past several years have witnessed a growth in the number of REITs falling into a middle-capitalization range. Exhibit 14–11 depicts a measure of the trading volume of three of the biggest REITs relative to the trading volume of three large-capitalization issues traditionally favored by institutional investors: AT&T, General Motors, and IBM. This exhibit shows that the shares of the REITs are fairly heavily traded relative to their market size. However, when we consider the dollar size of the issues, they are relatively less liquid than the large-capitalization stocks. This is meant to be not a lopsided contest between big and small but a look at what securitization offers in terms of relative liquidity. On a positive note, we find the general trend in the trading time for REITs decreasing over the past several years. However, the bound associated with the decreasing at a decreasing rate curve captures the limitations of this trend given the size of the issues (see Exhibit 14–12).

Corporate Governance and Liquidity

In the United States, the typical institutional investor's portfolio contains hundreds of stocks, each held for about a year (Bhide, 1993). This form of portfolio management is very consistent with an investment style that dictates that investors should sell stocks if they are unhappy with management. However, the trend over the last several years for the institutional investor has been characterized by a movement toward a relational-oriented investment style. In fact, some of

EXHIBIT 14–11
Average Daily Volume: Percentage of Shares Outstanding, 1982–92

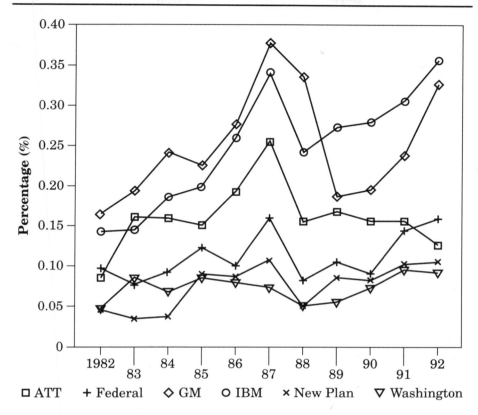

Note: "Federal" is Federal Realty Investment Trust; "New Plan" is New Plan Realty Trust; "Washington" is Washington Real Estate Investment Trust.

Source: CRSP data file.

the biggest pension funds are finding that they can no longer afford to just sell a stock when they are not happy (Bowman, 1993).

Along this line, several recent publications discussing the advantages of REIT investments suggest that this vehicle gives investors the ultimate form of liquidity, the ability to vote with their feet. This statement is unfortunately misleading, for a couple of reasons. First, it implies that investments in REITs may be dominated more through

EXHIBIT 14–12
Average Trading Volume: Days to Trade $1 Million, 1982–92

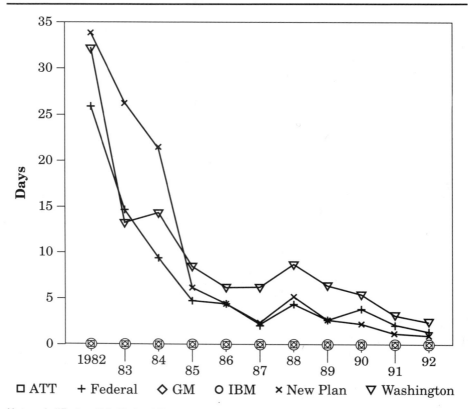

□ ATT   + Federal   ◇ GM   ○ IBM   × New Plan   ▽ Washington

Notes: 1. "Federal" is Federal Realty Investment Trust; "New Plan" is New Plan Realty Trust; "Washington" is Washington Real Estate Investment Trust.
2. Although difficult to see, AT&T, GM, and IBM lie along the horizontal axis. That is, on average, it takes well under a day for $1 million in these securities to trade.

Source: CRSP data file.

the perceived strength of management than through a longer-term commitment to the underlying asset. Second, this investment style ignores the potential benefits relational investing provides in the governance of corporations. Bhide (1993) argues that liquidity of this nature reduces the exit costs of unhappy shareholders and therefore actually discourages the valuable function of monitoring.

Bernstein (1993) provides yet another perspective on liquidity.

The essence of his argument is that liquidity is economically synonymous with the notions of systematic risk. At one end of the liquidity spectrum is money, and at the other end are assets like real estate. Because real estate is location specific, it arguably exhibits the least systematic risk of the institutional investments (Hartzell, Hekman, and Miles, 1986; Miles and McCue, 1984). However, by imposing liquidity on real estate investment, the idiosyncrasies of its performance and the performance of its management are ignored. The potential result is that the REIT vehicle begins to look as systematic as any other stock and not like real estate.

Relative Liquidity

A study of 451 stocks included in the S&P 500 and traded on the NYSE showed a marked decrease in liquidity across the month of October 1987 (Amihud and Mendelson, 1986). Consistent with theory, this decrease in liquidity was accompanied by a decrease in share price. However, the impact of the change in liquidity was not experienced proportionally across all securities. This observation supports the notion that liquidity changes have differential impacts on liquidity premia across assets. The significance of changes in liquidity on the return performances of securities is an important concept in finance and for investors. Theory and empirical evidence support the notion that the more liquid an asset, the more sensitive the asset is to a change in liquidity. As liquidity decreases, the demand for the stock drops, along with the price. However, the decrease in demand, and in price, is more drastic for more liquid securities. Stated slightly differently, a decrease in liquidity has less of a price effect on a thinly traded stock than on a very liquid security.

Clearly, the chaotic trading of the October 1987 stock market caused investors to reassess the liquidity of these exchanges. In fact, one might speculate that the marked decrease in the broader indexes over that month was, to a large degree, due to the lower expectation of market liquidity.

However, "during the 1987 stock market crash, REIT share prices dropped one-third as much as the Dow Jones" (National Association of Real Estate Investment Trusts, 1989). This statement reflects an interesting application of the theory that less liquid assets are less sensitive to changes in liquidity. Arguments suggesting that REITs were less volatile than common stocks during the tumultuous crash of 1987 may also be consistent with the explanation that REITs were, at least at that time, simply less liquid than the stocks that comprise the Dow Jones index.

A separate and preliminary inquiry into the liquidity of REITs, as measured by bid-ask spreads, finds that REITs do not look very different from common stocks (Nelling et al., 1994). The average spread for NYSE-traded REITs in 1990 was $0.20, which is comparable to the median spread on all NYSE stocks.

Liquidity and Information

One final comment on liquidity relates to the release of public information. Liquidity in asset markets is often associated with factors that improve informational flows: the number of analysts who follow a particular issue, the number of traders making a market in the issue, rating agencies, and so on. On the other hand, most of these factors can represent economic costs to the managers. For REITs, the costs may include obtaining and reporting external appraisals, elaborating on financial performance, and communicating tactical and strategic issues to investors.

A current crusade among the followers of the REIT industry is a general raising of reporting and disclosure standards (for example, see Parsons [1993]). Granted, many real estate–experienced managers who run REITs are accustomed to operating in private information circles. Yet these managers need to acknowledge the impact information has on liquidity. The public investor relies on the timeliness of information and its full disclosure. Firms can invest in liquidity through standardization of securities, presentations to stock market analysts, audits by reputable accountants, and listing on national rather than regional exchanges (Amihud and Mendelson, 1986).

As an interesting side note, the *REIT Handbook* (National Association of Real Estate Investment Trusts, 1993) lists the assets of equity REITs by property type, geographic location, and other classifications. For the state-by-state breakdown of property locations, the *REIT Handbook* reports 20 percent of the total assets as not disclosed.

A second issue concerns the reporting of current market values for REIT properties. The notion of marking to market the REIT provides the investor with a potentially critical piece of information. Only a fraction of REITs provide supplemental information on the current appraisal values of properties carried on their books. Admittedly, it can be extremely difficult to analyze and evaluate public real estate securities. The boom in the REIT industry is destined to attract more analysts. In some sense, the analysts will potentially have no better opportunity to value the underlying properties than appraisers. In the end, the analysts may be left to assess management to the exclusion of the underlying asset.

The tax laws ensure that REITs hold rather than continually buy and sell properties. This long-term investment strategy allows REITs to take advantage of property appreciation and reduce their exposure to the effects of short-term market changes. Of course, the investor that is best suited for a long-term investment strategy is the institutional investor. The question is whether the REIT is the best vehicle. Real estate, whether held in a public (securitized) form or a private (direct or commingled) form is difficult to evaluate. The very nature of the analyses and the resulting actions for private and public real estate may be the genesis of the assets' differences. The ability to trade real estate as a securitized asset can accommodate the philosophy of walking away, but it certainly inhibits the opportunity to time the real estate market (better than average) or obtain private information on properties. To this end, securitized real estate investors may rely to a high degree on standard equity-security analysis.

CONCLUSION

In recent years, due to dissatisfaction with traditional means of investing in real estate, institutional investors have looked for other vehicles to gain exposure to this asset class. Given that traditional benefits of real estate investment have not been generated by commingled real estate fund investments and that it is difficult to liquidate CREF holdings in a declining market, investors are naturally searching for alternative vehicles that offer the best of both worlds. That is, they want superior risk-adjusted returns, an inflation hedge, and diversification benefits, but they also want the liquidity that comes from active trading. Additional concerns regarding private holding of real estate surround the fees and costs of the commingled real estate funds (based on acquisition costs and appraised values) and the tremendous degree of control that is delegated to the investment manager.

As CREFs have fallen out of favor with investors, real estate investment trusts have recently become a sector of the stock market that has attracted a great deal of capital. While the market totaled only $8.5 billion of assets in 1991, new and secondary issues, combined with strong performance, lifted the total asset value of REITs to over $20 billion at the end of 1993. In an era characterized by a dearth of debt financing for the development or purchase of income-producing properties, developers and owners of real estate have rushed to raise capital by selling shares backed by their properties in the public stock markets. Combined with an increased ability of Wall Street firms to bring new issues to the market and an apparently strong appetite for holding REIT shares by individual and institutional investors because of current yields relative to bond and stock holdings, the REIT industry has become a favorite topic for articles in the popular press and in practitioner and academic journals.

REITs, which were originally structured to allow small-investor participation in real estate investment, have grown in popularity with institutional investors. Because of the special exemptions allowed at the corporate and taxpayer levels, institutions such as pension funds, endowments, and others have shown an increased interest in REITs. These tax-exempt investors potentially benefit from the exemption of REIT distributions from unrelated business taxable income (UBTI). The REIT vehicle offers investors the potential for or access to income, growth, professional management, quality real estate investment, liquidity, and limited liability. As discussed here, some of the important aspects of REITs for the institutional investor's consideration include the following:

- Liquidity is often cited as the biggest distinguishing feature of REITs from other real estate investments.
- Investor interest in REITs that began in mid-1992 was spurred by the emphasis on value-added management. This resulted in significant share price premiums and was a manifestation of the continuing flexibility of the investment vehicle.
- Pension funds that lack the expertise to invest directly in real estate and are unable to make the commitment to raise staff or that do not have the necessary credit and market analysis should consider the REIT security as a form of public ownership of real estate.

However, obvious questions arise as to the appropriateness of the REIT vehicle in providing real estate exposure to institutional investors. On the one hand, the underlying assets held by equity

REITs are individual real estate properties, and the cash flows passed through to shareholders are indeed residual income streams obtained from lease payments. On the other hand, it appears that changes in the prices of REITs have been closely related to the performance of the stock market as a whole, although the relationship has weakened over time. Therefore, the important issue of whether REITs provide exposure to real estate or additional exposure to the stock market should be of interest to the institutional investor. This will have important asset allocation implications as institutional investors continue to attempt to determine whether real estate is indeed a separate asset class or simply another sector of the stock market. Again, this has strong implications regarding the level of diversification offered by REITs in the context of institutional investment in real estate.

With regard to pension fund investment in real estate, the REIT does seem to be an appropriate vehicle for the large proportion of funds in the small and moderate-size ranges to gain exposure to the asset class. In addition, because of REIT specialization in certain regions and property types, these investors can pursue their own diversification strategies much as they can in the stock market. With the traditional methods of investing in real estate, this is not necessarily possible. For larger plans that already have exposure to direct investment in real estate, the REIT may provide an opportunity for tactical asset allocation to increase or decrease exposure to various sectors of the real estate market while maintaining a core portfolio. In some cases, this may create some redundancy if the equity managers are already exposed to REITs as a sector of the overall stock market. These internal adjustments are factors that will have to be considered as the REIT market continues to grow.

At this stage, it is too early to tell whether the growing equity REIT market will provide the overall benefits of real estate investment, plus the liquidity currently valued by institutional investors. As individual and institutional investors continue to absorb the new shares that are coming to market, and as the pipeline of new issues continues to swell as developers, owners, and investment managers alike attempt to capitalize on the apparent difference between public and private real estate pricing, the market will continue to evolve into some form of equilibrium. Whether this is represented by a total equity REIT asset value of $25 billion or $100 billion is anyone's guess, but certainly the infrastructure is in place for the market to grow further. One estimate of total pension fund exposure to real estate is $120 billion, which currently is much higher than the total equity REIT market, hence limiting a large move into REITs by the largest pension funds. Events occurring in the REIT market in 1994 indicate that the investor appetite for shares has declined. Rising interest rates have made REIT yields less attractive relative to those earned in fixed-income markets, and the REIT market has experienced declines in prices. As the number of investors willing to allocate more funds into the REIT market has declined, the growth of the market through initial public offerings and secondary offerings has stalled. Analysts are divided as to whether the price decline represents an opportunity for further investment to take advantage of continuing improvement in the underlying real estate market, or alternative investments have become more attractive given interest rate pressures. In any event, the public market remains one of the only sources of capital to a capital-starved sector of the economy and should continue to attract a great deal of interest from both the buy and sell sides of the marketplace.

APPENDIX 14A REIT CLASSIFICATION

REITs are most easily defined as tax-favored companies that specialize in real estate investment by pooling the funds of investors. Beyond this common denominator, however, REITs can be classified along many different dimensions.

The first distinction that can be made is between privately placed and publicly traded REITs. Most REITs are publicly traded. Private placements of REITs are less common because of the requirement to have at least 100 shareholders. The following is a sample of common distinctions for REITs.

Asset Mix. REITs that invest primarily in equity real estate are classified as equity REITs (EREITs). Likewise, if the assets of the REIT are principally real estate mortgages, the company falls into the mortgage REIT category. The lines of demarcation for equity and mortgage REITs are somewhat arbitrary; however, NAREIT (National Association of Real Estate Investment Trusts) uses a 75-percent-of-assets cutoff for each. Those REITs that fall into the middle ground are called hybrids. In addition, some REITs have been formed to issue collateralized mortgage obligations (CMOs) and other mortgage-related securities.

Property Type.   Although some REITs invest in several types of properties, others focus on a particular sector—office buildings, shopping centers, apartments, or warehouses, for example. In 1992, the distribution of equity REITs across property types was 27 percent retail, 19 percent offices, 14 percent industry, and 11 percent residential, with hotels and other properties comprising the balance. Health care properties represented 18 percent of the total.

Health Care REITs.   These REITs specialize in health care facilities such as hospitals, medical office buildings, and assisted living centers. Health care REITs often use a purchase/leaseback arrangement with the previous owner. Because of the special relationship that often exists between the REIT management and the tenants, these REITs are generally treated separately from other publicly traded, equity REITs.

Geographic Concentration.   Many REITs invest in properties across the country. However, most REITs have some geographic focus, even if it is in a single state or several noncontiguous states. The states with the highest concentration of REIT investment are California, Florida, New York, and Texas.

Operating Time Frame.   *Perpetual REITs* are formed to operate indefinitely, consistent with the objectives of the traditional corporate form. Finite-life REITs (FREITs) are formed for a prespecified period of time and are often referred to as self-liquidating REITs. The advantage of this form is the assurance of a realized gain within a known investment horizon. The disadvantage is the potential for poor timing, and accordingly some finite-life REITs have adopted provisions to extend their lives or convert to perpetual REITs.

Investment Policy.   A REIT may be identified as a blind pool or a planned-investment REIT. This qualification is based on whether or not the investments of the REIT are specified at the time of the investment offering.

Property Management.   REITs may contract out for external or independent management of their properties. A REIT may choose to use an internal structure to operate the properties or to operate through a wholly owned subsidiary. Some REITs use a combination of property managements.

Advisor.   Traditionally, about one-third of REITs carried out their administrative and management functions through their own employees. The others employed an independent or external management firm. This trend seems to be shifting toward a greater emphasis on self-managed REITs. The board of trustees contracts with the management, whether it be internal or external, to supervise the corporation's day-to-day operations. The trustees serve a special and important role in monitoring the advisor's performance and negotiating compensation.

APPENDIX 14B REIT QUALIFICATIONS

The REIT was established to offer the individual investor a fractional share in an economically oriented and professionally managed real estate investment. The purpose of the trust is to hold and operate institutional grade real estate investments. A side benefit of this form of investment is the liquidity offered by fractional shares that can be traded in public or private form.

What is a REIT? A REIT is a special investment vehicle, since it pays no federal tax on income or gains, provided it complies with the following specific requirements of the Internal Revenue Codes. The organization and operation rules for REITs stipulate that they be organized as corporations, business trusts, or associations. Unlike partnerships, the Internal Revenue Code requires that REITs be treated as corporations for tax purposes. However, if certain requirements are met, the income is taxed only at the shareholder level.

In addition, the REIT must:

- Be managed by a board of directors or trustees.
- Have shares that are fully transferable.
- Have a minimum of 100 shareholders.
- Have no more than 50 percent of the shares held by five or fewer individuals during the latter half of each taxable year. This restriction, popularly referred to as the five-or-fewer rule, was recently revised to allow domestic pension funds the same "look-through" treatment that was afforded foreign pension funds.

Following this, two principal tests of a REIT are the income and asset tests. The intention of the income test is to ensure that the REIT's income is principally the result of passive investment in real estate. The following points provide floor and ceiling requirements:

- At least 75 percent of income must derive from real estate.
- At least 95 percent of income must come from qualifying 75 percent

sources plus other passive sources (e.g., dividends, stock sales, interest).

- No more than 30 percent of income may result from the sale of real property held less than four years, securities held less than six months, or other restricted transactions.

Specific exclusions accompany each of these tests. One set of particular exclusions allows for the sale of properties obtained as a result of foreclosure.

The asset test stipulates that 75 percent of the value of the REIT's total assets at the close of each quarter of the taxable year be represented by real estate assets, cash, and government securities. The remaining 25 percent may comprise no more than 5 percent of the securities of any one issuer and no more than 10 percent of the outstanding voting securities of a particular issuer.

The REIT must pay dividends on 95 percent of its taxable income, although it may (and often does) pay a higher percentage. REIT dividends generally do not constitute unrelated business taxable income (UBTI) for tax-exempt investors. This is the case even if the REIT's income is derived from leveraged investments in real estate as long as the REIT abides by the five-or-fewer restriction. Distributions in excess of a REIT's earnings and profits are treated as a return of capital to the shareholder. This defers the tax otherwise due on the distribution and treats the distribution as a decrease in the taxable basis of the investment (resulting in a higher tax liability when the REIT shares are sold). REIT tax provisions do not require the distribution of capital gains realized on the sale of property to maintain standing as a qualified REIT. If the REIT retains any portion of the gain, it pays a capital gain tax similarly to a corporation. Otherwise, the distribution is taxed at the shareholder level. A REIT cannot pass losses from operations through to shareholders; however, it may carry losses forward to reduce taxable income in future years.

Finally, REITs must also comply with state rules, many of which are covered by the NASAA (North American Securities Administrators Association) guidelines pertaining to REITs. In essence, these rules require that the majority of the REIT's trustees be independent from the REIT. The trustees are usually experienced professionals from the fields of real estate, finance, law, and academia.

REFERENCES

Allen, P. R., and C. F. Sirmans. "An Analysis of Gains to Acquiring Firms' Shareholders: The Special Case of REITs" *Journal of Financial Economics*, March 1987, pp. 174–84.

Amihud, Y., and H. Mendelson. "Asset Pricing and the Bid-Ask Spread." *Journal of Financial Economics,* December 1986, pp. 233–49.

Bernstein, P. "Sourdough Is Hardly Pumpernickel." *Journal of Portfolio Management,* Spring 1993.

Bhide, A. "The Hidden Costs of Stock Market Liquidity." *Journal of Financial Economics,* August 1993, pp. 31–51.

Bowman, D. "New Directions for Institutional Investors." In "FM Real World: Issues and Solutions." *Financial Management,* Autumn 1993.

Burns, W., and D. Epley. "The Performance of Portfolios of REITs and Stocks." *Journal of Portfolio Management,* Fall 1983, pp. 37–42.

Chan, K. C.; P. Hendershott; and A. Sanders. "Risk and Return on Real Estate: Evidence from Equity REITs." *Journal of the American Real Estate and Urban Economics Association,* Winter 1990, pp. 431–52.

Chen, K. C., and D. D. Tsang. "Interest Rate Sensitivity of Real Estate Investment Trusts." *Journal of Real Estate Research,* Fall 1988, pp. 13–22.

Damodoran, A., and C. Liu. "Insider Trading as a Signal of Private Information." *Review of Financial Studies,* Spring 1993, pp. 79–119.

Davidson, H. A., and J. E. Palmer. "A Comparison of the Investment Performance of Common Stocks, Homebuilding Firms, and Equity REITs." *Real Estate Appraiser,* July–August 1978, pp. 35–39.

Eagle, B. "The Clearinghouse." *Real Estate Finance,* Spring 1994.

Eichholtz, P., and D. Hartzell. "Real Estate Investment Trusts, Appraisals, and the Stock Market: An International Perspective." Working paper, University of North Carolina, 1994.

Fama, E., and W. Schwert. "Asset Returns and Inflation." *Journal of Financial Economics,* November 1977, pp. 115–46.

Firstenberg, P.; S. Ross; and R. Zisler. "Real Estate: The Whole Story." *Journal of Portfolio Management,* Spring 1988, pp. 22–34.

Garrigan, R., and J. Pagliari. "The Impact of Supply Changes on Real Net Operating Income: The Multi-Family Perspective." *Real Estate Issues,* Spring–Summer 1992, pp. 24–32.

Gau, G., and K. Wang. "A Further Examination of Appraisal Data and the Potential Bias in Real Estate Return Indexes." *Journal of the American Real Estate and Urban Economics Association,* Spring 1990, pp. 40–48.

Giliberto, S. M. "Equity Real Estate Investment Trusts and Real Estate Returns." *Journal of Real Estate Research,* Summer 1990.

Gorlow, R.; D. Parr; and L. Taylor. "The Securitization of Institutional Real Estate Investments." *Real Estate Review,* Spring 1993.

Gyourko, J., and D. Keim. "What Does the Stock Market Tell Us about Real Estate Returns?" *Journal of the American Real Estate and Urban Economics Association,* Winter 1992, pp. 457–85.

Hartzell, D.; J. Hekman; and M. Miles. "Real Estate Returns and Inflation." *Journal of the American Real Estate and Urban Economics Association,* Summer 1986.

Hartzell, D., and A. Mengden. "Real Estate Investment Trusts: Are They Stocks or Real Estate?" *Salomon Brothers Real Estate Research,* August 1986.

Hartzell, D., and A. Mengden. "Another Look at Equity Real Estate Investment Trust Returns." *Salomon Brothers Real Estate Research,* September 1987.

Hartzell, D., and B. Webb. "Commercial Real Estate and Inflation During Periods of High and Low Vacancy Rates." Working paper, University of North Carolina, 1993.

Howe, J., and J. Shilling. "Capital Structure Theory and REIT Security Offerings." *Journal of Finance,* September 1988, pp. 983–93.

Howe, J., and J. Schilling. "REIT Advisor Performance." *Journal of the American Real Estate and Urban Economics Association,* Winter 1990, pp. 179–89.

Khoo, T.; D. Hartzell; and M. Hoesli. "An Investigation of the Change in Real Estate Investment Trust Betas." *Journal of the American Real Estate and Urban Economics Association,* Summer 1993, pp. 107–130.

Kuhle, J., and C. Wurtzebach. "The Financial Performance of Real Estate Investment Trusts." *Journal of Real Estate Research,* Spring 1986, pp. 67–75.

Liu, C.; D. Hartzell; W. Greig; and T. Grissom. "The Integration of the Real Estate Market and the Stock Market: Some Preliminary Evidence." *Journal of Real Estate Finance and Economics,* Fall 1990, pp. 261–82.

Liu, C., and J. Mei. "The Predictability of REITs and Their Co-movement with Other Assets." *Journal of Real Estate Finance and Economics,* Winter 1992, pp. 401–18.

Miles, M., and T. McCue. "Commercial Real Estate Returns." *Journal of American Real Estate and Urban Economics Association,* Fall 1984, pp. 355–77.

National Association of Real Estate Investment Trusts. *REIT Fact Book: The REIT Concept.* 1989.

National Association of Real Estate Investment Trusts. *REIT Handbook.* 1993.

Nelling, E.; J. Mahoney; T. Hildebrand; and M. Goldstein. "Real Estate Investment Trusts, Small Stocks and Bid-Ask Spreads." *Journal of the American Real Estate and Urban Economics Association,* Spring 1995.

Park, J.; D. Mullineax; and I. Chew. "Are REITs Inflation Hedges?" *Journal of Real Estate Finance and Economics,* Spring 1990, pp. 91–103.

Parsons, J. "Marketing REITs to Institutional Investors: Investor Relations Is the Key to Success." *The REIT Report,* Spring 1993.

Sagalyn, L. "Real Estate Risk and the Business Cycle: Evidence from the Security Markets." *Journal of Real Estate Research,* Summer 1990, pp. 203–20.

Scott, L. "Do Prices Reflect Market Fundamentals in Real Estate Markets?" *Journal of Real Estate Finance and Economics,* Summer 1990, pp. 5–23.

Smith, K., and D. Shulman. "The Performance of Equity Real Estate Investment Trusts." *Financial Analysts Journal,* September–October 1976, pp. 61–66.

Solt, M., and N. Miller. "Managerial Incentives: Implications for the Financial Performance of Real Estate Investment Trusts." *Journal of the American Real Estate and Economics Association,* Winter 1985, pp. 404–23.

Titman, S., and A. Warga. "Risk and the Performance of Real Estate Investment Trusts: A Multiple Index Approach." *Journal of the American Real Estate and Urban Economics Association,* Fall 1986, pp. 414–31.

Wurtzsach, C. H.; G. Mueller; and D. Macchi. "The Impact of Inflation and Vacancy on Real Estate Returns." *Journal of Real Estate Research,* Summer 1991, pp. 153–68.

CHAPTER 15

LEVERAGED INVESTMENTS FOR TAX-EXEMPT INVESTORS: THE FINANCIAL PERSPECTIVE

Joseph L. Pagliari, Jr.
Citadel Realty, Inc.

Richard T. Garrigan
Kellstadt Graduate School of Business
DePaul University

This chapter examines the financial impacts of using mortgage indebtedness to finance a portion of the real estate investments owned by tax-exempt investors[1] such as pension, endowment, and Taft-Hartley funds. While the impacts of income taxes on taxable investors may alter the conclusions contained herein, the Tax Reform Act of 1986 greatly reduced the tax shelter aspects generally associated with leveraged real estate investments for these investors.[2] Thus, the material in this chapter should also be of interest to taxable investors.

This chapter utilizes a base case through which such financial factors as capitalization rates, inflation levels, interest rates, and inflation pass-through rates can be examined. But first, it is desirable to explore a few definitions and concepts central to this examination.

---

[1] The legal and tax implications of engaging in leveraged transactions, particularly with regard to unrelated business taxable income (UBTI), should be discussed with an investor's legal/tax advisor.

[2] Recent tax reform proposals may mitigate some of the passive loss limitations applied to individuals and corporations actively engaged in real estate development and management.

OPERATING VERSUS FINANCIAL LEVERAGE

Traditional corporate finance draws the distinction between operating and financial leverage. *Operating leverage* is defined as the degree to which a firm's business is characterized by fixed costs in relation to total costs. Firms with higher fixed costs have higher break-even points and, accordingly, more business risk. The degree of business risk is also affected by the predictability of sales. *Financial leverage* is defined as the degree to which a firm's capitalization is provided by debt as opposed to equity.

Firms with low operating leverage often include service firms. Conversely, firms with high operating leverage are typically found where substantial fixed, capital investments are required, such as the telecommunications industry. Conventional wisdom posits that firms with low operating leverage can safely use more financial leverage than those with high operating leverage. Of course, the predictability of the revenue stream, another source of business risk, is also a critical component.

A real estate analogue would be an existing industrial building leased to one or more high-credit tenants on a long-term, triple-net basis in comparison to a speculatively developed office complex with no signed leases at the time of its proposed construction. While a high degree of financial leverage might be justified for the industrial property, a substantially lower degree of financial leverage might be justified for the office building.

A firm with high operating leverage and a high degree of uncertainty regarding its revenue stream may experience periods when the rate of return on its assets is lower than the cost of its indebtedness. If this pattern existed, the return on equity would decline, and progressively so for higher degrees of financial leverage. Thus, the risk from the use of financial leverage can be thought of as the difference between the variances in the return on equity and the return on assets. These relationships can be expressed as follows:[3]

$$\text{Risk from financial leverage} = \sigma_{\text{ROE}} - \sigma_{\text{ROA}}$$

where σ_{ROE} = Firm's (or project's) variance in return on equity.

σ_{ROA} = Firm's (or project's) variance in return on assets.

---

[3] Adapted from Eugene F. Brigham, *Financial Management: Theory and Practice,* 3rd ed. (Hinsdale, IL: The Dryden Press, 1982), pp. 598–606.

In the real estate examples that follow, asset (or portfolio) cash flows are treated generically. While the ratio of fixed to total operating costs and the variability of revenue streams are not explicitly incorporated into the following analyses, it is important to keep these fundamental principles in mind when assessing the potential for using financial leverage.

ASSET RETURN VERSUS COST OF INDEBTEDNESS

It is axiomatic that the decision to leverage an investment (real estate or otherwise) hinges on the assumption that the unleveraged return on the invested asset is expected to exceed the cost of the indebtedness. In this context, total returns and total costs are used.[4]

In a simplified setting, the return on assets for a real estate investment can be viewed as the sum of the capitalization rate plus the growth in cash flow:[5]

$$\text{ROA} = k_a = \text{Capitalization rate} + \text{Growth}$$

$$k_a = \frac{CF_0(1 + g)}{P_0} + g \tag{1}$$

$$= \frac{CF_1}{P_0} + g$$

where k_a = Return on assets (ROA).
  P_0 = Today's asset price.
  CF_n = Cash flow received at end of period n.
  g = Periodic growth in cash flow.

This simplified setting includes the following assumptions: no transaction costs or income taxes, constant growth, and the sale of the property at the same capitalization rate at which it was purchased. Though these assumptions do not conform to the real world's real

---

[4] The focus on total returns ignores short-run issues of insolvency, that is, periods of time when net operating income cannot sufficiently service the property's debt. In the context of institutional investors, many have an allocation to real estate that is below 10 percent of their total investment portfolio. Thus, the issues of insolvency and bankruptcy appear to be more theoretical than pragmatic, as the ability to meet any debt service requirements and repay any mortgage debt upon its maturity would likely exist should these investors believe that asset's long-run prospects merit such a financial commitment.

[5] Joseph L. Pagliari, Jr., "Inside the Real Estate Yield," *Real Estate Review,* Fall 1991; also see Chapter 3.

estate behavior, the model does provide a useful framework for initially projecting an asset's future return. Additional complications will be introduced later in the chapter.

For fixed-rate, fixed-payment mortage loans, the cost of mortgage debt (k_d) can be calculated[6] by determining the effective interest rate (i) that equates the net loan proceeds to the present value of periodic debt service payments and the unamortized loan balance, if any, at the time the loan matures:[7]

$$\text{Net loan proceeds} = \sum_{n=1}^{N} \frac{\text{Pmt}}{(1 + i)^n} + \frac{LB}{(1 + i)^N}$$

$$= \text{Pmt} \left[\frac{1 - \dfrac{1}{(1 + i)^N}}{i} \right] + \frac{LB}{(1 + i)^N} \tag{2}$$

where i = The periodic, effective interest rate (k_d).
    LB = Amortized loan balance upon maturity.
      n = Number of n periods through loan maturity (N).
    Pmt = Amount of the periodic (level) debt service payment.

Whether the use of financial leverage enhances or diminishes an investor's return on equity is determined by the interplay of the asset's unleveraged return and the effective cost of debt capital. The magnitude of this enhancement (or diminution) is directly effected by the degree of leverage. These relationships are depicted in Exhibit 15–1.

A more formal statement can be made using a one-period model:[8]

---

[6] Frank J. Fabozzi, "Bond Pricing and Return Measures," in F. J. Fabozzi, ed., *The Handbook of Fixed Income Securities,* 3rd ed. (Homewood, IL: Business One Irwin, 1991).

[7] In the case of zero-coupon mortgage indebtedness, the computation of the effective interest rate is simplified to

$$\text{Net loan proceeds} = \frac{LB}{(1 + i)^N}$$

In this case, the loan balance (LB) represents the accreted loan balance that incorporates the negative principal amortization associated with zero-coupon loans.

[8] Adapted from: Franco Modigliani and Merton H. Miller, "The Cost of Capital, Corporation Finance and the Theory of Investment," *American Economic Review,* June 1958, pp. 261–97. However, note two potential divergences from this model. First, this formulation implicitly assumes the return on assets (k_a) is unaffected by the degree of leverage. We believe that at some high degree of leverage, this assumption is untenable. Loan covenants generally become more restrictive with increasing leverage ratios; this may adversely affect the owner's ability

EXHIBIT 15–1

Comparison of Return on Assets under Varying Degrees of Leverage

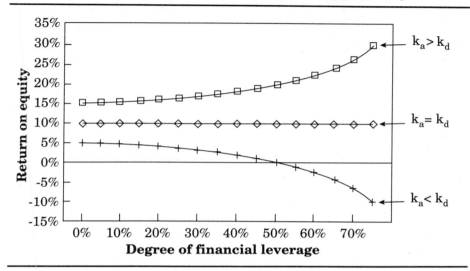

$$ROE = (ROA - i \times DOL)/(1 - DOL)$$
$$k_e = (k_a - k_d \times DOL)/(1 - DOL)$$
$$= \frac{\dfrac{CF_0(1 + g)}{P_0} + g - k_d \times DOL}{1 - DOL} \qquad (3)$$

where k_e = Return on equity (ROE).

DOL = Degree of financial leverage.

In the case of longer holding periods, equation (3) provides an approximation of the return on equity; the discounting process generates a

---

to manage the asset and, accordingly, may create a drag on projected earnings. Second, the effective interest rate is assumed to remain constant across all loan-to-value ratios. We believe that at some higher degrees of leverage, this assumption is also untenable. Lenders will want compensation for increasing default risk as the loan-to-value ratio increases. Because the analyses contained in this chapter generally use 70 percent as the upper end of the loan-to-ratio range, we believe these divergences are of little practical concern. Nevertheless, investors and lenders operating at higher loan-to-value ratios would be well served to keep these divergences in mind.

slightly different—and usually lower—return as the holding period lengthens.[9]

We will now explore the relationships of asset returns to mortage indebtedness in a more explicit way. To do this, we will construct a "base case" utilizing increasing levels of financial leverage and then make adjustments to the key asset assumptions to assess their impact on the equity position's leveraged return.

BASE CASE

Our simple base case has the following key assumptions:

Real Estate Parameters	
Initial cap rate (CF_0/P_0)	8.0%
Inflation rate (ρ)	4.0%
Inflation pass-through rate (λ)	100.0%
Capitalization rate shift (∇)	100.0%
Mortgage Loan Parameters	
Interest rate (i)	10.0%
Loan origination fees (c)	0%
Maturity (n)	10 years

The initial capitalization rate (CF_0/P_0) represents the property's initial unleveraged cash-on-cash yield. The inflation rate (ρ) represents the economywide annual change in the rate of inflation. The inflation pass-through rate (λ) represents that percentage of the inflation rate that the property captures and recognizes as increases in net operating income. Accordingly, the growth in cash flow is the product of the inflation rate and the property's inflation pass-through rate (or $g = \rho \times \lambda$). The mortgage loan is assumed to be priced at 10 percent per annum with no "points" (i.e., the loan origination fees

---

[9] As subsequently shown in Exhibit 15–2, we have computed the investor's equity return over the assumed 10-year holding period using an IRR-based approach. This approach will generally lead to a lower return than that indicated by the one-period model. Generally, the return on equity (k_e) declines from the one-period model rate of return as the holding period lengthens, even though real k_a and k_d remain constant.

and costs are reflected in the interest rate). For these analyses, we have used a 30-year amortization schedule to compute the debt service payments[10] and a 10-year loan maturity, which is coterminous with our assumed investment horizon.[11]

As a frame of reference, unleveraged real estate, using the Russell/NCREIF index as representative of institutional portfolios, yielded the following components over the 14 years ended December 31, 1991:[12]

Initial yield	8.66%
Growth in earnings	1.02
Changes in capitalization rates	0.62
Total return	10.29%
Inflation pass-through rate	17.76%
Capitalization rate shift	83.86%

There is, of course, no reason to expect the future to perfectly replicate the past. For example, it is unlikely that the 1990s will experience the overbuilding boom of the 1980s.

For a variety of leverage ratios, the base case assumptions are then integrated into a 10-year investment analysis. An example using 50 percent leverage is presented in Exhibit 15–2.

From this example, we can observe the following:

- The return on the asset (k_a) is the sum of the first year's capitalization rate ($CF_0 \times [1 + g]/P_0$) plus the growth rate (g), or $8\% \times (1 + .04) + 4\% = 12.32\%$.
- The cost of indebtedness (k_d) is equal to the interest rate—as

---

[10] We have assumed annual debt service payments, as opposed to the industry norm of monthly, to be consistent with the assumed receipt of net operating income, which is also assumed to be yearly. The conversion to monthly payments would not substantively alter the conclusions and relationships presented herein.

[11] The use of a 10-year investment horizon appears to be entirely consistent with the typical holding period assumed by institutional investors. See CB Commercial, *National Investor Survey,* vol. 2, no. 1, 1992.

[12] Joseph L. Pagliari, Jr., and James R. Webb, "Past and Future Sources of Commercial Real Estate Returns," *Journal of Real Estate Research,* Fall 1992, pp. 387–421.

EXHIBIT 15–2

Major Assumptions

Acquisition and financing:

Purchase price	$10,000,000
Mortgage indebtedness	5,000,000
Equity investment	$5,000,000

Leverage ratio	50.00%
Interest rate	10.00%
Amortization	30 years
Loan maturity	10 years
Loan constant	10.61%

Operations:

Initial cap rate $\left(\dfrac{CF_0}{P_0}\right)$	8.0%
Inflation rate	4.0%
Pass-through rate	100.00%

Disposition:

Cap rate shift	100.0%
Investment horizon	10 years

Spread Relationships

Interest rate/cap rate spread	2.00%
Interest/inflation rate spread	6.00%
Inflation pass-through	100.00%

One-Period Model

Capitalization	Weight	Nominal Return/Cost
Asset	100.0%	12.32%
Debt	50.0%	10.00%
Equity	50.0%	14.64%

	Product
Asset	12.320%
Debt	5.000%
	7.320%

Multi-Period Model

Asset return:

Nominal (k_a)	12.320%
Real (k_a)	8.000%

Cost of debt:

Nominal (k_d)	10.00%
Real (k_d)	5.769%

Equity return:

Nominal (k_e)	14.018%
Real (k_e)	9.633%

Investor Cash Flows

Year	Investment	Net Operating Income	Interest	Principal	Net Income	Sale Price	Mortgage Balance	Sale Proceeds	Net Cash Flow
0	($5,000,000)								($5,000,000)
1		$ 832,000	$ 500,000	$ 30,396	$ 301,604				301,604
2		865,280	496,960	33,436	334,884				334,884
3		899,891	493,617	36,779	369,495				369,495
4		935,887	489,939	40,457	405,491				405,491
5		973,322	485,893	44,503	442,926				442,926
6		1,012,255	481,443	48,953	481,859				481,859
7		1,052,745	476,547	53,849	522,349				522,349
8		1,094,855	471,163	59,234	564,459				564,459
9		1,138,649	465,239	65,157	608,253				608,253
10		1,184,195	458,723	71,673	653,799	14,802,443	4,515,562	10,286,881	10,940,680
	($5,000,000)	$9,989,081	$4,819,525	$484,438	$4,685,119	$14,802,443	$4,515,562	$10,286,881	$ 9,971,999

we assumed the loan origination fees and costs to be "priced" into the rate—of 10 percent.

- A simple, one-period model would suggest that the investor's return (k_e) is equal to the asset return $(k_a$ @ 12.32%) minus the weighted cost of indebtedness $(k_d \times \text{DOL} = 10\% \times 50\%)$ divided by the equity ratio (or 1 minus the degree of financial leverage). This results in an estimated yield of

$$14.64\% = \frac{12.32\% - 10\% \times 50\%}{1 - 50\%}$$

- When the time value of money is more exactly considered over the 10-year investment horizon, the investor's return on equity (k_e) is reduced to 14.02 percent. The difference (as compared to the 14.64 percent estimated above) is attributable to the annual compounding process, which, particularly at higher discount rates, leads to (usually) small adjustments from the one-period model. (A solution to this discrepancy would be to restate all rates in a continuous, exponential fashion.)

- When the assumed inflation rate of 4 percent is removed from each of the return numbers,[13] we find the following real (i.e., inflation-adjusted) figures:

$$r_a = 8.00\%$$
$$r_d = 5.77\%$$
$$r_e = 9.63\%$$

Exhibit 15–3 depicts the investor's real return over leverage ratios ranging from 0 to 70 percent. We used real returns to construct this graph to remove the inflationary impacts associated with our assumed nominal price changes (i.e., a 4 percent per annum inflation rate). The graph shows a real return that is increasing at an increasing rate; that is, it shows convexity. This convexity of returns is magnified at even higher leverage ratios; however, institutional investors have typically sought to leverage their assets at ratios of less than 75 percent.

---

[13] The inflation component is removed by

$$\frac{1 + k}{1 + \text{Inflation}} - 1 = \text{Real return } (r) \qquad (4)$$

EXHIBIT 15–3
Effects of Leverage on Real Returns: Base Case

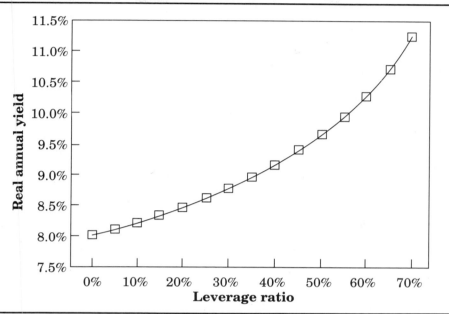

This hypothetical example demonstrates the potential allure of debt-financed real estate equity investments. In this example, the unleveraged investment is projected to provide a real return of 8 percent. By increasing the leverage ratio to 50 percent, the investor is expecting to add 163 basis points of yield, increasing the projected real yield to 9.63 percent. At 70 percent leverage, the yield enhancement doubles to 328 basis points, resulting in a projected real yield of 11.28 percent. The specific returns used to construct the graph presented in Exhibit 15–3 are identified in Exhibit 15–4.

Leverage ratios under 50 percent do not substantially enhance the investor's yield. For example, at 25 percent leverage, the yield enhancement is only 59 basis points. Of course, this is another way to describe the yield convexity noted above.

The preceding returns are predicated on four fundamental relationships:

- Interest/cap rate spread ($i - CF_0/P_0$): As noted previously, the rela-

EXHIBIT 15–4
Base Case Yields

Leverage Ratio	Real IRR	Yield Due to Leverage	
		Incremental	Cumulative
0%	8.00%	0.00%	0.00%
5	8.10	0.10	0.10
10	8.20	0.10	0.20
15	8.32	0.12	0.32
20	8.45	0.13	0.45
25	8.59	0.14	0.59
30	8.75	0.16	0.75
35	8.93	0.18	0.93
40	9.14	0.21	1.14
45	9.37	0.23	1.37
50	9.63	0.26	1.63
55	9.94	0.31	1.94
60	10.31	0.37	2.31
65	10.74	0.43	2.74
70	11.28	0.54	3.28

tionship between the interest rate and the capitalization rate is a critical first step in assessing the appropriate degree of leverage.

• Interest/inflation rate spread $(i - \rho)$: Since we are concerned with real returns, the general level of inflation and how it compares to the interest rate are critically important.

• Inflation pass-through rate (λ): In estimating the growth in cash flow (g), it is necessary to estimate the percentage of the inflation rate that the property will be able to pass through in the form of increased cash flow $(g = \lambda \times \rho)$.

• Capitalization rate shifts (∇): For our simple asset return model $(k_a = CF_1/P_0 + g)$ to work, one constraint is that the property must be sold for the same capitalization rate at which it was purchased $(CF_0/P_0 = CF_N/P_N)$. However, capitalization rates do shift, and therefore it is necessary to examine their impact $(CF_0/P_0 \times \nabla = CF_N/P_N)$.

The following sections explore each of these fundamental relationships. These analyses hold the mortgage terms (which can be known with relative certainty before the leverage decision is made) constant and test the sensitivity of the real estate assumptions (which have substantially greater uncertainty).

INTEREST/CAP RATE SPREAD

The base case has an interest/cap rate spread of

Interest rate (i)	10%
Capitalization rate (CF_0/P_0)	8
Interest/cap rate spread	2%

In Exhibit 15–5, we systematically vary this spread in increments of 200 basis points in either direction by changing the assumed capitalization rate. As a result, the interest/cap rate spread varies from −2 to 6 percent. The sensitivity of this change causes a substantial widening of the distribution of possible outcomes. Whereas the real return under the base case ranges from 8.00 to 11.28 percent, the range now runs from 1.61 to 21.90 percent. Generally, the impact of a 200-basis-point change in the initial capitalization rate equates to

EXHIBIT 15–5
Effects of Leverage on Real Returns: Interest/Cap Rate Spread

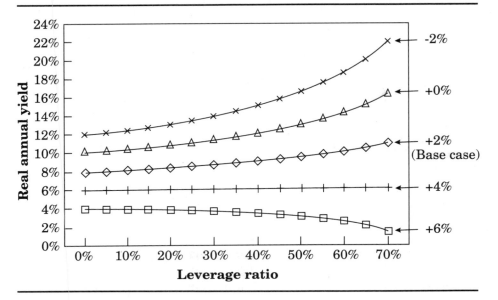

roughly a 500-basis-point change in the real return at 70 percent leverage, scaling down to a 200-basis-point change (i.e., point for point) in the real return at 0 percent leverage.

To understand the impact of these changing spreads, it is necessary to examine what is happening with the expected asset return (k_a). For example, in the case where the interest/cap rate spread is expected to rise to 400 basis points (i.e., a capitalization rate of 6 percent), the asset return is expected to drop (from the base case of 12.32 percent) to

$$
\begin{aligned}
k_a &= CF_0/P_0 \times (1 + g) + g \\
&= 6\% \times (1 + .04) + 4\% \\
&= 10.24\%
\end{aligned}
$$

In this case, the asset return about equals the cost of indebtedness $(k_a \approx k_d = .10)$. Therefore, the impact of leverage is essentially neutral, which gives rise to the nearly straight line for the spread of $+4$ percent shown in Exhibit 15–5. Thus, the line for r_e indicates a real return of nearly 6 percent after giving effect to the assumed 4 percent inflation rate.

Similarly, in the case where the interest/cap rate spread is expected to decrease to -200 basis points (i.e., a capitalization rate of 12 percent), the asset return is expected to increase to

$$
\begin{aligned}
k_a &= CF/P_0 \times (1 + g) + g \\
&= 12\% \times (1 + .04) + 4\% \\
&= 16.48\%
\end{aligned}
$$

On an unleveraged basis, the asset is expected to provide a real return of 12 percent. When leverage is introduced, at a real cost of slightly less than 6 percent, the investor's real return is expected to increase exponentially in the fashion described earlier.

Conversely, where the interest/cap rate spread increases to 6 percent (i.e., a capitalization rate of 4%), the asset return is expected to drop to

$$
\begin{aligned}
k_a &= CF_0/P_0 \times (1 + g) + g \\
&= 4\% \times (1 + .04) + 4\% \\
&= 8.16\%
\end{aligned}
$$

As the 8.16 percent nominal asset return falls beneath the nominal cost of indebtedness $(k_d = i = 10\%)$, the leveraged equity returns decrease at an accelerating rate. For example, at 50 percent leverage, a simple, one-period model suggests the following:

Capitalization	Weight	Nominal Return/Cost	Product
Asset	100%	8.16%	8.16%
Debt	50%	10.00%	5.00%
Equity	50%	6.32%	3.16%

The 6.32% nominal return on equity suggests an approximate 2.23 percent real return. When the more exacting method is used, the actual return is calculated to be 2.76 percent.

The other example, in which the capitalization rate equals the interest rate, suggests a nominal asset return of 14.40 percent (based on a capitalization rate of 10 percent and growth of 4 percent) or a 10 percent real return. As the leverage ratio increases, so does the return on equity.

INTEREST/INFLATION RATE SPREAD

To assess the impact of the inflation/interest rate spread (i.e., $i - \rho$), we again systematically alter the real estate assumptions while holding the nominal mortgage assumptions constant. In the base case, this spread equals

Interest rate (i)	10%
Inflation rate (ρ)	4
Interest/inflation rate spread	6%

As before, we vary the spread in increments of 200 basis points, resulting in a spread ranging from 2 to 10 percent. Interestingly, these changes in the assumed inflation rate affect the real cost of mortgage indebtedness (i.e., a fixed nominal interest rate less the assumed future inflation rate approximates the real cost of mortgage indebtedness) while leaving the real return on assets unchanged (by virtue of the assumed 100 percent pass-through of inflation, $g = \rho$, and therefore $r_a = CF_0/P_0$). Thus, the impact of changing inflation rates is to lower or raise the real cost of mortgage indebtedness while the asset's real return remains constant (for an inflation pass-through rate equal to 100 percent) at its initial yield (CF_0/P_0).

The equity returns (see Exhibit 15–6) display an interesting pattern. With no leverage, all five scenarios converge at an equity return of 8 percent. And, generally speaking, from 0 to 20 percent leverage, the equity return varies by about 1.5 percentage points, from 7.52 to 9.08 percent. Thus, one might conclude that at relatively low leverage (say, less than 20 percent), the impact of various inflation rates is somewhat benign. Beyond these low leverage ratios, the range of leveraged equity returns displays a pattern similar to that in the interest/cap rate spread analysis depicted in Exhibit 15–5.

As noted earlier, the impact of changing inflation is to alter the level of real (i.e., inflation-adjusted) interest rates. As the inflation rate rises, the real cost of indebtedness (r_d) drops, which in turn enhances the yield to the leveraged equity position. For example, the 4 percent interest/inflation rate spread implies an inflation rate of 6 percent. With nominal interest rates at 10 percent, this suggests a real interest cost of slightly less than 4 percent; in fact, the interest/inflation rate spread is a rough approximation of the real cost of

EXHIBIT 15–6
Effects of Leverage on Real Returns: Interest/Inflation Rate Spread

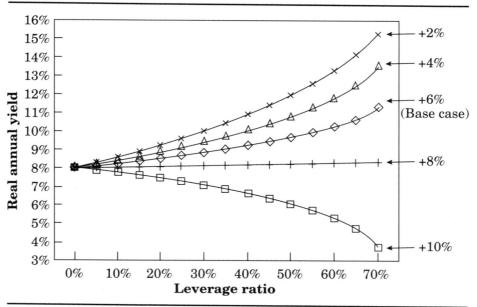

indebtedness. With the asset returning a real rate of return of 8 percent (again assuming a 100 percent inflation pass-through rate), any amount of borrowing at approximately 4 percent (real) will favorably lever the equity return. A simple, one-period example using the case of 50 percent leverage and the 4 percent interest/inflation rate spread indicates the following:

Capitalization	Weight	Nominal Return/Cost	Product
Asset	100%	14.48%	14.48%
Debt	50%	10.00%	5.00%
Equity	50%	18.96%	9.48%

Given an assumed inflation rate of 6 percent, this estimated nominal return to the investor (k_e) of 18.96 percent translates into an estimated real return (r_e) of approximately 12.2 percent. Alternatively, this return can be viewed in the context of an asset generating a real return of 8 percent and the real cost of indebtedness at slightly less than 4 percent; when levered to 50 percent, this increases the real equity return to slightly more than 12 percent. When the analysis is expanded to more completely incorporate the time value of money and the assumed 10-year holding period, the real return is calculated to be 10.8 percent.[14]

At an 8 percent interest/inflation spread (which implies a 2 percent inflation rate), the total nominal asset return approximately equals the nominal cost of indebtedness:

$$k_a = \frac{CF_0}{P_0}(1 + g) + g$$
$$= 8.00\%(1.02) + 2\%$$
$$= 10.16\%$$

---

[14] The reason this rather large discrepancy results from the increasing variance between the simple, one-period model and the more accurate 10-year IRR calculation is that the size of the difference increases as the discount rate increases. In the present case, the one-period model suggests a return of 18.96 percent; however, when a 10-year holding period is analyzed, the return drops to 17.45 percent. This nominal return is then converted to its real return of 10.80 percent ($1.1745/1.06 - 1 = .108$).

This relationship provides for a fairly steady real return to the investor (r_e)—since borrowing at a rate approaching the asset return has little effect on the investor's return—of approximately 8 percent.

In addition, it is interesting to note that the spread on leveraged equity returns widens as the inflation rate declines. Using the example of 70 percent leverage, note the difference in the leveraged, real equity returns at an interest/inflation rate spread of 2 percent versus 4 percent compared to 8 percent versus 10 percent. In the former case, the spread is approximately 170 basis points; in the latter case, it is approximately 450 basis points. Another interesting comparison is that between the 6 percent interest/inflation rate spread and the 10 percent spread: At an 8 percent spread, the real cost of debt $(r_d = 7.84\%)$ about equals the real asset return $(r_a = 8.0\% = CF_0/P_0$, given $\lambda = \nabla = 1.00)$, and accordingly levered equity returns are fairly flat. Thus, the 6 and 10 percent spreads are about equally distant from this break-even spread of 8 percent. However, the cost of being wrong about the use of leverage (i.e., contracting a fixed rate of interest in a reduced-inflation environment), as measured by the distance between the 8 and 10 percent spreads at 70 percent leverage, is greater than the benefit of being right about the use of leverage (i.e., contracting a fixed rate of interest in a heightened-inflation environment), as measured by the distance between the 6 and 8 percent spreads at 70 percent leverage.

INFLATION PASS-THROUGH RATES

Obviously, the asset's ability to pass through inflation as reflected in increased net income is a function of the supply of and demand for space within the submarket in which the property is occupied, the nature of the lease contracts written for the property, and the property's changing operating characteristics as the building ages. Accordingly, inflation pass-through rates may vary by location and property type.[15] Apartments, for example, have demonstrated a fairly strong ability to pass through inflationary increases,[16] while the ability of

---

[15] Pagliari and Webb, "Past and Future Sources."

[16] Richard T. Garrigan and Joseph L. Pagliari, Jr., "The Impact of Supply Changes on Real Net Operating Income: The Multi-family Perspective," *Real Estate Issues,* Spring–Summer 1992, pp. 24–32.

the office and industrial sectors to pass through inflation has been tied to vacancy rates.[17] In recent years, office buildings have experienced poor pass-through rates.

Thus, the need to model various inflation pass-through rates is critical. For this purpose, we have systematically varied the pass-through rates by 250 basis points so that they range from 25 to 125 percent of the inflation rate. In so doing, we have modified the asset returns to reflect growth (g) as a function of the inflation rate (ρ)—which is assumed to be 4 percent for purposes of this analysis—and the pass-through rate (λ).

Accordingly, the asset return can generally be written as

$$k_a = \frac{CF_0}{P_0}(1 + \lambda \times \rho) + (\lambda \times \rho) \tag{5}$$

In the case of the 50 percent inflation pass-through rate, this equates to an asset return of

$$
\begin{aligned}
k_a &= \frac{CF_0}{P_0}(1 + \lambda \times \rho) + (\lambda \times \rho) \\
&= 8.00\%(1 + .5 \times 4\%) + (.5 \times 4\%) \\
&= 10.16\%
\end{aligned}
$$

As in the case of the 8 percent interest/inflation rate spread (which also resulted in $k_a = 10.16\%$, because the assumed inflation rate of 2 percent and the pass-through rate of 100 percent resulted in effectively the same growth rate), the nominal asset return approximates the nominal cost of indebtedness. Therefore, there is little advantage (or disadvantage) to borrowing, and accordingly the real (and nominal) return on equity is nearly constant, as shown in Exhibit 15–7.

At lower pass-through inflation rates, the asset return falls beneath the cost of indebtedness, and accordingly the equity return drops with increasing leverage. As an example, the case of an assumed 25 percent inflation pass-through rate combined with 50 percent leverage results in a simple, one-period model return of

---

[17] Charles H. Wurtzebach, Glenn R. Mueller, and Donna Macchi, "The Impact of Inflation and Vacancy of Real Estate Returns," *Journal of Real Estate Research*, Summer 1991, pp. 153–68.

EXHIBIT 15–7
Effects of Leverage on Real Returns: Inflation Pass-Through Rate

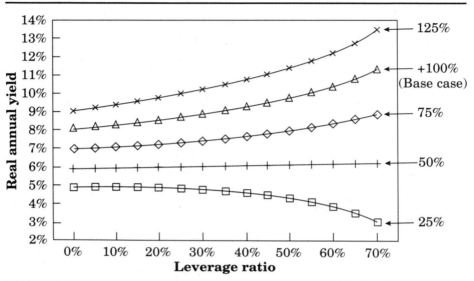

Capitalization	Weight	Nominal Return/Cost	Product
Asset	100%	9.08%	9.08%
Debt	50%	10.00%	5.00%
Equity	50%	8.16%	4.08%

$$k_a = \frac{CF_0}{P_0}(1 + \lambda \times \rho) + (\lambda \times \rho)$$
$$= 8.00\% \ (1 + .25 \times 4\%) + (.25 \times 4\%)$$
$$= 9.08\%$$

Based on an estimated 8.16 percent nominal equity return and a 4.00 percent inflation rate, this roughly translates into an approximate 4.0 percent real equity return. Clearly, the investor in this case would be better served by not leveraging the investment.

Conversely, with inflation pass-through rates in excess of 50 percent, the asset return (k_a) exceeds the cost of indebtedness (k_d), and accordingly equity returns are enhanced through the use of leverage.

Using the example of a 75 percent inflation pass-through rate combined with a 50 percent leverage ratio, these assumptions result (under the simple, one-period model) in the following:

$$k_a = \frac{CF_0}{P_0}(1 + \lambda \times \rho) + (\lambda \times \rho)$$
$$= 8.00\% (1 + .75 \times 4\%) + (.75 \times 4\%)$$
$$= 11.24\%$$

Capitalization	Weight	Nominal Return/Cost	Product
Asset	100%	11.24%	11.24%
Debt	50%	10.00%	5.00%
Equity	50%	12.48%	6.24%

In this case, the investor would be better served by leveraging the investment, because he or she can borrow at a cost that is less than that earned on the asset. When the analysis is expanded to more precisely incorporate the time value of money and the assumed 10-year building period, the real return is calculated at 7.88 percent.

Compared to the interest/inflation rate spread examples (Exhibit 15–6), the inflation pass-through rate examples (Exhibit 15–7) show more consistent differences between the high and low cases. That is, at 70 percent leverage, the differences between the high (125 versus 100 percent) and low (50 versus 25 percent) inflation pass-through rates are approximately 250 and 300 basis points, respectively, as compared to the high and low interest/inflation rate spreads, which were approximately 170 and 450 basis points, respectively.

CAPITALIZATION RATE SHIFTS

Because properties age and real estate transaction costs are high, market-clearing capitalization rates change over time. Therefore, it is important to assess the impact of changing capitalization rates on rates of asset returns and then compare these rates to the nominal and real costs of indebtedness.

Unlike our earlier assumption changes, the assumption of capitalization rate shifts violates the rules of our simplified approach to estimating asset returns. Therefore, to determine the impact of capitalization rate shifts on asset returns, we must iteratively solve for the discount rate (k_a) that equates the operating cash flows and the revisionary proceeds to the asset's acquisition cost.[18] We have examined cap rate shifts in basis point increments ranging from 90 to 150 percent. Our definition of a capitalization rate shift is

$$\nabla = \frac{\dfrac{CF_N}{P_N}}{\dfrac{CF_0}{P_0}}$$

where ∇ = Capitalization rate shift.

In the case of the 90 percent capitalization rate shift, the asset's return (k_a) is enhanced by virtue of a decrease in capitalization rates at the end of the holding period (as compared to the beginning). In this case, the real asset return increases from 8.00 percent (for the base case) to 8.74% (under the 90 percent capitalization rate shift assumption). The affect is to improve the leveraged equity return, as shown in Exhibit 15–8.

Because of the impacts of property aging and transaction costs, we believe the more likely scenario is increasing capitalization rates. In the most extreme case shown here, that of the 150 percent capitalization rate shift, the asset's real return (r_a) declines to 5.40 percent compared to the base case at 8.00 percent. Not surprisingly, the effect on leveraged equity is slightly negative, as the asset's real return $(r_a = 5.40\%)$ is less than the real cost of indebtedness $(r_d = 5.77\%)$. The other possibilities shown have a range between these two outcomes. As an aside, a capitalization rate shift of approximately 140 percent would result in the asset return (k_a) equaling the cost of indebtedness (r_d).

---

[18] In a general form, this equates to solving for k_a in the context of

$$P_0 = \sum_{n=1}^{N} \frac{CF_0 (1 + \lambda \times \rho)^n}{(1 + k_a)^n} + \frac{CF_0 (1 + \lambda \times \rho)^N}{(1 + k_a)^N} \times \left(\frac{P_0}{CF_0} \times \frac{1}{\nabla} \right) \qquad (7)$$

EXHIBIT 15–8
Effects of Leverage on Real Returns: Capitalization Rate Shift

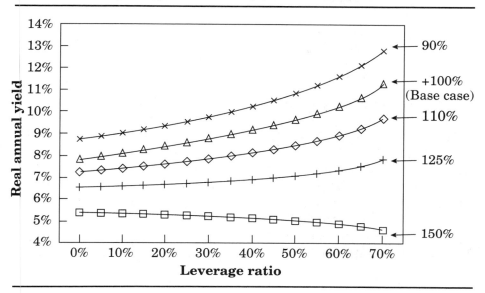

INTERPLAY OF ECONOMIC VARIABLES:
A RESTATEMENT

We have tried to demonstrate that the question of whether or not to leverage a real estate investment essentially boils down to one's confidence that the asset's expected total return will exceed the cost of the mortgage indebtedness. In our simplified context, the question can be answered in light of the asset's expected growth in cash flow vis-à-vis the differential between the cost of the indebtedness and the property's initial capitalization rate. This question can be formulated as

$$\text{Growth} \stackrel{?}{=} \text{Interest cost} - \text{Initial yield}$$

$$\lambda \times \rho \overset{?}{=} i - \frac{CF_0}{P_0} \times (1 + \lambda \times \rho) \qquad (8)$$

$$\lambda \times \rho \overset{?}{=} \frac{i - \dfrac{CF_0}{P_0}}{1 + \dfrac{CF_0}{P_0}}$$

The left-hand side of the equation, future growth, is inherently "unknowable" at the time of the leverage decision. The right-hand side, total mortgage cost less the initial yield (as adjusted by $1 + CF_0/P_0$), is "knowable." Therefore, real estate investors need to assimilate what they view as the reasonable prospects for growth in cash flow and compare them to the "known" hurdle of the current interest/cap rate spread as adjusted by $1 + CF_0/P_0$. In so doing, the investor can create graphically (see Exhibit 15–9) an "indifference line" where combinations of growth ($\lambda \times \rho$) are equal to the adjusted interest/cap rate spread ($[i - CF_0/P_0]/[1 + CF_0/P_0]$).

EXHIBIT 15–9
Indifference Line for Adjusted Interest/Cap Rate Spread at Various Spreads
(Holding All Other Parameters Constant)

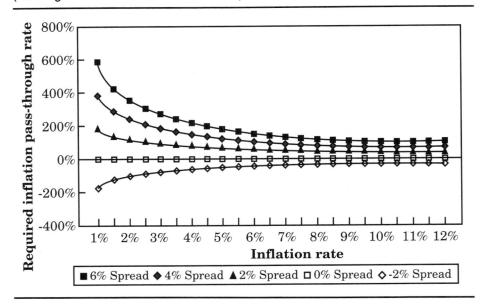

In these instances, the expected asset return equals the cost of the indebtedness, and accordingly the use of leverage does not affect the investor's return. If the investor believes the asset's growth prospects lie above the line for a given level of adjusted interest/cap rate spread, the investor should consider leveraging the property investment. Conversely, if the investor believes the asset's growth prospects lie beneath the line, he or she should not consider leveraging the property investment.

Using the base case assumptions would result in an adjusted interest/cap rate spread of

$$\text{Adjusted interest/cap rate} = \frac{i - \dfrac{CF_0}{P_0}}{1 + \dfrac{CF_0}{P_0}}$$

$$i = \frac{.10 - .08}{1 + .08}$$

$$i = .0185$$

For leverage to enhance the equity position's return, cash flow growth (assuming constant growth and capitalization rates) must exceed 1.85 percent per annum. This growth will reflect the interplay of the inflation rate (ρ) and the real estate's ability to pass through inflationary increases (λ). If an investor foresees future inflation of 4 percent per annum, a pass-through rate of less than 46.25 percent (i.e., $g = \rho \times \lambda = .04 \times .4625 = .0185$) would result in leverage detracting from the investor's return. Other forecasted rates of inflation would require a corresponding movement in the required inflation pass-through rate. The combination of the forecasted inflation rates and required inflation pass-through rates results in a continuum of possibilities. Exhibit 15–9 presents this continuum along with similarly constructed continua for the other interest/cap rate spreads previously discussed.

While this simplistic approach ignores potential shifts in the revisionary capitalization rate[19] and the other factors mentioned in the following sections, we suggest that the approach presented in Exhibit 15–9 captures the essence of the leverage question for long-

---

[19] Examples using various capitalization rate shifts can be constructed for each of the adjusted interest/cap rate spreads.

term real estate investors who are financing a portion of their properties with fixed-rate mortgage indebtedness.

"REAL-WORLD" VARIANCES FROM THE SIMPLIFIED MODEL

Several complications experienced in the real world of property investing warrant examination.

Aging/Property Obsolescence.   As a property ages, all other things being equal, its ability to generate inflation-adjusted net operating income often declines as its relative market position fades and/or the costs of maintenance increase. Though we have indirectly addressed this possibility in terms of potential capitalization rate shifts, we have not done so with regard to the growth (or decay) in real net operating income.[20]

Long-Term, Fixed Leases.   We have assumed continuous growth in cash flow. By definition, this excludes those properties characterized by long-term fixed-rate leases. Conceptually at least, the model is better suited to situations that avoid the step function associated with properties leased on a long-term, fixed-rate basis. The instances that may well fit the model include (1) apartment and hotel properties with short-term leases, (2) properties with a constant percentage of its tenants' leases expiring each year, and/or (3) properties with CPI-based rent adjustments and expense stops. Nonetheless, the comparison of asset return (k_a) to the cost of indebtedness (k_d) is still of paramount concern.

To accommodate those properties characterized by long-term, fixed-rate leases, we suggest utilizing a variation of the Income Differential model[21] to estimate asset returns:

---

[20] For newer properties (i.e., most institutional properties), the effects of aging and obsolence of over less than, say, a 20-year holding period are *de minimis*. See Pagliari and Webb, "The Impact of Aging/Obsolence: A 'Decay' Paradigm," working paper, 1994.

[21] Wylie D. Greig and Michael S. Young, "New Measures of Future Property Performance and Risk," *Real Estate Review*, Spring 1991, pp. 17–25.

$$P_0 = \frac{CF_0}{k_a} + \frac{\dfrac{CF_0 (1 + \lambda \times \rho)^N - CF_0}{k_a - \lambda \times \rho}}{(1 + k_a)^N} \qquad (9)$$

where N = Time until lease matures.

Given the initial value (P_0) and cash flow (CF_0) along with estimates of future inflation (λ) and the property's pass-through rate (λ), the asset's return (k_a) can be computed. Once the expected asset return has been computed, it can be compared to the cost of the indebtedness to determine whether or not leverage is appropriate.

Events Are Neither Mutually Exclusive nor Stationary. In systematically analyzing the impact of various fundamental economic relationships (e.g., the interest/cap rate spread and the interest/inflation rate spread), the analysis may imply that these events are mutually exclusive. They are not. Exhibits 15–5 through 15–8 portray the sensitivities of these various relationships. However, as we pointed out in Exhibit 15–9, the confluence of these relationships is the essence of the leverage question.

As but one example of the interplay among these various forces, consider the competing influences of (1) the interest/cap rate spread and (2) the inflation pass-through rate. A matrix of these joint influences on the real annual rate of return is presented in Exhibit 15–10. In examining the investor's real annual return, changes in the interest/cap rate spread (for a given inflation pass-through rate) generally resulted in a range of 1,400 basis points, whereas changes in the inflation pass-through rate (for a given interest/cap rate spread) generally resulted in a range of 700 basis points. Naturally, these ranges are a result of our assumed parameters (with regard to the leverage ratio, initial capitalization rate, inflation rate, etc.).

Investors might consider the interaction of these forces in three-dimensional space as presented in Exhibit 15–11. More accurately, the matrix represents selected points on a three-dimensional surface of possible returns. This particular surface is predicated on 50 percent leverage. As the leverage ratio decreases (increases), the range (and/or surface) of returns also decreases (increases).

Similarly, one should not assume that the relationships are constant over the holding period. They are dynamic—constantly changing. Moreover, these variables tend to move in relation to both the

EXHIBIT 15–10
Calculated Real Annual Returns Based on the Impact of Combining Various Interest/Cap Rate Spreads and Inflation Pass-Through Rates, Assuming 50% Leverage

Inflation Pass-Through Rate	Interest/Cap Rate Spread					Range
	6%	4%	2%	0%	−2%	
25%	−3.08%	0.50%	4.11%	7.76%	11.44%	14.52%
50	−1.00	2.50	6.05	9.64	13.28	14.28
75	0.94	4.38	7.88	11.44	15.04	14.10
100	2.76	6.17	9.63	13.16	16.74	13.98
125	4.49	7.87	11.31	14.82	18.39	13.90
Range	7.57%	7.37%	7.20%	7.06%	6.95%	21.48%

Note: Assumes an annual inflation rate of 4 percent.

general business cycle and the specific property markets cycle. Consider, for example, a relatively healthy property market in which (because of supply-demand equilibrium) inflation pass-through rates (λ) are high and, correspondingly, investors are more willing to accept lower current returns (i.e., a lower capitalization rate, CF_0/P_0) in return for this strong, inflation-adjusted growth in cash flow. Further, assume these markets move to disequilibrium (due to excess supply and/or slowing demand) such that inflation pass-through rates fall and in turn investors demand higher current returns to compensate them for their reduced growth prospects. Clearly, it would be plausible that those two factors (λ and CF_0/P_0) are negatively correlated with each other. This implies that an investor buying into the high side of this cycle and selling into the low side would experience a "double whammy" (investors might rationally expect lower pass-through inflation rates and in turn demand higher capitalization rates) that might drive the asset's return [k_a] beneath the cost of indebtedness [k_d].

Operating Frictions. In a world filled with substantial "free rent," leasing commissions, and tenant buildouts, the omission of

EXHIBIT 15–11

Calculated Real Annual Returns Based on the Impact of Combining Various Interest/Cap Rate Spreads and Inflation Pass-Through Rates (with 4% Inflation) at 50% Leverage

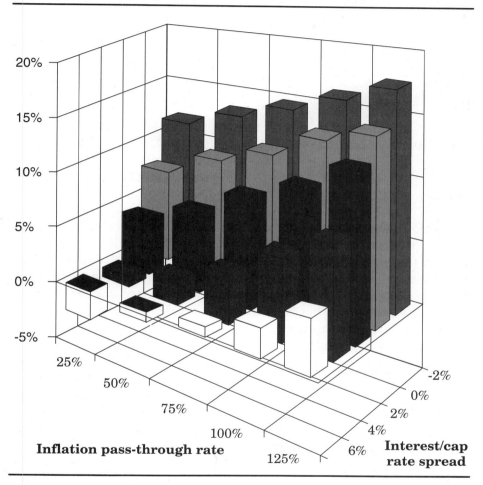

these and other operating frictions from the calculation of the asset's expected return would be devastating. Accordingly, we advise their incorporation into any worthwhile analysis of expected asset returns. Moreover, the calculations presented herein for cash flow (CF_n) are assumed to be made after having taken these costs (including advisory fees) into consideration.

Loan Rollovers. These analyses have assumed the loan maturity coincides with the investor's holding period. This too is an oversimplification. Investors face a multitude of refinancing options. Appendix 15A presents an approach for analyzing the alternative of financing long-term real estate investments with shorter-term debt.

Thus, the models presented herein should be used as an initial screen for the appropriateness of leverage. If the prospects for leverage appear favorable, the next level of detailed analysis should be pursued.

ADDITIONAL PROS AND CONS REGARDING LEVERAGE

We offer three reasons for and two reasons against the use of financial leverage.

Pro 1: Mortgage Debt as a Put Option. The use of nonrecourse mortgage financing provides the borrower with a put option: Should the property value fall beneath the loan balance, the investor may elect to "hand back the keys" by tendering a deed for the property to the lender in satisfaction of the indebtedness. It is open to question whether lenders and borrowers have historically priced this option properly. Surely, a number of lenders today believe they had underpriced the value of this option.

From the borrower's point of view, the value of this option decreases with a decline in the leverage ratio. In other words, as the borrower puts more equity at risk (i.e., the leverage ratio is declining), the likelihood of the borrower exercising this option declines.

Therefore, at relatively low levels of leverage—say, under 60 percent—the value of this option may be declining rapidly. Nevertheless, there are examples of transactions that were once thought to be moderately leveraged but the borrower did, in fact, elect to hand back the keys.[22]

Pro 2: Increased Diversification Possibilities. Like other investments, well-constructed, diversified real estate portfolios can

---

[22] Steve Hemmerick, "Randsworth Investments Wiped Out," *Pensions and Investments,* March 16, 1992, p. 1.

reduce portfolio risk without forsaking portfolio return.[23] The use of leverage enables an investor to expand the number of properties in which an institution is diversified. For example, the use of a 50 percent leverage ratio would double the number of (same-valued) properties as compared to a 0 percent leverage strategy, while 75 percent leverage would quadruple the number of properties owned. This diversification element may be important because real estate investments tend to come in large chunks. Commingled funds are an alternative; however, they sometimes carry their own set of problems.

An interesting question is: How do the portfolio benefits resulting from an increase in the number of properties compare to the risks associated with leverage?

Pro 3: Adjustments to Duration.   Duration is a concept designed to measure the sensitivity of assets and liabilities to a change in the level of interest rates. All other things being equal, an increase in interest rates decreases the present value of an asset's cash flow stream or a liability's payment stream, and, conversely, a decrease in interest rates increases the present value of either.

One approach to pension fund management (as well as the broader question of institutional liability management) is to match the duration of the pension's retirement liabilities with assets of identical duration.[24] In this way, the pension fund's surplus is considered to be immunized such that a change in the value of the pension fund's liabilities caused by a change in interest rates is completely offset by a change in the value of the pension fund's assets.

In this setting, the estimated duration of real estate assets can be used to immunize a liability structure. Generally, the duration of real estate ranges from very short for those properties with short-term leases to very long for those properties with long-term, fixed leases.[25] Accordingly, real estate duration can be adjusted by varying the length of the fixed-lease obligations of the property (or properties).

Unfortunately, the length of the lease is most often dictated by

---

[23] Glenn R. Mueller, "Refining Economic Diversification Strategies for Real Estate Portfolios," *Journal of Real Estate Research,* Winter 1993, pp. 55–68.

[24] Martin L. Leibowitz, "Total Portfolio Duration: A New Perspective on Pension Fund Asset Allocation," *Financial Analyst Journal,* September–October 1986.

[25] David J. Hartzell, David G. Shulman, Terrence C. Langetieg, and Martin L. Leibowitz, "A Look at Real Estate Duration," *Journal of Portfolio Management,* Fall 1988, pp. 16–24.

local market conditions. Therefore, it is unlikely that an investor can dictate the lease length necessary to meet a specific duration target. However, an investor can use mortgage financing to alter the duration of the leveraged real estate investment. Essentially, the duration of fixed-rate mortgage debt offsets the asset's duration. Consequently, for a variety of lease structures, it can be shown that (1) the use of mortgage debt reduces the investment's duration and (2) duration decreases as the loan-to-value ratio increases.[26] Moreover, investors obviously can control both the use and the extent of mortgage leverage in their realty investments, thereby avoiding the problems of using the lease length to target specific duration figures.

Con 1: Alteration of Mixed-Asset Allocations. The decision to leverage a real estate portfolio should be made in the context of the investor's entire mixed-asset portfolio. The use of mortgage debt to help capitalize real estate investments leads to a reduction in the investor's allocation to fixed-income securities. In effect, the use of mortgage debt has shorted the bond portfolio by the amount of the mortgage. To see why this is true, consider the following example. Initially the investor's portfolio (in $000s) is constructed as follows:

Stocks	$ 50,000
Bonds	40,000
Real estate (unleveraged)	10,000
Total	$100,000

Subsequently, the investor decides to increase his or her exposure to real estate by $5,000, half of which is to be provided by mortgage debt and the other half by liquidating a portion of the stock portfolio. The asset mix now looks like this:

Stocks	$ 47,500
Bonds	37,500
Real estate	15,000
Total	$100,000

[26] S. Michael Giliberto, "Managing Real Estate Duration: A New Perspective on the Use of Leverage" (Salomon Brothers Inc., October 1989).

The bond allocation is reduced because the use of a mortgage in effect represents the fact that for the mortgage amount ($2,500), the institution was a bond seller.

If one considers mortgages to be bondlike instruments for which the collateral happens to be real estate,[27] the use of mortgage indebtedness effectively means that the institution has sold bonds. In turn, this effectively reduces the value of the bonds it has previously bought. Though some might argue that the real estate would be $12,500 and the bonds remain at $40,000, this would misstate the underlying economics. The investor has $15,000 of real estate assets, and the $2,500 of mortgages sold is considered a reduction in the bonds/mortgages bought. To clarify with an intentionally extreme example, think of the institution as having originated this $2,500 mortgage from its bond fund; to have the money to do so, it would have to liquidate a $2,500 bond. Obviously, the impact on the bond allocation would have been more severe had it, rather than the stock allocation, been used to fund the $2,500 equity requirement for the $5,000 leveraged real estate investment.

The important point to consider is that the use of mortgage leverage can alter the portfolio's mixed-asset allocation. As a result, the portfolio may be suboptimal (i.e., it has moved off the efficient frontier), the investor now faces a different risk-return trade-off than previously accepted (at the old portfolio allocation), and/or the portfolio is no longer immunized as it was once considered to be.

Con 2: Increased Equity Yield Fallacy. The allure of increasing equity yields via leverage can lead to suboptimal property acquisitions if investors attempt to increase returns by selecting acquisitions that have a greater expected return than the cost of indebtedness but have a capitalization rate that is less than the market for the class of property acquired. This is a corollary to the preceding point (con 1) regarding altering the mixed-asset allocation.

To illustrate the fallacy of yield chasing via leverage, consider the following example.[28] Assume the appropriate capitalization rate

---

[27] While the characteristics of the mortgage market may differ from the government and corporate bond markets (assuming investment grade instruments in all cases) with regard to event risk, default risk, principal amortization, prepayment risk, and so on, we believe these differences are priced into their respective risk premia.

[28] Adapted from Merton H. Miller and Franco Modigliani, "Dividend Policy, Growth, and the Valuation of Shares," *Journal of Business,* October 1961, pp. 411–33.

for a particular property type is 10 percent (and this rate is also appropriate for all other properties in the investor's portfolio). However, a property with cash flow (CF_0) equal to, say, $1.0 million can be acquired at an 8 percent capitalization rate (i.e., $P_0 = \$12.5$ million) and the seller of the property is willing to accept a 50 percent purchase money mortgage, in the amount of $6.25 million, at a market interest rate of, say, 9 percent per annum. Moreover, the investor expects the property's income stream to grow at approximately 3 percent per annum—as is also the case for the other properties in the investor's portfolio—such that the property's total return is expected to be approximately 11 percent. Since the expected asset return ($k_a = 11.24\%$) exceeds the cost of indebtedness ($k_d = 9\%$), the investor's return ($k_e = 13.48\%$) is expected to exceed the property's unleveraged return and, also in this example, the market's capitalization rate of 10 percent.

However, the inclusion of the property into the investor's preexisting portfolio of, say, $100 million will reduce the portfolio's value on a relative basis as follows:

	With New Property	Without New Property
Portfolio cash flow*	$11,000,000	$10,000,000
Market capitalization rate	10%	10%
Market value	$111,000,000	$100,000,000
Investor's basis†	(112,500,000)	(100,000,000)
Investor's surplus (shortfall)	$(2,500,000)	$ 0

* From real estate operations.
† Gross of any mortgage indebtedness.

Thus, the inclusion of this property actually causes the investor to incur a loss, should the portfolio be liquidated, even though the expected return on leveraged equity is high. As before, the mortgage indebtedness really represents the shorting of the mixed-asset portfolio's fixed-income securities.

The key point is that if the property's capitalization rate is less than the market's capitalization rate for similar properties (assuming equivalent growth prospects), an investment in such a property will reduce the current value of the portfolio relative to the market value.

"Hence, the cost of capital or cut-off criterion for investment decisions is simply [the market capitalization rate]."[29]

CONCLUSION

As noted throughout this overview of the impacts of financial leverage on real estate investments, the paramount concern is that the asset's unleveraged return (k_a) exceed the costs of mortgage indebtedness (k_d). In these instances, the benefit of leverage is magnified as the degree of leverage increases.

While all investors will attempt to maximize this simple relationship ($k_a > k_d$), the inescapable truth is that, at the time a leverage decision is made, the asset return is inherently uncertain. Thus, the question becomes whether this unknown quantity exceeds the known (or at least relatively less uncertain) cost of mortgage indebtedness (k_d). The path of analysis taken here is to examine four key relationships/factors and their impact on leveraged equity returns (k_e):

1. *Interest/cap rate spread.* Narrowing this initial spread should provide real estate investors with some comfort that earnings growth will eventually produce a total asset return (k_a) in excess of mortgage costs (k_d).

2. *Interest/inflation rate spread.* As the spread between the future rate of inflation (ρ) and the cost of mortgage debt (k_d) narrows, the real (i.e., inflation-adjusted) cost of the debt (r_d) decreases. To the extent that real asset returns (r_a) remain relatively constant (under various inflation rates), the impact of increasing inflation rates is to increase the real leveraged equity return (r_e).

3. *Inflation pass-through rates.* As the inflation pass-through rate (λ) rises, the asset's real return (r_a) increases. Given a steady cost of debt (r_d), holding constant inflation and interest rates, this increasing real asset return will generate higher real returns on leveraged equity (r_e).

4. *Capitalization rate shifts.* That capitalization rates change over time leads to yet another uncertain element of future asset returns. Obviously, a decrease in capitalization rates would lead to

---

[29] Ibid.

an increase in asset returns, thereby improving the chances that $k_a > k_d$.

Absent the complications of capitalization rate shifts, the essential leverage question becomes: Will the property's growth in cash flow ($\lambda \times \rho$) exceed the spread between the cost of debt (i) and the property's initial yield? In notational form, this question can be expressed as

$$\text{Growth} \stackrel{?}{=} \text{Interest cost} - \text{Initial yield}$$

$$\lambda \times \rho \stackrel{?}{=} i - \frac{CF_0}{P_0} \times (1 + \lambda \times \rho)$$

$$\lambda \times \rho \stackrel{?}{=} \frac{i - \dfrac{CF_0}{P_0}}{1 + \dfrac{CF_0}{P_0}}$$

(8)

While the left-hand side of the equation is inherently unknowable at the time of the leverage decision, the right-hand side is known with some certainty. Therefore, real estate investors need to estimate the asset's growth prospects to determine whether or not the use of leverage appears reasonable. In fact, an indifference line can be generated (see Exhibit 15–9) that isolates the combinations of growth and the adjusted interest/cap rate spread where investors would be indifferent toward the use of leverage. If capitalization rate shifts are introduced into the analysis, the indifference line will move upward with an increase in capitalization rates (in other words, earnings growth will have to increase to offset the decline in total asset return attributable to an increase in capitalization rates) and will move downward with a decrease in capitalization rates.

There are several real-world complications to the simplified analysis presented here. These complications include:

- Property aging and obsolescence.
- Long-term, fixed-rate leases.
- The various relationships analyzed above are neither mutually exclusive nor stationary.
- Operating frictions (e.g., "free rent," leasing commissions, tenant improvements).
- Loan rollover possibilities.

In addition to the positive leverage question highlighted here, the use of debt financing includes several advantages and disadvantages:

Advantages

1. Nonrecourse mortgage debt provides the borrower with a put option.
2. The use of mortgage debt increases the diversification possibilities within the real estate portfolio.
3. Mortgage debt can be used to alter the duration of the real estate asset, thereby allowing for greater alignment between the duration of the investor's assets and liabilities.

Disadvantages

1. Financing real estate with debt is tantamount to shorting a portion of the investor's fixed-income portfolio and therefore alters the investor's portfolio allocations.
2. An increased equity yield fallacy is possible when investors focus on the leveraged yield (k_e) rather than on the asset return (k_a) in making their acquisition decisions.

Therefore, the prudent use of leverage should be viewed as a way to increase equity returns (k_e). However, the decision to use leverage should be made in the context of uncertain asset returns and the portfolio implications of the leverage decision.

APPENDIX 15A
IMPLIED FORWARD RATES

Most examples presented in this chapter used a 10-year, conventional fixed-rate mortgage loan. This assumed 10-year maturity coincides with our assumed 10-year investment horizon. However, nothing precludes an investor from selecting a shorter maturity and taking on the risk (reward) that interest rates will move higher (lower) during the refinancing period.

One way to examine the risks associated with utilizing loans of a shorter maturity than the assumed investment horizon is to examine the implied rates necessary in the refinancing period that equate to the longer-maturity loan's rate. An example may best serve to clarify this point.

Assume investors can choose one of the following two mortgage loans to assist in the capitalization of a real estate asset:

Loan Maturity	Interest Rate*
7 years	9.5%
10 years	10.0%

* As before, these rates are based on the "all-in" financing costs.

The level of interest rates in the uncovered three-year period will determine which loan provides the borrower with a cheaper source of funds. Using the following equation,[30] the interest rate that equates these alternatives can be determined:

$$r_f = x \sqrt{\frac{(1 + r_t)^t}{(1 + r_s)^s}} - 1 \tag{10}$$

where r_f = Implied forward rate.
   r_t = Interest rate on the long-maturity loan.
   t = Number of periods to maturity on r_t.
   r_s = Interest rate on the short-maturity loan.
   s = Number of periods to maturity on r_s.
   $x = t - s$.

Using the present example yields:

$$r_f = 3 \sqrt{\frac{(1 + .10)^{10}}{(1 + .095)^7}} - 1$$

$$= \underline{\underline{11.18\%}}$$

This suggests that if interest rates for 3-year mortgage loans were to rise above 11.18 percent at the start of the investor's uncovered 3-year period, the borrower would have been better served by choosing the 10-year mortgage loan. Conversely, if interest rates stayed below this 11.18 percent

---

[30] Adapted from Frank J. Fabozzi and T. Dessa Fabozzi, "Treasury and Stripped Treasury Securities," in F. J. Fabozzi, ed., *The Handbook of Fixed Income Securities,* 3rd ed. (Homewood, IL: Business One Irwin), 1991.

threshold, the borrower would have been better served by "rolling over" the loan at the end of the seventh year.

This somewhat simplistic example (ignoring liquidity preferences, yield curve slopes, etc.) illustrates but one of the many choices investors face when they consider the use of leverage.

PART 4

ELEMENTS OF REAL ESTATE INVESTMENT

CHAPTER 16

APPRAISAL PRACTICES
AND ISSUES

Frank P. Liantonio
Cushman & Wakefield

Roy L. Gordon
Cushman & Wakefield

INDUSTRY BACKGROUND

Initially, real estate appraising was a fragmented, cottage industry with no recognized professional organization or trade group. In response to the banking crisis of the Great Depression, two principal professional organizations were formed in the 1930s: (1) the American Institute of Real Estate Appraisers, which was founded under the auspices of the National Association of Real Estate Boards (later the National Association of Realtors) and whose members were primarily appraisers of commercial and industrial properties, and (2) the Society of Real Estate Appraisers, which was closely aligned with the savings and loan industry and whose main focus was the appraisal of residential properties.

Both organizations pursued their primary goal of training appraisers through educational courses and seminars and awarding professional designations. Professional designations such as MAI (Member, Appraisal Institute) and SRA (Senior Residential Appraiser) were awarded to those members of the organizations who had attained prescribed levels of competence measured in terms of course attendance, examination, and the preparation of demonstration appraisal reports that were submitted for grading. In addition, candidates submitted actual examples of field work for peer review, and experience credits were awarded, with a minimum of five years of field experience required for the MAI designation. Over the years, these two organizations grew large and influential, and the curriculum leading to the awarding of the designations became increasingly structured. Notwithstanding their growth in size and influence, the American Institute of Real Estate Appraisers and the Society of Real Estate Appraisers, even up to the time of their merger into a single organization called the Appraisal Institute on January 1, 1991, represented a relatively small percentage (probably less than 20 percent) of the practitioners (estimated at 200,000 to 300,000) who consider themselves as real estate appraisers in the United States.

However, the influence of these two organizations was far greater than their number of members suggested. The vast majority of major real estate appraisal assignments in the past 20 years have been performed by MAIs, while most residential appraisals for lending purposes have been conducted by SRAs. Most major users of appraisal services, including agencies of the federal government, looked to the Appraisal Institute to provide appraisal education and a pool of knowledgeable and experienced practitioners.

The greatest contribution to the general public benefit made by these two predecessors of the present-day Appraisal Institute was the adoption and enforcement of a Code of Professional Ethics and Standards of Professional Practice. Over time, the users of appraisals came to look to the Appraisal Institute as the arbiter of appraisal ethics and standards.

CODE OF PROFESSIONAL ETHICS

The Code of Professional Ethics requires the members of the appraisal organization to adhere to certain canons of conduct. The appraiser must develop and communicate the appraisal in an unbiased and impartial manner. It is unethical to knowingly act in a manner that is misleading or fraudulent, issue a misleading appraisal report, communicate an appraisal report in a misleading manner, or contribute to or participate in an appraisal opinion that reasonable appraisers would not believe to be justified. An appraisal cannot be based on a hypothetical condition unless (1) a careful investigation indicates that it is likely to be realized in the foreseeable future and that reasonable persons, given the same information, would reach the same conclusion; (2) the appraisal report clearly describes the investigations made and the basis for the conclusions; and (3) the appraisal report explains the hypothetical condition and its effect on the value of the conclusion.

In addition, the Code of Professional Ethics requires every appraisal report, whether written or oral, to be supported by a written appraisal memorandum in the file that contains sufficient detail to permit peer review. The appraiser is expected to treat the client's information as strictly confidential. All appraisal files must be retained for at least five years.

STANDARDS OF PROFESSIONAL APPRAISAL PRACTICE

The standards of practice establish certain minimums for the performance of an appraisal assignment. These requirements are listed in Appendix 16A. Moreover, the appraiser is required to certify to those items presented in Appendix 16B.

THE UNIFORM STANDARDS OF PROFESSIONAL APPRAISAL PRACTICE (USPAP) OF THE APPRAISAL FOUNDATION

In 1987, the Appraisal Foundation was formed and became the umbrella organization for all other appraisal organizations in the United States. The foundation established the Appraiser Qualifications Board to promulgate minimum education and experience requirements for appraisers. The Appraisal Standards Board adopted the Uniform Standards of Professional Appraisal Practice, to which all major appraisal organizations, including the Appraisal Institute, now subscribe. The Appraisal Standards Board meets regularly to discuss current issues relating to appraisal standards, to elicit public comment, and to issue revisions to the standards.

TITLE XI OF THE FINANCIAL INSTITUTIONS REFORM, RECOVERY AND ENFORCEMENT ACT (FIRREA)

Title XI of FIRREA, passed by the U.S. Congress in 1989 as an outgrowth of the virtual collapse of the savings and loan industry, is far and away the most significant piece of legislation affecting real estate appraisers ever adopted. One of the most important aspects of the FIRREA legislation was the provision for licensing and certification of real estate appraisers by the individual states.

The stated purpose of Title XI of FIRREA is to "provide that Federal financial and public policy interests in real estate related transactions will be protected by requiring that real estate appraisals utilized in connection with Federally related transactions are performed in writing, in accordance with Uniform Standards, by individuals whose competency has been demonstrated and whose professional conduct will be subject to effective supervision."

To this end, Title XI created the Appraisal Subcommittee of the Federal Financial Institutions Examination Council consisting of designees of the heads of federal financial institutions' regulatory agencies to monitor appraisal licensing and certification requirements established by the states for appraisers qualified to perform appraisals in connection with federally regulated transactions, including a code of professional responsibility. In addition, the Appraisal Subcommittee monitors the activities of the Appraisal Foundation, a broader industry group composed of representatives from major appraisal organizations and government regulatory agencies.

Regulatory agencies prescribe appropriate standards for the performance of real estate appraisals in connection with federally related transactions. These real estate appraisals are required to be performed in accordance with generally accepted appraisal standards as promulgated by the Appraisal Standards Board of the Appraisal Foundation.

Title XI of FIRREA became effective on January 1, 1993 and the various states have adopted legislation regulating the appraisal industry. Basically, appraisers of residential properties are required to be licensed, and appraisers of commercial, industrial, and income-producing properties are required to hold a general certification. The states have adopted minimum educational and field experience requirements as suggested by the Appraiser Qualifications Board of the Appraisal Foundation. All appraisers performing appraisals for federally regulated financial institutions must hold a license or certification from the state in which he or she is domiciled and must obtain a temporary permit to practice in any state in which he or she may perform an appraisal. All state-licensed and certified appraisers are subject to the Uniform Standards of Professional Appraisal Practice (USPAP) of the Appraisal Foundation, as shown in Appendix 16A.

Even though this legislation ostensibly pertains only to appraisals made for federally regulated financial institutions, the practical effect is state regulation of the practice of the real estate appraisal industry. All state-certified and licensed appraisers are or soon will be bound by the Appraisal Foundation's Uniform Standards.

The state requirements for licensing and certification have been established at a minimal level of experience and education to provide a pool of appraisers that is large enough to not impede lending practices of regulated financial institutions. The Appraisal Institute continues to promote the MAI and SRA designations as connoting a much higher level of education and experience than state minimums for licensing and certification.

The federal regulatory agencies, such as the Federal Deposit Insurance Corporation, the Office of Thrift Supervision, and the Office of the Comptroller of the Currency, have also adopted appraisal guidelines. While incorporating the Uniform Standards of Professional Appraisal Practice as a minimum, these agencies provide specific guidelines for preparing real estate appraisals. Generally, the guidelines tend to expand the reporting requirements, encourage the use of specific valuation techniques, and mandate minimal levels of analysis and supporting documentation. Many banks and other financial institutions regulated by these agencies have also adopted guidelines providing for increasing levels of specificity so that the appraiser typically encounters a hierarchy of guidelines, including:

- Uniform Standards of Professional Appraisal Practice (required of all Appraisal Institute members as well as all state-licensed and certified appraisers).
- Regulatory agency guidelines (required of all appraisers working for a federally regulated financial institution).
- Client guidelines.

If the client is not a federally regulated financial institution, the appraiser must comply with USPAP first and then with client-specific requirements.

NATIONAL COUNCIL OF REAL ESTATE INVESTMENT FIDUCIARIES (NCREIF) GUIDELINES

NCREIF has adopted guidelines for the preparation of appraisal reports to be used in monitoring pension fund portfolios. These guidelines seek to promote uniformity and consistency in the valuation process.

NCREIF members usually employ real estate appraisers to prepare full narrative appraisal reports under the reporting provisions of the Uniform Standards of Professional Appraisal Practice (USPAP) of the Appraisal Foundation. However, the Departure Provision of the Uniform Standards of Professional Appraisal Practice permits the appraiser to prepare limited appraisals as long as the client agrees in advance that something less than the level of research and analysis that would be performed in a complete appraisal will meet its current needs and provided the report meets certain specified minimal reporting criteria. The results of an appraisal may be reported in a self-contained, summary or restricted report; however, a report cannot be so limited in scope as to be misleading or be subject to reader misunderstanding. (The Departure Provision does not apply to appraisals prepared for federally regulated financial institutions.)

NCREIF guidelines require the appraiser to describe the methods and procedures used in the appraisal process in sufficient detail for the client to determine that the appropriate and necessary professional standards were employed, to use the discounted cash flow method of analysis in the income approach for all commercial properties, and to fully discuss and analyze all assumptions and projections utilized in the discounted cash flow analysis.

NCREIF has published an outline for the preparation of a full narrative appraisal report. This outline, presented in Appendix 16C, basically tracks the Uniform Standards of Professional Appraisal Practice of the Appraisal Foundation.

APPROPRIATE VALUATION APPROACHES

The appraiser is charged with reflecting the actions of informed market participants. During periods of illiquidity, this is a particularly challenging task. The three approaches to value, namely, the cost, sales comparison, and income approaches, do not account for periods of severe illiquidity. Consequently, each approach has its limitations during such periods.

An appraisal is defined in *The Dictionary of Real Estate Appraisal* as:

> The act or process of estimating value [USPAP, January 1, 1989]. An opinion of the nature, quality, value, or utility of specified interests in, or aspects of, identified real estate [Supplemental Standard 1, USPAP, January 1, 1989].

Given this definition, there has been a long-standing debate over whether or not the appraisal process is an art or a science. As a result of computer advancements, discounted cash flow and multiple regression analyses have contributed to the scientific aura of the appraisal process. But the fragmentation of real estate markets across the country and the lack of a central database with which to measure historical performance make a truly scientific approach impossible. Contrasting real estate with the stock and bond markets serves only to heighten the argument in favor of art over science. While sophisticated analyses and greater access to data will ultimately improve the appraisal process from a quantitative perspective, it will take considerable time and changes in the way real estate markets function before the appraisal process can become more scientific in its orientation.

However, appraisals of income-producing properties can never be reduced to the mechanistic and deterministic systems of a scientist. It is precisely because of real estate's "open" system (in scientific parlance) that the appraisal function rests on the appraiser's judgment, experience, and interpretative capabilities. The appraiser adds value by injecting his or her insights into a process that too many think should be mechanistic but never can be. Unfortunately, the frequent emphasis, especially among regulated financial institutions, on the formulaic elements of the appraisal is raising the cost of appraisals without necessarily enhancing their accuracy. Nonregulated users of appraisals would be well served by dealing with seasoned practitioners and encouraging them to exercise professional judgment and share insights in the less structured format now permitted by USAP. The appraiser's ability to contribute valuable insights should be encouraged, not stifled.

HISTORICAL VERSUS ANTICIPATORY PERSPECTIVE

Anticipation is one of the primary economic principles affecting the appraisal process. Anticipation is particularly important in the income approach, where the appraiser attempts to measure income as the present worth of future benefits. In theory, value should be a measure of the future income prospects an investor anticipates from a particular property. It should take into account the prospective dynamics of supply, demand, rent levels, concessions, and vacancy and truly capture the motivations of active market participants. The appraiser is not expected to have perfect foresight as to the intrinsic value of a property's cash flow. The goal of an appraisal is to attempt to estimate the most likely price at which a property would sell by attempting to simulate the bargaining and analytical behavior of the most probable buyer.

All too often, the appraisal process looks like a history lesson because it focuses on what happened yesterday. Although comparable sales can provide a meaningful measure of value, appraisers are not always as informed as they could be on a particular sale and often lack the insight needed to assess the true motivations of the buyer and the seller. Appraisals should evaluate the potential benefits a property will produce over time in a manner similar to that used by active market participants. Frequently the appraiser looks to history as a benchmark for future action. While appraisers are charged with estimating value, measuring value should not be an exercise solely in historical research; rather, it should be a focused attempt to understand a market and the dynamics that drive it. The key to the efficacy of these efforts is the depth of the appraiser's understanding of investor's expectations and analytical techniques.

THE COST APPROACH

The cost approach enables the appraiser to develop a value estimate by first estimating the value of the land and adding to it the depreciated value of the improvements. This approach has its greatest validity when improvements are relatively new and depreciation is limited. In illiquid markets, the first shortcoming of this approach lies in estimating land value. Non-income-producing by nature, land tends to trade even less frequently than improved properties during periods of illiquidity. The second problem lies in accurately estimating accrued depreciation, which is difficult to assess even in active markets. The cost approach, however, provides a value indication that establishes upper value limits. During periods of weak and illiquid markets, many investors peg their purchases at a fraction of replacement cost.

In more normalized markets, the cost approach is the test of economic feasibility. Market value should be equal to or greater than the sum of all agents of production: labor, materials, land, engineering fees, architectural fees, leasing, financing, and developer's profit.

The appraiser estimates land value by direct sales comparison, usually based on price per square foot of land area or price per square foot of permitted density. Construction costs are usually estimated by reference to published sources or actual costs of similar buildings. Contractors' estimates, if available, are one of the best sources of replacement cost new. Depreciation may be attributable to physical, functional, or external factors. Functional obsolescence is associated with poor design or construction features that exceed economic utility. External or economic obsolescence is attributable to conditions lying outside the property itself, such as soft market conditions. Measuring the various forms of depreciation becomes increasingly subjective as depreciation increases as a proportion of replacement cost new.

THE SALES COMPARISON APPROACH

The sales comparison approach develops a value conclusion through an analysis of similar properties that have been sold, adjusting for differences between properties sold and the property being appraised. The obvious problem with this approach in an illiquid market is the paucity of meaningful sales activity. Another limiting factor is the distressed nature of many of the sales (foreclosures, bankruptcies, etc.) that occur. The key to this approach is the availability of sales that are contemporaneous to the valuation date between parties that are not under duress. The appraiser should strive to understand buyers' and sellers' motivations, and, to the extent meaningful activity is found, informed value conclusions can be reached. When valuing a leased fee interest in income-producing properties, the pattern of future income flows is usually the most significant value determinant. Therefore, economic indicators derived from sales comparisons are more important than physical units of comparison such as sales price per square foot.

In more stabilized markets, the appraiser develops units of comparison from the sale of comparable properties. Physical units of comparison, such as price per square foot or price per apartment unit, are sometimes meaningful if all properties have similar rent levels and expense ratios and all are operating at stabilized levels of occupancy.

However, for income-producing properties, economic units of comparison of the effective gross income multiplier (sales price divided by effective gross income) or overall capitalization rate (net operating income divided by sales price) are usually more helpful. To be meaningful, these units of comparison require stabilized operation and a high degree of uniformity among properties. As comparables become more and more dissimilar, the appraiser's judgment becomes increasingly important.

The sales comparison approach has limited use in the appraisal of complex assets such as office towers and regional shopping malls. Here market value tends to be a function of the investors' expectations of future income flows, which are largely determined by leases in effect.

THE INCOME APPROACH

The income approach is the most meaningful approach in valuing income-producing properties. A value conclusion is developed by converting a property's anticipated income stream into value through the capitalization process. Although income can be converted into value through direct capitalization, income-producing real estate is bested suited to a discounted cash flow analysis. Even during times of illiquidity, many of the variables involved in developing a discounted cash flow analysis are more readily available than truly comparable sales. Evidence of gross and effective market rents, vacancy levels, concessions, and operating expenses are more readily obtainable than sales, and these data enable the appraiser to construct a cash flow model that simulates investor expectations.

Obvious shortcomings in the income approach lie in the areas of estimating absorption and forecasting market performance over time.

Questions such as when will markets stabilize and how quickly concessions fade and rents increase must reflect informed judgments based on reliable and realistic demographic forecasts, combined with knowledge of investor criteria. There is no substitute for regular communication with informed market participants, who should be queried with a specific focus on the type of property being appraised. No one approach to value provides all of the answers, but the income approach offers the most realistic and market-oriented view in what can only be characterized as an imperfect market.

Most investors in institutional grade income-producing real estate tend to rely most heavily on the income approach to value, specifically discounted cash flow analysis. The appraiser uses computer software to model the pattern of future income flows, usually over a period of 10 years with presumed property sale in the 11th year. Value at resale is forecast by capitalizing the 11th year's net income at an overall capitalization rate, called the *terminal cap rate*. This rate is selected based on the appraiser's judgment of the property's probable status at that time, taking into consideration leases in effect, age, condition, and expected competition.

Many assumptions go into the cash flow forecast, for example, lease-up of space vacant on the appraisal date, market rent, concessions, and expenses. The appraiser must also forecast trends and select an appropriate discount rate commensurate with the risk inherent in the realization of these assumptions.

The appraiser's task is to measure and mirror the expectations of informed market participants when formulating the discounted cash flow analysis.

DEALING WITH A CHANGING CAPITALIZATION ENVIRONMENT

Real estate markets are dynamic and constantly in flux. For example, markets were thrown into disarray by significant changes made in federal tax laws in 1986. The heady optimism of the mid-1980s gave way to pessimism in the late 1980s as real estate portfolio values declined in response to rising vacancies and falling rents. It is widely believed that readily available short-term financing for development projects in the early to mid-1980s led to a spate of overbuilding. In this environment, many projects were driven more by the availability of credit than by consumer demand. Overbuilding contributed in no small measure to a crisis in the banking industry.

Several factors conspired to bring illiquidity to real estate markets: The Tax Reform Act of 1986, the economic recession of the 1990s, and the illiquidity in the nation's banking system. It is now clear that the construction boom of the 1980s was unsustainable even if the preceding events had not taken place. Much of the market illiquidity can also be attributed to investors repricing the perceived risks of real estate. The economic recession of the early 1990s resulted in a shrinkage of demand as companies downsized their office space requirements and trimmed the ranks of middle management. Manufacturing jobs fell victim to the globalization of U.S. industry and retail jobs disappeared as consumer spending patterns adapted to the new realities. Jobs in the banking, insurance, and real estate sectors contracted as companies struggled to maintain profitability in the face of shrinking revenues. "Downsizing" became the corporate buzz word of the early 90s.

The chasm between buyer and seller expectations became almost unbridgeable in early 1990. Many owners were locked into properties by debt that had been put in place when rent levels and occupancies were forecast to reach levels that were never attained. Many buyers, on the other hand, sensing seller desperation, were looking for bargains and were only willing to purchase at truly distressed prices. The large inventory of real estate assets then in the hands of lending institutions and government agencies further depressed the market.

This recessionary environment presented a difficult challenge to the real estate analyst and made it imperative that the appraiser be informed of buyer and seller expectations. The reduced number of sales that do occur in an unstable market have to be carefully scrutinized to ascertain buyer and seller motivations. Meaningful interaction between the appraiser and the institutional investor/client is of the utmost importance. The appraiser should always maintain an ongoing dialogue with market makers, but this is especially true in times of illiquidity and market disarray.

Several appraisal firms, investment banks, and advisory firms publish periodic surveys of investors in which these firms attempt to chart trends in capitalization rates, discount rates, income and expense growth rates, and marketing periods in addition to investor preferences by property type and geographical location. However, these surveys present relatively broad parameters and cannot take the place of frequent interaction between active market participants.

Many developments, even attractive, well conceived ones, foundered on their inability to service debt during this period of instability that lasted from about 1989 to about late 1993. Some foreclosed properties were offered at prices that would have been unthinkable just a few years previously and, in hindsight, appear quite favorable to the buyers now that most markets are emerging from the doldrums. For the most part, buyers of these "distressed" assets were not passive investors seeking bond-like returns; they were more likely to be risk takers who expected to reap healthy entrepreneurial profits in turning these assets around during the recovery phase of the cycle. Timing is everything.

What is "market value" in an unsettled environment like the one that existed in the early 1990s? The definition of market value assumes that the "price is not affected by undue stimulus." The definition of "undue stimulus" may be open to some interpretation, although undue stimulus should not be confused with market makers' bearish outlook. Undue stimulus carries the connotation that the seller is being forced to sell by circumstances beyond his control.

For example, in the early part of this decade, financial institutions were under increasing pressure to shore up their balance sheets, reduce their exposure to troubled real estate assets, and rid themselves of REO properties. This situation had a dampening effect on real estate markets in general. A spirited debate took place in the financial community and within federal regulatory agencies as to whether restrictive lending policies were creating a "credit crunch" that was excessively depressing real estate values and causing a damaging downward spiral.

In November 1991, the Department of the Treasury attempted to deal with this problem by issuing an Interagency Policy Statement on the Classification of Commercial Real Estate Loans. This document directed regulatory examiners to take a long-term view and not to automatically require the write-down of performing assets. Regulatory review appraisers were encouraged to look to the discounted cash flow method of analysis and to consider discount rates that might be applicable in normal markets and to not place undue weight on liquidation-type market sales.

While undoubtedly a laudable goal in the context of maintaining some semblance of order in real estate markets from the perspective of the banking system, this policy does not solve appraisal dilemmas. What are normal discount rates? What is a reasonable marketing period? When is it appropriate to ignore recent sales because of "undue stimulus"? Is there a difference between "investment value" for a long-term hold and "liquidation value" for more immediate disposition? Does either "investment value" or "liquidation value" meet the test of market value? Is there one value for an investor who wants to sell immediately and another value for an investor willing to hold for the longer term?

Institutional investors, regulators, and appraisers continue to debate these issues as no definitive answers emerged from the market turbulence. However, the dialogue proved useful in defining some of the concepts underlying the appraisal process.

PERIODS OF MARKET ILLIQUIDITY AND THE RELIABILITY OF APPRAISALS

Because part of the appraisal process involves historical research, there is a tendency for appraised values to lag the market to some extent. In either a rising or falling market, this partial reliance on the past will cause appraised values to trail (or lag) the market—only in a static market will the problem be eliminated.

An interesting study entitled "An Empirical Evaluation of the Reliability of Commercial Appraisals, 1978–1990" was recently published by NCREIF. The data, taken from the Russell/NCREIF Property Index, show, in the opinion of the study's authors, that appraisals tend to have the greatest reliability in stable market environments. Periods of great volatility produce the greatest disparity between appraised value and sale price. Appraised values of high-value properties at stabilized levels of occupancy tend to be more accurate than appraisals of low-value properties or properties operating below stabilized levels.

The expansion and contraction of mortgage capital obviously affects value, as does the ebb and flow of equity capital. Equity capital consists of domestic sources, composed of individuals and institutions, and foreign sources, primarily institutional. It is the shifts in these market participants' collective view of the future and how they price that future that determines "value." As the views of these capital market sources change, so do "values."

MARKET VALUE VERSUS LIQUIDATION VALUE

The definition of *market value* found in the Uniform Standards of Professional Appraisal Practice of the Appraisal Foundation is as follows:

> The most probable price which a property should bring in a competitive and open market under all conditions requisite to a fair sale, the buyer and seller, each acting prudently and knowledgeably, and assuming the price is not affected by undue stimulus. Implicit in this definition is the consummation of a sale as of a specified date and the passing of title from seller to buyer under conditions whereby:
>
> 1. Buyer and seller are typically motivated;
> 2. Both parties are well informed or well advised, and acting in what they consider their own best interests;
> 3. A reasonable time is allowed for exposure in the open market;
> 4. Payment is made in terms of cash in U.S. dollars or in terms of financial arrangements comparable thereto; and
> 5. The price represents the normal consideration for the property sold unaffected by special or creative financing or sales concessions granted by anyone associated with the sale.

The *Dictionary of Real Estate Appraisal* defines *liquidation value* as follows:

> The price that an owner is compelled to accept when a property must be sold without reasonable market exposure.

The key words distinguishing liquidation value from market value are "compelled to accept" and "sold without reasonable market exposure." Market value is the benchmark against which appraisers have traditionally estimated value, and liquidation value was really meant to reflect distressed circumstances such as sales in bankruptcy and/or foreclosure. Investment grade real estate in the hands of institutional owners typically has not been the focus of liquidation value estimates.

The Appraisal Standards Board of the Appraisal Foundation has taken the position that under the definition of market value, reasonable exposure in the open market is a past event as of the effective date of the appraisal. This is consistent with the sales comparison approach to value, wherein sales prices obtained in the market represent transaction prices negotiated after "reasonable exposure."

Marketing time is presumed to be a future event that represents the period of time required to realize the estimated market value. Marketing time will depend on the type of property and the state of the market on the effective date of the appraisal.

Times of illiquidity introduce great volatility into markets. When traditional sources of mortgage funds dry up and foreign investors retrench, great downward pressure is exerted on the market. When markets destabilize and transactions become infrequent, the disparity between the bid and ask prices represents the lack of readily available mortgage financing as well as the unwillingness of institutional investors to realize substantial losses or buy into a market that is on the way down.

MARKET VALUE VERSUS NET REALIZABLE PROCEEDS

It is important to distinguish between market value and net realizable proceeds. No estimate of value, whether market value or liquidation value, reflects the time value of money and the corresponding diminution that occurs between the date of value and the date on which proceeds are actually received. Transaction costs are much greater in real property trades than those common to other forms of securitized investments, which obviously affects the investor's ultimate yield. However, the perspective of the appraisal is the price the buyer paid and not the seller's net receipts.

There seems to be agreement among most practitioners that the market value reported as of the effective date of the appraisal should represent the most probable selling price on that date assuming "reasonable exposure to the market" and that the anticipated marketing period cannot be so attenuated as to permit market conditions (and values) to change during that time. Whether or not one year is an appropriate marketing time depends on the circumstances of both the market and the property being appraised. The appraiser should seek the best market data available to substantiate his or her estimate of a probable marketing time.

CONCLUSION

The appraisal process has evolved over the years, but many client insensitivities are no different today from what they were in the 1970s or before. Although less frequently than in prior years, many clients view an appraisal as a file stuffer, a requirement of a particular deal or transaction and one of little importance. In such circumstances, the appraisal is meaningful principally from the perspective of value conclusion, with little else being important.

Then there are those clients who suffer from the "Taj Mahal" syndrome. These clients have a perception of value that transcends the realities of the market. Their particular property is in theory worth more than a competitive product, will rent more quickly, and produce higher values. Accepting well-supported, realistic values and assumptions is difficult for some clients, especially those who have a vested interest in the outcome of the appraisal. In recognition of this problem, many pension funds are restructuring advisors' compensation to avoid this potential conflict.

Many users in the market sometimes view appraisal fees as a necessary evil. Users also tend to equate the cost of an appraisal with other commodities that must be purchased. Purchasing the most for the least is the general rule. However, few users give sufficient thought to the appraisal process and what it entails in time. Many are quick to criticize, but few are willing to acknowledge the time and expertise necessary to perform at a level consistent with client expectations. This will ultimately take time and a better understanding between appraiser and client.

Even though most state laws require certified appraisers to adhere to USPAP, there is still considerable flexibility to respond to clients' needs. Clients should encourage seasoned practitioners to convey their judgments based on experience especially now that limited appraisals are permitted by the Departure Provision and appraisals may be reported in Self-Contained, Summary, or Restricted formats. Institutional investors should consider asking the appraiser for an opinion, in addition to the traditional estimate of market value, of the most probable price within a range. Upper and lower limits could be coupled with estimates of confidence levels.

Appraised values should be not static point value estimates but a range of probabilities along a scale. It is obvious that the assumptions regarding lease-up, growth in income and expenses, and the trend in discount rates and capitalization rates will have a marked impact on the final value estimate. All of these threads are part of the fabric of the forecast of future performance.

Appraisal practices have changed over time, and the pace of change within the industry has accelerated significantly since the enactment of FIRREA in 1989. The Uniform Standards of Professional Appraisal Practice have been endorsed by a single industry voice, the Appraisal Foundation, and the profession is starting to resemble other professions like accounting and law. While many issues remain unresolved at this writing, the groundwork has been laid for forging a consensus through the Appraisal Foundation.

APPENDIX 16A
OUTLINE OF UNIFORM STANDARDS OF PROFESSIONAL APPRAISAL PRACTICE

In the Uniform Standard of Professional Appraisal Practice, the Appraisal Standards Board of the Appraisal Foundation makes a distinction between a Complete Appraisal and a Limited Appraisal. The following standard rules guide the appraiser in the preparation of a Complete Appraisal.

Standard Rule 1–1. In preparing a real property appraisal, an appraiser must:

a. Be aware of, understand, and correctly employ those recognized methods and techniques that are necessary to produce a creditable appraisal;

b. Not commit a substantial error of omission or commission that significantly affects an appraisal;

c. Not render appraisal services in a careless or negligent manner, such as a series of errors that, considered individually, may not significantly affect the results of an appraisal, but which, when considered in the aggregate, would be misleading.

Standard Rule 1–2.   In developing a real property appraisal, an appraiser must observe the following specific appraisal guidelines:

  a. Adequately identify the real estate, identify the real property interest, consider the purpose and intended use of the appraisal, consider the extent of the data collection process, identify any special limiting conditions, and identify the effective date of the appraisal;

  b. Define the value estimate being considered; if the value to be estimated is market value, the appraiser must clearly indicate whether the estimate is the most probable price:
    i. In terms of cash; or
    ii. In terms of financial arrangements equivalent to cash; or
    iii. In such other terms as may be precisely defined; if an estimate of value is based on submarket financing or financing with unusual conditions or incentives, the terms of such financing must be clearly set forth, their contributions to or negative influence on value must be described and estimated, and the market data supporting the valuation estimate must be described and explained;

  c. Consider easements, restrictions, encumbrances, leases, reservations, covenants, contracts, declarations, special assessments, ordinances, or other items of a similar nature;

  d. Consider whether an appraised fractional interest, physical segment, or partial holding contributes pro rata to the value of the holding.

  e. Identify and consider the effect on value of any personal property, trade fixtures or intangible items that are not real property but are included in the appraisal.

Standard Rule 1–3.   In developing a real property appraisal, an appraiser must observe the following specific appraisal guidelines:

  a. Consider the effect on use and value of the following factors: existing land use regulations, reasonably probable modification of such land use regulations, economic demand, the physical adaptability of the real estate, neighborhood trends, and the highest and best use of the real estate;

b. Recognize that land is appraised as though vacant and available for development to its highest and best use and that the appraisal of improvements is based on their actual contribution to the site.

Standard Rule 1–4. In developing a real property appraisal, an appraiser must observe the following specific appraisal guidelines, when applicable:

a. Value the site by an appropriate appraisal method or technique;

b. Collect, verify, analyze, and reconcile:

    i. Such comparable cost data as are available to estimate the cost new of the improvements (if any);

    ii. Such comparable data as are available to estimate the difference between cost new and the present worth of the improvements (accrued depreciation);

    iii. Such comparable sales data, adequately identified and described, as are available to indicate a value conclusion;

    iv. Such comparable rental data as are available to estimate the market rental of the property being appraised;

    v. Such comparable operating expense data as are available to estimate the operating expenses of the property being appraised;

    vi. Such comparable data as are available to estimate rates of capitalization and/or rates of discount.

c. Base projections of future rent and expenses on reasonably clear and appropriate evidence;

d. When estimating the value of a lease fee interest or a leasehold estate, consider and analyze the effect on value, if any, of the terms and conditions of the lease;

e. Consider and analyze the effect on value, if any, of the assemblage of the various estates or component parts of a property and refrain from estimating the value of the whole solely by adding together the individual values of the various estates or component parts;

f. Consider and analyze the effect on value, if any, of anticipated public or private improvements located on or off the site, to the extent that market actions reflect such anticipated improvements as of the effective appraisal date;

g. Identify and consider the appropriate procedures and market information required to perform the appraisal, including all physical, functional, and external market factors as they may affect the appraisal;

h. Appraise proposed improvements only after examining and having available for future examination:
   i. Plans, specifications, or other documentation sufficient to identify the scope and character of the proposed improvements;
   ii. Evidence indicating the probable time of completion of the proposed improvements; and
   iii. Reasonably clear and appropriate evidence supporting development cost, anticipated earnings, occupancy projections, and the anticipated competition at the time of completion.
i. All pertinent information in items (a) through (h) above shall be used in the development of an appraisal.

Standard Rule 1–5. In developing a real property appraisal, an appraiser must:

a. Consider and analyze any current agreement of sale, option, or listing of the property being appraised, if such information is available to the appraiser in the normal course of business;
b. Consider and analyze any prior sales of the property being appraised that occurred within the following periods:
   i. One year for 1-2-4 family residential properties; and
   ii. Three years for all other property types.
c. Consider and reconcile the quality and quantity of data available and analyze within the approaches used and the applicability or suitability of the approaches used.

Departure Provision

The standard rules cited above pertain to a complete appraisal. The appraiser may enter into an agreement to perform an assignment that calls for something less than, or different from, the work that would otherwise be required by the specific guidelines, provided that prior to entering into such an agreement:

1. The appraiser has determined that the appraisal or consulting process to be performed is not so limited that the resulting assignment would tend to mislead or confuse the client or the intended users of the report;
2. The appraiser has advised the client that the assignment calls for something less than, or different from, the work required by the

specific guidelines and that the report will clearly identify and explain the departure(s), and;

3. The client has agreed that the performance of a limited appraisal or consulting service would be appropriate.

Exceptions to the following requirements are not permitted: Standard Rules 1–1, 1–5, 2–1, 2–2, and 2–5.

Reporting Options

The Appraisal Standards Board permits complete and/or limited appraisals to be reported in one of three formats:

Self-contained

Summary

Restricted

The level of detail presented varies with each report type. The self-contained report contains all the data and reasoning in support of the appraiser's opinion. A summary report presents the highlights of the appraisal in an abbreviated format and the restricted report basically states what was done with little or no supporting detail. (The restricted report cannot be so brief as to be misleading and its use is restricted to only one user.)

APPENDIX 16B
CERTIFICATION OF APPRAISER

The appraiser is required to sign a certification in this form:
I certify that, to the best of my knowledge and belief:

- The reported analyses, opinions, and conclusions are limited only by the reported assumptions and limiting conditions, and are my personal, unbiased professional analyses, opinion, and conclusions.

- I have no present or prospective interest in the property that is the subject of this report, and I have no personal interest or bias with respect to the parties involved.

- My compensation is not contingent on an action or event resulting from the analyses, opinion, or conclusions in, or the use of, this report.

- My analyses, opinion, and conclusions were developed, and this report has been prepared, in conformity with the Uniform Standards of Professional Appraisal Practice.

- I have (or have not) made a personal inspection of the property that is the subject of this report. (If more than one person signs the report, this certification must clearly specify which individuals did and which individuals did not make a personal inspection of the appraised property.)

- No one provided significant professional assistance to the person signing this report. (If there are exceptions, the name of each individual providing significant professional assistance must be stated.)

APPENDIX 16C
NCREIF'S TEMPLATE FOR FULL NARRATIVE APPRAISAL REPORTS

Letter of Transmittal

Summary of Salient Facts

Purpose of Appraisal

Property Identification

Legal Description of Property Rights Appraised

Value Definition

Effective Date of Appraisal/Date of Inspection

Regional/City Analysis

Site Analysis

Real Estate Tax and Assessment Analysis

Sale History of the Property

Zoning/Land Use Controls

Description of Improvements

Highest and Best Use

Valuation Process

Cost Approach

Description of approach and its applicability.

Minimum of 3 land comparables to establish land values; adjustments for comparability should be explained.

Cost of improvements should reflect depreciated replacement cost.

Source of cost and basis of depreciation information should be identified and explained.

Sales Comparison Approach

Description of approach and its applicability.

Discussion of applicable units of comparison for this type of property.

Selection rationale and adequate description of properties used for comparison.

Justification and explanation of adjustments for comparability.

Income Capitalization Approach

Description of approach and its applicability.

Selection rationale and adequate description of approach used, i.e., discounted cash flow analysis.

Income Analysis

Review of existing leases (scope to be determined by appraiser).

Review of market conditions for rent and terms.

Review of expected occupancy levels.

Operating Expense Analysis

Review of historical expenses.

Review of market expenses.

Reconciliation and establishment of first-year budget (note: savings availability only to current owner, e.g., purchasing power, favorable insurance premiums, California tax base, do not carry forward).

Capital Improvements and Reserves

Review of planned capital improvements and reserves for replacement of short-lived items over projected holding period.

Net Operating Income before Debt Service

Impact of Favorable Financing

Capitalization Process

Description of approach and its applicability.

Direct Capitalization

Review of selected market transactions, extraction of pertinent first-year overall capitalization rates, and application of capitalization rate to net income of property.

Discounted Cash Flow

Review of outline of assumptions: discount rates, length of holding period, growth of income and expenses, renewal probabilities, market rent, leasing concessions, brokerage commissions, timing and cost of capital improvement programs, reversionary capitalization rate, and cost of sale.

Reconciliation of Final Value Estimate

Limiting Conditions

Certification of Appraisal

Addendum

Exhibits

Legal Description

Lease Abstracts

Zoning Ordinance

Photographs of Property

Qualifications of Appraiser

CHAPTER 17

ENVIRONMENTAL ISSUES

Aileen M. Hooks
Jones, Day, Reavis & Pogue

Mary Ellen Kris
Jones, Day, Reavis & Pogue

INTRODUCTION

The old maxim that three factors—location, location, and location—should be considered in evaluating a potential real estate investment is no longer true.[1] Environmental considerations are becoming an increasingly important risk factor that must be evaluated when making a real estate investment decision. Environmental cleanup costs for sites where contamination is found can range from tens of thousands to hundreds of millions of dollars and not be considered unusual.[2] Consequently, today's investor must take into account the potential for environmental liabilities when weighing the economics of a prospective real estate investment or assessing the continued viability of an existing investment.

Overstating the importance of a thorough environmental investigation of a property is difficult to do; even a property with a relatively low market value can result in substantial environmental liabilities for an investor. A thorough analysis of how environmental liabilities associated with a property could affect its economic value is also critical. Although the nature of the liability may differ, depending on the type of investment and property, virtually all investments in real property create some potential for environmental liability.

In today's business climate, the prudent investor cannot ignore

---

[1] John Heath, Jr., *Environment, Improvements, Taxes: New Factors in Real Estate Investment; Asset Management,* 32 National Real Estate Investor 52 (1990).

[2] See, for example, *Toxic Law Reporter* (BNA) 723 (November 25, 1987).

703

the potential environmental liability that may attach to a real estate investment. As the rate of property appreciation has diminished in recent years, the margin for error in real estate investment has grown smaller; as the magnitude of environmental liabilities attached to real property grows, the importance of considering such liabilities in investment decisions increases. This chapter is intended to help the investor understand how environmental liabilities can affect real estate investments and to provide guidance on incorporating actual and potential environmental liabilities into the investment decision-making process.

ENVIRONMENTAL LIABILITY CONSIDERATIONS

Regulatory Overview

Although a real estate investor cannot be expected to have complete knowledge of all of the environmental statutes and regulations giving rise to environmental liabilities, familiarity with the statutory and regulatory scheme can help in evaluating environmental risks associated with an investment. This section presents an overview of the regulatory scheme at the federal, state, and local levels that can create environmental liability and briefly discusses the types of liability that may arise.

To understand the regulations that govern environmental liability associated with real property, the investor must first understand that environmental regulation is achieved through a dynamic, complex network of environmental regulations derived from many sources. Sources of environmental regulation include federal, state, and local laws, regulations, and ordinances and judicial decisions interpreting these laws and regulations. The United States Congress, the Environmental Protection Agency, state legislatures and agencies (often more than one agency in a single state), regional administrative agencies, city and county governments, and city and county agencies all play a part in shaping environmental policies, legislation, and enforcement.

Much of the environmental regulatory activity in the United States originated with the advent of federal environmental, health, and safety legislation. Such legislation included: the Clean Air Act, as amended by the Clean Air Act Amendments of 1990; the National Environmental Policy Act; the Safe Drinking Water Act; the Federal

Water Pollution Control Act (the Clean Water Act [CWA]; the Resource Conservation and Recovery Act (RCRA); the Comprehensive Environmental Response, Compensation, and Liability Act, as amended by the Superfund Amendment and Reauthorization Act of 1986 (CERCLA or "Superfund"); the Endangered Species Act; the Toxic Substances Control Act (TSCA); the Federal Insecticide, Fungicide, and Rodenticide Act; and the Occupational Safety and Health Act (OSHA).

Generally, environmental statutes set out broad goals and requirements and empower agencies to promulgate specific rules and regulations to carry out the legislative purpose. The result is a detailed set of federal and state rules and regulations governing various matters having potential environmental impacts. Many states have passed analogues to the federal statutes as well as supplemental statutes. In addition, a growing number of local governments are adopting ordinances regulating environmental matters. The result is a very complex scheme of local, state, and federal statutes and regulations, the violation of which can result in civil and/or criminal liability and require the expenditure of large sums of money for corrective action at contaminated sites and for modification or replacement of equipment required to meet regulatory standards. Although a detailed review of each federal statute is beyond the scope of this chapter, the more significant statutes are discussed briefly here.

Perhaps the most significant, and the most notorious, federal statute imposing liability for cleaning up contamination in soil and groundwater is CERCLA. Under CERCLA, the U.S. Environmental Protection Agency (EPA) may undertake or require potentially responsible parties (known as *PRPs*) to undertake response actions when there is a release or a threatened release of any hazardous substance, pollutant, or contaminant that may present an imminent and substantial danger to the public.[3] CERCLA also establishes a comprehensive liability scheme for hazardous substance contamination. A broad range of costs incurred by the EPA or parties authorized by the EPA may be recovered from PRPs. CERCLA broadly defines PRP to include the following four classes of persons:

(1) The owner and operator of a vessel or facility [current owner and operator].

---

[3] 42 U.S.C. §§ 9604, 9606.

(2) Any person who at the time of disposal of any hazardous substance owned or operated any facility at which such hazardous substances were disposed of [prior owner or operator].

(3) Any person who by contract, agreement, or otherwise arranged for disposal or treatment, or arranged with a transporter for transport or disposal or treatment of hazardous substances owned or possessed by such person, by any other party or entity, at any facility or incineration vessel owned or operated by another party or entity and containing such hazardous substances [generator/arranger].

(4) Any person who accepts or accepted any hazardous substances for transport to disposal or treatment facilities, incineration vessels or sites selected by such person, from which there is a release, or a threatened release which causes the incurrence of response costs of a hazardous substance [transporter].[4]

The definition of *facility* contained in CERCLA includes any building, structure, or parcel of real estate at which a hazardous substance has come to be located.[5]

A PRP's defenses to liability under CERCLA are very narrow. The statute limits the defense to liability to a showing by a preponderance of the evidence that the release or threat of release of hazardous substances and related damages were caused *solely* by either (1) an act of God; (2) an act of war; (3) the act of an *unrelated* third party despite due care on the part of the defendant and the defendant's taking precautions against foreseeable acts or omissions of such party and the foreseeable consequences thereof; or (4) any combination of the foregoing.[6] Third parties with whom the defendant has a direct or indirect contractual relationship (including landlords, tenants, and previous owners) are not considered "unrelated" third parties. However, the definitions set forth in CERCLA allow a PRP to establish a defense derived from the unrelated third-party defense known as the *innocent landowner* or *innocent purchaser* defense. The definition of *contractual relationship* in CERCLA is crucial to an understanding of the scope and availability of the innocent landowner defense. This definition includes:

---

[4] 42 U.S.C. § 9607.

[5] 42 U.S.C. § 9601(9).

[6] 42 U.S.C. § 9607(b).

Land contracts, deeds or other instruments transferring title or possession, unless the real property on which the facility concerned is located was acquired by the defendant after the disposal or placement of the hazardous substance on, in, or at the facility, and one or more of the circumstances described in clause (i), (ii) or (iii) is also established by the defendant by a preponderance of the evidence:

  (i) At the time the defendant acquired the facility the defendant did not know and had no reason to know that any hazardous substance which is the subject of the release or threatened release was disposed of on, in, or at the facility.

 (ii) The defendant is a government entity which acquired the facility by escheat, or through any other involuntary transfer or acquisition, or through the exercise of eminent domain authority by purchase or condemnation.

(iii) The defendant acquired the facility by inheritance or bequest.[7]

To establish that an alleged PRP had "no reason to know" of the presence of the hazardous substance, CERCLA provides that "the defendant must have undertaken, at the time of acquisition, *all appropriate inquiry* into the previous ownership and uses of the property consistent with good commercial or customary practice in an effort to minimize liability."[8] CERCLA identifies the following five factors to consider in judging the appropriateness of inquiry:

  1. Any specialized knowledge or experience on the part of the defendant.
  2. The relationship of the purchase price to the value of the property, if uncontaminated.
  3. Commonly known or reasonably ascertainable information about the property.
  4. The obviousness of the presence or the likely presence of the contamination at the property.
  5. The ability to detect any such contamination by appropriate inspection.[9]

---

[7] 42 U.S.C. § 9601(35)(A) (emphasis added).

[8] 42 U.S.C. § 9601(35)(B) (emphasis added).

[9] Ibid.

However, there is no clear guidance on what steps need to be undertaken for a pre-acquisition inquiry to constitute "all appropriate inquiry." Arguably, if a problem was not discovered during a pre-acquisition assessment, the government could contend that all appropriate inquiry was not taken and essentially place the PRP in a catch-22 situation.

If the pre-acquisition investigation discloses environmental conditions that could give rise to liability, the purchaser then has knowledge of the conditions and cannot utilize the innocent landowner defense. Further, the innocent landowner defense is not available if the defendant obtains actual knowledge of the presence of the hazardous substance while he or she owns the property and subsequently transfers ownership without disclosing this knowledge to the purchaser.[10]

From time to time, Congress has introduced legislation that would create a presumption that "all appropriate inquiry" has been undertaken if a pre-acquisition assessment meets certain criteria. These criteria generally include a review of title information for the past 50 years; a review of reasonably obtainable aerial photographs; determination of the existence of government liens; a review of reasonably obtainable federal, state, and local government records; and visual inspection of the real property and immediately adjacent property.[11] Until such legislation is passed or the language establishing the innocent landowner defining CERCLA is clarified, there is no bright-line test for determining whether a pre-acquisition investigation would be considered to constitute all appropriate inquiry.[12]

Because judicial interpretation of CERCLA's definition of PRP has tended to be very broad and the defenses to liability are extremely limited, the real estate investor must be aware of and, to the extent feasible, avoid activities that could bring the investor within the statute's coverage as a PRP. CERCLA (which is discussed in greater

---

[10] 42 U.S.C. § 9601(35)(C).

[11] See, for example, H.R. 2787, 101st Cong., 1st Sess. (1989); H.R. 1217, 102d Cong., 1st Sess. (1991).

[12] In an effort to develop a practice standard for "all appropriate inquiry" and to standardize the elements of what is typically referred to as a *Phase I assessment,* a committee composed of environmental professionals organized under the Association of Testing and Materials (ASTM) has developed an ASTM Standard Practice for Environmental Site Assessments, which was adopted by the ASTM on March 15, 1993.

detail in subsequent sections) and its state counterparts are often the statutes of greatest concern to real estate investors because of the broad net of no-fault liability these statutes cast. However, other environmental statutes regulating hazardous waste, the storage of petroleum products in underground and above-ground storage tanks, water discharges, air emissions, and development on land that is classified as a wetland or an endangered species habitat can also affect the value of a real estate investment or result in unanticipated expenditures. Five of these statutes—the Resource Conservation and Recovery Act (RCRA), the Clean Water Act (including wetlands regulations), the Clean Air Act, the Endangered Species Act, and the National Environmental Policy Act—are outlined briefly below.

The EPA can impose substantial remediation obligations on responsible individuals under the provisions of RCRA. While CERCLA was enacted to address abandoned or inactive sites where hazardous substances had been disposed in the past—in response to sites such as the now infamous Love Canal site—RCRA was intended to establish a cradle-to-grave scheme to address the generation, storage, treatment, and disposal of hazardous waste at active facilities. RCRA authorizes actions against persons contributing to an imminent and substantial endangerment resulting from the handling, storage, treatment, transportation, or disposal of any solid or hazardous waste to compel them to abate the danger.[13] The 1984 amendments to RCRA authorize the EPA to issue corrective action orders to waste management facilities that are permitted to operate under RCRA, requiring cleanup when a release of hazardous waste into the environment has occurred.[14] RCRA also regulates underground storage tanks containing petroleum products.[15]

Another statute that contains both remedial and permitting provisions is the Clean Water Act. The Clean Water Act, which is the principal federal law regulating water pollution, includes a more limited liability scheme for dealing with oil or hazardous substance spills in navigable waters and regulates wastewater discharges.[16] The Clean Water Act also regulates discharge of stormwater from point

---

[13] 42 U.S.C. §§ 6973, 6972.

[14] 42 U.S.C. § 6928(h).

[15] 33 U.S.C. § 6991 *et seq.*

[16] 33 U.S.S. § 1321.

sources.[17] In addition, Section 404 of the act regulates the discharge of dredged or fill material into waters of the United States, which include wetlands.[18] The wetlands regulations require a permit from the U.S. Army Corps of Engineers prior to the placement of fill material into wetlands. Any such placement without a permit would violate Section 301 of the Clean Water Act and give rise to the EPA's civil and criminal enforcement powers. Proposed real estate development activity therefore should include an evaluation of whether wetlands will be affected and, if so, whether the proposed activity is covered under the Clean Water Act, whether any regulatory exemptions apply or the activity can be authorized under an existing nationwide or general permit, or whether an individual permit is required. Obtaining an individual permit can be an expensive and time-consuming process.

The Clean Air Act authorizes the federal government to impose significant restrictions on the emission of air pollutants. The act calls for federal and state implementation of programs that will result in significant regulatory activity and place a considerable administrative burden on the owners and operators of facilities that emit air pollutants, including extensive monitoring and reporting of the emission of a number of air pollutants. The Clean Air Act places responsibility on state agencies to develop satisfactory programs to limit emissions of air pollutants. The investor should be aware that each state's implementation of the programs mandated by the Clean Air Act will differ and should consider such differences in making an investment decision on property affected by the act.

The Endangered Species Act prohibits the taking of threatened or endangered species of fish, wildlife, or plants. *Taking* includes harassing, harming, pursuing, hunting, shooting, wounding, killing, trapping, capturing, or collecting any threatened or endangered species.[19] Consequently, if property constitutes a habitat for an endangered or threatened species, development on that property may be restricted or prohibited.

Although a detailed review of these statutes is beyond the scope of this chapter, it is important to note that each statute can impose

---

[17] 33 U.S.C. § 1342(p).

[18] 33 U.S.C. § 1344.

[19] 16 U.S.C. § 1532(19).

significant duties and obligations on investors in real property and may impose significant restrictions on how such property may be transferred or used. Failure to comply with these statutes can result in substantial environmental liabilities, and the cost of continued compliance with environmental regulations promulgated pursuant to these and other applicable environmental statutes may greatly reduce the value of a real estate investment. Proper evaluation of the investment potential of real property should include an analysis of how environmental regulations put into effect pursuant to these and other applicable environmental statutes may affect the value of the real estate investment, including operating costs, required capital expenditures, and possible development restrictions.

The National Environmental Policy Act (NEPA) requires a detailed environmental impact statement (EIS) on "every recommendation or report on proposals for legislation and other major Federal actions significantly affecting the quality of the human environment."[20] *Federal action* includes projects financed, assisted, conducted, regulated, or approved by federal agencies[21] and therefore includes decisions on whether to grant federal approvals such as permits. If an EIS is required, the process can be very lengthy and can substantially delay, if not preclude, a project.

Direct and Indirect Liability

In analyzing how environmental regulations may affect an investment decision, the real estate investor should be aware that environmental regulations can have both direct and indirect impacts. Environmental regulations can result in the imposition of direct liabilities on the investor by virtue of the property's noncompliance with federal and state regulations or the need for corrective action at the property. Even if the investor is not personally liable directly for penalties or remediation costs, he or she may incur liability indirectly to the extent that the regulations impose liability on the investment vehicle entity, impair the value of the property, and/or increase the costs associated with property operations.

Noncompliance with environmental regulations can result in di-

---

[20] 42 U.S.C. § 4332(c).

[21] 40 C.F.R. § 1508.18(a).

rect liability not only in the form of fines or penalties pursuant to various statutes but also in the form of significant costs of remediation of contaminated property, liens, and superliens against the property arising from government-funded cleanups and tort liability associated with exposure of the public to hazardous substances and migration of hazardous substances across property boundaries. In this regard, although several statutes impose direct liability on violators, the most important statute giving rise to direct liability is CERCLA (and its state analogues).

CERCLA creates a scheme of both strict (regardless of fault) and joint and several (responsibility for all costs irrespective of percentage of contribution) liability requiring certain categories of persons associated with the properties, known as PRPs, to pay for the cleanup costs. Under CERCLA, PRPs include the current owner or operator and past owners or operators of real property from which there has been a release or threat of release of a hazardous substance. PRPs may be held directly liable for the costs of investigation, removal, and remediation, natural resources damages and damage assessments, and required human health assessments. Also, as previously discussed, the defenses to liability under CERCLA are extremely limited. However, recent cases indicate a possible trend toward the application of equitable considerations in assessing and allocating liability among PRPs.[22]

Would a real estate investor be considered an owner or an operator? The answer depends on the factual circumstances. The definition of the term *owner or operator* contained in Section 101(20)(A) of CERCLA sheds little light on who is considered to be an owner or operator, providing merely that the term *owner or operator* means "any person owning or operating [a] facility."[23] Courts have construed this definition broadly to include various individuals who are or have been associated with a contaminated real property. Consequently, depending on the circumstances, lenders, guarantors, shareholders,

---

[22] See, for example, *United States* v. *Alcan Aluminum Corp.*, 964 F.2d 252 (3d Cir. 1992), observing that damages should be apportioned if distinct harms are shown or a reasonable basis exists for allocation; *United States* v. *Atlas Minerals & Chemicals, Inc.*, 797 F. Supp. 411 (E.D. Pa. 1992), noting that the amount and type of substances generated by the PRP, the degree of care exercised by the PRP, and traditional principles of equity should be considered to ensure that the individual PRP pays its fair share of cleanup costs.

[23] 42 U.S.C. § 9601(20)(A).

venture capitalists, investors, parent corporations, real estate syndicators and developers, real estate portfolio managers, partners, officers, directors, and managers of corporations or other entities associated with contaminated property might find themselves caught in
the net of potential liability. Because the cost of remediation of contaminated property may exceed the value of the property, the investor
must consider what direct liabilities are associated with a property
and the likelihood that such direct liabilities will be imposed before
the investor can properly evaluate the property.

It is conceivable under CERCLA that the real estate investor
could be held personally liable for removal and remediation costs.
Direct liability, however, will be rare for a passive real estate investor
without a direct ownership interest in or operational control of the
property. If direct liability is found, it can be financially devastating.
Therefore, the potential should always be evaluated.

Personal liability under CERCLA can arise if the investor personally owns or operates real property and therefore falls under the
definition of PRP. Owning any direct interest in the property obviously would result in the investor being an owner subject to potential
liability merely by virtue of his or her status as an owner without
any affirmative act or omission. Unlike ownership, operation of the
property and classification as an *operator* generally require some
exercise of control over the property.[24] *Control* over the property is
defined as "the exercise of decision-making control over environmental compliance, including taking responsibility for the waste disposal
or hazardous substance practice which results in an actual or threatened release; or the exercise of control at a management level that
encompasses environmental compliance, where the control is comparable to that of a manager of the enterprise."[25]

The real estate investor should always be aware that attempts
to influence the management of investment property, particularly in
a way that could affect the environmental decision-making process,
could expose the investor to personal liability as an operator for

---

[24] Although some courts have held that direct liability may arise from the mere unexercised
power to control hazardous material management at a facility, *United States* v. *Fleet Factors
Corp.*, 901 F.2d 1550 (11th Cir. 1990), *cert. denied*, 111 S. Ct. 752 (1991), the recent trend has
been to find liability only where the actual exercise of control over such activities has occurred
(*In re Bergsoe Metal Corp.*, 910 F.2d 668 [9th Cir. 1990]).

[25] 40 C.F.R. pt. 300.

the environmental condition of the property, including liability for cleanup costs under CERCLA. If the investor does not have a direct ownership interest in the real estate and treats the investment as an investment without exercising any control over management or operations, especially with respect to decisions critical to the proper handling of hazardous materials associated with the property, the investor generally should not be exposed to personal liability for the environmental conditions of his or her real property investments.

Avoidance of direct exposure to environmental liabilities, however, does not end the prudent real estate investor's consideration of environmental liabilities. The investor must also consider how environmental regulations may indirectly affect the real property and hence the property's investment value. Indirect environmental liabilities include costs of compliance, that is, capital and operating costs associated with attaining and maintaining environmental compliance; diminished property values due to the presence of contamination on the property or to restrictions on how the property may be used; and increased financing costs due to lenders' hesitancy to fund projects where the value of the collateral may be at risk.

The cost of attaining compliance with environmental regulations may be significant. Environmental regulatory requirements can affect a project's feasibility and existing condition or proposed use. Several federal programs impose considerable regulatory requirements on owners of real property that can affect virtually any real property, regardless of use. For example, the underground storage tank program under RCRA imposes regulatory requirements on owners and operators of such tanks relating to the design, construction, and installation of the tanks, operating and release detection requirements, and financial assurance requirements. Other regulations include the National Emission Standards for Hazardous Air Pollutants (NESHAPS) for asbestos pursuant to the Clean Air Act, which impose regulatory requirements relating to the demolition or excavation of buildings containing asbestos; the stormwater regulations promulgated pursuant to the Clean Water Act, which regulate certain stormwater discharges, including those associated with particular real estate construction activities; and Section 6(e) of TSCA, pursuant to which EPA regulates polychlorinated biphenyls (PCBs), found in transformers, capacitors, and other mechanical equipment.

These and other environmental programs can result in significant expenditures to establish and maintain compliance. Such costs may range from a few dollars to cover the cost of a permit fee to dispose of wastewater under the Clean Water Act to a multimillion-dollar investment in new technology to comply with the best available technology standard set by the latest amendments to the Clean Air Act. Obviously, if substantial investments in technology are necessary to meet the compliance requirements under the various environmental regulations, the return on capital anticipated from a project will be reduced.

In addition, the investor must realize that once compliance with federal and state environmental regulatory programs has been attained, a project may continue to incur significant administrative and technological costs for maintaining compliance. These costs can be considerable and should be factored into an analysis of a project's cash flow.

An example of an environmental statute that can impose significant administrative burdens is the Clean Air Act. This act requires monitoring, recording, and reporting emissions of any air pollutant emitted from the facility. The extent to which these activities must be performed will depend on the type of pollutant emitted, the location of the facility, and the air quality in the region where the facility is located. But in most cases, the administrative costs of such activities, especially the costs of adding competent personnel to monitor pollutant emissions, can be substantial. For most large facilities (especially industrial facilities), these administrative costs will be an important factor in forecasting the project's cash flow; if ignored, the economics of the project may look more favorable than they really are. Although the Clean Air Act's monitoring and reporting requirements are more extensive than those of other federal and state programs, most government programs can place some administrative burden on residential and commercial developers and owners of real property. The administrative costs of such programs should be considered in evaluating real estate investments.

An accurate economic analysis of a proposed investment requires an evaluation of how continued administrative costs, as well as capital expenditures, associated with ongoing compliance with environmental regulations will increase the cost of day-to-day operations and thereby reduce the return on investment. In addition, environmental regulations may influence the timing of cash flow from an investment, often causing significant delays in the investor's realized return on investment. For example, the construction of a manufacturing facility may be delayed several months or even years as attempts are made to obtain the necessary permits. Many federal and state programs require a significant investment of time and effort before a permit for a particular project will be issued and construction begun. Permit programs may require public hearings before a permit to build and operate a facility is issued. The time a major facility needs to obtain a permit can range from several months to several years.

The investor should also be aware that delays to a development project are not limited to industrial facilities or other projects typically thought to be environmentally sensitive. Extensive delays may occur in the development of vacant tracts of land as the residential or commercial developer attempts to meet land use regulations or comply with the wetlands regulations or the EIS requirement under NEPA. Extensive and costly studies may be required before development of vacant land will be approved. These studies typically focus on how development of the land will affect the ecological balance in the area, such as surface or underground water supplies or any endangered species inhabiting the area. In some cases, the development of land may be halted completely. If, for example, the development would destroy the habitat of an endangered species, the project can be stopped.[26]

In general, these studies are not trivial undertakings and may require considerable time and expense to complete. In most cases, the results of studies are made public, sometimes leading to extensive public debate and discussion. In environmentally sensitive areas, public opposition to residential or industrial development can completely halt a large development effort. Although it is nearly impossible to quantify how public opinion may influence the development process, the investor should still attempt to understand a community's general outlook on development before making a significant investment in land within that community. Delays in the development of land in environmentally sensitive areas should be expected. It is axiomatic that a longer development process also will prolong the time it will take for investors to realize a return on their capital.

Environmental regulations may also cause a diminution in the value of the investment property. For example, restrictions on how the property may be developed can prevent it from being put to its

---

[26] See 16 U.S.C. §§ 1531–1544 (1988); 42 U.S.C. § 300f–300j–11 (1988).

highest economic use. This form of indirect liability is most frequently encountered when development of property is curtailed or completely proscribed, as can occur under NEPA, the Endangered Species Act, the National Historic Preservation Act, or Section 404 of the Clean Water Act (regulating development of wetlands). Likewise, property value can be diminished due to the presence of hazardous substances in buildings located on the property or in soil or groundwater. Assigning a dollar amount to the impact of environmental conditions or regulations on the value of the property can be problematic. It may be difficult to find a truly comparable property to use as a measure of market value. The other obvious methodology, subtracting the cost to remediate from the value, also can produce unsatisfactory results.[27]

Despite the difficulty in calculating the precise degree to which environmental factors affect market value, the investor should evaluate how direct and indirect environmental liabilities will affect the project's economic feasibility. Failure to consider such factors may result in unrealistic forecasts of the timing and amount of the project's expected return.

The Investment Vehicle

Virtually every investment in real estate has the potential to be affected by environmental regulation. As previously discussed, the potential for direct exposure to the environmental liability associated with an investment in real property should be avoided to the greatest extent feasible. Because the cost of remediation of an affected property may far exceed the property's value and personal liability may attach by virtue of ownership of the property, the investor should take steps to minimize the impact of such liabilities. The choice of investment vehicle may limit the investor's liability to the amount of the initial investment.

If the real estate investment vehicle is a corporation or a limited partnership, the shareholders or limited partners are best positioned to limit potential personal liability for environmental conditions. Absent participation by a shareholder or limited partner in the management of a facility, the shareholder in a corporation or the limited

---

[27] For a discussion of the valuation dilemma, see David J. Freeman and Deborah W. Newborn, "Valuing Contaminated Property," *Real Estate/Environmental Liability News,* May 22, 1992.

partner in a limited partnership that owns real estate should be limited to the amount of the investment.[28] Conversely, investment in a general partnership, serving as a general partner in a limited partnership, or direct property ownership exposes the investor to direct liability and can result in liabilities that far exceed the value of the initial investment. To minimize the risk of liabilities in excess of the planned investment, direct ownership of property and participation in general partnerships should be avoided. Instead, the investor should endeavor to participate in real estate investment by becoming a shareholder in a corporation, becoming a limited partner in a limited partnership, or otherwise getting involved in a limited liability vehicle.

State Property Transfer Laws

Over the past decade, a number of states have enacted property transfer laws addressing the environmental condition of property.[29] These laws can affect the transferability of contaminated property, as buyers and sellers are required to take certain steps before a transfer of an interest in property may take place. The requirements imposed by the various state statutes range from disclosure requirements between the parties to the transaction to pretransfer cleanup obligations with state agency oversight.

Under some state statutes, such as New Jersey's Industrial Site Recovery Act (ISRA), formerly known as the Environmental Cleanup Responsibility Act (ECRA), the seller of contaminated property will be required to clean up or commit to cleaning up contaminated property

---

[28] If, however, the corporate veil of the corporation is pierced, the shareholders can be held directly liable. Likewise, if limited partners engage in activities that would cause them to be considered general partners, they will also be exposed to personal liability. Further, active participation by the investor in the management of a facility may cause the investor to be liable for amounts far in excess of the initial investment. See, for example, *United States* v. *McGraw-Edison Co.,* 718 F. Supp. 154 (W.D.N.Y. 1989) (a corporation that is a minority shareholder in a corporate subsidiary may be liable when the shareholder actively participates in the management of the subsidiary).

[29] For example, see the Industrial Site Recovery Act, New Jersey Stat. Ann. §§ 13:1k-6 *et seq.;* N.J. Admin. Code tit. 7, § 26B *et seq.;* the Connecticut Transfer Act, Conn. Gen. Stat. Ann. §§ 22a–134 (i) *et seq.;* California Health & Safety Code § 2535 9.7(a); the Illinois Real Property Transfer Act, Ill. Ann. Stat. Ch. 30, para. 901 *et seq.;* the Indiana Hazardous Disclosure and Responsible Party Transfer Law, Ind. Code Ann. § 13-7-22.5-10 *et seq.;* W. Va. Code, § 20-5E-20.

before the property may be legally transferred to a willing buyer.[30] Under other statutes, such as Section 25359.7(a) of the California Health & Safety Code, the owner of contaminated property, although not required to clean up contaminated property, must disclose to potential buyers or renters of the property that it has been contaminated with hazardous waste. Connecticut requires that the transferor of real property make a negative declaration to the effect that no on-site discharge or spillage of a hazardous substance has occurred or that any such discharge or spillage has been properly cleaned up. In the absence of such a declaration, the transferor or transferee must certify that the hazardous substances have been cleaned up to the satisfaction of the state or will be cleaned up in the future. In any event, the transferor remains strictly liable for the cost of cleanup if the hazardous substances are not properly removed from the property.

State disclosure laws may also affect the transferability and, consequently, the market value of real property. The investor should be aware of a state's disclosure statutes when considering an investment in real property in that state. Disclosure statutes, such as New Jersey's ISRA, that require the owner to clean up contaminated property before transferring it may result in a lower return on investment. Pure notification statutes, such as the California statute, ultimately may have a similar effect, as fully informed buyers, upon notice of a contamination problem, will reduce the price they are willing to pay for the property by the anticipated cost of cleaning it up. In addition, because it is frequently difficult to estimate the cost of cleanup with certainty, some buyers simply will not consider purchasing property known to be contaminated at any price. In this instance, the property will have to be cleaned up prior to transfer, if the economics warrant.

State disclosure laws can also negatively affect the marketability of commercial rental properties. For example, California's disclosure law requires that a building owner who knows or has reason to know a property has been contaminated with a hazardous substance must notify any potential lessee of this fact.[31] The effect of the notice requirement on the rental value of the property may be difficult to determine and will depend in part on the intended use of the property. But it is reasonable to conclude that in many cases, the investor can

---

[30] New Jersey Stat. Ann. §§ 13:1k-6 *et seq.*
[31] California Health & Safety Code § 25359.7.

expect a reduction in the rental rates potential renters are willing to pay and that this reduction may be exaggerated in the case of residential property. The net effect may be to lower cash flow projections from investments in contaminated rental property as potential tenants are notified of the property's contamination and are less willing to pay market rental rates.

To summarize, state disclosure laws place certain duties on the owner of contaminated property. These laws can result in a dramatic reduction in the marketability of and/or increased costs associated with the property with respect to both the sale and lease of the property.

IDENTIFICATION AND MINIMIZATION OF ENVIRONMENTAL RISK

Environmental Site Assessment

To evaluate a prospective investment's potential for environmental liability, a pre-investment environmental investigation must be undertaken. Such an investigation should address the prior and current conditions of the property as well as ongoing compliance considerations and any improvements or planned improvements to the property. A central part of a pre-investment investigation is a proper environmental site assessment.

A site assessment is commonly performed in two phases. Phase I usually focuses on information pertaining to the site's history, a visual inspection of the property and the surrounding area, and a check of regulatory files regarding the property and adjacent sites. Although the scope of phase I assessments differs among properties, certain factors, such as whether the site is vacant or developed, the nature of facilities or activities on the site, and evidence of noncompliance with environmental regulations, will be critical to any phase I investigation. If the phase I assessment of the site indicates a likelihood of contamination by hazardous substances, a phase II assessment is typically performed to confirm the existence and extent of such contamination. A phase II assessment should include a technical and engineering assessment of the type and extent of any soil or groundwater contamination, an evaluation of potential public and environmental concerns, and a preliminary estimate of cleanup or mitigation costs.

Any site assessment will be limited by the scope and quality of the investigation(s) and the expertise and competence of the individual(s) who will analyze and interpret data generated by such investigation(s). Of course, whether or not an extensive investigation (using highly trained consultants) is warranted will depend largely on the nature of the real estate asset.[32]

Nature of Real Estate Assets

Certain types of real estate investments carry a greater risk of environmental liability than others. Accordingly, such investments warrant a more extensive environmental site assessment than less risky investments. Further, where a particular site has been used for commercial or industrial activities raising an environmental red flag, the investigation should be broadened to ensure that all aspects of environmental liability relevant to the site are examined. Following is a brief discussion of environmental liabilities associated with particular types of real estate investments.

Certain types of real estate investments, such as office buildings, apartment buildings, and hotels and motels, pose relatively limited concerns regarding the nature of environmental liability associated with the current use of the site. With these property types, the biggest concern generally is the presence of asbestos-containing materials in the structure. Although the presence of such materials may not by itself pose a health risk, degeneration of such materials may result in friable (i.e., airborne) asbestos, which does pose known health risks. More important, lenders often insist on the removal of asbestos even if it is not damaged, and the public's fear of asbestos in some cases may depress the value of real property containing asbestos. The cost of asbestos removal may exceed the value of the building itself.

Asbestos can be a major environmental concern in retail centers as well. Many older shopping centers were constructed with asbestos-containing products that, as the buildings age, release friable asbestos. These products typically include insulation, ceiling and floor tiles, and mastic used for floor tiles. As with office buildings, apartments, and hotels, the cost of asbestos removal at a shopping center may be very high. Also of potential concern at retail centers are USTs from

---

[32] See Mary Ellen Kris and Aileen M. Hooks, "Role of Environmental Counsel in Scoping and Budgeting Environmental Consulting Services," in David S. Machlowitz, ed., *Legal Guide to Working with Environmental Consultants* (1992).

emergency generators and tires and batteries from automotive facilities. The investor in a retail center also needs to consider other environmental liabilities, depending on the type of tenant in the facility. For example, if the retail center contains a dry-cleaning or a photo-processing establishment, it is possible that volatile organic compounds (VOCs) have been stored, spilled, or improperly disposed of on the property. Proper disposal of such materials and the cleanup of contaminated soil or water can be very costly. Because the mix of tenants at a retail center may change over time, a more extensive investigation is warranted to ensure that current or past activities on the site have not resulted in a significant and unanticipated environmental liability.

The investor in a health care facility must also perform a more extensive investigation of certain environmental issues. With health care facilities, the major source of environmental liability is the disposal of medical waste. Whether such disposal is in the form of solid waste or by on-site incineration, important environmental concerns exist. Improper disposal or storage of medical waste may result in significant cleanup costs, while proper disposal of such materials is becoming more and more costly. Because commercial disposal of medical waste is very expensive, many facilities have turned to on-site incineration. This alternative, however, is not without problems. First, significant costs are associated with installation and maintenance of an on-site incinerator. Second, the ongoing effort to comply with air quality regulations under the Clean Air Act entails administrative costs. Third, because many health care facilities are located in residential areas, applications for the permits required for an on-site incinerator frequently meet substantial opposition by the community. The investor in a health care facility therefore must be aware that such facilities generate medical waste that is difficult to dispose of and that such waste will be an ongoing environmental liability concern as the facility attempts to comply with regulations restricting its disposal.

Industrial facilities generally pose the greatest environmental risk and warrant the most extensive investigation to avoid unexpected liabilities. Most manufacturing facilities utilize and store hazardous materials. Many industrial facilities handle and store large quantities of hazardous materials and may generate air emissions and wastewater discharges, as well as hazardous wastes, which need to be properly managed.

Assessment of industrial facilities must focus on several important considerations. First is the history of the site. The investor must know whether prior occupants employed hazardous materials in their manufacturing processes or generated hazardous wastes. The older the site and the greater the number of prior tenants, the greater the possibility that hazardous materials or wastes were disposed of in a manner that would violate current requirements and thus pose a potential liability. The assessment must also include an evaluation of the facility's current compliance with the latest federal and state regulations. As noted above, in some cases the cost of new technology to meet current federal regulatory requirements under the Clean Air Act can be extremely high. Finally, the assessment should also consider whether environmental regulation will limit growth of the facility. A good example of this is the Clean Air Act and the limitations it places on the emission of certain air pollutants. If a facility is located in particular areas of the country, the Clean Air Act may mandate a reduction in the emission of certain pollutants. In some cases, this can completely eliminate the growth potential for facilities that emit that pollutant in their manufacturing process.

Evaluation of the Site Assessment

To fully understand the environmental risks associated with a potential investment property, a full evaluation of the information produced by a site assessment of the property is necessary. Gathering information on a site is of little practical use if the information is not organized and compiled into an understandable format. The investor should insist on a formal environmental report on the results of any site assessment.

The environmental report should be written in an understandable and useful manner.[33] It should identify areas of concern, but should avoid legal conclusions. Legal conclusions resulting from the report findings should be made in consultation with an environmental lawyer as the findings are reported. The report should describe in detail the steps taken in the investigation to document that all appro-

---

[33] For a discussion of considerations in reviewing environmental reports, see Carol A. Surgens, "Editing the Consultant's Report," in David S. Machlowitz, ed., *Legal Guide to Working with Environmental Consultants* (1992).

priate inquiry has been made, and all findings should be fully explained. In addition, in a situation where environmental liabilities are expected, the investigator should quantify the probability of the existence of such liabilities and provide an estimate of the range of associated costs for the various liabilities. Finally, to be effectively used, the information the investigator provides should also indicate the degree of certainty of the estimates provided. As with any analytical process, an environmental report and its conclusions are only as good as the data on which they are based.

If an environmental report has been prepared properly, the investor can incorporate the information in the report into his or her decision-making process. It is critical that the investor fully understand the potential magnitude of an environmental liability and the probability that such a liability will occur. If the site assessment report properly reduces these factors to hard numbers, the investor can incorporate them into the decision-making process. At this point, much of the uncertainty in evaluating environmental risk and liability begins to fade. A properly prepared site assessment report will greatly assist in the investment decision even if the investor is not fully conversant in the scientific analyses supporting the report.

Safeguards to Minimize Risks

Once the investor is fully informed of the environmental risks that may be associated with a real property transaction or a particular asset in the portfolio, the investor should take appropriate steps to minimize and, where possible, eliminate the risks. Such steps might include structuring the acquisition or leasehold transaction to limit the investor's liability and taking steps to ensure that any investment property is properly managed with respect to environmental liabilities.

Structuring the Investment

Given the increased risk of exposure for environmental liabilities attached to the status of owner or operator, it is advisable, wherever possible, to structure real estate investment transactions to avoid any direct ownership or responsibility for operation of the property. Consequently, an investment as a limited partner in a limited partnership would be less risky than an investment as a general partner.

Similarly, ownership of an interest in a corporation that holds title to or manages a real estate asset would be preferable to direct owner-ship or operation of that property from an environmental liability perspective. Other structuring techniques that can serve to minimize exposure for environmental liability include (1) requiring that any environmental issues discovered during the due diligence process be addressed and remediated prior to closing; (2) if the transaction includes a number of assets, excluding those properties that pose environmental concerns; and/or (3) requiring a financially backed indemnification from the transferor with respect to environmental matters. Contractual protections can also be negotiated.

Several types of contractual provisions can affect the liabilities associated with a real property transaction. With regard to the pur-chase contract, provisions related to economic responsibility (i.e., seller versus buyer) for environmental liability include representa-tions and warranties, indemnification obligations, and conditions to closing. Although the institutional investor is frequently removed from the transaction and not a party to the contract, the investor should make sure, if possible, that the actual party to the contract is aware of and utilizes these protections. Further, the investor may investigate existing contracts to better understand how environmen-tal liabilities have been addressed in properties already in its port-folio.

Representations and warranties allow the purchaser of property to establish current conditions and known liabilities. A well-drafted contract, from the purchaser's perspective, should require the seller to represent and warrant that all required permits, licenses, and approvals have been obtained and that the site is in compliance with such permits and with all other statutory and regulatory require-ments. Further, the purchaser may use representations and warrant-ies to require the seller to disclose the existence of pending or threat-ened suits or proceedings, past uses of the property, and past waste disposal practices at the site. An indemnity can be used to allocate economic responsibility for environmental liabilities between the par-ties to the transaction. The indemnity arrangement can be a straight-forward shift of responsibility or can include monetary floors and/or ceilings and/or a sliding scale percentage allocation between the parties over time. Conditions to closing can be used to ensure that an acceptable environmental assessment is received to trigger the closing obligation.

Property Management

Once a real estate asset becomes part of the investment portfolio, the investor should continue to take steps to minimize exposure for existing conditions, avoid the creation of new conditions of environmental concern on the property, and respond to any changes in environmental law. This can be accomplished through the development of an overall environmental management program. Sophisticated property management companies have begun to institute environmental management programs for the properties they manage to minimize the risk that environmental liabilities will be imposed on either themselves or the property owners and investors.

Depending on the number of properties and their nature, an environmental management program can consist of preleasing questionnaires concerning a prospective tenant's activities and exit questionnaires regarding a tenant's vacancy of the premises, including in each case a detailed identification of potentially environmentally sensitive activities and uses of hazardous substances; training of management personnel and development of an environmental procedures handbook to ensure that property management personnel know how to identify and respond to environmental issues and crises; an ongoing periodic inspection and audit program; and the implementation of operation and maintenance programs. Property owners and managers can develop long-term programs to address areas of current and anticipated environmental concern. For example, many companies are systematically removing or abating all asbestos-containing materials or systematically removing all underground storage tanks. Expenditures on these items now reduce the potential for exposure to environmental liability in the future.

For properties that are leased to third parties, in addition to checking whether a prospective tenant is a good credit risk, the environmental track record of the prospective tenant, the tenant's proposed activities on the property, and the tenant's general attitude toward environmental compliance (which can be gleaned from preleasing questionnaires, cursory investigations, and tenant interviews) should be considered in determining whether the tenant is an acceptable "environmental" risk. In addition, tenants can be required in their leases to adhere to strict environmental covenants and submit periodic certifications that they are in compliance with those covenants.

In implementing any environmental management program,

however, care must be taken to avoid crossing the line of "owner/ operator" as defined by CERCLA.[34] If the actions taken amount to an exercise of control over hazardous material management, the risk of being deemed an operator increases. However, this risk must be balanced against the risks associated with having no environmental management program in place.

CONCLUSION

Understanding the environmental issues that can affect a real estate investment decision and the management of real estate assets in an investment portfolio will greatly enhance the investor's ability to make informed decisions with respect to real estate investments and to minimize and possibly avoid unanticipated environmental liabilities. Given the complexity and ever-changing nature of environmental regulations, investors should consider the use of environmental professionals to assess and manage potential environmental liabilities. The environmentally educated investor will be able to factor environmental considerations into the investment decision and the portfolio management process by structuring transactions and developing asset management programs that take environmental considerations into account and to develop projected returns with an understanding of the impact environmental issues can have. Further, taking environmental considerations into account in the real estate investment process will enable the investor to manage the portfolio in a manner designed to minimize the risk of environmental liabilities and unanticipated environmental expenditures.

REFERENCES

American Society for Testing and Materials. *ASTM Practical Guide on Environmental Site Assessments* (1993).

Civins, Jeff. "Environmental Law Concerns in Real Estate Transactions." *Southwestern Law Journal* 43 (1982), pp. 819, 824.

---

[34] See footnote 24 and the accompanying text.

Freeman, David J., and Deborah W. Newborn. "Valuing Contaminated Property." *Real Estate/Environmental Liability News,* May 22, 1992.

Kris, Mary Ellen, and Aileen M. Hooks. "Role of Environmental Counsel in Scoping and Budgeting Environmental Consulting Services." In David S. Machlowitz, ed., *Legal Guide to Working with Environmental Consultants* (1992).

Miller, Lisl E., "Indemnification Agreements under CERCLA." *Environmental Law* 23 (1993), p. 333.

Surgens, Carol A. "Editing the Consultant's Report." In David S. Machlowitz, ed., *Legal Guide to Working with Environmental Consultants* (1992).

CHAPTER 18

DUE DILIGENCE IN REAL ESTATE TRANSACTIONS

Stephen E. Roulac
The Roulac Group

Institutional investors expect the organizations that advise and represent them to walk the talk of commitment to a prudent real estate investing process. This means adopting the appropriate strategic approach, combined with the prudent acquisition, operation, and disposition of property investments. The due diligence process, which confirms that the transaction meets general standards of prudence and the particular criteria of the investor, is integral to the original decision to invest in a fund, acquire a property, or retain a manager. Without effective due diligence prior to an acquisition, no amount of strategic insight and/or operational/dispositional brilliance can overcome the debilitating risk associated with a marginal (or worse) property acquisition and the consequences of overlooking a major infirmity in the property, market, manager, or investment structure.

As a senior real estate officer of a major pension fund put it, "I expect to have implicit trust in my advisors, and then I want complete assurance and confirmation that everything that is supposed to be done is in fact done." The message is that trust is a necessary but by no means a sufficient precondition for institutional real estate investing. Explicit substance must back up the implicit confidence of the advisor-investor relationship. Effective implementation of the due diligence priority is the explicit substance of prudent investing in the fiduciary context.

In a real estate market where the majority of investors have been materially disappointed by deals that fell far short of projections, if

The author wishes to thank Michael M. Caron, Jack P. Friedman, Andrew F. Fusscas, Barry E. Hinkle, Dan Kohlhepp, Jeffrey Lewis, Scott R. Muldavin, Joseph L. Pagliari, Jr., Miles Ruthburg, and James R. Webb for their comments.

not resulting in substantial financial reverses, risk aversion is the watchword. Some investors reacted to their apparent inability to discriminate between good and bad deals by determining to do no deals. Those institutional investors still active in the market, however, insist on approaches to identify, mitigate, and contain risk. The due diligence study is a transaction-specific procedure that can serve both to identify, measure, and control risk and to confirm that the attributes of the subject investment comply with articulated investment parameters.

The purpose of due diligence is to identify, organize, and, to the extent possible, quantify risk—not eliminate it—in order to assist acquisition negotiators and investment committee decision makers. Determining the appropriate due diligence cannot be prescribed by formula; it must be determined based on the investment structure, property type, and level of responsibility or authority of the individuals or entities commissioning and conducting the due diligence.

DUE DILIGENCE DEFINED

Due diligence in an institutional real estate setting is defined as an evaluation of the policies, procedures, and results of an organization's structure and staffing, portfolio construction, and monitoring and selection of specific real estate investments. The appropriate procedures and level of due diligence for a specific real estate opportunity will vary based on the critical success factors of the investment, the investment structure, the specific property type and attributes of the asset, the time period in which the analysis is conducted, and the specific fiduciary and contractual responsibilities of the entity or organization conducting the due diligence.

The due diligence imperative seeks to replicate that process that a prudent person would employ prior to a major financial commitment. The process does not necessarily involve a decision or a recommendation; rather, at a minimum it confirms that requisite tasks have been performed, addresses pertinent issues, and identifies and discloses critical information. Thus, the due diligence investigation confirms that designated standards, including acquisition policies and criteria as well as legal and regulatory guidelines, have been complied with, and that the decision process has been appropriately adhered to. In a sense, a due diligence investigation is analogous to what pilots do prior to take-off to ensure that all systems are functioning and the plane is ready to fly. The role of the board of trustees of the pension fund is to ensure that the pilots understand the procedures and that appropriate systems are in place to ensure compliance with these procedures.

A due diligence study is neither a roadblock nor a transaction facilitator, but a means to offer an objective, and preferably independent, view of the merits of the investment. Accordingly, the third-party due diligence study is not a substitute for a full investigation by those originating the investment opportunity. Rather, it is an independent confirmation that the appropriate questions have been asked and satisfactorily answered.

These questions should consider those elements of the proposed investment that will influence its future financial performance. Specifically, primary attention must be directed to important aspects of the fund or investment program, the investment manager that has oversight for the program or is representing the investor's interests, and a number of property-specific issues. Among the property's specific issues of concern are the local economy; supply-demand balance; the subject property's competitive position; neighborhood factors; site attributes; condition of improvements; planned and/or needed capital expenditures; lease review; tenant information, including financial strength; tax factors; historical financial operating information; reasonableness of assumptions in financial analysis; validity of the computer model; accuracy of calculations; property operations economics; key suppliers and contracts; title issues; physical environment risks; environmental compliance review; regulatory compliance; and key player review.

A comprehensive due diligence study also involves a review and an inspection of virtually every document pertaining to the property, including financial and economic reports generated by third-party professionals; all pertinent legal documents involving the contractual relationships among tenants, suppliers, and employees; all financial documentation relating to debt and equity investors; and all documents concerned with regulatory compliance, including tax returns.

Major objectives of a due diligence process are to assess regulatory compliance, perform appropriate financial and other analyses, detect sources of potential problems, and gain insights crucial to managing the property. Often the independent third-party due diligence is sought by organizations that lack the internal resources or expertise to analyze one or more critical issues that could have a major impact on the potential investment.

The emphasis of due diligence can be considered from both a results and a process perspective. A focus on results is necessarily prospective, in as much as the due diligence study is conducted *prior* to the captial commitment decision. Among the results issues that might be addressed in a due diligence investigation are the following:

1. *Investment performance.* How does projected investment performance compare to reasonable expectations over the indicated time horizon?

2. *Portfolio composition.* Portfolio composition can be viewed both quantitatively and qualitatively, in terms of the degree to which a contemplated investment will complement identified standards for the composition of the portfolio concerning parameters such as

   a. Property type.
   b. Geographic region.
   c. Property attributes.
   d. Property dimensions.
   e. Tenant characteristics.

   These and other factors may, in the aggregate, be considered in terms of a desired standard that the properties be of "institutional quality."

3. *Property attributes.* In addition to the quantitative and qualitative assessment of how a particular property might affect the composition of the overall portfolio, a summary assessment may be made of each property decision that considers additional factors such as

   a. Risk control mechanisms, including undertakings and commitments by sellers, tenants, managers, and third parties.
   b. Financial ratios.
   c. Other property-specific measures.

Beyond the prospective results orientation an emphasis on the *process* of making the decision is central to due diligence made. Here, the due diligence concern addresses questions such as:

- What are the decision procedures?
- Are these decision procedures adequate?
- Were these decision procedures adhered to?

This process review involves considering what information is employed in the decision, how the information is developed, who evaluates and/or confirms the information, and how the decision is made. Of particular concern is whether the overall decision process by the various parties involved is consistent with established procedures generally and the authority of the various parties to the investment decision specifically. Thus, the process aspect of due diligence emphasizes a review of the steps and procedures that were used to confirm what was done and how it was done. Some of this work is reflected in the proposed transaction's documentation, which should be appropriately reviewed in the due diligence process. The advantage of a third-party involvement is the opportunity to obtain an independent confirmation that the due diligence process was adhered to before any financial commitment is made.

Just as it is a mistake to view the due diligence investigation as primarily involving legal compliance, so too is it inappropriate to think that due diligence consists of a traditional program of accounting and auditing procedures. In only the narrowest construction of the scope of the due diligence responsibility would an accounting-based set of procedures be sufficiently prudent due diligence prior to a significant financial commitment.

Some view the due diligence function as being equivalent to traditional mortgage underwriting. In fact, due diligence shares many elements common to a comprehensive and conscientious mortgage underwriting. As long as the emphasis is on conscientious and comprehensive, the approach will likely embrace a number of elements that are part of the due diligence process. But since a mortgage underwriting specifically involves confirming a narrower array of documents and information elements than a comprehensive due diligence investigation would include, not all of the elements fundamental to accompaniments of due diligence investigation will necessarily be considered in most mortgage underwriting processes.

Others view due diligence as entailing a detailed evaluation of the physical condition of the site and structure, including consideration of current condition, expected life, component replacement costs, needed ongoing maintenance expenses, and likely future capital expenditures. Certainly these issues are necessary conditions of a competent due diligence study, but they are insufficient to achieve the full scope of due diligence in a prudent investing context.

Still others view due diligence as being essentially equivalent to the competent appraisal. To be sure, the contents of a competent appraisal—an appropriate description of the property, a discussion of the economy of the region where it is located, evaluation of the site and neighborhood, assessment of demand and competing facilities, calculation of the site's value as if vacant and the cost of reproducing the improvements, a comparative analysis of the property in terms of sale prices for similar properties, a forecast of probable future financial performance, and a composite calculation of value—touch on elements that are all part of a competent due diligence study.

But an appraisal falls short of a due diligence study in several critical ways. First, an appraisal generally provides a generic and generalized assessment of a property, whereas a due diligence study is more effective if done from the point of view of a designated investor. The orientation of the due diligence study should be particular to the specific investor and its objectives and criteria. Further, the due diligence study will likely investigate in greater depth issues that an appraisal only touches on. Also, several of the considerations critical to a due diligence study are beyond the scope of an appraisal. An appraisal can serve as one component of a due diligence study, but it is not the essence of such a study.

It is important to consider what due diligence should not do. For example, a pension fund may allocate X dollars to real estate; but once that is decided, it is not the purpose of due diligence to flatly countermand that decision by not recommending real estate because the consultant expects a general market decline. Similarly, once allocations are made to specific geographic areas or property types, it is not the role of a due diligence report to argue with that strategy, though it should note any major concerns.

The due diligence study can serve as a key element of an integrated planning and control system for real estate investment decision making. It can be the means of ensuring that the managerial actions following from the investment plan are consistent with the plan. To this purpose, the due diligence study can organize the information needed for assessment and provide the means to facilitate the decision-making process.

THE RATIONALE FOR THOROUGH DUE DILIGENCE

Recent real estate investing performance has been less than distinguished, due to unprecedented and largely unanticipated market declines and because due diligence historically has not received a high priority within the institutional investing community. Too many companies placed more emphasis on deal making and self-promotion than on investigation and disciplined analysis to ensure that representations made were realized. But in the 1990s, with markets characterized by supply surpluses and depressed and declining effective rents, institutional investors are seeking high performance standards from the managers and consultants with whom they work. Because the due diligence study is the means to confirm whether investors' expectations are likely to be achieved, the importance of due diligence has increased significantly as investors demand greater confidence that the expectations on which they make their financial commitments will be realized.

One purpose of the due diligence investigation is to increase the likelihood that the actual results will be consistent with expectations and that shortfalls from expected results are not attributable to a lack of compliance with the acquisition policy. More specifically, the due diligence process seeks to minimize reasons for performance shortfalls that might have been discovered had a more careful assessment of the potential investment been made prior to the decision to go forward.

Due diligence of prospective acquisitions is crucial irrespective of whatever investment strategy is pursued. For top-down investors concentrating on larger strategic issues concerning portfolio composition, due diligence is a critical safeguard to ensure that each individual transaction placed in the portfolio is consistent with overall strategic objectives and requisite quality standards. For the bottom-up tactician, disavowing any grand scheme and concentrating on assembling a collection of good deals, due diligence is imperative to ensure that each deal acquired meets minimum quality standards.

Not only must the asset acquisition pass the prudent investing standard, its appropriateness as an institutional investment must also be considered. This test is often subsumed within the concept of a so-called institutional grade asset, a much used but little understood and rarely defined term. Even if an asset is determined to have been prudently acquired and is consistent with an institutional grade standard, its appropriateness for the particular investor must be considered in the context of the aggregate portfolio. While the responsible institutional investor should have explicit portfolio composition guidelines in place, in their absence a point of reference is provided by cases in which the U.S. Department of Labor has prevailed in prosecuting alleged violations of the diversification standard of the prudent investing mandate of the ERISA legislation and thereby created case precedent of commitment levels that are deemed inappropriate. Thus, what could be an acceptable investment in isolation may be imprudent in the context of other investments and the overall circumstances of the investor.

Today's fiduciaries recognize that yesterday's good ol' boy style is no longer acceptable. Instead, astute fiduciaries are aggressively putting in place the strategies, systems, and controls needed to survive and maybe prosper in the current turbulent real estate investment market. In a market characterized by risk aversion and uncertainty, discriminating investors are insisting on an appropriate due diligence study as a precondition to any acquisition. Those advising institutional investors who do not proactively initiate sophisticated due diligence will inevitably find themselves at a competitive disadvantage as their market position erodes. Moreover, a due diligence study most likely will not and should not be just a pro forma closing requirement but a precondition to the investment approval decision.

Beyond the contributions that a due diligence study can make to improved investment performance, both implicit and explicit regulatory requirements, issues of legal liability, and responsibilities as a fiduciary and to other involved parties, as well as credit enhancement considerations, contribute to the increasing importance of the due diligence responsibility. The due diligence responsibility is expected to be implemented by the investment manager overseeing a real estate involvement in the fiduciary context. Some managers elect to perform the entire due diligence process, others employ third-party professional firms to implement specific components of the process, and still others turn exculsively to third-party firms to implement it. When due diligence is bought rather than made, managers may coordinate the multiple specialist talents or elect to have a single third-party professional firm coordinate and oversee the entire due diligence process. Because of the increasing importance of due diligence together with potential for conflicts of interest when due diligence is performed exclusively by the manager, those most sensitive to fiduciary concerns favor the use of third-party professional firms to implement the due diligence priority. This chapter adopts this latter view.

LEGAL INFLUENCES AND REQUIREMENTS

Much of the origin of due diligence obligation is traceable to the Securities Act of 1993, which champions the full disclosure mandate for communication between promoters of and prospective investors in a securities offering. The essence of full disclosure embraces the presentation of information in a manner that is not flawed by a misleading statement, a material falsehood, or the failure to disclose a material fact at the time the investment is sold, which in securities parlance is defined as the time when the registration statement becomes effective.

In preparing registration statements, the attorneys working on behalf of those selling the securities undertake certain procedures to ensure that the offering materials meet the full disclosure standard. These procedures are collectively known as due diligence and embrace a standard of reasonable care to investigate sufficiently that there is no reason to believe any omission of a material fact or any misstatements occurred. This reasonable-care standard is consistent with that "required of a prudent man in the management of his own property." Thus, due diligence and prudent investing practices are integrally and inextricably intertwined.

Because of the legal basis of the due diligence process, largely applied by attorneys concerned with ensuring that the registration documents and the offering materials are consistent with the full disclosure standard, due diligence has historically had more legal form than economic substance emphasis. But since legal and economic considerations are interdependent in the investing process, economic considerations influence the evolution of legal requirements. At the same time, the legal requirements shape the economic essence of the investment processes. Accordingly, given its initial legal origins, the due diligence obligation has continued to evolve to embrace an ever-growing economic primacy.

Whereas many have reviewed due diligence as the domain of the lawyer in a securities transaction to confirm that the appropriate documents are in place as well as to investigate the reliability of representations made by the parties to the transaction, in truth due diligence involves not merely pro forma legal compliance but, more important, the fundamental economic integrity of a contemplated capital commitment.

The traditional view of due diligence from the legal perspective focuses on confirming compliance with full disclosure standards with the objective of shielding the securities issuer from liability. Accordingly, it is critical to recognize that compliance with a full disclosure securities regulatory standard may have only the most peripheral relationship to the economic issues of concern to the investor.

As a consequence of the disclosure compliance emphasis of legally oriented due diligence, the prospectus contains considerable material that has only a peripheral relationship to the investment's ultimate outcome, is written from such a negative perspective that few who read it would ever dare invest, and omits much of the information of most concern to the investor. Specifically, the investor is very interested in knowing that all of the relevant research was performed, the economics of the proposed investment appear to meet or surpass articulated investment objectives, and there are no "fatal flaws" that might prevent realization of the investment objectives.

In an investment decision involving a fiduciary, which characterizes the preponderance, if not all, of institutional real estate investment involvements, the implications of the fiduciary standard embrace the concept of prudent investing. Thus, the common-law duty of the fiduciary requires him or her to "observe how men of prudence, discretion and intelligence manage their own affairs, not in regard to speculation, but in regard to the permanent disposition of their funds, considering the probable income, as well as the probable safety of the capital invested" [*Harvard College* v. *Amory* 9 Pick. 26 Mass. 446 (1830)]. This standard of "prudence, discretion and intelligence" involves due diligence as a precondition for major capital commitments.

Indeed, the concept of due diligence is fundamental to regulation of securities transactions. Basic to a securities transaction is the concept of the investment contract. In transactions where the investment is sold on the basis that there will be continuing management, by either the sponsor or a third party, and where investors buy for the purpose of achieving a return on their investment, the essential attributes of an investment contract are present. The investor relies on the sponsoring management in a fiduciary relationship. *Black's*

Law Dictionary defines a fiduciary as "a person having duty, created by his undertaking, to act primarily for another's benefit in matters connected with such undertaking." A fiduciary relationship exists where one party looks to another to act on his or her behalf in a business matter. Due diligence is fundamental to the fiduciary's responsibility for prudent investment decision making.

While securities regulations may not explicitly apply to every institutional real estate investment, the essence of the standards is relevant to all of those concerned with prudence and the responsibility associated with fiduciary involvements. Classification as a security is significant, since such classification brings into effect Rule 10-b-5, commonly known as the *primary antifraud provision* of the Securities and Exchange Act of 1934. Titled "Employment of Manipulative and Deceptive Devices," the specific language of Rule 10-b-5 provides:

> It shall be unlawful for any person, directly or indirectly, by the use of any means or instrumentality of interstate commerce, or of the mails, or of any facility of any national securities exchange, (1) to employ any device, scheme, or artifice to defraud, (2) to make any untrue statement of a material fact or omit to state a material fact necessary in order to make the statements made, in the light of the circumstances under which they were made, not misleading, or (3) to engage in any act, practice, or course of business which operates or would operate as a fraud or deceit upon any person, in connection with the purchase or sale of any security.

The due diligence study has the purpose of confirming the economic integrity of the investment, the veracity of the representations, the completeness of the information included, and the general compliance with prudent investing standards. Consequently, responsible due diligence is, at a minimum, an effective means of confirming that the contemplated investment commitment is neither fraudulent nor deceitful.

Conditions that create a security based on the federal definition apply at the state level as well. While some states employ a full disclosure standard as does the SEC, others apply a subjective test to determine whether or not the security in question may be offered to the public. Illustrative of this substantive law approach to regulating real estate securities is Section 10280 of the Real Estate Syndicate Act of the State of California, which applies to offerings involving

100 or fewer investors and is administered by the Department of Real Estate:

> The commissioner may refuse to issue a permit under Section 10271 unless he finds that the proposed plan of business of the applicant and the proposed issuance of real estate syndicate securities are fair, just and equitable, that the applicant intends to transact its business fairly and honestly, and that the real estate syndicate securities which it proposes to issue and the methods to be used by it in issuing them are not such as, in his opinion, will work a fraud on the purchaser thereof.

Independently of whether or not the securities are formally registered, the disclosure requirements and subjective standards still apply. Consequently, a disappointed purchaser can rely on these grounds in suing for recovery.

When a broker-dealer offers an investment security, prospective investors can rely on the expectation that the broker-dealer has implemented an appropriate due diligence investigation. The essence of this expectation was captured in a landmark Securities and Exchange Commission ruling:

> By associating himself with a proposed offer, the underwriter impliably represents that he has made such an investigation in accordance with professional standards. The investors properly rely on this added protection which has a direct bearing on their appraisal of the reliability of the representations in the prospectus [*The Richmond Corporation*, 41, SEC 398 (1963)].

Beyond the inherent investment merit and quality of a particular transaction on a generalized basis, the suitability of that transaction for a specific investor is considered. The concept of suitability is explicitly articulated in the National Association of Securities Dealers' specific suitability rule, spelled out in Section 2 of Article III of the NASD *Rules of Fair Practice,* as follows:

> In recommending to a customer the purchase, sale, or exchange of any security, a member shall have reasonable grounds for believing that the recommendation is suitable for such customer upon the basis of the facts, if any, disclosed by such customer as to his financial situation needs.

Thus, the due diligence responsibility embraces concerns for both the investment opportunity generally and its appropriateness for the investor specifically.

An important influence on the expectations of standards of due diligence in real estate transactions in the institutional setting is the broad language of ERISA concerning the definition of a fiduciary and the expectation of the fiduciary's duties. Specifically, Section 404 (a) (1) (B) addresses the expectation of a fiduciary in carrying out his or her duties as follows:

> With the care, skill, prudence, and diligence under the circumstances then prevailing that a prudent man acting in a like capacity and familiar with such matters would use in the conduct of an enterprise of a like character and with like aims.

Thus, the diligence expected is the central thrust in the determination of the appropriate level of due diligence in a real estate transaction by an institutional investor.

ORGANIZATIONAL CONTEXT

Since decision making occurs in an organizational setting, the roles of the different participants and their functions within the organization in creating the real estate investment are crucial to understanding the context of the due diligence study. Consideration of the context in which due diligence occurs is fundamental to determining how the due diligence function affects the realization of investment objectives. Crucial to the effectiveness of a due diligence study are the circumstances governing its preparation, especially the motives and qualifications of those involved in creating and reviewing its contents.

The due diligence study provides information that can be the basis for an investment decision to be made by persons other than those who prepared the study. Consequently, the due diligence study does not normally include a decision recommendation, although in some instances an investor retaining a third-party professional firm may extend the range of issues beyond those customarily considered in a due diligence study to ask for recommendations concerning certain aspects of the investment decision. To the extent that the assignment involves recommendations, the willingness of those who might act on the recommendations can influence the probable future investment outcome.

Here it is helpful to consider that the acquisition process in the fiduciary context is logically separated into three distinct and preferably independent phases: (1) origination of the opportunity, which may include structuring and negotiating the acquisition; (2) evaluation of the proposed investment; and (3) approval of the investment commitment. Typically, the origination function is the purview of an acquisition group, while evaluation is performed by a different department specializing in such assessments, often with the involvement of other functions such as property management, portfolio management, investor relations, legal, and accounting. The ultimate approval should be by the board and/or senior management, with no person responsible for the previous activities having a deciding vote in the decision.

Some organizations view the second step, the evaluation of the investment following its origination and prior to its approval, as the essence of due diligence. In some settings, due diligence involves an investment evaluation. In other settings, due diligence consists of the review and confirmation of an analysis that has already been prepared. Where an investing organization has a separate unit that reviews the investment proposals, the task should be considered due diligence by individuals not directly involved in creating the investment. Also, a third-party professional firm is often involved in this process as well. Thus, a fundamental issue for a due diligence study is the organizational relationship by whom and how the study is created and used.

Consequently, the due diligence study can be implemented in varying combinations of the division or group responsible for originating the investment opportunity, another business unit within the same organization that is not involved in the origination of the investment opportunity, and/or third-party professionals that deal with a single, a few, many, or all of the issues that influence the investment's probable future performance as broadly defined. Critical factors to consider are:

- Who is to be involved?
- What are their qualifications?
- What are the specifications for their roles and responsibilities?
- Which issues are being addressed?
- What types of investigations will be pursued?
- What depth of investigation is needed?
- What is the role of third-party professionals?

- What documentation is desired?
- What form of final work product is desired?
- Are any recommendations—yes/no, modify, pursue further investigations—desired?

Most organizations performing due diligence work are more vague than specific on these and related issues. Over time, the real estate investing sector will likely become more specific concerning these issues.

When real estate securities programs are offered to the public, an array of issues concerning the due diligence responsibility for such offerings are raised. In the past, those responsible for marketing a real estate securities product through a large securities firm's sales system often conducted or directed the due diligence activity. Those who recognize that this dual responsibility creates a conflict of interest have assigned the due diligence assessment to a department other than the sales force, perhaps the corporate finance or the financial consulting department.

In a broker-dealer network composed of largely independent securities salespersons, who often represent themselves as financial planners, the individual selling the securities relies on the principals of the firms with which they are affiliated to conduct the due diligence activity. But since many of these firms are themselves rather small, a comprehensive due diligence study can be uneconomical, which leads them to rely on standardized due diligence reports. Also, for purposes of economy, various smaller broker-dealer firms and regional brokerage firms may combine forces to conduct due diligence on a more economical shared-cost basis. Among the possible resolutions to these organizational issues are an integrated due diligence approach by the sponsor that competently addresses the critical issues, independent investigation involving third-party professionals, standardization of the due diligence format, and the formation of alliances of multiple firms to conduct due diligence.

Although the due diligence study should not be viewed as implicit assurance that the appropriate tasks have been undertaken, as a practical matter, third-party professionals effective in implementing due diligence may serve organizations whose internal departments and operations may lack the resources or expertise to study an issue that could have a major impact on the potential investment.

DUE DILIGENCE STANDARDS

While some elements of the due diligence study are amenable to objective quantification, others are more qualitative, subjective, and judgmental. Certainly due diligence is an evolving discipline. The literature on the subject often reflects a legal perspective concerning the compliance with disclosure, the adequacy of representations, and confirmation that required documents are included rather than addressing elements of economic integrity. Thus, the emphasis of due diligence has historically been more on form than on substance. Increasingly, however, the concern is with substance rather than merely form.

Organizations must think through how extensive and thorough a due diligence procedure to implement. Consequently, a key issue for due diligence is scarcity of resources. Accordingly, in determining how thorough due diligence should be, a more exhaustive due diligence study is necessary due to the historically disappointing performance of real estate during the last several years, the excellent cost-benefit ratio achieved by spending money up front versus at the end of an engagement, significant regulatory risk due to ERISA and the SEC, and the economic argument that substantial profit opportunities exist due to the inefficient market.

In assessing the pertinent standards of due diligence, especially since it is an evolving discipline, it is important to draw a distinction between aspirational standards, which might embrace what is desired in an ideal world—one not limited by resources, information reliability and availability, time pressures, or any other constraint—and the practicalities of the contemporary marketplace, which is subject to all of the pressures, constraints, and competing interests that characterize contemporary business generally and investing specifically. At the same time, it is important to recognize that practice is defined not as the lowest common denominator, as represented by the most cavalier or least sophisticated investor, but as what prudent fiduciaries consider reasonable decision-making procedures by prudent fiduciaries at that point in time under the specific circumstances.

Addressing the pertinent standards for due diligence involves multiple considerations, including:

1. *Industry standards:* What are the standards of investment decision making for participants in real estate transactions overall?

2. *Fiduciary responsibility:* What are the implications of a fiduciary and its decision-making authority on behalf of a beneficiary?

3. *Regulatory compliance:* How do regulatory standards influence the decision making by participants in the investment marketplace? (Among the pertinent regulatory standards are those concerned with securities regulations, financial institutions, and pension investment.)

4. *Investor policies:* How do the specific policies and procedures of the investor on whose behalf the investment decision is being made influence the procedure by which that decision should be made?

5. *Investment manager procedures:* How do the investment manager's procedures influence responsibilities vis-à-vis the clients it represents?

6. *Specific contract:* How do the particular provisions of the contract between the investor and the investment manager influence how decisions are made?

Due diligence must be considered at these multiple levels from the very general to the particulars of the specific transaction.

DUE DILIGENCE IMPLEMENTATION

The degree to which the investor's investment policy, strategy, portfolio composition, and property acquisition criteria are articulated influences the implementation of due diligence in real estate transactions. If an investment is to be evaluated in the abstract, not in the context of particular investment policies and procedures, the due diligence assessment necessarily is more general than precise. The greater the specificity of the investor's criteria and guidelines, the more precise the due diligence investigation can be. Indeed, in the desirable but highly unusual circumstance where the particular scope, depth of investigation, and parameters for the due diligence assessment are expressly articulated, implementation of due diligence can be especially focused.

The practicalities of implementing due diligence require the cooperation of various parties who have varying relationships to the property, access to a large and diverse collection of documents, and physical access to the property, including spaces occupied and controlled by tenants under leases. The effective due diligence study involves significant preplanning and preparation to identify what information is needed from whom, in what format, and during what time frame. In this process, the due diligence analyst identifies what information is needed, communicates those information needs to the appropriate client/decision maker, and obtains the support of the client/decision maker in implementing the assignment. Usually the client/decision maker will delegate collection and organization of requested information to certain individuals within his or her organization as well as to various outside professional advisors. In addition, the client/decision maker will introduce, usually through a letter, the due diligence consultant to those persons with whom the consultant must interact and authorize them to provide full information and cooperation to the due diligence consultant. Then the consultant will contact these individuals directly to conduct interviews, examine the relevant books and records, and make physical inspections of the property. Since engineering and construction specialists are often involved in these inspections, the due diligence consultant must anticipate appropriate coordination of these specialty disciplines.

Implementation of due diligence can be on a generalized basis, essentially involving a third-party professional firm reviewing the transactions according to certain general standards. Alternatively, and preferably, it can incorporate this review plus a determination that the proposed acquisition meets with pre-identified acquisition criteria. These criteria would include explicit, general policy statements concerning a property's attributes and specifications, tenancy composition and lease provisions, prior financial performance, property management structures, financial characteristics, projected investment performance, compliance with government regulations, and competitive position in its submarket and region.

Data identification, collection, and confirmation are critical to the implementation of due diligence. Compiling this information involves dealing with multiple departments within and multiple advisors to the organization that previously owned and operated the building, as well as their counterparts in the prospective purchaser's organization. Certain information needed for the due diligence process must be generated independently of those involved with the current and prospective operations of the property. Some of this information is obtained from secondary sources; other information may involve primary research, either contracted to a specialist organization or conducted by the organization performing the due diligence assessment.

Because multiple specialties and subspecialties are involved, increasingly the challenge is to have the full due diligence study led by professionals with strong capabilities and a broad business orientation. Unless all reports and analyses are integrated into a comprehensive assessment of the property, the ultimate decision may fall short of the investor's objectives, criteria, and desires.

A fundamental challenge to implementing the due diligence assessment is the diversity of issues and professional specialties that must be addressed prior to a reasoned and confident decision. For example, the environmental specialist is equipped to identify certain chemical implications of a site's past, present, and prospective condition, while assessment of the legal risk associated with the purchaser's response to the environmental consultant's recommendations is in the purview of a lawyer who combines a general real estate and business orientation with an environmental specialization. Assessment of specific provisions in tenant leases and complex financial relationships falls within the legal discipline generally, but the issues involved draw on legal subspecialties rather than on the general real estate specialty. Among other issues involving multiple disciplines and specialties are land use controls pertaining to public jurisdiction, private jurisdiction over the subdivision or special district in which the property is based, and unique restrictions on allowable uses, activities, and promotional identification pertaining to the entire property or particular units within it.

The comprehensiveness of due diligence investigation is evolving; there is no standard imposed by regulations, endorsed by professional associations, or generally accepted by the real estate investing community. What might be considered adequate by one investor or manager could be considered totally insufficient by another. Thus, due diligence can be considered to embrace a general orientation to question and confirm critical assumptions and information through a comprehensive investigation of those factors that influence an investment program's and property's prospective financial performance.

As noted previously, a comprehensive due diligence assessment involves a review and inspection of virtually every document pertaining to the property, including financial and economic reports generated by third-party professionals; all pertinent documents involving contractual relationships among tenants, suppliers, and employees; all financial documentation relating to debt and equity investors; and all documents concerned with regulatory compliance. Beyond inspection of documents specific to the property, the due diligence study investigates information concerning the environment in which the property operates, some of which is contained in documents and much of which must be accessed through interviews. This environmental information relates to economic conditions in general and to factors influencing the demand for the property's space in particular; the competition for the property's space, both existing and prospective new facilities; the economics of property operations, including labor, utilities, taxes, services, and supplies; financial market conditions, especially those relating to costs of capital and financing terms; regulatory factors concerning the property's operations broadly defined; and physical considerations relating to the property's improvements as well as the land on which the improvements are placed.

The implementation of a comprehensive due diligence process involves consideration of issues at the levels of the investment fund or program, the manager of the investment program, and the particular property(ies) that comprises the portfolio. To begin, it is critical to gain a clear understanding of precisely which interests the proposed investment contains. The assessment of the particular investment fund or program involves consideration of seven critical elements:

1. Management.
2. Property.
3. Compensation.
4. Investment criteria.
5. Portfolio composition.
6. Rights, responsibilities, and decision making.
7. Liquidity and exit strategy.

Each element is discussed briefly next.

Management.   The organization and people that will be responsible for managing the investment is critical to its success. Specific management issues are discussed later in this section.

Property.   Property considerations generally involve micro knowledge of the building per se, macro knowledge of the market in which the property is based, and an analysis of the financial attributes of the investment. Several property-specific elements are also discussed later in this section.

Compensation.   Compensation should be assessed in the context of the particular investment program structure and strategy, the services to be provided, the involvement and role of third parties, compensation arrangements, and the implications of those arrangements for realizing the investment goals. Of concern is not only the relative and absolute levels of compensation but also how the compensation arrangements may motivate key managers to work to realize the investor's objectives.

Investment Criteria.   The degree to which the subject investment meets the investor's particular criteria and objectives, including location, property size, property features, financial ratios, return on investment, time horizon, and risk issues, merits careful assessment.

Portfolio Composition.   How the contemplated investment will influence the overall composition of the portfolio generally and its expected risk also requires careful consideration.

Rights, Responsibilities, and Decision Making.   The provisions of the contractual arrangements between the manager and the investor concerning the relative rights, responsibilities, and decision-making involvements are crucial. These issues embrace concerns of corporate governance, accountability, and authority. The relative involvement by different decision makers, as well as understanding who is expected to do what and how participants' performance may influence realization of the investment goals, must be addressed.

Liquidity and Exit Strategy.   How the investment might be terminated, what influence the investor can have on termination timing and decisions, and the means by which the investor might transfer his or her interest if desiring to terminate his or her involvement with the property at an early date are crucial considerations.

Following the assessment of the terms of the investment program or fund, attention is directed to the investment manager and subsequently the property(ies) that comprises the portfolio. Since the purchase of an investment involves not just the tangible elements of the real property but also the enterprise that selects and manages the property on the investor's behalf, the due diligence investigation involves a number of considerations related to the investment manager's capabilities, including:

1. Business background.
2. Ownership.
3. Organization structure.
4. Staffing.
5. Corporate governance and decision making.
6. Compensation and incentives.
7. Information systems.
8. Research.
9. Property acquisition.
10. Portfolio management.
11. Property management.
12. Investor communications.
13. Financial reporting and accounting.
14. Marketing and client relations.
15. Facilities.
16. Financial review.
17. Legal review.
18. References.
19. Conflicts and self-dealing.

Each of these items is briefly discussed next.

Business Background. The history, evolution, and background of the business are of concern, since these factors can influence business performance. How other business involvements by the manager may complement, be unrelated to, or compete with the basic investment management undertaking on behalf of the investor is important. Understanding the enterprise's objectives and the strategies to pursue them can yield insights as to its probable approach to managing a particular investment situation.

Ownership. Who owns the company, their standing in the business community, their financial strength, objectives, commitment to the business strategy, and commitment to the particular real estate investing activity, and what support and/or synergy the ownership may provide are important points to consider in the due diligence investigation.

Organization Structure. How the business is organized, whether it operates on a centralized or a decentralized basis, whether different activities are carried out through divisions or subsidiaries, the degree to which suppliers or alliances are utilized, and other factors all influence the approach the company may take to managing real estate investments.

Staffing. Staffing considerations include the composition of the company's staff, their training and previous experience, and how long they have been with the organization.

Corporate Governance and Decision Making. The role of management and/or the board in various decisions, identities and backgrounds of board members, their active involvement in key decisions versus passive concurrence, single decision-making authority versus concurrence by multiple persons, and informal style versus formal documentation are considerations here.

Compensation and Incentives. How the company's staff are compensated, what incentive programs exist, and the implications of those incentive programs are items to include in the due diligence process.

Information Systems. How information is processed, the degree and type of computerization, sources of information, and information sophistication are key points in this area.

Research. Considerations here include the role of research in the real estate investing process, how the function is organized and staffed, what information sources are utilized, what issues are the subject of the research function, and the role research plays in the decision-making process.

Property Acquisition. This area addresses how the acquisition function is organized, the articulation of investment policy, how opportunities originate, the role of internal staff and/or outside brokers, relationships with outside brokers, how the acquisition analysis is conducted, the use of third-party professionals, and the acquisition decision process.

Portfolio Management. The approach to portfolio management, how the function is organized and staffed, the scope of concerns, the degree to which certain tasks and activities are performed internally or contracted out, and the role of portfolio management in key decisions are issues to address here.

Property Management. Considerations here are how intensively acquired properties are managed, internal function versus external contracting, orientation to adding value through property improvements, tenant relations programs, and other factors.

Investor Communications. This area addresses how the investor communication function is organized, what type of information is communicated, and with what frequency.

Financial Reporting and Accounting. The internal accounting and bookkeeping procedures, how the function is organized, the role of third-party accounting firms, and whether financial information is used purely for reporting purposes or also for decision-making purposes are important considerations.

Marketing and Client Relations. This area focuses on how relationships are created, how the function is organized, the involvement of marketing professionals in business decision making, and the types and cost effectiveness of the firm's marketing activities.

Facilities. The functionality and efficiency of the space in which the business operates, its flexibility, its economics, and what message it sends are key considerations here.

Financial Review. This area includes financial statements, tax returns, bank balances, and other confirmation of the company's financial standing.

Legal Review. This area deals with confirmation of legal form, compliance with licensing registration, assessment of litigation, including incidence and disposition, what disputes are pending and what are potential disputes, and their possible outcomes and implications.

References.   References include clients, service providers, tenants, and current and former employees.

Conflicts and Self-Dealing.   The investigation should review existing and possible future interests on the part of the business and/or its employees that could conflict with the proposed investing activity.

The comprehensive due diligence investigation of a particular property entails a number of considerations, including:

1. Property definition and description.
2. Site analysis.
3. Design and functionality.
4. Assessment of physical components and their condition.
5. Property use and activity.
6. Building services and amenities.
7. Access and transportation services.
8. Neighborhood analysis.
9. Market size.
10. Demand source.
11. Competitive market supply analysis.
12. Financing and ownership.
13. Financial structure.
14. Tenants.
15. Lease arrangements.
16. Property operations.
17. Management.
18. Financial performance.
19. Health, safety, and environmental quality.
20. Legal issues.
21. Risk assessment.

Property Definition and Description.   Fundamental to the real estate investment decision is specification and comprehension of the property interests being acquired. Beyond identification of the physical asset involved, it is critical to articulate clearly and precisely which specific interests are being obtained. To the extent that the investment does not involve acquisition and control of all of the interests associated with the property, careful investigation of those interests not being acquired, the nature of the interest possessed by third parties, the particular terms of those contracts, and their circumstances and motivations are fundamental to understanding the proposed transaction. Thus, definition and description involve addressing title issues, surveys, property profiles, easements, rights of way, encroachments, and related considerations that influence the property's utility and other parties' current and prospective claims to the asset and its income.

Site Analysis.   Basic to the assessment of a real estate investment is consideration of the land. Among the areas of investigation are dimensions, topography, soil conditions, vegetation, views, utilities, drainage, safety, and impacts of adjacent properties and their uses. Also of particular concern are potential physical risks, including flooding, earthquake, and fire, all of which have been major sources of calamity and financial loss in recent years. The implications of the sites' physical characteristics for the functionality, economics, and risk of space-using activities, including parking, in both the present and the future, need to be carefully considered. The impacts of adjacent properties on the subject property that should be considered include present or prospective noise from activities, traffic, and other structures; views, from present or possible improvements, as allowed under current or prospective land use control; and odor and adverse air quality impacts from emissions from manufacturing or processing activities on nearby parcels. Particularly if future improvements to a site are contemplated, it is important to consider how the site's attributes influence the physical and financial feasibility of such improvements.

Design and Functionality.   Properties characterized by superior design and a high degree of functionality inherently have greater appeal to tenants and therefore possess more enduring value than do those that are aesthetically displeasing and unresponsive to user needs. Space whose functionality promotes the purposes for which it is designed will be more valued than space whose design and layout promote dysfunctionality.

Allowing for the truism that beauty is in the eyes of the beholder, every physical element, and especially large, tangible elements such as properties, conveys a message. The shape, proportion, color, texture, spatial arrangements, materials, workmanship, and design style all communicate. These building communications influence the moods, productivity, comfort, and receptiveness of those who work in and visit the space. The more positive these communications are, the more appreciated and successful the social and business interactions conducted in that space will be, and therefore the more valuable the space will be.

Assessment of design and functionality provides insights into the relative appeal of the property to tenants, and therefore into its value. Superior design in all elements commands a premium, and therefore the market assigns higher rents to such buildings. When space is functional, less of it is needed to accomplish a particular purpose, and therefore that particular space is more valuable.

Assessment of Physical Components and Their Condition. Elements of the property to be included in an assessment of physical condition include site grading, paving, landscaping, basic structure, roofs, exterior and interior surfaces, signage, lighting, mechanical systems, plumbing systems, electrical systems, HVAC systems, elevators and related vertical and horizontal transportation systems, fire protection systems, security and life safety systems, and drainage systems. The dimensions of the property, floor sizes, numbers of floors, ceiling heights, and average unit sizes also are of concern.

The objective is to address current condition, expected useful life, the cost associated with replacing components, and the cost of maintainance over time and, in so doing, identify general quality, how that quality affects the building's appeal and its ability to provide and support space-using activities, and how those factors relate to financial performance. The comprehensive building evaluation seeks to identify potential problems and determine the related costs of resolving them. A careful building due diligence assessment will identify code and safety issues as well as compliance considerations.

Beyond assessing the particular components of the property, special emphasis is placed on the functionality, obsolescence, and comparative implications of these components. Specifically, how the building may accommodate contemporary office and communications equipment has important implications for its appeal to tenants and therefore for its ultimate investment value. Further, the flexibility and associated economics of the building system to reconfigure tenant spaces has important implications for the property's appeal and value. In addition, the overall quality, health, and safety aspects of mechanical and HVAC systems are of primary importance. The building's overall adaptability to changing space layouts and introduction of new technology is critical to defining tenant appeal and value over time.

The building evaluation often involves specialized engineering and technical knowledge and employing particular testing equipment and on-site surveys of the property. The results are presented in various reports and appropriate technical documents, along with photographs depicting the property's condition and associated problems (if any).

Property Use and Activity. A review of how the property is used generally and relative to its intended uses, as well as activities that take place at and close to the property, is basic to the comprehensive due diligence investigation. This review of property use and activity is important not only because its considerations have implications for the property's appeal to tenants and those who would transact business at the property, but also because significant potential legal risks are associated with uses that occur at a particular property. To the extent that a property attracts those who engage in activities that are contrary to fostering a positive ambiance or, of greater concern, that violate various laws, not only does the property's appeal and value diminish, but the owner may incur substantial legal liability as a consequence of such activities. Specifically, property owners may be liable for illegal activities, such as drug trafficking, that are conducted on their property. While the liability may apply to all property types, it is of greatest concern for apartments and hospitality properties.

The review of property use and activity involves observation and inspection at different times of the day over an extended time period. It also involves interviews with tenants, people who interact with them, and people who are on or within the general vicinity of the property. A comprehensive due diligence investigation will inform the investor about what is happening at the property and how that affects the probable future performance of and risks associated with the investment.

Building Services and Amenities.   Of concern are how information and goods are delivered to the building and the tenants' spaces and how various forms of waste product are removed. The nature, type, frequency, and quality of various services that enable the overall functioning of the building and that support particular tenants are also of concern. Among the building's services are garbage collection, including recycling, mail delivery and pickup, and delivery services. Building amenities include interior art and seating arrangements in public areas, newsstand and convenience stores, banking and ATM outlets, convenient food service, and restaurants and lounges. Whether these services and amenities are contained within the building or readily accessible from without can influence the appeal of the space. Also of concern are the number, quality, and location of restrooms, as well as the convenience and ease of handicap access. Lobby reception, security staff, and on-site maintenance can enhance tenants' and their customers' experience of the building.

Access and Transportation Services.   The means by which users of space and consumers of services offered by tenants occupying the building gain immediate access to the site as well as access to the surrounding neighborhood strongly influence the site's relative appeal and therefore its rent levels and ultimately value. As a rule, for sites designed to accommodate a large number of people for work-related and similar purposes, easy access is an important attribute of the property's appeal. In contrast, for sites that emphasize exclusivity, by contrast, overly eager access may be a negative attribute. Thus, a site's access to walkways, roads, and public transit facilities in its immediate vicinity is a crucial consideration and must be assessed in the context of its intended use and the objectives of both occupants of the property and their clients/visitors.

Access to the neighborhood in which the site is located is also a primary concern. An assessment of the transportation system servicing the immediate neighborhood is an important determinant of the property's relative appeal. Specific consideration needs to be given to train, subway, and bus services, private van and taxi services, road systems, bike paths, and public walkways. The capacity of such systems, the portion of present capacity that is utilized, factors that might constrain capacity, the potential to expand capacity, and possible changes that might affect transit services all need to be considered in a comprehensive due diligence investigation.

Neighborhood Analysis. Parcels close to the subject property have a major impact on the relative appeal of the subject property. Consequently, consideration of present and prospective uses of adjacent parcels is an integral element of due diligence. This investigation involves an inventory of those properties located within the subject property area, and consideration of current uses, and particularly prospective uses, that could alter the environment of the subject property. While some of these uses are positive, such as providing services or creating a physical environment that enhances the subject property, other uses may be presently or potentially negative. The objective is to understand the neighborhood and how what is happening or might happen there affects the quality of life for current—and, importantly, prospective—occupants of the subject property.

Market Size. The size of the market in which the property is located is another factor in determining the property's probable future performance. Important in assessing the market is how the market is defined, not only by absolute population figures and numbers of companies but also by the composition of the overall market. Here attention to particular market segments and their attributes, both in general and how they relate to the target market for the subject property, is critical. Further, the relationship of the size of the property to the market in which it is located influences both anticipated capture rates needed to achieve performance targets and the relative dominance that property might achieve in the market. This assessment inherently involves a trade-off: A property that is large relative to its market can be more visible and prominent within that market, but it must also capture a larger market share than a smaller property. Further, understanding how the market is defined in terms of physical dimensions, psychographics, and segment attributes is fundamental to the assessment process. Market size is assessed through information derived from market data organizations, as well as primary research to which information-specific analysis is applied.

Demand Source. Basic to an assessment of an investment opportunity is understanding the source of the demand for the space the property offers. Certainly, to the extent that the property is fully occupied, the source of demand assumes less apparent importance, although understanding why the current tenants originally chose that site is basic to determining the prospect that they will remain there. Also, given the ever-changing contemporary economic environment, failure to anticipate change in space-using preferences and patterns is myopic. So, even if the space is currently fully occupied, the discriminating analyst considers the fundamental source of demand for the property. This analysis involves asking and answering such questions as:

- Why do people desire to locate their business and/or live in this particular region?
- What is a profile of these prospective tenants, including their circumstances, financial resources, space use needs, and objectives?
- To what degree is this demand subject to change?
- What could cause this demand to diminish or even disappear?
- Does this particular area have an inherent appeal, or is the attraction primarily a function of a major employer or economic segment?
- If the demand is largely dependent on a major employer or economic segment, what risks are those entities subject to?
- To what degree does the subject property satisfy the attributes that these sources of demand desire?

Answers to these questions provide insight into the demand source, its strength, and the probable future performance of the subject property.

Competitive Market Supply Analysis.   While consideration of larger-scale market conditions for the particular property type and the metropolitan region in which it is located is highly relevant, also important is micro-level research on demand and pricing conditions in the property's immediate submarket. This research involves appraisals, market analyses, and feasibility studies, as well as interviews with local real estate brokers, other real estate professionals, and tenants. The due diligence process seeks to identify the property's general market and submarket as well as assess its competitive position in those markets. The thrust of this phase of the due diligence process is to confirm the potential revenue the property will generate as a consequence of the quantity of its space that will be demanded in the market at particular rent levels. To the extent that there is a marketing plan for the property as well as analyses of how the property compares to the competition, these materials should be reviewed to determine the property's likely performance.

Financing and Ownership.   A review of the property's financing and ownership logically begins with identifying all investors, owners, financial partners, lenders, and lenders' agents and representatives of these parties. The documents concerning financial ownership arrangements, including notes, loans, revolving credit agreements, mortgages, deeds of trust, security agreements, other documents relating to property indebtedness, ground leases, and the like, need to be obtained and reviewed. All communications to investors and lenders over the previous several years should be examined. Any recent transactions concerning the acquisition or disposition of interest in or components of the property(ies) should be reviewed. Also appropriate for consideration are all documents relating to partnership and joint venture arrangements concerning the property.

It is particularly important to consider the relationships among different parties that have financial interests in and/or provide services to the property. Were these relationships created, and do they now exist on the basis of a third-party, arm's length, objective negotiation? Or does one or more of the parties providing services and/or participating in the venture's financial performance have a prior family, friendship, supplier, client, or business involvement that introduces a consideration other than their purely professional involvement with the project? At worst, self-dealing and/or preferential treatment could materially compromise the investment outcome. The appearance of potential impropriety, especially in the institutional fiduciary investing context, may create problems among certain constituencies. The due diligence process is concerned with determining the existence of these actual or potential conflicts, considering whether they have been appropriately disclosed, and assessing how they may affect the ultimate outcome of the investment.

Financial Structure.   The relationships among the financial participants in the project have a crucial impact on the potential investment return. The objective of this phase of the due diligence process is to discover the financial commitments, claims, and priorities of the different parties to the financing of the property. In addition to standard and specialized debt financing arrangements, the role of land leases, master leases, condominium interests, options, and other financing arrangements needs to be considered. The thrust of the analysis is both the disposition of income from operations and the distribution of proceeds of refinancing or sale of the property. Thus, understanding claims and their priorities on cash flow operations, refinancing, and sale is critical. This process involves specification of such factors as fixed interest, contingent or participating interest, index interest, guaranteed payments, priority payments, subordinated participations, and other specialized profit-sharing arrangements. The objective is to determine who gets what under different scenarios and in what priority.

Tenants.   Since investment returns are dependent on the property's appeal to the tenants who will occupy it, careful assessment of the property's tenants is an integral element of the comprehensive due diligence investigation. Just as no business can succeed without successful customers, no real estate investment can succeed without successful tenants. Consequently, having strong tenants that are motivated and capable of paying rent and whose expanding businesses create the need for additional space is integral to a prosperous real estate investment. But although these factors are necessary conditions, they are not sufficient, for tenants' satisfaction and desire to remain in the space are crucial. Too often, buildings attract successful, growing tenants whose growth creates a demand for additional space, which then motivates these growing tenants to move to a competing property. Consequently, a successful tenant whose growth causes it to move represents a financial exposure to a building just as does a tenant whose adverse business performance makes it unable to pay rent.

Tenants are investigated on both an individual and an aggregate basis. At the individual tenant level, among the factors to address are the tenant's identity, its business, how that business complements or detracts from the building, the tenant's financial position, how the tenant is using the space, the tenant's basic business direction and future plans, the implications of the tenant's future business in terms of space requirements, its satisfaction with the building, and the likelihood that it will renew.

At the aggregate level, the investigation considers the following:

- What are the tenants' common attributes?
- What differentiates the tenants from one another?

- What is the relative composition of tenant occupancy by different types of businesses?
- Does the building attract smaller or larger companies?
- If larger companies, does the building attract headquarters, regional offices, or satellites?
- Do the tenant decision makers reside in the space or in some other location?
- How does the composition of the tenant mix influence the building's stature in the community as perceived by existing tenants? By prospective tenants?

This understanding of tenants' circumstances, future plans, desires, and motivations allows the due diligence investigator to draw conclusions about the property's probable performance.

Lease Arrangements. The financial and contractual arrangements between building ownership and tenants are reflected in leases, whose features define current income, prospective value, and risk. A critique of lease arrangements involves abstracting the basic financial provisions and primary rights, obligations, and responsibilities of tenant and landlord. Beyond the fundamentals of basic rent, adjustments to rent over time, and provisions for reimbursement of certain costs and changes in costs are such provisions as renewal options, limitations and what types of tenants might be allowed in the building, most-favored-nations clauses (which specify that no subsequent tenant shall enjoy more favorable lease terms) concerning future lease rates and adjustments thereto, and the like. It is important that the process extract critical financial information from leases to determine the component building blocks of the property's revenue over time. Thus, a careful analysis of leases provides the basis information concerning year-by-year cash flow and occupancy.

Among the documents of concern are copies of all leases, abstracts of leases, parking and storage agreements, the rent roll and lease summary, the list of security deposits, lease amendments, lease escalation letters, side letter agreements, all correspondence concerning current leasing activity and outstanding leasing proposals, the standard lease form, specialized equipment financing, and operating leases.

Property Operations. The economics of the property's operations should be evaluated in terms of both the details of historical performance and prospective future performance. If expectations for the future diverge substantially from past results, the reasons for the divergence should be identified, evaluated, and confirmed. Among the elements of property operation to consider are salaries for personnel, building supplies, HVAC costs, water and sewer costs, repairs and maintenance, elevator repair, decorating and painting, administrative costs, special assessments and taxes, real estate taxes, management costs, marketing and promotional expenses, leasing commissions, insurance, security, and other types of expenses.

The evaluation process involves consideration of what these expenses have been, including a review of invoices, contracts, purchase orders, service agreements, and related contractual documents. The document review should be supplemented through interviews with providers of those services, as well as with competitors and others knowledgeable about the economics of such services, to confirm their reasonableness. Insurance policies, labor contracts, collective bargaining agreements, employment agreements, and employee benefit plans, including various types of insurance, profit-sharing, and deferred compensation plans, should all be reviewed.

Capital expenditure plans and budgets should be evaluated, and a detailed assessment of all capital expenditures made within the last several years should be made. Operating statistics for the property should be reviewed on a historical basis to compare cost per foot and unit over time, as a function of occupancy and on a seasonal basis, with emphasis on how the economics of the subject property compare to standards for other properties.

Management.   Investigation of property management involves identification of all parties that provide services to and/or have an oversight responsibility for the property. Pertinent information on such organizations includes determination of business scope, specifically the range of business involvements of such organizations, what services they provide to what types of customers, their primary client and customer relationships, their organizational structure, biographical information on key executives and other members of the company, and a review of historical and financial statements and related considerations. Particularly important is understanding what services each organization provides or proposes to provide to the property and the financial arrangements for such services. In addition to the historical information specific to the management organization, all documents concerning the company's relationship to the property should be identified and evaluated. In addition, interviews with senior executives of that organization, as well as those members of the firm that are actively providing the services, should be conducted.

Among the management organizations to consider are all those with major contracts to provide building services, including property management, building and elevator maintenance, cleaning, security, and window washing. A particularly important consideration is existing and potential conflicts among companies providing services to the property. If the property employs individuals directly to provide services, copies of the relevant employment agreements, noncompetition agreements, indemnification agreements, bonding arrangements, and similar contracts should be identified and reviewed.

Financial Performance. The investigations discussed above are synthesized in the property's financial performance. This analysis includes detailed consideration of the historical operating and financial statements for the property. It involves application of the accounting analyses of current operations, sources and uses of funds, and the statement of financial position. Of concern are revenues expended, expenses incurred, and income generated. The analysis needs to be made on both a cash and an accrual basis, since different realization and timing considerations can exert major influences.

It is important to understand what cash was generated by the property and how that cash was allocated or disbursed. It is critical to determine what capital expenditures have been made, how they were funded, and their impacts on the property's value. Since alternative interpretations can determine whether an expenditure is an expense related to current operations or a capital improvement recorded on the balance sheet, it is important to understand the economics of such expenditures, their accounting treatment, and their implications for the property's value.

Since tax motivations can often influence how certain expenditures are classified, it is important to carefully consider how tax motivations may have influenced the classification of such expenditures. Expenditures for properties owned by private investors with strong tax-planning motivations may differ from those for properties held by institutional, largely tax-exempt investors.

Among the documents employed in assessing financial performance are historical operating and financial statements, detailed offering statements and budgets, leasing and operating plans, cash flow performance, audited and unaudited financial statements, tax returns, listings of accounts payable and accrued liabilities, listings and agings of accounts receivable, financial projections and budgets, and investor communications concerning financial performance. If third parties, such as pension consultants, have evaluated the property's financial performance, copies of those evaluations should be obtained. It is desirable to obtain the financial information for the last three years or, preferably, the last five years.

Health, Safety, and Environmental Quality.   Enhanced public awareness and increased regulation of health and safety issues specifically and environmental quality factors generally have raised the importance of these considerations in the comprehensive due diligence investigation of a particular property. While the assessment of the site, as well as its physical components and their condition, embraces numerous health, safety, and environmental quality considerations, an explicit review of how these factors influence a property's appeal to present and prospective tenants and to those who might transact business at the property is an integral part of a comprehensive due diligence investigation. This investigation should include compliance with particular regulations, as well as an assessment of potential risks derived from an owner's overall responsibility.

While regulations have proliferated concerning the environmental, health, and safety consequences of materials used to build a property, as well as pollutants generated by activities conducted at the property, the operations of the property generally and safety issues specifically involve important legal factors. Any conditions that contribute to a less than safe environment could create liability and thereby diminish the value of the property. Consequently, the comprehensive due diligence investigation addresses health, safety, and environmental quality considerations.

Legal Issues.   As discussed previously, the legal aspects of due diligence were traditionally its central thrust. The concerns include confirming compliance with a plethora of legal considerations at the local, county, special district, regional, state, and federal levels, as well as verifying that all requisite documentation for the property investment is available and in an appropriate form. The compliance considerations involve not only public regulations but also private regulations associated with a particular property and the development district in which it is located.

Legal review includes investigating current and pending litigation and contingent liabilities, including vendor/supplier and tenant disputes. Copies of relevant communications with federal, state, and local taxing authorities related to the property should be obtained. Copies of all agreements concerning the property's use are also needed.

Risk Assessment.   Each of the 20 due diligence elements discussed above have associated risk considerations. The objective of the risk assessment phase of the due diligence process is to identify all of these risks in an integrated, coordinated, and objective assessment. The risk assessment process involves consideration of the following:

- What are the potential adverse outcomes?
- What is the likelihood of the outcomes occurring?
- What factors might influence these outcomes?
- To what degree can those factors be predicted and/or controlled?
- What is the potential magnitude of these adverse consequences?
- What is the financial exposure associated with each of these consequences?
- To what degree can these adverse consequences be mitigated through risk management techniques and/or insurance?
- Does the subject investment as it is now presented sufficiently incorporate appropriate risk management features and insurance?
- Is the risk explicitly recognized and appropriately priced?

Ultimately, the risk assessment phase of the due diligence process involves identifying and evaluating the economic consequences of risk to determine that the investment as presented has incorporated the appropriate risk management techniques and reasonably reflects the risks in its pricing. Particularly important is to identify the existence of insurance policies, the amount of coverage, deductibles and limits, and any other special provisions that may influence probable financial recovery.

Although real estate investors historically have thought in terms of future expectations expressed in terms of single-point estimates of probable investment performance, the reality of the investing process, especially for real estate in today's dynamic and uncertain economic environment, is that future investment results are inherently uncertain. A due diligence process that explicitly recognizes the manifold risks of real estate investing offers greater insights than one that presumes a single, most-likely-case outcome. As the consequences of adverse risk outcomes are ultimately translated into impacts on the financial performance of the property, an analytical methodology that directly accommodates assessment of such risks is fundamental to effective due diligence. A probabilistic analysis of multiple scenarios reflecting the alternative outcomes of different sets of investment results is one means of quantifying the consequences of risk and uncertain futures.

A property's future financial performance is uncertain for the very reason that its revenue, expenses, and needed capital expenditures cannot be forecast with absolute precision. Among the multiple forces influencing a property's probable future revenues are the business prospects and plans of existing tenants, which prospective tenants may desire to occupy space, what lease terms competing properties offer existing and prospective tenants, tenants' expectations for improvements, tenants' preferences for lease duration and terms, and what revenues may be achieved from such lease provisions as cost pass-through, inflation indexing, and participation in tenant revenues. Similarly, on the expense side, each line item is subjected to a multitude of factors that influence what expenses may be incurred in operating the property. The nature, amount, timing, cost, and frequency of improvements and enhancement to the structure itself are a function of economic conditions, competitive forces, tenant demands, volatile weather patterns, natural disasters, and shifting regulatory requirements.

The interplay of forces influencing a property's revenues, operating expenses, and capital expenditures cause the projection of probable future cash flows to be inherently uncertain. The uncertainty associated with projections of future operating results is compounded by the multiple forces that influence what a property's future value might be, which in turn influences proceeds that might be realized from the sale or refinancing of an asset.

When the uncertainty associated with a given property is coupled with the collective and combined uncertainties of all the properties that comprise a portfolio of real estate, the forecasting of probable future cash flows for an institutional investor is best viewed in the context of ranges, multiple scenarios, and probabilities rather than a single-point estimate. Consequently, those analytical presentations to support decision making that incorporate a probabilistic treatment of future property and portfolio investment results will provide more realistic and insightful information for the purposes of decision making. While some due diligence approaches have incorporated sensitivity analyses, essentially considering the consequences of stated adjustments to certain critical variables on the overall investment performance, sufficient consideration has too seldom been given to the inherent uncertainty and volatility of future investment performance. Over time, a probabilistic treatment of future property and portfolio cash flow will become more integral to the competent due diligence study.

EVOLVING EXPECTATIONS

Industry standards for due diligence have tightened substantially since the mid-1980s. In the past, the expectations of continued positive market momentum contributed to decisions being made with less intensive review, often based on relationships and subjective rather than objective criteria. Driving acquisition and lending decisions at this time was the necessity to outbid another prospective bidder to acquire a property and/or maintain long-term relationships, as well as the expectation that market value increases would forgive an overvaluation, since investors and lenders expected property values would increase some 5 to 10 percent within 6 to 12 months of funding.

The fact that today's underwriting standards are more stringent than those in the mid-1980s was conclusively confirmed by the Due Diligence Practices Survey of the mortgage lending industry that the Roulac Group performed in 1993. Institutional investors familiar with making financial commitments in a fiduciary context were asked 30 questions requiring their opinions on a total of 242 elements in the real estate investment decision process. Investors were asked to assess the relative importance of different sources of information for real estate decision making, the reliance placed on different types of information in the decision process, and changing investing standards from 1987 to the present.

More than 83 percent of the survey respondents indicated that more rigorous due diligence is performed today than in 1987. Responses showed dramatically that many aspects of due diligence are more or much more rigorous today than they were in 1987. Responses to a series of questions regarding changes in due diligence practices from 1987 to today are summarized below:

	More or Much More
Time devoted to overall due diligence practice	88%
Level of expertise of person responsible for due diligence	80
Emphasis on thorough review and critique of appraisal report	67
More in-depth investigations of borrower's/seller's representations	84
More careful and conservative financial analysis of property and borrower/seller	78

Not only are today's standards for evaluating real estate investments much more stringent, but so are requirements for documenting the effort. Some 88 percent of the survey respondents said that more or much more documentation is required today than in 1987. This enhanced documentation emphasis is largely attributable to greater market sophistication and concern over future litigation. In the mid-1980s, past relationships, creativity, and accommodation characterized real estate financing by lenders. As a consequence, flexibility dominated rigor in the loan underwriting process. The conditions prevalent in the mid-1980s are very different than those that prevail in the mid-1990s.

Awareness of environmental issues today is much advanced over what it was in the 1980s, when pension funds' advisors were insufficiently knowledgeable of environmental investigation compliance requirements of federal Superfund and California state legislation. These fiduciaries did not always investigate environmental compliance issues with as much initiative and thoroughness as is the norm today.

On the federal level, as a consequence of the 1986 Superfund amendment to the Comprehensive Environmental Response, Compensation and Liability Act of 1980, buyers who learn, subsequent to their acquisition, that a property is contaminated can avail themselves of the innocent landowner defense, provided they undertook "at the time of acquisition, all appropriate inquiries into the previous ownership of the property consistent with good commercial and customary practice."

The significance of appropriate pre-acquisition due diligence of environmental issues is underscored by the consideration that the costs associated with environmental cleanup can exceed a property's value. The broad definition of the "potential responsible parties" charged with responsibility for such cleanup costs includes anyone who is associated with generating or disposing of hazardous substances at the property, including current and prior operators of the facility, as well as current and prior owners, which can include lenders as well as equity owners. Not surprisingly, most lenders insist on environmental review as a precondition to advancing funds.

Direct work by the Roulac Group on behalf of institutional investors and the real estate managers that work with them suggests that environmental awareness is insufficient generally and especially in the present risk-averse investment climate. This conclusion is confirmed by the results of a survey of pension advisors and developers to test the awareness of institutional investors concerning their due diligence responsibility and how their advisors are implementing that responsibility. All pension fund advisors surveyed require a full environmental review as a precondition for investment in multifamily projects. Surprisingly, 48 percent of pension advisors who, under ERISA legislation, are fiduciaries charged with adhering to the "prudent investor" standard were unaware of California's 1987 requirement of seller disclosure of environmental contamination.

Interestingly, developers proved to be more informed than institutional investors about the implications of the 1987 California law requiring seller disclosure by an 83 to 52 percent margin, even though pension advisors have fiduciary responsibility for institutional investors' substantial assets, and accordingly their responses reflect inherent risk aversion.

Since a due diligence study will most probably be a precondition to the investment approval decision rather than a perfunctory closing requirement, sellers should recognize that initiating due diligence preparation can facilitate the transaction and enhance the prospects of a deal with advantageous timing and terms. Indeed, some savvy sellers of properties retain independent advisors to prepare a due diligence study of the transaction so that what is offered is not just real estate but a package composed of real estate together with a third-party professional study of issues that will be of concern to a prospective buyer. It should be noted, however, that in circumstances in which a seller retains a due diligence study in anticipation of its use by a prospective purchaser, special care needs to be taken to ensure independence.

CONCLUSION

In today's world, due diligence in real estate transactions certainly is different than in the past, given the character of investments, lower and still declining property prices, sometimes marginal assets, and bottom-fishing strategies pursued by various investors. These troubled market conditions cause due diligence to take on a much more stringent financial orientation. As a consequence, institutional investors and their advisors must take care that a rigid due diligence system does not eliminate properties that fail to meet designated property standards but nonetheless have excellent financial results with even the most conservative assumptions.

One probable future trend of due diligence in real estate transactions will be a greater emphasis on assessing managers' capabilities. Because of the significant discontinuity that has characterized the real estate market, highly variable performance of real estate investments over the last several years, and the great uncertainly about the future prospects of real estate, selecting managers who are adaptable to changing market conditions and responsive to investor needs and specifications will be increasingly important.

Many perceive due diligence as encompassing the objective of translating information concerning the property in the market in which it operates into a forecast of future financial performance and then performing the appropriate investment analysis of that probable future performance. Although an emphasis on financial results is basic to the due diligence study, it alone is insufficient. An important benefit of an independent due diligence assessment provided by independent real estate professionals is the identification of a proposed transaction's risk. Thus, a due diligence study that can effectively highlight and communicate the significant risks to a decision maker represents a major contribution. At the same time, it should be recognized that in many instances, the proliferation of documents and comprehensive reports may tend more to obfuscate than clarify the factors that are critical to the investment's probable future success.

Thus, a major challenge of the due diligence study is to be both comprehensive in coverage, yet succinct and focused in ultimate communication.

The due diligence process can range materially in terms of the issues that are explored, the scope of such explorations, the range and types of analyses pursued, the role of third-party professionals, and the depth of analysis. Each market participant must address where it stands on a continuum of resource commitment to the due diligence process. Certainly the size, complexity, and perceived risk of a proposed transaction, both generally and relative to the investor's overall portfolio, are instrumental in determining the appropriate financial commitment to and sophistication of the associated due diligence process. While the specific elements of an investment exert a major influence on this determination, the decision can be made more effectively if an investor is quite clear about its approach to and philosophy of due diligence in real estate transactions.

While the scope, comprehensiveness, and sophistication of due diligence in real estate transactions have evolved considerably over the last decade and will continue to do so, even the most competent due diligence study is not an insurance policy. The process of due diligence in real estate transactions confirms the reasonableness of the assumptions on which the transaction is premised, that appropriate investigations have been undertaken, that the documentation and process by which the investment was created are in compliance with both regulations and investor-specific standards, and that the investment offers a reasonable risk-adjusted return in the context of the market and circumstances in which it was created.

PART 5

HOW DO WE GET THERE FROM HERE?

CHAPTER 19

EFFECTIVE USE OF REAL ESTATE CONSULTANTS FOR INSTITUTIONAL REAL ESTATE INVESTING

Stephen E. Roulac
The Roulac Group

Scott R. Muldavin
The Roulac Group

INTRODUCTION

Once largely passive, unsophisticated, and implicitly trusting, institutional real estate investors today insist that the strategies and management actions by those who represent them be characterized by expertise and objectivity. Today's institutional real estate investors insist on dramatically higher standards from their professional staff, senior management and board, investment managers, and real estate consultants.

From earliest times, the role of objective expert advice by a knowledgeable but disinterested third party has been recognized. The Greek philosopher Plautus sagely observed:

> Every man, however wise, needs the advice of some sagacious friends in the affairs of life.

The real estate consultant has assumed a role as the most important, and perhaps the only, independent and objective real estate advisor to institutional investors. Since their compensation is not determined

Certain portions of this paper are adapted from articles by the author that previously appeared in *Appraisal Review Journal* (co-authored with Richard D. May and Daniel T. Vigano), *Real Estate Investing,* and *Real Estate Issues* (see references for full citations). The authors would like to acknowledge the contributions of Gil Castle and Jack P. Friedman.

by investment performance and they are typically removed from the political pressures faced by the senior management and board, real estate consultants can provide critically needed independence.

The role and effective use of real estate consultants by institutional investors need to be reconsidered in light of market uncertainty, higher performance expectations, demanding regulatory compliance burdens, and the historical performance of the real estate sector during the last several years. Most important, given consultants' unique independence and objectivity, institutional investors need to consider a more expanded definition of the real estate consultant's role that puts a priority on strategic assistance.

The essence of the dilemma is highlighted by the difference between effectiveness and efficiency, as well as that between leadership and management. Leadership and effectiveness involve selecting the right things to do, whereas efficiency and management encompass doing whatever you happen to be doing the right way. Consequently, if the focus of the real estate consultant search and definition is on efficiency and management, some leadership and effectiveness may be sacrificed, which can have critical consequences in today's real estate marketplace.

This chapter aims to assist institutional real estate investors in the effective use of real estate consultants. To acomplish this, it provides some background on the definition of real estate consulting and the factors influencing its use. It discusses when to use consultants, how to select them, and how to get the most out of them once they are selected. Finally, it discusses future trends in the use of real estate consultants.

REAL ESTATE CONSULTING DEFINED

General Definition

In contrast to certain disciplines and professions that have recognized definitions and boundaries, *real estate consulting* is an ambiguous term. Indeed, Jared Shlaes opens *Real Estate Counseling in a Plain Brown Wrapper—A Practical Guide to the Profession* (published by the American Society of Real Estate Counselors, 1992) with the observation that "Real estate counseling is such a new profession that few

Americans have ever heard of it, even those who make a living in the land-and-buildings business."

The term *consultant* is adopted to serve many purposes:

- A label for the status of someone who is between jobs and is seeking project work until a full-time job becomes available.
- An entrepreneurial-based firm that seeks agency/contingent compensation-type business under the cloak of providing advice.
- An investment manager who provides fiduciary asset management services for substantial fees.

These and other definitions use the term consultant as a label to describe something other than what consulting really involves. There is a plethora of definitions of consulting, all of which emphasize one or more features such as:

- Independence.
- Objectivity.
- Expertise.
- Special training and qualifications.
- An advisory role emphasizing assistance as opposed to performing management duties.
- Problem identification and analysis.
- Problem solving.
- Change facilitation.
- Implementation.
- Innovation and creativity.

In their authoritative *Consulting to Management,* Greiner and Metzger (1983) define *consulting* as follows:

> Management consulting is an advisory service contracted for and provided to organizations by specially trained and qualified persons who assist, in an objective and independent manner, the client organization to identify management problems, analyze such problems, recommend solutions to these problems, and help, when requested, in the implementation of solutions.

Reasons consultants are hired, beyond those identified above, include introducing new ideas and a fresh approach, acting as a catalyst for change, supplementing the organization's resources, bringing greater specificity and higher levels of skill, designing and implementing new systems, and training and professional development.

Traditional thinking about real estate consulting is reflected in the American Society of Real Estate Counselors' definition of real estate counseling:

> Providing competent, disinterested, and unbiased advice, professional guidance, and sound judgment on diversified problems in the broad field of real estate involving any or all segments of the business such as merchandising, leasing, management, planning, financing, appraising, court testimony, and other similar services. (Shlaes, 1992)

Interestingly, this definition is unchanged from a 1962 booklet of the American Society of Real Estate Counselors, which was described as "the first in a series of publications to be issued on real estate counseling for the information and benefit of those interested in this new type of professional service."

To illustrate how real estate consulting is distinct from other real estate services, Exhibit 19–1 shows the relative market shares of the overall real estate professional services market. Real estate consulting is one of a number of professional services that support

EXHIBIT 19–1
Real Estate Professional
Services Revenues

Service Category	Percent
Consulting	2%
Sales and leasing brokerage	33
Mortgage origination	16
Property management	23
Architecture, engineering, and planning	6
Legal	7
Investment management	11
Accounting	2
Total	100%

Source: Roulac Group.

the planning, designing, building, financing, investing, documenting, reporting, and managing of a property involvement. Real estate consulting represents approximately 2 percent of a professional services market of at least $100 billion.

Differences among Real Estate Brokerage, Appraisal, and Consulting

As an aid to better understanding the distinct services real estate consultants provide, Exhibit 19–2 identifies the differentiating attributes of the services provided by real estate brokers, appraisers, and consultants. Real estate brokers' services are characterized by contingent compensation, advocacy, an undefined work product, and a short time horizon. Real estate appraisers' services are characterized by noncontingent compensation that is typically on a fixed-fee basis, a focus on a specific property value and value date, providing little additional advice, and a standard work product. Real estate consultants often work on an hourly or a retainer basis, are objective, and emphasize solving problems and facilitating change for an organization as well as an asset, and consequently their work product is customized to meet client needs.

Real Estate Consulting in a Pension Fund Context

Pension funds, particularly public pension funds, use real estate consultants primarily on a retainer basis to assist them in their selection of investment managers, establishment and review of investment policy and strategies, and performance monitoring and reporting. Real estate consultants play a unique role in that they are a layer between the real estate investment managers, who are responsible for the selection and acquisition of specific assets and day-to-day property management, and the pension fund. They are also uniquely positioned in that they often report directly to senior management and boards of directors while having an ongoing day-to-day relationship with the pension fund's professional real estate staff. This traditional use of real estate consultants is not the only way pension funds use consultants, for many are used on a more ad hoc basis for specific situations that require expertise. But in general, most pension funds view real estate consultants in the limited role discussed above.

EXHIBIT 19–2
Differentiating Attributes of Real Estate Professional Services

Attribute	Broker	Appraiser	Consultant
Compensation basis	Percentage of transaction	Fixed fee	Varies: hourly, fixed fee, retainer
Advocacy	Yes—make the deal happen	No—unbiased opinion	No, unless in implementation role
Contingency on outcome	Yes—transaction proceeding	No	No
Objectivity	No	Yes	Yes
Emphasis	Complete transaction	Specify property value	Provide guidance, solve problems, facilitate change
Time horizon	Immediate	Value date	Present *plus* future
Form of professional service	Transaction facilitation	Opinion	Analysis, advice, implementation
Role of advice	Provided without charge as a means of attracting new business	Not part of appraisal; seldom offered	Essence of what is offered and what is paid for
Form of work product	Whatever it takes to get the deal	Generally standardized report	May be standardized, but often customized to client needs

Clients

The clients employing real estate consulting services have changed dramatically over time. In the quarter-century following World War II, builder-developers, financial institutions, and the public sector were dominant users of real estate consulting services. With the advent of securitization, first in the form of real estate investment trusts and then in the form of limited partnerships and mortgage securities, investment managers have emerged to become the dominant consumers of real estate consulting services. During the 1980s, builder-developers were major users of consulting, followed by financial institutions and financial services firms. Presently, real estate investment managers continue to be among the most important consumers of consulting services, with builder-developers in a much less prominent role than before.

FACTORS INFLUENCING CONSULTANT USE

The effective use of real estate consultants, discussed in detail in later sections of this chapter, can be aided by an understanding of the emergence of the consulting market, the changing demand for consultants, and the impacts of technology on consulting in the real estate sector.

Emergence of Consultants

Although the recognition of the role of the consultant in institutional real estate investing has moved to the forefront in recent years, the role of specialists in real estate has a long history. In recent years, *feng shui,* the ancient Chinese art of geomancy and an absolute requirement in the design of any contemporary Hong Kong facility, has been the subject of considerable attention in Western cultures, to the point that many progressive organizations in the United States have adapted these concepts in the design of their living and working spaces.

More recently, real estate consulting has evolved into a separate and distinct professional service. Once offered as a secondary adjunct to real estate brokerage and appraisal, leading real estate consultants now provide a level of professional service that is fully comparable to that provided by leading professionals in such established disciplines as law, accounting, and advertising. Still, real estate consulting is not nearly as well known and understood by the broad public as are these other disciplines. Because of the newer status of real estate consulting, it is helpful to have a perspective on the evolution of this specialty.

The real estate broker emerged to fill the need for a formal market of specialists to facilitate bringing buyers and sellers of property together, with individuals specializing in that function on a full-time basis replacing those who previously provided such assistance as an adjunct to other activities or merely as an accommodation. Appraisal, in turn, evolved out of real estate brokerage, in response to the need of market participants for more rigorous and thorough analyses of issues as well as objectivity and accountability, to replace the informal value comments previously provided by brokers as part of their overall package of services.

Over time, there was increasing recognition that the appraisal report neglected to address many clients' information decision requirements. Thus, the real estate counseling process evolved in the latter half of this century from real estate professionals who elected to charge for services they provided, particularly for advice on what a decision maker might do following completion of an appraisal report.

A third of a century ago, thoughtful commentators on the real estate process recognized that modern real estate problems frequently required disassociation from the promotional aspects of the transaction (Shattuck, 1962). Indeed, prior to the advent of the American Institute of Real Estate Appraisers, brokers furnished appraisals without charge, but this practice has changed. Still, real estate brokers continue to offer advice on various types of real estate matters without charge as a public relations gesture.

Today discriminating consumers of financial services recognize the inherent problems of advice provided by someone who receives a commission for a sale that depends on that advice. Further, and equally important, diligent, competent work to support a major decision is not probable on a public relations basis, since there is an inherent tendency to be less rather than more conscientious, probing, and comprehensive in the approach. Thus, advice on a major decision that is offered in relation to a transaction-contingent involvement is inconsistent with an independent consulting approach.

On a broad basis, in a market characterized by considerable

expansion and forward momentum, tying advice to compensation for transactions consummated is perhaps not unreasonable. If the practitioner has confidence that a transaction will be completed, it is only a matter of which one; then advice not to buy a given property but to buy a different property may work for all involved. But as the inherent thrust of the brokerage relationship is for the broker to be compensated for transactions consummated, a fundamental bias predisposes a transaction being made. Further, few people want to be told not to proceed with doing something they desire and plan to do. Consequently, consultants must deal with people's basic reluctance to pay for advice that is unrelated to action.

The institutionalization of the real estate business has caused the emergence of a new genre of firms that provide real estate asset management services. A quarter-century ago, few organizations had any meaningful responsibilities for overseeing real estate assets on a substantial scale. But today at least several hundred organizations provide real estate asset management services. This rapid emergence of institutional real estate investing has imposed extraordinary demands on organizations, managers, and their advisors. Real estate's substantial acceptance and recognition in the institutional community impose pressure for professionalism on the part of those delivering services and also the particular need to bridge the traditional world of real estate and the cultures of the new participants. Consultants can be a critical resource for responding to these demands for a higher professional standard and quality of investment management services.

Increasingly, organizations that in the past promoted their business by emphasizing the tangibility of properties and their ability to make deals happen are adopting a consulting posture linked to implementation. Whereas in times past the emphasis was on action, with little attention paid to the rationale for such action, today a more deliberate, even reflective approach is promoted. Illustrative of this orientation is a recent promotion by Equitable Real Estate Investment Management, presented in Exhibit 19–3. Interestingly, Equitable readily offers to unbundle its services offering, providing either the traditional disposition brokerage function or, alternatively, the up-front consulting-based strategy, or the integrated package of strategy-management-disposition.

Traditionally, real estate consulting has been dominated by property-specific assignments with non-property-specific assign-

EXHIBIT 19–3

Illustrative Promotion: Reflecting Investment Manager's Unbundling of Asset Management Services

More Help.
More Hope.
For More Hotel Investors.

Equitable Real Estate's Hospitality Asset Management Group has a proven, successful process for turning around "problem" hotels and resorts. Today's hospitality market is a new game with new rules—and we know what it takes to succeed.

1. Analysis Phase: We start Phase I by analyzing what's really going on at your hotel and within its market. We work quickly but comprehensively in preparing a Strategic Business Analysis.

2. Asset Management Phase: We then move to the hotel asset management phase. Unlike hotel consultants, we go from hard-hitting asset management, employing nuts-and-bolts remedies, to solving problems at your property. On either a short- or long-term basis, we will direct every function from operations and accounting to marketing and refurbishment.

3. Disposition Phase: Finally, at an agreed-upon time our internal sales team sells the property. We will handle the total disposition as your representative. The goal: Recover maximum asset value.

You can hire Equitable Real Estate's Hospitality Asset Management Group to do any one phase or all three. Either way, you'll be the winner.

Source: Equitable Real Estate Investment Management, Inc., promotion.

ments representing only a very small share of the total market. Non-property-specific consulting has grown from approximately 10 percent of the market in the mid-1980s to more than 15 percent of the market in the mid-1990s. Significantly, non-property-specific real estate consulting work was virtually nonexistent as recently as a quarter-century ago. Just as organizational and strategic consulting have become dominant themes (replacing more mundane consulting engagements such as time and motion studies) in the overall consulting market, so are issues of organization and strategy assuming ever greater priority to real estate market participants.

The future of real estate consulting may best be viewed as a virtual corporation. While the idea of virtual corporation was introduced about three years ago, today it is a phrase commonly employed in business. The virtualization of corporate America is the creative application of technology and dynamic organization relationships in ways that enable even the smallest companies to deliver services over a time and quality horizon that heretofore even the largest organizations could not match. The ultimate virtual enterprises are consultants, whose role and function should be increasingly recognized as the leading, if not defining, engine of economic vitality and expansion.

Changing Demand for Consultants

By virtually every measure the real estate markets have experienced revolutionary change, with transformation from simple to complex, limited to broad, basic to sophisticated, predictable to discontinuous, and local to global. Exhibit 19–4 compares the extraordinary changes from yesterday to today for some key attributes defining the real estate market.

The forces of change that are realigning the environment in which the real estate executive operates are similar to the dynamic changes occurring within the country's overall economic system and the financial services markets in particular. Current forces contributing to the increasing demand for consulting expertise generally and shaping the particular type of consulting services needed broadly include:

- Information-communications technology advances.
- Business moves from central business districts to suburban, exurban, and foreign locations.

EXHIBIT 19–4
Changing Real Estate Markets

Attributes	Yesterday	Today
Focus	Transaction	Strategy, policy
Economic environment	Solid growth	Uncertain, dynamic
Change predictability	Stable	Discontinuous
Change pace	Slow, long lead time	Fast, dynamic
Communications	Slow	Instantaneous
Business space market demand	Strong, predictable	Volatile
Tenant orientation	Passive, unsophisticated	Aggressive, strategic, sophisticated
Tenant mobility	Stable, limited	High
Capital access	Residual user	Primary, direct access
Finance source	National	Global
Investor source	Local	Global
Investment form	Direct	Securities
Investor sophistication	Low	High
Investment orientation	Entrepreneurial deal mentality	Fiduciary, institutional
Manager orientation	Opportunistic, deal making	Strategic, value creation
Professional service providers	Local	National
Property market data	Local	National
Analytic tools	Slide rule	Computers
Information sophistication	Low	High
Information availability	Modest	Overwhelming
Building complexity	Simple	High
Academic programs	Modest, limited, rigid	Extensive, flexible, responsive

Source: Adapted from Stephen E. Roulac, "ARES: A Cost-Effective Research Resource for Changing Real Estate Markets," *Real Estate Finance*, Winter 1993, pp. 75–78.

- Organizational downsizing and rightsizing.
- Elimination of middle management staff positions.
- Growing proportion of work being done on a contractor and outsourcing basis.
- More specialization and sophistication.
- Increased global competition.
- Globalization of financial services and capital.

- Increased environmental awareness.
- Proliferating regulatory involvement in business.

Significantly, specialized enterprises are increasingly meeting the service needs of formerly large corporations whose staffs have been reduced to skeletons through rightsizing, downsizing, and layoffs. By terms such as outsourcing, contracting, alliances, and virtualizing, companies are increasingly seeking third-party, specialist firms to provide functions and services previously performed internally. The role of consulting continues to expand. Increasingly, the idea is emerging that the largest, most dominant job classification in advanced economies will be consultants. *Today, Inc.* magazine reports that some 20 million Americans make their primary living as solo operators.

A perspective on how changes in the real estate sector have influenced the demand for real estate consulting in the second half of the 20th century is provided in Exhibit 19–5. Most clearly, the focus of real estate consulting is quite adaptable, based on the key issues in the industry at the time. In the current environment, work-outs, securitization, and strategic reorganizations are key priorities.

Influence of Enhanced Computer Capabilities

Technology trends affecting real estate have created a significant need for expert assistance to cope with software and hardware advances as well as the organizational issues created by these advances. The proliferation of software generally and software design for real estate applications specifically challenges even those whose sole concern is to track and evaluate new product introductions. Among the pertinent categories for classifying real estate software are:

- Spreadsheets and templates.
- Database management systems.
- Word processing/desktop publishing.
- Illustration/drawing programs.
- Various hypermedia/presentation practices.
- Geographic information systems.
- Artificial intelligence/expert systems.
- Animation, CPM, sound processing, other miscellaneous tools.
- Software packages developed specifically for real estate analyses.

EXHIBIT 19-5

Real Estate Sector Changes and Implications for the Demand for Consulting, 1951–95

Issue	1951–60	1961–70	1971–75	1976–80	1981–85	1986–90	1991–95
Economic and investment environment	Stable growth	Rapid growth	Recession	Rapid growth	Dramatic changes	Uncertainty	Recession
Commercial property markets	Balanced	Balanced	Overbuilt	Balanced to tight	Tight to seriously overbuilt	Seriously overbuilt	Seriously overbuilt
Real estate capital markets	Uncomplicated	Stable	Diversification	Growth	Excess	Balance	Restricted to improving
Real estate financial services emphasis	Traditional	Stable	Expansion	Sophistication	Integration	Refinement	Focused
Consulting market growth outlook	Emphasis on property-related transactions	Steady growth in property-specific consulting as	Non-property-specific consulting market grows;	Rapid growth in property and non-property-	Securitization and economic uncertainty	Non-property-specific consulting remains strong	Workouts, reorganization, restructuring; appraisal for

and basic organizational issues; limited client or consulting sophistication

private and government property investment grows; management consulting and real estate investment analysis techniques improve as property size and real estate complexity increase

client decisions grow more complicated as financial services expand and capital markets diversify

specific consulting as property markets boom, financing increases in complexity, and financial services potential is recognized

generate strong non-property-specific demand; property analysis demand also up due to institution-alization of markets and record levels of construction

as workouts, legal economics, systems analysis, and mergers and acquisitions continue; property-specific consulting growth slows as building declines, but new attention to "economics" keeps demand steady

regulatory compliance; repricing; recapitalization; securitization expansion; risk control and due diligence; strategy services

Source: The Roulac Group.

The accelerating advances in software have been matched by comparable real estate hardware developments. Notably, in the half-century since the first mega-size computer was introduced, computational power has increased by an extraordinary 32 orders of magnitude, an exponential gain unprecedented in human history. Among the important manifestations of this accelerating computational power are:

- Miniaturization of computers (e.g., from laptops to notebooks to palm-size).
- Ever larger databases due to ever cheaper storage costs.
- Ever greater communication flows across ever cheaper local, regional, and national information networks.
- Enhanced presentation techniques—more colors, images (e.g., high-resolution aerial, grade-level, and interior photographs), and business graphics.
- Simple user interface (e.g., computers that recognize handwritten messages and even voices are already available).
- Incredible speed; the user's productivity is never diminished due to waiting for the computer to process a command.

WHEN TO USE REAL ESTATE CONSULTANTS

Knowing when to use, or when not to use, a real estate consultant is key to the effective use of consultants for institutional real estate investing. Critical to this decision is a strong understanding of both the organization and the types of services real estate consultants can provide. This section first looks at how consultants add value, then discusses the general services real estate consultants provide and the specific types of situations where institutional investors can use real estate consultants. Finally, it examines the organizational factors within a particular company that influence the decision on when to use a consultant.

How Consultants Add Value

Real estate consultants can be used (1) offensively to initiate ideas, chart a new course, or implement actions; (2) defensively to reduce mistakes and confirm that prudence was employed; and (3) as scorekeepers to measure results and introduce objectivity. All three activities add value.

Many pension funds view the consultant's function as primarily to protect the board of trustees from making mistakes and to assist in achieving stated goals and objectives. Although these roles are important, they inherently limit and constrain contributions the consultant might otherwise make. If the consultant's emphasis is to support the realization of previously articulated goals and objectives, the ultimate result will be defined largely in terms of those goals and objectives rather than possibilities the consultant might contribute that would *extend* the investor's thinking to new approaches, new horizons, or new possibilities. Institutional investors should be open to all of the valuable contributions consultants can make.

In addition to coping with the profound changes inherent in the nature of the real estate markets as described above and outlined in Exhibit 19–5, the importance of bringing a real estate consultant's expertise and objectivity into institutional real estate investing decisions is underscored by the implications of the relative inefficiency of the real estate markets generally and in comparison to corporate securities specifically. The many factors contributing to a comparatively inefficient real estate investing market include transaction infrequency, property uniqueness, information unavailability, limited and unsophisticated investment analyses, unpackaged investments, confrontational pricing negotiations versus impersonal auction markets for corporate securities, extended execution time horizons, and management responsibilities and influence on investment performance.

One example of how real estate consultants add value is their production of high-quality property analyses. As a particular property may come to the market only every 5 to 10 years, little information is readily available. An analyst cannot readily obtain an S&P tearsheet on the building, since such information does not exist in the public domain. Much of the information needed for investment decisions must be custom prepared for the time, place, and circumstances of the particular transaction. Transaction infrequency is a major constraint to a cumulative broad "market intelligence" of real estate transaction information concerning price and value, thus ensuring a role for real estate consultants.

Significantly, the broad public is generally unfamiliar with the range of services real estate consultants offer. Partly for this reason and partly because of the inherent behavioral barriers to clear self-perception, many people who need real estate counseling lack a clear insight into their problem. Consequently, a fundamental function of the real estate consulting process is education as well as needs definition. Thus, diagnostic skills and the ability to explain the problem, the suggested approach, and why that approach is justified are valuable additions to effective consulting relationships.

General Consulting Services

Real estate consulting services cover three primary components:

- **Enterprise direction and financing.** Enterprise direction includes business planning, securitization, investment strategies, marketing, investment decisions, and such investment banking–related work as arranging financing for debt and equity and facilitating real estate transactions such as leasing, purchase, and disposition of property.
- **Management consulting.** Services traditionally offered by general management consulting firms and the management advisory services business units of public accounting firms, including financial projections, management information systems, accounting-related and computer-based services, and organizational and compensation studies.
- **Property and portfolio analysis.** Such analysis includes market studies, development feasibility, appraisal, portfolio valuation, financial and economic analysis, and a wide variety of property-specific studies concerning public sector involvement in the real estate markets.

Institutional Needs for Real Estate Consulting

Beyond the three primary classifications of real estate consulting services just described, descriptions of which tend to reflect the types of firms offering such services, another approach to defining real estate consulting services, which has more direct application to institutional investing, is to identify specific strategic decisions and issues that institutional investors face. The key issues and decisions outlined below provide an overview of the types of non-property-specific issues with which real estate consultants get involved:

1. Investment policy
   a. Should the investor participate in real estate?
   b. What portion of the portfolio should be committed to real estate?
   c. What are the investor's time horizon, risk tolerance, and liquidity requirements?
   d. Should the involvement be direct or indirect?
   e. What are the investor's circumstances and objectives?
   f. How does real estate investing contribute to the realization of these investment objectives?
   g. What legal, regulatory, and institutional policy guidelines affect the real estate allocation decision?
   h. What legal, regulatory, and institutional policy guidelines affect the real estate strategy and its implementation?
2. Investment strategy
   a. What are the investor's particular investment goals and criteria for the real estate portfolio?
   b. Specification of portfolio composition guidelines, including investment form, diversification requirements, size parameters, property types, geographic location, age and condition, and manager relationship.
   c. Specification of management relationships, including investment vehicles.
   d. Organization design, including addressing the relationship among board and senior management, staff, managers, and subprofessionals.
3. Investment procedures
   a. Property acquisition criteria.
   b. Decision-making structures and systems.
   c. Organizational issues and work content.
   d. Management information systems.
   e. Market-monitoring systems.
   f. Compensation systems.
4. Portfolio management systems
   a. Appraisal management.
   b. Portfolio management.

      c. Asset management.
      d. Manager oversight.
      e. Performance measurement.
      f. Financial reporting.
  5. Portfolio implementation
      a. Investment manager evaluation, screening, and selection.
      b. Investment opportunity origination.
      c. Due diligence.
      d. Capital commitment decisions.
      e. Portfolio performance monitoring.
      f. Investment performance measurement.
      g. Problem property resolution: diagnosis for problem identification, strategic assessment, formulation of workout plan, implementation support.
  6. Financial review and compliance
      a. Financial reporting.
      b. Investor communications.
      c. Regulatory agency relationships.

In addition, consultants may be used for a variety of specialized projects to address issues of concern to the investor's board, senior management, and staff.

Organizational Factors Influencing Use

Whereas in the past certain traditional and old-line financial institutions, especially insurance companies and commercial banks, operated largely independently from third-party, external resources, today the majority of institutional real estate investors actively employ specialized professional services in their ongoing business. Significantly, these specialized capabilities are provided by both a diverse array of outside professional firms and, increasingly, internal advisory specialists, often operating as a research department whose charter may extend to all facets of the organization's activities. The internal professionals and the enterprise's research department may functionally operate as internal consultants, taking on assignments, issues, and problems associated not only with properties and investors' portfolios but also with the enterprise's organization, systems, and strategies.

Prior to consideration of which consultant to employ, the institutional investor would do well to identify how it wishes to use consultants, for which particular tasks, and on what terms. A fundamental consideration in institutional real estate investing is the allocation of responsibilities among the investor's professional staff of fiduciary investment managers it retains to implement its investment program, and real estate consultants it retains to advise on the overall investment program. This is the classic, albeit more subtle and complex, make-or-buy decision of business management, which has escalated in priority and prominence given the contemporary trend toward outsourcing, intimate customer-supply relationships, strategic alliances, and other specialized arrangements. There is no single, uniform preferred answer; the investor's indicated action is a function of circumstances, opportunities, constraints, and motivations.

While some investment managers believe they possess all of the capabilities the investor's staff and consultants would offer, and therefore staff and consultants are at least redundant, probably irrelevant, and possibly disruptive to what and how the manager wishes to do its job, some staff believe that everything the investment manager does could be done without it. Similarly, most services the investment manager provides could be separately offered by firms that provide brokerage, asset management, and/or real estate consulting services exclusively or as part of or an adjunct to their other business.

Multiple considerations influence how the division of responsibility among staff, outside managers, and consultants might best be determined. Among the considerations are:

- Size and qualifications of internal investment staff.
- Overall size of investment portfolio.
- Volume of investment transactions.
- Current status and quality of internal performance evaluation systems, decision-making structure, and overall quality of information and data access.
- Required level of independence and objectivity in both strategy- and property-level decisions.
- Familiarity and experience with the particular investment options being considered.

Clearly, there is no one right answer to this decision. However, where major investment dollars are at risk, a combination of professional staff, outside investment managers, and independent consultants can provide a good mixture of strategic insight, oversight, and practical experience that is necessary for success in the real estate industry.

HOW TO EFFECTIVELY SELECT REAL ESTATE CONSULTANTS

The Strategic Approach

Perhaps the most important step an institutional investor can take to ensure the effective use of its real estate consultants is to make a specific determination up front about the role and objectives for the consultant. This type of strategic approach would encompass all the issues discussed above, including how consultants add value, the types of services consultants can provide to institutions, and organizational factors that influence the type of consultant that would be most appropriate. A strategic approach, including an explicit delineation of the responsibilities of professional staff, investment managers, and real estate consultants, is fundamental to the successful use of a real estate consultant.

Crucial to determining the strategy for consultant selection is to address the need for consulting services, specifically by articulating questions to be answered and problems to be solved. Then alternative ways to meet those needs should be explored, including working with a bundled package of services versus the unbundled approach of multiple service providers, exploring outsourcing service contract arrangements, and addressing an explicitly desired approach for single versus multiple service providers, including consideration of whether to use firms with a general orientation or firms with more specialized talents. Once the type of consulting services needed and the terms are determined, the requirements for the particular consulting firms to deliver such services should be specified. Then the universe of prospective consultants can be addressed.

Another fundamental issue in selecting a real estate consultant is to what degree real estate consulting is perceived to be a commodity in contrast to a specialized professional service. Certainly some integrated services, particularly compliance-based activities such as some aspects of property inspection and appraisal, have many attributes of commodities, and certain components of even the most sophisticated, comprehensive, and complex services involve commodity elements.

It is critical to determine when a more generalized commodity-based service is appropriate and when a more personalized, specialized service is needed.

Larger firms, particularly accounting firms, may tend to perceive themselves as being more in the commodity business than in the specialized personal service business. Such forces as heavy fee pressure, high volume, short turnaround, and standard formats suggest a commodity orientation more than does more personalized and customized professional work that depends heavily on the senior principals' professional involvement in creation and service.

Certainly many real estate consulting services that institutional investors need have substantial, if not predominant, commodity attributes. These types of services can be delivered more cost effectively by those service providers that have in place the appropriate data, personnel, and/or systems required to produce such commodity products.

The complexity of the acquisition and management process and the increasing number of real estate service firms plying their wares suggest that explicit policies and strategies for retaining service firms need to be developed. Such an orientation is really an extension of an effective, forward-looking strategic management approach to the business. This approach involves consideration of the issues and challenges the business faces, putting in place the appropriate decision models to guide those decisions, identifying the systems and information needs to support those decision models, specifying decision-making participation, and accountability and documentation. Such an approach for employing professional services could be designed entirely by an outside firm or entirely internally, and, depending on the institutional investor's circumstances, such approaches may be adequate. In some settings, however, the involvement of an outside firm that has broad knowledge of the real estate markets, institutional real estate investing, and professional real estate services specifically, combined with the active involvement of the investment organization's senior management and staff specialists, could develop a superior system for utilizing real estate professional services.

Types of Real Estate Consulting Firms

Once the specific attributes and requirements of a real estate consulting firm have been identified through the strategic approach outlined above, the next task is to identify potential real estate consulting firms to hire. To begin that process, it is important to understand the different categories of real estate consulting firms. As Exhibit 19–6 shows, there is a plethora of real estate consulting firms, and accordingly clarity and precision in specifying professional service needs will facilitate a more informed, appropriate, and confident decision.

As shown in Exhibit 19–6, if information and statistics are required rather than analytic and communications talent, many economic and data companies and nonprofit organizations can provide data. The specialist real estate consulting firms, which are typically smaller but in some cases have a national presence, can provide concentrated knowledge and specialization on a particular segment of the market or insightful strategic planning from a strong real estate perspective.

The real estate consulting units of professional services firms, including the large CPA firms, general management consulting firms, and the large multi-asset class pension consultants, also provide an array of services, including systems and organizational analysis, strategic planning, portfolio allocation, performance measurement, and, perhaps most important, the reputations of their organizations. These firms have a lot to offer, but in using them it is particularly important to focus on techniques to get the most out of the consultant. These techniques are discussed later in this chapter.

The other real estate businesses, such as institutional property advisors, real estate brokerage companies, and development companies, provide a wide variety of services that are often transaction related but also rely on a large degree of specialization. These firms can also be very helpful for specific, well-defined assignments, but typically are not as strong in the problem-solving process and skills as are more focused consulting firms.

Identifying Consulting Firms

Contrary to many industries where the classification of firms providing services is reasonably homogeneous, firms providing real estate consulting services are characterized by considerable heterogeneity. As noted earlier, while many perceive real estate consulting as primarily embracing property analysis, in fact the strategic planning/ investment advisory segments of the market and the management consulting component are quite important. While a select number of firms are active in all three components of consulting to advise real estate organizations, the majority of firms concentrate on a particular, often narrowly defined segment of one component.

Exhibit 19–7 provides perspective on the property analysis consulting market. Certain important consulting attributes, including pricing, clients, property attributes, and engagement implementation, reflect the different emphases of the local, regional, national, and institutional consulting firm market segments. As highlighted by the comparative market segment information presented in Exhibit 19–8, extraordinary differences exist between local and institutional practices.

Consultants may be identified from a variety of sources, including individuals and firms known to the client; speakers at conferences and meetings; contributors to professional journals; organizations and individuals profiled and/or written about in the financial press; referrals from other institutional investors, investment managers, other consultants, attorneys and accountants; and various directories, including *Consultant's Compendium, Money Market Directory, Urban Land Institute Source Book, Nelson's Directory, Pensions and Investments,* and *Consultant's News Directory of Management Consultants.*

Consultant Selection Criteria

Critical to the selection of a real estate consultant is the understanding that real estate is not a monolithic market but is made up of multiple components and segments.

Fundamental to evaluating a prospective consultant is understanding that consultant's orientation. Among the issues to consider are the following:

- Is real estate consulting the primary emphasis of the consultant?
- If real estate consulting is not the primary emphasis, what other services does the consultant offer?
- Are these other services complementary, potentially conflicting, or distracting from the primary service needed?
- If the consultant is not primarily in the real estate consulting business, does it possess the requisite talent, commitment, and resources to deliver superior consulting services?
- Is the consultant concentrating on a particular segment of the real estate market, or on a broad-based orientation?

EXHIBIT 19–6
Classification of Real Estate Consulting Firms

Consulting Firm Type	Differentiation–Distinctive Competence	Primary Service Areas	Representative Firms
Information			
Economic and data companies	Information creation, manipulation, and delivery	Market studies, investment outlook, comparative geographic market analysis, general data provision	Data Resources, Inc., REIS Reports, Comps
Nonprofit Organizations			
Research departments of trade associations	Industry statistics	Capital markets, financing trends, investment outlook, comparative geographic analysis	Urban Land Institute, National Association of Home Builders
University real estate centers	Academic research	Theoretical and empirical research on public policy and certain specialized micro real estate decision issues	Harvard–MIT Joint Center for Urban Studies
Economic development organization	Optimistic orientation, can-do attitude	Market selection, economic data, planning assistance	Regional organizations to encourage business location and expansion, chambers of commerce

Government agencies	Authoritativeness, objectivity, unique access to data	Information and data on demographic and other measures of real estate supply	U.S. Department of Commerce, county planning departments

Real Estate Specialists

Small (one- to five-person) firms—by far the most numerous real estate consulting firms	Focus on local market knowledge and involvement, plus personal service	Market studies, appraisals, development planning, property analysis, capital placement	Real Estate Counseling Group of Connecticut, The Dorchester Group
Segment specialists: hospitality, pensions, financial institutions, retail	Concentrated knowledge of and specialization in particular segment	Strategic planning, organizational analysis, compensation studies, diagnostic studies, manager selection, performance measurement	Hospitality Valuation Consultants
Large real estate consulting firms	Broad market coverage	Appraisal, property analysis, market analysis, financing strategies, strategic planning	Landauer, Real Estate Research Corp.

Units of Professional Services Firms

Real estate consulting divisions of CPA firms	Letterhead, recognized name, insurance policy, quality control, tax/financial reporting expertise	Systems, organizational analysis, deal structuring, appraisal, market studies, industry studies, financing	Arthur Andersen, Kenneth Leventhal & Co.

(continued)

EXHIBIT 19–6 (concluded)

Consulting Firm Type	Differentiation–Distinctive Competence	Primary Service Areas	Representative Firms
General management consulting firms	Disciplinary expertise in management and knowledge of multiple industries that are customers of real estate services	Strategic planning, organizational analysis, systems, compensation studies	McKinsey, Boston Consulting Group
Multi-asset pension consultants	Broad knowledge of pension investing and relationship of real estate to other asset classes	Portfolio allocation, manager selection, performance measurement	Frank Russell, Callan, Wilshire
Other Real Estate Businesses			
Institutional property advisors	Fiduciary investment management	Strategic planning, portfolio analysis, capital placement, investment outlook, due diligence, property analysis	Richard Ellis Co., LaSalle Partners

Real estate brokerage companies	Access to information on market transactions; give out free market data	Appraisal, site identification, property analysis, development and transaction analysis, capital placement	Coldwell Banker, Grubb & Ellis, Cushman & Wakefield
Mortgage brokers and bankers	Information on investor preferences, criteria, and strategies	Capital placement, due diligence, transaction support, portfolio planning and advisory work	Sonnenblick-Goldman Corp., Brooks Harvey, Eastdil
Development companies	Hands-on real estate involvement	Outsourcing corporate real estate services, development planning, market studies, property design and marketing, property management, property analysis	Many firms have entered consulting to capitalize on skills as new construction has declined

Source: The Roulac Group.

EXHIBIT 19–7
Attributes of Property Analysis Consulting

Property Analysis Consulting Assignment	Precipitating Events/ Circumstances	Primary Purposes	Complexity/ Sophistication	Number of Properties	Work Product Form/Format
Cost segregation	Construction or transaction	Information for cost allocation and asset classification	Low	One or few	Input to accounting entry
Purchase price allocation	Transaction initiated	Establishing accounting systems and tax bases	Varies	Varies	Summary schedule
Appraisal reports	Compliance	Financings, reportings, loan/lost reserves (financial institution/ RTC)	Generally low	Usually one	Long narrative report
Value verification assistance	Leverage staff in terms of heavy workload; provide objective/ independent value attestation; bring complementary expertise to client	Help management develop value estimates	Low	Multiple	Narrative report, working papers, value opinion letter

Appraisal reviews	Financial reporting and/or regulatory compliance	Verify quality of appraisal report and the liability of value conclusion	Medium	One or few	Critique of appraisal report, value conclusion
Portfolio valuations	Transaction, regulatory compliance	Financial reporting, establish trading value	High	Many	Letter, *not* long report
Specialized valuation issues	Major transaction	Decision making	High	Varies	Short report
Market analysis	Decision: development, investment, marketing, disposition	Information on supply-demand relationship of rental space and for-sale property	Medium	Usually one	Narrative report with market information and analyses
Highest and best use	Proposed development	Determine appropriate development concept	Medium to high	Usually one	Recommendations supported by information and analysis in a narrative report as to development concept that provides highest financial return

(continued)

EXHIBIT 19–7 (concluded)

Property Analysis Consulting Assignment	Precipitating Events/ Circumstances	Primary Purposes	Complexity/ Sophistication	Number of Properties	Work Product Form/Format
Feasibility	New development or financial commitment	Provide assurance that the proposed project is financially feasible: generate risk-adjusted financial returns sufficient to justify capital investment	High	Usually one	Narrative report with market information and analyses, plus financial analysis
Strategic use	New development project	Determine development strategy that will respond to concerns/ interests of multiple stakeholders	High	Usually one	Narrative report with market information and analyses, plus strategies for project success
Due diligence	Financial commitment	Confirm that investors' objectives and criteria are being met	High	One or more	Letter to narrative report
Litigation	Litigation and related conflicts	Information to facilitate dispute resolution	High	Varies	Expert testimony, process, consultation

Source: The Roulac Group.

EXHIBIT 19–8
Property Analysis Consulting Market Segmentation

	Market Segments			
Attribute	Local	Regional	National	Institutional
Pricing				
Hourly rates	Under $100	$100–$125	To $200	$200 and up
Fee per report	Under $5,000	Approaching $15,000	$15,000–$25,000	$25,000 plus, often approaching six figures
Clients				
Nature of client	Small, local business	Medium-size business	Large corporation, MNC, financial institution	Large corporation, MNC, financial institution
Primary purpose	Financing	Financing	Transaction and financial reporting	Reporting, regulatory compliance, transaction
Market penetration	Minimal	Sporadic	Comprehensive	Highly specialized
Selection criteria	Price and result meet client purposes	Price, consistency, responsiveness	Reputation, responsiveness, price	Expertise, reputation, responsiveness
Client satisfaction criteria	Flexibility	Timely delivery	Timely delivery	Quality of analysis and consulting presentation

(continued)

807

EXHIBIT 19–8 (concluded)

Attribute	Market Segments			
	Local	Regional	National	Institutional
		Consulting Firms		
Geographic orientation	Local	Regional, some specialization	Regional to national, some firms in multiple offices	National, large professional staff
Number of offices	One	Fewer than 5	As many as 50	Up to 15
Office location	Suburbs or out of home	Suburbs or maybe downtown	Downtown	Multiple downtown in first-tier financial centers
Number of property analysts	1–5	5–10	25 plus	25 plus
Number of MAI-designated appraisers	1–2	3–5,	3–5	3–5
Style	"Cottage industry" format	Master craftsperson	Franchise	Managerial: systemization, standardization, hierarchy, quality control
Primary competitive firms	Solo practitioners and small firms	Regional firms and some national firms	Regional firms and national firms	Highly specialized regional firms and national firms
Representative firms	"Mom and pop" fee shop	American Appraisal	Cushman & Wakefield, RERC	Arthur Andersen

	Single properties	Single properties	Single to multiple properties, multiple tenants	Complex single properties to large portfolios, multiple tenants
Number	Single properties	Single properties	Single to multiple properties, multiple tenants	Complex single properties to large portfolios, multiple tenants
Leases	Noncomplex	Multiple leases	More complex leases	Multiple complex lease arrangements
Financing	Noncomplex	Noncomplex	Noncomplex	Specialized institutional financing structures
Value	Under $5 million	Up to $10 million	Up to $50 million, most much less	$50 million plus
Engagement Implementation				
Specialization knowledge	Minor	Moderate	Critical	Essential
Methodology	Simplistic	Moderate	Intermediate	Sophisticated
Data access	Unsophisticated	Marginally organized	Partially computerized	Comprehensive, integrated, computerized
Modeling expertise	Not applicable	Moderate	Intermediate	Complex, advanced
Analytic content	Low	Moderate	Moderate	High
Report form	Simple	Boilerplate	Standardized	Customized
Report length	Short	Usually long narrative	Long narrative	Varies: short form to narrative
Quality control	Minimal	Minimal	Emphasis on form	Critical priority

Source: The Roulac Group.

- Does the consultant have more a local/regional or national/global orientation?
- Does the consultant emphasize property analysis or accounting-based consulting or financial or strategic services consulting?
- Does the consultant deliver a common work product of similar style, orientation, and quality throughout the organization, or is it highly variable, reflecting the personalities of the particular consultants working on a specific engagement?

Some investors employ a formulaic, structured evaluation system, assigning points and weightings to different criteria, then choosing the consultant with the highest score or choosing from among those that score at a certain designated level. Others favor a more informal, impressionistic decision style.

Of particular concern in retaining a consulting organization is whether the investor is retaining (1) an organization, which is often the approach of the major accounting firms; (2) a team of professionals who propose to work together on the investor's particular assignment; or (3) an individual who will concentrate his or her energies on the assignment. Each approach has advantages and disadvantages. Ideally, the investor obtains consulting services from an established, recognized organization that dedicates a strong team of professionals led by a highly qualified consultant who is highly motivated to work with the client.

Among the elements to consider in evaluating the prospective consultant are the firm's prior experience generally and experience in doing similar type of work specifically; the general business backgrounds and education of the consultants who work on the engagement; the ability of both the firm and the individuals to deal with unstructured problems; and the firm's commitment and access to information and research resources, which can be reflected by its past work, library resources, research orientation, and involvement in professional associations. Further, it is helpful to work with consultants who have already done considerable thinking about the issues the client faces, as evidenced by the consultants' professional contributions to the discipline in the form of journal articles, books, and speeches.

In assessing the ability of a consultant to provide expertise and objectivity to support institutional real estate investing decisions, a number of critical attributes might be considered. Among these

attributes are market knowledge, strategic outlook, MBA-like technical skills, entrepreneurial initiative, institutional style, managerial
orientation, marketing flair, personal skills, and people orientation.

   Market Knowledge.   As discussed previously, an understanding of the "territory" is fundamental to successful participation in
any business, particularly in the real estate sector.

   Strategic Outlook.   Given the rapidly accelerating pace of
change within the structure of the real estate business, which is
causing traditional relationships to crumble and new power alliances
to emerge, positioning oneself and one's organization strategically is
extremely important.

   MBA-Like Technical Skills.   The skills that are honed
through the MBA learning experience (or something similar), particularly the analytical methods for problem solving, systems, and procedures to achieve economies of operation and control of performance
and forecasting techniques to plan future operations and facilitate
capital budgeting decisions, have an important role in the "tool kit"
of the real estate consultant.

   Entrepreneurial Initiative.   The real estate business is inherently entrepreneurial in that it marshals resources and influences
behavior patterns in settings that are largely unstructured and have
few, if any, precedents.

   Institutional Style.   The integrated trends in the maturation
of the business and the increasing dominance of the role of capital
control by institutions mean that an important prerequisite for effective operation in the real estate sector will be appropriate "presence"
in the institutional settings. This requirement is a departure from
past practices and is alien to many practitioners involved in various
facets of the real estate business.

   Managerial Orientation.   More competitive conditions, larger
organizations, and higher expectations of more sophisticated participants place a premium on a managerial orientation to the business.
A structured approach that emphasizes planning systems and controls
is becoming increasingly important.

Marketing Flair.   The real estate business is ultimately concerned with the merchandising of space, which reflects a practical application of the process of supply and demand. Answers to critical questions such as the following define a consultant's ability to perceive the unrecognized opportunity, structure creative purchase terms, and perform effectively the many functions involved in the real estate process:

- What do people want?
- What factors influence decisions?
- What else is available?
- How does our space compare to that of the competition?
- How can we differentiate our product and merchandise it to achieve a premium return?

Marketing flair can be instrumental in promoting space and achieving superior returns.

Personal Skills and People Orientation.   While the "people factor" is important in a number of businesses, it is especially important in real estate, given the influence real estate decisions have on one's personal and organizational life, as well as the role emotional factors play in many real estate decisions. Thus, creating the appropriate personal rapport is often fundamental to achieving good real estate results. At the same time, such basic personality traits as creativity, integrity, persistence, persuasiveness, diligence, and attention to detail are all factors that increase one's likelihood of success in the real estate business.

Critical to a consultant's effective application of these attributes is an organization that is effective and committed to delivering high-quality professional services.

Alternative Approaches to Acquiring Property Analysis Services

The most prevalent form of real estate consulting involves property analysis services. These services are concerned with a specific property or collection of properties. Property analysis consulting can take many forms, including cost segregation, purchase price allocation, appraisal compliance reports, value verification assistance, appraisal reviews, portfolio valuations, specialized valuation issues, market analysis, highest and best use, feasibility, strategic use, due diligence, and litigation. Each of these types of property analysis consulting serves particular purposes in response to precipitating events and circumstances. Their complexity and sophistication can vary greatly, as can the form and format of the work product, especially in terms of length and quality. These attributes of property analysis consulting are summarized in Exhibit 19–7.

Institutional investors have employed five alternative methods to meet their needs for property analysis and appraisal services. Through the use of one or more of these alternatives, an institutional investor can satisfy its requirements according to its own particular circumstances. The alternatives are:

1. Internal appraisal staff.
2. Correspondents.
3. Local appraisal or consulting firms.
4. National appraisal or consulting firms.
5. Modern systems approach.

The following sections describe the characteristics, advantages, and disadvantages of each method. The relative merits of the methods are listed in Exhibit 19–9.

Internal Staff

One early solution to the property analysis and appraisal problem was the creation of large, internal appraisal staffs that also acted as mortgage loan underwriters. This choice was entirely appropriate for efficiently processing large numbers of mortgage loan applications according to specific underwriting guidelines or investment criteria. Another historical reason for this approach was that the appraisal profession as we know it today did not exist, at least not in a consistent form, in all sections of the country. By incurring heavy overhead commitments and training costs, those institutions were reasonably assured of consistent application of their appraisal and underwriting criteria. A national perspective of real estate markets was acquired by operations located throughout the country, and knowledge of local markets was obtained through the use of field offices or coordination with mortgage loan correspondents.

As a result of intensive effort within the framework of the institu-

EXHIBIT 19-9
Comparative Elements of Sources of Appraisal Services

	Internal Staff	Correspondent	Local Appraisal Firms	National Appraisal Firms	Modern Systems Approach
Overhead	High	Low	Low	Low	Very low
Compensation arrangements	Salary plus Benefits	Commissions	Fees	Fees	Fees
Understanding of institutional investment goals	High	Medium	Low	Medium	High
Responsiveness to change	Low to medium	Low to medium	High	High	High
Knowledge of local markets	Medium	Medium to high	High	Low to medium	Medium
National perspective	Medium to high	Low to medium	Low	High	High
Independence as to value conclusion	No	No	Yes	Yes	Yes
Exposure to a variety of transactions	Low	Medium	Medium	Medium to high	Medium to high
Sophistication	Low to medium	Medium	Low to medium	Medium	High

Source: The Roulac Group.

tion's investment criteria, the majority of the internal staff was relatively unexposed to other types of real estate transactions. A side effect of this form of organization was that internal staffs developed inertia and became unresponsive to changes in investment criteria. The life insurance companies discovered this in the late 1970s, when disintermediation and other changes in the financial markets made long-term mortgages a poor investment. The changes occurring in the real estate capital markets forced considerable reorganization and retraining of internal staffs, and in some cases this is still going on. The recent creation of separate real estate investment subsidiaries reflects large institutions' attempts to remain competitive in today's more entrepreneurial investment climate.

Correspondents
Correspondents have traditionally been used in combination with in-house staffs of review appraisers or underwriters employing their expertise to achieve the best of both worlds (i.e., to provide the more entrepreneurial outlook, which has generally been lacking in in-house staffs, and generate a volume of potential investments for consideration by the institution).

Theoretically, correspondents should be well versed in the institutions' investment criteria so that potential acquisitions meet with a high likelihood of ultimate approval. Correspondents are not used as often as they used to be, and their relationships with institutions have greatly changed, largely because of changes in the way real estate investment is conducted. A variety of investments now available to many institutions are beyond the evaluation capacity of many mortgage and real estate brokers. Bulk purchases of mortgages or mortgage-backed securities and the sheer size of many investments available today create economies of scale for institutions that far surpass the economies achieved through the correspondent system.

However, for many smaller institutions, particularly those that make most of their investments in mortgages, the use of correspondents can be a viable method of avoiding the need to maintain large internal staffs in an environment in which the volume of potential investments is highly cyclical. For example, thrift institutions often lay off staff to cut expenses when their lending volume is down. At the other end of the cycle, when mortgage rates are low, they are overwhelmed by more loan applications than they can keep up with.

A disadvantage of using correspondents is that because they are compensated by closing deals, they are not independent as to value conclusions. Consequently, their appraisals should not be relied on without thorough review.

Local Appraisal Firms

A well-respected local appraisal firm has a distinct advantage because it is active in the market where the potential investment is located. The local appraiser possesses (or has access to) a comprehensive database on the local market, as well as intimate knowledge of its history, including its trends, the forces acting within it, and the major players. Such knowledge can greatly benefit an institution that utilizes a small, centralized acquisitions staff. An appraiser that is knowledgeable about a local market can provide information that would take an in-house staff or other out-of-town party weeks to uncover. If the appraisal process is a dynamic one, the local appraiser can function as adjunct staff and provide information for acquisition analysis (in addition to the appraisal report itself), any appraisal updates that may be required, and ongoing information about changing conditions in the market.

One potential disadvantage of a local appraisal firm is that the staff may lack a national market perspective on the types of investments the institution desires. Unless the local firm is knowledgeable about these investments, its approach to investment analysis may be rather provincial and may not best serve the client. Another potential problem is that a local firm may lack sufficient staff to perform the necessary tasks in a timely fashion.

National Appraisal Firms

A national appraisal firm is likely to have a nationwide perspective on investment analysis, but may lack insight into the local markets. If an out-of-town appraiser must collect the data necessary for an appraisal, delays may result and the quality of the information may not be as good as that generated by a local appraiser. The local office of a national appraisal firm may provide the best of both worlds; however, the quality of appraisals provided by a local office will vary according to the capabilities of the staff. An additional variable is that the nationwide perspective on investment analysis will vary both with the overall experience of the firm and with the comprehensiveness of its interoffice communication.

Modern Systems Approach

A fifth alternative, and the method we recommend, takes a modern systems approach to acquiring appraisal services. The system should be designed to meet the institution's needs and capabilities. To design and implement a systems approach, the institution engages a local appraiser or the local office of a national appraisal firm and an independent third-party consultant. The services provided by the consultant will vary according to the needs of the institution, its investment goals, and the size and capabilities of its in-house appraisal and acquisitions staffs. Examples of services the consultant could provide include:

- Ascertaining the needs of the institution.
- Drafting appraisal specifications that respond to those needs.
- Designing a system for appraiser selection.
- Assisting in appraiser selection.
- Acting as liaison between appraiser and institution.
- Providing a nationwide perspective on investment analysis to local appraisers.
- Reviewing the appraisals and judging the accuracy, reliability, and credibility of the appraisal reports.
- Estimating the values of investor positions.

The essence of the consultant's involvement is to supply the institution with the best possible information for decision making, reporting, and due diligence, as well as to facilitate the appraisal process so it runs smoothly and allows the institution to receive comprehensive information and analysis within its own time constraints. In each of the aforementioned categories, the consultant's involvement will vary according to the circumstances. The consultant could be assigned to comprehensive oversight of the entire process or only to specific tasks, assigned to spot check to ensure quality control in appraisals and appraisal reviews, or simply be available as a troubleshooter on an as-needed basis. The right combination of internal and external resources can achieve high quality and the desired results for an institution.

GETTING THE MOST OUT OF YOUR CONSULTANTS

Knowing What You Want

Hiring a consultant is closely parallel to hiring accounting and legal services. Firms can be retained for a discrete project, for the initial phase of a multipart assignment, to provide a designated service on an ongoing basis, and/or to provide a collection of services over time. Some investors favor sole-source arrangements, looking to one professional firm to provide all of their needs. Other investors prefer hiring several firms to provide different types of needs on an ongoing basis. Still others employ an ever-changing portfolio of outside advisors. Each approach has advantages and disadvantages.

Most important, to get the most out of your consultant, you must know what you want, which you can best determine by reviewing the strategic approach outlined in the preceding section. Once you know what you want and set up a system to measure whether you are getting it, you can be sure you will be getting the most out of your consultant.

Distribution among Consultants

Hiring a single firm may be viewed as more efficient in that the consultant assumes responsibility for solving the client's problems rather than the client taking the initiative to determine which consultant is appropriate in which situation and then proceeding through the search, engagement specification, negotiation, and selection processes for each needed task. When a client concentrates the bulk of its professional services with a single firm, it becomes a more important client of that firm and therefore can reasonably have higher expectations about the firm's commitment of its capabilities generally and its best talent specifically to serve the client's needs.

An advantage of using a consultant over an extended period of time is that a longer-lasting relationship allows the consultant to gain greater knowledge about the company, its circumstances, and its capabilities. Thus, the consultant becomes a valued resource that, if properly used, can materially enhance the company's business results. To the extent that a consulting firm has broad, diverse, and deep talent and the ability to access and apply that talent to the client's particular needs, as certain major law firms do, the client benefits accordingly.

In practice, very few real estate consulting firms have the breadth of talent to meet all of a client's diverse service requirements. Consequently, most investors work with multiple consultants. In some instances, certain investors may find that a single consultant can provide an effective leading, coordinating role, perhaps addressing the client's overall strategic and specialized property analysis needs while supporting the client in the retention of other consultants to address specialized technical issues as well as provide compliance-based property analyses and financial reporting services.

Contractual Relationships

Some institutional investors, particularly public funds, favor a formal consultant solicitation process involving requests for proposal. This prospect features the expectation that prospective consultants will provide detailed background information on the firm and its clients, prior experience, and personnel and also prepare a comprehensive work program detailing how the consultant proposes to provide the services it would offer. Following a review of these written submissions, one or more rounds of interviews, personal evaluations, and presentations are held before a decision is ultimately made. Although this approach yields considerable information and thereby may enhance the investor's confidence in its decision as to which consultant to retain, the approach by necessity is extraordinarily resource intensive, and certain consultants, including some of the most qualified, decline to participate in this type of hiring process. Consequently, formal solicitation has the benefits of competitively reducing consulting fees and allowing the client to get to know prospective consultants, but it may also eliminate the best consultants to serve a particular client's needs.

Access to Top Talent

A key issue in selecting and contracting with a consulting firm is to know who will be assigned to the engagement and actually perform the work. During the selection of a consulting firm, you need not only to review the overall credentials and reputation of the firm to determine that it is a top-level organization, but also to review the credentials and experience of the principals and staff who will be involved.

It is important to look at the level of depth of the senior principals as well as the structure of the organization. If a collaborative problem-solving approach is key to the engagement, which is generally the case for strategy and policy consulting engagements, you should confirm that the organizational structure supports this approach. Often this approach is strived for as an ideal, but is not achieved due to the structure of the organization.

It is also recommended that the consulting contract specify the level of commitment anticipated from the senior principals and supporting staff members.

Measuring Success

Measuring the success of a real estate consultant employed in an institutional setting is clearly more difficult than measuring the success of an investment manager where specific performance measures can be defined up front and evaluated annually. The consultant is often involved in proposing new investment strategies and making recommendations based on the interpretation of trends; consequently, performance results are difficult to measure in the short run. However, if a consultant is used only for tasks that can be easily measured, the true benefits of strategy and trend advice will be severely limited.

Although specific evaluation of the consultant's performance will depend on the particular consulting assignment and the scope of services provided, key performance review criteria include the following:

- Responsiveness, frequency, and effectiveness of communications.
- Ability to articulate through verbal and written communications to multiple audiences (i.e., investment board members, professional staff, and investment managers).
- Active involvement of senior principals.
- Dedication and continuity of consulting principals and staff.
- Quality of support and research behind opinions and recommendations.
- Demonstration of objectivity and independence.

- Continuous review of strategy and objectives based on interpretation of trend information.

FUTURE DIRECTIONS

Future trends in the use of real estate consultants include greater involvement in the area of real estate securitization and an increased responsibility to address real estate decisions in a larger societal context.

A profound trend in the real estate industry in general and in the institutional real estate investment arena in particular is a move toward greater securitization of real estate products. The consultant's role in this area is expected to increase accordingly. Increased property securitization will produce a vast array of investment vehicles, options, futures, and derivative instruments combining real estate assets. Real estate consultants will be needed to assist investors in understanding and evaluating the pricing, risks, and investment benefits of these new vehicles. Increasingly, real estate investment analysis will focus on portfolios of properties (e.g., REITs) as well as analysis of the securitized entities' market position, their capital structure, and the competence of their key executives. Real estate consultants will be called on to assist investors in applying the new technology of securitization to the specifics of real estate investing.

Although many consultants have a rather narrow scope of concern and a limited perception of their larger societal role, consultants are singularly positioned and uniquely qualified to address real estate issues in a larger context, to incorporate multiple perspectives into their work and introduce a measure of responsibility to real estate decisions that is not always present. Consultants therefore are responsible in the larger sphere to provide leadership to enhance the quality of real estate decisions in their multiple facets. Just as former Harvard president Derek Bok advocated in his 1983 *Report to the Board of Overseers* that lawyers emphasize productive endeavors to enhance society rather than limit their concerns to distribution issues such as how to carve up the pie, overproduction, how to make their share grow larger—so too can it be asserted that real estate consultants have a similar higher purpose.

In terms of social utility, there is the classic question of whether the architect retained to design a new structure should faithfully execute the specific ends already decided on by the client in a pursuit of his or her work or be guided by higher values. Society's increasing discomfort with a predominantly materialistic emphasis in economic and business realms is reflected in the American Bar Association rule that "in rendering advice, a lawyer may refer not only to law but to other considerations such as moral, economic, social and political factors, that may be relevant to a client's situation (American Bar Association, 1983).

While today many professional firms have a predominantly business emphasis, largely at the expense of any public purpose priority, there is strong sentiment within society, as well as in the thoughtful leadership of these professions, that the financial objectives are overly dominant relative to public purpose. Since legal forces influence the demand for real estate consulting and real estate consultants address issues similar to those lawyers confront, but from a managerial and economics rather than a legal perspective, the themes that define the role and terms of legal practice are relevant harbingers of real estate consulting's future direction.

REFERENCES

American Bar Association. *Model Rules of Professional Conduct* (1983), rule 2.1.

American Society of Real Estate Counselors. *What Is Real Estate Counseling?* Chicago: American Society of Real Estate Counselors, 1992.

Greiner, Larry E., and Robert O. Metzger. *Consulting to Management.* Englewood Cliffs, NJ: Prentice Hall, 1983.

Kagan, Robert, and Robert Rosen. "On the Social Significance of Large Law Firm Practice." *Stanford Law Review* 37 (1985), p. 399.

Lewis, Elliott. "Living with a Buyer's Market—Part I." *Touche Ross Real Estate Review,* January 1982.

Roulac, Stephen E. "Games the Stock Market Didn't Teach You." In *Real Estate Investing,* pp. 36–42. Monograph published by the Institute of Chartered Financial Analysts and Dow Jones-Irwin, 1985.

Roulac, Stephen E. "Management Challenges in an Era of Institutional Transformation." *Real Estate Issues,* Spring–Summer 1984.

Roulac, Stephen E.; Richard D. May; and Daniel T. Vigano. "Appraisal Management and Review Systems for the Institutional Investment Sector." *Appraisal Review Journal* 9, no. 3 (Winter 1986), pp. 9–19.

Shattuck, Charles B. "The Realtor in Real Estate Counseling." *Appraisal Journal,* January 1962.

Shlaes, Jared. *Real Estate Counseling in a Plain Brown Wrapper—A Practical Guide to the Profession.* Chicago: American Society of Real Estate Counselors, 1992.

CHAPTER 20

STRUCTURING A PLAN SPONSOR'S REAL ESTATE DEPARTMENT

John F. C. Parsons
MacGregor Associates

INTRODUCTION

Real estate is the most management-intensive asset in a pension fund portfolio. A wide variety of organizational formats exist for pension funds active in real estate. The precise structure of real estate investment operations depends on the fund's investment philosophy, portfolio size and complexity, legal composition, geographic diversity, and investment activity level. Real estate professionals play a critical role in maximizing the performance of pension fund real estate investments. Hiring the right people, allocating responsibilities, managing and monitoring the activity of advisors and consultants, and responding to the needs of trustees and beneficiaries are essential activities that can be enhanced by the appropriate choice of organizational design. Since pension funds are relatively recent entrants into the real estate investment field, human resource issues are just now entering a phase of rigorous examination. Pension funds are now developing professional personnel standards to hire, train, manage, and motivate their internal real estate staff. This chapter is intended to add to the body of knowledge pertaining to this important subject.

INTERNAL VERSUS EXTERNAL STAFF

Pension fund trustees must make the philosophical decision about whether to manage investments through external firms acting in an advisory capacity or use investment professionals acting as employees of the fund who are dedicated to the task of investment management, or, most commonly, a combination of both internal and external human resources. For all forms of assets, including equities, fixed-income instruments, real estate, and alternative investments, the decision to employ internal versus external staff hinges on the issues of performance vis-à-vis cost and the expertise required to successfully implement an investment program. The responsibility for formulation of personnel strategy resides with the trustees and chief investment officer. The responsibility for execution of the investment strategy resides with professionals directly employed by the pension fund and with advisors. The determination of specific roles for trustees, investment directors, internal real estate staff, and advisors and consultants is a critical element for the pension fund organization.

The strategic decision to develop an in-house real estate management capability is influenced by several factors. Typically, the most important factor is the size of the real estate portfolio. The scatter diagram in Exhibit 20–1 plots the number of dedicated real estate professionals against the total base of real estate equities and commercial mortgages for several of the largest corporate and public real estate funds in North America. As a general rule, pension funds tend to dedicate at least one real estate professional upon reaching the $250 million level in real estate investments. As the portfolio grows beyond $500 million, the real estate staff typically grows with specialist functions for acquisition and asset management. Thereafter, as the real estate portfolio grows in complexity, additional functions may be added in the areas of research and analysis, accounting, and other coordination functions to manage real estate advisors.

In the early years of real estate investment, pension funds often adopted a product-oriented approach to investment programs. Today the emphasis is on strategic investment decision making. Therefore, the organizational evolution of a plan sponsor's real estate department is highly dependent on the investment strategy chosen by the trustees, who act on the advice and counsel of advisors, consultants, and real estate staff.

The decision to add real estate staff to the pension fund investment department is based largely on the following considerations:

1. *Investment management philosophy.* Pension plan sponsors often adopt an overall policy regarding the internal versus external management of assets. Pension fund trustees commonly recommend internal management capability for stocks and bonds as the fund

EXHIBIT 20–1
Real Estate Portfolio Size versus Professional Staff (Selected North American Public and Corporate Plan Sponsors)

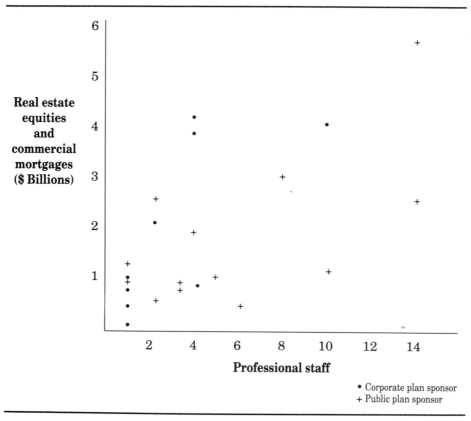

Source: MacGregor Associates.

grows in size. This pattern holds true for real estate investments to some extent. Funds that internalize management of stocks and bonds commonly organize real estate on an internal basis as well.

2. *Costs.* Many pension fund trustees believe that as the portfolio grows, the fees paid to advisors tend to become excessive relative to the benefits of advisory services. These trustees may choose to hire dedicated professionals for real estate assets, believing the cost of their salaries, bonuses, and benefit programs to be less than the external fees. Real estate advisors, however, normally continue to play an integral role in the investment management process, particularly for corporate plan sponsors who are subject to ERISA.

   3. *Control.* Rather than rely on advisory firms, trustees seek to acquire greater control over real estate assets as they gain sophistication in the asset class. As the pension fund matures, trustees commonly become willing to get involved in direct property investments rather than relying on commingled real estate investments. Direct forms of investment require sophisticated internal real estate staff.

   4. *Management of advisors.* Many pension fund trustees believe their real estate portfolio performance will be enhanced by even a very small internal staff who constantly demands top performance from advisors. Trustees find the advisors are more attentive when they receive proper feedback and guidance.

   5. *Better communication.* The communication link between real estate advisors and the plan sponsor can become cumbersome as the real estate portfolio grows in size. The ability of internal staff to manage and monitor real estate assets, with direct communication channels to the trustees, gives the trustees added assurance of prudent management.

   6. *Experience.* As trustees gain experience with real estate, they become comfortable assigning responsibilities to internal staff. Few first-time investors in real estate would adopt this approach, but as the funds gain experience, they often discover that bringing aboard experienced real estate talent to execute their investment strategies ultimately enhances value.

   7. *Turnover costs.* Pension funds prefer minimal turnover in the real estate staff dedicated to handling their investment portfolios. While there is no statistical record of the turnover experience of advisors vis-à-vis internal staff, direct control of internal staff may minimize turnover possibilities.

   8. *Conflict of interest.* Real estate advisors commonly are responsible for a large number of clients who have invested through them. The advisor must allocate resources according to the needs of clients. However, many funds want direct attention paid to their portfolios. Therefore, they may hire internal staff members who are free from potential conflicts of interest with other clients.

   While these are compelling reasons to develop an internal real estate capability, a number of counterbalancing arguments can be made for the ongoing use of external real estate advisors. In reality, the vast majority of pension funds that have internal real estate capability also rely heavily on advisors to perform and implement real estate strategies. In most instances, advisors are an integral part of the real estate investment management strategy. Typically, pension fund real estate staff work jointly with advisors to originate acquisitions, handle asset and property management, and deal with dispositions. The benefits of such a joint approach to real estate investment management include:

- *Professional expertise.* Few pension funds could directly match the extensive professional real estate expertise available from advisory firms. Most pension funds do not have the budget, or frequent need, for top acquisition, asset management, and disposition staff. Instead, this talent can be accessed through advisor relationships. This also provides pension funds access to professional expertise without directly incurring the salaries required to attract such top talent. Finally, career paths tend to be more attractive within advisory firms, since an individual can progress through several levels of job responsibilities that may not be available by working directly for the pension fund.
- *Flexibility.* The employment of advisors can be adjusted to match the needs of the pension fund. Real estate advisors can be hired—and dismissed—on the basis of their actual performance. This flexibility is not directly available with internal real estate staff. The dismissal of staff has complex implications from a human resources standpoint.

Therefore, the use of internal staff is frequently complemented by the activities of external real estate advisors who are highly skilled in certain property types, geographic regions, investment structures, and mangement of property portfolios.

STAGES OF INVESTMENT SOPHISTICATION

Pension fund trustees commonly reorganize their investment departments as they become more sophisticated in real estate investment. The level of sophistication of the organizational design of real estate operations is directly related to the stage of growth of a pension fund. The stages of growth for a pension fund's real estate investment portfolio are (1) the initial investment in real estate, (2) portfolio growth, (3) portfolio maturity, (4) the employment of functional staff, and (5) the creation of an investment subsidiary. In select circumstances, the largest pension funds may act as an advisor to third parties. This five-stage pattern of growth may vary for certain funds that skip early stages of development in favor of establishing an internal real estate department at the outset of their investment program.

The rate of growth for the pension fund that invests in real estate is largely a function of the various types of real estate products that the fund utilizes in its investment strategy. Exhibit 20–2 indicates the relationship between the stages of growth for a real estate portfolio

EXHIBIT 20–2
Real Estate Plan Sponsor Stages of Investment Sophistication

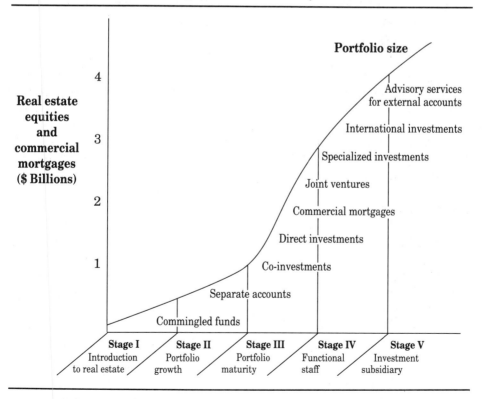

Source: MacGregor Associates.

and the various vehicles used to invest in real estate, which in turn affect the basic form of organizational design to be employed by the fund. Exhibit 20–3 outlines how the organizational design of real estate operation can be modified as the real estate portfolio grows through five stages of investment sophistication.

Stage I: Introduction to Real Estate

Pension funds generally make their initial investments in real estate through commingled funds and equity REITs. In this stage, pension funds typically manage their real estate assets through an advisor acting with discretion and reporting to the investment director of the fund. The role of the pension fund advisor(s) for these new investors in real estate is to provide strategic advice, implementation services, and discretionary advice on acquiring and managing real estate assets.

   The organization of this activity within the pension fund is generally quite simple. The chief investment officer acts alone under the supervision of trustees, but works with the advisor(s) to handle real estate transactions (see Exhibit 20–4). We can refer to this organizational format as a *stage I organizational design*.[1] This format is attractive to companies that cannot afford dedicated real estate staff and expertise, particularly since their real estate investments may be relatively small—say, under $200 million. The stage I organizational format is utilized by ITT Corp., where the pension trust director has responsibility for real estate investments.

Stage II: Portfolio Growth

As pension funds gain experience with commingled funds, they frequently hire a real estate director who is responsible for managing relationships with pension fund advisors. The real estate director acts under the supervision of the chief investment officer, managing and monitoring real estate advisors. Real estate directors rely heavily on advisors to source and manage real estate investments, since they have no other internal real estate staff to whom to assign tasks. The

---

[1]See Bruce R. Scott, *The Stages of Corporate Development—Part I* (International Commodities Clearing House, 1971).

EXHIBIT 20–3

Stages of Organizational Development for Real Estate Investment Management

Stage of Organizational Development	Size Range of Real Estate Portfolio	Organization of Real Estate Investment Operations
I. Introduction to real estate	$0–$250 million	Chief investment officer
II. Portfolio growth	$250 million–$500 million	Real estate director
III. Portfolio maturity	$500 million–$2.5 billion	Acquisition/asset management staff
IV. Internal staff	$2.5 billion–$3.5 billion	Full real estate staff
V. Investment subsidiary	$3.5 billion and over	Real estate operations for internal and external accounts

Source: MacGregor Associates

real estate director serves as the fund's internal expert and as a liaison between the chief investment officer and pension advisors and consultants who provide real estate services. In this capacity, real estate consultants may play an important role in assisting with decisions pertaining to asset allocation, advisor selection, and ongoing performance measurement of the advisor.

Pension funds in a growth phase often adopt a *stage II organiza-*

EXHIBIT 20–4

Stage I Organizational Design: ITT Corporation, Pension Trust Department

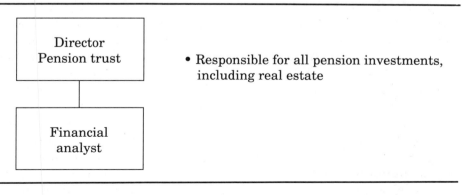

- Responsible for all pension investments, including real estate

Source: ITT Corporation.

tional design, which consists of a single real estate director who reports to the chief investment officer, who in turn is responsible to the pension fund trustees. The dominant responsibility of the real estate director is to manage the services provided by external real estate advisors, focusing initially on acquisition of real estate assets as the fund strives to attain its real estate allocation. This form of organizational structure is utilized by the Commonwealth of Pennsylvania State Employees' Retirement System (see Exhibit 20–5).

In this growth phase, pension funds may move into separate accounts and joint ventures, adopting a more direct form of investment than commingled funds. Real estate pension advisors and consultants remain heavily involved in strategy formulation, helping the real estate director with implementation services for the chosen real estate strategy. In some cases, a plan sponsor initiating a real estate investment program may move directly into a stage II format, depending on the sophistication of the investment program. The common element of real estate management in stage II is that the activities of the pension advisor typically become less discretionary as the pension fund grows in sophistication. As the real estate director becomes more heavily involved in strategy formulation, the advisors act more on the instructions of the real estate officer rather than with discretion. The fiduciary role the advisors play remains, but the real estate director begins to assume moderate liability for decision making.

Stage III: Portfolio Maturity

As pension funds mature in terms of real estate sophistication, they typically adopt more direct forms of real estate investment. These large pension plans augment their commingled real estate investments with separate account relationships with advisors, co-investments with other pension funds, and joint ventures with insurance companies and other experienced real estate investors, as well as commercial mortgages. In some instances, funds acquire direct ownership interests in a development company. Pension funds with real estate assets in excess of $500 million typically rely on *stage III organizational design,* which consists of a chief real estate director, who acts in a leadership role and coordinates functions in the areas of acquisition and asset management. A variation on this form of organization is employed by Ameritech Corp., as shown in Exhibit

EXHIBIT 20–5

Stage II Organizational Design: Commonwealth of Pennsylvania State Employees' Retirement System

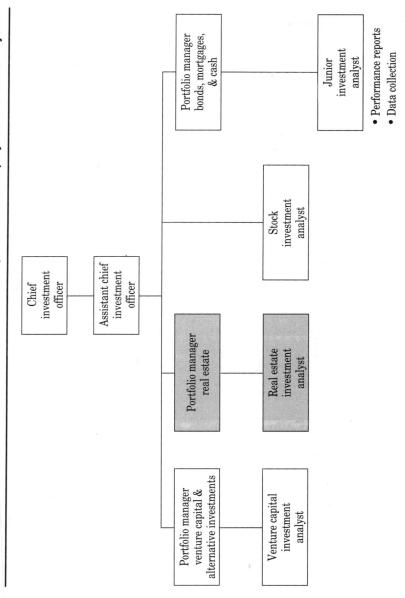

Source: Commonwealth of Pennsylvania State Employees' Retirement System.

EXHIBIT 20–6   Stage III Organizational Design: Ameritech Corp.

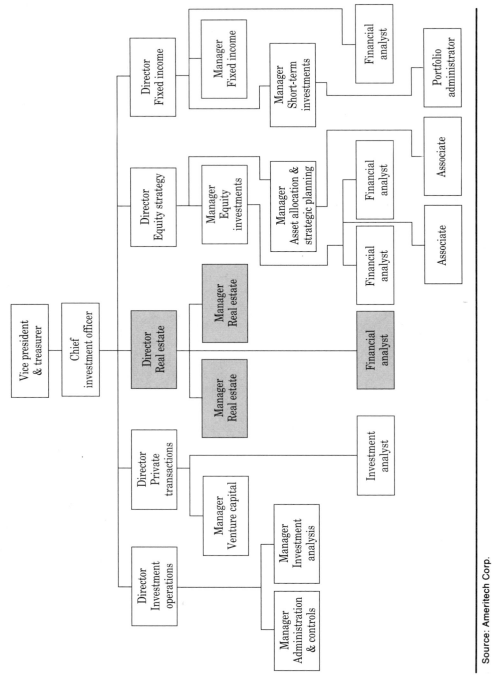

Source: Ameritech Corp.

20–6. Ameritech operates with a real estate director who is supported by two managers who share responsibilities for both acquisitions and asset management.

Stage IV: Internal Functional Staff

When the real estate portfolio of a plan sponsor grows beyond $1 billion, a progression tends to occur whereby staff are added to handle mortgage origination and mortgage servicing, research and valuations, accounting and MIS, engineering and physical inspections, cash management, and environmental reviews. Once a plan sponsor's real estate operation reaches stage IV, organizational evolution tends to accelerate, and staff may grow dramatically, particularly in areas such as asset management. Pension plan sponsors with a *stage IV organizational design* utilize internal functional staff to assist in the acquisition and management of real estate assets. This staff may perform a few of the activities previously performed by advisors. The California Public Employees' Retirement System uses this form of organizational design to manage a real estate equity portfolio in excess of $6 billion (see Exhibit 20–7).

The responsibilities of the real estate staff for these large pension funds also include the management and monitoring of real estate advisors, who service the plan sponsors in a core capacity and/or as sector specialists, providing access channels to the various classes of real estate assets such as office, retail, industrial, and residential properties. At present, fewer than 5 percent of the top 200 pension funds invested in real estate have such large real estate staffs. However, these entities control a large portion of institutionally owned real estate assets.

The role of the pension advisor for these large funds is to execute the strategy formulated by the pension fund's real estate staff. These advisors implement the strategic decisions of the pension fund staff, who in turn report to the pension fund trustees. The ongoing responsibilities of these advisors are heavily oriented toward excellent asset management services that enhance the value of the real estate portfolio. The fiduciary role pension fund advisors play remains in place, but the formulation and execution of real estate strategy are largely under the domain of the real estate staff and consultants hired by the pension fund trustees. Pension fund real estate directors responsible for managing mature real estate portfolios are charged with devel-

EXHIBIT 20–7

Stage IV Organizational Design: Functional Staff for Real Estate, California Public Employees' Retirement System Investment Office

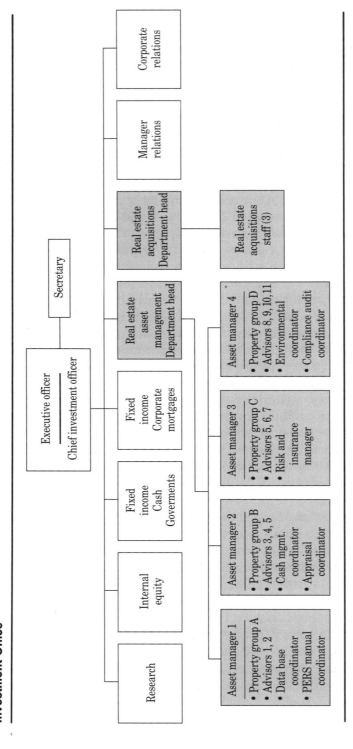

Source: California Public Employees' Retirement System.

oping strategic investment plans and allocating human resources in a manner that meets the needs of the trustees and plan participants.

Stage V: Investment Subsidiary Phase

A pension fund with experience in the direct acquisition and management of real estate assets may develop a fully integrated real estate investment subsidiary to handle its real estate. The *stage V organizational design* is adopted only by the largest plan sponsors, such as those that have real estate assets in excess of $3 billion. Investment subsidiaries are relatively expensive to maintain due to the costs of salaries, benefits, facilities, and related office expenses. Insurance companies that provide real estate investment management services are usually structured in a subsidiary format. These entities invest funds on behalf of the general account of their insurance company parent organizations, and also for third-party pension clients.

Real estate investment subsidiaries are responsible for money management for the pension fund, but they also raise funds and manage assets on behalf of less sophisticated third-party clients. Small pension funds that invest with larger plan sponsors that have investment subsidiaries enjoy the comfort of having the large funds co-invest with them. This coinvestment arrangement is thought to ensure prudent investment management.

In addition to a staff to handle real estate asset management functions, these organizations may have executives to market investment services to other funds. In this manner, a large corporate fund, for example, can lever its investment capabilities among other corporations. Frequently, these other corporate pension investors have close business ties to the sponsor of the investment management subsidiary. For example, they may be an equipment supplier or purchaser in an industrial business. The fully integrated real estate investment subsidiary of General Electric Investment Corp. is shown in Exhibit 20–8.

As pension funds grow in sophistication, they take control over the destiny of their real estate investments through internal real estate staff. The largest plan sponsors develop their own mission statements and business plans to handle the responsibilities of real estate investment strategies. Sophisticated pension funds continue to use advisors for specialty or niche areas where they have little

EXHIBIT 20—8
Stage V Organizational Design: General Electric Investment Corp.

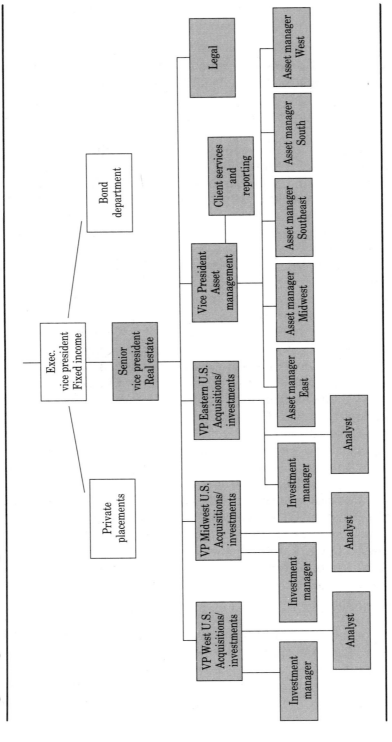

Source: General Electric Investment Corp.

expertise. From an organizational perspective, pension fund staff provide the expertise previously offered by advisors who earlier served their real estate investment management needs.

FUNDAMENTAL JOB FUNCTIONS

The job functions to be executed within a plan sponsor's real estate department are best described by analyzing the critical tasks to be performed by a large, sophisticated pension fund with a mature real estate portfolio. Position descriptions are essential to define the roles and responsibilities of each member of the plan sponsors' real estate staff. Annual work plans are also critical to directing behavior and judging performance of real estate staff. Very few plan sponsors are organized with employees in all of the following positions; however, some derivative of these positions are commonly in place at many sophisticated pension funds.

Trustees

The trustees of the pension fund are ultimately responsible for investment decisions pertaining to real estate. Trustees are responsible for four critical areas in real estate investment management: (1) allocating a portion of the fund's total portfolio to real estate, (2) setting a real estate investment strategy, (3) selecting real estate advisors, and (4) approving specific real estate investments. As custodians of the fund, trustees receive recommendations from the chief investment officer and the real estate director, with input from the real estate staff, and then vote on whether to proceed with acquisitions, dispositions, the hiring or firing of managers and advisors, and other matters that come before the board of directors.

The relationship between the trustees and the fund managers can take many forms. In certain circumstances, trustees coordinate all real estate acquisition activity through their real estate staff rather than receiving or giving communication to real estate advisors. Other funds have quite active boards of trustees who communicate directly with the real estate advisory community. A preferred approach is to manage the investment process through the real estate department, where trustees operate with a high level of respect for the real estate staff professionals.

Advisory Boards

Real estate advisory boards can provide tremendous expertise to a pension fund, and on a relatively inexpensive and ad hoc basis, as funds consider major strategic issues. Advisory boards may be composed of leading industry professionals and academics who regularly meet to review the activities of the pension fund's real estate staff. Advisory boards can provide a system of checks and balances for the chief investment officer, who gains a second opinon by consulting the advisory board.

The composition of advisory boards is often limited to six or eight senior industry professionals. Advisory board members commonly have at least 15 years' experience in the real estate industry and an extensive track record with real estate equity and mortgage investments. Advisory boards can help adjudicate investment decisions by analyzing the data presented by the real estate department to the chief investment director and trustees, thus making the real estate investment process more efficient.

Real Estate Director

Reporting to the chief investment officer, the real estate director acts in a leadership role to guide the pension fund toward maximizing performance of its real estate portfolio. Since many chief investment officers are unfamiliar with real estate and the complexities of managing this relatively illiquid asset, the real estate director must act as a liaison between the real estate assets and the chief investment officer on behalf of the trustees of the fund. The real estate director's most critical task is to manage the performance of real estate advisors who provide services to the fund in an acquisition and asset management capacity. The real estate director of a large portfolio may accomplish this task with a staff of internal asset managers who are assigned to specific property types, investment types, or geographic regions. In total, real estate staffs can be as large as 12 people, so a director may have substantial supervisory responsibilities. As the real estate portfolio grows in size, the real estate director may be required to develop certain skills in the management of real estate staff.

Acquisitions

The success of a real estate investment program is largely determined at the point of acquisition. Once pension funds reach the level of $250 million in real estate assets, they commonly hire an acquisitions officer. At this stage, it is also likely that an asset management executive will be added. The critical function of the acquisitions officer is to manage the "pipeline" of deals presented to the pension fund. Upon screening these deals, the acquisitions officer prepares summaries analyzing the critical factors of each promising real estate investment for the pension plan trustees. These acquisition proposals are best prepared on a uniform basis to simplify the decision-making process.

The process of acquiring property should incorporate a physical and an engineering review. This can be accomplished by outside consultants with engineering backgrounds who examine the physical aspects of real estate investments. Outside consultants responsible for due diligence analyses may report directly to the real estate director rather than the acquisitions officer, who may have a personal interest in completing a transaction.

Acquisitions officers are also frequently charged with disposition responsibilities. Given that pension funds are relatively new entrants into the real estate field, disposition activities have been handled by acquisition staff or advisors. As the real estate portfolio matures, however, the disposition function grows in importance. At large funds, the most common approach to disposition has been to delegate this task to external real estate intermediaries with strong marketing skills. These disposition experts work in concert with the pension fund's internal acquisitions staff.

Asset Management

Individuals charged with asset management are primarily responsible for the formulation, execution, and monitoring of agreements with advisors and real estate management firms. Asset management staff are typically responsible for a portfolio of property. For each property in the portfolio, they are responsible for (1) operating budgets, (2) capital budgets, and (3) leasing guidelines. Asset managers ensure that budgets are prepared to address annual operating performance and other critical issues such as capital improvements. Asset managers handle sensitivity analyses, preparing pro forma analyses to challenge the assumptions provided by advisors. Advisor performance measurements may also fall under the domain of the asset manager.

It is common to assign responsibilities to asset managers according to the relationships the pension fund has with its advisors and co-investors. Another typical approach is to assign asset managers to particular categories of real estate investments, such as office properties, regional malls, and industrial buildings. Asset management responsibilities may also be assigned according to geographic regions, particularly in a format that employs junior asset managers who report to a senior officer with product responsibilities, such as office or industrial properties.

A critical role of the asset manager is to monitor the advisor's ongoing performance with specific properties in the pension fund portfolio. The asset manager must be positioned to make forward-thinking recommendations to the senior executives of the advisor that protect and enhance the value of properties in the fund's portfolio. A primary objective of the asset manager is to add value to the property by formulating and executing strategies for major capital, leasing, and marketing decisions in conjunction with outside property management firms and advisors. An asset manager must play the role of a prudent owner. As part of this activity, many of the largest plan sponsors are giving asset managers responsibility for lease administration, since leasing performance directly affects cash flow performance. Lease administration details are commonly delegated to analysts and accounting support staff. Issues pertaining to property risk and insurance may also fall under the domain of the asset manager. For a corporate plan sponsor, insurance requirements are frequently analyzed by the staff executive responsible for the corporation's overall insurance program. For a public plan sponsor, a blanket insurance policy may be utilized.

Asset managers may also be responsible for special projects that arise in the areas of cash management, database management, appraisal coordination, environmental reviews, compliance auditing, and coordination of policy manuals.

Mortgage Operations

While the scope of real estate investing for most pension funds is predominantly of an equity nature, mortgage investments are also an important asset within a balanced portfolio. Many pension funds manage mortgages as fixed-income instruments rather than as real estate assets. This is reasonable, since real estate asset management is the responsibility of the holder of the equity interest. Traditionally, the major life insurance companies have provided external services to offer debt products to pension funds. However, a few of the largest public plan sponsors have established internal operations for mortgage origination and servicing. Relatively large staffs are required to handle such activities, whether they are conducted directly or through mortgage correspondents. Mortgage activities tend to be time consuming, since significant time is required to successfully underwrite, close, and service commercial mortgages on a nationwide basis.

The internal origination and servicing of commercial mortgage instruments is a relatively labor-intensive process given the requirement that funds obtain national diversification in their investment programs and work closely with real estate mortgage brokers to source product. Mortgage underwriting can take place as an adjunct function to the acquisition role for real estate equities. Servicing functions can be placed within the realm of asset managment or handled by commercial mortgage correspondents. As with equity investment operations, the fund's ability to analyze specific debt opportunities and market characteristics can be divided into (1) an acquisition/origination function and (2) an investment/asset management function.

Appraisals

Appraisals are mandatory for pension funds and typically must be completed by an objective third-party appraiser, such as a Member of the Appraisal Institute (MAI). The hiring of appraisers is coming increasingly under the control of the pension fund rather than the advisor, who might have a vested interest in overstating appraised values. Coordination of data for the appraisal process is essential. This activity is commonly becoming a responsibility of asset managers. The paperwork involved in handling the provisions of lease details and other property information can become extremely onerous. To facilitate the appraisal process, appraisal data requirements can be coordinated by an internal real estate staff member.

Cash Management

Cash management is a major issue for the largest pension funds, which can benefit by having cash accounts swept on a daily basis. A money center bank can provide national cash management services to receive funds and wire these amounts to a central account. The liquid investment department of the pension fund can then access the cash for its own purposes. Cash management activities can effectively be assigned to a member of the asset management staff as an ancillary responsibility.

Research

Increasingly, pension funds are adding research analysts to help in strategy formulation. A critical aspect of research is that it must be focused to yield maximum benefit for the time spent. The research function is typically charged with determining the most profitable asset classes on a geographic basis to develop acquisition preferences. In addition, the research function may have broader responsibility to assess the impact of economic variables on a balanced real estate portfolio to limit the plan sponsor's risk exposure, avoid economic down cycles, and trigger disposition programs.

Legal Services

Real estate is complex from a legal standpoint. Commonly, corporate pension funds turn to in-house legal counsel to assist with acquisition and contract negotiations. Similarly, public pension funds look to internal counsel for their needs. Third-party legal firms are also brought on board as a matter of course to assist in the investment and due diligence procedures required for real estate investments. However, since legal services are required on an infrequent basis, pension funds rarely have full-time professionals dedicated solely to real estate. This activity is handled by lawyers, internal and external, who also have responsibilities for other categories of investments.

MIS/Accounting

As the real estate portfolio grows, management information systems (MIS) and accounting activities grow proportionally. Investment accounting, financial policies, manuals, and reporting systems are the responsibility of accounting staff. In the corporate plan setting, staff from the corporation's internal audit department can be transferred to the real estate function on an ad hoc basis. In the public setting, it is common to dedicate internal resources to this effort or use external auditors for accounting needs. A single experienced accounting officer should be able to handle real estate assets in excess of $1 billion in association with external auditors.

International

The acquisition and management of international real estate assets are of interest to the largest and most sophisticated pension funds. Typically, large pension funds treat international real estate investments as within a "regional sector" rather than dedicating specific staff to handle this activity. However, as large U.S. pension funds execute international investment strategies, foreign investment operations may be managed by internal staff, similar to the approach taken by European funds that are active in the United States. European investors often set up local operations to handle their real estate portfolios. Currently, many public funds are legislatively prohibited from making international investments. These restrictions are likely to be relaxed as international investing becomes a core strategy of portfolio diversification.

CRITICAL ORGANIZATIONAL ELEMENTS

A number of key organizational elements must be addressed when structuring the organization of real estate investment operations. Each of these elements is discussed briefly next.

Fiduciary Responsibilities

Employees working within a pension fund's real estate investment department must be cognizant of the fiduciary responsibilities they have when conducting their duties. Normally, the "prudent person rule" applies for all activities pertaining to the acquisition and management of real estate investments. To a certain extent, pension fund employees are protected by the fiduciary role of advisors and consultants, but as pension funds increase their investment activity and provide input into implementation activities, fiduciary lines tend to blurr. Fiduciary liabilities for real estate staff can be managed in a number of ways. For example, real estate properties can be held as separate corporations to limit liability. In addition, insurance can be arranged to handle liabilities at the property level.

Experience Levels

For the key positions of real estate director, acquisitions officer, and asset management officer, a minimum of 10 years' experience is normally required for a sophisticated pension fund. Real estate staff are typically drawn from a background in real estate finance, banking, or law. University degrees at the master's level have become the industry norm. Real estate staff are often promoted from other areas of the corporate or public organization, where their talents and abilities have been proven.

Levels of Authority

The board of trustees of a pension fund active in real estate has the authority to delegate levels of authority pertaining to investment management decisions. For example, at large funds, a board of trustees may delegate decisions up to a certain dollar amount, such as $10 million for acquisition and property management decisions. In effect, given the fact that real estate assets typically have high values, these discretionary levels of authority do not necessarily result in significant levels of power to the executive. Trustees remain involved in virtually all important decisions. However, the delegation of authority frequently facilitates decision making.

Career Planning

Several career tracks are viable for real estate executives working in the pension fund environment. A typical career path might begin with an analytical role in asset management, such as a junior asset management officer learning the nuts and bolts of the real estate business. Thereafter, the individual might move to a market analysis or mortgage underwriting position prior to moving into the real estate equity department. The career ladder from analyst to asset management to acquisitions to director of the department normally occurs over a 10- to 15-year time frame. A second form of career track is to rotate an executive through various pension fund departments, such as benefits, administration, finance, personnel, and investor relations, as part of a path to heading the real estate function.

It is also increasingly common for pension funds to recruit seasoned real estate executives from the real estate advisory community. Top real estate pension fund executives working at many of the large pension funds today have had previous experience with large life companies or advisory firms that provide services to the pension funds. These high-calibre real estate executives have the ability to utilize their experiences from the advisory side of the business.

Communication

The real estate organization within a pension fund is generally quite tightly knit. Formal means of communication are not normally required, other than weekly staff meetings, for example, to analyze possible investment decisions. Trustees commonly meet on a monthly basis to analyze prospective property acquisitions and review asset management reports.

Training

Expertise is gained by exchanging knowledge at industry seminars, such as the Pension Real Estate Association or the National Association of Real Estate Investment Trusts. These associations typically hold annual or semiannual meetings to provide for an exchange of ideas on important issues faced by the industry.

Salaries and Perquisites

Generally speaking, the internal real estate staff at a pension fund receives less compensation than employees with equal skills who work in the advisory community. Public plan employees with similar skill sets can earn up to 50 percent less than their peers in the advisory industry. Corporate plan employees are usually paid more, but their compensation levels remain below those of employees working for advisors. The discrepancy between corporate plan employees and the advisory community can be upwards of 35 percent.

Pension plan real estate employees are well aware of the discrepancy in compensation from their brethren in the advisory community. But a number of factors may compensate for this disparity, including greater responsibility, greater job security, a better quality of life, and comprehensive benefits.

Responsibility

The responsibility for managing multibillion-dollar portfolios is an attractive job element for pension fund staff. As advisors, real estate professionals may not feel the same sense of accomplishment as fund employees. The consultation role is appealing to some real estate pros, but others find being a key decision maker at a fund to be much more satisfying professionally.

Job Security

Pension fund staff have relative job security, acting as fiduciaries to professionally manage the portfolio and report performance to the board of trustees. There is relatively low turnover in the community of pension fund directors who are responsible for real estate investments due to the importance of personnel stability in handling large volumes of monies. For this reason, selecting the appropriate individuals for these positions is critical.

Quality of Life

Pension fund managers responsible for real estate assets often have the opportunity to enjoy a high standard of living in the communities in which they work. Professionals associated with public funds, for example, have the benefit of working in their respective state capitals. State capitals are frequently less congested than larger cities, have high-quality educational facilities, and are scenically endowed. Visitors to state capitals such as Sacramento, Madison, Tallahassee, Richmond, Austin, and Columbus appreciate the natural amenities associated with these cities. In addition, because these cities tend to have a lower cost of living, the compensation paid to the real estate employee has more local buying power.

Comprehensive Benefits

In addition to relative job security, pension fund directors normally receive comprehensive health and retirement benefits, similar to those enjoyed by the plan participants whom they represent for investments.

PUBLIC PLAN SPONSORS

The organization of a public plan sponsor is subject to applicable federal, state, and municipal laws that govern public investment management. These regulations determine the responsibilities of trustees and plan administrators. Generally, public funds must address the issue of organizational growth prior to corporate plans, since the assets of public funds are growing more rapidly. Public funds are also not subject to ERISA regulations, which have hindered corporate plans from making and managing direct real estate investments.

Public plan sponsors face unique challenges in managing investments, particularly real estate. At the state government level, legislators typically serve on a part-time basis, and many may be unfamiliar with the process or the technicalities of investing in real estate. In addition, legislators tend to be frugal with budgets for investment administration. Budgets for real estate staff, travel, office facilities, and general administrative expenses can be quite small. Employees working in a state environment are also often restricted from entertainment programs offered by the real estate advisory community. Lunches, dinners, golf outings, and other "perks" are often strictly prohibited by government regulation.

The addition of new staff to a public fund can be a difficult task, especially if the investment agency is a state department subject to civil service hiring constraints. Quasi-governmental bodies typically find it easier to manage staff needs and terminations. Job posting and notification of new positions within the government agency are normally required.

State employee unions are also a fact of life that must be understood and properly managed within the real estate department. To avoid the complexities of unionized environments and lengthy hiring times, independent contractors may be used to manage real estate assets.

Large state funds often benefit from close alliances with educational institutions sponsored by their governments. For example, the state university may run a real estate program as part of its business curriculum. Many research and analysis activities can be conducted jointly with a state university. This is of great benefit to the faculty and students, since it gives them real-world experience. The pension fund benefits by having bright young people analyze some of its most critical issues at reasonable cost.

The political dynamics associated with public pension plans must be managed as they relate to real estate investments. This is particularly true in the case of members of the board of trustees who tend to circumvent their real estate staff in making investment decisions for real estate. Marketing efforts by the private real estate community are often targeted at these trustees. This marketing activity must be properly managed to avoid undermining the authority of real estate staff, since their expertise in reviewing investment decisions is crucial to the fund.

CORPORATE PLAN SPONSORS

As a general rule, corporations with pension fund assets invested in real estate prefer to work with real estate advisors. Therefore, staffing and organizational issues are kept to a minimum, since real estate investment activity is handled by external parties. Only the largest corporations have dedicated professionals to manage real estate investments. Typically, a corporation will hire real estate talent only after reaching a portfolio size of $500 million or more.

The reluctance of corporations to add staff to manage real estate stems largely from a perception that investment management is an expense rather than a source of income. Major public corporations must operate under the scrutiny of their shareholders, and expense control is always a priority. Many large corporations are reluctant to add staff in the investment area given their overall desire to limit growth of their work force. Therefore, a small staff is most common. In addition, compensation levels at corporations may not be high enough to attract the highest calibre of professionals who find employment with advisors.

However, as a corporate pension plan grows beyond the level of $1 billion invested in real estate, it usually requires dedicated staff to manage and monitor the performances of advisors. This is frequently accomplished by recruiting a real estate director, who reports to the chief investment officer of the pension fund. Referring to our maturity model (see Exhibit 20–2), we would view these types of corporate plan sponsors as attaining a stage II level of organizational design.

The most sophisticated corporate pension fund departments are equipped to manage portfolios well in excess of $1 billion, handling complicated joint ventures as well as direct investments, frequently with the assistance of real estate advisors. These major corporations tend to prefer direct relationships with the real estate community. In certain instances, corporations with large real estate investment management departments (like General Electric) sell real estate investment services to other corporations, in essence acting as a competitor to the real estate advisory community by co-investing with third parties. Using this strategy, a corporation may spread the cost of its operations to third-party clients while giving smaller plan sponsors the opportunity to co-invest.

Many tasks required to acquire and manage real estate occur on an infrequent or irregular basis; therefore, professionals dedicated to these activities can be often shared from other parts of the corporate organization. For example, large corporations with pension funds active in real estate can draw on their staff resources in the areas of accounting, legal, engineering, environmental, corporate real estate, and even underwriting, if the corporation is a financial institution active in real estate lending. Cash management activities can also be shared by the real estate investment department.

ORGANIZATIONAL IMPLICATIONS FOR REAL ESTATE ADVISORS AND CONSULTANTS

Real estate advisors and consultants must be cognizant of the maturity and sophistication of their pension fund clients. Real estate products, marketing programs, reporting documents, and additional services provided by advisors and consultants must be tailored to the needs of pension fund clients and their particular levels of sophistication. The increasing maturity of the pension fund investment community and the changing needs of specific clients mandate organizational changes at the advisory and consultant levels.

Frequently, 3 to 10 core advisors are utilized by the sophisticated pension plan, in addition to sector specialists who act as conduits to the particular real estate asset class, such as office, industrial, or retail properties. The opinion of a pension fund's real estate staff must be solicited on a regular basis and respected by the advisor providing service. Advisors who sell skills must adapt to meet the demands of sophisticated pension plans. For the most mature and sophisticated pension funds, advisors must maintain excellent reporting relationships to convey information on a property-by-property basis.

Advisors and consultants to sophisticated pension funds need to be prepared to negotiate fees and make knowledgeable fee bids. In the future, asset management fees may become correlated with property cash flows as well as overall property performance. Fee negotiations will be common among the largest funds, since they have sophisticated real estate staff who understand the "service for value" relationship. Sales decisions to dispose of assets will become more prevalent as pension funds become fully funded and reallocate investments among their portfolios. Advisory and consulting organizations must be prepared to adapt to the needs of clients seeking to dispose of property to reallocate their real estate portfolios.

Co-investment situations are also likely to become more commonplace among U.S. pension funds, as they are among European pension funds. Large corporate and public pension funds may seek joint investment positions with major U.S. insurance companies or with foreign investors to access real estate transactions without having to add professional staff. Pension funds operating with this approach benefit from being a part of a large network with their joint partners to access product.

Advisors seeking business from mature pension funds should concentrate their marketing programs on gaining acceptance from the real estate staff and then consult with trustees. In the corporate setting, real estate staff are responsible for making recommendations to the trustees. With less mature public pension fund entities, a direct sales approach at the trustee level frequently succeeds. But as pension funds grow in size and sophistication, real estate staff become critical in gaining approval to proceed with an investment decision.

CONCLUSION

The organizational design of a pension fund sponsor's real estate department is largely dependent on the size and sophistication of the pension fund. The decision to use external versus internal staff is a strategic issue that is based on the investment philosophy of the pension fund trustees. Once pension funds achieve a level of $500 million or more invested in real estate, dedicated professionals are commonly hired to handle, monitor, and manage real estate advisors and consultants. Beyond the $1 billion level, additional real estate staff are often recruited to manage the portfolio as it grows.

As pension funds' real estate investment programs mature, they move from a stage I organizational format, where the fund relies totally on external advisors. At the stage II level of maturity, funds hire a dedicated professional to handle real estate investments. At stage III, asset management is added as an internal responsibility. Thereafter, plan sponsors move to a stage IV format, where a more extensive internal staff handles the wide range of activities required to manage real estate investments. In certain circumstances, a large fund may advance to a stage V format and begin selling its real estate investment management services to other investors. Throughout this process of organizational maturity, pension funds begin to assume organizational responsibilities previously handled by their advisors. Advisory organizations serving sophisticated pension funds react to the changing requirements of their clients and the sophistication of real estate professionals handling pension fund assets. This is accomplished by modifying reporting structures and disposition services, while also acting as a conduit to real estate assets in a core and sector specialist capacity.

Public plan sponsors and corporate plan sponsors vary significantly in their organizational formats. Typically, public pension plans tend to hire more staff than their corporate brethren. This is due to the very large size of the public portfolios, but also to the fact that corporations seem more concerned about expense control and accordingly prefer to use advisors. Large corporations, however, once they achieve a significant size, will selectively co-invest with and market to third parties, a tactic usually prohibited in the public environment. Corporations also share functions from their legal, environmental, and insurance departments, since these services are available within the corporate hierarchy, whereas public funds typically must have this capacity resident full time within the fund department or hire it on an ad hoc basis.

The success of a pension fund's real estate investment program depends on the people charged with responsible management of the portfolio. High-calibre professionals, coupled with the right organizational design and a well-thought-out strategic investment program, can contribute to maximizing real estate investment returns. Advisors and consultants working with pension funds must be cognizant of the sophistication of their clients, which grows with the pension fund's experience in real estate investing.

CHAPTER 21

STRUCTURING A REAL ESTATE ADVISORY FIRM

Michael A. Herzberg
FPL Associates

INTRODUCTION

The tremendous growth in plan sponsor real estate portfolios in recent years has been facilitated in part by a large number of advisory firms that have helped establish the foundation for today's sophisticated real estate pension fund industry. The organizational form of a real estate advisory firm depends greatly on the needs of its pension fund clients and the real investment strategy chosen by the advisor. An advisor's strategy is based on such factors as the geographic location for investments, property types, and legal structures, as well as investment management style. Each of these important strategic factors have a bearing on the type of organization an advisor will adopt. Since the plan sponsor community's needs are diverse, a wide variety of organizational designs exists for advisors. The real estate advisory industry currently is composed of firms ranging from small, specialized boutiques to internationally diversified firms controlled by large financial institutions. The diverse needs of pension funds have spawned an industry of close to 100 firms offering particular investment strategies that are executed through a wide variety of organizational forms.

A BRIEF HISTORY OF REAL ESTATE ADVISORY FIRMS

In the early 1970s, Prudential offered the first large-scale commingled, open-end real estate fund, known as PRISA. This marked the

The author wishes to recognize John F. C. Parsons for his assistance in the preparation of this chapter.

first serious foray of institutional investor into the world of real estate equity investments through a commingled account, advisory relationship. Other insurance companies, money managers, and bank trust departments followed suit, as this was a natural extension of the stock and bond services already offered by these companies.

During the late 1970s and early 1980s, a sustained increase in inflation combined with weakened performance in the stock and bond markets. As "necessity is the mother of allocation," these factors led to increased interest by institutional investors in real estate equity investments.[1]

By the early 1980s, the institutional market saw the introduction of advisory firms that were thought to be more entrepreneurial than the insurance companies. Firms like RREEF, JMB, and Aldrich, Eastman & Waltch began to gain significant market share. Some insurance companies responded by organizing their real estate advisory services as subsidiary operations to provide for greater autonomy.

The insurance companies were also followed by other organizations that had been in the real estate business in one fashion or another but did not have access to pension fund relationships. These companies were typically in the acquisition, syndication, or lending business and therefore had an organizational infrastructure that allowed then to serve pension funds. Money management firms also had access to pension fund capital and desired to enter the real estate arena. During the formative stages of the industry, the principal hurdle for the pension fund was gaining confidence in the role of real estate equities in a diversified portfolio.

Commercial mortgage banking firms, such as Heitman, that were familiar with sourcing institutions for debt financing followed the insurance and money management firms into real estate equity management for pension funds. These commercial mortgage firms had the advantage of existing relationships with the real estate investment and development community. For the most part, corporate plan sponsors led the way in utilizing the services of these early advisory firms.

During the early 1980s, a few visionary real estate syndication firms (which primarily served individual investors) switched their strategic business focus toward public and corporate pension funds.

---

[1] Joseph L. Pagliari, Jr., "Real Estate in 3-D—See It Now!", *Real Estate Issues,* Fall–Winter 1990, p. 16.

Several of the large, national commercial real estate brokerage firms also established pension advisory organizations around this time. During the latter half of the 1980s, the pension plan sponsors became more sophisticated in their demands. Accordingly, dozens of specialist boutique firms entered the business. Typically, these organizations tended to be relatively small and focused on a particular product type or geographic region. This time period also witnessed the first serious introduction of separate account and co-investment vehicles as alternatives to commingled funds, which led to increased complexity in the organizational design of advisory firms.

TYPES OF REAL ESTATE ADVISORY ORGANIZATIONS

Real estate advisory firms might best be described as belonging to a particular segment along a spectrum of organizational types (see Exhibit 21–1). The frame of reference for this organizational spectrum is total assets under management. At one end of the spectrum, advisory firms that are associated with large American insurance companies, domestic and foreign banks, investment firms and other money management advisors represent the most significant share of assets under management. These firms manage billions of dollars in finan-

EXHIBIT 21–1
Spectrum of Organizational Types for Real Estate Pension Advisors

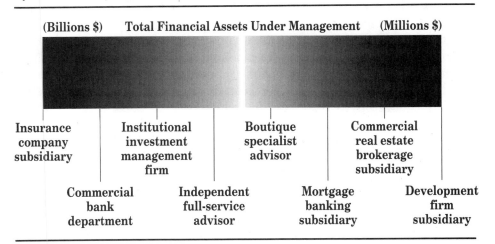

Source: FPL Associates.

cial assets in the form of stocks, bonds, and other financial instruments in addition to their real estate advisory activities. In the middle of this organizational spectrum are firms that are associated with old-line mortgage banking companies and vertically integrated, full-service real estate advisory firms. These firms serve as advisors to pension fund clients strictly in the field of real estate. Toward the opposite end of the organizational spectrum are nationally recognized commercial real estate brokers, affiliates of development firms, and smaller boutique entities that cater to a particular geographic, product, or client segment. A wide variety of organizational designs exist for each type of advisory firm along this spectrum. Within the category of larger firms, there are very few totally independent real estate advisory organizations. Most advisors are controlled by entities that have ancillary services in general money management, insurance, banking, syndication, development and brokerage, or mortgage banking.

As pension funds have gained experience in real estate, advisors have reconfigured their organizations and staffs to satisfy a maturing investment market. Evidence of this maturity of pension funds that invest in real estate can be found by assessing several fundamental trends in the pension real estate industry, such as (1) slower growth, (2) increased sophistication, (3) an emphasis on cost and service, and (4) high levels of competition.[2] In response to the trends in industry maturity, the organizational forms of real estate advisors have gravitated toward two ends of a spectrum. The large firms that offer a national presence with full-scale capabilities dominate one end of the spectrum. At the opposite end, smaller boutique firms offer specialized services catering to a particular market niche, such as a specific property type or geographic location. Advisory firms that currently reside in the middle of this spectrum often face the choice of moving toward becoming full-service or downsizing to become a boutique operation.

As in other areas of the financial services industry, the movement of firms toward either end of the spectrum creates an "hourglass" profile.[3] Mid-size firms find it difficult to compete against the industry giants on one side and the small, entrepreneurial firms on the other.

---

[2] Michael E. Porter, "The Transition to Industry Maturity." In *Competitive Strategy—Techniques for Analyzing Industries and Competitors* (New York: The Free Press, 1980).

[3] Joseph J. Ori, "Real Estate Strategies for Profitability in the 1990s," *Real Estate Review,* Spring 1990.

REAL ESTATE NEEDS OF PLAN SPONSORS

Within the overall framework of achieving portfolio diversification, plan sponsors are attracted to real estate as a complement to their equity and fixed-income investments. The real estate needs of plan sponsors are satisfied by a wide range of advisors who provide acquisition, asset management, property management, disposition, and reporting services through a variety of real estate vehicles. These products are designed to help the plan sponsor achieve diversification with minimal risk and with an emphasis on long-term capital growth.

Relative to traditional pension fund investments in equity and fixed-income instruments, real estate is a complex asset to acquire, manage, and dispose. Furthermore, this asset is relatively new to the pension fund portfolio. To satisfy the complex real estate requirements of plan sponsors, real estate advisory firms' services and products continue to evolve. In addition to the basic services of property acquisition, management, and disposition, capabilities in the areas of research, client reporting, and portfolio management are an integral part of satisfying plan sponsor real estate requirements. As noted previously, another critical factor is the issue of discretion over real estate decision making. Some plan sponsors require fully integrated real estate advisory firms that control the entire process of acquisition, management, and disposition, while others are positioned to work with real estate advisors who are not full-service but have unique attributes that give their organizations a competitive advantage in satisfying plan sponsor needs.

STRATEGIC MISSION OF THE REAL ESTATE ADVISOR

Strategic focus is essential for success in the competitive world of real estate advisors. Because of the varied and complex nature of the plan sponsor community, real estate advisors have developed different strategies to satisfy their clientele. Today real estate pension advisory firms are more client driven than in the past. Each firm's strategic mission is oriented toward satisfying the real estate demands of its clients. In outlining the strategic mission of the real estate advisor, senior management must address who the firm's principal clients will be, what products and services will be offered to pension funds, and what particular market segments will be serviced. In addition, senior management must determine which marketing approaches and in-

vestment vehicles will be most effective in raising new capital. The
driving force behind strategy formulation for the advisory firm is the
ability of the advisor to add value to the real estate investment process
over and above the capabilities of competition in the industry. The
organizational design the advisory firm chooses depends on the firm's
strategic direction and abilities, while successful implementation of
this strategy depends on the skills of professional staff working within
an appropriate organizational framework, as indicated in Exhibit
21–2.

From time to time, the organizational design of an advisory firm
should be modified to respond to the changing needs of pension fund
clients. Over the past several years, as pension funds have moved
from discretionary, commingled funds to nondiscretionary, separate
accounts and co-investment vehicles, organizational changes have
occurred among advisory firms. Organizational form therefore is not
a static element in the investment services strategy of an advisory
firm. For example, in recent years, two of the more prominent changes
in organizational form have occurred in the areas of portfolio management and market research. These important functions have been

EXHIBIT 21–2
Critical Factors in Organizational Design

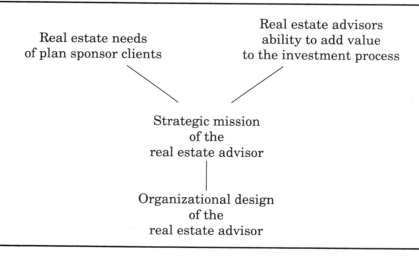

Source: FPL Associates.

added by many advisors to assist pension fund investors in administering their increasingly large portfolios, utilizing proactive research to support decision making for acquisitions, asset management, and disposition. Functions such as portfolio management and market research also serve to distinguish advisors vis-à-vis the competition. These critical aspects of an advisor's organization are essential ingredients for achieving competitive advantage in the pension real estate industry.

ORGANIZATION OF THE ADVISOR

Successful real estate advisory firms are composed of experienced professionals working in a variety of functional responsibilities. Larger advisory firms tend to have high degrees of specialization within each functional area. Smaller advisory firms typically combine certain functional areas, such as acquisitions and dispositions, within a single department.

As shown schematically in Exhibit 21–3, large real estate pension advisory firms typically have several functional positions. These positions are described in the following sections.

Chairperson and Chief Executive Officer

The chairperson of the firm, who is often the founding member of the organization, is responsible for overall strategic direction and general leadership. Often the chair is also a major force in long-term planning for the firm, as well as a key motivating agent for all employees. The chair is also responsible for reporting the results of the firm's performance to the board of directors of the organization. Since many of the large advisory firms are owned by parent organizations, the chairperson must be adept at interpreting the results of the firm's performance for the owners, who may not have real estate backgrounds.

President and Chief Operating Officer

The president is primarily responsible for the implementation of the strategy chosen by the chairperson and the board of directors. The president's role is heavily oriented toward the execution of the firm's

EXHIBIT 21-3   Organizational Design of a Large Real Estate Advisory Firm

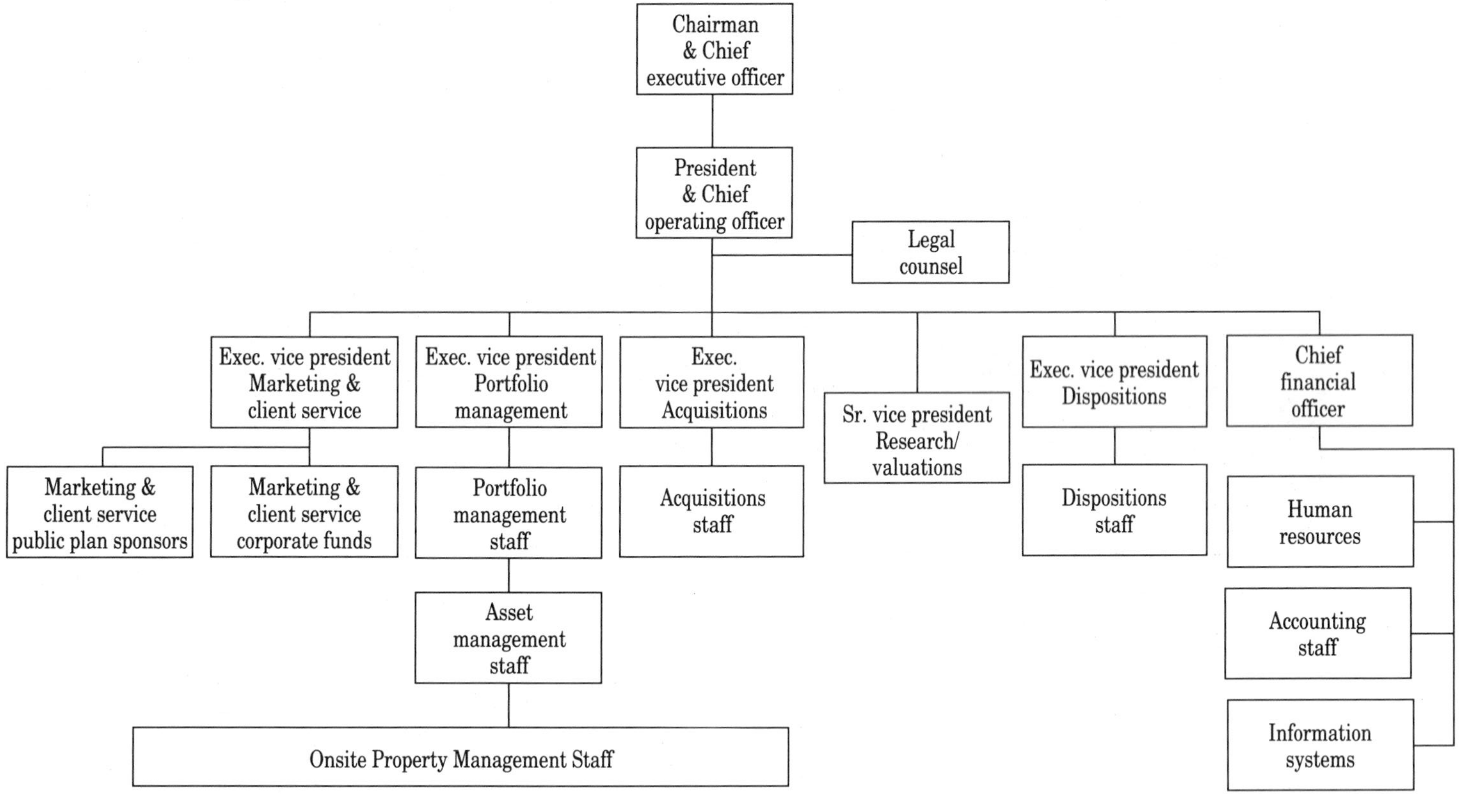

Source: FPL Associates.

strategy through a senior role in client relationships, as well as the coordination of all functional responsibilities. In the formative years of the pension advisory industry, company presidents tended to have a high degree of financial experience relative to the acquisition of real estate property. In recent years, it has become essential that the president of a firm also have strong capabilities in leading the portfolio and asset management disciplines within the firm. In addition, the effective president possesses excellent team-building skills to form and manage teams of professionals with the requisite skills to service pension fund accounts.

A number of private advisory firms are based on the principles of partnership. Therefore, the CEO/COO role may to some extent be shared by a number of senior principals. These firms often have management committees that govern firm policy. They usually have one or two principals who serve as the final arbiters of internal, unresolved matters as well as setting the firm's strategic direction. Private firms tend toward this partnership structure, while firms that are subsidiaries of larger organizations tend toward a more traditional corporate hierarchy.

Acquisitions

The acquisitions function is typically managed by a very senior executive with expertise in the acquisition process. This individual usually reports to and works with the president. Depending on the size of the organization, the head of acquisitions is supported by an acquisitions team to originate and structure the financial details of an acquisition, negotiate the documentation, and efficiently close the transaction. Acquisition professionals may be assigned to specific geographic regions and/or property types within which they are responsible for sourcing attractive properties. Acquisition professionals maintain relationships with property owners who control assets that meet the investment needs of plan sponsor clients as well as those of the broader real estate brokerage community. Since there tends to be significant competition for the highest-quality real estate assets, acquisitions professionals with the closest relationships to vendors of the best properties are in a position to have early knowledge of product availability. This can create a competitive advantage for the advisory firm.

Marketing and Client Service

Marketing professionals have two principal responsibilities: raising new funds to grow the advisor's assets under management and servicing the ongoing needs of plan sponsors, such as providing information on the status of their real estate investments. Marketing professionals tend to spend a great deal of time traveling to meet with corporate pension fund executives, public plan sponsors, university and endowment funds, and union funds. Real estate investments tend to be made by the larger pension plans, which also tend to be more sophisticated. Therefore, marketing staff must be comfortable dealing with sophisticated pension plan professionals.

Pension plans find the most attractive marketing professionals to be those who can communicate well, are persistent (but not obnoxious) in their calling activity and, most important, have detailed product knowledge.[4] It is critical that marketing professionals have an ongoing understanding of their customers' portfolios. Senior marketing executives must also be able to coordinate the full range of services their firms offer. Increasingly, marketing is becoming a team effort. In many instances, client relationship managers will join with marketing staff to generate new business through team presentations. Pension funds want to know the experience and backgrounds of key employees. Therefore, acquisition, portfolio management and research professionals frequently join the marketing staff of an advisory firm to make joint presentations. In advance of these meetings, detailed preparation and rehearsal of presentations is essential to coordinate speaking roles for all team members. This activity is commonly managed by senior marketing executives.

Marketing professionals are often the leading spokespeople for their firms at industry conferences; thus, public speaking abilities are an attractive attribute. As marketing executives mature, they become more adept at communicating their firm's message to both the real estate staff of the pension fund and the trustees who ultimately are responsible for the investment decisions made by the fund. There are different schools of thought when it comes to marketing issues relative to the staff versus the trustees. Though it is vital to

---

[4] Based on interviews with real estate directors of the 20 largest U.S. real estate equity portfolios conducted by FPL Associates, in 1991.

create and maintain relationships with trustee members, it is also critical to have a strong operating relationship with the pension fund's staff. It is the pension fund staff who will make the recommendations to the board of trustees and be responsible for the implementation of the decisions. Therefore it is important not to alienate the staff by concentrating marketing efforts solely on trustees.

Junior marketing executives tend to focus on certain specifics of the client group, such as corporate pension plans or public plan sponsors. In addition, many have a specific geographic focus, such as an eastern or western regional emphasis. It is the role of the junior marketing person to not only support the senior marketing person but, in those organizations with a large base of clients, to also provide additional services to a specific group of clients. Certain organizations have a client base in excess of 200 clients and are required to provide high-quality services to them. Junior marketing people provide much of this support.

Marketing professionals are generally responsible for presenting quarterly and annual financial results. In addition, they should have input into ongoing portfolio management decisions, along with other members of the firm. The interpretation of client feedback for the CEO is also the responsibility of marketing staff. Therefore, in addition to communicating well, these professionals must be able to listen well to client concerns and calls to action to correct problems.

Portfolio Management

Along with decisions pertaining to acquisitions, portfolio management represents the highest level of strategic decision making for the real estate portfolio (followed by asset management and property management). The responsibility for strategic portfolio decisions to preserve and enhance the value of a real estate portfolio falls within the realm of the portfolio manager. Typically, these portfolio managers are responsible for a multiple-property portfolio that is likely to be geographically diverse but may have a specific real estate product focus, such as retail properties or hotels. Portfolio management responsibilities can be centralized (on a national basis) or localized, depending on the properties' management intensity and the impact of local and regional economics on ongoing investment performance. The overall goal of the portfolio manager is to enhance and improve the long-term performance of the total portfolio, helping to make decisions on the types of properties to include in the portfolio as well as being involved in decisions relative to capital investment, property (re)positioning, and selling decisions. Issues such as the balance between income and capital appreciation are important components of the portfolio manager's universe.

Asset Management

Asset managers are dedicated to preserving and enhancing the value of real estate investments in a more limited sense than portfolio managers are. They are commonly responsible for one large asset or a pool of assets in a particular region. Asset managers are responsible for both strategic decisions and implementation activities that have a long-term impact on asset values. Typically, these decisions relate to major capital expenditures, approvals of major leases, marketing strategy, renovations, budgeting, mortgage negotiations, insurance and risk management, and tenant retention programs. Traditionally, asset management professionals have a financial background and a familiarity with issues pertaining to real estate financial management. Increasingly, asset management professionals are being drawn either from leasing backgrounds (given the importance of value enhancement of real estate assets through increased marketing efforts and tenant retention programs) or from property management (given their experience in budgeting, construction/renovation, leasing, and tenant retention). These asset management skills have taken on a new significance in recent years due to falling real estate values. During the growth of pension fund real estate assets in the early to mid-1980s, the focus was primarily on the acquisition function. With the poor performance of real estate equities in the late 1980s and early 1990s, asset and portfolio management have become areas of increased importance.

Property Management

Property management capabilities can reside within the advisory firm or be contracted to external third-party organizations that have expertise in the property type as well as in the region where the asset is located. The selection of internal versus external management is a function of a number of often conflicting issues such as sufficient geographic and/or property type concentration, access to local market information, and the strengths and weaknesses of a particular firm.

Real estate advisors that are involved in regional mall investments tend to have vertically integrated staffs to handle property management. Many of the large national advisors also have internal staff to manage other types of property. Hotel management is typically contracted to outside third parties. Advisory firms that are national in scope have gravitated to internal property management departments. Since leasing is such a critical factor in the performance of office properties, local professionals will work with the firm's professionals to provide leasing expertise. Property management staff within the advisory firm are responsible for custodial functions. These professionals handle property maintenance, purchasing, traffic and parking, waste management, collection of rent, and tenant security. Property management staff also work side by side with asset managers to provide feedback on repositioning the asset for higher value.

Research and Valuations

Among sophisticated real estate advisory firms, the research function is integrated into a senior mangement position to assist the decision-making process for acquisitions, management, and dispositions. Generally, two types of research are common in the industry. Some firms employ research professionals who provide a macro overview of demographic and economic trends with insights on how these trends affect various geographic regions and property types. This information is provided to plan sponsor clients to help them make decisions relating to the ongoing management of the real estate portfolios.

Other firms tend to stress a micro or "street-level" approach to research. These firms employ research staff who emphasize local market information to determine, for example, the direction of market rents or the performance of a competing regional mall or other direct influences on the properties they manage in the immediate area. Property sales, leasing data, absorption of space, traffic counts, and other local analyses are used by these research professionals.

The research function is a key element of the marketing mix of the sophisticated advisor. Research serves to educate clients in complex real estate situations. Similarly to research conducted for equity and fixed-income investments, quantitative analysis is emphasized to support decisions pertaining to investment style and management.

Plan sponsor clients have a growing appetite for research to support decision making beyond the acquisition of a property, particularly decisions relating to ongoing asset management as well as property dispositions.

Pension funds require frequent valuations of their real estate investments. These valuations are normally conducted by internal staff working for the pension fund advisor. Internally prepared valuations are verified by external appraisers, who usually have a Member of the Appraisal Institute (MAI) designation. A tremendous amount of property and market data must be collected on a regular basis to estimate the value of properties under management by the advisor. Normally, these valuations are completed on an annual basis, then property values are marked up or down accordingly. An advisor's research and valuations capability can be a distinguishing factor in achieving a competitive advantage.

Chief Financial Officer

The chief financial officer of the advisory firm is usually responsible for all accounting functions in addition to all debt-related activities for the firm and the portfolio. In this regard, the CFO will undertake to secure financing, both short and long term, for the general needs of the firm and the specific needs of the properties. This often requires maintaining relationships with Wall Street and the banking community in addition to overseeing all financial negotiations in the effort to secure debt or debt-related products. Other oversight functions may include exchange rate programs, hedging programs, bank syndication, and other related responsibilities, including cash management to sweep surplus cash accounts from each property into a central pool of funds that can be invested in money market accounts. The CFO is also responsible for the preparation of all financial reports in conjunction with portfolio and asset managers. In this manner, the CFO assists the COO with day-to-day administration of the firm, enabling the CEO to focus on client relationships and execution of long-term strategies. To accomplish these myriad tasks, the CFO may have a department head to handle each of the functional areas of human resources, systems, and accounting. The CFO may also provide asset and portfolio managers with financial performance information in the form of written quarterly and annual financial statements for pension fund clients. The CFO may also help asset managers with insurance policies and risk management.

Legal Counsel

Depending on the size of the real estate advisor, real estate counsel may be obtained through attorneys hired by the firm on an ad hoc basis, particularly to assist with property acquisitions. Alternatively, legal counsel may reside within the firm in the form of full-time legal professionals who not only assist in the acquisition process but also are involved in the day-to-day legal tasks of the property portfolio and the firm. The principal responsibility of legal counsel is to support the CEO and COO in a staff capacity, working in concert with other members of the firm. Legal counsel is responsible for the firm's compliance with federal legislation, including ERISA- and SEC-related matters. Most acquisition-related legal work tends to be performed by third-party counsel due to the scope and complexity of certain legal issues.

International Operations

Several of the largest U.S. real estate advisors have international offices to house professionals who source foreign capital as well as acquire properties for international funds. Foreign operations complicate the management of the overall firm due to differences in approach as well as to the conduct of business across time zones. Usually either foreign nationals are transferred overseas to run these offices, or local experts are hired to provide leadership to foreign operations.

Dispositions

Once a decision is reached to dispose of a property from a portfolio managed by the advisor, the firm may give this task to external third-party marketing agents such as commercial property brokers and investment banks or use internal staff for disposition activity. The characteristics of professionals charged with this responsibility are normally similar to those of professionals involved with acquisitions. Dispositions professionals must maintain a wide network of potential buyers and possess the sales acumen to communicate the investment opportunity to interested parties. In those advisory firms that do not employ full-time dispositions professionals, portfolio and asset managers frequently team up with the CFO to market properties.

CRITICAL SUPPORT ELEMENTS OF
THE ORGANIZATION

The pursuit of the strategic mission of the advisory firm requires not only an effective organizational form but also a number of key support elements to ensure success. These support elements often have an intangible nature, but are nevertheless essential. The most critical support elements for the real estate advisor are:

- Dynamic leadership.
- Culture and values.
- Performance measurement.
- Managerial development.
- Recruitment and training policies.
- Information systems.

Dynamic Leadership

The chairperson and the president are generally responsible for fostering a positively charged work atmosphere for all members of the advisory firm. This positive environment can then be shared by the firm's plan sponsor clients. Leadership of the advisory firm normally takes the form of communicating a broad strategic mission to all levels of the organization to imbue a common sense of purpose, with a goal of satisfying client needs. The chairperson typically plots the course for the firm and instills a vision among employees as to future growth. Communication from the senior management team to employees can take many forms, but a combination of regular staff meetings and annual meetings and social events for employees can be some of the more effective ways to spread the word about the firm's strategic mission.

Culture and Values

The culture and value system of the advisory firm is fostered and communicated by the senior management team through its daily activities and leadership by example. Senior management is responsible for instilling a work ethic and an esprit de corps for the entire organization. A positive culture is extremely beneficial to the firm as it seeks to form new relationships through its marketing efforts. The most successful firms are obsessed with serving the client.

Performance Measurement

Goal setting on both a corporate and a personal basis is essential to maximizing the performance of the advisory organization. The goals must be motivational in nature and allow for future measurement against actual performance. Because there is such a wide variety in the types of functions performed within the advisory organization, each job function should have a specific set of performance measurement standards. These standards should be communicated to the staff on an annual basis at a minimum, and preferably semiannually, to enable the staff to make course corrections in their work plans. By paying attention to the details of individual performance measurement, the senior management of the advisory firm can ensure an integrated performance in pursuit of the corporate strategic mission.

Managerial Development

From time to time, senior managers within the advisory organization should receive educational exposure outside the workplace to support their job activities. This instruction might pertain to leadership and team-building abilities, sales presentation training, or general industry knowledge. In addition, managerial development can be achieved by allowing lower-level managers to participate in ongoing strategic planning sessions conducted on an annual basis by the firm. Attendance at industry conferences can also help broaden the scope and awareness of issues faced by plan sponsor clients. These conferences can provide managers with the information they need to make strategic changes to their particular areas of expertise.

It is critical that managers update themselves on issues confronting the institutional real estate industry. These issues may pertain to government regulation of pension funds, trends in corporate governance, demographic shifts that affect real estate utilization, or the changing demands for various types of real estate investment products. By obtaining this knowledge outside the work force, the managers in training are unencumbered by the day-to-day pressures of their particular areas of responsibility. This arrangement enables them to focus on solutions that they can later apply to their daily working activities.

Recruitment and Training Policies

Professional competency and proficiency can be achieved at every level within the organization with strict recruiting and training procedures. As a general rule, it is usually best to promote employees from within the firm to more senior levels of responsibility. From time to time, however, special expertise may be required, and this can be obtained outside the firm. The introduction of new employees can reinvigorate the organization to pursue positive new directions, but the selection process for new employees should involve a rigorous screening and interview procedure involving a team of senior managers.

Ongoing training of current employees can minimize the need to recruit external talent. Training programs in the disciplines of marketing, property management, computer skills, and so on will ensure the growth of the professional ability of the organization in concert with the demands of pension fund clients.

Information Systems

State-of-the-art information systems are essential to enable the advisory firm to satisfy plan sponsor needs for up-to-date financial information and ongoing property status reports. These systems are also critical to managing database information that supports the research function provided by the firm. In addition, information systems can be used to support databases for marketing activity. These marketing systems can keep track of a large number of existing and potential clients of the organization and the many trustees and real estate professional staff with whom the marketing people must remain in frequent contact. Information systems also allow for the frequent mailing of marketing materials to keep the name of the company in front of existing and potential clients.

The complex nature of real estate investments creates a tremendous need to manage and maintain up-to-date information. This is particularly true for those advisors that provide separate account and direct investment management services, which must meet the demands of the sophisticated real estate professionals who are their clients. Commingled funds are also information intensive, particularly since many plan sponsors require detailed property-by-property information on the performance of assets within the commingled fund. Good information systems are also essential to managing the accounting function.

COMPENSATION SYSTEMS

The fees generated by today's advisory firms are quite different in terms of both magnitude and structure than in the early days of the advisory business. In the early 1980s, fees were typically based on the gross asset value of the portfolio managed by an advisor. The determination of the value of the portfolio was based on appraised value. Fees in the range of 125 basis points of the appraised portfolio value, paid annually, were the standard. Recently fees have decreased as advisory firms have adopted competitive pricing to attract and retain pension fund clientele. Total fees now tend to fall in the range of 60 to 75 basis points, with a portion of the fee deferred and paid upon performance. Commonly, the performance fee is structured to provide the client with a minimum real return, say, 5 percent. Thereafter, the advisor may participate in some portion of the total return above and beyond the minimum level. These incentive fees are paid to the advisor at the end of the contract period.

As the pension real estate industry has matured in recent years, competitive forces have put downward pressure on fees. This has created an environment that favors the consolidation of small advisors into larger entities to achieve certain economies of scale and strengthen their revenue streams. As this consolidation stabilizes with the strongest and most efficient firms remaining, the advisory fees paid per annum may increase to cover actual costs plus a small profit, with the remaining portion of the fees to be paid on a performance basis.

Executive Compensation

A wide range of compensation programs exists for the various types of employees who work in a real estate advisory firm. Commonly, the senior executive team, including the chairperson, president, and heads of the specific functions, have compensation packages that provide a base salary, an annual cash bonus based on the firm's performance, and some form of share ownership incentive. Marketing professionals also receive a base salary as well as a year-end annual cash bonus, which is normally dependent on the funds raised throughout the year. Bonuses are paid at year-end. Acquisitions professionals also have received significant bonuses at year-end in addition to their base salary packages. These bonuses are dependent on their success in acquiring properties on behalf of the advisor's clients. In the aggregate, acquisitions and marketing professionals may receive bonuses upwards of 50 percent of their base salary packages to provide an incentive for top performance. Exhibit 21–4 provides basic compensation data pertaining to key positions within an advisory firm.

Executives who have responsibility for asset and portfolio management typically receive a greater portion of their compensation packages in the form of base salary. Bonuses are provided at year-end based on the asset manager's performance against predetermined objectives. Several sophisticated advisory firms are also basing asset managers' bonuses on their ability to enhance the value of their managed assets.

Executives working in the areas of finance, accounting, systems, research and valuations, and other support functions normally receive

EXHIBIT 21–4
Compensation Levels for Key Positions in a Real Estate Pension Advisory Firm, 1991*

Position	Base Salary	Bonus
Chairperson/president	$300,000	25%–50%
Head of acquisitions	190,000	25%
Head of marketing	200,000	25%–50%
Head of asset management	215,000	50%
Head of research	210,000	50%

* Figures indicate average compensation levels for a major pension fund advisor with over $500 million in real estate assets under management.

Source: FPL Associates, *1991 Compensation Review of Real Estate Organizations.*

the bulk of their compensation in the form of a base salary, with a subjective bonus based on teamwork and personal performance. The level of base salaries paid in the advisory firm depends on the employees' experience, compensation levels in the cities where the firm operates, and salaries for comparable positions at other firms. The primary goal of the compensation program should be to promote close teamwork among members of the firm, but also to enable each professional in the organization to strive toward personal excellence within his or her particular area of responsibility.

In addition to base salary and bonus, advisory firms commonly offer partnership equity interests to executives who have met certain standards of tenure, performance, peer review, and leadership. These equity interests promote long-term commitment to the organization, which is essential to servicing investor relationships that have performance-based fee agreements. Through these equity holdings, employees share a common interest in focusing on long-term performance, which benefits both the pension fund client and the advisory firm. The determination of an award of an equity interest is most commonly based on subjective rather than objective factors. The process of making an employee a "partner" in an advisory organization is often analogous to the process of achieving partner status in a major law firm.

CONCLUSION

The strategy of a real estate advisory firm is driven by the real estate needs of the plan sponsors. The organization of the real estate advisor is a support mechanism for the chosen strategic mission of the firm. The success of a real estate advisory firm is highly dependent on its organizational structure and critical support elements such as strong leadership, performance standards, information systems, and effective compensation arrangements.

A real estate advisory firm will have a number of functional areas to cater to the needs of plan sponsors, specifically in the fields of marketing and client services, acquisitions, portfolio management, asset management, property management, research and valuations, dispositions, finance, and administration. These functional responsibilities will be handled by highly talented real estate professionals who constantly seek to attune themselves to the demands of their clients and strive to improve their personal skills in support of corporate goals.

Revenue derived from pension fund advisory clients in the form of fees is the life blood of the real estate advisor. Performance fees are becoming critical to giving the advisory firm upside potential to reward excellent investment performance. Executive compensation systems within the advisory firm should motivate professional staff to work in a concerted fashion to satisfy client objectives. For senior executives, performance programs that provide for attractive base salaries and subjective bonuses based on team performance and personal goals, supported by ownership in the advisory firm, all combine to maximize the performance of the advisory organization.

The successful real estate advisory firm will adapt to the changing needs of pension fund clients. By reacting to change in advance of the competition, the responsive real estate advisory firm will be positioned to pursue new pension fund relationships while continuing to maintain excellent relationships with existing clients.

PART 6

PORTFOLIO MANAGEMENT REVISITED

CHAPTER 22

THE EVOLVING ROLE OF REAL ESTATE RESEARCH

Jacques N. Gordon
LaSalle Partners

The professional management of real estate portfolios has placed greater emphasis on research than ever before. The first section in this chapter discusses the sources of this increasing demand for both market and portfolio research. The second section reviews the types of market monitoring and financial research that have become indispensable to today's portfolio or asset manager. The third section describes the various ways research has been integrated into the real estate investment process.

The growing reliance on analyses and forecasts has raised new questions regarding the quality, applicability, and payback of research as part of the overall investment management effort. Now that more resources are being devoted to research, it is appropriate to examine the research function within the framework of a real estate investment organization. The fourth section of this chapter takes a critical look at the limitations of market research as well as future directions in the field.

THE DEMAND FOR RESEARCH

Market knowledge has always played an important role in the real estate investment process. However, the lack of any standards prior to the 1970s created an environment where abuses could and did occur. The importance of a systematic research approach was emphasized after the passage of the Employee Retirement and Income Security Act of 1974 (ERISA). This legislation required the sponsors of retirement plans to exercise their fiduciary duties in a "prudent" manner. After ERISA, a certain amount of research was deemed necessary to demonstrate that an investor had acted with "care, skill, prudence and diligence."[1] Today's institutional investors, including those not bound by ERISA, demand levels of research that exceed a narrow interpretation of the original ERISA directive. While these requirements set a vague standard for a minimum level of effort by a fiduciary, additional considerations have emerged.

Larger Portfolios

The sheer size of institutional real estate portfolios has created a need for systems that capture, analyze, and disseminate market information in an organized fashion. The growth of the Russell/NCREIF index (see Exhibit 22–1) gives a clear indication of the rapid expansion of U.S. pension funds' real estate holdings in the 1980s. The size of lending institutions debt and REO (real estate owned) portfolios has also grown dramatically in recent years (see Exhibit 22–2). Many large investors, advisors, and insurance companies have established research departments simply to keep abreast of the diverse markets where their assets are located.

The Aftershocks of Poor Performance

Uneven past performance and uncertain future performance have increased the demand for research. Most portfolio managers have now experienced at least one full real estate cycle. Investors who made acquisitions during the early 1980s have watched rental income and capital values rise and then fall precipitously. One of the most important repercussions of this poor performance has been the extension of research efforts to all phases of the investment cycle. During the 1980s, it was common practice to concentrate research energies on the capital placement phase while ignoring the asset management, financing, and disposition phases of the investment cycle. Today investors rely on market research at all stages of the investment cycle (see Exhibit 22–3).

---

[1] Employment Retirement and Income Security Act Sec. 404(a) (1).

EXHIBIT 22–1
Russell/NCREIF Equity Index

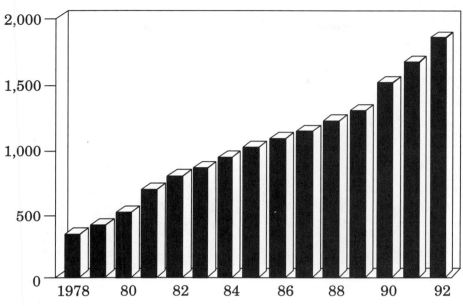

Number of properties

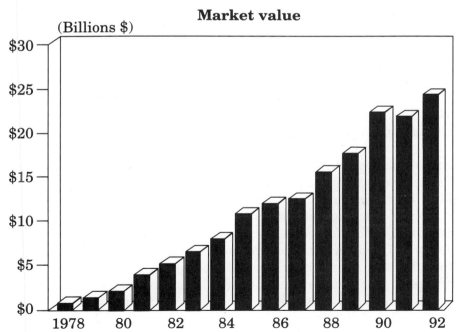

Market value

(Billions $)

EXHIBIT 22-2
Other Real Estate Owned by Insured Commercial Banks

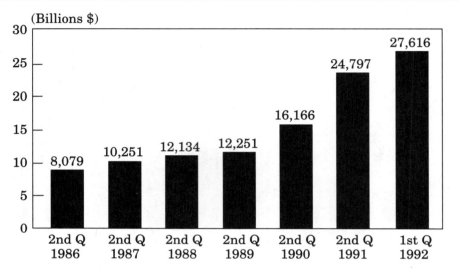

Banks' REO has mushroomed over the last two years.

Source: Comptroller of the Currency.

Competition from Other Asset Classes

Experienced portfolio managers ask tougher questions, and they want honest and informed answers. Moreover, institutions expect the same level of sophisticated market analysis and financial research from real estate managers that they are accustomed to seeing from their stock and bond managers. Pressure has been put on real estate managers to develop performance measures and use financial engineering techniques that are already commonplace in other investment capital markets. As a result, researchers are often cast in the role of mediator or interpreter between the world of modern finance and an asset class that is often disinclined to view itself through the prism of the broader capital markets.

EXHIBIT 22–3
Research Plays an Important Role Throughout the Investment Cycle

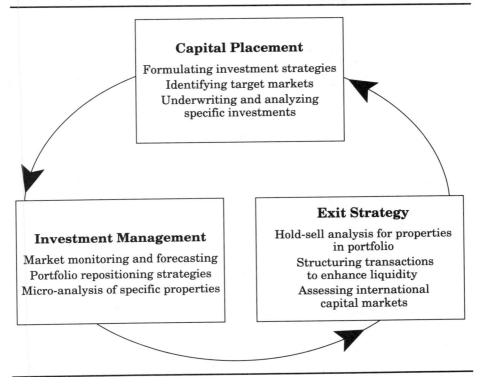

Exploiting Market Inefficiencies

Real estate is often described as a classic example of an inefficient market. Efficient markets, of course, are characterized by many buyers, many sellers, a steady flow of transactions, and readily available information on current prices. The returns from assets traded in efficient markets are expected to be commensurate with the risks assumed. Inefficient markets, on the other hand, reward specialized knowledge because price and market information is not readily available. Research should exploit these inefficiencies in two ways. First, opportunities to earn excess returns can be uncovered, particularly in emerging or untested markets. Second, market risks can be managed and, in some cases, reduced once they have been clearly identified. These two concepts are examined separately next.

The Search for Higher Returns

Among the most important tasks of a researcher is to investigate investment opportunities in new markets, examine new financial structures, and, in short, perform an R&D function similar to that undertaken in any other industry. Researchers cannot be expected to initiate every new investment idea or predict every ascending market, but they should have the tools to evaluate such opportunities as they arise. This type of investigative research is not used solely during the placement of new capital. Exhibit 22–3 gives examples of ways research is used throughout the investment cycle. For instance, portfolio managers have made extensive use of highly focused strategic research in deciding how to reposition properties in competitive markets and in making hold-sell decisions.

Risk Management

One of the main contributions research can make is its ability to instill a disciplined approach to investment management. Investors and advisors can be seduced by a "deal-oriented" approach that loses sight of broader market movements or portfolio considerations. Researchers need to remain balanced and circumspect, able to steer capital away from situations where investors are inadequately compensated for their risk taking. The research discipline is often inclined to identify prospective risks and ranges of likely outcomes rather than providing simple point estimates of future returns or rental income streams. An astute portfolio manager welcomes this probabilistic approach, because it highlights where a property's vulnerabilities might lie. Once market-related risks have been identified, many (though not all) risks can be reduced through pre-acquisition negotiations or active asset management.

Diversification is another important risk management tool that can reduce volatility across an entire portfolio. By assembling assets whose performances are likely to be uncorrelated or weakly correlated, portfoliowide risks can be lowered without sacrificing portfolio return. These diversification strategies can be quite research intensive, because estimation of future correlations usually begins with sifting through large amounts of historical data.

Improving Research Standards

A proponent of Say's law[2] would point out that the rising demand for real estate research may be driven in part by an increase in the supply of high-quality real estate researchers. Advances in the field have come about through the expansion and improvement of real estate educational programs (see Exhibit 22–4), the creation and expansion of professional groups devoted to the subject (such as NCREIF, PREA, AREUEA and ARES)[3], access to higher-quality data, and a proliferation of publications and journals devoted to real estate topics (see Exhibit 22–5).

Until the mid-1970s, real estate was ignored as a subject suitable for serious study in all but a handful of American universities. Now over 53 universities offer graduate real estate programs, and 66 offer undergraduate real estate curricula.[4] Many graduates of these programs, not to mention the academics themselves, are entering the real estate investment field and putting their newly acquired research tools to work. Improvements in the quality of real estate research are probably more an *effect* than a *cause* of increasing demand. However, as described in the final section of this chapter, the links among academia, industry researchers, and portfolio managers are tremendously important for the future of institutional real estate.

Additional Rationales

An alternative way of thinking about the demand for systematic research would be to focus on the "consumers" of the analysis. Exhibit 22–6 identifies three very general categories of customers:

- Sources of institutional capital (e.g., pension plan sponsor, endowment fund, insurance company, general account, or lending institution).

---

[2] Named for 18th-century French philosopher J. B. Say, who observed that supply always creates its own demand. In modern economists' terms, it may well be that investment research has been treated as an inferior good, one whose demand goes up when real estate earnings fall.

[3] National Council of Real Estate Investment Fiduciaries. Pension Real Estate Association, American Real Estate and Urban Economics Association and American Real Estate Society.

[4] Gayle Berens, "Teaching Real Estate Today," *Urban Land,* April 1992. See also Katherine Stadtmueller, "1992 National Real Estate Center Survey," Center for Real Estate and Urban Economic Studies, University of Connecticut, July 1992.

EXHIBIT 22–4

Growth in Academic Real Estate Research, University Real Estate Centers Created after 1980*

University	Center
American University	The Real Estate Center
California State University at Fresno	Real Estate Center
California State University at Sacramento	Real Estate & Land Use Institute
Cleveland State University	Center for the Study of Real Estate, Brokerage and Markets
Florida State University	Homer Hoyt Center for Land Economics and Real Estate
Fordham University	Fordham G.B.A. Real Estate Center
Indiana University	Center for Real Estate Studies
John Hopkins University	Allan L. Berman Real Estate Institute
Lehigh University	M.H. Goodman Center for Real Estate
Louisiana State University	LSU Real Estate Institute
Massachusetts Institute of Technology	MIT Center for Real Estate
Northwestern University	Center for Real Estate Research
Pennsylvania State University	Institute for Real Estate Studies
San Diego State University	Real Estate and Land Use Institute
University of California at Los Angeles	Center for Finance and Real Estate
University of Central Florida	Real Estate Center
University of Cincinnati	Real Estate Program
University of Illinois	Office of Real Estate Research
University of Kentucky	Center for Real Estate Studies
University of Nevada at Las Vegas	Lied Institute for Real Estate
University of New Orleans	Real Estate Market Data Center
University of Northern Iowa	Real Estate Education Program
University of Pennsylvania	The Wharton Real Estate Center
University of South Carolina	Center for Real Estate and Urban Economics Studies
University of Southern California	Lusk Center for Real Estate
Virginia Commonwealth University	Virginia Real Estate Research Center
Washington State University	Center for Real Estate Research

Source: *1992 Real Estate Center Survey,* Center for Real Estate and Urban Economic Studies, University of Connecticut, July 1992. Approximately 20 academic real estate research centers existed prior to 1980; most were established within graduate business schools or finance departments.

- A capital manager (e.g., investment advisor, equity fund manager, or loan portfolio manager).
- A third-party consultant (e.g., actuary, appraiser, or consultant specializing in manager search and evaluation).

Exhibit 22–6 presupposes that all three categories are concerned with

EXHIBIT 22-5
Major U.S. Real Estate Periodicals First Published after 1980

Publication*	First Published
Russell/NCREIF Real Estate Performance Report	1981
Land Use Digest	1982
Real Estate Finance	1984
Real Estate Finance Journal	1985
Journal of Real Estate Research	1986
Pension Real Estate Association Quarterly	1987
Journal of Real Estate Finance and Economics	1988
Commercial Property News	1989
Institutional Real Estate Letter	1990
Real Estate Capital Markets Report	1992
Journal of Real Estate Literature	1993
Journal of Shopping Center Research	1994
Commercial Mortgage Alert	1994
Journal of Real Estate Portfolio Management	1995

* Research reports by companies (e.g., Salomon Brothers and Goldman Sachs), regional real estate publications (e.g., *New England Real Estate News*) and academic working paper series (e.g., working papers of the Wharton Real Estate Center) are excluded.

using research to improve risk-adjusted returns. However, this list draws attention to the other ways research has taken on important functions *external* to the investment management firm and sometimes not directly related to financial performance. Chief among these is a research group's role in the reporting function. Today's investors want to know the *why* as well as the *what* when hearing about performance. Institutions such as pension funds are no longer content to be passive observers of the investment process. As institutions' understanding of the market has grown, so has their ability to take action in response to rapid market changes.

Another external source creating demand for specialized research efforts are regulatory agencies. These include the SEC, the EPA, the Department of Labor, the OCC, the Justice Department, and a long list of other state and local commissions and authorities. Regulatory compliance rarely relies on market research per se, but actions of these agencies can have profound effects on specific assets or entire markets. Regulators are looking for accurate indicators of the industry's health in light of the costs of the mortgage losses incurred by S&Ls and commerical banks. Individual firms support these efforts through their participation in national organizations that produce industrywide statistics and research.

EXHIBIT 22–6
Additional Sources of Demand for Research*

Pension Plan or Financial Institution
Keeping trustees/directors informed of market trends
Reporting broad trends to plan participants/stockholders
Understanding comparative performance
   (one's own performance versus a market index)
Allocating funds among various asset classes
Making allocations within real estate
Complying with ERISA, OCC requirements, or other regulatory standards

Investment Advisor or Portfolio Manager
Keeping professional staff and clients informed about market trends
Developing new products or a specialist niche
Demonstrating the firm's expertise
Complying with fiduciary obligations and regulatory requirements

Third-Party Consultants
Actuary: Estimating long-term financial attributes of the asset class (such as
   risk, real returns, and liquidity) for asset allocation studies
Appraiser: Making accurate valuations based on realistic market assumptions
Search consultants: Evaluating managers' strategies and performance

*In addition to a strict focus on improving risk-adjusted returns.

Independent consultants are also interested in research, because they advise pension funds asset allocation issues and manager hirings. Accurate historical performance data are an essential part of the asset allocation exercise. Industry researchers have devoted much time and effort to producing and interpreting these benchmarks, most notably through two organizations that publish well-known performance indexes, the National Council of Real Estate Investment Fiduciaries (NCREIF) and the National Association of Real Estate Investment Trusts (NAREIT).

One task of the pension fund consultant is to differentiate among management firms for their clients. Evaluation of a firm's research capacity is one way of doing so. Research is often used to help establish areas of special expertise, an essential step when the capacity of the firms vying for management dollars is greater than the amount of funds entering the market. Consequently, research plays an explicit marketing role in communicating to potential clients and consultants that a management firm understands the workings of real estate markets and can use this knowledge to a client's advantage.

The embedded theme throughout this demand-side section is that research plays an increasingly important role when markets become competitive. Real estate competes directly with other asset classes for funds. If real estate analysts cannot explain likely causes of past and future performance, the asset class is unlikely to attract new capital. Moreover, during the booming property markets of an earlier postwar era, it was possible to make profitable real estate investments in a great many different locations with little, if any, reliance on research. Overbuilding, a slowing economy, and less rapid population growth all suggest that greater research efforts will be required to earn competitive returns in today's real estate markets.

APPROACHES TO INVESTMENT RESEARCH

Just as the demand for research is multidimensional, so too are the tasks researchers perform. The following two sections examine the emergence of research specialists and the various methods they employ.

A brief look at the evolution of real estate research in an investment setting can be helpful. The idea that research activities add value is *not* a new concept to the industry. Resources and techniques have evolved considerably, but the purchase of investment grade real estate has always required a certain amount of investigative work. Prior to the mid-1980s, these investigations were typically carried out by acquisition teams during the due diligence phase of a property purchase. The time and energy put into acquisitions research varied tremendously from one investor or advisor to another. For managers of discretionary accounts, the standards were ultimately set by whatever efforts were necessary to convince an internal investment committee to proceed. Market research efforts, if any, were focused on the acquisition stage. This information was helpful when asset managers took over a property, but the shelf life of the data was rarely longer than a year. This left portfolio managers at the mercy of on-site leasing agents and property managers in judging the movement and direction of local markets.

On-site property managers may have reasonably accurate current information on rental rates and sales activity. However, their jobs typically do not require them to analyze or understand longer-term trends. Moreover, the time horizons and motivations of local agents often diverge significantly from those of the institutional investors. For example, a leasing broker has a strong disincentive to divulge any market information that might jeopardize a transaction-based fee, and similarly a property management firm is unlikely to convey any information likely to trigger a sale, thereby putting itself out of work. Thus, many portfolio managers found they needed a reliable source of independent market analysis to make leasing and capital improvement decisions that were more closely aligned with owners' interests.

The Research Specialist

By the early 1980s, the pressures for independent data, as well as many of the other factors described earlier, led portfolio managers to increase their efforts devoted to market research activities. Insurance companies and the larger investment advisors were the first to start hiring trained specialists to assist operations people with their research-oriented tasks. Yet in nearly all of these firms, market monitoring never became the exclusive domain of these research specialists. The gathering and interpretation of market data have remained a collaborative effort. Today the flow of information back and forth among transaction staff, portfolio managers, property managers, and researchers is increasing. In the case of investment management firms, clients have also been placed in the information flow, as indicated in Exhibit 22–7.

The responsibility for carrying out research can be divided among existing personnel, as many smaller firms successfully do. Yet the specialized skills required of researchers and the benefits of a division of labor have led larger investment firms to create separate research groups. Many organizations now rely on research specialists to elevate the market awareness of all participants in the investment process.

The research abilities required in an industry setting are quite different than those found in an academic environment. Applied market research relies on a wide spectrum of disciplines and types of information. While academics are urged to demonstrate proficiency in a single discipline, industry researchers must often adopt a multidisciplinary approach. Unlike an academic researcher who is rewarded more for highly detailed, original work than timely results, the industry analyst must work within tight deadlines. In the absence of any industry-defined GARP (Generally Accepted Research Prin-

EXHIBIT 22–7
Information Flows to and from a Research Group

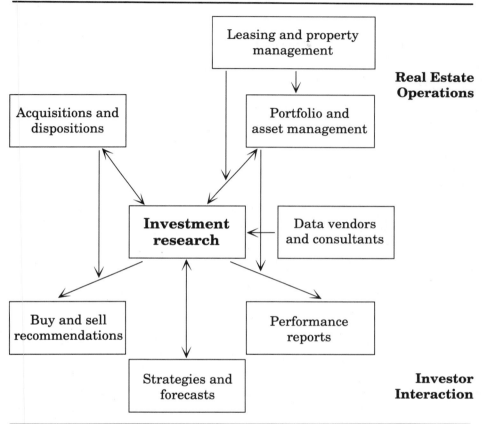

Leasing and property management

Real Estate Operations

Acquisitions and dispositions

Portfolio and asset management

Investment research

Data vendors and consultants

Buy and sell recommendations

Performance reports

Strategies and forecasts

Investor Interaction

ciples), investment analysts must walk a fine line, upholding high standards while serving the pressing needs of the investment decision-making process.

In the final analysis, when research efforts are viewed simply as overhead or cost centers, they are likely to have a short life in any profit-oriented venture. Rather, a research group should be expected to add value to the investment process by participating fully in major investment decisions. While the integrity of an independent research function lies with its ability to influence decisions, researchers must be held accountable for their forecasts and analyses. The creation of a separate research function can introduce a degree of tension within an investment firm, but this function must be guided by the same business plan as the rest of the organization. In time, when other professionals see how investment services can be improved through the use of research, these tensions should ease. If they don't, the collaborative process researchers depend on will be threatened. Once research groups have gained acceptance, one of the most difficult problems they face is finding the best way to meet all the demands on their time across an entire organization.

What Do Researchers Do?

This chapter is testimony to the diverse types of analyses undertaken in the service of institutional real estate investment and portfolio management. The sections that follow serve as an overview rather than a definitive description of the various types of research being used today. This list is broken into two categories, market research and financial research, although in practice the two are closely intertwined.

Market Research
Exhibit 22–8 illustrates the hierarchical nature of market research. Analysts do not necessarily undertake original research within all the concentric rings illustrated in the exhibit. To provide portfolio managers access to all levels of research, from the macro down to the micro, analysts must be able to assimilate the findings of other specialists. The "value added" by good researchers is their ability to make sense of disparate sources of market information and then suggest the implications for portfolio investment decisions.

Monitoring Macroeconomic Trends. Real estate investments are subject to the forces of both the national and international economies. The exposure of each asset class to so-called systematic risks—those that affect an entire market—must be monitored. Property performance is linked to macroeconomic forces such as the business cycle, inflationary expectations, changes in the value of the dollar on international currency markets, and interest rate movements. The real estate researcher must explore the potential effects of these national and global forces on real estate portfolios.

EXHIBIT 22–8
A Macro to Micro View of Real Estate Research

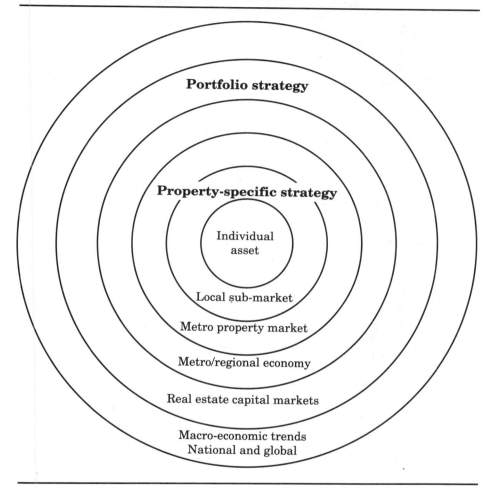

Portfolio strategy

Property-specific strategy

Individual
asset

Local sub-market

Metro property market

Metro/regional economy

Real estate capital markets

Macro-economic trends
National and global

Tracking Real Estate Capital Markets.   As mentioned earlier, real estate competes as an asset class with other financial instruments for investment capital. Just as researchers must track supply and demand from an occupier's point of view, they must also be aware of supply and demand from an investor's point of view. Investors' preferences determine capitalization rates, liquidity, and future performance. Moreover, financial markets do not always move in close synchronization with property markets. The capital market's treatment of real estate is often influenced by factors that are exogenous to the property sector. Real estate may still be a locally produced and consumed good, but financial markets are truly global. An investor's ability to place debt on a property or execute a sale may hinge on movements in LIBOR or the state of the currency swap market. Moreover, the resurgence in the public markets' appetite for real estate securities has added many new variables to the real estate capital market equation.

Monitoring Metropolitan and Regional Economies. Economists consider real estate to be a factor of production alongside labor and other capital goods (such as machinery or office equipment). In this view of the world, property markets *serve* economic growth and cannot be viewed in isolation. An analyst who understands what drives a metropolitan area's economy is much closer to understanding the nature of that region's demand for real estate. In an economy as diverse as the United States, many regions and metropolitan areas move independently of one another. As a result, real estate economists have learned to track a variety of subnational indicators most closely associated with real estate markets. These might include job growth (broken down by occupation or industry), business activity statistics, demographics, income growth, and other key variables.

Researchers' understanding of how these indicators are linked to absorption and rental rate movements, not to mention overall financial performance, is still far from perfect.[4] But there is little doubt that strong links do exist, albeit with complex leads, lags, and intervening factors that can dominate the performance of a specific asset at any given time. Further advances in this nascent field are likely to improve the quality of real estate demand forecasting in the years to come.

Property Market Research. This has been the traditional turf of a real estate research group. Many analysts cut their teeth assembling competitive market inventories and gathering effective rental rate data. These studies typically focus on the supply side. Ten

---

[4] Gayle Berens, "Teaching Real Estate Today," *Urban Land,* April 1992. See also Katherine Stadtmueller, "1992 National Real Estate Center Survey," Center for Real Estate and Urban Economic Studies, University of Connecticut, July 1992.

years ago, researchers spent most of their time gathering, organizing, and verifying microdata on property markets. Today secondary sources (data developed by others) are available from a wide number of sources. The use of such data allows researchers to spend more time on analysis and less time counting buildings. Nevertheless, the use of secondary sources is no substitute for on-site inspections of the competitive inventory or detailed interviews delving into the prospects for future supply and the dominant sources of current demand. Moreover, the reliability of many sources is highly variable, and researchers must take into account any biases that lurk in the data when completing a market analysis.

In sum, reliance on any single source for vacancy rates, rental rates, absorption statistics, or forecasts of supply and demand can render highly misleading results. Confirmation of market trends should be sought from several independent sources whenever possible. By working closely with researchers, portfolio managers have learned to ask tougher questions from their sources of market intelligence: Does the vacancy rate include sublet space? Do absorption statistics truly measure the *net* increase in occupied space, and what inventory was used as the basis of the estimate? How does an inventory break out in terms of quality? How was the "effective rent" of a quoted deal calculated?

Despite a growing body of literature on property market forecasting,[5] the links between supply-side data, demand-side trends, and forecasts of market rents are still being forged. The application of these forecasts to portfolio decisions often requires managers and research specialists to work together quite closely. For example, a hold versus sell decision requires, by its very nature, a comparison of present and future prospects for a specific market. By the same token, a researcher's prediction of the timing and nature of a recovery in an overbuilt area has specific implications for leasing, reinvestment, or selling strategies.

---

[5] Several anthologies describing the techniques of real estate market research are available. These include the *Journal of the American Real Estate and Urban Economics Association*, special issue on office markets, Summer 1992; the *Journal of Real Estate Research*, special issue on the determinants of demand for real estate, Fall 1991 special issue on retail research, Winter 1994; John Clapp, *Handbook of Market Analysis* (Englewood Cliffs, NJ: Prentice Hall, 1987); James D. Vernor, ed., *Readings in Market Research for Real Estate*, (Chicago: American Institute of Real Estate Appraisers, 1985).

Asset-Specific Research. Inquiries into the prospects of a specific building have traditionally been the domain of an asset manager or an appraiser rather than a market researcher. However, researchers are making contributions to asset-specific issues as well. Examples of the types of questions that lend themselves to a researcher's expertise are:

- How does a specific building compare with others in its category? What physical improvements would improve a building's competitiveness?
- How do local planning regulations or infrastructure changes affect a building?
- What is the future creditworthiness of a specific tenant?
- How well does a retail center's tenant mix match the demographics of its trade area?
- Are on-site property managers achieving competitive rents?

As these questions illustrate, there can be considerable overlap between inquiries that focus on a specific building and marketwide issues. Research is most effective when asset managers are making use of market analyses and forecasts when preparing budgets, estimating future cash flows, and making hold/reinvest/sell decisions. Astute portfolio managers will not use a forecast unquestioningly but will probe to determine the analyst's confidence in his or her own forecasts. Finally, portfolio managers must add market knowledge and intuition from their own experience with property markets to the probabilistic forecast supplied by the researcher.

The researcher's contribution to a problem must also be weighed against the time and learning costs of getting portfolio managers fully informed about all the details of a specific asset. When a portfolio or asset manager considers whether or not to consult a research specialist, the following guidelines are useful:

- Does an issue require a market specialist, or does the asset manager already have all the information needed to make an asset-specific decision?
- What are the implications of a decision for a client's holdings? If the decision involves a large capital expenditure, it may be well worth getting a researcher's point of view on the issue.
- Is the portfolio manager looking for confirmation of a conclusion

or for an entirely new insight? Is original research necessary, or can the researcher simply check the logic of someone else's analysis?

Financial Research

The application of modern financial theory has also become the domain of many investment researchers. Investment finance encompasses a broad family of concepts, including the efficient markets hypothesis, capital asset and option pricing models, portfolio optimization, asset allocation, duration matching, hedging, and performance measurement. These concepts, many of which were developed for the securities markets, are now being applied to real estate. Investment professionals are finding that real estate must justify its place in a mixed-asset portfolio with the standard yardsticks used for other financial assets. Analytical tools such as beta, systematic and unsystematic risk, duration, and the standard deviation and covariance of time-series returns are all being applied to real estate.[6]

Devising Portfolio Strategies. This task deals with the analysis of risks and returns of an entire portfolio rather than the individual elements. In theory, portfolio risk can be lowered—without forsaking portfolio returns—if assets can be assembled that are unlikely to perform in lockstep. Portfolio hedging and trading techniques used for finely tuned stock and bond portfolios have limited application to unsecuritized property holdings. However, research at the portfolio level can illuminate diversification issues and raise the efficiency of a client's holdings. The chapters that follow describe the elements required to develop a portfolio strategy. As mentioned earlier, nearly all of these methods require a significant amount of data manipulation and familiarity with the nuances of real estate financial statistics.

Securities Research. The emergence of the public markets as a source of real estate equity and debt financing has accelerated the application of stock and bond research to real estate. The rapid growth of the domestic real estate securities markets in 1992 and 1993 increased the number of securities analysts tracking both debt and

---

[6] S. Michael Giliberto, "The Allocation of Real Estate to Future Mixed-Asset Portfolios," *Journal of Real Estate Research,* Fall 1992.

equity issues. For equities, fundamental and technical research is used to evaluate initial and secondary REIT offerings as well as to make earnings and dividend forecasts for outstanding REIT shares. On the debt side, rating agencies and underwriters are now analyzing mortgage-backed securities with many of the same techniques commonly used in other fixed-income markets.

Portfolio managers are using securities research to help them invest capital in the public markets as well as invest in private offerings. Moreover, research is being used to develop new securitized products and hedging instruments. The first commercial real estate derivatives were introduced to the U.S. market in 1993, and other financially engineered products are being developed in both the equity and mortgage-backed securities markets with amazing speed. As a prerequisite to tapping these public markets, nearly all of these products are built on a platform of in-depth financial research. Issuers use sell-side research to help "make the market" for their securities. Independent, buy-side research is also important in serving the growing demand for impartial opinions on pricing and performance.

Performance Measurement.   In the 1980s, large amounts of investment capital were raised for real estate investments based on assumptions about the asset class's low volatility, high returns, and ability to hedge inflation. Yet these assumptions had not been rigorously tested through all phases of the construction cycle. When the commercial property markets began to fall in the early 1990s, regulatory agencies and private organizations such as the Association for Investment Management and Research (AIMR) urged holders of real estate debt and equity to adopt a mark-to-market discipline that more closely resembles the valuations available in daily auction markets. Because direct real estate investments often rely on periodic appraisals, a tightening of appraisal practices has been the primary focus of these efforts. Certified appraisers are trained in the fundamentals of market research, but the appraisal process, by its very nature, tends to produce values that lag the market and "smooth out" the volatility evident in arm's-length transactions.

Researchers have made an important contribution by pointing out the understated volatility inherent in appraisal-based performance data and interpreting the performance data that are currently available.[7] More important, professional organizations such as NCREIF and AIMR have proposed ways to improve real estate performance data through uniform accounting standards and the publication of industry benchmarks. Researchers have been at the forefront of efforts to bring the industry's measures of income and appreciation into the mainstream of financial reporting as conducted for all asset classes.[8]

Putting It All Together

Each organization will strike a different balance between where the portfolio or asset manager's duties leave off and the market or financial researcher's responsibilities pick up. There is no one correct way to organize the research function, but several prototypes are described in the next section. In some firms, the researcher is responsible for many of the types of information contained in Exhibit 22–9. This exhibit outlines a typical multidisciplinary approach to the micro-analysis of real estate markets. The portfolio or asset manager often has the responsibility to ensure that these findings are fully reflected in a discounted cash flow analysis, which relies on assumptions about future market conditions and asset performance.

ORGANIZING THE RESEARCH FUNCTION

Where should the research function reside? How does it interact with the rest of an organization? The answers to these questions start with the size and scope of an organization's investment activities, the skills of its professional staff, and the research resources at its disposal. From there, three factors typically determine the ultimate shape of the research function:

1. The organization's investment philosophy.

---

[7] Stephen Ross and Randall Zisler, "Risk and Return in Real Estate," *Journal of Real Estate Finance and Economics,* June 1991; David Geltner, "Smoothing in Appraisal-based Returns," *Journal of Real Estate Finance and Economics,* September 1991; S. Michael Giliberto, "Measuring Real Estate Returns: The Hedged REIT Index," *Journal of Portfolio Management,* Spring 1993.

[8] For instance, the AIMR Performance Presentation Standards (AIMR, 1993).

EXHIBIT 22-9
Microanalysis of Real Estate Markets

I. **Market Area Characteristics**
  A. Demographics
    1. Population characteristics and trends.
    2. Migration patterns.
    3. Income and occupational patterns and trends.
  B. Economic base
    1. Exporting industries.
    2. Labor force characteristics.
    3. Support services.
    4. Diversification of economy.
  C. Local government and regulatory environment
    1. Quality of local government.
    2. Zoning and approval process.
    3. Quality of local public services (especially schools).
  D. Quality-of-life issues
    1. Crime and perceptions of safety.
    2. Environmental factors: climate, pollution, etc.
    3. Cultural and recreational amenities.
    4. Availability of affordable housing.
  E. Infrastructure issues
    1. Transportation: roads, parking, mass transit.
    2. Water, sewer, and electrical capacities.
    3. Access to airport and interstates.
  F. Detailed analysis of microenvironment
    1. Description of site and environs.
    2. Historical neighborhood trends.
    3. Influence of adjacent uses.
    4. Transportation access.

II. **Demand Analysis**
  A. Identify target market(s)
    1. What is the universe of consumers/potential tenants?
    2. What are past and present growth patterns?
  B. Identify trade area(s)
    1. How are the markets distributed over the landscape?
    2. How are these markets currently served?
  C. Techniques for estimating market penetration
    1. Market segmentation models.
    2. Survey research.
    3. Develop profiles of consumers/tenants.
  D. Demand analysis tailored to property type
    1. Office and industrial property: economic sector approach.
    2. Residential and retail: demographic emphasis.
    3. How sensitive are tenants/buyers to rent/price levels?
    4. Develop scenarios to be used in pro forma.
  E. Projection of future demand
    1. Correlate historical absorption rates with historical demographic and economic trends.
    2. Has demand led or followed supply?

    3. Translate demographic and economic projections into demand for space.

III. Supply Analysis
  A. Inventory of competitive supply
    1. Identify markets and submarkets.
    2. Document characteristics of competitive buildings.
    3. Determine occupancy and absorption.
  B. Components of inventory change
    1. New construction.
    2. Absorption (negative or positive).
    3. Planned developments.
    4. Removals from the stock.
    5. Conversions to other use.
  C. Price/rent data
    1. How are rents and prices quoted (gross, net, etc.)?
    2. Quoted versus effective rents/prices.
    3. Types of concessions offered.
    4. Confirmation of price/rent data.
  D. Expense data
    1. How are competitive buildings marketed and managed?
    2. What are real estate tax assessment practices?
    3. Estimate operating expenses: insurance, maintenance, leasing commissions, tenant alterations, etc.
  E. Projection of future supply
    1. Correlate historical prices, supply cycle, and business cycle.
    2. Develop scenarios of future supply.
    3. Develop scenarios for pricing and absorption.

IV. Evaluation of Micromarket Research
  A. Accuracy of market forecasts
    1. Has the local economy performed as expected?
    2. Was absorption in the market close to projections?
    3. How accurate were the forecasts of supply?
    4. Which buildings that were planned never got built?
    5. Were there unanticipated additions to the inventory?
  B. Review of property assumptions (as performance data become available)
    1. How did rental income and expenses vary from projections?
    2. Which tenants have stayed and which have left?
    3. What has the market response been to the building over time?
    4. Has the building's investment value changed in ways that were not anticipated?

---

  2. The organization's corporate culture.
  3. The organization's skills and personalities of the organization's researchers.

The following sections discuss several different ways research has been structured in investment advisory firms, pension funds, insurance companies, commercial banks and securities firms. Elements of each of these models may be present in any single organization.

A Top-Down Approach

A centralized research function has been adopted by some of the larger life insurance companies and fund managers faced with allocating capital to a network of regional offices. The findings of the research group are used to set priorities that are then implemented by local operations personnel. To work effectively, the field staff must understand the rationale behind the mandates or guidelines coming out of the headquarters office. At the same time, the central research staff must be aware of the particular market realities faced by regional offices. Nevertheless, a top-down approach has been effectively used to set regional allocations of capital and coordinate decisions that have an impact at the portfolio level. In this way, researchers have helped define national or international strategies and have also set up systems intended to direct transactions toward meeting these portfoliowide objectives.

A Decentralized Approach

Many research functions are more appropriately conducted in a decentralized fashion. The collection of transaction-oriented property data, such as asking and achieved sales prices, effective lease rates, and changes in the competitive inventory, are best monitored by active participants in the market. Nevertheless, unless an organization sets up consistent methods for capturing and using this information, most of it will remain buried in someone's file drawer. In some firms, centralized systems have been set up to coordinate and standardize the collection of the data, even if the responsibility for maintaining the system remains decentralized. In other firms, property market monitoring remains purely the domain of portfolio managers, while the research group concentrates on portfoliowide issues such as diversification strategies or capital market trends.

A Specialized Approach

Mid-size and smaller firms that do not need national coverage are also using research to develop specialized databases and market expertise in specific markets. Institutional investors who have built core portfolios are now seeking higher yields in specialized areas. The higher risks associated with investing in relatively untested markets all demand a deeper level of research. By developing a thorough knowledge of a niche market, a portfolio manager can do a superior job of investing its own or its client's capital. In these firms, the principals of the organization can all be closely involved in research activities, even though a research group may coordinate the effort.

External Source Liaison

The capabilities of a research group are often drawn from a wide variety of external sources. Access to expertise in the fields of economics, finance, demographics, urban planning, environmental law, and structural engineering (to name but a few) is essential for institutions investing in real estate today. Moreover, no research department can develop an intimate familiarity with all disciplines or all major markets. Independent consultants with specific areas of expertise offer a cost-effective alternative for detailed market analyses. Consequently, some portfolio managers rely on outside consultants far more than on their in-house staff to stay on top of various markets. In some firms, as noted shortly, the researchers act as the firm's liaison with external sources of market information. In others, operations staff use their own discretion.

Information Broker/Data Manager

Another role the research function can play is to act as a liaison among different departments in a large organization as well as among organizations. Large institutions are notoriously poor at sharing information internally. Market information can be used to great advantage, but it must be in the right place at the right time if an investor is to benefit from its use. For this model to work effectively, the research staff must engender a climate that allows information to be shared collaboratively. Colleagues need assurance that sensitive information will be treated confidentially and, equally important, that they can be beneficiaries of as well as contributors to a system of information exchange. In some firms, the research function is organized like a management information systems group. In these instances, the emphasis is on the timely reporting of organized market statistics rather than in-depth analysis.

Check and Balance

In some organizations, the research groups take on an oversight role by providing an independent check against the analyses of portfolio managers or transactions staff. When investment decisions come up for review, the research group critiques the assumptions made by others and may present its own independent market analysis. The disadvantages of this method are that it can engender an adversarial rather than a cooperative spirit, and that one or both sides may end up building elaborate financial models without the full benefit of complete market data. The advantage is that it can provide an internal check against faulty assumptions.

Marketing Research: Joint Efforts

The ties between the marketing and research functions are quite close in investment institutions, especially advisory firms. Researchers are often called on to help draw attention to an organization's market knowledge through publications and presentations. There is nothing inherently inappropriate about placing a researcher in the role of helping to attract new business. However, marketing activities can be quite time consuming. If a research group spends most of its time meeting with prospective clients or working on marketing materials, it is doubtful that very much serious research is getting done. Meetings with potential sources of capital can, of course, constitute research into the criteria and concerns of investors. Yet marketing staff are usually already carrying out this type of research on a systematic basis, and capital market analysts simply need to be kept informed. In many advisory firms, the most useful collaborations between marketing and research personnel lie in the development of new products or services.

EVALUATING RESEARCH

Research, like any other part of the investment process, benefits from critical evaluation. Clearly, there are limitations to all research efforts. Investment committees and boards of trustees have learned painful lessons about what research cannot accomplish. While it is unrealistic to expect researchers' insights to be correct all the time, it is reasonable to monitor their performance. Researchers are often in the best position to check the accuracy of their own databases and forecasts. The senior directors of an investment organization should also be fully aware of their research group's track record in alerting staff to current market conditions and forecasting future trends. The purpose of a performance review is not to engage in self-flagellation but to improve internal communications and enhance everyone's understanding of the behavior of real estate markets. Researchers are fallible, but like all other real estate professionals, they can learn from their mistakes.

The drive to develop a research capacity quickly in the late 1980s and early 1990s undoubtedly led to some misguided efforts. For example, while computers have become important tools for all real estate practitioners, the purchase of software and databases does not guarantee that thoughtful and useful analysis of real estate markets will be conducted. Much of the work has to be done in the field, as it always has been. In today's competitive property markets, occupiers' and investors' preferences cannot be discerned by a computer terminal. Quantitative measures of supply and demand must be tempered by a qualitative understanding of local market conditions. The answers to such questions as "Which properties are attracting the best tenants? Do all competitive planned buildings stand an equal chance of getting built?" can be found only through a close ear to the ground style of research.

Ultimately, the research process may be more important than the final report. The network of relationships established during the course of a market study often proves invaluable for future inquiries. Real estate markets consist of *people* as well as buildings. Pouring money into databases and national econometric forecasting models may not be appropriate, given the scale of a company's operations or the geographic distribution of assets under management. In the final analysis, some kinds of information cannot be purchased from a vendor, nor can they be deduced from a computer screen.

Pitfalls and Black Holes

Several years ago, the research capacity of the institutional real estate industry was raised to a higher level. It is time to take a look back with a critical eye. First, as Exhibit 22–10 indicates, it is not immedi-

EXHIBIT 22–10
Researchers in Advisory Firms versus Russell/NCRIEF Property Index

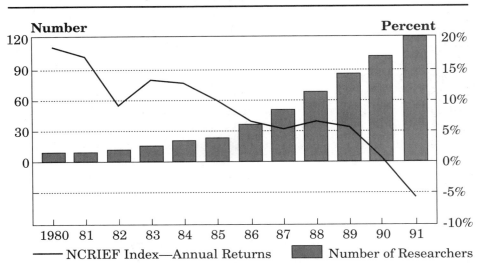

Number / Percent

NCRIEF Index—Annual Returns ▪ Number of Researchers

ately clear that research has had much of an effect on performance. To be fair, poor performance in recent years probably has had more to do with decisions made 5 or 10 years ago, when research efforts were minimal. Nevertheless, the apparent inverse correlation between the recent growth of research efforts and deteriorating performance highlights several weaknesses with the research process.

First, as in any industry, an investment in research takes time to bear fruit. A time lag between the immediate, hard costs of devoting more resources to research and the subsequent, difficult-to-measure benefits that should derive from attempts to lower risk and raise returns is inevitable.

Second, analysts are generally poor at predicting inflection points (when markets change direction), and their prophetic powers may have been oversold. Researchers need to communicate fully the uncertainties associated with their data and forecasts (which is not always an easy thing to do). Failure to do this may result in overreliance on "point" estimates rather than a more complex, probabilistic approach.

Third, like meteorologists, researchers are often powerless to do anything about the conditions they describe or foretell. Most researchers have been acutely aware of oversupplied office markets for some time, but not all of them have had the power within their own organizations to recommend action. Moreover, no real estate researcher has yet shown the ability to influence broad market outcomes through his or her own pronouncements. The self-fulfilling prophecy may exist in other markets, but real estate is not one of them.

Fourth, many researchers have been guilty of producing marvelous, academic-quality studies that have limited application in a business setting. In most organizations, it will be incumbent on the researchers to fully explain the implications of their research for operations people, who may be too busy to absorb the significance of abstruse research.

Fifth, not all researchers have had experience in working within tight budget constraints. Uncontained research costs have undoubtedly surfaced as a problem for some organizations. Research is particularly vulnerable to cost cutting because it is not directly responsible for its own revenue stream. Consequently, research practitioners must state the case clearly for the amount of resources needed to meet their obligations. These costs must be weighed against the benefits research can provide. Then, like any other professionals, researchers must adhere to their budgets.

Sixth, some research efforts have undoubtedly been directed toward generating new business at the expense of studying problems in existing portfolios. The misallocation of research resources within an organization can be the fault of both researchers and senior management. Competing demands on the research group's time must be carefully managed so that no essential tasks are neglected.

QUO VADIS: WHITHER RESEARCH?

Definitive proof that a fully integrated research effort makes a measurable contribution to investment performance, whether in terms of risk reduction or higher returns, is likely to prove elusive. Nevertheless, institutions are placing new demands on investment research both before and after funds are placed in the market. As a result, what was always an essential part of a fiduciary's role—financial and market research—has become one of the most important services an investment manager can provide to its clients.

Institutional sources of capital have learned through experience

EXHIBIT 22–11
Cutting-Edge Real Estate Research Topics

1. The underlying components of demand for space:
   - Linking metropolitan economic analysis, real estate demand, and investment performance.
   - Linking consumer research with real estate markets (e.g., demographics and psychographics).
   - Links between investor demand and occupier demand.
   - Demand elasticities: What is the slope of the demand curve? (i.e., what effect do falling or rising rents have on demand?).
2. The heterogeneity of supply:
   - Obsolescence and depreciation rates in overbuilt markets.
   - Supply elasticities: What is the slope of the supply curve? (e.g., when do rents justify new construction?).
   - Physical/locational quality gradients.
   - Cyclicality of supply.
3. Financial structures:
   - Performance of debt, equity, and hybrid instruments.
   - Private and public securities markets and real estate (e.g., issues of liquidity and control).
   - The influence of ownership structure on performance.
   - Corporate finance and real estate.
4. Tactics and strategies:
   - Applications of market timing and hedging to real estate.
   - Applications of modern portfolio theory.
   - Identification of market risks and unsystematic risks in real estate.
   - Synthetic real estate using index-linked derivatives.
5. International markets:
   - Developed countries: Western Europe, Canada, Hong Kong, Japan.
   - Emerging markets: Eastern Europe, Southeast Asia, Latin America.
   - International property securities markets.
6. Performance measurement:
   - Asset valuation and transaction prices.
   - Market indices corrected for appraisal smoothing.
   - Correcting for accounting versus financial reporting.
7. New research tools:
   - Geographic information systems.
   - On-line databases.
   - Neural networks.
8. Diversification categories in real estate:
   - New looks at "naive" categories.
   - Economic location taxonomies.
   - Ex ante asset allocation modeling.

9. Linking capital markets and space markets:
   * Real estate's correlations with other asset classes.
   * Real estate and inflation: asymmetrical relationships.
   * Hurdle rates required to bring real estate into a mixed-asset portfolio.
   * The relationship between debt markets and real estate liquidity.
10. Agency theory:
    * The incentives of participants and their impact on the market's behavior (e.g., brokers, advisors, appraisers, legal counsel).

---

that informed investment decisions are preferable to those made without the benefit of careful study. While uncertainty cannot be eliminated, careful research can help reveal the degree and nature of risks associated with any given investment. By the same token, portfolio managers have learned that investment advice that focuses on returns and ignores risks is given at a client's peril. Moreover, they have come to view research as much more than a mere information service. Raw market data are now readily available at a reasonable cost through a variety of vendors. A good researcher applies analytical techniques, experience, and judgment to these data sources. The results of these studies are being used in attempts to improve portfolio performance and to match investors' objectives with prevailing opportunities in the market.

In short, the research discipline has become a fully accepted part of the real estate investment process, as it has in other asset classes. Portfolio managers have benefited from new research techniques and expanded research capacity. As one of the primary consumers of research, portfolio managers are also in an excellent position to help direct the future contributions of research.

CONCLUSION

In his introduction to *Capital Ideas,* an account of the concepts that helped shape modern financial theory, Peter Bernstein (the founding editor of the *Journal of Portfolio Management*) recalls the role that the 1974 bear market for securities played in the acceptance of academic research:

Had it not been for the crisis of 1974, few financial practitioners would have paid attention to the ideas that had been stirring in the ivory towers for some twenty years. But when it turned out that improvised strategies to beat the market served only to jeopardize their clients' interests, practitioners realized that they had to change their ways. Reluctantly, they began to show interest in converting abstract ideas of the academics into methods to control risk and to staunch the losses their clients were suffering.[9]

Real estate investors and advisors may have found themselves at a similar juncture in the mid-90s. Crashing real estate values in 1991–92 may provide the same stimulus for new ideas that the 40 percent drop in stock prices had on Wall Street after the 1973–74 bear market. However, the recent flowering of academic research on real estate markets and financial theory has yet to be fully applied to most investment portfolios. In 1989, one pundit speculated that after 25 years of interplay between real estate practitioners and academics, real estate investment theories are finally "approaching the status of a paradigm."[10] This was not a very sound endorsement for the state of applied real estate research, because the analysis of other financial assets had already experienced several "paradigm shifts."

Nevertheless, the world of real estate research is moving rapidly toward an integration of academic ideas and practical applications. This chapter cannot do justice to all of the topics that practitioners and academics are investigating. However, Exhibit 22–11 gives an indication of some of the most exciting work just getting under way. The exciting part about these research topics is that many attempt to test empirically our theoretical understanding of the way financial and property markets work. Moreover, many of these topics are being worked on jointly by practitioners and academics. In fact, the university-industry distinction has been blurred due to the growing numbers of scholars who now work directly for investors or advisors.

The real estate portfolio manager of the year 2010 is likely to look back on the period from 1985 to 1995 as a seminal era when

---

[9] Peter Bernstein, *Capital Ideas: The Improbable Origins of Modern Wall Street* (New York: Free Press, 1992).

[10] Mike Miles, "Real Estate as an Asset Class: A 25-Year Perspective," *Salomon Brothers Bond Market Research,* January 1989.

academic theory, applied research principles, and professional practice came together. These advances are likely to raise the efficiency of some real estate markets. Eventually, real estate may fall into the Catch-22 of all efficient financial markets. As described by Marshall Blume and Jeremy Siegel in their seminal study of the New York Stock Exchange . . .

> A market can be efficient only if some people think it isn't, because those are the people who, believing they can beat the market, will invest their energy and resources in obtaining the information that makes a market efficient.[11]

In the meantime, a weak form of the efficient markets hypothesis is likely to persist. Thus, property investing will continue to reward highly focused research efforts.

---

[11] Marshall Blume and Jeremy Siegel, *Revolution on Wall Street: The Rise and Decline of the New York Stock Exchange* (New York: W. W. Norton & Co., 1993), p. 94.

CHAPTER 23

PORTFOLIO DIVERSIFICATION CONSIDERATIONS

Joseph J. Del Casino
New York State Common Retirement Fund

INTRODUCTION

For years, real estate investors have hidden in the shadows of their counterparts in other investment fields, most notably stocks and bonds.[1] A plethora of theories explaining investment behavior in the securities markets have evolved over the past several decades. These theories have armed securities advisors with numerous rigorous and scientific approaches and strategies to optimally manage their portfolios. In contrast, only recently have the techniques of modern portfolio

---

[1] For decades, real estate was considered the exclusive province of individual entrepreneurs driven by instinct and intuition and prone to back-of-the-envelope decision making. Consequently, real estate was perceived as a substandard investment class by institutional investors and business academics, who believed its fragmented, localized markets and dearth of standardized, reliable data were serious obstacles to consideration of real estate as a legitimate addition to institutional portfolios. In fact, an old joke has been bandied about real estate conferences and professional seminars for years. It goes something like this. A customer walks into a novelty shop and sees a strange display on the shelf behind the cashier's counter. On the display is a sign that reads "Brains for Sale," behind which are three glass containers, each with a different price tag: $50, $75, and $500. The customer begins studying the contents of the three containers and, after a while, turns to the shopkeeper and asks why one container is priced so much higher than the other two. The shopkeeper replies that the two less expensive brains had been taken from former stock and bond investors, and the very expensive one was the brain of a real estate investor. The puzzled customer said he really didn't understand why a real estate investor's brain would cost more than that of a stock or bond investor, since he believed these two brains had to have proven to be at least comparable to the third brain by virtue of education, training, and years of experience. The shopkeeper exclaimed that the answer was really very simple: Whereas the stock and bond investors' brains were really quite worn out, the real estate investor's brain had never been used!

During the 1980s, real estate captured a place within the global institutional investment marketplace, and, for better or worse for the investment industry, it is likely to remain there for years to come.

theory (MPT) and other rigorous scientific methods gained favor as effective management tools in real estate.

This chapter provides an overview of the elements of real estate diversification strategy and specifically discusses how an investor might diversify a portfolio of real estate investments. In addition, the chapter highlights the findings of some of the major work in the field pertaining to economic/geographic diversification and provides some guidance to investors pursuing a more in-depth inquiry into diversification topics of specific importance to them.

This chapter should be read as a primer on diversifying a U.S. real estate portfolio. It is written in a nontechnical format designed to briefly introduce a broad range of topics to readers. Consequently, it might be viewed as either a map for directing further inquiry or a blueprint for building a base of knowledge about real estate diversification. It is not, nor is it intended to be, a comprehensive, in-depth study of this vast and complex subject.

ELEMENTS OF SOPHISTICATED PORTFOLIO DIVERSIFICATION

Encouraged by the well-documented advantages of adding real estate to an investment portfolio, investors face some obvious and important questions. For example, an investor must decide what type of investment vehicle to use (direct investment, real estate investment trusts, etc.), what type of deal structure to use (100 percent equity, 50/50 joint venture, participating loan, etc.), what type of property to buy (office, hotel, retail, industrial), where to buy it (region, subregion, state, city), when to buy, and how long to hold an investment. Simultaneously with making these decisions for individual transactions, the investor needs to consider the manner in which these investments will perform together in a portfolio, that is, develop a diversification strategy.

Before considering decisions at either level (i.e., transaction or portfolio), the investor needs to learn about the variety of investment opportunities afforded by the real estate marketplace and their corresponding risks and returns, which directly affect investment and portfolio decisions. All too often, real estate investors hold two fundamental misconceptions about this marketplace. First, they believe real estate is a homogeneous product, that is, that all real estate is the same (especially investors who have traditionally invested in securities markets and have long referred to the real estate market without differentiating property characteristics within this broad investment class). Second, they believe generalizations about the entire marketplace can be extrapolated from experiences and knowledge of a few fragmented market segments. As a result, new real estate investors set out to develop a comprehensive and clear view of the marketplace, but instead become confused by inconsistent and conflicting opinions and assessments. This situation is similar to that in the ancient Indian tale of the four blind men who feel an elephant's leg, tail, ear, and body, respectively, and conclude that the elephant is like a log, a rope, a fan, and something without a beginning or an end. Clearly, our perspectives and vantage points greatly affect our perceptions and opinions about the things we observe and study.

Real estate is not a homogeneous product. In fact, the real estate marketplace is an amalgamation of at least hundreds, if not thousands, of specific market segments that have their own conditions, problems, and opportunities. Conceptually, real estate can be viewed as having three basic defining characteristics: geographic location, property type, and quality/age (life cycle) considerations.[2] These attributes are depicted in Exhibit 23–1. Each cell in this three-dimensional block of real estate types possesses unique risks and rewards. Like stocks, properties are considered to be composed of systematic and unsystematic risk. The former is applicable to the entire property market and cannot be diversified away. The latter is specific to the particular property and can be diversified away in the setting of a large portfolio of efficiently diversified buildings. While such a presentation conveys the fundamental heterogeneity of real estate, it oversimplifies the distinctions within property types (e.g., in retail, regional mall versus community center versus strip mall), geographic locations (e.g., in the East, New York versus Boston versus Washington, DC), and life cycle (e.g., there are no commonly accepted definitions delineating class A from class B buildings).

The need for and the complexity of an efficiently diversified real estate portfolio will be discussed in greater detail in this and other

---

[2] See Joseph L. Pagliari, Jr., "Real Estate in 3-D: See it Now!" *Real Estate Issues,* Fall–Winter 1990, pp. 16–19.

EXHIBIT 23–1

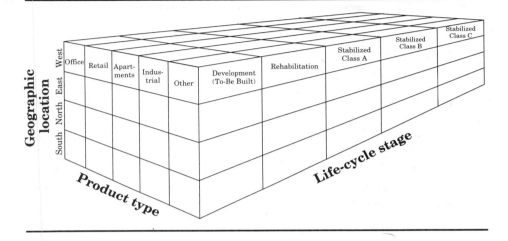

chapters. For the moment, simply note that a poorly diversified real estate portfolio will entail investors taking unnecessary risks.

Another level of complexity is revealed when the question of financial leverage is raised. Many institutional investors have historically been reluctant to invest in real estate with less than 100 percent equity. This is in part attributable to the taxation problems caused by the possible presence of unrelated business taxable income (UBTI) when financial leverage is utilized. No amount of leverage will resuscitate a poorly performing portfolio of properties. In fact, quite the contrary is true: Financial leverage will exacerbate the problems of a poorly performing portfolio of properties or enhance the returns of well-performing portfolio of properties (see Chapter 15).

Layered on top of the real estate portfolio allocation and the leverage decisions is the variety of legal/economic forms in which real estate investments can be held—the "packages." A partial listing of these formats would include limited partnerships, general partnerships, open-end commingled trust accounts, closed-end accounts, REITs, and corporate formats. This (partial) menu of choices, all entailing their own unique advantages and disadvantages, is further complicated by the question of whether the vehicle is publicly traded or privately registered. The combination of legal format and public versus private venue can lead to a bewildering set of choices. Moreover, this array of choices should not obscure the importance of the underlying real estate. As with financial leverage, no amount of sophisticated financial engineering at the packaging level can resuscitate a poorly performing portfolio of properties.

These latter two components, the questions of leverage and the legal package, filter the risk-return characteristics of the underlying real estate before they reach the investor. While bad leverage and/or packaging decisions can harm an otherwise good decision on the underlying real estate allocation, the converse is not true: Good leverage and/or packaging decisions will not help an otherwise poor decision on the underlying real estate allocation.

The following sections analyze in greater detail the real estate investment marketplace according to a variety of characteristics, including geographic markets, property types, lease structures, life cycle stages, investment structures, and investment vehicles. These characteristics illustrate the rich variety of returns and risks available in real estate that play an important role in individual investment and portfolio construction decision making.

Economic/Geographic Markets

Where should investors purchase property? The choices are multidimensional and involve regional, state, metropolitan, and city considerations as well as downtown versus suburban trade-offs. As a result, investors need to consider the challenges and opportunities inherent in various geographic regions of the United States. A traditional approach defines these regions as Northeast, South, Midwest, and West (as used by the Russell/NCREIF index). Other approaches use a socioeconomic dimension: the Energy Belt (Texas, Oklahoma, Colorado, Wyoming, and Utah), the Rust Belt (the heavy manufacturing midwestern states), the Hi-Tech Belts (the Northeast, Southwest, and West), and the Food Belt (the North Central states.)

Investors also need to consider the advantages and disadvantages of particular metropolitan areas and cities. Such considerations might be distinguished with respect to a variety of characteristics—old cities versus new, growing cities versus declining ones, large cities versus small ones, Eastern versus Western cities, cities with restrictive zoning policies versus those without zoning policies, dense cities versus sprawling ones, and so forth.

In general, regardless of the geographic areas selected for investment, investors should plan to diversify their investments with respect to geographical and regional economic vulnerabilities and opportunities. For example, in recent years the Frost Belt had been more severely affected by our national recession than the Sun Belt. In addition, Houston and Denver, as well as other cities largely dependent on the petroleum industry, have been economically depressed relative to most other large cities. The dimensions of economic/geographic diversification are discussed in greater detail later in this chapter.

Property Types

Despite the diverse physical characteristics among different property types (and varying aesthetics within any particular property category), investors often reduce property characteristics to two common denominators: returns and risks. Investors often conceptualize real estate projects as brick-and-mortar envelopes that generate streams of cash flow. Consequently, the discussion that follows focuses on comparing and contrasting factors that create market demand for various property types and on some of the salient characteristics that enable them to generate income, create value, and appeal to investors.

It is difficult to comprehend the enormous size and wealth of the U.S. real estate market. One recent *Wall Street Journal* estimate placed the value of all U.S. real estate at more than $9 trillion in 1991. Despite the tremendous size and wealth of the residential real estate market, commercial real estate—office buildings, retail centers, apartment complexes, industrial properties, hotels—is the focal point of institutional real estate investment in the United States. Various sources indicate that the value of commercial real estate expanded significantly during the 1970s and 1980s, from approximately $100 billion in the early 1970s to roughly $2.6 trillion in 1991. Also, within the broad commercial real estate classification, investment grade property (a very small subcategory) has been in greatest demand among institutional investors. An investment grade property is usually at least 50,000 square feet, is well located, constructed, and managed, and possesses high-quality credit tenants. The expansion in the investment real estate marketplace is a direct result of the unprecedented construction spree that occurred among all property types in the late 1980s.

What types of real estate should investors purchase? The primary categories of choice are office buildings, shopping centers, industrial properties, hotels and motels, apartment buildings, predeveloped land, agricultural and undeveloped land, and specialty-use properties. Investors also need to consider existing properties, new developments, and older properties with rehabilitation potential.

Before selecting a property type, investors should be aware of the range and variety of characteristics attributable to each category. It is also important to understand the investment and ownership characteristics of the various property types. The traditional framework for viewing these characteristics (which is being challenged in the current depressed market environment) generates the following comparisons among property types: Office building cash flows, in general, are considered average in comparision to the cash flows of shopping centers and hotel properties, which are considered to be superior because they are responsive to inflation over the short as well as the long term. However, office buildings and shopping centers are generally comparable with regard to capital appreciation over the long term and are typically superior to industrial properties in this regard. Office buildings and shopping centers are generally considered to be more liquid and easier to sell than hotels, and industrial properties can be difficult to sell unless they have long-term leases to high-credit tenants. In addition, because of their inherent higher business and operating risks, hotels tend to be owned by hotel operating companies or, when owned by others, are often leased to hotel operating companies. However, office buildings and shopping centers are usually owned by major investors such as financial institutions, corporations, and real estate investment trusts (REITs). Although these examples illustrate general characteristics and tendencies, they can not be applied in every comparative situation. Suffice it to say that the key question facing real estate investors is: What is the pricing (usually in terms of capitalization rates) at which a property should be purchased (or valued) for the investor to accept the market's current risks? These risks can include "soft" markets, rising capitalization rates, overleveraged tenants, changing tenant (and tenant's customers') behavior, and a stagnating economy, among other factors.

Moreover, these risks must be evaluated for each property type (each of which differs with regard to socioeconomic factors, management intensity, ease of sale/refinancing, etc.).[3]

Other differences among property types relate to the time and expertise necessary to manage them as investments. Office buildings are generally considered to be among the easiest and least time-consuming types of properties to manage properly, although the negotiation of office leases usually requires substantial experience and expertise. Hotels provide a sharp contrast to office buildings and require an extraordinary amount of management time and expertise. Hotel management involves constant tenant (i.e., customer) contact and continuous customer turnover and demands a broad knowledge of a wide variety of hotel services and functions. Shopping centers are also management intensive and require constant promotion and attention to maintenance and tenant satisfaction. Lease negotiations for shopping centers also require a high level of experience and expertise.

Regardless of the particular property types favored, as investors' real estate holdings increase, investors should consider diversifying their assets with a mix of property types to avoid excessive exposure to particular market conditions. Fluctuations in the national economy affect property types differently; for example, increases in consumer spending tend to enhance the performance of shopping centers. Gross domestic product (GDP) growth favorably affects the demand for office space. The devaluation of the dollar tends to increase tourism, which in turn tends to increase the occupancy rates of certain types of hotels.

Lease Diversification: Term, Quality, and Tenancy

Lease structure diversification, a topic that has received considerable attention from some investors in recent years, can be a useful alternative or supplement to the diversification strategies embodied in geography and property type. Many investors conceptualize real estate investments as bond portfolios, noting bondlike attributes in the tenant leases that encumber these investments. Consequently, investors

---

[3] For each of the major property types, these issues are addressed in Chapters 7 through 13.

often analyze leases with regard to tenants' credit ratings, tenants' businesses, lease length, and the value of the leaseholds.

Tenant credit ratings are typically evaluated according to the senior corporate debt of the lessees and usually to Moody's and/or Standard and Poor's ratings. Tenants' businesses are typically analyzed in terms of government-generated standard industrial classification (SIC) codes that differentiate between manufacturing and service-oriented companies and allow further differentiation of specific types of manufacturing (e.g., electronic equipment) and service organizations (e.g., finance, professional services). Leases are also compared with regard to their length (including renewal options), which may vary considerably, typically from 3 to 20 years. Investor attitudes toward lease lengths often vary with the market cycle. Generally, in a rising market investors prefer shorter leases (which provide an opportunity for tenant renewals at higher rents), while in falling markets they prefer longer leases (which provide some downside protection; unfortunately, falling markets sometimes lead tenants to "put" their lease obligation). The value of leasehold interests compares lease contract rent payments to market rents. It is useful in evaluating the probability that tenants will attempt to "buy out" or default on their leases in advance of their expiration.

The lease structure of a property or a portfolio of properties has a significant bearing on the property's or portfolio's inherent risk and return profile. Diversification of tenant mix (in terms of credit quality and business) and lease maturities can be effective strategies for minimizing a property's or portfolio's operating risks. For example, an office property portfolio heavily weighted with noncredit tenants, tenants in similar or complementary businesses, or leases expiring in any short period of time may be prone to higher operating risks than more thoughtfully diversified portfolios.

Timing: Life and Investment Cycles

Timing considerations include the life cycle and investment holding period of the particular real estate in question. Many investors doubt their ability to time markets and also question the net returns attainable, giving due consideration to real estate's high transaction costs from such a strategy. Consequently, institutional investors generally hold their realty investments for a long period of time, typically 10 and 20 years. A period of several years is usually required for leases to roll over and for investors to realize the value of the property in current cash flows (assuming rising markets). However, individual investors may have had important reasons (at least prior to the Tax Reform Act of 1986) for limiting the investment holding period to an interval of between 8 and 12 years in that the tax and leverage benefits associated with an investment usually taper off rapidly in later years. In addition, such investors may enjoy a rapid buildup of their leveraged equity, which motivates them to sell or refinance their investments in order to liquify this equity buildup.

Some real estate investments are relatively short-term investment plays. For example, developers often acquire, construct, and sell new developments within a period of two to three years. In addition, some investors acquire existing properties that they rehabilitate and improve within a few years and sell for substantial profits. In either case, such investors are attempting to capture their "value added" soon after its creation and to redeploy their investment and/ or profit in similar, high-yielding ventures.

The life cycle of a property involves several stages: planning, land acquisition, pre-development (or horizontal development), super-structure (or vertical development), and lease-up. Once stabilized in its market, the property begins to depreciate in an economic (versus a tax or an accounting) sense. The property's revenue potential—the combination of its occupancy and real (inflation-adjusted) rental rates—declines, and its operating costs increase. Eventually, the improvements are either substantially renovated (thereby starting the process over again) or razed (thereby converting the investment to its land value.)

This pattern is no different than the assets utilized by the corporation in which stockholders invest. They also go through a three-phase (start-up, maturity, decline) life cycle. The major difference between real estate and corporate assets is that real estate tends to have a much longer useful life.

The life cycle stage of a property has as significant an effect on its investment characteristics as the market cycle stage and other attributes such as geography and property type. The type and level of risk vary according to a property's life cycle. For example, real estate acquired during the development stage may involve environmental risks relating to land use regulations, zoning ordinances, infrastructure requirements, and the physical risks associated with new construction, such as labor strikes, construction material shortages, vandalism, and so on. Alternatively, properties acquired upon completion may involve only financing and marketing (lease-up) risks. Not surprisingly, minimum required development returns are higher than returns for fully leased existing properties to compensate investors for the greater risks associated with development.

Investment Structures

Investment structure usually relates to how equity and debt are combined in capitalizing a transaction and, as a result, usually affects the position of the investor (i.e., his or her rights, responsibilities, and risks) with respect to an investment. (As noted previously, Chapter 15 contains a detailed discussion of the use of leverage by tax-exempt investors.)

What are typical investment structures? Real estate investments may involve either an ownership (equity) interest in properties or a creditor (debt) interest; in the latter case, the investment is made in the form of a mortgage loan. In recent years, there has been a proliferation of debt-equity interests that are actually hybrids of the "pure debt" and "pure equity" structures. An example of a pure equity structure is the 100 percent ownership of a property, free and clear of all debt. An example of a pure debt structure is a fixed-rate mortgage in which the investor lends money to a property owner at a constant interest rate (and constant debt service) for a specified term, such as 10 years.

Examples of debt-equity structures are participating mortgages, shared appreciation mortgages (SAMs), and convertible mortgages. With a participating mortgage, an investor-lender receives a percentage of property cash flow in addition to debt service payments. SAMs provide investors with debt service and a percentage of cash flow, as well as a percentage of the residual value of the property at the time of sale. A convertible mortgage typically gives the investor-lender the option to convert the debt to an equity ownership in the property after a certain period of time, usually five years. If the property performs favorably, these hybrid structures can increase the yield to the investor-lender and offer some hedge against inflation.

Another type of hybrid structure that has become popular in recent years is the sale/leaseback. A typical sale/leaseback occurs when a major business corporation with a high credit rating sells a facility it occupies (often its headquarters) and simultaneously signs a long-term (15- to 20-year) "bondable" net lease. The lease convenants usually provide substantial security to the rent payments and require the corporation to pay all operating expenses in addition to rent. Sale/leasebacks provide owners with a hybrid of debt and equity returns: (1) The term of the lease provides a fixed (or periodically graduated) coupon return similar in quality to the tenant's corporate bonds, and (2) at lease expiration, there is an equity residual attributable to the owner's fee simple interest in the real estate that may be realized through a sale or refinancing of the facility. Generally, the equity residual component of the return is mostly profit, because lease payments are usually structured to amortize or recover at least 75 percent of the original investment during the lease term.

These examples illustrate that real estate investments can be structured to suit an investor's requirements and objectives. Depending on the manner in which an investment is structured, it may exhibit the qualities (i.e., returns and risks) of traditional debt or equity or a combination of both.

Investment Vehicles

The term *investment vehicle* refers to the ownership format of an investment. Whether a property is owned individually, as a partnership, as a corporation, or some other form has a significant effect on its return and risk characteristics. Securitized real estate investments, such as real estate investment trusts, often exhibit multiple return and risk characteristics, some attributable to real estate and some to the securities markets.

What vehicles are available for investing in real estate? Real estate investments can be made directly or indirectly, actively or passively. Direct investments usually require investors to manage real estate actively or delegate this responsibility to a professional real estate advisor for a fee. Indirect investments are carried out by means of an intermediary. A general description of several direct and indirect real estate investment vehicles, together with some of their advantages and disadvantages, follows.

Direct Investments
Direct investment vehicles include the direct purchase or financing of existing properties, properties under construction, and new developments by single investors or joint ventures. In the case of direct

equity investments, investors are directly involved in the day-to-day acquisition, leasing, management, financing, and disposition of real estate. The direct control over the selection of properties and the timing of acquisitions and dispositions can lead to high returns. However, return performance is heavily dependent on the skill and experience of the investor or his or her real estate advisor. As a result, along with high returns, direct equity investments usually mean higher risks, have lower liquidity than some other types of real estate investments, and require numerous skilled acquisition and property management personnel. In addition, the large dollar value of quality properties generally precludes proper diversification unless an investor can allocate a substantial amount of equity (i.e., buy several properties).

Commingled Funds
Commingled funds are open- and closed-end funds and can be either equity-oriented investments or mortgage funds. Both open- and closed-end funds give investors the opportunity to purchase units in a pool that owns real estate (in the case of equity-oriented funds), a variety of mortgage instruments (in the case of debt-oriented mortgage funds), or a combination of equity and debt investments. These funds allow investors to diversify investments by property type and geographical area without allocating an enormous amount of capital to real estate and to own property without the management burden. However, they do not allow individual investor-participants direct control over the real estate they purchase; for example, investors cannot make management decisions to sell or hold a property, and so forth.

The liquidity of fund shares or units has been an important concern and the subject of considerable debate since the emergence of real estate commingled funds in the early 1970s. The earliest funds were insurance company–sponsored open-end funds, which encouraged additional ongoing investment of fund operating distributions from existing participants and investment from new investor-participants. Consequently, these funds, which expanded in size as new investors entered the market, provided investors with the appearance of liquidity until the early 1980s, when the market began to soften and some investors found it difficult to redeem their units. During this period, the illiquidity of open-end funds became apparent and was attributed primarily to their enormous size (some exceeded $1 billion in assets), their varied asset base (e.g., property types, geographic markets), and, of course, their infinite lives. Consequently, by the late 1980s, closed-end funds with finite lives (typically 10 to 20 years), limited size, and focused investment strategies were perceived to offer greater liquidity (with fixed fund termination dates), even though closed-funds by design would limit the reinvestment potential of existing participants and the entry of new participants during the funds' term. The 1990s brought the realization that all commingled funds, open and closed, were illiquid investments. The lack of an established market or exchange/trading mechanism, depressed and stagnant market conditions, and uncertain investor sentiment continue to hinder the share/unit valuation and redemption processes. Consequently, today's investment managers/advisors and investors are focusing on improving the liquidity of these funds and are engaged in efforts ranging from the establishment of a secondary market to mechanisms for the conversion of existing funds to publicly traded, securitized vehicles.

REITs

REITs constitute another form of indirect investment vehicle. They are generally structured to allow investors to purchase publicly traded shares of an investment trust that pays no federal income taxes if at least 95 percent of taxable income is distributed to shareholders. Accordingly, one advantage of the REIT format is that it avoids the "double taxation" associated with a corporate structure. Another major advantage of the REIT is that it provides liquidity and daily market-quoted prices if it is publicly traded. A disadvantage of REITs is that REIT stock prices generally follow stock market price movements, and as a result REITs may exhibit volatility characteristics of both the stock and real estate markets.

Statistically, little correlation exists between the returns of equity REITs and those of unsecuritized real estate investments. Recent research suggests that approximately 60 percent of equity REITs' total variability is explained by stock and bond variability. When this variability is removed from the equity REIT returns, there is significant amount of covariance between equity REITs and unsecuritized real estate returns (as measured by the Russell/NCREIF/ index).[4]

---

[4] See S. Michael Giliberto, *Equity Real Estate Investment Trusts and Real Estate Returns* (New York: Salomon Brothers, 1990).

Syndications

Real estate syndications generally allow investors to purchase limited partnership interests in real estate that may be sold privately or publicly. These vehicles are structured to allow taxable income and losses of the partnerships to pass through to partners, with no tax liability affecting the partnership entities. Syndications have traditionally been tax shelter oriented, a characteristic that has diminished in importance since the Tax Reform Act of 1986, which greatly limited the ability of partners to deduct losses (often created by the combination of high leverage and depreciation deductions) against other sources of income. In addition, syndications charge substantial fees and tend to be undiversified compared to other pooled investment vehicles. Syndicated partnership interests also tend to be highly illiquid investments.

Listed Securities

Investments in capital market instruments provide yet another possibility for indirect investment. For debt instruments, these securities include Government National Mortgage Association (GNMA) pass-throughs, conventional pass-throughs, and mortgage-backed bonds, which are mortgages or bonds that are purchased in the secondary market. These instruments are originated by financial institutions, serviced through an intermediary, and then sold in packages in the marketplace. These investments provide a relatively high annual cash flow return and a low risk of default. However, they create high exposure to market inflation and generally do not provide for call protection and/or prepayment penalties (because many relate to single-family residential loans).

The common stock of publicly traded real estate companies provides the most indirect form of real estate investment. These firms engage in a variety of fields, such as housing production, building products, manufactured housing, real estate development, and finance. This type of investment provides liquidity, diversification, and daily market-quoted prices. However, it is subject to stock market–induced volatility, double taxation, and the presumption that the stock market generally does not recognize or adequately measure the value of the underlying real estate assets.

TYPICAL DIVERSIFICATION STRATEGIES

Considering the range and variety of real estate investment opportunities, investors need to focus on identifying real estate investments that meet their specific return and risk requirements and assist them in achieving their overall investment and portfolio diversification goals and objectives.

Real estate diversification strategies can take many forms. Some focus on diversifying according to particular segments of the real estate marketplace or particular phases of the real estate investment cycle. Sometimes strategies combine various market segments and investment phases. This section identifies and describes some of the most popular diversification strategies currently used by institutional investors and considers the effects of each strategy at the real estate portfolio level and the overall investment portfolio level.

Economic/Geographic Diversification

Economic/geographic diversification is based on the idea that the returns and risks of real estate investments vary according to their location, even if all other aspects, such as transaction structure, property type, and size, are similar. Geographic diversification is often pursued on a variety of levels, including national, regional, metropolitan area, and even smaller spatial definitions. For example, international investors often fulfill their economic/geographic diversification requirements at a national level by making investments in a few large cities of a particular nation, irrespective of the extent to which the cities represent national economic trends. Domestic investors view diversification on a much smaller scale. Some have a particular regional orientation and diversify by placing investments in a variety of metropolitan areas. For example, an investor with a Northeast orientation might select properties in Boston, Providence, Hartford, and Stamford to achieve some diversification. Other investors approach diversification with a much broader or narrower perspective. For example, investors with a narrower perspective—say, the New York metropolitan area—might diversify their holdings among several submarkets, such as northern New Jersey, Westchester, Greenwich, and Manhattan.

Investors utilizing the economic/geographic diversification approach are hopeful that the ebb and flow of the various markets are somewhat uncorrelated, thereby reducing the portfolio's volatility. However, investing in properties that are spatially separated does not necessarily ensure proper diversification. For example, although New York and Los Angeles are separated by more than 2,500 miles, their economies are similarly affected by events in the financial and other service industries. At the same time, the relative spatial proximity of Philadelphia and Washington, DC, has not mitigated the fundamental differences in their economies.

Recent evidence indicates that effective economic/geographic diversification results from selecting investments in areas that have fundamentally different economies. Some previous efforts to achieve geographic portfolio diversification were unsuccessful because they diversified according to the four basic geographic regions of the United States—Northeast, South, Midwest, and West—instead of according to regions possessing economic differences such as the Energy Belt, the Farm Belt, the Industrial Belt, and so on. The economic similarities among the four basic regions may have precluded effective diversification, depending on the particular subregions chosen for investment.

Although careful geographic selections can effectively diversify real estate portfolios, users of this approach must be careful to consider the effects that certain geographic selections might have on other investment classes (such as stocks and bonds) in their portfolios. For example, the returns of a portfolio of real estate investments dispersed throughout the Midwest in cities such as Detroit, Chicago, and Pittsburgh may be positively correlated with the returns of stocks in auto, steel, and other heavy manufacturing companies. Similarly, an overall investment portfolio with significant stock holdings in energy-related industries should probably avoid real estate holdings in Dallas, Denver, Houston, and other Oil Patch economies.

Property Type Diversification

The basic concept behind property type diversification is that returns and risks vary according to the particular industries utilizing various types of property. Diversification by property type, like geographic diversification, is usually attempted on several levels. Some investors diversify their real estate holdings at the broadest level by selecting a mix of residential and nonresidential properties or a mix of developed and undeveloped real estate holdings. Institutional real estate investors usually diversify at a more detailed level by differentiating among basic business categories such as office, industrial, retail, and hotel uses. Other investors, particularly those who deal in only one particular business category, such as office or retail properties, make further refinements. For example, retail property investors often differentiate their holdings according to the regional or local markets they serve and the products they sell. Industrial property investors often differentiate among light and heavy manufacturing facilities, warehouses, and distribution plants. Office property investors sometimes distinguish between downtown high-rise properties and suburban business parks, as well as among different quality classes (class A, class, B, class C, etc.) of properties.

Diversifying a real estate portfolio by property type is similar to diversifying a securities portfolio by industry. Different property types cater to different sectors of the economy. For example, office property generally responds to the needs of the financial and services-producing sectors; industrial property to the goods-producing sectors; retail property to the retail sector; and hotels to the travel and tourism sectors, employment growth, and the business cycle. Understanding the return and risk factors attendant to different property types requires understanding the factors affecting each property type's user groups. See Chapters 7 through 13 for more detailed descriptions of these linkages.

There has been much less research in the area of property type diversification than in geographic diversification, and the findings on the effectiveness of the former, though preliminary, have been much less compelling. Nonetheless, research in this area supports certain possibilities for true diversification. For example, some studies have shown that office property investment returns have been negatively correlated with retail property returns on a national basis over the past two decades, which suggests that a portfolio already containing primarily office investments can reduce risk by adding retail investments. Conversely, at the national level, hotels have been positively correlated with offices and certain industrial property types, suggesting that there may be minimal diversification benefits associated with adding hotels or warehouses to a predominantly office property portfolio. On a local or metropolitan area level, some opportunities exist for effective property type diversification, especially in mature cities such as New York and Chicago. And, if an investor is limited to a few locations, property type diversification may be a particularly appropriate and important strategy alternative.

Like geographic diversification, property type diversification must be sensitive to the diversification requirements of an investor's overall portfolio. For example, an overall investment portfolio heavily invested in the stocks of financial institutions and securities firms is already vulnerable to some of the same risks affecting office property investments in the financial center cities of New York, Los Angeles, and Chicago. Similarly, the value of industrial real estate holdings is sometimes adversely affected by changes in environmental legislation, and such holdings should probably be limited in overall investment portfolios heavily invested in environmentally sensitive industries. Portfolios concentrated in the securities of consumer product, apparel, and department store retailers should probably limit shopping center holdings because of similarities in their risk-return factors.

Timing: Investment/Life Cycle Diversification

Some investors attempt to capitalize on the presumption that a real estate investment's returns and risks change as it moves through an investment holding period cycle and through the various phases of the life cycle: planning, acquisition, pre-development, development, financing, leasing, management, and ultimately disposition.

"Value-Added" Approaches
In general, overall return and risk levels fall after the development process is successfully completed. Some investors and investment advisors have developed expertise in one or more phases of the life cycle and investment cycle and have cultivated investment programs that focus on investments in those phases. For example, some investors are confident of their strategic planning and investment research capabilities and of their ability to identify emerging opportunities, that is, to "pick 'em right." Others focus on their expertise in transaction underwriting analysis and in effect emphasize their ability to "buy 'em right." The traditional approach to real estate investment emphasizes the ongoing management of an asset, in which leasing and property management and property rehabilitation were the critical factors affecting investment performance (i.e., the ability to create property value by managing expenses and enhancing revenue through sound leasing strategies—the ability to "run 'em right").

In recent years, particularly because of the escalated involvement of the investment banking community in the real estate investment marketplace, some investors have focused on sophisticated financing techniques and emphasize their ability to arrange favorable financing for their acquisitions to enhance investment returns. Still others emphasize the property disposition process as the critical element and focus on their ability to "sell 'em right." Usually these investors depend on an ability to access global capital markets to structure a sale that maximizes the sale price, which is done through a combination of targeting the right buyers, arranging favorable financing, and creating the right ownership format for a sale. Obviously, a minimum level of expertise in handling all phases of the investment cycle is prerequisite to the successful implementation of each of these approaches.

"Opportunity" Approaches

One of the controversial investment and market-timing strategies of the early 1990s, which arose from the overbuilt condition of most major markets, is to purchase quality properties in "temporarily" depressed markets at heavily discounted prices and aggressively manage them in anticipation of a turnaround in market conditions. Many proponents of this strategy eagerly point to Olympia & York's purchase of the Uris portfolio in 1977, just about the time New York City's economy began rising from its mid-1970s doldrums. (O&Y had purchased nearly 12 million square feet of prime Manhattan office properties for approximately $30 per square foot, or, conservatively estimated, 10 percent of its value in 1988, a little more than a decade later!) Although O&Y's success with its New York acquisitions should be viewed as exceptional at the very least, the strategy has steadily gained popularity, particularly among institutional investors who have made substantial capital commitments to "vulture" funds (more euphemistically known as *opportunity* funds) that target the acquisition of quality real estate in "temporarily" and "moderately depressed" market areas nationally (not merely in very depressed markets such as Texas, Colorado, and elsewhere in the Oil Patch).

Land "Plays"

A common variant of the real estate investment timing strategy just described involves acquiring land beyond (but directly in the path of) current development, at or near the bottom of a real estate cycle, to capitalize on appreciating land values during a subsequent construction boom. Several investors and managers/advisors have geared up to meet the growing institutional appeal of this strategy.

Certain parallels can be drawn between investing in various phases of the real estate cycle and other investment classes. For example, an investment in raw, undeveloped land has characteristics similar to venture capital investments or collectibles, at least to the extent that current income is forgone for substantial future appreciation potential. Investment in an existing, fully leased office building often has return and risk characteristics similar to those of the stocks of mature, well-established companies. Investors focusing on the disposition phase of the real estate cycle will purchase property to profit from its immediate flip or sale, which is similar to certain types of commodity trading. Consequently, investors should consider their real estate investment timing strategies within the broad context of their other investments to effectively diversify their overall holdings from the timing perspective.

Investment Structure Diversification

Unlike geographic and property type diversification, investment structure diversification has little to do with searching for return and risk differences intrinsic to the real estate itself. It does, however, have much to do with the structure of real estate transactions. It is the structure of transactions that often enables investors to tailor investment performance to achieve their goals and objectives. Investment structure can materially affect the amount and timing of various types of investment returns, such as income, appreciation, equity build-up, and tax benefits. It can also affect various types of risk, such as interest rate and inflation risk, liquidity risk, and so on.

It is conceivable that several real estate investment structures that are in the same geographic market and similar in property type might exhibit very different return performances and risk profiles. For example, a portfolio of Manhattan office properties with alternative investment structures—one mortgage, one all-cash-equity investment, one convertible mortgage, one leasehold, one sale/leaseback, and so on—may provide a blend of risk-return characteristics. For example, its mortgage would be vulnerable to interest rate, inflation, and default risks and perform strictly as a fixed-income investment; its equity investment might provide an effective inflation hedge but be vulnerable to certain business risks; and its convertible mortgage would perform as a hybrid, showing returns and risks characteristic of each "pure" form of investment.

When diversifying a real estate portfolio according to investment structures, it is important to consider the percentage allocations of the overall portfolio to other classes of investment—common stocks, long-term bonds, U.S. Treasuries, venture capital, and so forth. Portfolios heavily concentrated in long-term corporate bonds may not find significant portfolio diversification advantages to investing in real estate in the form of mortgages, which have returns and risks similar to those of corporate bond investments. However, hybrid real estate investments, such as participating and convertible mortgages or pure equity real estate, might be attractive additions to an otherwise fixed-income-based portfolio. Moreover, certain types of bondlike real estate investments, such as sale/leasebacks, might provide better risk-adjusted returns than comparable corporate bonds.

Investment Vehicle Diversification

To the extent that investment vehicle diversification has more to do with how the real estate is owned by investors than the real estate itself, this approach is very similar to the investment structure diversification approach.

The ownership format for a real estate investment affects the extent to which an investor has a passive or an active role in managing the investment and often materially affects investment returns and risks. At one extreme, direct ownership usually offers investors the greatest potential returns, but also usually exposes them to the greatest risks. More passive ownership, such as that achieved through private real estate limited partnerships, limits the business liability risks attendant to real estate investments, but also limits the investor's participation in management decisions. Extremely passive ownership formats, such as publicly traded REITs and real estate mutual funds, reduce the liquidity risks associated with real estate, but preclude investors from individually managing their investments to suit their own financial objectives and requirements; for example, the decision to return capital flowing from the sale of assets in fund portfolios is made by fund managers, not investors.

The proliferation in the number and variety of real estate investment vehicles has made it easier for real estate investors to eliminate certain types of risks that were traditionally characteristic of real estate investments, such as limited liquidity, but has increased or injected stock market risks into real estate investments. Thus, although REITs may be used to diversify a direct equity real estate portfolio, they may, from an overall portfolio perspective, result in too heavy an allocation to securities investments. Consequently, diversifying a real estate portfolio through vehicle diversification must be done within the context of an overall investment portfolio strategy.

Diversification Dynamics

It is important to recognize that the various categories comprising the elements of diversification are constantly changing according to a dynamic marketplace. The dynamics of the U.S. real estate investment marketplace can be measured not only by its rapid evolution and change in recent years but also by the frequency with which investors challenge norms with innovative investment transactions. Witness the changes in geographic preferences over the last decade. Houston, Dallas, and Denver were among the strongest and most promising real estate markets in the early 1980s, but by 1990 they were among the least preferred by investors. In contrast, the Rust Belt of the Midwest, considered hopelessly depressed in the 1970s, began showing signs of economic resilience in the late 1980s, enabling older, mature urban areas such as Columbus, Ohio, to catch the eyes of investors. Oil prices have had other profound effects on geographic preferences; low oil prices in the late 1950s and the 1960s fostered the expansion of suburban business centers in the same way the high oil prices (and the consequent reliance on mass transit) of the mid-1970s encouraged the redevelopment and revitalization of urban cores.

Dramatic changes can also be seen with respect to property types. Much of the excitement generated for office building and hotel investments during the late 1970s and early 1980s has since been transferred to shopping centers, industrial properties, residential properties, and, along the way, several other specialized types of properties such as golf courses, resort hotels, congregate care housing, timberland, and even wine vineyards!

In addition, it is not surprising that substantial changes in investment structures and vehicles have also emerged. The current popularity of straightforward, "pure" debt and "pure" equity transactions notwithstanding, several hybrid debt-equity structures, such as participating and convertible mortgages, have become commonplace in recent years. Furthermore, it is expected that more companies will use the sale/leaseback structure (removing the real estate from their balance sheets and becoming tenants) in the years ahead in an effort to raise capital to operate, revamp, and expand their businesses.

The investment vehicles for owning these assets have also shifted in priority and increased in variety. Commingled funds, syndications, and limited parternships diminished in popularity during the 1980s. Undoubtedly, the uncertainty surrounding these vehicles brought about by tax reform has been at least partly responsible for investors' preference shift toward "public" versus "private" partnerships, quite the reverse of the trend earlier in the 1980s. In addition, by the mid-1980s, real estate investment trusts regained the popularity they enjoyed prior to the collapse of the mortgage REITs in the mid-1970s, and real estate master limited partnerships emerged as competitors of the trust format for many investors.

Strategy Implementation

Real estate investors often implement diversification strategies in a two-stage process. First, a diversified "core" real estate portfolio is assembled, either one property at a time or all at once through an investment in a commingled diversified fund or the acquisition of an existing property portfolio. Many real estate investors believe the relative scarcity of institutional grade real estate available for acquisition in recent years has encouraged large investors to purchase property in bulk as a method of reducing competition, since few investors can afford to purchase, say, half a billion dollars worth of real estate at a time. The seller's motivation for selling property in bulk is often part of a defensive strategy against a corporate takeover; that is, companies realize that by spinning off their real estate holdings, they become less attractive takeover candidates.

Among the most highly visible recent company acquisitions involving substantial real estate holdings is Campeau Corp.'s $6.6 billion acquisition of Federated Department Stores in 1988 and its $3.9 billion acquisition of Allied Stores Corp. in 1986, which made Campeau a major owner of retail investment property. These types of transactions indicate a two-sided investment approach: a value as an ongoing operating entity and as a real estate "play."

During the past several years, various investors have been expanding and complementing their real estate holdings through the strategic acquisition of a variety of companies. In 1988, for nearly $1 billion, JMB acquired Amfac, Inc., whose real estate holdings, including some 60,000 acres of land in Hawaii, were valued at approximately $400 million. JMB's acquisition of Toronto-based Cadillac Fairview Corp., Ltd., for $5.8 billion in 1987 expanded its holdings at that time by more than 60 million square feet of retail, office, and multi-use properties. Other recent JMB acquisitions include Alcoa's Century City portfolio in Los Angeles for $600 million; Walt Disney's Arvida unit, a developer of planned communities, for $400 million; and Aetna Life's Urban Investment and Development unit for approximately $1 billion.

Other major acquisitions in recent years include Kohlberg, Kravis, Roberts & Co.'s purchase of Jim Walter Corp., a Florida development and investment concern, for approximately $2.5 billion in 1987 and the $1.5 billion sale of the Westin Hotel chain, which included more than 60 hotels, to a joint venture of the Robert M. Bass Group and Aoki Corp. of Japan. A steady and dramatic increase occurred in the sizes of real estate transactions during the last decade, owing primarily to the portfolio acquisition strategies of major investors.

Almost by definition, the core portfolios of investors are usually diversified with regard to geographic markets and property types and sometimes also in terms of investment structures and vehicles.

During the second stage of implementation, diversification is enhanced by assessing portfolio biases and adjusting portfolio asset allocations. Readjustments are accomplished through individual acquisitions or through the acquisition of units in niche or specialty funds that emphasize the types of investments required for additional diversification. For example, core portfolios assembled a decade ago tended to be highly concentrated in office properties in energy cities such as Dallas and Houston. These core portfolios have since been supplemented with retail and industrial properties with a broader geographic representation. Sometimes specialty funds are used to enhance or fine-tune portfolios to take advantage of current hot trends and opportunities. It is not uncommon, for example, for an existing core portfolio containing substantial retail property holdings to be further supplemented with investments in fad or theme retail centers or other types of specialty malls.

During the past few years, several new niche funds have emerged to meet the needs of institutional investors. Funds specializing in property redevelopment or rehabilitation or other "value enhancement" strategies are becoming popular, as are funds specializing in particular property types such as apartments and land. Traditional funds, which feature a geographical mix of existing, substantially leased properties, are becoming less attractive by comparison, particularly among investors with substantial real estate holdings.

Each investor needs to determine the diversification approach that best suits his or her investment preferences and constraints. Geographic and property type diversification will appeal to those investors most interested in maximizing the income and appreciation potential of their real estate investments while eliminating or reducing exposure to local market risks and business risks. At the same time, only investors and/or their advisors with experience in managing several types of property and with knowledge of many geographic markets will be sufficiently equipped to implement these strategies.

Alternatively, investment structure and vehicle diversification strategies generally appeal to investors seeking the optimal combination of tax consequences, leverage, interest rate risk, inflation risk, and liquidity risk. Investors pursuing these strategies are most likely to possess expertise in legal, accounting, tax, and other technical areas that are essential to a thorough understanding of investment structures and vehicles. As mentioned earlier, the various timing strategies will naturally appeal to investors with the requisite skills; for example, construction companies will focus on physical value creation in the development phase, property management companies will focus on value enhancement in the operating phase, and so on.

DIMENSIONS OF ECONOMIC/GEOGRAPHIC DIVERSIFICATION

The remainder of this chapter examines in detail the dimensions of economic/geographic diversification, which investors believe is potentially the most effective strategy for diversifying portfolios.

An old adage says that the three most important factors in real estate are location, location, and location. This maxim was primarily site specific. The current twist on the old adage (from a portfolio perspective) has real estate investors viewing location as the correlation among markets. Analyzing real estate markets usually involves segmenting or partitioning the geography of the United States into three stages: (1) *multi-state regions,* (2) *metropolitan areas,* and (3) *submetropolitan areas.*

Newcomers to the U.S. real estate market usually start with the regional level and work their way into the nuances of intrametropolitan locational characteristics. However, it is not uncommon for investors with real estate holdings in particular submarkets of a metropolitan area to expand outward to other markets in a larger region. For example, many foreign investors initially invested only in downtown areas of major U.S. cities such as New York, Houston, Los Angeles, and Washington, DC, but over time expanded their geographic investment selection criteria to include surrounding suburban areas and even neighboring metropolitan areas such as Philadelphia, Boston (i.e., near New York), Dallas, Austin, and San Antonio (i.e., surrounding Houston), San Diego (i.e., near Los Angeles), and Baltimore (i.e., near Washington, DC).

Multistate Regional Choices

The United States has been segmented in numerous ways to serve a variety of purposes, including

1. Time zones (e.g., Eastern Standard, Central, Mountain, Pacific).
2. Political zones (e.g., states, cities, counties).
3. Climate zones (e.g., Sun Belt, Frost Belt, hurricane zones).
4. Topographic/geologic zones (e.g., earthquake areas, the Great Plains, the Rocky Mountains).
5. U.S. Census zones (e.g., Mid-Atlantic states, East South Central states).
6. Urbanized zones (e.g., Northeast [Boston–Washington] corridor, Southwest [San Francisco–Houston] corridor).
7. Economic zones (e.g., multistate regions such as the Rust Belt, Energy Belt, and Food Belt, metropolitan areas, etc.).

For the purposes of real estate analysis, the urbanized and economic zones are usually most relevant. The other zones occasionally enter the market selection process. For example, investors are often concerned with probabilities of natural disasters such as earthquakes in California, hurricanes in Florida, tornadoes in Kansas, flooding in some coastal states, droughts in Arizona and Texas, or forest fires in some of the western states. In addition, investors may find dealing with the governments of some municipalities and states easier than others, or may even find managing investments in different time zones inconvenient (particularly if you are a U.S. representative of a European institution who is stationed in New York with investments in Los Angeles and Honolulu and is trying to engage in a conference telephone call with the home office and your on-site property managers!).

The economic geography of the United States is often described in terms of seven regions (see Exhibit 23–2): New England, the Northeast corridor, the South, the Rust Belt, the Food Belt, the Energy Belt, and the Pacific Rim. Each region has a distinct economic identity and unique return and risk characteristics, although regional boundaries overlap in many cases.[5]

The *New England region* includes Maine, New Hampshire, Vermont, Rhode Island, Massachusetts, and the eastern portion of Connecticut. Historically one of the oldest manufacturing regions of the nation, this region has in recent decades shifted to high-technology manufacturing and business, financial, and educational services. Boston, Hartford, and Providence are the major economic focal points in New England.

The *Northeast corridor* extends 450 miles from Boston to Washington, DC. Because of its size and functional complexity, its center is easier to identify than its functional boundaries. New York is the corridor's focal point and is surrounded by Boston, Providence, Hartford, Philadelphia, Baltimore, and Washington, DC. As one of the densest financial, industrial, cultural, communications, and transportation corridors in the nation, the corridor also possesses several concentrated nodes of international business, culture, and

---

[5] The economic geography of the United States is discussed in substantial detail in David J. Hartzell, David G. Shulman, and Charles H. Wurtzebach, *Refining the Analysis of Regional Diversification for Income-Producing Real Estate* (New York: Salomon Brothers Real Estate Research, February 1988); David Shulman and Robert E. Hopkins, *Economic Diversification in Real Estate Portfolios* (New York: Salomon Brothers Real Estate Research, November 1988); and *Real Estate Stocks Monitor* (Baltimore, MD: Third Quarter, 1988. Alex. Brown & Sons, Inc.). An interesting method for quantifying diversification is discussed in Merlin M. Hackbart and Donald A. Anderson, "On Measuring Economic Diversification," *Land Economics,* November 1975.

EXHIBIT 23–2   Economic Regions of the United States

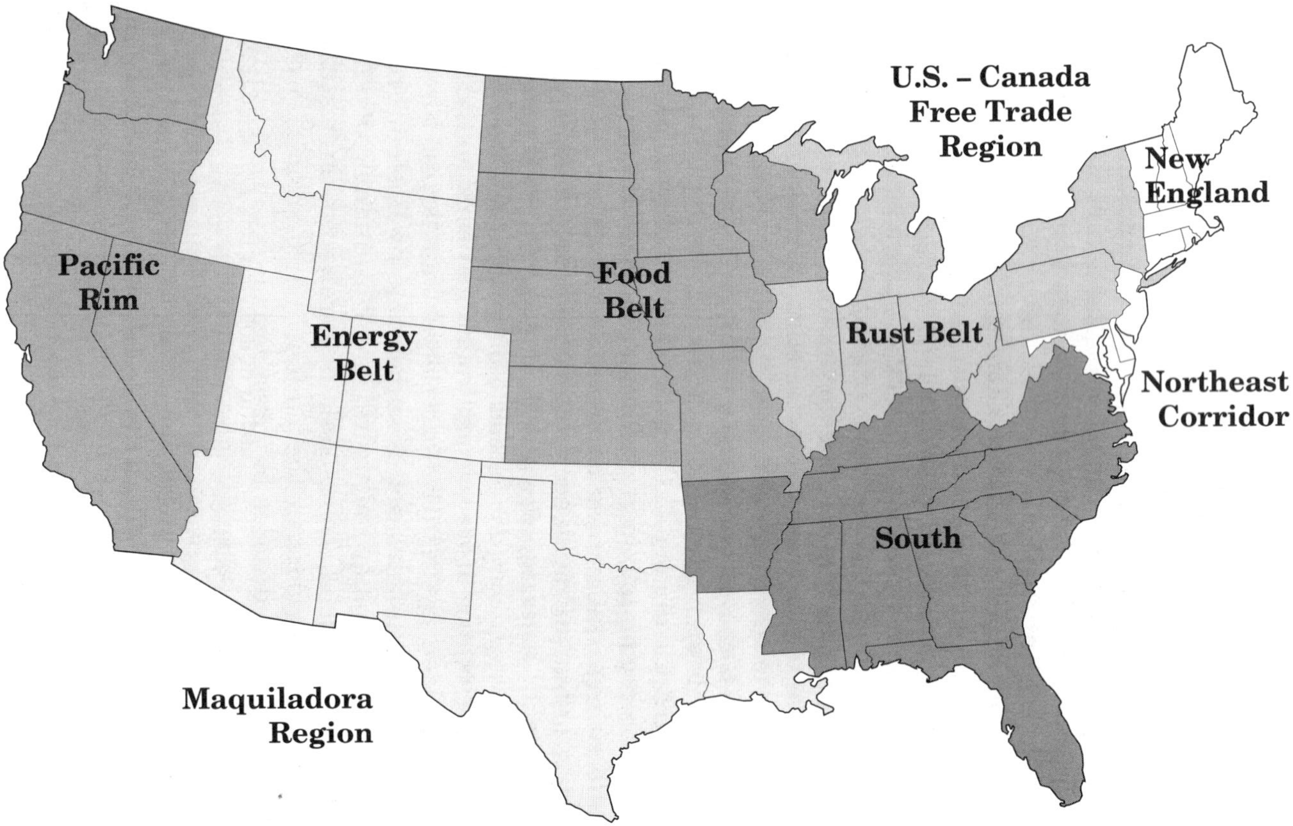

New England

Northeast Corridor

U.S. – Canada Free Trade Region

Rust Belt

South

Food Belt

Energy Belt

Pacific Rim

Maquiladora Region

politics. The size, density, and maturity of many of the property markets in this region continue to attract many investors to this area.

The *South* extends from Kentucky and Virginia on the north, southward to Florida, and westward to states bordering on the west bank of the Mississippi River. The growth of the southern economy in the 1960s and 1970s resulted from its transformation from agriculture to manufacturing. In recent years, its services-producing industries have also emerged. In addition to Atlanta, Miami, and Tampa, there are several other important business centers in the South, including Charlotte, Louisville, and Memphis.[6]

The *Rust Belt* is the focal point of heavy manufacturing industries (steel, autos, machinery) in the nation and extends from Michigan and Illinois eastward to New York and Pennsylvania. Obsolete manufacturing plants and the region's orientation toward the production of durable goods led to its economic vulnerability during the recession of the 1970s. With U.S. economic and trade policy focusing on making the United States more competitive in world markets for manufactured goods, the 1980s witnessed a rebirth in manufacturing and resilience in the Rust Belt's major cities, including Chicago, Detroit, Cleveland, and Pittsburgh.

The *Food Belt* is composed of eight contiguous states located in the center of the nation, an area often referred to by its topography as the Great Plains. The area is bounded within North Dakota, Wisconsin, Missouri, and Kansas and, as its regional name suggests, has an economy dominated by the production of agricultural products. St. Louis, Minneapolis, and Kansas City are the major cities of this region.

The *Energy Belt* extends from Canada through Mexico roughly parallel to the Rocky Mountains. In the continental United States, the Energy Belt is a corridor that extends from Idaho and Montana in the north, south to Louisiana. Clearly, the focal point of the U.S. energy industry in general and the oil industry in particular is Texas, Oklahoma, and Louisiana. One striking characteristic of the Energy Belt economy is that it has been generally countercyclical to that of the United States, as exemplified by its unprecedented boom during

---

[6] For a detailed study of the industrial structure of southern metropolitan areas and the growth of southern cities, see Larry C. Ledebur, *Southern Cities: Economies in Transition* (Washington, DC: The Urban Institute, October 6, 1980).

the national economic doldrums precipitated by the energy crises of the 1970s. Houston, Dallas, and Denver are the major cities of the Energy Belt.

The *Pacific Rim* is the crescent-shaped region that extends from Washington State to Arizona, which substantially borders on the Pacific Ocean. Its preoccupation with the rapidly expanding economies of Southeast Asia—Japan, China, and Taiwan—is the unique characteristic linking the vast and economically diverse states comprising this region. The focal points of this region are Los Angeles and San Francisco. Seattle, San Diego, and Phoenix are other important cities.

Canada and Mexico

Two other regions are emerging as the result of U.S. economic activities with Canada and Mexico. The U.S.–Canada free trade agreement of the late 1980s liberalized the world's largest trading relationship by, among other actions, phasing out tariffs over the next decade, modifying the 1965 U.S.–Canada agreement to allow increased free trade in automobiles and trucks, and removing some restrictions on cross-border investment. The agreement may have some major long-term implications for the economies of cities located on both sides of the northern U.S. border, especially since 80 percent of Canada's population resides within 100 miles of the United States.

A new economic region has also emerged along the U.S.–Mexican border, which extends some 2,000 miles from San Diego on the Pacific Coast to Brownsville, Texas, near the Gulf Coast. Maquiladora industries have encouraged enormous investment in the region and have been a major factor leading to increased trade with Mexico. The number of companies involved in these activities increased from 600 in 1980 to more than 1,500 by 1990. The maquiladora program, initiated in 1965 by the Mexican government, allows U.S. and other foreign companies to establish subsidiaries in Mexico that produce exclusively for export. Mexico provides cheap labor and allows duty-free imports of machinery, parts, and raw materials for the assembly and finishing of products, which are re-exported to the United States and abroad. Maquiladora industries are primarily light manufacturing oriented, although heavy manufacturing industries, including major automakers, have recently established plants in the region. While Mexican law allows these industries to be created throughout Mexico, 90 percent of the plants have been located within the six Mexican states that border the United States.

In addition, direct foreign investment, particularly from the United States, Germany, Japan, and other European nations, is expected to increase substantially in the years ahead, especially if Mexico can secure foreign investor confidence by continuing to cope effectively with its foreign "bad loan" portfolio as it has done with its debt-equity swap program. Increased investment will effect profound changes in the region for Mexico as well as for the four U.S. states that form its border—California, Arizona, New Mexico, and Texas.

Metropolitan Area Choices

Recent research suggests that it may be more efficient to characterize metropolitan areas based on their dominant economic employment categories[7] (i.e., the metropolitan area is categorized by comparing that area's employment patterns to the country's). In essence, this approach removes the physical boundaries of contiguous regions and views metropolitan areas (rather than regions) as similar (or dissimilar) regardless of location, proximity, and contiguity. For example, those areas considered to be financial services cities include Fort Lauderdale, Phoenix, San Francisco, and Boston. This type of economic diversification has been found to provide better risk-return trade-offs than other attempts at geographic diversification.

Most investors faced with selecting metropolitan areas for investment usually develop an intimate knowledge of several areas for comparative purposes. Their research typically consists of qualitative and quantitative analyses of real estate markets as well as economic, political, social, and cultural conditions. The method of investigation usually consists of a cold, hard statistical analysis of historical data, combined with personal intuition and judgment based on observations made during a series of field visits.[8]

Regardless of the differences in their analytical methods, most investors initiate their inquiries by attempting to understand what makes various metropolitan areas tick. What factors led to their

---

[7] See Glenn R. Mueller, Barry A. Ziering, and Donna Machi, "Real Estate Portfolio Diversification Using Economic Diversification," *Journal of Real Estate Research*.

[8] Some interesting work in this area includes "Commercial Mortgage Backed Securities: Real Estate Market Risk Analysis for Five U.S. Cities," *Focus on Structured Transactions* (Moody's Investors Service, March 1987); and Robert E. Hopkins and David Shulman, *Ranking Metropolitan Growth: A Real Estate Tool to be Used with Caution* (New York: Salomon Brothers Real Estate Research, November 25, 1987).

initial creation? What is their current stage of development? What factors are likely to guide their future evolution?

Numerous locational and regional economic growth theories have been proposed over the past several decades to explain the existence and structure of metropolitan areas.[9] These theories have described regional economic growth in terms of a series of development stages, from subsistence farming to industrialization and on through the development of industries producing for export. Unlike many European cities that gradually evolved from a feudalist system through each development stage until eventually becoming export-based market economies, American cities and regions evolved under different circumstances. Several regions of America were initially created because of their export potential and developed by the search for and exploitation of goods to be marketed in world markets. As a result, and as a general rule, the growth of U.S. regions throughout history has depended on the success of the regions' export bases. Even today, an understanding of metropolitan economies necessarily requires an understanding of the economic relationships between metropolitan areas and the larger regional and national economies within which they operate. Important economic linkages among geographic areas have emerged because of goods and services imported from and exported to other regions of the United States and abroad. Based on these theories, a variety of simple economic indicators have been derived to assist investors in the metropolitan area selection process. The following discussion pertains to regional economic factors affecting user demand for real estate, primarily office space.

---

[9] Some of the most notable work in this field includes Alfred Weber's *Theory of the Location of Industries,* originally published in German in 1909 and translated into English in 1928 (Chicago: University of Chicago Press), followed by several other major works, most notably. Edgar M. Hoover, *The Location of Economic Activity* (New York: McGraw-Hill, 1948); August Lösch, *The Economics of Location* (New Haven, CT: Yale University Press, 1954); Walter Isard, *Location and Space Economy* (New York: The Technology Press and John Wiley & Sons, 1956) and *Methods of Regional Analysis* (New York: John Wiley & Sons, 1960); Raymond Vernon, *Metropolis 1985* (Cambridge, MA: Harvard University Press, 1960); and J. Friedman and W. Alonso, eds., *Regional Development and Planning* (Cambridge, MA: MIT Press, 1964). Also see John R. Meyer, "Regional Economics: A Survey," *American Economic Review,* and A. M. Weimer, "A Note on the Early History of Land Economics," *AREUEA Journal,* Fall 1984.

Demand Considerations

Five major economic aspects of a metropolitan area are normally considered in selecting areas for investment: (1) its size, density, and maturity; (2) its general and long-term economic growth potential; (3) the extent to which its economic/industrial base is diversified; (4) how much of its economy is composed of services-producing industries; and (5) the magnitude of its manufacturing base. Many of the return and risk characteristics attendant to the selection of a metropolitan area for real estate investment flow from these five aspects.

Size, Density, and Maturity.

Investors often group metropolitan areas according to physical characteristics, the most obvious of which are size, density, and maturity (i.e., the area's age or stage of development). This classification has an emotional as well as an analytical basis. In general, investors are comfortable with large, dense, mature metropolitan areas. Size and age engender a sense of stability, and high density creates a strong sense of identity and focus of activity that seems inexorable and permanent. There is an additional reason that applies to many foreign investors, especially European and Japanese investors. Large, dense, mature urban areas such as New York, Chicago, Philadelphia, Boston, and San Francisco are spatially very familiar to investors from cities like London and Tokyo.

Exhibit 23–3 shows the variety of size and density characteristics of major U.S. metropolitan areas. New York, Los Angeles, and Chicago are clearly the nation's largest areas and, compared with most other major metropolitan areas, contain more than twice as many people. A visual analysis of New York, San Francisco, and Phoenix demonstrates some of the differences in density. New York, for example, covers approximately the same square mileage as San Francisco, but has more than five times the population. Phoenix has approximately the same population as San Francisco but covers more than nine times its land area. Completing the comparison of extremes, New York, with approximately 7,400 people per square mile, is approximately 35 times denser than Phoenix, which has approximately 200 people per square mile!

One indicator of the maturity of metropolitan areas is population growth, particularly as it relates to the historical population base of an area. Mature metropolitan areas tend to register modest (if not slow) growth relative to their existing populations. For example, in

EXHIBIT 23–3
Population Size and Density of Selected Metropolitan Areas

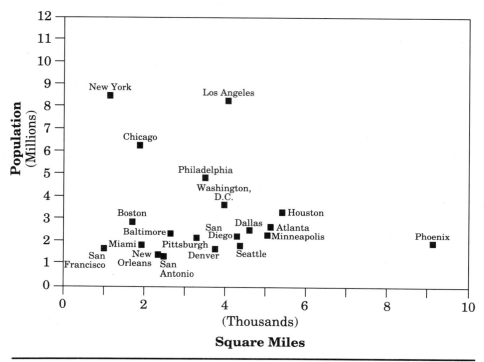

Source: U.S. Bureau of the Census.

terms of aggregate population growth, New York and Chicago have been virtually stable since 1960. In sharp contrast, Houston and Phoenix have nearly tripled in population since 1960 (see Exhibit 23–4).

Economic Growth Potential. Investors normally favor metropolitan areas that lie within regions that are continuing to experience rapid secular population growth, because these areas are most likely to experience the greatest expansion in business investment over the long term.

Shifts in regional economies have been predicted, observed, and

EXHIBIT 23–4

Historical Population as a Percentage of Current Population for Selected Metropolitan Areas, 1930–86

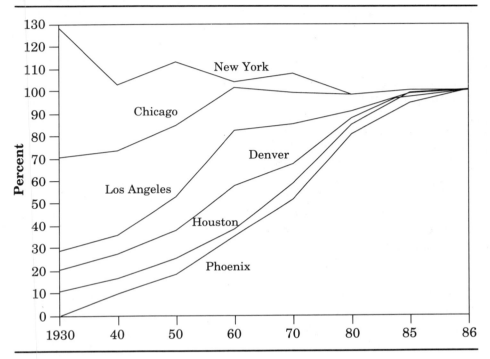

Source: U.S. Bureau of the Census.

most recently characterized as an important national megatrend.[10] Three shifts that have important consequences for metropolitan areas and their real estate markets are (1) the shift of the U.S. population from North to South (and East to West),[11] (2) the gradual replacement of the New York–Chicago axis by the Los Angeles–Houston axis as

---

[10] See John Naisbitt, *Megatrends* (New York: Warner Books, 1982).

[11] The 1980 census indicated a spatial redistribution in the nation's population from the North and East to the South and West. In 1980, the geographic center of the U.S. population was situated in Missouri. (The *center of population* is the point at which an imaginary flat, weightless, and rigid U.S. map would balance if weights of identical value were placed so that each weight represented the location of one person.)

the dominant financial and economic corridor in the United States, and (3) the relative concentration of economic activity in certain states. For example, four states—California, New York, Texas, and Illinois—account for approximately one-third of U.S. gross domestic product, and the 10 largest—including Pennsylvania, Florida, Ohio, New Jersey, Michigan, and Massachusetts—account for more than half the national economic output.[12]

More important, the accompanying shift in the economy is still gaining momentum, and the United States is continuing to experience the result of the mass population movement during the last two decades. Since the mid-1970s, approximately two-thirds of the total amount of construction in the United States has occurred in the West and South. Although high rates of growth do not guarantee either long or short business cycles, there is a tendency toward greater economic expansion in areas of rapid secular development. During periods of business recession, high-growth economies are hit as hard as others. However, when the economy improves, these areas generally recover faster and stronger.

Historical and forecasted employment growth patterns for the United States and selected metropolitan areas are illustrated in Exhibit 23–5. The horizontal and vertical dotted lines intersecting the United States dissect the rectangular field into four quadrants, which can be used for making growth comparisons relative to the country as a whole. For example, metropolitan areas in quadrant I continue to expand employment faster than the United States, while those within quadrant III continue to expand at a slower rate. Not surprisingly, quadrant I is composed primarily of metropolitan areas situated in the southern and western regions, whereas quadrant III contains mostly northeastern and midwestern areas. Quadrants II and IV show metropolitan areas that may be in transition. For example, Denver and Miami, which experienced above-average growth during the past decade, are expected to lag U.S. employment growth over the next decade. In addition, it is interesting to note that each of the major Oil Patch office markets—Dallas, Denver, and Houston—demonstrates characteristically different overall historical and future growth patterns.

---

[12] See Eugene Carlson, "Regions," *The Wall Street Journal*, September 6, 1988, p. 33.

EXHIBIT 23–5
Change in Nonagricultural Employment for Selected Metropolitan Areas

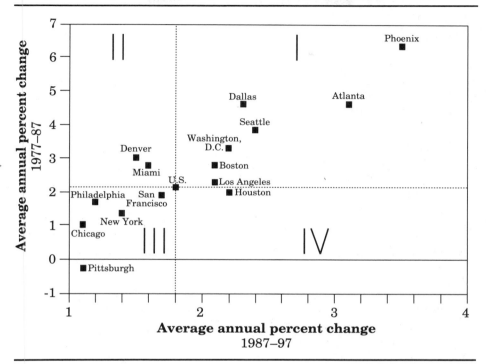

Source: Wharton Econometrics.

Economic/Industrial Base. Investors normally favor economically diversified areas, since they tend to be more stable and less vulnerable to shifts in the economy. Employment concentration ratios (also known as *location quotients*) are a convenient method for analyzing the breadth and diversity of an economy. These ratios compare the concentrations of employment in each local sector with the economy of the entire nation. The concentration ratios for 20 metropolitan areas, shown in Exhibit 23–6, indicate that when an industry's ratio is *greater than 1* (1.0), the area employs more workers in that industry than the national average. Similarly, if the concentration ratio for an industry is *less than 1,* the area employs fewer workers in that industry than the national average. Since many of the metropolitan areas in Exhibit 23–6 have concentration ratios near 1.0, their em-

EXHIBIT 23–6
Employment Concentration Ratios for Selected Metropolitan Areas

	Mining	Construction	Manufacturing	Transportation, Communications, Utilities	Wholesale/ Retail	FIRE	Services	Government
Atlanta	0.00	1.31	0.73	1.55	1.21	1.13	0.97	0.80
Baltimore	0.00	1.35	0.66	1.05	1.00	1.10	1.11	1.15
Boston	0.00	0.79	1.04	0.85	0.95	1.15	1.26	0.77
Chicago	0.10	0.77	0.99	1.20	1.05	1.36	1.12	0.70
Dallas	2.05	1.23	0.91	1.22	1.12	1.58	0.95	0.62
Denver	2.87	1.14	0.63	1.48	1.07	1.34	1.06	0.84
Houston	6.95	1.38	0.58	1.28	1.06	1.23	1.06	0.76
Los Angeles	0.38	0.64	1.21	0.98	0.98	1.10	1.12	0.73
Miami	0.00	1.00	0.61	1.63	1.13	1.35	1.17	0.76
Minneapolis	0.00	0.82	1.07	1.07	1.03	1.17	1.08	0.79
New Orleans	4.19	0.99	0.44	1.62	1.13	1.02	1.10	0.96
New York	0.05	0.73	0.62	1.18	0.80	2.18	1.31	0.93
Oklahoma City	4.25	0.79	0.63	0.97	1.05	1.04	0.90	1.37
Philadelphia	0.00	0.89	0.98	0.87	0.99	1.12	1.22	0.82
Phoenix	0.08	1.85	0.77	0.92	1.08	1.28	1.08	0.77
Pittsburgh	1.03	1.01	0.79	1.01	1.07	0.97	1.30	0.74
San Antonio	0.72	1.49	0.52	0.73	1.09	1.23	1.00	1.28
San Diego	0.12	1.24	0.78	0.75	1.02	1.06	1.12	1.09
San Francisco	0.19	0.77	0.45	1.65	0.99	1.90	1.27	0.86
Seattle	0.00	1.06	1.01	1.25	1.05	1.18	0.98	0.84
Tulsa	8.01	0.91	0.90	1.37	1.03	0.91	1.01	0.67
Washington, DC	0.00	1.28	0.22	0.85	0.84	0.92	1.35	1.67
U.S. Total	1.00	1.00	1.00	1.00	1.00	1.00	1.00	1.00

These concentration ratios are calculated as follows:

$$\text{Ratio} = (e_i^m / E^m) \div (e_i^n \div E^n)$$

where
- e_i^m = Metropolitan area employment in sector i.
- E^m = Total metropolitan area employment.
- e_i^n = National employment in sector i.
- E^n = Total national employment.

Sources: Wharton Econometrics; Cushman & Wakefield, Inc., 1987.

ployment composition reflects the well-diversified U.S. economy. (While approaches to employment diversification may be more robust, Exhibit 23–6 concisely demonstrates the concept of employment diversification patterns.) In some instances, an area shows a strong dependence on a particular industry. For example, Dallas, Denver, Houston, New Orleans, Tulsa, and Oklahoma City are very dependent on mining, including the petroleum and other energy-related industries; Washington, DC, is dependent on government; and New York is dependent on finance, insurance, and real estate.

Generally, an investor should favor broad, diversified metropolitan areas. However, when a particular area, such as Houston or Denver, is selected, an investor should, as a precaution, minimize his or her exposure in other areas with the same economic dependency.

Services-Producing Industries.   In recent decades, investors have been known to favor metropolitan areas with services-producing industries. These industries are a significant part of the U.S. economy, and in recent years they have accounted for more than half the national income and a similar proportion of employees on nonagricultural payrolls. Broadly defined, the service sector industries consist of businesses whose output is intangible, such as transportation and communications, utilities, wholesale and retail trade, finance, insurance, and real estate, and personal and business services, which are among the largest and fastest growing.

As indicated in Exhibit 23–6, some metropolitan areas reflect this economic transformation. For example, New York, San Francisco, Miami, Chicago, Boston, and Dallas have heavy concentrations in the finance, insurance, and real estate industries, and Boston, Washington, DC, New York, Pittsburgh, and Philadelphia are dominant centers for services. These areas are well positioned to grow as the United States continues its evolution into a services-based economy.

As indicated in quadrants I and IV of Exhibit 23–7, Atlanta, Houston, Los Angeles, Miami, Seattle, Phoenix, and Washington, DC, are expected to expand faster than the U.S. average in finance, insurance, and real estate. Many northeastern and midwestern metropolitan areas are expected to lag. Exhibit 23–8 generally shows that although services employment growth is likely to slow down in the future in all major metropolitan areas, future growth is likely to be proportional to past growth; that is, areas that grew faster than the United States in the past are likely to continue doing so,

EXHIBIT 23–7

Change in FIRE Employment for Selected Metropolitan Areas

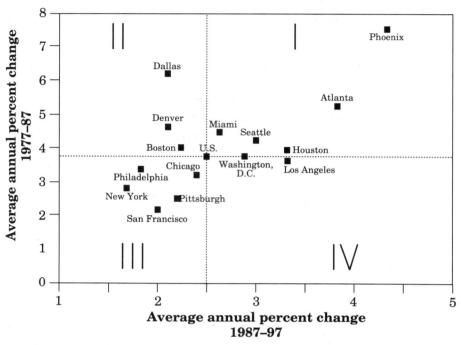

Source: Wharton Econometrics, Spring 1988.

and similarly areas that grew slower than the United States in the past are likely to grow slower in the future. Consequently, most of the metropolitan areas are shown to fall within quadrants I and III.

Manufacturing Base. Investors have also been known to favor metropolitan economies that have small concentrations of durables manufacturing employment. Many investors believe that a metropolitan economy that is dependent on the production of durables is most sensitive to changes in the business cycle.

Employment in manufacturing, particularly durables manufacturing, represents a small percentage of the total employment in most major metropolitan areas (see Exhibit 23–9). Manufacturing employment accounts for approximately 19 percent of total employ-

EXHIBIT 23–8
Change in Services Employment for Selected Metropolitan Areas

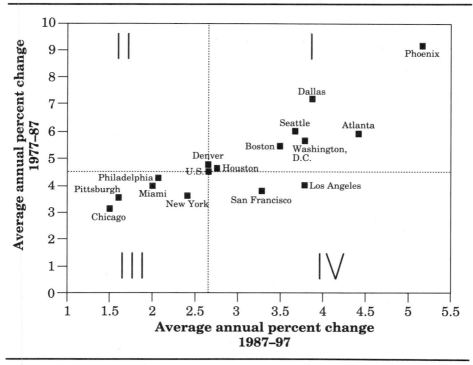

Source: Wharton Econometrics (Spring 1988).

ment in the United States, and a similar percentage of employment in some of the heavy manufacturing metropolitan areas, such as Los Angeles (23 percent), Minneapolis (20 percent), Seattle (20 percent), Chicago (18 percent), Philadelphia (17 percent), Dallas (17 percent), and Boston (16 percent). Durables manufacturing employment represents 11 percent of the nation's employment and a similar share of the employment of Seattle (16 percent), Los Angeles (15 percent), Minneapolis (12 percent), Boston (12 percent), Phoenix (12 percent), San Diego (12 percent), and Dallas (11 percent).

The emerging pattern of manufacturing employment is more complicated than the others just discussed. In addition to comparing the past and future metropolitan area patterns with the United States, four additional quadrants become relevant, that is, the quad-

EXHIBIT 23–9
Manufacturing Employment as a Percentage of Total Employment, 1987

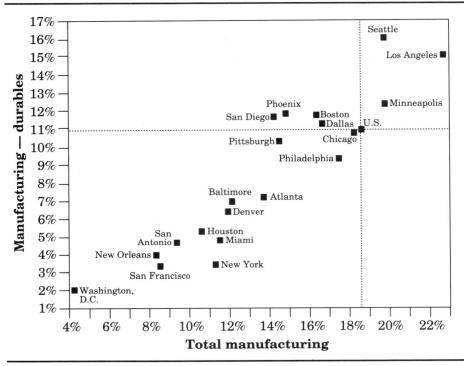

Source: U.S. Bureau of Labor Statistics.

rants formed by the solid horizontal and vertical lines that distinguish between rates of growth and decline for the past and future periods (see Exhibit 23–10). These two overlapping sets of quadrants show, for example, that although New York, Chicago, and Pittsburgh continue to lag behind the United States in manufacturing employment growth, these metropolitan areas are expected to register employment gains during the next decade compared to the previous decade of decline. Other areas are expected to continue along the same trend. Atlanta and Phoenix, for example, are expected to continue their growth in the manufacturing sector, and San Francisco and Philadelphia will likely continue to decline.

Few property markets will meet all five of the requirements detailed above. For example, while Houston and Denver are situated

EXHIBIT 23–10
Change in Total Manufacturing Employment for Selected Metropolitan Areas

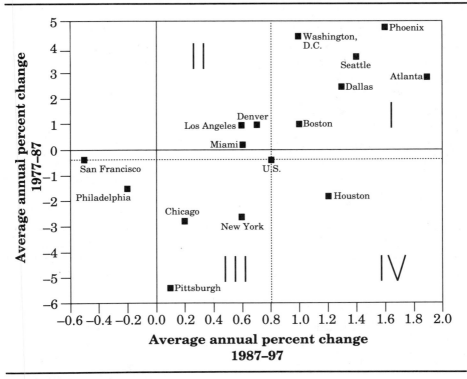

Source: Wharton Econometrics, Spring 1988.

in the fastest-growing regions of the United States, they are heavily dependent on the mining (i.e., petroleum) industry. Similarly, the economies of New York and Boston are heavily concentrated in services but lie in the slower-growing Northeast. The selection of property markets cannot be reduced to a simple mechanical process. Nevertheless, the use of market criteria is helpful in the selection process and for making market comparisons.

Supply Considerations
Demand is only half the story. Only recently has the importance of the supply-side portion of the equilibrium equation begun to re-emerge in earnest. The recent illiquidity of the marketplace (due in part to the

problems of the S&Ls, commercial banks, developers, and syndicators) has led many to conclude, perhaps justifiably, that a new period of decreased construction portends strong rates of increase for rental rates and appreciation. Greater constraints placed on new construction should in time restore the attributes of the real estate equities (inflation hedge, high return, low risk, low covariance) that investors (particularly institutions) thought they were buying in the 1980s.

Of course, many of these real estate prophets were also demand-siders (those placing too great an emphasis on socioeconomic trends and not enough on the supply side) when that part of the equation was more in vogue (pre-1990). The enthusiasm of these demand-siders led in part to a major construction boom in almost all real estate sectors, the result of which has been the steadily eroding performance of real estate equities.

While Phoenix, as one example, is by most measurements characterized as a city of very high (past and future) growth, the rapid pace of new construction has led to disappointing results (as measured in inflation-adjusted rents) for many of its real estate apartment investors.[13] Conversely, Denver, which grew much less quickly (and lost almost 23,000 employees in 1986) experienced a greater increase in its real rents than did Phoenix.

The metropolitan Houston office market during the 1970s and early 1980s (before oil prices plunged) is another example of what happens when unrestrained construction occurs, even in an economy experiencing robust demand growth. During its heyday, despite unprecedented demand growth, demand lagged the pace of new construction, which resulted in relatively high vacancy rates and slow rental growth. Of course, the decline in oil prices during the mid-1980s dramatically reduced demand growth and exacerbated the market's overbuilt condition.

What factors affect the amount of new construction in a given market? Although the demand for space is an important factor affecting supply, there are other important factors that relate to the availability of resources required to accommodate demand growth and create new properties, including humanmade resources such as public infrastructure (airports, highways, mass transit, water, gas, elec-

---

[13] See Marc Andrew Louargand, "Apartment Earnings and Regional Economic Diversification" (Working paper FP#4, MIT Center for Real Estate Development, June 1989).

tric, and telephone utilities, etc.) and the most obvious natural resource, land. Land can be tricky, however. In addition to the physical
availability of developable land, local attitudes toward growth, development, and environmental issues, usually manifested in regional
development plans (at a macro level), and zoning ordinances (at a
micro level) must be considered. Regardless of the physical availability of land, political attitudes toward development often substantially
influence development patterns.

Although a propensity for growth is usually a desirable characteristic of the demand side of the market equation, investors have mixed
feelings when it comes to growth as it pertains to the supply side.
Although supply must be somewhat flexible for a real estate market
to continue to grow and evolve, many investors prefer markets that
have some natural and/or artificial barriers to new construction.
These investors believe that constrained growth in development keeps
rents, and consequently property values, higher than would otherwise
be achieved.

Due to the risks attendant to unconstrained supply, investors
often seek markets possessing a variety of artificial and natural barriers to new supply. There are numerous examples. New York's central
business district (Manhattan) has both types of barriers. The growth
of its midtown and downtown markets along an east-west axis is
limited by rivers, and growth along its north-south axis is somewhat
constrained by its natural geologic conditions, the availability of public infrastructure, and zoning and environmental requirements.
Downtown San Francisco is constrained for similar reasons, plus
additional development restrictions due to its location within an active earthquake area. In addition, Washington, DC, and Philadelphia
have height restrictions for new development that relate to monu-
ments with historical significance to these cities (e.g., the Washington
Monument and the statue of William Penn, respectively). Recently
other cities, such as Seattle and West Los Angeles, have imposed
more stringent development restrictions to preserve the environment
and limit the burden on existing infrastructure.

Submetropolitan Area Choices

Downtown versus Suburbs
An investor would hope that once metropolitan areas have been selected, locational decisions relating to investment selection will be

readily apparent. However, while some investors argue persuasively for suburban investments, many others favor downtown areas. To understand their preferences, it is important to understand suburbanization itself and the opportunities and risks associated with downtown and suburban areas.

Several theories have been developed to explain the massive suburbanization of U.S. urban areas during the past 40 years. These theories relate to a variety of "push" and "pull" factors. The major pull factors most often cited have been the secular rise in the use of the automobile as the primary means of travel and the availability of inexpensive suburban land, which together have enabled businesses and residences to flee outward from urban centers. Some have attributed the movement to a basic American preference for low-density living and see the suburbs as the fulfillment of this preference for the most affluent segments of the population. Still others have described the poor social conditions of central cities, such as poor schools, crime, neighborhood deterioration, and the proximity of low-income people and minorities as exerting a push toward suburban living.

Proponents of the suburban lifestyle point to factors relating to the evolutionary cycle of urban areas that suggest why suburbanization may be inevitable. For example, because urban centers are already densely developed, they tend to grow proportionally less than their surrounding suburbs; that is, metropolitan areas tend to distribute their development densities outward from their centers and over a wider area. In the case of declining metropolitan areas, urban centers tend to lose population at a faster rate than the area as a whole because they contain the oldest facilities, such as infrastructure and housing. In addition, and in general, the gradual but continuous decline in transportation costs relative to other living costs causes a central location to lose its advantage and, consequently, lose some of its natural economic appeal.

The case for increasing suburbanization is eloquently made in *Edge Cities* by Joel Garreau[14] (the same author who wrote *The Nine Nations of North America,* which voiced the underpinnings for much of the regional diversification considerations discussed earlier). By definition, an edge city must have in excess of 5 million square feet of office space and 600,000 square feet of retail space, have more jobs

---

[14] Joel Garreau, *Edge City: Life on the New Frontier* (New York: Doubleday, 1991).

than bedrooms, be perceived by the population as one place, and have been perceived as nothing like a "city" as recently as 30 years ago. Garreau asserts that edge cities will continue to become an increasingly important element of the American landscape. However, he also asserts that most CBDs will also continue to hold important places as well; it is not a zero-sum game.

Investors who prefer downtown areas usually subscribe to the theory that some critical point occurs in the suburbanization process after which city living will once again become more desirable than suburban living. That is, there is some point at which the growing attractiveness of the suburbs and the decline of cities will level off. From the outset, it seems plausible that the close geographic proximity of cities and suburbs will, in the long run, cause each to acquire its counterpart's attributes. There has also been some recent evidence suggesting that city decline and suburban growth will not continue indefinitely. First, the evidence refers to a variety of urban long-run corrective mechanisms. In particular, the growing fiscal crises in many cities has led to the increased recognition that in the past, cities have borne various welfare costs disproportionately. This, in turn, has led state and federal governments to rethink policies and to share these costs more fairly. Second, as suburban municipalities develop their own problems—that is, as more suburban problems emerge to cancel out the city problems avoided by those moving to the suburbs—businesses and individuals will come to appreciate central locations for things that cannot be matched by suburbs, such as the concentration of financial institutions, legal and accounting firms, and certain cultural advantages. Therefore, there is reason to expect that as the pluses and minuses begin to cancel out, balance between city and suburban growth will result.[15]

---

[15] A recent study conducted for Cushman & Wakefield, Inc., by Louis Harris and Associates, Inc., showed that business headquarters' relocation patterns have stabilized in recent years (see *Headquarters Relocation,* 1987). During 1987, the Harris firm interviewed top executives at 400 organizations nationwide that relocated their headquarters during the previous five years. These organizations were screened from a sample of public and private corporations, partnerships, nonprofit organizations, and government entities with 50 or more employees at their headquarters location.

The study showed that 85 percent of organizations that relocated their headquarters during the previous five-year period moved to the same type of place (big city, suburb of a big city, smaller city, small town, or rural area). In addition, the study made the following observations: Although the nation's largest cities are seen as *worst* on four of the five most important criteria, the image of the nation's largest urban centers seems to be improving. It's not easy to say *why*

Although it is difficult to predict long-term intrametropolitan growth patterns, one fact is certain: Development patterns do not change overnight. Major changes in land use patterns at the metropolitan area scale take place after many decades. Consequently, existing land patterns can be expected to dominate for most of the foreseeable future. In addition, the fact that economic growth in the United States will be slower in future years should cause metropolitan land use patterns to evolve at a slower rate than in the past. Also, inasmuch as major commercial real estate contracts often involve very-long-term commitments, usually ranging from 10 to 25 years, there is an inertia to real estate development and relocation patterns that almost ensures that a review of near-term developments should afford a reasonable picture of land pattern trends likely to emerge in the next couple of decades.[16]

Despite the inherent stability of development patterns and all the theories to explain intraurban growth, intrametropolitan area investment choices can be tricky. And, unfortunately, intrametropolitan area growth and development patterns are difficult, if not impossible, to predict. During the past 30 years, however, great strides have been made in understanding these growth dynamics. Some of the work in this field has centered on microdescriptive modeling efforts, which focus on understanding the locational decision-making process of millions of individual households and businesses and how and why those individual decisions create the variety of spatial development patterns that characterize urban areas. The macrodescriptive models

---

this is. Although in some instances those who moved a year ago or less are not as demanding as those who moved two to five years ago, the two groups are about equally likely to see the all-important attributes of ample space and room to expand as important—yet the more recent relocators give the cities better marks.

The study findings indicate that among more recent relocators the industry mix swings slightly toward service-oriented organizations and government entities, which as a group are more likely than industrial, wholesale, and retail organizations to have moved to one of the largest cities; other findings show that those currently headquartered in the cities tend to rate them highly.

If these explanations for the apparent improvement in the image of the big cities make any sense, it is possible that either increasing space availability or continuing relocation on the part of organizations in the service industry will ensure that the nation's leading urban centers are not going out of style as headquarters locations. (p. 41)

[16] For example, another finding of the Cushman and Wakefield study was that only approximately 4 percent of the organizations screened for the survey nationwide relocated their headquarters within the 1982–87 period.

have dealt with similar behavioral processes, but have described behavior at a broader level of detail.[17]

A major innovation in these efforts came about with the creation of the first prototype version of an integrated transportation and land development model package during the early 1970s. Also, certain areas, such as the San Francisco metropolitan area, have been used to test new theories and models in this field. Although the model was initially developed as a tool to improve highway construction planning, it is clear that the evolution of a region's transportation system has a significant and profound effect on real estate development patterns. Considering the strong linkages between regional transportation development and local development patterns, perhaps in the future these models will be used to enrich our understanding of the dynamics of local real estate markets and clarify intrametropolitan area investment choices.

Downtown and suburban real estate investments differ with regard to their returns and inherent risks. These differences are readily observed in office property investments.

Downtown.   Downtown office properties have been most popular among institutional investors, especially European investors, who find them easy to compare with properties in their own major cities. Downtown areas are usually the largest, oldest, densest, and single most important office submarkets within their respective metropolitan areas and, consequently, usually serve as good barometers for metropolitan area office property conditions. Downtown areas also tend to have the best-documented histories, which are particularly useful in analyzing and projecting future conditions—a characteristic that appeals to generally risk-averse institutional investors.

Downtown areas and the office properties within them have traditionally been viewed as investments providing solid real returns, for several reasons. The considerable maturity and size of downtown markets generally translate into a stable and diversified tenant base, thus enabling properties to substantially maintain secure income streams and their value during economic downturns. Due to their central location and importance to their regional economies, down-

---

[17] Interested readers should see Stephen Putman, *Urban Residential Location Models* (Boston: Martinus Nijhoff Publishing, 1979).

town areas also consist of properties that are generally well positioned for income growth and value appreciation during economic expansions. Furthermore, because of their general appeal to lenders and investors, downtown properties also tend to be easier to refinance and sell than properties in other markets. However, the last several years have demonstrated that despite these strengths, a period of sustained new construction can lead to considerable weakness in these fundamental assumptions.

Special kinds of risks are also associated with downtown properties. Individual properties tend to be larger and more costly (on a per-square-foot basis) than others, which makes portfolio diversification difficult unless substantial investment funds are available or leverage is used. One extreme example would be prime Manhattan office properties, which have become prohibitively expensive for all but the largest institutional investors to finance or purchase. Some large property owners, cognizant of the problem faced by lenders and investors in this market, have resorted to selling and refinancing their properties via securitization methods and pooled investment vehicles.

Deteriorating infrastructure, the rising cost of public services, and rising local income and real estate taxes in many urban centers pose another threat to the long-term viability and profitability of downtown office property investments. The necessary use of mass transportation for access to downtown areas, combined with the (perceived) American preference to drive automobiles, creates another risk when gasoline prices fall; low gas prices permit the dispersal of economic activities, hasten suburbanization, and encourage the use of automobiles. When oil prices rise, however, high-density downtown areas served by mass transportation systems reassume their important role in regional office markets; that is, downtown properties may be less vulnerable to energy crises and the policies of OPEC.

Suburbs. The massive suburbanization of employment and residences during the past several decades has led to the growth and development of many suburban office markets. The centripetal forces that created concentrated urban centers in the past have, in some measure, given way to compelling corporate objectives to pay lower taxes, pay cheaper rents, and maintain proximity to a skilled labor market. Over time, many suburban markets have become regional focal points for certain business activities, exceeding their role as markets for back-office and administrative functions of firms head-quartered downtown.

What investment opportunities do suburban office properties provide? Suburban office properties generally cost less than downtown properties, primarily because land is less expensive, properties are smaller, and low-rise buildings tend to be less expensive to build. Consequently, real estate portfolio diversification is easier for modest institutional investors. New suburban markets tend to offer the significant property value appreciation associated with the early stages of a market's creation and its development of a critical mass. The development of a few properties strategically located along a major suburban highway often creates a market with a distinct identity. Consequently, office property owners possessing rights to develop adjoining parcels as the market expands are well positioned to enjoy substantial appreciation in property values.

However, the above-average appreciation potential of certain suburban properties carries with it some substantial risks. Due to their location in relatively new and small office markets, suburban properties have less secure income streams. This stems primarily from the perceived substitutability of suburban properties and the difficulty corporate tenants have in differentiating among them. The locational amenities of suburban properties are generally less site specific than downtown properties. For example, the locational amenities associated with properties situated north of the MetLife Building (200 Park Avenue) in midtown Manhattan differ substantially from those to the south, whereas differentiation among suburban sites usually occurs over greater distances.

Suburban markets also tend to be less economically diversified and more vulnerable to the relocation decisions of a few large tenants or the economic conditions facing a few industry groups, which makes these markets vulnerable to cyclical economic downturns.

It is also difficult to argue persuasively for the ability of suburban properties in general to preserve their value. Given the limited histories and often undiscernible presence of these markets within the surrounding suburban sprawl, unforeseen factors can cause the inertia of development patterns to shift away from newly emerging suburban nodes with greater ease than other, better-established markets. (For example, the energy crises and high gasoline prices of the 1970s redirected growth from some new, remote suburban areas to older suburban areas located close to downtown within mass transportation corridors.)

Finally, the lack of experience of many foreign investors with suburbanized development on such a grand scale in their own countries and their unfamiliarity with our suburbs in general have contributed to their reluctance to undertake suburban investments in the United States in the past. Downtown areas in major U.S. cities such as New York, Chicago, Los Angeles, and Washington, DC, on the other hand, have been popularized by American films and television for years. Consequently, because of this blind spot, suburban properties are generally less visible internationally and less liquid as investments in the global real estate marketplace.

CONCLUSION

Not one homogeneous real estate marketplace but several heterogeneous markets should be delineated and segmented according to various characteristics. This chapter identified several characteristics that are particularly useful in segmenting the market, including locational and property characteristics, lease structures and life cycles, and investment vehicle and structure types.

Considering the range and variety of real estate investment opportunities and the advantages of real estate for overall investment portfolios, investors should not have to question the validity of including real estate in their investment portfolios. Rather, they should be able to focus on identifying segments of the real estate market that meet their specific return and risk requirements and on selecting real estate opportunities that will assist them in achieving their overall investment goals and objectives.

REFERENCES

Carlson, Eugene. "Regions." *The Wall Street Journal,* September 6, 1988, p. 33.

Clark, Dave. "Proprietary Demographic Projections Are Unreliable." *Real Estate Review,* Fall 1988.

"Commercial Mortgage Backed Securities: Real Estate Market Risk Analysis for Five U.S. Cities." *Focus on Structured Transactions*. Moody's Investors Service, March 1987.

Garreau, Joel. *Edge City: Life on the New Frontier*. New York: Doubleday, 1991.

Giliberto, S. Michael. *Equity Real Estate Investment Trusts and Real Estate Returns*. New York: Salomon Brothers, 1990.

Hackbart, Merlin M., and Donald A. Anderson. "On Measuring Economic Diversification." *Land Economics,* November 1975.

Hartzell, David J.; David G. Shulman; and Charles H. Wurtzebach. *Refining the Analysis of Regional Diversification for Income-Producing Real Estate*. New York: Salomon Brothers Real Estate Research, February 1988.

Harvey, Robert O., and W. A. V. Clark. "The Nature and Economics of Urban Sprawl." *Land Economics,* February 1965.

Headquarters Relocation. Study conducted for Cushman & Wakefield, Inc., by Louis Harris Associates, Inc., 1987.

Hoover, Edgar M. *The Location of Economic Activity*. New York: McGraw-Hill, 1948.

Hopkins, Robert E. *The Regional Impact of the Slowdown in Defense Spending*. New York: Salomon Brothers Real Estate Research, November 25, 1987.

Hopkins, Robert E., and David Shulman. *Ranking Metropolitan Growth: A Real Estate Tool to Be Used with Caution*. New York: Salomon Brothers Real Estate Research, June 1987.

Isard, Walter. *Location and Space Economy*. New York: The Technology Press and John Wiley & Sons, 1956.

Isard, Walter. *Methods of Regional Analysis*. New York: John Wiley & Sons, 1960.

Ledebur, Larry C. *Southern Cities: Economies in Transition*. Washington, DC: The Urban Institute, October 6, 1980.

Ledebur, Larry C., and Ronald L. Moomaw. *The Productivity Paradox: Slow Growth/High Growth among Regions and Metropolitan Areas*. Washington DC: The Urban Institute, October 9, 1981.

Lösch, August. *The Economics of Location*. New Haven, CT: Yale University Press, 1954.

Louargand, Marc Andrew. "Apartment Earnings and Regional Economic Diversification." Working paper FP#4, MIT Center for Real Estate Development, June 1989.

Meyer, John R. "Regional Economics: A Survey." *American Economic Review*.

Mueller, Glenn R.; Barry A. Ziering; and Donna Machi. "Real Estate Portfolio Diversification Using Economic Diversification." *Journal of Real Estate Research,* forthcoming.

Naisbitt, John. *Megatrends.* New York: Warner Books, 1982.

Pagliari, Joseph L., Jr. "Real Estate in 3-D: See it Now!" *Real Estate Issues,* Fall–Winter 1990.

Putman, Stephen H. *Urban Residential Location Models.* Boston: Martinus Nijhoff Publishing, 1979.

Real Estate Stocks Monitor. Baltimore, MD: Alex. Brown & Sons, Inc. Third Quarter, 1988.

J. Friedman and W. Alonso, eds. *Regional Development and Planning.* Cambridge, MA: MIT Press, 1964.

Shulman, David, and Robert E. Hopkins. *Economic Diversification in Real Estate Portfolios.* New York: Salomon Brothers Real Estate Research, November 1988.

Vernon, Raymond. *Metropolis 1985.* Cambridge, MA: Harvard University Press, 1960.

Weber, Alfred. *Theory of the Location of Industries.* English translation. Chicago: University of Chicago Press, 1928.

Weimer, A. M. "A Note on the Early History of Land Economics." *AREUEA Journal,* Fall 1984.

Wiseman, Michael, and Pravin Varaiya. "Reindustrialization and the Outlook for Declining Areas." *Research in Urban Economics* 3 (1983).

CHAPTER 24

DEVELOPING A
PORTFOLIO STRATEGY

Glenn R. Mueller
La Salle Advisors, Ltd., and Johns Hopkins University

Marc A. Louargand
Cornerstone Real Estate Advisers, Inc.

INTRODUCTION

This chapter addresses the development of a real estate portfolio strategy for institutional investors. Given the affirmative decision to allocate a portion of the investment portfolio to real estate, another series of questions arises. How should we do it? What kinds of vehicles are available? What should we expect from it? How should we manage the process? Unless the investor starts with a clear vision of what the real estate strategy should be, these questions will be answered on an ad hoc basis. This chapter examines the issues that drive the development of a strategy, including the size of the investment portfolio, the sophistication of the investor, the goals and objectives of the total portfolio, human and money capital resources available to the investor, the visibility of real estate and associated liabilities, the current investment environment, investment vehicles, new developments in the field, and the importance of exit strategies. Next, the chapter describes some basic portfolio strategies, including core portfolios, sector plays, rotational strategies, and other specialized strategies. It concludes by discussing the monitoring of a portfolio strategy, measuring asset and manager performance, and budgeting for performance.

The Role of Portfolio Strategy

Portfolio strategy results from a set of decisions about how best to accomplish the *goals* and *objectives* that have been set out for the portfolio. These may be direct reflections of a mixed-asset portfolio's mission or vision statement, or they may flow from the real estate portfolio's goal statement. Often, however, portfolios have strategy statements that appear as free-floating ideas, not connected to any particular portfolio goal or objective. Investors will create better portfolios if they are able to ground the strategy in their portfolio objectives. At the same time, they are limited in the development of a strategy by the constraints of organizational goals and character-istics.

CRITICAL ISSUES IN STRATEGY DEVELOPMENT

Planning a portfolio strategy is like developing a strategic business plan. Initial considerations include who and what are we, how big are we, what is our mission, what resources do we command, and what are the goals for the organization? Developing a portfolio strategy requires an understanding of these issues to be able to sift through the alternative approaches and vehicles to find those most appropriate for the specific goals and constraints of the portfolio. For investment portfolios, timing of cash in and cash out requirements is often an important consideration.

Most portfolios are created for one of two purposes: to create wealth or to fund future liabilities. Wealth creation is sometimes thought of as a personal goal, while funding future liabilities is often considered to be either a personal or a business goal. In fact, these two purposes are inextricably linked. For example, consider these purposes in the context of a pension fund. Understanding pension fund portfolio management involves understanding the conflicting nature of the claims against the fund. Bernstein[1] puts forth these issues in the context of a corporate pension plan, but they are also relevant to public and Taft-Hartley funds, endowments, foundations, and other institutional investors such as insurance companies, where similar conflicting motivations can be identified. Bernstein writes, "The employees are the beneficiaries of the plan, which gives them a senior claim on the [pension plan] assets. In addition, the employees have lent their deferred wages to the corporation and have a further

---

[1]Peter L. Bernstein, "Asset Allocation: Things Are Not What They Seem," *Financial Analysts Journal,* March–April 1987.

contractual claim on future compensation; the assets of the pension fund are collateral to secure these claims." Quite naturally, employees are concerned primarily about the safety of the plan and are "willing to minimize return in exchange for the comfortable feeling that the plan is, first and foremost, minimizing risk." These employee concerns are at odds with the company's stockholders, who "want to maximize the size of the assets and to minimize the pension expense. This is the only one consistent with the stockholders' objective of maximizing the long-run value of the corporation." Consequently, "[t]he stockholders are thus willing to accept higher risk than the employees would accept, because the stockholders rather than the [pension plan] beneficiaries will enjoy the fruits of higher expected returns." Yet another level of complexity/conflict is senior management: "The pension officer, the chief financial officer, the chief executive officer, and often the board of directors have a stake in the performance of the pension fund. And they—not the employees and not the stockholders—are the ones who determine the risk-reward tradeoffs in the pension fund."[2]

How these conflicting interests are resolved is far from uniform and results in a blurring array of portfolio allocation, management styles, risk-return temperament, and so on. These choices are often influenced, if not determined, by the cultural characteristics of the pension plan sponsor.[3]

Notwithstanding these conflicts, it is axiomatic that any investor's net worth is determined by the interplay of its assets and liabilities. Thus, while much discussion of pension fund management focuses on the asset side of the equation, the relationship between assets and liabilities ultimately governs a plan's surplus (or net worth). With this in mind, we'll take an investment focus on wealth creation over a given time period to fund future needs or liabilities. The timing of those future needs or liabilities is also critical to the overall strategy. The time available to the investor, the beginning endowment, and the monetary return goals will determine the level of risk the portfolio must bear and hence its potentially suitable strategies.

Investors often view the establishment of a risk tolerance level

---

[2]Ibid.

[3]William M. O'Barr and John M. Conley, *Fortune and Folly: The Wealth and Power of Institutional Investing* (Homewood, IL: Business One Irwin), 1992.

for a portfolio as a choice driven by individual preferences and tastes for risk. But there is a risk-return trade-off. In many cases, major pension funds are defined benefit plans that must be able to fund preset cash flow obligations. The major trade-off is the plan sponsor's fear of losing capital against the need for returns high enough to grow the fund internally through investment instead of asking the corporation or public entity that funds the pension to cover shortfalls in cash outlay needs.

Size of the Portfolio

Most businesses and governments create separate entities to invest monies that will create wealth outside the core business or fund liabilities such as pension benefits for workers. In the early days of pension fund management, investments were limited to the highest-quality-rated debt and portfolio management was predominantly passive. With their entry into common equity (stocks) in the postwar era, pension fund investors began to adopt more active management styles. But they were active only in the selection and monitoring process, not in the managerial decision-making role that is often required in real estate. For an overview of institutional real estate investing, see Chapter 1, "The Evolution of Institutional Investment in Real Estate."

This operations component of real estate raises issues of liability for pension plan sponsor staff which may not be part of the picture in other asset classes. Real estate, more than other major asset classes, requires its investors to be operations managers at some level. Direct investment in real estate requires managerial decision making with respect to the daily life of the asset and its optimization strategy. The alternative is to purchase tradable security vehicles that invest in real estate. These include real estate operating companies and real estate investment trusts (REITs).

Portfolio size is more critical in real estate than in other asset classes due to the indivisibility of the asset itself and to discontinuities in the spectrum of available investment vehicles. Consequently, the size of the total investment portfolio is even more important, since real estate is typically relegated to a minority allocation among other assets.

Estimates of real estate's share of the total wealth portfolio vary from 50 to 75 percent, depending on the source. Globally, the share is probably toward the higher end of the range and likely toward the lower end in the United States. About 70 percent of U.S. real estate is residential. That leaves between 15 and 20 percent of U.S. wealth to commercial property, with the remaining 10 to 15 percent in other forms of real estate such as farm and timberland. The current 4 percent average U.S. pension allocation to real estate is well below the U.S. asset proportion and is small compared to much higher foreign pension allocations in the 20 to 30 percent range, life company allocations in the 15 to 30 percent range, and commercial bank portfolios in the 30 percent range. Life companies and banks invest in real estate debt more often than in equity. According to an analysis of the 200 largest pension plans, if the pension portfolio's exposure to commercial mortgages is included, their allocation is approximately 10 percent. Adding mortgage-backed securities (MBSs) raises the real estate exposure to 15 percent. In contrast, most estimates of pension investment in common stocks fall in the range of 30 to 40 percent.[4]

Since certain types of real estate investment vehicles carry substantial entry costs, there is a strong link between total portfolio size and the range of feasible options for developing a portfolio strategy. In addition to entry costs, some vehicles may have substantial human capital requirements that preclude their use in some organizations. It is also important that the portfolio strategy be based on a clear understanding of the portfolio's objectives and constraints, which should generally be independent of the investment vehicles used. However, in some cases, such as the use of real estate securities in a portfolio that has substantial liquidity needs, the nature of the vehicle may be closely related to the portfolio objective.

Goals and Objectives of the Investment Program

Most investment programs look for a combination of cash flow and appreciation to fund their liabilities. Historically, bonds supplied cash flow and stocks brought appreciation. Real estate has the ability to produce both income and appreciation, albeit in cyclical patterns. As real estate is added to the portfolio, the timing of the cash flow and

---

[4]See Marc Andrew Louargand, "Pension Fund Investment in Housing," working paper, WP #34, MIT Center for Real Estate Development, November 1991. If we examined the smaller pension plans, we would find their total exposure to real estate is smaller and would likely be biased toward mortgage-backed securities and other, more liquid and divisible real estate interests.

ultimate asset sale must be considered due to the illiquid nature of the asset.

Since real estate has both stock- and bondlike characteristics, one reason for adding it to a portfolio is to achieve greater diversification. Real estate's low correlation with other asset types is well demonstrated in the literature and in practice, much to the regret of the investor of the late 1980s (i.e., real estate returns failed to keep pace with the long bull run in the stock and bond markets in the late 1980s and early 1990s). Despite the current cyclical effects, real estate continues to be a vehicle for creating additional diversification in a mixed-asset portfolio. In the pension fund arena, the Employee Retirement Income Security Act of 1974 (ERISA) requires corporate pension funds to provide prudent care in the management of pension reserves. Part of the mandate was to diversify the investment portfolio, which provided an impetus for the addition of real estate to pension portfolios.

Within the real estate portfolio itself, diversification models have evolved from property type to geographic location to economic location. While each piece of real estate is unique and may perform differently than its market in the short term, history has shown that over the long term, individual properties tend to follow local market movements. Thus, the long-term investor must examine local market economics and diversify the economic risks found there. Current research[5] shows that locational diversification by standard industrial code (SIC) employment dominance in a metropolitan statistical area (MSA) provides risk-return characteristics superior to those of geographical diversification strategies, which are actually less than perfect proxies for economic diversification. However, investors may find it difficult to diversify efficiently with small real estate portfolios, and consequently they need to weigh the benefits of diversification against the costs of administering a complex portfolio of properties.

One of the main functions of an investment portfolio is to preserve value over the investment holding period. Bonds lose value when interest rates rise (with interest rate movement tied to expected inflation rate movement) and have fixed principal values upon maturity;

[5]Glenn R. Mueller, "Refining Economic Diversification Strategies for Real Estate Portfolios," *Journal of Real Estate Research,* Winter 1993, pp. 55–68, provides a review of this progression and current views of diversification.

therefore, bonds are not considered inflation hedges. Stock returns have fluctuated widely over the years and generally have had low correlations with inflation; therefore, stocks are generally not considered an inflation hedge, at least in the short term. Real estate as a physical "hard" asset has historically been considered an inflation hedge. A recent study[6] found that real estate was an inflation hedge in the 1970s and 1980s until the market fell out of balance (with market balance defined by vacancy rates). Office buildings were an inflation hedge in the 1970s and early 1980s but lost their hedging effectiveness when large amounts of new supply were built without a corresponding amount of new demand, thus pushing vacancy rates above their equilibrium levels. Over the same time period, industrial properties consistently retained their inflation-hedging characteristics as their vacancy rates stayed below or near equilibrium levels. In general, we can say that real estate is likely to provide inflation hedging when markets are in equilibrium and inflation is accompanied by real growth in demand, as was the case in the 1970s and early 1980s. Absent real growth in demand, or absent market equilibrium, real estate is not likely to provide a meaningful hedge against inflation.

Investments compete for dollars in the capital market based on their risk-adjusted returns. Throughout the 1970s, real estate equity investment came mainly from private individuals and debt came from local sources such as banks and S&Ls. In the 1980s, large amounts of capital from institutions flowed to equity real estate, changing the face of the industry. Initially yields were good, but the demand for investment product in the real estate capital market outstripped the growth in demand for occupancy in the real estate space market. Unfortunately, forces combined to satisfy investment demand instead of responding to the dampening of occupancy demand. Many properties were purchased for appreciation potential rather than current income. This situation created an oversupply of product in the asset class. The oversupply exists in many markets in the mid-1990s; prices of office buildings, for example, have dropped by as much as 50 percent from their peak. Recently real estate's current yields have once again

---

[6]Charles H. Wurtzebach, Glenn R. Mueller, and Donna Macchi, "The Impact of Inflation and Vacancy Rates on Real Estate Returns," *Journal of Real Estate Research,* Summer 1991, pp. 153–68.

become attractive relative to other investments in the capital markets, since they offer wider spreads off the treasury curve than most alternative investment assets.

Real estate's historical appreciation behavior can be looked at as either a wealth-enhancing mechanism or an inflation-hedging mechanism. Future appreciation potential for real estate must be assessed based on a property's potential to produce an increasing income stream, its relative competitiveness in the market, the equilibrium of supply and demand in the local marketplace, and real estate's relative position in the capital marketplace. Market corrections in real estate last much longer than those in the stock or bond markets, and only patient investors with a long-term time horizon should consider real estate for its appreciation potential.

Human Capital Resources

Real estate is unique in the capital markets. It is a real, physical asset that is immovable. It has the potential to deliver continuous cash flows over long holding periods with appropriate maintenance expenditures. But real estate is one of a few asset classes that require managerial oversight on the part of the investor. A common equity holder finds management built into the investment. If the investor is sufficiently large and activist, management may listen to the investor's wants, but in general the investor is active in the asset selection process and passive in the holding phase of a stock investment. In real estate, the investor must marshal the resources of the asset manager to develop a business strategy for each property, implement that strategy, monitor the results, and redefine the plan on a regular basis.

Institutional investors realize that while investment decisions are made in the context of the capital markets, operational decisions are made in the context of the space markets. Someone must allocate the experienced human capital required to make and monitor these space market decisions. Investors have to evaluate the degree to which they want to be involved in the management of real estate. The degree of involvement may relate to the type of investment vehicle chosen. A passive investment would be one made in publicly traded securities or commingled funds (similar to stock mutual funds). A semipassive investment might be in a discretionary account managed by an advisor in which goals and criteria are set by the investor, but the advisor has discretion to function within those parameters. An active investment might be a nondiscretionary account in which acquisition, asset management, and disposition decisions of the advisor are monitored and approved by the investor. A fully active management style may be one where internal pension fund staff acts as asset and/or property managers.

Investor monitoring of advisors' real estate decisions increased in recent years as more investors moved toward nondiscretionary accounts. Some believe this move is a response to the dissatisfaction with commingled fund performance. Many believe this increase in control and participation is the result of the market producing returns that have been lower than originally projected, concerns about appraisal-based fees, advisor fees, liquidity, and other issues. The result is that real estate advisors are now more heavily scrutinized on their acquisition assumptions and their asset management capabilities. This oversight takes increased time and effort by investors and asset managers. Some larger pension plan sponsors are responding to these pressures by adding to their real estate staffs generalists who have the ability to provide closer oversight of managers and consultants. Recently, some investors have begun to return to discretionary approaches.[7]

Visibility and Potential Liability

Visibility

Because real estate is a large, immobile asset, it is an easy focal point for public scrutiny, protest, or political action. Pension investors in real estate have a special set of concerns that other investors may not raise. Whether public or private, most pension real estate investors are large, well-known institutions in their communities, in their states, or on a national or international level. Routine real estate decisions—rent increases and evictions for residential properties, for example—can have a far-reaching impact on an institution's image, political stature, or ability to generate public sector business in light of unfavorable publicity. Imagine the response if a state employee pension plan were put in the position of evicting the elderly parent of a current plan participant. These issues are not limited to equity positions in real estate. As many pension investors have learned

---

[7]As reported in the 1991 *Plan Sponsor Survey* conducted for the Pension Real Estate Association by Marc Louargand.

during the current real estate cycle, mortgages can also become equity positions overnight.

Liability

The visibility issue is less serious than the liability issue. Real estate investments by institutional players tend to be in large, complex properties. The potential liabilities associated with a fire, structural damage, a terrorist attack, or toxic exposure can far exceed the total investment value. One case illustrates the point. A European pension fund invested $150 million in a U.S. high-rise office building that was destroyed by fire. The deaths of firefighters, interruptions of businesses, damage to adjacent structures, and long-term impact on the neighborhood have generated civil suits with an estimated payout of $2 billion.[8] That amount doesn't even begin to measure the indirect and direct costs associated with the disaster in terms of investor and consultant time, reformulation of portfolio strategy, and new risk management standards for the balance of the portfolio, which will result in higher asset management costs. The potential third-party liability for toxic substances in high-rise, temperature-controlled buildings is unknown as of yet, but appears to be climbing every year (see Chapter 17, "Environmental Issues"). Legal counsel should be sought whenever unusual measures or problems are undertaken.

The Current Investment Environment

Investors like to examine historical trends when determining future investment potential. In the stock and bond markets, historical information is readily available. In real estate, however, information is much more difficult to obtain, especially long-term historical information. Real estate should first be assessed from its position relative to other investments in the capital markets. If expected total returns in real estate move above those of alternatives such as stocks and bonds, investors should consider the asset class attractive for new investment. The problem with investment in real estate is that each local market, submarket, and individual property may move differently than the asset class as a whole; thus, local knowledge is important to the investment decision. The investor must assess the past,

---

[8]See the *Meridian Plaza* case prepared by Professor Lawrence Bacow, MIT Center for Real Estate Development, 1992, for a description of the disaster.

present, and prospective demand and supply and their effects on individual transactions. In other asset classes, such as stocks and bonds, such analysis is fairly standardized, as the classes are homogeneous. In real estate, each piece of property is more or less unique, making comparative analysis difficult. Appraisers have developed a methodology for adjusting the dissimilar features of properties to make them more comparable in terms of likely selling prices, but the process tends to be narrowly focused with respect to property type and submarket. Thus, it may not be a useful tool for broad-based decisions about when to enter or when to exit the asset class. One way to think about the issue is to accept the possibility that a prudent portfolio manager can allocate across different markets to benefit from differences across regional economic cycles, but it is unlikely that a manager can successfully "time" the asset class as a whole.[9]

Real estate is a long-term investment. Therefore, investments can be made at any time, since over the long term, value increases may occur as an increasing population and its productive activities raise the demand for shelter. In the short term, the real estate market goes through cycles just as every other asset class does. Entering near the bottom of a cycle should improve overall long-term returns to investors, but choosing the exact bottom of a cycle is always difficult, and perhaps even more so in the more efficient stock and bond markets. In real estate, the investor may have to experience significant negative cash flow periods to ride out the bottom of a cycle. The investor must consider current pricing relative to historical levels and the availability and quality of potential investments. Unlike the stock and bond markets, where investments are traded daily, real estate investments are less readily available and less homogeneously priced; thus, the selection process is much more labor intensive.[10] With real estate, as with stocks, an individual purchase does not

---

[9]The one exception to this rule, of course, may be the present real estate market of the mid-1990s, where many believe the cycle has come to or near its bottom in many regional real estate markets at the same time. The flood of money into public and private market real estate transactions in 1992 and 1993 was the result of this belief that it is time to bet on real estate.

[10]For institutional real estate investment, the time required to complete a transaction has risen from a few weeks to something approaching a year for most investors. Increases in the rigor of the due diligence process are due partly to regulatory oversight of the investment process but mostly to the myriad complexities in any given investment. Toxic materials on site, safety standards, access standards, a lengthy appraisal process, and the need to guard against ancillary liabilities all combine to make a complete "round trip" take up to two years for a single asset.

reflect the overall market, and each purchase must be made within a long-term portfolio strategy context.

In an overall investment strategy, allocations to each asset class seldom go to zero but are kept within a target range. Most investors look at a 25 to 60 percent range for stocks, a 20 to 40 percent range for bonds, and a 5 to 20 percent range for real estate. In each asset class, investors move to the low end of the range during perceived down cycles and increase their allocations during up cycles. With real estate being a new entrant into portfolio strategies, very few investors have ever moved to the top of their allocation range, and many have only gotten started. Disposing of real estate in any market is not as easy as placing a telephone order with a stockbroker. Moreover, real estate down cycles create substantially decreased market liquidity. Many investors were advised to sell during the high-growth up cycle of the late 1980s but refused to let go of such high yields; most have now lost much, if not all, of their appreciation in the current down cycle. Thus, a disciplined approach that looks at real estate trends relative to other capital market returns is imperative to an overall exit strategy. In addition, each asset must be constantly reassessed for its current and future performance, especially its relative competitive position in its local marketplace. Aging physical characteristics that will require major capital improvements, new technology that will make current investments obsolete, and new supply that will directly compete must be constantly monitored in the disposition decision for each asset. In addition, the allocation target should be reviewed on a semiannual or annual basis to reflect changes in the capital markets as well as the real estate markets.

While hedging has not been available historically in the real estate field, a number of hedging opportunities were recently created by major New York financial institutions such as Bankers Trust and Salomon Brothers. These opportunities allow the investor to buy or sell against the Russell/NCREIF index but do not involve the actual sale or exchange of properties. Thus, the hedge position exposes the investor to the return risk but not to the liquidity risk in real estate investments. Hedging should be considered when the investor believes its current allocation in the asset class is too high or too low and wishes to lower the risk of its over- or underallocated position. Hedging strategies may become one of the most effective methods of making this illiquid investment class more acceptable to investors in the future. For a further discussion of these issues, see Chapter 27, "Applications of Derivative Instruments."

Investment Vehicles

Institutional investors can choose between direct and indirect real estate vehicles. Indirect vehicles include REITs, limited partnerships, real estate operating companies, securitized mortgage interests, and open-end and closed-end commingled real estate funds. Direct investment—actually selecting a property or properties for ownership—has traditionally been a private market choice, although current securitization initiatives are providing tradable interests in single properties. Direct investment vehicles can be discretionary (where managers make the decisions), nondiscretionary (where investors make all major decisions and some minor ones as well), or a hybrid of the two approaches. Direct investments can also be separate accounts (wholly owned by the investor), commingled accounts (multiple investors), or coinvestments (a small number of investors or an investment in which the investment manager also has a significant stake).

Since the mid-1980s, direct investments have been the preferred type of vehicle for many pension investors. Early experiences with commingled open-end and closed-end funds were not satisfying for many. Returns were lower than expected, and management's priorities often were not aligned with a particular investor's needs. Consequently, these disappointments led to investors' desire for increased involvement and control and therefore to an increased appetite for direct investment. Early vehicles of this type were discretionary separate accounts, where the manager had authority to buy and sell assets and make asset management decisions within a set of agreed-upon guidelines. Increased investor experience in the asset class, combined with disappointing results in the 1980s, helped produce the desire for nondiscretionary accounts in which the manager executes decisions that the investor approves.

Commingled funds are similar to mutual funds in that a manager pools investors' money and purchases a portfolio of properties. Open-end funds have no termination date; thus, investors cash out by selling their shares. These funds have a variable number of shares that the investors purchase and sell at the portfolio's appraised net asset value. Closed-end funds have a defined termination date, and investors receive their investment returns through the sale of properties and hence termination of the fund. A set number of shares can be traded on a bid-ask basis, and prices can fluctuate. These funds can also be blind pools, where no properties have been selected at the start (thus leaving the discretion for purchase up to the fund manager), or specific (where properties have already been purchased or specified), or a combination of the two. Real estate limited partnerships (RELPs) are another form of commingled fund where the manager is the general partner and the investors are "limited" in their involvement to removing and replacing the general partner (this form of fund was popular in the 1970s and 1980s, when REITs were out of favor with both taxable and nontaxable investors). REITs are a special creation designed to meet specific IRS codes that allows these investment trusts to pass through earnings without being taxed at the entity level (for a more detailed discussion, see Chapter 14, "Real Estate Investment Trusts"). Individual investors have typically invested in public offerings of REITs and RELPs, while institutional investors have ventured into both publicly and privately placed vehicles. The Omnibus Budget Reconciliation Act of 1993 allows pension investors to take much larger positions in REITs than in the past; thus, these vehicles may earn an increasing share of pension allocations in the future.

The largest portion of institutional investing was concentrated in commingled funds in the 1970s, when many firms followed the lead of Wachovia National Bank and the Prudential Insurance Co., which developed the first widely subscribed, open-end commingled funds. Closed-end funds with finite lives emerged as an alternative in the mid-1970s. During the late 1980s downturn in real estate, closed-end funds found it difficult to dispose of properties, and many had to lengthen their original life spans. Open-end funds have also experienced problems as investors submitted their shares for repurchase to reduce their real estate holdings, but the commingled funds were unable to sell properties in illiquid markets. During the growth years of the late 1970s and early 1980s, most funds were able to fund redemption requests from new investors coming in or from cash flows generated on existing investments. As a result, these funds gave the appearance of liquidity and continued to grow in size, even while the market's fundamentals deteriorated in the mid-1980s. This investment growth turned negative in the late 1980s as investors saw the real estate market turn negative and values decline. In many cases, queues of investors formed since the charters of many of these funds called for disbursement based on the date of redemption request. The redemption problem has caused many fund managers to rethink their sales strategies, as selling top-quality properties to pay redemption requests may leave the remaining investors with less desirable properties in the future. Most fund managers have worked toward an equitable plan that can accommodate all investors.

Real estate limited partnerships grew in popularity in the 1970s and 1980s for both individual and institutional investors. The public RELPs began to have problems beginning in the mid-1980s as the heavy front-end fees and high degree of leverage hurt return performance. Many investors also found they could not sell their units easily, and the illiquid investments lost a great deal of value. The Tax Reform Act of 1986 was the final blow to the syndication business, making "tax-leveraged" partnerships virtually worthless overnight and creating dormant tax liabilities for investors in properties not supported by market fundamentals. These problems prompted a number of small partnership exchanges to emerge. These exchanges typically found that unit prices varied widely and the bid-ask spread was too wide to facilitate expeditious trades. As of this writing, two similar exchanges, the Clearinghouse and SMART, are being developed for institutional investor fund units. The size of the investments and recovering real estate fundamentals may result in a different outcome.

REITs began as investors in newly developed properties in the late 1960s, but suffered major losses. In the early 1970s, many REITs went into the mortgage lending business often with questionable underwriting and standards, and thereby created an imbalance between medium-term assets and short-term liabilities. In the late 1970s and early 1980s, REITs were out of favor with investors who remembered the problems of the early 1970s. But in the late 1980s, REITs that invested in existing properties with a specific focus on property type or geographic region began to emerge as the dominant vehicle in the securitized marketplace. These equity REITs performed very well in the early 1990s, with both strong dividend growth and price appreciation. Institutional investor interest was limited due to the small size of the REIT marketplace and the laws that prohibited any one investor from owning more than 5 percent of a single REIT's stock. As noted earlier, modification of this investor restriction allowed pension investors to expand into this more liquid investment vehicle as of 1994. Some people believe the growth in REITs can eventually securitize the entire U.S. real estate market this prophecy is highly unlikely, as a REIT requires existing properties of a reasonable size and in-place management expertise with a reasonable track record. However, this has not stopped many entrepreneurs from attempting to form new REITs, and some worry that the same problem that emerged with the early 1970 REITs and the 1970–80 RELPs will re-emerge. The REIT sell-off in 1994 underscored the capital-market flavor and interest-rate sensitivity that many REITs have taken on.

Investors still need to analyze the locations of properties, types and quality of properties, and management's expertise and track record when they make investments in commingled funds of any type. Historical returns should be compared to overall market trends and appreciation potential analyzed based on future expectations.

New Developments

Changing Tenants

Space users that seek greater flexibility in lease rates and terms and wanting to leverage their current positions in weak, overbuilt markets are exerting continuous downward pressure on effective rents in many markets in the mid-1990s. At the same time, a fundamental change is taking place in the way the corporation defines itself. The most startling result of this change is substantial reductions in the quantity and quality of real estate used by all types of corporations. The driving force behind the change is accountability. Real estate in the corporation is changing from a subsidy operation to a directly priced factor input. When business unit managers find they have the power and authority to reduce overhead through real estate decisions, they redefine their needs downward very quickly.[11]

New Real Estate Synthetics

Financial engineers have recently looked to new ways to break down the components of real estate into separate financial instruments. Currently this consists of separating the cash flow component from the appreciation of value. These instruments are synthetics or derivatives that allow the investor to separate the contractual lease income stream from the underlying physical asset. The concept is similar to "stripping" a Treasury bond into two instruments, a self-amortizing income stream instrument, and a zero-coupon bond. Similar ideas

---

[11]See Michael Joroff, Marc Louargand, Sandra Lambert, and Franklin Becker, *Strategic Management of the Fifth Resource: Corporate Real Estate* (Industrial Development Research Foundation, 1993), for a detailed discussion of these changes.

are being floated on the user side by large corporations that would like to see their lease payment streams become tradable capital market instruments.

Another movement currently afoot involves the creation of a large volume of securitized commercial mortgage instruments that can be traded like the residential mortgage-backed products now found on Wall Street. Many observers believe this vehicle will be a major force in recapitalizing and liquefying the real estate portfolio through the turn of this century. The existence of large pools of commercial mortgages in life insurance companies that will be coming under new, risk-based capital standards indicates there will be a sufficient feedstock for this new business activity. We envision that Wall Street and real estate firms will create new synthetics and derivatives, some of which will look like equity investments even though they are based on mortgage obligations.

New Market Makers

As noted previously, many pension investors in open- and closed-end funds found that these vehicles lacked promised liquidity once new subscriptions trailed off. Lawsuits and restructurings have been only partly successful as a means of acquiring liquidity. The fund managers took the position that in poor market conditions, they would be forced to sell the better properties at substantial discounts to provide liquidity to some investors, leaving the others with a damaged corpus. They argued that it was a question of equity that could be solved only by not allowing redemptions. At the time of this writing, one group is close to starting up a secondary market operation called the Clearinghouse, which intends to make a market in unit interests in existing open- and closed-end funds. If they are successful, we expect that the relative attractiveness of these vehicles will increase. We also believe their continued presence will allow "middle tier" investors to try the asset class. These smaller pension plans have been limited in their ability to invest in real estate because of the high minimum investment required.

The Importance of Exit Strategies

The downturn in the late 1980s to early 1990s has pointed to the need for a well-planned and well-executed exit strategy. Those investors who believed the strong real estate markets would continue forever and there would always be another investor willing to pay the current market price for their appreciating asset have been sorely disappointed by a dearth of "greater fools." The capital markets eventually realized that production of more space than was needed would weaken the real estate investment market. In a recent NCREIF survey of pension plan sponsors, the number one area of research interest among these investors was the topic of market cycles. Future investments should have strong grounding in real estate market cycles theory due to two factors: (1) the lag between the growth of employment and the response of the development pipeline providing new space, and (2) the ease of entry into the pipeline, causing potential oversupply in response to new demand. This traditional situation is only exacerbated by the increasing velocity of capital and production technology in a truly global economy. The result may be a much greater sensitivity and volatility on the demand side in the future.

Future investment strategy will also have to be more responsive to the need for timely infusions of capital. Institutional-quality real estate typically requires far more renovation, remodeling, or competitive repositioning than many investors realized when they entered the asset class. Investors must continue to recognize that real estate is one of the most illiquid investments in their portfolios and that the investment horizon should be long term and the disposition strategy one of patience. Each piece of real estate is like a small business that must be sold in a private market with incomplete information. Illiquidity places a greater burden on the investor to create and adhere to a disciplined exit strategy.

BASIC PORTFOLIO STRATEGIES

Investors can choose from many different strategies or invent their own, but certain constants regarding portfolio management apply to almost every situation and strategy.

Allocation to real estate is the first step. An investor with substantial funds may face an allocation among multiple advisors or vehicles or elect to create an in-house staff to run (some or all of) the investment. A smaller investor must also choose a real estate manager and a vehicle.

The relationship between institutional real estate investors and their managers is a troubled one today. Advisors have been under severe pressure to lower fees, especially in the face of poor performance in the marketplace. Allocations to real estate managers may not stay with the managers in the case of a sale. This is not a problem for most stock and bond managers, but real estate managers may be inherently torn between the desire to retain income and their fiduciary duty to do their best for their clients. Incentive arrangements are currently changing and may be more in line with both parties' interests in the future.

Which ever path is followed, additional issues must be resolved. The amount of discretion granted a manager, the measurement of property and manager performance, and the basis for compensation all loom as potential hazards to a smooth journey.

Core Portfolio Strategy

A core portfolio strategy is designed to provide the investor with a return that is approximately equal to the overall real estate market. Obviously, the choice of a reference point for the overall market is an important and problematic starting point. Investors define core property differently. Some investors define it by the stability and quality of the cash flow. Others define it by the quality of the bricks and boards. Still others define it by product type (office, regional mall, etc.). These product type definitions have tended to shift the most over the years. Unlike in years past, most pension investors today define an office building as an opportunistic or high-risk investment play. In the 1980s, apartment properties were not considered core, but new evidence about their risk and return characteristics have changed the minds of many investors, and today they are being added to many core portfolios.[12]

We should point out here that holding a core portfolio is not the same as holding an index portfolio in the stock market. It is possible today to actually purchase a portfolio of common stocks or shares in a mutual fund portfolio that represent a capitalization-weighted microcosm of a large segment of publicly traded stocks such as the S&P 500 or the Wilshire 5000. These portfolios are virtually the same

---

[12]Lynn Sagalyn and Marc Louargand, "Real Estate and the Next Recession," MIT Center for Real Estate, Citicorp Real Estate Finance Working Paper Series FP 1, 1989, offered an early argument about the relative returns and volatility of apartments versus other product types.

as the market and are true index portfolios. In the real estate world, the vast majority of properties would not be considered "institutional grade" investments. In addition, the total portfolio of institutional grade commercial real estate is extremely small compared to the total portfolio of commercial and residential real estate equity. Therefore, it is unlikely that a "core" portfolio will ever be an "index" portfolio, meaning that the benchmark for performance of a given portfolio is open to interpretation. This issue remains unresolved at present.

What are the size implications of a decision to hold a core portfolio? Real estate is not easily divisible unless special sharing agreements are instituted. These sharing agreements, sometimes called *agency costs,* are typically complex and costly to administer. Due to the lumpy nature of the asset class, many small pension investors are unable to invest in this arena. Most pension investors in real estate have at least $500 million in total assets, but the major players are significantly bigger. As an illustration, assume a pension investor defines core property as the portfolio reported by the Russell/NCREIF index. To build an "index" portfolio to match (i.e., a value-weighted allocation across property, but not necessarily geographic, types), an investor would need to invest approximately $200 million. At a 5 percent real estate allocation, this investor would be a $4 billion pension plan. As of early 1994, only 122 such funds existed in the U.S. market.[13] In addition to the divisibility problem, there are scale economies in asset management and minimum investment amounts in many vehicles. For instance, the separate account investor probably has a real estate allocation of at least $100 million. Investors with only a few million dollars for real estate may look to REIT portfolios, limited partnerships, or commingled funds to meet their needs.

Diversification Considerations

In the latter half of the 19th century, portfolio diversification (commonly referred to as *modern portfolio theory*) was developed as a means of reducing investors' risks in stocks and bonds.[14] As real estate

---

[13]According to *Pensions and Investments,* annual survey, "Largest Pension Funds," *Pension and Investments,* January 24, 1994, p. 19.

[14]See Harry M. Markowitz, "Portfolio Selection," *Journal of Finance,* March 1952, pp. 77–91, and William F. Sharpe, "A Simplified Model of Portfolio Analysis," *Management Science,* 1963, pp. 277–93.

investors build portfolios of assets, they too should consider finding returns of individual assets with different co-movements over time. The research on real estate portfolio diversification began in earnest in the early 1980s with the presumption that a properly diversified real estate portfolio should partially overcome the illiquidity and immobility problems inherent in real estate. In the early 1980s, diversification strategies that consisted of dividing the country into four geographic regions were tested against a strategy that diversified the portfolio by property type. This work found that diversification by property type showed better risk-return characteristics than did a four-region geographic strategy.[15] When the previous data set was extended farther into the mid-1980s and enriched with the additional property characteristics, regional characteristics were shown to be more important.[16]

The research continued to evolve with later findings suggesting that significant locational effects acted on asset pricing between two cities in the same state.[17] While previous geographic diversification research divided contiguous geographic areas along state lines, Hartzell, Shulman, and Wurtzebach[18] refined the geographic categorization by combining U.S. regions of similar economic character to create "economic regions" similar to those described in the popular book, *The Nine Nations of North America*.[19] This economic region concept was also tested on real estate limited partnerships.[20] The premise for this work was that when regional boundaries conformed more closely to economic specialties, the distinctions among real estate in the regions would become more important.

The latest step of linking real estate portfolio performance to

[15]Mike E. Miles and T. E. McCue, "Historic Returns and Institutional Real Estate Portfolios," *AREUEA Journal,* Summer 1982, pp. 184–98.

[16]David J. Hartzell, J. S. Hekman, and M. E. Miles, "Diversification Categories in Investment Real Estate," *AREUEA Journal,* Summer 1986, pp. 230–54.

[17]Terrence Grissom, J. L. Kuhle, and C. H. Walther, "Diversification Works in Real Estate, Too," *Journal of Portfolio Management,* 1987, pp. 66–71.

[18]David J. Hartzell, David G. Shulman, and Charles H. Wurtzebach, "Refining the Analyses of Regional Diversification for Income-Producing Real Estate," *Journal of Real Estate Research,* Winter 1987; pp. 85–95.

[19]Joel Garreau, *The Nine Nations of North America* (New York: Avon Books, 1981).

[20]Glenn R. Mueller, S. A. Kapplin, and A. F. Schwartz, "A Study of Geographical Diversification on Real Estate Asset Management," paper presented at the Financial Management Association meeting, New Orleans, October 1988.

local economic conditions was taken by Wurtzebach[21] in 1988 and then refined by Mueller[22] in 1993, when they shed the constraints of geography altogether and placed cities in economic categories based on their dominant base industry employment type (a base industry is one that exports goods from the local economy, thus bringing in money, which is usually considered the engine for local economic growth).

This concept conforms to the idea that real estate is a delayed mirror of the economy and that the economic fortunes of the major base industry help to drive local economic fortunes and thus real estate demand. Economic diversification groups cities together that have similar base industries producing their growth,—for example, San Diego (California) and Norfolk (Virginia) have more in common due to their dependence on military employment than they have with the particular geographic regions of the country in which they reside. Although economic diversification is now considered a standard for real estate portfolio management, most investment researchers differ on the economic categories they use for diversification groupings. Only time will tell which strategy is the most effective.

Sector Plays

If investors make a sector investment in the stock market, they need only call their brokers. In real estate, however, making a sector investment requires a number of decisions. Sector bets can be by property type, by city, by submarket, or by economic orientation (export demand–sensitive distribution warehouses, for instance). For example, if office properties, which are/were out of favor, are thought to be attractive investments, investors may wish to purchase properties that can improve their positions through marketing, management, and physical alteration in their local markets or simply buy quality properties in markets that are expected to improve.

The first choice is a manager-style strategy (i.e., intensive asset management with a repositioning strategy). The second choice is a

---

[21]Charles H. Wurtzebach, "The Portfolio Construction Process" (Newark: Prudential Real Estate Investors, 1988).

[22]Glenn R. Mueller, "Refining Economic Diversification Strategies for Real Estate Portfolios," *Journal of Real Estate Research,* Winter 1993, pp. 55–68.

sector play to the extent that the investor expects office buildings to do better in general.

Appropriate Investment Vehicles
Investing in funds that are focused on a sector strategy puts all decisions in the hands of the fund manager, whereas direct investments allow the investor a higher level of control over how the investment is played.

Correct and Incorrect Approaches to Diversification
Sector investments must be carefully analyzed in relation to the entire portfolio, as too large an investment may create undue risk in a particular category.

Economics of Core Property Types
Sector plays are normally made when an investor or manager has particular expertise in a given area or when the investor believes the sector is particularly undervalued and will recover within a reasonable investment time frame. The economics of a sector play usually include stronger than average demand growth, restricted supply, and/or mispricing (e.g., even with average demand and unrestricted supply, the capital markets might over- or underprice a particular sector).

Sector investments require portfolio managers to modify their overall portfolio strategies and justify the increased allocation to the sector(s) that has been invested in. Often an expert in the sector must be hired or consulted to monitor sector activity, new developments, and future directions of the sector. The portfolio manager must find a benchmark against which to measure sector performance, as well as make sure that standard accounting methods are followed so that comparisons can be made with other assets in the portfolio.

Rotational Strategies

In common equity markets, many managers follow a "rotational" strategy that responds to fundamental economic conditions. At the beginning of an expansion, they shift into consumer durables. As the expansion picks up speed, they shift into capital goods companies that will benefit from the need to grow productive capacity. Finally, as the expansion matures or slows, they shift into consumer nondurables, which are less sensitive to the business cycle since they represent basic need products that are consumed in poor times as well as good.

Some managers have very narrowly defined rotations that rely on much more subtle distinctions than expansion or contraction. In real estate, these strategies have had little credence to date, for a few reasons. First, managers ran the risk of losing an allocation if they sold property. Second, during the expansion of pension portfolios, unspent allocations were common, so there was little incentive to sell during an acquisition campaign. Third, the sophistication level in regional economics is much higher today than it was in the early 1980s, when most managerial strategies were first developed. The concept of rolling regional recessions was only vaguely understood in the late 1980s, whereas today we have a much better grasp of how regional economies differ and how they react to systematic stimuli. In real estate, the differing regional cycles are analogous to the durable/nondurable cycle in common equities. Managers who have a good insight into the dynamics of regional economies will develop strategies that include both buy and sell disciplines based on the relationships between local real estate markets and regional economies. A second set of rotational strategies will emerge from the understanding of capital market influences on pricing. In recent years, more than one observer came to realize that real estate is not isolated from capital market influences any more than stocks or bonds are. The local and regional economies and real estate markets determine the quantity and quality of income flows. The capital markets determine the value of those flows. By following capital market movements, managers may develop rotational strategies that are based on or informed by the changes in capital market expectations.

Appropriate Investment Vehicles
As of this writing, (in the mid-1990s) a few investment managers are beginning to develop investment strategy models based on regional cycles. The appropriateness of a vehicle is a function of the investor and its objectives. These strategies lend themselves to commingled funds and separate accounts alike as a function of investment and portfolio size. An interesting twist on these strategies is to build a portfolio of rotational managers through REITs and other securitized interests. At least one global investor has done this using REITs, property trusts, and property companies in about 20 countries. A brief look at the property company indices from around the world will reveal the potential for global diversification in real estate.

Economics of Rotational Strategies

The rotational strategy can be viewed as an extension and a refinement of the "replacement cost play." Many investors rely on the concept that buying an asset below replacement cost ensures a strong return. But the very existence of a below-replacement-cost price does not guarantee a good result. In fact, it implies the opposite: that market makers see poor future prospects for the asset. Only if the economic fundamentals are in place to indicate a level of growth in demand for the space will demand for the real estate rise above its current level. Thus, the rotational strategy may begin from a replacement cost benchmark or from some other market measure. The important part, however, is a rational forecast of growth in demand in the local real estate market due to fundamental economic factors such as growth in population, households, employment, regional exports, or some other engine of growth. By understanding regional cycles, the rotational manager establishes buy and sell disciplines that are mapped onto the local real estate cycle.

Portfolio Management Issues

Investors that pursue rotational strategies face all of the traditional portfolio-level issues that come up in any other type of strategy, plus one more. A rotational strategy, like the sector-bet strategy, may be contrary to generally accepted ideas about diversification in real estate portfolios. Traditional portfolio theory says we should diversify across economies (economic location theory) to diversify away from specific local cycles. Rotational strategies imply that we should hold a collection of upmarkets and avoid the downmarkets. Here is where the common stock analogy breaks down. Stock diversification is driven by the concepts of systematic and specific risk. Markowitz and Sharpe won the Nobel Prize for their ideas about efficient diversification and the use of systematic risk to appropriately price risky assets. If a stock manager has a well-diversified portfolio of stocks within a particular rotation, the portfolio will bear the systematic risk of the market and, in all likelihood, some risks specific to the strategy but little company-specific risk. Recent work, however, suggests that individual real estate assets bear mostly specific and little systematic risk. Real estate is a factor input for productive activity (i.e., housing for workers and workplaces). If we think of the regional economy as the unit of analysis instead of the individual asset or asset class, we can see that the rotational strategy is played out in terms of a particular building type in a set of particular markets that change over time. So the portfolio implication is that the investor should think in terms of an allocation to the strategy and the manager, not to particular properties. For the strategy to be effective, the investor has to let the manager practice buy and sell disciplines without fear of losing the account. Even more important, those strategies require the manager and investor to move beyond an exit strategy to an exit discipline.

Specialized Strategies

Duration Strategy
Many managers are beginning to look at the durations of the cash flows in their portfolios. Pension funds are interested in the durations of their assets and liabilities (More detailed discussions of duration appear in Chapter 2, "Portfolio Management Concepts and Their Application to Real Estate" and Chapter 4, "Leases as a Key to Performance and Value"). In addition, the timing of lease expirations can affect the portfolio's exposure to changes in market rental rates as well as changes in capital markets. Thus, many managers look to stagger their lease expirations by building and by market—but also need to look at the portfolio as a whole.

Another set of questions arises with respect to real estate's duration. Like a bond portfolio, a building can be thought of as a set of fixed-income investment decisions. The asset manager faces a fixed amount of capital (space) to invest by selecting from the universe of available bonds (tenants), each of which will have distinctive characteristics of term, current yield, yield to maturity, and riskiness. Like stocks and bonds, real estate bears the capital market risk that its income stream will be repriced due to changes in the market price of risk or the time value of capital. The duration of the fixed-income portfolio is the weighted-average duration of each bond in it. The duration of the real estate is the weighted-average duration of each of its leases—essentially fixed-income contracts—plus the weighted-average duration of the residual value of the space represented by the expiring leases. Given the differences among product-type leases, we can see that some types of real estate have longer durations than others. Net-leased, single-tenant properties, for instance, typically have long durations similar to those of tenants' debt obligations, while apartment properties have durations shorter than a year in many cases. The duration concept can be applied at both the property level and the portfolio level. If the investor has a preference for a longer or shorter duration at any point, a review of the product mix in the portfolio will help to establish leasing targets in those properties where the market and custom allow for flexibility in lease terms. In the same vein, the property type mix in a portfolio can be seen as a rough indicator of the portfolio's duration. One must consider, of course, the implications of juggling a set of lease durations which are all shorter than the investor's liability duration. It may be impossible to "balance the book" after all.

Bulk Purchase Strategies

Bulk purchases of properties have previously been considered only by venture capital–type entrepreneurs. In the 1990s, institutional investors began to enter this area. Typically bulk purchases include a mix of properties from high quality with reasonable cash flows to low quality with little or no cash flows. Investors must perform an analysis of all properties in the bulk purchase and determine which properties have the characteristics that provide strong, long-term return potential and which properties should be liquidated quickly as they will have little or no appreciating value in the future. Valuing the entire portfolio asset by asset is a major key to long-term performance. It may be that a number of assets in a bulk purchase are valued at zero or even a negative value, thus offsetting some of the inherent value in the high-quality properties. Expertise in disposition as well as asset rehabilitation and management are necessary to handle bulk purchases successfully. Some institutional investors have found that the bulk purchasers that are bought for the purpose of unbundling and flipping properties are good sources of quality property purchases; however, these sellers have no historical knowledge of the property and are usually unaware of any problems that might exist in the asset. Purchasers must perform extra due diligence and expect to spend additional time trying to construct historical performance on the buildings. One problem in this area is that the supply of bulk transactions is shrinking as the Resolution Trust Corporation (RTC) and the Federal Deposit Insurance Corporation (FDIC) work their way through the backlog of failed financial institution portfolios. The emerging shortage is compounded by an increase in the number of investors in these markets. Some believe that the latter 1990s will bring a new set of portfolios to the bulk sale market, primarily those of life insurance companies.

Pipeline Interests

A strategy that appeared at the end of the last cycle may prove to be popular in the future. California Public Employees Retirement System (CalPERS), the largest public pension plan real estate investor in the United States, acquired controlling interests in two development companies in the West. By making a common equity purchase, the investor has acquired a means of accessing the pipeline for new real estate projects. The well-known volatility of real estate companies relative to real estate investment trusts and other property plays puts this strategy in the high-risk category.

MONITORING PORTFOLIO STRATEGY

Portfolio management is dynamic. It requires constant monitoring and updating, including feedback of asset and manager performance as well as changing circumstances of the investor and capital markets.

Performance measures should reflect the investment objectives. Pension investors need to hit real return targets rather than nominal return targets. Pension real estate investors tend to be dominated by defined benefit plans, which are driven by a need to increase some percentage of terminal earnings. Those earnings will reflect inflation, and some participants won't be annuitants for another 20 or 30 years. Therefore, actuarial prudence demands that inflation not be counted as part of the return. Most investors have targets in the neighborhood of 5 or 6 percent real annual returns, compounded over their holding periods. As a result, their investment managers must share those targets. The problem is that no one knows how long it will be—if ever—before real estate provides an inflation hedge as investors believed it did during the 1970s and 1980s. When markets are in disequilibrium, substantial excess supply overhangs the market, and users report a fundamental downsizing trend, real estate will not provide a hedge against inflation.

Measuring Asset Performance

Most investors look to their asset advisors to provide them with asset performance information. As investors have become more sophisticated, they continue to ask for more information. Total returns are usually divided into income and appreciation components. Portfolio information is broken down by location, property type, property age, building age, tenant profile, and other measures that might indicate deviations from normal expected patterns. Even the durations of leases can be analyzed and compared.

Measuring performance and establishing benchmarks is a difficult and changing area in the institutional real estate investment business. Traditionally, managers managed against a "bogey," usually the Russell/NCREIF index. But dissatisfaction with the index itself has led to the proposal of alternatives, such as the Wilshire Real Estate Securities Index and the NAREIT Equity Index, which are based on public market pricing of real estate portfolios. Most research shows that managers themselves believe their institutional real estate portfolios are about as risky as the stock market in general, while traditional index volatility has been extremely low.[23]

Another controversial issue is the definition of property performance itself. Is it net operating income? Cash flow from operations? Net or gross of management fees? Net or gross of the capital improvement line? Investors are increasingly interested in resolving these questions. A parallel effort on the part of the Association for Investment Management Research will likely result in a uniform reporting format for real estate investment managers in the near future. Cash flow from operations, after capital improvements, leasing commissions, tenant improvements, and operating expenses, will probably emerge as the most meaningful measure of performance.

Accounting methods are normally dictated by a given policy or by the direct needs of the client investor. Unfortunately, there are still too many ways to account for a number of items in the return analysis. Should tenant improvements, capital expenditures, and major repairs be expenses, or should they be amortized? Should nonpayments of leases be shown as bad debts or as accrued payments, and for how long? As noted previously, these issues are in the process of resolution by leading industry groups, but the eventual form of their solution is still unknown.

---

[23]Marc Louargand, "A Survey of Pension Fund Real Estate Portfolio Management Practices," *Journal of Real Estate Research*, 7:4, Fall 1992, pp. 361–74, provides a discussion of this issue.

Measuring Manager Performance

There is much debate over the proper way to measure manager performance or whether it is possible to measure such performance at all. In the case of a commingled fund, the fund as a whole can be compared to an industry index such as the Russell/NCREIF index. But with separate accounts, it is difficult to look at manager performance when managers' asset decisions are constrained or guided by the investor's discretion. In the case where investors retain discretion, managers may be unable to make the capital improvements deemed necessary, sign the leases they believe are appropriate, or determine the disposition timing or set the selling price, as the institutional investor may have the final word on these decisions. Accordingly, true manager performance can only be realized when the manager has full discretion.

In many cases, the most relevant test of manager performance should be a comparison of actual to budget. When the manager is given the latitude to determine the budget for a property, the opportunity to compare actual results to this budget can be considered equitable for all parties. Another possibility is to compare to an industry index, but the composition of assets managed by a manager is typically different than an index and thus is difficult to use on an equitable basis. However, a manager with portfolio composition discretion is best measured against the index.

Perhaps a reasonable alternative is to measure a manager's performance against a target established by the investor and the manager in collaboration. After all, the investor establishes a portfolio strategy based on a set of constraints and objectives that lead to a required rate of return. The ability to satisfy this requirement is the most reasonable test of performance.

The budgeting process should be a dynamic, not a static, process; changes need to be made as soon as circumstances change. Unexpected market movements, bankruptcy of a tenant, or major physical damage, either natural or humanmade, should cause the budget to be revised. If a particular asset management strategy also fails to produce the intended results, the strategy can be reviewed and modified. When a major change in a market occurs, leasing strategies need to be revised so that returns can be maximized. Leasing agents must be informed of new pricing, and the negotiating stance they take can be modified to give the owner better positioning. In the downturn of the late 1980s, many managers found that lack of service, inflexibility in lease rates, and aggressive negotiating tactics were causing them to lose tenants. In the early 1990s, asset managers found out what it is like to work from a disadvantaged position. Monitoring markets and reevaluating strategies is an important part of running a successful asset management operation.

Periodic Review

Finally, the vision behind the strategy needs to be constantly questioned. More than one major pension investor has a "portfolio strategy" document that has not been re-examined since it was written in the mid-1980s. What were the portfolio's goals and objectives that led to the creation of a strategy? Are these targets still relevant today? Have the goals changed sufficiently to require a new strategy? Is the current strategy performing in such a way that we can expect it to bring us to our goals? These are some of the questions an investor might want to bring to an annual re-examination of the portfolio and property strategy.

CHAPTER 25

THE REAL ESTATE PORTFOLIO MANAGEMENT PROCESS

Frederich Lieblich
Metlife Realty Group, Inc.

What is born will die,
What has been gathered will be dispersed,
What has been accumulated will be exhausted,
What has been built up will collapse,
And what has been high will be brought low.

Buddhist saying on impermanence

INTRODUCTION

The last several years have wrought dramatic changes in the real estate industry, the likes of which have not been seen since the Great Depression of the 1930s. The tremendous increase in supply and subsequent reduction in demand and capital inflows for real estate have caused lease pricing and ultimately property values to collapse. Few investors contemplated such dramatic changes, and fewer still repositioned their portfolios in anticipation of such changes. Exhibit 25–1 identifies some current uncertainties in the real estate market.

Where will these uncertainties take us? What can we do to properly assess ever-changing market risks and position our portfolios to be on the winning side of these changes? The answer to the first question is simple: *No one fully knows.* The answer to the second

I wish to express my deep appreciation to Joseph L. Pagliari, Jr. (editor), for his encouragement and his significant contribution in the chapter's development and refinement. I also wish to thank Michael Giliberto and Peter Colwell (consulting editors) for their many thoughts, ideas, and suggested improvements to the chapter.

EXHIBIT 25–1
Uncertainty in the Real Estate Markets

Capital Markets	Space Markets

• Global integration of capital markets; competition among asset classes
• Growth of international trade
• Growth of real estate securities
• Development and use of real estate derivatives
• High to low inflation environment
• High to low interest rate environment
• Tax Code revisions
	• Existing oversupply of space
	• Global competition:
	   Corporate downsizing
	• Electronic revolution:
	   Working at home, virtual company, and hoteling (office and apartment)
	   Home shopping (retail)
	   Just-in-time inventory (industrial)
	• Shifting demographics:
	   Aging of the population
	   Increased ethnic diversity
	   Continued shift to South and West
	   CBD to edge city to small town
	• Environmental issues

question, which is the theme of this chapter, is found in *the creation, integration, and implementation of a systematic and disciplined portfolio management process.* While investors can't change the past, they can hope to learn from it.

THE PARADIGM SHIFT

The need to implement a portfolio management process has caused a shift in the paradigm of real estate investment management. The old paradigm is represented by firms using an asset-by-asset process, whereas the new paradigm is represented by firms using a disciplined portfolio management process. This fundamental evolution has transformed real estate investment.

Until very recently, the asset-by-asset process dominated real estate portfolio allocation, construction, and management. From this perspective, the investment decision is based on the *individual* property's fundamentals (location, physical, economic, and legal characteristics, etc.), its sensitivity to local supply and demand market conditions, and the market's pricing of risky assets. In essence, portfolio allocation under this approach is determined by an ad hoc selection of assets that meet singular property criteria. It focuses the investment decision on the risk-return relationship of an individual property, with little or no understanding of how it influences the risk-return relationship of the entire portfolio.

The portfolio management process, on the other hand, concentrates on the aggregation of individual properties that, when combined into a *portfolio,* exhibit risk return characteristics. While the asset-by-asset investment analysis remains an essential element of a disciplined portfolio management process, it becomes an intermediate step in a more encompassing process.

Institutional real estate investors are now making this paradigm shift for several reasons: (1) the need to restore credibility lost in the recent industry collapse; (2) the lower cost and increased availability of national, regional, and local real estate market supply and demand information made possible by the proliferation of low-cost, computer-related applications; (3) asset class competition for capital inflows; (4) increased sophistication of real estate professionals corresponding to their attainment of advanced degrees and designations (e.g., MBA, PhD, CFA); and (5) their application of financial technologies initially developed for the bond and stock markets.

To address these market forces, most real estate investment management firms have adopted their own real estate portfolio approach or style, probably no fewer than one for each firm. However, equally important is the firm's dedication to a disciplined portfolio management approach. Only those firms that can develop a disciplined portfolio management process and can integrate and implement it within their organizations will have completed the paradigm shift. By creating a framework for understanding the changing real estate market, these firms can expect to have the upper hand in assessing market/portfolio opportunities and risks. Without this discipline, the firm loses perspective on the inherent risks in its portfolio, lacks the tools and techniques to identify opportunities for higher returns and risk reduction through diversification, and possibly becomes susceptible to the latest investment fad.

Also important to the real estate investment firm is its ability to remain flexible while adhering to a disciplined portfolio management process. The portfolio manager must understand the limitations and applications of many of the analytical tools and techniques (some of which are presented in this chapter) and must recognize that *judgment* must be applied and used as a "reality check" at all times.

It is this balance between the adherence to a disciplined portfolio management process and the need for flexibility and judgment that must be sought by the investment decision maker.

To introduce the steps involved in a disciplined portfolio management process this chapter overviews both the portfolio management process and the role of the portfolio manager. This chapter provides investors/portfolio managers with a pragmatic approach to creating, integrating, and implementing their own portfolio management process. To focus on the process itself, the chapter simply introduces several of the techniques and tools that accompany it. These analytical mechanisms are amply covered in other chapters of this book (for example, see Chapter 2, "Portfolio Management Concepts and Their Application to Real Estate"). In addition, the chapter does not dwell on the subtle, and sometimes not so subtle, differences created by the form of investment vehicle (e.g., direct investments such as joint ventures and (non)discretionary separate accounts and indirect investments such as commingled funds and REITs) on the portfolio management process. See Chapter 24, "Developing a Portfolio Strategy," for discussion of each form of investment vehicle, though the portfolio management process described below is generally independent of the form of the investment vehicle(s).

THE PORTFOLIO MANAGEMENT PROCESS

The concept, definition, and implementation of a portfolio management process has been evolving for many years. Like many new ideas, it has grown and evolved at different rates, depending on the market forces acting on it. The two main forces that have acted on the portfolio management process are (1) technological advances in computers, statistics, and theoretical finance and (2) the tremendous growth in institutional assets under a fiduciary framework. Both forces have greatly contributed to its evolution.

Technological Advances and Modern Portfolio Theory

The theoretical foundation underlying the portfolio management process began in earnest with Harry Markowitz. His seminal work in the early 1950s formalized the concept of diversification and, consequently, the importance of asset allocation to portfolio performance.

Moreover, Markowitz introduced the mathematical/statistical framework for identifying these efficient portfolios, which later became known as *modern portfolio theory (MPT)*. However, had it not been for the advances in the computer industry (in terms of speed, cost, accessibility, etc.), it is unlikely that Markowitz's framework for optimizing a portfolio would enjoy the wide use and acceptance that it does today.

Modern portfolio theory identifies sets of efficient portfolios. An *efficient portfolio* is one in which no other portfolio offers a higher expected return for the same or lower risk (or lower risk with the same or a higher expected return). The set of all efficient portfolios derived from a portfolio group of assets is called the *efficient frontier* (see Exhibit 25–2). As the portfolio manager moves up along the efficient frontier, two things happen: The asset mix of the portfolio changes, and the portfolio's expected return and risk change.

EXHIBIT 25–2
The Efficient Frontier

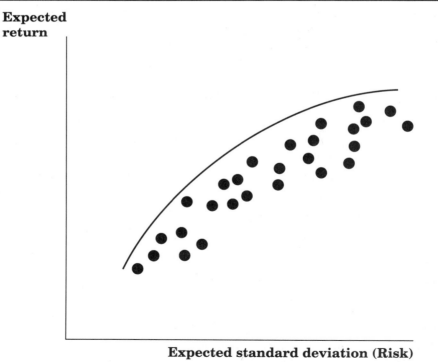

To derive the efficient frontier, estimates of the following three inputs are required for each asset over a specified time period:

1. *Expected return,* which is the summation of each of the asset's potential return conditions multiplied by the probability of that condition occurring.
2. *Expected standard deviation,* which is the variation of potential returns around the expected return.
3. *Expected correlation of returns,* or the degree to which each asset's returns are expected to move together over time with the returns from all other assets in the portfolio.

The investor's goal then becomes to move the portfolio to a point on the efficient frontier that fulfills the investor's objectives and constraints. However, the required inputs, and hence the efficient frontier, are constantly in flux. Consequently, the job of the investor/portfolio manager is to monitor these changing inputs and rebalance the portfolio accordingly. This rebalancing must be performed in light of the transaction costs involved, which in the case of real estate can be substantial. Therefore, a long-term view of these required inputs (and consequent portfolio construction) is usually taken.

Growth of Institutional Assets under a Fiduciary Framework

Around the same time Markowitz developed MPT, institutional investors (composed primarily of pension funds and insurance companies) began their phenomenal growth (see Exhibit 25–3). Furthermore, the enactment of the Employee Retirement Income Security Act of 1974 (ERISA) required the fiduciaries of private pension plans to use the same care, skill, prudence, and diligence in making investments that a prudent person who is familiar with such matters would use under similar circumstances (the "prudent man" rule). Along with the prudent man rule, ERISA required diversification of investment to minimize large losses. These fiduciary provisions of ERISA caused plan trustees to become much more focused on available portfolio management technologies (e.g., MPT) and the means to implement them.

Until ERISA's passage, real estate occupied a minuscule portion of institutional mixed-asset portfolios. However, many saw the passage of ERISA as a mandate to more completely diversify institutional

EXHIBIT 25–3
Institutional/Ownership of U.S. Financial Assets, 1950–90

Year	Owned by Institutions (millions)	Percent of Total
1990	$6,520	20.5%
1985	3,298	15.5
1980	1,769	13.5
1975	914	12.9
1970	569	12.3
1965	392	11.5
1960	256	10.8
1955	170	9.5
1950	107	8.4

Sources: Adapted from W. O'Barr and J. Conley, *Fortune and Folly: The Wealth and Power of Institutional Investing* (Homewood, IL: Business One Irwin, 1992). Data from the Federal Reserve, Columbia Institutional Investor Project, and New York Stock Exchange.

portfolios, which is consistent with the concepts of prudent behavior. Beginning in the late 1970s and early 1980s, institutional investors began to allocate a more meaningful portion of their assets to real estate. In fairness, note that this allocation to real estate was also spurred by the poor performance concurrently experienced in the stock and bond markets as inflation rose to unexpectedly high levels.

In essence, the real estate portfolio manager was the last to come to the party. During the last several decades, portfolio managers in the stock and bond markets have continued to develop and implement sophisticated tools, techniques, and processes to understand the dynamics of their markets and fulfill the needs of their investors. Meanwhile, the real estate investment manager, not subject to the same forces and not privy to the same wealth of historical data, was able to remain competitive without these technological improvements.

Steps in the Portfolio Management Process

Presently, the real estate portfolio manager faces many of the same forces that previously caused stock and bond portfolio managers to embrace a disciplined portfolio management process. That is, the collapse in stock and bond values (especially on an inflation-adjusted basis) led many stock and bond managers to abandon their old ways of doing business and adopt more sophisticated techniques (such as MPT) in a more integrated and disciplined fashion.

Exhibit 25–4 illustrates the dynamics of the real estate portfolio management process. The process is broken down into the following six steps:

1. Investor objectives and constraints.
2. Real estate market conditions and expectations.
3. Target portfolio determination.
4. Portfolio strategy determination.
5. Monitoring of investor objectives and constraints, market conditions and expectations, and portfolio rebalancing.
6. Portfolio performance measurement.

Each of these steps, along with the role of the portfolio manager, is discussed in detail in the remaining sections of this chapter.

EXHIBIT 25–4
Real Estate Portfolio Management Process

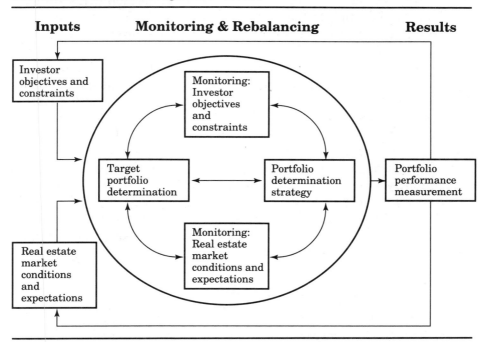

INVESTOR OBJECTIVES AND CONSTRAINTS

The most fundamental business precept is to understand and fulfill the needs of your customer. Real estate portfolio management is no different. Its first precept is "know thy investor." Therefore, before constructing a portfolio or repositioning an existing portfolio, it is essential to thoroughly understand the investor's objectives and constraints and develop a formal investment policy that encompasses them.

An investment policy is a statement of the investor's investment objectives and constraints, along with the method(s) by which they will be attained. Different investors will have (sometimes radically) different investment needs. Accordingly, as a means of more accurately understanding the investor's preference, the portfolio manager will interview the investor to determine the investor's specific needs. For example, defined benefit pension plans have significantly different investment needs depending on such factors as ratio of active to retired individuals, over- or under-funded benefits obligations, percentage of vested benefits, and so on. Likewise, insurance companies have their own internal lines of business (e.g., personal insurance, group insurance, and pensions), each requiring portfolios (i.e., portfolio segmentation) tailored to properly match its financial products and liabilities.

Although few portfolio managers would dispute the importance of developing and continuously updating an investment policy, they often do not give the policy the attention it deserves. Once initially developed, if developed at all, the investment policy often becomes a dormant document gathering dust on someone's back shelf instead of the effective and dynamic communication tool it is meant to be. By their nature, investors' investment needs are always changing. Consequently, even if portfolio managers satisfy the investor's initial objectives, they may unknowingly stray from the investor's changing investment needs if they do not constantly monitor those needs. The following sections briefly identify some areas that are typically addressed in an investment policy statement.

Portfolio Size

How much money does the investor want to allocate to equity real estate? Typically, investors use an optimization model that includes each major asset class (e.g., bonds, stocks, real estate) to determine the appropriate allocation to equity real estate. Thus, the equity real estate portfolio size is often known (or bounded by a range), and the real estate portfolio manager can then focus on the allocation within equity real estate.

Return Requirements

What are the required level and form of the return? Is there a minimum return requirement that must be met? Should the return level be measured in nominal or real terms? Should the form of return be mostly in current income or long-term capital gains? For example, income tax considerations and the durations of the fund's corresponding liabilities often influence the desired trade-off between current return and appreciation.

Risk Tolerance

How much volatility can the investor accept in his or her portfolio returns? Given the strong positive relationship between risk and return, the investor's risk tolerance will be a defining force behind the portfolio's long-term return. Exhibit 25–5 subjectively illustrates equity real estate's risk-return spectrum by core real estate property type. Furthermore, since factors other than property type have a powerful impact on portfolio return, they are often defined in the investment policy. For example, the investment policy of a *conservative* investor may specify relatively fixed percentages (i.e., little or no market timing) of the portfolio to be allocated to specific property types and require the properties to be fully leased, located in diversified and stable markets, and purchased without leverage. The investment policy of an *aggressive* investor may allow greater flexibility (i.e., market timing) in the allocation of the portfolio to various property types and allow the properties to be exposed to significant lease rollover, located in nondiversified markets with high vacancy rates, and/or purchased with substantial leverage.

Liquidity and Time Horizon Requirements

Given the inherent poor liquidity (e.g., 6 to 12 months to execute a trade) and lumpiness (i.e., the size of investment) in real estate private market transactions, it is essential that investors and portfolio man-

EXHIBIT 25–5
Estimate of Current Equity Real Estate Risk-Return Spectrum

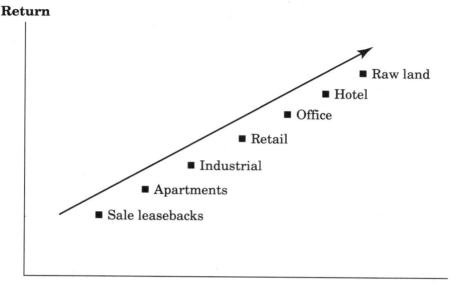

agers define the liquidity needs of the portfolio and continually reassess its cash requirements over an extended time horizon. For example, does a portion of the portfolio need to be liquidated to meet upcoming obligations? Most investors have come to understand (many the "hard way") the poor liquidity and extended time horizon requirements of investing in real estate and have already considered this when making their allocation decisions.

Given the recent explosion of real estate equity securities, many institutional investors are further partitioning their real estate allocations to include the traditional illiquid real estate investment vehicles along with some portion of liquid real estate equity securities from the emerging public market.

Tax and Legal Considerations

Assuming the investor is a taxable entity, the portfolio manager's goal is to maximize the investor's after-tax return. Legal considerations may include limiting the investor's liability from property-level incidence (environmental, personal injury, etc.) and regulatory considerations (e.g., ERISA).

To summarize, an understanding of the investor's investment objectives and constraints is the essential starting point in the portfolio management process. When the portfolio manager begins the process with a solid understanding of the investor's needs (portfolio size, return requirements, risk tolerance, liquidity, time horizon, and tax and legal considerations) and the knowledge that these needs are distinct and continually changing, the chance of success is greatly enhanced.

REAL ESTATE MARKET CONDITIONS AND EXPECTATIONS

Once the investor's objectives and constraints are understood, the portfolio manager's attention focuses on real estate market conditions. The real estate market is constantly evolving and changing, with discount rates and capitalization rates rising and falling along with investor sentiment for particular markets and property types. In the context of identifying the combination of properties that will lead to a portfolio located near or on the efficient frontier, which is consistent with the investor's objectives and constraints, the portfolio manager must *identify and analyze markets within the targeted investment universe.*

Investors and portfolio managers require an objective and analytical approach to identifying the factors that contribute to equity real estate return and risk. Accordingly, substantial time and resources are now being spent on the creation of "real estate market expectation models" that assist in estimating the inputs into the optimization process. Remember: Portfolio construction is based on estimates of future risk-reward parameters, which are inherently uncertain. Thus, portfolio managers are left with the unsettling task of subjectively—albeit heavily steeped in quantitative analysis—estimating these parameters. The question is how to do this.

Before beginning our discussion, it is imperative to mention the difficulty of obtaining high-quality, inexpensive, and consistent real estate market data. This shortcoming is especially apparent when comparing the availability of real estate market data to the abundance of data available for the bond and stock markets. However, there are hopeful signs that this is changing. Now a small number of real estate market information vendors and econometric firms have been able to assemble historical databases that capture the relevant local, regional, and national market conditions systematically through time. A systematic approach (i.e., employing a consistent, unbroken methodology) to gathering these data is essential to properly analyze property type and market performance over time. In addition, there is growing industry awareness that real estate investors, advisors, and managers need to share data to better understand real estate's risks and returns.

Another aspect of this lack of quality real estate market data merits mentioning. An increased amount of quality, inexpensively available data offers no guarantee of superior investment performance. For example, the availability of the vast amounts of market data is one of the primary reasons why the bond and stock portfolio managers have a very difficult time beating their respective portfolio benchmarks (e.g., market indices)—the crux of "adding value." Therefore, the real estate portfolio manager with access to "relatively" superior market information has the upper hand in beating the market indices, thereby adding the most value.

Given the preceding caveats, we now begin our discussion of real estate market conditions and expectations by introducing different portfolio/property analysis approaches and a general framework for analyzing real estate market conditions and expectations. Furthermore, we will attempt to explain the linkages among the approaches, tools, and techniques presented in this section and the portfolio process itself. This section is broken down into the following areas:

1. Market efficiency.
2. Portfolio management approaches.
3. Real estate market analysis.
4. Market segmentation.
5. The return factor model.
6. Fundamental analysis.
7. Scenario analysis/probabilistic forecasting.
8. Portfolio optimization: reconciliation and judgment.

Much of what follows focuses on the returns-generating process. Since risk-adjusted returns are typically considered the main determinant of portfolio performance, it seems to be a proper focus for portfolio managers.

Market Efficiency

At the start, portfolio managers must determine how they themselves view the question of market efficiency. How efficient is the market? Ultimately, how investors and portfolio managers view this question determines how the portfolio is to be managed: passively or actively. Once the portfolio manager answers this question, the portfolio/property analysis approaches to be employed become clearer.

An *efficient market* is a market with many participants in which market information is quickly and efficiently disseminated and asset prices adjust rapidly in accordance with the new information. In such markets, there is little benefit (net of transaction costs) to asset selection and/or market-timing approaches intended to identify mispriced opportunities. Exhibit 25–6 provides a spectrum of market efficiency and places both active and passive market approaches within this spectrum.

An *active portfolio approach* assumes low to moderate market efficiency, and thus mispriced market segments and properties are worth seeking out. A *passive portfolio approach* assumes moderate to high market efficiency, and consequently the costs of finding mis-

EXHIBIT 25–6
Market Efficiency Spectrum

Low	Moderate	High

Active Market Approach	**Passive Market Approach**
Goal: Over/under allocate portfolio in certain market segments or individual properties in order to outperform broad market index	Goal: Allocate portfolio to match broad market index
Assumes: Low to moderate market efficient; mispriced market segments and properties are worth seeking out	Assumes: Moderate to high market efficient; mispriced market segments and properties are not worth seeking out

priced market segments and properties are not justified. Under the passive portfolio approach, the portfolio manager should focus his or her energies on constructing and maintaining a low-cost index or index proxy portfolio that matches the investor's objectives and constraints.

Given the lesser quality and availability of real estate market information, few believe the real estate market is efficient. Thus, for real estate, an active portfolio approach that attempts to provide the potential to obtain "excess" or premium returns above what is justified by the risk assumed seems appropriate. However, as the real estate market becomes relatively more efficient, perhaps through real estate equity securities (REITs), and the cost of constructing and maintaining a passive portfolio decreases, passive equity real estate portfolio approaches will become more viable.

If investors and portfolio managers conclude that the equity real estate market is efficient and accordingly a passive portfolio approach is appropriate, they should focus their attention on ways to construct and monitor an index proxy portfolio. The balance of this section is for those investors and portfolio managers who have concluded that the equity real estate market is inefficient and for whom an active portfolio management approach is therefore appropriate. Consequently, we will now introduce portfolio management and asset selection approaches used within an active portfolio framework.

Portfolio Management Approaches
As in the stock and bond markets, the real estate portfolio manager will typically favor either a top-down or a bottom-up investment approach. For real estate, the *top-down approach* focuses the investment decision on the national market first. Then regions and local markets that are expected to outperform the overall market based on their forecasted economic cycle, current market strength, current pricing levels, and so on are identified. Finally, properties are selected in the local market based on their expected excess return. The *bottom-up approach* focuses the investment decision on the return and risk relationship of an individual property to determine if it is priced attractively. The goal is to purchase properties that can be bought at below their estimated intrinsic value and sell properties that can be sold above their estimated intrinsic value. If taken to its extreme, the bottom-up approach constitutes the asset-by-asset process perspective discussed earlier. The portfolio manager disregards what is

happening in national and regional economies and how the property fits in within a portfolio context, and is content to receive the positive excess returns due from finding a mispriced asset.

In real estate portfolio management, more so than for stocks and bonds, the investor is to some degree directly responsible for the management of the asset (unless investing through a REIT or a similar vehicle). Therefore, it is essential that the portfolio managers also maintain accurate and timely information from the property/asset managers so that informed decisions can be made.

Exhibit 25–7 depicts an *interactive top-down/bottom-up approach* to real estate portfolio management. The local market is where both approaches interact, as this is where the real estate portfolio manager's knowledge of the market typically dissipates and the manager can no longer (nor should he or she attempt to) be expert in the

EXHIBIT 25–7
Interactive Top-Down/Bottom-Up Portfolio Management Approaches

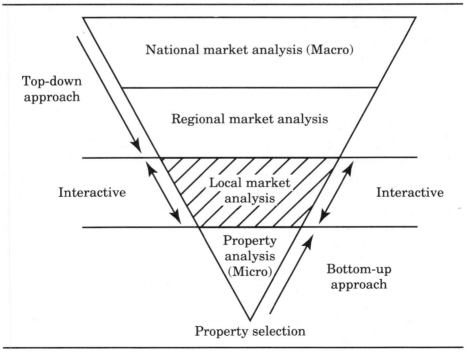

dynamics of all markets and the properties they contain. Accordingly, the portfolio manager must rely on the knowledge and experience of the internal organization (e.g., acquisition/disposition, property/asset management, architectural/engineering, and legal or external advisors) to obtain an understanding of local market and property dynamics. Likewise, the field organization (either internal or external) must rely on the portfolio manager to communicate and monitor investor objectives and constraints, capital market conditions and expectations, the portfolio strategy, and portfolio performance. Thus, as we can see, top-down and bottom-up approaches in real estate are not mutually exclusive; rather, they are interdependent.

Asset Selection Approaches

The property-level investment decision focuses on determining whether an existing property should be held or sold and whether a potential acquisition should be purchased or passed over. Active investors in the common stock arena have developed two approaches to making this decision: fundamental analysis and technical analysis.

Fundamental analysis assumes the markets are not efficient and mispriced assets[1] exist. This approach assumes an asset is worth the present value of all future cash flows. It therefore becomes the job of the investment analyst to assess the asset's (or, company's) fundamentals to estimate the amount and timing of cash flows, along with the appropriate discount rate to apply, to arrive at an estimate of the asset (or, stock) value. This value estimate is then compared to the current market price of the asset to determine whether it should be purchased or sold.

Technical analysis also assumes the market is not efficient and asset mispricing exists. This approach is based primarily on past prices and transaction volumes to determine the asset (or, stock's) future price behavior. Its basic assumption is that there are repeatable patterns and momentum in the market that persist over time that the investment analyst can identify and use in selecting under- and overpriced assets (or, stocks).

---

[1] Throughout this chapter, the term *mispriced assets* is used to identify assets (specifically properties) that have a positive expected net present value (i.e., their "intrinsic" value exceeds the current market price), either because investors' expectations differ substantially from the capital market's aggregate view or because the heterogeneity of investors causes them to price asset characteristics differently.

Since the fundamental approach is more compatible with accepted real estate analytics, we will now focus on it. However, this does not imply that, in the less efficient real estate market, all forms of technical analysis are without merit.

Real Estate Market Analysis

Determining real estate market condition and expectations and, accordingly, expected returns, volatility, and correlation is a complicated undertaking, but it can be made a little easier by developing a general framework for the real estate market. This framework, or model, helps us understand the many factors that interact to determine a market and/or property's return expectation.

Comparison between Stock and Real Estate Market Analysis
Exhibit 25–8 gives an overview of the stock market and real estate analysis process. As you can see, both analytical processes employ

EXHIBIT 25–8
Comparison of Stock Market and Real Estate Market Analysis

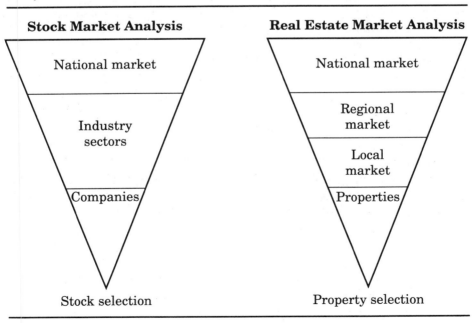

very similar approaches. Both stock and real estate returns are affected by changes in the capital markets and by specific company or property factors that define the asset. The main difference is due to the fixed/contractual nature of real estate leases. In essence, a property is a factory that provides "space" for sale or rent to its surrounding local market. Consequently, property performance can be viewed as having a bondlike component (relating to the lease contract[s]) and a reversionary value (upon the expiration of the lease[s]) that is directly linked to local supply and demand conditions. Companies, on the other hand, have greater flexibility in both the mobility of their factories and the markets they wish to supply. Therefore, a company's performance is directly linked to the industry (or industries) in which it competes, while a property's performance is directly linked to the market in which it competes.

Real Estate Markets, Linkages, and Potential Risk Factors

As shown in Exhibit 25–8, the stock market and real estate market analysis process is very similar. In comparison, Exhibit 25–9 focuses solely on real estate. It provides an overview of the unique nature of the real estate markets, the linkages among them, and the potential risk factors for each. Much of a portfolio manager's attention is given to understanding the risks inherent in the real estate market and how these risks can be managed. This section divides risk into its two components: *systematic risk* (factors that are not diversifiable) and *unsystematic risk* (factors that are diversifiable). Those firms that develop a framework with which to understand and manage risk factors will have a competitive advantage in assessing the market's opportunities and risks.

Systematic Risks

As noted above, systematic risk factors affect all assets in the market. Consequently, it is impossible for the portfolio manager to diversify these risk factors away completely. However, if the portfolio manager can determine the portfolio's sensitivity to these systematic risk factors and can reposition the portfolio according to its anticipated movements (up or down), the portfolio's risk-return performance can be improved.

National Market.   It is well documented that fiscal and monetary policies influence the national economy and the assets that are traded in them. Changes in fiscal policy (increases or decreases in

EXHIBIT 25–9
Real Estate Market Analysis, Risk Factors, and Diversification

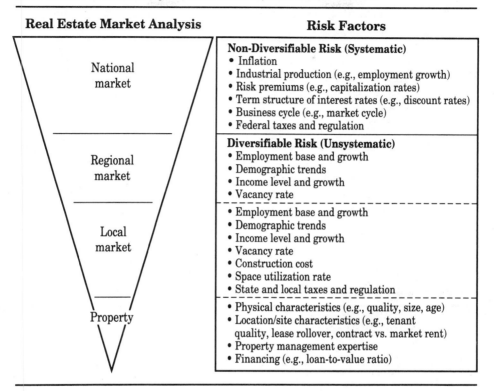

Real Estate Market Analysis	Risk Factors
National market	**Non-Diversifiable Risk (Systematic)** • Inflation • Industrial production (e.g., employment growth) • Risk premiums (e.g., capitalization rates) • Term structure of interest rates (e.g., discount rates) • Business cycle (e.g., market cycle) • Federal taxes and regulation
Regional market	**Diversifiable Risk (Unsystematic)** • Employment base and growth • Demographic trends • Income level and growth • Vacancy rate
Local market	• Employment base and growth • Demographic trends • Income level and growth • Vacancy rate • Construction cost • Space utilization rate • State and local taxes and regulation
Property	• Physical characteristics (e.g., quality, size, age) • Location/site characteristics (e.g., tenant quality, lease rollover, contract vs. market rent) • Property management expertise • Financing (e.g., loan-to-value ratio)

government taxes or spending) can have an impact on the entire national market and all the properties contained therein or a disproportionate impact on one area of the country. A poignant example is the impact of recently decreased federal spending on defense on southern California's property values. Similarly, the Tax Reform Act of 1986 (TRA '86) may have been more damaging (merely from a tax-advantaged viewpoint) to apartments than most other commercial property types. However, changes in monetary policy (increases or decreases in the supply of funds in the economy) that affect business cost of capital (interest rates) can have a broad impact on a variety of property types. Consequently, monetary policy affects "all" aspects of the economy, including the pricing of all assets. Furthermore, inflation, industrial production, risk premiums, and interest rates

have broad implications for all asset pricing, with real estate potentially posing additional systematic risks for market cycles (vacancy
rates), employment growth, and high information, transaction, and
liquidity costs.

Unsystematic Risks

Unsystematic risks do not affect all properties in the market. Consequently, it is possible for the portfolio manager to diversify many of
these risk factors away by properly combining properties. Exhibit
25–10 shows how the addition of properties (assuming their returns
are less than perfectly correlated) reduces total portfolio risk. As
mentioned earlier, this is the most cost-effective way to reduce overall
portfolio risk without reducing portfolio return. Therefore, a diligent
portfolio manager will always be looking for ways to combine real
estate assets to maximize the benefits of diversification. Accordingly,
diversification can become one of the dominant forces in the determi-

EXHIBIT 25–10
Portfolio Risk Reduction through Diversification

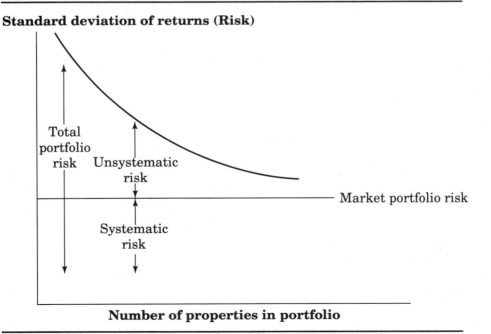

Standard deviation of returns (Risk)

Total portfolio risk

Unsystematic risk

Market portfolio risk

Systematic risk

Number of properties in portfolio

nation of the real estate portfolio's allocations to various property types and geographic locations.

Regional Market.   The national real estate market is often broken down into regional markets that define a specific area of the country by some distinguishing economic characteristics, most typically by its underlying business activities (e.g., employment base). For example, the industrial Midwest region would encompass the cities and states around the Great Lakes that have a high dependence on the industrial employment sector. Behind this regional market breakdown is the hypothesis that economic regions behave very differently over time than the national market due to differences in their existing employment base, employment growth, demographics, income trends, market vacancy levels, and other factors. These differences provide the portfolio manager with the potential to identify regional opportunities for increases in real estate returns along with the diversification benefits of owning properties in several economic regions, thereby reducing regional risks in the portfolio.

The concept of the economic region is evolving away from the grouping of contiguous states and/or metropolitan areas to the grouping of metropolitan areas based on their respective economic concentrations (e.g., employment base). This allows for the grouping of non-contiguous areas into economic clusters. For example, metropolitan areas with a preponderance of jobs in the financial services sector may be grouped together even though they are located in divergent parts of the country.

Local Market.   While the health of national and regional markets can have a significant impact on local property returns, they often seem a diluted force when compared to the dynamics of the local market. It is here where buyers and sellers of space consummate transactions and hence determine rent and property pricing. These transactions are based on the interaction of several factors, including current and expected local supply and demand, cost of new construction, and local taxes and regulations, along with a general knowledge of required rates of return in the capital markets.

Property.   At the property level, the old axiom "no two properties are alike" applies. A property's own individual characteristics have a very significant impact on its returns over time. Property factors like physical condition, location, lease characteristics, and property management all affect a property's return. One way to view how a property is linked to its local market is to think of the local market as a "stream" of real estate cash flow determined by the national, regional, and local market factors described above. How affected the property is by this stream of cash flow depends on its sensitivity to the surrounding market.

Exhibit 25–11 lists some determinants of a property's sensitivity to local market conditions (see also Chapter 4, "Leases as a Key to Performance and Value"). Most of the sensitivity of a property's asset value is a function of the property's lease characteristics. The shorter the property's average lease term, the more equitylike its cash flows and, accordingly, the more sensitive it is to local market conditions. The longer the property's average lease term, the more bondlike its cash flows and the less sensitive its value is to local market conditions. For example, consider two adjacent class A office buildings. One is a multitenant building with an average remaining lease term of 1.5 years, and the other is a single-tenant building recently contracted on a 20-year, long-term lease. As the leases in the building with the average lease term of 1.5 years expire, the space is "marked to market," thus giving the building a high market sensitivity. The building with the long-term lease, assuming quality tenancy, has no exposure to the market for another 20 years and thus has low market sensitivity, but it does have high sensitivity to movements in interest and inflation rates.

From the preceding framework, we can see that one of the main goals of the portfolio manager is to identify and predict which risk factors will influence real estate returns and position the portfolio

EXHIBIT 25–11
Sensitivity of Property Value Determinants to Changing Market Conditions

Property Characteristic	Change in Characteristic	Property Value Sensitivity to Changing Market Conditions
Average time to lease rollover	Increase	Decrease
Difference between contract rent and effective market rent	Increase	Increase
Tenant quality	Increase	Decrease

accordingly. As the real estate market changes over time, the significance of each risk factor also changes. As we look back over the 1980s, we see the significant *macro* risk factors for office properties included the reduction in office employment growth, continued growth in office construction, and unjustifiably positive investor sentiment (as manifested by low capitalization rates). As we look forward into the remaining half of the 1990s, we see the significant risk factors may have again changed, perhaps to many of the uncertainties listed in Exhibit 25–1. This illustrates the potential pitfalls of using historical trends to forecast the future, along with underscoring the importance of diversification as the only prudent way to protect the portfolio against unexpected changes in market conditions.

Market Segmentation

To analyze the domestic real estate investment universe, we need to break it down into manageable, homogeneous pieces called *market segments,* or *diversification categories.* Essentially, market segmentation means the aggregation of individual assets into categories with similar return behavior over time. Statistically, a market segment should constitute an aggregation of assets with high correlations of returns but low correlations of returns to other market segments over time. Market segmentation has been used by stock market portfolio managers to help them capitalize on market trends and investment styles. Some stock market examples are industry sectors (utilities, automotive, technology, etc.), firm size (small, medium, and large capitalization), and cyclical (consumer, durable, etc.) goods. For real estate, some market segments that have been used are property type, geographic region, economic region, economic cluster, metropolitan area employment growth, type of tenancy, average lease rollover, density of land use, and property life cycle. (See also Chapter 23, "Portfolio Diversification Considerations.")

Once the market segments have been identified, the portfolio manager needs to understand as much as possible about what drives the returns for each segment. This understanding can be obtained from several complementary sources; including (1) a historical review of applicable data series and research literature; (2) interviews and discussions with other portfolio managers, researchers, and asset/property managers; and (3) creation of the investment firm's own knowledge base through analysis and development of market explanatory models. Once these steps have been completed, the investor/

portfolio manager will be better equipped to understand each market segment.

We now introduce some of the basic tools, techniques, and models that may enhance understanding of the dynamics of the real estate markets.

The Return Factor Model

While an in-depth discussion is beyond the scope of this chapter, we will briefly introduce the concept and benefits of return factor models. Factor models can be an effective analytical tool in identifying an asset's (or portfolio's) return-generating process and, accordingly, its potential risk (as measured by the standard deviation of its returns). For our purposes, we begin by discussing the components of the required rate of return and then introduce single- and multifactor return models.

Required Rate of Return

The *required rate of return* is the return an investor requires to be fairly compensated for assuming the risks of the asset or portfolio being acquired. For reasons described earlier, we have broken the real estate market into manageable, homogeneous market segments. Consequently, we will use market segments as our fundamental unit for market analysis.

To determine a real estate market segment's required rate of return, recall that a nominal rate of return has three components: (1) the rate of inflation, (2) the real risk-free rate, and (3) the risk premium. These relationships are multiplicative and are shown in equation (1):

$$k = (1 + p)(1 + r' + r'') - 1 \tag{1}$$

where k = Nominal, required rate of return.
       p = Inflation rate.
       r' = Real risk-free rate.
       r'' = Risk premium.

This return can be viewed on either an ex ante or ex post basis. On an ex ante basis, this input represents the investor's expectations. On an ex post basis, the inflation rate is known as is the nominal return (k) earned by the asset; accordingly, the real risk-free and risk premium rates can be determined.

As discussed earlier, all assets are affected by the real risk-free and inflation rates (i.e., the nominal risk-free rate). What differs for each asset is the uncertainty of the size and timing of expected cash flows. This uncertainty needs to be quantified in a market risk factor model to determine the market segment's risk premium and, accordingly, the required rate of return the investor needs to be fairly compensated for the inherent risk in the market segment.

A return factor model uses a single- or multiple-regression equation to measure risk and explain real estate returns. It can be used at the national, regional, local, and/or property level to estimate expected returns and identify the factors that are responsible for real estate returns. Essentially, it attributes real estate returns to factors that influence returns, thereby acting as a tool with which to further understand real estate risk and return and identify a property's (or portfolio's) sensitivities to these risk factors.

The two types of factor models used to determine an asset's expected return are the single-factor model and the multifactor model. The *single-factor model,* which has become one of the major paradigms in finance, is commonly referred to as the *capital asset pricing model (CAPM).* Its basic premise is that the required rate of return of an asset (or a portfolio) is dependent on the rate of return of the market and its sensitivity to changes in the market's return. The CAPM also states that the asset's (or portfolio's) return is based solely on its systematic risk (beta), since it is unsystematic risk (e_i) which can be diversified away. The market model form of the CAPM is presented in equation (2):

$$E(R_i) = R_f + B_i \times [E(R_m) - R_f] + e_i \qquad (2)$$

where $E(R_i)$ = Required rate of return on ith asset (or portfolio).
R_f = Risk-free rate of return.
B_i = Sensitivity of the ith asset's (or portfolio's) return to the market return.
$E(R_m)$ = Expected return on the market.
e_i = Error term, or non-market-related (unsystematic) return.

The *multifactor model* is an extension of the single-factor model. Essentially, it includes additional factors to measure an asset's (or portfolio's) risk and commensurate expected return. The multifactor model is referred to as the *arbitrage pricing theory (APT).* Whereas the CAPM relies solely on a single factor, how the asset moves with the market portfolio (as measured by beta), APT asserts that an asset's return, and thus its riskiness, is a function of its "sensitivities" to unanticipated changes in several factors. A standard representation of a multifactor return model is presented in equation (3):

$$R_i = b_{i,0} + b_{i,1} \times F_1 + b_{i,2} \times F_2 + \ldots + b_{i,n} \times F_n + e_i \qquad (3)$$

where R_i = Return on the ith asset (or portfolio).
   $b_{i,0}$ = Constant (or intercept) term.
   $b_{i,n}$ = Sensitivity of the asset's return to factor n.
   F_n = Value of factor n.
   e_i = Error term, or non-factor-related (unsystematic) return.

A traditional applicaton of APT would include identifying unexpected changes in the following four economic factors that have been shown to influence returns on all assets: (1) inflation, (2) industrial production, (3) risk premiums, and (4) the term structure of interest rates. Because of real estate's unique nature, the portfolio manager may want to include factors specific to real estate, such as the influence of market cycles (vacancy rates), employment growth, and high information, transaction, and liquidity costs. (As with CAPM, the ex-ante version of APT assumes that the expected return to unsystematic risk equals zero.)

Following are some basic characteristics of a good factor model: First, when examining ex-post returns, the error term (e_i) should not be correlated to other significant factors in the model, for if it is, the factors may suffer from multicollinearity. Second, when examining ex-post returns, the error term (e_i) of the asset (or portfolio) should not be correlated with the asset's (or portfolio's) return; if it is, the factor model may be missing a significant systematic risk factor. Third, the model is parsimonious; that is, the selection of very few risk factors explains most of the return (a high R-squared).

Despite the apparent rigorousness of these models, several practical problems should be noted:

1. Which factors should be used? The absence of one or more significant factors might seriously impair the model.
2. These models are often developed using historical data. Their application to projecting future returns implicitly assume these factors (F_n) can be accurately predicted over time. This

may be a large leap of faith (e.g., can the future value of the factors driving the supply of and demand for CBD office space be accurately forecasted?).

3. The models assume the sensitivity (b_n) of these factors will remain constant (or nearly so) in the future (e.g., will the demand for CBD office space continue to be explained by the same factors, with the same relative magnitude, as those observed in the past?).

4. A scenario/probabilistic approach (expected factors and probability of outcome) is still needed to determine the variance and covariance of returns (which are needed inputs in the MPT process).

Assuming the portfolio manager has developed a multifactor model that has the required positive characteristics and has kept in mind the very practical problem with all factor models described above, the model may provide the portfolio manager with two potential uses. First, it may assist in developing a portfolio diversification, or allocation, strategy based on the portfolio's current factor "sensitivities" and market factor expectations. Second, it may generate the required inputs (i.e., expected return, standard deviation, and correlation) for each market segment for portfolio optimization.

Fundamental Analysis

We now move from single- and multifactor models to a market analysis model. We begin by exploring the concepts of intrinsic value and market value. *Intrinsic, or investment, value* (V_0) is the value an individual investor places on an asset. *Market value* (M_0) is the price the market places on the asset. As both a basic valuation model and one of the central tenets in finance, equation (4) states that the intrinsic value of any asset equals the present value of the asset's expected cash flows over the holding period:

$$V_0 = \sum_{n=1}^{N} \frac{CF_n}{(1 + k)^n} \qquad (4)$$

where V_0 = Current intrinsic value.
   CF_n = Cash flow (including sales price) in period n.
   N = Holding period.
   n = Equal, discrete time periods.
   k = Discount rate.

The discount rate can be determined through the multiplicative approach and/or the return factor models discussed earlier. In addition, equation (4) can be expressed in a form to which real estate practitioners (specifically real estate appraisers/underwriters) are more accustomed:

$$V_0 = \frac{CF_0(1 + g_1)}{(1 + k)^1} + \frac{CF_1(1 + g_2)}{(1 + k)^2} + \cdots$$
$$+ \frac{CF_{N-1}(1 + g_N)/(k - g_N)}{(1 + k)^N}$$

(5)

where $\quad g_n$ = Growth in cash flow in period n.
$(k - g_N)$ = Reversionary capitalization rate (assuming long-term equilibrium).

Equation (5) expands equation (4) by breaking cash flow out to include growth rates and sales price. Equation (5) represents the *multistage dividend discount model,* which is often used by stock analysts to determine intrinsic stock prices. However, its use requires that cash flows grow at a constant rate (g_N) once equilibrium is experienced after the Nth period.

To determine whether a market is overpriced, underpriced, or fairly priced, an investor must derive his or her best estimate of the market's (1) expected cash flow, (2) growth in cash flows, (3) exit capitalization rate, and (4) required rate of return. If an investor's estimate of intrinsic value differs from the market value, in effect the investor is disagreeing with some or all of the market's consensus opinion of CF_n, g_n, or k.

Market Segment Pro Forma

To determine a real estate market segment's expected return, it is necessary to build an income and expense pro forma for the market segment and include these estimates in equation (4) and/or (5). This has only recently become possible with improvements in the gathering of real estate market information. Depending on the size of one's investment organization, one can obtain the needed market segment information from various vendors, the investor's field organization, or both.

A market segment pro forma is then established based on an average unit measure for the targeted market segment (e.g., average class A office space per square foot). The market segment pro forma would contain estimates of current market rent, occupancy, operating expenses (fixed and variable), and capital expenditures (leasing commissions, tenant improvements, etc.), along with growth rates in income and expenses, going-in/going-out capitalization rates, and the expected rate of return. Exhibit 25–12 presents an example of cash flow pro forma and assumptions for a hypothetical market segment. Potential rent and expense growth rates, changes in market vacancy, and exit capitalization rates are derived by forecasting changes in the space and capital markets.

This process culminates in a ranking of property markets by estimated returns. This ranking can be summarized as:

$V_0 > M_0$; market is underpriced (buy)
$V_0 < M_0$; market is overpriced (sell)
$V_0 = M_0$; market is fairly priced (hold)

However, estimates of the variance and covariance of returns are still needed as inputs to the MPT-based portfolio optimization approach.

Scenario Analysis/Probabilistic Forecasting

The scenario approach takes a probabilistic view of the market segment's anticipated performance rather than the single-point estimate approach presented in Exhibit 25–12. Scenario analysis applies estimated probabilities to a variety of asset (or portfolio) potential outcomes and can then be used to determine expected return, standard deviation, and correlation. It more accurately reflects the uncertain nature of future asset returns and can generate all three portfolio optimization inputs (expected return, standard deviation, and correlations).

Given the cost, sophistication, and capacity of today's computer hardware and software, the benefits of using a scenario approach to understand the dynamics of the real estate market can no longer be readily dismissed on the basis of excessive cost and/or time requirements. Today a scenario analysis can be performed inexpensively. Accordingly, there is very little justification for continuing to use the old, single-point estimate approach when a scenario approach provides substantially more insight. Moreover, the process of thinking through the different scenarios and how they affect each market segment's expected returns adds considerably to the portfolio

EXHIBIT 25–12
Hypothetical Retail Market Pro Forma

	Market Cash Flow Projections					Reversionary Proceeds	Growth Rate Assumptions					Comments
	Year 1	Year 2	Year 3	Year 4	Year 5	End of Year 5	Year 1	Year 2	Year 3	Year 4	Year 5	
Potential rent	$15.53	$16.23	$16.29	$17.20	$17.98	$17.98	0.0%	1.0%	-3.0%	2.0%	1.0%	Year-over-year percentage increase.*
Occupancy	86.0%	87.0%	85.0%	86.0%	85.0%	85.0%	1.0	1.0	-2.0	1.0	-1.0	Change in occupancy percentage points
Net rent	$13.35	$14.12	$13.85	$14.79	$15.28	$15.28						
Operating expenses:												
Variable expenses	1.05	1.11	1.09	1.16	1.20	1.20	7.8	7.8	7.8	7.8	7.8	Percentage of net rent
Fixed expenses	3.11	3.21	3.33	3.44	3.56	3.56	3.5	3.5	3.5	3.5	3.5	Year-over-year percentage increase†
Total	4.16	4.32	4.42	4.60	4.76	4.76						
Net operating income	$9.20	$9.80	$9.44	$10.19	$10.52	10.52						

Reversionary capitalization rate					.09					
Capital expenses:										
Leasing commissions	0.52	0.54	0.54	0.55	0.55	3.5	3.5	3.5	3.5	3.5	Year-over-year percentage increase.†
Tenant improvements	1.04	1.07	1.07	1.11	1.11	3.5	3.5	3.5	3.5	3.5	Year-over-year percentage increase.†
Other	0.31	0.32	0.33	0.34	0.36	3.5	3.5	3.5	3.5	3.5	Year-over-year percentage increase.†
Total	1.87	1.93	1.94	2.00	2.02						
Net cash flow and reversionary proceeds	$7.34	$7.87	$7.50	$8.18	$8.50	$116.91					

Summary assumptions:

Initial purchase price	$100.00
Going-in capitalization rate	8.75%
Going-out capitalization rate	9.00%

Results:

Expected annual growth in cash flow	4.11%
Expected annual rate of return	10.56%

* Percentage change in real rents.
† Assumed inflation rate.
Note: Numbers may not add due to rounding.

manager's appreciation of the intricacies and relationships of the various market segments. Good portfolio managers will use these insights to exploit market opportunities and minimize portfolio risk.

On the other hand, the accuracy of this approach is only as good as the user's capabilities. It is subject to arbitrariness in the selection of the scenarios and in the weights assigned to each. Moreover, it may be difficult to forecast the correlation among assets if the scenarios are incorrectly framed. For example, a rising market in one area of the country may be attributable to, say, the recent passage of a plethora of trade agreements (e.g., NAFTA, GATT), while another part of the country may suffer a falling market due to the same causes. Other examples might include military buildup versus reduction, tax law changes, and other market uncertainties listed in Exhibit 25–1. Accordingly, great care must be taken in framing these scenarios.

To illustrate how scenario/probabilistic forecasts can be used, we have extended the market pro forma presented in Exhibit 25–12 into a probabilistic forecast. Exhibit 25–13 summarizes initial market-based financial information and probability matrix and market expectations for each of six market outcomes for a hypothetical market segment. More specifically, there are three conditions for market vacancy—rising, steady, and falling—and two conditions for inflation—low and high. Thus, we have a 3×2 joint-probability matrix, or, in other words, a six-scenario analysis.

Exhibit 25–14 shows the return distribution resulting from weighting each of the six scenarios by its estimated probability of occurrence. Once the expected return is calculated, the standard deviation can be completed. Assuming that the expected return is normally distributed, the frequency distribution shown in Exhibit 25–14 can be plotted. Exhibits 25–15 through 25–20 show the derivation of expected return for each of the six scenarios. Finally, Exhibit 25–21 shows the computation of the scenario-based expected return and standard deviation for the hypothetical retail market segment.

Similar benefits can be obtained by using a Monte Carlo simulation approach to generating returns under uncertainty for which the mean return, standard deviation, and correlation parameters can be estimated. Fundamentally similar to a scenario-based approach, Monte Carlo simulation requires the portfolio manager to estimate the distribution of each significant variable (rental rates, vacancy,

EXHIBIT 25–13   Overview of Market Assumptions: Hypothetical Market Segment

Initial Market-Based Financial Information			Probability Matrix of Market Conditions			
	Actuals from Prior Year	Inflation Rate	Rising	Steady	Falling	Total
Potential rent	$15.00	Low	20.0%	40.0%	20.0%	80.0%
Occupancy	85.0%	High	5.0	10.0	5.0	20.0
Net rent	$12.75	Total	25.0%	50.0%	25.0%	100.0%
Operating expenses:						
Variable expenses	1.00	*Market Expectations*				
Fixed expenses	3.00		Real Changes in Rents			
Total	$4.00					
Net operating income	8.75		*Year 1*	*Year 2*	*Year 3*	*Year 4*	*Year 5*
Capital expenses:						
Leasing commissions	0.50	Rising	0.5%	1.0%	0.5%	1.0%	1.0%
Tenant improvements	1.00	Steady	0.0	1.0	−3.0	2.0	1.0
Other	0.30	Falling	−0.5	−1.0	−0.5	−1.0	−1.0
Total	1.80		(Year-over-year percentage increase.)				
Net cash flow	$6.95		Changes in Occupancy				
Summary assumptions:						
Initial purchase price	$100.00		*Year 1*	*Year 2*	*Year 3*	*Year 4*	*Year 5*
Going-in capitalization rate	8.75%	Rising	0.5%	1.0%	1.5%	1.0%	0.5%
Going-out		Steady	1.0	1.0	−2.0	1.0	−1.0
capitalization rate (at disposition)	9.00%	Falling	−0.5	−1.0	−1.5	−1.0	−0.5
			(Change in occupancy percentage points.)				
Scenario-Based Expected Result		Inflation Rate				
Return	11.12%	Low	3.5%			
Standard deviation	2.54%	High	7.0			

growth rate, etc.) to the return-generating process. From these distributions, a series of simulated "draws" are recorded and used to create a distribution of returns. However, space limitations preclude an extensive treatment here. Interested readers are referred to any graduate-level textbook on quantitative analysis with a thorough treatment of simulation technologies.

Portfolio Optimization: Reconciliation and Judgment

We now focus on obtaining the inputs into the optimization process in order to create an efficient frontier that formally represents the return, risk, and diversification expectations for each segment of the

EXHIBIT 25–14

Overview of Return Distribution: Hypothetical Market Segment

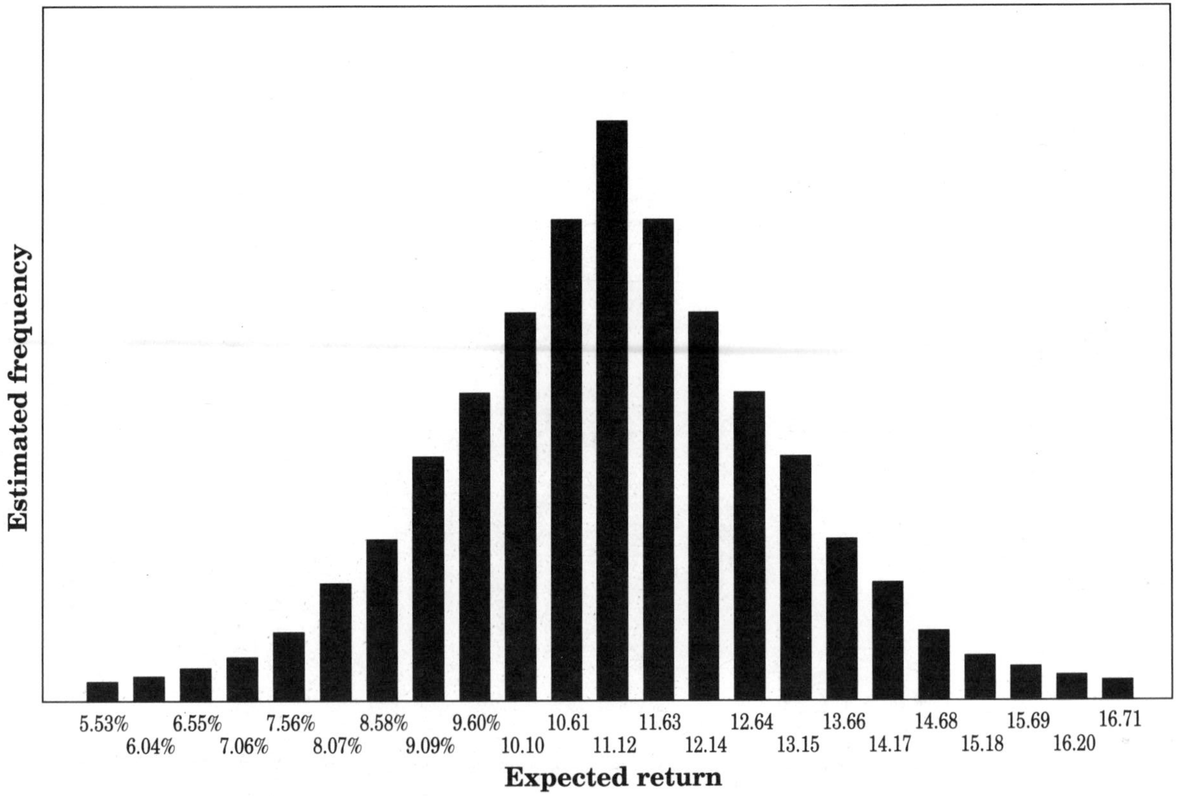

EXHIBIT 25–15   Probability 20% (Rising Market/Low Inflation): Hypothetical Market Pro Forma

	Market Cash Flow Projections					Reversionary Proceeds
	Year 1	Year 2	Year 3	Year 4	Year 5	End of Year 5
Potential rent	$15.60	$16.31	$16.97	$17.73	$18.54	$18.54
Occupancy	85.5%	86.5%	88.0%	89.0%	89.5%	89.5%
Net rent	$13.34	$14.11	$14.93	$15.78	$16.59	$16.59
Operating expenses:						
Variable expenses	1.05	1.11	1.17	1.24	1.30	1.30
Fixed expenses	3.11	3.21	3.33	3.44	3.56	3.56
Total	4.16	4.32	4.50	4.68	4.86	4.86
Net operating income	9.19	9.79	10.43	11.10	11.73	$11.73
Capital expenses:						
Leasing commissions	0.52	0.54	0.54	0.55	0.55	
Tenant improvements	1.04	1.07	1.07	1.11	1.11	
Other	0.31	0.32	0.33	0.34	0.36	
Total	1.87	1.93	1.94	2.00	2.02	
Reversionary capitalization rate						.09
Net cash flow and reversionary proceeds	$7.33	$7.86	$8.49	$9.10	$9.71	$130.31
Summary assumptions:						
Initial purchase price			$100.00			
Going-in capitalization rate			8.75%			
Going-out capitalization rate			9.00%			
Results:						
Expected annual growth in cash flow			6.91%			
Expected annual rate of return			13.03%			

Note: Numbers may not add due to rounding.

targeted market. However, we have a problem, and the problem is called *uncertainty*. There is little question that on an ex post basis, the efficient frontier creates nothing less than the exact answer. But as a tool to construct ex ante portfolios, the efficient frontier is only as good as its inputs. This is also why the efficient frontier has been nicknamed the "fuzzy" frontier by practitioners and academics alike. To improve our chances of deriving the best inputs to the optimization process, we employ four approaches, a reconciliation, and a strong dose of judgment. To recognize the inherent uncertainty of the inputs in addition to the lumpy nature of real estate private market transactions, target allocation ranges have been instituted.

EXHIBIT 25–16 **Probability 5% (Rising Market/High Inflation): Hypothetical Market Pro Forma**

	Market Cash Flow Projections					Reversionary Proceeds
	Year 1	Year 2	Year 3	Year 4	Year 5	End of Year 5
Potential rent	$16.13	$17.43	$18.75	$20.26	$21.89	$21.89
Occupancy	85.5%	86.5%	88.0%	89.0%	89.5%	89.5%
Net rent	$13.79	$15.08	$16.50	$18.03	$19.59	$19.59
Operating expenses:						
Variable expenses	1.08	1.18	1.29	1.41	1.54	1.54
Fixed expenses	3.21	3.43	3.68	3.93	4.21	4.21
Total	4.29	4.61	4.97	5.34	5.75	5.75
Net operating income	9.50	10.46	11.53	12.68	13.85	$13.85
Capital expenses:						
Leasing commissions	0.54	0.57	0.57	0.61	0.61	
Tenant improvements	1.07	1.14	1.14	1.23	1.23	
Other	0.32	0.34	0.37	0.39	0.42	
Total	1.93	2.05	2.08	2.23	2.26	
Reversionary capitalization rate						.09
Net cash flow and reversionary proceeds	$7.57	$8.40	$9.44	$10.45	$11.59	$153.89

Summary assumptions:
Initial purchase price $100.00
Going-in capitalization rate 8.75%
Going-out capitalization rate 9.00%

Results:
Expected annual growth in cash flow 10.77%
Expected annual rate of return 16.88%

Note: Numbers may not add due to rounding.

In his seminal paper "Portfolio Selection," Markowitz notes the difficulty in determining the correct inputs for portfolio optimization:

> [W]e must have procedures for finding reasonable [means] and [variances]. These procedures, I believe, should combine statistical techniques and the judgment of practical men. My feeling is that the statistical computations should be used to arrive at a tentative set of [means] and [variances]. Judgment should then be used in increasing or decreasing some of these [means] and [variances] not taken into account by the formal computations.[2]

---

[2] Harry Markowitz, "Portfolio Selection," *Journal of Finance,* March 1952, p. 91.

EXHIBIT 25–17   Probability 40% (Steady Market/Low Inflation): Hypothetical Market Pro Forma

	Market Cash Flow Projections					Reversionary Proceeds
	Year 1	Year 2	Year 3	Year 4	Year 5	End of Year 5
Potential rent	$15.53	$16.23	$16.29	$17.20	$17.98	$17.98
Occupancy	86.0%	87.0%	85.0%	86.0%	85.0%	85.0%
Net rent	$13.35	$14.12	$13.85	$14.79	$15.28	$15.28
Operating expenses:						
Variable expenses	1.05	1.11	1.09	1.16	1.20	1.20
Fixed expenses	3.11	3.21	3.33	3.44	3.56	3.56
Total	4.16	4.32	4.42	4.60	4.76	4.76
Net operating income	9.20	9.80	9.44	10.19	10.52	$10.52
Capital expenses:						
Leasing commissions	0.52	0.54	0.54	0.55	0.55	
Tenant improvements	1.04	1.07	1.07	1.11	1.11	
Other	0.31	0.32	0.33	0.34	0.36	
Total	1.87	1.93	1.94	2.00	2.02	
Reversionary capitalization rate						.09
Net cash flow and reversionary proceeds	$7.34	$7.87	$7.50	$8.18	$8.50	$116.91

Summary assumptions:

Initial purchase price	$100.00
Going-in capitalization rate	8.75%
Going-out capitalization rate	9.00%

Results:

Expected annual growth in cash flow	4.11%
Expected annual rate of return	10.56%

Note: Numbers may not add due to rounding.

Given the historically poor quality of real estate market information and the short time these tools have been employed in the real estate market, Markowitz's warning seems particularly appropriate. In part because of these problems, there has been much debate regarding the usefulness of these approaches, including the benefits of applying MPT to real estate at all. Notwithstanding the shortcomings of using an MPT-based approach, the benefits of adhering to a disciplined portfolio optimization process, including multiple approaches reconciled with judgment, provide the practitioner with many benefits that cannot be easily dismissed.

EXHIBIT 25–18 **Probability 10% (Steady Market/High Inflation): Hypothetical Market Pro Forma**

	Market Cash Flow Projections					Reversionary Proceeds
	Year 1	Year 2	Year 3	Year 4	Year 5	End of Year 5
Potential rent	$16.05	$17.35	$18.00	$19.65	$21.23	$21.23
Occupancy	86.0%	87.0%	85.0%	86.0%	85.0%	85.0%
Net rent	$13.80	$15.09	$15.30	$16.90	$18.05	$18.05
Operating expenses:						
Variable expenses	1.08	1.18	1.20	1.33	1.42	1.42
Fixed expenses	3.21	3.43	3.68	3.93	4.21	4.21
Total	4.29	4.61	4.88	5.26	5.63	5.62
Net operating income	9.51	10.47	10.43	11.64	12.43	$12.43
Capital expenses:						
Leasing commissions	0.54	0.57	0.57	0.61	0.61	
Tenant improvements	1.07	1.14	1.14	1.23	1.23	
Other	0.32	0.34	0.37	0.39	0.42	
Total	1.93	2.05	2.08	2.23	2.26	
Reversionary capitalization rate						.09
Net cash flow and reversionary proceeds	$7.58	$8.41	$8.34	$9.41	$10.17	$138.06
Summary assumptions:						
Initial purchase price			$100.00			
Going-in capitalization rate			8.75%			
Going-out capitalization rate			9.00%			
Results:						
Expected annual growth in cash flow			7.91%			
Expected annual rate of return			14.34%			

Note: Numbers may not add due to rounding.

Forecasting Approaches

To summarize, we have discussed several possible approaches to forecasting the three inputs (expected return, standard deviation, and correlation) needed to derive the efficient frontier. The first is based primarily on historical relationships, while the remaining three are based on subjective estimates about the future (which might be substantially influenced by historical relationships):

1. Factor models.
   a) single-factor,
   b) multi-factor
2. Fundamental analysis.

EXHIBIT 25–19   Probability 20% (Falling Market/Low Inflation): Hypothetical Market Pro Forma

	Market Cash Flow Projections					Reversionary Proceeds
	Year 1	Year 2	Year 3	Year 4	Year 5	End of Year 5
Potential rent	$15.45	$15.83	$16.30	$16.70	$17.11	$17.11
Occupancy	84.5%	83.5%	82.0%	81.0%	80.5%	80.5%
Net rent	$13.05	$13.22	$13.37	$13.53	$13.78	$13.78
Operating expenses:						
Variable expenses	1.02	1.04	1.05	1.06	1.08	1.08
Fixed expenses	3.11	3.21	3.33	3.44	3.56	3.56
Total	4.13	4.25	4.38	4.50	4.64	4.64
Net operating income	8.92	8.97	8.99	9.03	9.13	$9.13
Capital expenses:						
Leasing commissions	0.52	0.54	0.54	0.55	0.55	
Tenant improvements	1.04	1.07	1.07	1.11	1.11	
Other	0.31	0.32	0.33	0.34	0.36	
Total	1.87	1.93	1.94	2.00	2.02	
Reversionary capitalization rate						.09
Net cash flow and reversionary proceeds	$7.06	$7.04	$7.05	$7.02	$7.11	$101.48

Summary assumptions:
Initial purchase price	$100.00
Going-in capitalization rate	8.75%
Going-out capitalization rate	9.00%

Results:
Expected annual growth in cash flow	0.47%
Expected annual rate of return	7.31%

Note: Numbers may not add due to rounding.

3. Scenario analysis.
4. Monte Carlo simulation.

The difficulty with the historical relationships is the potential naive extension of historical statistics into the future, which runs contrary to the notions of the inevitability of change, investor fads, and so on.

While the factor models rely extensively on history, fundamental, scenario, and Monte Carlo analyses rely on forecasting to reflect the uncertain nature of future asset returns. The difficulty with these approaches is that their accuracy is only as good as the user's capabili-

EXHIBIT 25–20   Probability 5% (Falling Market/High Inflation): Hypothetical Market Pro Forma

	Market Cash Flow Projections					Reversionary Proceeds
	Year 1	Year 2	Year 3	Year 4	Year 5	End of Year 5
Potential rent	$15.97	$16.92	$18.01	$19.08	$20.21	$20.21
Occupancy	84.5%	83.5%	82.0%	81.0%	80.5%	80.5%
Net rent	$13.49	$14.13	$14.77	$15.45	$16.27	$16.27
Operating expenses:						
Variable expenses	1.06	1.11	1.16	1.21	1.28	1.28
Fixed expenses	3.21	3.43	3.68	3.93	4.21	4.21
Total	4.27	4.54	4.84	5.14	5.49	5.49
Net operating income	9.23	9.58	9.94	10.31	10.79	$10.79
Capital expenses:						
Leasing commissions	0.54	0.57	0.57	0.61	0.61	
Tenant improvements	1.07	1.14	1.14	1.23	1.23	
Other	0.32	0.34	0.37	0.39	0.42	
Total	1.93	2.05	2.08	2.23	2.26	
Reversionary capitalization rate						.09
Net cash flow and reversionary proceeds	$7.30	$7.52	$7.85	$8.08	$8.53	$119.84

Summary assumptions:
Initial purchase price $100.00
Going-in capitalization rate   8.75%
Going-out capitalization rate   9.00%

Results:
Expected annual growth in cash flow   4.17%
Expected annual rate of return   10.98%

Note: Numbers may not add due to rounding.

ties and are subject to arbitrariness in the selection of the scenarios, weights, distributions, and so on.

Having completed several approaches, the portfolio manager must now determine the best inputs to use to create the efficient frontier. This compares to the "mosaic" approach used by security analysts and the three approaches to value (cost, market, and income) reconciliation used by real estate appraisers. It is at this point that judgment must come into play in the selection of the inputs, or range of inputs, to derive the efficient frontier. It is hoped, however, that portfolio managers, through the completion of each approach and the thought process that accompanies it, will have gained additional knowledge and insight that will enhance their ability to select the

EXHIBIT 25–21
Computation of Expected Return and Standard Deviation for Hypothetical Market Segment

Market Conditions	Inflation Rate	Expected Return	Estimated Probability of Occurrence	Weighted Expected Probability Return	Deviation from the Mean	Squared Deviations	Estimated Probability of Occurrence	Weighted Squared Probability Deviations
Rising	Low	13.0%	20.0%	2.61%	1.91%	0.0365%	20.0%	0.0073%
Rising	High	16.9	5.0	0.84	5.76	0.3319	5.0	0.0166
Steady	Low	10.6	40.0	4.22	−0.56	0.0031	40.0	0.0012
Steady	High	14.3	10.0	1.43	3.22	0.1037	10.0	0.0104
Falling	Low	7.3	20.0	1.46	−3.81	0.1451	20.0	0.0290
Falling	High	11.0	5.0	0.55	−0.14	0.0002	5.0	0.0000
			100.0%	11.12% Mean			100.0%	0.0645% Variance

2.54% Standard deviation

best inputs. Thus, the process of completing multiple approaches and reconciliation has the benefit of forcing a more explicit thought process, which should enhance the selection of the portfolio optimization inputs.

Other Optimization (MPT) Related Problems

In addition to the limitations and difficulties of each approach, at least two other MPT problems merit discussion. First, the results of MPT-generated efficient frontiers also depend on the classification scheme used (i.e., market segments). As the classification of market segments is not an exact science, the portfolio manager risks classifying them too broadly or too narrowly. Too broad a classification system will mask important (risk reduction) differences in the portfolio, while too narrow a classification system may result in an overly cumbersome analytical process. Second, the nature of the portfolio optimization process is such that if two assets offer nearly identical mean/variance characteristics but one is slightly more attractive, the optimization process will place a very large portfolio allocation on the one asset that is slightly more attractive to the virtual exclusion of the other asset. However, common sense tells us that the uncertainty of the inputs for both assets makes it foolish to make such a dominant allocation to one asset at the expense of another offering nearly identical but slightly less attractive characteristics.

We have now completed the second step in the real estate portfolio management process. We began by examining market efficiency and portfolio management approaches. We then identified the real estate investment universe and partitioned (or, segmented) it into manageable, fairly homogeneous clusters. Each cluster (or, market segment) was then examined for its risk/return characteristics through the use of various analytical tools and approaches. Finally, these results were compared, contrasted, and then reconciled with the practioner's judgments in order to arrive at the inputs needed to optimize a portfolio using MPT (i.e., to create the efficient frontier).

TARGET PORTFOLIO DETERMINATION

We began our portfolio management process by defining the investor's investment objectives and constraints. We then analyzed the real estate market conditions and expectations and derived the input estimates (i.e., expected return, standard deviation, and correlations) using several different approaches for each market segment and, through a reconciliation process, derived an efficient frontier. We are now ready to integrate these two fundamental aspects, investor needs and market conditions, into a target portfolio. The target portfolio and how it is determined is the topic of this section.

Exhibit 25–22 graphically depicts the integration of the investor's investment objectives and constraints (represented by investor risk-return indifference curves) and market conditions and expectations (represented by the efficient frontier). The investor's risk-return indifference curves are combinations of expected returns and standard deviations (risk) to which the investor is indifferent. Investors prefer higher indifference curves, as they offer greater utility (i.e., for any given risk, a higher indifference curve provides a higher return). In addition, the investor's risk-return indifference curves are upward

EXHIBIT 25–22
Target "Optimal" Portfolio Selection

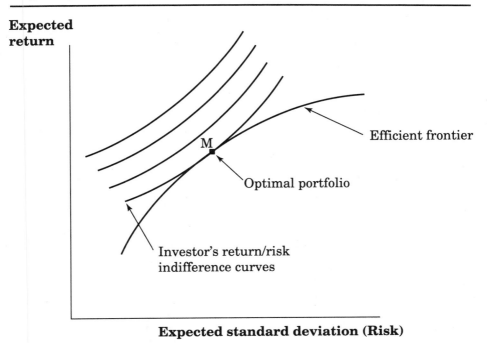

sloping to reflect the need for expected return to grow rapidly to offset increasing risk.

The tangential intersection of the investor's risk-return indifference curve and the efficient curve, at the optimal point *M*, represents the portfolio allocation that provides the investor with the greatest possible utility. Point *M* represents an exact market segment allocation. For example, if property type market segment were being allocated, it might represent a 15 percent office, 20 percent retail, 25 percent industrial, and 40 percent apartment portfolio allocation. However, to account for the uncertainty of forecasting the inputs for the efficient frontier along with the investor's objectives and constraints, allocation ranges are used to both reflect this uncertainty and provide the flexibility needed to properly manage property-level investment decisions.

Exhibits 25–23 and 25–24 show allocation ranges by both property type and economic region and a hypothetical portfolio's current allocation to each of these market segments. These allocation ranges

EXHIBIT 25–23
Hypothetical Property Type Allocation Ranges

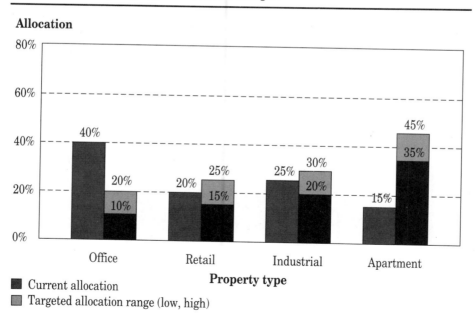

Current allocation
Targeted allocation range (low, high)

EXHIBIT 25–24
Hypothetical Economic Region Allocation Ranges

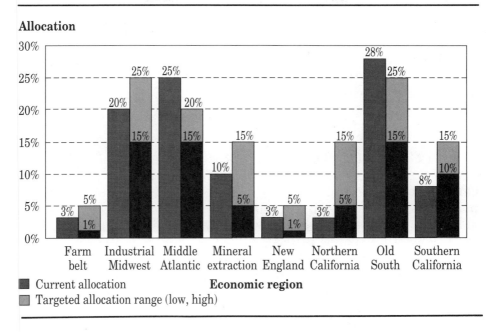

Allocation

- ■ Current allocation
- ▨ Targeted allocation range (low, high)

Economic region

now become the guidepost the investor/portfolio manager uses when making individual property-level investment decisions. For example, from Exhibit 25–23, we can see that the hypothetical current portfolio is substantially overallocated in office and substantially underallocated in apartment, while falling within the allocation range for retail and industrial. From Exhibit 25–24, we can see that the hypothetical current portfolio is overallocated in the Middle Atlantic and Old South and underallocated in Northern and Southern California, while falling within the desired ranges for the remaining economic regions.

By taking the hypothetical portfolio example depicted in Exhibits 25–23 and 25–24 (the initial repositioning of an existing portfolio) a step further, the investor/portfolio manager now faces a very practical set of problems, specifically, the balancing of the property's existing position in the market (e.g., leasing, capital improvements, property management changes) and the market's position within its investment cycle (i.e., peak to trough to peak) within the target portfolio's designated allocation ranges. This is an important balance, because if the investor/portfolio manager allows the portfolio to stray too far from the designated allocation ranges, he or she runs the risks of losing the return, risk, and diversification benefits of the target portfolio. Likewise, if the investor/portfolio manager does not maintain an understanding of properties and the markets in which they are located, the portfolio runs the risk of generating lower returns due to an inopportune time for property sales. This balance is determined and then executed as part of the portfolio strategy determination, our next step.

PORTFOLIO STRATEGY DETERMINATION

Once the target portfolio is identified, the investor/portfolio manager must develop a portfolio strategy that will be consistent with the allocation ranges of the target portfolio and the current and expected conditions of properties in the portfolio.

If the first three steps of the portfolio management process have been completed diligently, the broad goals of the portfolio strategy should have become readily apparent (return, risk, diversification, liquidity, financing, etc.). However, the challenge now becomes translating these broad goals to be both definable and measurable. If, for example, the investor/portfolio manager has an internal real estate organization, the acquisition, asset/property management, and disposition groups will each require this translation to take place. For this type of real estate organization, Exhibit 25–25 depicts the process by which the target portfolio is translated into a single portfolio strategy and then into sub-strategies for each of the firm's functional disciplines.

It is essential that the development of each functional group's strategy be completed in conjunction with the functional group that will be responsible for its execution (i.e., an interactive, team approach). By not doing so, the investor/portfolio manager runs the risk that the functional disciplines will lack commitment and/or "buy-in" to the implementation strategy proposed. Furthermore, he or she will also miss out on a needed reality check by the individuals in the firm with the best knowledge of property and market conditions.

Each functional group's strategy thus becomes the document that communicates portfolio goals and objectives and establishes benchmarks and performance measurements, thereby providing the framework for motivating and rewarding the organization. For example,

EXHIBIT 25–25
Portfolio Strategy Determination

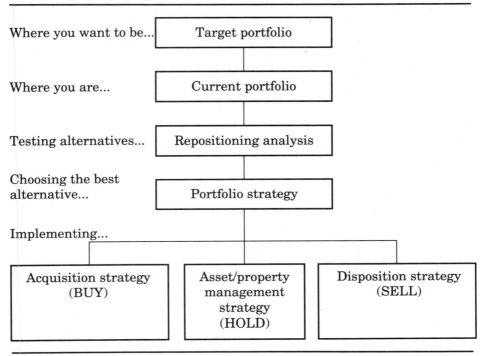

the acquisition strategy would outline acquisition goals and objectives for each portfolio (e.g., property type, location, size, age, lease structure, financing), and the performance of the acquisition group would be measured on its ability to acquire properties with these characteristics and perform as underwritten. The asset/property strategy would outline the goals and objectives for the property (market and property risk analysis, leasing objectives and guidelines, operating and capital budget, etc.). Likewise, the disposition strategy would outline the goals and objectives for the sale of properties.

For the real estate public market (i.e., REIT) investor/portfolio manager, the implementation and execution of the portfolio strategy are much simpler and more straightforward. Typically, they entail the placement and execution of a trade, which can be accomplished, depending on the liquidity of the issue, in a few minutes to a few days.

MONITORING AND REBALANCING

The concept of and need for monitoring and rebalancing goes to the very root of portfolio management. It acknowledges that the only certainty is that things will change in unexpected ways. Consequently, even the most passive investment management styles require some monitoring and rebalancing.

Monitoring and rebalancing also introduce the dimension of time into the portfolio management process. The portfolio management steps discussed thus far (investor objectives and constraints, market conditions and expectations, target portfolio determination, and portfolio strategy determination) are completed by analyzing all available information as of a point in time. The introduction of monitoring and rebalancing converts the portfolio management process from this static snapshot into a continuous, dynamic process.

This section provides a very general overview of monitoring and rebalancing. It begins with a definition and discussion of both monitoring and rebalancing, then touches on the cost of rebalancing, and concludes by examining the psychology involved in this process.

Definitions

Monitoring is the act, or process, of analyzing and understanding change and its potential impact on the performance of the portfolio. The monitoring process is represented graphically in Exhibit 25–4. That exhibit clearly shows that the monitoring process focuses on the two inputs into the portfolio management process: investor objectives/constraints and market conditions/expectations. These two inputs, knowledge of the investor and knowledge of the market, come together to determine the most appropriate target portfolio and portfolio implementation strategy.

Monitoring is also the reason we view the portfolio management process as dynamic. Essentially, monitoring captures the dynamics of change. What should be monitored for the investor? Recall the categories contained in the investment policy: portfolio size, return requirements, risk tolerance, liquidity, time horizon, and tax and legal considerations. In more technical terms, monitoring for the investor should include anything that affects the shape of the investor's risk-return preference indifference curves and their tangential intersection with the efficient frontier (see Exhibit 25–22). What should be monitored for market conditions and expectations? Recall the potential risk factors listed in Exhibit 25–9. All of these have the potential to change the risk-return trade-off for each market segment, which in effect will change the shape and composition of the efficient frontier. If conditions and/or expectations change significantly enough, the investor/portfolio manager will initiate a rebalancing of the portfolio.

Rebalancing is the process of modifying the assets within the portfolio to make them better fit the changing needs of the investor and market conditions and expectations. Rebalancing can take one of three forms: (1) allocation changes between market segments (e.g., Chicago office to Atlanta retail), (2) category or emphasis changes in a market segment (e.g., regional malls to power centers), and (3) selling a property and replacing it with another of like kind. The determination of when to rebalance and when to hold tight with the current portfolio is the operative question. To help us understand when rebalancing is worthwhile, we now introduce the concepts of rebalancing costs and psychological factors.

Rebalancing Costs

The cost of rebalancing a portfolio can take the form of trading or not trading. The costs of not trading include (1) holding onto a property that is overpriced (i.e., $V_0 < M_0$) and/or (2) holding onto a property that no longer fit the needs of the investor (e.g., changing risk tolerance). The costs of trading include (1) commissions and associated fees and (2) the impact on the market, where the impact is very difficult to measure.

Although all of the costs of rebalancing a portfolio are important, depending on the market one is trading in, they are not all equal. For example, selling and purchasing private market equity properties are expensive and time-consuming endeavors. Trading costs range from 100 to 700 basis points, depending on the size and complexity of the transaction. However, public market equity transactions (i.e., REITs) are more in line with other equity trades in the capital markets. Also, although they are just becoming available in the real estate equity market, derivatives provide an inexpensive way to change the return, risk, and diversification dynamics of a portfolio (see Chapter 27, "Application of Derivative Instruments").

Psychology of Portfolio Rebalancing

The psychology of the portfolio rebalancing decision can have a powerful impact on what the investor/portfolio manager does. In the uncertain world of investments, it is all too easy to make rebalancing decisions based on emotions and the latest investor fad. Furthermore, the investor/portfolio manager may be influenced by the portfolio rebalancing decisions of others (i.e., the herd mentality) if the portfolio is managed in a fiduciary context. The reason for this is the fiduciary constraints the portfolio manager may be required to follow (recall ERISA's "prudent man" rule). Therefore, given the substantial costs of rebalancing an equity real estate portfolio, the investor/portfolio manager must always be certain that portfolio rebalancing is being executed not for psychological reasons but for sound, fundamental reasons. Otherwise, the result is needless erosion of returns by transaction costs.

Monitoring and rebalancing are costly and time-consuming endeavors that require the dedication of the entire organization. While each firm will have its own particular method or process, the suggested approach (and theme of this chapter) is the creation, integration, and implementation of a systematic and disciplined portfolio management process. Through a disciplined approach, one moves from being overly influenced by the latest event(s) and fads to a framework that helps to identify and systematically measure how the investor and the market have fundamentally changed. Monitoring and rebalancing then become a natural part of this disciplined process.

PORTFOLIO PERFORMANCE MEASUREMENT

How skillful was the portfolio manager? Did the portfolio manager meet the investor's objectives? Were the time and resources spent on analyzing market conditions and expectations, determining the target portfolio, and completing property analysis worthwhile? More specifically, in what areas did the portfolio manager perform well, and what areas need improvement? To answer these questions, the investor/portfolio manager needs an objective means to assess the portfolio's performance.

This section provides an overview of portfolio measurement by briefly discussing (1) the ways a portfolio manager can add value, (2) return measures, and (3) performance attribution.

Adding Value

Active portfolio management can add value, via excess risk-adjusted returns, to the portfolio in one of three ways: market allocation (timing), property selection, and diversification. In essence, portfolio managers are measured on their ability to provide these three functions.

Market allocation is the percentage of the portfolio invested in each market segment (property types, economic regions, etc). When the market allocation deviates from the benchmark portfolio, it is called *market timing*. The *benchmark portfolio* is an unmanaged, or passive, portfolio (e.g., Russell/NCREIF return series) with risk equal to that of the managed, or active, portfolio. When portfolio managers engage in market timing, they assume they can affect portfolio performance by identifying and acquiring (selling) properties in markets that are expected to out- or underperform the overall market on a risk-adjusted basis.

Property selection is the impact the properties owned (or selected) have on portfolio performance. Property selection assumes the portfolio manager can affect portfolio performance by acquiring (selling) properties that are expected to outperform (underperform) the overall market segment benchmark. Here the portfolio manager is being measured on the ability to identify mispriced properties within a market segment.

Finally, *diversification* measures how completely the portfolio is diversified compared to the market portfolio. The level of diversification is important, as portfolio theory states that investors are willing to pay only for systematic (market) risk. Consequently, the portfolio manager's return performance must be adjusted for risk to provide a proper portfolio performance comparison. The degree of portfolio diversification can be determined by comparing the return of the portfolio and the returns of the market portfolio. Perfect correlation means the portfolio is completely diversified (no unsystematic risk remains).

The measurement of market allocation and property selection will be discussed more fully in the section "Performance Attribution."

Return Measures

Return measures are either historical or forecast measures of performance. Historical returns are sometimes called *performance returns,* while forecast returns are often called *expected returns.* For purposes

EXHIBIT 25–26
Various Single-Period Return Measures

1. Russell/NCREIF

Unleveraged

$$R_{inc} = \frac{I_t}{MV_{t-1} + .5(CI_t - PS_t) - .33I_t}$$

$$R_{app} = \frac{(MV_t - MV_{t-1}) + PS_t - CI_t}{MV_{t-1} + .5(CI_t - PS_t) - .33I_t}$$

$$R_{total} = R_{inc} + R_{app}$$

Where
R_{inc} = Income return.
R_{app} = Appreciation return.
R_{total} = Total return.
I_t = Income during period t.
MV_{t-1} = Market value at beginning of period t.
MV_t = Market value at end of period t.
CI_t = Capital improvement in period t.
PS_t = Partial sales during period t.

2. Cash-on-cash (average book cost)

$$R_{CC,BC} = \frac{CF_t}{(BC_{t-1} + BC_t)/2}$$

Where
$R_{CC,BC}$ = Cash-on-cash return on book cost.
CF_t = Cash flow during period t.
BC_{t-1} = Book cost at beginning of period t.
BC_t = Book cost at end of period t.

3. Cash-on-cash (market value)

$$R_{CC,MV} = \frac{CF_t}{MV_{t-1}}$$

Where
$R_{CC,MV}$ = Cash-on-cash return on market value.
CF_t = Cash flow during period t.
MV_{t-1} = Market value at beginning of period t.

4. Capitalization rate (market value)

$$R_{cap} = \frac{NOI_t}{MV_{t-1}}$$

Where
R_{cap} = Capitalization rate.
NOI_t = Net operating income during period t.
MV_{t-1} = Market value at beginning of period t.

of portfolio measurement, performance returns are used. Performance returns can be determined for a single period or multiple periods.

Returns can also be calculated using one or more of several generally accepted alternative methodologies. Exhibit 25–26 summarizes several of the more commonly used single-period performance return measures: Russell/NCREIF unleveraged return, cash-on-cash (using average book cost), cash-on-cash (using market value), and capitalization rate.

Performance returns may also be either time weighted, or dollar weighted. *Time-weighted* returns are computed for each period, multiplied together across time, and then annualized to measure portfolio performance. The *dollar-weighted* return is an internal rate of return formula that solves for the return that equates the present value of the cash flows to the initial investment. Since dollar-weighted returns are affected by the size and timing of cash flows into and out of the portfolio over the holding period, time-weighted returns are used as a measure of portfolio performance because they are independent of the timing of significant cash flow into and out of the portfolio.

Performance Attribution

The goal of performance attribution is to identify the portfolio impact of the portfolio manager's allocation and property selection decisions. Following Brinson et al. (1986), Exhibit 25–27 provides an example of a hypothetical portfolio's performance as benchmarked against the Russell/NCREIF return series for each property type.

The allocation effect measures the impact of the portfolio allocation deviating from the benchmark portfolio. It is measured as the difference between the actual portfolio return and the benchmark portfolio return. In Exhibit 25–28, the market timing effect is computed to be −3.70 percent. Using the attribution grid, it becomes readily apparent that the portfolio manager's decision to be overweighted in office and underweighted in apartments, as compared to the benchmark portfolio, has caused a significant reduction in the portfolio's overall return.

The property selection effect measures the impact of the properties actually owned in comparison to the benchmark portfolios. It measures the sum of the difference between the actual portfolio market segment returns and the returns of the appropriate benchmark portfolio. In Exhibit 25–28, the property selection effect is computed to be 2.90 percent. This reflects the portfolio manager's superior abil-

EXHIBIT 25–27
Performance Attribution: Market Timing and Property Selection

<table>
<tr><td rowspan="2"></td><td colspan="2" align="center">Property (security)
selection</td></tr>
<tr><td align="center">Active</td><td align="center">Passive</td></tr>
<tr><td>Market
timing Active</td><td align="center">I
$\sum W_{a,i} R_{a,i}$</td><td align="center">II
$\sum W_{a,i} R_{p,i}$</td></tr>
<tr><td>Passive</td><td align="center">III
$\sum W_{p,i} R_{a,i}$</td><td align="center">IV
$\sum W_{p,i} R_{p,i}$</td></tr>
</table>

<table>
<tr><td>Market
timing Active</td><td align="center">I
−4.05%</td><td align="center">II
−7.80%</td></tr>
<tr><td>Passive</td><td align="center">III
−1.20%</td><td align="center">IV
−4.10%</td></tr>
</table>

I–IV = *Returns to active management*
II–IV = *Returns to market timing*
III–IV = *Returns to security selection*

ity to acquire and manage office, warehouse, retail, and apartment properties and inferior ability to acquire and manage properties compared to the benchmark portfolio.

The importance of return attribution becomes apparent when comparing the overall return for both the active portfolio (−4.05 percent) and the passive (benchmark) portfolio (−4.10 percent). Without completing a return attribution grid, one would most likely conclude the portfolio manager performed at the level of the benchmark

EXHIBIT 25–28
Example—Performance Attribution: Market Timing and Property Selection

Market Segment (Property Type)	Market Index (Benchmark)	Portfolio Allocation		Property Returns		Return Types			
		Active(A)	Passive(B)	Active(C)	Passive(D)	I(A × C)	II(A × D)	III(B × C)	IV(B × D)
Office	Russell/NCREIF (office)	55%	35%	–11%	–15%	–6.05%	–8.25%	–3.85%	5.25%
Retail	Russell/NCREIF (retail)	20	25	3	6	0.60	1.20	0.75	1.50
Warehouse	Russell/NCREIF (warehouse)	20	15	6	–4	1.20	–0.80	0.90	–0.60
Apartment	Russell/NCREIF (apartment)	5	25	4	1	0.20	0.05	1.00	0.25
		100%	100%			–4.05%	–7.80%	–1.20%	–4.10%

Performance Attribution Results

Passive return (IV)	–4.10%
Effects of property selection (III–IV)	2.90
Effects of market timing (II–IV)	–3.70
Joint effects	0.85
Active return (I)	–4.05%
Effects of active management (I–IV)	0.05%

portfolio and, consequently, would fail to obtain the additional insight and benefit of understanding how the underlying investment decisions affected the portfolio's performance.

THE ROLE OF THE PORTFOLIO MANAGER

Implicit in any discussion of the real estate portfolio management process is the role of the portfolio manager. The portfolio manager provides the energy, focus, discipline, and, most importantly, the investment decisions to make the portfolio management process a reality.

Exhibit 25–29 identifies the role of the portfolio manager as one of facilitator and communicator. More specifically, at each respective step of the portfolio management process, the portfolio manager:

1. *Identifies* the investor's objectives and constraints.

EXHIBIT 25–29
Portfolio Manager's Role as Facilitator, Communicator, and Monitor

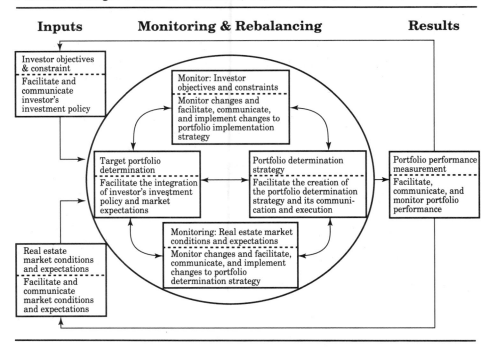

2. *Analyzes* market conditions to understand each market segment's expected return, risk, and correlations within the specified investable universe.
3. *Integrates* the investor's investment policy with market conditions and converts them into target portfolio allocation ranges.
4. *Creates* the portfolio strategy and *communicates* its goals and objectives to those responsible for its implementation.
5. *Monitors* the investor's investment objectives and constraints and market conditions, communicates these changes, and facilitates any necessary changes to the target portfolio and portfolio strategy.
6. *Measures* and *communicates* the portfolio's performance.

Moreover, the real estate investor/portfolio manager who invests in equity real estate directly, unlike the investor/portfolio manager for bonds and stocks, leads an organization and/or third-party vendors with direct management responsibilities for the properties. This requires that the portfolio manager also be an effective leader and manager. Recall Exhibit 25–7, which depicts an interactive top-down/bottom-up approach in which both approaches are interdependent. Thus, the success of the portfolio is inextricably linked to how well the portfolio manager can create a sense of mutually defined goals and esprit de corps with those responsible for implementing the real estate strategy.

CONCLUSION

This chapter attempted to show real estate portfolio management as a process, one that has individual functions (steps) that are interrelated and dynamic. The chapter began by discussing the inherent uncertainty in the market and consequent need for a disciplined portfolio management process. Then it described the industry's paradigm shift from an asset-by-asset view to a portfolio process view of investment decision making and the two market forces that act jointly to create this shift: (1) technology advances and modern portfolio theory and (2) the growth of institutional assets under a fiduciary framework.

The chapter then provided an overview of each of the six steps in the portfolio management process: (1) investor objectives and constraints, (2) real estate market conditions and expectations, (3) target portfolio determination, (4) portfolio strategy determination, (5) monitoring and rebalancing, and (6) portfolio performance measurement. Finally, the chapter discussed the role of the portfolio manager as one of communicator, implementor, monitor, and most important, investment decision maker.

As a final note, the only thing certain in the real estate market is the inevitability of change. The investor/portfolio manager thus needs to improve the chances of constructing, or repositioning, his or her real estate portfolio in anticipation of these changes. Without such a disciplined process, the investor/portfolio manager lacks the proper foundation and framework to analyze the ever-changing needs of the investor and market conditions and expectations. This chapter asserted that the best way to accomplish this is through creating, integrating, and implementing a systematic and disciplined portfolio management process.

REFERENCES

Association for Investment Management and Research. *Performance Reporting for Investment Managers: Applying the AIMR Performance Presentation Standards*. AIMR, 1991, p. 29.

Bodie, Zvi; Alex Kane, and Alan J. Marcus. *Investments*. Homewood, IL: Richard D. Irwin, 1989.

Booth, David G.; Daniel M. Cashdan, Jr.; and Richard A. Graff. "Real Estate: Hybrid of Debt and Equity." *Real Estate Review* 19 (Spring 1989), pp. 54–58.

Brinson, Gary; L. Hood; and G. Beebower. "Determinants of Portfolio Performance." *Financial Analysts Journal*, July/August 1986, pp. 38–44.

Ennis, Richard M., and Paul Burik. "The Influence of Non-Risk Factors on Real Estate Holdings of Pension Funds." *Financial Analysts Journal*, November–December 1991, pp. 44–55.

Firstenberg, Paul B.; Stephen A. Ross; and Randall C. Zisler. "Managing Real Estate Portfolios." *Real Estate Research*, November 16, 1987.

Firstenberg, Paul B., and Charles H. Wurtzebach. "Managing Portfolio Risk and Reward." *Real Estate Review* 19 (Summer 1989).

Fisher, Jeffrey; Susan Hudson-Wilson; and Charles Wurtzebach. "Equilibrium in Commercial Real Estate Markets: Linking Space and Capital Markets." *Journal of Portfolio Management*, Summer 1993, pp. 101–107.

Geltner, David Michael. "Smoothing in Appraisal-Based Returns." *Journal of Real Estate Finance and Economics* 4, no. 4 (September 1991), pp. 327–45.

Giliberto, S. Michael. *Thinking about Real Estate Risk.* New York: Salomon Brothers, Inc., May 26, 1989.

Giliberto, S. Michael. *Real Estate Risk and Return: 1991 Survey Results.* New York: Salomon Brothers, Inc., March 31, 1992.

Gold, Richard B. "Asset Allocation: The Importance of Uncertainty in Optimizing Illiquid Assets or Why the Efficient Frontier Is 'Fuzzy.'" Paper presented at the American Real Estate Society Conference, April 15, 1994.

Graff, Richard A., and Daniel M. Cashdan, Jr. "Some New Ideas in Real Estate Finance." *Journal of Applied Corporate Finance* 3 (Spring 1990), pp. 77–89.

Greig, D. Wylie, and Michael S. Young. "New Measures of Future Property Performance and Risk." *Real Estate Review* 21 (Spring 1991), pp. 17–25.

Hartzell, David; John Hekman; and Mike Miles. "Real Estate Returns and Inflation." *AREUEA Journal,* Spring 1987.

Hartzell, David; John Hekman; and Mike Miles. "Diversification Categories in Investment Real Estate." *AREUEA Journal,* Summer 1986.

Hartzell, David J.; David G. Shulman; and Charles H. Wurtzebach. "Refining the Analysis of Regional Diversification for Income-Producing Real Estate." *Journal of Real Estate Research* 2, no. 2 (Winter 1987), pp. 85–95.

Levine, Sumner N., ed. *The Financial Analyst's Handbook.* Homewood, IL: Business One Irwin, 1988.

Liang, Youguo; F. C. Neil Myer; and James R. Webb. "The Bootstrap Efficient Frontier for Mixed-Asset Portfolios." Paper presented at the American Real Estate Society Conference, April 15, 1994.

Maginn, John L., and Donald L. Tuttle, eds. *Managing Investment Portfolios: A Dynamic Process.* Boston/New York: Warren, Gorham & Lamont, 1990.

Miles, Mike, and Tom McCue. "Commercial Real Estate Returns." *AREUEA Journal,* Fall 1984.

Pagliari, Joseph L., Jr. "Inside the Real Estate Yield." *Real Estate Review* 21, no. 3 (Fall 1991), pp. 48–53.

Pagliari, Joseph L., Jr., and James R. Webb. "Past and Future Sources of Real Estate Research." *Journal of Real Estate Research* 7, no. 4 (Fall 1992), pp. 387–421.

Reilly, Frank K. *Investment Analysis and Portfolio Management.* Fort Worth, TX: The Dryden Press, 1989.

Shulman, David, and Robert E. Hopkins. *Economic Diversification in Real Estate Portfolios.* New York: Salomon Brothers Real Estate Research, November 1988.

Webb, James R., and Jack H. Rubens. "The Effect of Alternative Return Measures on Restricted Mixed-Asset Portfolios." *Journal of the American Real Estate and Urban Economics Association* 16 (Summer 1988).

White, John Robert, ed. *The Office Building from Concept to Investment Reality*. Joint Publication of the Counselors of Real Estate, the Appraisal Institute, and the Society of Industrial and Office Realtors Educational Fund, 1993.

Zisler, Randall, and Robert A. Feldman. *Real Estate Report*. New York: Goldman Sachs & Co., 1985.

CHAPTER 26

STRATEGIC ASSET ALLOCATION: A COMPARATIVE APPROACH TO THE ROLE OF REAL ESTATE IN A MIXED-ASSET PORTFOLIO

Joseph L. Pagliari, Jr.
Citadel Realty, Inc.

James R. Webb
Real Estate Research Center
James J. Nance College of Business
Cleveland State University

INTRODUCTION

Some researchers (see Brinson et al. [1986, 1991]) have suggested that a portfolio's asset allocation is the single most important determinant of the portfolio's total return and, as a corollary, that the security selection (i.e., choosing the underlying securities for each asset class) is considerably less important. At the very least, the strategies that generate these allocations are important and unavoidable.

In the context of ex ante portfolio allocations, Chapra and Ziemba (1993) suggest that generating estimates of future returns has the most significant impact on mixed-asset portfolio performance, with successively lesser impacts attributable to variances and covariances. Moreover, the nature of ex ante investment performance is largely characterized by uncertainty. Ex post performance may, at best, be only a starting point for projecting future performances of the asset classes available to the portfolio. Thus, the need for some framework that forecasts future performance, especially, returns, is critical to optimal portfolio management. Inherently, these forecasts will be subjective (i.e., will emphasize qualitative as well as quantitative aspects). In his seminal paper "Portfolio Selection," Markowitz (1952) perhaps best summarized the ambiguous nature of the forecasts needed for the selection of asset classes or securities:

> [W]e must have procedures for finding reasonable [means] and [variances]. These procedures, I believe, should combine statistical techniques and the judgment of practical men. My feeling is that the statistical computations should be used to arrive at a tentative set of [means] and [variances]. Judgment should then be used in increasing or decreasing some of these [means] and [variances] on the basis of factors or nuances not taken into account by the formal computations. (p. 91)

Interestingly, Markowitz's paper also contemplated the use of market aggregates for bonds, stocks, and real estate to maximize the portfolio's mean/variance efficiency (though he noted that care must be used when using and interpreting relationships among market aggregates).

Consequently, this chapter overviews a disciplined approach designed to estimate future returns on real estate in comparison to bonds and stocks. This approach attempts to identify and isolate the fundamental factors of the return-generating (or pricing) process. Some of these factors are known with relative certainty at the time the allocation decision is made; others are inherently uncertain. This chapter's approach is to utilize those factors with (relatively) known parameters and focus on the sensitivities of the unknown factors. This can be approached with successive generality:

• *A point estimate approach.* All but one of the parameters are assumed to be known with relative certainty. The analysis then focuses on the single value for this parameter such that the real estate offers an equal risk-adjusted return to bonds or stocks. Generally, this approach assumes that pricing multiples (capitalization rates, coupon yields, and P-E ratios) remain constant over the holding period.

• *A linear approach.* All but two of the pricing parameters are assumed to be known with relative certainty. One of the parameters applies to real estate's return-generating process and the other to bonds' or stocks' return-generating process. The analysis then focuses on the combination of values that, when plotted over the range of possibilities, forms a line with real estate offering an equal risk-adjusted return to bonds and stocks. Here too the pricing multiples are assumed to remain constant over the holding period.

• *A matrix approach.* This approach broadens the linear approach by incorporating shifts in the pricing multiples over the holding period.

While the approach still focuses on the combination values that generate equivalent risk-adjusted returns, the range of such values, when plotted over the range of possibilities, forms a three-dimensional surface or plane.

In all of these approaches, the portfolio manager is asked to compare his or her expectations for the uncertain parameter(s) against the computed value(s). The result is qualitative; no mechanistic allocation rules are generated by the use of this approach. Rather, the intention is to adjust the portfolio's weights (to and from real estate) within a range of normal policy weights. This is a dynamic strategy that can be thought of as an "active" one with reference to a static norm. In other words, this chapter's view of strategic portfolio management implies some intermediate position along the portfolio management spectrum. At one end of the spectrum is a static, buy-and-hold strategy that determines portfolio allocations infrequently. At the other end are the various dynamic strategies, which can effectively be divided into two competing approaches: (1) tactical asset allocation and (2) portfolio insurance (where tactical asset allocation can essentially be thought of as selling portfolio insurance). See Brown and Kritzman (1990), Perold and Sharpe (1988), and Sharpe (1990).

Specifically, strategic asset allocation, as discussed herein, may offer its greatest contribution in its attempt to identify major market movements. Alternatively, this version may be viewed as a "weak form" of tactical asset allocation (the "strong form" being a more aggressive market timing approach). When such movements are expected to occur, a moderate shift from the portfolio's normal weights would be indicated. However, absent a strong, reasoned expectation of such a move, investors may be best served by utilizing their static (or normal) portfolio weights. Moreover, the inclusion of real estate[1] in the mixed-asset portfolio is thought to provide investors with more efficiently diversified portfolios (than those that exclude real estate) over the long run; see Karnosky (1988) and Webb et al. (1988). This chapter discusses real estate in the context of a portfolio containing three risky assets—stocks, bonds, and real estate—along with a risk-free asset (Treasury bills). This constraint is not made to suggest

---

[1] For purposes of this chapter, *real estate* is defined to be equity investments as opposed to investments in mortgages (i.e., bonds for which the collateral is real estate).

limiting the mixed-asset portfolio to these three risky assets; rather, they represent three of the largest asset classes.

From the perspective of a portfolio manager, this chapter discusses a strategy designed to exploit relative mispricing among asset classes by tilting the portfolio to the asset(s) that appears undervalued (an approach commonly used by major money management firms for stock/cash and stock/bond/cash portfolios). Specifically, this chapter advocates using the initial yields currently offered for each of these asset classes and examining the underlying growth, inflation, and pricing assumptions that are needed to offer competitive total real returns for each asset class over the investor's time horizon. This approach is intended to augment traditional modern portfolio theory (again, see Markowitz [1952]), providing a framework for examining, on an ex ante basis, the asset inputs necessary to optimize mean/variance efficiency:

1. Likely future asset returns (by identifying the underlying components of an asset's total return).
2. Potential variance and covariance relationships of these asset returns.

In addition, the approach suggested here can be similarly used to augment a portfolio management style that involves the forecasting of multiple scenarios; for example, see Diermeier (1990). The relationships identified herein may be used to help formulate the linkages among these various scenarios.

Much research (for example, see Sharpe [1975], Jeffrey [1984], and Samuelson [1989]), has suggested that market timing (or dynamic) strategies have failed to outperform (adjusted for trading and transaction costs) a simple buy-and-hold (or static) strategy. While others (for example, see Grossman [1989] and Sy [1990]) have debated this conclusion, it is imperative that any dynamic strategy avoid excessive trading that would incur substantial transaction costs. Moreover, Ibbotson Associates (1993) dramatically notes the substantial dangers of attempting to "time" the stock market. For example, $1.00 continuously invested in common stocks at the end of 1925 would have grown to $727.38 by the end of 1992. However, had investors missed the 30 best months (representing less than 4 percent of the total number of months) over this time period, they would have experienced a gain to only $11.16, a level of return that would have been exceeded by simply investing in Treasury bills. Similar results were experienced in the 1979–92 period. At that time, $1.00 would have grown to $6.85 had it been continuously invested in the stock market. However, had investors missed the 10 best months (representing less than 7 percent of the total number of months), they would have received only $2.70, which again would have been exceeded by simply investing in Treasury bills.

Finally, the suggested use of strategic asset allocation, as discussed herein, is intended to neither override an efficiently diversified portfolio within each asset class nor avoid examining potential correlations between the asset classes within the portfolio (e.g., a real estate investment program with an emphasis on energy-dependent cities and/or energy-related tenants, combined with a high common stock exposure to energy-related corporations).

THE REQUIRED RATE OF RETURN

An investor's required rate of return (k) can be viewed as having several components:

$$k = (1 + r + \delta)(1 + \rho) - 1 \qquad (1)$$

where k = Investor's required nominal, gross return.
   r = Investor's required real, net return.
   δ = Advisory fees and transaction costs.
   ρ = Anticipated inflation rate.

It is axiomatic that any assessment of prospective returns (for any asset class) should be made in the context of (1) net returns and (2) real (inflation-adjusted) returns.

Net returns should be calculated after including an estimate of advisory fees and transaction costs (δ). In the calculations that follow, it is assumed (unless otherwise noted) that these costs are:

Asset Class	Estimated Advisory and Transaction Costs (Percentage of Investment Value)
Real estate (δ)	1.00%
Bonds (δ')	0.25
Common stocks (δ'')	0.45

(To distinguish the real estate parameters from the bond parameters, the latter will bear a "prime" symbol where and when needed. Similarly, the common stock parameters will be distinguished from the real estate and bond parameters by the use of a double prime symbol.)

Nominal returns (represented by k) are meaningful only in the context of the inflation rate. Moreover, net real returns (r) are important to those investors whose liabilities are linked (directly or indirectly) to inflation[2] and to the extent that advisory fees and transaction costs vary by asset class. For example, if real estate investors seek a net, real return of 7 percent and assume the inflation rate to be 4 percent, they will seek property investments priced to yield 12.32 percent $(k = [1 + .07 + .01] \times [1 + .04] - 1 = .1232)$.

BONDS: A THEORETICAL FRAMEWORK

In the context of this chapter, bonds consist of long-term, fixed-income securities (without equity conversion or participation features). The distinction from equities in general and real estate in particular involves the senior claim bonds[3] have against the asset(s) and their nominal-based payment streams. The nature of these income streams has important implications for comparatively assessing the future performance of real estate vis-à-vis bonds. (Again, we use a prime symbol—e.g., k', δ', etc.—to distinguish the paramters of fixed-income securities from those of real estate.)

The bondholder's return can be conceptualized as

$$P_0 = \sum_{n=1}^{N} \frac{C_n}{(1 + k')^n} + \frac{P_N}{(1 + k')^N} \qquad (2)$$

where P_0 = Today's asset price.
C_n = Periodic coupon payments.
k' = Required gross, nominal return to bondholders.
T = Maturity date of bonds.
P_N = Bond's principal value upon maturity.

---

[2] The impact of income taxes should also be considered. However, the current tax code makes no substantive distinction between ordinary income and capital gains, and income tax brackets are relatively flat. Accordingly, real estate lacks its formerly privileged tax status.

[3] For purposes of this chapter, mortgages are considered to be bonds for which the collateral happens to be real estate.

If equation (1) is used to rewrite equation (2) in a more generalized version—recognizing that the nominal, gross discount rate represents the interplay of the real required, net return (r'), advisory fees and transaction costs (δ'), and the inflation rate (ρ)—an expanded form of the bondholder's return can be expressed as follows:

$$P_0 = \sum_{n=1}^{N} \frac{C_n}{(1 + r' + \delta')^n(1 + \rho)^n} + \frac{P_N}{(1 + r' + \delta')^N (1 + \rho)^N} \quad (3)$$

Because the amount and timing of payments to bondholders is known with relative certainty, the nominal return (k), or yield to maturity, is also known with relative certainty. The primary risk for the holder of an investment grade bond is the actual inflation rate over the holding period.[4] Accordingly, a premium is built into the pricing of bonds that includes the anticipated rate of inflation and the uncertainty about the actual rate of inflation over the maturity period of the bond. Unfortunately, the relationship between the anticipated inflation rate (ρ) and the risk premium (r) is not separately observable; the capital markets indicate only the product of these figures:

$$k' = (1 + r' + \delta') (1 + \rho) - 1 \quad (1)$$

This discussion begins by first assuming constant interest rates across the investor's holding period and then drops this assumption later. In the simplistic case of constant interest rates and bonds selling at par, the general valuation bond model (equation [3]) can be simplified to

$$P_0 = \frac{CF'_0}{(1 + r' + \delta') (1 + \rho) - 1} = \frac{CF'_0}{k'} \quad (4)$$

where $CF'_0 = C_n$ = Initial cash flow.

The terms of this equation can also be restated to isolate the expected return:

$$r' = \frac{1 + CF'_0/P_0}{1 + \rho} - (1 + \delta') \quad (5)$$

---

[4] Also, if the bond's maturity extends beyond the investor's holding period, the market's perception of future inflation rates (after the holding period is ended) will also alter the bond's value.

Equation (4) also represents the valuation of bonds with an infinite maturity, sometimes known as *consul bonds,* and it is used in the following sections to simplify the mathematics of comparing bonds to real estate (though, as noted above, the simplifying assumptions supporting the use of this equation will be dropped later).

As with the general valuation bond model, the individual components of the denominator are aggregated in the capital market's pricing mechanism. In the case of constant interest rates, we can observe only that

$$k' = \frac{CF_0'}{P_0} \tag{6}$$

It is left to the portfolio manager to determine whether the capital market's estimates of future inflation (ρ) and the risk premium (r') are sufficient inducements to tilt the mixed-asset portfolio toward bonds.

REAL ESTATE INVESTMENTS:
A THEORETICAL FRAMEWORK

The value of a real estate investment can be conceptually stated as

$$P_0 = \sum_{n=1}^{N} \frac{CF_n}{(1 + k)} + \frac{P_N}{(1 + k)^N} \tag{7}$$

where CF_N = Cash flow to be received at the end of period n.
P_N = Asset price at end of holding period (N).
N = Length of investor's holding period.

In terms of strategically allocating investment funds between real estate and bonds, the framework of the dividend discount model (DDM) (see Gordon [1962]) is helpful. Subject to the assumptions noted below, equation (7) can be simplified to

$$P_0 = \frac{CF_0 \times (1 + g)}{k - g} = \frac{CF_1}{k - g} \tag{8}$$

where CF_0 = Initial cash flow.
g = Periodic growth in cash flow.

The model assumes constant growth, stable capitalization rates, and no trading costs or income taxes. More specifically, these latter constraints require that

$$CF_n = CF_0(1 + g)^n \qquad (9)$$

and that

$$\frac{CF_0}{P_0} = \frac{CF_N}{P_N} \qquad (10)$$

Obviously, the assumptions with regard to trading costs and income taxes are better suited to large, tax-exempt investors than to small, individual investors. While still employing the same simplifying assumptions, the model can be further generalized to capture the underlying elements of the growth rate.

Some analysts (see Asikoglu and Ercan [1992] and Estep et al. [1984]) suggest that growth reflects the firm's or asset's ability to increase cash flow as it compares to economywide movements in domestic prices. These approaches generally view growth as

$$g = \lambda \times \rho \qquad (11)$$

where λ = Inflation pass-through rate.
    ρ = Anticipated inflation rate.

When the inflation pass-through rate (λ) exceeds 1.0, real (i.e., inflation-adjusted) growth is expected to occur in the firm's (or asset's) earnings. When the rate equals 1.0, the firm's (or asset's) earnings will act as a perfect inflation hedge. When the rate is less than 1.0, the firm's (or asset's) real earnings will decline.

For the moment, at least, we have assumed capitalization rates are constant (this restriction is also dropped in a subsequent section). Thus, the only source of return is via increased cash flow, which also manifests itself as price appreciation given the constant pricing multiple.

To provide a more precise estimate of the parameters, the DDM, as shown in equation (8), can be expanded to incorporate equations (1) and (11) as follows:

$$P_0 = \frac{CF_0(1 + \lambda \times \rho)}{(1 + r + \delta)(1 + \rho) - (1 + \lambda \times \rho)} \qquad (12)$$

Equation (12) indicates that the value of an asset (or firm) is determined in part by its ability to generate earnings growth in relation to inflationary forces. It can also be reformulated to identify any of the six parameters (P_0, CF_0, λ, ρ, r, and δ) that it contains. If, for example, a portfolio manager wanted to identify the required return (r), equation (13) would do so:

$$r = \left(\frac{1 + \lambda \times \rho}{1 + \rho}\right) \times \left(1 + \frac{CF_0}{P_0}\right) - (1 + \delta) \tag{13}$$

Given the elements of initial yield (CF_0/P_0), inflation (ρ), and its pass-through rate (λ), the investor's required return (r) can be viewed as shown in equation (13).

In the special case of a 100 percent inflation pass-through rate ($\lambda = 1.0$), equation (13) simplifies to

$$r = \frac{CF_0}{P_0} - \delta \tag{14}$$

In this special case (equation [14]), the required real return is equal to the property's initial capitalization rate (CF_0/P_0) less the advisory and transaction fees (δ) associated with the investment. Alternatively stated, the property's required initial capitalization rate (CF_0/P_0) is equal to the required return (r) plus the advisory and transaction costs. Thus, if the property is to generate a net 6 percent real return (r) and the inflation pass-through rate is 100 percent ($\lambda \neq 1.0$), the property must be purchased at an initial capitalization rate equal to 6 percent plus the 1 percent estimate of annual advisory and transaction costs, or 7 percent in total, regardless of the expected inflation rate.

In the more typical case (equation [13]), where the inflation pass-through rate differs from 100 percent ($\lambda = 1.0$), the investor's return moves directly with changes in the inflation pass-through rate and inversely with changes in advisory and transaction costs (δ). For example, assuming a 25 percent inflation pass-through rate ($\lambda = .25$) in the context of a 4 percent annual inflation rate ($\rho = .04$), equation (12) suggests that the initial capitalization rate (CF_0/P_0) must be approximately 10.2 percent compared to the 7.0 percent discussed above.

REAL ESTATE VERSUS BONDS: A COMPARISON

By comparing the yield to maturity on investment grade bonds (k') to the initial yield on real estate (CF_0/P_0), the portfolio manager can compare a nominal yielding security to a real yielding security[5] and in this way make a first approximation of the capital market's consensus inflation expectation. However, this approach assumes that real estate offers a perfect inflation pass-through rate ($\lambda = 1.00$), that advisory fees and transaction costs are equivalent for real estate and bonds ($\delta = \delta'$), and that earnings-to-price multiples are constant (this assumption will also be relaxed later). The fact that real estate offers something other than a perfect inflation hedge ($\lambda \neq 1.0$) is well documented (see, among others, Pagliari and Webb [1992] and Wurtzebach et al. [1991]). In addition, real estate's advisory fees and transaction costs are substantially higher than those for bonds. Accordingly, the valuation equations for real estate (equation [12]) and for bonds (equation [4]) can be utilized to isolate the inflation rate (ρ), which is, of course, common to both asset classes:

$$\rho = \frac{CF_0/P_0 - r - \delta}{(1 + r + \delta) - \lambda(1 + CF_0/P_0)} = \frac{CF_0'/P_0) - r' - \delta'}{1 + r' + \delta'} \quad (15)$$

This approach more precisely incorporates the possibility that real estate's inflation pass-through rate (λ) will differ from 1 and that the advisory fees and transaction costs will vary substantially.

Before moving on to the refinements of these models, let us consider how this interplay between nominal and real returns might manifest itself in the marketplace. Available are two investments: one a long-term Treasury bond and the other a brand-new office building leased to a federal agency on a long-term, triple-net lease with full CPI escalations. In this extremely hypothetical case, the bond investor receives a nominal-based risk-free return, while the real estate investor receives a real, risk-free return.[6] The difference between the two must then equal the market's consensus view of anticipated inflation and the risk premia associated with each asset.

If we instead assume the lease is risky (i.e., the tenant is not a federal agency, the lease term is shortened, and the lease is written on a gross[7] basis), the risk premium for the real estate investor increases

---

[5] An earlier version of this argument was applied to bonds versus common stocks; see Bernstein (1983).

[6] One could argue that the real estate investor takes on additional risks, such as releasing repairs and improvements (which may be covered under the lease as a tenant expense), and so on. If, however, the lease were very long say, 40 to 50 years—these risks would be of no real economic significance. The main point is simply isolating the inflation-related risk premia.

[7] That is, the landlord (as opposed to the tenant in a net lease) is responsible for the payment of the operating expenses.

substantially. This increase in the risk premium for real estate significantly changes the observed difference between the bond's yield to maturity (k') and the real estate's capitalization rate (CF_0/P_0).

Finally, if we strip away the inflation indexation of the lease (i.e., remove the CPI escalations, move to a fixed-rate lease, and/or assume excess supply constrains the property from reaching 100 percent inflation pass-through), real estate will (or should) also be priced to reflect this lack of indexation. The pricing will take the form of a higher current return to compensate for the lack of inflation pass-through. In fact, buildings leased on a long-term, fixed-rate basis are often priced as bondlike investments.

REAL ESTATE VERSUS BONDS: A POINT ESTIMATE APPROACH

As noted previously, the key to an asset allocation strategy designed to entrepreneurially exploit market mispricing lies in the investor's ability to estimate elements of future return that may vary considerably from the market's consensus viewpoint. Isolating those components contributing to total return begins by examining the conditions under which the real estate investor's ex ante return ($r_{RE} = r$) relates to the bond investor's ex ante return ($r_B = r'$). This comparison is based on the typical assumption of $r_{RE} > r_B$, reflecting the greater risk associated with equities in general and real estate in particular.

Given the bondholder's requirement for the ex ante real net return (r') increases, the nominal return requirement (k') increases as the ex ante estimate of the inflation rate increases. As the inflation rate increases, the required inflation pass-through rate (λ) for real estate investments also increases (and vice versa), though, generally speaking, λ is more sensitive to the spread between the investment's capitalization rate (CF_0/P_0) and its gross real costs ($r + \delta$).

An example may best illustrate these points. Based on the market values at the end of 1993, the indicated initial cash flow yield (CF_0/P_0) for real estate (based on the Russell/NCREIF index) was 9.15 percent[8] and the coupon yield for long-term, fixed-rate bonds selling

---

[8] As described in Webb and Pagliari (1994).

at par (based on 30-year Treasury bonds) was 6.17 percent.[9] If bond investors expect a 2.5 percent[10] real net return, they are implicitly forecasting an inflation rate of approximately 3.3 percent. This figure was computed by rearranging the terms of equation (4) to restate inflation (as shown previously in equation [15]):

$$\rho = \frac{CF'_0/P_0 - r' + \delta'}{1 + r + \delta}$$

$$= \frac{.0617 - .025 - .0025}{1 + .025 + .0025} \tag{15}$$

$$= .0333$$

Since the economywide domestic rate of inflation must be the same for real estate as it is for bonds, this estimated rate of inflation can be substituted into the real estate equation solving for the expected inflation pass-through rate (λ). If real estate investors are expecting a 6.0 percent real net return[11] combined with an anticipated inflation rate of 3.3 percent, they are implicitly forecasting an inflation pass-through rate of approximately 38.8 percent, again assuming no change in the pricing multiple (or capitalization rate) over the holding period. This was computed by rearranging the terms of equation (12) to isolate the inflation pass-through rate (λ) parameter, as follows:

$$\lambda = \left[\frac{(1 + r + \delta)(1 + \rho)}{1 + \dfrac{CF_0}{P_0}} - 1 \right] \times \frac{1}{\rho}$$

$$= \left[\frac{(1 + .06 + .01)(1 + .0333)}{1 + .0915} - 1 \right] \times \frac{1}{.0333} \tag{16}$$

$$= .3885$$

This approach generates a single combination ($\rho = .0333$, $\lambda = .3885$) that satisfies equivalent risk-adjusted returns between real estate and

---

[9] Based on Federal Reserve annualized yields, adjusted for constant maturity, as reported in *Barron's*, December 20, 1993.

[10] Over the subperiods 1802–1990, 1871–1990, and 1926–90, the long-term U.S. government bonds generated real compounded annual returns of 3.4, 2.5, and 1.4 percent, respectively. See Siegel (1992).

[11] This approximates the net real return required by institutional real estate investors for newly acquired properties. See Giliberto (1992).

bonds. From the perspective of strategically allocating the portfolio between real estate and bonds, the question becomes: How do these implicit capital market expectations of ρ and λ compare to the expectations of the portfolio manager? If, for example, the portfolio manager believes real estate's inflation indexing ability, as measured by its inflation pass-through rate (λ), will be substantially beneath 39 percent and the inflation rate is reasonably expected to be approximately 3.3 percent, the portfolio manager should increase the portfolio's allocation to bonds at the expense of real estate.

REAL ESTATE VERSUS BONDS: A LINEAR APPROACH

A more general approach (which augments the single-point estimate approach discussed above) to strategically allocating the portfolio between real estate and bonds is to examine the spectrum of combinations that result in satisfying equivalent net real return differentials for each asset class. However, note that while these return differentials will remain equivalent, they will be higher or lower than the real net returns initially sought by the portfolio manager. Once these combinations are identified, the portfolio manager compares his or her individual perceptions of key investment parameters for each asset class to the market consensus.

This examination can be accomplished by setting equation (12), the price of real estate, equal to equation (4), the price of bonds, as shown in Appendix 26A. The key parameters of total expected return can then be compared.

From the perspective of strategic asset allocation, it is perhaps most telling to create an indifference line (or, more accurately, an indifference curve) based on the required gross risk premium of real estate versus bonds (i.e., $[r + \delta]$ versus $[r' + \delta']$) in conjunction with utilizing implied expectations about inflation (ρ)[12] and real estate's

---

[12] The derivation of ρ is shown in Appendix 26A. It was derived by using the quadratic formula, which more completely solves for two possible values of ρ:

$$\rho_1 = \frac{-b + \sqrt{b^2 - 4ac}}{2a} \text{ and } \rho_2 = \frac{-b - \sqrt{b^2 - 4ac}}{2a} \tag{17}$$

In the present context, only the former (ρ_1) has economic significance.

ability to adequately pass through (λ) these inflationary increases. Exhibit 26–1 illustrates this approach.

As the risk premium differential ($[r + \delta] - [r' + \delta']$) increases, the indifference line moves upward, though not in a parallel fashion. The spread widens as the inflation rate decreases for a given change in the risk premium differential. The indifference line, based on the net risk premium selected, indicates the combinations of points representing λ and ρ that satisfy the investor's expectation of real net returns, as shown in Exhibit 26–1.

However, if the portfolio manager strongly believes that the combination of real estate's inflation pass-through rate (λ) and the economywide inflation rate (ρ) results in a point above the indifference line, the investor should tilt the mixed-asset portfolio toward real

EXHIBIT 26–1

Real Estate versus Treasury Bonds: Portfolio-Weighting Approach Based on Expected Inflation and Real Estate's Inflation Pass-Through Rate

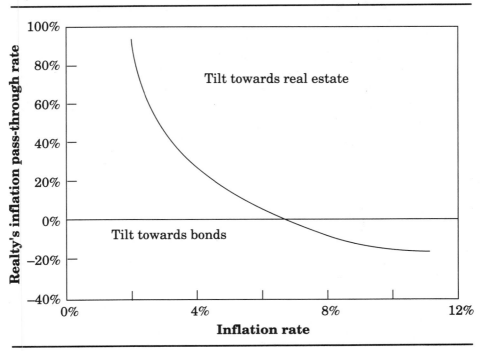

estate and away from bonds.[13] Conversely, if the combination of the investor's estimates results in a point beneath the indifference line, the portfolio should be tilted toward bonds and away from real estate.

It should be noted that much of the information needed to make the real estate/bond comparison is known at the time of the investment decision. For example, the initial yields (CF_0/P_0 and CF'_0/P_0) are known with relative certainty, as are the estimated advisory and transaction costs (δ and δ'). Less certain are the estimates of required net risk premia (r and r').

REAL ESTATE VERSUS BONDS: A HISTORICAL OVERVIEW

It is perhaps instructive to review the historical relationship between bond yields (k') and real estate's capitalization rates (CF_0/P_0). Over the period 1978 through 1993 (see Exhibit 26–2), capitalization rates for real estate (as estimated by the Russell/NCREIF index) have trended downward through most of the observed time period until recently, when they have started a significant upward trend. In addition, the path of capitalization rates tends to exhibit less volatility than bond yields. Thirty-year Treasury bonds were used in these analyses because they are noncallable and default risk is generally considered to be nonexistent. Other types of bonds would require extending the analysis to incorporate these differences.

The difference between the two lines shown in Exhibit 26–2 represents changing investor sentiment with regard to anticipated inflation (ρ), inflation uncertainty and real risk premium differences ($r - r'$), estimates of real estate's inflation pass-through rates (λ), and the differences in the advisory and transaction costs ($\delta - \delta'$).

REAL ESTATE VERSUS BONDS: A MATRIX APPROACH

The preceding models assume earnings multiples for real estate and coupon yields for bonds remain constant. However, history indicates

---

[13] This can also be accomplished by adding leveraged real estate to the portfolio, where the mortgage debt essentially represents "shorting" a portion of the bond portfolio.

EXHIBIT 26–2
Comparison of Quarterly Income Yields: Real Estate versus Bonds,
1978:1–1993:4

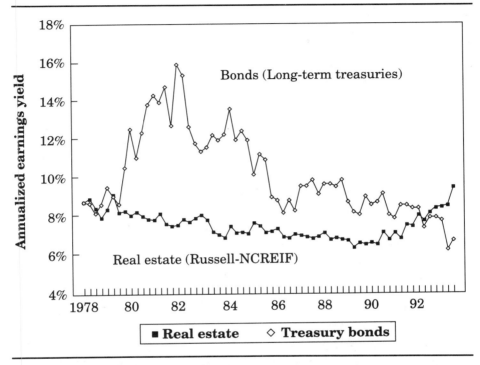

Sources: Updated from Pagliari and Webb (1992); Ibbotson Associates (1993).

(as shown in Exhibit 26–2) that these simplistic assumptions are untrue. The shifts in valuation multiples come in two forms: changing real estate capitalization rates and/or changing long-term interest rates.

The volatility of these valuation multiples suggests that an astute portfolio manager should examine the impact of changing valuation multiples. One method is to expand the linear approach to incorporate a matrix of potential shifts in valuation multiples for both real estate and fixed-income investments in which the total estimated risk-adjusted yield is equal for the two investment classes.

To incorporate shifting valuation multiples, the earlier models of constant growth must be modified. For real estate, bonds, and common stocks, this can be accomplished by modifying the earlier models to explicitly incorporate a factor that acknowledges these shifts, as follows:

$$\nabla = \frac{CF_N/P_N}{CF_0/P_0} \tag{18}$$

where ∇ = Shift in initial valuation multiple at end of holding period.

   N = Expected length of holding period.

As a simple example of the impact of shifting valuation multiples, consider a property with an initial capitalization rate (CF_0/P_0) of 8.0 percent and a constant growth rate of 4.0 percent per annum. In the case of constant capitalization rates (i.e., $\nabla = 1.00$), the property should be expected to generate an annual (nominal) return of 12.32 percent (i.e., $k = CF_0/P_0 \times [1 + g]$), regardless of the investor's holding period (N). However, if capitalization rate shifts do occur over the holding period, annual return will be influenced by two forces: (1) Changes in the annual return will vary inversely with changes in the capitalization rate shift, and (2) the impact of such shifts ($\nabla \neq 1.00$) will decline as the holding period lengthens. These forces are illustrated in Exhibit 26–3.

Exhibit 26–3 illustrates the extreme sensitivity of annual returns to capitalization rate shifts ($\nabla \neq 1.00$) when accompanied by a short holding period. For example, with a capitalization rate shift of 1.20 (and, accordingly, $CF_N/P_N = 9.6\%$) and a one-year holding period, the total return is -5.01 percent; with a two-year holding period, the return becomes 3.64 percent; with a three-year holding period, the return becomes 6.69 percent; and so on. By the 15th year, the annual return is 11.65 percent. Moreover, for all levels of capitalization rate shifts, the annual returns begin to converge substantially on 12.32 percent—the case of constant capitalization rates—as the holding period lengthens.

These capitalization rate shifts represent the manifestation of investor sentiment and, perhaps, historical performance. That is, when investors expect real estate to offer inflation pass-through rates approaching 1, they should be more inclined to accept a lower current return (CF_0/P_0). (Conversely, a lower expected inflation pass-through rate would indicate an increase in the required current return.) The expectations may, in large part, be formed by the asset class's recent

EXHIBIT 26–3
Total Annual Return Based on Capitalization Rate Shifts and Holding Periods

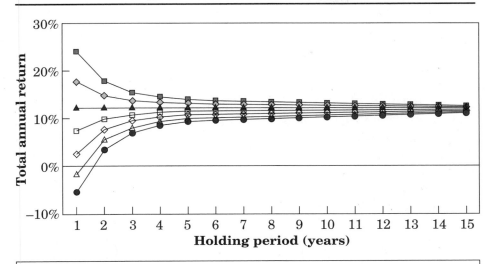

.90 cap rate shift ◇.95 cap rate shift ▲ 1.00 cap rate shift □ 1.05 cap rate shift
◇ 1.10 cap rate shift △ 1.15 cap rate shift ● 1.20 cap rate shift

performance. Obviously, a similar illustration could be prepared for shifts in the coupon yields of bonds (and in the earnings-to-price ratios of common stocks).

A separate shift factor is modeled in equation (19) for both real estate (∇) and bonds (∇'). For real estate, the modification results in

$$P_0 = \sum_{n=1}^{N} \frac{CF_0(1 + \lambda \times \rho)^n}{(1 + r + \delta)^n (1 + \rho)^n} + \frac{CF_0(1 + \lambda \times \rho)^N \div [CF_0/P_0 \times \nabla]}{(1 + r + \delta)^N (1 + \rho)^N} \qquad (19)$$

where N = Length of investor's holding period.

Equation (19) recognizes that the portfolio manager may believe it is more appropriate to forecast explicitly expected growth ($\lambda \times \rho$) in cash flow (CF_N) over his or her expected holding period and, at the conclusion of the holding period (N), estimate how the marketplace will capitalize ($CF_N/P_N = CF_0/P_0 \times \nabla$) the asset's then current income stream ($CF_N = CF_0(1 + \lambda \times \rho)^N$]. Because equation (19) still utilizes the assumption of constant growth, it can be reduced further to

$$P_0 = \frac{CF_0(1 + \lambda \times \rho)}{(1 + r + \delta)(1 + \rho) - (1 + \lambda \times \rho)} \times \left[\frac{1 - \dfrac{(1 + \lambda \times \rho)^N}{[(1 + r + \delta)(1 + \rho)]^N}}{1 - \dfrac{1}{\nabla} \times \dfrac{(1 + \lambda \times \rho)^N}{[(1 + r + \delta)(1 + \rho)]^N}} \right] \quad (20)$$

In the special case of constant capitalization rates (i.e., $\nabla = 1.0$), equation (20) can be further simplified to equation (12).[14] Mathematically, this results (when $\nabla = 1.0$) from the right-hand side of the denominator in equation (20) equaling the right-hand side of that equation's right-hand-side numerator, thereby canceling each other out. Conceptually, this results from constant capitalization rates rendering the holding period irrelevant.[15] Consequently, this set of assumptions is identical to that which produced equation (12).

Accordingly, the linear approach can be expanded to incorporate changing valuation multiples. This process begins by constructing a matrix of inflation (ρ)/inflation pass-through rate (λ) trade-offs based on varying shifts in these valuation multiples. An example of this matrix is shown in Exhibit 26–4.

By incorporating shifts in long-term interest rates as changes in the required coupon yield for bonds, the previous methodology can be utilized for capturing these shifts by rewriting equation (18) as follows:

$$\nabla' = \frac{CF_N/P_N}{CF_0'/P_0} = \frac{k_N'}{k_0'} \quad (18)$$

In the case of bonds, the shift in coupon yields (∇') may be a function of a variety of interrelated components such as changing risk premia,

---

[14] In the even more specialized case of $\nabla = \lambda = 1.0$, equation (20) can be further reduced to a version of equation (14):

$$P_0 = \frac{CF_0}{r + \delta} \quad (21)$$

[15] The combination of constant valuation multiples and growth rates (basic assumptions of the DDM) results in the present value of any future price (P_n) equaling the current price:

$$P_0 = \frac{P_n}{(1 + k)^n} \quad (22)$$

EXHIBIT 26—4

Real Estate versus Treasury Bonds: Required Shift in Bond's Coupon Rate Necessary to Generate Risk-Adjusted Price Equal to Real Estate Given Real Estate's Shift in Capitalization Rate and Inflation Pass-Through Rate

Real Estate's Shift in Capitalization Rate	Bond's Shift in Coupon Rate for Given Real Estate Inflation Pass-Through Rate								
	25.0%	37.5%	50.0%	62.5%	75.0%	87.5%	100.0%	112.5%	125.0%
0.80	0.91	0.88	0.84	0.81	0.79	0.76	0.74	0.72	0.70
0.85	0.95	0.91	0.88	0.85	0.82	0.79	0.77	0.74	0.72
0.90	0.98	0.94	0.91	0.87	0.84	0.82	0.79	0.77	0.74
0.95	1.01	0.97	0.94	0.90	0.87	0.84	0.82	0.79	0.77
1.00	1.05	1.00	0.97	0.93	0.90	0.87	0.84	0.81	0.79
1.05	1.08	1.03	0.99	0.96	0.92	0.89	0.86	0.83	0.81
1.10	1.11	1.06	1.02	0.98	0.94	0.91	0.88	0.85	0.83
1.15	1.14	1.09	1.04	1.00	0.97	0.93	0.90	0.87	0.85
1.20	1.16	1.11	1.07	1.03	0.99	0.95	0.92	0.89	0.86
1.25	1.19	1.14	1.09	1.05	1.01	0.97	0.94	0.91	0.88

changing inflationary expectations, and changing advisory and trans-action costs.[16] Notwithstanding the reason(s) for the shift (∇') in coupon yields, equation (3) can be modified to reflect potential shifts in coupon yields as follows:

$$P_0 = \sum_{n=1}^{N} \frac{CF'_0}{[(1 + r' + \delta')(1 + \rho)]^n} + \frac{CF'_0 \times P_0/CF'_0 \times \frac{1}{\nabla'}}{[(1 + r' + \delta')(1 + \rho)]^N} \quad (23)$$

As with equation (19), equation (23) can be simplified to

$$P_0 = \frac{CF'_0}{(1 + r' + \delta')(1 + \rho) - 1} \times \left[\frac{1 - \frac{1}{[(1 + r' + \delta')(1 + \rho)]^N}}{1 - \frac{1}{\nabla'} \times \frac{1}{[(1 + r' + \delta')(1 + \rho)]^N}} \right] \quad (24)$$

This approach to shifting coupon yields implicitly assumes the investor has invested in perpetual (or consul) bonds. For bonds with distant maturities (say, greater than 20 years), this assumption will normally result in a *de minimis* variation in computed reversionary price (P_N). For bond investors with shorter maturities, such reversionary prices may need to undergo additional adjustments.[17]

A three-dimensional depiction of the interplay between real estate's inflation pass-through rate (λ) and shifting valuation multiples between real estate and bonds (∇, ∇') is generated to overcome the sometimes stifling (depending on length of holding period and magnitude of the shift in pricing multiples) assumption of constant capitalization and coupon rates. This interplay is captured in Exhibit 26–5. The result is an indifference plane or surface. If the portfolio manager believes the ex ante coordinates of real estate's pass-through rate (λ)

---

[16] If applicable, changes can be incorporated into real net risk premia to compensate for the seemingly increasing frequency with which the tax laws are changed.

[17] When a shorter maturity is anticipated, equation (24) must be modified as follows:

$$P_0 = \sum_{n=1}^{N} \frac{CF'_0}{[(1 + r' + \delta')(1 + \rho)]^n} + \sum_{t=N+1}^{T} \frac{CF'_0}{[(1 + r'_t + \delta'_t)(1 + \rho_t)]^t} \quad (25)$$

$$+ \frac{P_T}{[(1 + r'_T + \delta'_T)(1 + \rho_T)]^T}$$

where t = Period(s) following investor's holding period (N).

EXHIBIT 26–5
Real Estate versus Treasury Bonds: Portfolio-Weighting Approach Based on Shifts in Pricing Multiples and Real Estate's Inflation Pass-Through Rate

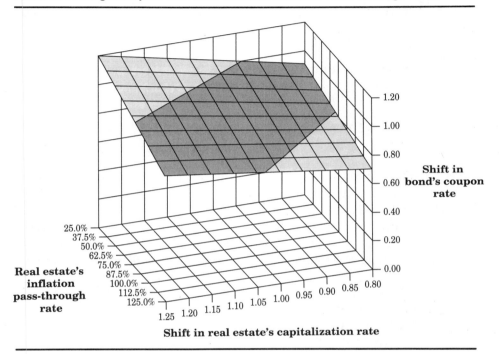

and valuation shifts (∇, ∇') result in a point above the plane, the mixed-asset portfolio should be tilted toward real estate and away from bonds. Conversely, if the coordinates result in a point beneath the plane, the portfolio should be tilted toward bonds and away from real estate.

However, two notes should be made.

Holding Period Dependency.   These matrix analyses are sensitive to the length of the investor's holding period (see Exhibit 26–3). As the holding period lengthens, the impact of changing valuation multiples diminshes substantially, and vice versa. The result is a flattening of the "indifference" plane as the holding period lengthens. Accordingly, those investors with long-term orientations should avoid fixating on yield rate shifts, unless they believe such rates are about to undergo a substantial cyclical or secular change.

Net Risk Premium: Real Estate versus Bonds. For purposes of these analyses, the gross risk premium of real estate vis-à-vis bonds equaled a spread of:

$$
\begin{aligned}
\text{Risk premium differential} &= (r + \delta) - (r' + \delta') \\
&= (.06 + .01) - (.025 + .0025) \qquad (26) \\
&= .0425
\end{aligned}
$$

There is nothing to support this spread as reflecting prior or future ex ante spreads.

When market signals are at odds with the portfolio manager's reasoned views of future returns, a tilting of the portfolio toward the favored asset class(es) is advised. Accordingly, when market-based valuation multiples result in pricing an asset class too high, some profit taking in this asset is probably warranted. However, a full-scale liquidation of any asset class is rarely justified.

COMMON STOCK INVESTMENTS: A THEORETICAL FRAMEWORK

Common stock investments require an expansion of the DDM to recognize the ability of corporations to reinvest a portion of their earnings (or issue new debt and/or stock) in new assets. Whether or not the return on these assets exceeds the firm's cost of capital determines the prudence of this reinvestment activity.

Growth via Reinvested Earnings

In the context of a firm, Babcock (1970), Durand (1989), and Miller and Modigliani (1961), among others, have suggested that the only sustainable and meaningful source of growth is through reinvesting a portion of the firm's income in assets that generate a rate of return exceeding the firm's cost of capital. The firm's ability to earn a rate of return (k^*) on its reinvested earnings that exceeds its cost of capital (k'') will translate into earnings that will generate a premium price for the equity holders. These approaches (see Miller and Modigliani [1961]) can essentially be generalized as[18]

$$P_0 = \sum_{n=1}^{N} \frac{\overline{CF}_0}{(1 + k'')^n} + \sum_{n=1}^{N} \frac{k^* - k''}{k''} \times b \times \overline{CF}_0 \times \frac{(1 + b \times k^*)^{n-1}}{(1 + k'')^n} \quad (28)$$

where $\overline{CF}_0$ = Uniform perpetuity of earnings based on inital asset base.

b = Firm's reinvestment rate.

k^* = Firm's net, nominal return on invested assets.

In the case of constant growth rates, as represented by $b \times k^*$, and either an infinite holding period or constant E-P ratios, equation (28) can be simplified to the following:

$$P_0 = \frac{\overline{CF}_0 (1 - b)}{k'' - b \times k^*} \quad (29)$$

The right-hand-side denominator of this model indicates that the firm will grow based on earnings that are retained (b) for reinvestment at a rate of return equal to k^*. Further, it is assumed transaction and advisory costs, if any, have already reduced the firm's return (k^*) on reinvested assets.

This approach to valuation assumes a "uniform perpetuity" (or annuity), which has been defined as $\overline{CF}_0$. This assumption is not restrictive in the context of investor certainty, "since it is always possible by means of a simple, present-value calculation to find an equivalent perpetuity for any project, whatever the time shape of its actual returns" (Miller and Modigliani [1961]). Notwithstanding the rigidity of "perfect certainty," subsequent sections will utilize this conversion process.

---

[18] Using the notation described herein, Miller and Modigliani (1961) derived equation (4) from the following:

$$P_0 = \sum_{n=1}^{\infty} \frac{\overline{CF}_0}{(1 + k'')^n} + b \times \overline{CF}_0 \left(\frac{k^* - k''}{k''} \right) \sum_{n=1}^{\infty} \frac{(1 + b \times k^*)^{n-1}}{(1 + k'')^n} \quad (27)$$

This equation assumes the firm has a "uniform perpetual" earnings stream ($\overline{CF}_0$) and elects to reinvest a constant percentage (b) of its total earnings in assets that yield a return (k^*) beginning in the period following investment. All such earnings are discounted at the firm's cost of capital (k'').

Cash Flow versus Earnings

While real estate analysts most typically talk about cash flow, common stock analysts most typically talk about earnings. In fact, both terms should describe the same economic production. In either case, "the earnings figure should be interpreted as the maximum amount of money the firm could pay out each year in perpetuity without deleting its productive capacity. For this reason, the net earnings number may be quite different from the accounting earnings figure that the firm reports in its financial statements" (Bodie et al., 1992). Accordingly, for real estate it is important that all of the "friction" costs (tenant improvements, leasing commissions, "free" rent, etc.) be accurately amortized to determine net operating income (CF_n).

APPLYING VERSIONS OF THE VALUATION MODELS

So far, this chapter has identified two generalized equity valuation models (equations [8] and [29]) and has embellished on some of the components (see equations [1] and [11]) found in these models. These models provide a theoretical framework for comparing the relative attractiveness of one asset class to another (e.g., real estate to common stocks). Whereas real estate represents an investment in a single (albeit long-lived) asset, the DDM (see equation [8]) best captures the essence of real estate investments. Whereas common stock ownership represents an equity claim against (what is hoped to be, at least) an ever-evolving amalgamation of assets, the Miller and Modigliani model, or the MMM (see equation [29]), best captures the essence of common stock investments. An example perhaps best clarifies this distinction. Consider an R&D/office facility fully leased to ABC Co. (a member of the Fortune 500), its sole tenant, versus an ownership interest in ABC's stock. The real estate investor owns a single building that will, over time, decline in productivity (as wear and tear, obsolence, and other factors conspire to limit the building's useful life). Upon the expiration of the initial lease, subsequent lessors (ABC or otherwise) will incorporate this decline into their rental rate negotiations. Eventually, the value of the building will revert to the underlying land value (less demolition costs).[19] Conversely, the shareholders of ABC Co. have presumably invested in a corporation committed to carefully and continuously introducing new products to the marketplace. While each of these products (e.g., computers) may have a useful life considerably shorter than that of the R&D/office building, the corporation is expected to prolong its economic life by the continued generation and amalgamation of many shorter-lived assets. The corporation has to continually reinvest some portion of its profits to create these new products.

Accordingly, the return on real estate assets can best be modeled using the DDM, in which returns are considered in the context of (and in relation to) inflation ($\lambda \times \rho$) and it is implicitly assumed that the asset's (or firm's) reinvestment rate (b) is zero. Note that this is exclusive of normal reinvestment in building upgrades and improvements. Conversely, the return on common stocks can best be modeled using the MMM, in which returns are considered in the context of management's ability to reinvest earnings (b) and the rate of return (k^*) earned on these investments.

To provide more precise estimates of the parameters, the MMM is restated after having incorporated equation (1) into equation (29) as follows:

$$P_0 = \frac{\overline{CF}_0\,(1 - b)}{[(1 + r'' + \delta'')(1 + \rho) - 1] - b[(1 + r^*)(1 + \rho) - 1]} \quad (30)$$

where r^* = Firm's net, real return on reinvested assets.

With a little manipulation, equation (30) can be simplified to

$$P_0 = \frac{\overline{CF}_0\,(1 - b)}{(r'' + \delta'' - br^*)(1 + \rho) + \rho(1 - b)} \quad (31)$$

The MMM explicitly recognizes that firms can choose to reinvest a portion (b) of their earnings, and such firms should expect to earn a net rate of return (r^*) on these assets that exceeds their real cost of capital ($r'' + \delta''$). Among other assumptions, the MMM assumes earnings are a uniform perpetuity and the present value equivalent of a growing earnings stream ($CF_n = CF_0\,[1 + g]^n$) can be converted

---

[19] For newer properties with long useful lives, the present value of any of the property's reversion to its underlying land value upon the expiration of the improvement's useful life is negligible.

to a pseudo-annuity $(\overline{CF}_0)$ for purposes of the valuation formula (equation [29]), which is the MMM.

The conversion of a nonannuity cash flow to a pseudo-annuity $(\overline{CF}_0)$ is quite simple. It is based on the premise that the price (P_0) under the constant growth model (using equation [12]) must be equal to the price $(\overline{P}_0)$ of earnings where represented by a uniform annuity in perpetuity. In this case (where $g = \lambda \times \rho = 0$), the DDM can be restated as follows:

$$\overline{P}_0 = \frac{\overline{CF}_0}{k''} = \frac{\overline{CF}_0}{(1 + r'' + \delta'')(1 + \rho) - 1} \qquad (32)$$

where $\overline{P}_0 = $ Initial price based on perpetual annuity.

The conversion to a pseudo-annuity $(\overline{CF}_0)$ simply makes use of the fact that some perpetual annuity can be found such that the initial price is identical under either the constant growth model (equation [12]) or the no-growth model (equation [32]). In other words, $P_0 = \overline{P}_0$. Given this verity (again, under the conditions of riskless cash flow), conversion to a pseudo-annuity is simply a matter of multiplying the price (P_0) computed under the constant growth model by the discount rate (k''):

$$\overline{CF}_0 = P_0 \times k'' = P_0 \times [(1 + r'' + \delta'')(1 + \rho) - 1] \qquad (33)$$

An example of this conversion process and the impact of various inflation pass-through rates (λ'') will illustrate the point. Assume $CF_0'' = \$7.45$, $\rho = 4.0\%$, $r'' = 7.0\%$, and $\delta'' = 0.45\%$. Then the calculated values of P_0'' from (equation [33]) for various levels of inflation pass-through rates are as follows:

Assumed λ''	Calculated P_0''	Pseudo earnings $(\overline{CF}_0)$
1.5	$137.39	$16.14
1.0	100.00	11.75
0.5	77.95	9.16
0.0	$63.42	$7.45

In this way, the pseudo-earnings $(\overline{CF}_0)$ can be incorporated into the MMM without violating the assumption of a uniform perpetuity, while at the same time focusing on real (i.e., inflation-adjusted) results.

In the special case of a 0 percent inflation pass-through rate ($\lambda'' = 0.0$), expected earnings (CF_n''') and the pseudo-earnings ($\overline{CF}_0$) are identical. This could also occur if the inflation rate were 0 percent ($\rho = 0.0$).[20]

While inflation pass-through rates can vary significantly by industry and across time (see Asikoglu and Ercan [1992]), the historical growth in dividends relative to the inflation rate for the companies comprising the S&P 500 has, on average, been in excess of 100 percent, as shown later in this chapter. Consequently, in most of the common stock examples that follow, it is assumed the inflation pass-through rate is 1. In those cases where the inflation pass-through rate is 100 percent ($\lambda'' = 1.0$), the constant growth income stream (CF_n''') can be translated into a pseudo-annuity ($\overline{CF}_0$) via the following conversion:

$$\overline{CF}_0 = CF_0''' \left(1 + \rho + \frac{\rho}{r'' + \delta''} \right) \tag{37}$$

Equation (37), which assumes a 100 percent inflation pass-through rate ($\lambda'' = 1.0$), will be used in subsequent numerical examples.

As with the firm's initial earnings (CF_0''') and its conversion to a pseudo-annuity ($\overline{CF}_0$), the return (r^*) on reinvested assets is a function of (1) the asset's initial yield and (2) its inflation pass-through rate (λ^*). Given these factors, the firm's real, net return (r^*) on reinvested assets can be determined.

---

[20] A potential problem with this approach is that the impact of the inflation pass-through rate is negated when the inflation rate is exactly equal to zero. A solution is to treat the growth rate and its components in an exponential fashion:

$$e^{gt} = e^{it} \times e^{\lambda t} \tag{34}$$

where e^{gt} = Exponential growth rate of CF_n over t periods.
   i = Growth rate of inflation.
   λ = Inflation pass-through rate.

The use of continuous compounding for growth rates would, for purposes of consistency, require that the valuation paradigm for the case of constant growth ($g_1 = g_2 = \ldots = g_n$) and constant capitalization rates ($V = 1.00$) be revised accordingly:

$$P_0 = \int_{t=0}^{\infty} CF_0 \times e^{gt} \times e^{-kt} \tag{35}$$

$$P_0 = \int_{t=0}^{\infty} CF_0 \times e^{(g-k)t} \tag{36}$$

Other variations of the standard valuation paradigm would be adjusted similarly.

From the standpoint of comparatively forecasting asset returns, equation (31) can be reformulated to identify any of the parameters (P_0, CF_0, b, r'', r^*, and δ'') it contains. As an example, assume a corporation's pseudo-annuity ($\overline{CF}_0$) relative to its price is 8.0 percent and reasonable parameters for those variables known with relative certainty include the following: The reinvestment rate (b) is 40 percent, the inflation rate (ρ) is 4.0 percent, the advisory fees and transaction cost (δ'') are 0.45 percent, and the corporation can earn a net, real rate of return (r^*) on its reinvested assets of 8.0 percent. Then shareholders could project their net, real return (r'') by restating equation (32) as follows:

$$r'' = \left[\frac{\overline{CF}_0}{P_0} - \rho\right] \times \left[\frac{1-b}{1+\rho}\right] + br^* - \delta''$$

$$= [.08 - .04] \times \left[\frac{1 - .4}{1 + .04}\right] + .4(.08) - .0045 \qquad (38)$$

$$= .0506$$

Given these assumptions, the shareholders are expected to receive a net, real return of approximately 5.1 percent. Alternatively, the gross, nominal return would be approximately 9.7 percent (i.e., $k = [1 + .0506 + .0045] [1 + .04] - 1$). Let's assume the shareholders instead seek a 6.0 percent net, real return (r''). Again, by restating equation (32), shareholders can determine (using equation [39]) the minimum rate of return (r^*) that the reinvested assets must earn to achieve this 6.0 percent return:

$$r^* = \left[\rho - \frac{\overline{CF}_0}{P_0}\right] \times \left[\frac{1-b}{(1+\rho)b}\right] + \frac{r'' + \delta''}{b}$$

$$= [.04 - .08] \times \left[\frac{1 - .4}{(1 + .04)(.4)}\right] + \frac{.06 + .0045}{.4} \qquad (39)$$

$$= .1036$$

Consequently, the corporation must earn a net, real rate of return (r^*) of approximately 10.4 percent on its invested assets to deliver the 6.0 percent real return to its shareholders.

More generally, given adjusted initial earnings ($\overline{CF}_0$) and an investor's required return (r''), the price (P_0) moves directly with changes in the firm's reinvestment rate (r^*) and inversely with changes in advisory and transaction costs (δ''). In those instances where management invests in assets earning less than its real cost of capital (r)—that is, $r^* < (r'' + \delta'')$—management's activities increasingly detract from the value of the firm as the reinvestment rate (b) increases.

REAL ESTATE VERSUS COMMON STOCKS: A POINT ESTIMATE APPROACH

The important components of an asset's total return can now be identified. In the present case, real estate versus stocks, the problem involves isolating those components contributing to return. This involves comparing the real estate investor's ex ante return $(r_{RE} = r)$ to the common stock investor's ex ante return $(r_{CS} = r'')$. As noted previously, the key to an asset allocation strategy designed to exploit market mispricing lies in the investor's ability to estimate accurately elements of future returns that may vary considerably from the market's consensus viewpoint.

Both the DDM and the MMM stipulate six parameters. For the DDM, they are P_0, CF_0, λ, ρ, r, and δ. For the MMM, they are P_0'', CF_0'', b, r'', r^*, and δ''. If the expected price on real estate (using the DDM) is set equal to the expected price on common stocks (using the MMM), most of the variables are known with relative certainty at the time the investment decision is made. For both assets, the initial pricing $(CF_0/P_0$ and $\overline{CF}_0/P_0)$ is known, as are the advisory and transaction costs $(\delta$ and $\delta'')$. Similarly, the portfolio manager often knows the magnitude of the real net returns $(r$ and $r'')$ sought by the portfolio. For corporations, the reinvestment rate (b) is usually known and historically has been fairly constant. Obviously, the economy's inflation rate (ρ) is identical for both assets. This leaves only the inflation pass-through rate (λ) as unknown in the DDM and the firm's net real return on invested capital (r^*) as unknown in the MMM.

By assuming values for all other parameters in either valuation model, the unspecified parameter can be identified. For the reasons stated above, it seems that examining the required levels (to meet the required return) for the inflation pass-through rate (λ) in the DDM and the return on reinvested assets (r^*) in the MMM would be most insightful with regard to strategically allocating the portfolio mix.

Perhaps examples will best illustrate this point. Based on the market values at the end of 1993, the indicated initial cash flow yield

(CF_0/P_0) for real estate (based on the Russell/NCREIF index) was 9.15 percent[21] and the dividend yield was 2.72 percent[22] ($CF_0/P_0[1 - b]$), with a reinvestment rate (b) of 37.9 percent for common stocks (based on the S&P 500). Earlier we demonstrated that if real estate investors are seeking a 6.0 percent real net return, the required inflation pass-through rate is 38.8 percent ($\lambda = .3885$).

If common stock investors are also seeking a 6.0 percent real net return[23] (and assuming a constant reinvestment rate of 37.9 percent, along with a 100 percent inflation pass-through rate), they are implicitly forecasting that management can generate real reinvestment returns (r^*) of approximately 11.5 percent. To do so requires three steps: First, remove the reinvestment portion from the dividend yield:

$$.0272 = \frac{CF_0''}{P_0}(1 - b)$$

$$= \frac{CF_0''}{100}(1 - .379) \tag{33}$$

$$CF_0 = \$4.38$$

Second, convert the (assumed) constant growth yield (CF_0''/P_0) to a pseudo-annuity yield ($\overline{CF}_0/P_0$) (again, based on the assumption that $\lambda'' = 1.0$) using equation (37):

$$\overline{CF}_0 = CF_0''\left(1 + \rho + \frac{\rho}{r'' + \delta''}\right)$$

$$= 4.38\left(1 + .0333 + \frac{.0333}{.06 + .0045}\right) \tag{37}$$

$$= \$6.79$$

Third, using equation (39), solve the MMM in terms of the firm's required reinvestment return:

$$r^* = \left[\rho - \frac{\overline{CF}_0}{P_0}\right]\left[\frac{1 - b}{(1 + \rho)b}\right] + \frac{r'' + \delta''}{b}$$

---

[21] See Webb and Pagliari (1994).

[22] See *Barron's* Market Laboratory, December 20, 1993.

[23] This approximates the long-term real return provided by the New York Stock Exchange, which was relatively stable over the subperiods 1802–70, 1871–1925, and 1926–90. The real compounded annual returns on equity were 5.7, 6.6, and 6.4 percent, respectively. See Siegel (1992).

$$= \left[.0333 - \frac{6.79}{100} \right] \left[\frac{1 - .379}{(1 + .0333).379} \right] + \frac{.06 + .0045}{.379} \quad (39)$$

$$= .1154$$

As computed previously, the inflation (ρ) is assumed to equal 3.33 percent. Accordingly, the required nominal rate of net return (k^*) on invested assets can be computed: $k^* = 15.2\%$ (i.e., $k^* = [1 + r^*]$ $[1 + \rho] - 1$).

This combination of isolated parameters $(\lambda = .3885$ and $r^* = .1154)$ represents the only combination of these two parameters that generates equivalent risk-adjusted returns to real estate and common stocks. Nevertheless, from the perspective of strategically allocating the portfolio between real estate and common stocks, the question becomes: How do these implicit capital market expectations of λ and r^* (or k^*) compare with the expectations of the portfolio manager? If, for example, the portfolio manager believes real estate's inflation indexing ability, as measured by its inflation pass-through rate (λ), is to be substantially beneath 40 percent and corporate firms are likely to generate a real (net) rate of return in excess of 11.5 percent, the portfolio manager should increase the portfolio's allocation to common stocks at the expense of real estate.

Several caveats should be made with regard to this presentation.

Inflation Pass-Through Rates. While the estimate of the requisite inflation pass-through rate (λ) may change only slightly for large increases in the anticipated inflation rate (ρ),[24] it is important to keep in mind that the pass-through rates depend on the level of inflation in at least three ways: (1) whether the user market for the asset's (or firm's) goods and services is in or out of balance (a market operating in equilibrium is more likely to reach a 100 percent inflation pass-through rate), (2) the existence of fixed-payment contracts, and/ or (3) the property's rate of obsolescence or decay. While the middle case is more prevalent with real estate, it is often true, to varying degrees, of capital-intensive companies contracting for future delivery of goods and services (e.g., certain manufacturers and financial intermediaries).

---

[24] For example, a 100 percent increase in the assumed inflation rate—from 4 to 8 percent—results in less than a 2 percent increase in the required inflation pass-through rate for the first numerical example shown in this section.

The Petersburg Paradox. When growth rates ($\lambda \times \rho$ in the case of real estate or $b \times k^*$ in the case of common stocks) approach or exceed the cost of capital (k), nonsensical prices can appear. This situation is most often related to growth companies and is sometimes referred to as the *Petersburg paradox*. See Durand (1957).

As an example, consider the variation in price (P_0) when computed by using the MMM under three slightly different sets of assumptions:

	Assumption		
Parameter	1	2	3
$\overline{CF_0}$	$ 5.00	$ 5.00	$ 5.00
b	.80	.85	.90
k	.07	.07	.07
k^*	.08	.08	.08
Computed P_0	$233.33	$525.00	$-$350.00

With small adjustments in the assumed reinvestment rate (e.g., from 80 to 85 percent and 85 to 90 percent) and holding all other parameters constant, the price (P_0) can fluctuate widely. Extremely high reinvestment rates (b) and rates of return (k^*) on such investments are associated with growth companies, which in turn makes the valuation of these firms more problematic. Accordingly, the use of these models is better suited to market aggregates than to specific growth companies (or industries). If these models are applied to growth companies (or industries), it is better to estimate a finite period of extraordinary growth in a multistage model. See Durand (1957) and Miller and Modigliani (1961).

Equivalent Total Returns. The preceding analyses explicitly assumed real estate and stock investments are expected to yield equivalent, real net returns. This, however, need not be true. Adjustments can and should be made where varying risk premia are warranted.

REAL ESTATE VERSUS COMMON STOCKS: A LINEAR APPROACH

The preceding approach isolates a single point (i.e., the combination of λ = .3885 and r^* = .1154) that offers equivalent risk-adjusted real net returns for real estate and common stocks. Another approach to isolating the implied returns of real estate vis-à-vis common stocks is to examine the spectrum of combinations that result in both asset classes generating equivalent risk-adjusted real net returns. Again, while these returns will be equivalent, they will be higher or lower than the real net returns initially sought by the portfolio manager. Once these combinations are identified, the portfolio manager compares his or her individual perceptions of future growth for each class in relationship to the market's consensus viewpoint.

This examination can be accompanied by setting the DDM and MMM (i.e., equations [12] and [29]) equal to each other and rearranging the terms of each model. Thus, the key parameters of total expected return can be comparatively set forth as

$$r_{RE} = r_{CS} \qquad (40)$$

Setting equations (12) and (29) equal to each other results in reformulated equations in which either real estate's inflation pass-through rate (λ) or common stock's reinvestment return (r^*) can be isolated. (See Appendix 26B for the calculations supporting this linear approach.) When this risk-adjusted equality is achieved, real estate will provide a real, net return (r) identical to that provided by common stocks (r''). In other words, this equality will hold for a variety of assumed real estate and common stock parameters. This collection of points can be translated into an "indifference line" as shown in Exhibit 26–6. This graph indicates that for the combination of points lying along the indifference line, real estate and common stock investors will realize identical real, net returns. However, if the portfolio manager strongly believes the combination of real estate's inflation pass-through rate (λ) and common stock's reinvestment rate of return (r^*) results in a point above the indifference line, the investor should tilt the mixed-asset portfolio toward common stocks and away from real estate. Conversely, if the combination of the manager's estimates results in a point beneath the indifference line, the investor

EXHIBIT 26–6

Real Estate versus Common Stocks: Portfolio-Weighting Approach Based on Real Estate's Expected Inflation Pass-Through Rate and Stock's Net, Real Reinvestment Return

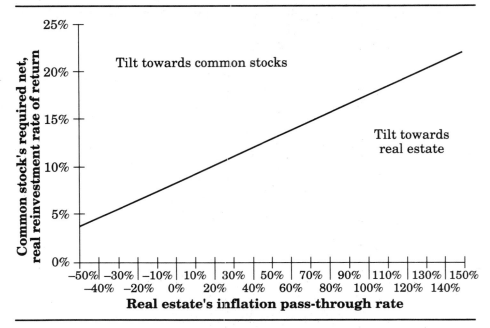

should tilt the portfolio toward real estate and away from common stocks.

For example, if a portfolio manager believes real estate's future inflation pass-through rate (λ) is to average 50 percent over a predetermined holding period and the real, net reinvestment return from common stocks (r^*) is to average 5 percent over the same holding period, this combination would place the portfolio manager with a point as determined by the coordinates (.5, .05) significantly beneath the indifference line. Consequently, the portfolio manager should increase the portfolio's strategic allocation (relative to some static norm) to real estate at the expense of the common stock allocation (i.e., sell common stock and buy real estate).

As noted above, only one point along the indifference line satisfies the investor's real net return requirements. It is given by the coordinates $\lambda = .3885$ and $r^* = .1154$. Points along the indifference line that lie above this single point will generate greater returns, while points beneath will generate lesser returns. If substantially lower returns are forecasted by the portfolio manager's estimates of future growth (λ and r^*) for both asset classes, caution should be exercised in the allocation of funds to either class.

REAL ESTATE VERSUS EQUITY REITs

The preceding discussion (as well as those that follow this section) examines real estate in terms of unleveraged, single assets held in an unsecuritized format. As such, the Russell/NCREIF index might well represent the institutional performance of this asset class.

The nature of equity real estate investment trusts (REITs) differs from that described earlier. Equity REITs generally consist of a leveraged portfolio of real properties held in a securitized format, with management having discretion over reinvestment policies (b) and the rates of return (r^*) these invested assets earn. Therefore, equity REITs may be better modeled using the MMM.

Throughout this chapter, real estate is used in the context of the unleveraged, unsecuritized, single-asset format. Though this chapter will not endeavor to do so, any extension to equity REITs would begin with these asset returns (calculated using the DDM) and then incorporate the impacts of financial leverage (see Chapter 15), volatility attributable to securitized instruments, and the "management" premium (if any, attributable to the interplay of b and r^* vis-à-vis r) highlighted in the MMM.

REAL ESTATE VERSUS COMMON STOCKS: AN HISTORICAL OVERVIEW

Given that expectations of future growth play a large role in any strategic asset allocation approach, it may be helpful to review the historical behavior of real estate and common stocks. Since real estate and common stocks are both equity interests, they represent residual claims on earnings and offer the possibility of indexing their returns to inflation. However, the historical performances of both asset classes relative to inflation have been mixed. Moreover, the ability of the underlying income streams to pass through inflationary increases is often clouded by changing earnings multiples, which in turn affect total returns.

Real Estate's Recent Experience

For example, throughout much of the early 1980s, real estate was widely touted as an inflation hedge (see Wurtzebach et al. [1991]). This was corroborated by comparing real estate's total return to the inflation rate. However, further inspection has revealed that much of real estate's total return was generated by falling capitalization rates (or increasing price-earnings multiples); see Pagliari and Webb (1992). For the three-year periods ending in 1980, 1983, and 1986, compare these sources of annualized returns (for the Russell/NCREIF index) to the annual inflation rate:

	1978–80	1981–84	1985–86	1987–89
Current yield (CF_1/P_0)	8.66%	7.71%	6.80%	6.92%
Growth in earnings ($\lambda \times \rho$)	4.87	1.47	1.51	−2.06
Change in pricing multiples	3.35	3.03	0.73	1.03
Total return	16.18%	12.22%	9.04%	5.89%
Inflation rate (ρ)	11.11%	5.40%	2.91%	4.42%
Inflation pass-through rate (λ)	43.88%	27.31%	51.88%	−46.64%

Source: Pagliari and Webb (1992).

It is evident that real estate's income failed (as measured by the inflation pass-through rate) to fully keep pace with inflation, since the inflation pass-through rate averaged only 41 percent over the nine-year period ended in 1986. As the decade concluded, the inflation pass-through rate worsened. While the overbuilding of the 1980s was (and is) largely responsible for the real (i.e., inflation-adjusted) declines in net income, the central point is to avoid focusing solely on total returns, which may obscure the underlying ability of the asset to act as an inflation hedge. No asset can permanently rely on decreasing capitalization rates as a source of total return in the face of earnings that fail to keep pace with inflation. Accordingly, the inflation-hedging effectiveness of the income stream is the key component in the assessment of an asset's long-term inflation-hedging effectiveness.

Common Stock's Recent Experience

In many ways, the stock market has experienced the converse of the real estate market experience. Consider the growth of dividends compared to inflation (see Exhibit 26–7). In this context, the underlying income streams were fairly closely correlated with inflation (see Exhibit 26–8). Yet falling price-to-earnings multiples (or increasing capitalization rates in the parlance of the real estate practitioner) in the 1970s led to declining total rates of return (see Malkiel [1990]). This led some analysts to conclude that common stocks are poor inflation hedges (for example, see Modigliani and Cohn [1979]). How-

EXHIBIT 26–7
Growth Comparison of S&P 500's Dividend to Inflation, 1926–90

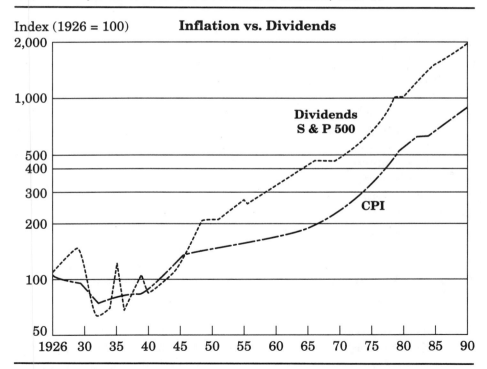

Source: Malkiel (1990), p. 319.

EXHIBIT 26–8
P-E Multiples for the S&P 500, 1959–91

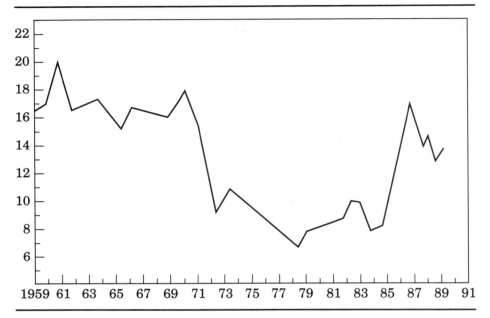

Source: Malkiel (1990), p. 320.

ever, this need not be the case. To wit, much of the bull market of the 1980s resulted from the cyclical nature of price-earnings ratios, which plummeted from their highs in the 1960s to their lows in the 1970s and back to their highs in the 1980s (again see Malkiel [1990]).

As noted previously, the importance of examining underlying earnings growth and the relationship of the current E-P multiple (or capitalization rate) to historical norms must be stressed.

REAL ESTATE VERSUS COMMON STOCKS: A MATRIX APPROACH

The preceding models assume an infinite holding period. Clearly, this is not the case for all portfolios (and certainly not for portfolio managers). Thus, earnings multiples for real estate and common stocks at the end of some expected holding period must be estimated. History suggests that a simplistic assumption about stagnant earnings multiples is untrue. Exhibit 26–9 displays the indicated capitalization rates for the properties comprising the Russell/NCREIF index and the earnings-price ratios for the S&P 500. Of course, any variations between the earnings-price ratios and the dividend yield variation can be partly attributed to changing dividend payout ratios.[25]

As with real estate and bonds, the volatility of the valuation multiples associated with real estate and common stocks suggests that an astute portfolio manager should incorporate changing valuation multiples into the pricing calculus. For real estate, the modifications in pricing have been discussed previously. For common stocks, the modification results in

$$
P_0 = \sum_{n=1}^{N} \frac{\overline{CF}_0}{(1 + k'')^n} + \frac{\dfrac{P_0}{\nabla''}}{(1 + k'')^N} + \sum_{n=1}^{N} \frac{(1 + bk^*)^{n-1}}{(1 + k'')^n}
$$

$$
\times \frac{k^* - k''}{k''} \times b\overline{CF}_0 + \frac{\dfrac{P_0}{\nabla''}(1 + bk^*)^N}{(1 + k'')^N} \tag{41}
$$

More generalized forms of equations (41) and (42), with the inflationary component (ρ) specifically identified, can be found in Appendix 26C.

Like equation (19), equation (41) recognizes that the reversionary value of the asset may be based on a pricing multiple that differs from that when the security was purchased. Because of the way the pseudo-annuity and the constant reinvestment rate are constructed (see Miller and Modigliani [1961]), it is more workable to break the reversionary value into two components that are attributable to the pseudo-annuity ($\overline{CF}_0$) and to the constant reinvestment portion ($\overline{CF}_0 \times [1 + bk^*]^N$) and then apply the then current E-P ratio ($\overline{CF}_N/P_N$) to each. Accordingly, equation (41) can also be further reduced to:

---

[25] The same conversion of earnings to dividends should be made for real estate. Unfortunately, Russell/NCREIF historically has not disclosed the tenant improvement component of its series. Accordingly, only net income can be utilized. To this extent, the lack of tenant improvement expenditures biases the present analysis in favor of real estate.

EXHIBIT 26–9

A Comparison of Quarterly Earnings Yield (E-P) Rates: Real Estate versus Common Stocks, 1978:1–1993:4

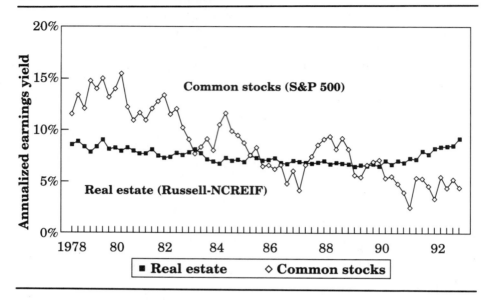

Sources: Updated from Pagliari and Webb (1992); Standard & Poor's Corp., *The Analysts Handbook,* 1993.

$$P_0 = \frac{\overline{CF_0}}{k''} \times \left[\frac{1 - \frac{1}{(1 + k'')^N}}{1 - \frac{1}{\nabla''} \times \frac{1}{(1 + k'')^N}} \right] + \frac{\overline{CF_0}}{k''} \qquad (42)$$

$$\times \frac{b[k^* - k'']}{k'' - bk^*} \times \left[\frac{1 - \frac{(1 + bk^*)^N}{(1 + k'')^N}}{1 - \frac{1}{\nabla''} \times \frac{(1 + bk^*)^N}{(1 + k'')^N}} \right]$$

Similar to the reduction of equation (20) to equation (12), in the special case of constant earnings multiples ($\nabla'' = 1.0$), equation (42) can be further reduced to equation (29).

Given these equations and the initial parameters (CF_0/P_0), r, ρ, b, and δ), the interplay of the requisite real estate growth (λ) and common stock growth (r^*) can be viewed against the backdrop of changing valuation multiples. A matrix of the required shift in the (pseudo) E-P rate for common stock investments can be computed for a given level of real estate inflation pass-through (λ) and shifts in capitalization rates. An example of such a matrix is presented in Exhibit 26–10. As before, these combinations of the shifts in real estate's and common stock's pricing multiples, along with real estate's inflation pass-through rates (λ), result in equivalent ex ante real net yields for real estate vis-à-vis common stocks. More broadly, this matrix approach can be extended to any three parameters of the real estate and common stock pricing models (DDM versus MMM). This trade-off in terms of equivalent ex ante real net yields can also be viewed as a three-dimensional surface (or plane) as shown in Exhibit 26–11. This three-dimensional depiction captures real estate's inflation pass-through rate (λ) as real estate and common stock valuation multiples fluctuate. As before, if the portfolio manager believes the ex ante coordinates of real estate's inflation pass-through rate (λ), combined with the relative changes in real estate and common stock valuation multiples (∇, ∇''), result in a point below the indifference

EXHIBIT 26–10
Real Estate versus Common Stocks: Required Shift in Common Stock's (Pseudo) E-P Yield Necessary to Generate Risk-Adjusted Price Equal to Real Estate Given Real Estate's Shift in Capitalization Rate and Inflation Pass-Through Rate (%)

Real Estate's Shift in Capitalization Rate	Common Stock's Shift in Coupon Rate for Given Real Estate Inflation Pass-Through Rate (%)								
	25.0	37.5	50.0	62.5	75.0	87.5	100.0	112.5	125.0
0.80	0.91	0.87	0.84	0.82	0.80	0.78	0.76	0.75	0.74
0.85	0.94	0.91	0.87	0.85	0.82	0.80	0.78	0.77	0.75
0.90	0.98	0.94	0.90	0.87	0.84	0.82	0.80	0.78	0.77
0.95	1.02	0.97	0.93	0.90	0.87	0.84	0.82	0.80	0.78
1.00	1.05	1.00	0.96	0.93	0.89	0.86	0.84	0.82	0.80
1.05	1.09	1.04	0.99	0.95	0.92	0.89	0.86	0.84	0.81
1.10	1.13	1.07	1.02	0.98	0.94	0.91	0.88	0.85	0.83
1.15	1.16	1.10	1.05	1.00	0.96	0.93	0.90	0.87	0.85
1.20	1.20	1.13	1.08	1.03	0.99	0.95	0.92	0.89	0.86
1.25	1.23	1.16	1.11	1.06	1.01	0.97	0.94	0.91	0.88

EXHIBIT 26–11

Real Estate versus Common Stocks: Portfolio-Weighting Approach Based on Shifts in Pricing Multiples and Real Estate's Inflation Pass-Through Rate

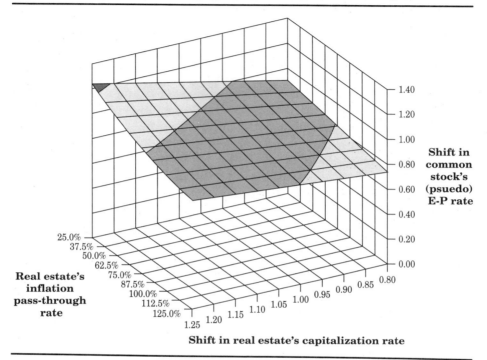

Shift in real estate's capitalization rate

plane, he or she should tilt the portfolio toward common stocks and away from real estate. Conversely, if the growth and valuation coordinates lie above the indifference plane, the portfolio should be tilted toward real estate and away from common stocks.

Several caveats should be noted before moving on.

Holding-Period Dependency. Like Exhibits 26–4 and 26–5, Exhibits 26–10 and 26–11 assume a 10-year investment horizon. The earlier comments about the length of the holding period and the impact of changing valuation multiples apply here as well (see Exhibit 26–3). Accordingly, those investors with long-term orientations should avoid fixating on yield rate shifts, unless they believe such rates are about to undergo a substantial cyclical or secular change.

Relative Volatility of Valuation Multiples. The preceding calculations assumed changes in real estate's valuation multiples are less volatile than those of common stocks. This assumption is predicated on the results portrayed in Exhibit 26–9), wherein the historical volatility of these multiples (CF_n/P_n) can be summarized as follows:

| | Quarterly Earnings-to-Price Multiples, 1978:1–1991:4 | | |
	Mean* (1)	Variance* (2)	Coefficient of Variation (2 ÷ 1)
Real estate	7.28%	0.65%	8.86%
Common stocks	9.06	3.11	34.53

* Annualized

However, while common stock earnings-to-price multiples have clearly been more volatile than those for real estate, there is no certainty that this pattern will continue.

Cyclicality in Valuation Multiples. The marketplace will determine future valuation multiples (CF_n/P_n) based on the optimism or pessimism with which investors in the aggregate view each asset class. These consensus views are rooted in the market's average expectations of real returns (r), advisory and transaction costs (δ), inflation (ρ), internal growth $(b \times r^*)$, and inflation pass-through rates (λ). The market, however, can be wrong. These swings may cause excess volatility between optimism and pessimism (see Shiller [1981]), and/or there may be an excessive pattern of bidding up the winners and writing down the losers (see DeBondt and Thaler [1985]). In any event, the fluctuations in valuation multiples may or may not align themselves with the portfolio manager's expectations. To the extent that these expectations vary, the portfolio manager should alter his or her portfolio weightings accordingly. For example, if the portfolio manager believes the current valuation multiples (CF_n/P_n) price an asset class too high, such an investor should realize some of the gain in this asset class and redeploy this capital in asset classes that are fundamentally more attractive.

Correlation of Shifts in Pricing Multiples. As is evident from Exhibits 26–4 and 26–10, the shifts in pricing multiples (whether it be real estate versus bonds or real estate versus common stocks) necessary to generate equivalent risk-adjusted prices are highly correlated. Therefore, a portfolio manager who expects the shift in such multiples to move inversely (say, an increase in real estate's capitalization rates accompanied by a decrease in bonds' coupon rates and/or common stocks' E-P rates) should be especially cognizant of the divergence in pricing this will cause. Conversely, a portfolio manager who believes risk premia will remain relatively constant across time and changes in the ex ante estimate of future inflation rates are the primary determinant of changes in nominal discount rates is best served by focusing on the determinants of real growth, λ and r^*, for real estate and common stocks, respectively.

All of the foregoing discussion merely suggests that incorporating valuation shifts (∇) into the analysis enables the portfolio manager to more explicitly estimate the expected holding period return. This does not, however, relieve the portfolio manager of the responsibility to subjectively assess the market's optimism or pessimism for each asset class and act accordingly.

ALLOCATION TO THE RISK-FREE ASSET

The models advocated herein are also useful for determining the confluence of parameters within each asset class necessary to deliver the investor's desired real return. If the expected values of the underlying components (CF_0/P_0, λ, r^*, b, etc.) are believed to be unlikely to deliver the required return (r)—for example, if the parameters lie substantially outside their long-term historical values—the portfolio manager may be best served by increasing the portfolio's allocation to the risk-free security (cash and its near equivalents).

HETEROGENEITY WITHIN ASSET CLASSES

For the sake of brevity, the asset classes of real estate, stocks, and bonds have been discussed as though the securities within each class were homogeneous. This is not the case. Various sectors within each of these asset classes may offer substantially different initial yields, reinvestment rates, risk premia, and so on. Thus, the model delineated herein may also be used to exploit intra-class opportunities.

OTHER STRATEGIC COMPARISONS

This chapter's comparison of real estate to stocks and bonds can be extended to a variety of settings. Most obvious is a comparison of stocks to bonds, but other possibilities also exist, such as international securities (real estate, stocks, and bonds), venture capital, oil and gas ventures, and so forth. The purpose of this chapter is to introduce the technique of fundamental comparisons, not to extend the technique to all possibilities.

CONCLUSION

With due consideration for the transaction costs related to portfolio turnover, a strategic asset allocation approach designed to identify significant mispricings among asset classes may improve portfolio performance for some investment managers. Absent a significant level of mispricing, the portfolio should be maintained at its normal, policy weights (the determination of which can be augmented with the approach advocated herein).

To identify periods of significant mispricing, the portfolio manager should carefully analyze the information provided and implied by the capital markets with regard to future yields, real and nominal growth rates, payout ratios, inflation pass-through rates, and so on. More specifically, the assets' implied growth rates can be compared and analyzed in the context of a single-point estimate, a line, or a plane. If, for example, the portfolio manager believes the combination of real estate's and common stocks' future growth is represented by a point (or a group of points) above the indifference line (or plane, if pricing multiples are considered), he or she should tilt the portfolio accordingly.

Since many of the required parameters (CF_0/P_0, r, b, and δ) are known with relative certainty for most asset classes, the future growth rates and changes in pricing multiples will ultimately determine their yields (the changes in pricing multiples have progressively smaller impacts as the holding period lengthens). The portfolio manager must then subjectively determine whether these relationships are consistent with his or her own view of these key relationships.

For real estate and bonds, the variables of importance are the imbedded inflation expectation (ρ), real estate's net risk premium

$([r + \delta] - [r' + \delta])$, and real estate's inflation pass-through rate (λ). For real estate and common stocks, the variables of importance are net risk premia (r versus r''), reinvestment patterns (b), real returns (r^*) on reinvested earnings, the inflation rate (ρ), and real estate's inflation pass-through rate (λ). These relationships can be calculated and displayed graphically to assist portfolio managers in identifying the various combinations of assumptions necessary to tilt the portfolio away from or toward real estate. In all cases, the impact on total return of a shift in pricing multiples (∇) diminishes with increases in the holding period (N).

While this chapter has focused on specific parameters (e.g., λ versus r^*) as offering the most telling insights, portfolio managers are free to isolate any set of variables (e.g., λ versus $b \times r^*$) that they think will lead to profitable insights. The sensitivity of the key variables (as chosen by the portfolio manager) should be thoroughly examined.

This process involves subjectively estimating the key components of future returns. There are no mechanistic trading rules that emit buy/sell signals. Therefore, the process is inherently ambiguous and discomforting. The portfolio manager should be exposed to (and rewarded for) the accuracy of his or her forecasts, guile, and grace under pressure.

APPENDIX 26A SUPPORTING CALCULATIONS TO REAL ESTATE VERSUS BONDS: A LINEAR APPROACH

The linear approach discussed in the chapter involved a comparison of bonds vis-à-vis real estate that begins with identifying the combinations that yield equivalent risk-adjusted prices:

$$P_B = P_{RE}$$

$$P_B = \frac{CF_0'}{(1 + r' + \delta')(1 + \rho) - 1} \tag{4}$$

$$P_{RE} = \frac{CF_0(1 + \lambda \times \rho)}{(1 + r + \delta)(1 + \rho) - (1 + \lambda \times \rho)} \tag{12}$$

Therefore, $P_B = P_{RE}$ can be related as:

$$\frac{CF_0'}{(1 + r' + \delta')(1 + \rho) - 1} = \frac{CF_0(1 + \lambda \times \rho)}{(1 + r + \delta)(1 + \rho) - 1 + \lambda \times \rho} \tag{43}$$

While equation (43) can be solved in terms of any of its potential parameters, for the purposes of this appendix we are most interested in isolating potential values for λ and ρ. As such, equation (43) has been restated in terms of λ:

$$\lambda = \frac{1}{\rho} \times \left[\frac{CF_0'(1 + r + \delta)(1 + \rho)}{CF_0[(1 + r' + \delta')(1 + \rho) - 1] + CF_0'} - 1 \right] \tag{44}$$

and in terms of ρ:

$$\rho = \frac{-b + \sqrt{b^2 - 4ac}}{2a} \tag{45}$$

where
$$a = \lambda \times CF_0 \times (1 + r' + \delta')$$
$$b = (1 + \lambda)CF_0(1 + r' + \delta') + \lambda(CF_0' + CF_0)$$
$$\quad - CF_0'(1 + r + \delta)$$
$$c = CF_0(r' + \delta') - CF_0'(r + \delta)$$

With assumed values for all parameters but λ and ρ, the indifference curve shown in Exhibit 26–1 is generated by assuming a range of λ values and then solving for the resulting ρ values.

APPENDIX 26B SUPPORTING CALCULATIONS TO REAL ESTATE VERSUS COMMON STOCKS: A LINEAR APPROACH

The linear approach involving a comparison of real estate vis-à-vis common stocks begins with identifying the combinations that yield equivalent risk-adjusted returns:

$$r_{RE} = r_{CS}$$

$$r_{RE} = \left[\frac{1 + \lambda \times \rho}{1 + \rho} \right] \times \left[1 + \frac{CF_0}{P_0} \right] - (1 + \delta) \tag{13}$$

$$r_{CS} = \left[\frac{\overline{CF_0}}{P_0} - \rho\right] \times \left[\frac{1-b}{1+\rho}\right] + br^* - \delta'' \tag{38}$$

$$\left[\frac{1 + \lambda \times \rho}{1 + \rho}\right] \times \left[1 + \frac{\overline{CF_0}}{P_0}\right] - (1 + \delta) \tag{46}$$

$$= \left[\frac{\overline{CF_0}}{P_0} - \rho\right] \times \left[\frac{1-b}{1+\rho}\right] + br^* - \delta''$$

While equation (46) can be solved in terms of any of its parameters, for the purposes of this appendix we are most interested in isolating potential values for λ and r^*. As such, equation (46) has been restated in terms of λ:

$$\lambda = \frac{1}{\left(1 + \dfrac{CF_0}{P_0}\right)\rho}\left[\left(\frac{\overline{CF_0}}{P_0} - \rho\right)(1 - b)\right. \tag{47}$$

$$\left. + (1 + br^* - \delta'' + \delta)(1 + \rho) - \left(1 + \frac{CF_0}{P_0}\right)\right]$$

With assumed values for all parameters but λ and r^*, the indifference line shown in Exhibit 26–3 is generated by assuming a range of r^* values and then solving for the resulting λ values.

APPENDIX 26C GENERALIZED VERSION OF SHIFT IN THE PRICING MULTIPLES OF COMMON STOCKS

Revising equation (41) to accommodate a specified inflation parameter (ρ) involves the following expansion:

$$P_0 = \sum_{n=1}^{N}\frac{\overline{CF_0}}{[(1 + r'' + \delta'')(1 + \rho)]^n} + \frac{\overline{CF_0} \times \left[\dfrac{P_0}{CF_0 \times \dfrac{1}{\nabla''}}\right]}{[(1 + r'' + \delta'')(1 + \rho)]^N}$$

$$+ \sum_{n=1}^{N}\frac{(1 + b[(1 + r^*)(1 + \rho) - 1])^{n-1}}{[(1 + r'' + \delta'')(1 + \rho)]^n}\left(\frac{r^* - (r'' + \delta'')}{r'' + \delta''}\right) \times b \times \overline{CF_0}$$

$$+ \frac{\overline{CF}_0[1 + b(1 + r^*)(1 + \rho) - 1]^N \times \left[\dfrac{P_0}{\overline{CF}_0} \times \dfrac{1}{\nabla''} \right]}{[(1 + r'' + \delta'')(1 + \rho)]^N} \qquad (48)$$

Similarly, revising equation (42) involves the following expansion:

$$P_0 = \frac{\overline{CF}_0}{(1 + r'' + \delta'')(1 + \rho) - 1}$$

$$\times \frac{\left[1 - \dfrac{1}{[(1 + r'' + \delta'')(1 + \rho)]^N} \right]}{\left[1 - \dfrac{1}{\nabla} \times \dfrac{1}{[(1 + r'' + \delta'')(1 + \rho)]^N} \right]}$$

$$+ \frac{\overline{CF}_0}{(1 + r'' + \delta'')(1 + \rho - 1)}$$

$$\times \frac{b[(1 + \rho)(r^* - r'' \times \delta'')]}{\rho(1 - b) + (1 + \rho)(r'' + \delta'' - br^*)}$$

$$\times \left[\frac{1 - \dfrac{[1 + b[(1 + r^*)(1 + \rho) - 1]]^N}{[(1 + r'' + \delta'')(1 + \rho)]^N}}{1 - \dfrac{1}{\nabla} \times \dfrac{[1 + b[(1 + r^*)(1 + \rho) - 1]]^N}{[(1 + r'' + \delta'')(1 + \rho)]^N}} \right] \qquad (49)$$

REFERENCES

Asikoglu, Yaman, and Metin R. Ercan. "Inflation Flow-Through and Stock Prices." *Journal of Portfolio Management*, Spring 1992, pp. 63–68.

Babcock, Guilford C. "The Concept of Sustainable Growth." *Financial Analysts Journal*, May–June 1970.

Bernstein, Peter L. "Capital Market Expectations: The Macro Factors." In J. L. Maginn and D. L. Tuttle, eds., *Managing Investment Portfolios: A Dynamic Process*. Boston: Warren, Gorham & Lamont, 1983).

Bodie, Zvi; Alex Kane; and Alan J. Marcus. *Essentials of Investments*. Homewood, IL: Richard D. Irwin, 1992, pp. 422–23.

Brinson, Gary P.; L. Randolph Hood; and Gilbert L. Beebower. "Determinants of Portfolio Performance." *Financial Analysts Journal,* July–August 1986.

Brinson, Gary P.; Brian D. Singer; and Gilbert L. Beebower. "Determinants of Portfolio Performance II: An Update." *Financial Analysts Journal,* May–June 1991.

Brown, Stephen J., and Mark P. Kritzman. "Quantitative Methods in Asset Allocation." In S. J. Brown and M. P. Kritzman, eds., *Quantitative Methods for Financial Analysis.* 2nd ed. Homewood, IL: Dow Jones-Irwin, 1990.

Chapra, Vijay K., and William T. Ziemba. "The Effects of Errors in Mean, Variance and Covariances on Optimal Portfolio Choice." *Journal of Portfolio Management,* Winter 1993, pp. 6–11.

DeBondt, Werner F. M., and Richard Thaler. "Does the Stock Market Overreact?" *Journal of Finance* 40, no. 3 (July 1985), pp. 793–805.

Diermeier, Jeffrey J. "Capital Market Expectations: The Macro Factors." In J. L. Maginn and D. L. Tuttle, eds., *Managing Investment Portfolios: A Dynamic Process.* New York: Warren, Gorham & Lamont, 1990.

Durand, David. "Afterthoughts on Controversy with MM, Plus New Thoughts on Growth and the Cost of Capital." *Financial Management,* Summer 1989, pp. 12–18.

Durand, David. "Growth Stocks and the Petersburg Paradox." *Journal of Finance,* September 1957, pp. 348–63.

Estep, Tony; Nick Hanson; and Cal Johnson. "Sources of Value and Risk in Common Stocks." New York: Salomon Brothers, Inc., May 1984.

Giliberto, S. Michael. "Real Estate Risk and Return: 1991 Survey Results." New York: Salomon Brothers, Inc., March 31, 1992.

Gordon, Myron J. *The Investment, Financing and Valuation of the Corporation.* Homewood, IL: Richard D. Irwin, 1962.

Grossman, Sanford J. "Asset Allocation Strategies and Risk Premium Phenomenon." W. F. Sharpe and K. F. Sherred, eds., *Quantifying the Market Risk Premium Phenomenon for Investment Decision Making.* Seminar proceedings published by the Institute of Chartered Financial Analysts, 1989.

Hartzell, David J.; David G. Shulman; Terrance C. Langetieg; and Martin L. Leibowitz. "A Look at Real Estate Duration." *Journal of Portfolio Management,* Fall 1988.

Ibbotson Associates. *Stocks, Bonds, Bills and Inflation: 1993 Yearbook.* Chicago, 1993.

Jeffrey, Robert H. "The Folly of Stock Market Timing." *Harvard Business Review,* July–August 1984, pp. 102–10.

Karnosky, Denis S. "Management of the Asset Allocation Decision." In S. Hudson-Wilson, ed., *Real Estate: Valuation Techniques and Portfolio*

Management. Seminar proceedings published by the Institute of Chartered Financial Analysts, 1988.

Malkiel, Burton G. *A Random Walk Down Wall Street.* 5th ed. New York: W. W. Norton & Company, 1990.

Markowitz, Harry. "Portfolio Selection." *Journal of Finance,* March 1952, pp. 77–91.

Miller, Merton H, and Franco Modigliani. "Divided Policy, Growth, and the Valuation of Shares." *Journal of Business,* October 1961, pp. 411–33.

Modigliani, Franco, and Richard Cohn. "Inflation and the Stock Market." *Financial Analysts Journal,* March–April 1979.

Pagliari, Joseph L., Jr. "Inside the Real Estate Yield." *Real Estate Review,* Fall 1991.

Pagliari, Joseph L., Jr., and James R. Webb. "Past and Future Sources of Commercial Real Estate Returns." *Journal of Real Estate Research,* Fall 1992, pp. 387–421.

Perold, Andre F., and William F. Sharpe. "Dynamic Strategies for Asset Allocation." *Financial Analysts Journal,* January–February, 1988.

Samuelson, Paul A. "The Judgment of Economic Science on Rational Portfolio Management, Indexing, Timing and Long-Horizon Effects." *Journal of Portfolio Management,* Fall 1989, pp. 4–12.

Sharpe, William F. "Asset Allocation." In J. L. Maginn and D. L. Tuttle, eds., *Managing Investment Portfolios: A Dynamic Process,* 2nd ed. New York: Warren, Gorham & Lamont, 1990.

Sharpe, William F. "Likely Gains from Market Timing." *Financial Analysts Journal,* March–April 1975, pp. 60–69.

Shiller, Robert J. "Do Stock Prices Move Too Much to Be Justified by Subsequent Changes in Dividends?" *American Economic Review* 71, no. 3 (June 1981), pp. 421–36.

Siegel, Jeremy J. "The Equity Premium: Stock and Bond Returns Since 1802." *Financial Analysts Journal,* January–February 1992, pp. 28–38.

Sy, Wilson. "Market Timing: Is It a Folly?" *Journal of Portfolio Management,* Summer 1990, pp. 11–16.

Webb, James R.; Richard J. Curcio; and Jack H. Rubens. "Diversification Gains from Including Real Estate in Mixed-Asset Portfolios." *Decision Sciences,* Spring 1988, pp. 434–52.

Webb, James R., and Joseph L. Pagliari, Jr. "Past and Future Sources of Commerical Real Estate Returns: A Regional Approach." Working paper, 1994.

Wurtzebach, Charles H.; Glenn R. Mueller; and Donna Macchi. "The Impact of Inflation and Vacancy on Real Estate Returns." *Journal of Real Estate Research,* Summer 1991, pp. 153–68.

CHAPTER 27

APPLICATIONS OF DERIVATIVE INSTRUMENTS

Adam K. Gehr, Jr.
DePaul University

INTRODUCTION

The rapid emergence of derivative instruments (forwards, futures, swaps, and options, among others) has changed portfolio management in the 1990s. These instruments have opened the door to a variety of management and risk control techniques. Some of these techniques are

- *Synthetic asset allocation.* A portfolio can be switched from stocks to bonds or from bonds to bills without buying or selling the underlying instruments.
- *Risk management.* The exposure of a portfolio to given sources of risk (interest rates, market risk) can be controlled.
- *Portfolio insurance.* A lower limit (floor) may be set on the value of a portfolio or a portion of a portfolio.
- *Creation of new payoff patterns.* For example, a portfolio can be created that will pay off if a price makes a large move *in either direction.* Alternatively, a portfolio can be created that pays off only if prices don't move.

In the following section, we describe some of the available derivative instruments. We then turn to how the prices of these instruments are determined. The following section describing pricing is somewhat more technical than the rest of the chapter and can be skipped by anyone interested only in what derivative instruments are and how they are used in portfolio management. In the next section, we look at some applications of existing instruments in portfolio management. Then we describe their potential and evolving use in real estate portfolio mangement. Finally, we discuss how real estate–based derivative instruments could be designed and how these instruments might be used by real estate portfolio managers.

A CATALOG OF DERIVATIVE INSTRUMENTS

A *derivative instrument* is a contract whose payoff depends on the price of some underlying asset. The value of the derivative instrument depends on the value of the underlying asset. The following sections describe a few of the more common instruments.

Forward Contracts

A *forward contract* is simply an agreement to deliver a financial instrument or a commodity for a fixed price some time in the future. For example, a gold producer agrees to deliver 10,000 ounces of gold in five years for a price of $400 an ounce. No cash changes on the initiation of the contract. In five years, the producer will deliver 10,000 ounces of gold and receive $4 million.

Note that the only cash flow that occurs comes at the end of the contract. The contract may be unique. In other words, the terms of the contract (fineness of the gold, place of delivery, physical form of the gold, date of delivery) may be determined solely for this contract. For some forward markets, however, standards organizations exist and most contracts traded are simply variations on some standard contract developed by the standards organization.

If either party to the contract defaults when the term of the contract is over, the counterparty must take legal action to recover damages. Thus, when forward contracting it is important to know your counterparty. Markets for large forward contracts—for example, for forward foreign exchange—are typically between large, well-known institutions. Thus, a company that wishes to purchase 1 million deutsche marks for delivery in six months to pay for a delivery of German goods will have to enter a forward contract through its bank. The bank enters a forward contract with a bank counterparty and enters an offsetting forward contract with the company. In other words, it agrees to buy deutsche marks from another bank and to deliver them to the company. The bank is willing to deal with the company because the firm is a known customer. Most companies cannot, however, enter a forward contract with another bank as counterparty.

Most parties entering a forward contract typically expect to carry out their duties at maturity. If either party changes its mind about the contract, some other party must be persuaded to take or make delivery instead. This may involve a cash payment. Suppose, for example, the gold producer decides not to make delivery of the gold. The producer must find (in some markets, aided by a dealer) some other party willing to make the delivery. If the forward price of gold has risen in the meantime to, for example, $425, a new party will demand a payment to take over the contract—to deliver gold for $400 instead of $425. If, on the other hand, the forward price of gold has fallen to, say, $375, the company will receive a payment from a party that wishes to deliver gold for $400 instead of $375.

Futures Contracts

Futures contracts are similar to forward contracts in that they involve future delivery of a good for payment. They differ, however, in many important respects.

First, futures are *exchange traded*. To trade gold futures in the United States, for example, it is necessary to trade on the Commodity Exchange in New York. The transactions can be carried out only between exchange members. If a nonmember wishes to buy or sell a contract, he or she must do so through a broker who is an exchange member.

Second, the contracts are *standardized*. The amount to be delivered, size of the contract, quality of the good to be delivered, and location of delivery are determined by the exchange. This standardization means the contracts can be *settled by offset*. The long party to a contract (i.e., the party who has agreed to accept delivery) can fulfill all responsibilities by taking the short side of a contract for the same commodity in the same delivery month (i.e., an agreement to make delivery that offsets the agreement to take delivery).

Third, futures contracts are *marked to market* every night. This means each contract is effectively renegotiated at the end of a trading day. For example, suppose a trader takes a short position in February gold at $350 an ounce. At the end of the day, February gold closes at $355. The trader will have to pay $5 per ounce, or $500 for each 100-ounce contract, and in return take on an obligation to deliver gold for $355 an ounce instead of the originally contracted $350 an ounce.

If gold closes the next day at $348, the trader will receive a cash inflow of $7 per ounce, or $700 per contract. In return for the cash payment, the trader has effectively agreed to make delivery of the gold for $348. Now suppose the price is still $348 per ounce when the gold is delivered. The total amount paid for the gold is

$$\$348 + \$7 - \$5 = \$350$$

In a sense, the trader receives the originally agreed-upon price. Some of the price, however, was in the form of mark-to-market payments. In other words, in taking a short futures position, the trader has agreed to sell gold for a series of payments, randomly timed, some positive and some negative, totaling $350. The mark-to-market payments drive the value of the contract to zero every night. This eliminates the incentive for either party to the contract to default and also makes possible the settlement by offset referred to above.

Fourth, both sides of a futures position, short and long, must post *margin*. The margin, which may be posted in earning assets (e.g., T-bills) or with letters of credit, guarantees the ability of the trader to pay mark-to-market. The size of the margin is small relative to the size of the contract, usually about the size of one large mark-to-market.

Finally, a *clearinghouse* is associated with each futures market. The clearinghouse effectively takes the opposite side on all futures contracts. It is long against the short side and short against the long side.[1] Thus, it is the ultimate guarantor of the contract. Therefore, it is possible to trade on a futures market without worrying about who your counterparty is; your counterparty is always the clearinghouse.

In most conventional futures markets, the contract calls for the eventual delivery of the commodity traded—gold, oil, wheat, and so on. In fact, these deliveries are made for only a fraction of the contracts. Because the contracts are standardized, anyone holding a futures contract can get out of the contract simply by taking an offsetting position. Thus, a trader who is long June corn is relieved of the duty

---

[1] More precisely, each member of the exchange must either be a member of the clearinghouse or clear trades through a clearinghouse member. The clearinghouse guarantees clearing member to clearing member, and the clearing members guarantee performance of the contracts entered into by the members who clear through them.

of making mark-to-market payments and any other obligations by taking a short position in June corn. In effect, someone else has taken over the obligations of the contract. If the other party was also executing an offsetting trade, the amount of *open interest*—the number of contracts in existence—falls by 1.

In many futures markets, however, there is no delivery obligation. These are called *cash delivery* markets. The Eurodollar futures market and the stock index futures market are the largest cash delivery markets; there is simply a final mark-to-market payment on the last day of the contract. However, instead of paying the difference between yesterday's futures price and today's futures price, traders pay the difference between yesterday's futures price and today's *spot price*. The spot price may be either an observed spot price or an index. In the S&P 500 futures market, for example, the final payment is the difference between the previous day's futures price and the closing value of the S&P 500 index. The introduction of cash delivery has made futures trading possible in many areas in which actual, physical delivery would be difficult or impossible. When real estate–based futures contracts come into existence, they will be cash delivery contracts.

Options: A Basic Typology

There are two basic types of options: puts and calls. We will see that many variations exist on these simple instruments.

Calls

A *call option* is the right, but not the obligation, to purchase a financial instrument or commodity at a fixed price for a fixed period of time. For example, a call option on oil might give the holder the right to buy 1,000 barrels of light, sweet crude for $18 a barrel any time during the next three months.

For every option purchased, there must be someone who sells (or *writes* or *grants*) the option. That is, the option seller in the above example stands ready to deliver 1,000 barrels of oil on demand and accept $18 a barrel. In return for this, the seller receives the price of the call option (sometimes called the *premium*).

Because there is no obligation to exercise the option, the holder of the option will exercise it only if the price of oil is above $18 a barrel. If the price of oil is less than or equal to $18 a barrel, the option will expire worthless.

Puts

A *put option* is the right, but not the obligation, to sell a financial instrument or commodity at a fixed price for a fixed period of time. For example, a put option on gold might give the holder the right to sell gold for a price of $375 an ounce. If the price of gold fell to $360 an ounce, the holder would exercise the option and receive $375 instead of $360 for the gold.

Once again, on the other side of the contract is an option writer who receives the put price in return for standing ready to buy gold at $375 at the request of the option purchaser. If the price of gold does not fall, the option will not be exercised and the put price will be earned with no offsetting action. If the price of gold falls, the seller of the put must buy the gold at $375 instead of the (lower) market price and resell it at the market price in order to liquidate the position.

European versus American Options

Options that can be exercised at any time during their life are called *american options* (note the use of lowercase *a*). Options that can be exercised only at the end of the option period are called *european*. The geographical designation does not imply that american options are traded in America and european options are traded in Europe. In fact, most options traded in both Europe and the United States are american options.

Some options can be exercised only at distinct points during their lives. In other words, there may be three or four times during the life of the option at which it can be exercised. These options are sometimes called *mid-atlantic* or *bermuda options*.

Exchange-Traded and Over-the-Counter Options

Options were traded long before the existence of options exchanges. Indeed, the famous tulip bubble in Holland was actually a speculative bubble in options on tulip bulbs. Nonetheless, trading in options of all types experienced its most rapid growth after the Chicago Board Options Exchange (CBOE) opened to trade options on stocks. The CBOE and all other options exchanges are organized very much like the futures exchanges described earlier. Only members of the exchange can trade on the exchange floor. Members of the exchange must be members of the clearinghouse or clear their trades through a member of the clearinghouse. Only one clearinghouse clears trades for all stock options exchanges: the Option Clearing Corp.

The clearinghouse guarantees both sides of the trade. There is no mark-to-market for the purchaser of exchange-traded options. The short side, however, must post margin. If equity in the position falls too low because of changing market value of the optioned asset, the seller must add to it. Exchange-traded options exist for stocks, stock indexes, futures (futures options will be discussed next), foreign exchange, and some fixed-income instruments.

A wider variety of options are traded over the counter (OTC). OTC options can be custom designed for the purchaser. One disadvantage of these options is that there is no organized secondary market. Sometimes the firms dealing in the options are willing to make a (usually thin) secondary market. To the extent that the over-the-counter contracts become standardized, the secondary market will grow.

Like futures, options can call for either physical or cash delivery. For example, a stock index call does not require the option writer to actually deliver a portfolio of stocks; rather, the option writer must pay, if asked, the difference between the closing value of the stock index and the exercise price of the option. This gives the owner of the option the same profit he or she would have if the stocks had been actually delivered and resold on the open market, but eliminates the transaction costs associated with stock trading.

Fancy Options

Options on Futures
Futures exchanges have introduced options on the futures contracts that they trade. The instruments are similar to options on physical commodities or on financial instruments. A call option on a futures contract gives the holder the right to take a *long* position in the underlying futures contract at the exercise price of the option. For example, suppose a trader buys a call on February gold futures with an exercise price of $370. If the February futures contract subsequently rises to $380, the trader can exercise the option. The trader receives a long position in February gold futures and an inflow of $1,000 ($380 − $370, a profit of $10 an ounce, times 100 ounces per contract) into his or her margin account. Note that the trader must now mark the futures position to market every day until an offsetting position is taken or delivery is made. If the February gold futures contract remains at or below $370 through the expiration date of the option, the option expires worthless.

A put option on a futures contract gives the holder the right to take a *short* position in the underlying futures contract at the exerice price of the option. Suppose a trader buys a put on March crude oil futures at $18 a barrel. If the price of the March crude futures contract subsequently falls to $17, the trader can exercise the option. On exercise, the trader receives a short position in the March futures contract and a cash flow of $1 per barrel into the margin account. Again the trader will take or make mark-to-market payments until an offsetting long position is taken or delivery is made.

Futures options typically expire the month before the futures contracts on which they are written. For example, the option on March crude would expire in February. This guarantees that the option can be held to maturity and exercised while still giving the holder time to get out of the underlying futures contract before delivery is required.

Asian Options

An *asian option* is an option on an average price over a period. (Once again, the name of the option has nothing to do with where it is written.) Usually a cash delivery instrument, it pays off the difference between the average price over a period (the sum of the prices recorded each day divided by the number of days) and the exercise price of the option. To see why anyone would want such an instrument, consider an airline that purchases fuel at a rate of 100,000 barrels per month. In buying oil on the spot market over the next three months, the cost of oil will equal the average spot price of oil over the period. Suppose the airline buys an asian call option on the price of jet fuel with an exercise price of $19 per barrel for 300,000 barrels. If the average price of oil over the following three months is $20.50, the airline will receive $450,000 on exercise of the option, thereby reducing its cost to $19.00 per barrel. Note the convenience of exercise into cash: The airline can buy fuel wherever and whenever it needs to and still be able to exercise the option if it ends up in the money (the average price of oil is above the exercise price).

On the other hand, consider a gold mining concern that produces 150,000 ounces of gold per year. The mine sells the gold at the spot price. The mine could guarantee a minimum level of revenue by buying an asian put. If it buys a put on 150,000 ounces at an exercise price of $375 and the average price of gold is $371, the mine collects $600,000 upon exercise of the option. It receives revenues of $375 per ounce.

Asian options are less expensive than regular, european options because the average price is less volatile than the ending price.

Another, less common variety of averaging option pays off the difference between the average price and the ending price.

Lookbacks

Now we turn to the real esoterica in the options markets. A *lookback* is a european option. However, its exercise (strike) price is the maximum (for a put) or the minimum (for a call) price. Thus, a lookback call allows the owner to purchase the optioned asset at the minimum price achieved during the period. For example, suppose you purchase a lookback call on gold. If the low reached during the life of the option was $350 and the end-of-period price was $357, you would have a profit on exercise of $7 per ounce.

Similarly, the owner of a lookback put on gold would have been able to exercise at the high price reached during the option period. Had this price been $360, the profit on exercising the put at the end of the option period would have been $3 per ounce. Notice that *both* the put and the call owners can exercise their options profitably in this case. Lookback options are much more expensive than standard options—up to 100 percent more expensive in some cases.

Barrier Options

Barrier options are european options that either are good only if the price reaches a certain level (ins) or are canceled if the price reaches a certain level (outs). They can be either puts or calls. Thus, we could have a down-and-out call option. It would be an ordinary, european call, but if the price of the underlying asset reached a certain level during the period, the option would be canceled. Alternatively, we could have an up-and-in put on gold with an exercise price of $400 and a trigger (or knock-in) price of $410. Thus, at the end of the option period, we would have the right to sell gold at $400 an ounce only if the price of gold reached $410 sometime during the period.

Swaps

The market in swap arrangements has grown by leaps and bounds during the past 10 years. The rules for most swaps are set by the International Swap Dealers Association. This standardization means there is a small secondary market for swaps and, more important, makes it possible for swap dealers to make a market in swaps. No exchange trades swaps, although efforts have been made from time to time to create a futures market in swaps.

Interest Rate Swaps

Using an *interest rate swap,* a borrower who is paying interest on a fixed-rate loan can convert the payments to payments on a floating-rate loan. Alternatively, the payer on a floating-rate loan can swap to paying a fixed-rate loan.

The two parties to a swap are the fixed-rate payer and the floating-rate payer. The two parties agree on the notional principal of the loan—the amount on which the interest payments are to be based—the fixed rate, the basis (or index) for the floating rate, and the duration of the swap. For example the payments may be based on a notional principal of $100 million, a fixed rate of 8 percent, a floating rate equal to six-month LIBOR, and a five-year swap. The notional principal is never exchanged; it's simply an amount on which the interest payments are based.

To continue the example, suppose that at the beginning of the swap, six-month LIBOR is at 7 percent. Six months later, the fixed-rate payer will pay the floating-rate payer $500,000, or the 1 percent difference between the fixed and floating rates times the $100 million notional principal of the swap for one-half year. The next payment for the swap is now determined by the current value of LIBOR, say, 7.75 percent. One year after the swap is contracted, the fixed-rate payer will pay the floating-rate payer $125,000 = (8% − 7.75%) × $100,000,000 × 0.5. Suppose LIBOR in one year is 8.25 percent. The 18-month payment will therefore be from the floating-rate payer to the fixed-rate payer in the amount of $125,000.

Exhibit 27–1 continues this scenario for two more periods. The payments column shows payments from fixed to floating. Thus, a negative number in the payments column shows a cash flow from floating payer to fixed payer.

The effect of the swap is to allow the fixed-rate payer to convert a floating-rate loan into a fixed-rate loan and allow the floating-rate payer to convert a fixed-rate loan into a floating-rate loan. Every period, the fixed-rate payer will pay the interest on a floating-rate loan and make or receive payment on the swap. If the swap and the floating loan rates are based on the same index (usually LIBOR,

EXHIBIT 27–1
Payments on Interest Rate Swap

Month	Six-Month LIBOR	Payment From Fixed to Floating
0	7.00%	—
6	7.75	$500,000
12	8.25	125,000
18	8.00	− 125,000
24	8.50	0
30	9.00	− 500,000

although other rates can be used in setting swaps), the total payments will be the same every month. On the other hand, the floating-rate payer makes a fixed-rate payment on the loan, plus a swap payment that varies up and down with the interest rate. The result is a set of payments that simulates the payments of a floating-rate loan.

Foreign Exchange Swaps

Foreign exchange swaps convert a set of cash flows denominated in a foreign currency into a set of cash flows denominated in another currency, such as dollars. For example, a swap might match a party receiving foreign yen but wishing to receive dollars with a counterparty receiving dollars but wishing to receive yen. The parties simply exchange the cash flows they receive.

Alternatively, it is possible to convert a loan in, for example, deutsche marks to a loan in dollars by swapping loan proceeds and repayments with a counterparty who wishes to borrow dollars and convert to deutsche marks.

Equity Swaps

An *equity swap* swaps the return on a standardized equity portfolio for a fixed payment. This can be used to convert a fixed-income portfolio to an equity portfolio, or vice versa, for the duration of the swap.

Commodity Swaps

A *commodity swap* allows a spot purchaser of a commodity to lock in the price of the commodity or allows a seller to lock in the commodity price. The swap does not actually involve an exchange of the commodity; rather, payment is determined by the difference between the spot price and the agreed-upon fixed price.

For example, the basis for a swap might be 100,000 barrels of light, sweet crude oil. One side of the contract, perhaps a refinery attempting to control its costs, will pay the fixed price less the spot price. The other side of the swap, say, an oil-producing company attempting to lock in a fixed price for output, will pay the spot price less the fixed price.

Exhibit 27–2 shows the payments for the fixed-payment side assuming a fixed price of $18 per barrel. In period 1, the spot price is $17. The fixed payer buys oil in the spot market and pays $100,000 (i.e., [$18 − $17] × 100,000 barrels per contract) to the floating payer, making the total cost of oil $18. The floating payer receives the spot price in the market and receives $100,000 under the swap agreement to make the total price received $18 per barrel.

In period 4, the cash flows reverse. The spot price of oil has risen to $19. The fixed payer now receives $100,000 from the floating payer. Since the fixed payer is now paying $19 per barrel in the spot market for oil, this brings the cost per barrel down to $18. The floating payer receives $19 in the spot market, but pays out $100,000, which brings the amount received per barrel down to $18.

Other Instruments

A variety of other derivative instruments are traded in the over-the-counter markets. Space permits discussing only a few here.

Commodity Loans and Synthetic Commodity Loans
In the gold and oil markets, it is useful to contract for loans denominated not in currency but in the commodity itself. Consider a gold miner who wishes to open a new mine. The miner knows the amount of gold to be produced, but the future price of gold is uncertain. The

EXHIBIT 27–2
Payments on a Commodity Swap

Period	Spot Price	Payment From Fixed to Floating
1	$17.00	$100,000
2	17.50	50,000
3	18.00	0
4	19.00	− 100,000
5	18.50	− 50,000

miner would like to borrow gold, sell the gold to get money to fund mining operations, and pay off the loan principal and interest with output from the mine. This is a gold loan. Similar loans are constructed in the oil market.

Alternatively, the loan could be synthesized by borrowing dollars and selling gold forward. Delivering gold against the forward contracts provides the cash to repay the loan. Absent transaction costs, the benefits to the miner are the same.

Options on Swaps

Options on swaps, or *swaptions,* give an investor the right, but not the obligation, to enter into a swap agreement at fixed terms. This essentially means the swap can be entered with a fixed rate different than the market rate. For example, suppose the current fixed rate for five-year swaps is 8 percent. An investor might purchase a swaption allowing payment of 8 percent fixed and receiving LIBOR. If the interest rates rise, the investor can switch from a floating-rate obligation to paying a fixed rate of 8 percent. The swaption creates a ceiling on the loan rate.

The other type of swaption would allow an investor to receive 8 percent fixed. Thus, an investor might borrow at the current fixed rate of 8 percent and buy a swaption. If rates go up, the investor continues to pay off the 8 percent loan. If rates go down, the investor exercises the swaption. The fixed payments of the swaption turn the fixed-rate loan into a variable-rate loan at the current value of LIBOR.

PRICING DERIVATIVE ASSETS

For derivative assets to trade successfully, both parties to each transaction must have some assurance that the price at which they are trading is reasonable. One of the most important factors contributing to the growth of derivative asset markets during the past several years has been the development of pricing models that apply to a wide variety of assets.

Pricing Options

The market value of all derivative instruments is calculated using *arbitrage* arguments. An arbitrage is simply simultaneously buying and selling the same thing at two different prices. For example, if I can buy apples on one street corner for 25 cents and sell them on the next corner for 30 cents, I am conducting an arbitrage. Arbitraging causes prices to adjust so that the arbitrage disappears. Others will be attracted to arbitraging apples, and the price differential will be competed away. The prices of apples on both street corners will quickly become equal.

Because the payoffs from derivative instruments depend on the value of the underlying asset, mispricing of the derivative instrument creates an arbitrage opportunity. If a derivative asset is mispriced, it will generally be possible to buy and sell some combination of the derivative asset and the underlying asset to create a risk-free, zero-investment profit opportunity. Such profit opportunities do not exist long in well-functioning markets. The buying and selling that takes place to exploit the arbitrage will drive the relative prices of the derivative instrument and the underlying asset back to equilibrium.

A One-Stage Case

To see how this works in the case of options, consider the simple example in Exhibit 27–3. Point A shows the current price of the optioned asset, $10, and the current interest rate, 6 percent. Points B and C show that the asset has two possible values next period, $12 and $8. We want to know the value of a one-period call option on the asset with an exercise price of $10. The values of the option at payoff are given at points B and C in the diagram: $2 if the price of the optioned asset rises and $0 if the price of the asset falls.

From the information given, we can calculate the only possible arbitrage-free price of the option. The key to pricing the option is to see that a proper combination of the option and a risk-free security will give the same payoffs as the underlying asset next period. The price of this combination must equal the price of the asset if no arbitrage opportunities are to exist. From this and the proportions of the combination, we can deduce the price of the option.[2] To find the price of the option, we first need to know the quantity of the option, x, and the quantity of the risk-free security, y, we need to buy

---

[2] This argument can be presented in other ways. The option and the asset can be combined to give a risk-free security. The asset and the risk-free security can be combined to give payoffs equal to the option. Any of these relationships can be used to deduce the arbitrage-free price of the option.

EXHIBIT 27–3
A Simple Option

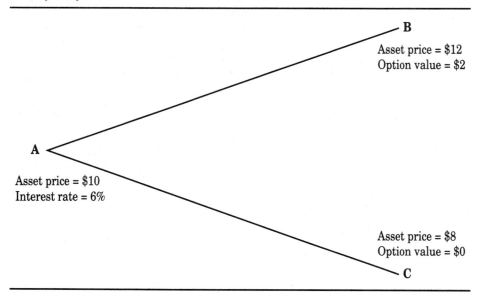

B
Asset price = $12
Option value = $2

A
Asset price = $10
Interest rate = 6%

Asset price = $8
Option value = $0
C

to replicate the value of the asset. To do this, we must solve the following simultaneous equations:

$$2x + 1.06y = \$12$$
$$1.06y = \$8$$

The first equation says that if the asset price rises, the value of the options—the $2 payoff times the number of calls purchased, x—plus the value of the risk-free asset—the number of dollars invested, y, times 1 plus the interest rate—must equal the value of the asset, $12. The second equation says that if the value of the asset falls, the value of the risk-free asset purchased must equal the value of the asset, since the option is valueless.

Solving these equations yields $y = 7.55$ and $x = 2$. In other words, if we hold two options and invest $7.55 at 6 percent, we will get $8.00 if the asset price goes down or $12.00 if the asset price goes up.

Since the asset price is now $10, the value of the portfolio of the risk-free security and the option must also be $10. We can find the value of the call price, c, by solving

$$\$7.55 + 2c = \$10$$

In words, the amount we invest in the risk-free asset ($7.55) plus the amount we invest in the calls (2 times the price of a call) must equal the price of the asset. Solving this equation, we find that c, the price of the call, is $1.23.

To see why this must be the price, consider what would happen were the call price $1.00. In this case, we can sell the asset for $10.00 and buy the portfolio containing calls and the risk-free asset for only $9.55. We get a net cash inflow of 45 cents and get the same payoffs next period. In buying options to take advantage of this profit opportunity, however, arbitrageurs will drive the price of the option up to its fair value.

If the call were priced at more than $1.23—say, $2.00—we could sell the call and create a combination of stock and risk-free security that has the same payoffs. The portfolio would cost $1.23, and we would get $2.00 for writing the call. We would have a risk-free position and a 77 cent cash inflow.

Multistage Options

The previous example may seem unduly simplified. However, it gives us a technique for solving far more complicated problems. Consider the situation in Exhibit 27–4. This exhibit differs from Exhibit 27–3 because we have let the stock change price twice. First, the stock will jump to either point B or point C. From B it will jump to either D or E. From C it will jump to either E or F. We thus have a model that allows the asset price to take three values at maturity. We now set the option strike price at $9. Consequently, the option will have three possible payoffs: $3, $1, and $0.

We want to know the arbitrage-free price of the option at point A. Note that the technique we used above will give the price of the option at B (using the values at D and E) or at C (using the values at E and F). To get the price of the option at A, we just use the prices at B and C to find the arbitrage-free value. We proceed through each of these steps in turn.

First, we find the value of the option at C. We set up two equations that say that the value of an arbitrage portfolio must equal the price of the asset in either state E or state F. Keeping the annual interest rate at 6 percent, we now use an interest rate of 3 percent.[3] The equations are

---

[3] This leads to a slight inaccuracy, because 3 percent compounded semiannually is slightly higher than 6 percent. In practice, it's easier to use continuous compounding and discounting.

EXHIBIT 27–4
A Two-Stage Option

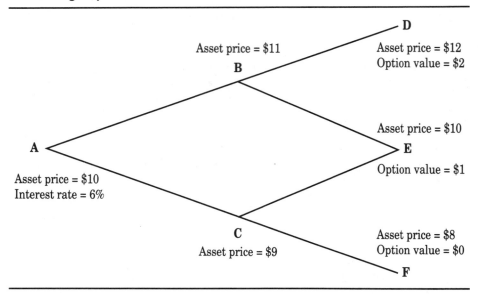

$$1x + 1.03y = \$10$$
$$1.03y = \$8$$

Here x equals 2 and y equals \$7.77. We now ask what option price makes this portfolio equal to the price of the asset at E:

$$7.77 + 2c = \$9$$

The price of the option is approximately 62 cents.

We now follow the same procedure to get the value of the option at B. First, we find the arbitrage portfolio:

$$2x + 1.03y = \$12$$
$$1x + 1.03y = \$10$$

Once again, x equals 2 and y equals \$7.77. To find the value of the option, we solve

$$\$7.77 + 2c = \$11$$

The option price, c, is \$1.615.

We can now solve for the value at A. We set up two equations that say that an arbitrage portfolio must equal the value of the asset at both B and C:

$$1.615x + 1.03y = \$11$$
$$0.615x + 1.03y = \$9$$

Again, the number of options, x, equals 2 and the investment in the risk-free asset, y, equals $7.54.

Finally, we ask what option value makes the price of the arbitrage portfolio equal to the asset price at A:

$$\$7.54 + 2c = \$10$$

The call price is now $1.23.

We could continue to allow for smaller jumps until we got as many states as we wished at the end of the option's life. It is also relatively easy to modify the model so that it works with puts, american options, and a variety of other complications.

In this example, for purposes of simplicity, the price jumps are of a constant amount, $2 in the first example and $1 in the second. In practice, we would use constant *proportions*. For example, the price might jump up by a factor of 1.1 or jump down by a factor of 1/1.1. If we make the number of subperiods large in the constant-proportion model, the price we get for a european call approaches the price given by the Black-Scholes model.

The Black-Scholes Model

Black and Scholes analyzed the price of an option when the price of the underlying asset varies continuously.[4] The math of this model is much more complicated, but the logic is the same as the logic in the preceding sections: In equilibrium, the price of the option should be a price that makes arbitrage profits impossible to achieve.

The Black-Scholes model gives the value of a european call option as:

$$c = AN(d_1) - Xe^{-rT}N(d_2)$$

$$\text{where} \quad d_1 = \frac{\ln(A/X) + (r + \sigma^2/2)T}{\sigma\sqrt{T}}.$$

$$d_2 = d_1 - \sigma\sqrt{T}.$$

---

[4]Fisher Black and Myron Scholes. "The Pricing of Options and Corporate Liabilities," *Journal of Political Economy*, 1973, pp. 351–68.

A = Asset price.

X = Exercise price of the call.

r = Continuously compounded interest rate.

T = Time remaining until the option matures.

σ = Standard deviation of the rate of return on the underlying asset.

N = Cumulative normal distribution function; for example, $N(.5)$ gives the probability of drawing a value of 0.5 or less from a normal distribution, a bell-shaped curve with a mean of 0 and a standard deviation of 1.

Both the Black-Scholes model and the two-state model suggest that a call option price depends on five variables.

- The greater the asset price (A), the greater the value of the call.
- The greater the exercise price (X), the lower the price of the call.
- The greater the interest rate (r), the greater the price of the call.
- The greater the time to maturity, the greater the price of the call.
- The greater the riskiness (σ in the Black-Scholes model, jump size in the two-state model), the greater the price of the option.

Pricing Puts

The preceding examples showed how to price calls. Clearly, in the two-state example, we could have substituted in the payoffs for a put and solved for its value using the same techniques that gave us the value of a call. Alternatively, we can use the price of a european call (given, say, by the Black-Scholes model) to find the price of a european put.

If we invest in a call, sell a put, and buy enough T-bills to pay off an amount equal to the exercise price when the option matures, we have something that behaves very much like the underlying asset. If the price of the asset goes up, we make money (on the call). If the price of the asset goes down, we lose money (the put is exercised against us). To solve for the price of the put, we calculate the price of the call and then ask what price makes the value of the portfolio described above (long call, short put, long T-bills) equal to the value of the optioned asset.

For example, consider Exhibit 27–3 again. Suppose we buy a call, short a put (both of which have an exercise price of $10), and invest in enough T-bills to give us $10 in the second period. We have the following possible outcomes:

	Ending Price of Optioned Asset	
	$12	$8
Call value	$2	$0
Put value	0	−2
T-bill value	10	10
Total	$12	$8

Since the portfolio has the same payoff as the optioned asset, it must have the same value today. We can write this relationship as:

Asset value = Call price − Put price + Present value of strike price

Manipulating this a bit gives the value of the put in terms of the value of the call, the value of the asset, and the present value of the strike price:

Put price = Asset value − Call price − Present value of strike price

This relationship is known as *put-call parity*. It shows that once we know the value of a european call, we can easily calculate the value of a european put. Although the relationship does not hold exactly for american options, it gives a very useful approximation.

Pricing Forward and Futures Contracts

Like option prices, forward and futures prices are calculated as the price that prevents an investor from earning profits by arbitrage. Also like option prices, if a forward or futures price differs by much from its equilibrium value, arbitrageurs will take advantage of the profit opportunity. The resulting trading will drive the forward or futures price back to its equilibrium value.

Although the previous section emphasized the differences between futures and forward contracts—futures have mark-to-market cash flows every day, and forward contracts have a cash flow only at maturity; futures require posting margin, and forward contracts do not require margin—the same model that provides forward prices turns out to work well for futures prices as well. Because the margin on a futures contract can be satisfied by posting an earning asset and therefore does not require a cash outflow, it does not enter into the calculation of the futures price. The mark-to-market payments can be shown to matter in a world of uncertain interest rates, but empirical studies have found that the actual market prices of futures contracts are indistinguishable from forward prices.

For many commodities, called *carry-cost* commodities, the futures price is determined by the cost of holding the commodity. For financials and quasi-financial commodities like gold, the cost of carry is simply the interest forgone by holding the commodity. We will examine the forward prices on carry-cost commodities.

Consider gold. Using a combination of a spot position in gold and a short position in the forward market, we can create a synthetic money market instrument. Suppose we can buy gold for $350 an ounce. If we buy gold and simultaneously sell a one-year forward contract on gold, we have something very much like a T-bill. We have a cash outflow (to buy the gold), followed by a sure cash inflow in the future (when the gold is delivered against the forward contract). If the prevailing interest rate is, for example, 10 percent, the synthetic money market instrument should yield the same rate. This will happen only if the forward price is 10 percent higher than the spot price, that is, if the forward price is $385.

Suppose the forward price is above $385—say, at $400. In that case, an arbitrage opportunity is available. Traders could sell money market instruments and get an increase in return by buying spot gold and selling forward gold. But this buying and selling of gold would drive the forward price down relative to the spot price. The pressure on prices would continue until equilibrium was restored. A similar arbitrage would occur if the forward price were too low relative to the spot price.

Complications can occur if the asset itself generates cash flows during the period of the forward contract. For example, suppose we have a forward contract on a financial instrument, perhaps a bond, that generates cash flows before the end of the forward contract. To make a synthetic T-bill, an investor buys the bond and sells a forward contract. Now someone making a synthetic loan will earn both the difference between the price of the forward contract and the spot price of the bond and the cash flows from the coupon payments.

The price of the forward contract must take into account the coupon payments on the bond if the rate on the synthetic T-bill is to equal the rate on the real T-bill (i.e., if equilibrium is to be arbitrage free). If the cash flow occurs at the end of the forward contract, it is simply subtracted from the full-carry price. For example, suppose the risk-free interest rate is 6 percent and the forward contract is a one-year contract on a bond with a 4 percent yearly coupon that is now priced at $950. The forward price would be

$$\$950 \times 1.06 - \$40 = \$967$$

A lender can buy the bond for $950. In one year, the lender receives $967 for delivering against the forward contract and a $40 coupon payment for a total of $1,007. This is exactly principal plus 6 percent interest on $950.

If cash flows from the bond take place during the period, they must be compounded out to the end of the forward contract before being subtracted from the price. For example, suppose the bond in the above example paid two semiannual coupon payments instead of a single year-end coupon payment. In that case, the forward price would be

$$\$950 \times 1.06 - \$20 \times 1.03 - \$20 = \$966.40$$

An investor who bought a synthetic T-bill by buying a bond, selling a one-year forward contract, and investing the cash flow from the bond at 6 percent[5] would end up with a 6 percent return on the initial investment.

Because futures contracts are marked to market every day, the value of a futures contract is always zero.[6] The end-of-day change in the futures price always restores the value of the contract to zero. This is not true for forward contracts. The terms of a forward contract stay the same throughout its life. As market prices change, the value of the forward contract can become positive or negative.

Consider a forward contact on gold. If the forward contract is for

---

[5] This approximation again ignores semiannual compounding.

[6] Although margin must be posted when a futures contract is entered, the margin can be in the form of a letter of credit or an earning asset and therefore does not constitute a cash outflow.

two years, the risk-free interest rate is 7 percent, and the current price of gold is $370 per ounce, the zero-arbitrage forward price is

$$\$370 \times (1.07)^2 = \$423.61$$

Suppose that one year from the inception of the contract, the spot price of gold has fallen to $360 per ounce. The right to be paid $423.61 in one year for gold is now valuable. If interest rates are unchanged, the current one-year forward price for gold is

$$\$360 \times 1.07 = \$385.20$$

A holder of the old forward contract can take a short position at the current price and guarantee an inflow of

$$\$423.61 - \$385.20 = \$38.41$$

in one year. The present value of this cash flow is

$$\frac{\$38.41}{1.07} = \$35.90$$

Thus, the value of an off-market forward contract equals the difference between the current forward price and the off-market forward price discounted back to present value. Note that this value could be negative.

Swap Prices

A swap can be regarded as a series of identically priced forward contracts or as back-to-back loans. For example, suppose we want the fixed-payment side of a five-year gold swap with annual payments. We are contracting to make a set of fixed payments and receive the spot price of gold. We could do something similar by buying a sequence of five forward contracts (a one-year contract, a two-year contract, etc.). Alternatively, we could combine a long position in gold with the floating pay side of a swap to construct a synthetic term loan. We pay money out today for the gold. Each year for five years, we sell one-fifth of the gold and the money we receive from the sale, combined with the money we receive or pay on the swap, gives us a cash flow equal to the fixed side of the swap.

This suggests the way we must calculate the zero-arbitrage swap price. The fixed side must equal the payments on a five-year term loan whose present value equals five times the current spot price of gold. If the current spot price of gold equals $380 and the risk-free interest rate is 8 percent, the fixed side of the swap must be priced at $475.87. The present value of five annual payments of $475.87 is $1,900, which is five times $380. At any other value for the fixed side of the swap, it would be possible to combine a swap and a term loan to earn a pure profit. Doing so would, of course, help drive the swap price back to its zero-arbitrage equilibrium.

Just as a forward contract will become an off-market forward during its life, so will a swap, when prices change, become an off-market swap. Just as an off-market forward has a nonzero (possibly negative) price, so will an off-market swap have a nonzero value. To calculate the value of an off-market swap, we calculate the difference between the fixed side of the off-market swap and the fixed side of a current swap. The present value of this series of cash flows is the value of the off-market swap.

Suppose, for example, we have an interest rate swap with a $1 million notional principal. The swap has three years remaining, and the fixed side of the contract pays 8 percent. The fixed side of an at-the-market three-year swap would pay 6 percent. The difference between the two payments is

$$0.08 \times \$1,000,000 - 0.06 \times \$1,000,000 = \$20,000$$

The present value of $20,000 per year for three years at 6 percent (the current interest rate inferred from the swap contract) is $53,460.24, the value of our swap.

Some Caveats on Pricing Models

We have seen that the potential for arbitrage gives us a powerful tool for analyzing the prices of derivative instruments. To the extent that market frictions inhibit arbitrage, however, these models will fail. Transaction costs, for example, may make an apparent arbitrage unprofitable. Illiquidity in some markets may make it impossible to create an arbitrage portfolio. This is especially true in dealing with real estate. When facing transaction costs or illiquidity, we have not a single price at which an asset should trade but a band of prices within which arbitrage is unprofitable. Thus, we might be unable to arbitrage against the futures market when gold futures trade in a range of $395.50 to $396.00, but be able to trade profitably if futures move out of that range (assuming the spot price stays constant).

Furthermore, certain assumptions were made in describing the option model. Interest rates were assumed to be constant, and the jump sizes were also constant. In fact, of course, interest rates change, and the market volatility also changes. Models have been developed that attempt to deal with these problems, but they are much more complicated and are forced to make very specific assumptions about the way interest rates and volatility can move. Simpler models, such as the Black-Scholes model, can be used to give ballpark estimates of prices and are also useful in estimating the proper number of options to use to hedge a given position, but an observed difference between the market price and the model's price does not necessarily mean an arbitrage opportunity.

Finally, even the best model will work only if it is fed the correct numbers. Some of the numbers the models require—for example, the volatility of the asset price for option pricing models—must be estimated; they cannot be observed directly. The quality of the numbers produced by the model is only as good as the estimates it is provided. Once again, we can view the model as providing a probable trading range. By trying various plausible values for asset volatility, we can determine how sensitive the model's price is to the data it uses and how certain we can be about the quality of its estimates.

USING EXISTING DERIVATIVE ASSETS IN PORTFOLIO MANAGEMENT

The set of derivative assets discussed above can play a variety of roles in current portfolio management. In this section, we look at some of these uses.

Buying and Selling Synthetic Assets

We have seen that much of the trading in derivatives can be treated as dealing in "synthetic" assets. In this section, we look at a few examples useful in portfolio management.

Synthetic Stock
A manager with a portfolio in cash (perhaps invested in T-bills) can invest in synthetic stock simply by buying a stock index futures contract. The combination of the return on the cash portion of the portfolio, the gain in price locked into the futures contract, and the

gains and losses from the mark-to-market payment will simulate the returns to the market (S&P 500 if those futures are used), including both the dividend return and the change in price.

One obvious difference for taxable entities would be the different tax treatment of futures and cash stock. Futures are marked to market for tax purposes at year end. Gains on stock, of course, are not taxable until the stock is sold.

On the other hand, a portfolio manager with a portfolio of stocks could sell stock index futures to create a synthetic cash portfolio. By selling short stocks in an amount determined by the size of the portfolio and the portfolio's beta, the manager effectively shorts synthetic stock and removes the risk of movements in the stock market from the portfolio. This can be more beneficial to the portfolio than simply selling the stocks outright.

Consider a fund manager who has a portfolio of carefully chosen stocks. While the manager may be bearish on the market, he or she may still be bullish on the performance of the individual stocks in the portfolio relative to the market. Without derivatives, the manager must either sell the stocks and forgo their anticipated performance or keep the portfolio knowing that the extra-market performance of the stock portfolio may well fail to offset the decline in the market. If using derivative assets, these problems do not occur. The manager keeps the stocks in the portfolio. If they perform no better than the market, the manager receives the return on a synthetic money market instrument. If they do outperform the market, the manager gets the benefit of this performance as well. If they underperform the market, the manager's return on the synthetic money market instrument is reduced accordingly.

Buying and Selling Synthetic Bonds

A manager with a cash position can create a portfolio of synthetic bonds simply by buying bond futures. The combination of the return on the cash portion of the portfolio, the difference between the spot price of bonds and the futures price, and the payment and receipt of mark-to-market payments will cause the value of the manager's assets to move as though the portfolio really contained bonds.

On the other hand, a manager with a bond portfolio could, by selling bond futures, convert the price behavior of the bond portfolio to imitate the performance of a portfolio of cash. In other words, the duration of the portfolio could effectively be reduced to zero. The amount of bonds to sell short would be determined by the size and duration of the bond portfolio and the duration of the bond futures contract.

Asset Allocation Using Derivatives

The most common use of derivatives is in asset allocation. Shifting the contents of an asset portfolio in response to changing prices in different sectors of the market can be slow and expensive. Existing assets must be disposed of, new assets must be chosen and acquired, and, on both parts of the transaction, transaction costs must be paid. Furthermore, as we saw earlier, shifting asset classes can result in disruption of a carefully chosen portfolio. Transaction costs in the futures market are low, and the asset allocator need not touch the existing portfolio.

If the only assets in the portfolio are bonds, stocks, and bills, asset allocation can be done using the techniques described previously. Suppose, for example, that a portfolio manager wishes to shift a portion of a portfolio from bonds to stocks. This is done in two steps. First, the bonds are turned into synthetic cash by selling bond futures. Second, the synthetic cash is turned into synthetic stock by buying stock index futures. The amount of stock index futures purchased determines the portfolio's sensitivity to the market—its beta. The portfolio is now sensitive to movements in the stock market and insensitive to movements in the bond market. If a rise in the stock market is accompanied by a rise in interest rates, the portfolio will increase in value, even though the bonds—which, after all, the manager still owns—decrease in value.

Shifting from stock to bonds simply involves the reverse operation. Stock index futures are sold short against the portfolio and bond futures are purchased. The amount of bond futures purchased determines the portfolio's sensitivity to interest rates.

Using Options to Create Payoff Patterns

Options may be used instead of futures contracts to create more complicated payoff patterns. Futures can change the sensitivity of a portfolio to the stock market. Options can change the sensitivity in one direction only. For example, the purchase of index put options can limit the downside risk of a portfolio. If the market declines, the profit from the puts will offset the losses from the portfolio. If the market increases, the price of the puts will be lost, but no further losses will occur.

An alternative way to do the same thing is to combine a cash portfolio with index call options. If the market increases, the call options will earn a profit. If the market decreases, the price of the calls will be lost, but no further losses will occur.

Combining options and futures can dramatically change the pay-off pattern of a portfolio. For example, suppose a bond portfolio manager sells bond futures and buys stock index call options. The sale of the bond futures turns the portfolio into synthetic cash. The purchase of the options means the portfolio will be sensitive to upward movements in the stock market, but not to downward movements.

Spreads

Managers can use option spreads to express their opinions about the future course of the market in substantial detail. For example, suppose a manager believes the stock market will fall, but by a limited amount. In this case, the manager could buy an at-the-money put (a put with a strike equal to the current asset price) and sell an out-of-the-money put (a put with a strike less than the current asset price). The spread would provide protection against any fall in price that did not go past the exercise price of the out-of-the-money option. The money raised by selling the out-of-the-money option would reduce the cost of the protective put strategy. As long as the asset's price does not fall below the strike of the out-of-the-money option, the manager's loss will be limited to the cost of the option position.

Alternatively, suppose a portfolio manager believes the market will move, but is uncertain of the direction. The manager could (if the stock position were zero) purchase a straddle—a put and a call. If the market goes up, the put will pay off. If the market goes down, the call will pay off.

If the manager starts with an initial position in stock, the same outcome could be achieved by buying two puts. In this case, if the market goes up, the stock will pay off and the puts will expire worthless. If the market goes down, one put will protect the portfolio and the other will provide profit.

A manager who believes the market will not move may act on this belief by buying an in-the-money call, selling two at-the-money calls, and buying an out-of-the-money call. This position, called a *butterfly,* will pay off most if the market is flat, and profit will tail off if the market makes a large move in either direction.

APPLICATION OF EXISTING ASSETS TO REAL ESTATE PORTFOLIO MANAGEMENT

Even though currently trading assets are rarely backed by real estate and therefore can rarely affect the returns on the real estate portion of the portfolio directly, possible uses still exist for currently trading derivative assets for real estate portfolio management.

Changing from Fixed- to Variable-Rate Financing

Suppose a real estate project has been financed with a fixed-rate loan at 10 percent. Cash flows from the project are divided up among owners. Floating-rate loans are currently available at 8 percent. A portfolio manager who owns a proportion of the project believes floating rates will be below 10 percent for the foreseeable future. The manager therefore would prefer to have a share of the same project with floating-rate financing.

This can be accomplished with a swap arrangement. The portfolio manager enters an interest rate swap receiving fixed payments and paying a floating rate. The size of the swap should equal the portfolio's pro rata share of the project's debt. The payments to and from the swap, combined with the payments from the project, will equal the payments from a floating-rate-financed project.

Note that the managers of the project itself need not even know that this transaction has occurred. They will continue to make payments on the loan before sending the remainder of the cash flows from the project to the equity holders. The swap merely changes the size of the net cash flows received by one particular portfolio manager and also changes his or her sensitivity to interest rate fluctuations.

Changing from Variable- to Fixed-Rate Financing

The example in the preceding section could be reversed. Suppose a portfolio manager owns a share of a project financed by floating-rate loans. The manager is either pessimistic about the future course of interest rates or averse to bearing interest rate risk. The effective financing of the project could be changed by entering a swap receiving floating rate and paying fixed rate. The floating-rate payments would rise with a rise in interest rates, offsetting the reduction in cash flow from the project due to higher interest rates. The manager would, however, be required to make fixed-rate payments.

Note that not all of the interest rate risk from the project has been offset. If the project goes bankrupt because of an excessive debt burden combined with a rise in interest rates, the loss in cash flows will not be entirely offset by the cash inflows from the swap. Nonetheless, if interest rates rise by enough to put the financial viability of the project in jeopardy, the manager will, as a partial offset, have a valuable off-market swap that can be resold.

Guarding against Adverse Rate Movements with a Swaption

In contrast to the preceding examples, suppose a manager wants to take advantage of favorable movements in interest rates but be protected against adverse rate movements. This can be done with a swaption. A portfolio manager investing in a floating-rate-financed project could buy a swaption to enter a swap paying fixed and receiving floating. If rates fall, the swaption will expire worthless. If rates rise, the manager will exercise the swaption and begin paying fixed and receiving floating rate on the previously arranged terms.

Hedging Currency Risk

Investors who purchase foreign real estate face not only the usual risks associated with real estate investment but also an exposure to risk of price change in foreign exchange. For example, suppose an investor from the United States purchases an interest in property in Germany. Cash flows from the property will be received in deutsche marks, which must be converted into dollars. If the value of the deutsche mark falls, the profitability of the project to the U.S. investor will be reduced. If the value of the deutsche mark rises, the profitability of the project will increase.

Part of this risk can be offset by the use of derivative instruments. Using swaps or forward contracts, an investor can agree to exchange a fixed amount of cash flows received from an investment for a fixed amount of dollars. The drawback is that the exchange must be set up for a fixed cash flow. If the cash flow varies from period to period, only a portion of the risk will be offset. For example, suppose an investor agrees to deliver DM 1,000,000 per year for a fixed amount of dollars. If the investor receives DM 1,200,000, the 200,000 extra is unprotected. Alternatively, if the investor receives DM 800,000, he or she must purchase DM 200,000 at the spot price to fulfill the contract. This may lead to either higher or lower profits, depending on the spot price of the deutsche mark.

Options also provide a useful tool for hedging against currency risk. Suppose an investor purchases a put option on yen to protect the cash flows from a Japanese investment. If the value of the yen rises, the put will expire worthless. If the value of the yen falls, the profit from the put will offset the loss in value of the yen received from the investment.

Protection of capital value, as opposed to cash flows, from currency fluctuation is more difficult to achieve. Suppose an investor purchases a foreign property and plans to sell it after a fixed period of time. If the holding period is long enough—say, 10 years—it is unlikely that the investor will be able to purchase any instrument with which to hedge foreign exchange exposure. Even for shorter term exposure, the risk can't be hedged completely. The investor might take on a five-year forward agreement. The agreement, however, will call for a fixed amount of currency. Because the investor cannot know today what the selling price will be in five years, no fixed hedge can remove all of the currency risk.

DESIGN OF REAL ESTATE–BASED INSTRUMENTS

The only real estate–based derivatives that have traded in the United States have been the GNMA futures contracts, which have traded in various guises on the Chicago Board of Trade. These contracts, of course, are more interest rate contracts that real estate contracts. A variety of innovative contracts have been suggested, however, and some of them should see the light of day during the next few years.

The difficulty in designing real estate–based instruments is finding a proxy for real estate prices. Physical delivery of real estate against a futures or options contract is impractical. In other cases where delivery is impractical, cash-delivery contracts have been used, with the amount of the final settlement based on the value of an index. Most proposals for real estate–based derivative instruments have been based on some index of real estate prices. To the extent that the value of the index correlates with the prices of the assets whose prices are to be hedged, these derivatives will be useful in laying off risk.

The problem, however, is how to construct such an index. There are four apparent alternatives:

- An index of total return on income-producing properties based in part on the appraised values of the properties.
- An index of sale prices of properties.
- An index of rents or vacancies.
- An index of real estate–backed stock prices.

We will examine each of these alternatives in turn.

Total Return Index of Appraised Property Values

While the Russell/NCREIF index could be used as a total return index for income-producing commercial real estate, it suffers from a number of faults that limit its use.

First, much of the index's total return is based on the appraised values of the underlying properties. These appraisals have come under a number of attacks; see Chapter 3. Appraised values can lag actual property value movements. Therefore, if such an index were to back a futures contract or a swap contract, the payoffs from the contract may not reflect the prevailing price. Furthermore, appraised values not only lag market values but are also sluggish in a sense. They tend to fall by less than market values fall and to rise by less than market values rise. Payoffs from futures or options contracts based on an appraised value index would tend to be less volatile than the prices of the underlying assets. To some extent, hedgers could adjust for this lack of volatility by increasing the size of the hedge positions they take.

Second, the Russell/NCREIF index also has a changing asset mix. That is, the proportion of various property types (office, retail, apartments, etc.) and geographic locations has varied over the life of the index. Thus, the weighting of various property type and/or geographical characteristics is changing over time and may not reflect the desired mix for hedging purposes.

Third, the returns of the Russell/NCREIF index are self-reported by the investors and advisory firms that are members. Such self-reporting, in addition to a changing profile, may be subject to selection bias and/or lack of outside scrutiny.

Finally, the differing accounting and reporting treatments available to member firms can lead to nonstandardized reporting results.

The London Fox real estate futures market was based on appraisals of property values.[7] It failed in short order due to lack of liquidity, and subsequent investigation showed that the greatest percentage of the transactions on the exchange had been initiated by the exchange itself.

Index of Sale Prices

In the stock market, indexes are constructed based on the last-sale price of stocks in the index. This usually provides an unambiguous measure of the value of the assets underlying the index.[8]

In the stock market, almost all stocks trade nearly every day. In the commercial real estate market, however, most properties do not change hands in most years. Constructing an index, even annually, based on the prices of a given set of buildings is therefore impossible. However, it is possible to construct an index based on the prices of buildings that do sell during a given period. By constructing a *hedonic* index, the price of an idealized building can be constructed using actual building sales prices. For example, the prices of apartment buildings might be determined by the number of apartments, size of apartments, location, age, and so forth. The impact of these values on price could be used to construct the price of a hypothetical apartment building with constant characteristics that is evaluated every month. Each month, the actual sale prices from current transactions would be used to construct the index.

The advantages of this technique are that it uses observable market prices to calculate the index value and removes the problem

---

[7] See Kenneth Posner, "Are We Ready for a Futures Contract in Real Estate?" *Insight,* September 1992, pp. 21–24, and London Fox, "The London Fox Property Futures Market" (Futures and Options Exchange, undated).

[8] But not always. On the morning of October 19, 1987, the day of the stock market crash, so many sell orders flooded the specialists that many of the stocks in the S&P 500 index opened very late. The index continued to be calculated during this time with last-trade prices from the previous Friday. Thus, though the index dropped during the first hour of trading that morning, its drop gave no indication of the magnitude of the crash that was actually taking place.

of comparing the prices of properties with different physical characteristics (location, size, age, etc.). The disadvantages are the complexity of the calculation and the fact that changes in the method of evaluating the hedonic index could lead to different values for the index. Furthermore, it is unlikely, even in large cities, that enough sales will be made to construct this index more than once per month. Even if it is constructed monthly, it will reflect values of buildings traded at all times during the month. Therefore, it will give not a snapshot of building values at one time but something more like a mid-month average of building prices.

Alternatively, an index based on repeat sales of given properties can avoid the problems of a hedonic index. If we compare the most recent sales price of a property with its price when purchased, we have a measure of the increase in value over the period. If we have repeat sales of many assets, it is possible to construct an index that is a good representation of value across a particular market. Case and Shiller[9] have developed a particularly elegant version of this index and applied it to sales of single-family houses. They have suggested basing futures contracts on the value of the index. This will not have direct hedging application to institutional investors in real estate, most of which do not hold equity claims on single-family properties. However, it may provide an interesting way for them to make synthetic investments in residential real estate by combining default-free securities and a long position in residential real estate futures.

To maintain an active futures market, frequent reporting of the index on which final settlement is made is necessary. Traders will not be willing to take a position in a contract that could lead to a large end-of-contract surprise. The only contract based on a monthly reported index, a CPI futures contract, was a dismal failure.[10]

On the other hand, monthly reports might be sufficient for a swap-type contract that is not exchange traded and therefore need not be marked to market every day.

---

[9] Karl E. Case and Robert J. Shiller, "The Efficiency of the Market for Single-Family Homes," *American Economic Review,* March 1989, pp. 125–37.

[10] Most futures contracts that are introduced fail, so other factors may have been at work as well.

Indexes of Rents and Vacancy Rates

To avoid the estimation problem associated with an appraisal-based index, an alternative index form would be a survey of rents and vacancies. A large number of property owners could be surveyed each month to determine the average rent per square foot and vacancy rate. Ideally, the survey would determine the effective rents received per square foot (taking into account both rental rate and vacancy rate for each property). The resulting index could be used to settle futures or swaps contracts. Derivative instruments based on this index would allow investors to hedge revenues received from property investment, but not any changes in the value of the property.

Unfortunately, an index of rents and/or vacancy rates is subject to the same consistency problems as the sales price index. To the extent that the characteristics (elevator access, water views, floor height, etc.) of the physical space (even within the same building) vary over time and from lease to lease (tenants' credit standing, space requirements), some hedonic form of an index must be created to maintain consistency. The solution has the same problems as those discussed with regard to the sales price index.

Index of Real Estate–Based Stock Prices

Since stock prices are reported every day, an alternative way to construct a hedging instrument is to use an index of real estate–based stocks, for example, an index of equity REIT stock prices. These stocks are actively traded and give the market's evaluation of the company every day. Construction of such an index is simple, and the mechanics of trading a futures or options contract based on stock indexes are well established.

Experimentation with REIT indexes has shown that they are very volatile compared to appraised value indexes. This may show the inadequacy of appraisals discussed above or an excess of volatility on the stock exchange. In any case, it can mean that an investor attempting to hedge a real estate investment will find the value of the hedge vehicle changing much more rapidly than the appraised values of the underlying property. While this may be more a measurement problem than an economic one, it may be serious enough to block the use of the instruments.

Nevertheless, this approach would overcome the problems associated with the other indexes. Given the burgeoning growth recently experienced by REITs, it is entirely likely that Wall and LaSalle streets' financial engineers will make a serious run at creating such a traded index.

Moreover, the NAREIT index, as an example, can be broken down into several property type and/or geographic subindexes. This may facilitate the use of such an index in a variety of applications. In addition, given the problem of appraisal versus market volatility, constructing asian options—using the moving average of REIT prices—could mitigate the difference in observed volatility.

Other Problems in Asset Design

Still more problems in designing assets arise because of the nature of property investment.

Regional Price Differences

Real estate prices in different parts of the country can vary dramatically, not only in their level but, more important, in the rate and even direction of change. Office building prices can be rising in Dallas and falling in New York or rising in Miami and falling in Chicago.

Because real estate investment tends to be localized—an investor might have a substantial investment in Chicago but no investment at all in San Francisco—a considerable part of the risk of a typical real estate investor could not be hedged away using instruments based on nationwide price levels.

Alternatively, instruments could be constructed based on regional price indexes. Such instruments would be unlikely to trade on organized exchanges because of the lack of liquidity of such a limited instrument. It might be possible, however, for investment bankers to make such instruments available for over-the-counter trading.

Differences in Asset Type

Another problem has to do with the variability of asset types within a given property market. Apartment building price experience, for example, might be quite different from office building price history. To the extent that a local index is constructed based on a broad range of property types, it becomes less suitable for hedging the risk associated with an individual property. To the extent that the index is constructed from a narrow range of property types, it becomes a less desirable asset to trade because of a lack of liquidity. A plethora of narrowly based contracts are unlikely to trade frequently.

Property-Specific Risk
Finally, a large amount of the risk of an individual property is property specific. It can't be hedged away using any kind of an index-backed derivative tool. It is often possible to hedge the risk associated with portfolios, whether of stocks, bonds, or other assets. It is rarely possible to hedge away the risk of an individual asset.

APPLICATION OF DERIVATIVE INSTRUMENTS TO REAL ESTATE PORTFOLIO MANAGEMENT

We now turn from the problem of instrument design to the question of how real estate–backed instruments could be used by the portfolio manager.

Asset Allocation

One of the major uses of existing derivative instruments is asset allocation. Just as bond and stock index futures can be used to transform a fixed-income position to a stock position, and vice versa, real estate–backed derivative instruments can be used to shift asset allocation synthetically.

Creating Synthetic Real Estate
Portfolio managers can use real estate–backed futures or swaps to create an investment in synthetic real estate. Synthetic real estate is simply an investment that has the economic characteristics of real estate investment (absent some of the tax consequences) but does not involve direct ownership of the underlying assets.

A combination of the purchase of a futures or swap contract in real estate and the purchase of a fixed-yield instrument with a life equal to the life of the derivative asset would create an investment in synthetic real estate. For example, the purchase of a 90-day futures contract and 90-day T-bills would give the portfolio manager 90-day ownership of synthetic real estate. The T-bills would compensate the portfolio manager for the time value of money. The real estate futures contract would mimic the price movement of real estate and also give any additional return to risk bearing available in the real estate market. To maintain an investment in real estate, the position would have to be rolled over when the futures contract and the T-bills matured.

For investors who prefer longer-term investment, a combination of a multiyear real estate swap and a longer-term fixed-income instrument would be more desirable. This position would not have to be rolled over as often as the T-bill and futures mix.

Changing Stock into Synthetic Real Estate

A portfolio manager wishing, for tactical purposes, to reduce a portfolio's exposure to stock and increase its exposure to real estate could do so with a combination of stock index futures and real estate futures. A short position in stock index futures would convert the stock position into a synthetic T-bill. A long position in a real estate futures contract would convert the synthetic T-bill into a synthetic real estate position.

The manager could get a longer-term investment in real estate by selling an equity swap and buying a real estate swap. Once again, this obviates the need to roll the position over. This position is interesting for the portfolio manager who desires an exposure to real estate but believes his or her analytical strength is in picking strong stocks. The manager could continue to buy potentially undervalued stocks. The impact of the market on these stocks would be offset by the short position in the equity swap. If the stocks do outperform the market, the manager still gets the benefit of return to effective stock selection, while obtaining an exposure to the broad returns in the real estate market.

Changing from Real Estate into Synthetic Bonds

Suppose a real estate portfolio manager wishes to reduce the portfolio's exposure to real estate and increase its exposure to interest rates. The first step would be to short real estate futures, thus converting the real estate into synthetic T-bills. The addition of a long position in T-bond futures would give the investor an exposure to long-term interest rate movements and turn the synthetic T-bills into synthetic T-bonds.

Alternatively, shorting a real estate swap of, say, five years' duration would give the investor an effective exposure to five-year interest rates.

Switching among Types of Real Estate Investments

The richer the variety of instruments available, the broader the array of strategies the portfolio manager can employ. For example, if real estate derivative contracts are available for different property types, a real estate portfolio manager can invest directly in some property types and indirectly in others.

For example, suppose a manager wishes to specialize in direct investment in office buildings, perhaps because of prior successful experience in that area. The manager would also like, however, to have the benefits of diversification into other property types. By taking a short position in office-based swaps and a long position in, for example, apartment swaps, the manager could create a position in synthetic apartment buildings. In addition, the manager would retain the possibility of above-market performance in the specific office buildings in the portfolio, while removing the market performance of office buildings as an asset class.

Alternatively, because of the very regionally specific nature of real estate price movements, it should be possible to create regionally specific real estate–based derivative instruments. For example, swaps could be based in the New York real estate market, the Chicago real estate market, or the Denver real estate market. These swaps would allow a real estate portfolio manager to obtain nationwide diversification of investments without having to make direct investments in every market.

For example, a real estate portfolio manager based in Chicago might feel most comfortable investing in the local market. Knowledge of the vagaries of the market, the individuals involved in the deals, and, indeed, local politics may give the manager a decided edge in choosing properties in which to invest. However, the manager would also like the risk-reducing effect of diversification into other regional markets. A combination of selling a Chicago-based real estate swap to reduce the exposure to the local market and the purchase of real estate swaps from other areas gives diversification without necessitating direct investment in other markets.

Once again, the manager does not lose the value of his or her expertise in the Chicago market by making these transactions. The short position in Chicago real estate–based swaps removes only the Chicago-wide portion of the return on the property. If the projects in which the manager invests outperform the Chicago market as a whole, the portfolio will still realize the benefits of the manager's expertise.

Risk Management and the Use of Options

At the cost of an additional investment in options, options on real estate swaps or futures can provide a real estate portfolio manager with controlled exposure to markets. The manager could position the portfolio to accrue the benefits of an increase in the market and control exposure to decreases in the market.

For example, suppose a manager wants to guard against a decrease in value of real estate. The purchase of a real estate–based put (a put on a real estate–based futures or swap contract) could provide the needed protection. If the market increases, the manager's investments will benefit, but the put will expire worthless. If the real estate market decreases, the put will pay off, which will offset the decline in the value of the property.

Alternatively, suppose a manager wishes to make an investment in a segment of the real estate market, but is concerned about downside risk. The simultaneous purchase of fixed-income instruments and a call option on real estate futures or swaps will give exposure to the upside of the real estate market and control of the downside.

Whether to invest directly in the property and use put options to protect value or invest indirectly in call options and fixed-income instruments would be determined by the manager's expertise in the area. The direct investment and put option approach would be used for geographical areas and property types in which the manager has special confidence in investing. The fixed-income and call option approach would be appropriate for geographical areas and property types in which the manager has no particular comparative advantage in investments.

If the manager believes the upside potential of real estate is currently limited, he or she can protect against drops in the market at lower cost by using spreads. The manager could combine a long position in real estate with the purchase of a put option and the sale of an out-of-the-money call option. The amount received for the call option offsets part of the cost of the put option. If the value of real estate falls, the put will pay off, thus offsetting the loss on the property investment. If the market advances modestly, the property value will rise and the manager will reap the benefit. The manager does, however, forgo the potential benefit of a rise in the market beyond the exercise price of the call option. If the market rises into that area, the gain in the manager's property value will be offset by the cost of paying off the exercised option.

CONCLUSION

The introduction of a variety of derivative instruments has increased the range of strategies available to the portfolio manager. The manager has much more flexibility in asset allocation and risk control and at the same time can reduce transaction costs by trading in the synthetic rather than in the underlying assets. The existing assets based on interest rates and stocks provide some potentially interesting strategies for the real estate portfolio manager.

If similar derivative instruments are introduced in the real estate area, many additional strategies will open up. The manager will be able to shift the portfolio's asset allocation, be able to synthetically diversify, and have greater capacity for risk control.

The problem still to be mastered is how these new instruments are to be designed. Financial engineers have yet to solve myriad technical issues that arise when attempting to apply existing derivative instrument technology to the real estate market. The special complexities of the real estate market—the regional nature of the market and the illiquidity of the assets traded—make designing real estate–based swaps futures and options especially difficult.

But it has been just these difficulties that have, in the past, limited the willingness of some institutional investors to take positions in real estate. If the issues can be resolved—and current work suggests that this is about to happen—many new investors will be attracted to direct or indirect investment in real estate, and existing investors will be granted an abundance of new investment strategies.

CHAPTER 28

REAL ESTATE CYCLES AND ANIMAL SPIRITS

Werner F. M. De Bondt
University of Wisconsin–Madison

INTRODUCTION

During the last decade, real estate markets around the world have been characterized by high price volatility. This volatility has taken investors, lenders, developers, and policymakers by surprise. However, it is less extraordinary when seen in the context of the volatility of other financial markets today and in the past. A general theory of booms and busts cannot be derived from institutional explanations that depend on time and place, such as taxes or regulation. However, it may be based on investor psychology. The literature on heuristics and biases suggests that at times, many people fall victim to predictable cognitive errors, such as excessive optimism or overconfidence. When the errors are widely shared, they lead to speculative bubbles and market inefficiencies. Expert investors, acting with discipline, can likely profit from the disparities between price and value.

OVERVIEW

Was it the day before yesterday when everyone was extolling the unbeatable investment characteristics of real estate? "Wealth without risks," we were told, and experience seemed to confirm it in many parts of the country. Today Americans by and large continue to believe that buying a home is the investment with the highest return and

I thank Joseph Pagliari (the editor) for encouragement and for numerous comments. I also thank Walter Barnes, Richard Ennis, Richard Green, Paul Schoemaker, Jim Shilling, Alex Triantis, and James Webb.

the lowest risk a household can make. For many people, real estate still represents a significant fraction of their personal investment portfolios. But the unbridled optimism has vanished.

Academic studies helped to build the excitement concerning commercial real estate. These studies stressed (1) the high returns of real estate, (2) the low return variability (Webb and Sirmans, 1980); (3) the diversification benefits derived from the low correlation with stock and bond prices (Burns and Epley, 1982; Froland et al., 1986; Firstenberg et al., 1988), and (4) the value of real estate as a hedge against inflation. Other selling points included tax benefits and the pride and pleasure of property ownership.[1]

Historically, the evidence suggested annual nominal returns somewhere between 10 and 20 percent (Sirmans and Sirmans, 1987). With the dramatic rise in inflation during the late 1970s and early 1980s, the volatility in short-term interest rates and bond prices, and a relatively unrewarding stock market, many investors were "ripe for real estate religion."[2] Institutional investors raced to diversify their portfolios. Deregulated savings and loans, commercial banks,

---

[1] Later studies have questioned these views. First, while the data confirm "excess" real estate returns in the framework of the capital asset pricing model, the evidence tends to evaporate in multifactor models (Chan et al., 1990). Second, it is true that the standard deviation of annual returns on the S&P 500 stock index is more than five times greater than that of the Russell/NCREIF Property Index. But it is also widely believed that the risk of real estate is underestimated. The source of the problem is that the returns are based on appraisals rather than transaction prices. This method smooths the return data (among others, see Firstenberg et al. [1988]). Third, the diversification benefits may have been overestimated for pension funds with elderly beneficiaries who own a home. Finally, several papers dispute whether real estate is a hedge against unexpected inflation. For example, Chan et al. (1990) conclude that real estate investment trusts (REITs) are indistinguishable from stocks in this regard. Damodaran et al. (1992) found that during the 1972–88 period, the hedging characteristics of REITs varied with vacancy rates (i.e., the ability of owners to step up rents) and changing tax regimes.

[2] The attractiveness of real estate followed in part from the interaction of the tax system with inflation and its effect on the real rate of return investors could earn on nonresidential fixed investment. Feldstein (1983) offers a detailed analysis. In brief, the argument says that tax rules distort capital formation when inflation exists. On the one hand, inflation distorts the correct measurement of capital gains and corporate profits. The effective tax rate investors pay on corporate stock increases because fictitious (nominal) capital gains are taxed. Also, because of historical cost depreciation and first-in/first-out inventory accounting, corporate profits are overstated (and overtaxed). On the other hand, inflation warps the measurement of true interest expense. Because nominal interest is deductible in calculating taxable income, "what appears to have been a rising interest rate . . . was actually a sharply falling real after-tax cost of funds" (Feldstein, 1983, p. 10). In addition, the implicit rental income and capital gains on owner-occupied housing go virtually untaxed. As a result of all of the above, the real tax burden on business capital rises with inflation, but the burden on housing capital falls.

insurance companies, and pension funds all poured large sums into mortgage loans and equity positions. Foreign investors, joined by the likes of Donald Trump, helped to bid up the prices of "trophy" properties. All the while, property values and returns were on a stable upward path. It looked almost too good to be true.

BOOM AND BUST

And it was. During the 1980s, more office space was built in the United States than ever before. Valued in real dollars, the additional space created each year never fell below *twice* the average annual addition during the 1970s. The results of this expansion were immediate and dramatic. For example, between 1978 and 1991, the net rentable area of commercial space in downtown Chicago rose from 65 million to nearly 110 million square feet. The vacancy rate rose from 6 to 16 percent. The U.S. downtown office market vacancy rate was above 16 percent for the entire second half of the 1980s. The suburban vacancy rate was above 20 percent. Not surprisingly, rental income and real estate values plunged.

It all adds up to what some now call the worst commercial real estate debacle since the Great Depression. Hendershott and Kane (1992) estimated that $130 billion in U.S. resources have been wasted in the process.[3] However, the property malaise is not uniquely American. It extends to Europe and Japan. Consider, for instance, Canary Wharf in London's Docklands, built by Olympia & York (Foster, 1993). In Scandinavia, the governments of Norway, Sweden, and Finland have spent over $16 billion propping up commercial and savings banks. Entire banking systems, as well as the insurance

---

[3] Because of overbuilding, about $100 billion was tied up in vacant commercial real estate. If the vacancy rate returns to normal (8 percent) by the year 2001, the present value of the opportunity losses is about $130 billion (in 1991 dollars).

Another way to gauge the consequences of the overbuilding is by its effect on real estate values. Hendershott and Kane (1992) put the decline in value at $220 billion to $300 billion. The drop in value adds to the financial troubles of U.S. depository institutions, as well as insurance companies and pension funds. The insurance industry holds $240 billion in commercial real estate mortgages. Standard & Poor's estimates that these companies may be forced to write off about $9 billion. Pension funds have roughly $120 billion invested in commercial real estate. Most funds contributed money to pools managed by real estate advisors. Pension funds that participated in leveraged property investments have lost most of their equity (*Fortune,* December 14, 1992).

industry, are at risk because of bad property debts.[4] In Japan, property casualties represented a third of all bankruptcies in 1991. In mid-1993, commercial land prices in Tokyo tumbled nearly 50 percent from their peak.[5] Mitsubishi Estate expects negative cashflows for the next decade on the Landmark Tower in Yokohama, Japan's biggest building. Its foreign investments are not doing much better. The value of Mitsubishi's equity share in New York's Rockefeller Center is estimated to have fallen by $500 million. Developers like Mitsui Fudosan and Kumagai Gumi now replace loans to foreign subsidiaries with equity because they can no longer pay interest. Japan's fragile banks may well be holding the grand total of about $500 billion of unacknowledged bad property loans (*The Economist,* February 13, 1993).[6]

The booms and busts of real estate have been most spectacular for office buildings, shopping malls, warehouses, and undeveloped land.[7] In many places, however, the U.S. market for single- and multi-family homes has also been characterized by unusually large price fluctuations. For example, in the Boston area, the median price of existing single-family homes rose about $100,000, from $83,000 to

---

[4] Another interesting case study in Europe is Rodamco, a Dutch real estate investment fund. Rodamco managed its stock price by repurchasing shares at the "appraised value" of its portfolio. (This is legal practice in the Netherlands.) However, it was forced to abandon the policy on September 24, 1990. The share price immediately fell by 25 percent. For an analysis, see De Wit (1991).

[5] In 1990–91, the total land value in Japan was about $20 trillion, that is, double the amount of all corporate capital listed on the world's equity markets. The land under the emperor's palace in Tokyo (three-quarters of a square mile) was worth about the same as all the land in California. See Stone and Ziemba (1993).

[6] Estimates differ widely. According to *The Wall Street Journal* (July 29, 1993, p. A1), Japan's 21 major banks reported nonperforming loans totaling $110 billion at the end of March 1993, with about a third of the bad loans property related. However, "judged by U.S. standards, troubled loans may be twice the reported amount."

[7] It is interesting to "unbundle" aggregate real estate returns. Pagliari and Webb (1992) studied the different Russell/NCREIF indexes that apply to the (1) office, (2) retail, (3) R&D/office, (4) warehouse, and (5) apartment sectors. They attribute the quarterly returns for each series to (1) initial yield, that is, net operating income (NOI) divided by price; (2) expected growth in NOI; and (3) changes in capitalization rates. Across real estate categories, NOI did not keep pace with inflation for much of the 1980s. Returns benefited, however, from declining capitalization rates. Thus, investors bought "laggardly earnings at higher and higher multiples" (Pagliari and Webb, 1992, p. 419).

In addition, Barkema (1987) and Colling and Irwin (1988) describe the rise and fall in farmland values. There was a dramatic runup in real prices during the 1970s and a collapse in the 1980s.

$183,000, between 1983 and 1987.[8] The collapse that followed is nearly legendary.

Real estate cycles can be painful. They involve sharp swings in building activity, vacancies, rents, and real dollar property values that can have a strong impact on the economy of the region. A period of excess building is followed by contraction. Case (1991) estimates that the price rises and the building boom of the mid-1980s increased the wealth of homeowners and real estate investors in Massachusetts by $160 billion. For the regional economy, this led to an annual increase in consumption of at least $3.25 billion, adding nearly 100,000 jobs. The demand for labor rose, but the growth in the labor supply did not keep up. High home prices simply discouraged people from moving to the state. Between 1987 and 1991, annual home sales dropped from 105,000 to about 60,000, a number comparable to sales for 1983 and 1984. The construction industry lost 70,000 jobs and, as is widely known, the local economy and the financial condition of regional banks suffered. While real estate is only one factor that contributed to the recession in New England, it seems certain that the real estate cycle amplified the business cycle.

As a second example, consider Houston (Harris County).[9] Between 1982 and 1984, the housing stock increased by 164,000 units (16 percent). Soon the supply of housing exceeded demand. Then, following the downturn in the oil and gas industry, the population declined, but only modestly. By 1985, 18.4 percent of the housing stock within the metropolitan area was vacant. (During the 1970s, the residential vacancy rate was typically around 9 percent.) The glut in housing caused a real price decline of 30 percent. Condominium prices fell by as much as 60 percent. In 1987, foreclosures reached 3,000 per month, more than 20 times their historical level. Most vacant houses either were never occupied or had outstanding mortgage debt in excess of market value. Between 1970 and 1985, upper-end housing increased in value at an annual rate of 9 percent. But by 1987, real dollar prices had fallen back to their 1970 levels.

---

[8] This discussion of housing prices in Massachusetts is based on Case (1986, 1991) and Case and Cook (1989).

[9] The account that follows is largely based on Smith and Tesarek (1991).

BOUNDED RATIONALITY

What are we to make of the booms and busts in the real estate market? One possible reaction is solemn indifference. From a societal perspective, the financial consequences are serious. However, the buildings are in place and, at the correct price, will be used in the productive process. Some mistakes of commercial judgment will always be made in a market economy.

A second reaction is to look for a rational interpretation so that investors, lenders, operators, and policymakers do not repeat past mistakes. Maybe the problems with commercial real estate were the predictable outcome of government-distorted incentives. The issue is: With deregulation, did competitive forces push federally insured depository institutions into mispricing real estate debt, in effect shifting part of their deposit insurance subsidies to borrowers? (See, for example, Hendershott and Kane [1992].)[10] Not only was the debt too cheap relative to the true investment risk; it was also extremely large. Lenders often provided mortgages of 100 percent or more of cost, and development companies claimed a share of future appreciation as their equity stake. Perhaps, with little at stake, many developers lost sight of supply and demand and built projects in cities they knew little about. In addition, the 1981 tax package, which was designed to stimulate the economy, allowed generous depreciation deductions. With high leverage, an initial equity investment could be recouped within the first few years through tax losses alone. But in 1986, most tax breaks were eliminated. The 1989 legislation to help the S&L bailout also contributed to real estate's woes. For example, higher capital requirements associated with mortgage loans severely cur-

---

[10] Thus, federal deposit insurance is blamed for the problems in the financial sector as well. See Benston et al. (1991) for a discussion of the failures of thrifts. To illustrate these problems, consider how in 1991, for U.S. banks with over $300 million in assets, 8.4 percent of real estate loans were nonperforming. But one subcategory, construction and development loans, had a nonperforming rate of 20.2 percent. (The rate for mortgages was only 3.2 percent.)

Corrigan (1991) and Gorton and Rosen (1992) offer competing points of view. Corrigan (1991) calls it a "myth" that because of moral hazard, deposit insurance is "fatally and irreversibly flawed." Among other elements, he points to the fact that troubled banks typically lose deposits. Thus, many large depositors "do not accept the notion of full insurance" (p. 51). Gorton and Rosen (1992) argue that managerial entrenchment is the true culprit. The entrenchment predicts overly aggressive risk taking.

tailed real estate lending even for soundly operated properties seeking to refinance maturing debt.[11]

While misguided government policies may have triggered or contributed to the latest debacle in real estate, it should be patently clear that institutional factors *alone* do not add up to a full explanation. First, booms and busts in property and land values have occurred for many decades, if not centuries! Consider, for instance, the overbuilding associated with the emergence of REITs during the late 1960s and 1970s or Malkiel's (1990) discussion of the Florida land craze in the 1920s. Second, as described earlier, the current crisis in real estate has spread to many countries outside the United States. Third, within the United States, the problems are spread rather unevenly. They are most severe in just a few regions, such as California, Texas, and New England. Finally, the bursting of the speculative bubble extends beyond commercial real estate and undeveloped land to single- and multifamily homes.

To interpret real estate cycles, I would argue instead for a more fundamental explanation, one that has to do with human nature itself. This new approach introduces investor psychology. It is built around *descriptive theories of financial decision making* that are perhaps less elegant than the austerity of the optimization principle dominant in economics. The research question is: What do people do? (As opposed to: What would rational people want to do?) To achieve progress, we have to stop reducing all human behavior to the normative concept of rationality defined by *homo economicus,* that is, expected utility maximization, risk-aversion, rational expectations, and Bayesian updating.[12]

---

[11] A more detailed list of institutional factors would include four categories: (1) changes in the federal income tax (in 1981, 1982, 1984, and 1986); (2) changes in federal securities laws (Regulation D); (3) financial innovation, particularly, the creation of staged pay-ins of equity investment in real estate limited partnerships; and (4) changes in capital requirements for financial institutions. See Garrigan and Pagliari (1992).

[12] Ingersoll (1987) presents an introduction to the building blocks of neoclassical economics and modern finance. Thaler (1987) offers a systematic critique. (For a philosophical appreciation of the optimality principle in science, see Schoemaker [1991].) Methodologically, behavioral theories are attractive because they impose the discipline of descriptive realism (i.e., the approach does not permit unending ad hoc "rational" theorizing). But economists such as Milton Friedman reply that the lack of realism of the standard axioms and their simplicity are strengths so long as the theory predicts well.

In finance, behavioral asset pricing theories are part of the "noise trader approach" (Black,

Before moving on, the reader may protest: Why should we take this step? There are two reasons. First, the predictions of the standard economic models often gain little support from the data. This is most clearly seen in empirical studies of financial valuation theory. In finance, we come closest to studying the ideal of frictionless markets, rational arbitrage is more likely to be a potent force than in any other market, and we have access to high-quality data. In rational and perfect markets, asset prices—whether for stocks, bonds, or commodities—should at all times equal "intrinsic values." This is the so-called efficient markets hypothesis (EMH) (Fama, 1970). The hypothesis says that, with the competition from expert traders, investor psychology can play no systematic role in market pricing. Just one thing matters: the objective financial outlook—exclusively.

The EMH always troubled practical people on Wall Street because in its extreme "strong-form" version, it denies that competent analysts can consistently identify assets that are overpriced and others that are bargains. (The 1987 stock market crash did not help the efficiency crowd!) Nonetheless, during the 1970s and early 1980s, academics generally stood by the EMH. Since that time, numerous anomalies have been discovered.[13] For example, stock prices are too variable relative to the dividends shareholders receive later (Shiller, 1989). Stock returns also vary in unexplained seasonal patterns. Small-capitalization companies and those with low price-to-earnings ratios seem underpriced . After the usual correction for risk, excess

---

1986; De Long et al., 1990a; Shleifer and Summers, 1990). The theory assumes two classes of traders: (1) rational information traders, and (2) less than fully rational "noise traders." Noise traders base their decisions on uninformative "noise" (e.g., the prediction of a stock market guru) as though it were valuable information. Noise trader models are meant to justify possible deviations between price and value as well as the high price volatility and high trading volume actually observed in markets. The models also examine the incentives of rational traders in an irrational world (De Long et al., 1990b).

[13] See Keim (1986) or Fama (1991) for a review of the pricing anomalies. Fama emphasizes that, since the EMH cannot be tested independently of models of the risk-return trade-off, the stock market may yet be rational. For example, risk premia may vary with time or institutional factors may be responsible for the predictability in returns.

Another old puzzle has to do with the massive volume of trading in financial markets. In a fully rational world, people would buy or sell shares only for consumption purposes or to adjust the risk and tax exposures of their portfolios. In fact, much trading is speculative, that is, motivated by past price movements or presumed access to superior information. But how could people rationally give so much weight to their own insights and so little to the knowledge of other traders?

returns do not look as random as the EMH would have it. Instead, excess returns show mean reversion, especially in the long run (De Bondt and Thaler, 1985, 1989). In other words, initial big price movements, up or down, are followed by price reversals that can be interpreted as "a return to fundamentals." (Within the context of the EMH, it remains a puzzle why the contrarian strategies that exploit these price corrections would be profitable.)

The market rationality debate will continue. Observers from across the spectrum can agree, however, that the surprising volatility of financial markets is poorly understood. Past, contemporaneous, and future public information simply does not account for much of the variation in prices (Roll, 1988; Shiller, 1989). Also, the restrictions imposed by rationality—say, in the context of the capital asset pricing model—are either rejected (Fama and French, 1992) or, in the end, deemed untestable (Fama, 1991). In sum, the data certainly do not stop us from telling a story where, in equilibrium, the irrational beliefs of millions of unsophisticated investors affect stock prices.[14] The popular image offered by the news media—that investing in shares has more to do with psychology than with economics—may well be true. But if this story goes for the stock market, it should apply more strongly to markets with large transaction costs, as in the case of real estate.

The second reason to consider an alternative to the rational-economic approach is that the underlying behavioral assumptions are descriptively wrong. For instance, risk taking is at least as much a function of situational factors as it is driven by personality characteristics (Slovic, 1972a, 1972b). Or, contrary to the "principle of invariance," alternative versions of the same decision problem frequently give rise to different preferences (Tversky and Kahneman, 1986).[15] The defects of the pure logic of choice are probably demonstrated most convincingly by experimental research (Thaler, 1987). But results gathered with other research methods, such as surveys or field studies, are just as disappointing.

As a way out, Herbert Simon (1957) launched the concept of

---

[14] On the other hand, one should keep in mind that our ignorance is not to be construed as evidence in favor of a behavioral explanation!

[15] But neoclassical financial theory simply ignores framing issues as well as situational determinants of decision making under uncertainty. See, for example, Ingersoll (1987).

bounded rationality.[16] In general, the bounded rationality perspective looks on people as reasonable beings, but it accepts the limitations of human intelligence. It directs our attention to the psychology of actual decision processes. For many problems, decision makers are not capable of finding the answers that are truly optimal in a normative sense. They may be satisfied with a given solution and stop searching for improvement. The actions taken typically depend on the way the issue is framed. (Here task complexity invites reliance on simplifying strategies.) Put bluntly, the concept of bounded rationality reintroduces the human factor to economic modeling. We have to investigate the quality of judgment.

The quality of judgment is a function of the inherent difficulty of the valuation problem. In *The General Theory,* John Maynard Keynes (1936) reminds us of "the extreme precariousness of the basis of knowledge" on which cash flow forecasts are made. "If we speak frankly, we have to admit that our basis of knowledge for estimating the yield ten years hence of a railway, a copper mine, . . . , a building in the City of London amounts to little and sometimes to nothing; or even five years hence" (pp. 149–50). In this context, the consensus forecast (or the state of "business confidence") looms large, and perceptions of risk and return may be subject to crowd psychology, that is, conformist behavior and fashion (Shiller, 1989). Keynes refers to "animal spirits."[17]

Newspaper accounts of the troubles of real estate agree with this assessment. An analysis of local events in the *Chicago Tribune* concludes that "the basics of real estate were forgotten in the 1980s" (Steve Kerch, August 9, 1992). To some extent, the mentality of the 1980s was shaped by the stock market. Stocks are bought and sold

---

[16] George Katona (1951) is another pioneer of this line of research. For more discussion, see Simon (1983) and Loewenstein and Elster (1992, Chapter 1).

[17] Other prominent old-time macroeconomists shared this view with Keynes. See, for example, Pigou (1929) or Mitchell (1913). In *Business Cycles,* Wesley Mitchell (1913) wrote, "Most men find their spirits raised by being in optimistic company . . . [When] the first beneficiaries of a trade revival develop a cheerful frame of mind about the business outlook, they become centers of infection, and start an epidemic of optimism . . . As it spreads, the epidemic of optimism helps to produce conditions that both justify and intensify it" (p. 5).

More recently, Malabre (1987) also defended a psychological theory of the business cycle: "Economic developments are deeply rooted in human nature. People tend to overextend themselves . . . Banks invariably will run down liquidity by bidding more and more aggressively for deposits, accepting lower-quality credits, and shaving loan charges. Corporations invariably will overexpand if they think they can accelerate earnings growth . . . Politicians invariably will mortgage more and more of the future . . ." (p. 101).

daily, but property is less liquid. The article quotes Blaine Kelley, chair of Landmarks Group, an Atlanta-based real estate firm, admitting that "we overreached the market, and like many just got carried away with what we thought were boundless opportunities. It didn't work out that way." Chicago developer J. Paul Beitler, whose proposed "World's Tallest Building" project is on hold, puts it, "We were victims of a herd instinct."

As another example, consider the following quote from *The Economist* in its survey of the Japanese economy (March 6, 1993):

> In 1989 . . . industrial enterprises were behaving like financial intermediaries—raising finance in order to accumulate financial assets . . . The overall expansion of bank lending and financial activity fuelled, and then was fuelled by, rising asset prices. That is why the term "bubble" is not . . . misplaced. Driven by expectations that the price of land and equities would keep rising, firms and households borrowed to invest in them, thus causing their expectations to be fulfilled; at the same time, the rising value of asset portfolios served as collateral for more borrowing, giving the circle another vigorous turn . . . While the bubble was inflating, it was easily mistaken for a miracle . . . Then, all of sudden, the market psychology shifts. Soon the majority was rushing as fast as it could in the opposite direction. Asset prices began to fall sharply . . . (pp. 8–9)

Apart from their reliance on trader psychology, what are the common elements in the various interpretations of real estate cycles and market volatility? It is useful to go back to Kindleberger's (1989) scenario of the canonical financial crisis. (See also Summers [1991].) In the prelude to crisis, Kindleberger distinguishes three stages: (1) an economic shock that objectively justifies higher prices; (2) rising investor confidence, leading to the increased use of leverage; and (3) a bandwagon or herding effect, where demand increases because prices are going up. Similarly, when the bubble bursts, an outside shock first reduces speculative demand. Next, market prices drop more as demand slows because even lower prices are expected in the future.[18]

---

[18] In addition, falling prices restrain new borrowing because of the lower value of the properties used as collateral. At the same time, the supply of real estate may increase if lower prices force some investors to liquidate their holdings. These feedback mechanisms sometimes operate between asset classes. In Japan, stock prices peaked in December 1989, roughly one year before the peak in land prices. For a discussion, see Kobayashi (1993).

Kindleberger's scenario has all the drama of a self-fulfilling prophecy. In real estate cycles in particular, an eventual crash seems inevitable as additions to supply overwhelm demand and adversely affect both rental payments and occupancy levels. *The central puzzle is the excessive optimism and overconfidence that start the cycle, as well as the so-called positive feedback trading that keeps it going.* Corrigan (1991) addresses the last point. Unrealistic hopes for rapid wealth accumulation, he believes, draw naive players into the market, usually at the wrong time. They duplicate strategies that produced high profits in the past. (See also Rose [1993].) As a result, the profits are short-lived. An interesting aspect of herding behavior is the apparent illusion of universal liquidity, that is, the belief of any individual trader that, in a downturn, he or she will be able to get out while others take losses.

Weak investment performance is so common that overoptimism may well characterize investors in closed-end mutual funds, commodity funds, and initial public offerings of equity (IPOs); see, for example, Ritter (1991). Overoptimism agrees with the continued popularity of active stock portfolio management. More important, overoptimism may also explain the never-ending influx of entrepreneurs in industries with high bankruptcy risk, such as restaurants. In his 1921 classic *Risk, Uncertainty, and Profit*, Frank Knight argued strongly that entrepreneurs, as a class, earn less than the competitive rate of return. One view of this is excessive risk taking or, stated less politely, recklessness. Knight emphasizes, however, that the risk does "not relate to objective external probabilities, but to the value of the judgment and executive powers of the person taking the chance . . . Most men have an irrationally high confidence in their own good fortune, and that is doubly true when their personal prowess comes into the reckoning . . . To these considerations must be added the stimulus of the competitive situation, constantly exerting pressure to outbid one's rivals . . . Another . . . factor is the human trait of tenacity . . . once committed, . . . the general rule is to hold on to the last ditch" (pp. 365–66).[19] Thus, we must return to the issue of the quality of judgment.

---

[19] In this context, Daniel Kahneman uses the phrase "bold forecasts, timid choices." See also Arrow (1982).

THE PSYCHOLOGY OF JUDGMENT

A simple way to think about investment decision making is as a series of present value calculations. Which projects are worthwhile and which ones are not? Everything depends on (1) the expected future cash flows and (2) the opportunity cost of capital. Of course, it may be exceedingly difficult to get an accurate estimate of, say, the net operating income of a shopping center two to five years from now. So the deeper question becomes: How do people handle such assignments? How are intuitive forecasts made?

To formulate the beginnings of an answer, we turn to cognitive experimental psychology. Because of space limitations, the following discussion is rather brief. Useful references include Bazerman (1986), Hogarth (1987), Nisbett and Ross (1980), Kahneman et al. (1982), and Russo and Schoemaker (1989). The important conclusion of this research is that, in many circumstances, individual errors are predictable. And, because we all tend to make the same logical mistakes, average opinion may be systematically biased.

Heuristics and Biases

Heuristics are intuitive mechanisms for coping with complexity. Generally, heuristics are useful shortcuts that produce the desired outcome. Sometimes, however, they lead to foreseeable errors in judgment. People are typically not aware of these biases. In a series of classic papers, Amos Tversky and Daniel Kahneman analyzed three major rules of thumb: (1) representativeness, (2) availability, and (3) anchoring-and-adjustment. Hereafter, I define these heuristics and use examples to illustrate potential losses in the quality of judgment. But, to repeat, one should not forget that heuristics produce far more adequate than inadequate decisions.

Judgment by *representativeness* occurs when people assess the chances of an event by its similarity to a well-known stereotype. In other words, the subjective probability of a certain event rises because it displays the salient features of other events in the same category, but the increase ignores, or gives too little weight to, the base rates for the category. For example, when people are told about Isabelle, "a senior at Wellesley interested in classical music, old paintings, and antiques," the predicted likelihood that she will enter a graduate program in arts management is typically a very large multiple of the fraction of all graduate students who in fact pursue this type of education.[20] Thus, the unjustified neglect of base rates leads to intuitive forecasts that are too extreme. Representativeness has many other consequences, such as the discovery of patterns in random-walk data or a failure to appreciate the phenomenon of regression-to-the-mean. Many stock market investors naively extrapolate past price patterns (De Bondt, 1993b). Even financial analysts' forecasts of corporate earnings show a systematic tendency to be too extreme, that is, either too high or too low (De Bondt and Thaler, 1990).[21]

Judgment by *availability* takes place whenever a probability is judged by vividness and by the ease with which an event is brought to mind, that is, retrieved from memory. For example, many drivers put on their seatbelts right after witnessing a bad road accident. In 1991, tens of thousands of American tourists canceled their vacations in Europe even though the danger to life of well-publicized terrorist attacks does not compare to the risks of street crime in many U.S. cities.[22]

The *anchoring-and-adjustment* heuristic is used when people start from an initial value and adjust it to yield a final inference. Adjustments from the starting value tend to be insufficient so that different anchors produce different conclusions. A good example is the "first-impression-syndrome." After meeting someone for the first time (say, at a dinner party), we may be slow to adjust our opinion at a later date, even if the context completely changes (say, to a job interview).

---

[20] Yet when people are asked for this fraction, their responses indicate an awareness that there are few such students.

The effects of representativeness can be demonstrated as follows. Subjects (1) rank order the chances that Isabelle chooses to become a graduate student in various fields (arts management, biology, business, etc.) and (2) rank order the similarity between Isabelle and "typical" students in those fields. Usually both judgments are highly correlated, but, as we know, they should not be.

[21] Other expert predictions, such as the macroeconomic forecasts of professional economists, appear to be subject to the same cognitive bias (Ahlers and Lakonishok, 1983).

[22] In his study of crowd sentiment (1895), Le Bon provides the following example: "The epidemic of influenza, which caused the death . . . of five thousand persons in Paris alone, made very little impression on the popular imagination. The reason is that this veritable hecatomb was not embodied in any visible image, but was only learnt from statistical information . . . An accident which should have caused the death of only five hundred . . . persons, but on the same day and in public, as the outcome of an accident appealing strongly to the eye, by the fall, for instance, of the Eiffel Tower, would have produced, on the contrary, an immense impression . . . It is not, then, the facts in themselves that strike the popular imagination . . . It is necessary that . . . they should produce a startling image which fills and besets the mind" (pp. 70–71).

Tversky and Kahneman (1974) rely on the anchoring heuristic to explain *overconfidence* in judgment. For instance, when subjects were asked to produce high and low forecasts of the Dow Jones so that, two weeks later, in only 10 percent of the cases the stock price index actually turned out higher or lower, almost 50 percent of the realizations fell outside the confidence interval (De Bondt, 1993b). Presumably, people started with a point forecast and then adjusted it to develop the confidence interval. But the poor calibration of the forecasts means the adjustments were insufficient. This result generally typifies the overconfidence literature (see Lichtenstein et al. [1982] for a review).

As mentioned earlier, perhaps the central question that needs to be answered by a psychological theory of real estate cycles concerns the sources of the excessive optimism that starts the overbuilding. Unrealistic optimism about future life events is, in fact, common behavior. In an experimental study, Weinstein (1980) asked 258 college students to estimate the difference (in percent) between the chances that a particular event would happen to them and the average chances for other people. Clearly, if there were no forecast bias, the mean value of this difference score ought to be zero. However, many subjects acted as if they were "invulnerable." For example, when asked about the chances that the value of their homes would double in five years, nearly two-thirds believed their own chances were greater than average. The mean difference score was +13.3 percent. In general, a substantial majority of people believe negative events (e.g., being fired) are less likely to happen to them than to others but positive events (e.g., living past 80 years) are more likely to happen to them than to others.

Weinstein (1980) blames the optimism bias on wishful thinking as well as cognitive mechanisms. The motivational explanation simply suggests that the more desirable or undesirable the outcome, "the stronger the distortion of reality" (p. 807). In other words, predictions tend to coincide with preferences. The cognitive explanation relies on availability and representativeness. In comparative assessment, an individual is likely to pay too much attention to his or her own actions and circumstances and too little to those of other people.[23]

---

[23] Feldstein's (1991) view of nonperforming real estate loans held by commercial banks partly echoes this perspective. He states, "although each prospective project seemed attractive on the basis of the existing stock of real estate and the associated level of rents, when all the new buildings became available the rent levels were depressed" (p. 13).

For instance, previous personal experience makes it easy to recall a given event, imagine its repetition, or construct a new causal sequence that suggests its future occurrence. When the event is partly controllable, it is also natural for people to find reassurance in their current plans to deal with it. Thus, the imagined chances of a positive (or a less negative) outcome rise with the perceived controllability of the situation. In addition, there may be a familiar stereotype of the kind of person to whom certain events happen, for example, "male blue-collar workers over 55 who have smoked for many years often get lung cancer." Since people easily discern the differences between themselves and the stereotype (who does little to improve her or his chances), they become more optimistic about their own prospects.[24]

Another important question is whether the cognitive biases that are documented in the laboratory survive in a real-world setting (Hogarth, 1981). Northcraft and Neale (1987) addressed this issue with a clever study of the effect of the anchoring-and-adjustment heuristic on property pricing decisions. Forty-eight business students ("amateurs") and 21 real estate agents with an average of seven years of experience ("experts") individually toured and appraised a house for sale in Tucson, Arizona. The actual listing price and appraised value was $74,900. Subjects had a standard Multiple Listing Service (MLS) listing sheet for the property and for other houses currently for sale in the neighborhood. In addition, they had the MLS summary of real estate sales for the last six months, as well as more detailed information on houses that recently sold or that were previously listed but did not sell. Every subject had the same information, with one exception: The listing price mentioned on the MLS sheet was either $65,900 ("low price condition"), $71,900, $77,900, or $83,900 ("high price condition").

The hypothesis that the listing price would bias the subjects' appraisals was strongly confirmed. For example, for amateurs, the average responses to the lowest offer "that the subject would accept if he or she were the seller" were, respectively, $62,571 in the low price condition and $69,785 in the high price condition. For experts,

---

[24] Thus, for negative events, the representativeness heuristic produces optimism. (But for positive events, it leads to pessimism.)

the respective numbers were \$65,000 and \$72,590.[25] Thus, from this research, it appears that the cognitive errors found in laboratory experiments are not wholly due to an "artificial" context. A second interesting finding is that even experts are susceptible to decisional bias. In Northcraft and Neale's study, they were not aware of the bias. In a follow-up survey, only 14.3 percent of the real estate agents even admitted to listing price as one of their "top three" considerations.

Social Cognition, Fashion, and Conformity

I have described some of the nonreflective and automatic strategies people use in making intuitive judgments. However, judgment and decision making further depend on a rich repertoire of knowledge structures, that is, familiarity with objects, issues, and events and their characteristic relationships.[26] People are *active* interpreters of new information; that is, they constantly go beyond the data given to them. Heuristics can be seen as taking part in the selection of knowledge structures. For example, the similarity of new data to a stereotype (e.g., Isabelle) may result in its application. As explained earlier, the acute or transient availability of a schema also encourages its use. Also, because of anchoring effects, once a particular cognitive construct is in place, attempts to integrate new data are frequently inadequate. Hence, human cognition is conservative. Beliefs tend to sustain themselves despite evidence to the contrary (Nisbett and Ross, 1980).

Cognitive schemas and intuitive theories are widely shared. Precisely because our own perceptions and actions are influenced by what others say and do, we are "social animals" (Aronson, 1992). An

---

[25] Northcraft and Neal repeated the experiment with a property in Tucson listed at \$135,000. Fifty-four business students and 47 real estate agents participated. The flavor of the results remained the same. For the low and high price conditions, the lowest acceptable offers were, on average, \$12,682 (amateurs) or \$28,898 (experts) apart.

[26] For more details, see Nisbett and Ross (1980, Chapters 1 and 2). Knowledge structures include cognitive schemas (e.g., concepts such as "umbrella," "breakfast," or "mowing the lawn") as well as theories and beliefs, ranging from simple generalizations to broad conceptions of the universe (e.g., "X is a good neighbor," "high taxes hurt the economy"). Knowledge structures influence people's attitudes toward behavior and ultimately behavior itself (Ajzen and Fishbein, 1980).

interesting application to real estate is the so-called land myth in Japan. In one of its reports, the Council on Tax Reform, set up by the Japanese government, defined the land myth as "the popularly held belief that nothing beats land as a lucrative asset" (Kobayashi, 1993).

A critical point is that with time, many ideas go in and out of fashion. Consider changing popular attitudes toward "a fair tax system" or "butter and a healthy diet." People's beliefs further vary in the cross-section, for example, in terms of socioeconomic factors or personal experience. Their theories clearly differ in complexity and sophistication. In response to the question "What is the effect of the dollar-yen exchange rate on economic activity?", a hairstylist, a restaurant owner, and a business economist may formulate answers that range from just a couple words (a media sound bite?) to a one-hour lecture!

Clearly, then, no persuasive rationale exists to equate average opinion at a point in time—as expressed in markets, organizations, or political processes (Le Bon, 1895)—with objective truth. Rather, the time-series and cross-sectional variations in social cognition suggest that the market determination of economic value must also be seen as a (potentially faulty) social phenomenon (Klausner, 1984).[27] Janis (1972) describes the dangers of groupthink. He lists many instances of collective misjudgment that are "laughed off in a clubby atmosphere of relaxed conviviality." In this condition, investment success may be defined by good forecasts of novel cognitive frames that are about to "catch on." This is Keynes' beauty contest. Certainly, in the stock market, examples of institutional investors becoming obsessed with a specific sector of an industry abound. For example, IPOs typically occur in industry waves. More recently, in real estate, institutions have also emerged as a major force. But the property types favored by institutions have shifted over time. Now and then,

---

[27] With true diversity of opinion (Harris and Raviv, 1992), even the experts are at odds about the proper interpretation of the same data, so low-cost rational arbitrage cannot save market rationality. Most troubling, however, is the fact that the world overflows with superstitions of all kinds; see, for example, MacKay (1841) or Bertrand Russell's (1950) famed essay "An Outline of Intellectual Rubbish." Evolutionary arguments do not satisfy either. Is this the best of all possible worlds? Among others, Voltaire (1759) offers a poignant critique of Leibnizian optimism.

mass movements occur from one type to another. For instance, in the mid-1970s, large shopping malls were the most sought-after properties. But toward the end of that decade and in the early 1980s, office buildings were the most favored properties.[28]

Herding and belief perseverance are consistent with several stylized empirical facts of security pricing, including (1) the inverse link between three-to-five-year past and subsequent stock returns (or the inverse link with past price-to-book value ratios) and (2) the anomalous "slow" reaction of prices to past earnings surprises (Bernard and Thomas, 1990). Whereas the first fact agrees with prolonged disparities between price and value, the second confirms that popular labels for company XYZ as either a "growth firm" or as part of a "mature industry" may take months or even years to wear off.

Herding may also be partly attributable to pressures originating from the fiduciary nature of portfolio management. By law and business custom, certain standards of prudent behavior are to be maintained. These standards promote conventional thinking. Faced with frequent performance reviews and rankings, managers may prefer tactical moves that make them look good, such as the purchase of current favorites or a niche strategy that offers a recognizable management style.[29] In addition, the psychological theory of regret predicts that, in ambiguous decision situations, individuals often "choose not to choose." Ex ante, people anticipate the regret that accompanies a bad decision, in particular the awareness of "what could have been." Thus, when thorny decisions are to be made, the natural tendency to follow consensus opinion may be a convenient mechanism with which to shift responsibility for the outcome, ex post (De Bondt, 1993a).

---

[28] Fogler et al. (1985) and Statman (1985) raise the possibility that the high aggregate returns on real estate during 1978–83 were explained by changing fashions.

Similarly, Hunter and Coggin (1988) suggest that security analysts tend to accept and to overuse the leading financial theories of their time, such as the capital asset pricing model. Because the theories are employed as knowledge structures, consensus analyst opinion is greatly influenced by them.

[29] The problem also reflects the mathematical certainty that, irrespective of investment skill, luck will anoint some portfolio managers with a false aura of genius. In truth, future success is weakly related to past returns (if at all), but it is common for investors to detect such "patterns" nonetheless. Thus, we observe that the flow of funds in and out of money management companies and their financial viability heavily depend on past performance.

PRICE VERSUS VALUE

Building on evidence from psychology, I have suggested that systematic valuation errors are a likely possibility in all financial markets. But for real estate, the problem looks especially severe because of (1) high transaction and information costs, limiting quick arbitrage, and (2) the length of the building cycle, or the period between the signal to go ahead with a project and the project's time of completion. Thus, it is no surprise, if society's investments in new real estate are not coordinated among developers but are the macro-result of their individual plans, and if significant adjustments to the regional balance of supply and demand are a matter of years, that we find occasional large gaps between the market value of properties and their replacement cost.[30] Nor is it surprising in this context that an astute portfolio manager may be capable of earning "excess profits." This final section of the chapter therefore concludes with a review of empirical studies of real estate market efficiency as well as some practical lessons for real estate valuation.

Real Estate Market Efficiency: Empirical Studies

From a statistical viewpoint, it is difficult to assess the efficiency of real estate markets. A serious problem is the lack of adequate price indices.[31] A second problem is that the empirical tests are unavoidably

---

[30] When demand falls because of exogenous factors, the inability to quickly withdraw supply results in a "buyer's market." Similarly, an unexpected increase in demand creates "a seller's market" because additional space cannot be quickly built. Wheaton (1987) explores the extent to which lags in construction and in the adjustment of rents to changing demand conditions are responsible for cycles in the office market.

[31] For instance, market prices of commercial real estate are not readily available. (See also footnote 1.) Financial economists, suspicious of the quality and timeliness of appraisals, usually rely on REIT returns. One problem is that, contemporaneously, REIT returns are more closely correlated with the stock market, particularly the returns earned by small firms, than with appraisal-based return series. (Are REITs real estate or stocks? See Corgel et al. [1993] for a discussion.) Another problem is that REITs represent only about 1 percent of U.S. commercial real estate. On the other hand, Gyourko and Keim (1992) show that equity REIT returns are good predictors of subsequent changes in the Russell/NCREIF Property Index.

As a second example, consider the National Association of Realtors (NAR) monthly reports of median sales prices for existing single-family homes in 54 cities. These reports do not control for changes in the characteristics of homes actually sold. But the quality of real estate depends on funds spent on maintenance and improvements. Case and Shiller (1987) discuss different methods to address this measurement problem.

joint tests with a valuation model. Short of a correct model of the risk-return trade-off, excess return predictability may always be seen as evidence of rational time-varying risk (Fama, 1991). A third problem is that the usual autocorrelation tests for excess returns have low power; that is, large misvaluations may occur, but the test statistics do not detect it (Shiller, 1989, Chapter 1).[32]

Nevertheless, it is fairly clear that the volatility in real estate values is not easily explained by movements in economic fundamentals. For example, bearing in mind what has happened to vacancy and rental rates, can we really say straight-faced that the United States *needed* to have half of its office space now standing built after 1980? (As mentioned before, commercial property returns were propped up by declining capitalization rates. See Pagliari and Webb [1992].) With respect to residential housing, a similar cry for understanding may be heard. How does one explain the extraordinary price volatility in some regional markets when the major demand factor is demographics (Mankiw and Weil, 1989; Garner, 1992)? Surely, population growth and migration occur only gradually, thus allowing for adjustments in the supply of housing.

For the 1965–86 period, Darrat and Glascock (1989) studied whether the returns of a portfolio of real estate firms listed on the NYSE and AMEX are predicted by past changes in macroeconomic variables. Among other measures, they tried the unemployment rate, changes in industrial production, and changes in the consumer price index. As it turns out, past growth in the monetary base and past returns on a stock market index are significantly related to future real estate returns.

The most credible studies of efficiency were done by Case and Shiller. Their 1989 paper examined the market for single-family homes in four metropolitan areas: Atlanta, Chicago, Dallas, and San Francisco. They constructed their own indices based on actual sales prices for homes that were sold twice with no apparent quality change. (The data were provided by the Society of Real Estate Appraisers.) Perhaps most striking, there is persistence (i.e., positive autocorrela-

---

[32] The roadblocks to formally proving inefficiency are perhaps best illustrated by Stone and Ziemba's (1993) work on Japan (see footnote 5). In the end, these authors conclude that as to the question of "whether a speculative bubble occurred," in the way the academic literature defines *bubbles,* the answer involves "rather subtle matters of definition" (p. 163).

tion) in housing returns. A price change in a given year and city is typically followed by a price change of the same sign from one-quarter to one-half as large. In addition, real per capita income growth, increases in the adult population, and the ratio of construction costs to prices predict excess returns (Case and Shiller, 1990). Interestingly, the price indices show prolonged periods of real decline in property values—in San Francisco, for example, from 1980 to 1983. However, nominal declines are "rare" (Case and Shiller, 1987, p. 53). With falling prices, many homes are taken off the market and the number of completed sales slows down.[33]

What causes the inefficiencies? At this time, the most reasonable explanation is that on occasion, a significant percentage of transactions in the housing market are driven by investment considerations rather than the consumption of housing services. The risk-return forecasts themselves may reflect conformist behavior or "fads" that are consistent with destabilizing speculation. For instance, in an up market, demand may rise merely because buyers, afraid to miss the boom and be "priced out" of the market, accelerate the purchase of a home.

Case and Shiller (1988) analyzed the results of about 900 surveys of people who, during May 1988, bought homes in Boston (a "post-boom" market), Milwaukee (a "normal" market), and Anaheim and San Francisco (two "boom" markets). In San Francisco, a whopping 37 percent of the respondents said they made their purchases "strictly for investment purposes." Nearly 70 percent agreed with the statement "unless I buy now, I won't be able to afford a home later." On average, home buyers in that city expected the value of their property to rise by 13.5 percent over the next 12 months and 14.8 percent each year over the next 10 years! While predicting substantial price increases, 56 percent of the respondents saw "little or no risk," 40 percent believed there was "some risk," and only 4 percent worried about "a great deal of risk."[34] On the whole, the results for Anaheim

---

[33] People tend to hang on to losing investment positions because they do not like to make losses "definite." Shefrin and Statman (1985) offer a psychological interpretation of loss aversion.

[34] To appreciate these answers, it is relevant to consider what happened to home prices over the period prior to the survey. In 1983, the median sales price of existing single-family homes in San Francisco was $129,500. In the second quarter of 1988, the median sales price was $196,300. In contrast, for Milwaukee, the corresponding figures were $68,000 (1983) and $71,500 (1988).

and San Francisco were similar. However, in Boston, where a crash was to follow soon, the average expected price changes were about half of those in boom markets. Still, the perceived risk of buying a home remained small (only 5 percent of the respondents saw "a great deal of risk"). In Milwaukee, people were least optimistic about future price appreciation and most concerned with risk.

Case and Shiller attempted to evaluate people's intuitive theories of housing price booms. The stories they collected reflect only a marginal understanding of market fundamentals. Often the stories are superficial, for example, "there is not enough land" or "it's a nice place to live" (1988, p. 39). Case and Shiller conclude that "the suddenness of booms has to be understood in terms of investor reactions to one another [and] to past price increases, . . . , rather than to economic fundamentals" (1988, p. 43).

Implications for Real Estate Investors

To repeat, the ups and downs of the real estate market are less surprising when put in the context of the volatility of other financial markets. However, real estate has peculiar attributes that logically make it more likely that the market is inefficient. Buildings are durable goods with a long economic life. They are fixed in location. Each property is essentially unique, and as a result the value depends on local circumstances such as the nearness of other properties, zoning regulations and building codes, or economic conditions. Transaction costs for real estate are high. One reason is that many different parties may be involved; for instance, the owner of a property may lease the land on which the building is situated. Another issue is the need to manage the property. (This burden tends to be especially heavy for apartments.) It discourages real estate investments by pension funds, which usually prefer to be passive investors.

In an inefficient real estate market, the skill with which properties are acquired, managed, and disposed is responsible for a major part of total return. In other words, the quality of judgment and decision making is critical. Definitely, much can be learned from studying the decision traps discussed earlier.[35] Conceptually, real

---

[35] The book by Russo and Schoemaker (1989) is ideal reading for this purpose. The authors discuss the psychology of judgment from a managerial point of view.

estate valuation is similar to security analysis. The term *valuation* implies estimating a market value for the property at hand. For this purpose, the analyst uses a variety of analytical and appraisal processes. A simple model of real estate decisions says that every decision involves three components: the property, the financial transaction, and the participants (Stevenson, 1978, p. 152). Most analysts would agree that valuation is as much art as it is science. Formal methods of security analysis may eventually pay off, however, if a structured and disciplined framework, such as cash flow discounting, is consistently applied (Graham and Dodd, 1934). Such a framework certainly improves the organizational controllability of the portfolio management process.

Investment success is based largely on the ability of the analyst to engage in independent investigation and logical thought. Consensus thinking is to be avoided. But this advice, of course, runs counter to a fundamental psychological need to seek acceptance by other people (Aronson, 1992). Portfolio managers easily alienate their clients if they are out of phase with the popular investment concepts of the day, and eventually they may even doubt themselves. Since bull markets cause widespread investor optimism and bear markets pessimism, there is always a natural tendency to "buy high and sell low." The pressure to conform may be greatest when it can be least afforded, that is, when short-term performance is lagging.

The difficulty with placing contrary bets is that the strategy looks imprudent as well as financially unsound. Yet many real estate tycoons, including the Reichmann family and Donald Trump, have built fortunes precisely by playing on the shifting emotions of the crowd as manifested in market volatility. For patient investors, contrarian stock market strategies seem to pay off (De Bondt and Thaler, 1985, 1989). There is plenty of anecdotal evidence to suggest that the same is true for real estate. Returning sanity to the property market likely requires that the public accept old-fashioned values, such as a "long-term perspective." But that hope is unrealistic and without basis in history.[36]

Recent events provide an excellent example. During the first seven months of 1993, an unprecedented $5.3 billion of REIT shares were sold as IPOs. (During the same period, REITs were star perform-

---

[36] For a discussion, see, for example, Loewenstein and Elster (1992).

ers relative to the S&P index.) But in a period of declining interest rates, the investment craze appears to have been driven by yield-hungry individual investors, the same people who were also pouring billions into bond funds. The financial press warns that REIT prices may already have risen beyond the underlying value of the property. "It's another Wall Street promotional fiasco. The real estate isn't worth what it's being sold for," says one industry veteran (*The Wall Street Journal,* August 24, 1993, p. C1).[37] Toward the end of 1994, the REIT public offering market had considerably cooled off.

REFERENCES

Ahlers, D., and J. Lakonishok. "A Study of Economists' Consensus Forecasts." *Management Science* 20, no. 10 (1983), pp. 1113–25.

Ajzen, I., and M. Fishbein. *Understanding Attitudes and Predicting Social Behavior.* Englewood Cliffs, NJ: Prentice Hall, 1980.

Aronson, E. *The Social Animal.* 6th ed. New York: W. H. Freeman, 1992.

Arrow, K. J. "Risk Perception in Psychology and Economics." *Economic Inquiry* 20 (January 1982), pp. 1–9.

Barkema, A. D. "Farmland Values: The Rise, the Fall, the Future." *Federal Reserve Bank of Kansas City Economic Review,* April 1987, pp. 19–35.

Bazerman, M. H. *Judgment in Managerial Decision-Making.* New York: John Wiley & Sons, 1986.

Benston, G. J.; M. Carhill; and B. Olasov. "The Failure and Survival of Thrifts: Evidence from the Southeast." In R. G. Hubbard (ed.), *Financial Markets and Financial Crises.* Chicago: University of Chicago Press, 1991.

Bernard, V. L., and J. K. Thomas. "Evidence That Stock Prices Do Not Fully Reflect the Implications of Current Earnings for Future Earnings." *Journal of Accounting and Economics* 13 (1990), pp. 305–40.

Black, F. "Noise." *Journal of Finance* 41 (July 1986), pp. 529–43.

Burns, W. L., and D. R. Epley. "The Performance of Portfolios of

---

[37] Another aspect of recent events is that some investors are betting that a recovery will occur soon. Investment banks, including Goldman Sachs and Merrill Lynch, have set up property funds. U.S. banks are cutting their commercial property holdings. Of those holdings (loans and other property), perhaps more than $30 billion are nonperforming. The banks have sold assets at big discounts (30 to 50 percent or more) from their nominal value. BankAmerica sold commercial properties and mortgages with a book value of $1.7 billion to Morgan Stanley for less than half that sum.

REITS + Stocks." *Journal of Portfolio Management,* Spring 1982, pp. 37–42.

Case, K. E. "The Market for Single Family Homes in Boston." *New England Economic Review,* May–June 1986, pp. 38–48.

Case, K. E. "The Real Estate Cycle and the Economy: Consequences of the Massachusetts Boom of 1984–87." *New England Economic Review,* September–October 1991, pp. 37–46.

Case, K. E., and L. Cook. "The Distributional Effects of Housing Price Booms: Winners and Losers in Boston, 1980–88." *New England Economic Review,* May–June 1989, pp. 3–12.

Case, K. E., and R. J. Shiller. "Prices of Single Family Homes Since 1970: New Indexes for Four Cities." *New England Economic Review,* September–October 1987, pp. 45–56.

Case, K. E., and R. J. Shiller. "The Behavior of Home Buyers in Boom and Postboom Markets." *New England Economic Review,* November–December 1988, pp. 29–46.

Case, K. E., and R. J. Shiller. "The Efficiency of the Market for Single Family Homes." *American Economic Review* 79, no. 1 (1989), pp. 125–37.

Case, K. E., and R. J. Shiller. "Forecasting Prices and Excess Returns in the Housing Market." *AREUEA Journal* 18, no. 3 (1990), pp. 253–73.

Chan, K. C.; P. H. Hendershott; and A. Sanders. "Risk and Return on Real Estate: Evidence from Equity REITs." *AREUEA Journal* 18, no. 4 (1990), pp. 431–52.

Colling, P. L., and S. H. Irwin. "Has the Farm Asset Market Been Too Volatile?" Working paper no. 1350, Department of Agricultural Economics and Rural Sociology, Ohio State University, 1988.

Corgel, J. B.; W. McIntosh; and S. H. Ott. "Real Estate Investment Trusts: A Review of the Financial Economics Literature." Working paper, School of Hotel Administration, Cornell University, June 1993.

Corrigan, E. G. "The Risk of a Financial Crisis." In M. Feldstein (ed.), *The Risk of Economic Crisis.* Chicago: University of Chicago Press, 1991.

Cutler, D.; J. M. Poterba; and L. H. Summers. "Speculative Dynamics and the Role of Feedback Traders." *American Economic Review,* May 1990, pp. 63–68.

Damodaran, A.; C. H. Liu; and J. E. Pinto. "Real Estate Securities as a Hedge Against Unanticipated Inflation." Working paper, Stern School of Business, New York University, December 1992.

Darrat, A. F., and J. L. Glascock. "Real Estate Returns, Money, and Fiscal Deficits: Is the Real Estate Market Efficient?" *Journal of Real Estate Finance and Economics* 2 (1989), pp. 197–208.

De Bondt, W. F. M. "What Are Investment Advisors Paid for? The Shefrin-Statman and Competing Views." In J. B. Guerard, Jr., and M. N. Gultekin (eds.), *Handbook of Security Analyst Forecasting and Asset Allocation*. Greenwich, CT: JAI Press, 1993a.

De Bondt, W. F. M. "Betting on Trends: Intuitive Forecasts of Financial Risk and Return." *International Journal of Forecasting*, forthcoming 1993.

De Bondt, W. F. M., and R. H. Thaler. "Does the Stock Market Overreact?" *Journal of Finance* 40, no. 3 (1985), pp. 793–805.

De Bondt, W. F. M., and R. H. Thaler. "A Mean-Reverting Walk Down Wall Street." *Journal of Economic Perspectives* 3, no. 1 (1989), pp. 189–202.

De Bondt, W. F. M., and R. H. Thaler. "Do Security Analysts Overreact?" *American Economic Review*, May 1990, pp. 52–57.

De Long, J. B.; A. Shleifer; L. H. Summers; and R. J. Waldmann. "Noise Trader Risk in Financial Markets." *Journal of Political Economy* 98, no. 4 (1990a), pp. 703–38.

De Long, J. B.; A. Shleifer; L. H. Summers; and R. J. Waldmann. "Positive Feedback Investment Strategies and Destabilizing Rational Speculation." *Journal of Finance* 45, no. 2 (1990b), pp. 379–95.

De Wit, D. P. M. "The Performance of Real Estate and Real Estate Investment Trusts: The Effect of Appraisals on Perceived Risk" (in Dutch). *Financiering and Belegging*. Rotterdam, Netherlands, 1991.

Fama, E. F. "Efficient Capital Markets: A Review of Theory and Empirical Work." *Journal of Finance*, May 1970, pp. 383–417.

Fama, E. F. "Efficient Markets: II." *Journal of Finance*, December 1991, pp. 1575–1617.

Fama, E. F., and K. R. French. "The Cross-Section of Expected Stock Returns." *Journal of Finance*, June 1992, pp. 427–65.

Feldstein, M. *Inflation, Tax Rules, and Capital Formation*. Chicago: University of Chicago Press, 1983.

Feldstein, M., ed. *The Risk of Economic Crisis*. Chicago: University of Chicago Press, 1991.

Firstenberg, P.; S. Ross; and R. Zisler. "Real Estate: The Whole Story." *Journal of Portfolio Management* 14 (1988), pp. 22–34.

Fisher, J. D. "Portfolio Construction: Real Estate." Chapter 11 in J. L. Maginn and D. L. Tuttle (eds.), *Managing Investment Portfolios: A Dynamic Process*. New York: Warren, Gorham & Lamont, 1983.

Fogler, H. R.; M. R. Granito; and L. R. Smith. "A Theoretical Analysis of Real Estate Returns." *Journal of Finance*, July 1985, pp. 711–19.

Forrestal, D. J., III. "Management Skills for Investment Managers." Chapter

15 in J. L. Maginn and D. L. Tuttle (eds.), *Managing Investment Portfolios: A Dynamic Process*. New York: Warren, Gorham & Lamont, 1983.

Foster, P. *Towers of Debt*. London: Hodder & Stoughton, 1993.

Froland C.; R. Gorlow; and R. Sampson. "The Market Risk of Real Estate." *Journal of Portfolio Management*, Spring 1986, pp. 12–19.

Garner, A. "Will the Real Price of Housing Drop Sharply in the 1990s?" *Federal Reserve Bank of Kansas City Economic Review* 77, no. 1 (1992), pp. 55–68.

Garrigan, R. T., and J. L. Pagliari, Jr. "The Impact of Supply Changes on Real Net Operating Income: The Multi-Family Perspective." *Real Estate Issues*, Spring–Summer 1992, pp. 24–32.

Gorton, G., and R. Rosen. "Corporate Control, Portfolio Choice, and the Decline of Banking." Working paper, Wharton School, University of Pennsylvania, December 1992.

Graham, B., and D. Dodd. *Security Analysis*. New York: McGraw-Hill, 1934.

Gyourko, J., and D. B. Keim. "What Does the Stock Market Tell Us about Real Estate Returns?" *AREUEA Journal* 20, no. 3 (1992), pp. 457–85.

Harris, M., and A. Raviv. "Differences of Opinion Make a Horse Race." Working paper, Graduate School of Business, University of Chicago, June 1992.

Hendershott, P. J., and E. Kane. "Causes and Consequences of the 1980s Commercial Construction Boom." *Journal of Applied Corporate Finance*, 1992, pp. 61–70.

Hogarth, R. M. "Beyond Discrete Biases: Functional and Dysfunctional Aspects of Judgmental Heuristics." *Psychological Bulletin* 90, no. 2 (1981), pp. 197–217.

Hogarth, R. M. *Judgment and Choice*. 2nd ed. New York: John Wiley & Sons, 1987.

Hunter, J. E., and T. D. Coggin. "Analyst Judgment: The Efficient Market Hypothesis versus a Psychological Theory of Human Judgment." *Organizational Behavior and Human Decision Processes* 42 (1988), pp. 284–302.

Ingersoll, J. E, Jr. *Theory of Financial Decision-Making*. Totowa, NJ: Rowman & Littlefield, 1987.

Janis, I. L. *Victims of Groupthink*. Boston: Houghton Mifflin, 1972.

Kahneman, D.; P. Slovic; and A. Tversky. *Judgment under Uncertainty: Heuristics and Biases*. Cambridge, MA: Cambridge University Press, 1982.

Kahneman, D., and A. Tversky. "On the Psychology of Prediction." *Psychological Review* 80 (1973), pp. 237–51.

Katona, G. *Psychological Analysis of Economic Behavior*. New York: McGraw-Hill, 1951.

Keim, D. B. "The CAPM and Equity Return Regularities." *Financial Analysts Journal,* May–June 1986, pp. 19–34.

Keynes, J. M. *The General Theory of Employment, Interest, and Money.* New York: Harcourt Brace Jovanovich, 1936.

Kindleberger, C. *Manias, Panics, and Crashes: A History of Financial Crisis.* Rev. ed. New York: Basic Books, 1989.

Klausner, M. "Sociological Theory and the Behavior of Financial Markets." In P. A. Adler and P. Adler (eds.), *The Social Dynamics of Financial Markets.* Greenwich, CT: JAI Press, 1984.

Knight, F. H. *Risk, Uncertainty, and Profit.* Chicago: University of Chicago Press, 1971. First published by Houghton Mifflin, 1921.

Kobayashi, H. "Price Volatility in the Japanese Real Estate Market." Working paper, Dai-ichi Kangyo Bank, Ltd., Tokyo, September 1993.

Le Bon, G. *The Crowd.* New York: Penguin Books, 1977. First published in 1895.

Lichtenstein, S.; B. Fischhoff; and L. D. Phillips. "Calibration of Probabilities: The State of the Art to 1980." In D. Kahneman et al. (eds.), *Judgment under Uncertainty: Heuristics and Biases.* Cambridge, MA: Cambridge University Press, 1982.

Loewenstein, G., and J. Elster. *Choice over Time.* New York: Russell Sage Foundation, 1992.

MacKay, C. *Extraordinary Popular Delusions and the Madness of Crowds.* London: Bentley, 1841.

Malabre, A. L., Jr. *Beyond Our Means.* New York: Vintage Books, 1987.

Malkiel, B. *A Random Walk Down Wall Street.* 5th ed. New York: W. W. Norton, 1990.

Mankiw, G., and D. Weil. "The Baby Boom, the Baby Bust, and the Housing Market." *Regional Science and Urban Economics* 19, no. 2 (1989), pp. 235–58.

Mitchell, W. C. *Business Cycles and Their Causes.* Philadelphia: Porcupine Press, 1989. First published in 1913.

Nisbett, R., and L. Ross. *Human Inference: Strategies and Shortcomings of Social Judgment.* Englewood Cliffs, NJ: Prentice Hall, 1980.

Northcraft, G. B., and M. A. Neale. "Experts, Amateurs, and Real Estate: An Anchoring-and-Adjustment Perspective on Property Pricing Decisions." *Organizational Behavior and Human Decision Processes* 39 (1987), pp. 84–97.

Pagliari, J. L., Jr., and J. R. Webb. "Past and Future Sources of Commercial Real Estate Returns." *Journal of Real Estate Research* 7, no. 4 (1992), pp. 387–421.

Pigou, A. C. *Industrial Fluctuations*. 2nd ed. London: Macmillan, 1929.

Ritter, J. R. "The Long-Term Performance of Initial Public Offerings." *Journal of Finance*, March 1991, pp. 3–27.

Roll, R. "R^2." *Journal of Finance* 43, no. 2 (1988), pp. 541–66.

Rose, H. "The Changing World of Finance and Its Problems." Working paper no. 167-93, Institute of Finance and Accounting, London Business School, 1993.

Ross, S., and R. Zisler. "Risk and Return in Real Estate." *Journal of Real Estate Finance and Economics* 4, no. 2 (1991), pp. 175–90.

Russell, B. *Unpopular Essays*. New York: Simon and Schuster, 1950.

Russo, J. E., and P. J. H. Schoemaker. *Decision Traps*. New York: Simon and Schuster, 1989.

Schoemaker, P. J. H. "The Quest for Optimality: A Positive Heuristic of Science?" *Behavioral and Brain Sciences* 14, no. 2 (1991), pp. 205–45.

Shefrin, H., and M. Statman. "The Disposition to Sell Winners Too Early and Ride Losers Too Long: Theory and Evidence." *Journal of Finance*, July 1985, pp. 777–92.

Shiller, R. J. *Market Volatility*. Cambridge, MA: MIT Press, 1989.

Shleifer, A., and L. H. Summers. "The Noise Trader Approach to Finance." *Journal of Economic Perspectives*, Spring 1990, pp. 19–33.

Simon, H. A. *Models of Man: Social and Rational*. New York: John Wiley & Sons, 1957.

Simon, H. A. *Reason in Human Affairs*. Stanford, CA: Stanford University Press, 1983.

Sirmans, G. S., and C. F. Sirmans. "The Historical Perspective of Real Estate Returns." *Journal of Portfolio Management*, Spring 1987, pp. 22–31.

Slovic, P. "Psychological Study of Human Judgment: Implications for Investment Decision-Making." *Journal of Finance* 27, no. 4 (1972a), pp. 779–99.

Slovic, P. "Information Processing, Situation Specificity, and the Generality of Risk-Taking Behavior." *Journal of Personality and Social Psychology* 22, no. 1 (1972b), pp. 128–34.

Smith, B. A., and W. P. Tesarek. "House Prices and Regional Real Estate Cycles: Market Adjustments in Houston." *AREUEA Journal* 19, no. 3 (1991), pp. 396–416.

Statman, M. "Discussion of 'A Theoretical Analysis of Real Estate Returns.'" *Journal of Finance*, July 1985, pp. 719–21.

Stevenson, H. H. "Equity Real Estate Investments of Life Insurance Companies." In J. D. Cummins (ed.), *Investment Activities of Life Insurance Companies*. Homewood, IL: Richard D. Irwin, 1978.

Stone, D., and W. Ziemba. "Land and Stock Prices in Japan." *Journal of Economic Perspectives* 7, no. 3 (1993), pp. 149–65.

Summers, L. H. "Planning for the Next Financial Crisis." In M. Feldstein (ed.), *The Risk of Economic Crisis*. Chicago: University of Chicago Press, 1991.

Thaler, R. H. "The Psychology of Choice and the Assumptions of Economics." In A. E. Roth (ed.), *Laboratory Experimentation in Economics: Six Points of View*. New York: Cambridge University Press, 1987.

Tversky, A., and D. Kahneman. "Judgment under Uncertainty: Heuristics and Biases." *Science* 185 (1974), pp. 1124–31.

Tversky, A., and D. Kahneman. "Rational Choice and the Framing of Decisions." In R. M. Hogarth and M. W. Reder (eds.), *Rational Choice: The Contrast between Economics and Psychology*. Chicago: University of Chicago Press, 1986.

Voltaire (F. M. Arouet). *Candide*. Geneva: Cramer, 1759.

Webb, J. R., and C. F. Sirmans. "Yields and Risk Measures for Real Estate, 1966–1977." *Journal of Portfolio Management,* Fall 1980, pp. 14–19.

Weinstein, N. D. "Unrealistic Optimism about Future Life Events." *Journal of Personality and Social Psychology* 39, no. 5 (1980), pp. 806–20.

Wheaton, W. C. "The Cyclic Behavior of the National Office Market." *AREUEA Journal* 15, no. 4 (1987), pp. 281–99.

INDEX